WEBSTER'S DICTIONARY

Edited by

John Gage Allee, Ph.D.

*Professor of English Philology,
The George Washington University*

This book is not published by the original publishers
of WEBSTER'S DICTIONARY, or by their successors.

D0954887

 Harbor House Publishers Inc.

Baltimore, MD 21204

A
B
C
D
E
F
G
H
IJ
K
L
M
N
O
P
Q
R
S
T
U
V
W
X
YZ

KEY TO THIS DICTIONARY

The entries in this Dictionary are arranged in groups, derived and related words being placed under the main entry.

A. Each main entry, in bold-faced type, is syllabized. The part of speech, in italics, follows; then the definition.

    Ex.: **cross** *a.* intersecting; interchanged. . . .

B. Sub-entries are shown in bold-faced type following the definition of the main entry.

  1. If a hyphen precedes the sub-entry, the ending is added to the main entry.

    Ex.: **-ing** (crossing)

  2. If a dash precedes the sub-entry, a hyphenated word is indicated.

    Ex.: **—examination** (cross-examination)

  3. If a dash and a space precede the sub-entry, this indicates words that are commonly found together.

    Ex.: **— reference** (cross reference)

  4. If the sub-entry is spelled out, this may indicate differences from the main entry. (In some instances, sub-entries are spelled out where confusion may otherwise develop).

Note: Irregularities of verb forms, plurals and comparisons are included as sub-entries to facilitate word usage.

ABBREVIATIONS USED IN THIS DICTIONARY

a. adjective
abbrev. abbreviation
ablat. ablative; ablatival
Aborig. Aboriginal
acc. accusative
A.D. Anno Domini
  (in the year of Our Lord)
adv. adverb
Aero. Aeronautics
Afr. Africa; African
Agric. Agriculture
Alg. Algebra
alt. alternative
Amer. America; American
Anat. Anatomy
Anglo-Ind. Anglo-Indian
Anthropol. Anthropology
Ar. Arabic
Arch. Archaic
Archaeol. Archaeology
Archit. Architecture
Arith. Arithmetic
Astrol. Astrology
Astron. Astronomy
aux. auxiliary
Aviat. Aviation

Bacter. Bacteriology
B.C. before Christ
Bib. Biblical
Biol. Biology
Bot. Botany
Br., Brit. British
Braz. Brazilian
Bret. Breton
Build. Building

c. about (L. = *Circa*)
C. Centigrade; Central
Can. Canada; Canadian
Cap. capital letter
Carib. Caribbean
Carp. Carpentry
Celt. Celtic
cent. century
Cent. Central
cf. compare (L. = *confer*)
ch. Chapter
Chem. Chemistry
Chin. Chinese
Class. Myth. Classical
  Mythology
Colloq. Colloquial;
  Colloquialism
Comm. Commerce;
  Commercial

comp. comparative
conj. conjunction
conn. connected
contr. contraction
corrupt. corruption

Dan. Danish
dat. dative
def. art. definite article
demons. demonstrative
der. derivation; derived
Dial. Dialect; Dialectal
Dict. Dictionary
dim. diminutive
Dut. Dutch
Dyn. Dynamics

E. East; English
Eccl. Ecclesiastical
e.g. for example (L. =
  exemplia gratia)
E.Ind. East Indian
Elect. Electricity
Embryol. Embryology
Engin. Engineering
Entom. Entomology
esp. especially
Ethnol. Ethnology
etym. etymology

F., Fahr. Fahrenheit
fem. feminine
fig. figuratively
Finn. Finnish
Flem. Flemish
Fort. Fortification
fr. from
Fr. French
freq. frequentative

Gael. Gaelic
gen. genitive
Geog. Geography
Geol. Geology
Geom. Geometry
Ger. German
Gk. Greek
Gk. Myth. Greek Mythology
Gram. Grammar

Heb. Hebrew
Her. Heraldry
Hind. Hindustani
Hist. History
Hort. Horticulture
Hung. Hungarian

i. intransitive
Ice. Icelandic
i.e. that is (L. = *id est*)
imit. imitation; imitative
imper. imperative
impers. impersonal
Ind. Indian
indef. art. indefinite article
indic. indicative
infin. infinitive
interj. interjection
interrog. interrogative
Ir. Irish
It. Italian

Jap. Japanese

L. Latin
l.c. lower case letter
L.Ger. Low German
lit. literally
Lit. Literature
L.L. Low (Late) Latin

masc. masculine
Math. Mathematics
M.E. Middle English
Mech. Mechanics
Med. Medicine
Metal. Metallurgy
Meteor. Meteorology
Mex. Mexican
M.H.Ger. Middle High German
Mil. Military
Min. Mineralogy
Mod. Modern
Mus. Music
Myth. Mythology

n. noun
N. North; Norse
Nat.Hist. Natural History
Naut. Nautical
neg. negative
neut. neuter
nom. nominative
Norw. Norwegian
n.pl. noun plural
n.sing. noun singular
N.T. New Testament

obj. object; objective
obs. obsolete
O.E. Old English
O.Fr. Old French
O.H.Ger. Old High German
O.L.Ger. Old Low German
O.N. Old Norse

Onomat. Onomatopoeic
opp. opposite; opposed
Opt. Optics
orig. originally
Ornith. Ornithology
O.T. Old Testament

Paint. Painting
pa.p. past participle
pass. passive
pa.t. past tense
Path. Pathology
perh. perhaps
pers. person
Pers. Persian
pert. pertaining
Peruv. Peruvian
Pharm. Pharmacy
Philol. Philology
Philos. Philosophy
Phon. Phonetics
Photog. Photography
Phys. Physics
Physiol. Physiology
pl. plural
Poet. Poetry; poetical
Pol. Polish
Port. Portuguese
poss. possessive
pref. prefix
prep. preposition
pres. present
Print. Printing
prob. probably
pron. pronoun
Pros. Prosody
Prov. Provincial
pr.p. present participle
Psych. psychology

q.v. which see (L. = *quod vide*)

R. River
R.C. Roman Catholic
recip. reciprocal
redup. reduplication
ref. reference; referring
refl. reflexive
rel related; relative
Rhet. Rhetoric
Rom. Roman
Rom.Myth. Roman Mythology
Russ. Russian

S. South
S.Afr. South African
S.Amer. South American

Sans. Sanskrit
Scand. Scandinavian
Scot. Scots; Scottish
Sculp. Sculpture
sing. singular
Singh. Singhalese
Slav. Slavonic
Sp. Spanish
St. Saint
superl. superlative
Surg. Surgery
Sw. Swedish
Syn. Synonym

t. transitive
Teleg. Telegraphy
Teut. Teutonic

Theat. Theatre
Theol. Theology
Trig. Trigonometry
Turk. Turkish

U.S.(A.) United States (of America)
usu. usually

v. verb
var. variant; variation
v.i. verb intransitive
v.t. verb transitive
vulg. vulgar

W. Welsh; West

Yid. Yiddish

Zool. Zoology

a *indef. art.* meaning *one.*

aard•vark *n.* animal resembling the anteater, found in parts of Africa.

aardvark

A.B. Bachelor of Arts.

ab- *pref.* meaning from, away, off.

ab•a•ca *n.* Manila hemp, or the plant producing it.

a•back *adv.* backwards; *(Naut.)* against the masts, of sails pressed back by the wind.

ab•a•cus *n.* an instrument with parallel wires on which arithmetical calculations are made with sliding balls or beads; *(Archit.)* a tablet crowning a column and its capital.

a•baft *adv.* and *prep. (Naut.)* at or towards the stern; behind.

ab•a•lo•ne *n.* the name of several species of limpet-like mollusks or "earshells," yielding mother-of-pearl.

a•ban•don *v.t.* to give up wholly and finally; *n.* careless freedom. **-ed** *a.* deserted; unrestrained; given up entirely to, esp. wickedness. **-edly** *adv.* **-ment** *n.* the act of abandoning, or state of being abandoned.

a•base *v.t.* to bring low; to cast down; to humble.

a•bash *v.t.* to strike with shame or fear.

a•bate *v.t.* to beat down, lessen; *v.i.* to decrease, subside, decline.

ab•at•toir *n.* a slaughterhouse.

ab•ba•cy *n.* the office or dignity of an abbot; the building under the control of an abbot; an abbey. **abbey** *n.* a church establishment forming the dwelling-place of a community of monks or nuns. **abbot** *(fem.* abbess) *n.* the head of an abbey or monastery.

ab•bre•vi•ate *v.t.* to shorten, reduce by contraction or omission. **abbreviation** *n.* the act of abbreviating; a shortened form. **abbreviator** *n.* abbreviatory *a.*

ab•di•cate *v.t.* and *v.i.* formally to give up power or office. **abdication** *n.*

ab•do•men *n.* the lower part of the trunk of the body; the belly.

ab•duct *v.t.* to take away by fraud or force; to kidnap. **-ion** *n.*

a•beam *adv. (Naut.)* at right angles to a ship's length.

a•bed *adv.* in bed.

a•bele *n.* the white poplar tree.

ab•er•rate *v.i.* to deviate from the right path or normal course. **aberrant** *a.* deviating from the normal. **aberration** *n.*

a•bet *v.t.* to encourage or aid, esp. in doing wrong.

a•bey•ance *n.* a state of suspension or temporary inactivity; the condition of not being in use or action.

ab•hor *v.t.* to hate extremely. **-rent** *a.* detestable; abominable; repugnant. **-rer** *n.*

a•bide *v.i.* to stay; reside; continue firm or stable; *v.t.* to tolerate; bear. **abidance** *n.* **abiding** *a.*

a•bil•i•ty *n.* quality, state, or condition of being able.

ab•i•o•gen•e•sis *n. (Biol.)* the theory of spontaneous generation from nonliving matter.

ab•ject *a.* base; degraded; mean and worthless; contemptible; miserable. **-ly** *adv.* **-ion, -ness** *n.* degradation; abasement; servility.

ab•jure *v.t.* to renounce upon oath. **abjuration** *n.*

ab•la•tive *a.* (used as *n.*) the sixth case of Latin nouns and pronouns expressing *time when.*

ab•laut *n. (Philol.)* variation of root vowel in certain related words, as *sink, sank, sunk.*

a•blaze *a.* on fire; aglow; gleaming.

a•ble *a.* having skill, strength to perform a task; competent; talented; vigorous. **ability** *n.* being able. **-ness** *n.* **ably** *adv.*

a•bloom *adv.* or *a.* in bloom.

ab•lu•tion *n.* cleansing or washing; (usually plural) the purification of the body or of sacred vessels before certain religious ceremonies, e.g., Eucharist; the wine and water used. **-ary** *a.*

ab•ne•gate *v.t.* to deny; surrender; relinquish. **abnegation** *n.*

ab•nor•mal *a.* contrary to rule or system; deviating from a recognized standard. Also **-ity, -ism** *n.* the state of being abnormal. **-ly** *adv.*

a•board *adv.* and *prep. (Naut.)* on board; within a vessel; on a train.

a•bode *n.* residence, a dwelling place.

a•bol•ish *v.t.* to do away with; to repeal; to obliterate. **-ment** *n.*

ab•o•li•tion *n.* the act of abolishing, as of laws, taxes, etc. **-al** *a.* **-ist, -ism** *n.*

A-bomb *n.* atomic bomb.

a•bom•i•nate *v.t.* to loathe; detest extremely; abhor. **abominable** *a.* **abominableness** *n.* **abominably** *adv.* **abomination** *n.* the act or object of loathing.

ab•o•rig•i•nes *n.pl.* the original inhabitants of a country. **aboriginal** *a.*

a•bort *v.i.* to miscarry in giving birth. **-ifacient** *a.* capable of producing abortion. **-ion** *n.* **-ionist** *n.* **-ive** *a.* prematurely produced; undeveloped; imperfect; rudimentary. **-ively** *adv.*

a•bound *v.i.* to be in great plenty (used with preps. *with* and *in*). **-ing** *a.* plentiful.

a•bout *adv.* and *prep.* on every side; concerning; approximately; (before an infin.) on the point of.

a•bove *adv.* and *prep.* and *a.* higher than; more in number, quantity or degree.

ab•ra•ca•dab•ra *n.* corruption of sacred Gnostic term, derived from ancient Egyptian magical formula; a catchword; gibberish.

a•brade *v.t.* to rub or wear off; to scrape or grate off; to graze (as of skin). **abradant** *n.* a substance, e.g. emery powder, for polishing. **abrasion** *n.* **abrasive** *a.*

ab•re•ac•tion *n.* in psychoanalysis, elimination of a morbid complex by expression through conscious association with the original cause. **abreact** *v.t.*

a•breast *adv.* side by side; on a line with.

a•bridge *v.t.* to shorten; curtail; reduce; diminish; epitomize. -ment *n.*

a•broad *adv.* and *a.* at large, over a wide space; overseas.

ab•ro•gate *v.t.* to annul; repeal (a law); do away with; put an end to; cancel. abrogation *n.*

a•brupt *a.* broken off; steep; precipitous; curt; unceremonious; brusque. -ly *adv.* -ness *n.*

ab•scess *n.* gathering of pus in any infected organ or tissue of the body.

ab•scind *v.t.* to cut off; pare away; separate; rend apart.

ab•scond *v.i.* to take oneself off; to flee from justice. -ence, -er *n.*

ab•sence *n.* being absent. absent *a.* not present; inattentive. absent *v.t.* to withdraw (oneself); deliberately to fail to appear. absentee *n.* one who is not present. absently *adv.* casually; forgetfully.

ab•sinthe, ab•sinth *n.* a green-colored liqueur flavored with wormwood and other aromatics.

ab•so•lute *a.* unconditional; without restraint; *(Gram.)* not dependent; pure. -ly *adv.* positively; very; entirely. -ness *n.* absol:tion *n.* a remission of sin after confession, pronounced by the R. C. Church; formal acquittal by a judge. absolutism *n.* unrestricted and unlimited rule; arbitrary government. absolutist *n.* absolutory, absolvatory *a.*

ab•solve *v.t.* to set free from an obligation, guilt, debt, penalty; to pardon; acquit. -r *n.*

ab•sorb *v.t.* to swallow up; drink in; soak up; to engage one's whole attention. -ability *n.* -able, -ing *a.* -ent *a.* absorbing; *n.* anything which absorbs. -ency *n.*

ab•sorp•tion *n.* the act of absorbing. absorptive *a.* able to absorb.

ab•stain *v.i.* to forbear; to refrain. -er *n.*

ab•ste•mi•ous *a.* showing moderation in the use of food and drink. -ly *adv.* -ness *n.*

ab•sten•tion *n.* the act of abstaining or refraining from. -ist *n.*

ab•sti•nence *n.* voluntary forbearance from using or doing something. Also abstinency. abstinent *a.* temperate; refraining from. abstinently *adv.*

ab•stract *v.t.* to separate from; remove, summarize; reduce. -ed *a.* -edly *adv. a.* not concrete, theoretical. *n.* that which comprises in itself the essential qualities of a larger thing, or of several things; a summary. -ion *n.* abstracting or separating; a theoretical idea.

ab•struse *a.* hidden; difficult or hard to be understood. -ly *adv.* -ness *n.*

ab•surd *a.* contrary to reason; ridiculous; silly. -ly *adv.* -ity *n.*

a•bun•dance *n.* ample sufficiency; great plenty. abundant *a.* abundantly *adv.*

a•buse *v.t.* to make a wrong use of; to ill-treat; to violate; revile; malign; *n.* ill-usage; improper treatment; a corrupt practice; rude language. abusive *a.* abusiveness *n.*

a•but *v.i.* to end; to touch with one end; to border on; to adjoin. -ting *pr.p.* -ted *pa.p.* -ment *n.* *(Archit.)* the support at end of an arch or bridge.

a•byss *n.* any deep chasm; a gulf. abysmal *a.* bottomless; vast; profound. abysmally *adv.* -al *a.* inhabiting, or characteristic of, the depths of the ocean.

a•ca•cia *n.* thorny, leguminous tree or shrub, yielding gum arabic.

a•cad•e•my *n.* a place of education or specialized training; a society of men united for the promotion of the arts and sciences. academic, academical *a.* academician *n.* a member of an academy or society for promoting the arts and sciences.

a•can•thus *n.* a prickly plant, also called "bear's breech" or "brank-ursine."

a•cat•a•lec•tic *a.* not stopping short; complete in syllables; *n.* a verse that has the complete number of syllables.

a•cat•a•lep•sy *n.* incomprehensibility; acatalepsia *n.* acataleptic *a.*

a•cat•a•pha•si•a *n.* difficulty or inability in expressing ideas logically.

ac•cede *v.i.* to agree; assent; consent; to arrive at a certain state or condition; to succeed as heir. -r *n.*

ac•cel•er•ate *v.t.* and *v.i.* to cause to move faster; to become swifter. acceleration *n.* accelerative *a.* accelerator *n.* acceleratory *a.*

ac•cent *n.* stress on a syllable or syllables of a word; a mark to show this; inflection of the voice; manner of speech. *v.t.* to utter, pronounce, or mark with accent; to emphasize; to stress. -ual *a.* -uate *v.t.* to accent; to stress; to make more prominent. -uation *n.*

ac•cept *v.t.* to take; receive; admit; believe; to agree to. -able *a.* welcome; pleasing; agreeable. -ably *adv.* -ability, -ance *n.* -ation *n.* the usual meaning of a word, statement, etc. -ed *a.* -er, -or *n.*

ac•cess *n.* a coming to the means or way of approach; admission; entrance; attack; fit. -ible *a.* -ibility *n.* -ion *n.* increase; a coming to, esp. to a throne, office, or dignity. -ory, -ary *a.* aiding; contributing; additional; *n.* an additional, secondary piece of equipment.

ac•ci•dence *n.* the part of grammar dealing with changes in the form of words, e.g. plurals, etc.

ac•ci•dent *n.* chance; a mishap; a casualty; contingency; a quality not essential. -al *a.* -ally *adv.*

ac•claim *v.t.* and *v.i.* to receive with applause, etc.; cheer; to hail as; acclamation *n.* general applause. acclamatory *a.*

ac•cli•ma•tize *v.t.* to accustom to a new climate. Also acclimate. acclimatization *n.* Also acclimatation, acclimation *n.*

ac•cliv•i•ty *n.* an upward slope.

ac•co•lade *n.* a ceremony used in conferring knighthood, consisting now of a tap given on the shoulder; award, praise.

ac•com•mo•date *v.t.* to render fit or suitable; adapt; adjust; reconcile;

A

provide room for. **accommodating** *a.*
accommodation *n.* (usually pl.) a loan of money; convenience; room or space for; lodgings. **accommodative** *a.*

ac•com•pa•ny *v.t.* to go with. **accompaniment** *n.* that which goes with; *(Mus.)* the instrumental parts played with a vocal or other instrumental part. **accompanist** *n.*

ac•com•plice *n.* a companion in evil deeds; an associate in crime.

ac•com•plish *v.t.* to carry out; to finish; to complete; to perform. **-ed** *a.* complete; perfect; having accomplishments; hence, talented. **-ment** *n.* completion; finish; that which makes for culture, elegant manners, etc.

ac•cord *n.* agreement; harmony; *v.t.* to grant; settle; compose; *v.i.* to agree; to agree in pitch and tone. **-ance** *n.* **-ant** *a.* corresponding. **-ing** *a.* in accordance; agreeing; suitable. **-ingly** *adv.*

ac•cor•di•on *n.* wind instrument fitted with bellows and button keyboards.

ac•cost *v.t.* to speak first to; to address; to approach.

ac•count *n.* a reckoning; a record; a report; a statement of debts and credits in money transactions; *v.t.* to reckon, judge; *v.i.* to give a reason; to give a financial reckoning. **-able** *a.* **-ably** *adv.* **-ability** *n.* **-ancy** *n.* the profession of an accountant. **-ant** *n.* **-ing** *n.* or *a.*

ac•cou•tre *v.t.* to furnish with dress or equipment, esp. military; to equip. **-ments** *n.pl.* dress; military dress and equipment.

ac•cred•it *v.t.* to give trust or confidence to; to vouch for; to recommend; to furnish with credentials, as an envoy or ambassador. **-ed** *a.* **-ation** *n.*

ac•crete *v.i.* to grow together; *v.t.* to add by growth. **accretion** *n.* **accretive** *a.*

ac•crue *v.i.* to increase; to result naturally; to come as an addition, e.g. interest, profit, etc. **accrual** *n.*

ac•cu•mu•late *v.t.* to heap up; to collect; *v.i.* to grow into a mass; to increase. **accumulation** *n.* **accumulative** *a.* **accumulatively** *adv.* **accumulator** *n.*

ac•cu•rate *a.* correct. **-ly** *adv.* **-ness** *n.*

ac•curse *v.t.* to doom to destruction; to curse. **-d** *a.* under a curse. **-dness** *n.*

ac•cuse *v.t.* to charge with a crime or fault; to blame. **-d** *a.* *n.* one so charged. **-r** *n.* **accusation** *n.* **accusative**, **accusatory** *a.*

ac•cus•tom *v.t.* to make familiar by use; to familiarize; to habituate. **-ed** *a.*

ace *n.* a card with only one spot; a single point; the best, highest; an outstanding fighter pilot.

ac•er•bate *v.t.* to make bitter; to exasperate; *a.* embittered; severe; exasperated. **acerbity** *n.* sourness of taste, with bitterness and astringency; hence bitterness, or severity in persons.

a•ce•tic *a.* pert. to acetic acid, the acid in vinegar. **acetate** *n.* *(Chem.)* a salt formed by acetic acid; also a rayon material. **acetify** *v.t.* and *v.i.* to turn into vinegar. **acetification** *n.* **acetous** *a.* sour.

a•cet•y•lene *n.* a highly inflammable gas used as an illuminant.

ache *n.* a continuous dull, heavy pain; *v.i.* to be in pain. **aching** *a.* and *n.*

a•chieve *v.t.* to bring to a successful end; to accomplish. **achievable** *a.* **-ment** *n.* performing; a performance; an exploit; a feat. **-r**, *n.*

ach•ro•ma•si•a *n.* *(Med.)* absence of color. **achromate** *a.*

ach•ro•ma•tic *a.* *(Opt.)* free from color. **-ity**, **achromatism** *n.* **achromatize** *v.t.* **achromatous** *a.*

ac•id *a.* sour; sharp to the taste; having the taste of vinegar; *n.* a sour substance; *(Chem.)* a substance which contains hydrogen replaceable by a metal. **-ify** *v.t.* and *v.i.* **-ity** *n.* **-ulate** *v.t.* to make slightly acid or sour; *(Fig.)* to embitter. **-ulated**, **-ulous** *a.*

ac•knowl•edge *v.t.* to admit as true; to give a receipt for; to give thanks for; to reward. **acknowledgment** *n.*

ac•me *n.* the highest point, the top; perfection.

ac•ne *n.* a skin disease characterized by hard, reddish pimples often appearing as blackheads.

ac•o•lyte *n.* a candidate for priesthood in the R. C. Church; a lesser church officer; an assistant; a novice.

ac•o•nite *n.* *(Bot.)* wolfsbane or monkshood.

a•corn *n.* the seed or fruit of the oak.

a•cous•tic *a.* pert. to the sense of hearing. **acoustics** *n.pl.* the science of sounds; the estimation of audibility in a theater, etc.

ac•quaint *v.t.* to make fully known or familiar; to inform. **-ance** *n.* familiar knowledge; a person known slightly. **-anceship** *n.* **-ed** *a.*

ac•qui•esce *v.i.* to agree in silence; to assent without objection. **-nce** *n.* **-nt** *a.*

ac•quire *v.t.* to gain; to obtain; to get. **acquirable** *a.* **-ment** *n.* **acquisition** *n.* the act of acquiring; the thing acquired. **acquisitive** *a.* grasping; greedy for gain. **acquisitiveness** *n.*

ac•quit *v.t.* to set free; release; declare innocent; to conduct oneself; to discharge a debt. *pr.p.* **-ting**, *pa.p.* and *pa.t.* **-ted. -tal, -tance** *n.*

a•cre *n.* a measure of land containing 4840 square yards. **-age** *n.*

ac•rid *a.* bitter; sharp; pungent; harsh; ill-tempered. **-ly** *adv.* **-ness**, **-ity** *n.*

ac•ri•mo•ny *n.* bitterness of temper or of language. **acrimonious** *a.* **acrimoniously** *adv.*

ac•ro•bat *n.* one skilled in gymnastic feats; a ropedancer; a tumbler. **-ic** *a.* **-ics** *n.pl.* skill of an acrobat.

ac•ro•nym *n.* a word formed from initials, e.g., *radar.*

ac•ro•pho•bi•a *n.* a morbid fear of heights.

a•crop•o•lis *n.* the fortified summit of a Greek city; a citadel, esp. the citadel of Athens.

a•cross *adv.* and *prep.* from side to side; transversely; athwart.

a•cros•tic *n.* a composition in verse, in which the first, and sometimes last, letters of the lines read in order form a name, a sentence, or title.

act *v.t.* to perform, esp. upon stage; to behave as; *v.i.* to exert energy; to fulfil a function; to operate. *n.* deed; performance; actuality; action; a decree, law, edict, or judgment; principal division of a play. **-ing** *a.* **-or** *n.* one who performs. **-ress** *n.* a female actor.

ac•tin•i•a *n.* the sea anemone. *pl.* actiniae.

ac•tin•ism *n.* the radiation of light or heat; the property possessed by the sun's ray, of producing chemical changes, as in photography. **actinic, actiniform** *a.*

ac•tin•i•um *n.* a radioactive element.

ac•ti•nol•o•gy *n.* that branch of science concerned with chemical action of light.

ac•ti•no•ther•a•py *n.* the treatment of disease by natural or artificial light rays; often known as "sunlight treatment."

ac•tion *n.* a thing done; behavior; physical movement; function; a battle; the development of events in a play, etc.; legal proceedings; *(Chem.)* effect. **-able** *a.* affording grounds for legal proceedings. **-ably** *adv.*

ac•ti•vate *v.t.* to make active. **activation** *n.*

ac•tive *a.* having the power to act; agile; busy; alert. **-ly** *adv.* vigorously. **activism** *n.* policy of those who, by energetic action, seek to fulfil the promises of a political program. **activist, activity, -ness** *n.*

ac•tu•al *a.* existing now or as a fact; real; effectual. **-ize** *v.t.* to make real in fact or by vivid description. **-ist** *n.* a realist. **-ity** *n.* reality, existence. **-ly** *adv.*

ac•tu•a•ry *n.* registrar or clerk. **actuarial** *a.* **actuarially** *adv.*

ac•tu•ate *v.t.* to put into action; incite; motivate; influence. **actuation, actuator** *n.*

a•cu•men *n.* quickness of perception or discernment; sharpness; penetration. **acuminous** *a.*

a•cute *a.* sharp; pointed; sagacious; subtle; penetrating. **-ly** *adv.* **-ness** *n.*

A.D. in the year of our Lord.

ad•age *n.* saying or maxim that has obtained credit by long use; a proverb; a byword. **adagial** *a.*

ad•a•mant *n.* a stone of impenetrable hardness; the diamond; *a.* very hard; unyielding. **-ine** *a.*

Ad•am's ap•ple *n.* projection of cartilege at the front of one's throat.

a•dapt *v.t.* to make fit or suitable; to make to correspond. **-ability, -ableness** *n.* **-able** *a.* **-ation** *n.* **-er** *n.* any appliance which makes possible a union of two different parts of an apparatus. **-ive** *a.* **-ively** *adv.* **-iveness, -or** *n.*

add *v.t.* to join, unite to form one sum or whole; to annex; to increase; to say further. **-able, -ible** *a.* **-er** *n.* a machine which adds; a comptometer. **-ibility, -ition** *n.* **-itional** *a.* supplementary; extra. **-itionally** *adv.* **-itive** *a.*

ad•dend *n.* number to be added.

ad•den•dum *n.* a thing to be added; an appendix; *pl.* **addenda.**

ad•der *n.* a venomous serpent.

ad•dict *v.t.* to apply habitually; habituate; *n.* one addicted to evil habit, e.g.

drug-taking. **-ed** *a.* **-ion** *n.*

ad•dle *v.t.* to corrupt; putrify; confuse; to make addled. **addle, addled** *a.*

ad•dress *v.t.* to direct in writing, as a letter; to apply (oneself); to make a speech; to present a congratulatory message or petition; accost; *n.* a formal speech; manner of speaking; direction of a letter; skill. **-es** *n.pl.* attentions in courtship. **-ee** *n.* person to whom a communication is sent. **-er** *n.*

ad•duce *v.t.* to bring forward as proof; to cite; to quote. **-nt** *a.* **-r** *n.* **adducible** *a.* **adduction** *n.* **adductive** *a.* **adductor** *n.* **adducent muscle.**

ad•en (ə) a combining form. **-itis** *n.* inflammation of the lymphatic glands. **-oid, -oidal** *a.* glandular; gland-shaped. **-oids** *n.pl.* a swelling of tissue between nose and throat.

ad•ept *n.* one skilled in any art; an expert; *a.* well-skilled; expert.

ad•e•quate *a.* equal to; sufficient. **adequacy. -ness** *n.* **-ly** *adv.*

ad•here *v.i.* to stick fast; to be devoted to; to hold to (an opionion). **-nce** *n.* **-nt** *a.* and *n.* supporter of person or cause. **adhesion** *n.* act of adhering. **adhesive** *a.* sticky; tenacious; *n.* an agent which sticks things together. **adhesively** *adv.* **adhesiveness** *n.*

ad•hib•it *v.t.* to use or apply; to attach.

a•dieu *interj.* good-bye; farewell; *n.* a farewell; a leave-taking. *pl.* **adieus, adieux.**

ad•i•pose *a.* pert. to animal fat; fatty. **adiposity** *n.* fatness **adipic** *a.*

ad•it *n.* horizontal or inclined entrance into a mine.

ad•ja•cent *a.* lying close to; adjoining; bordering on. **-ly** *adv.* **adjacency** *n.*

ad•jec•tive *n.* a word used with a noun to qualify, limit, or define it; *a.* pert. to an adjective. **adjectival** *a.* **adjectivally** *adv.*

ad•join *v.t.* to join or unite to; to be next or contiguous to; *v.i.* to be next to. **-ing** *a.*

ad•journ *v.t.* to put off to another day; to postpone. **-ment** *n.*

ad•judge *v.t.* to settle judicially; to pronounce judgment. **adjudgment** *n.* **adjudicate.** *v.t.* to settle judicially; *v.i.* to pronounce judgment. **adjudication** *n.* **adjudicator** *n.* a judge.

ad•junct *n.* something joined to another thing, but not essential to it; *a.* added to; united with. **-ive, -ively** *adv.*

ad•jure *v.t.* to charge or bind, under oath; to entreat earnestly. **adjuration** *n.* a solemn command on oath; an earnest appeal. **adjuratory** *a.*

ad•just *v.t.* to adapt; to put in working order; to accommodate. **-able** *a.* **-ment, -er, -or** *n.*

ad•ju•tant *n.* an assistant; staff officer who helps the commanding officer issue orders. **adjutancy** *n.*

ad•min•is•ter *v.t.* to manage public affairs or an estate; to dispense, as justice or relief; to give, as medicine; to apply, as punishment or reproof; *v.i.* to give aid (to). **administrable** *a.* **administrant** *a.* **executive;** *n.* one who administers. **administration** *n.* the executive part of a government. dispensation; direction. **administrative** a. **administrator** n. (*fem.* **administratrix**) one who directs; executes affairs of any kind.

administrator n. (*fem.* **administratrix**) one who directs; executes affairs of any kind.

ad·mi·ral n. a naval officer of the highest rank. **-ty** n.

ad·mi·ral n. a species of butterfly, esp. the red admiral.

ad·mire v.t. to regard with wonder and approval, esteem, or affection; to prize highly; v.i. to wonder; to marvel. **-r** n. **admiring** a. **admiringly** adv. **admirable** a. excellent; praiseworthy. **admirably** adv. **admiration** n.

ad·mis·si·ble a. allowable. **admissibly** adv. **admissibility** n. **admission** n. permission to enter; the price paid for this.

ad·mit v.t. to grant entrance; to concede as true; to acknowledge. pr.p. **-ting.** pa.p. and pa.t. **-ted. -tance** n. permission to enter.

ad·mix v.t. to mingle with something else. **-ture** n.

ad·mon·ish v.t. to reprove gently; to instruct or direct. **-er** n. **admonition** n. rebuke. **admonitory** a.

a·do n. fuss; bustle; trouble.

a·do·be n. sun-dried brick.

ad·o·les·cence n. stage between childhood and manhood; youth. **adolescent** a. and n.

a·dopt v.t. to receive the child of another and treat it as one's own; to select and accept as one's own, e.g. a view. **-er** n. **-able** a. **-ion** n. **-ive** a.

a·dore v.t. to worship; to love deeply; **-r** n. **adorable** a. **adorably** adv. **adorableness**, **adoration** n.

a·dorn v.t. to decorate; to deck or ornament; to set off to advantage. **-ing** a. **-ment** n.

ad·re·nal n. a small, ductless gland situated close to upper end of each kidney (same as *suprarenal*). **-in** n. the hormone of the adrenal glands.

a·drift adv. and a. floating at random; at mercy of the wind and tide.

a·droit a. dexterous; skillful; ingenious; adept. **-ly** adv. **-ness** n.

ad·sorb v.t. said of solids, to condense and hold a gas on the surface. **adsorption** n.

ad·u·late v.t. to praise or flatter in a servile manner; to fawn; to cringe. **adulation**, **adulator** n. **adulatory** a.

a·dult a. grown to maturity, or to full size and strength; appropriate for a grown-up; n. a grown-up person. **-ness, -hood** n.

a·dul·ter·ate v.t. to debase by addition of inferior materials; to vitiate; to corrupt. a. debased; guilty of adultery. **adulteration** n.

a·dul·ter·y n. violation of the marriage vows. **adulterer** n. (*fem.* **adulteress**). **adulterous** a. **adulterously** adv.

ad·um·brate v.t. to shadow forth; to give faint outline of; to forecast; to typify. **adumbral** a. shady. **adumbrant**, **adumbrative** a. **adumbration** n.

ad·vance v.t. to bring or push forward; to raise in status, price, or value; to propose as a claim; to supply beforehand, esp. money; v.i. to go forward; to improve; to rise in rank, etc. a. before the time. n. a forward movement; gradual approach; a paying out of money before due; an increase in price; expansion of knowledge. **-d** a. **-ment, -r** n.

ad·van·tage n. any state or means favorable to some desired end; v.t. to benefit, to promote the interests of; to profit. **-able** a. able to be turned to advantage. **-ous** a. **-ously** adv.

ad·vent n. arrival; approach; the anticipated coming of Christ; **-ual** adv.

ad·ven·ti·tious a. accidental; out of the proper place; extraneous. **-ly** adv.

ad·ven·ture n. risk; bold undertaking; chance; v.t. to risk. v.i. to venture; to dare. **-r** n. (*fem.* **adventuress**). **-some** a. **-someness** n. **adventurous** a. **adventurously** adv.

ad·verb n. a word used to modify a verb, adjective, or other adverb. **-ial** a. **-ially** adv.

ad·ver·sar·y n. an opponent.

ad·ver·sa·tive a. expressing opposition; not favorable.

ad·verse a. contrary; opposite in position; unfortunate; opposed. **-ly** adv. **-ness**, **adversity** n.

ad·vert v.i. to turn the mind or attention to. **-ence, -ency** n.

ad·ver·tise v.t. and v.i. to give public notice of. **-ment, -r** n. **advertising** n. and a.

ad·vice n. opinion offered as to what one should do; counsel.

ad·vise v.t. to give advice to; to counsel; to give information to; to consult (with). v.i. to deliberate. **advisability, advisableness** n. expediency. **advisable** a. prudent; expedient. **advisably** adv. **-d** a. judicious. **-dly** adv. purposely. **-r** or **advisor** n. **advisory** a.

ad·vo·cate n. a vocal supporter of any cause; v.t. to recommend; to maintain by argument. **advocacy, advocator** n.

adz, adze n. a carpenter's tool for chipping.

adze

ae·gis n. orginally the shield of Jupiter; (*Fig.*) protection.

ae·on, eon n. an infinitely long period of time; an age.

aer·ate v.t. to charge with carbon dioxide or other gas; to supply with air. **aeration, aerator** n.

aer·i·al a. pert. to, consisting of, air; n. and a. (*Radio and Television*) an insulated wire or wires, generally elevated above the ground and connected to a transmitting or receiving set. **-ly** adv.

aer·i·al·ist n. high-wire acrobat.

a·e·rie, a·e·ry n. the nest of a bird of prey, esp. of the eagle.

aer·o·dy·nam·ics n.pl. the science that treats of gases in motion.

aer·o·lite n. a meteorite; a meteoric stone. Also **aerolith, aerolithic** a. **aerology** n. the science which treats of the air and its phenomena.

aer·om·e·ter n. an instrument for measuring the weight or density of air and other gases. **aerometry** n. this science.

aer·o·naut n. a balloonist. **-ic** a. **-ics** n. the science of flight.

aer·o·sol n. a smoke, suspension of insoluble particles in a gas.

aer·o·stat n. a generic term for all lighter-than-air flying machines. **-ics** n. the science that treats of the equilibrium of gases, or of the buoyancy of bodies sustained in them.

aes·thet·ics n. the laws and principles determining the beautiful in nature, art, taste, etc. **aesthetic, aesthetical** a. **aesthetically** adv. **aesthete** n. a lover of the beautiful. **aestheticism** n.

a·far adv. from, at, or to a distance.

af·fa·ble a. ready to converse; easy to speak to; courteous; friendly. **affably** adv. **affability** n.

af·fair n. what is to be done; a business or matter; a concern; a thing.

af·fect v.t. to act upon; to produce a change in; to put on a pretense of; to influence. **-ed** a. inclined or disposed; not natural. **-edly** adv. **-edness** n. **-ing** a. moving; pathetic. **-ingly** adv. **-ation** n. a striving after artificial appearance or manners. **-ive** a. **-ively** adv.

af·fec·tion n. disposition of mind; goodwill; tender attachment; disease. **-ate** a. loving. **-ately** adv.

af·fer·ent a. conveying to, esp. of nerves carrying sensations to the centers.

af·fi·ance n. plighted faith; bethrothal; the marriage contract; reliance; confidence; v.t. to betroth.

af·fi·da·vit n. (Law) a written statement of evidence on oath.

af·fil·i·ate v.t. to adopt as a son; to receive into fellowship; to unite a society, firm, or political party with another, but without loss of identity. **affiliation** n.

af·fin·i·ty n. relationship by marriage; close agreement. **affined, affinitive** a.

af·firm v.t. to assert positively; to confirm; to aver; **-able** a. **-ably** adv. **-ance, -ant, -er** n. **-ative** a. ratifying; n. positive. **-atively** adv.

af·fix v.t. to fasten to; to attach; to append to. n. addition to either end of word to modify meaning or use.

af·fla·tus n. inspiration; impelling inner force.

af·flict v.t. to give continued pain to; to cause distress or grief to. **-ed, -ing** a. **-ingly** adv. **-ion** n. **-ive** a. **-ively** adv.

af·flu·ence n. abundance, esp. riches. **affluent** a. wealthy; flowing to; n. tributary of river. **affluently** adv. **afflux, affluxion** n.

af·ford v.t. to yield, supply, or produce; to be able to bear expense.

af·for·est v.t. to plant trees on a big scale. **-ation** n.

af·fran·chise v.t. to enfranchise; to free from slavery; to liberate. **-ment** n.

af·fray n. a noisy quarrel or fight in public; v.t. to frighten; to startle.

af·fright, af·fright·en v.t. to impress with sudden and lively fear.

af·front v.t. to confront; to meet face to face; to insult one to the face; to abash. **-ed** a.

a·field adv. to or in the field; abroad; off the beaten track.

a·fire adv. and a. on fire.

a·flame adv. and a. flaming; on fire.

a·float adv. and a. borne on the water.

a·flut·ter a. fluttering.

a·foot adv. on foot; astir.

a·fore adv. and prep. before.

a·foul adv. in collision, in a tangle.

a·fraid a. filled with fear; frightened.

a·fresh adv. anew; over again.

aft adv. or a. (Naut.) toward, or at, the stern.

af·ter prep. behind; later; in pursuit of; in imitation of; according to; adv. behind; a. in the rear; succeeding. **-ward (s)** adv. later; subsequently.

a·gain adv. another time; once more; in return; moreover.

a·gainst prep. in contact with; opposite to; in opposition to; in preparation for.

a·gape a. or adv. open-mouthed, as in wonder, expectation, etc.; gaping.

ag·ate n. a precious stone, composed of layers of quartz of different colors.

age n. the length of time a person or thing has existed; a period of time; periods of history; maturity; v.t. to cause to grow old; v.i. to grow old; pr.p. **aging. -d** a. of the age of **-dness** n. **-less** a.

a·gen·cy n. instrumentality; a mode of exerting power.

a·gen·da n. literally, things to be done; the items of business to be discussed at a meeting.

a·gent n. a person or thing that exerts power or has the power to act; one entrusted with the business of another.

ag·glom·er·ate v.t. and v.i. to collect into a mass; a. heaped up; n. (Geol.) a mass of compacted volcanic debris. **agglomeration** n. **agglomerative** a.

ag·glu·ti·nate v.t. to unite with glue; a. united, as with glue. **agglutination** n. **agglutinative** a.

ag·gran·dize v.t. to make greater in size, power, rank, wealth, etc.; to promote; to increase; to exalt. **-ment** n.

ag·gra·vate v.t. to make more grave, worse. **aggravating** a. making worse; provoking. **aggravatingly** adv. **aggravation** n.

ag·gre·gate v.t. to collect into a total; to accumulate into a heap; n. a sum or assemblage of particulars; the sum total; a. collected together. **aggrevation** n. **aggregative** a.

ag·gress v.i. to attack; to start a quarrel. **-ion** n. a first act of hostility; an unprovoked attack. **-ive** a. **-ively** adv. **-iveness, -or** n.

ag·grieve v.t. to give pain or sorrow to; to bear heavily upon; to vex; to afflict. **-d** a.

a·ghast a. struck with amazement, horror, terror.

ag·ile a. having the power of quick motion;

nimble. -ly *adv.* -ness, agility *n.*

ag•i•tate *v.t.* to throw into violent motion; to stir up; *v.i.* to cause a disturbance. -dly *adv.* agitation *n.* agitator *n.*

a•gleam *adv.* and *a.* gleaming.

a•glow *adv.* and *a.* glowing.

ag•nate *n.* any male relation on the father's side. *a.* related on the father's side; akin; allied. agnatic *a.* agnation *n.*

ag•no•men *n.* an additional name.

ag•nos•tic *n.* one who believes that God, life hereafter, etc., can neither be proved nor disproved. -ism *n.*

a•go, a•gone *adv.* and *a.* past; gone; in time past.

a•gog *a.* and *adv.* eagerly excited.

a•gon•ic *a.* not forming an angle.

ag•o•ny *n.* extreme physical or mental pain. agonize *v.t.* to distress with great pain; to torture. *v.i.* to writhe in torment. agonizing *a.* agonizingly *adv.*

ag•o•ra *n.* forum, public square, or market of ancient Greek towns. -phobia *n.* fear of open spaces.

a•gou•ti *n.* a genus of rodents or gnawing animals, natives of S. America.

a•grar•i•an *a.* relating to lands, their management and distribution; *n.* one who favors an equal division of property. -ize *v.t.* -ism *n.*

a•gree *v.i.* to be of one mind; to acquiesce; to resemble; *(Gram.)* to correspond in gender, case, or number. -ing *pr.p.* -d *pa.p.* -able *a.* consenting; favorable; suitable; pleasant; congenial. -ably *adv.* -ableness, -ment *n.*

ag•ri•cul•ture *n.* the science and practice of the cultivation of the soil. agricultural *a.* agriculturist or agriculturalist *n.*

a•gron•o•my *n.* rural economy; husbandry. agronomial, agronomic, agronomical *a.* agronomics *n.pl.* the science of management of farms. agronomist *n.*

a•ground *adv.* and *a.* on the ground; stranded; run ashore; beached.

a•gue *n.* *(Med.)* intermittent malarial fever. -d, aguish *a.*

a•head *adv.* farther forward; in advance; in front; head foremost.

aid *v.t.* and *v.i.* to help; to relieve. *n.* help; assistance; the person or thing which aids; auxiliary; assistant. aide *n.*

ai•guille *n.* *(Geol.)* a sharp, slender rock; a drill for boring rock. -tte, -t *n.* the tag of a shoelace.

ail *v.t.* to trouble; disturb; to pain; afflict. *v.i.* to feel pain; to be ill. -ing *a.* -ment *n.* illness.

ai•le•ron *n.* adjustable flaps near the tips of the wings of an airplane.

aim *v.t.* to point at; to direct; to endeavor after; to intend; *n.* direction; end; purpose; intention. -less *a.* -lessly *adv.* -lessness *n.*

air *n.* the atmosphere; a gas; a light breeze; a tune; manner, bearing of a person; carriage; appearance; mien. *v.t.* to expose to air or heat, for drying or warming; to parade before the public. -s *n.pl.* an affected manner. -ing *n.* a ride or walk in the open air. -y *a.* of air; exposed to the air; lighthearted. -ily *adv.* gaily; merrily;

lightly. -iness *n.* openness to the air; gaiety. —condition *v.t.* to provide a building, etc. with air through a filtering apparatus. — conditioning *n.* -craft *n.* all kinds of machines for flying. -drome *n.* an airport. -field *n.* tract of land, used for accommodation and maintenance of aircraft. -foil *n.* any surface wing, etc. to help in lifting or controlling an aircraft. -plane *n.* a heavier-than-air aircraft. -port *n.* a terminal station for passenger airplanes. air sacs *n.pl.* air cells in the bodies of birds. -ship *n.* lighter-than-air machine, developed from balloon. -sick *adj.* ill from air travel. -strip *n.* concrete runway on an airfield. -tight *a.* admitting no air. -way *n.* a prepared route for travel by airplane.

aire•dale *n.* a kind of large terrier, with a close, wiry coat of tan and black.

aisle *n.* the wing of a building; any lateral division of a church; the passageways between rows.

aitch•bone *n.* the rump bone of an ox; the cut of beef surrounding it.

a•jar *adv.* partly open, as a door.

a•kim•bo *adv.* with a crook; bent.

a•kin *a.* related by blood; allied by nature; having the same properties.

al•a•bas•ter *n.* gypsum; a semitransparent kind of soft marble-like mineral; *a.* made of, or white as, alabaster. alabastrine *a.*

a•lac•ri•ty *n.* cheerful readiness; eagerness; briskness.

a•lar *a.* winglike; pert. to wings; having wings.

a•larm *n.* sound giving notice of danger; a mechanical contrivance to rouse from sleep; *v.t.* to fill with apprehension; to call to arms. -ingly *adv.* -ist *n.* one given to exciting alarm, esp. needlessly.

a•las *interj.* an exclamation of sorrow, pity, etc.

a•late *a.* having wings; winged. Also -d *a.*

alb *n.* a vestment of white linen, reaching to the feet, worn by R.C. clergy.

al•ba•core *n.* tunny fish.

al•ba•tross *n.* a large web-footed seabird commonest in the South Seas.

al•be•it *conj.* although; even though.

al•bi•no *n.* a person, or animal, with an abnormal whiteness of the skin and hair, and a pink color in the eyes. albinism *n.*

al•bum *n.* a book for autographs, photographs, stamps, etc.; a book of selections.

al•bu•men *n.* white of egg; a similar substance found in the tissues of animals and plants. albumin *n.* any of a class of proteins, necessary for growth in the body. albuminoid *n.* albuminous *a.*

al•bur•num *n.* sapwood, part of tree under bark and outside heart up which sap rises.

al•che•my *n.* the forerunner of modern chemistry. Its chief aims were (*a*) transmuting the baser metals into gold, and (*b*) discovery of an elixir of life. alchemic *a.* alchemist *n.*

al•co•hol *n.* pure spirit; a liquid of strong pungent taste, the intoxicating element in fermented or distilled liquor. -ism *n.*

a morbid condition caused by overindulgence in alcoholic liquor. -ic *a.* *n.* one addicted to the immoderate use of alcohol.

al•cove *n.* a recess in a room.

al•de•hyde *n.* a liquid produced by the oxidation of alcohol.

al•der *n.* a tree of birch family, growing in marshy soil.

al•der•man *n.* a civic dignitary.

ale *n.* liquor made from malt by fermentation.

a•lem•bic *n.* a vessel of glass or metal formerly used in distillation.

a•lert *a.* watchful; vigilant; brisk; nimble; active; *n.* a signal by sirens of air attack; period of air raid. -ly *adv.* -ness *n.*

al•ex•an•drine *n.* a verse of six iambic feet.

a•lex•i•a *n.* inability to understand written language.

al•fal•fa *n.* plant of the pea family.

al•fres•co *a.* and *adv.* in the fresh air.

al•ga *n.* (*Bot.*) one of the algae *pl.* plants found in seawater, and in slow-moving fresh or stagnant water. algal, algoid, algous *a.* algology *n.* scientific study of marine plants.

al•ge•bra *n.* a branch of mathematics. -ic(al) *a.* -ically *adv.* -ist *n.*

al•gid *a.* cold. -ity, -ness *n.* algific *a.*

a•li•as *adv.* otherwise; *n.* an assumed name.

al•i•bi *n.* (*Law*) a plea that the prisoner was elsewhere when the crime was committed; excuse.

al•ien *a.* of another country; foreign; different in nature; estranged; *n.* a non-naturalized foreigner. -able *a.* -ability *n.* -ate *v.t.* -ation, -ator *n.* -ism *n.* study of mental diseases. -ist *n.*

a•lif•er•ous *a.* having wings.

a•light *adv.* or *a.* on fire; illuminated.

a•light *v.i.* to dismount; to finish one's journey; to fall; to descend.

a•lign *v.t.* to adjust by a line; to line up; to range; *v.i.* to form in a line; to fall in, as troops. Also aline, -ment *n.*

a•like *a.* having likeness; similar; *adv.* similarly; equally.

al•i•ment *n.* nourishment; nutriment; (*Law*) provision for maintenance. *v.t.* to maintain. -al *a.* -ally *adv.* -ary *a.* -ation *n.* the process of introducing nutriment into the body.

al•i•mo•ny *n.* means of living, esp. an allowance made to a wife out of her husband's income.

al•i•quant *a.* (of a number) not dividing without remainder.

al•i•quot *a.* dividing exactly, or without remainder.

a•live *a.* having life; existent; active; alert.

al•ka•li *n.* one of a class of chemical compounds which combine with acids to form salts. alkalify, -ze *v.t.* and *v.i.* to become alkaline; *pa.p.* -fied. -fiable *a.* -metry *n.* the quantitative estimation of the strength of alkalis. -ne *a.* -nity *n.* alkaloid *n.* nitrogenous organic compound; *a.* resembling an alkali in properties.

all *a.* the whole of; every one of; *n.* whole amount; whole duration of; *adv.* wholly; entirely.

al•lay *v.t.* to lighten; to make quiet; to lessen grief or pain. -er, -ment *n.*

al•le•ga•tion *n.* affirmation; that which is positively asserted. allege *v.t.* to bring forward with positiveness; to plea, or excuse; to declare; affirm; cite. allegeable *a.* allegedly *adv.*

al•le•giance *n.* the duty of a subject to his government or superior; loyalty; an oath of homage. allegiant *a.* loyal; *n.* one who owes allegiance.

al•le•go•ry *n.* a narrative in which abstract ideas are personified; a description to convey a different meaning from that which is expressed; a continued metaphor. allegoric (-al) *a.* allegorically *adv.* allegorist *n.*

al•le•lu•iah *n.* song of praise to the Almighty.

al•ler•gy *n.* hypersensitivity to particular substances; susceptibility to ill effects from eating some foods. allergen *n.* a substance which induces allergy. allergic *a.*

al•le•vi•ate *v.t.* to make light; to lighten; to ease; to afford relief; to mitigate. alleviation *n.* alleviative *a.* alleviator *n.*

al•ley *n.* a narrow passage between buildings; a garden path.

al•li•ance *n.* persons, parties, or states allied together for a common purpose.

al•li•ga•tor *n.* a reptile distinguished from crocodile by a broad flat head, depressed muzzle and unequal teeth.

alligator

al•lit•er•ate *v.i.* to begin each word with the same letter or sound. alliteration *n.* alliterative *adj.*

al•lo•cate *v.t.* to distribute; to assign to each his share; to place. allocation *n.*

al•lo•cu•tion *n.* a formal address, esp. of the Pope to his clergy.

al•lot *v.t.* to divide by lot; to distribute as shares. -ting *pr.p.* -ted *pa.p.* and *pa.t.* -ment *n.* what is allotted; distribution; a share.

al•lot•ro•py *n.* property of some chemical substances of being found in two or more different forms. allotropic *a.* allotropism *n.*

al•low *v.t.* to acknowledge; to permit; to give; to set apart; *v.i.* to provide. -able *a.* -ance *n.* -edly *adv.*

al•loy *v.t.* to melt together two or more metals; to reduce the purity of a metal by mixing with a less valuable one; to debase; *n.* any mixture of metals.

A

al•spice n. a spice.
al•lude v.i. to refer indirectly to; to hint at; to suggest.
al•lure v.t. to tempt by a lure, offer, or promise. -ment n. alluring a. alluringly adv.
al•lu•sion n. a passing or indirect reference; a hint; a suggestion. allusive a. referring to indirectly; symbolical. allusively adv.
al•lu•vi•on n. land formed by washed-up earth and sand. alluvium n. waterborne matter deposited on low-lying lands.
al•ly v.t. to join by treaty, marriage, or friendship; pr.p. -ing; pa.p. and pa.t. allied. ally n. a person, family country, etc., bound to another, esp. of nations in wartime; a partner.
al•ma•nac n. a calendar of days, weeks and months, to which astronomical and other information is added.
al•might•y a. all-powerful; omnipotent. almightiness n.
al•mond n. the kernel of the nut of the almond tree.
al•mon•er n. one who distributes alms or bounty. almonry n.
al•most adv. very nearly; all but.
alms n. gift offered to relieve the poor; a charitable donation.
al•oe n. a bitter plant used in medicine; a purgative drug, made from the juice of several species of aloe.

aloe

a•loft adv. on high; (Naut.) on the yards or rigging.
a•lone a. solitary; single; adv. by oneself; singly.
a•long adv. in a line with; throughout the length of; lengthwise; onward; in the company of (followed by with); prep. by the side of. -side adv. by the side of.
a•loof a. reserved in manner, almost unsociable; adv. at a distance; apart. -ness n.
al•o•pe•cia n. disease causing loss of hair.
a•loud adv. with a loud voice or noise; loudly; audibly.
alp n. a high mountain; mountain pastureland. Alps n.pl. the mountains of Switzerland. alpine a. pert. to the Alps; n. a plant that grows on high ground. -inist n.
al•pac•a n. a sheeplike animal of Peru; a thin kind of cloth made of the wool of the alpaca.
al•pen•horn, alp•horn n. a long wooden horn curving towards a wide mouthpiece, used by Swiss herds. alpenstock n. a long, stout staff, shod with iron, used by mountaineers.
al•pha n. the first letter of Greek alphabet.
al•pha•bet n. letters of a language arranged in order; first principles. -ic, -ical a. -ically adv. -ize v.
al•read•y adv. before this; even now; even then; previously to the time specified.
al•so adv. and conj. in like manner; likewise; further.
al•tar n. a table or raised structure in a place of worship.
al•ter v.t. to change; v.i. to become different. -ably a -ability n. -ation n.
al•ter•cate v.i. to contend in words; to wrangle. altercation n. a dispute.
al•ter•nate a. occurring by turns; one following the other in succession. -ly adv. alternate v.t. to cause to follow by turns; v.i. to happen by turns. alternation n. alternative a. offering a choice of two things; n. a choice of two things. alternatively adv. alternator n. (Elect.) a dynamo for producing alternating current.
al•though conj. admitting that; notwithstanding that.
al•tim•e•ter n. an instrument for taking altitudes; in aviation, barometer to show height.
al•ti•tude n. height; perpendicular elevation above a given level.
al•to n. (Mus.) part sung by lowest female voice.
al•to•geth•er adv. wholly, entirely, quite; on the whole.
al•tru•ism n. the principle of living for the good of others (opp. to egoism). altruist n. altruistic a. unselfish. altruistically adv.
al•um n. a double sulfate of alumina and potash.
a•lu•mi•num n. a whitish metal produced largely from bauxite; it is strong, light, malleable. alumina, alumine n. an oxide of aluminum; the clay, loam, etc., from which alum is obtained. aluminate v.t. to impregnate with alum. aluminic a. aluminiferous a. containing alum or alumina. aluminite n. a sulfate of alumina.
al•ve•o•lar a. pert. to or resembling the sockets of the teeth. alveolate a. pitted; honeycombed. alveolus n.
al•ways adv. at all times; perpetually; invariably; regularly.
a•lys•sum n. a species of rock plant.
am the first person sing. pres. indic. of the verb to be.
a. m. before noon.
a•mal•gam n. a compound of mercury with another metal; a mixture of different substances. -ate v.t. to mix a metal with quicksilver; to compound; to consolidate; to combine (esp. of business firms); v.i. to coalesce; to blend; to fuse. -ation n. -ative a. -ator n.
a•man•u•en•sis n. one who writes what another dictates, or copies what another has written; a secretary. pl. amanuenses.
am•a•ranth n. an imaginary purple flower which never fades; a purplish color; also

a real flower. **amaranthine** *a.*

am•a•ryl•lis *n.* a plant, the belladonna lily.

a•mass *v.t.* to heap up; to collect; accumulate.

am•a•teur *n.* one who cultivates any study, art, or sport for the love of it, and not for money. -ish *a.* unskilled; clumsy. -ism, -ishness *n.*

am•a•tive *a.* pert. to love; amorous.

am•a•tol *n.* explosive of ammonium nitrate of trinitrotoluene (**T.N.T.**).

am•a•to•ry *a.* pert. to or causing love. **amatorial** *a.* **amatorially** *adv.*

a•maze *v.t.* to fill with astonishment or wonder; to confound; to perflex. **-dly** *adv.* **-ment** *n.* astonishment, surprise. **amazing** *a.* **amazingly** *adv.*

Am•a•zon *n.* one of a mythical race of female warriors of Scythia; a masculine woman. **Amazonian** *a.*

am•bages *n.pl.* circumlocution; subterfuge; evasion; used in *pl.*

ab•bas•sa•dor *n.* an envoy of highest rank sent to a foreign country. **ambassadress** *n. fem.* **-ial** *a.* **-ship** *n.*

am•ber *n.* a yellowish, brittle fossil resin of vegetable origin, used in making jewelry, etc.

am•ber•gris *n.* a fragrant, ash-colored, waxy substance, derived from a biliary secretion of the spermaceti whale.

am•bi•dex•ter *n.* one able to use either hand with equal dexterity; a double-dealer. **-ity** *n.* **ambidextrous** *a.* **ambidextrously** *adv.*

am•bi•ent *a.* encompassing on all sides.

am•bi•gu•i•ty *n.* any statement that may be interpreted in more than one way. **ambiguous** *a.* **ambiguously** *adv.* **ambiguousness** *n.*

am•bit *n.* circuit or compass; sphere of action; scope.

am•bi•tion *n.* an eager desire for the attainment of honor, fame, or power; aim; aspiration. **ambitious** *a.* **ambitiously** *adv.*

am•biv•a•lence, am•biv•a•len•cy *n.* in psychoanalysis, the simultaneous operation in the mind of two conflicting wishes. **ambivalent** *a.*

am•ble *v.i.* to move along easily and gently; *n.* a peculiar gait of a horse; a stroll. **-r** *n.* **ambling** *a.* **amblingly** *adv.*

am•bro•sia *n.* (*Myth.*) the food of the ancient Greek gods which conferred immortality; an exquisite dish. **-l** *a.*

am•bu•lance *n.* a covered vehicle for the transport of the injured or sick.

am•bu•lant *a.* walking. **ambulate** *v.i.* to walk backwards and forwards. **ambulation** *n.* walking. **ambulatory** *a.* having power of walking; *n.* a cloister for walking exercise.

am•bush same as ambuscade. *n.* a surprise attack; the place of ambush; *v.i.* to lie in wait; *v.t.* to attack from a concealed position.

a•me•lio•rate *v.t.* and *v.i.* to make better; to improve. **amelioration** *n.* **ameliorative** *a.*

a•men *adv.* or *interj.* so be it; truly; verily.

a•me•na•ble *a.* liable to be brought to account; easily led; willing to yield or obey. **amenability, -ness** *n.* **amenably** *adv.*

a•mend *v.t.* to change for the better; to improve; *v.i.* to grow better. **-able** *a.* **-atory** *a.* **-ment** *n.* **-s** *n.pl.* reparation for loss or injury; compensation.

a•men•i•ty *n.* pleasantness in situation, climate, manners, or disposition.

a•merce *v.t.* to punish by a fine. **amerciable** *a.* liable to a fine. **-ment** *n.*

A•mer•i•can *n.* in, of, or characteristic of the United States or America. *n.* a native, citizen or resident of America or the United States. **-ism** *n.* **-ize** *v.t.* and *v.i.* **-ization** *n.*

am•e•thyst *n.* a kind of quartz; violet, purple, or blue color. **-ine** *a.*

a•mi•a•ble *a.* worthy of love or affection; sweet-tempered. **amiably** *adv.* **amiability** *n.* Also **-ness.**

am•i•ca•ble *a.* friendly; peaceable. **amicably** *adv.* **amicability** *n.* Also **-ness.**

a•mid, a•midst *prep.* in the middle of; among.

am•i•no ac•ids a group of nitrogenous organic compounds, basic constituents of proteins.

a•miss *a.* wrong; faulty; improper; *adv.* in a faulty manner.

am•i•ty *n.* friendship.

am•me•ter *n.* an instrument used to measure the strength of an electric current.

am•mo•ni•a *n.* a pungent, alkaline gas, very soluble in water; a solution of this gas in water, for household use. **-c, -cal, -d** *a.* **ammonium** *n.* hypothetical base of ammonia.

am•mu•ni•tion *n.* military projectiles and missiles of all kinds.

am•ne•sia *n.* memory loss.

am•nes•ty *n.* an act of oblivion; a general pardon of political offenders.

a•moe•ba *n.* a minute animalcule of the simplest structure constantly changing in shape. *pl.* **amoebae, amoebas. amoeboid, amoebic** *a.*

amoeba

a•mok See amuck.

a•mong, a•mongst *prep.* mixed with; making part of; amidst.

a•mor•al *a.* nonmoral; heedless of morals.

ambulance

am•o•rous *a.* having a propensity for love and sexual enjoyment; in love. **-ly** *adv.* **-ness** *n.*

a•mor•phous *a.* without regular shape; shapeless; irregular; uncrystallized.

am•or•tize *v.t.* to pay off a debt, usually by periodic payments. **amortization** *n.*

a•mount *v.i.* to come to (in value or meaning); to be equal to; *n.* the sum total; the whole, or aggregate.

am•pere *n.* the unit of electric current. **amperage** *n.*

am•per•sand *n.* the name given to the sign &.

am•phib•i•a *n.pl.* animals that can live either on land or in water, as frogs, toads, newts, etc. **-n**, **amphibious** *a.*

am•phi•brach *n.* in prosody, a foot of three syllables, the middle one long, the first and last short.

am•phi•the•a•ter *n.* an edifice, having tiers of seats, encircling an arena, used for sports or spectacles.

am•pho•ra *n.* a two-handled earthenware vessel or jar, used by the ancient Greeks and Romans; 6 gallons.

amphora

am•ple *a.* of adequate size; copious. **amply** *adv.* **-ness** *n.*

am•pli•fy *v.t.* to extend; to enlarge; *v.i.* to dilate; to expatiate upon. **amplification, amplifier** *n.*

am•pli•tude *n.* largeness; extent; abundance; *Radio* (of a wave) vertical distance between its highest and lowest levels; amplitude modulation (AM) radio transmission by changing the amplitude of waves (contrasted with frequency modulation, FM); *(Elect.)* maximum value of an alternating current.

am•poule *n.* also **ampule**, a small sealed glass container holding hypodermic dose.

am•pul•la *n.; pl.* **ampullae**; a sacred vessel for holding oil; cruet holding wine and water for Mass.

am•pu•tate *v.t.* to cut off, as a limb of the body. **amputation** *n.* **amputee** *n.* one who has lost a limb through amputation.

a•muck, **a•mok** *adv.* to rush about frantically or murderously.

am•u•let *n.* a talisman; a charm.

a•muse *v.t.* to entertain agreeably; to occupy pleasantly; to divert. **-ment** *n.* **amusing** *a.*

an *a.* the form of the indefinite article used before a vowel sound.

An•a•bap•tist *n.* one who denies the validity of infant baptism and advocates rebaptism of adults.

a•nab•o•lism *n. (Physiol.)* the constructive form of metabolism; the building-up of tissues by plant or animal.

a•nach•ro•nism *n.* a chronological error. **anachronistic, anachronous** *a.*

an•a•con•da *n.* a gigantic, nonvenomous snake of tropical S. America.

an•a•glyph *n.* a figure or ornament cut in low relief; a cameo. **-ic** *a.*

an•a•gram *n.* a transposition of the letters of a word or phrase to form a new word or phrase. **-matic, -al** *a.* **-matically** *adv.* **-matize** *v.t.* **-matism** *n.*

a•nal *a.* pert. to or near the anus.

an•a•lects, an•a•lec•ta *n.pl.* an anthology of short literary fragments. **analectic** *a.*

an•a•lep•sis *n. (Med.)* restoration of strength after disease. Also **analepsy.** **analeptic** *a.*

an•al•ge•sia *n. (Med.)* absence of pain while retaining tactile sense; painlessness. **analgesic** *a.* insensible to or alleviating pain; *n.* a drug which relieves pain.

a•nal•o•gy *n.* resemblance in essentials between things or statements otherwise different. **analogic, analogical** *a.* **analogically** *adv.* **analogize** *v.t.* to explain by analogy. **analogism** *n.* an argument proceeding from cause to effect. **analogist** *n.* **analogous** *a.* **analogously** *adv.* **analogue** *n.* a word or thing resembling another.

a•nal•y•sis *n.* the resolution, separating, or breaking up of anything into its constituent elements; a synopsis. *pl.* **analyses. analyzable** *a.* **analyzation** *n.* **analyze** *v.t.* to take to pieces; to examine critically part by part. **analyst** *n.* one skilled in analysis. **analytic, analytical** *a.* **analytically** *adv.* **analytics** *n.pl.* the technique of logical analysis.

an•a•pest, an•a•paest *n.* in prosody, a foot of three syllables, two short or unaccented followed by one long or accented syllable. **-ic** *a.*

an•ar•chy *n.* want of government in society; lawless disorder in a country; a political theory, which would dispense with all laws, founding authority on the individual conscience. **anarchic, anarchically** *adv.* **anarchize** *v.t.* **anarchism, anarchist** *n.*

a•nath•e•ma *n.* the word used in the R.C. church as part of the formula in excommunication; something highly distasteful to one; **-tic** *a.* **-tization** *n.* **-ize** *v.t.*

a•nat•o•my *n., pl.* **anatomies,** art of dissecting an animal or a plant; study of form or structure of an animal; the body; a skeleton. **anatomic, anatomical** *a.* **anatomically** *adv.* **anatomize** *v.t.* **anatomist** *n.*

an•ces•tor *n.* forefather; forebear. **ancestral** *a.* **ancestry** *n.*

an•chor *n.* a heavy iron instrument by which a ship is held fast to the sea bottom; *v.t.* to weight down; **-age** *n.* a sheltered place where a ship may anchor. **-ed** *a.* to cast anchor, to let down anchor. to weigh anchor, to raise anchor.

an•chor•ite, an•chor•et *n.* one who lives apart, renouncing the world for religious reasons; a hermit. **anchoress, -ss** *n.* anchorage *n.*

an•cho•vy *n.* small fish of the herring family.

an•cient *a.* very old; antique; venerable; one who lived in olden times. **-ly** *adv.* **-ness** *n.* **-ry** *n.*

an•cil•lar•y *a.* giving help to; attending upon.

and *conj.* added to; together with.

an•dan•te *a.* or *adv.* moving rather slowly, but in a steady, flowing manner.

and•iron *n.* a utensil for supporting logs in a fireplace.

an•dro•gen *n.* male sex hormone.

an•drog•y•nous *a.* having the characteristics of both sexes; hermaphrodite. Also **androgynal. androgyny** *n.*

an•ec•dote *n.* a brief account of any fact or happening (often amusing); **anecdotage** *n.* **anecdotal** *a.* **anecdotist** *n.*

an•e•lec•tric *a.* nonelectric; *n.*

a•ne•mia *n.* also **anaemia**, disease characterized by a deficiency of blood or of hemoglobin. **anemic** *a.*

a•nem•o•ne *n.* plant of crowfoot family; wind flower. **sea anemone** *n.* name given to certain plant-like marine animals.

a•nent *prep.* concerning; about; as to.

an•e•roid *a.* denoting a barometer depending for its action on the pressure of the atmosphere on a metallic box almost exhausted of air, without the use of mercury or other fluid.

an•es•the•sia, an•aes•the•sia *n.* absence of sensibility to external impressions, particularly touch. Also **anesthesis. anesthetic** *n.* a drug which induces insensibility to pain; *a.* producing loss of feeling and sensation. **anesthetically** *adv.* **anesthetize** *v.t.* **anesthetist** *n.*

an•eu•rism *n.* (*Med.*) a local widening or dilatation in the course of an artery.

a•new *adv.* in a new form or manner; newly; over again; afresh.

an•gel *n.* a heavenly messenger; a spirit who conveys God's will to man. **angelfish** *n.* a bright-colored tropical fish. **ic (al)** *a.* **-ically** *adv.*

an•ge•lus *n.* a short devotional service in the R.C. Church held morning, noon, and sunset.

an•ger *n.* a strong passion or emotion excited by injury; rage; *v.t.* to excite to wrath; to enrage. **angry** *a.* roused to anger; displeased; enraged; inflamed. **angrily** *adv.* **angriness** *n.*

an•gi•na *n.* (*Med.*) inflammation of the throat, e.g., quinsy. **angina pectoris**, a heart disease.

an•gi•o•sperm *n.* (*Bot.*) a plant whose seeds are enclosed in a seed vessel.

an•gle *n.* a fishhook; a rod and line for fishing; *v.i.* to fish with rod, line, and hook; **-r** *n.*

an•gle *n.* a corner; the point at which two lines meet.

An•gli•can *a.* English: of, or belonging to,

Church of England; *n.* a member of Church of England. **-ism** *n.*

an•gli•cize *v.t.* to make or express in English idiom. **anglicism** *n.* **anglify** *v.t.*

An•glo- *prefix*, an angle, combining to form many compound words. **Anglophile** *a.* favoring anything English; *n.* a supporter of English customs, manners, or policy.

An•go•ra *n.* a Turkish province in Asia minor, famous for a breed of goats; cloth made from hair of these goats.

an•guish *n.* acute pain of body or of mind; grief; anxiety; moral torment. **-ment** *n.*

an•gu•lar *a.* having angles; sharp-cornered; (of people) not plump; gawky; irascible. **-ity** *n.* **-ly** *adv.* **angulate** *a.*

an•hy•dride *n.* (*Chem.*) a compound formed from an acid by evaporation of water. **anhydrous** *a.* entirely without water.

an•il *n.* a West Indian shrub from the leaves and stalks of which indigo is made. **-ine** *n.* a product used in the manufacture of brilliant dyes, colored inks, soaps, explosives, etc.

an•ile *a.* like an old woman; imbecile. **anility** *n.* senility.

an•i•mad•vert *v.t.* to consider disparagingly; to comment on censoriously; to reprove. **animadversion** *n.*

an•i•mal *n.* a living creature having sensation and power of voluntary motion; a living organism, distinct from plants; *a.* **-cule** *n.* a very minute animal (*pl.* **-cules** or **-cula**). **-culine** *a.* **-ism** *n.* sensuality.

an•i•mate *v.t.* to give natural life to; to endow with spirit or vigor; to energize; to inspire; to make alive; *a.* living or organic. **-d** *a.* **-dly** *adv.* **animating** *a.* animation, animator *n.*

an•i•mism *n.* the belief that all forms of organic life have their origin in the soul. **animist** *n.* **animistic** *a.*

an•i•mos•i•ty *n.* violent hatred; active enmity.

an•i•mus *n.* animosity; temper; grudge.

an•ise *n.* an herb with pungent smell and bearing aromatic seeds. **aniseed** *n.* seed of anise.

an•kle *n.* the joint connecting the foot with the leg. **-t** *n.* a sock which reaches just above the ankle; an ornament for the ankle.

an•nals *n.pl.* history of events recorded each year; a yearly chronicle. **annalize** *v.t.* **annalist** *n.*

an•neal *v.t.* to heat, and then cool slowly, for the purpose of rendering less brittle.

an•nex *v.t.* to unite at the end; to subjoin; to bind to; to take additional territory under control; *n.* something joined on. **-ation, -ion, -ment** *n.*

an•ni•hi•late *v.t.* to reduce to nothing; to destroy; to make null and void. **annihilable** *a.* **annihilation, annihilator** *n.*

an•ni•ver•sa•ry *a.* yearly; annual; *n.* day on which event is yearly celebrated.

an•no•tate *v.t.* to mark in writing; to write explanatory notes, esp. upon literary text. **annotation, annotator** *n.* **annotatory** *a.*

an•nounce *v.t.* to give first public notice of;

to proclaim; to promulgate; to publish. -ment, -r *n*.

an·noy *v.t.* disturb continually; to torment; tease. -ance *n*.

an·nu·al *a*. yearly; *n*. a periodical published once a year; a plant which completes its life cycle within a year. -ly *adv*.

an·nu·i·ty *n*. a fixed sum of money payable each year for a number of years, or for life. annuitant *n*.

an·nul *v.t.* to make void; to nullify *pr.p*. -ling; *pa.t*. and *pa.p*. -led. -ment *n*.

an·nu·lar *a*. ring-shaped; like a ring. annulated *a*. annulet *n*. annularly *adv*. annulose *a*. annulation *n*.

an·num *n*. year.

an·nun·ci·ate *v.t.* to announce; to proclaim. annunciation, annunciator *n*. annunciatory *a*.

an·ode *n*. positive electrode of a voltaic current; (*Radio*) plate of an electron tube.

an·o·dyne *n*. a drug or measures which relieve pain.

a·noint *v.t.* to pour oil upon; to rub over with an ointment or oil. -ed *a*. -ment *n*. the Lord's anointed.

a·nom·a·ly *n*. deviation from the common rule; irregularity. anomalism *n*. anomalistic, anomalous *a*.

a·non *adv*. quickly; at once. ever and anon.

a·non·y·mous *a*. applied to a writing or work of which the author is not named. anonym *n*. -ly *adv*. anonymity *n*.

a·noph·e·les *n*. the mosquito carrying the parasite which causes malaria.

an·oth·er *a*. not the same; one more; *pron*. anyone else.

an·swer *v.t.* to speak or write in return; to vindicate. -able *a*. -er *n*. to answer for.

ant *n*. a small mebranous-winged insect living in colonies in wood or the ground.

ant

-bear *n*. the great anteater of South America. anteater *n*. one of several quadrupeds. -hill *n*.

ant- *prefix* a combining form, against, used to form compounds. antacid *a*. counteracting acidity.

an·tag·o·nize *v.t.* to contend violently against; to act in opposition. antagonism, antagonist *n*. antagonistic *a*. antagonistically *adv*.

ant·arc·tic *a*. relating to southern pole or region near it.

an·te *n*. in poker, a player's stake.

an·te- *prefix* meaning *before*. antebellum *a*. before the war. antecedent *a*. going before in time, place, rank, etc. *n*. that which goes before.

an·te·date *v.t.* to date before the true time; to precede in time.

an·te·di·lu·vi·an *a*. pert. to before the Flood.

an·te·lope *n*. (*pl*. -lope, -lopes) a hoofed ruminant.

an·te·me·rid·i·an *a*. before noon (abbrev. a.m.)

an·ten·na *n*. feeler of an insect, crustacean, etc. *pl*. antennae. antenna *n*. (*Radio*) a wire for sending or receiving electric waves.

an·te·pe·nult *n*. last syllable but two of word. -imate *a*.

an·te·ri·or *a*. before; occurring earlier. -ity *n*.

an·te·room *n*. a room giving entry to another.

an·them *n*. a hymn sung in alternate part; church music adapted to passages from the scriptures; song of praise.

an·ther *n*. the little sac in a flower containing the pollen or fertilizing dust. -al *a*.

an·thol·o·gy *n*. orig. a collection of flowers; a collection of literary passages or poetry. anthologist *n*.

an·thra·cene *n*. product from distillation of coal tar, used in manufacture of dyes. anthracite *n*. coal, nearly pure carbon.

an·thrax *n*. a carbuncle; a malignant disease in cattle and sheep.

an·thro·po- *prefix* meaning man, combining to form derivatives. anthropogency *n*. science of development of man. anthropoid *a*. manlike.

an·thro·pol·o·gy *n*. study of man, including all aspects of his evolution, physical and social. anthropological *a*. anthropologically *adv*. anthropologist *n*.

an·thro·pom·e·try *n*. the scientific measurement of the human body.

an·thro·po·mor·phism *n*. the conception of God as a human being with human attributes. anthropomorphist *n*. anthropomorphize *v.t.* to invest with human qualities. anthropomorphic *a*.

an·thro·po·mor·pho·sis *n*. transformation into human shape.

an·ti- *prefix* meaning *against, opposite, instead of*, combining to form derivations; contracted to ant- before a vowel.

an·ti·bi·ot·ic *n*. substance which acts as an antibacterial agent.

an·ti·bod·y *n*. a substance in blood which counteracts growth and harmful action of bacteria.

an·tic *a*. odd; fanciful; grotesque; *n*. a comical trick or action.

An·ti·christ *n*. a name given in the New Testament to various incarnations of opposition to Christ.

an·tic·i·pate *v.t.* to be beforehand in thought or action; to forestall. anticipant *a*. anticipation *n*. anticipative *a*. anticipatively, anticipatorily *adv*. anticipatory *a*.

an·ti·cli·max *n*. a sentence or figure of speech in which ideas are arranged in descending order of importance.

an·ti·cy·clone *n*. an outward flow of air in a spiral movement from an atmospheric area of high pressure, tending to produce steady weather.

an·ti·dote *n.* a remedy which counteracts the effects of a poison. **antidotal** *a.*

an·ti·freeze *n.* a substance added to a liquid (as in automobile radiators) to prevent freezing.

an·ti·gen *n.* a substance which can produce the formation of antibodies in the bloodstream.

an·ti·his·ta·mine *n.* any of several drugs used to treat allergies.

an·ti·log·a·rithm *n.* the complement of a logarithm or of a sine, tangent, or secant.

an·til·o·gy *n.* a contradiction in terms, or in two separate passages of a book. **antilogous** *a.*

an·ti·ma·cas·sar *n.* an ornamental covering for chair backs, etc.

an·ti·mo·ny *n.* a whitish, brittle chemical element; a bad conductor of heat; used as an alloy in medicine and the arts. **antimonial** *a.* **antimoniate** *n.* **antimonic,** **antimonious** *a.* **antimonite** *n.*

an·ti·pas·to *n.* an appetizer course; hors d'oeuvres

an·tip·a·thy *n.* opposition; aversion; dislike. **antipathetical** *a.* **antipathic** *a.* hostile to. **antipathist** *n.*

an·ti·phon, an·tiph·o·ny *n.* the chant, or alternate singing, in choirs. **-al** *a.;* **-ally** *adv.* **-ic, -ical** *a.*

an·tiph·ra·sis *n.* use of words in a sense opposite to their proper meaning. **antiphrastic,** **antiphrastical** *a.* **antiphrastically** *adv.*

an·tip·o·des *n.pl.* those living on opposite sides of globe; regions directly opposite any given point on globe.

an·ti·pope *n.* one who usurps the papal office; rival to pope properly elected by cardinals. **antipapal** *a.*

an·ti·py·ret·ic *n.* any agent which lowers temperature in fevers; *a.* counteracting fever.

an·tique *a.* ancient; old-fashioned; obsolete; aged; *n.* relic of bygone times. **antiquarian** *n.* student of antiquity or antiquities. *a.* pert. to old times or objects; out-of-date; obsolete. **antiquarianism** *n.* study of antiquities. **antiquary** *n.* an antiquarian. **antiquate** *v.t.* to render obsolete. **antiquated** *a.* very old; out of date. **antiquity** *n.* ancient times. **antiquities** *n.pl.* the remains and relics of ancient times.

an·ti·Sem·i·tism *n.* widespread outburst of hatred against members of the Hebrew race leading to persecution. **anti-Semite** *n.* **anti-Semitic** *a.*

an·ti·sep·sis *n.* prevention of sepsis; destruction or arresting of growth of living microorganisms which cause putrefaction. **antiseptic** *n.* a disinfectant.

an·ti·so·cial *a.* averse to social intercourse; opposed to social order.

an·ti·the·ism *n.* opposition to the belief in the existence of God. **antitheist** *n.* **antitheistic** *a.*

an·tith·e·sis *n.* a direct opposition of words or ideas. *pl.* **antitheses. antithetic,** **antithetical** *a.*

an·ti·tox·in *n.* a toxin which neutralizes another toxin in the blood serum. **antitoxic** *a.*

an·ti·trust *a.* opposed to trusts or monopolies.

ant·ler *n.* a horn of an animal of the deer family. **-ed** *a.*

antler

an·to·nym *n.* a word of contrary meaning.

an·trum *n.* a cavity, esp. sinus of the upper jaw. *pl.* **antra.**

a·nus *n.* the lower orifice of the alimentary canal.

an·vil *n.* an iron block, usually steel-faced, upon which blacksmith's forgings are hammered and shaped. **-led** *a.*

anx·i·e·ty *n.* distress of mind; disquietude; uneasiness. **anxious** *a.* **anxiously** *adv.*

an·y *a.* one out of many; some; *adv.* to any extent; at all. **-body** *n.* any person. **-one** *pron.* any person. **-thing** *n.* any one thing, no matter what.

a·or·ta *n.* the great artery leading from the left ventricle of the heart. **-l, aortic** *a.*

a·pace *adv.* at a quick pace; hastily; swiftly; fast.

A·pach·e *n.* one of a tribe of American Indians.

a·part *adv.* separately; aside.

a·part·heid *n.* racial segregation.

a·part·ment *n.* a room in a house; a suite of rooms; lodgings.

ap·a·thy *n.* indifference. **apathetic** *a.* indifferent.

ape *n.* a monkey, esp. one without a tail; one of the larger species, e.g. chimpanzee, gorilla, etc.; a mimic; *v.t.* to imitate. **-r, -ry** *n.* apish *a.*

a·pe·ri·tif *n.* alcoholic drink taken before meals.

ap·er·ture *n.* an opening; a hole.

a·pex *n.* the top, peak, or summit of anything. *pl.* **apexes** or **apices.**

a·pha·sia *n.* loss of power of expressing ideas in words, often due to brain disease; loss of power of remembering words. **aphasic** *a.*

a·phe·li·on *n.* point of planet's orbit most distant from sun.

aph·o·rism *n.* a maxim. **aphoristic** *a.* **aphoristically** *adv.* **aphorize** *v.t.* and *v.i.* **aphorist** *n.*

a·phra·sia *n.* inability to use connected language; speechlessness.

Aph·ro·di·te *n. (Myth.)* the Greek goddess of love and beauty. **aphrodisiac** *a.* exciting sexual desire.

a·pi·ar·y *n.* place where bees are kept. **apiarian** *a.* **apiarist, apiculture** *n.*

a·piece *adv.* for each one.

a·plomb *n.* perpendicularity; uprightness; *(Fig.)* self-assurance; coolness.

A

a·poc·a·lypse n. an unveiling of hidden things; revelation; disclosure. **Apocalypse** n. (Bib.) the last book of the New Testament, called the Revelation of St. John. **apocalyptic** a., **apocalyptically** adv.

a·poc·ry·pha n.pl. originally hidden or secret things not suitable to be seen by the uninitiated. -l a.

a·pod·o·sis n. (Gram.) the clause, in a conditional sentence, which expresses result as distinct from the protasis. pl. **apodoses.**

ap·o·gee n. that point in the orbit of a heavenly body at the greatest distance from the earth (opposed to perigee); the culmination; zenith. **apogeal, apogean** a.

ap·o·logue n. a parable; a fable.

a·pol·o·gy n. something spoken in defense; expression of regret at offense. **apologize** v.i. **apologist** n. **apologetic, apologetical** a. **apologetically** adv. **apologetics** n. the branch of theology charged with the defense of Christianity. **apologia** n. a defense in writing of the author's principles, etc.

ap·o·plex·y n. a sudden loss of consciousness, sensation, and voluntary motion, due generally to rupture of a blood vessel in the brain. **apoplectic** a.

a·pos·ta·sy, a·pos·ta·cy n. the act of renouncing one's faith, or principles, desertion of a cause. **apostate** n. renegade; traitor; deserter; a. false; traitorous. **apostatic, apostatical** a. **apostatize** v.i.

a·pos·tle n. one sent out to preach or advocate a cause; one of the twelve disciples of Christ. **apostolate** n. the office or dignity or mission of an apostle. **apostolic, apostolical** a. **apostolically** adv. **apostolicism** n.

a·pos·tro·phe n. an address delivered to the absent or the dead, as if present; a mark (') indicating possessive case, or omission of one or more letters of a word. **apostrophic** a. **apostrophize** v.t. and i. to address by, or to use, apostrophe.

a·poth·e·car·y n. one who prepares or sells drugs for medicines.

ap·o·thegm n. a short, pithy saying, a maxim; a proverb. **apothegmatic, apothegmatical** a.

a·poth·e·o·sis n. the act of raising a mortal to the rank of the gods; deification. **apotheosize** v.t.

ap·pall v.t. to overwhelm with sudden fear; to confound; to scare; to terrify; -ing a. shocking.

ap·pa·ra·tus n. things provided as a means to an end; collection of implements or utensils for effecting an experiment, or given work. s. and pl.

ap·par·el n. clothing; dress; garments; (Naut.) rigging, etc.; v.t. and pr.p. to dress.

ap·par·ent a. visible; evident; obvious. -ly adv.

ap·pa·ri·tion n. appearance (esp. inexplicable); ghost. -al a.

ap·peal v.i. to invoke; to call to witness; to solicit aid; (Law) to reopen a case before a higher court; to be pleasing to mind or senses. n. an urgent call for sympathy or aid; personal attraction. -able, -ing a. -ingly adv. -ingness n.

ap·pear v.i. to come in sight; to become visible; to seem. -ance, -er n.

ap·pease v.t. to quiet; to calm; to pacify; to dispel anger or hatred. **appeasable** a. -ment n. pacifying; -r n.

ap·pel·lant n. (Law) one who appeals to a higher court against the verdict of a lower tribunal; **appellancy** n. **appellation** n. name; title; designation. **appellational, appellative** a. **appellatively** adv.

ap·pend v.t. to hang or attach to; to add. -age n. something added. -ant n. an adjunct or unessential thing; a. hanging to; annexed.

ap·pen·di·ci·tis n. (Path.) inflammation of the appendix vermiformis. **appendectomy** n. surgical removal of appendix.

ap·pen·di·cle n. a small appendage. **appendicular** a.

ap·pen·dix n. thing added; an adjunct; supplement at end of book. pl. -es, **appendices.**

ap·per·cep·tion n. (Philos.) an act of voluntary consciousness; a mental perception of self as a conscious agent.

ap·per·tain v.i. to belong by nature; to relate. -ing a. -ment n. **appertinent** a.

ap·pe·tite n. desire as for food, drink, rest, etc. **appetitive** a. **appetize** v.t. to create an appetite. **appetizer** n. **appetizing** a.

ap·plaud v.t. and v.i. to praise by clapping; to acclaim; commend; extol. -er, **applause** n.

ap·ple n. fruit of the apple tree; the apple tree.

ap·pli·cant n. one who applies; a candidate; a petitioner. **applicability** n. the quality of being suitable. **applicable** a. **applicableness** n. **applicably** adv. **applicate** a. applied or put to some use. **application** n. **applicatory** a.

ap·plied pa.p. and pa.t. of apply.

ap·ply v.t. to place one thing upon another; to employ for a particular purpose; v.i. to agree with; to be relevant; to have recourse to; to become a candidate. **appliance** n. act of applying; thing applied; an instrument or tool.

ap·point v.t. to set apart; to assign; to ordain; to decree; to designate for an office; to fix (a date); to equip. -ed a. established, furnished. -ee, -ment n. -ments n.pl. equipment; furnishings; fittings.

ap·por·tion v.t. to divide and share in just proportion. -ment n.

ap·po·site a. appropriate; well-adapted. -ly adv. -ness n. **apposition** n. the act of placing beside. **appositional** a.

ap·praise v.t. to put a price upon; to fix the value of. **appraisal**, -ment, -r n. **appraising** a.

ap·pre·ci·ate v.t. to value justly; v.i. to rise in value. **appreciation** n. a rise in value. **appreciative, appreciatory** a. **appreciatively** adv. **appreciable** a. that may be estimated. **appreciably** adv.

ap·pre·hend v.t. to seize; to arrest; to fear.

apprehensible *a.* **apprehension** *n.* **apprehensive** *a.* filled with dread; suspicious. **apprehensively** *adv.*

ap•pren•tice *n.* one bound to another to learn a trade or art; beginner; *v.t.* **-ship** *n.*

ap•prise *v.t.* to inform; to give notice.

ap•proach *v.i.* to come near; *v.t.* to enter into negotiations with. **-es** *n.pl.* **-able** *a.* **-ability** *n.*

ap•pro•ba•tion *n.* approval; sanction. **approbate** *v.t.* **approbative, approbatory** *a.*

ap•pro•pri•ate *v.t.* to take as one's own; to set apart for a particular purpose; to claim; *a.* suitable; fitting. **-ly** *adv.* **-ness,** **appropriation** *n.* **appropriative** *a.* **appropriator** *n.*

ap•prove *v.t.* to be pleased with; to commend; to accept; to sanction officially. **approval** *n.* **approving** *a.*

ap•prox•i•mate *v.t.* to come near to; *a.* near to; nearly correct; not quite exact. **-ly** *adv.* **approximation** *n.* a close estimate.

ap•pur•te•nance *n.* that which appertains or is annexed to another thing; adjunct. **appurtenant** *a.*

a•pri•cot *n.* an oval, orange-yellow fruit.

A•pril *n.* the fourth month of the year.

á pri•o•ri from cause to effect.

a•pron *n.* a covering or protection worn in front to protect the clothes.

a•pro•pos *adv.* at the right time; *adj.* apt, relevant.

apse *n.* semicircular recess at east end of church. **apsidal** *a.*

ap•sis *n.* the point at which a planet is nearest to, or farthest from, the sun; *pl.* **apsides. apsidal** *a.*

apt *a.* fit; suitable. **-ly** *adv.* **aptitude** *n.* faculty for learning. **-ness** *n.*

aq•ua *n.* water.

aq•ua•ma•rine *n.* a semiprecious stone; *a.* of a sea-green color.

aq•ua•plane *n.* a plank or boat towed by a fast motorboat.

a•quar•i•um *n.* a glass tank in which is kept living specimens of water animals and plants; *pl.* **-s,** or **aquaria.**

A•quar•i•us *n.* (*Astron.*) the Water Bearer, the 11th sign of the zodiac.

a•quat•ic *a.* growing or living in water; practiced on, or in, water.

aq•ua•tint *n.* and *v.i.* an etching process.

aq•ue•duct *n.* a course, channel, or bridge for conveying water either under- or aboveground.

a•que•ous *a.* watery; made of, or from, water. **-ly** *adv.*

aq•ui•line *a.* belonging to the eagle; curving; hooked like the beak of an eagle.

Ar•ab *n.* native of Arabia; an Arab horse. **Arabian** *n.* **Arabic** *n.* the language of the Arabians.

ar•a•besque *n.* an ornament after the Arabian manner, with intricate interlacing of foliage, fruits, etc **-d** *a.*

ar•a•ble *a.* fit for plowing or tillage.

a•rach•nid *n.* one of the *Arachnida*, the spiders, scorpions, mites, etc. **arachnoid, arachnoidal** *a.*

ar•bi•ter *n.* (*fem.* **arbitress**) an umpire; a judge in a dispute. **arbitrable** *a.* **arbitrage** *n.* **arbitral** *a.* **arbitrament** *n.* decision; authoritative judgment. **arbitrary** *a.* guided by will only; high-handed; despotic; absolute. **arbitrarily** *adv.* **arbitrariness** *n.* **arbitrate** *v.t.* and *v.i.* to hear and give an authoritative decision in a dispute. **arbitration** *n.* a method of settling disputes between persons, parties and nations by an agreement on both sides to accept the findings of a third party. **arbitrator** *n.* (*fem.* **arbitratrix**) a referee; an umpire.

ar•bor *n.* a garden seat sheltered or enclosed by trees.

ar•bo•re•tum *n.* botanical garden for special planting and growing of trees; (*pl.* **arboreta**). **arborous** *a.*

ar•bu•tus *n.* evergreen shrub with scarlet berries.

arc *n.* a curved line or any part of a curve forming segment of a circle.

ar•cade *n.* a series of arches, generally supported by pillars; a walk, arched above.

Ar•ca•di•a *n.* region in the Peloponnesus conceived by poets to be a land of shepherds and shepherdesses. **Arcadian** *a.* **Arcady** *n.* an ideal rustic place.

ar•ca•num *n.* a secret; mystery. *pl.* **arcana.**

arch *a.* cunning; sly; mischievous; roguish. **-ness** *n.*

arch *prefix* used as *a.* chief; first of a class, as in *arch*bishop, etc. **-angel** *n.* an angel of supreme order.

arch *n.* a structure for support; *v.t.* or *v.i.* to form an arch; to bend into an arch. **-ed** *a.*

arch

ar•chae•ol•o•gy, archeology *n.* the study of human antiquities. **archaeologist** *n.* **archaeological** *a.*

ar•cha•ic *a.* antiquated; ancient; obsolete. **-ally** *adv.* **archaism** *n.* a word, expression or idiom out of date. **archaist** *n.* an antiquary. **archaistic** *a.*

ar•che•an *a.* pert. to the oldest period of geological time.

arch•er *n.* one who shoots with a bow; a bowman. **-y** *n.* art and practice of shooting with bow and arrow.

ar•che•type *n.* the original pattern or model from which a thing is made or copied; prototype. **archetypal** *a.*

ar•chi•pel•a•go *n.* a group of islands. *pl.* **-es. archipelagic** *a.*

ar•chi•tect *n.* one skilled in the art of building; designer. **-ural** *a.* **-urally** *adv.* **-ure** *n.* the art of building.

ar•chives *n.pl.* place in which public or historical records are stored; public records. **archivist** *n.* a keeper of archives.

arc•tic *a.* pert. to the regions near the N. Pole.

ar•dent *a.* burning; passionate; eager. **-ly** *adv.* ardency, ardor *n.*

ar•du•ous *a.* high and lofty; steep; difficult to overcome; strenuous. **-ly** *adv.*

are present indicative plural of the verb to **be.**

are *n.* metric unit of land measure containing 100 square meters, about 119.6 square yards.

a•re•a *n.* an open space; total outside surface of a thing; superficial extent.

a•re•na *n.* any place of public contest. **-ceous** *a.* like sand; sandy.

ar•e•om•e•ter *n.* an instrument for measuring the specific gravity of fluids.

a•rete *n.* a sharp mountain ridge; a rocky spur.

ar•gent *a.* made of, or like, silver.

ar•gil *n.* pure clay; potter's earth.

ar•gon *n.* an inert gas used for filling electric light bulbs.

ar•go•sy *n.* a large, richly laden merchant ship.

ar•gue *v.t.* to prove by reasoning; to discuss; to persuade by debate; *v.i.* to prove; to offer reasons; to dispute. **arguable** *a.* **-r** *n.* argument *n.* a reason offered in proof for or against a thing; the subject of a speech, etc. **argumentation** *n.* **argumentative** *a.* **argumentatively** *adv.* **argumentativeness** *n.*

a•ri•a *n.* (*Mus.*) a melody as distinct from harmony; a solo part in a cantata, opera, oratorio, etc.

ar•id *a.* dry; parched; barren; (*Fig.*) uninteresting. **-ity** *n.*

a•right *adv.* rightly.

a•rise *v.t.* to come up; to stand up; to get up; to come into view; to spring up; to occur; *pr.p.* arising. *pa.p.* arisen. *pa.t.* arose.

ar•is•toc•ra•cy *n.* originally the rule of the best; later, the rule of a hereditary upper class; privileged class in a state; the nobility; upper classes. **aristocrat** *n.* a member of the aristocracy. **aristocratic** *a.* **aristocratically** *adv.*

Ar•is•tot•le *n.* (384-322 B.C.) a great Greek philosopher, pupil and disciple of Plato. **Aristotelian** *n.* a follower of Aristotle.

a•rith•me•tic *n.* the science of numbers; the art of reckoning by figures; a work on this subject. **-al** *a.* **-ally** *adv.* **-ian** *n.* one skilled in arithmetic.

ark *n.* the large floating vessel in which Noah lived during the Flood (Genesis 6-8); vessel of bulrushes in which the infant Moses was placed (Exodus 2).

arm *n.* the limb extending from shoulders to hand; anything projecting from main body, as a branch; *v.t.* to give an arm to for support. **-less** *a.* without arms. **-ful** *n.* as much as the arms can hold.

arm *n.* a weapon; a branch of the army, e.g. infantry, artillery, etc.; *pl.* all weapons; *v.t.* to equip with weapons; *v.i.* to take up arms. **-ed** *a.* equipped with, or supported by, arms; fortified; strengthened.

ar•ma•da *n.* a fleet of armed ships.

ar•ma•dil•lo *n.* an animal, having the body encased in armor-like covering of small, bony shell plates.

Ar•ma•ged•don *n.* the scene of the last battle between the powers of good and evil.

ar•ma•ment *n.* forces equipped for war; munitions; the process of equipping forces in time of war.

ar•ma•ture *n.* armor; protective covering (of plants); part of magnet or dynamo which rotates in electrical generator; coil of wire in electric motor which breaks magnetic field.

ar•mi•stice *n.* a temporary or lasting cessation of hostilities; a truce.

arm•let *n.* band worn around arm.

ar•mor *n.* defensive covering for the body in battle. **—bearer** *n.* **—clad** *a.*

armor

ar•mor•y *n.* place where arms are stored; building for headquarters and drill area of National Guard unit; arsenal; (*Arch.*) science of heraldry.

ar•my *n.* a body of men trained and equipped for war; a military force; an organized body for some special purpose; large number of people.

a•ro•ma *n.* fragrance. **-tic** *a.*

a•round *adv.* in a circle; near; *prep.* on all sides of; about.

a•rouse *v.t.* to excite to action; to awaken; *v.i.* to wake. **arousal** *n.*

ar•peg•gi•o *n.* (*Mus.*) the sounding of notes of a chord in quick succession.

ar•que•bus *n.* an ancient form of handgun.

ar•raign *v.t.* to call or set a prisoner at the bar; to call to account; to accuse publicly. **-ment** *n.*

ar•range *v.t.* to put into order; to settle terms; to prepare; to adapt; to adjust; *v.i.* to make agreement; to take steps. **-ment,** **-r** *n.* **-ly** *adv.*

ar•rant *a.* notorious.

ar•ras *n.* tapestry; large tapestries, used as wall hangings.

ar•ray *v.t.* to set in order; to draw up, as troops for battle; to equip; *n.* order; equipment; fine apparel.

ar•rear *n.* the state of being behind. **-s** *n.pl.* moneys still owing; work still to be overtaken. **-age** *n.*

ar•rest *v.t.* to stop; to check; to hinder; to

seize by authority of law; to engage the attention; n. the apprehending of a person by the authority of law. -ation, -er, -or n. -ing a. impressive; striking. -ive a. calculated to draw attention. -ment n.

ar•rive v.i. to reach a point; to come to; to attain to any aim or object. **arrival** n.

ar•ro•gance n. insolent pride; intolerable presumption; overbearing manner. **arrogant** a. **arrogantly** adv. **arrogate** v.t. to claim unduly; to take upon one's self without authority.

ar•row n. a barbed missile shot from a bow; a sign to show direction. **-y** a. of, like an arrow. **— grass** n. small, erect, grasslike plants.

ar•row•root n. a nutritious starch used in puddings, cookies, etc.

ar•se•nal n. factory for military and naval arms and stores; an armory.

ar•se•nic n. a semimetallic element; the poisonous, whitish, or steel-gray powder of white oxide of arsenic. **arsenic, -al, arsenous** a.

ar•son n. the crime of intentionally setting on fire houses, buildings, ships, or other property.

art n. skill; human skill as opposed to nature; skill applied to music, painting, poetry, etc.; any of the subjects of this skill; a profession or craft; cunning; trick. **-s** n.pl. certain branches of learning, languages, history, etc. as distinct from natural science. **-ful** a. exhibiting art or skill; crafty; cunning. **-fully** adv. **-fulness** n. **-less** a. guileless. **-lessly** adv. **-lessness** n.

ar•ter•y n. a vessel carrying blood from the heart. **arterial** a. **arterialize** v.t. to change venous blood into arterial blood by oxygenization. **arterialization** n. **arteriole** n. a small artery. **arteriosclerosis** n. (Med.) a hardening of the arteries.

ar•te•sian well n. a well bored deep enough so that water rises to the surface of the ground by internal pressure.

ar•thri•tis n. inflammation of a joint; gout. **arthritic(al)** a.

ar•thro•pod n. an animal with segmented body and jointed limbs, e.g. a spider, crustacean, etc. **-al** a.

ar•ti•choke n. a plant with thistlelike head.

ar•ti•cle n. a clause or term in a contract, treaty, etc.; a literary composition in a journal, etc.; a rule or condition; an item; a commodity or object; (Gram.) one of the words a, an and the.

ar•tic•u•lar a. pert. to the joints.

ar•tic•u•late v.t. to connect by a joint; to utter clearly defined sounds; v.i. to be connected by joints; to speak in distinct syllables or words; a. jointed; of speech, clear, distinct. **-ly** adv. **-ness**; **articulation** n.

ar•ti•fact n. object made by man.

ar•ti•fice n. an artful or skilful contrivance; a ruse; a trick; cunning. **-r** n. a skilled workman; an inventor. **artifical** a. made by art; manufactured; affected in manners. **artifically** adv. **artificiality** n.

ar•til•lery n. cannon; troops trained in the use of guns.

ar•ti•san n. a craftsman.

art•ist n. one who practices one of the fine arts; applicable to any craftsman whose work is of high standard. **-ic(al)**, a. **-ically** adv. **artistry** n. artistic ability or effect.

Ar•y•an n. the progenitors of the Indo-European group, i.e. Celtic, Teutonic, etc.

as adv. like; in like manner; similar to; for example; conj. since; because; when; while; pron. that.

as•bes•tos n. a fibrous noninflammable mineral.

as•cend v.t. to climb, to mount; to walk up; v.i. to rise; to arise; to soar; to climb; to mount; to go back in time. **-able, -ible** a. **-ancy, -ency** n. superior or controlling influence; authority; domination.

as•cent n. the act of rising; the way by which one rises; a slope.

as•cer•tain v.t. to get to know; to find out for a certainty. **-able** a. **-ment** n.

as•cet•ic a. sternly self-denying; austere; strict; n. one who practices rigorous self-denial. **-ism** n. **-ally** adv.

as•cot n. a kind of scarf or broad tie.

as•cribe v.t. to attribute; to impute; to assign. **ascribable** a. **ascription** n.

a•sep•sis n. freeing from bacteria by use of antiseptics. **aseptic** a.

a•sex•u•al a. without sex; lacking sexual instinct or reproductive organs. **-ity** n.

ash n. a genus of trees of the olive family. **-en** a.

ash n. the dry white or grayish dust left after a substance has been burned. **-en** a. of the color of ashes; pale. **-tray** n. receptacle for cigarette ash. **-y** a.

a•shamed a. affected by shame.

a•shore adv. on or to shore.

A•sian, A•si•at•ic a. pert. to Asia or to the people of Asia.

a•side n. something said in an undertone, esp. on stage by an actor and supposed not to be heard by the other actors; adv. on or to one side; apart.

as•i•nine a. pert. to an ass; stupid.

ask v.t. to seek information; to interrogate; v.i. (for, about) to request.

a•skance, a•skant adv. towards one corner of the eye; awry; with disdain.

a•skew adv. askant; awry.

a•slant adv. in a slanting direction.

a•sleep adv. and a. in a state of sleep.

a•slope a. tilted; oblique.

a•so•cial a. not social.

as•par•a•gus n. a succulent vegetable with tender shoots.

as•pect n. look; appearance; view.

as•pen n. a tree known also as the trembling poplar.

as•per•ate v.t. to make harsh or uneven; to roughen.

as•per•i•ty n. roughness of surface, manner, or speech; harshness.

as•perse v.t. to slander; to defame; to vilify. **aspersion** n. slander. **aspersive, aspersory** a.

as•phalt n. a black, hard, tar-like substance,

used for paving, roofing, etc.; *v.t.* to cover with asphalt.

as•phyx•i•a, as•phyx•y *n.* suspended animation due to lack of oxygen in the blood; it is caused by obstructed breathing. **-te** *v.t.* to suffocate. **-tion** *n.*

as•pic *n.* the asp; *(Bot.)* the great lavender.

as•pic *n.* savory jelly containing pieces of fish, fowl, egg, etc.

as•pi•rate *v.t.* to pronounce with a full breathing sound. **aspiration** *n.*

as•pire *v.i.* to desire with eagerness; to strive towards something higher (usually followed by *to* or *after*). **aspirant** *a.* **aspiration, -r** *n.*

as•pi•rin *n.* a drug used for relief of headache, fever, etc.

ass *n.* a quadruped of the horse family; a donkey; *(Fig.)* a stupid person.

as•sail *v.t.* to leap or fall on; to attack; to ply with arguments, reproaches, etc. **-able** *a.* **-ant** *a.* and *n.*

as•sas•sin *n.* one who murders by secret or treacherous assault. **-ate** *v.t.* to murder by guile or by sudden violence. **-ation, -ator** *n.*

as•sault *n.* a violent onset or attack; *v.t.* to attack violently; to storm. **-able** *a.* **-er** *n.*

as•say *n.* trial; test; examination. *v.t.* to test. **-er** *n.*

as•sem•ble *v.t.* to bring or call together; to collect; to fit together the parts, e.g. of a machine; *v.i.* to meet together. **assemblage** *n.* a group, gathering. **assembly** *n.* a meeting; a company gathered; the putting together of parts.

as•sent *v.i.* to agree; to admit; to concur; *n.* acquiescence; approval. **-ation** *n.* servile assent; obsequiousness. **-er, -or** *n.* **-ient** *a.* giving assent; *n.* one who assents.

as•sert *v.t.* to declare strongly; to maintain or defend by argument. **-er, -or, -ion** *n.* **-ive** *a.* positive; self-confident. **-ively** *adv.* **-iveness** *n.* **-ory** *a.*

as•sess *v.t.* to fix the amount of a tax or fine; to tax or fine; to estimate for damage, taxation, etc.; to rate; to appraise. **-able** *a.* **-ment, -or** *n.*

as•sets *n.pl.* funds or property available for payment of debts, etc.; *n.sing.* an item of such property; a thing of value.

as•sev•er•ate *v.t.* and *v.i.* to assert positively or solemnly; to aver. **asseveration** *n.*

as•sid•u•ous *a.* constant in application or attention; diligent; hardworking. **-ly** *adv.* **-ness, assiduity** *n.*

as•sign *v.t.* to allot; to apportion; to give out; to fix; to transfer; to ascribe. **-able** *a.* **-ation** *n.* **-ment** *n.* an allotting to a particular person or use; a transfer of legal title or interest; a task assigned.

as•sim•i•late *v.t.* to make similar; to change into a like substance; to absorb into the system; to digest; *v.i.* to become similar; to be absorbed. **assimilation** *n.* **assimilative** *a.*

as•sist *v.t.* to help; to aid; to give support to; *v.i.* to lend aid; to be present. **-ance** *n.* **-ant** *a.* helping; acting under the direction of a superior; *n.* one who assists.

as•size *v.t.* to fix the rate of; to assess. **-ment** *n.* inspection of weights and measures. **-r** *n.*

as•so•ci•ate *v.t.* to join with as a friend, colleague, or partner; to class together; *v.i.* (foll. by *with*) to keep company; *n.* a companion; a coadjutor; a junior member; *a.* affiliated. **associable, associative** *a.*

as•so•nance *n.* a resemblance of sounds; imperfect rhyme in which vowel sounds are same, but consonants following are different, e.g. *blunder, slumber.*

as•sort *v.t.* to classify; to arrange; *v.i.* to suit or agree or match. **-ed** *a.* varied. **-edness, -ment** *n.*

as•suage *v.t.* to soften; to allay; to mitigate. **-ment, -r** *n.* **assuasive** *a.*

as•sume *v.t.* to take upon oneself; to take for granted; to usurp; *v.i.* to claim unduly. **assumable, -d** *a.* **-dly** *adv.* **assuming** *a.* **assumingly** *adv.* **assumption** *n.* the act of taking to or upon oneself by force or right; the act of taking for granted. **assumptive** *a.*

as•sure *v.t.* to make sure or certain; to affirm. **assurable** *a.* **assurance** *n.* promise; self-confidence; presumption. **-dly** *adv.*

as•ter *n.* a genus of plants so-called because the expanded flowers of various hues are like stars.

as•ter•isk *n.* the mark (*) used in printing to indicate words for reference or words omitted. **asterism** *n.* small cluster of stars.

a•stern *adv.* in, at, or toward the hinder part of ship.

as•ter•oid *n.* one of the smaller planets; *(Zool.)* starfish. **-al** *a.*

asth•ma *n.* a chronic disorder of the respiratory organs, marked by cough, labored breathing and feeling of suffocation. **-tic** *a.*

a•stig•ma•tism *n.* a defect of eye, attended with dimness of vision, due to malformation of lens of eye. **astigmatic** *a.*

a•stir *adv.* or *a.* on the move; alert.

as•ton•ish *v.t.* to impress with sudden surprise, wonder or admiration. **-ed, -ing** *a.* **-ingly** *adv.* **-ment** *n.*

as•tound *v.t.* to strike dumb with terror or amazement; to astonish greatly. **-ing** *a.*

as•tra•khan *n.* the skin of the young Persian lamb with soft, curling ringlets of wool; a cheap fabric, made in imitation.

as•tral *a.* pert. to the stars; star-shaped.

a•stray *adv.* out of the right way.

a•strict *v.t.* to bind fast; to confine; to restrict; to contract. **-ion** *n.* **-ive** *a.* astringent.

a•stride *adv.* straddling; with the legs apart; *prep.* with one foot on each side of an object.

as•tringe *v.t.* to bind together; to draw together. **-ncy** *n.* **-nt** *a.* binding; strengthening; *n.* a drug which causes contraction of the muscular fiber tissues. **-ntly** *adv.*

as•tro- *prefix* used in the construction of compound words having some reference to stars.

as•tro•labe *n.* instrument for finding altitude of stars, etc.

as•trol•o•gy n. science which professes to interpret the influence of heavenly bodies on human affairs. **astrologer** n. **astrologic, astrological** a.

as•trom•e•try n. the determination of the magnitudes of the fixed stars.

as•tro•naut n. a space traveler; **-ical** a. **-ics** n.

as•tron•o•my n. the science which studies the heavenly bodies. **astronomer** n. **astronomic, astronomical,** a. pert. to astronomy; boundless, countless, prodigious. **astronomize** v.i.

as•tro•phys•ics n. (Astron.) the study of the physical components of the stars.

as•tute a. cunning; shrewd; **-ly** adv. **-ness** n.

a•sun•der adv. apart; into different pieces; in a divided state.

a•sy•lum n. a sanctuary; refuge for criminals, debtors and others liable to be pursued; an institution for the deaf and dumb, the blind, or the insane; the protection afforded by such places.

a•sym•me•try n. want of symmetry. **asymmetric, asymmetrical** a.

a•syn•chro•nism n. lack of synchronism; want of correspondence in time. **asynchronous** a. not simultaneous.

at prep. denoting rest in a place, presence or nearness; near to, by, in; engaged on.

at•a•vism n. the recurrence in living organisms of hereditary characteristics, diseases, etc. which have skipped one or more generations. **atavistic** n.

a•tax•i•a n. (Med.) irregularity of bodily functions. **ataxic** a.

ate past tense of the verb eat.

a•the•ism n. disbelief in the existence of God. **atheist** n. **atheistic, atheistical** a. **athiestically** adv.

A•the•na, A•the•ne n. (Myth.) Greek goddess of wisdom, art, industries, and prudent warfare. **Athenian** n. native of Athens.

a•thirst a. thirsty; eager.

ath•lete n. one trained to physical exercises, feats or contests of strength, etc. **athletic** a. pert. to physical exercises, contests, etc.; strong; vigorous; muscular. **athletics** n.pl. athletic sports.

a•thwart prep. across; from side to side; adv. crosswise in oppositon.

a•tin•gle a. tingling.

At•lan•tic a. pert. to the ocean separating Europe and Africa from America; n. the ocean itself.

At•las n. (Myth.) a Titan, condemned by Zeus to carry the world on his shoulders. **atlas** n. a book of maps.

at•mo•sphere n. the mass of air, clouds, gases, and vapor, surrounding the earth or other heavenly body; any similar mass; atmospheric pressure; the air in any place, esp. if enclosed, e.g. in a theater. **atmospheric, atmospherical** a.

a•toll n. a ring-shaped coral reef.

at•om n. constituent of a chemical element; (Fig.) anything very small; a tiny bit. **-ic, -ical** a. **-ize** v.t. to reduce to atoms. **-izer** n. an instrument for reducing

liquid to the form of spray.

a•ton•al a. (Mus.) without tone. **atonic** a. without tone; unaccented; (Med.) lacking tone or energy.

a•tone v.t. to appease; v.i. to make amends or reparation for an offense. **-ment** n. amends; reconciliation.

a•top a., adv. on or at the top; prep. on top of.

a•tri•um n. the principal room of an ancient Roman house; (Anat.) an auricle of the heart.

a•tro•cious a. savagely brutal; extremely cruel; very wicked. **-ly** adv. **-ness** n. **atrocity** n. extreme wickedness; a brutal act.

at•ro•phy n. a wasting away through lack of nutrition or use; emaciation. Also v.t. and v.i. to waste away; to cause to waste away. **atrophic, atrophied** a.

at•ro•pin, at•ro•pine n. a poisonous alkaloid.

at•tach v.t. to bind, fasten, or tie; to take by legal authority; to bind by affection; v.i. to adhere; to be ascribed to. **-able** a. **-ed** a. fixed; fond of. **-ment** n.

at•tack v.t. to fall on with force; to assail with hostile criticism in words or writing; to set to work on; n. a violent onset or assault.

at•tain v.t. to reach by exertion; to obtain by effort; to accomplish; to achieve. **-able** a. **-ability, -ableness, -ment** n.

at•taint v.t. to stain or disgrace; to accuse of; to find guilty; to deprive of civil rights for treason; n. a taint or disgrace. **attainder** n. loss of civil rights after sentence of death or outlawry for treason or felony. **-ment** n.

at•tar n. a fragrant oil.

at•tempt v.t. to try; to endeavor to do; to attack; n. trial; an effort, esp. unsuccessful; an assault.

at•tend v.t. to accompany; to be present with or at; to give medical care to; v.i. to be present; to pay attention; to take care of; to wait on. **-ance** n. **-ant** a. **attention** n. careful observation; watching; act of civility; command issued, as in a military sense, to ensure readiness to act. **attentions** n.pl. courtship. **attentive** a. **attentively** adv.

at•ten•u•ate v.t. to make thin or fine, to make slender; to weaken the potency of; a. slender; thin; (Bot.) tapering. **attenuant, -d** a. **attenuation, attenuator** n.

at•test v.t. and v.i. to bear witness to; to vouch for; to certify. **-able, -ative** a. **-ation** n.

At•tic a. pert. to Attica or Athens. **attic** n. a room under the roof of a house.

at•tire v.i. to dress; to array in splendid garments; n. apparel; dress. **-ment,** **attiring** n.

at•ti•tude n. posture of a person; pose (in portrait).

at•tor•ney n. one put in the turn or place of another; one legally authorized by another to transact business; lawyer; solicitor. **attorn** v.t. to transfer; v.i. to transfer homage; to acknowledge a new landlord. **-ship, -dom** n.

A

at‧tract *v.t.* and *v.i.* to draw toward; to cause to approach. -able *a.* -ile *a.* attractive. attraction *n.* -ive *a.* -ively *adv.* -iveness *n.*

at‧tri‧bute *v.t.* to consider as belonging to; to ascribe to; *n.* something inherent in a person or thing.

at‧tri‧tion *n.* the act of wearing away by friction; state of being worn. attrite *a.* worn away by rubbing or friction; (*Theol.*) penitent through fear.

at‧tune *v.t.* to put in tune; to make musical; (*Fig.*) to bring into spiritual harmony.

a‧typ‧i‧cal *a.* not typical; abnormal. -ly *adv.*

au‧burn *a.* reddish brown; *n.* rich chestnut color.

auc‧tion *n.* a method of public sale whereby the object for sale is secured by highest bidder; *v.t.* to sell by auction. -eer *n.* one licensed to sell by auction; *v.i.* to sell by auction.

auc‧tion bridge *n.* a card game in which the players bid.

au‧da‧cious *a.* bold, fearless; impudent; -ly *adv.* audacity *n.* boldness, effrontery, impudence.

au‧di‧ble *a.* capable of being heard. audibly *adv.* audibility *n.*

au‧di‧ence *n.* the act of hearing; an assembly of hearers or spectators; a ceremonial reception. audient *a.* listening.

au‧di‧o *a.* electronic apparatus using audible frequencies (between 15-20,000 cycles).

au‧dit *n.* an examination, by qualified persons, of accounts of a business, public office, or undertaking; *v.t.* to test and vouch for the accuracy of accounts; listen. -ion *n.* the act, or sense, of hearing, hearing given to a performer as test. -orium *n.* the body of a concert hall or theater where the audience are seated; the nave of a church. -ory *a.* pert. to the sense of hearing; *n.* a lecture room; an audience.

au‧ger *n.* a boring tool for woodwork, like a large gimlet.

auger

aught *n.* anything; any part; zero; *adv.* to any extent.

aug‧ment *v.t.* to increase; to add to; *v.i.* to grow larger; *n.* an increase; a prefix added to the past tense of verbs to distinguish them from other tenses.

au‧gur *n.* a soothsayer; a diviner; *v.t.* to foretell; to presage; to prognosticate.

au‧gust *a.* majestic; imposing; sublime; magnificent; sacred.

Au‧gust *n.* the eighth month of the year.

Au‧gus‧tine *n.* a member of a monastic order which follows rules framed by St. Augustine.

auk *n.* a marine bird, of the Arctic regions.

aunt *n.* a father's or a mother's sister.

au‧ra *n.* a subtle invisible essence or fluid said to emanate from human and animal bodies, and even from things. -l *a.*

au‧ral *a.* pert. to the ear, or sense of hearing. -ly *adv.*

au‧re‧ole, au‧re‧o‧la *n.* a radiance around a sacred figure, in art.

au‧ric *a.* pert. to gold. aureate *a.* golden.

au‧ri‧cle *n.* the external ear; each of the two upper cavities of the heart. auricula *n.* a part like an ear. auricular *a.* auriculate, auriform *a.* ear-shaped.

au‧rif‧er‧ous *a.* yielding gold.

Au‧ro‧ra *n.* (*Myth.*) the Roman goddess of the dawn. aurora *n.* the dawn; the rosy tint in the sky before the sun rises; an orange-red color.

aus‧cul‧ta‧tion *n.* (*Med.*) listening to the movement of heart and lungs. ausculate *v.t.* and *v.i.*

aus‧pice *n.* favoring influence; an omen based on observing birds; augury; divination; *n.pl.* -s, protection; patronage. auspicate *v.t.* to predict; to inaugurate in favorable conditions. auspicious *a.* giving promise of success; favorable; propitious. auspiciously *adv.* auspiciousness *n.*

aus‧tere *a.* harsh; severe; strict; simple and without luxury. -ly *adv.* -ness, austerity *n.*

aus‧tral *a.* southern.

au‧tar‧chy *n.* absolute power; despotism; dictatorship. autarchic *a.*

au‧then‧tic *a.* genuine; real; not of doubtful origin; trustworthy; of attested authority. Also -al. -ally *adv.* -ate *v.t.* to prove to be genuine; to confirm. -ation, authenticity *n.*

au‧thor *n.* (*fem.* authoress) the beginner or originator of anything; the writer of a book, article, etc. -ial *a.*

au‧thor‧i‧ty *n.* legal power or right; accepted source of information; the writer himself; permission; a body or group of persons in control (often *pl.*). authoritarian *a.* advocating obedience to authority as opposed to individual liberty. authoritative *a.* having the weight of authority; justified. authoritatively *adv.*

au‧thor‧ize *v.t.* to empower; to make legal. authorization *n.*

au‧to *n.* (*Colloq.*) abbrev. for automobile. -ist *n.* a motorist. -mobile *n.* a road vehicle driven by mechanical power. -motive *a.*

au‧to‧bi‧og‧ra‧phy *n.* the story of a person's life, written by himself. autobiographer *n.* autobiographic *a.*

au‧to‧crat *n.* monarch who rules by his own absolute right; despot. -ic *a.* -ically *adv.* autocracy *n.*

au‧to‧gi‧ro *n.* airplane using horizontal revolving wings for vertical ascent and descent.

au‧to‧graph *n.* a person's signature; *a.* written in one's own handwriting; *v.t.* to write with one's own hand; to write one's signature.

au‧to‧mat‧ic *a.* self-acting; mechanical; not voluntary; done unconsciously; automat *n.* a restaurant which serves food using automatic devices.

au•to•mo•bile. See auto.

au•ton•o•my *n.* the right of self-government; independence; autonomous, autonomic *a.*

au•top•sy *n.* the dissection and examination of a dead body; a postmortem examination.

au•to•sug•ges•tion *n.* a mental process similar to hypnotism but applied by the subject to himself.

au•tumn *n.* the third season of the year, generally applied to September, October, and November; fall; the season of decay; the time of declining powers. -al *a.*

aux•il•ia•ry *a.* assisting; subsidiary; *n.* a helper; a verb which helps to form moods, tenses, or voice of another verb.

a•vail *v.i.* to profit by; to take advantage of; *v.t.* to benefit; to profit; *n.* advantage; profit; benefit; utility. -able *a.* capable of being used to advantage; procurable. -ability *n.*

av•a•lanche *n.* mass of snow and ice moving down from a height and gathering momentum in its descent; *(Fig.)* tremendous downpour.

av•a•rice *n.* greed; miserliness. avaricious *a.*

a•vast *interj.* cease! hold! stop! enough!.

a•ve *interj.* hail! farewell.

a•venge *v.t.* and *v.i.* to take satisfaction for an injury to; to punish a wrongdoer; to seek retribution. -ful *a.* -ment, -r *n.*

av•e•nue *n.* a wide street with houses and trees down each side.

a•ver *v.t.* to declare positively; to avouch; to assert; to allege. -ring *pr.p.*; -red *pa.p.* -ment *n.*

av•er•age *a.* containing a mean proportion; ordinary; normal; *n.* a medial estimate obtained by dividing the sum of a number of quantities by the number of quantities; *v.t.* to reduce to a mean.

a•verse *a.* reluctant (to do) or disinclined for; unwilling; set against (foll. by *to*). -ly *adv.* -ness *n.* aversion *n.* a strong dislike.

a•vert *v.t.* to turn away from or aside; to ward off. -ed *a.* -edly *adv.* -ible *a.*

a•vi•an *a.* pert. to birds. aviary *n.* an enclosed space for breeding, rearing and keeping of birds.

a•vi•a•tion *n.* the art of flying aircraft. aviate *v.i.* to fly. aviator *n.*

av•id *a.* eager; greedy; desirous. -ity *n.* hunger.

a•vo•ca•do *n.* the alligator pear.

av•o•ca•tion *n.* a distraction; a minor plausable occupation; a hobby; a side interest; avocative *a.* calling off; *n.* a dissuasion.

a•void *v.t.* to shun; to elude; to keep clear of; to eschew; to abstain from; to escape. -able *a.* -ance *n.*

a•vouch *v.t.* to declare positively.

a•vow *v.t.* to declare openly; to own; to confess freely; to acknowledge. -able *a.* -al *n.* an open declaration or admission.

a•wait *v.t.* to wait for; be in store for; attend; be ready for.

a•wake *v.t.* to rouse from sleep; *v.i.* to cease from sleep; *pa.t.* awoke; *pa.p.* awoke, -d; *a.* not asleep; alert; vigilant; alive. -n *v.t.* and *v.i.* to rouse from sleep; to awake; to excite. awak(en)ing *n.* a revival of interest or consciousness.

a•ward *v.t.* to adjudge; to decide authoritatively; to assign judicially; *n.* judgment; the recorded decision of an arbitrator in a court of law; thing awarded; prize.

a•ware *a.* watchful; mindful; conscious of; possessing knowledge of; sensible. -ness *n.*

a•wash *adv.* *(Naut.)* level with the surface of the water.

a•way *adv.* absent; apart; be gone!.

awe *n.* wonder mingled with veneration and dread; *v.t.* to inspire with awe. -some *a.* -struck, -stricken *a.* awful *a.* full of awe; filling with fear and admiration; impressive; awfulness *η.*

a•weigh *adv.* *(Naut.)* when a ship's anchor is just broken out of the ground; atrip.

aw•ful. See awe.

a•while *adv.* for a while.

awk•ward *a.* ungainly; difficult to manage; inconvenient; embarrassing. -ly *adv.* -ness *n.* awkward age, adolescence.

awl *n.* a small pointed instrument for boring holes in leather.

aw•ning *n.* a covering of canvas, etc. to shelter from the sun's rays.

a•woke. See awake.

a•wry *adv.* and *a.* twisted to one side; crooked (See wry).

ax, axe *n.* a tool for cutting, chopping or hewing.

axe

ax•es plural form of axe and axis.

ax•i•om *n.* a necessary and self-evident proposition, requiring no proof. -atic, -atical *a.* self-evident. -atically *adv.*

ax•is *n.* imaginary line around which a solid body rotates. *pl.* -s. axial *a.* forming the axis. axially *adv.*

ax•le, ax•le•tree *n.* a bar of wood or iron rod on which a wheel, or a system of wheels, turns.

a•za•lea *n.* a genus of pl ants allied to the rhododendron.

a•zo•ic *a.* pert. to that part of geologic time before animal life existed.

Az•tec *n.* a member of a people dominant in Mexican Empire at the time of the Sp. conquest.

az•ure *n.* sky blue; *a.* sky-blue.

Ba•al *n.* a false deity. *pl.* **Baalim. Baalist** *n.* a worshipper of Baal.

bab•ble *v.t.* and *i.* to chatter senselessly; to prate; *n.* prattling; idle talk; murmuring of running water. **-r** *n.* **babbling** *n.*

babe *n.* an infant; a young child.

ba•boon *n.* a species of monkey with large body, big canine teeth and capacious cheek-pouches.

baboon

ba•by *n.* an infant; a young child; *a.* pert. to a baby; small, as in — **grand** (piano), etc. **-hood** *n.* the period of infancy. **-ish** *a.* infantile; behaving like a young child.

bac•ca•lau•re•ate *n.* the university degree of bachelor.

Bac•chus *n.* (*Myth.*) the god of wine.

bach•e•lor *n.* an unmarried man; one who has taken the first degree at a university. **-hood, -ism, -ship** *n.*

ba•cil•lus *n.* microscopic, rod-like organisms, capable of causing certain diseases. *pl.* **bacilli, bacillar, bacillary** *a.* **bacilliform** *a.* of a rod-like shape.

back *n.* the upper or hinder part of the trunk of an animal; the hinder part of an object; a football player whose position is behind the line of scrimmage; *a.* at the rear of; not current (as a magazine); reversed; *adv.* to or toward a former place, condition, or time; away from the front; in return; *v.t.* to force backward; to support; to endorse, *v.i.* to move or go back. **-bone** *n.* the spine or vertebral column; firmness; courage. **backboned** *a.* **-er** *n.* supporter; **-field** *n.* the backs as in football who play behind the line. **-fire** *n.* in internal combustion engines, premature ignition of fuel, *v.i.* to do this; to go awry; **-ground** *n.* part behind foreground of a picture or stage setting; knowledge gained by experience. **—hand** *n.* writing sloped from left to right; a stroke in tennis with the hand turned backwards. **-handed** *a.* with the back of the hand; deceitful. **-lash** *n.* the jarring reaction of a machine due to the degree of play; **-log** *n.* an accumulation, a reserve amount. **-side** *n.* back or hinder part; the buttocks. **-slide** *v.i.* to slide backwards; to lapse from a high moral standard. **-stage** *adv.* behind the stage, in the wings, etc. **—talk** *n.* insolent reply; impertinence. **-track** *v.i.* to retreat; to return over the same route. **-ward** *adv.* with the back in advance; towards, or on, the back; in a reverse direction; *a.* directed to the back or rear; dull; shy; late. **-wash** *n.* backward current. **-water** *n.*

water held back by a dam; water thrown back by a paddle-wheel. **-woods** *n. pl.* outlying forest districts or remote undeveloped country. **-woodsman** *n.*

back•gam•mon *n.* a game played by two with 15 pieces each on a special board.

ba•con *n.* back and sides of hogs after being salted and smoked.

bac•te•ri•um *n.* group of nonspore forming bacteria. *pl.* **bacteria. bacterial** *a.* **bactericide** *n.* any agent capable of destroying bacteria. **bactericidal** *a.* **bacteriology** *n.* the study of bacteria.

bad *a.* ill or evil; wicked. **-ly** *adv.* **-ness** *n.* **bad blood,** ill feeling. **bad lands** *n. pl.,* badly eroded, barren land esp. in the Dakotas.

bade past tense of the verb **bid.**

badge *n.* an emblem, usually symbolic, worn to distinguish members of societies, regiments, etc.; mark; symbol.

badg•er *n.* a greyish-brown hibernating animal; *v.t.* to follow hotly as dogs do the badger; to tease, by persistent questioning.

badger

bad•min•ton *n.* a game similar to tennis with the substitution of shuttlecocks for tennis balls.

baf•fle *v.t.* to frustrate; to confuse. **-r** *n.* **baffling** *a.* disconcerting; confusing.

baf•fle *n.* a plate for regulating the flow of a liquid or gas; a metal plate used between the cylinders of an air-cooled motor engine to break up a stream of heated gases.

bag *n.* a sack or pouch; content of a sack; results of one's fishing or hunting; *v.t.* to put into a bag; *v.i.* to hang loosely. *pr.p.* **-ging.** *pa.p.* **-ged. -gage,** *n.* luggage. **and baggage,** with all one's belongings. **-giness** *n.* the state of being baggy (as trousers). **-gy** *a.* hanging loosely. **in the bag,** certain, assured. **to let the cat out of the bag,** to reveal a secret unwittingly.

bag•a•telle *n.* a thing of little worth; a game played with balls and a cue on a board.

ba•gel *n.* a doughnut-shaped roll.

bag•pipe *n.* musical reed instrument, common to Scotland. **-r** *n.*

bail *n.* (*Law*) security taken by the court that a person charged will attend at a future date to answer to the charge; one who furnishes this security; *v.t.* to obtain the release of a person from prison by giving security against his reappearance. **-able** *a.* **— bond** *n.* a bond given by a person who is being bailed and his surety. **bail out** *v.i.* to jump from an aircraft and descend by parachute.

bail *n.* a shallow vessel for clearing water out of a boat; *v.t.* to empty of water with some kind of water scoop. **-er** *n.*

bail• iff *n.* a minor officer of a court.

bail•i•wick n. bailiff's jurisdiction; (Fig.) one's special domain.

bait n. food set to entice fish or an animal; a lure; snare; v.t. to put food on a hook or in a trap as a lure. -er n. -ing a. and n.

bake v.t. to cook in an oven or over a fire; v.i. to work at baking. -house n. bakery n. a bakehouse. baking n. a batch of bread, etc. **a baker's dozen**, thirteen.

Ba•ke•lite n. a hard, strong synthetic resin used as a substitute for wood, bone, celluloid, etc., a trade name.

bal•ance n. an apparatus for determining the weight, or comparing the masses, of bodies; a poised beam with two opposite scales; part of a watch or clock which regulates the beats; payment still due, or cash in hand; v.t. to weigh, as in a balance; to render equal in proportion, etc.; to adjust, as an account; v.i. to be of the same weight. **— sheet** a. statement of the assets and liabilities of a company.

bal•co•ny n. a platform or gallery projecting from a building; a gallery in a theater or concert hall.

bald a. destitute of hair or feathers on the crown of the head; bare; without literary style. -head, -pate n. one destitute of hair. -ly adv. -ness n.

bal•er•dash n. a jargon of meaningless words jumbled together; nonsense.

bale n. that which causes sorrow or ruin. -ful a. -fully adv.

bale n. a package, compactly compressed, and wrapped in a protecting cover; v.t. to pack in bales. -r n. one employed in baling goods.

balk n. a crossbeam or rafter, of squared timber, stretching from wall to wall; an unploughed ridge of land; a barrier or check; a disappointment; a part of a billiard table; in baseball, an uncompleted pitch, entitling base runners to advance one base; v.t. to frustrate; to bar the way; v.i. to stop abruptly; refuse to move. -y a.

ball n. any round body; a sphere; the earth; bullet or shot; a delivery outside the strike zone by a pitcher; the heavy piece of a pendulum; v.t. and i. to form into a ball. **— bearings** n. hardened steel balls interposed in channels or 'races' between the rotating and stationary surfaces of a bearing to lessen friction. **— point pen** n. fountain pen with a tiny ball point leaving a fine trace of ink on the paper. **—race** n. the grooves in which the balls of a ball bearing run. **ball and socket**, a joint formed by a ball partly enclosed in a cup and so adjusted that it can move freely in all directions.

ball n. a social gathering for the purpose of dancing. -room, n.

bal•lad n. a story in verse, of popular origin, generally patriotic and sung orig. to the harp. -ist n. a composer or singer of ballads. -ry n. collected ballads; folk songs. -eer n.

bal•last n. heavy material taken on board ship to increase the vessel's draft and steadiness; sandy material dredged from river beds used for concrete; that which renders anything steady; v.t. to load with ballast; to steady.

bal•le•ri•na n. a female ballet dancer.

bal•let n. a representation, consisting of dancing and miming, aiming to express an idea or tell a story, to the accompaniment of music.

ballistic a. pert. to a projectile and its flight.

bal•lis•tics n.pl. scientific study of motion of projectiles.

bal•lon n. bag designed to float in the air and unequipped for mechanical propulsion; anything inflated. -ing n. -ist n.

bal•lot n. secret voting; slip of paper used in secret voting; v.t. to draw lots.

balm a fragrant plant; any fragrant or healing ointment; anything which soothes pain. -iness n. -y a. fragrant; bearing balm.

bal•sa n. the extremely light wood of a W. Indian tree.

bal•sam n. a name applied to many aromatic resins and oils with stimulant and tonic properties; a healing agent. -ic n. soothing, oily. -ous a. soothing. -y a.

bal•us•ter n. a stone or wooden shaft turned and molded, used to support a handrail. -ed a. provided with balusters. **balustrade** n. a row of balusters supporting a railing.

bam•boo n. a genus of immense grasses in the tropics.

ban n. proclamation; a sentence of outlawry; a prohibition; v.t. to prohibit; to curse; pr.p. -ning. pa.t. and pa. p. -ned.

ba•nal a. trite, trivial, petty, commonplace, -ity n.

ba•nan•a n. the edible fruit of a tropical plant.

banana

band n. a cord, tie or fillet; an endless belt used for driving wheels or rollers. -box n. a light cardboard box for millinery.

band n. players of musical instruments in combined performance; a company united for common purpose; v.t. to bind together; v.i. join together. -master n. director of a military or brass band. -stand n. an open-air structure suitable for musical performances.

band•age n. a strip of cloth, used for binding up wounds, etc. v.t. to bind with a bandage.

ban•dan•na, ban•dan•a a large patterned silk or cotton handkerchief.

ban•it *n.* robber; outlaw; *pl.* -s, -ti. -ry *n.*

ban•dy *a.* crooked; bent; *v.t.* to toss from one to another, as 'to bandy words.' **bandied** *a.* — **legged** *a.* having crooked legs, bending outwards.

bane *n.* any cause of ruin; mischief; poison. -ful *a.* -fulness *n.*

bang *v.t.* to beat, as with a club; to make a loud noise; *n.* a blow with a club or a fist; a loud noise. -ing *n.*

bang *v.t.* to cut the front hair square across; *n.* a straight fringe over the forehead.

ban•gle *n.* an ornamental ring worn round arm or ankle.

ban•ish *v.t.* to condemn to exile; to drive away; to expel; to cast from the mind. -ment *n.* exile.

ban•is•ter *n.* Same as **baluster.**

ban•jo *n.* a stringed musical instrument.

bank *n.* a ridge of earth; the edge of a stream or lake; a mass of heavy clouds or fog; *v.t.* to raise a mound; to cover a fire with small coal to procure slow combustion. **to bank on** *v.t.* to depend on.

bank *n.* an establishment where money is received for custody and repaid on demand; the money at stake in games of chance; *v.t.* to deposit money in a bank. -book *n.* a pass book in which a customer's dealings with a bank are recorded. -er *n.* one employed in banking. — note *n.* a promissory note on bank of issue promising to pay its face value to bearer on demand. — rate *n.* the rate of discount, fixed by a bank or banks.

bank•rupt *n.* insolvent person compelled to place his affairs in the hands of creditors; *v.t.* to cause to go bankrupt; *a.* insolvent, unable to pay debts. -cy *n.*

ban•ner *n.* a flag or ensign. -ed *a.*

ban•quet *n.* a feast; something specially delicious. -ing *n.*

ban•shee *n.* in Ireland and W. Highlands of Scotland, a fairy-elf who, by shrieks and wailing, foretells the approaching death of a member of a family.

ban•tam *n.* a variety of the small, common domestic fowl; *a.* of very light weight. -weight a boxer weighing less than 118 lbs.

ban•ter *v.i.* to make good-natured fun of someone; to joke. *n.* wit at expense of another. -er *n.*

Ban•tu *n.* an African language.

ban•yan *n.* the Indian fig; a tree whose branches, bending to the ground, take root and form new stocks, till they become a forest.

bap•tize *v.t.* to christen; give a name to. **baptism** *n.* sacrament by which a person is initiated into the membership of the Christian Church. **baptismal** *a.* **Baptist** *n.* one who insists that the rite of initiation is duly administered only by immersion upon personal profession of faith.

bar *n.* a long piece of any solid material, used as barrier; the bolt of a door; part of a tavern with a counter for the sale of liquor; members of the legal profession allowed to plead in court; *(Mus.)* a perpendicular line drawn across the stave immediately before the primary accent; *v.t.* to mark with a bar; to obstruct; to exclude; *prep.* except. -maid, -man, -tender *n.* a bar attendant. -ring *prep.* excepting; *n.* exclusion of any kind. *pr. p.* -ring. *pa. p.* -red.

barb *n.* the spike of an arrow, fish-hook, etc.; *v.t.* to furnish with barbs or prongs, as an arrow; to trim the beard. -ed *a.* bearded; furnished with a barb or barbs. -ed wire *n.* a wire armed with sharp points used for defensive purposes.

bar•bar•i•an *n.* an uncivilized being without culture; a cruel, brutal man; *a.* savage; rude. **barbaric** *a.* uncivilized. **barbarize** *v.t.* to render barbarous. **barbarism** *n.* want of civilization. **barbarity** *n.* cruelty; savagery. **barbarous** *a.* uncivilized or savage.

bar•be•cue *n.* a grid-iron on which meat is roasted over an open fire; a lavish open-air feast.

bar•ber *n.* one who shaves or trims and dresses the hair; a hair-dresser.

bar•ber•ry *n. (Bot.)* a shrub with clusters of red berries.

bar•bi•tu•rates *n. (Med.)* derivatives of barbituric acid, non-habit forming, hypnotic and sedative drugs.

bare *a.* without covering; naked; empty; *v.t.* to strip off or uncover. -ly *adv.* openly; scarcely. -ness *n.* -facedness *n.* sheer impudence.

bar•gain *n.* an agreement between parties in buying and selling; something purchased cheaply. *v.i.* to make a contract. -er *n.* one who haggles over the price.

barge *n.* flat-bottomed boat; *v.i.* to push forward roughly. -man *n.*

bar•i•tone *n.* the male human voice between tenor and bass.

bar•i•um *n.* metallic element (symbol *Ba*). **baric** *a.*

bark *n.* the outer covering of a tree; *v.t.* to strip off bark.

bark *v.t.* to utter a cry like a dog; to yelp.

bar•ley *n.* a cereal, the grain being used for malt-making, bread, and food for cattle. -corn *n.* a grain of barley.

barm *n.* the froth on fermenting malt liquors, used in making bread; yeast. -y *a.* light-headed, flighty, or giddy.

barn *n.* a covered farm-building for storing grain, hay, etc. and for stabling live stock; *v.t.* to store in a barn. -yard *a.* pert. to domestic fowls. *n.* open enclosure attached to barn.

bar•na•cle *n.* a shell-fish which attaches itself to the bottoms of ships and to rocks. -d *a.*

ba•rom•e•ter *n.* an instrument for recording the weight or pressure of the atmosphere which indicates impending weather changes. **barometric, barometrical** *a.*

bar•on *n.* a title of nobility, the lowest of the British peerage to sit in the House of Lords.

ba•roque *n. (Art.)* a florid style of the late Renaissance; *a.* over-lavish;

extravagantly ornamented.

bar·o·scope n. an instrument giving rough indications of variations in the atmospheric pressure.

bar·rack n. a building for the accomodation of soldiers.

bar·ra·cuda n. a large edible pike-like fish, found in the Atlantic.

bar·rage n. an artificial bar erected across a stream to regulate its flow; a screen of continuous military fire produced to protect the advance of troops or to stop hostile attacks.

bar·rel n. a cylindrical wooden container consisting of staves bound by hoops; a measure of capacity; anything cylindrical, as a gun-barrel; v.t. to stow in barrels. — **organ** n. street-organ played by rotating a wooden barrel.

bar·ren a. incapable of producing offspring or fruit; empty, lacking. -ly adv. -ness n. sterility.

bar·rette n. small bar or clasp worn to hold hair in place.

bar·ri·cade n. an obstruction which hinders free passage; v.t. to build this.

bar·ri·er n. a chain of military posts to protect frontiers; a railing, fence or wall; a line of separation.

bar·row n. a small kind of light frame provided with two shafts, for carrying loads.

bar·ter v.t. to exchange or give in exchange; v.i. to traffic by exchange of one kind of goods for another; n. direct exchange of commodities.

bas·al See base n.

ba·salt n. an igneous rock of greenish-black color. -ic a.

bas·cule n. a balancing lever. **bascule-bridge** n. a counterpoise bridge.

base a. morally low. -ly adv.

base n. bottom; part of a thing on which it rests; foundation; fixed point; supply point of an army; station at baseball; (Chem.) a substance capable of combining with an acid to form a salt; v.t. to put on a base; to found. **basal** a. situated at the base. -less a. having no foundation. -lessness n. -ly adv. -ment n. the lowest story of a building. **basic** a. -board n. a skirting board covering the lower part of a wall.

base·ball n. ball game, played by two teams of nine players in which a player after batting must make the complete circuit of four bases to score a run; the ball used.

bash v.t. (Colloq.) to smash in; to knock out of shape; n. a severe blow; a dent. -ing n. a thrashing.

bash·ful a. shy; not desiring to attract notice. -ly adv. -ness n.

ba·sic a. relating to or serving as a base; primary. **English**, simplification of English.

bas·il n. aromatic culinary plant; sweet basil.

ba·sil·i·ca n. a public building or hall of the Romans, later often converted into a church by early Christians. **basilican** a.

ba·sin n. a wide, hollow, bowl-shaped container; a sink; the whole tract of country drained by a river.

ba·sis n. that on which a thing rests; foundation. pl. **bases**.

bask v.i. to lie in warmth or sunshine.

bas·ket n. a container made of willow, cane, rushes, or other flexible materials, interwoven. -**ball** n. a game where a ball has to be thrown through a basket. -**ful** n. -**ry**, -**work** n. wickerwork.

Basque n. a native or the language of the Basque country (Western Pyrenees); a. relating to the Basques.

bass n. name applied to any perch-like fish.

bass, base n. (Mus.) the lowest part of harmony, whether vocal or instrumental; the deepest quality of the human voice or a stringed instrument; a. low. — **clef** n. the sign on the fourth line of the bass stave. **doublebase** n. the largest of the stringed instruments.

bas·set n. a hound formerly used in badger hunting; (Geol.) emergence of strata at the surface. — **horn** n. a rich-toned wind instrument.

bas·so n. a bass singer; the bass part of a harmony.

bas·soon n. a wood-wind musical instrument with a double reed mouthpiece; organ reed stop of that name. **double** —, one which sounds an octave lower. -ist n.

bast n. inner bark of a tree, used for binding purposes.

bas·tard n. a child born out of wedlock; an impure, coarse brown refuse product of sugar-refining, used to color beer; a. illegitimate; counterfeit; -ize v.t. to render illegitimate.

baste v.t. to sew loosely with long stitches; to moisten (meat) with butter, drippings, etc. while cooking.

bas·tille n. originally a tower or bastion. **The Bastille**, the famous state prison of Paris.

bat n. a club or stick; a shaped club used in cricket or baseball; v.i. to strike or hit with a bat; pr.p. -ting; pa.p. -ted, -ter, -man n.

bat n. nocturnal, flying mammal. -ity a.

bat v.t. (Colloq.) to wink. **never batted an eyelid**, showed no emotion whatever.

batch n. a number of articles received or dispatched at one time; a set of similar articles.

bate v.t. to lessen; to abate.

bath n. a vessel or place to bathe in; the water in which to bathe; a solution in which photographic plates are immersed; v.t. to wash oneself. -s n.pl. hot or mineral springs resorted to by invalids. -house n. -room n. blood — n. a massacre. **Turkish bath**, steam bath followed by massage. **sitz bath**, a shallow bath, for bathing hips and buttocks.

bathe v.t. to wash by immersion; v.i. to be immersed; to swim; pr.p. **bathing**. -r n. **bathing** n. **bathingpool** n.

ba·thet·ic See under **bathos**.

bath·i·nette n. portable folding bathtub for babies.

ba·thom·e·ter n. a spring balance for

determining the depth of water.

ba·thos *n.* a term which indicates a ludicrous descent from the sublime to the ridiculous in speech or writing; anti-climax. **bathetic** *a.*

ba·tiste *n.* a fine kind of linen cloth from Flanders.

ba·ton *n.* a short staff or club. in music, wand used by conductor in beating time.

batt, batting *n.* fiber wadded into sheets.

bat·tal·ion *n.* a military tactical and administrative unit of command consisting of three or more companies or similar units. **-s** *n.pl.*

bat·ten *n.* a piece of wood nailed on a surface to give it strength; *v.t.* to fasten with battens.

bat·ter *v.t.* to strike or beat continuously; *n.* a mixture moistened to a paste and briskly beaten up. **-ing ram.** *n.* a suspended beam used to breach walls.

bat·ter·y *n.* a division of artillery; electric cells which store electric current; the pitcher and catcher in baseball.

bat·tle *n.* an encounter between enemies; *v.i.* to fight on a large scale. **— axe** *n.* primitive weapon; **— cry** *n.* a war-shout; a slogan. **-field, -ground** *n.* scene of battle. **-r** *n.* one who takes part in a battle. **-ship** *n.* the largest and most heavily armed of fast warships.

bau·ble *n.* a trifling piece of finery.

baux·ite *n.* the principal source of aluminum.

bawd *n.* a procurer of procuress of women for immoral purposes. **-ily** *adv.* **-iness** *n.* **-ry** *n.* **-y** *a.* unchaste. **—house,** *n.* a brothel.

bawl *v.t.* to proclaim; *v.i.* to shout out with a loud voice; *n.* a loud, prolonged cry. **bawl out** (*Colloq.*) reprimand.

bay *n.* an inlet of the sea.

bay *n.* the subdivision longitudinally of a building by piers, arches, girders, etc. **— window** *n.* a window projecting beyond the wall. **sick —**, ship's hospital.

bay *n.* the laurel tree. **-s** *n.pl.* the victor's crown. **— rum** *n.* an aromatic liquid used as a perfume and cosmetic for the hair.

bay *n.* barking, esp. of hounds in pursuit of prey; *v.t.* to bark at. **at bay,** said of a hunted animal, when all escape is cut off.

bay·ber·ry *n.* evergreen shrub, used for making bay rum; one variety used in candle making.

bay·o·net *n.* a short spear-like weapon attached to the muzzle of a rifle; *v.t.* to stab with a bayonet.

ba·zaar, bazar *n.* a sale where articles are sold for charity.

ba·zoo·ka *n.* a portable light rocket-gun.

B.C. before Christ.

be *v.i.* and *aux.* (*pres. indic.* **am**; *past indic.* **was**; *past part.* **been**), to exist; to live; to have a state, existence, or quality; to belong.

be- *prefix* used in the construction of compound words, as *becalm*, etc.

beach *n.* the shore of the sea or of a lake, esp. where sandy or pebbly; the shore; *v.t.* to run or haul a boat up on to a beach. **-comber** *n.* a lounger who frequents beaches or seaports; scrounger. **-head** *n.* a footing gained on hostile shores by an army.

bea·con *n.* a fire lit on a high eminence, usually as a warning; a warning light.

bead *n.* any small spherical object; *v.i.* to string beads. **-s** *n.pl.* a rosary, a necklace; **-ed** *a.* in bead form. **-ing** *n.* a small rounded molding imitating beads. **-y** *a.* bead-like.

bea·gle *n.* the smallest hound used in hunting.

beak *n.* the horny bill of a bird, turtle, etc.

beak·er *n.* a tumbler-shaped vessel of thin glass used by chemists.

beam *n.* a strong, horizontal piece of timber or reinforced concrete for spanning and supporting weights; a sharply defined ray of light; the sparkle in a person's eyes manifesting extreme pleasure or interest; *v.t.* to emit beams of light; *v.i.* to send forth rays of light; to smile benignly. **-ing** *a.* radiantly happy; *n.* rays of light; manifestation of pleasure by smiling. **-less** *a.*

bean *n.* the flat, kidney-shaped seed of various plants, chiefly of the genus *Phaseolus;* **-bag** *n.* a toy, a small cloth bag partly filled with beans.

bear *v.t.* to support or to carry; to endure; to give birth to; *v.i.* to produce (as fruit); to endure; *pa.t.* bore; *pa.p.* **borne** or **born.** **-able** *a.* tolerable. **-ably** *adv.* **-er** *n.* messenger. **-ing** *n.* the manner in which a person behaves; **-ings** *n.pl.* machine surfaces carrying a moving part and bearing friction. **to bear out,** to corroborate. **to bear with,** to endure patiently. **to bring to bear,** to apply pressure. **to lose one's bearings,** to lose all sense of direction.

bear *n.* a carnivorous mammal of the Ursidae order; a rough, boorish person; (*Astron.*) one of two constellations in the northern hemisphere called respectively the **Great Bear** and the **Lesser Bear.** **-like** *a.* **skin** *n.*

beard *n.* the hair that grows on the chin and cheeks. **-ed** *a.* **-less** *a.*

beast *n.* any inferior animal as opposed to man; a four-footed animal especially if wild. **-ly** *a.* like a beast in nature; displeasing. **-liness** *n.*

beat *v.t.* to strike repeatedly; to pommel; to defeat; to mark time in music; *v.i.* to throb; *pa.t.* beat; *pa.p.* **-en**; *n.* a recurrent stroke; a pulse throb; (*Mus.*) the divisions in a bar, the movement of a conductor's baton; *a.* (*Colloq.*) exhausted. **-en** *a.* hammered into shape by a tool; worn by continual use. **-er** *n.* **-ing** *n.* act of giving blows. **-nik** *n.* (*Colloq.*) one who rebels against the conventions of society. **to beat about the bush,** to approach a subject in a round about way.

be·at·i·fy *v.t.* to render supremely blessed or happy. **beatification** *n.*

be·at·i·tude *n.* highest form of heavenly happiness.

beau *n.* suitor. *pl.* beaux.

beau·ty *n.* the inherent quality in an object

of pleasing the eye, ear, or mind; a fine specimen. **beauteous** *a.* very handsome. **beauteously** *adv.* **beauteousness** *n.* **beautician** *n.* expert in use of cosmetics. **beautifier** *n.* a cosmetic; a decorator. **beautiful** *a.* highly pleasing to eye, ear, or mind. **beautifully** *adv.* **beautifulness** *n.* **beautify** *v.t.* to make beautiful. **beautiless** *a.* lacking beauty. — **spot** *n.* a patch placed on the face to heighten beauty.

bea•ver *n.* an amphibious, four-footed rodent valued for its fur and for castoreum, an extract from its glands used in medicine; *a.* made of beaver fur.

be•calm *v.t.* to make calm or quiet.

be•came past tense of **become**.

be•cause *adv.* and *conj.* for the reason that; since.

beck *n.* gesture of the head or hand; a nod; *v.i.* to make such a gesture; *v.t.* to call by a nod; to beckon. **at one's beck and call**, entirely at someone's disposal.

beck•on *v.t.* and *v.i.* to make a sign with the hand or head.

be•come *v.t.* to pass from one state to another; to be suitable to; *pa.t.* **became**; *pa.p.* **become**. **becoming** *a.* appropriate.

bed *n.* a couch on which to sleep or take a rest; a plot of ground in which plants are cultivated; a layer of rock; *v.t.* to place in bed; to arrange in layers; *pr.p.* **-ding**; *pa.p.* **-ded**. **-bug** *n.* bloodsucking insect. **-clothes** *n.pl.* bed coverings, clothes worn to bed. **-ding** *n.* materials of a bed. **-fellow** *n.* one who sleeps in the same bed with another. **-pan** *n.* pan used as toilet. **-post** *n.* one of the upright supports of a bed. **-rid, -ridden** *a.* permanently confined to bed by age or infirmity. **-rock** *n.* the solid rock beneath loose material as sand, etc.; fundamentals. **-room** *n.* a room for sleeping. **-sore** *n.* ulcer caused by constant pressure on a part of the body of a bed-ridden patient. **-spread** *n.* a covering of fine material for a bed. **-ticking** *n.* the cloth case for holding the feathers, hair, etc. of a mattress.

be•daub *v.t.* to smear.

be•daz•zle *v.t.* to overpower by employing too strong a light or by a magnificient show.

be•deck *v.t.* to adorn.

be•dev•il *v.t.* to beat with devilish malignity; to bewitch.

bed•lam *n.* a scene of uproar; pandemonium.

Bed•ou•in *n.* Arab; nomad.

be•rag•gle *v.t.* to soil by trailing in the wet or mud. **-d** *a.*

bee *n.* highest form of insect belonging to the order Hymenoptera; gathering for

bee

amusement or mutual help, e.g. a spelling-bee. **culture** *n.* the rearing of bees, apiculture. **-hive** *n.* a case or box where the bees are housed; *a.* shaped like a bee-hive. **-keeper** *n.* **-line** *n.* the shortest route from one place to another. **-wax** *n.* the wax secreted by bees.

beech *n.* a tree of the temperate and sub-frigid zones, greatly valued for its wood. **-coal** *n.* charcoal made from beechwood. **-en** *a.* made of beech. **beechnut** *n.* the triangular, edible nut of the beech.

beef *n.* the flesh of an ox, bull, or cow; muscular strength; *a.* consisting of beef; **beeves** *n.pl.* oxen. **-iness** *n.* tendency to put on flesh. **-steak** *n.* a thick slice of beef. **-y** *a.* stolid; stout.

been *pa.p.* of the verb **be**.

beer *n.* an alcoholic beverage made by brewing and fermentation of cereals.

beet *n.* a garden or field plant having a succulent tap root, the red variety being used as a vegetable, the white yielding sugar. — **sugar** *n.* crystallized sugar extracted from beetroot.

bee•tle *n.* name of a large order of insects, Coleoptera.

be•fall *v.t.* to happen to; *v.i.* to come to pass; *pr.p.* **-ing**; *pa.t.* **befell**; *pa.p.* **-en**.

be•fit *v.t.* to be suitable to; to become; *pr.p.* **-ting**; *pa.t.*, *pa.p.* **-ted**. **-ting** *a.* **-tingly** *adv.*

be•fog *v.t.* to envelop in a fog; perplex. *pr.p.* **-ging**. *pa.t.* **-ged**.

be•fore *prep.* preceding; in the presence of; *adv.* in front of; already. *conj.* sooner than; rather than. **-hand** *adv.* previously. **-time** *adv.* of old; formerly.

be•foul *v.t.* to foul, dirty.

be•friend *v.t.* to act as a friend to; to help a stranger.

be•fud•le *v.t.* to confuse.

beg *v.t.* to ask humbly; to beseech; *pr.p.* **-ging**; *pa.t.* and *pa.p.* **-ged**. **-gar** *n.* one who solicits alms; *v.t.* to ruin financially. **-garliness** *n.* **-garly** *a.* like a beggar; poor; worthless; *adv.* meanly. **-gary** *n.* extreme poverty. **-ging** *n.* soliciting alms; *a.* soliciting.

be•gan *pa.t.* of **begin**.

be•get *v.t.* to generate; give rise to. *pr.p.* **-ting**; *pa.t.* **begot**, **begat**; *pa.p.* **begot**, **begotten**.

be•gin *v.t.* to start, to commence; *v.i.* to set about. *pr.p.* **-ning**. *pa.t.* **began**; *pa.p.* **begun**. **-ner** *n.* novice. **-ning** *n.* source; first part.

be•gird *v.t.* to bind with a girdle or band; *pa.t.* **begirt** or **-ed**.

be•gone *interj.* depart! woebegon *a.* gloomy and miserable.

be•go•ni•a *n.* a genus of tropical plants.

be•got begotten *pa. p.* of **beget**.

be•grime *v.t.* to soil with grime.

be•grudge *v.t.* to allow reluctantly. **begrudgingly** *adv.*

be•guile *v.t.* to cheat or deceive by trickery; to delude. **-ment** *n.* **-r** *n.* **beguilingly** *adv.*

be•gun *pa. p.* of **begin**.

be•half *n.* favor; benefit; defense.

be·have v.t. and v.i. to conduct oneself; to act. **behavior** n. deportment. **behaviorism** n. theory that man's actions are automatic responses to stimuli and not dictated by consciousness.

be·head v.t. to sever the head from the body. **-al, -ing** n.

be·held pa.p. of behold.

be·hest n. that which is ordered.

be·hind prep. at the back of; in the rear (of); after; n. rump; posterior. **-hand** adv. and a. backward; in arrears.

be·hold v.t. to fix the eyes upon; v.i. fix the attention. pa.t. and pa.p. **beheld. -en** a. owing a debt of gratitude (to). **-er** n. an on-looker; spectator.

be·hoof n. advantage; benefit; use. **behoove, behove** v.t. to be necessary, convenient for.

beige n. very light brown color of unbleached wool.

be·ing n. existence.

be·la·bor v.t. to beat soundly; to assail verbally.

be·late v.t. to cause to be late.

be·lay v.t. to make fast a rope, by winding it round a fixed pin or cleat; n. in mountaineering, a rock to which a climber anchors himself by a rope. **-ing-pin** n. a pin or cleat to which running rigging may be belayed.

belch v.t. to emit wind from the stomach by way of the mouth; n. eructation.

bel·fry n. a bell-tower, or a part of a steeple, where bells are hung.

be·lie v.t. to speak falsely of; to misrepresent; pr.p. **belying.**

be·lieve v.t. to regard as true; to trust; v.i. to have faith (in); to suppose. **belief** n. full acceptance of a thing as true; a firm persuasion of the truth of a body of religious tenets. **believable** a. credible. **-r** n. to make believe, to pretend.

be·lit·tle v.t. to think lightly of; to disparage. **-ment** n.

bell n. a hollow, cup-shaped metal vessel which gives forth a clear, musical note when struck. **bells** n.pl. (Naut.) half hours of a watch at sea, struck on a ship's bell. **-boy** n. page-boy in hotel. **-buoy** n. a buoy which by its swaying rings a bell attached.

bell n. the cry of an animal. Also **-ing**; v.i. to bellow; to roar.

bel·la·don·na n. deadly nightshade from which drugs, hyoscine and atropine, are obtained.

bel·li·cose a. pugnacious; quarrelsome. **-ly** adv. **bellicosity** n.

bel·lig·er·ence n. the state of being at war; warlike attitude. **belligerency** n. a state of war. **belligerent** n. a nation, party, or person taking part in war; a. waging war; pugnacious.

bel·low v.i. to roar like a bull; to shout loudly; to make an outcry.

bel·lows n.pl. an instrument for producing a strong blast of air (to stimulate a fire, to work an organ, etc.)

bel·ly n. part of the body which contains bowels; abdomen; a. abdominal; v.i. to bulge. **-ache** n. abdominal pains. **-band** n.

a band under the belly of a horse to secure saddle. **-ful** n. sufficiency of food, etc.

be·long v.i. to be connected with; to be property of. **-ings** n.pl. possessions.

be·loved a. greatly loved; n. one very dear to others.

be·low prep. beneath; of inferior rank or status; adv. in a lower place; beneath.

belt n. a band used for encircling; a zone given over to the raising of one plant, e.g. wheat—v.t. to encircle, as with a belt; to thrash with a belt. **-ed** a. thrashed with a belt. **conveyor**—n. an endless belt used for conveying material from one place to another. **-ing** n. material for skirt or bodice bands.

be·moan v.t. to express deep grief for, by moaning.

be·muse v.t. to put into a state of confusion; to daze. **-d** a.

ben n. a geographical term, a mountain peak, as Ben Lomond.

bench n. a long seat; a table on which wood work is done; collective name for the body of judges sitting in judgment.

bend v.t. to curve; to turn out of direct course; to subdue or make submissive; to tie, make fast—of ropes and sails v.i. to be moved out of a straight line; to yield; pa.t. **bent,** pa.p. **bent** or **-ed;** n. a curve; turn. **-er** n. an instrument for bending; a drinking spree. **the bends,** aenoembolism.

be·neath prep. under; lower than; unworthy of; adv. below.

Ben·e·dict n. the founder of Western monasticism. **Benedictine** a. pert. to St. Benedict or his monastic order; n. a Black Friar; a cordial or liqueur originally distilled by the Benedictine monks.

ben·e·dic·tion n. the blessing at the end of a religious service. **benedictory** a. imparting a blessing.

ben·e·fac·tion n. act of doing good; donation. **benefactor** n. (fem. **benefactress)** one who helps others; a patron. **benefactory** a.

ben·e·fice n. an ecclesiastical living. **-d** a. in enjoyment of a benefice.

be·nef·i·cence n. habitual practice of doing good; charity. **beneficent** a. kindly disposed; generous **beneficently** adv.

ben·e·fi·cial a. advantageous; helpful. **-ly** adv. **-ness** n. **beneficiary** n. one who benefits from the act of another.

ben·e·fit n. an act of kindness; a favor conferred; a theatrical or other exhibition, the proceeds of which go to charity or an individual; v.t. to do good to; v.i. to gain advantage (from).

be·nev·o·lence n. disposition to do good; generosity. **benevolent** a. of a kindly nature.

be·night·ed a. enveloped in moral and mental darkness; unenlightened.

be·nign a. of a kindly disposition; not malignant (of disease). **-ancy** n. **benignant** quality. **-ant** a. kind; beneficial. **-antly** adv. **-ity** n. **-ly** adv. in benign fashion.

ben·ja·min n. benzoin, a kind of resin or gum used as a medicine.

bent pa.t. and pa.p. of bend.

bent n. (of mind), leaning, bias, or inclination for.

be·numb v.t. to make numb, through cold or fear; to deaden. -ed a.

Ben·ze·drine n. amphetamine, a synthetic drug.

be·queath v.t. to leave by will, said of personal property; to leave to those who follow on, as a problem, trouble, etc. **bequest** n. legacy.

be·rate v.t. to scold vigorously.

be·reave v.t. to deprive of; pa.p. -d or **bereft**. -d a. robbed by death, esp. of a relative. -ment n. loss, esp. by death.

be·ret n. a soft, round, tightfitting cap without any peak.

berg n. a large mass or mountain of ice.

ber·i·ber·i n. a nervous disease due to deficiency of vitamin B.

ber·ry n. a small, pulpy, juicy fruit; strictly a simple fruit with succulent pericarp. -ing n. **berried** a.

ber·serk, **ber·serk·er** n. a battle-frenzied Norse warrior; a. frenzied. **to go berserk**, to go mad with fury.

berth n. the place where a ship is anchored; a sleeping-place on a ship, etc. v.t. to bring to anchorage. -age n. dock or harbor dues.

ber'yl n. a group of green or bluish-green precious stones of exceptional hardness. -lium n. a rare metal of the magnesium group.

be·seech v.t. to ask or entreat earnestly; pa.t. and pa.p. besought. -er n. -ing a.

be·seem v.t. to be fit for; to become. **beseeming** a.

be·set v.t. to place on, in, or around; pr.p. -ting. pa.t. and pa.p. beset, -ment n. -ter n.

be·shrew v.t. to wish some slight evil to befall one.

be·side prep. and adv. at the side of; over and above; distinct from. -s adv. moreover; prep. over and above. **— oneself**, out of one's wits.

be·siege v.t. to surround with armed forces; to pay court to. -ment n. -r n. **besieging** a. **besiegingly** adv.

be·smear v.t. to smear over; to soil.

be·spat·ter v.t. to sprinkle or splash with mud, ink, etc.

be·speak v.t. to order, speak for, or engage beforehand; pa.t. bespoke. pa.p. bespoke and bespoken. **bespoke**, **bespoken** a. ordered beforehand.

be·speck·le v.t. to mark with speckles or spots.

best a. superl. good in the highest degree; most suitable, advantageous, or appropriate; adv. in the most excellent manner; n. perfection. **— man**, chief attendant to the groom at a wedding. **— seller**, a current popular book with an enormous sale. **to make the best of**, to resign oneself to conditions, etc.

bes·tial a. having the instincts of a beast. -ity n. beastly depravity.

be·stir v.t. to rouse into vigorous action; to stimulate. pr.p. -ring. pa.t. -red.

be·stow v.t. to lay up in store; to give ceremoniously. -al n. -er n. -ment n. what is bestowed.

be·strew v.t. to scatter over. pa.p. -ed, -n.

be·stride v.t. to stand or sit with the legs extended across. pr.p. bestriding; pa.t. **bestrode**, **bestrid**; pa.p. **bestrid**, **bestridden**.

bet n. a stake or wager on some problematical event; v.t. to stake money upon some contingency; pr.p. -ting; pa.p. bet or -ted. -ter, -tor n.

be·ta n. the second letter of the Greek alphabet, printed thus, β. **— particles**, fast electrons emitted when certain atoms undergo radioactive breakdown. **— rays**, streams of beta particles emanated by radioactive substances.

be·take v.t. to have recourse to; to make one's way; pr.p. betaking; pa.t. betook; pa.p. -en.

be·think to remind oneself; to cogitate. pa.t. bethought.

be·tide v.t. to happen to; v.i. to occur.

be·took pa.t. of betake.

be·tray v.t. to be disloyal to; to disclose (a secret); deceive. -al n. -er n. a traitor; a seducer.

be·troth v.t. to promise to give or take in marriage. -al n. an agreement with a view to marriage. -ed n. a person engaged to be married; fiancé, (fem.) fiancée.

bet·ter a. (compar. of good), showing a greater degree of excellence; improved in health; adv. (compar. of well), in a more excellent or superior manner; v.t. and i. to raise one's worldly position. -ment n. improvement. -s n.pl. one's superiors in rank or wealth. **— off**, in more prosperous circumstances.

be·tween prep. in the middle of two (of space, time, etc.); adv. midway. **go-between** n. an intermediary.

be·twixt prep. between; midway.

bev·el n. an adjustable instrument used in building, etc. for testing angles; a. having the form of a bevel; slanting; v.t. to cut to a bevel angle. -led a. -ing, -ment n.

bev·er·age n. a refreshing liquid suitable for drinking.

bev·y n. a flock of birds; a collection or group.

be·wail v.t. to express grief for; mourn over.

be·ware v.i. to be on one's guard; to take care (lest).

be·wil·der v.t. to lead astray or into confusion; puzzle. -ed a. -ing a. confusing. -ment n.

be·witch v.t. to gain power over, by sorcery; to charm. -er n. -ery, -ment n. power to bewitch; enchantment. -ing a.

be·yond prep. on the farther side of; out of reach of; past in time; adv. farther off; n. the future life.

bi-, prefix used in the construction of compound nouns, indicating two, twice, or double.

bi·an·nu·al a. happening twice a year. -ly adv.

bi·as n. prejudice; prepossession that sways the mind; a diagonal line of direction; *v.t.* to prejudice; *pa.t.* and *pa.p.* -sed or -ed.'

bib *n.* piece of cloth worn mainly by children over the breast when eating; part of a workman's overalls to protect chest.

Bi•ble *n.* the volume which contains the Scriptures of the Old and/or New Testament. biblical *a.* scriptural.

bib•li•o- *prefix* from Gk. *biblion*, a book, used in the formation of compound words referring to books. -graphy *n.* a list of books on a specific subject. -grapher *n.* one who compiles lists of books for further study of a subject; one interested in various editions of certain books. -graphic(al) *a.* -logy *n.* knowledge of the production and distribution of books. -mania *n.* a mania for possessing rare books. -maniac *n.* -phile *n.* a lover of books. -pole, -polist *n.* a dealer in books, esp. rare books. -poly *n.* -theca *n.* a library. -thecary *n.* a librarian.

bi•car•bon•ate *n.* a salt or compound containing two equivalents of carbonic acid to one of a base—usually applied loosely for 'bicarbonate of soda.'

bi•ceps *n.* two-headed muscle of arm or leg. biciptial *a.*

bick•er *v.i.* to wrangle; to move quickly and lightly. -ing *n.* -ment *n.*

bi•cus•pid *n.* a tooth with two fangs; *a.* having two cusps or fangs. Also -ate.

bi•cy•cle *n.* a vehicle with two wheels, one in front of the other, propelled by pedals; *v.i.* to cycle. bicyclist *n.* one who rides a bicycle. bike *n.* (*Colloq.*)

bicycle

bid *v.t.* to ask; to order or direct; to offer a price; *pr.p.* bidding; *pa.t.* bid or bade; *pa.p.* bid, -den; *n.* an offer of a price, esp. at auctions; an attempt. -dable *a.* compliant. -der *n.* -ding *n.* command; series of bids at cards.

bide *v.i.* to dwell permanently; reside. *v.t.* to endure.

bi•en•ni•al *a.* happening once in two years; lasting for only two years; *n.* a plant which requires two seasons to bloom. -ly *adv.*

bier *n.* a frame or carriage for conveying the dead to the grave.

bi•fo•cal *n.pl.* spectacles with a small lens for reading, set into a larger lens for distant vision.

bi•fo•li•ate *a.* (*Bot.*) having two leaflets springing from the same point.

big *a.* bulky; massive. — hearted *a.* -ness *n.* bulk; importance.

big•a•my *n.* the crime of having two wives or husbands at one time. bigamist *n.* bigamous *a.* bigamously *adv.*

big•horn *n.* a Rocky Mountain wild sheep.

big•ot *n.* one obstinately and unreasonably wedded to a particular belief or creed. -ed *a.* -ry *n.* the blind zeal of a bigot.

bi•ki•ni *n.* a scanty two-piece bathing suit.

bi•lat•er•al *a.* having two sides; affecting two parties. -ly *adv.*

bile *n.* a greenish, viscous, bitter fluid secreted by the liver; general disorder of health due to faulty secretion of bile. biliary *a.* pert. to the bile. bilious *a.* pert. to the bile; ill-humored. biliousness *n.* a disturbance of the digestive system associated with an excess of bile.

bilge *n.* the broadest part of a ship's bottom nearest the keel, acting as a sump.

bi•lin•gual *a.* speaking, or writing, in two languages. Also bilinguar. bilinguist *n.* a person who can speak fluently in two languages.

bilk *v.t.* to defraud, to swindle. -er *n.*

bill *n.* a kind of axle with two sharp pointed spikes mounted on a long staff.

bill *n.* an account of money owed; the draft of a proposed law; *v.t.* to announce by posters; to send a statement of money owed. -board *n.* a signboard for advertising. -fold *n.* a wallet. -ing *n.* invoicing.

bil•let *n.* the quarters occupied by soldiers in private houses, etc.; *v.t.* to lodge troops.

bil•liard *a.* pert. to billiards. billiards, *n.* a table game played with three balls which are hit by a cue.

bil•lion *n.* a thousand millions (10^9). -aire *n.* a fabulously wealthy person. -th *a.*

bil•low *n.* a great, swelling wave of the sea; a surge of flame, smoke, cloud, etc.; *v.i.* to swell or roll, as waves. -ed, -y *a.*

bil•ly•goat *n.* a he-goat.

bi•met•al•lism *n.* in currency, the use of both gold and silver coins at a fixed relative value.

bi•month•ly *a.* once in two months or twice in a month; *n.* a periodical which appears once in two months or twice a month.

bin *n.* a box or enclosed place with a lid, for corn, bread, etc.; *v.t.* to store in a bin. *pr.p.* -ning *pa.t.* -ned.

bi•na•ry *a.* composed of two; double; *n.* a double star. binate *a.* growing in pairs.

bind *v.t.* to tie together as with a band, cord, etc.; to be obligatory; to constipate; *pa.t.* and *pa.p.* bound. -er *n.* a person who binds; a machine for binding, as sheaves, books, etc. -ery *n.* a book-binding establishment. -ing *a.* obligatory; constipating; *n.* act of fastening.

binge *n.* concerted eating and especially drinking, to celebrate an occasion.

bin•o•cle *n.* a telescope fitted with two tubes. binocular *a.* adapted for the use of both eyes; *n.* a binocular telescope. binoculars *n.pl.* field-glasses. binoculate *a.* adapted for the use of two eyes.

bi•nom•i•nal *a.* (*Bot.*) having two names,

the first indicating the genus, the second indicating the species.

bi•o- a *prefix* used in the construction of compound terms, to express having organic life.

bi•o•chem•is•try *n.* physiology considered from the chemical point of view; the chemistry of living things.

bi•o•dy•nam•ics *n.pl.* the science which investigates the vital forces.

bi•o•gen *n.* a hypothetical protein molecule assumed to be the primary source of all living matter. **biogenesis** *n.* the theory that life develops only from living organisms.

bi•og•ra•phy *n.* the detailed story of a person's life and achievements; the section of literature devoted to the writing of the life-stories of individuals. **biographic, -al.**

bi•ol•o•gy *n.* the science of life, whether animal or vegetable. **biologic, biological** *a.* **biologically** *adv.* **biologist** *n.* **biological warfare**, a method of fighting in which disease bacteria would be used.

bi•o•nom•ics *n.* study of influence of environment on organisms; ecology.

bi•o•phys•ics *n.* physics of living organisms.

bi•op•sy *n.* the excision of a piece of living tissue for diagnosis.

bi•ot•ic *a.* (*Biol.*) relating to life. **biotics** *n.* the functions, properties, and activities of living things.

bi•par•ti•san *a.* pert. to, or composed of, members of two parties.

bi•par•tite *a.* consisting of two corresponding parts. **bipartition** *n.*

bi•plane *n.* an airplane or glider having two main wings.

bi•pod *n.* a two-legged stand. —cf. **tripod.**

bi•po•lar *a.* having two poles.

bi•quad•rate *n.* (*Math.*) the value of the fourth power of a number. **biquadratic** *a.*; *n.* the fourth power.

birch *n.* a tree with slim branches and silvery bark-scales; *v.t.* flog with a birch-rod. **birch, -en** *a.* of birch. **-rod** *n.* a rod of birch twigs for inflicting punishment.

bird *n.* a feathered animal with wings. — **cage** *n.* a cage made of wire and wood for keeping birds. **-call** *n.* the sounds made by a bird.

bird•ie *n.* (*Golf*) holing a ball in one stroke under par.

birth *n.* act of coming into life or of being born; origin. — **control** *n.* restriction of conception. **-day** *n.* the anniversary of that day. **-mark** *n.* peculiar mark on the body at birth. **-place** *n.* the place where a person is born. — **rate** *n.* the ration of births to the total population. **-right** *n.* anything to which one is entitled by birth.

bis•cuit *n.* a quick bread in small soft cakes.

bi•sect *v.t.* to divide into two equal parts. **bisection** *n.* one of two equal parts. **-or** *n.* a bisecting line. **bisegment** *n.* one of two segments of a bisected line.

bi•sex•u•al *a.* having the organs of both sexes.

bish•op *n.* a clergyman of high rank, chess man moving diagonally. **-ric** *n.* diocese, jurisdiction, or office of a bishop.

bi•son *n.* the large buffalo of Western N. Am.

bisque *n.* a thick soup made with shellfish or game.

bi•sul•phate *n.* a salt of sulphuric acid in which one-half of the hydrogen in the acid is replaced by a metal.

bit *pa.t.* of **bite.**

bit *n.* small piece of anything; a boring tool generally for use in brace; part of bridle

bits

which is placed in a horse's mouth; *v.t.* to put the bit in the mouth of a horse.

bitch *n.* the female of the dog, wolf, or fox.

bite *v.t.* to cut, seize, or wound with the teeth; to pinch with cold; *v.i.* to be given to biting; to be pungent; *pr.p.* **biting;** *pa.t.* **bit;** *pa.p.* **bit** or **bitten** *n.* act of biting; a portion bitten off; the nibble of a fish at a hook; **-r** *n.* **biting** *a.* sarcastic; caustic; chilling.

bit•ter *a.* biting or acrid to the taste; causing pain to the feelings; *n.* bitter beer. **-ly** *adv.* **-ness** *n.* the quality of being bitter to the taste; animosity. **-s** *n.* alcoholic liquor containing bitter flavorings. **-sweet** *n.* the woody nightshade whose root, when chewed, tastes first bitter then sweet.

bi•valve *a.* having two valves; *n.* an animal with a shell of two parts opening like a hinge. **bivalvous** *a.*

biv•ou•ac *n.* an encampment in the open air, without any cover; *v.i.* to encamp without covering. *pr.p.* **bivouacking;** *pa.t.* and *pa.p.* **bivouacked.**

bi•week•ly *a.* occurring once in every two weeks; occurring twice in each week; *n.* a periodical issued twice a week or once in two weeks.

bi•zarre *a.* eccentric; strange.

blab *v.t.* to imprudently reveal secrets entrusted to one; *v.i.* to tell tales; *pr.p.* **-bing;** *pa.t.* and *pa.p.* **-bed** *n.* a tell-tale. Also **-ber.**

black *a.* of the darkest color; nightlike; *n.* the darkest color; *v.t.* to make black. **-en** *v.t.* to make black; to defame; *v.i.* to turn black. **-ly** *adv.* **-ness** *n.* **-ball** *v.t.* to reject a candidate for admission to a club. **-berry** *n.* a fruit-bearing shrub, the bramble. **-bird** *n.* any of a number of birds which have predominantly black plumage. **-board** *n.* a slate, or any dark surface to write on with chalk. **-bread** *n.* rye bread.

— eye n. discoloration due to a blow.
-flag n. flag popularly associated with
pirates. -guard n. a low scoundrel; a. vile;
v.i. to act in a vile manner. -guardism n.
-guardly a. -head n. a small black-topped
mass which plugs the mouths of the
follicles of the skin. -jack n. a short,
leather-covered club with a heavy head
on an elastic shaft. — lead n. graphite, a
form of nearly pure carbon and used in
the manufacture of lead pencils. —list n.
any list of undesirable persons; v.t. to
place on such a list. -mail n. extortion of
money by threats of denunciation.
— mark n. a mark of failure. — market n.
a clandestine market for the sale of goods
whose distribution is regulated, and
which are not on free sale. — out n. a
total cutting off of all light.

blad·der n. a thin musculo-membranous
bag, in the pelvis, serving as a reservoir
for urine. -ed a. swollen like a bladder. -y
a. thin and inflated.

blade n. the leaf, or flat part of the leaf, of a
plant; the cutting part of a knife, or tool;
a sword. -bone n. the upper bone in
shoulder, scapula. -d a.

blame v.t. to express disapprobation of; n.
fault. -less a. -lessness n.

blanch v.t. to whiten; v.i. to become white;
to turn pale.

bland a. mild; affable. -ly adv. -ness n.

blank a. without writing or any marks;
empty; n. an empty space. -ly adv.
— verse, unrhymed heroic.

blan·ket n. a loosely woven woolen
bedcover; a thick canopy of cloud; v.t. to
cover with a blanket; to toss in a blanket.
-ing n. thick material for blankets; tossing
in a blanket. a wet blanket, one who
depresses others.

blare v.t. and v.i. to sound loudly; to
trumpet; n. a long, prolonged noise.

blar·ney n. coaxing, cajoling talk;
outrageous flattery.

bla·sé a. absolutely bored; sophisticated.

blas·pheme v.t. to speak irreverently of
God; v.i. to take God's name in vain. -r n.
blaspheming n. impious talk.
blasphemous a. blasphemously adv.
blasphemy n. irreverence in speaking of
sacred matters.

blast n. a gust or puff of air; an explosion of
gunpowder in rending rocks. v.t. to
injure, as by a noxious wind; to blight; to
split as by gunpowder. -ed a. blighted;
accursed; -er n. — furnace n. a
smelting-furnace in which hot air is
furnished by bellows or other apparatus.
-ing n. a blast; explosion.

bla·tant a. offensively noisy; loud-(voiced);
obtrusive. blatancy n. -ly adv.

blaze n. bright flame; outburst of activity or
zeal; v.i. to burn brightly. -r n. sports
jacket of bright color.

blaze n. white mark upon a horse's
forehead; v.t. to mark a trail.

bla·zon v.t. to make known to everybody;
n. art of drawing coats of arms. -er n.
-ment n. -ry n. art of describing coats of
arms.

bleach v.t. to whiten by exposure to
sunlight and air, or by chemical action;
v.i. to become whiter; n. a decolorizing,
chemical agent. -er n. one who, or that
which, bleaches. bleachers n.pl. outdoor,
uncovered seat for a spectator in a
stadium.

bleak a. without color; desolate and
exposed. -ly adv. -ness n.

blear a. dim or watery, due to inflammation
of the eye, or tears; v.i. to blur. -y a. dim.

bleat v.i. to cry as a sheep; to talk in a
whining fashion; n. the sound made by a
sheep.

bleed v.t. to draw blood surgically; v.i. to
lose blood; pa.t. and pa.p. bled. -er n. a
person who is afflicted by hemophilia,
excessive bleeding. -ing n.

blem·ish n. any deformity, physical or
moral; v.i. to mark with a flaw; to
disfigure.

blend v.t. to mix allied articles together
smoothly and inseparably; v.i. to mingle
well; pa.p. -ed or blent; n. a mixture. -er
n. -ing n.

bless v.t. to consecrate; praise; invoke
happiness on. pa.p. -ed or blest. blessed,
blest a. favored with blessings; hallowed.
-edness n. happiness; heavenly joy. -ing
n. a source of happiness or gratitude;
prayer.

blew pa.t. of blow.

blight n. disease of plants caused by certain
fungi or parasitic bacteria; v.t. to affect
with blight.

blimp n. a small non-rigid airship.

blind a. destitute of sight; unaware of;
concealed; v.t. to deprive sight; to
deceive; n. a window-covering or screen.
— date n. a date arranged with someone
not previously known; the person
involved. -ed a. rendered sightless;
oblivious to all other factors. -ers n.pl. a
horse's blinkers. -fold a.; v.t. to cover the
eyes with something. -ing a. — landing n.
grounding an aircraft by depending on
radio signals. -ly adv. -ness n. lacking
power of sight.

blink v.i. to wink; to look with the eyes
half-shut; v.t. to shut out of sight, as a fact
or question; n. a glance. -ers n.pl. pieces
of leather preventing a horse from seeing
to either side.

bliss n. the acme of happiness; heavenly
rapture. -ful a. supremely happy. -fully
adv. -fulness n. -less a.

blis·ter n. a vesicle of the skin filled with a
clear or blood-stained serum.

blithe a. gay; jolly; sprightly. -ly adv. -ness
n. -some a. cheerful.

blitz n. a heavy, sudden attack by enemy
bombers; v.t. to bomb from the air. -ed a.

bliz·zard n. a blinding snowstorm.

bloat v.t. to swell or puff out; to cure fish
by salting and smoking. -ed a. swollen.
-edness n. bloater n. a herring—salted,
smoked, and dried.

blob n. anything small and globular.

block n. a solid mass of matter; a roughly
squared piece of wood, stone, etc.; a
number of buildings forming one
compact mass; v.t. to enclose; to shape (a
hat). -buster n. a heavy explosive bomb.

-head *n.* a dullard. **-house** *n.* an improvised fort made of logs. **— letters** *n.* a form of script where the letters are printed instead of. in the usual cursive style.

block•ade *n.* prevention of imports into countries usually during a war; *v.t.* to prevent trade with a hostile country. **— runner** *n.* a vessel employed to slip through to a blockaded country.

blond *n.* a person of fair complexion *a.* fair.

blood *n.* the red, viscid fluid which circulates in the body of men and animals; relationship, kindred; **— bank** *n.* a store of blood for use in a transfusion. **— count** *n.* the number of red and white cells in a specific quantity of blood. **-curdling** *a.* terrifying. **-hound** *n.* a hound, with keen sense and

bloodhound

perseverance. **-ily** *adv.* **-less** *a.* without blood; spiritless. **-lessness** *n.* **-mobile** *n.* a mobile unit for collecting blood for blood banks. **— plasma,** the fluid part of blood. **— poisoning** *n.* a condition due to circulation of bacteria in blood stream. **— pressure** *n.* the pressure exerted by the blood on the walls of the arteries. **— red** *a.* crimson. **— serum** *n.* the fluid part of the blood after the fibrin and the corpuscles have been eliminated. **-shed** *n.* the shedding of blood. **-shot** *a.* of the eyes, red or congested with blood. **-stain** *n.* the dried and darkened stain left on clothing, floors, etc. after contact with blood. **-sucker** *n.* an animal which sucks blood, esp. the leech. **-test** *n.* an examination of the blood often to determine to which of the four groups it belongs. **-thirsty** *a.* eager to shed blood. **— transfusion** *n.* the transference of blood from one person to another. **— vessel** *n.* an artery or vein through which blood flows. **-y** *a.* stained with blood.

bloom *n.* a blossom; state of freshness and vigor; to flow with youthful vigor; *v.t.* to cause to blossom or flourish.

blos•som *n.* the flower of a plant, esp. a tree; *v.i.* to flourish. **-ed** *a.* **-y** *a.* rich in blossoms.

blot *v.t.* to spot esp. with ink; to obliterate; to dry with blotting-paper; *pr.p.* **-ting;** *pa.p.* **-ted;** *n.* a spot or stain, as of ink; disgrace, **-ter** *n.* a blotting-pad. **-ting-paper** *n.* a kind of unsized paper for drying ink.

blotch *n.* an irregular, colored spot; an eruption upon the skin; *v.t.* to mark with blotches; to make spotted. **-y** *a.*

blouse *n.* a light, loose upper garment; *v.i.* and *v.t.* to drape loosely.

blow *n.* a stroke; a smack; sudden calamity.

blow *v.i.* to produce a current of air; to

breathe hard or quickly; *v.t.* to direct a current of air on; to sound a wind instrument; *pa.t.* **blew;** *pa.p.* **-n;** *n.* a high wind. **-lamp** *n.* a portable lamp for applying intense local heat. **-n** *a.* out of breath; tainted. **-out** *n.* a burst tire. **— pipe** *n.* an instrument for concentrating the heat of a flame on some point by blowing. **-y** *a.* windy.

blub•ber *n.* the fat of whales and other marine animals; *v.i.* to weep unrestrainedly. **-ed** *a.* swollen by weeping. **-ing** *n.*

bludg•eon *v.t.* to knock out with a club.

blue *n.* the color of the clear sky; one of the seven primary colors; *n.pl.* a very slow jazz dance of Negro origin. **blue** *a.* of the color blue; melancholy; *v.t.* to make or dye blue. **bluish** *a.* slightly blue. **-bell** *n.* the wild hyacinth. **-berry** *n.* a shrub with edible small berries. **-bird** *n.* a migratory bird of N. Am. belonging to the thrush family. **— blood** *n.* an aristocrat. **— book** *n.* a directory of socially prominent people; a college examination book. **Blue Cross,** a system of nonprofit health insurance. **-grass** *n.* meadow grass of Kentucky which forms thick turf. **-heat,** about 550° F. **-jay** *n.* a crested bird of the eastern U.S. and Canada. **— laws** *n.* laws restricting activities on Sunday. **— pencil** *v.t.* to edit. to alter. **-print** *n.* a simple photographic reproduction of technical drawings leaving white lines of plan on a blue background. **— ribbon,** first prize.

bluff *a.* frank and hearty in manner; *n.* a high bank or cliff presenting a steep front. **-ness** *n.* steepness; a frank, blunt manner of speech.

bluff *n.* an attempt to mislead in regard to one's real purpose; *v.t.* to mislead one by giving a wrong impression. **-er** *n.* **-ing** *n.,* *a.*

blun•der *v.i.* to make a gross mistake; *n.* a gross mistake. **-er** *n.* **-ing** *n.* and *a.* continually making mistakes; fumbling. **-ingly** *adv.*

blunt *a.* having a dull edge or point; brusque in speech; *v.t.* to render less sharp. **-ly** *adv.* **-ness.**

blur *n.* smudge; whatever dims without effacing; *v.t.* to make indistinct. *pr.p.* **-ring;** *pa.t.* and *pa.p.* **-red.**

blurb *n.* an advertisement, esp. extravagant in praise.

blurt *n.* a sudden outburst. **to blurt out** *v.t.* to give information suddenly, indiscreetly, or tactlessly.

blush *v.i.* to redden in the face, from shame, modesty, or confusion; *n.* a red color suffusing the face. **-ing** *n.* a rosy glow on the face; *a.* coy; bashful. **-ingly** *adv.*

blus•ter *v.i.* to blow in boisterous gusts, of wind; to talk with violence and noise; *n.* fitful noise and violence. **-er** *n.* **-ous** *a.* **-y** *a.* stormy.

bo•a *n.* a genus of constricting, nonvenomous serpents. **— constrictor** *n.* a serpent which crushes its victims.

boar *n.* the male of the swine. **— hound** *n.* a large dog used in hunting boars.

board *n.* a long, narrow strip of timber; a table, hence food or diet; a thick paper made by pasting together several layers; *v.t.* to cover with boards; to supply with meals and lodging for payment; to embark on a ship, airplane, etc.; *v.i.* to be a lodger. **-s** *n.pl.* the covers of a book. **-er** *n.* one receiving food and lodging. **-ing** *n.* obtaining food and lodging. **-ing-house** *n.* a house in which boarders are accomodated. **-ing-school** *n.* a school in which the students are in residence.

boast *v.t.* to be unduly proud of; *v.i.* to praise oneself extravagantly; *n.* a statement, expressive of vain glory. **-er** *n.* **-ful** *a.* **-fully** *adv.* **-fulness**, **-ing** *n.* indulging in boasting. **-ingly** *adv.*

boat *n.* a small vessel moved by oars or sails or small motor; *v.i.* to row or sail about in a boat. **boatswain** *n.* a ship's officer.

bob *n.* a short, jerking motion; *v.t.* to move with a jerk; *v.i.* to dangle; to move up and down or in and out; *pr.p.* **-bing**; *pa.p.* **-bed.**

bob-bin *n.* a spool on which thread is wound.

bob-o-link *n.* a common North American songbird.

bob-sled, bob-sleigh *n.* two small sleds coupled together; *v.i.* to use a bobsled.

bode *v.t.* and *v.i.* to foretell; to be an omen of. **-ful** *a.* **-ment** *n.* an omen. **boding** *a.* ominous; *n.* an omen.

bod-ice *n.* that part of a woman's dress above the waist, with or without sleeves, and close-fitting.

bod-y *n.* the frame of a human being or of an animal; the main part of anything; a solid substance; consistency of a liquid; *v.t.* to produce in definite shape; *pa.t.* and *pa.p.* **bodied. bodied** *a.* used in compounds, e.g. able-bodied. **bodiless** *a.* possessing no body. **bodily** *a.* pert. to the body; *adv.* physically, in the body, in the flesh; in the mass. **-guard** *n.* an escort.

bo-gey *n.* (*Golf*) one over par for hole.

bog-gle *v.i.* to shrink back through fear; to hesitate.

bo-gle *n.* a fearsome apparition, imp, or hobgoblin associated with the nursery. **bogey, bogy** *n.* the devil; a goblin.

bo-gus *a.* sham; counterfeit.

Bo-he-mi-an *a.* unconventional *n.* one who leads a loose and unsettled life.

boil *v.t.* to bring to a seething condition, by heating; *v.i.* to be agitated by the action of heat. **-er** *n.* a vessel for boiling. **-ing point**, the temperature at which a liquid boils.

boil *n.* local inflammation of the skin round a hair follicle.

bois-ter-ous *a.* noisy; turbulent. **-ly** *adv.* **-ness** *n.*

bold *a.* daring; ready to meet danger; valorous. **— faced** *a.* impudent; printed with heavy thick strokes. **-ly** *adv.* **-ness** *n.*

bo-le-ro *n.* a short jacket, usually without sleeves, worn over a blouse.

boll *n.* a seed capsule of cotton, flax, etc. **-weevil**, **-worm**, larvae of various moths destructive of cotton crops.

bo-lo-gna *n.* a large smoked, seasoned type of sausage.

Bol-she-vik *n.* a member of the Communist Party. **bolshevism** *n.* theory and practice of Russian or other communism. **bolshevist** *n.* and *a.* **bolshevistic** *a.* **bolshevize** *v.t.*

bol-ster *n.* a long round bed-pillow; anything designated as a support; *v.t.* to prop. **-er** *n.* **to bolster up**, to support a weak person.

bolt *n.* a bar for fastening a door, window, etc.; part of a lock which engages with the keeper; a metal pin with a head at one end and screw threads at the other to receive a nut; a roll of cloth; *v.t.* to fasten with a bolt; to swallow food hurriedly; *v.i.* to rush away; to start suddenly forward.

bomb *n.* a cast-iron container filled with high explosives, gas, incendiary contents or smoke-producing substances exploding by percussion or by a timing mechanism. **-er** *n.* an airplane for bombs. **-proof** *a.* secure against small bomb splinters. **-shell** *n.* a bomb; something devastating. **atom(ic) bomb**, a bomb depending on the release of atomic energy. **bomb sight**, instrument for aiming bombs.

bom-bard *n.* an early mortar with a wide bore, using stone-shot. **bombard** *v.t.* to batter with heavy artillery fire. **-ier** *n.* a gunner in the artillery. **-ment** *n.* a sustained attack with guns, bombs, etc.

bom-bast *n.* inflated, high-sounding language. **-ic** *a.* **ically** *adv.*

bo-nan-za *n.* a profitable enterprise.

bond *n.* that which binds, a band, a link, a tie; an oath or promise. **-s** *n.pl.* chains; captivity. **-age** *n.* slavery.

bond *n.* a legal engagement in writing to fulfill certain conditions; a certificate of ownership of capital lent to a government, municipality, etc.; *v.t.* to put dutiable articles on or under bond. **-ed** *a.* mortgaged. **-ed warehouse**, a warehouse for holding goods in bond.

bone *n.* the hard tissue which forms the skeleton of mammals, birds, reptiles and fishes. *v.t.* to remove the bones; to filet (fish). **-s** *n.pl.* human remains. **— ash** *n.* calcined bones. **-black** *n.* finely ground animal charcoal. **— china** *n.* china in which bone ash is used. **-dry** *a.* absolutely dry. **— meal** *n.* a fertilizer for dry soils, made from ground bones. **boniness** *n.* **bony** *a.* full of bones.

bon-fire *n.* orig. a fire for burning bones.

bon-net *n.* a woman's head-gear. **-ed** *a.*

bo-nus *n.* something over and above that which is due.

boo *interj.* an exclamation of contempt, often used to startle. **-es** *n.pl. v.t.* and *v.i.* to show disapproval; *pr.t.* (he) **booes**; *pa.t.* **-ed.**

book *n.* a number of sheets of paper, etc. bound together; a literary composition written or printed; *v.t.* to obtain business order, ticket. **-s** *n.pl.* record of business transactions, especially financial. **-binder** *n.* one who binds books. **-binding** *n.*

-**case** n. a case with shelving for books.
— **club** n. a club to distribute specially chosen books to subscribers. — **ends** n.pl. weighted props to keep books upright on a shelf. -**ing** n. an engagement to perform. -**ing clerk** n. a clerk who issues railway, etc., tickets. -**ish** a. found of books. -**ishness** n. — **jacket** n. an attractively printed outer paper wrapper of a book. -**keeper** n. -**keeping** n. the art of keeping a systematic account of financial transactions. — **learning, -lore** n. knowledge acquired by extensive reading. -**let** n. a pamphlet. -**maker** n. a professional betting-man who accepts bets. -**mark** n. something placed in a book to mark a particular page. **the Book of Books,** the Holy Bible. -**seller** n. one who sells books. -**selling** n. -**shelf** n. a shelf for displaying books. -**shop, -stall, -stand** n. a place for exhibiting books for sale. -**worm** n. one who reads intensively.

boom v.i. to make a deep hollow sound; to flourish; n. a hollow roar; economic prosperity. -**er** n. -**ing** a.

boom•er•ang n. a curved wooden missile used by the natives of Australia.

boomerang

boor n. a peasant; bumpkin. -**ish** a. -**ishly** adv. -**ishness** n.

boost v.t. to raise by pushing from beneath; to increase the output or power of a machine; n. a push up. -**er** n.

boot n. a covering for the foot and leg; a kick; v.t. to put on boots; to kick. -**black** n. one who polishes the shoes of passers-by. -**ee** n. a knitted boot. -**leg** v.t. to sell illicitly alcoholic liquor. -**legger** n. -**legging** n.

booth n. a temporary structure of boards or other materials; a small restaurant compartment.

bo•rax n. hydrated sodium borate, used in the manufacture of enamels and glazes, as a softener for hard water. **boracic** a. **boracic acid,** white powder used as an antiseptic or for checking excessive perspiration. **borate** n. a salt of baracic acid.

bor•der n. the outer edge of anything; a frontier; an ornamental design around the outside edge of anything; v.t. to adorn with a border; v.i. to come near. -**ing** n. material for a border. -**land** n. land contiguous to a frontier. -**line** a. on the verge of.

bore v.t. to make a hole in; to weary by uninteresting talk; n. the hole made by boring; a person that wearies one. -**dom** n. the state of being bored; ennui. -**r** n. tool for drilling.

bore pa.t. of **bear.**

born pa.p. of **bear,** to bring forth; a.

natural. **borne** pa.p. of **bear,** to carry.

bor•ough n. an incorporated town.

bor•row v.t. to obtain on loan or trust. -**ed** a. -**er** n. -**ing** n.

bos•om n. the breast of a human being; v.t. to press to the bosom; a. intimate.

boss n. a prominent circular projection on any article; v.t. to emboss; to provide with bosses. -**ed** a. embossed.

boss n. employer; one in charge; v.t. to manage; -**iness** n. -**y** a. fussy and masterful. -**ism** n.

bot•a•ny n. that branch of biology which is concerned with the structure and growth of plants. **botanic, botanical** a. pert. to botany. **botanically** adv. **botanic garden,** a garden where plants are scientifically studied. **botanist** n.; **botanize** v.i. to study plants; to search for and collect plants for further study.

botch n. a clumsy patch of a garment; bungled work; v.t. to bungle; to patch clumsily; to blunder; spoil. -**er** n. a bungler. -**ery, -work** n. -**ily** adv. -**y** a.

both a. and pron. the one and the other.

both•er v.t. to annoy; tease; plague; v.i. to fuss; to be troublesome; n. trouble; annoyance; fuss; worry; interj. an exclamation of annoyance. -**ation** n. trouble and worry; a mild imprecation. -**some** a. troublesome.

bottle n. a vessel with a narrow neck for holding liquids; a thermionic valve; v.t. to put in bottles; to restrain; to curb. -**d** a. enclosed in bottles; of a bottle shape. -**d-up** a. confined; not allowed to speak. — **green** a. of a dark-green color. **bottling** n. and a. -**neck** n. a narrow outlet which impedes the smooth flow of traffic or production of goods. -**nose** n. a whale with a beaked snout. -**party** n. one where the guests provide the liquid refreshments. -**r** n.

bot•tom n. the lowest part of anything; the posterior of human body; origin; v.t. to put a bottom on an article; -**less** a.

bot•u•lism n. a rare and dangerous form of food poisoning caused by spoiled foods.

bou•cle n. a woven material with raised pile; a. pert. to such material.

bou•doir n. a lady's private room.

bouf•fant a. puffed out, full, as in draperies, skirts, hair.

bough n. an arm or large branch of a tree.

bought pa.t. and pa.p. of **buy.**

bouil•lon n. broth; stock **bouillabaisse** n. a Provençal fish soup or stew.

boul•der n. a rock torn from its bed, and rounded by water.

boul•e•vard n. a street or promenade planted with trees. -**ier** n. one who haunts the boulevards.

bounce v.i. to move with a bound and rebound; to leap or spring suddenly; v.t. to cause to rebound, as a ball; n. a sudden spring or leap; **bouncing** a. vigorous; big.

bound pa.t. and pa.p. of **bind.**

bound v.i. to leap; spring; n. a leap; jump.

bound a. tending to go or on the way, as in homeward bound.

bound n. usually in pl. limit or boundary;

confines; *v.t.* to restrain; to set bounds to. -ed *a.* restricted; cramped. -less *a.* without limits; infinite. -lessness *n.*

bound·a·ry *n.* a border or limit; barrier.

boun·ty *n.* a payment formerly made to men enlisting voluntarily in the army or navy; a premium offered by a government. bounteous, bountiful *a.* ample; plentiful. bounteously, bountifully *adv.*; bounteousness, bountifulness *n.*

bou·quet *n.* a bunch of flowers; a perfume; the aromatic flavor and aroma of wine.

bour·bon *n.* a whisky distilled from corn and rye.

bour·geois *n.* a member of middle-class society; *a.* middle-class; conventional. bourgeoisie *n.*

bout *n.* a turn; a conflict.

bou·ton·nier *n.* a flower or flowers worn on a lapel.

bo·vine *a.* pert. to cattle; ox-like; stolid.

bow *v.i.* to bend body in respect, assent, etc.; to submit; *v.t.* to bend downwards; *n.* an inclination of head or body; the rounded forward part of a ship. -line *n.* a rope used to keep the weather edge of the sail tight forward; knot used for tying a rope to a post. -man *n.* the one who rows the foremost oar in a boat.

bow *n.* anything bent or curved; weapon from which an arrow is discharged; a ribbon tied in a slip-knot. -ed *a.* bent like a bow. -er *n.* -legged *a.* having crooked legs. -man *n.* an archer. — tie *n.* a small bow-shaped tie.

bow·el *n.* an entrail; the entrails; the inside of everything. -s *n.pl.* the intestines.

bow·er *n.* (*Poetic*) a small country dwelling. -y *a.* shady.

bow·ie-knife *n.* a long hunting-knife, the point double-edged, the blade straight and single-edged at the hilt.

bowl *n.* a round vessel; a drinking-cup; a stadium.

bowl *n.* a ball rolled in certain games; *pl.* a game played on a bowling-green with bowls; *v.t.* to roll, as a bowl; *v.i.* to play with bowls; to deliver a ball. -er *n.* one who bowls. -ing *n.*

box *n.* a small case or chest, generally with a lid; a compartment. — kite *n.* a kite consisting of a square frame strength. —office *n.* ticket office at a theater. —pleat *n.* a double fold with material turned under on both sides with knife edges.

box *n.* a small evergreen shrub. — berry *n.* the wintergreen. -en *a.* made of or like boxwood. -wood *n.* a tree.

box *n.* a blow on the head or the ears; *v.t.* to buffet; *v.i.* to fight with the fists. -er *n.* a pugilist. -ing *n.* the sport of fighting with fists.

boy *n.* a male child; a lad. -hood *n.* -ish *a.* boy-like. -ishly *adv.* -ishness *n.* the natural actions of a boy.

boy·cott *n.* a method of coercion by refusing to deal with; *v.t.* to ostracize. -er *n.* -ing *n.*

bra See brassiere.

brace *n.* a rod or bar crossing a space diagonally to connect two structural parts; a support; *v.t.* to furnish with braces; to support. -s *n.pl.* . suspenders; wires for straightening teeth. and bit, small interchangeable boring tool fitted into the socket of a brace. -r *n.* a wrist-guard of leather used esp. by archers. bracing *a.* invigorating; refreshing.

brace·let *n.* an encircling ornament for the wrist.

brack·en *n.* a large coarse species of fern.

brack·et *n.* a projecting support fastened to a wall; one of two hooks, used to enclose explanatory words; *v.t.* to couple names together as of equal merit, etc.

bract *n.* a leaf in the axil of which a flower arises. -eal *a.* of the nature of a bract. -eate *a.* having bracts.

brad *n.* a cut nail tapering in width with a small head projecting at one end. -awl *n.* a small hand-boring tool.

brag *v.i.* to praise oneself or one's belongings; *pr.p.* -ging *pa.t.* and *pa.p.* ged; *n.* boasting. -gart *a.* boastful; *n.* a boaster. -ging *a.*, *n.* -gingly *adv.*

braid *v.t.* to plait, or interweave; *n.* a narrow ribbon used as a dress-trimming; a tress of hair. -ed *a.* -ing *n.*

braille *n.* a system of printing books in relief to be read by the blind; also the letters used, consisting of raised dots in combination.

brain *n.* the whitish, soft mass in the skull in which are the nerve centers; mental capacity; *v.t.* to dash out the brains of. -ed *a.* having the brains beaten out. -less *a.* stupid. — storm *n.* (*Colloq.*) a sudden idea, inspiration. -wash *v.t.* (*Colloq.*) to effect a radical change in beliefs by intensive indoctrination. -y *a.* highly intellectual.

braise *v.t.* to cook meat by browning in fat and simmering in a covered dish with a small amount of liquid.

brake *n.* instrument for breaking flax or hemp; any device for checking speed; *v.t.* to pound or crush flax, hemp, etc., by beating; to check by applying a brake. braking *n.* — shoe *n.* the surface of a block brake.

bram·ble *n.* a prickly hedge-plant; the wild blackberry.

bran *n.* the ground husk of wheat and other grain, separated in milling from the flour.

branch *n.* a limb of a tree or shrub; a department of a business, etc.; an off-shoot; *a.* pert. to a subsidiary section of any business; *v.t.* to divide, as into branches; *v.i.* to spread, in branches; -ed *a.* -ing *a.* shooting out. -y *a.*

bran·chi·ae *n.pl.* the breathing organs of fishes, the gills. branchial *a.* pert. to gills. branchiate *a.* furnished with gills.

brand *n.* an iron used for burning marks on; a mark made by a hot iron; a trade-mark; *v.t.* to burn a mark on; to designate a commodity by a trade-mark; to reproach. -ed *a.* -er *n.* -ing-iron *n.*

bran·dish *v.t.* to wave, as a weapon.

bran·dy *n.* a spirit distilled from wine.

brash *a.* insolent; **-ness** *n.*

brass *n.* a yellow alloy of two parts of copper to one of zinc; *a.* brazen; made of brass. **-es** *n.pl.* the brass instruments of an orchestra. — **band** *n.* musicians who perform on brass instruments. — **hat** *n.* (*Colloq.*) staff-officer (from gold braid on hat). **-iness** *n.* bold; impudent. **-y** *a.* pert. sole. — **knuckles** *n.pl.* metal pieces fitted across the knuckles, used in fighting.

bras·si·ere *n.* a woman's undergarment supporting the breasts; short form, **bra.**

brat *n.* a child (used contemptuously).

bra·va·do *n.* showy bravery.

brave *a.* courageous; fearless; *n.* an Indian warrior; *v.t.* to encounter with courage. **-ly** *adv.* **-ry** *n.* heroism.

bra·vo *interj.* an expression of applause; *pl.* **-es.**

brawl *v.i.* to squabble noisily; *n.* a noisy quarrel. **-er** *n.*

brawn *n.* muscular strength esp. of the arms and legs. **-iness** *n.* **-y** *a.* muscular; robust.

bray *n.* the harsh noise of a donkey; *v.i.* to utter a harsh noise, like a donkey.

bray *v.t.* to pulverize; to grind small.

braze *v.t.* to make or ornament with brass. **brazing** *n.*

bra·zen *a.* pert. to, or made of, brass; impudent; *v.t.* to face a situation in a bold, impudent manner. **-ly** *adv.*

bra·zier *n.* a portable iron container to hold burning coals; a worker in brass.

Bra·zil·i·an *n.* a native of Brazil, in S. America; *a.* pert. to Brazil.

breach *n.* a break or opening, esp. in a wall; non-fulfillment of a contract. *v.t.* to make a breach in something. — **of promise,** the nonfulfillment of a promise, esp. of marriage.

bread *n.* form of food prepared by baking dough made from a cereal. — **winner** *n.* one who earns a living for his dependents.

breadth *n.* distance from side to side.

break *v.t.* to shatter by force; to tame; *v.i.* to divide into several parts; curl over (as waves); to crack or falter; to make the first stroke at billiards; *pa.t.* broke; *pa.p.* broken.

break *n.* the act of being broken; a fracture; separation; a breathing space. **-able** *a.* fragile. **-age** *n.* act of breaking; an allowance for articles broken. **-down** *n.* loss of health; an accident to machinery; suspension of negotiations; *v.t.* to divide into small categories. **-er** *n.* a long wave as it breaks into foam. **-fast** *n.* the first meal of the day. **-neck** *a.* dangerous to life and limb. **-up** *n.* disintegration; separation. **-water** *n.* a strong structure to break the force of the waves.

breast *n.* the external part of the thorax or chest between neck and abdomen; *v.t.* to oppose boldly. **-s** *n.pl.* the milk or mammary glands of women and female animals. **-bone** *n.* the sternum, the flat narrow bone to which the first seven ribs are attached. **-plate** *n.* a piece of armor for protecting the chest. — **stroke** *n.* a long-distance stroke in swimming.

breath *n.* air respired by the lungs; life; fragrance. **-less** *a.* out of breath; panting; expectant. **-lessness** *n.* **under one's breath,** in a low voice or whisper. **with bated breath,** breath held from fear or excitement.

breathe *v.t.* to draw in and give out air from the lungs; *v.i.* to be produced; to increase air—hence to live. **breathable** *a.* **-d** *a.* (*Phon.*) uttered with breath only. **-r** *n.* a short spell of rest. **breathing** *n.* respiration; **breathing-space, breathing-time,** a pause.

bred *pa.t.* and *pa.p.* of breed.

breech *n.* the hinder part, esp. of a gun-barrel; *v.t.* to whip; to flog. **-es** *n.pl.* trousers, esp. those which fit tightly around knees. **-ing** *n.* that part of the harness which passes round a horse's haunches.

breed *v.t.* to beget; to engender; to train or bring up; *v.i.* to be produced; to increase in number; *pa.t.* and *pa.p.* bred; *n.* a race of animals from the same stock; sort. **-er** *n.* one who breeds cattle or other live stock. **-ing** *n.* producing; the rearing of live stock; deportment

breeze *n.* a wind of moderate strength. **breezy** *a.* windy; of a person, animated and brisk.

breth·ren *n.pl.* members of the same society or profession [See brother].

breve *n.* a mark distinguishing short vowels.

brev·i·ty *n.* conciseness; terseness.

brew *v.t.* to prepare a fermented liquor, from malt, hops, etc.; concoct; *v.i.* to be impending; *n.* something brewed. **-er** *n.* **-ery** *n.* a place where brewing is carried on.

bribe *n.* anything bestowed, to influence judgment and conduct; *v.t.* to influence by gifts; *v.i.* to practice bribery, **bribable** *a.* **bribery** *n.*

bric·a·brac *n.* ornamental articles.

brick *n.* a building material made from a special clay molded into a rectangular block and hardened by drying in the sun or firing in a kiln; *v.t.* to lay with bricks. **-kiln** *n.* a kiln in which bricks are baked or burnt. **-layer** *n.* one who is skilled in building with bricks. **-laying** *n.*

bride *n.* a woman about to be, or just, married. **bridal** *n.* wedding; *a.* pert. to a bride or a wedding; nuptial. **bridal-suite** *n.* apartments set aside for a honeymoon couple. **-groom** *n.* a man newly-married, or about to be married. **-s maid** *n.* an unmarried woman who acts as attendant on a bride.

bridge *n.* a structure spanning a river or a valley, etc., in order to afford passage; the bone of the nose, etc.; mounting for false teeth; (*Mus.*) connecting passage; *v.t.* to build a bridge. **-head** *n.* a footing gained by an attacking force on the far bank of a river.

bridge *n.* a card game for four players.

bri·dle *n.* the headgear of a horse; *v.t.* to put a bridle upon; control. — **path** *n.* a narrow track used by riders on horseback.

brief *a.* short in duration; using few words; *n.* an abridged statement of a case; to inform personnel of the details of an impending action. — **case** *n.* a small flat case for carrying papers. **-ly** *adv.* **-ness** *n.* **-s** *n.pl.* undershorts.

bri•er *n.* any prickly bush; a tangled mass of them.

brig *n.* a sailing-ship with two masts, both square-rigged.

brig

bri•gade *n.* a sub-division of an army under the command of a general officer; a group of people organized for a specific purpose, such as a *fire brigade.* **brigadier-general** *n.*

bright *a.* shining; full of light or splendor; cheerful; intelligent. **-en** *v.t.* to make bright; *v.i.* to grow bright. **-ly** *adv.* **-ness** *n.*

bril•liant *a.* glittering; sparkling; distinguished; *n.* a polished diamond cut to a definite pattern. **-ly** *adv.* **-ness** *n.* **brilliance** *n.* **brilliancy** *a.*

brim *n.* rim or border; *v.i.* to be full to the brim. **-ful** *a.* **-med** *a.* **-ming** *a.*

brine *n.* water containing an admixture of salt; the sea. **brinish** *a.* salty, like brine. **briny** *a.*

bring *v.t.* to fetch, to convey from one person or place to another; to transport; *pa.t.* and *pa.p.* brought.

brink *n.* margin of a steep slope; verge.

brisk *a.* full of activity; *v.t.* and *i.* to enliven; to cheer up. **-ly** *adv.* **-ness** *n.*

bris•ket *a.* part of animal's breast which lies next to ribs.

bris•tle *n.* a very stiff, erect, coarse hair, as of swine; *v.t.* to erect the bristles of; *v.i.* to stand up erect, like bristles; to show anger **-d** *a.* provided with bristles.

Brit•ish *a.* of or pertaining to Britain; *n.* the inhabitants of Britain. **-er** *n.* a British subject.

brit•tle *a.* easily broken; fragile.

broach *n.* a tapered, hardened-steel bit for enlarging holes in metal; *v.t.* to pierce; to approach a subject.

broad *a.* wide, ample, open; liberal-minded; plain, unmistakable (hint); full (daylight). **broad, -ly** *adv.* **-brim** *n.* a wide-brimmed hat, much affected by Quakers, and so a Quaker. **-cloth** *n.* a finely woven woollen, cotton, or rayon cloth for clothing. **-en** *v.t.* and *v.i.* to grow broad. — **jump** *n.* (*Sports*) a horizontal jump from rest or from a run. **-loom** *n.* woven on a wide loom, of carpets and rugs. — **minded** *a.* tolerant.

-ness *n.* **-side** *n.* the whole side of a ship above water-line; a volley from the gun on one side of a naval craft; violent abuse.

broad•cast *n.* a transmission by radio; *a.*; *v.t.* to disseminate by radio-telephone transmitter, news, music, etc., by receiving apparatus. **-er** *n.* a person or organization broadcasting.

bro•cade *n.* a fabric woven with elaborate design; *v.t.* to ornament a fabric with raised designs. **-d** *a.*

broc•co•li *n.* a variety of the cauliflower.

bro•chure *n.* a printed work of a few sheets of paper; a pamphlet.

brogue *n.* a mode of pronunciation peculiar to Irish speakers.

broi•der *v.t.* to adorn with figured needlework.

broil *n.* a noisy quarrel; altercation.

broil *v.t.* to cook under gas or electric heat in a stove; *v.i.* to be overheated.

broke *pa.t.* and old *pa.p.* of **break**; *a.* (*Colloq.*) penniless; degraded. **-n** *pa.p.* of **break**; *a.* shattered; parted; impaired; exhausted; spent. **-n English**, imperfect English, as spoken by a non-native. **-n hearted** *a.* crushed with grief; inconsolable. **-nly** *adv.* intermittently. **-nness** *n.*

brok•er *n.* a person employed in the negotiation of commercial transactions between other parties in the interests of one of the principals; a dealer in second-hand goods. **-age, brokerage,** *n.* the business of a broker.

bro•mide *n.* a compound of bromine with some other element; a sedative drug.

bro•mine *n.* one of the elements, related to chlorine, iodine, and fluorine. **bromic** *a.*

bron•chi, bron•chi•a *n.pl.* the two tubes forming the lower end of the trachea. **-al** *a.* pert. to the bronchi. **bronchitis,** *n.* inflammation of the bronchial tubes.

bron•chus *n.* one of the bifurcations of the windpipe; *pl.* see **bronchi**.

bron•co *n.* an unbroken, or partly broken horse. — **buster** *n.*

bronze *n.* an alloy of copper, tin, and zinc; the color of bronze; *a.* made of or colored like bronze; *v.t.* to give the appearance of bronze to; to harden. **Bronze Age,** pre-historic period between the Stone and Iron Ages. **bronzy** *a.*

brooch *n.* an ornamental clasp with a pin for attaching it to a garment.

brood *v.t.* to sit upon, as a hen on eggs; to ponder; *v.i.* to sit upon to hatch; to meditate moodily; *n.* a family of young, esp. of birds; a race. **-er** *n.* an appliance for rearing incubator-hatched chickens by artificial heat. — **mare** *n.* a mare kept for breeding. **-y** *a.* wishing to sit, as a hen; sullen.

brook *n.* a small stream.

brook *v.t.* to bear; to support.

broom *n.* implement for sweeping.

broth *n.* water in which meat has been boiled with vegetables.

broth•el *n.* house of prostitution.

broth•er *n.* a male born of the same parents; fellow-member of a corporate body; *pl.* -s, **brethren.** -**hood** *n.* an association of men of the same religious order, profession, or society; the mutual regard resulting from this association. — **in-law** *n.* the brother of one's husband or wife; a sister's husband. — **like,** -**ly** *a.* affectionate. -**liness** *n.*

brought *pa.t.* and *pa.p.* of **bring.**

brow *n.* the ridge over the eyes; the forehead. -**beat** *v.t.* to bully a person by over-bearing speech. -**beater** *n.*

brown *n.* a dark color inclining to red or yellow; a mixture of black, red, and yellow; *a.* of a brown color; sunburnt; *v.t.* to sunbathe; to roast brown. — **betty** *n.* a spiced, bread and apple pudding. -**stone** *n.* a reddish-brown sandstone used in building. — **sugar,** unrefined or partly refined sugar.

brown•ie *n.* a member of the junior section of Girl Scouts; a chocolate cookie.

browse *v.t.* and *i.* to glance through a book shop, etc. **browsing** *n.*

bruise *v.t.* to injure by striking or crushing; to pound or pulverize; *n.* a contusion. -*r n.* a prize-fighter.

brunch *n* (*Colloq.*) breakfast and lunch combined.

bru•nette *n.* a woman with dark brown hair.

brunt *n.* the force of a blow.

brush *n.* an implement made of bristles, twigs, etc., bound together and used for removing dust, dressing the hair, applying paint, and the like; the smaller trees of a forest, brushwood; the bushy tail of a fox or squirrel; *v.t.* to remove dust, etc., with a brush; to touch lightly in passing; *v.i.* to touch with light contact. -**wood** *n.* thicket of small trees and shrubs. -*y a.* rough, shaggy.

brusque *a.* blunt; abrupt in speech. -**ness** *n.*

brute *a.* irrational; ferocious; *n.* a beast. **brutal** *a.* savage; inhuman. **brutalism** *n.* brutality. **brutality** *n.* inhumanity; savagery; **brutalize** *v.t.* to make brutal, cruel, or coarse; to treat with brutality; *v.i.* to become brutal. **brutally** *adv.* **brutish** *a.*

bry•ol•o•gy *n.* the science of mosses.

bub•ble *n.* a hollow globe of water or other liquid blown out with a globule of air or gas in liquid or solid substances; a small bladder-like excrescence on surface of paint, metals, etc.; *v.i.* to rise in bubbles; to effervesce; to gurgle; *v.t.* to cause to bubble. **bubbly** *a.*

bu•bo *n.* lymphatic swelling of the glands in the groin or armpit. **bubonic** *a.; pl.* **buboes, bubonic plague,** the Black Death of the 14th cent.

buc•ca•neer *n.* a pirate; *v.i.* to play the buccaneer.

buck *n.* the male of the rabbit, hare, sheep, goat, and deer; (*Colloq.*) a male Indian; *v.i.* to attempt to unseat a rider by jumping vertically with arched back and head down; to foil all attempts at improvement. -**shot** *n.* large leaden shot for killing big game. -**skin** *n.* a soft leather made of deerskin or sheepskin. -**tooth** *n.* a tooth which protrudes. **buck**

up! (*Colloq.*) cheer up!

buck•board *n.* a four-wheeled vehicle in which a long elastic board takes the place of steel springs.

buck•et *n.* a vessel for carrying water. -**ful** *n.* the quantity held by a bucket.

buck•le *n.* a metal clasp for fastening straps, bands, etc.; a bend or kink; *v.t.* and *v.i.* to clasp with a buckle; to bend.

buck•ram *n.* a coarse linen or cotton cloth stiffened with sizing; *a.* made of buckram.

buck•wheat *n.* an herb, the seeds of which are ground into flour or fed to animals.

bud *n.* the sprout on a plant containing an unexpanded leaf, branch, or flower; *v.i.* to begin to grow; *v.t.* to graft by budding. -**ding** *n.* the act of inserting the bud of one tree under the bark of another, for propagation. **to nip in the bud,** to destroy at the beginning. *pr.p.* -**ding.** *pa.t.* -**ded.**

Bud•dhism *n.* the chief religion of E. Asia. **Buddhist** *n.* a worshipper of Buddha.

bud•dy *n.* a bosom friend.

budge *v.t.* and *i.* to move; to stir.

budg•et *n.* a plan for systematic spending; *v.t.* to plan one's expenditures.

buff *n.* a soft, yellow leather prepared from the skin of the buffalo, elk, and other animals; a revolving wooden disc covered with layers of leather used with an abrasive for polishing; a light yellow-tan color; a fan; *a.* made of buff leather; *v.t.* to polish with a buff. -*y a.* of a buff color.

buf•fa•lo *n.* a ruminating, horned animal, resembling an ox, but larger and more powerful.

buf•fer *n.* a resilient cushion to deaden the concussion between a moving body and one on which it strikes; a polisher. — **state,** a country lying between two powerful and rival nations.

buf•fet *n.* a cupboard for displaying fine china. *a.* (a meal) spread on tables from which guests serve themselves.

buf•fet *n.* a blow with the fist; *v.t.* to strike with the fist. -**s** *n.pl.* hardships.

buf•foon *n.* a person who acts the clown by his clumsy attempts at humor. -**ery** *n.* the silly antics of a buffoon. -**ish** *a.*

bug *n.* name applied to various insects; a concealed microphone. -**gy** *a.* swarming with bugs.

bu•gle *n.* a wind instrument used because of its penetrating note for conveying orders. sound a call. -*r n.*

build *v.t.* to erect a structure; to raise (hopes); *v.i.* to exercise the work of building; to depend with *on, upon; pa.t.* and *pa.p.* built; *n.* form; physique; style of construction. -**er** *n.* -**ing** *n.*

bulb *n.* a modified leaf-bud emitting roots from its base and formed of fleshy leaf scales containing a reserve supply of food; a dilated glass tube containing filament for electric lighting; *v.i.* to form bulbs; to bulge. -**aceous,** -**ar,** -**ed,** -**ose,** -*y a.* pert. to bulbs. -**iform** *a.* -**osity** *n.* the state of being bulbous. -**ous** *a.* having the appearance of a bulb; growing from bulbs.

bulge *n.* anything rounded which juts out; *v.i.* to swell out. **bulgy** *a.*

bulk *n.* size, the main body; the largest portion; *v.i.* to pile up; *v.i.* to be of some importance. **-age** *n.* roughage. **-iness** *n.* **-y** *a.* clumsy in shape, so difficult to handle. **in bulk**, unpackaged, in large quantity.

bulk·head *n.* a partition in a ship made with boards, etc., to form separate compartments; a horizontal or sloping cover to outside step leading to the cellar of a building.

bull *n.* the male of any bovine; the male of numerous animals as elephant, whale, seal, moose, elk, deer; *a.* to denote a male animal. **-baiting** *n.* an ancient sport of setting ferocious dogs on a bull tied to a stake. **-dog** *n.* a breed of dog formerly used for bull-baiting; **-dozer** *n.* a tractor with an attached horizontal blade in front. **-fight** *n.* the national sport of certain Latin races, esp. in Spain and consisting of a combat between men and specially bred bulls. **-finch** *n.* a bird of the thrush family with a thicker head and neck. **-frog** *n.* a large, dusky-brown frog. **-headed** *n.* headstrong. **— pen**, fenced enclosure; *(Sports)* where baseball pitchers practice. **— ring** *n.* the arena in which a bull-fight is held. **bull's-eye** *n.* a shot that hits the center of the target. **— session** *(Colloq.)* informal discussion. **— terrier** *n.* a cross between bulldog and terrier.

bul·let *n.* a small projectile to be discharged from a gun.

bul·le·tin *n.* a periodical publication; a brief statement of facts issued by authority. **-board** *n.*

bul·lion *n.* uncoined, refined gold or silver; the precious metals, including coined metal, when exported or imported.

bul·ly *n.* over-bearing person who tyrannizes the weak; *v.t.* intimidate; *v.i.* to bluster.

bul·wark *n.* an outwork for defense; *pl.* a railing round the deck of a ship; *v.t.* to fortify with a rampart.

bum *n.* an idle, dissolute person; *a.* worthless; *v.i.* to loaf.

bum·ble-bee *n.* a large, hairy, social bee.

bum·bling *a.* noisy and blundering [See **bumble-bee**].

bump *n.* a dull, heavy blow; a swelling resulting from a blow; one of the protuberances on the skull, said by phrenologists to give an indication of mental qualities, character, etc.; *v.t.* to strike against; *v.i.* to collide. **-y** *a.* covered with bumps.

bump·er *n.* *(Auto.)* a horizontal bar in front and rear of a car; *a.* very large; excellent.

bump·kin *n.* an awkward, stupid person; a country lout.

bump·tious *a.* rudely self-assertive; self-important. **-ness** *n.*

bun *n.* a kind of bread roll, light in texture and slightly sweetened; hair twisted into a knot at the back of a woman's head.

bunch *n.* a cluster of similar things, tied or growing together; a bouquet of flowers; *v.t.* to gather together; to crowd; *v.i.* to swell out like a bunch. **bunched** *a.* crowded together. **-y** *a.* growing in bunches.

bun·dle *n.* a number of things bound together; a definite number of things; *v.t.* to make up into a bundle or roll; *v.i.* to dress warmly.

bun·ga·low *n.* small detached one-storied house.

bun·gle *v.t.* to manage clumsily; *v.i.* to act awkwardly; *n.* a blundering performance. **-r** *n.* **bungling** *a.*

bun·ion *n.* an inflamed swelling occurring on the foot.

bunk *n.* a box-like structure used as a seat by day and a bed at night; a sleepingberth on board ship; in a camp, etc.; *v.i.* to sleep in a bunk.

bunk·er *n.* an underground fortification.

bun·ny *n.* a pet name for a rabbit.

Bun·sen burn·er *n.* a gas burner in which a strong current of air produces a weakly luminous, but very hot, flame.

bunt *v.t.* to butt with horns or head; *(baseball)* to bounce ball a short distance off the bat.

buoy *n.* any floating body of wood or iron employed to point out the particular situation of a ship's anchor, a life-buoy; *v.t.* to fix buoys. **to buoy up**, to keep afloat. **-age** *n.* a series of buoys in position; the providing of buoys. **-ancy** *n.* capacity for floating in water or air; cheerfulness. **-ant** *a.* floating lightly; hopeful.

bur *n.* the rough, sticky seed-case of certain plants with hooked spines to help in its distribution; a burr. See **burr**.

bur·ble *v.i.* to gurgle, as of running water; *(Colloq.)* to talk idly.

bur·den *n.* anything difficult to bear, as care, sorrow, etc.; *v.t.* to oppress; to encumber.

bu·reau *n.* a small chest of drawers; a government department.

bu·reau·c·ra·cy *n.* administration by bureaus, often excessively numerous and powerful; the officials engaged in such an administration. **bureaucrat** *n.* one who advocates such a system of government. **bureaucratic** *a.*

bur·geon *v.i.* to sprout; to put forth branches.

bur·glar *n.* one who is guilty of house-breaking. **-y** *n.* breaking and entering into a dwelling-house.

Bur·gun·dy *n.* name given to various wines, red or white.

bur·i·al *n.* interment; entombment. **—ground**, a cemetery. [See **bury**].

burl *n.* a knot in wood, thread or yarn. **-ed** *a.*

bur·lap *n.* a coarsely woven canvas of flax, hemp, or jute, used for packing and as a wall covering, etc.

bur·lesque *n.* exaggerating, and ridiculing a work of art; theatrical performance featuring vulgar comedy and dancing; *a.* comical; ludicrous; *v.t.* to turn into burlesque.

bur·ly *a.* of stout build; big and sturdy.

burliness n.

burn v.t. to consume with fire; to subject to the action of fire; to char; v.i. to be on fire; to flame; blaze; pa.t. and pa.p. -ed or -t; n. injury or damage caused by burning. -er n. part of a gas jet from which the flame issues. -ing n. act of consuming by fire; a. flaming; parching. -ing-glass n. a convex lens which causes intense heat by bending the rays of the sun and concentrating them upon a single point. burning question, a topic of universal discussion. burnt-offering n. a sacrifice of a living person or animal by burning.

burnt pa.t. and pa.p. of burn.

burr n. a tool for cutting or drilling; a rough edge left on metal by a cutting tool. Also bur.

bur•ro n. a donkey.

bur•row n. a hole dug in the ground by certain small animals to serve as an abode; v.i. to tunnel through earth.

bur•sa n. a sac or cavity, especially between joints; -l a.; bursitis n.

bur•sar n. a treasurer of a college.

burst v.t. to break into pieces; to break open violently; to break suddenly into some expression of feeling; v.i. to shatter; pa.t. and pa.p. burst; n. a bursting; an outbreak; spurt.

bur•y v.t. to inter in a grave; to hide by covering; pa.p. buried. -ing n. burial; interment. to bury the hatchet, to restore friendly relations.

bus, 'bus n. a vehicle for public conveyance of passengers; pl. -es.

bush n. a shrub; a thicket of small trees and shrubs; v.i. to grow thick or bushy; v.t. to plant bushes about. — fighting n. guerilla warfare where advantage is taken of trees and bushes. -iness n. the quality of being bushy. -man n. a settler in the backwoods. -master n. a large venemous snake. -y a. thick and spreading.

bush n. the internal lining of a bearing, to form a plain bearing surface for a pin or shaft. -ing n. a removable lining to reduce friction.

bush•el n. a dry measure of 4 pecks, for corn, fruit, etc.

busi•ness n. employment; any occupation for a livelihood; firm. -like a. systematic; methodical. -man n.

buss n. a hearty kiss; v.t. to kiss, esp. boisterously.

bust n. sculptured representation of a person from the waist upwards; the upper part of the human body.

bus•tle v.i. to busy oneself with much movement; n. great stir. -r n.

bus•tle n. a stuffed pad worn by ladies to support and elevate the back of the skirt just below the waist.

bus•y a. active and earnest in work; industrious; v.t. to keep busy; to occupy (oneself). busily adv. -body n. a person who meddles in other people's business. -ness n. state of being busy.

but conj. yet; unless; nevertheless; prep. except; without; adv. only. all but, nearly.

bu•tane n. a natural gas used in refrigeration and as a fuel.

butch•er n. one who slaughters animals for food or retails the meat; v.t. to slaughter animals for food; to murder in cold blood. -ing n. killing for food. -y n. wanton slaughter.

but•ler n. a male servant.

butt n. the lower end of a tree-trunk providing the strongest timber; one continually subject to ridicule; v.t. to strike by thrusting the head downwards. n.pl. a mound with targets where shooting is practiced. to butt in (Colloq.) to intervene without permission.

but•ter n. the fatty ingredients of milk, emulsified by churning; v.t. to spread with butter. -cup n. plant with cup-shaped, yellow flowers. -fingers n. (Colloq.) one who drops things easily. -milk n. the fluid residue after butter has been churned from cream. -scotch n. a kind of taffy with butter as an ingredient. -y a.

but•ter•fly n. the common name of all diurnal, lepidopterous insects.

but•tock n. rounded, lower, posterior part of the body (usually in pl.)

but•ton n. a stud for fastening clothing; an emblem of membership; v.t. to fasten with buttons; v.i. to be fastened by a button. -hole n. the loop in which a button is fastened; -hook n. a hook for pulling a button through a buttonhole.

but•tress n. a projecting support to a wall; v.t. to support.

bu•tyl n. a highly elastic synthetic rubber, made from butane, a natural gas.

bux•om a. full of health; lively.

buy v.t. to obtain by payment; to purchase; pa.t. and pa.p. bought. -er n. a purchaser.

buzz v.i. to make a humming sound; v.t. to spread news secretly. -er n. an apparatus used for telephonic signaling. -ingly adv.

buz•zard n. a genus of birds of the hawk family.

by prep. beside; in the neighborhood of; adv. near; close; beyond. by and by, in the near future. -name n. a nick-name. -pass n. a road for the diversion of traffic from crowded centers; v.t. to avoid a place by going round it. — path n. a side path. -play n. action carried on apart from the main part of a play; diversion. — product n. secondary product obtained during manufacture of principal commodity. -road n. a less frequented side road. -stander n. an onlooker. -way n. a secluded road. -word n. a common saying.

bye n. having no opponent in a round of competition. -bye (Colloq.) good-bye.

by•law, bye-law n. a local law made by an association.

Byz•an•tine relating to Byzantium, the original name for Constantinople.

cab n. a taxicab; driver's accomodation on a truck. -**by** n. a taxi driver.

cab·a·la, cabbala n. occultism. **cabalism** n. **cabalist, cabalistic(al)** a. mysterious; occult.

cab·a·ret n. restaurant providing entertainment and space for dancing.

cab·bage n. a garden vegetable of Brassica family.

cab·in n. a small house; an apartment in a ship; the space in an airplane for the pilot and passengers; v.t. to confine in a cabin; v.i. to live in a cabin. — **boy** n. a boy who waits on the officers of a ship.

cab·i·net n. a council of ministers who advise the chief executive; a chest for displaying objects; — **maker** n. a maker of cabinets and other furniture.

ca·ble n. a large, strong chain; a stranded insulated conductor of electricity; a

cable

submarine telegraph line; a message sent by such line; v.t. to send a message by cable. — **car** n. a car pulled by a moving cable. — **gram** n. a telegram sent by cable.

ca·boose n. a car attached to a freight train for the crew.

ca·ca·o n. a tropical tree from the seeds of which cocoa and chocolate are prepared.

cacao

cache n. a hole in the ground for hiding provisions, etc.; articles so hidden; v.t. to conceal.

cack·le v.i. to make a noise like a hen or goose; n.

ca·cog·raphy n. bad writing or spelling.

ca·coph·o·ny n. a harsh or disagreeable sound; a use of ill-sounding words. **cacophonous** a.

cac·tus n. an American desert plant with thick, fleshy, prickly stems, generally no leaves but frequently producing showy flowers. pl. -es, or cacti.

cad n. a mean, vulgar fellow. -**dish** a. ill-bred, mean.

ca·dav·er n. (Med.) a corpse. -**ous** a. corpse-like; sickly-looking.

cad·die, cad·dy n. an attendant who carries a golfer's clubs; v.i.

cad·dis, cad·dice n. worm-like aquatic larva of caddis-fly.

ca·dence n. a fall of the voice in speaking; the beat of any rhythmical action; (Mus.) the subsiding of a melody towards a close. -**d** a. rhythmical. **cadency** n.

ca·den·za n. (Mus.) an ornamental passage for a voice or solo instrument.

ca·det n. a youth in training for commissioned ranks in the army or air force; -**ship** n.

cadge v.t. and i. to peddle goods; to beg. -**r** n. a peddlar.

cad·mi·um n. (Chem.) a soft, bluish-white metal of zinc group. **cadmia** n. an oxide of zinc.

ca·du·ce·us n. the staff carried by Mercury, messenger of the gods; the emblem of the medical profession.

cae·cum n. (Med.) the first part of the large intestine, opening into the colon; pl. **caeca. caecal** a.

Cae·sar n. one who acts like Julius Caesar (100-44 B.C.), Roman emperor and dictator. **Caesarean. Caesarian** a. pert. to Julius Caesar. **Caesarian section** (Med.) delivery of child through an opening cut in abdominal wall.

cae·si·um See cesium.

cae·su·ra, cesura n. a break in a line of poetry.

ca·fé n. a restaurant, usually licensed for the sale of light refreshments only.

caf·e·te·ri·a n. a restaurant where the customers help themselves.

caf·feine n. the stimulating alkaloid in coffee and tea.

cage n. a box-like enclosure, with bars of iron or wire, for keeping animals or birds; v.t. to imprison. -**ling** n. a bird kept in a cage. -**work**, n. open frame-work. -**y** a. cautious, wary.

cais·son n. an ammunition wagon; (Engineering) a water-tight chamber of sheet-iron or wood, used for workmen in laying the foundations of piers or bridges, quay-walls, etc.

ca·jole v.t. to persuade by flattery; to wheedle. -**r** n. -**ry** n. the act of cajoling.

cake n. a piece of dough baked; a flattish mass of matter, esp. soap, tobacco, etc.; v.t. to make into a cake; v.i. to become a flat, doughy mass. **caky** a.

cal·a·bash n. the bottle-gourd tree; a species of pear.

cal·a·mine n. a silicate of zinc, used as a pigment in skin ointments.

ca·lam·i·ty n. any great misfortune. **calamitous** a. producing distress and misers. **calamitously** adv.

cal·car·e·ous a. chalky.

cal·cif·er·ol n. crystalline vitamin D used in fortifying margarine. **calciferous** a. containing carbonate of lime.

cal·ci·fy v.t. and i. to harden or petrify, by a deposit of lime. **calcification** n.

cal·ci·mine n. a white or tinted wash for ceiling and walls.

cal·cine v.t. to expel water and other volatile substances by heat; v.i. to be turned into powder. **calcinable** a. **calcination** n. **calcinatory** n. a vessel used in calcination.

cal·ci·um *n.* the metallic base of lime. calcic *a.* containing calcium. calcite *n.* native carbonate of lime.

cal·cu·late *v.t.* to estimate; to compute; to expect; *v.i.* to make a calculation. calculable *a.* -d *a.* intended to produce a certain effect. calculating *a.* shrewd in matters of self-interest. calculation *n.* calculative *a.* tending to calculate. calculator *n.* a machine which does automatic computations.

cal·cu·lus *n.* a branch of higher mathematics concerned with the properties of continuously varying quantities; *n.* a hard concretion which forms, esp. in kidney, bladder, etc. usually called stone or gravel; *pl.* calculi. calculose, calculous *a.* hard, like stone; gritty.

cal·dron, cauldron *n.* a large metal boiler.

cal·a·fac·tion *n.* the act of heating, the state of being heated. calefacient *a.* making warm; *n.* a heat-giving remedy. calefactor *n.* that which gives heat. calefactory *a.*

cal·en·dar *n.* a table of days, months or seasons. *v.t.* to enter in a list.

calf *n.* the young of the cow, and of some other mammals, such as elephant, whale, etc.; *pl.* calves —skin *n.* a fine, light-colored leather made from the skin of a calf. calve *v.i.* to bring forth a calf.

calf *n.* the thick, fleshy part of the leg below the knee; *pl.* calves.

cal·i·ber *n.* the diameter of the bore of a cannon, gun, etc.; *(Fig.)* quality of mind; character. calibrate *v.t.* to determine the caliber of a firearm tube or other cylindrical object. calibration *n.*

cal·i·co *n.* white cotton cloth, first made in *Calicut* in India; *a.* made of calico.

cal·i·pers, callipers *n.* a two-legged instrument for measuring diameters.

ca·liph, ca·lif *n.* a title given to the successors of Mohammed.

ca·lix See calyx.

calk, caulk *v.t.* to fill or close joints or crevices to make air- or water-tight. -er *n.* -ing *n.*

call *v.t.* to summon; to name, as for office; to utter in a loud voice; *v.i.* to cry out; to make a brief visit; *n.* a summons or invitation; a short visit; authorized command; the characteristic cry of a bird or animal. -er *n.* one who calls. -ing *n.* a person's usual occupation. at call, on demand. on call, of a person, ready if summoned. -boy *n.* a boy who calls actors to go on the stage; a bellboy. to call down, to rebuke. to call up *(Mil.)* to summon to military service.

cal·ligra·phy *n.* penmanship. calligrapher, calligraphist *n.* calligraphic *a.*

cal·lis·then·ics *n.pl.* light gymnastic exercises to promote beauty and grace of movement. callisthenic *a.*

cal·lous *a.* hardened; unfeeling. -ly *adv.* -ness *n.* callosity *n.* a horny hardness of the skin.

cal·low *a.* pert. to the condition of a young bird; unfledged; *(Fig.)* inexperienced. -ness *n.*

cal·lus *n.* a hardened part of the skin.

calm *a.* still; at rest; *n.* the state of being calm; *v.t.* to make calm. -ly *adv.* -ness *n.*

ca·lor·ic *n.* heat; *a.* heat-producing. caloricity *n.* the power of animals to develop heat. calorifacient *a.* heat-producing. calorific *a.* heat-producing. calorification *n.* the production of heat.

cal·o·rie, calory *n.* the unit of heat or energy produced by any food substance. calorimeter *n.* a scientific instrument for determining the amount of heat produced by any substance.

ca·lum·ni·ate *v.t.* to accuse falsely; *v.i.* to utter slanders. calumniation *n.* slanderous representations. calumniator *n.* calumniatory, calumnious *a.* slanderous. calumniously *adv.* calumny *n.* a flase accusation; libel.

calve See calf.

Cal·vin·ism *n.* the doctrines of John Calvin. Calvinist *n.* Calvinistic *a.*

calx *n.* the crumbly substance that remains after the calcination of a metal or mineral; *pl.* calxes, calces.

ca·lyp·so *n.* an improvised song in native rhythm from the West Indies.

ca·lyx, ca·lix *n.* the outer covering or leaf-like envelope of a flower.

calyx

cam *n.* a projecting part of a wheel used to give an alternating or variable motion to another wheel or piece. -shaft *n.* the shaft on which cams are formed for opening the valves.

cam

cam·ber *n.* a slight convexity of an upper surface, as of a ship's deck, a bridge, a road surface.

Cam·bri·an *a.* pert. to Cambria or Wales; *n.* a Welshman.

cam·bric *n.* a fine white linen fabric first made at *Cambrai*, in N. France.

came *pa.t. of the verb* come.

cam·el *n.* a large ruminant animal of Asia and Africa, with one or two humps, used as a beast of burden. -eer *n.* a camel driver.

ca·mel·lia *a.* a species of Asiatic shrub with showy flowers and elegant dark-green, laurel-like leaves.

cam·e·o *n.* a gem stone of two layers cut in ornamental relief.

cam·e·ra *n.* device for taking photographs. -man *n.* a professional motion picture or press photographer.

cam·ou·flage *n.* a method of visual

deception of the enemy by disguising; *v.t.* to cover with camouflage material; to disguise.

camp *n.* the area of ground where soldiers are lodged in huts or tents; permanent barracks near a suitable exercise ground; *v.t.* and *i.* to pitch tents. -er *n.* one who lives in a camp in open country, esp. living in a tent. -ing *n.* the act of living in camp. — chair *n.* a light, portable chair with folding legs. — meeting *n.* a religious meeting in the open air. — out *v.* to live without conveniences.

cam-paign *n.* in politics, business, etc. an organized series of operations (meetings, canvassing, etc.); *v.i.* to conduct, or assist in political, etc. operations. -er *n.*

cam-phor *n.* a whitish substance with an aromatic taste and smell, obtained from

camphor

the camphor laurel-tree. -aceous *a.* resembling camphor. -ate *v.t.* to impregnate with camphor. -ate, -ic *a.* pert. to camphor.

cam-pus *n.* the grounds of a college or school.

can *pres. indic.* of a defective, intransitive verb meaning, to be able, to be allowed. *pa.p., pa.t.* could.

can *n.* a metal container for holding liquids, etc.; *v.t.* to put into a can for the purpose of preserving; *pr.p.* -ning. *pa.p.* and *pa.t.* -ned. -nery *n.* a factory where foods are preserved by canning.

Ca-na-di-an *n.* an inhabitant of Canada; *a.* pert. to Canada.

ca-nal *n.* an artificial watercourse for transport, drainage or irrigation purposes. canalize *v.t.* to make a canal through.

can-a-pé *n.* a small piece of bread, with anchovies, etc. on it served as an appetizer.

ca-nar-y *n.* a yellow singing bird, a species of finch; a pale-yellow color.

ca-nas-ta *n.* a card game played with two packs.

can-can *n.* a kind of dance, once popular in music-halls in France.

can-cel *v.t.* to blot out; to annul; (*Math.*) to strike out common factors; to offset. -lation *n.* the act of canceling.

can-cer *n.* (*Med.*) a malignant growth or tumor. -ate *v.i.* to grow into a cancer. -ation *n.* -ous *a.* pert. to cancer.

can-de-la-brum *n.* a branched and highly ornamented candle-stick. candelabra *n.sing.* and *pl.*

can-did *a.* fair; frank. -ly *adv.* -ness *n.* frankness; ingenuousness.

can-di-date *n.* one who seeks an appointment, office, honor, etc.

candidature, candidacy *n.* the position of being a candidate.

can-dle *n.* a stick of tallow, wax, etc. with a wick inside, used for light. — power, the unit of luminosity. -stick *n.* an instrument for holding a candle.

can-dor *n.* candidness; frankness.

can-dy *n.* a kind of sweetmeat made of sugar; *v.t.* to form into crystals, as sugar; *v.i.* to become candied. candied *a.*

cane *n.* the stem of a small palm or long, strong reed; the sugar-cane; a walking-stick; *v.t.* to beat with a cane. -brake *n.* a dense growth of canes. — sugar *n.* sugar from the sugar-cane.

ca-nine *a.* of, or pert. to a dog. — teeth, the two pointed teeth in each jaw, between the incisors and the molars.

can-is-ter *n.* a small case or box for holding tea, coffee, etc.

can-ker *n.* ulceration of the mouth; a disease affecting horses' feet; *v.t.* to gnaw at; *v.i.* to decay, to become cankered. -ed *a.* corrupted; malignant. -ous *a.* corrupting like a canker. -y *a.* cankered. -worm *n.* a destructive caterpillar.

can-nel-coal *n.* a kind of coal, burning with a clear, smokeless flame, used in the manufacture of gas. Also **candle-coal.**

can-ni-bal *n.* one who eats human flesh; *a.* relating to this practice. -ism *n.* the practice of eating human flesh. -istic *a.* cannibalize *v.t.* to dismantle in the hope of getting spare parts to be used for re-conditioning.

can-non *n.* a large gun; *v.i.* to cannonade. -ade *n.* an attack with cannon; the firing of cannon; *v.t.* to bombard. -eer, -ier *n.* one who loads or fires cannon; an artilleryman. — ball *n.* an iron ball to be discharged by cannon. -shot *n.* a cannon ball; the range of a cannon.

can-not combination of *can* and *not*, therefore, = not to be able.

ca-noe *n.* a light, narrow boat propelled by a hand paddle. -ist *n.*

can-on *n.* the books of the Scriptures accepted by the Church as of divine authority. -ess *n.* a member of a religious association of women. canonic, canonical *a.* canonicals *n.pl.* official dress worn by a clergyman. canonically *adv.* -ization *n.* -ize *v.t.* to place in the list of saints. -ist *n.* one skilled in canon law. -ry *n.* the office of canon.

can-o-py *n.* a covering fixed above a bed, or a dais, or carried on poles above the head.

cant *n.* an inclination from the level; a tilted position; *v.t.* to tilt; *v.i.* to have, or take a leaning position.

can-ta-loupe, can-ta-loup *n.* a variety of muskmelon, having a furrowed rind.

can-tan-ker-ous *a.* quarrelsome. -ly *adv.*

can-ta-ta *n.* a short musical composition in oratorio or lyric drama form.

can-teen *n.* a small container for carrying water; a store and refreshment-room.

can-ter *v.i.* to move at an easy gallop; *n.* an easy gallop or gait.

can‑ti‑lev‑er n. a bracket for supporting a balcony. cantilever bridge. a bridge built on the same principle.

can‑to n. a part of a poem. -r n. the leader of the singing, esp. in a synagogue.

can‑ton n. a small district administered by a separate government; v.t. to divide into districts, as territory. -al a. -ment n. quarters for troops.

can‑vas n. a coarse cloth made of hemp, for sails, tents, etc.; a special prepared material for painting on.

can‑vass v.t. to examine thoroughly; to solicit support, or votes, or contributions; v.i. to solicit votes; n. solicitation; a seeking to obtain votes. -er n.

can‑yon n. a ravine; a deep gorge.

cap n. a brimless covering, for the head; a small lid used as a cover; v.t. to cover the top or end of; to confer a degree on; pr.p. -ping. pa.p. and pa.t. -ped.

ca‑pa‑ble a. competent; skillful. capably adv. -ness n. capability n. power.

ca‑pa‑cious a. roomy; spacious. -ly adv. -ness n.

ca‑pac‑i‑ty n. power of holding or grasping; room; ability; cubic content. capacitate v.t. to render capable.

ca‑par‑i‑son n. a covering laid over a horse; v.t. to cover with a decorated cloth.

cape n. a covering for the shoulders.

cape n. a point of land running out into the sea; a headland.

ca‑per v.i. to leap about like a goat, in a sprightly manner.

cap‑il‑lar‑y n. one of the microscopic blood-vessels connecting the arteries and veins. capillarity n. capilliform a. hair-shaped.

cap‑i‑tal a. involving the forfeiture of life; first in importance; principal; n. the city or town which is the seat of government in a state or nation; the estimated total value of a business. — punishment n. the death penalty; -ize n. to take advantage of. -ization n. to provide with capital letters; to supply with capital.

cap‑i‑tal‑ism n. form of economic, industrial, and social organization of society involving ownership, control, and direction of production by privately owned business organizations. capitalist n.

cap‑i‑ta‑tion n. a census; a tax or grant per head.

Cap‑i‑tol n. the building used by the U.S. Congress in Washington for its sessions; a state legislature building.

ca‑pit‑u‑late v.i. to draw up terms of an agreement. capitulation n. capitulator n.

ca‑pon n. a young castrated cock fed for the table. caponize v.t.

ca‑price n. illogical change of feeling or opinion; a whim; a fancy. capricious a.

cap‑si‑cum n. a genus of tropical plants, whose fruits when dried and ground give Cayenne pepper.

cap‑size v.t. and i. overturn.

cap‑stan n. a heavy cable-holder revolving on an upright spindle.

cap‑sule n. a small gelatinous case containing medicine; a. condensed.

cap‑tain n. in the army, an officer commanding a company of infantry; in the navy, an officer in command of a man-of-war; the master of a merchant ship or other vessel; in sport, the leader of a team; v.t. to command; -cy n. the rank or commission of a captain.

cap‑tion n. the heading of a newspaper, chapter, page, etc.

cap‑tious a. apt to find fault; difficult to please. -ly adv. -ness n. fault-finding.

cap‑ti‑vate v.t. to capture the fancy of. captivating a. winning, charming. captivation n.

cap‑tive n. a prisoner; one held in captivity; a. made prisoner. captivity n. imprisonment. captor n. one who takes a prisoner or a prize. capture n. the act of seizing by force or stratagem; arrest; the thing seized; the prize; v.t. to take possession of.

car n. any kind of vehicle on wheels; automobile.

ca‑rafe n. a glass decanter.

car‑a‑mel n. burnt sugar, used for coloring and in cooking; a kind of candy.

car‑at n. a measure of weight for gold and precious stones, the standard carat being 3.16 grains troy.

car‑a‑van n. parties of merchants or others traveling together for greater security, esp. across deserts. -eer n. the leader of a caravan.

car‑a‑way n. a biennial aromatic plant; its seed, used as a flavoring for bread, cakes, etc.

car‑bide n. a compound of carbon with certain elements, including calcium, manganese, iron, etc.

car‑bine, carabine n. a short rifle. carbineer, carabineer n. a soldier armed with a carbine.

car‑bo‑hy‑drate n. a substance, such as sugar, starch, cellulose, etc. composed of carbon, hydrogen, and oxygen.

car‑bol‑ic a. derived from carbon; n. carbolic acid. carbolated a. treated with or containing, carbolic acid. carbolic acid, a poisonous acid distilled from coal tar.

car‑bon n. a non-metallic element existing pure in nature as diamond, graphite, charcoal, etc. and as a compound of animal and vegetable substances; a copy made by using carbon paper. -aceous a. pert. to, or composed of, coal. -ize v.t. to make into carbon; to coat with carbon. -ization n. — paper, type of paper used for duplicating written work.

car‑bo‑run‑dum n. silicon carbide, a black crystalline substance, of exceptional hardness.

car‑bu‑ret‑or n. an apparatus in an internal-combustion engine to convert liquid gasoline into vaporized form. carburation n. carburize v.t. cause to unite with carbon.

car‑cass, carcase n. the dead body of man or animal, esp. of the latter; the framework of anything.

car‑ci‑no‑ma n. a cancer.

C

card n. a small piece of pasteboard often with figures, pictures, etc. on it for playing games; a piece of pasteboard having on it a person's name and address; an ornamented piece of paper or cardboard with a greeting, such as a birthday card; -board n. finely finished pasteboard. -sharp n. one who cheats at cards.

car•di•ac See cardio-

car•di•gan n. a knitted jacketlike sweater.

car•di•nal a. of great importance; (Color) deep scarlet. -ly adv. — numbers, 1, 2, 3, 4, 5, etc.

car•di•nal n. the highest rank next to the Pope, in the Catholic Church. -ate, -ship n. the office of a cardinal.

car•di•o- the heart, combining to form derivatives. cardiac a. pert. to the heart; n. a heart stimulant. -gram n. the graphic tracing of the movements of the heart as recorded by an instrument called the cardiograph. cardiology n. (Med.) the branch of medicine which deals with the functions and diseases of the heart.

care n. concern or anxiety; caution; v.i. to be anxious, concerned; to be affected with solicitude. -ful a. full of solicitude; watchful; painstaking. -fully adv. -fulness n. -less a. heedless; thoughtless; regardless. -lessly adv. -lessness n. -worn a. showing the wearing effects of care. -taker n. one who takes over the care of anything or anyone.

ca•reen v.t. to turn a ship over on one side; v.i. to lean over.

ca•reer n. profession; conduct in life, or progress through life. -ist n. one who makes his personal advancement his one aim in life.

ca•ress v.t. to treat with affection; to fondle; n. a loving touch; an embrace. -ing a.

car•et n. a mark (∧) which shows where something should be inserted.

car•go n. the freight of a ship; the merchandise carried.

car•i•bou n. the N. American reindeer.

car•i•ca•ture n. a ludicrous exaggeration (usually in picture form) of peculiar personal characteristics; v.t. to exaggerate in words or in pictorial form. caricaturist n.

car•il•lon n. a set or peal of bells of different tones.

car•mine n. a brilliant crimson, prepared from cochineal. Also a.

car•nage n. massacre; bloodshed.

car•nal a. pert. to the flesh; sensual. -ize v.t. to make carnal. carnality n. fleshly lust. -ly adv. — knowledge sexual intercourse.

car•na•tion n. a variety of the clove-pink, noted for its beauty and sweet scent.

car•ni•val n. a traveling show with amusements such as merry-go-rounds, etc.

car•niv•o•ra n.pl. animals that feed on flesh. carnivore n. a flesh-eating animal. carnivorous a. carnivorously adv. carnivorousness n.

car•ol n. a song of joy, esp. a Christmas hymn; v.i. to sing a carol.

ca•rot•id n. each of the two main arteries in the neck conveying blood to the head; a. pert. to these.

ca•rouse v.i. to revel; to hold a drinking-party. carousal n. a noisy drinking-party. -r n.

car•ou•sel See carrousel.

carp v.i. to find fault petulantly and without reason.

carp n. a fresh-water fish.

car•pel n. (Bot.) the seed-bearing part of a plant; part of a compound ovary. -lary a.

car•pen•ter n. a worker in lumber as used in building of houses, ships, etc. carpentry n.

car•pet n. a woven covering for floors; -ing n. a covering similar to a carpet. -bagger n. a political adventurer.

car•ra•way See caraway.

car•riage n. a vehicle for passengers; a wheeled conveyor; one's posture or bearing. -able a. carriable; passable for carriages.

car•ri•er n. one who carries; one who carries goods for hire, often called a 'common carrier'; a receptacle for carrying objects; (Med.) one who, without showing symptoms of disease, can convey infection to others.

car•rot n. a plant cultivated for its edible root. -y a. reddish-yellow.

car•rou•sel, car•ou•sel n. a merry-go-round.

car•ry v.t. to transport; to impel; to transfer.

cart n. a two-wheeled vehicle used for the transport of heavy goods; a small four-wheeled vehicle pulled by hand; v.t. to convey in a cart. -age n. carting; the price paid for carting. -er n. -wright n. maker of carts.

car•tel n. an international industrial combination for regulating volume and price of output.

car•ti•lage n. a strong, transparent tissue in the body, very elastic and softer than bone. cartilaginous a.

car•tog•ra•phy n. the art of making charts or maps. cartographer n.

car•ton n. a pasteboard box.

car•toon n. a pictorial caricature; a comic strip; movie comics. -ist n.

car•tridge n. a case made of metal, cardboard, etc. to contain the charge for a gun.

carve v.t. and i. to fashion artistically by cutting; to cut in pieces or slices, as meat, etc.; to divide. -r n. one who carves; a large knife for carving. carving n.

cas•cade n. a waterfall; a wavy fall of lace; v.i. to fall in cascades.

case n. a receptacle; anything which encloses or contains; a box and its contents; (Print.) a frame for holding type; v.t. to put in a case. casing n. a case or covering. -room n. (Print.) the room in which type is set. — shot n. canister shot; small projectiles put in cases or canisters, to be shot from cannon. -harden v.t. to heat soft steel in contact with carbonaceous material, so that carbon is absorbed, and a surface of harder steel produced. **lower case** (*Print.*) denoting small letters. **upper case** (*Print.*) mew. — **burglary** a burglar who makes

case *n.* an event, occurrence, or circumstance; a question of facts requiring solution; (*Med.*) a patient under treatment; (*Gram.*) an inflection or terminal change in nouns, pronouns, etc. **casal** *a.* (*Gram.*) pert. to case.

ca·se·in *n.* the curd or cheesy part of milk, a protein.

case·ment *n.* a window, or part of a window, opening on hinges.

cash *n.* money, esp. ready money; *v.t.* to turn into, or exchange for, money. — **register** *n.* an automatic money-till which registers and indicates the amount paid for goods sold.

cash·ew *n.* a tropical American tree whose fruit, the cashew-nut, is eaten raw or roasted.

cash·ier *n.* one who has charge of the cash.

cash·ier *v.t.* to dismiss from office in disgrace; to discard.

cash·mere *n.* a shawl made from the hair of the Kashmir (Cashmere) goat; the material; *a.*

ca·si·no *n.* a public assembly-room for dancing, gambling, etc.

cask *n.* a large wooden vessel for holding liquor; a barrel; *v.t.* to put in a cask.

cas·ket *n.* a coffin; a small box.

cas·se·role *n.* a covered baking dish in which food is both cooked and served.

cas·sia *n.* a genus of plants, including senna, whose pods are used medicinally as a laxative; a cheap kind of cinnamon.

cas·sock *n.* a long, close-fitting black gown worn by clergymen.

cast *v.t.* to fling; to direct or bestow, as a glance; to shed, as a skin; to distribute the parts of a play among the actors; to throw a line in angling; to forecast (to cast a horoscope); to give (a vote); *n.* the act of casting; the distance a thing is thrown; a change of direction; that which is shed or ejected; a forecast; the actors appearing in a play; squint (of the eye). — **down** *a.* depressed. **-ing** *n.* the act of foundling and molding. **-ing-vote** *n.* the vote of a chairman, which decides a question when votes are equally divided. — **iron** *a.* indefatigable; unshakable.

cas·ta·nets *n.pl.* two small concave shells fastened to the thumb and clicked in time to music of a Spanish type.

castanets

cast·a·way *n.* a shipwrecked person.

caste *n.* an exclusive social order.

cast·er, castor *n.* a small bottle with perforated top; a small swivelled wheel

on the foot of a chair-leg, etc.

cas·ti·gate *v.t.* to rebuke severly; to chastise. **castigation** *n.* severe chastisement; discipline. **castigator** *n.*

castle *n.* a fortified residence; a stronghold, esp. of nobleman; a piece (also called rook) in chess. **-d** *a.* having a castle; built like a castle.

cas·tor·oil *n.* an oil used as a cathartic.

cas·trate *v.t.* to deprive of the testicles; to emasculate. **castration** *n.*

cas·u·al *a.* incidental; occasional; offhand or careless; *n.* a casual worker, etc. **-ly** *adv.* **-ness** *n.* **-ty** *n.* an accident, mishap. **-ties** *n.pl.* (*Mil.*) losses caused by death, wounds, capture, etc.

cas·u·ist *n.* one versed in casuistry. **-ry** *n.* the science of dealing with problems of right or wrong conduct by applying principles drawn from the Scriptures. **casuistic, casuistical** *a.* **casuistically** *adv.*

cat *n.* a small domestic quadruped, of the family of felines; related carnivores such as the lion, tiger, leopard, lynx, etc. **-ty**, **-tish** *a.* spiteful. **-bird** *n.* a gray N. Am. songbird having a cry similar to a cat's mew. — **burglary** a burglar who makes his entry by climbing to windows, roofs, etc. **-call** *n.* a cat-like cry, used by audiences to express disapproval. — **eyed** *a.* able to see in the dark. — **nap** *n.* a very short, light sleep. **-'s-eye** *n.* a gem with reflections like those from a cat's eye. **cat-o-nine-tails** *n.* a whip with nine thongs or lashes. **tabby cat** a female cat; a striped cat. **tom cat** a male cat.

cat·a- a combining form meaning away, against, fully, used to form derivatives.

cat·a·clysm *n.* a social or political upheaval; a sudden and violent alteration in earth's surface. **-al** *a.* **-ic** *a.*

cat·a·combs *n.pl.* underground passage-ways with niches for tombs.

cat·a·lec·tic *a.* lacking a syllable at the end of a verse.

cat·a·lep·sy *n.* (*Med.*) suspension of senses and bodily powers, with muscular rigidity; a trance. **cataleptic** *a.*

cat·a·logue *n.* a list, usually alphabetical, of names, books, goods, etc.; a descriptive price-list; also **catalog.** *v.t.* to make such a list. **-r** *n.*

ca·tal·y·sis *n.* (*Chem.*) the chemical change effected in one substance by the aid of another which itself undergoes no change. **catalyst** *n.* a substance producing such a change. **catalytic** *a.*

cat·a·pult *n.* a siege engine for hurling stones, arrows, etc.; a device for launching airplanes from the deck of a ship; *v.t.*

cat·a·ract *n.* the flow of a large body of water over a precipice; (*Med.*) a disease of the eye, characterized by an opaque condition in the lens.

ca·tas·tro·phe *n.* a disaster; a calamity. **catastrophic** *a.*

catch *v.t.* to take hold of; to seize; to get a disease by contagion; to come upon unexpectedly; *v.i.* to seize, and keep hold; *pa.t.* and *pa.p.* **caught.** *n.* anything that holds, stops, etc.; that which is

C

caught. -able *a.* able to be caught. -er *n.*
-ing *a.* -y *a.* containing a hidden difficulty; captivating; attractive. -all *n.* a receptacle for miscellaneous objects.

catch•ment *n.* drainage area.

catch•pen•ny *n.* something of little value made to sell quickly; *a.* cheap and showy.

catch•up, catsup, ketchup *n.* a bottled sauce made from tomatoes, vinegar, sugar and spices.

catch•word *n.* a word that takes the popular fancy; a slogan; the first word in the column of a dictionary, etc., repeated above the column as a reference.

cat•e•chize *v.t.* to instruct by question and answer, esp. in Christian doctrine. catechism *n.* a set form of question and answer to teach the tenets of religion. catechist *n.* one who catechizes. catechetical *a.* consisting of question and answer. catechetically *adv.* catechesis *n.* oral instruction as given to catechumens.

cat•e•chu•men *n.* one being instructed in the fundamentals of a subject, esp. religion. (See catechize).

cat•e•go•ry *n.* a group, division; in logic, any fundamental conception. categorical *a.* pert. to a category; admitting no conditions; precise. categorically *adv.* categorize *v.t.* to place in a category.

ca•ter *v.i.* to provide food, entertainment, etc. -er *n.*

cat•er•cor•nered *a.* diagonal.

cat•er•pil•lar *n.* the larva of butterflies and moths.

ca•thar•tic *a.* (*Med.*) purgative; cleansing the bowels; *n.* a purging medicine. catharize *v.t.* to cleanse; to purify. catharsis *n.* purgation, also of the emotions, through art.

Ca•thay *n.* an old name for China.

ca•the•dral *n.* the principal church in a diocese, which contains the bishop's throne; *a.* pert. to a cathedral.

cath•ode *n.* the negative pole of an electric cell; the conductor by which an electric current leaves an electrolyte, and passes over to the negative pole; opp. of *anode.* — rays negative ions or electrons.

cath•o•lic *a.* pert. to Roman Catholics; comprehensive in understanding; *n.* a member of the R.C. Church. catholicism *n.* the faith and practice of Catholic Church, or of R.C. Church; liberality of opinion; catholicity. catholicity *n.*

cat•nip *n.* an aromatic plant with blue flowers, attractive to cats.

cat•sup See catchup.

cat•tle *n.pl.* domestic livestock, esp. cows and bulls.

Cau•ca•sian *a.* Indo-European, i.e. pert. to the white race. *n.*

cau•cus *n.* a meeting of leaders of a political party to decide policies, etc.

cau•dal *a.* pert. to a tail. caudate *a.* having a tail.

caught *pa.p.* and *pa.t.* of catch.

caul *n.* the membrane covering the head of some babies at birth.

caul•dron See caldron.

cau•li•flow•er *n.* a variety of cabbage.

caulk See calk.

cau•sal *a.* relating to a cause or causes. causality *n.* the relation of cause and effect. causation *n.* agency by which an effect is produced. causative *a.*

cause *n.* that which produces a result or effect; the motive of an action; principle supported by a person or party; *v.t.* to be the occasion of; to induce. -r *n.* -less *a.* without reason or motive.

cause•way *n.* a raised paved road.

caus•tic *a.* (*Fig.*) biting, bitter, satirical; *n.* a substance that corrodes and destroys animal tissue. -ally *adv.* causticity *n.*

cau•ter *n.* a hot, searing iron. -ize *v.t.* to burn animal tissue in order to destroy diseased tissue, or promote healing. -ization *n.* -y *n.* the act of cauterizing; a hot iron for searing.

cau•tion *n.* prudence; wariness; a warning; *v.t.* to advise to take care; to admonish. cautious *a.* wary; discreet. cautiously *adv.* -ary *a.* containing a warning. -er *n.*

cav•al•cade *n.* procession on horseback.

cav•a•lier *n.* a horseman; an attendant escort to a lady; *a.* gay and offhand; supercilious. -ly *adv.*

cav•al•ry *n.* horse-soldiery.

cave *n.* a small chamber hollowed out of the earth horizontally, either by nature or by man. — man *n.* a male of primitive ways. to cave in (of ground) to fall in, (*Fig.*) to admit defeat.

cav•ern *n.* a deep, hollow place under the earth; a large dark cave. -ed *a.* full of caverns. -ous *a.* hollow; deep-set.

cav•i•ar, caviare *n.* a delicacy made from the roes of the sturgeon.

cav•i•ty *n.* a hollow place of any size.

caw *v.i.* to cry like a crow or raven; the sound made by the crow.

cay•enne *n.* a pungent red pepper.

cease *v.t.* to put a stop to; *v.i.* to discontinue. -less *a.* without stopping. -lessly *adv.*

ce•dar *n.* species of coniferous, evergreen trees yielding durable, fragrant wood. -n, cedrine *a.*

cede *v.t.* to yield; to give up, esp. of territory.

ce•dil•la *n.* a small sign (ç), used, principally in French, as a pronunciation mark.

ceil•ing *n.* the interior part of the roof of a room; the maximum height to which a particular airplane can ascend.

cel•e•brate *v.t.* to mark by ceremony, as an event or festival; to observe with solemn rites. -d *a.* famous. celebration *n.* the act of celebrating. celebrant *n.* one who celebrates. celebrity *n.* fame; a person of distinction.

cel•er•y *n.* an edible plant cultivated for eating with salads or as a cooked vegetable.

ce•les•tial *a.* heavenly; *n.* an inhabitant of heaven. -ly *adv.*

cel•i•ba•cy *n.* the unmarried state. celibate *n.* one unmarried; *a.* unmarried.

cell *n.* a small room, as in a prison or monastery; the simplest unit in the structure of living matter; a division of a voltaic or galvanic battery. -ed a. furnished with, or containing, cells; contained in cells. -ular a. consisting of, or containing, cells, as cellular tissue. -ulated a. having a cellular structure.

cel•lar n. the lowest story under a building; a storeroom, esp. for wines, liquors.

cel•lo, 'cel•lo n. (Mus.) a contraction for violoncello, a stringed musical instrument. cellist, 'cellist n. a player on the violoncello.

cel•lo•phane n. a transparent, waterproof material used as wrapping tissue, etc.

cel•lu•loid n. name for a hard compound used in the manufacture of imitation ivory, coral, amber, etc.

cel•lu•lose n. a chemical substance, one of the carbohydrates, forming the chief constituent of the walls of plant cells; an essential part of wood, paper, linen, cotton, etc.

Celt, Kelt n. one of a race, including the Highlanders of Scotland, the Irish, Welsh, Bretons, Manx, and Cornish. Celtic, Keltic n. the language spoken by the Celts. a. pert. to the Celts.

ce•ment n. a material used in making concrete for building or paving; v.t. to unite by using cement; to join closely. -ation n. the act of cementing.

cem•e•ter•y n. a graveyard; a burying ground.

cen•ser n. a metal vessel in which incense is burned. cense v.t. to perfume with incense.

cen•sor n. one appointed to examine books, plays, newspaper articles, etc. before publication, and ban them if containing anything objectionable; also, in time of war or crisis, to examine letters, etc., and erase anything calculated to convey information to the enemy; one who finds fault; v.t. to blame or reprove; to subject to examination by the censor. -ial a. pert. to correction of morals; pert. to a censor. -ious a. apt to find fault. -iously adv. -iousness n. -ship n. the office of a censor; the act of censoring.

cen•sure n. the act of finding fault; v.t. to criticize adversely. censurable a.

cen•sus n. an official numbering of the inhabitants of a country. censual a.

cent n. a hundredth, as 10 per cent; a U.S. coin worth the hundredth part of a dollar.

cen•taur n. a fabulous being, half man and half horse.

cen•te•nar•y n. a period of a hundred years; the commemoration of a hundredth anniversary. centenarian n. a person a hundred years old.

cen•ten•ni•al a. pert. to a period of 100 years; happening once in a hundred years; n. a hundredth anniversary.

cen•ter n. the mid-point of anything; a point to which things are drawn; v.t. and i. to place in the center. -piece n. an ornament or cloth covering for the center of a table. centric(al) a. placed in middle. centrically adv. centricity n. the state of being centric. center of gravity, the point in a body about which it will balance.

cen•ti- a hundred, combining to form

derivatives. -grade a. divided into 100 degrees, as the centigrade thermometer on which freezing-point is marked 0° and boiling-point 100°. -meter n. 100th part of a meter = .394 inch.

cen•ti•pede n. an insect, of flat and elongated shape, with a segmented body.

cen•tral a. relating to, or placed in, the center; important. -ly adv. -ize v.t. to draw to a central point; to put under one control. -ization n. -ism n. centralization. esp. of government. centrality n. the state of being central. — heating, heating of a building or group of buildings from one central furnace.

cen•tri•fu•gal a. tending to move away from the center of a revolving body.

cen•trip•e•tal a. tending to move towards the center.

cen•tu•ry n. a period of a hundred years.

ce•phal•ic a. pert. to the head; n. a medicine for headaches.

ce•ram•ic a. pert. to pottery. ceramics n.pl. the art of molding, modelling, and baking clay.

cere v.t. (Obs.) to cover with wax. ceraceous a. waxy. cerate n. an ointment of wax, oil, etc. -cloth n. a cloth smeared with melted wax in which dead bodies used to be wrapped. -ment n. (usually pl.) graveclothes.

ce•re•al n. any edible grain (wheat, barley, oats, etc.); a breakfast food made of such grains.

ce•re•brum n. the upper and larger division of the brain. cerebellum n. the part of the brain behind and below the cerebrum. cerebral a. pert. to the brain. cerebral hemorrhage, rupture of an artery of the brain with a consequent escape of blood. cerebral palsy n. paralysis from cerebral lesion, chiefly characterized by spasms. cerebrate v.i. to have the brain in action. cerebration n. cerebrospinal a. pert. to both brain and spinal cord.

ce•re•mo•ny n. a sacred rite; formal observance; a public or private function. ceremonial a. formal; n. usage followed in performing rites. ceremonially adv. ceremonious a. full of ceremony; particular in observing forms. ceremoniously adv. ceremoniousness n. master of ceremonies n. at public functions, etc. one whose business it is to see that all rules, and courtesies are observed.

ce•rise n. and a. light clear red; cherry-colored.

cer•tain a. sure; constant; of moderate quantity, degree, etc. -ly adv. -ty n. the quality of being certain. certitude n. freedom from doubt; certainty. certes adv. in truth.

cer•ti•fi•cate n. a written testimony to the truth of a fact; written statement of qualifications v.i. to attest by a certificate; to furnish with a certificate. certify v.t. to vouch for the truth of. certifiable a. able to be vouched for. certification n. the act of certifying. certified a.

ce•ru•le•an a. sky-blue; deep blue.

ceruleous *a.* sky-blue.

ce•ruse *n.* white lead. **cerussite** *n.* a carbonate of lead.

cer•vi•cal *a.* pert. to the neck or neck of the uterus.

ces•sa•tion *n.* stoppage; discontinuance.

ces•sion *n.* act of surrendering, as by treated; something yielded, ceded.

cess•pool *n.* a pit for collection of drainage water or sewage.

chafe *v.t.* to wear away by rubbing; to irritate; *v.i.* to be worn by friction; to fret; *n.* friction; injury caused by rubbing. -*r n.* one who chafes. **chafing dish** *n.* a dish and heating apparatus for keeping food warm on the table.

chaff *n.* straw cut small for cattle-feeding.

chaff *n.* banter; *v.t.* to make fun of (without spite).

cha•grin *n.* ill-humor; vexation; *v.t.* to vex deeply.

chain *n.* a series of metal links connected and forming a flexible cable; a succession of events; *v.t.* to fasten or connect with a chain; to restrain. — **bridge** *n.* a suspension bridge. -**drive** *n.* the transmitting of driving-power by means of chain-gear. — **gang** *n.* a number of convicts chained together. — **reaction** *n.* in nuclear physics, a self-sustaining process in which some neutrons from one splitting atom are able to split more atoms, setting free still more neutrons which carry on the reaction indefinitely.

chair *n.* a seat with a back, legs, and sometimes arms, usually for one person; an official seat occupied by the president of a meeting, a university professor; *v.t.* to install in a chair or office. **to take the chair**, to act as chairman of a meeting. -**man** *n.* the presiding officer of a meeting. -**manship** *n.* -**woman** *n.*

chaise *n.* a light, one-horse carriage. — **longue** *n.* an elongated seat with backrest at one end and support for legs.

chal•ice *n.* a wine-cup; a goblet.

chalk *n.* a soft, white, carbonate of lime; a chalk-like material used for marking; *v.t.* to mark with chalk. -**y** *a.* containing or like chalk. -**iness** *n.* — **up** *v.t.* to score.

chal•lenge *n.* an invitation to a contest; *v.t.* to call upon a person to settle a dispute by fighting; to summon to answer; to call in question. -**able** *a.* -**r** *n.*

cham•ber *n.* a room, esp. one used for lodging or study; a place where an assembly, such as a legislature meets, and the assembly itself; *v.t.* to confine, as in a chamber; *v.i.* to occupy as a chamber. -**ed** *a.* -**s** *n.pl.* rooms where a judge hears cases not requiring action in court. -**maid** *n.* a woman servant who has the care of bedrooms, esp. in hotels, etc. — **music** *n.* music suitable for performance in a house or small hall.

cha•me•le•on *n.* a small lizard, which changes color with its surroundings.

cham•fer *v.t.* to cut a groove in; to bevel; *n.* a groove; a bevel. -**ed** *a.*

cham•ois *n.* a goat-like species of antelope; a kind of soft leather.

champ *v.t. and i.* to bite, chew, or munch noisily. **to champ at the bit** *(Fig.)* to be impatient; *n.*

cham•pagne *n.* a light effervescent, white wine, made in the province of *Champagne* in N.E. France, or elsewhere.

cham•pi•on *n.* one who fought in single combat to defend the honor of another; one capable of defeating his competitors in any form of sport; *a.* first-class; *v.t.* to defend; to maintain or support. -**ship** *n.* the position of a champion; defense; advocacy.

chance *n.* an unforeseen occurrence; risk; opportunity; possibility; *a.* accidental; *v.t.* to risk; *v.i.* to happen. **by —**, accidentally.

chan•cel•lor *n.* the title of various high officials in the state, and in the law; the head of a university. -**ship** *n.* the office of chancellor. **chancellery** *n.* the premises of a chancellor.

chan•cer•y *n.* the office of a chancellor; a chancellery; a court of equity.

chan•de•lier *n.* a branched framework for holding lights, esp. one hanging from the ceiling.

change *v.t.* to alter or make different; to shift; to exchange, as money; *v.i.* to become different; to change one's clothes; *n.* alteration; that which makes for variety; money of small denomination given in exchange for money of larger; balance of money returned after payment; fresh clothing; an exchange. -**able** *a.* variable; unsteady. -**ful** *a.* -**fully** *adv.* -**fulness** *n.* -**less** *a.* unchanging; constant.

chan•nel *n.* a waterway; the deeper part of a river, harbor, etc.; means of access; *a.* frequency band for transmission of radio, television, etc.; *v.t.* to form a channel; to direct in a particular course.

chant *v.t. and i.* to sing; to celebrate in song; *n.* a song; sacred words recited in a singing manner. -**er** *n.*

chant•i•cleer *n.* a cock, rooster.

cha•os *n.* chaotic *a.*

chap *v.t.* to split; to crack; *v.i.* to become cracked, red, and rough (as the skin in cold weather); *pr.t.* -**ping.** *pa.t.* -**ped.** *n.* a crack in the skin.

chap•el *n.* a private church; a division of a church with its own altar.

chap•e•ron *n.* a mature person who is in attendance at social gatherings of young

chameleon

people; *v.t.* to escort, accompany. **-age** *n.*

chap·lain *n.* a clergyman. **-cy** *n.*

chap·ter *n.* a division of a book or treatise; an organized branch of a society, fraternity, or military order; *v.t.* to divide into chapters.

char *v.t.* to reduce to charcoal; to burn to a black cinder; *pr.p.* **-ring.** *pa.p.* and *pa.t.* **-red. -coal** *n.* the residue of partially burnt vegetable matter, esp. wood.

char, chare *n.* work done by the day; *v.i.* to work by the day; to do small jobs. **-woman** *n.*

char·ac·ter *n.* a mark, letter, figure, sign, stamp; any distinctive mark; the total of qualities making up an individuality; moral excellence; a personage in a play or novel; *v.t.* to characterize; to represent. **-ize** *v.t.* to depict the peculiar qualities of; to give character to. **-istic** *a.* peculiar; distinctive; *n.* that which distinguishes a person or thing from another; **-istically** *adv.* **-ization** *n.* the act or characterizing literary or dramatic portrayal of character.

cha·rade *n.* a game, consisting of the interpretation (usually dramatic) of a word for others to guess.

chard *n.* leafy vegetable.

charge *n.* a burden; price or cost; care or trust; accusation or allegation; the amount of powder, etc., that a gun is fitted to hold; an impetuous onset or attack, or the signal for it; electrical contents of accumulator or battery; *v.t.* to lay a task, command, trust upon; to ask as payment; to load, as a gun; *v.i.* to make an onset. **-able** *a.* **-r** *n.* a war-horse.

char·i·ot *n.* in ancient times, a two-wheeled cart used in warfare. **-eer** *n.*

char·i·ty *n.* love and goodwill to men; any act of kindness; alms; a charitable cause or institution. **charitable** *a.* liberal to the poor; generous. **charitably** *adv.*

char·la·tan *n.* a quack or impostor.

charm *n.* a magic spell; anything supposed to possess magic power; a trinket worn on a bracelet; attractiveness; *v.t.* to subjugate by magic; to attract irresistibly; *v.i.* to be fascinating. **-er** *n.* **-ing** *a.* alluring; delightful.

chart *n.* a map of part of the sea, showing currents, depths, islands, coasts, etc.; a graph; *v.t.* to map; to delineate. **-er** *n.*

char·ter *n.* a formal document confirming privileges, titles, or rights; the hiring of a vessel; *v.t.* to establish by charter; to hire, as a ship. **-ed** *a.* **— member** *n.* one of the original members.

char·treuse *n.* a light yellowish-green color.

chase *v.t.* to pursue; *v.i.* to hasten; *n.* pursuit; hunting of enemy, game, etc. **-r** *n.* one who chases; a mild beverage taken after liquor.

chase *v.t.* to enchase; to engrave metal. **-r** *n.*

chase *n.* an iron frame to hold type when set up; a wide groove.

chasm *n.* a deep opening in the earth; a cleft.

chass·é *n.* in dancing, a rapid gliding step to the right or left.

chas·sis *n.* the framework and undercarriage of an automobile, including the engine.

chaste *a.* virtuous; pure and simple in taste and style. **-ly** *adv.* **-ness** *n.* **chastity** *n.* purity.

chas·ten *v.t.* to correct by punishment.

chas·tise *v.t.* to inflict pain in order to reform; to punish. **-ment** *n.*

chat *v.i.* to talk idly; *n.* light, informal talk; *pr.p.* **-ting;** *pa.p.* and *pa.t.* **-ted. -ter** *v.i.* to talk rapidly. **-terbox** *n.* one who chatters excessively. **-terer** *n.* one who chatters. **-tiness** *n.* **-ty** *a.* talkative; gossipy.

cha·teau *n.* a castle; a mansion.

chat·tel *n.,* usually in *pl.* **chattels,** any kind of property, except land and buildings. **— mortgage** *n.* a mortgage on personal property.

chat·ter See chat.

chauf·feur *n.* the paid driver of private automobile; *v.t.* to drive.

chau·vin·ism *n.* absurdly exaggerated patriotism; blind enthusiasm for a cause. **chauvinist** *n.* **chauvinistic** *a.*

chaw *n.* (*Dia.*) See chew.

cheap *a.* low in price; of low cost, as compared with the value, or the usual cost. **-ly** *adv.* **-ness** *n.* **-en** *v.t.* to bring down the price.

cheat *v.t.* to defraud; to trick; *v.i.* to practice trickery; *n.* a fraud; an impostor. **-er** *n.*

check *n.* a restraint; control or supervision, or one employed to carry out such; a mark placed against items in a list; an order to a bank to pay money; a term in chess to indicate that opponent's king must be moved or guarded; *v.t.* to restrain; to verify; to leave articles in the custody of another; in chess, to put in check; *v.i.* to pause. **-ers** *n.pl.* a board game, for two. **-book** *n.* book of blank orders on a bank. **-mate** *n.* the final movement in chess, when the king can be neither moved or protected. **-room** *n.* a place where articles may be left under the temporary protection of others. **-up** *n.* a medical examination.

check·er *v.t.* to variegate with cross lines; *v.i.* to produce a checkered effect, of alternate light and shade; *n.* a pattern like a chess-board; a piece in the game of checkers. **-ed** *a.*

Ched·dar *n.* a kind of hard, smooth cheese.

cheek *n.* the fleshy side of the mouth; each side of the face below the eyes. **-bone** *n.* the bone below the outer corner of the eye. **-y** *a.*

cheep *v.i.* to chirp, as a small bird; *n.* a small shrill sound.

cheer *n.* good spirits; expression of approval, or encouragement, by shouting; *v.t.* to render cheerful; to hearten or encourage; *v.i.* to shout hurrah. **-er** *n.* **-ful** *a.* having good spirits. **-fully** *adv.* **-fulness** *n.* **-ily** *adv.* with cheerfulness. **-iness** *n.* **-less** *a.* comfortless. **-lessness** *n.* **-y** *a.* in good spirits; promoting cheerfulness.

cheese *n.* a curd of milk, separated from

the whey, and prepared in several ways as food. **-cloth** *n.* a thin loosely woven cotton cloth, orig. used for wrapping cheese.

chee-tah *n.* the hunting leopard of India and Africa.

chef *n.* a head cook.

chem-i-cal *a.* pert. to chemistry; *n.* a substance produced by chemical processes. **-ly** *adv.* according to chemical principles.

chem-ist *n.* a person versed in chemistry or professionally engaged in it. **-ry** *n.* the study of the various substances which compose the universe and the processes by which they act one upon another.

chem-o-ther-a-peu-tics *n.* the use of chemical compounds in the treatment of disease. **chemotherapy** *n.*

che-nille *n.* a soft plush-like cord of silk, wool, worsted, etc. used for ornamental trimmings, fringes, etc.; a soft, velvety fabric.

cher-ish *v.t.* to hold dear; to treat tenderly.

cher-ry *n.* the bright red fruit of a tree akin to the plum; *a.* pert. to a cherry; red.

cher-ub *n.* a winged creature with a human face; an angel; a beautiful child; *pl.* **cherubim** or **-s. cherubic** *a.*

chess *n.* a game of Eastern origin played by two persons on a board containing

chess

sixty-four squares, with two differently colored sets of sixteen pieces or 'men.' **-man** *n.* a piece used in the game.

chest *n.* a large box; part of the body enclosed by ribs and breastbone; *v.t.* to place in a chest. **chest of drawers,** a piece of furniture fitted with drawers. **-y** *a.* having a large chest; conceited.

ches-ter-field *n.* a long overcoat, a heavily padded sofa.

chest-nut *n.* the nut of a forest tree; the tree itself, or its timber; a reddish-brown color; *a.* reddish-brown.

chew *v.t.* to bite and crush with the teeth; to masticate; *n.* action of chewing. **-ing gum** *n.* a sweet and flavored substance for chewing prepared from *chicle,* the gum of a Mexican rubber-tree.

Chi-an-ti *n.* an Italian red or white wine.

chic *n.* style and elegance; *a.* stylish; modish.

chi-cane *n.* trick or artifice; sharp practice, esp. in legal proceedings; *v.i.* to use trickery. **-ry** *n.* trickery. **-r** *n.*

chick, chicken *n.* the young of fowls, esp. of hen. **-en-hearted** *a.* cowardly; timid. **-en-pox** *n.* a mild, contagious, eruptive

disease. **-weed** *n.* weed with small white blossoms.

chic-le *n.* a gum-like, milky juice obtained from several Central American trees.

chic-o-ry *n.* a plant whose taproot when roasted and ground is used to mix with

chicory

coffee and whose greens are used for salad.

chide *v.t.* to scold; to rebuke; *v.i.* to find fault; *pr.p.* **chiding.** *pa.p.* **chided** or **chid.** *pa.t.* **chid.**

chief *a.* foremost in importance; principal; at the head; *n.* a head or leader; a principal person or thing. **-ly** *adv.* principally. **-tain** *n.* the head of a clan or tribe.

chif-fon *n.* a thin, soft, gauzy material.

chig-ger *n.* a flea.

chi-gnon *n.* a rolled-up bun of hair at the back of a woman's head or on the nape of the neck.

child *n.* a very young person of either sex; offspring; *pl.* **children** offspring, descendants. **-birth** *n.* the act of bearing a child. **-bearing** *n.* producing children. **-hood** *n.* the time during which one is a child. **-ish** *a.* pert. to a child; trifling. **-ishly** *adv.* **-ishness** *n.* **-less** *a.* **-lessness** *n.* **-like** *a.* innocent; trustful.

chil-i, chilli *n.* the red pepper, or fruit of the capsicum, called Cayenne pepper when dried and ground.

chill *a.* tending to cause shivering; cool in manner or feeling; *n.* a feeling of coldness, attended with shivering; illness caused by cold; *v.t.* to cool; to cause to shiver; to dispirit; to keep cold; *v.i.* to grow cold. **-y,** cold; creating cold; ungenial. **-iness** *n.*

chime *n.* the musical sound of bells; a set of bells tuned to the musical scale; *v.t.* and *i.* to be in harmony.

chim-ney *n.* the passage through which the smoke of a fireplace is carried off. **— sweep** *n.* one who removes the soot from chimneys.

chim-pan-zee *n.* a large African anthropoid ape.

chin *n.* the part of the face below the mouth.

Chi-na *n.* a vast country in E. Asia; *(l.c.)* a translucent, vitreous ceramic ware. **-man** *n.* a native of China. **Chinese** *n.* the natives, or the language of China; *a.* **-ware** *n.* dishes of china.

chin-chil-la *n.* a small animal, with very fine, soft fur; the fur itself.

C

chinchilla

chine *n.* the backbone or spine of an animal.

chink *n.* a small cleft or fissure; a crack; *v.t.* to open; *v.i.* to crack.

chink *n.* the sound of a piece of metal when struck; *v.i.* to ring.

Chi·nook *n.* a tribe of N.W. American Indians; a kind of Salmon.

chintz *n.* a printed cotton cloth.

chip *v.t.* to chop off into small pieces; to break little pieces from; *v.i.* to break off in small pieces; *pr.p.* -piping; *pa.p.* and *pa.t.* -ped; *n.* a piece of wood separated from a larger body by an axe, etc.; a counter, instead of money, used in gambling. -s *n.pl.* fried slices of potato. — **shot** *n.* (*Golf*) a short, lofted shot onto the green. — **in**, *v.t.* to contribute.

chipmunk *n.* a burrowing ground-squirrel or striped gopher.

chip·pen·dale *n.* a style of furniture.

chi·ro·man·cy *n.* divination by inspection of the hand; palmistry.

chi·rop·o·dist *n.* one skilled in the treatment of diseases of the feet. **chiropody** *n.*

chi·ro·prac·tic *n.* a method of healing which relies upon the removal of nerve interference by manual adjustment of the spine. **chiropractor** *n.*

chirp, chir·rup *n.* a short, sharp note, as of a bird or cricket; *v.i.* to twitter; to talk gaily.

chis·el *n.* a tool sharpened to a cutting edge at the end, used in carpentry, sculpture, etc.; *v.i.* to carve with this tool.

chit *n.* a voucher; a permit or pass.

chiv·al·ry *n.* the qualities of a knight, viz. dignity, courtesy, bravery, gallantry. **chivalric, chivalrous** *a.* pert. to chivalry. **chivalrously** *adv.*

chive *n.* a small herb of the onion kind.

chlo·rine *n.* a heavy gas of yellowish-green color used in disinfecting, bleaching, and poison-gas warfare. **chloral** *n.* a sleep-producing drug. **chlorate** *n.* a salt of chloric acid. **chloric** *a.* pert. to chlorine. **chloride** *n.* a compound of chlorine with another element. **chlorinate** *v.t.* disinfect, bleach, or combine with chlorine. **chlorination** *n.* **chlorite** *n.* a mineral of a green color. **chloroform** *n.* a colorless, volatile liquid used as an anesthetic; *v.t.* to make insensible by using chloroform. **chlo·ro·phyll** *n.* (*Bot.*) the green coloring matter of plants.

chock *n.* a wedge to steady a wheel. **-ful** *a.* packed.

choc·o·late *a.* a paste or hard cake made from the powdered seeds of the cacao plant, mixed with sugar, etc.; a beverage made by pouring boiling water or milk over this; candy; *a.* dark brown.

choice *n.* opportunity of choosing; selection; alternative; *a.* worthy of being chosen; superior.

choir *n.* a company of singers, belonging to a church.

choke *v.t.* to stop the breath by compression of the windpipe; *v.i.* to have the wind-pipe stopped; *n.* a valve regulating the proportion of gas to air in a motor. **-r** *n.* something worn closely about the neck.

chol·er *n.* bile; wrath. **choleric** *a.* easily angered. **cholera** *n.* deadly, epidemic, bilious disease, marked by purgings, vomiting and gripping pains.

cho·les·ter·ol *n.* a fatlike substance found in bile, gallstones, blood, and the brain, also in egg yolks, etc.

choose *v.t.* to take one thing in preference to another; *v.i.* to decide; to think fit. *pa.p.* **chosen.** *pa.t.* **chose.**

chop *v.t.* to cut into pieces; to mince, by striking repeatedly with a sharp instrument; *v.i.* to make strokes with a sharp instrument, as an axe; *n.* a thick slice of meat attached to a bone; a cutlet. *pr.p.* -ping. *pa.p.* and *pa.t.* -ped. **-per** *n.* one who chops; a large heavy knife; cleaver. **-py** *a.* of the sea, having short, broken waves.

chop sticks *n.* one of two small sticks of wood, ivory, etc. used by the Chinese in taking food.

cho·ral *a.* pert. or belonging to a choir or chorus. **-ly** *adv.* **choric** *a.* pert. to a chorus.

chorale *n.* a simple, dignified melody sung to religious words.

chord *n.* (*Mus.*) a series of tones having a harmonic relation to each other, and sounded simultaneously; (*Geom.*) a straight line between two points in the circumference of a circle.

chore *n.* any odd job, or occasional housework; (*pl.*) routine work.

cho·re·og·ra·phy *n.* the art of creating dance compositions for ballet. **choreographer** *n.* **choreographic** *a.*

cho·rog·ra·phy *n.* the art of making a map, or writing a description, of a region or country. **chorology** *n.* the study of the geographical distribution of plants and animals.

chor·tle *v.i.* to chuckle gleefully. **chortling** *n.*

cho·rus *n.* a combination of voices singing together; the refrain; *v.t.* to join in the refrain; to sing together. **choric** *a.* pert. to a chorus.

chose *pa.t.* of **choose.**

chosen *pa.p.* of **choose.**

chow·der *n.* a stew made of fish, pork, onions, etc.

Christ *n.* The Anointed — a name given to Jesus of Nazareth. **-like, -ly** *a.* resembling Christ.

chris·ten *v.t.* to give a name to. **Christendom** *n.* all Christian countries; the whole body of Christians. **-ing** *n.*

baptism.

Chris·tian *n.* a follower of Christ; a professed adherent of the Church of Christ; *a.* pert. to Christ or his religion. **-ize** *v.t.* to convert to Christianity. **Christianity** *n.* the religion of the followers of Christ. **— era,** the era counting from the birth of Christ. **— name,** individual name, as opposed to family name. **— Science,** a religious doctrine of faith-healing founded in America.

Christ·mas the annual celebration of the birth of Christ, observed on Dec. 25.

chro·mat·ic *a.* pert. to color; *(Mus.)* proceeding by semitones. **-s** *n.* the science of colors; *(Mus.)* chromatic notes. **-ally** *adv.*

chrome, chro·mi·um *n.* a metal, very resistant to corrosion, used generally for plating other metals. **chromic** *a.* pert. to, or obtained from, chrome or chromium. **chromate** *n.* a salt of chromic acid. **chromite** *n.* a mineral, the chief source of chromium.

chro·mo·some *n.* *(Biol.)* one of the gene-carrying bodies in the tissue of a cell, regarded as the transmitter of hereditary factors from parent to child.

chron·ic *a.* continuing for a long time; of disease, deep-seated and lasting. **-ally.**

chron·i·cle *n.* a register of events in order of time; *v.t.* to record in order of time. **-r**

chro·no- a combining form fr. Gk. *chronos,* time. **-graph** *n.* an instrument for measuring and recording time very exactly. **chronology** *n.* the science that treats of historical dates and arranges them in order; a table of events and dates. **chronologer, chronologist** *n.* one who records historical events, etc. **chronological** *a.* arranged in order of time. **chronologically** *adv.* **chronometer** *n.* a very accurate watch or time-keeper. **-metric, -metrical** *a.* **chronometry** *n.* the process of measuring time by instruments.

chrys·an·the·mum *n.* a mop-headed garden flower.

chub *n.* a fish of the carp family, small and fat. **-by** *a.* round and plump. **-biness** *n.*

chuck *n.* a cut of beef from the neck to the shoulder blade.

chuck·le *v.i.* to laugh in a suppressed manner; *n.* a short, quiet laugh.

chug *n.* an explosive sound made by an engine exhaust; *v.i.* to make an explosive sound. *pa.p., pa.t.* **-ged.** *pr.p.* **-ging.**

chum *n.* an intimate friend (with); to share a room (with). *pr.p.* **-ming.** *pa.p.* and *pa.t.* **med. -my** *a.* friendly; sociable.

chump *n.* a lump of wood.

chunk *n.* a short, thick piece of wood, etc. **-y** *a.*

church *n.* building for Christian worship; a denomination of the Christian religion; the clergy; the church service; *v.t.* to bring to church. **-goer** *n.* one who attends church regularly. **-ly** *a.* **-man** *n.* an ecclesiastic; a member of a church. **-warden** *n.* an officer entrusted with the

church

interests of the church or parish. **-yard** *n.* the ground adjoining a church.

churl *n.* a countryman. **-ish** *a.* **-ishly** *adv.* **-ishness** *n.*

churn *n.* a vessel in which cream is violently stirred to produce butter; *v.t.* to agitate cream so as to produce butter; to stir up violently; *v.i.* to produce butter.

chute *n.* a rapid descent in a river; a rapid; a sloping contrivance for transferring coal, rubbish, etc. to a lower level.

ci·ca·da, cicala *n.* an insect, the male of which emits a shrill, chirping sound.

ci·der *n.* a drink made from the juice of apples.

ci·gar *n.* tobacco leaf made up in a roll for smoking. **-ette** *n.* finely cut tobacco rolled in thin paper.

cil·i·a *n.pl.* the eyelashes; *(Anat.)* hair-like, vibratile processes. **ciliary, ciliate, ciliated, ciliferous, ciliform** *a.*

cinch *n.* a saddle-girth; *v.t.* to fasten a cinch around; to tighten (girth).

cin·cho·na *n.* a genus of trees from which quinine is extracted; the bark. **-ceous** *a.*

cinc·ture *n.* a belt; a girdle; a zone; *v.t.* to encircle. **-d** *a.*

cin·der *n.* any partially burned combustible substance.

cin·e·ma *n.* a theater where moving pictures are shown; a motion picture; **-scope** *n.* a wide, panoramic motion picture screen. **-tography** *n.* **-tographer** *n.*

cin·er·ar·y *a.* pert. to ashes; made to hold ashes. **cinerarium** *n.* *(pl.* **-raria)** *n.* a place for ashes after cremation. **cineration** *n.* a reducing to ashes; incineration.

cin·na·bar *n.* red sulphide of mercury used as a pigment; *a.* vermillion colored.

cin·na·mon *n.* the inner bark of a laurel tree of Ceylon; an aromatic substance obtained from the bark, used as a spice; *n.* and *a.* a light-brown color.

ci·pher, cy·pher *n.* the arithmetical symbol 0; a secret writing; the key to a code; *v.i.* to work at arithmetic.

cir·cle *n.* a plane figure bounded by a single curved line called its circumference, every point of which is equally distant from a point within called the center; a sphere; the company associated with a person; a never-ending series; *v.t.* to revolve round; to encompass, as by a circle; *v.i.* to move in a circle.

cir·cuit *n.* the space enclosed within a fixed limit; *(Law)* the round made by judges holding court; path of an electric current.

cir·cu·lar *a.* in the form of a circle; roundabout; *n.* a notice sent out in quantities. **-ly** *adv.* **circularity** *n.* **-ize** *v.t.* to send circulars to.

cir·cu·late *v.t.* to cause to pass round as in a circle; to spread abroad; *v.i.* to move around and return to the same point. **circulation** *n.* the flow of blood from, and back to, the heart; the money circulating in a country. **circulative, circulatory** *a.* circulating. **circulator** *n.*

cir·cum- meaning *round, about,* combining to form many derivatives as in **-ambient** *a.* enclosing. **-ambiency** *n.* environment. **-ambulate** *v.t.* and *i.* to walk around or about.

cir·cum·cise *v.t.* to cut off the foreskin. **circumcision** *n.*

cir·cum·fer·ence *n.* the line that bounds a circle; the distance around; area. **circumferential** *a.*

cir·cum·flex *n.* an accent mark placed over a vowel to denote length, contraction, etc.

cir·cum·flu·ent *a.* flowing round. **circumfluence** *n.*

cir·cum·ja·cent *a.* bordering on every side.

cir·cum·lo·cu·tion *n.* a roundabout manner of speaking. **circumlocutory** *a.*

cir·cum·nav·i·gate *v.t.* to sail around. **circumnavigable** *a.* capable of being sailed round. **circumnavigation** *n.* **circumnavigator** *n.* one who sails around.

cir·cum·scribe *v.t.* to draw a circle around; to enclose within limits. **circumscription** *n.* limitation. **circumscriptive** *a.* limited in space.

cir·cum·spect *a.* watchful on all sides; discreet. **-ly** *adv.* **circumspection** *n.* prudence; discretion; tact. **-ive** *a.*

cir·cum·stance *n.* a particular fact, event, or case; *v.t.* to place in a particular situation. **-s** *n.pl.* condition as to pecuniary resources; situation; details. **circumstantial** *a.* accidental; not essential. **circumstantially** *adv.* **circumstantiality** *n.* minuteness of detail. **circumstantiate** *v.t.* to detail exactly.

cir·cum·vent *v.t.* to get around by stratagem. **-ion** *n.* **-ive** *a.*

cir·cus *n.* a travelling company of performers, animals, etc.; a circular enclosure for performances.

cir·rho·sis *n.* (*Med.*) hardening and enlargement of the liver. **cirrhotic** *a.*

cir·rus *n.* a lofty, fleecy cloud; *pl.* **cirri**.

cis·tern *n.* a large tank for holding water.

cite *v.t.* to quote; to bring forward as proof. **citation** *n.* an official notice to appear; the mention of gallantry in military orders. **citator** *n.* **citatory** *a.*

cit·i·zen *n.* an inhabitant of a city; a member of a state; *a.* having the character of a citizen. **-ry** *n.* citizens collectively. **-ship** *n.* the rights and duties of a citizen.

cit·ron *n.* the fruit of the citron tree, resembling a lemon; a yellow color. **citrate** *n.* a salt of citric acid. **citric** *a.* extracted from the citron lemon, etc. **citrus fruits**, citrons, lemons, oranges, etc.

cit·ron·el·la *n.* a sharp smelling oil to keep insects away (See **citron**).

cit·y *n.* a corporate town; the business or shopping center of a town; *a.* pert. to a city.

civ·ic *a.* pert. to a city or a citizen. **-s** *n.pl.* the study of civic affairs, municipal or national.

civ·il *a.* pert. to city, state, or citizen; polite. **-ly** *adv.* **civilian** *n.* one whose employment is non-military; *a.* pert. to civilian life (e.g. civilian dress). **civility** *n.* politeness; *pl.* acts of politeness. **civil defense**, an organization to deal with civilians during air raids, etc. **civil engineer**, one who plans bridges, roads, dams, etc. **civil service**, the government positions obtained by examination. **civil war**, war between citizens of the same country.

civ·i·lize *v.t.* to reclaim from a savage state; to enlighten. **-d** *a.* **civilization** *n.* the act of civilizing, or state of being civilized.

clack *v.i.* to make a sudden, sharp noise, as by striking; *n.* a sharp, repeated, rattling sound; continual talk.

clad *pa.p.* and *pa.t.* of **clothe**; *a.* clothed.

claim *v.t.* to demand as a right, or as due; to assert as true; *n.* the demand of a right; a title; the thing claimed. **-ant** *n.* one who claims. **—jumper** *n.* one who seizes a piece of land marked out by a settler or miner.

clair·voy·ance *n.* the power of seeing things not normally perceptible to the senses; second sight. **clairvoyant** *n.* one who claims the power of clairvoyance. Also *a.*

clam *n.* an edible bivalve shellfish.

cla·mant *a.* crying out; clamorous. **clamancy** *n.*

clam·ber *v.i.* to climb with difficulty, holding on with the hands.

clam·my *a.* sticky and moist; cold and damp. **clamminess** *n.*

clam·or *n.* loud shouting; uproar; *v.i.* to shout loudly; to utter loud complaints or demands. **-ous** *a.*

clamp *n.* any appliance with parts brought together by a screw for holding anything; *v.t.* to make firm.

clan *n.* a tribe bearing the same surname, united under a chieftain; a set of persons having a common interest. **-nish** *a.* disposed to associate only with members of the same clique. **-nishly** *adv.* **-nishness** *n.*

clan·des·tine *a.* secret, and contrary to law, morals, etc. **-ly** *adv.* **-ness** *n.*

clang *v.t.* to strike with a ringing, metallic sound; *v.i.* to give forth a ringing, metallic sound; *n.* a sharp, ringing sound. **-ing** *n.* a clang.

clan·gor *n.* a loud harsh, ringing sound. **-ous** *a.* **-ously** *adv.*

clank *n.* a brief, hard, metallic sound; *v.t.* and *i.* to produce such a sound.

clap *v.t.* to strike the hands together in approval; *v.i.* to strike the hands together in applause; *n.* applause; *pr.p.* **-ping**. *pa.p.* and *pa.t.* **-ped**. **-per** *n.* one who claps; the tongue of a bell. **-board** *n.* thin board used to cover wooden houses.

clar·i·fy v.t. to make clear; to remove possibility of error; v.i. to become clear. **clarification** n. **clarity** n. clearness; lucidity of mind.

clar·i·on n. trumpet with shrill piercing note. **clarinet, clarionet** n. a wood wind instrument. **clarinettist** n.

clash v.t. to strike noisily together; v.i. to disagree; n. a loud noise; a conflict.

clasp v.t. to fasten together with a catch or hook; to cling to; n. a catch or hook for fastening; a grasping of the hands.

class n. an order or grouping of persons or things possessing the same characteristics or status; a group of students taught together; a grouping of plants or animals; rank or standing in society; v.t. to rank together; v.i. to rank. **-able, -ible** a.

clas·sic n. a work, writer of recognized worth; an ancient Latin or Greek writer or book; a. of model excellence in literature or art; conforming to standards of Greek and Roman art. **-s** n.pl. ancient Latin or Greek literature. **-al** a. **-ally** adv. **-ality, -alness** n. the quality of being classical. **classicism** n. classic principles in art and literature; a classical idiom. **classicist** n.

clas·si·fy v.t. to arrange in classes. **classifiable** a. **classification** n. the act of classifying.

clat·ter v.t. to strike and so make a rattling noise; v.i. to make rattling sounds; n. a repeated rattling noise.

clause n. (Gram.) a subordinate part of a sentence; (Law) an article or distinct portion of a document, contract.

claus·tral a. secluded. **claustration** n. the state of being confined in a cloister.

claus·tro·pho·bi·a n. (Med.) a morbid dread of confined spaces.

clav·i·cle n. the collarbone. **clavicular** a.

claw n. a sharp, hooked nail, as of a beast or bird; v.t. to pull, tear, or scratch with claws or nails.

clay n. soft earth, consisting of alumina and silica, with water used in making pottery, bricks, etc. **-ey** a. consisting of clay; like clay.

clean a. free from dirt, stain, or any defilement; v.t. to free from dirt; to purify; adv. so as to leave no dirt. **-er** n. one who, or that which, cleans. **-liness** n. freedom from dirt; purity. **-ly** a. habitually clean in persons and habits; pure. **-ly** adv. in a clean manner; neatly. **-ness** n. **—cut** a. well-shaped.

clear a. free from cloud; free from obstruction; without drawback; transparent; adv. wholly; v.t. to make bright or clear; to free from accusation; to pass over or through; to free from difficulty, obstruction, suspicion, etc.; v.i. to become clear, transparent, free. **-age** n. **clearance. -ance** n. a certificate that a ship has been cleared at the custom house. **-ing** n. a tract of land cleared of wood. **-ing-house** n. an office maintained by several banks for balancing accounts, exchanging checks, etc. **-ly** adv. **-ness** n.

—cut a. sharply defined. **—eyed, —seeing, —sighted** a. having acuteness of sight.

cleat n. a piece of metal fastened to a shoe.

cleave v.t. to split asunder; to cut in two; v.i. to crack asunder; pa.p. **cloven** or **cleft**. pa.t. **clove** or **cleft**. **cleavage** n. of rocks, the quality of splitting naturally; a rupture. **-r** n. one who, or that which, cleaves; a butcher's chopper.

cleave v.i. to adhere closely; to stick; to be faithful to.

clef n. (Mus.) a sign used to indicate the pitch.

cleft pa.p. and pa.t. of the verb **cleave**; n. a fissure or split; a chink.

clem·en·cy n. leniency; mildness; mercy. **clement** a. compassionate.

clench, clinch v.t. to close together tightly (the hands, the teeth); n. a firm closing; decisive proof; a firm grip. **-er** n. an unanswerable argument.

cler·gy n. the body of men ordained for religious service. **-man** n. a minister.

cler·ic n. a clergyman; a. clerical. **clerical** a. belonging to the clergy; pert. to a clerk or copyist.

clerk n. one who is employed to do correspondence, keep accounts, etc. in an office; salesman or saleswoman; v.i. to act as a clerk or secretary. **-ship** n.

clev·er a. ingenious; intelligent. **-ly** adv. **-ness** n.

clew, clue n. a ball of thread or cord; anything that helps to solve a mystery.

cli·ché n. (Print.) an electrotype or stereotype plate; a stereotyped or hackneyed phrase.

click n. a slight, short sound, as a latch in a door.

cli·ent n. one who employs another professionally as his agent; a customer. **clientele** n. customers collectively.

cliff n. a high rock-face; the sheer side of a mountain.

cli·mac·ter·ic n. a period in human life in which a change takes place in the constitution; any critical period; a. critical. **-al** a.

cli·mate n. the general atmospherical conditions (temperature, moisture, etc.) of a region. **climatic** a. **climatical** a.

cli·max n. an arrangement of words such that they rise in rhetorical force; the point of greatest excitement or tension. **climactic** a.

climb v.t. and i. to go up, ascent (as a hill, tree, etc.); to grow upward; n. an ascent. **-er** n.

clinch v.t. and i. struggle at close quarters in wrestling or boxing; n. a close holding in wrestling or boxing. **-er** n.

cling v.i. to adhere to; to be attached firmly to; pa.p. and pa.t. **clung**.

clin·ic n. an institution where non-resident patients attend for treatment. **-al** a.

clink n. a sharp, tinkling sound.

clip v.t. to grip tightly. pr.p. **-ping**. pa.t., pa.p. **-ped**. n. any device for holding a thing firmly.

clip v.t. to cut with scissors or shears; v.i. to move quickly; n. act of clipping; a season's shearing of wool; a rapid pace. *pr.p.* -**ping**. *pa.p.* and *pa.t.* -**ped**. -**per** *n.* one who clips; a fast sailing-vessel, with a long sharp bow. -**pers** *n.* a two-bladed instrument for cutting. -**ping** *n.* an item cut from a newspaper, etc.

clique *n.* a circle of persons with common interests. **cliquish** *a.* **cliquishness** *n.*

cloak *n.* a long, loose, outer garment; something that conceals; a pretext; *v.t.* to cover with a cloak; to hide. -**room** *n.* a room where coats, hats, etc. may be temporarily left.

clock *n.* a device which measures time. -**wise** *adv.* in the direction of the hands of a clock. **counterclockwise** *adv.* circling in the opposite direction. -**work** *n.* the machinery of a clock; regular movement as of clock; *a.* mechanically regular. **o'clock**, by the clock.

clod *n.* a lump of earth or turf; a dull, stupid fellow. -**hopper** *n.* a rustic; a boor.

clog *n.* an impediment; an obstruction; *v.t.* to hinder; to choke up; *v.i.* to become choked, encumbered. *pr.p.* -**ging**. *pa.p.* *pa.t.* -**ged**.

clois•ter *n.* a monastery or nunnery; a secluded spot; *v.t.* to confine. -**al**, **cloistral** *a.* -**ed** *a.*

close *v.t.* to shut up; to conclude; to complete (a wireless circuit); *v.i.* to unite; to end. **closing** *a.* ending; *n.* the conclusion. **closure** *n.* the act of shutting; a closing; the close of a debate.

close *a.* confined; tight; near at hand; intimate; crowded; *adv.* in a close manner or state; tightly; *n.* an enclosed place; (*Mus.*) a cadence. -**ly** *adv.* -**ness** *n.* — **by**, near. — **call**, a very narrow escape. — **fisted** or — **handed** *a.* miserly, penurious. — **mouthed** *a.* uncommunicative. — **quarters** *n.pl.* a crowded space. — **up** *n.* a close view of anything.

clos•et *n.* a small room for storing things; a lavatory; *v.t.* to take into a private room for consultation.

clot *n.* a coagulated mass of blood; *v.t.* to form into clots; *v.i.* to coagulate. *pr.p.* -**ting**. *pa.p.* and *pa.t.* -**ted**.

cloth *n.* any woven fabric of wool, silk, cotton; a cover for a table. *pl.* **cloths**.

clothe *v.t.* to put garments on; to wrap up in. *pr.p.* **clothing**. *pa.p.* and *pa.t.* -**d** or **clad**. -**s** *n.* *pl.* wearing apparel. **clothier** *n.* one who makes, or sells, clothes; an outfitter. **clothing** *n.* garments in general; raiment. **clotheshorse** *n.* one who likes clothes.

cloud *n.* a body of visible vapor floating in the atmosphere; a mass of smoke, flying dust, etc.; a state of impending trouble; *v.t.* to overspread with clouds; to darken; to defame; *v.i.* to grow cloudy; to be blurred. -**y** *a.* darkened with clouds; overcast; indistinct; gloomy. -**ily** *adv.* -**iness** *n.* -**burst** *n.* a violent downpour of rain; a deluge.

clout *n.* a slap or blow; to strike with the open hand.

clove *n.* the flower-bud of the clove-tree, used as a spice.

clove

clove *pa.t.* of **cleave**.

clo•ven *pa.p.* of **cleave**. Also *a.* divided into two parts.

clo•ver *n.* a common field plant of the trefoil family. -**leaf** *n.* a highway intersection in the shape of a four-leaf clover.

clown *n.* the buffoon in a play or circus; a boor; *v.i.* to behave like a fool. -**ishly** *adv.* -**ishness** *n.*

cloy *v.t.* to induce a sensation of loathing by overmuch of sweetness, or flattery; to satiate. -**ing** *a.* satiating.

club *n.* a heavy stick, thickening towards one end, used as a weapon; a stick used in golf; an association of people united in pursuance of a common interest; *v.t.* to beat with a club; to gather into a club; *v.i.* to unite for a common end. *pr.p.* -**bing**. *pa.p.* and *pa.t.* -**bed**. -**foot** *n.* a congenitally deformed or crooked foot.

clump *n.* a shapeless mass of any substance; a cluster of trees or shrubs; a tramping sound; *v.t.* to put in a group; *v.i.* to tramp heavily.

clumsy *a.* awkward; ungainly. **clumsily** *adv.* **clumsiness** *n.*

clung *pa.p.* and *pa.t.* of **cling**.

clus•ter *n.* a bunch; a number of things growing together, as grapes; *v.t.* to collect into a bunch; *v.i.* to grow, or be, in clusters.

clutch *v.t.* and *i.* to seize or grip with the hand; *n.* a tight grip; the coupling of two working parts, used in motor vehicles to connect or disconnect engine and transmission gear. -**es** *n.pl.* the hands; power.

clut•ter *n.* disorder; *v.t.* to crowd together in disorder.

coach *n.* a tutor who prepares students; a trainer in athletics; *v.t.* to tutor or train.

co•ac•tion *n.* compulsion.

co•ad•ju•tant *a.* assisting; *n.* an assistant. **coadjutor** *n.* an associate and destined successor.

co•ag•u•late *v.t.* to congeal; to solidify; *v.i.* to clot. **coagulant** *n.* a substance that causes coagulation. **coagulation** *n.* **coagulative** *a.*

coal *n.* a black substance used for fuel, composed of mineralized vegetable matter; *v.t.* to supply with coal; *v.i.* to take in coal. -**s** *n.pl.* glowing embers. — **bin** *n.* a recess for storing coal. — **field** *n.* a district where coal abounds. — **gas** *n.* gases produced from the distillation of coal or from burning coal. — **mine,** — **pit** *n.* the excavation from which coal is dug. — **oil** *n.* kerosene. — **tar** *n.* a thick, sticky substance, produced during the distilling of coal.

co·a·li·tion *n.* a union or combination of persons, parties, or states into one body; a league. **-ist** *n.*

coarse *a.* rough, rude; not refined; without grace or elegance; ill-mannered; vulgar; inferior. **-ly** *adv.* **-n** *v.t.* and *i.* to make or become coarse. **-ness** *n.*

coast *n.* land bordering the sea; the country near the shore; *v.t.* and *i.* to run shut off, or on a bicycle without pedaling; to toboggan. **-al** *a.* pert. to the coast. **-er** *n.* a small tray placed under glasses to protect a table. **-guard** *n.* a service organized orig. to prevent smuggling; since 1925, largely a life-saving service; **-line** *n.* the outline of a coast. **-wards** *adv.* toward the coast. **-wise** *adv.* along the coast.

coat *n.* an outer garment; the fur or skin of an animal; a layer spread over another, as paint; *v.t.* to cover with a coat to clothe. **-ed** *a.* **-ing** *n.* a layer; cloth for making coats.

coax *v.t.* to win over by fond pleading. **-ingly** *adv.*

cob *n.* a corn-cob; a male swan.

co·balt *n.* a metallic element classified with iron and nickel, and used as an ingredient of many alloys. — **blue** *n.* a pigment containing an oxide of cobalt; *a.* a dark-blue color. **-ic** *a.*

cob·ble *v.t.* to patch coarsely; to mend boots or shoes. **-r** *n.* a mender of shoes; a deep-dish fruit pie with a biscuit crust.

cob·ble *n.* a stone rounded by the action of water; *v.t.* to pave with cobbles. **-stone** *n.* a rounded stone used in paving.

co·bra *n.* the venomous 'hooded' snake of Africa and India. **-cobric** *a.*

cobra

cob·web *n.* a spider's web.

co·ca *n.* a Peruvian plant or its dried leaf, which is a nerve stimulant. **cocaine** *n.* a drug made from coca leaves, used as a local anesthetic.

coc·cyx *n.* the triangular bone ending spinal column. *pl.* **coccyges. coccygeal** *a.*

cock *n.* the male of birds, esp. of the domestic fowl; the hammer of a firearm; *v.t.* to draw back the hammer of a gun; to set erect, set at an angle, as a hat. **-erel** *n.* a swaggering youth. **-scomb** *n.* the comb of a cock; a flowering plant. **-tail** *n.* a drink concocted of liquor, bitters, sugar, etc.; a mixture of fruit, or of seafood, served as an appetizer. **-y** *a.* full of self-assurance. **-ily** *adv.* **-iness** *n.*

cock·a·too *n.* a kind of parrot with a crested head.

cock·a·trice *n.* a fabulous animal represented as a cock with a dragon's tail.

cock·er *n.* a small variety of spaniel, used for retrieving game.

cock·le *n.* a weed that grows among corn; the corn rose.

cock·le *n.* a bivalve shell-fish, with a thick ribbed shell; *v.t.* to cause to pucker; to wrinkle. **-shell** *n.* the shell of a cockle.

cock·pit *n.* in aircraft, a compartment in the fuselage for the pilot and controls.

cock·roach *n.* a black or brown beetle infesting houses.

cock·swain See coxswain.

co·co, co·coa *n.* a palm tree producing the coconut. **-nut,** the fruit of the coco palm.

cocoa

co·coa *n.* a powder made from the kernels of the cacao plant; a beverage from this.

co·coon *n.* the silky envelope which larvae spin for themselves before passing into the pupa stage.

cod, cod·fish *n.* a large fish from northern seas, used as food.

cod·dle *v.t.* to pamper or spoil.

code *n.* an orderly collection of laws; a system of words, symbols, or numbers adopted for secrecy; **codify** *v.t.* to collect laws, into a digest. **codification** *n.* act of collecting laws.

cod·i·cil *n.* a supplement to a will.

co·ed·u·ca·tion *n.* the education of boys and girls together in mixed classes. **-al** *a.*

co·ef·fi·cient *a.* cooperating; combining; *n.* that which unites with something else to produce a result; *(Math.)* a number or other factor placed before another as a multiplier; *(Phys.)* a constant number or factor measuring some specified property of a substance. **coefficiency** *n.*

co·e·qual *a.* of the same power as another; *n.* a person having equality with another.

co·erce *v.t.* to compel by force; to constrain; to restrain. **coercible** *a.* **coercive** *a.* having power to compel. **coercively** *adv.* **coercion** *n.* state of being coerced; compulsory force.

co·e·val *a.* of same age; *n.* contemporary.

co·ex·ist *v.i.* to exist at the same time or together. **-ence** *n.* **-ent** *a.*

cof·fee *n.* an evergreen shrub, valuable for its berries; a drink from this. **-bean** *n.* the

coffee

seed of the berry. -house n. a restaurant where coffee and other refreshments are supplied.

cof•fer n. a chest for valuables; v.t. to hoard (money, etc.).

cof•fin n. a casket in which the dead are enclosed before burial; v.t. to place in a coffin.

cog n. one of a series of teeth on a wheel; v.t. to fit a wheel with cogs. pr.p. -ging. pa.p. and pa.t. -ged.

co•gent a. having great force; convincing. -ly adv. cogence, cogency n. convincing power.

cog•i•tate v.i. to reflect deeply; to meditate. cogitable a. cogitation n. contemplation. cogitative a.

co•gnac n. a French brandy, so called from the town of Cognac in S.W. France.

cog•nate a. allied by blood or birth; from the same origin, formation, etc.; n. anything of the same origin, nature, or effect.

cog•ni•zance n. knowledge; perception. cognizable a. capable of being known. cognizably adv. cognizant a. having knowledge of.

cog•ni•tion n. awareness; state of being able to perceive objects or ideas. cognitive a.

co•ha•bit v.i. to live together as husband and wife. ation, -ant n.

co•here v.i. to stick together; to be connected; to adhere. -nce, -ncy n. -nt a. sticking together; consistent. -ntly adv. cohesible a. capable of cohesion. cohesion n. the act of sticking together. cohesive a. having the power of cohering. cohesiveness, cohesibility n.

co•hort n. a company of persons; an associate.

coif n. a headdress in the form of a close-fitting cap, worn by nuns. -feur n. a hairdresser. coiffure n. a style of dressing the hair.

coil v.t. to twist into a spiral shape; v.i. to take on a spiral shape; n. the spiral of rings into which anything is wound.

coin n. a piece of stamped metal issued by government authority to be used as money; v.t. to make into money; invent or fabricate, as a word or phrase. -age n. the act of coining; money coined; currency. -er n. one who makes coins; an inventor.

co•in•cide v.i. to happen at the same time; to agree (in opinion). coincidence n. correspondence in nature, circumstances, etc. coincident, coincidental a. simultaneous. coincidently adv.

co•i•tion n. sexual intercourse; copulation. Also coitus.

coke n. coal half burnt, and used as fuel; v.t. to turn into coke.

col•an•der n. a vessel with a perforated bottom, used for draining off liquids. Also cullender.

cold a. wanting in heat; deficient in the emotions; n. absence of warmth; chilliness; a disorder of the nose, throat and chest, characterized by running at the nose, hoarseness and coughing; -ly adv.

-ish a. somewhat cold. -ness n. —blooded a. having cold blood, like fish; callous or heartless. Also —hearted. — war, campaign carried on by means of economic pressure, press, radio, etc.

cole n. a name for plants of the cabbage family. —slaw n. a salad of finely sliced or chopped cabbage.

Co•le•op•ter•a n.pl. the order of insects, such as beetles, whose outer wings form a horny covering for the true wings.

col•ic n. severe pain in the abdomen.

co•li•se•um n. a stadium or large auditorium.

col•lab•o•rate v.i. to labor together; to act jointly. collaboration n. joint labor; willing cooperation with the enemy. collaborator n.

col•lapse v.i. to fall in; to break down; to give way under physical or mental strain; n. a falling in or down; a sudden and complete failure. collapsable, collapsible a.

col•lar n. something worn around the neck; the part of a garment that fits around the neck; v.t. to capture; to put a collar on. -bone n. the bone from the shoulders to the breast-bone; the clavicle.

col•late v.t. to arrange in order, as the sheets of a book for binding. collation n. the act of collating; a repast. collative a. collator n.

col•lat•e•ral a. running parallel; subordinately connected; additional (of a security); n. additional security. -ly adv. -ness.

col•league n. an associate or companion.

col•lect v.t. to gather; to receive payment of; v.i. to be assembled; to come together. -able, -ible a. -ed a. cool; self-possessed. -edly adv. -edness n. collection n. the act of collecting; a contribution or sum of money gathered at a meeting. -ive a. formed by gathering; gathered into a mass or body. -ively adv. -ivism n. a term embracing all systems on the Socialistic doctrine of the state of the economic life of the country. -ivist n. -or n. an officer appointed to receive taxes, customs, duties, tolls, etc.

col•lege n. an institution for higher education; the buildings of such an institution. collegial a. pert. to a college. collegian n. a member of a college; a student. collegiate a. pert. to or instituted like, a college.

col•lide v.i. to strike together; to clash; to come into conflict. collision n. a violent impact; a clash.

col•lie n. a breed of sheep dog.

col•lo•cate v.t. to place together; to arrange. collocation n.

col•loid a. gelatinous; n. a glue-like, non-crystalline substance unable to pass through animal membrances. -al a. like a colloid.

col•lo•quy n. dialogue; discussion; a debate. colloquial a. pert. to, or used in, ordinary conversation. colloquially adv. colloquialism n. an expression used in ordinary conversation, but not regarded as slang.

col•lu•sion *n.* a secret agreement between two or more persons for a fraudulent purpose. **collusive** *a.*

co•logne *n.* a perfumed toilet water.

co•lon *n.* a punctuation mark (:), separating parts of a sentence that are almost independent and complete in themselves; *(Anat.)* that part of the large intestine extending from the caecum to the rectum. **colonic** *a.*

colo•nel *n.* the officer ranking between lieutenant colonel and a brigadier general, usually commanding a regiment. **-cy, -ship** *n.* the rank of colonel.

col•on•nade *n.* a series of columns arranged symmetrically.

col•o•ny *n.* a body of people who settle in a new country but remain subject to the parent state; the country thus occupied; a group of animals or plants living and growing together. **colonial** *a.* pert. to a colony; *n.* a colonist. **colonize** *v.t.* to plant or establish a colony; *v.i.* to settle. **colonist** *n.* **colonization** *n.*

col•o•phon *n.* individual inscription used by publishers and printers on the title pages of books, etc.

col•or *n.* any hue as distinguished from white; a flush; vividness in writing; *v.t.* to tinge with color; *v.i.* to blush. **colors** *n.pl.* a flag or standard; a colored badge, device, etc. used as a distinguishing mark. **-able** *a.* capable of being colored; plausible. **-ably** *adv.* **-ful** *a.* having plenty of color. **—blind** *a.* unable to distinguish colors.

col•or•a•tion *n.* arrangement or disposition of colors in art. Also **coloration**.

co•los•sus *n.* a gigantic statue, esp. that of Apollo at Rhodes; hence any person of great stature or enormous strength. **colossal** *a.* of enormous size.

colt *n.* young horse, esp. a male.

Colt *n.* a repeating rifle; also a revolver invented by Samuel Colt.

col•umn *n.* a round pillar; a body of troops drawn up in deep files; a perpendicular

column

line of figures. **-ar** *a.* having the form of columns. **-ated, -ed** *a.* furnished with, or supported on, columns. **-ist** *n.* a writer who contributes articles to a newspaper.

co•ma *n.* *(Med.)* a stupor generally resulting from injury to the brain, alcoholic or narcotic poisoning; drowsiness. **-tose** *a.* lethargic; drowsy.

comb *n.* a toothed instrument for separating, adjusting, or fastening hair; a decoration for a lady's hair; a cock's crest; the cell structure in which bees store their honey. **-er** *n.* one who, or that which, combs. **-ing** *n.* **-ings** *n.pl.* hair, wool, etc. removed by combing.

com•bat *v.t.* to oppose by force; to contend with; *v.i.* to struggle; to contend; *n.* a fight; a struggle; a contest. **-ant** *a.* contending; disposed to content; *n.* one engaged in a fight. **-ive** *a.* quarrelsome.

com•bine *v.t.* to join together; to unite; *v.i.* to form a union;*(Chem.)* to unite and form a new compound; *n.* an association formed to further political or commercial interests; a syndicate. **combinable** *a.* capable of combining. **combinative, combinatory** *a.* tending to combine. **combination** *n.* union; association of persons; chemical union; series of letters or numbers for operating a lock.

com•bus•tion *n.* the act of burning; chemical action accompanied by heat and light. **combustible** *a.* inflammable; *n.* a substance that burns readily.

come *v.i.* to approach; to arrive at some state or condition; to move towards; to appear. *pr.p.* **coming.** *pa.p.* **come.** *pa.t.* **came. -back** *n.* a return to a former activity.

com•e•dy *n.* a play dealing with the lighter side of life; the humorous element in life, or an incident.

co•me•di•an *n.* an entertainer whose songs or stories are light and humorous; a comic. **comedienne** *n.* *fem.*

come•ly *a.* good-looking; graceful. **comeliness** *n.*

com•et *n.* a heavenly body consisting of a diffuse, nebulous head, a nucleus, and a tail.

com•fort *v.t.* to allay grief or trouble; to console, cheer, gladden; *n.* solace or consolation; ease of body or mind. **-s** *n.pl.* circumstances which give greater ease to life. **-able** *a.* enjoying comfort. **-ably** *adv.* **-er** *n.* one who comforts; a quilted bedcover. **-less** *a.*

com•ic *a.* pert. to comedy; mirth-provoking; *n.* that which induces laughter; a comedian; *(Colloq.) (pl.)* a comic magazine or newspaper strip. **-al** *a.* ludicrous. **-ally** *adv.* **-ality.**

com•ma *n.* a punctuation mark (,), used to mark the shortest pauses in the division of a sentence.

com•mand *v.t.* to order or demand with authority; to govern or control; *v.i.* to be at the head; *n.* an order; the body of troops under an officer; a region under a commander; a word of command; mastery or facility. **-ing** *a.* fitted to control; impressive or imperious. **-ant** *n.* officer in charge of a military station or a body of troops. **-eer** *v.t.* to seize for military purposes; to take forcible possession of. **-er** *n.* a commanding officer. **-ment** *n.* a command; precept.

-er-in-chief, the officer in supreme command of the forces of a state.

com·man·do n. (Mil.) a selected body of men, who undergo special training for particularly dangerous enterprises against the enemy.

com·mem·o·rate v.t. to call to remembrance; to celebrate the memory of someone or something by a solemn act of devotion. **commemoration** n. **commemorative, commemoratory** a.

com·mence v.t. to begin, to start, to originate; v.i. to begin. **-ment** n. the ceremony of conferring degrees in colleges and universities.

com·mend v.t. to speak favorably of; to entrust to. **-able** a. **-ably** adv. **-ableness** n. **-ation** n. the act of commending; praise; approval. **-atory** a.

com·men·su·rate a. proportionate; adequate. **-ly** adv. **-ness** n. **commensuration** n. **commensurable** a. suitably proportioned. **commensurably** adv. **commensurability** n.

com·ment v.t. and i. to make remarks, notes, criticisms; n. a critical remark; an observation. **-ary** n. a series of notes; an exposition of a book. **-ate** v.t. to interpret the meaning of. **-ator** n. an expositor; one who speaks a commentary, either on events for broadcasting, or with a film.

com·merce n. buying and selling; trade. **commercial** a. pert. to commerce; broadcast program paid for by an advertiser. **commercialism** n. business principles, methods, or viewpoint. **commercialize** v.t. **commercially** adv.

com·mis·er·ate v.t. and i. to have compassion for; to sympathize. **commiseration** n.

com·mis·sar·i·at n. the army department which supplies food, stores, equipment, transport.

com·mis·sa·ry n. one to whom duty is assigned; (Mil.) a store which supplies food and equipment. **commissarial** a.

com·mis·sion n. something entrusted to be done; payment by a percentage for doing something; a group of people authorized to deal with specified matters; a warrant of appointment, to the rank of officer in the army, navy, etc.; v.t. to authorize; to appoint to the rank of officer. **-ed** a. **-er** n. one holding a commission to act; the head of a governmental department.

com·mit v.t. to entrust; to give in charge; to be guilty of; to send for trial or confinement; pr.p. **-ting**, pa.p. and pa.t. **-ted**. **-tal** a. **-ment** n.

com·mit·tee n. a number of persons appointed to attend any particular business by a legislative body, court, society, etc.

com·mode n. a chest of drawers.

com·mo·di·ous a. spacious. **-ly** adv. **-ness** n. **commodity** n. an article of trade. **commodities** n.pl. goods.

com·mo·dore n. rank just below rear admiral; captain of a convoy of ships.

com·mon a. shared by or belonging to all, or to several; frequent; of low social status; n. a tract of land belonging to a community for public use. **commons** n.pl. the lower House of Parliament, called the House of Commons. **-er** n. one of the common people, i.e. not a member of the nobility. **-ly** adv. in a common manner; jointly. **-ness** n. **-place** a. ordinary; trite; n. a trite remark. — **sense** n. sound understanding; well-balanced judgment. — **law**, unwritten law as distinguished from statute law.

com·mon·weal n. the public welfare; the common good. **commonwealth** n. the whole body of people.

com·mo·tion n. violent motion; public disorder.

com·mune v.i. to have spiritual intercourse (with); (Eccl.) to receive the communion. **communion** n. (Christianity) the celebration of the Lord's Supper.

com·mune n. a small administrative district. **communal** a. pert. to a community; for common use. **communalize** v.t. to make over for common use. **communalism** n. a system by which small local governments have large powers. **communism** n. the theory of a social system in which everything is held in common. **communist** n. **communistic** a.

com·mu·ni·cate v.t. to impart information; v.i. to have connection with; to have dealings, correspondence, with. **communicable** a. **communicably** adv. **communication** n. intercourse by speech, correspondence, messages, etc.; information. **communicant** n. one who imparts information; one who receives communion. **communicative** a. ready to impart information; talkative.

com·mu·ni·ty n. a locality where people reside; the public, or people in general; common possession or enjoyment.

com·mute v.t. to mitigate a sentence; travel regularly between home and work. **commutable** a. exchangeable. **commutability** n. **commutation** n. **commutator** n. (Elect.) a device for reversing the direction of an electric current. **-r** n.

com·pact a. closely packed; condensed; v.t. to press closely together; to make firm. **compact** n. a pocket vanity-case. **-ly** adv. **-ness** n. **-ed** a. firmly united.

com·pact n. a mutual bargain; covenant.

com·pan·ion n. one who is in another's company, habitually or for the moment; comrade; **-able** a. fitted to be a companion; sociable. **-ably** adv. **-ability**, **-ableness** n. **-ship** n.

com·pa·ny n. a gathering of persons; an association of persons in business, etc.; visitors; a division of a regiment.

com·pare v.t. to notice or point out the likeness and differences of two or more things; (Gram.) to state the comparative and superlative of an adjective or adverb; v.i. to be like; to compete with. **comparable** a. of equal regard or value. **comparably** adv. **comparative** a. estimated by comparison; not absolute; (Gram.) expressing 'more'. **comparatively** adv. **comparison** n. the act of comparing.

com·part·ment *n.* a part divided off; a division of a railway car.

com·pass *n.* an instrument for showing directions; a circumference; measure-

compass

ment around; scope; *v.t.* to go round; to surround; to accomplish. **-es** *n.pl.* a mathematical instrument for drawing circles, measuring, etc.

com·pas·sion *n.* sympathy with the suffering of another; pity. **-ate** *a.* showing pity; merciful; *v.t.* to pity. **-ately** *adv.* **-ateness** *n.*

com·pat·i·ble *a.* agreeing with; capable of harmonious union. **-compatible** *adv.* **compatibility** *n.*

com·pa·tri·ot *n.* one of the same country; a fellow countryman.

com·pel *v.t.* to force; to overpower; to bring about by force; *pr.p.* **-ling.** *pa.p.* and *pa.t.* **-led. -lable** *a.*

com·pen·di·um *n.* an abridgement or summary. Also **compend.** *pl.* **-s,** or **compendia. compendious** *a.* abridged. **compendiously** *adv.*

com·pen·sate *v.t.* to recompense suitably; to pay; *v.i.* to make up for. **compensation** *n.* recompense; payment for some loss, injury, etc. **compensative, compensatory** *a.*

com·pete *v.i.* to strive against others to win something; to vie with. **competition** *n.* the act of competing; a contest. **competitive** *a.* **competitively** *adv.* **competitor** *n.* one who competes. **competitory** *a.*

com·pe·tent *a.* able; properly qualified; skillful. **-ly** *adv.* **competence, competency** *n.* the state of being capable.

com·pile *v.t.* to put together literary materials into one book or works; to collect or amass. **-r** *n.* **compilation** *n.*

com·pla·cent *a.* self-satisfied; gratified. **-ly** *adv.* **complacence, complacency** *n.* self-satisfaction.

com·plain *v.i.* to express distress, dissatisfaction; to grumble; to be ailing. **-ant** *n.* a complainer; one who beings an action against another. **complaint** *n.* the expression of distress, dissatisfaction, etc.; a malady or airment.

com·ple·ment *n.* that which supplies a deficiency; something completing a whole; the full number; *v.t.* to supply a deficiency. **-al, -ary** *a.* completing.

com·plete *a.* entire; finished; perfect, with no part lacking; *v.t.* to bring to a state of entirety; to accomplish. **-ly** *adv.* **-ness** *n.* **completion** *n.* the act of completing;

conclusion.

com·plex *a.* consisting of two or more parts; not simple; *n.* a complicated whole; *(Psych.)* a group of repressed emotional ideas responsible for abnormal mental condition. **-ly** *adv.* **-ness, -ity** *n.*

com·plex·ion *n.* color of the skin, esp. of the face; appearance.

com·pli·ance *n.* submission; a yielding; acquiescence. **compliant** *a.* yielding; obedient; civil. **compliantly** *adv.* **compliable** *a.* inclined to comply.

com·pli·cate *v.t.* to twist together; to make intricate. **-d** *a.* involved. **complication** *n.*

com·plic·i·ty *n.* the state of being an accomplice, of having a share in the guilt.

com·pli·ment *n.* an expression of admiration; flattering speech; *v.t.* to congratulate; to express respect for. **-ary** *a.* expressing praise, admiration; free, a *complimentary* ticket.

com·ply *v.i.* to yield to; to consent; to adapt oneself to. **complier** *n.*

com·po·nent *a.* making up; helping to form a compound; *n.* a part helping to make a whole.

com·pose *v.t.* to form by uniting parts; to arrange; to calm; *v.i.* to practice composition. **-d** *a.* sedate; calm. **-dly** *adv.* **-dness** *n.* **-r** *n.* one who composes; an author. **composite** *a.* made up of distinct parts or elements. **composition** *n.* literary, musical, work; the organization of the parts of a work of art. **compositor** *n.* a typesetter. **composure** *n.* calmness.

com·post *n.* a fertilizing mixture.

com·pote *n.* fruit stewed or preserved in syrup.

com·pound *v.t.* to put together, as elements or parts, to form a whole.

com·pound *a.* composed of elements, ingredients, or parts; not simple; *n.* a mixture; a word, made up of parts; *(Chem.)* a substance composed of two or more elements, which are always present in the same fixed proportions. **— fracture,** a fracture of a bone where a portion pierces the skin, making a surface wound. **— interest,** interest paid on capital plus accumulated interest.

com·pre·hend *v.t.* to understand; to grasp with the mind; to take in; to comprise. **comprehensible** *a.* understandable; conceivable. **comprehensibly** *adv.* **comprehensibility, comprehensibleness** *n.* **comprehension** *n.* the capacity of the mind to perceive and understand. **comprehensive** *a.* including much within narrow limits; extensive; inclusive.

com·press *v.t.* to press together; to condense. **-ed** *a.* **-ible** *a.* **-ibility** *n.* **-ion** *n.* the act or effect of compressing. **-ive** *a.* tending to compress. **-or** *n.*

com·press *n.* *(Med.)* a pad to make pressure on a wound.

com·prise *v.t.* to be composed of; to consist of.

com·pro·mise *n.* a settling of matters by mutual adjustment, each side making some concessions; *v.t.* and *i.* to settle by making mutual concessions.

comp·tom·e·ter n. a calculating machine.

comp·trol·ler n. a form of controller.

com·pul·sion n. the act of compelling; force; violence; (Psych.) an irresistible impulse. **compulsive** a. exercising compulsion. **compulsory** a. compelling; obligatory.

com·punc·tion n. remorse of conscience; scruple. **compuctious** a. conscience-stricken; remorseful.

com·pute v.t. to calculate; to estimate. **computable** a. computation n. calculation; reckoning.

com·rade n. a close friend or companion; an associate. **-ship** n. close friendship; **con** v.t. affectionate association.

con adv. against, e.g. in the phrase **pro and con**, for and against. **the pro and con** n. Also pl. **the pros and cons**, the advantages and disadvantages.

con·cat·e·nate v.i. to unite in a series. **concatenation** to unite in a series. **concatenation** n. a series of things depending on each other.

con·cave a. hollow and curved inwards. **concavity** n. hollowness.

) ( )

concave

con·ceal v.t. to hide or secrete; to disguise; to withhold from knowledge. **-ment** n.

con·cede v.t. to admit to be true; to surrender; v.i. to admit.

con·ceit n. over-estimation of self-vanity; fanciful thought. **-ed** a. vain. **-edly** adv.

con·ceive v.t. to form an idea in the mind; to imagine; v.i. to become pregnant; to have a notion. **conceivable** a. that may be believed, imagined, or understood. **conceivably** adv.

con·cen·trate v.i. to reduce to small space; to increase in strength; v.i. to come together; to devote all attention. **concentration** n. the act of concentrating; the fixation of the mind on something. **concentration camp**, a place of detention.

con·cept n. an abstract notion; a mental impression of an object. **conception** n. a mental picture; an idea; (Med.) the beginning of pregnancy. **conceptive** a. capable of conceiving. **conceptual** a. pert. to conception or to a concept.

con·cern v.t. to relate or belong to; to be of importance to; to make uneasy; n. that which relates or belongs to one; interest in, or care for, any person or thing; a business establishment. **-ed** a. interested; troubled; involved. **-ing** prep. regarding; with respect to. **-ment** n.

con·cert v.t. to plan together; to design. **-ed** a. mutually planned; (Mus.) arranged in parts. n. harmony; a musical entertainment. **concerto** n. a musical composition arranged for a solo instrument with orchestral accompaniment.

con·ces·sion n. the act of conceding; a special privilege; an admission. **-aire** n. one who holds a concession. **-ary** a.

conch n. a seashell.

con·chol·o·gy n. the scientific study of shells and shellfish. **conchologist** n.

con·cil·i·ate v.t. to win over to goodwill; to pacify. **conciliation** n. **conciliative** a. conciliatory. **conciliatory** a. tending to pacify.

con·cise a. condensed; comprehensive. **-ly** adv. in few words; tersely. **-ness** n.

con·clave any secret meeting.

con·clude v.t. to bring to an end; to make a final judgment of; v.i. to come to an end.

con·clu·sion n. the last part of anything; the final judgment; inference; result from experiment. **conclusive** a. final; convincing.

con·coct v.t. to make a mixture; to make up, esp. a story. **concoction** n.

con·com·i·tant a. accompanying; attending; n. an accompanying circumstance. **concomitance, concomitancy** n. the state of being concomitant; coexistence.

con·cord n. agreement; union between persons, as in opinions, etc.; consonance; v.i. to agree. **concordance** n. agreement; **concordant** a. harmonious.

con·cor·dat n. a pact; a treaty.

con·course n. a gathering together; a promenade in a park; a large space in a railroad station.

con·crete a. solid; not abstract; specific; n. a mixture of sand, cement, etc., used in building; anything specific; v.t. to form into a solid mass; v.i. to harden. **-ly** adv. **-ness** n. **concretion** n. the state of being concrete; a mass formed of parts pressed together.

con·cu·pis·cence n. violent sexual desire; lust. **concupiscent, concupiscible** a. lustful.

con·cur v.i. to agree; to express agreement; to coincide. pr.p. **-ring** pa.p. and pa.t. **-red. -rence** n. **-rent** a. acting in conjunction; agreeing; taking place at the same time; accompanying; n. a joint or contributory cause. **-rently** adv.

con·cus·sion n. act of shaking by sudden striking; shock; (Med.) a violent disturbance of the brain caused by a blow or fall.

con·demn v.t. to blame; to pronounce guilty; to sentence; to declare unfit for use. **-ation** n. **-atory** a.

con·dense v.t. to make more solid; to change a vapor or gas into liquid or solid; to pack into few words; v.i. to become more compact; to pass from vapor to liquid or solid. **condensation** n. the state of being condensed; conciseness. **-d** a. compressed; (of milk) evaporated and preserved in cans. **-r** n. one who, or that which, condenses; an apparatus for changing vapor or gas into liquid or solid.

con·de·scend v.i. to come down from one's position, rank, or dignity; to stoop; to deign; to be gracious or affable to inferiors; to patronize. **-ing** a. **condescension** n.

con·di·ment n. a relish; seasoning for food.

con·di·tion n. a thing on which a statement, happening, depends; state or circumstances of anything; a

C

prerequisite; *v.t.* to impose conditions on; to render fit and in good health; *v.i.* to make terms. -al *a.* not absolute. -ally *adv.* -ed *a.* conditioned reflex, in psychology, an automatic response.

con•dole *v.i.* to grieve with; to offer sympathy. condolence, -ment *n.* an expression of sympathy.

con•done *v.t.* to pardon; to overlook.

con•duce *v.i.* to lead to some result; to promote. conducive *a.* having a tendency to promote or forward. conduciveness *n.*

con•duct *n.* the act of guiding; behavior. conduct *v.t.* to lead; to manage; to behave. -ance *n. (Elect.)* the property of a body for conducting electricity. conductible *a.* conduction *n.* the transmission of heat from one body to another. conductive *a.* able to transmit heat, electricity, etc. conductivity *n.* the quality of being conductive. conductor *n.* the leader of a choir or orchestra; one in charge of a bus, train, who collects fares; a substance capable of transmitting heat, electricity, etc.

cone *n.* a solid body tapering to a point from a circular base; the fruit of the pine,

cone

fir, etc. conic, conical *a.* having the form of a cone. conically *adv.*

con•el•rad *n.* a system used by radio in time of war to prevent the enemy from locating cities by radio beams.

con•fec•tion *n.* the act of compounding different substances into one compound; candy, ice cream, etc. -ary *a.* -er *n.* one who makes or sells confections. -er's sugar *n.* finely powdered sugar. -ery *n.* a finely powdered sugar. -ery *n.* a shop where these are sold.

con•fed•er•ate *a.* bound by treaty; allied; *n.* an accomplice; *v.t.* and *i.* to unite in a league. confederacy *n.* an alliance. confederation *n.* the act of forming a confederacy; an alliance.

con•fer *v.t.* to bestow upon; *v.i.* to consult together; to take advice. *pr.p.* -ring. *pa.p.* and *pa.t.* -red. -ee *n.* recipient of an award. conference *n.* a meeting; a consultation.

con•fess *v.t.* to admit; to declare one's sins; to plead guilty. -edly *adv.* admittedly. confession *n.* avowal of sins; declaring one's sins to priest. confessional *n.* the stall where a priest sits to hear confessions; *a.* pert. to confession. -or *n.* a priest who hears confessions.

con•fet•ti *n.pl.* small bits of paper, for throwing at weddings.

con•fide *v.t.* to entrust to; to tell a secret to; *v.i.* to put faith in. confidant *n.* a person in whom one can confide.

con•fi•dence *n.* that in which faith is put; trust; feeling of security. confident *a.* having assurance; bold. confidently *adv.* confidential *a.* treated with confidence;

secret. confidentially *adv.*

con•fig•u•ra•tion *n.* outward form, or figure; outline; aspect.

con•fine *v.t.* to keep within bounds; to imprison; *v.i.* to have a common boundary; confine *n.* usually in *pl.* confines, boundary; limit. -ment *n.* imprisonment; restraint.

con•firm *v.t.* to settle; to make valid by formal assent; to verify. confirmation *n.* the act of making valid, certain, etc. -ative *a.* -atory *a.* -ed *a.*

con•fis•cate *v.t.* to seize by authority; to take possession of without compensation; *a.* forfeited. confiscation *n.* confiscator *n.* confiscatory *a.*

con•flict *v.i.* to clash; to be at odds with; to differ. conflict *n.* prolonged struggle; strong disagreement. -ing *a.* differing; contradictory.

con•flu•ence *n.* a flowing together; a large assemblage. confluent *a.* Also conflux.

con•form *v.t.* to make like; to bring into agreement; *v.i.* to comply; *a.* in accord. -able *a.* corresponding in form; submissive. -ably *adv.* -ation *n.* the manner in which a body is shaped; structure. -ist *n.* one who complies with custom. -ity *n.*

con•found *v.t.* to bring to confusion; to bewilder. -ed *a.* confused; baffled.

con•front *v.t.* to face boldly; to bring face to face. confrontation *n.*

Con•fu•cius *n.* Chinese philosopher.

con•fuse *v.t.* to mix up; to mistake one thing for another. -d *a.* mixed up; perplexed. confusedly *adv.* confusion *n.* the state of being confused; disorder; bewilderment.

con•fute *v.t.* to prove to be wrong. confutable *a.* confutation *n.*

con•geal *v.t.* and *i.* to freeze, as a fluid; to solidify; to coagulate; *v.i.* to become stiff or solidified, from cold. -able *a.* -ment *n.* a thing congealed; a clot. congelation *n.*

con•gen•ial *a.* allied in disposition and tastes; agreeable. -ly *adv.* congeniality *n.*

con•gen•i•tal *a.* existing at the time of birth.

con•gest *v.t.* to produce a hampering accumulation; to overcrowd. -ed *a.* overcrowded. congestion *n.*

con•glom•er•ate *a.* gathered into a mass; *v.t.* to bring together into a mass; *n.* *(Geol.)* rock composed of fragments of rock cemented together. conglomeration *n.* a mixed collection.

con•grat•u•late *v.t.* to wish joy to; to felicitate. congratulation *n.* felicitation. congratulatory *a.*

con•gre•gate *v.t.* to gather into a crowd or assembly; *v.i.* to meet together; *a.* collective. congregation *n.* an assemblage; a gathering of persons for worship. congregational *a.*

con•gress *n.* a formal assembly, e.g. of representatives of governments. Congress *n.* the legislative body of the United States. -man *n.* a member of the U.S. House of Representatives. congressional *a.*

con•gru•ent *a.* agreeing together;

corresponding. **congruence, congruency** *n.* suitableness. **congruity** *n.* **congruous** *a.*

con·ic See cone.

co·nif·e·rae *n.pl.* an order of trees bearing a cone-shaped fruit. **coniferous** *a.*

con·jec·ture *n.* opinion founded on insufficient proof; *v.t.* to guess; to infer on insufficient grounds. **conjecturable** *a.* **conjectural** *a.*

con·join *v.t.* to join together; *a.* united; associated.

con·ju·gal *a.* pert. to marriage; matrimonial. **-ly** *adv.* **conjugality** *n.* the married state.

con·ju·gate *v.t.* (*Gram.*) to write all the different parts of a verb. **conjugation** *n.* a class of verbs inflected in the same manner; (*Biol.*) the fusion of cells for reproduction.

con·junct *a.* joined together. **-ly** *adv.* **conjunction** *n.* union; (*Gram.*) a word used to join clauses, etc. **conjunctive** *a.* serving to connect.

con·junc·ti·vi·tis *n.* inflammation of the mucous membrane lining the eyelid.

con·jure *v.t.* solemnly to implore. **conjure** *v.i.* to practice magic; to imagine. **conjuration** *n.* the act of calling upon by a sacred name. **conjurer, conjuror** *n.* a magician.

con·nect *v.t.* to fasten together; to relate; to attach; *v.i.* to unite; to have a close relation. **-ed** *a.* joined; **-edly** *adv.* **connection** *n.* a link; state of being united. **-ive** *a.* binding; *n.* a connecting word. **-or** *n.*

con·nive *v.i.* to pretend not to see; to co-operate secretly (with 'at'). **connivance** *n.* consent in wrong-doing. **-r** *n.*

con·note *v.t.* to have a meaning in addition to the primary meaning. **connotate** *v.t.* to connote. **connotation** *n.* a secondary implied meaning. **connotative** *a.*

con·nu·bi·al *a.* pert. to marriage. **connubiality** *n.*

con·quer *v.t.* to overcome; to subjugate or subdue; *v.i.* to be victorious; to prevail. **-able** *a.* **-or** *n.* **conquest** *n.* the act of conquering; that which is conquered.

con·science *n.* the faculty by which we know right from wrong. **conscientious** *a.* governed by dictates of conscience. **conscientiously** *adv.* **conscientiousness** *n.* **conscionable** *a.* governed by conscience. **—stricken** *a.* seized with scruples. **conscientious objector**, a man who refuses to serve in the armed forces, on moral or religious grounds.

con·scious *a.* having inward knowledge (of); having the use of one's faculties. **-ly** *adv.* **-ness** *n.* the state of being mentally awake to one's surroundings.

con·script *v.t.* to enroll compulsorily for service in the armed forces. **conscript** *n.* one compelled to serve as a soldier. **conscription** *n.*

con·se·crate *v.t.* to set apart for sacred uses; to dedicate. **consecration** *n.*

con·sec·u·tive *a.* following one another in unbroken order; successive. **-ly** *adv.* **-ness** *n.*

con·sen·sus *n.* a general agreement.

con·sent *n.* agreement; permission; *v.i.* to agree. **consentient** *a.* united in opinion. **consentience.** *n.*

con·se·quent *a.* following as a result; *n.* effect. **-ly** *adv.* therefore; as a result; by logical sequence. **consequence** *n.* that which naturally follows; result; importance; value. **consequential** *a.*

con·serve *v.t.* to keep safe; to preserve; *n.* anything conserved. **conservation** *n.* preservation; safe-guarding; the official safe-guarding of forests, rivers, etc.; the area so protected. **conservative** *a.* tending to conserve; hostile to change; *n.* one opposed to hasty innovations. **conservatory** *n.* a greenhouse for plants; a school of music.

con·sid·er *v.t.* to reflect upon carefully; to be of opinion; *v.i.* to deliberate seriously. **-able** *a.* worthy of attention; moderately large. **-ably** *adv.* **-ate** *a.* thoughtful for others. **-ately** *adv.* **-ateness** *n.* **-ation** *n.* deliberation; fee or recompense; thoughtful regard for others. **-ed** *a.* carefully thought out. **-ing** *prep.* in view of.

con·sign *v.t.* to entrust to a carrier for transport; *v.i.* to agree. **consignee** *n.* the person to whom goods are consigned. **-er, -or** *n.* the person who consigns goods. **-ment** *n.*

con·sist *v.i.* to be composed of; to be compatible with. **-ence, -ency** *n.* a condition of being fixed; a degree of firmness or density; harmony. **consistent** *a.* compatible; constant in adhering to principles, etc.

con·sole *v.t.* to comfort in distress. **consolable** *a.* able to be consoled. **consolation** *n.* the act of comforting; solace; encouragement. **consolatory** *a.*

con·sol·i·date *v.t.* and *i.* to make solid; to make firm; to strengthen. **consolidation** *n.* the act of making or becoming compact and firm.

con·so·nant *a.* agreeing with; *n.* a non-vowel. **-ly** *adv.* **consonance, consonancy** *n.* agreement; harmony.

con·sort *n.* a companion. **consort** *v.t.* to join; *v.i.* to keep company; to associate.

con·sor·ti·um *n.* an association for a common end.

con·spec·tus *n.* a general outline of a subject; a synopsis.

con·spic·u·ous *a.* very noticeable. **-ly** *adv.* **-ness, conspicuity** *n.*

con·spire *v.i.* to plot together. **conspiracy** *n.* a combination of persons for an evil purpose; a plot. **conspirator** *n.* **conspiratorial** *a.*

con·sta·ble *n.* a peace officer.

con·stant *a.* fixed; invariable; *n.* that which is not subject to change. **-ly** *adv.* **constancy** *n.* steadfastness; fidelity.

con·stel·la·tion *n.* a group of fixed stars.

con·ster·na·tion *n.* amazement or terror that throws the mind into confusion. **consternate** *v.t.* to fill with alarm.

con·sti·pate *v.t.* to clog or make sluggish. **constipation** *n.* insufficient; irregular evacuation of the bowels.

con·sti·tute *v.t.* to establish; to set up; to

compose. **constitution** n. the natural state of body or mind; the system of laws under which a state exists. **constitutional** a. pert. to the constitution; n. a walk for the benefit of health. **constitutionally** adv. **constitutionalist** n. one who upholds constitutional government. **constitutionality** n. **constitutive** a. having powers to enact or establish. **constituent** a. serving to compose or make up.

con•strain v.t. to force or compel; to restrain; to limit. -t n. compelling force; unnaturalness or embarrassment of manner.

con•strict v.t. to cause to shrink or contract; to squeeze. **constriction** n. -ive a. that which constricts; the boa-constrictor.

con•struct v.t. to fabricate; to compile. **construction** n. erection; structure; interpretation or meaning. -ive a. -iveness n. -or n.

con•strue v.t. to interpret; to deduce; to translate. **construable** a. -r n.

con•sub•stan•ti•ate v.t. and i. to unite in one substance or nature. **consubstantial** a. **consubstantiation** n.

con•sul n. an officer appointed by a government to represent it in a foreign country. -ar a. -ate n. the offices of a consul. -ship n.

con•sult v.t. to ask advice of; to seek the opinion of; v.i. to confer. -ant n. one who gives expert advice. -ing a. -ation n. a council or conference. -ative a. advisory.

con•sume v.t. to use up; to eat or drink up; v.i. to waste away. **consumable** a. -r n.

con•sum•mate v.t. to complete; to perfect; (Law) to complete marriage by sexual intercourse. **consummate** a. complete. -ly adv. **consummation** n.

con•sump•tion n. the act of consuming; the amount consumed; pulmonary tuberculosis. **consumptive** a. wasteful; affected with, or inclined to, pulmonary tuberculosis; n.

con•tact n. a touching; a meeting; v.t. to get in touch with a person. -ual a. implying contact. — **lens**, an invisible eye-glass fitting over the eyeball.

con•ta•gion n. the transmission of a disease from one person to another. **contagious** a. communicable.

con•tain v.t. to hold; to comprise. -able a. -er n.

con•tam•i•nate v.t. to taint; to infect. **contaminable** a. **contamination** n. pollution; (War) the result of coming into contact with radioactive particles.

con•tem•plate v.t. to look at with attention; to meditate on; v.i. to reflect. **contemplation** n. **contemplative** a. **contemplatively** adv.

con•tem•po•ra•ne•ous a. happening at the same time. -ly adv. -ness n. **contemporary** a. living at the same time; present-day; n. a person approximately of one's own age.

con•tempt n. scorn; disregard; open disrespect to court orders. -ible a. despicable. -ibleness n. -ibly adv. -uous a. expressing disdain; scornful. -uously adv. -uousness n.

con•tend v.i. to struggle with; to assert strongly; -er n.

con•tent a. satisfied; v.t. to satisfy the mind of; n. freedom from anxiety. -edly adv. -edness n. -ment n. satisfaction; ease of mind.

con•tent n. that which is contained; volume. -s n.pl. an index of the topics treated in a book.

con•ten•tion n. strife; subject matter of discussion. **contentious** a. quarrelsome.

con•test v.t. to question or resist, as a claim; to dispute; v.i. to contend or vie (with). **contest** n. conflict; dispute; strike. -able a. -ant n. a competitor.

con•text n. that which comes immediately before or after a passage and helps to explain it. -ual a. pert. to the context. **contexture** n. the weaving of parts into one body; structure; style of composition in writing.

con•ti•gu•i•ty n. the state of being contiguous. **contiguous** a. touching; adjacent.

con•ti•nent n. one of the large divisions of unbroken land. -al a. pert. to a continent.

con•ti•nent a. temperate; moderate. **continence, continency** n.

con•tin•gent a. possible; dependent; n. quota, esp. of troops. -ly adv. **contingence, contingency** n.

con•tin•ue v.t. to prolong or extend in duration; to resume; v.i. to remain in a state or place; to last. **continual** a. without interruption; unceasing. **continually** adv. **continuance** n. a remaining in existence; uninterrupted succession. **continuant** a. **continuate** a. uninterrupted. **continuation** n. the act of continuing. **continuity** n. uninterrupted succession; close union. **continuous** a. united without break; constant. **continuously** adv.

con•tort v.t. to twist violently; to bend out of shape. **contortion** n. writhing. **contortionist** n. one who practices contortion. **contortive** a.

con•tour n. outline; v.t. to draw the contour of.

con•tra•band a. prohibited by law or treaty; n. goods, the exportation or importation of which is forbidden.

con•tra•cep•tion n. birth control. **contraceptive** a. and n. a drug or appliance for preventing conception.

con•tract v.t. to draw together; to reduce to a less volume; v.i. to become smaller; to become involved in. **contract** n. an agreement. -ed a. drawn together; narrow. -ible a. -ile a. tending to contract; producing contraction. -ility n. -ion n. shortening of a word by the omission of a letter. -or n. one who undertakes to work for a fixed sum. -ual a. implying, or connected with, a contract.

con•tra•dict v.t. to deny. **contradiction** n. denial; discrepancy of statements. **contradictious** a. inclined to contradict. -ive a. containing contradiction. -ory a. diametrically opposed; inconsistent.

con•tra•dis•tinc•tion n. direct contrast.

contradistinctive *a.* **contradistinguish** *v.t.* to note the difference between two things by contrasting their different qualities.

con·tral·to *n.* the lowest of the three female voices.

con·tra·ry *a.* opposed; opposing; different; adverse; self-willed; *n.* something the exact opposite of. **contrariety** *n.* something contrary. **contrarily** *adv.* **contrariness** *n.* **contrariwise** *adv.* on the contrary.

con·trast *v.t.* to set in opposition for the purpose of comparing; *v.i.* to stand in opposition. *n.* a striking difference; a comparison to show their relative excellence.

con·tra·vene *v.t.* to break or infringe, as a law. **contravention** *n.*

con·tri·bute *v.t.* to give to a common fund; to help to a common result; *v.i.* to lend assistance. **contributable** *a.* **contribution** *n.* that which is contributed. **contributive** *a.* **contributory** *a.*

con·trite *a.* remorseful. **-ly** *adv.* **-ness** *n.* **contrition** *n.* remorse.

con·trive *v.t.* and *i.* to plan; to bring about; to invent. **contrivance** *n.* the act of planning; mechanical invention. **-r** *n.*

con·trol *v.t.* to have under command; to regulate; to restrain; *n.* authority or power. *pr.p.* **-ling.** *pa.p.* and *pa.t.* **-led.** **-lable** *a.* **-ler** *n.* one who controls. **-lership** *n.* **-ment** *n.*

con·tro·vert *v.t.* to dispute by argument; to refute. **-ible** *adv.* **controversy** *n.* disputation; debate. **controversial** *a.* leading to controversy; likely to provoke argument. **controversially** *adv.* **controversialist** *n.*

con·tu·ma·cy *n.* contempt of authority; stubborn disobedience. **contumacious** *a.* rebellious. **-ly** *adv.* **-ness** *n.*

con·tu·me·ly *n.* insult; disdainful insolence. **contumelious** *a.* haughtily disdainful.

con·tuse *v.t.* to injure without breaking the skin. **contusion** *n.* a bruise.

con·va·lesce *v.i.* to recover from illness. **convalescent** *a.* **convalescence** *n.*

con·vec·tion *n.* the process of transmission of heat by means of currents in liquids or gases.

con·vene *v.t.* to call together; *v.i.* to assemble. **-r** *n.* **convenable** *a.*

con·ven·ient *a.* suitable; handy or easy of access. **-ly** *adv.* **convenience** *n.* that which is convenient; any appliance which makes for comfort.

con·vent *n.* a community devoted to a religious life; a nunnery. **conventual** *a.*

con·ven·tion *n.* a formal assembly of representatives; accepted usage, custom, or rule. **-al** *a.* formed by agreement or compact; customary. **-ally** *adv.* **-alism** *n.* that which is established by usage. **-ality** *n.*

con·verge *v.i.* to tend to one point; to approach. **convergent** *a.* **convergence**, **convergency** *n.* coming together.

con·verse *v.i.* to talk with. **conversable** *a.* affable. **conversably** *adv.* **conversance,**

conversancy *n.* the state of being acquainted with. **conversant** *a.* acquainted with by use. **conversation** *n.* talk. **conversational** *a.* **conversation(al)ist** *n.* one who excels in conversation.

con·verse *a.* opposite; turned around; *n.* the contrary. **-ly** *adv.*

con·vert *v.t.* to apply to another purpose; to cause to adopt a religion, an opinion, etc.; *v.i.* to be changed. **convert** *n.* **conversion** *n.* a change from one state to another. **-er** *n.* one who converts; *(Elect.)* a machine for changing alternating current into direct current, or altering the pressure of direct current. **-ible** *a.* capable of change; *n.* an automobile with a folding top.

con·vex *a.* curving outwards; bulging. **-ity,** **-ness** *n.*

convex

con·vey *v.t.* to transport; to communicate. **-able.** **-ance** *n.* the act of conveying; the transference of property. **-ancing** *n.* **-er,** **-or** *n.*

con·vict *v.t.* to prove guilty; *n.* a person serving a sentence. **-ion** *n.* a verdict of guilty; a firm belief.

con·vince *v.t.* to persuade by argument; to satisfy by proof. **convincible** *a.* **convincing** *a.* **convincingly** *adv.*

con·viv·i·al *a.* jovial; merry. **-ly** *adv.* **conviviality** *n.*

con·voke *v.t.* to call together. **convocation** *n.* the act of calling together; an assembly.

con·volve *v.t.* and *i.* to wind together; to coil. **convolute, convoluted** *a.* rolled together; spiral. **convolution** *n.* the act of rolling together; a turn of a coil.

con·voy *v.t.* to escort for protection, by land, sea, or air. **convoy** *n.* escorting protection.

con·vulse *v.t.* to affect with violent and irregular spasms. **convulsion** *n.* any violent agitation; *pl.* *(Med.)* violent and involuntary contractions of the muscles. **convulsive** *a.* spasmodic.

coo *v.i.* to make a low, melodius sound like the note of a dove.

cook *v.t.* to prepare food by boiling, roasting, baking, etc.; *v.i.* to prepare food by the action of heat; *n.* one whose occupation is to cook food. **-ery** *n.* the process of cooking. **-er** *n.* **-out** *n.* meal cooked and eaten outdoors.

cook·y, cook·ie *n.* a small sweet cake made of stiff dough which is rolled, dropped, or sliced, and baked.

cool *a.* slightly cold; self-possessed; impudent; *n.* a moderate state of cold; *v.t.* to cause to cool; to calm; *v.i.* to become cool; to lose one's affection. **-er** *n.* a container for cooling. **-ish** *a.* fairly cool. **-ly** *adv.* **-ness** *n.* **—headed** *a.* calm; self-possessed.

coop *n.* pen for poultry; *v.t.* confine.

co·op·er·ate *v.i.* to act jointly with another;

C

to unite for a common effort.
co-operation n. **co-operative** a.
co-operator n. **co-operative store,** the shop of a co-operative society, where members make their purchases and share the profits.

co-opt v.t. to choose or elect into a committee by the votes of its own members. **-ion, -ation** n.

co-or-di-nate a. equal in degree, rank, importance, etc.; v.t. to bring into order as parts of a whole; n. a person of the same rank, importance, etc. as another. **-ly** adv. in the same order. **-ness** n. **coordination** n. **coordinative** a.

co-part-ner n. an associate. **-ship** n.

cope v.i. to deal successfully (with).

Co-per-ni-can a. pert. to *Copernicus* the founder of modern astronomy.

cop-i-er n. See copy.

co-pi-ous a. abundant; plentiful. **-ly** adv. **-ness** n.

cop-per n. a red-colored metal; a. copper-colored; v.t. to cover with copper. **-y** a. like copper. **-head** n. a poisonous N. American snake.

cop-u-la n. a connecting link; (*Gram.*) the word uniting the subject and predicate. **copulate** v.i. to unite sexually. **copulation** n. **-tive** a. pert. to copulation.

cop-y n. an imitation of an original; a writing like another writing; an exact reproduction; the manuscript, placed in the compositor's hands; v.t. to write, print, etc. in imitation of an original; to imitate. **-ist** n. **copier** n. an imitator. **-book** n. a book in which copies are written for learners to imitate. **-writer** n. a writer of advertisements. **-right** n. the legal exclusive right which an author, musician, or artist has to print, publish, and sell his own works, during a certain period of time; a. protected by the law of copyright.

cor-al n. a hard reddish yellow, white, etc. substance growing on the bottom of

coral

tropical seas, and composed of the skeletons of zoophytes; a. coral-colored; made by coral.

cord n. a thick string or a thin rope of several strands; anything like a cord (e.g. spinal cord, vocal cord); a cubic measure esp. for fuel wood; v.t. to bind with a cord or rope. **-age** n. an assemblage of ropes and cords, esp. the rigging of a ship. **-ed** a. **-ing** n. ribbed surface.

cor-dial a. expressing warmth of heart; sincere; n. a refreshing drink or medicine. **-ly** adv. **-ity** n.

cord-ite n. a smokeless explosive.

cor-du-roy n. a thick cotton fabric, corded or ribbed on the surface. n.pl. trousers made of this fabric.

core n. the heart or inner part, esp. of fruit;

v.t. to take out the core.

co-res-pon-dent n. in a divorce suit the man or woman charged along with the respondent as guilty of adultery.

cork n. a stopper for a bottle; a. made of cork; v.t. to stop up with a cork; **-screw** n. a tool for drawing corks from bottles; a. shaped like a corkscrew, with a spiral twist.

corn n. a single seed of oats, wheat, rye, barley, maize, etc.; an inclusive term for grain of all kinds; v.t. to preserve meat by salting. **-cob** n. the head in which are encased the grains of the maize plant. **-flour** n. a foodstuff consisting of the finely ground starch granules of Indian corn (maize). **-flower** n. an annual weed growing in cornfields and bearing blue flowers. **-husk** n. the outer leaves enclosing an ear of corn. **-starch** n. a starch used for thickening.

corn n. a horny growth of the skin, usually on toes and feet. **-y** a. pert. to a corn.

cor-ne-a n. the transparent membrane which forms part of the outer coat of the eyeball.

cor-ner n. the point where two lines meet; the part of a room where two sides meet; an embarrassing position; v.t. to put into a position of difficulty, leaving no escape. **-stone** n. a corner foundation stone laid with ceremony; something of fundamental importance; **-wise** adv. diagonally; with the corner in front. **to corner the market,** to obtain a monopoly.

cor-net n. a kind of trumpet with valves.

cor-nice n. an ornamental molding around the top of the walls of a room.

cor-nu-co-pi-a n. the horn of plenty, an emblem of abundance.

cor-ol-lar-y n. an inference from a preceding statement; a consequence.

co-ro-na n. the flat projecting part of a cornice; a crown; **-l** a. pert. to a corona;

corona

n. crown. **coronary** a. resembling a crown; pertaining to the arteries which supply the heart tissues. **coronary thrombosis** (*Med.*) a heart condition caused by a blood clot in a coronary artery. **coronate** v.t. to crown. **coronation** n. the crowning of a sovereign. **coronet** n. a small crown worn by nobility.

cor-o-ner n. a legal officer appointed to hold an inquest in cases of death.

cor-po-ral n. non-commissioned officer of a troop, next below a sergeant.

cor-po-ral a. belonging or relating to the body. n. the state of having a body. **corporate** a. united legally in a body; pertaining to a corporation. **corporately**

adv. **corporateness** *n.* **corporation** *n.* a legal, municipal, or professional association.

corps *n.* a division of an army forming a unit. *pl.* **corps.**

corpse *n.* a dead body, esp. of a human being.

cor·pu·lence *n.* excessive fatness; stoutness. Also **corpulency** *n.* **corpulent** *a.*

cor·pus *n.* the main substance of anything. *pl.* **corpora.**

cor·pus·cle *n.* a minute particle; *(Anat.)* an organic cell, either moving freely, as in

corpuscle

the blood, or intimately connected with others, as bone-corpuscles.

cor·ral *n.* an enclosure for cattle; *v.t.* to drive into a corral.

cor·rect *a.* free from faults; *v.t.* to indicate the errors in; to punish. **-ly** *adv.* **-tion** *n.* a change to remedy a fault; punishment. **-itude** *n.* **-ional** *a.* **-ive** *a.* having power to correct; *n.* that which counteracts. **-ness** *n.* **-or** *n.*

cor·re·late *v.i.* to be mutually related; *v.t.* to place in reciprocal relations; *n.* either of two things necessarily implying the other. **correlation** *n.* reciprocal relation. **correlative** *a.* reciprocally related; *n.* one who, or that which, is correspondingly related to another person or thing. **correlativity** *n.*

cor·re·spond *v.i.* to exchange letters; to agree with in some respect; to be congruous. **-ence** *n.* exchange of letters; the letters themselves; suitability. **-ent** *a.* suitable; congruous; *n.* one with whom intercourse is maintained by exchange of letters. **-ing** *a.* **-ingly** *adv.*

cor·ri·dor *n.* a passage in a building.

cor·ri·gi·ble *a.* capable of being corrected.

cor·rob·o·rate *v.t.* to add strength to; to support a statement. **corroborant** *a.* giving strength. **corroboration** *n.* **corroborative** *a.* confirming; strengthening.

cor·rode *v.t.* to eat away by degrees (by chemical action, disease, etc.); to rust. **corrodent** *a.* corrosive; *n.* a substance which eats away. **corrodible, corrosible** *a.* capable of being corroded. **corrosion** *n.* **corrosive** *a.* having the power of corroding; *n.* any corrosive sbstance.

cor·ru·gate *v.t.* to form into folds or alternate furrows and ridges. **corrugation** *n.* **— iron,** sheet-iron, corrugated to increase its rigidity.

cor·rupt *v.t.* and *i.* to make rotten; to make evil; to bribe; *a.* depraved; tainted with sin; influenced by bribery. **-er** *n.* **-ible** *a.* capable of being corrupted. **corruption** *n.* **-ive** *a.* **-ly** *adv.* **-ness** *n.*

cor·sage *n.* a small bouquet worn by a lady.

cor·set *n.* undergarment; girdle.

cor·tex *n.* bark; sheath of a plant. *(Anat.)* the outer covering of an organ, esp. the outer layer of gray matter of the brain; *pl.* **cortices. cortical** *a.* **corticate, corticated** *a.*

cor·ti·sone *n.* a substance produced in the adrenal glands.

cor·us·cate *v.i.* to flash; to glitter; to gleam. **coruscation** *n.*

co·se·cant *n.* *(Trig.)* the secant of the complement of an angle.

co·sig·na·to·ry *a.* signing jointly; *n.* a joint signer of a document.

co·sine *n.* *(Trig.)* the sine of the complement o an angle.

cos·met·ic *a.* making for beauty, esp. of the skin; *n.* any substance helping to enhance the appearance.

cos·mic *a.* See **cosmos.**

cos·mog·o·ny *n.* a theory of the creation of the universe and its inhabitants.

cos·mol·o·gy *n.* the science of the laws which control the universe. **cosmological** *a.* **cosmologist** *n.*

cos·mo·naut *n.* a space traveler.

cos·mo·pol·i·tan *a.* relating to all parts of the world; *n.* a citizen of the world. Also **cosmopolite** *n.*

cos·mos *n.* the ordered universe. **cosmic, cosmical** *a.* pert. to the universe, or to the earth as a part of the universe; orderly. **cosmically** *adv.* **cosmic rays,** radiations of great penetrating power, coming to the earth from outer space.

cost *v.i.* to entail the payment, loss, or sacrifice of; *n.* price; the amount paid, or to be paid, for anything; suffering undergone for any end. **-liness** *n.* great cost or expense; expensiveness. **-ly** *a.* very expensive. **— price,** the wholesale, as opposed to the retail, price.

cos·tal *a.* pert. to the ribs or to the side of the body.

cos·tive *a.* having sluggish motion; constipated. **-ness** *n.*

cos·tume *n.* dress peculiar or appropriate, as to country, period, office, or character; a person's dress or attire. **-r** *n.* one who makes or deals in costumes.

co·sy See **cozy.**

cot *n.* a light, portable bed.

co·tan·gent *n.* *(Trig.)* the tangent of the complement of an angle.

cot·tage *n.* a small dwelling house, esp. in the country or at a resort. **-r** *n.* one who inhabits a cottage. **— cheese** *n.* a soft, white cheese.

cot·ter *n.* a pin or wedge used for tightening or fastening.

cot·ton *n.* a soft, downy, substance; cloth or thread made of cotton; *a.* made of cotton;

cotton

— gin n. a machine for separating the seeds from cotton. **-mouth** n. the water moccasin. **-wood** n. a type of American poplar tree. **-y** a.

couch v.t. to cause to lie down, esp. on a bed; v.i. to lie down; to crouch; n. a sofa; davenport. **couchant** a. lying down.

cou•gar n. the puma or American panther.

cougar

cough n. noisy, violent, explosive effort to expel irritating matter from the lungs; v.t. to expel from the lungs by a cough.

could p.at. of the verb **can**.

cou•lomb n. the quantity transferred by a current of one ampere in one second.

coun•cil n. an assembly summoned for advice; a municipal body. **-man** n. **-lor** n.

coun•sel n. opinion; one who gives advice, esp. legal; v.t. admonish; recommend. **-or** n. an adviser; a trial lawyer. **-orship** n.

count n. (fem. **countess**) a title of nobility.

count v.t. to number; to sum up; to recite the numerals in regular succession; v.i. to depend or rely (with 'on'); n. the act of reckoning; (Law) a charge in an indictment. **-able** a. **— down** n. the last check before a missile is launched. **-less** a. innumerable. **-er** n. one who counts; a token used in reckoning; a table on which money is counted, goods displayed or business transacted.

coun•te•nance n. the face; aspect; support; v.i. to support; to approve. **to keep one's countenance,** to preserve one's composure.

count•er a. contrary; opposite; adv. in opposition; n. that which is opposite; a return blow or parry; v.t. and i. to parry; to make a counter-move. **-attack** n. an attack launched to stop and drive back an enemy attack. **-attraction** n. rival attraction. **-clockwise** adv. revolving in a direction opposite to the movement of the hands of a clock. **-espionage** n. spying directed against the enemy's system of espionage. **-tenor** n. a man's voice singing alto.

coun•ter•act v.t. to act in opposition to.

coun•ter•bal•ance v.t. to act against with equal power or effect; n. a weight balancing another.

coun•ter•charge n. a charge brought in opposition to another.

coun•ter•check v.t. to check by an opposing check.

coun•ter•feit v.t. to copy without authority; to imitate with intent to deceive; a. forged; false; n. a forgery; an imposter. **-er** n.

coun•ter•mand v.t. to cancel an order; n. a contrary order.

coun•ter•march v.i. to march back; n. a marching back.

coun•ter•mine n. any scheme to frustrate the designs of an opponent.

coun•ter•pane n. a coverlet; a quilt.

coun•ter•part n. a duplicate; something complementary or correlative.

coun•ter•point n. (Mus.) the addition of a subsidiary melody to another so as to form a perfect melody.

coun•ter•poise v.t. to act against with equal weight or power; n. a weight sufficient to balance another.

coun•ter•sign v.t. to sign a document already signed by another; to attest authenticity; n. a password.

coun•try n. a region; the territory of a nation; land of birth, residence, etc.; rural districts as opposed to town; a. rural; rustic; pert. to territory distant from a city. **countrified** a. **countrify** v.t. to make rural. **— club** n. a club with grounds, a house, and facilities for outdoor sports. **-man** n. a rustic; a compatriot. **-side** n. any rural district.

coun•ty n. a division of a state for administrative purposes; the inhabitants of a county. **— seat,** the capital of a county.

cou•ple n. two things of the same kind taken together; a pair; husband and wife; v.t. to join together; v.i. to connect. **couplet** n. a pair of lines of verse. **coupling** n. a connection; that which

coupling

couples, esp. the device joining railroad cars.

cou•pon n. an interest certificate attached to a bond; a dividend warrant; a negotiable voucher.

cour•age n. fearlessness; daring. **courageous** a. full of courage. **courageously** adv. **courageousness** n.

cour•i•er n. a messenger; a tourist guide who accompanies travelers.

course n. the act of passing from one point to another; movement, both in space and in time; direction; the ground on which a race is run; each of the successive divisions of a meal; v.t. to chase; v.i. to run swiftly; to gallop. **-r** n. one who hunts.

court n. an uncovered area enclosed by buildings; a yard; a legal tribunal; the hall where justice is administered; (Sport) a space, usually rectangular, laid out for certain sports. **courteous** a. polite; well-bred. **courteously** adv. **courteousness** n. **courtier** one with the manners of a frequenter of courts. **-ly** a. elegant; with the manners of a courtier. **-liness** n. **— martial** n. a court of military officers for the trial of persons in the army or navy; pl. **-s-martial.**

court v.t. to try to gain the affections of; to seek in marriage; v.i. to woo; to play the lover. **-ship** n.

cour•te•sy n. politeness of manners; urbanity.

cou•sin n. formerly any kinsman; now, the son or daughter of an uncle or aunt.

cove n. a small bay.

cov•e•nant *n.* a mutual and solemn agreement; *v.t.* to agree to by covenant; *v.i.* to enter into an agreement. **-er** *n.* one who makes a covenant or agreement.

cov•er *v.t.* to be over the whole top of; to include; to point a revolver, gun, etc. at; to wager an equal sum of money; *n.* anything that covers; a lid; concealment; shelter. **-ing** *n.* **-let** *n.* a bedcover. **covert** *a.* covered over; concealed; veiled; *n.* a place sheltering game. **covertly** *adv.* secretly; in private. **coverture** *n.* shelter; defense.

cov•et *v.t.* to long to possess, esp. what belongs to another; to desire unlawfully; *v.i.* to have strong desire. **-able** *a.* that may be coveted. **-ous** *a.* very desirous; avaricious for gain. **-ously** *adv.* **-ousness** *n.*

cow *n.* the female of a bovine animal; **-ish** *a.* **-boy** *n.* on the western plains, a herdsman employed on a ranch to look after cattle. **-herd** *n.* one who herds cows. **-hide** *n.* leather made from the hide of a cow. **-lick** *n.* a tuft of hair not easily flattened.

cow *v.t.* to frighten into submission.

cow•ard *n.* one who lacks courage. **-ly** *a.* lacking in courage; afraid. **-ice** *n.* want of courage; fear.

cow•er *v.i.* to crouch down through fear, shame, cold.

cowl *n.* a hooded cloak; a hooded top for a chimney. **-ed** *a.*

cox•swain, cox *n.* the steersman of a boat. **to cox** *v.t.* and *i.* to act as coxswain.

coy *a.* shy; pretending to be shy. **-ly** *adv.* **-ness** *n.*

coy•o•te *n.* the Amer. prairie wolf.

coz•en *v.t.* to flatter in order to cheat; to defraud.

co•zy *a.* snug; comfortable; *n.* a covering to keep a teapot hot. Also **cosy, cozily** *adv.* **coziness** *n.*

crab *n.* an edible crustacean; a disagreeable person; *v.t.* to fish for crabs. *pr.p.* **-bing.** *pa.t.* **-bed. -biness** *n.* **-by** *a.* **— grass** *n.* rapid growing coarse grass.

crack *v.t.* to break with a sharp noise, either wholly or partially; to snap; *v.i.* to burst open in chinks; to give forth a sudden, sharp sound; *n.* a partial break; fissure; a break in the voice. **-ed** *a.* **-er** *n.* a thin crisp biscuit. **— up** *n.* a collision; a breakdown.

crack•le *v.i.* to produce slight but repeated cracking sounds; *n.* a noise composed of frequent, slight cracking sounds. **crackling** *n.* a succession of small sharp reports.

cra•dle *n.* a bed for infants that can be rocked; *v.t.* to place or rock in a cradle; to tend in infancy.

craft *n.* dexterity; a skilled trade; a vessel. **-y** *a.* cunning; artful. **-ily** *adv.* **-iness** *n.* **-sman** *n.* one engaged in a trade. **-smanship** *n.*

crag *n.* a steep, rugged rock or peak. **-ged** *a.* **-gy** *a.* full of crags; rugged. **-giness** *n.*

cram *v.t.* and *i.* to stuff; to pack tightly; (*Colloq.*) to prepare hastily for an examination. *pr.p.* **-ming.** *pa.t.* **-med.** *n.*

(*Colloq.*) a crowd of people.

cramp *n.* a painful contraction of muscles of the body; that which restrains; *v.t.* to affect with cramp; to hamper; to hold with a cramp; *a.* narrow; cramped; restricted.

cran•ber•ry *n.* a red, sour, berry.

crane *n.* a tall wading bird with long legs, neck, and bill; a machine for lifting and

crane

lowering heavy weights; *v.t.* to stretch out the neck to look at something.

cra•ni•um *n.* the skull. *pl.* **crania. cranial** *a.* pert. to the skull. **craniology** *n.* the study of skulls. **craniological** *a.*

crank *n.* a handle attached to a shaft for turning it; the bent portion of an axis, used to change horizontal or vertical into rotatory motion, etc.; an eccentric or crotchety person; *v.t.* to shape like a crank; to operate by a crank; *v.i.* to turn the crank as in starting an automobile engine (usually with 'up'). **-case** *n.* the housing for a crankshaft. **-shaft** *n.* (*Mach.*) a shaft driven by a crank. **-y** *a.* shaky or in bad condition of machinery; bad-tempered. **-iness** *n.*

cran•ny *n.* an open crack; a crevice.

crash *n.* a violent fall accompanied by loud noise; a sudden collapse; *v.i.* to collapse; *v.t.* to break into pieces. **— helmet** *n.* a padded helmet worn by racing motorists.

cra•sis *n.* (*Gram.*) union of two vowels into one long vowel or diphthong.

crass *a.* gross; stupid. **-ly** *adv.* **-ness** *n.*

crate *n.* a wicker hamper, or open-work packing-case.

cra•ter *n.* cup-shaped mouth of a volcano; cavity resulting from the explosion of a large bomb.

crave *v.t.* and *i.* to have a very strong desire for; to ask with earnestness, humility. **-r** *n.* **craving** *n.* an inordinate desire.

cra•ven *a.* cowardly; *n.* a spiritless fellow; a coward.

craw•fish, crayfish *n.* a fresh-water crustacean, resembling the lobster but smaller.

crawl *v.i.* to move along the ground on the belly or on the hands and knees; to swim with an overarm stroke; *n.* a crawling motion; swimming stroke.

cray•on *n.* a coloring pencil; *v.t.* to draw with crayons.

craze *n.* a strong, habitual desire or passion; a general or individual mania; *v.t.* to make crazy; (*Pottery*) to crackle. **-d**

a. weak in mind. **craziness** *n.* **crazy** *a.* insane; extremely foolish. **crazily** *adv.*

creak *n.* a harsh, grating sound; *v.i.* to make a sharp, harsh, grating sound. **-y** *a.*

cream *n.* the fatty substance that rises to the surface of milk; the best part of anything; *v.t.* to take off the cream; *v.i.* to become covered with cream. **-y** *a.* full of cream; resembling cream. **-ery** *n.* a center to which milk is sent for distribution. **-iness** *n.* — **cheese** *n.* a soft, smooth, white cheese.

crease *n.* a mark made by folding anything; *v.t.* to make a crease on; *v.i.* to become creased.

cre•ate *v.t.* to bring into existence out of nothing; to originate. **creation** *n.* the act of creating, of bringing the world into being; any original production of the human mind. **creative** *a.* original. **creator** *n.* one who creates; a maker. **Creator** *n.* God. **creature** *n.* anything created; any living being.

cre•dence *n.* trust; belief. **credentials** *n.pl.* testimonials showing that a person is entitled to credit. **credible** *a.* worthy of belief. **credibility** *n.*

cred•it *n.* belief; trustworthiness; amount at a person's disposal in a bank; in commerce, the system of buying, borrowing and lending based on good faith; *v.t.* to put trust in. **-able** *a.* meriting credit. **-ably** *adv.* **-ableness** *n.* **-or** *n.* one to whom money is due.

cred•u•lous *a.* too prone to believe. **-ly** *adv.* **-ness** *n.* **credulity** *n.* gullibility.

creed *n.* statement of principles. **credo** *n.* a creed.

creek *n.* a branch or small tributary of a river.

creep *v.i.* to move along with the body close to the ground, like reptile; to spread, like certain plants, by clinging. *pa.t.*, *pa.p.* **crept. -er** *n.* esp. a creeping plant. **-y** *a.* causing a creeping sensation on the skin.

cre•mate *v.t.* to consume by burning, the dead. **cremation** *n.* the act of cremating the dead. **cremator** *n.* **crematorium** *n.* an establishment for the cremation of bodies. **crematory** *a.* or *n.*

Cre•ole *n.* a native of Spanish America or the W. Indies, of European parentage.

crepe *n.* a thin crinkled fabric or paper; a kind of rough-surfaced rubber used for the soles of shoes, etc.

crept *pa.p.* and *pa.t.* of creep.

cre•scen•do *n.* (*Mus.*) a gradual increase in loudness; *adv.* with increase in loudness.

cres•cent *a.* like the young moon in shape; *n.* the moon in first quarter; a crescent-shaped object.

cress *n.* various salad greens.

crest *n.* the comb or tuft on a bird's head; the highest part of a wave; *v.t.* to reach the top of. **-fallen** *a.* dispirited; dejected.

cre•tin•ism *n.* condition caused by thyroid deficiency. **cretin** *n.* one suffering from cretinism. **cretinous** *a.*

cre•vasse *n.* a deep open chasm in a glacier; a fissure.

crev•ice *n.* a narrow fissure; a crack.

crew *n.* a group of workmen; a ship's company.

crew•el *n.* embroidery yarn, **-work** *n.*

crib *n.* a child's bed with barred sides; a key (used by students); an enclosure for storing grain.

crib•bage *n.* (*Cards*) a game played by two or four players.

crick *n.* neck or back spasm or cramp.

crick•et *n.* a small, brown, chirping insect.

crick•et *n.* a game played with bats, balls, and wickets.

cri•er *n.* See cry.

crime *n.* a violation of the law (usually of a serious nature). **criminal** *a.* guilty of, or pert. to, crime; wicked; *n.* one guilty of a crime. **criminality** *n.* guiltiness. **criminally** *adv.* **criminate** *v.t.* to charge with a crime. **crimination** *n.* **criminative**, **criminatory** *a.* accusing. **criminologist** *n.* **criminology** *n.* science dealing with the cause and treatment of crime.

crimp *v.t.* to form into curls or pleats; *n.* small waves, as in hair.

crim•son *a.* of a rich deep red color; *n.* the color itself.

cringe *v.t.* to shrink; to behave obsequiously.

crin•kle *v.t.* to make a series of twists in a surface; to rustle. **crinkly** *adv.*

crin•o•line *n.* a stiff, fabric petticoat.

crip•ple *n.* a person without the use of a limb or limbs; *a.* lame; *v.t.* to lame.

cri•sis *n.* the decisive moment; the turning point, esp. in an illness; *pl.* **crises.**

crisp *a.* brittle; breaking with a short snap; *v.t.* to make crisp; **-ly** *adv.* **-ness** *n.*

criss•cross *a.* arranged in crossing lines; *adv.* crossing in different directions; *v.t.* and *i.* to be marked with cross lines.

cri•te•ri•on *n.* a standard of judging; a rule by which opinions may be judged. *pl.* **criteria.**

crit•ic *n.* one who expressed a reasoned judgment on art or literature; one whose profession it is to write reviews; one given to finding fault. **-al** *a.* pert. to criticism; fault-finding; decisive. **-ally** *adv.* **criticism** *n.* the art of making a reasoned judgment. **criticize** *v.t.* and *i.* to pass judgment. **critique** *n.* review.

croak *v.t.* and *i.* to make a low, hoarse noise in the throat; *n.* the hoarse, harsh sound made by a frog. **-y** *a.*

cro•chet *n.* a kind of needlework consisting of loops; *v.t.* and *i.* to work in crochet.

crock *n.* an earthenware pot; a piece of broken earthenware. **-ery** *n.* dishes of all kinds, made of earthenware.

croc•o•dile *n.* a large, amphibious reptile of the lizard kind. — **tears**, sham grief.

crocodile

cro‑cus n. a bulbous plant; saffon.

cro‑ny n. an intimate friend.

crook n. any bend, or sharp turn; a thief; v.t. to curve; v.i. to be bent or curved. **-ed** a. bent; (Fig.) not straightforward. **-edly** adv. **-edness** n.

croon v.t. and i. to sing in a sentimental manner. **-er** n. **-ing** n.

crop n. the cultivated produce of any plants, in a farm, field, etc.; a harvest; closely‑cut head of hair; v.t. to reap the produce of a field. pr.p. **-ping**. pa.p. and pa.t. **-ped.** —**eared** a. with hair cut close to head. **-per** n. one who, or that which, crops. **to crop up**, to appear unexpectedly.

cro‑quet n. an outdoor game played with balls, mallets and hoops.

cro‑quette n. (Cookery) a ball of finely minced meat, fish, etc. seasoned and fried.

cross n. a stake used for crucifixion; a misfortune; v.t. to mark with a cross; to make the sign of the cross. **-wise** adv. in the form of a cross.

cross

cross a. transverse; intersecting; out of temper; n. an intermixture of breeds in cattle‑breeding; v.t. to place so as to intersect; to pass over; to modify the breed of animals, plants, etc. by intermixture; v.i. to intersect; to move or pass from one side to the other; adv. across. **-ing** n. the act of passing across; an intersection; the intermixture of breeds. **-ly** adv. —**action** n. (Law) an action brought by a defendant against a plaintiff on points pert. to the same case. **-bones** n.pl. two thigh bones crossed and surmounted by a skull, used as symbol of death, a sign of deadly danger, or the flag of a pirate ship. **-breed** n. a hybrid. —**examination** n. the examination of a witness by counsel on the other side. —**eyed** a. with eyes turned in toward the nose. — **reference** n. in a dictionary, the directing of the reader to another part for related information.

cross‑bill n. a bird of the Finch family, whose mandibles cross.

cross‑bow n. a medieval weapon. **-man** n.

crotch n. the angle where the legs branch off from the human body. **-ed** a.

crouch v.i. to huddle down close to the ground.

croup n. (Med.) acute inflammation of the windpipe, accompanied by a hoarse cough. **-y** a.

crou‑ton n. a small cube of toasted bread used in soups, etc.

crow n. a large bird, wholly black, of the

crow

genus Corvus; v.i. to give the shrill cry of the cock; to utter a sound of pleasure. **crow's‑foot** n. a wrinkle about the outer corners of the eyes in adults. **crow's‑nest** n. a perch for the lookout man near the top of the mast.

crowd v.t. to press together; to fill or occupy by crushing together; v.i. to be numerous; n. a number of persons collected into a close body.

crown n. the state headdress worn by a sovereign; royalty; the topmost part of the head; the summit; v.t. to bestow as a mark of honor; to surmount. — **prince** n. the heir apparent to the throne.

cru‑cial a. decisive; critical.

cru‑ci‑ble n. vessel capable of withstanding great heat, used for melting metals.

cru‑ci‑fy v.t. to put to death by nailing to a cross; to mortify. **crucifier** n. **crucifix** n. an image of Christ on the Cross. **crucifixion** n. **cruciform** a. cross‑shaped.

crude a. in the natural or raw state; unfinished. **-ly** adv. **-ness** n. **crudity** n.

cru‑el a. hard‑hearted. **-ly** adv. **-ty** n. the quality of being cruel (See **crude**). **cru‑et** n. a small stoppered bottle for holding vinegar, oil.

cruise v.i. to sail about without precise destination; in motoring to go at a normal operating speed; n. an organized pleasure‑sail. **-r** n.

crumb n. a small particle; v.t. to reduce to crumbs; to cover with crumbs. **-y** a.

crum‑ble v.t. to break into fragments; v.i. to fall into crumbs. **crumbly** a.

crum‑ple v.t. to wrinkle; to rumple; v.i. to become creased; to collapse.

crunch n. the sound made by chewing crisp food, treading on gravel, hard snow; v.t. and i. to chew, tread, with this sound.

cru‑sade n. a medieval Christian war to recover the Holy Land from the Saracens; a campaign against any evil or vice; v.i. to join in a crusade. **-r** n.

crush v.t. to press between two hard bodies to break; to squeeze out by pressure; to defeat utterly; v.i. to be compressed by force; n. violent pressure.

crust n. the hard outer covering of anything; the outer part of baked bread; pastry, forming the covering of a pie; v.t. to cover with a crust; v.i. to form a crust. **-ated** a. incrusted. **-ation** n. **-ily** adv. in a crusty manner; morosely. **-iness** n. **-y** a. like a crust; hard; surly.

Crus‑ta‑ce‑a n.pl. (Zool.) a class of mainly aquatic animals including lobsters, crabs, shrimps, etc. **-n** a. and n. pert. to the crustacea. **crustaceous** a. having a hard shell.

crutch n. a staff with a cross‑piece to go

under the armpit for the use of cripples. *v.t.* to aid.

crux *n.* a perplexing problem; the real issue.

cry *v.t. v.i.* to exclaim vehemently; to weep; *n.* a loud utterance; the shedding of tears. **crier** *n.* one who cries. **-ing** *a.*

crypt *n.* a cell underground, used for burial. **cryptic(al)** *a.* hidden; mysterious. **cryptically** *adv.*

cryp-to-gram *n.* a writing in secret characters. Also **cryptograph** *n.* **cryptology** *n.* a secret language.

crys-tal *n.* a transparent, colorless quartz; a superior sort of glass; *(Chem.)* a mineral body which has assumed a regular geometrical form; *a.* consisting of crystal; transparent. **-line** *a.* **-lize** *v.t.* to cause to assume a definite shape; *v.i.* to be formed into crystals. **-lizable** *a.* **-lization** *n.*

cub *n.* the young of the bear, fox, wolf; a junior Boy Scout.

cub-by hole *n.* a small place for storing things, or for hiding in.

cube *n.* *(Geom.)* a solid body with six equal sides; *(Math.)* the product of a number multiplied twice by itself; *v.t.* to raise to the third power. **cubic(al)** *a.* having the form of a cube. **cubic foot, cuboid** *a.* resembling a cube in shape. — **root** *n.* the number which gives the stated number if raised to the third power.

cu-bi-cle *n.* a small partitioned compartment.

cub-ism *n.* modern art based on geometrical forms. **cubist** *n.*

cu-bit *n.* a measure of length, about 18 inches. **-al** *a.*

cuck-old *n.* a man whose wife is unfaithful to him; *v.t.* to be unfaithful to a husband.

cuck-oo *n.* a migratory bird named from its call; the call of the bird.

cuckoo

cu-cum-ber *n.* plant of the gourd family and its fruit.

cud *n.* food brought up by ruminating animals, from their first stomach, and chewed a second time.

cud-dle *v.t.* to hug; to fondle; *v.i.* to lie close or snug; *n.* a close embrace. **-some** *a.*

cudg-el *n.* a short thick stick; *v.t.* to beat with a cudgel.

cue *n.* the last words of an actor's speech as a signal to the next actor to speak.

cue *n.* a long tapering rod used in billiards.

cuff *n.* a blow with the open hand; *v.t.* to strike with the open hand.

cuff *n.* the ending of a sleeve; the turned-up end of a trouser leg.

cu-li-nar-y *a.* pert. to the kitchen or cookery.

cull *v.t.* to select, or pick out.

cul-mi-nate *v.i.* to reach a climax.

culmination *n.* the attainment of the highest point; climax.

cu-lottes *n.pl.* knee length trousers resembling a skirt.

cul-pa-ble *a.* deserving blame or censure. **culpably** *adv.* culpability, **-ness** *n.*

cul-prit *n.* one accused of a crime; an offender.

cult *n.* a system of religious worship, and ceremonies.

cul-ti-vate *v.t.* to prepare for the raising of crops; to produce by tillage, labor. **-d** *a.*

cul-ture *n.* tillage or cultivation; mental development; refinement; the propagation of bacteria in artificial media; *v.t.* to cultivate. **cultural** *a.* pert. to culture. **-d** *a.* educated and refined.

cul-vert *n.* an arched drain for the passage of water under a road.

cum-ber *v.t.* to burden with a useless load. **-some** *a.* burdensome. **cumbrous** *a.*

cum-mer-bund *n.* a broad sash worn as a belt.

cu-mu-late *v.t.* to heap together; *a.* heaped up. **cumulation** *n.* **cumulative** *a.* becoming greater by successive additions. **cumulatively** *adv.*

cu-mu-lus *n.* a piled-up cloud mass with rounded outlines. *pl.* cumuli.

cu-ne-i-form, cuniform *a.* wedge-shaped.

cuneiform

cun-ning *a.* wily; sly; *n.* craft; guile; deceit. **-ly** *adv.*

cup *n.* a drinking vessel; an ornamental vessel given as a prize; *v.t.* to hold, as in a cup; to form into a cup shape. *pr.p.* **-ping.** *pa.t.* **-ped.** **-ful** *n.* the quantity that a cup holds, 8 fluid oz. **cupboard** *n.* a small closet with shelves for cups, plates, etc. **loving cup** *n.* trophy, given as a prize.

cu-pid-i-ty *n.* an eager desire for possession.

cu-pre-ous *a.* pert. to, or containing copper.

cur *n.* a dog of mixed breed; a mongrel.

cu-ra-tor *n.* a superintendent, as of a museum, library; a guardian. **-ship** *n.*

curb *n.* any means of restraint; an edging to a pavement or sidewalk; *v.t.* to restrain; to confine. **-ing** *n.*

curd *n.* the cheesy part of milk; coagulated milk. **-le** *v.t.* and *i.* to turn into curd; to coagulate.

cure *v.t.* to heal; to restore to health; to preserve fish, skins, by salting; *n.* the act of healing; remedy. **curable** *a.* **curative** *a.* **cure-all** *n.* a panacea.

cu-rette *n.* instrument for scraping body tissue. **-ment** *n.*

cur-few *n.* the time after which persons may not be out of doors.

cur-ie *n.* *(Chem.)* the standard unit of emanation from one gram of radium. **curium** *n.* a radioactive, inert, gaseous element.

cu-ri-o *n.* a rare or curious object.

cu-ri-ous *a.* eager to know; inquisitive;

strange. **-ly** *adv.* **curiosity** *n.* inquisitiveness; a novelty.

curl *v.t.* to twist into ringlets; to bend into spiral or curved shape; *v.i.* to take a spiral or curved shape or path; to turn into ringlets; to ripple; to play at the game of curling; *n.* a ringlet of hair; anything of a similar shape. **-y** *a.* having curls; tending to curl; full of ripples. **-icue** *n.* a lock of hair; a fancy curve in writing. **-iness** *n.* **-ing** *n.* a game like bowls played on ice with large, rounded stones. **-er** *n.* a pin used as a fastener to retain a curl.

cur•rant *n.* the fruit of various plants allied to the gooseberry.

cur•rent *a.* belonging to the present time; *n.* a flowing body of water or air in motion; transmission of electricity through a conductor. **-ly** *adv.* commonly. **currency** *n.* money in circulation.

cur•ric•u•lum *n.* a specified course of study at a school. *pl.* **curricula.**

cur•ry *n.* (*Cookery*) a highly-flavored condiment much used in the East. **— powder** *n.*

cur•ry *v.t.* to dress leather; to beat or thrash. **currier** *n.* one who dresses tanned leather. **to curry favor,** to try to win favor by flattery.

curse *v.t.* to utter a wish of evil against; to swear at; *v.i.* to utter blasphemous words; the invocation of evil upon a person; oaths. **cursed** *a.* hateful. **cursedly** *adv.*

cur•sive *a.* written with all the letters joined. **-ly** *adv.* **cursory** *a.* characterized by haste; superficial.

curt *a.* concise to the point of rudeness; terse. *n.*

cur•tail *v.t.* to abridge; to diminish. **-ment** *n.*

cur•tain *n.* a drapery; a screen in front of stage of a theater; anything that conceals; *v.t.* to enclose with curtains. **iron curtain** (*Fig.*) any hindrance to obtaining information about conditions in a country.

curt•sy, curtsey *n.* a gesture of respect.

curve *n.* a bending without angles; an arch; *a.* bent; *v.t.* and *i.* to bend. **curvate** *a.* curved. **curvature** *n.*

cush•ion *n.* any padded surface used as a rest or protector; *v.t.* to protect with a cushion.

cusp *n.* a prominence on a molar tooth; the point at which the two branches of a curve have a common tangent. **-id** *n.* a canine tooth. **-idal** *n.* ending in a point.

cus•tard *n.* a sweet dish made with milk and eggs.

cus•to•dy *n.* guardianship; imprisonment. **custodial** *a.* custodian, **custodier** *n.* a caretaker.

cus•tom *n.* fashion; business patronage; toll, tax, or tribute; **-s** *n.pl.* duties levied on imports. **-able** *a.* liable to duty. **-ary** *a.* established by common usage; habitual. **-arily** *adv.* **-er** *n.* one who enters a shop to buy. **-house** *n.* office where customs are paid.

cut *v.t.* to sever, penetrate, or wound with

an edged instrument; to intersect; to mow; to reduce; to abridge; (*Sports*) to hit the ball obliquely in order to impart spin to it. *pr.p.* **-ting.** *pa.p.* and *pa.t.* **cut** *n.* opening made with an edged instrument; a gash. **-ter** *n.* he who, or that which, cuts. **-ting** *n.* a small branch, cut from a plant, bush, etc.; *a.* sarcastic. **— glass** *n.* glass ornamented with cut designs. **-off** *n.* a device to shut off. **—rate** *a.* below usual price. **-throat** *n.* a murderer; *a.* merciless.

cu•ta•ne•ous *a.* belonging to, or affecting, the skin.

cute *a.* (*Colloq.*) attractive.

cu•ti•cle *n.* the epidermis around the fingernails and toenails.

cut•ler *n.* one who repairs, or deals in knives and cutting implements. **-y** *n.* cutting instruments, esp. tableware.

cut•let *n.* a piece of meat from the rib bones.

cy•a•nide *n.* a poisonous compound.

cy•an•o•gen *n.* (*Chem.*) a colorless, poisonous gas. **cyanic** *a.* blue.

cy•ber•net•ics *n.* the study of the mechanical brain.

cyc•la•men *n.* a tuberous plant of the Primrose family.

cy•cle *n.* a regularly recurring succession of events, or the time occupied by such a succession; a bicycle or tricycle; *v.i.* to pass through a cycle of changes. **cyclist** *n.* one who rides a bicycle or tricycle. **cycloid** *n.* (*Geom.*) a curve traced by a point in a circle when the circle revolves along a straight line.

cy•clone *n.* a violent storm characterized by strong winds. **cyclonic.**

cy•clo•pe•di•a See encyclopedia.

cy•clo•ram•a *n.* circular panorama.

cy•clo•tron *n.* a radio oscillator developed to disintegrate atoms, in order to study their internal structure.

cyl•in•der *n.* a roller-like body with straight sides, the ends being equal, parallel circles. **cylindric, cylindrical** *a.* **cylindriform** *a.*

cym•bal *n.* musical percussion instrument.

cyn•ic *n.* one who believes man's conduct is based on self-interest. **cynic(al)** *a.* distrustful of people's motives. **cynically** *adv.* **cynicalness** *n.* **cynicism** *n.* disbelief in goodness; misanthropy.

cy•no•sure *n.* (*Astron.*) the constellation of the Lesser Bear, containing the Pole-star; a guiding star.

cy•press *n.* a slender coniferous tree with evergreen foliage.

cyst *n.* (*Med.*) a membranous sac containing liquid secretion. **-ic** *a.* pert. to cysts.

Czar *n.* a title used by various Slavonic rulers, esp. by the Emperors of Russia. **Czarina** *n.* the wife of a Czar.

Czech *n.* a member of the Slavonic race of people inhabiting the western region of Czechoslovakia; *a.* pert. to the people or their language. **Czechoslovak, Czechoslovakian** *a.* pert. to the country, the people, or the language of Czechoslovakia; *n.* a native of the country; the language.

dab n. Eur. flatfish.

dab v.t. to pat gently and intermittently, -bing. pa.p. and pa.t. -bed. n. a gentle blow with a soft substance; a small lump of anything soft, as butter.

dab·ble v.t. to wet by little dips; to moisten; v.i. to play in water; to pursue a subject superficially.

dach·shund n. dog with long body, short legs, and drooping ears.

dac·tyl n. a metrical foot in poetry, consisting of one accented syllable followed by two unaccented syllables. -ic a. -iography n. the history of gem engraving. -ogram n. a finger print. -ography n. the science of finger prints. -ology n. the finger language of the deaf and dumb.

da·da·ism n. a school of art and literature which aims at suppressing all relation between thought and expression.

dad·dy-long-legs n. a flying insect; a harvestman.

da·do n. the part of a pedestal between the base and cornice; the lower part or wide skirting of the walls of a room.

dae·mon n. an inspiring influence; a divinity; genius. -ic a. more than human; supernatural.

daf·fo·dil n. a spring plant of the genus Narcissus; the yellow color of the daffodil.

daft a. insane; foolish. -ness n.

dag·ger n. a short, two-edged sword used in close combat; a mark of reference in typography (†) or (‡).

dag·gle v.t. to trail through mud; to bedraggle.

da·guerre·o·type n. in photography, an early method of taking pictures on plates of silver or silvered copper.

dahl·ia n. a genus of plants with large, brightly colored flowers.

dai·ly a. or adv. happening each day; n. a newspaper published each day or each weekday.

dain·ty a. pleasing to the taste; refined; pretty and delicate; scrupulous; n. a delicacy. daintily adv.

dair·y n. the shop where milk and its products are processed and sold; a dairy farm. -ing n. the business of conducting a dairy. -maid, -man n.

da·is n. the raised platform at the end of a room, esp. of dining hall.

dai·sy n. a common wild flower.

dale n. a low place between hills; a valley or vale; a glen.

dal·ly v.i. to waste time; to trifle. dalliance n.

Dal·ma·tian n. a breed of large white dogs with black or liver-colored spots.

dam n. a female parent — used of animals.

dam n. a barrier of earth, stones, etc. to obstruct the flow of water; v.t. to confine water by a dam; to block up.

dam·age n. any injury or harm to person, property, or reputation; v.t. to harm; to hurt. -s n.pl. legal compensation paid to injured party. -able a.

dam·ask n. a figured silk or linen fabric; a rose-pink color, like that of damask rose; a.

dame n. a noble lady; **Dame** n. (Br.) title of the wife of a knight or baronet.

damn v.t. to consign to everlasting punishment; to destroy the reputation of; n. an oath; a curse. -able a. -ably adv. -ation n. -ed a.

damp n. moist air; humidity; fog; noxious gases in coal mines; a. slightly moist; v.t. to retard combustion. -en v.t. -er n. a contrivance in a flue to regulate the draft; a device to minimize vibration. -ish a.

dam·sel n. a young unmarried woman.

dam·son n. a small dark plum.

dance v.t. and v.i. to move with measured steps; to move rhythmically; to caper; n. a social gathering for the purpose of dancing. -r n. St. Vitus's dance nervous disorder accompanied by twitching of muscles.

dan·de·li·on n. a plant with large yellow flowers, and tooth-edged leaves.

dan·der n. anger; passion; temper.

dan·dle v.t. to move up and down in affectionate play, as an infant; to pet; to caress.

dan·druff, dandriff n. a disease affecting the scalp and producing scurf or small scales of skin under the hair.

dan·dy n. one who affects special finery in dress; a. fine; first-rate. dandify v.t. dandified a.

Dane n. a native of Denmark; a breed of dog, large and smooth coated, usually great Dane. **Danish** a.; n. the language of the Danes.

dan·ger n. exposure to injury or evil; peril; jeopardy. -ous a. -ously adv. dangerousness n.

dan·gle v.t. to swing loosely or carelessly; (Fig.) to use as a bait; v.i.

dank a. unpleasantly damp or moist. -ness n.

dap·per a. neat; trim; smart.

dap·ple n. a spot; a. spotted, applied to horses and deer. -d a.

dare v.i. to have courage for; to venture (to); v.i. to defy; to challenge. daring n. a bold action; a. courageous; audacious. daringly adv. —devil n. a foolhardy, reckless fellow.

dark n. lacking light; black; somber; evil; unenlightened; n. absence of light; gloom; obscurity; evil. -en v.t. to obstruct light; to render dim, to cloud; to sully; v.i. -ish a. rather dark. darkly adv. -ness n. -y, -ey n. a Negro — horse n. one unexpectedly nominated for an office.

dar·ling n. a beloved or lovable one; a. cherished.

darn v.t. to mend; to repair a hole by weaving threads at right angles to one another; n. -ing-needle n.

dart n. a pointed arrow-like weapon; anything similar which pierces or wounds; a small seam or intake in garment to make it fit more closely; a sharp, forward movement; v.t. to send forward quickly. v.i. to run forward swiftly. -s n.pl. a popular game using darts and dartboard.

Dar·win·i·an a. pert. to Charles Darwin or

to his Theory of Evolution. *n.*

dash *v.t.* to throw violently; to cast down; to shatter; *v.i.* to rush forward or move violently. *n.* a rapid movement; a mark of punctuation (—); a small amount. **-ing** *a.* daring; spirited; showy. **-y** *a.* showy.

das•tard *n.* mean or cowardly fellow; *a.* cowardly. **-ly** *a.* **-liness** *n.*

da•ta *n.pl.* things known and from which inferences may be deduced.

date *n.* period of time of an event; epoch; duration. *v.t.* to note or fix the time of. *v.i.* to reckon back to a given time. **—line** *n.* approximately the 180° parallel of longitude on each side of which the date of the day differs.

date *n.* the stone fruit of the Eastern date palm.

da•tum *n.* a fact given; *pl.* **data.**

daub *v.t.* to smear with mud or plaster; to soil. *n.* a crude painting; a smudge. **-er** *n.* one who daubs.

daugh•ter *n.* a female child; *a.* like a daughter. **—in-law** *n.* the wife of one's son.

daunt *v.t.* to subdue the courage of; to dismay; to dishearten. **-less** *a.* fearless; intrepid.

dau•phin *n.* (*fem.* **dauphiness**) the French Crown prince.

da•ven•port *n.* a sofa.

dav•its *n.* uprights fitted with tackle for lowering life-boats over side of ship.

davits

Da•vy Jones *n.* a sailor's name for the Devil.

daw *n.* a bird of the crow family.

daw•dle *v.i.* to loiter; to move very slowly.

dawn *v.i.* to grow towards daylight; to begin to be visible; to come to the mind; *n.* daybreak; morning half-light; beginning.

day *n.* the period from sunrise to sunset; 24 hrs. **— bed** *n.* a divan. **-book** *n.* a book kept to record daily transactions. **-break** *n.* dawn. **-dream** *n.* a reverie; *v.i.*

daze *v.t.* to confuse; to bewilder; *n.* the state of being bewildered. **dazzle** *v.t.* to daze with sudden light; to confuse mentally; *n.* **dazzling** *a.*

dea•con *n.* an assistant to a priest or minister; a layman elected to certain duties in the church. **-ess** *n.* **-hood** *n.* **-ry** *n.* **-ship** *n.*

dead *a.* without life; *adv.* wholly; *n.* **-en** *v.t.* to benumb. **-ness** *n.* **—beat** *a.* without oscillation. **—end** *n.* a street with only one entrance. **-fall** *n.* a trap, esp. for large animals. **— heat** *n.* a race where two or more competitors reach the winning post at exactly the same time. **— language,** a language no longer spoken. **— letter** *n.*

an undeliverable letter. **-liness** *n.* **-lock** *n.* an impasse. **-ly** *a.* causing death; *adv.* completely. **— pan** *n.* an immobile face. **— reckoning** *n.* the steering of a vessel by, compass and not by the stars. **— weight** *n.* the unrelieved weight of inert objects.

deaf *a.* lacking partially or wholly the sense of hearing; heedless. **-en** *v.t.* **-ening** *a.* very loud. **-ly** *adv.* **—mute** *n.* one who is deaf and dumb. **—mutism** *n.* **-ness** *n.*

deal *v.t.* to divide; to dole out. *v.i.* to traffic. *n.* distribution of playing cards; a business transaction. *pa.p.* **dealt.** **-er** *n.* **-ing** *n.pl.* relations with others. **a raw deal,** iniquitously unfair treatment. **a square deal,** fair treatment.

dean *n.* a dignitary in cathedral or collegiate churches; an official of a college with disciplinary authority.

dear *a.* precious; highly esteemed or valued; costly. **-ly** *adv.*

dearth *n.* scarcity; lack.

death *n.* extinction of life; decease; dissolution. **— blow** *n.* a fatal stroke. **-less** *a.* immortal. **-lessness** *n.* **-like** *a.* **-ly** *adv.*; *a.* **— mask** *n.* a plaster cast of a person's face taken immediately after death. **— rate** *n.* **—throes** *n.pl.* last struggle before death. **— warrant** *n.* an official document authorizing execution of a criminal. **-watch** *n.* a vigil.

de•ba•cle *n.* a sudden collapse; the breaking up of ice in a river.

de•bar *v.t.* to cut off from entrance; to prohibit; to exclude; *pr.p.* **-ring.** *pa.t. pa.p.* **-red.** **-ment** *n.*

de•bark *v.t.* and *v.i.* to disembark, oppos. of *embark.* **-ation,** **-ment** *n.*

de•base *v.t.* to reduce to a lower state; to disagree; to degrade; to adulterate. **-ment** *n.* **debasing** *a.* corrupting, esp. in moral sense.

de•bate *n.* controversy; argument. *v.t.* to discuss; to argue in detail; *v.i.* to reflect. **debatable** *a.* **-r** *n.*

de•bauch *v.t.* to corrupt; to seduce; to pervert. *n.* excess in eating and drinking. **-ed** *a.* **-ee** *n.* a dissipated person. **-ery** *n.* moral corruption. **-ment** *n.*

de•ben•ture *n.* a certificate acknowledging a debt and guaranteeing repayment of loan with interest.

de•bil•i•tate *v.t.* to weaken; to make infirm; to enervate. **debilitation, debility** *n.*

deb•it *n.* an item entered on debtor side of an account (oppos. of *credit*); *v.t.*

deb•o•nair *a.* bearing oneself cheerfully and well; sprightly.

de•bris, dé•bris *n.* rubble; ruins.

debt *n.* something owed to another; an obligation. **-or** *n.*

de•but, dé•but *n.* a first appearance in public. **debutante** *n.* one, esp. a girl, making her first appearance in society; abbrev. **deb.**

dec•a- *prefix,* ten.

dec•ade *n.* a period of ten years.

de•ca•dence; decadency *n.* deterioration; degeneration; decay.

dec•a•dent *a.* deteriorating.

dec•a•gon n. a plane figure of ten sides and ten angles.

dec•a•gram(me) n. in the metric system, a weight of 10 grams, i.e. 0.353 oz.

dec•a•he•dron n. a solid figure of a body having ten sides. decahedral a.

de•cal•ci•fy v.t. to deprive bones of lime.

de•cal•i•ter n. a measure of capacity equal to 10 liters — about 2.64 imperial gallons.

Dec•a•logue n. the Ten Commandments.

dec•a•me•ter n. in the metric system a measure of ten meters, or 32.8 ft.

de•camp v.i. to move away from a camping ground; to move off suddenly or secretly.

de•cant v.t. to pour off liquid without disturbing sediment, esp. used of wines. -er n. a slender necked glass bottle into which wine is decanted.

de•cap•i•tate v.t. to cut off the head; to behead. decapitation n.

dec•a•pod n. a shellfish of the crab family having five pairs of legs; a. having ten legs. -al, -ous a.

de•car•bon•ize v.t. to deprive of carbon; to remove a deposit of carbon, as from a motor cylinder. Also **decarbonate**, decarburize. **decarbonization**, decarburization n.

dec•a•syl•lab•ic a. having ten syllables. decasyllable n.

de•cath•lon n. a group of ten different contests at Olympic games.

de•cay v.i. to rot away; to become decomposed; to deteriorate; v.t. to impair; n. gradual decline. -ed a.

de•cease n. death; v.i. to die. -d a. dead n. a dead person.

de•ceit n. fraud. -ful a. crafty; fraudulent. -fulness n. deceive v.t. to delude; to cheat. deceivable a. deceivably adv. deceiver. n.

de•cel•er•ate v.t. and v.i. to reduce speed.

De•cem•ber n. orig. the tenth month of the Roman calendar; the twelfth month of the year.

de•cen•nial a. lasting for ten years or happening every ten years. decennary n.

de•cent a. fitting or becoming; modest; suitable. decency n. -ly adv.

de•cen•tral•ize v.t. to remove from the center or point of concentration and distribute among small areas. decentralization n.

de•cep•tion n. the act of deceiving; fraud; illusion. deceptible a. deceptibility n. deceptive a. causing a false impression. deceptively adv.

dec•i•bel n. one transmission unit; the smallest variation in sound that the human ear can detect.

de•cide v.t. to determine the result of; to make up one's mind about; v.t. to come to a conclusion. -d a. not ambiguous; determined. decidedly adv. decision n. determination; settlement; judgement. decisive a. conclusive; resolute. decisively adv. decisiveness n.

de•cid•u•ous a. shedding leaves in autumn, oppos. of coniferous or evergreen; not lasting; liable to fall.

dec•i•mal a. pert. to tens. n. some power of 10. **-ization** n. **-ize** v.t. to reduce to the decimal system. — **fraction**, a fraction the (unexpressed) denominator of which is 10 or a power of 10.

dec•i•mate v.t. to kill every tenth man, chosen by lot, as punishment; to reduce the numbers of, very considerably. decimation n.

de•ci•pher v.t. to make out what is illegible, unintelligible or written in strange symbols.

de•ci•sion See decide.

deck v.t. to adorn; to dress up. n. a covering; the horizontal platform extending from one side of ship to the other; a pack of cards, or part of pack remaining after dealing. —**chair** n. a light-weight, collapsible chair, made partly of canvas. — **hand** n. a person employed on deck of ship. **-ing** n. hurricane-deck n. a half-deck. main-deck n. deck below the upper deck. quarter-deck n. part of the deck abaft the main mast. double-decker n. a vehicle with upper and lower passenger-decks.

deck•le n. the gauge on a paper-making machine. —**edge** n. untrimmed edge of paper. —**edged** a.

de•claim v.t. to recite; v.i. to make a formal speech. declamation n. a set speech; declamatory a. ostentatiously rhetorical.

de•clare v.t. to proclaim; to make clear; to state publicly; v.i. (at Customs) to admit possession of dutiable goods. declarable a. declaration n. a solemn statement. declaratory a. explanatory.

de•clen•sion n. the act of falling away; deterioration; the inflection of nouns, pronouns, adjectives; -al a.

de•cline v.t. to bend downward; to refuse; to avoid; v.i. to slope; to fall in value or quantity; to pine away; to languish; n. a downward slope; a falling off. declinable a. declination n. a sloping away.

de•cliv•i•ty n. a downward slope; a gradual descent. declivitous, declivous a.

de•code v.t. to translate a message in code into ordinary language.

de•col•le•tage n. the line of a woman's low cut evening dress. décollete a. low-necked.

de•com•pose v.t. to break up into elements; to separate the constituent parts of; v.i. to decay; to rot. decomposition n.

de•con•tam•i•nate v.t. to cleanse from effects of poison gas, etc. decontamination n.

de•con•trol v.t. to release from government or state control.

de•cor n. the decoration, or setting of a theater, stage, or room.

dec•o•rate v.t. to beautify; to honor a person by giving a medal or badge of honor. -d a. decoration n. an ornament; a badge of honor. decorative a. decorativeness n. decorator n.

dec•o•rous a. seemly; decent; staid. -ly adv. -ness n. decorum n. behavior, etc. in keeping with social conventions.

de•coy v.t. to lead into a snare; n. a device for leading wild birds into a snare; an enticement.

de•crease v.t. to lessen; to make smaller; to reduce gradually; v.i. to become less. n. gradual diminution; a lessening.

de•cree n. an order made by a competent authority; an edict; decision in a law court; an established law. v.t. to determine judicially. v.i. to decide authoritatively. **decretal** a. **decretive** a.

de•cre•ment n. the quantity lost by decrease.

de•crep•it a. worn out or enfeebled by old age; infirm; broken down; ramshackle. **-ude, -ness** n.

de•cres•cent a. becoming gradually less.

de•cry v.t. to bring into disrepute; to abuse. **decrial** n.

ded•i•cate v.t. to give oneself wholly to a worthy purpose; to inscribe a book or other object to someone as mark of appreciation or admiration. **-d** a. devoted. **dedication** n. **dedicatory** a. complimentary.

de•duce v.t. to reach a conclusion by deductive reasoning. **deducible** a. inferred. **deduct** v.t. to remove; to subtract. **deductible** a. **deduction** n.; the amount subtracted; the inference arrived at. **deductive** a. **deductively** adv.

deed n. an act; exploit; achievement; a legal document or contract; v.t. to convey by deed.

deem v.t. to believe on consideration.

deep a. extending far below the surface; dark; intense; low in pitch; adv. to a great depth; n. the sea. **-en** v.t. v.i. to become deeper. **-most** a. deepest. **-ness** n. depth. **—rooted** a. firmly established. **—seated** a. not superficial. **depth** n. the quality of being deep.

deer n. any of the ruminant quadrupeds.

deer

de•face v.t. to destroy or mar the external appearance of; to disfigure. **-able** a. **-ment** n.

de•fal•cate v.t. to misappropriate money; to embezzle. **defalcation** n. **defalcator** n.

de•fame v.t. to harm or destroy the good name or reputation of; to slander. **defamation** n. **defamatory** a.

de•fault n. failure to appear in a law court when summoned; failure to account for money held in trust; v.i. to fail to meet an obligation. **-er** n.

de•fea•sance n. defeat; a rendering null and void. **defeasible** a. capable of being annulled.

de•feat v.t. to overcome; to subdue; to conquer; n. conquest. **-ism** n. the attitude of mind of those who accept defeat as inevitable. **-ist** n.; a.

def•e•cate v.t. to clear or strain impurities from; v.i. to void excrement from the bowels. **defecation** n.

de•fect n. a want; an imperfection; absence of something necessary for completeness. **defection** n. the act of abandoning allegiance to a cause. **-ive** a. incomplete; imperfect; faulty. **-ively** adv. **-iveness** n.

de•fend v.t. to protect; to ward off attack; to maintain; to justify. **-able** a. **-ant** n. one who defends; the accused in a criminal case; the one prosecuted in a civil case. **-er** n.

de•fense n. that which shields or protects; (Law) a plea or reply to a charge. **-less** a. open to attack. **-lessly** adv. **-lessness** n. **Civil Defense**, an organization in World War 2 and since, for protection of civilians. **defensible** a. **defensibility** n. **defensive** a. resisting attack. **defensively** adv.

de•fer v.i. to submit; to yield or bow to the opinion of another. **deference** n. **deferential** a.

de•fer v.t. to put off; to postpone; v.i. **-ring**; pa.p. **-red. -able, -rable** a. **-ment** n.

de•fi•ance n. a challenge to combat; contempt; opposition. **defiant** a. aggressively hostile; insolent. **defiantly** adv.

de•fi•cient a. wanting; failing; lacking a full supply; incomplete. **deficiency**, **deficience** n. **-ly** adv. **deficit** n. excess of expenditure over income.

de•file v.t. to dirty; to desecrate. **-ment** n.

de•fine v.t. to determine the boundaries of; to state the exact meaning of; to circumscribe; to designate; to specify. **definable** a. **definite** a. **definitely** adv. **definiteness** n. **definition** n. description of a thing by its properties; explanation of the exact meaning of a word or term. **definitive** a. limiting; determining.

de•flate v.t. to empty of air or gas; to reduce inflated currency. **deflation** n.

de•flect v.t. to turn aside; to divert from the right direction; v.i. to swerve. **-ed** a. **deflection** n. **-or** n.

de•flow•er v.t. to deprive of flowers.

de•fo•li•a•tion n. the shedding of leaves. **defoliate** v.t. **defoliate, defoliated** a.

de•for•est v.t. to deprive of forests. **-ation** n.

de•form v.t. to mar or alter the form of; to make misshapen; to disfigure. **-ed** a. **-ation** n. **-ity** n.

de•fraud v.t. to deprive of; cheat.

de•fray v.t. to bear the cost of; to provide the money for. **-al** n.

de•frock v.t. to unfrock, as of a priest deprived of ecclesiastical status.

deft a. dexterous; handy. **-ly** adv. **-ness** n.

de•funct a. dead; deceased; obsolete; n.

de•fy v.t. to challenge; to resist authority.

de•gen•er•ate v.i. to decline; n. a person of low moral standards; a. having become less than one's kind. **degeneracy** n. **-ly** adv. **-ness** n. **degeneration** n. **degenerative** a.

de•grade v.t. to reduce in status; to lower the moral reputation of; to disgrace. **degradation** n.

de•gree n. a step upward or downward;

station or status; extent; rank to which one is admitted by a university; the 360th part of a revolution; a measured space on a thermometer, third degree (*U.S.*) a long, searching cross-examination by police of a suspect.

de·gres·sion *n.* a going down; a lowering of rate of taxation on certain wage levels.

de·hy·drate *v.t.* to remove water from; *v.i.* to lose water; dehydration *n.*

de·i·cide *n.* the killing of a god.

de·i·fy *v.t.* to make a god of; to exalt to the rank of divinity; to worship. deific, -al *a.* deification *n.* deiform *a.*

deign *v.i.* to condescend; to stoop; *v.t.*

de·ism *n.* belief, on purely rational grounds, in the existence of God without accepting the revelation implied in religious dogma. deist *n.* deistic, -al *a.* deity *n.* God, the Supreme Being; a pagan god or goddess.

de·ject *v.t.* to cast down; to dishearten; to depress. -ed *a.* downcast; moody; in low spirits. -edly *adv.* -edness *n.* -ion *n.*

de·lay *v.t.* to put off; to postpone; to stop temporarily; *v.i.* to dawdle; to procrastinate; *n.* tardiness. -er *n.*

de·lec·ta·ble *a.* highly pleasing; delightful; enjoyable. -ness *n.* delectably *adv.* delectation *n.*

del·e·gate *v.t.* to entrust authority to a deputy. *n.* a deputy; a representative. delegation *n.* body of delegates. delegacy *n.*

de·lete *v.t.* to erase; to strike out. delenda *n.pl.* things to be blotted out. deletion *n.*

del·e·te·ri·ous *a.* capable of harming or destroying health. -ly *adv.* -ness *n.*

delft *n.* glazed earthenware, orig. made at *Delft* in Holland. Also delf, delft-ware.

de·lib·er·ate *v.t.* to weigh in the mind; to discuss; *v.i.* to consider carefully; *a.* carefully considered; slow. -ly *adv.* -ness *n.* deliberation *n.* deliberative *a.*

del·i·cate *a.* dainty; frail; exquisitely wrought; nicely adjusted; highly sensitive or perceptive. delicacy *n.* -ly *adv.* -ness *n.*

del·i·ca·tes·sen *n.pl.* a shop selling cold cooked meats and other foods requiring little or no preparation.

de·li·cious *a.* extremely pleasing to the taste or sense of smell; delightful. -ly *adv.*

de·light *v.t.* to give great pleasure to; to charm; *v.i.* to take delight; *n.* the source of pleasure. -ed *a.* -edly *adv.* -ful *a.*

de·lim·it *v.t.* to fix the limit or boundaries of. -ation *n.*

de·lin·e·ate *v.t.* to draw an outline; to sketch; to portray; to describe clearly in words. delineation *n.* delineator *n.*

de·lin·quent *n.* one who fails in duty; an offender or criminal, esp. of a young person; *a.* failing in duty. delinquency *n.*

del·i·quesce *v.i.* to liquefy by absorbing moisture from the air. deliquescence *n.* deliquescent *a.*

de·lir·i·ous *a.* wandering in the mind; light-headed. deliration *n.* madness. -ly *adv.* -ness *n.* delirium *n.* mental disturbance caused by grave physical

illness or nervous shock. delirium tremens (*abbrev.* **D.T.**) violent delirium resulting from excessive alcoholism.

de·liv·er *v.t.* to liberate from danger, captivity, restraint; to save; to distribute; to pronounce (as a speech); to give birth to a child (used passively). -able *a.* -ance *n.* -er *n.* -y *n.*

dell *n.* a small, deep valley; a hollow.

Del·phic, Del·phian *a.* pert. to the town of *Delphia* in Ancient Greece, to the oracle of Apollo in that town; oracular.

del·phin·i·um *n.* a genus of flowering plants.

del·ta *n.* the fourth letter of the Greek alphabet, Δ (small letter = δ); a triangular tract of alluvium at the mouth of a large river. delta rays, rays from radioactive metals.

de·lude *v.t.* to lead into error; to mislead; to deceive. deludable *a.* -r *n.* delusion *n.* a mistaken belief. delusive *a.* delusory *a.*

de·luge *n.* a great flow of water; torrential rain; a flood; *v.t.* to flood; to inundate.

de·luxe *a.* sumptuous; of superlative quality.

delve *v.t.* and *v.i.* to carry on intensive research.

dem·a·gogue *n.* an unprincipled agitator. demagogic, -al *n.* demagogy *n.*

de·mand *v.t.* to ask authoritatively or peremptorily; to question; to require; *n.* earnest inquiry. -ant *n.* a plaintiff.

de·mar·ca·tion, demarkation *n.* the act of marking a line or boundary; a boundary. demarcate *v.t.*

de·mean *v.t.* to conduct or comport oneself. demeanor *n.* behavior; conduct.

de·mean *v.t.* to make mean; to debase; to degrade.

de·ment·ed *a.* insane; crazy; dement *v.t.* to drive mad. dementia *n.* incipient loss of reason; insanity marked by complete mental deterioration. dementia praecox, insanity in adolescence.

de·mer·it *n.* a fault; a mark against one's record.

de·mesne *n.* a manor house and the estate adjacent to it; private ownership of land.

dem·i· *prefix* signifying *half.*

dem·i·god *n.* a classical hero half human, half divine.

dem·i·john *n.* a glass bottle with large body, slender neck, and enclosed in wicker work.

dem·i·monde *n.* a class of women of doubtful reputation; prostitutes.

de·mise *n.* death; transmission by will to a successor; *v.t.* to bequeath.

dem·i·tasse *n.* a small-sized cup, esp. for after-dinner coffee.

de·mo·bi·lize *v.t.* to dismiss (troops); to disband. demobilization *n.*

de·moc·ra·cy *n.* a form of government for the people, by the will of the majority of the people; a state having this form of government. democrat *n.* one who adheres to democracy; member of Democratic party. democratic, democratical *a.*

de·mog·ra·phy *n.* science of vital and social statistics.

D

de·mol·ish v.t. to destroy; to pull down; to ruin. -er n. demolition n.

de·mon n. a spirit; a devil; **demoniac** a. devilish — also **demoniacal**; n. a human being possessed of an evil spirit. -olatry, -ism n. -olater n.

de·mon·e·ti·za·tion n. demonetize v.t. to diminish or deprive of monetary value.

dem·on·strate v.t. to prove by pointing out; to exhibit; to explain by specimens or experiment. **demonstrable** a. demonstrably adv. demonstration n. demonstrative a. demonstrator n.

de·mor·al·ize v.t. to injure the morale of; to corrupt.

de·mos n. the people.

de·mur v.i. to object. pr.p. -ring; pa.p. -red; n. -rable a. -rage n. undue detention of a ship, railroad car, etc.; compensation paid for such detention. -rer n. (Law) a plea that a case has insufficient evidence to justify its being pursued further.

de·mure a. grave; staid; shy; seemingly modest. -ly adv. -ness n.

den n. a cave or hollow place; lair or cage of a wild beast; a private sanctum.

de·nar·i·us n. a Roman silver coin; pl. denaril. denary a. containing ten.

de·na·ture v.t. to make unfit for eating or drinking by adulteration. denaturant n. denaturation n.

den·dri-, dendro- prefix from Gk. dendron, a tree, as in -form a. having the shape or appearance of a tree. -tic, -tical a. dendroid, dendroidal a.

de·ni·al n. a flat contradiction; a refusal.

den·i·gra·tion n. a blackening of; defamation of a person's character. denigrate v.t.

den·im n. a stout cotton twill cloth.

den·i·zen n. a dweller; anything successfully naturalized; v.t.

de·nom·i·nate v.t. to give a name to; to designate. denominable a. denomination n. a title; a religious sect; unit of measure. denominational a. denominative a. denominatively adv. denominator n. the number below the line in a fraction.

de·note v.t. to signify or imply; to be the symbol of. denotable a. denotation n.

dé·noue·ment n. the unraveling of the complication of a dramatic plot; the issue or outcome of a situation.

de·nounce v.t. to inform against; to accuse in public. -ment n. -er n.

dense a. compact; thick, crowded; (Fig.) stupid. -ly adv. -ness n. density n.

dent n. a small depression made (by a blow) in a surface; v.t.

den·tal a. pert. to the teeth or to dentistry; n. and a. a consonant sound (e.g. d or t) made by tip of tongue behind the upper front teeth. dentate a. toothed; sharply notched. dentiform a. dentifrice n. powder, paste, or liquid used to clean and whiten teeth. dentist n. a medically trained specialist in the care of the teeth. dentistry n. dentition n. arrangement of teeth. dentoid a. denture n. set or part set of teeth, esp. artificial teeth.

den·ti·cle n. a small tooth or projection.

denticular, denticulate, denticulated a. having notches or sharp projections.

de·nude v.t. to lay bare; to strip. denudation n.

de·nun·ci·ate v.t. Same as denounce. denunciation n. denunciator n.

de·ny v.t. to declare to be untrue; to refuse a request; to disavow; to disown.

de·o·dor·ize v.t. to deprive of odor. deodorant, deodorizer n.

de·ox·i·dize v.t. to remove oxygen from.

de·part v.i. to go away; to leave; to die; to deviate; v.t. to leave. -ed n. the dead. -ment n. a section of a business or administration; a special branch of the arts or science. -mental a. affecting only a section of a business, etc. -ure n.

de·pend v.i. to rely on; to be sustained by; to be contingent on. -able a. trustworthy. -ably adv. -ant, -ent n. one who is supported, esp. financially by another; a. hanging down; varying according to; -ence n. -ency n. -ently, -antly adv.

de·pict v.t. to portray; to present a visual image of; to describe in words. -tion n. -ive a.

dep·i·late v.t. to remove hair from. depilation n. depilatory n. agent for removing superfluous hair from body; a.

de·plete v.t. to empty; to diminish; to reduce. depletion n. depletive, depletory a.

de·plore v.t. to suffer remorse for; to regret. deplorable a. deplorably adv.

de·ploy v.t. to spread out; to extend troops in line; v.i. -ment n.

de·po·lar·ize v.t. to deprive of polarity.

de·pone v.t. to give evidence under oath, in a law court. deponent n.

de·port v.t. to carry away; to expel; to banish into exile; (reflex.) to behave; to bear oneself. -ation n. the compulsory removal of people from one country to another. -ment n. conduct of a person.

de·pose v.t. to remove from a throne; to oust from a high position; to degrade; (Law) to state upon oath. deposable a. deposal n. deposition n. removal of someone from a high position; (Law) a written declaration by a witness.

de·po·sit v.t. to lay down; to entrust; n. that which is deposited or laid down; sediment falling to the bottom of a fluid; money placed in safe-keeping of a bank; partial payment. -ary n. -or n. -ory n.

de·pot n. a railway station; a storage center for supplies and materials.

de·prave v.t. to make bad or worse; to corrupt; to pervert. depravation n. -d a. immoral. depravity n.

dep·re·cate v.t. to express disapproval of. deprecatingly adv. deprecation n. deprecative, deprecatory a. deprecator n.

de·pre·ci·ate v.t. to lower in value; v.i. to lose quality; to diminish in market value. depreciation n. depreciative, depreciatory a. depreciator n.

dep·re·date v.t. to plunder; to lay waste. depredation n.

de·press v.t. to deject or cast a gloom over; to press down; to lower; to diminish the vigor of. -ed a. -ible a. depression n. a hollow; despondency; in meteorology, an area of low barometric pressure. -or n.

de•prive v.t. to take away; to dispossess; deprivation n. deprivable a. depriver n.

depth n. deepness; distance measured downwards from surface; distance from front to back.

de•pute v.t. to send with commission to act for another; to delegate duties to another. deputation n. deputize v.i. deputy n.

de•range v.t. to put out of order or place; to upset; to make insane. -d a. -ment n.

der•by n. a man's felt hat, with stiff rounded crown and narrow brim.

der•e•lict a. forsaken; abandoned and disclaimed by owner; n. a ship abandoned by captain and crew; a person abandoned by society. dereliction n.

de•ride v.t. to ridicule; to mock; to laugh at with scorn. -r n. deridingly adv. derision n. derisive a. derisively adv. derisiveness n. derisory a.

de•rive v.t. to obtain or draw from a source; to trace the descent or origin; v.i. to have as an origin; to proceed. derivable a. derivation n. etymology. derivative n. a word derived from another; a.

der•ma, der•mis n. the true skin below epidermis. dermal a. dermatic a. -titis n. inflammation of the skin. -tology n. branch of medical science concerned with the skin and skin diseases. -tologist n.

der•o•gate v.i. to lessen. derogation n. derogatory a. tending to impair the value of; detracting. derogatorily adv.

der•rick n. an apparatus like a crane for hoisting heavy weights.

derrick

der•rin•ger n. a short-barrelled pistol with a large bore.

der•vish n. a member of one of the mendicant orders among the Mohammedans.

des•cant n. a melody harmonizing with and sung or played as accompaniment to a musical theme; a discourse on a theme; v.i. to sing. -er n.

de•scend v.t. to go down; v.i. to sink; to lower oneself or stoop to something. -ant n. offspring. -ent a. descending a. descent n. act of coming down; lineage.

de•scribe v.t. to represent the features of; to portray in speech or writing. describable a. description n. descriptive a. descriptively adv.

de•scry v.t. to discover by the eye; to perceive from a distance. descrier n.

des•e•crate v.t. to violate the sanctity of; to profane. -r, -or n. desecration n.

de•sert n. that which is deserved.

des•ert n. a wide, sandy waste region; a. uncultivated; solitary.

de•sert v.t. to abandon; to leave; v.i. to quit the armed forces without authorization. -ed a. -er n. desertion n.

de•serve v.t. to earn by service; to be entitled to; v.i. to be worthy of reward. deservedly adv. deserving a.

des•ic•cate v.t. to extract all moisture from; to dehydrate. desiccant a. n. substance capable of absorbing moisture. desiccation n.

de•sign v.t. to draw the outline of; to plan; v.i. to purpose; n. sketch in outline; a pattern. -able a. designate v.t. designation n. designative a. -edly adv. intentionally. -er n. -ful a. -ing a.

de•sire v.t. to yearn for the possession of; to request; n. anything desired; a longing. desirable a. desirably adv. desirableness, desirability n. desirous a.

de•sist v.t. to cease; to discontinue. -ance, -ence n.

desk n. a table for reading or writing; a lectem.

des•o•late v.t. to devastate; to make lonely or forlorn; a. waste; deserted. -ly adv. -ness n. -r n. desolation n. desolatory a.

de•spair v.i. to be without hope; n. despondency; hopelessness. -ing a. -ingly adv.

des•patch See dispatch.

des•pi•ca•ble a. contemptible; deserving to be despised. despicably adv. despicability n.

de•spise v.t. to look down upon; to hold in contempt. despisable a.

de•spite n. contemptuous treatment; prep. notwithstanding. -ful a. -fully adv.

de•spoil v.t. to take away by force; to rob. -er n. a plunderer. -ment, despoliation n.

de•spond v.i. to be cast down in spirit. -ence, -ency n. depression. -ent a. -ently adv. -ingly adv.

des•pot n. one who rules with absolute power; a tyrant. -ic a. -ically adv. -ism n.

des•sert n. a course served at end of a dinner.

des•tine v.t. to predetermine. destination n. the place to which one is traveling. destiny n. fate.

des•ti•tute a. in want; needy. destitution n.

de•stroy v.t. to turn to rubble; to put an end to. pa.p. -ed. -able a. -er n. a type of fast warship armed with guns and torpedoes.

de•struc•tion n. the act of destroying; state of being destroyed; ruin. destructible a. destructibleness, destructibility n. destructive a.

des•ue•tude n. discontinuance of a custom or practice.

de•sul•tor•y a. leaping from one thing to another; unmethodical. desultorily adv. desultoriness n.

de•tach v.t. to separate; to disunite; to detail for special service. -able a. -ed a.

D

standing alone; impersonal; disinterested. **-edly** adv. **-edness, -ment** n.

de·tail v.t. to relate minutely; to record every item; to appoint for a special duty. **detail** n. a minute part. **-ed** a.

de·tain v.t. to keep back or from; to prevent someone proceeding. **-er** n. **-ment** n. **detention** n.

de·tect v.t. to uncover; to discover. **-able, -ible** a. **-or** n. **-ion** n. **-ive** a., n. a member of the police force, not in uniform, who apprehends criminals and investigates cases.

de·ter v.t. to frighten from; to discourage; to restrain. pr.p. **-ring;** pa.p. **-red. -ment** n. **-rent** a., n. **deterrence** n.

de·terge v.t. to cleanse; to wipe off. **detergence, detergency** n. **detergent** a. cleansing n. cleansing substance.

de·te·ri·o·rate v.t. to make worse; to cause to depreciate; v.i. to degenerate. **deterioration** n.

de·ter·mine v.t. to fix the limits of; to define; to decide; v.i. to make a decision or resolution. **determinable** a. **determinant** a. serving to fix, or limit; n. **determinate** a. having fixed limits. **determinately** adv. **determination** n. resolution. **-d** a. unwavering. **-dly** adv. **determinism** n. the doctrine that man is not a free agent, and that his actions and mental activity are governed by causes or motives outside his own will.

de·test v.t. to dislike intensely; to hate. **-able** a. **-ableness, -ability** n. **-ation** n.

de·throne v.t. to remove from a throne; to depose. **-ment** n.

de·to·nate v.t. to cause to explode; v.i.; **detonation** n. **detonator** n. device to make another substance explode.

de·tour n. a roundabout way; a digression.

de·tract v.t. to take away a part from; to defame; v.i. **-or** n. **-ingly** adv. **detraction** n. depreciation; slander.

de·tri·ment n. injury; harm; loss. **-al** a.

de·trun·cate v.t. to lop off from the trunk; to shorten. **detruncation** n.

deuce n. a card or die with two spots; (Tennis) score of 40 all.

deuce n. the devil; bad luck.

deu·te·ri·um n. a form of hydrogen twice as heavy as the normal gas.

deu·ter·on·o·my n. the fifth book of the Pentateuch.

de·val·u·ate, devalue v.t. to reduce the value of. **devaluation** n.

dev·as·tate v.t. to lay waste. **devastation** n. destruction.

de·vel·op v.t. to cause to grow; to increase the resources of; to produce image on photographic plate or film by chemical application; v.i. to evolve by natural processes. **-er** n. a chemical for producing image on plate or film. **-ment** n. a gradual unfolding or growth.

de·vi·ate v.i. to diverge; to turn away from the direct line; v.t. **deviation** n.

de·vice n. that which is planned out or designed; contrivance; emblem on a shield.

dev·il n. the spirit of evil; Satan; v.t. to torment; to prepare with hot or savory seasoning. **-ish** a. **-ishly** adv. **—may-care** a. happy-go-lucky. **-ment** n. mischief. **-ry; -try** n. **-'s advocate,** one appointed by papal court to oppose a proposed canonization; one who maintains an argument with which he really disagrees. **give the devil his due,** give even the worst person credit for something.

de·vi·ous a. not direct; erring. **-ly, -ness** n.

de·vise v.t. to invent; to contrive; to scheme; to plan; v.i. to consider; n. (Law) the act of bequeathing. **devisable** a. **devisal,** n. **-r** n. **devisor** n. one who bequeaths by will.

de·vi·tal·ize v.t. to deprive of life or vitality. **devitalization** n.

de·void a. empty; free from; without.

dev·o·lu·tion n. delegation of powers to subsidiary or local bodies; opposite of evolution. [See **devolve**].

de·volve v.t. to transmit; to transfer; v.i. (Law) to pass, by inheritance, from one to another.

de·vote v.t. to give oneself wholly to; to dedicate. **-d** a. **-dly** adv. **devotedness** n. **devotee** n. a zealous supporter. **devotion** n. **devotions** n.pl. worship and prayer. **devotional** a.

de·vour v.t. to consume completely and wantonly; to destroy. **-ing** a.

de·vout a. **-ious;** passionately religious. **-ly** adv.

dew n. moisture in the atmosphere or in the soil itself, condensed on exposed surfaces, esp. at night; v.t. to moisten. **-fall** n. **-iness** n. **-y** a.

dex·ter a. pert. to the right hand. **dexterity** n. manual skill; cleverness. **-ous, dextrous** a. **-ously** adv. **-ousness** n. **dextral** a. right as opposed to left. **dextrality** n. right-handedness. **dextrally** adv.

dex·trin, dextrine n. a soluble gummy substance used for stiffening fabrics, sizing paper.

di·a·be·tes n. a disease marked by excessive flow of sugar-urine due to failure of pancreas to produce insulin.

di·a·bol·ic, diabolical a. devilish; fiendish. **-ally** adv.

di·ac·o·nal a. pert. to a deacon.

di·a·dem n. a headdress or crown significant of royalty. **-ed** a.

di·ag·no·sis n. a scientific discrimination of any kind; the identification of a disease from its signs and symptoms; pl. **diagnoses. diagnose** v.t. **diagnostic** a. symptomatic; n. a clue. **diagnostician** n.

di·ag·o·nal n. a straight line joining two opposite angles in a rectilineal figure; a. from corner to opposite corner; oblique. **-ly** adv.

di·a·gram n. a figure drawn to demonstrate a theorem; a drawing or plan in outline. **-matically** adv.

di·al n. any plate or face on which a pointer moves; v.t. to measure on a dial; to call a number on automatic telephone; pr.p. **-ling.** pa.p. **-led.**

di·a·lect n. a mode of speech peculiar to a district or social group; vernacular.

di·a·lec·tic, -al *a.* pert. to dialectics; *n.* the science of reasoning. **-ally** *adv.* **dialectician** *n.*

di·a·logue *n.* a conversation between two (or more) persons. **dialogistic** *a.* **dialogize** *v.i.*

di·al·y·sis *n.* separation of colloid (non-crystalline) from crystalline substances in solution, by filtration through a membrane; *pl.* **dialyses.** **dialytic** *a.*

di·am·e·ter *n.* a line passing through the center of a circle and terminated by the circumference; transverse measurement; unit of magnifying power of a lens. **diametric (-al)** *a.* directly opposite.

di·a·mond *n.* one of the crystalline forms of carbon and the hardest substance

diamonds

known; a popular gem stone; a four-sided figure with two acute and two obtuse angles; one of the four suits of playing-cards; playing field for baseball. *a.* —**wedding,** the sixtieth anniversary of a marriage. **black diamonds,** coal.

di·a·pa·son *n.* correct pitch; harmony; the two foundation stops of an organ.

di·a·per *n.* a baby's breechcloth; *v.t.* to change a baby's diaper.

di·aph·a·nous *a.* having the power to transmit light; transparent; translucent.

di·a·pho·ret·ic *n.* a medicine which induces perspiration; *a.*

di·a·phragm *n.* a dividing membrane; a dome-shaped muscular partition between chest and abdomen; vibrating disc in telephone or microphone; a disc with a circular hole used in telescope or camera to cut off part of a ray of light. **-atic, -al** *a.*

di·ar·chy *n.* a system of government in which power is held jointly by two authorities.

di·ar·rhe·a, diarrhoea *n.* an excessive and frequent looseness of the bowels. **diarrhetic** *a.*

di·a·ry *n.* a daily record; personal record of thoughts, actions, etc. **diarist** *n.*

di·a·stase *n.* an enzyme capable of converting starch into sugar, **diastasic** *a.*

di·as·to·le *n.* a rhythmical dilatation of the heart and arteries; the lengthening of a syllable usually short, before a pause.

di·a·ther·mal *a.* permeable by heat. **diathermanous, diathermous, diathermic** *a.* **diathermy** *n.*

di·a·tom *n.* one of an order of microscopic unicellular marine or vegetable organisms.

di·a·tom·ic *a.* consisting of two atoms.

di·a·ton·ic *a.* pert. to major or minor scales.

di·a·tribe *n.* a wordy denunciation. **diatribist** *n.*

dib·ble *n.* a pointed instrument used in

gardening for making holes. Also **dibber.** *v.t.; v.i.* to make holes. **-r** *n.*

dice *n.pl.* small cubes on each of the six faces of which are spots representing numbers 1-6; *Sing.* form **die;** *v.t.* to cut into small squares; *v.i.* to play with dice. **dicer** *n.*

di·ceph·a·lous *a.* having two heads.

di·chot·o·my *n.* (*Logic*) division of ideas into two classes. **dichotomize** *v.t.* and *v.i.* **dichotomous** *a.*

dick·er *v.t.* and *v.i.* to barter; to haggle; to quibble; *n.* a bargain; a deal.

dick·ey, dicky *n.* detachable shirt front; seat for servants at back of old-fashioned carriage.

dic·tate *v.t.* to read aloud a passage for another to transcribe; to give orders; *v.i.* to speak with authority; *n.* direction that must be obeyed. **dictation** *n.* that which is read aloud for another to write down. **dictator** *n.* one who holds absolute power. **dictatorial** *a.* tending to force one's opinions on another. **dictatorially** *adv.* **dictatorship** *n.*

dic·tion *n.* verbal style; enunciation.

dic·tion·ar·y *n.* a book containing, alphabetically arranged, the words of a language, their meanings and etymology.

dic·to·graph *n.* sound-recording telephonic instrument.

dic·tum *n.* a positive assertion; an authoritative statement or opinion; *pl.* **dicta.**

did *pa.t.* of verb **do.**

di·dac·tic *a.* designed to instruct; containing precepts or doctrines. **-ally** *adv.* **-s** *n.* the science of teaching.

did·y·mous *a.* twin.

die *n.* a small cube used in games of chance; *pl.* **dice. the die is cast,** one's fate is irrevocably settled.

die *v.i.* to cease to live; to become extinct; to wither. *pr.p.* **dying.** *pa.p.* **-d. dying** *a.* **to die for** to want desperately. **to die hard,** to resist stubbornly.

die *n.* a device for cutting in a press; an engraved metal block used for stamping a design; the cubical part of a pedestal; *pl.* **dies.** — **casting** *n.* method of making castings in permanent molds.

di·e·lec·tric *a.* non-conducting; *n.* name for a substance through or across which electric induction takes place.

di·er·e·sis, diaeresis *n.* a mark (¨) placed over the second of two consecutive vowels to indicate that each is to be pronounced separately, as in coöperate. *pl.* **diereses, diaereses.**

Die·sel en·gine *n.* an internal combustion engine.

di·e·sis *n.* (*Print.*) a mark of reference, the double dagger (‡); *pl.* **dieses.**

di·et *n.* what one habitually eats and drinks; a regulated allowance of provisions; *v.i.* to slim. **-ary** *n.; a.* **-etic** *a.* **-etics** *n.* the science and study of food values, and their effect on health. **-ician, -itian** *n.*

di·et *n.* a legislative assembly in certain countries; an international conference.

dif·fer *v.i.* to be unlike; to have distinctive

characteristics. **-ence** n. unlikeness; the amount by which one thing exceeds another in weight or number. **-ent** a. distinct; **-entia** n. the essential quality or characteristic distinguishing any one species from another in a genus; pl. **-entiae**. **-ential** a. characteristic; proceeding by increments infinitely small. **-entially** adv. **-entiate** v.t. to distinguish; v.i. to acquire different characteristics. **-entiation** n. **-ently** adv. **-ential gear**, a mechanism by which two sets of wheels are made to rotate at different speeds.

dif·fi·cult a. hard to do or understand; not easy. **-ly** adv. **-y** n. **-ies** n.pl. financial embarrassment.

dif·fi·dent a. timid; shy. **diffidence** n. lack of confidence. **-ly** adv.

dif·fract v.t. to break or separate into parts, esp. of rays of light and sound waves. **diffraction** n. the phenomenon caused by light passing through a narrow slit.

dif·fuse v.t. to spread; to scatter; v.i. to mix. **diffuse** a. widely spread. **diffusely** adv. **-ness** n. **diffusible** a. **diffusion** n. term applied to the intermixture of two gases or fluids without chemical combination. **diffusive** a. spreading. **diffusively** adv. **diffusiveness** n.

dig v.t. to break and turn up earth; to excavate; to delve; to poke or nudge someone; v.i. to till the soil; pr.p. **-ging**. pa.p., pa.t. **dug**. n. **-ger** n. **-gings** n.pl. areas where mining or other digging is carried on.

di·gest v.t. to convert into a substance which can be readily absorbed into the blood; to think over; v.i. **digest** n. a magazine containing condensed version of articles already published elsewhere. **-er** n. **-ible** a. **-ibility** n. **digestion** n. **digestive** a.; n. any medicine that aids digestion.

dig·it n. a finger; integer under 10. **-al** a. pert. to the fingers; n. one of the keys of piano or organ. **-alin** n. the drug obtained from leaves of digitalis. **-alis** n. a strong drug obtained from foxglove, and used medicinally as sedative, narcotic and as cardiac stimulant. **-ate, -ated** a. **-igrade** n. an animal which walks on its toes; a. walking on the toes.

di·glot a. speaking two languages.

dig·ni·fy v.t. to invest with dignity or honor; to exalt; to ennoble. **dignified** a.

dig·ni·ty n. state of being dignified; loftiness. **dignitary** n. one who holds a high position.

di·graph n. two vowels or two consonants combined to express one sound as ea in head.

di·gress v.i. to wander from the main theme, topic, or argument; to be diffuse. **digression** n. **digressional, -ive** a.

di·he·dral a. having two plane faces. **dihedron** n.

dike, dyke n. an artificial embankment to prevent inundation of low lying ground; igneous rock, once molten, which has filled up fissures of stratified rocks.

di·lap·i·date v.t. to pull stone from stone; to suffer to fall into ruin; v.i. to be in a condition of disrepair. **-d** a. **dilapidation** n.

di·late v.t. to swell out; to expand in all directions; v.i. to widen. **dilatable** a. elastic. **dilatancy, dilatation, dilation** n. **dilatant** a. **dilator, -r** n.

dil·a·tory a. tardy; inclined to procrastination. **dilatorily** adv. **dilatoriness** n.

di·lem·ma n. choice between alternatives equally undesirable; a predicament.

dil·et·tante n. a lover of the fine arts, esp. in a superficial way; a dabbler. pl. **dilettantes, -ti**. **dilettantish** a. **dilettantism, dilettanteism** n.

dil·i·gent a. steady and constant in application; industrious. **diligence** n. **-ly** adv.

dill n. a perennial yellow-flowered herb used in medicines and flavoring.

dil·ly-dal·ly v.i. to loiter; to delay.

di·lute v.t. to make thinner or more liquid; to reduce the strength of by addition of something; v.i. to become thin; a. reduced in strength; **diluent** a.; n. that which thins or weakens the strength, color, etc. **-ness** n. **dilution** n.

di·lu·vi·um n. a surface deposit of sand, gravel, etc. regarded as glacial drift. **diluvial, diluvian** a. pert. to or produced by a flood.

dim a. not bright or distinct; faint; shadowy; vague; v.t. to cloud; v.i. to become dull or indistinct. pr.p. **-ming**. pa.p., pa.t. **-med**. **-ly** adv. **-mer** n. in motoring, a device to dimish power of headlights. **-ness** n.

dime n. U.S. silver coin equal to 10 cents.

di·men·sion n. a measurement of extent in a single direction; usually pl. measurement in three directions; capacity; importance. **-al** a.

dim·e·ter n. a verse with two measures or accents.

di·min·ish v.t. to weaken; to reduce; v.i. to become smaller. **-ed** a. lessened; (Mus.) lowered by a semi-tone.

di·min·u·en·do n. (Mus.) a gradual decrease in volume of sound and marked >.

dim·i·nu·tion n. state of being reduced in size, quality, or amount. **diminutive** a. of small size; applied to a suffix expressing smallness; n.

dim·i·ty n. a thin cotton cloth ribbed or figured.

di·morph·ic a. existing in two forms; capable of crystallizing in two forms under different degrees of temperature. **dimorphism** n. **dimorphous** a.

dim·ple n. a slight indentation in any surface; v.t.; v.i.

din n. a loud, continuous noise; racket; clamor; v.t. to harass with insistent repetition. pr.p. **-ning**. pa.p., pa.t. **-ned**.

dine v.t. to entertain at dinner; v.i. to take dinner. **-r** n. a compartment on a railway train for serving meals to passengers. Also **dining car. dinette** n. a small dining room. **dinner** n. the principal meal of the day. **dinner jacket**, a black coat (without tails) worn as informal evening dress.

ding v.t. to ring. —**dong** n. the sound of bells continuously rung; a. monotonous.

din·ghy, dingy, dingey n. a small boat.

din·gy a. soiled; of a darkish color. **dinginess** n.

di·no·saur n. a gigantic extinct four-footed reptile of the Mesozoic age.

dint n. a mark or depression made by a blow; force or energy exerted; v.t. by **dint of,** by means of.

di·o·cese n. the district in which a bishop exercises ecclesiastical jurisdiction. **diocesan** a.; n.

di·oe·cious, diecious a. (Bot.) having the stamens and pistils borne by separate plants of the same species; (Zool.) having the male and female reproductive organs separate.

di·op·ter, dioptre n. the unit for measuring power of a lens.

di·o·ram·a n. a miniature, three-dimensional scene; varied effects of reality being realized by manipulation of lights.

di·ox·ide n. a substance the molecules of which comprise one part metal, two parts oxygen.

dip v.t. to immerse momentarily in a liquid; to dye; to lower and raise again; to wash; v.i. to sink below at a certain level; pr.p. -**ping.** pa.p., pa.t. -**ped.** n. a liquid into which something is dipped; immersion; inclination downward of rock strata. -**per** n. a semi-aquatic diving bird; (Astron.) the Great Bear; the Little Bear. -**py** a.

diph·the·ri·a n. epidemic disease affecting mainly throat and air passages. -**l, diphtheric, diphtheritic,** a.

diph·thong n. a union of two vowel sounds pronounced as one. -**al** a. -**ally** adv. -**ize** v.t. **diphthongization** n.

di·plex a. (Radio) pert. to the reception or transmission of two messages simultaneously.

dip·lo·car·di·ac a. having a double or divided heart.

di·plo·ma n. a document or certificate conferring some honor, privilege, or degree; v.t.

di·plo·ma·cy n. the art of conducting international negotiations; tact in dealing with people. **diplomat, diplomatist** n. **diplomatic, -al** a. **diplomatically** adv. **diplomatic corps,** the body of accredited foreign diplomatists resident in any capital.

di·po·lar a. having two poles. **dipolarize** v.t. to magnetize.

dip·so·ma·ni·a n. an uncontrollable craving for alcoholic stimulants. **dipsomaniac** n. **dipsomaniacal** a.

Dip·ter·a n. an order of insects which have only two wings. **dipteral** a. **dipteran** n. **dipterous** a.

dip·tych n. an ancient writing tablet hinged in the middle and folding together like a book; a pair of carvings or pictures similarly hinged.

dire a. dreadful; calamitous; disastrous. Also -**ful.** -**ly, -fully** adv.

di·rect a. straightforward; in line of descent; sincere; unambiguous; v.t. to manage; to prescribe a course or line of procedure; v.i. to act as a guide; adv. in a straight line. **direction** n. instruction; guidance; management; line taken by a moving body. **directional, -ing, -ive** a. -**ive** n. orders from a supreme authority. -**ly** adv. in a straight line; immediately after. -**ness** n. the quality of being unimpeded by extraneous details. -**or** n. (fem. -**ress**) one who directs. -**orate** n. a board of directors. -**orial** a. -**ory** a. containing directions; n. a book containing the alphabetically arranged names and addresses of the residents of a town or district. — **current** a current flowing in one direction. **direction finder** an aerial which determines direction of incoming radio signals.

dirge n. a funeral chant; a lament. -**ful** a.

dir·i·gi·ble a. capable of being directed or steered; n. a navigable balloon elongated in shape and propelled by engine-driven propellers.

dirk n. a short dagger; v.t.

dirn·dl n. a type of skirt.

dirt n. any filthy substance; loose soil; obscenity. —**cheap** a. uncommonly cheap. -**ily** adv. -**iness** n. -**y** a.; v.t. to befoul.

dis- pref. implying separation, as in dismiss; negation, as in disband; deprivation, as in disanimate; thoroughness, as in disannul.

dis·a·ble v.t. to make incapable or physically unfit; to disqualify. -**ment** n. **disability** n. incapacity.

dis·a·buse v.t. to free from misapprehension or error; to undeceive.

dis·ad·van·tage n. a drawback; a hindrance; a handicap; detriment; hurt. **disadvantageous** a. **disadvantageously** adv.

dis·af·fect v.t. to alienate the affection of; to fill with discontent. -**ed** a. -**edly** adv. -**edness, disaffection** n.

dis·af·firm v.t. to annul; to invalidate; to reverse a decision. **disaffirmation** n.

dis·a·gree v.i. to be at variance; to differ in opinion. -**able** a. -**ably** adv. -**ment** n.

dis·al·low v.t. to refuse to allow; to reject as untrue or invalid. -**able** a. -**ance** n.

dis·ap·pear v.i. to vanish; to become invisible; to cease to exist. **disappearance** n.

dis·ap·point v.t. to fail to realize the hopes of; to frustrate. -**ed** a. -**ing** a. -**ment** n.

dis·ap·pro·bation n. act of disapproving; censure.

dis·ap·prove v.t. to form an unfavorable judgment of; to dislike; v.i. **disapproval** n. **disapprovingly** adv.

dis·arm v.t. to deprive of arms; to render unable to attack; to conciliate; v.i. -**ament** n. -**ing** a. ingenuous.

dis·ar·range v.t. to disturb the order or arrangement of; to throw into confusion. -**ment** n.

dis·ar·ray v.t. to throw into disorder; to undress; n. disorder; confusion.

dis·as·so·ci·ate v.t. to disunite.

dis•as•ter n. an adverse happening; sudden misfortune; catastrophe. **disastrous** a.

dis•a•vow v.t. to refuse to acknowledge; to repudiate. **-al, -ment** n.

dis•band v.t. to break up an organization; to dismiss; v.i. **-ment** n.

dis•bar v.t. to expel a lawyer from the legal profession. pr.p. **-ring.** pa.p., pa.t. **-red. -ment** n.

dis•be•lieve v.t. to maintain to be untrue; to refuse to believe; v.i. **disbelief** n. **disbeliever** n.

dis•burse v.t. to pay out money. **-ment** n. **-r** n.

disc See disk.

dis•card v.t. and v.i. to put aside; to cast off; n. anything thrown out as useless.

dis•car•nate a. having no physical body.

dis•cern v.t. to distinguish clearly; to behold as separate. **-er** n. **-ible** a. **-ing** a. discriminating. **-ment** n. power or faculty of judging.

dis•charge v.t. to unload a cargo; to fire off the charge with which gun is loaded; to emit smoke; to perform a duty; to pay a debt; to demobilize soldiers; to dismiss; n. performance; matter which exudes, as from an abscess; the rate of flow of a liquid or waste matter through a pipe.

dis•ci•ple n. one who receives instruction from another; one who adheres to a particular school of philosophy, religious thought, or art. **-ship** n.

dis•ci•pline n. instruction; subjection to authority; self-control; v.t. to improve behavior by judicious penal methods. **disciplinarian** n. **disciplinary** a. **-r** n.

dis•claim v.t. to renounce claim to, or responsibility for; to disown; v.i. **-ant** n. **-er** n. denial; disavowal.

dis•close v.t. to reveal; to divulge. **-r** n. **disclosure** n.

dis•col•or v.t. to spoil the color of; to stain; v.i. **-ation, -ment** n. **-ed** a.

dis•com•fit v.t. to defeat; to foil. **-ure** n.

dis•com•fort n. uneasiness; pain; v.t. to make uneasy.

dis•com•mode v.t. to put to inconvenience; to disturb.

dis•com•pose v.t. to upset the self-possession of; to disturb. **discomposure** n.

dis•con•cert v.t. to embarrass. **-ment** n. state of disagreement.

dis•con•nect v.t. to sever. **-ed** a. separated.

dis•con•so•late a. forlorn; utterly dejected. **-ly** adv. **-ness, disconsolation** n.

dis•con•tent a. dissatisfied; n. dissatisfaction; v.t. to dissatisfy. **-ed** a. **-edly** adv. **-edness, -ment** n.

dis•con•tin•ue v.t. to interrupt; to break off; v.i. to cease. **discontinuance, discontinuation** n. **discontinuity** n. **discontinuous** a.

dis•cord n. want of agreement; lack of harmony; strife. **discord** v.i. to be out of tune. **discordance, discordancy** n. **discordant** a. dissonant. **discordantly** adv.

dis•count v.t. to deduct a sum or rate per cent from; to disregard; v.i. to lend money with discount. **discount** n. a deduction.

dis•coun•te•nance v.t. to refuse to give approval to.

dis•cour•age v.t. to dishearten; to deter. **-ment** n. dejection. **discouraging** a.

dis•course n. a formal speech; a sermon; a dissertation; conversation. **discourse** v.t. to utter; v.i. to converse.

dis•cour•te•ous a. lacking in courtesy; rude. **-ly** adv. **discourtesy** n.

dis•cov•er v.t. to find out; to bring to light. **-able** a. **-er** n. **-y** n.

dis•cred•it v.t. to bring into disrepute; n. loss of credit or of reputation. **-able** a.

dis•creet a. prudent; judicious; cautious. **-ly** adv.

dis•crep•an•cy n. inconsistency; variance; difference. **discrepant** a.

dis•crete a. separate; distinct. **-ly** adv. **-ness** n.

dis•cre•tion n. the quality of being discreet; prudence; discernment. **-al, -ary** a. **ally** adv.

dis•crim•i•nate v.t. to detect as different; v.i. to make a distinction in. **-ly** adv. **discriminating** a. able to observe subtle differences. **discriminatingly** adv. **discrimination** n. **discriminative** a.

dis•cur•sive a. passing from one topic to another; rambling. **-ly** adv. **-ness** n. **discursory** a.

dis•cus n. a circular plate of stone or metal, used in athletic contests.

dis•cuss v.t. to examine critically; to exchange ideas on; **-able** (or **-ible**) a. **discussion** n.

dis•dain v.t. to look down upon; to scorn; n. contempt. **-ful** a. **-fully** adv. **-fulness** n.

dis•ease n. an unhealthy condition of mind or body; malady; **-d** a.

dis•em•bark v.t. to put on shore; v.i. to land. **-ation, -ment** n.

dis•em•bod•y v.t. to free from the body or flesh. **disembodiment** n.

dis•em•bowel v.t. to gut; to eviscerate.

dis•en•chant v.t. to disillusion.

dis•en•fran•chise v.t. to deprive of the right to vote. **-ment** n.

dis•en•gage v.t. to unfasten. **-d** a. unattached. **-ment** n.

dis•en•tan•gle v.t. to unravel; to untwist.

dis•es•tab•lish v.t. to deprive of established position. **-ment** n.

dis•fa•vor n. disapproval; v.t. to regard unfavorably.

dis•fig•ure v.t. to mar the appearance of; to deface; to deform. **-ment** n.

dis•frock v.t. to unfrock; to deprive of the right to wear clerical garb.

dis•gorge v.t. to eject from the throat; to hand over. **-ment** n.

dis•grace n. dishonor; discredit; shameful conduct; v.t. to bring dishonor to. **-ful** a.

dis•grun•tled a. vexed; sulky.

dis•guise v.t. to change the outward appearance of; to misrepresent; n.

dis•gust n. loathing; nausea; aversion; repugnance; v.t. **-edly** adv. **-ing** a.

dish n. a plate or shallow concave vessel for serving food; the food in such a vessel. v.t.

dis•ha•bille n. partial undress. Also **deshabille**.

dis·har·mo·ny n. lact of harmony; discord.

dis·heart·en v.t. to deprive of courage, confidence, or hope; to depress.

di·shevel v.t. to cause the hair or clothes to be untidy or unkempt; v.i. to spread in disorder. -ment n.

dis·hon·est a. lacking in honesty. -ly adv. -ty n.

dis·hon·or n. loss of honor; shame; indignity; v.t. to disgrace; -able a. -ableness n. -ably adv.

dis·il·lu·sion v.t. to make the truth apparent; n. -ment n.

dis·in·cline v.t. to excite dislike or aversion. disinclination n. unwillingness.

dis·in·fect v.t. to destroy disease germs. -ant n. disinfection n. -or n.

dis·in·her·it v.t. to deprive of rights and privileges of an heir. -ance n.

dis·in·te·grate v.t. to break up; v.i. to crumble to pieces. disintegration n.

dis·in·ter v.t. to disentomb; to unearth.

dis·in·ter·est·ed a. free from self-interest; unprejudiced. -ness n.

dis·join v.t. to sever; to disunite. -t v.t. to separate at the joints; v.i. to fall to pieces. -ted a. incoherent.

dis·junct a. disjoined. disjunction n. disconnection; -ive a.

disk, disc n. a flat circular plate or surface. -al a. — jockey n. announcer of a radio program of recorded music.

dis·like v.t. to have an aversion to; n. distaste; antipathy.

dis·lo·cate v.t. to put out of place or out of joint. dislocatedly adv. dislocation n.

dis·lodge v.t. to remove from a position of rest; v.i. dislodg(e)ment n.

dis·loy·al a. failing in duty or allegiance; faithless; treacherous. -ly adv. -ty n.

dis·mal a. gloomy; dreary; depressing; bleak. -ly adv. -ness, -ity n.

dis·man·tle v.t. to strip of furnishings; to take apart.

dis·may v.t. to alarm; n. loss of courage.

dis·mem·ber v.t. to tear limb from limb; to mutilate. -ment n.

dis·miss v.t. to send away; to disperse. -al n.

dis·mount v.i.; v.t. to bring down from a place of elevation.

dis·o·bey v.t. to refuse to do what is commanded. disobedient a. disobediently adv. disobedience n.

dis·o·blige v.t. to refuse to grant a request to. disobliging a. ungracious.

dis·or·der n. muddle; confusion; discomposure; v.t. to upset. -ed a. -ly a.

dis·or·gan·ize v.t. to upset the structure or regular system of; disorganic a. disorganization.

dis·own v.t. to repudiate ownership.

dis·par·age v.t. to belittle; to lower in rank or reputation. -ment n. unjust comparison.

dis·pa·rate a. essentially different. -ness n.

dis·par·i·ty n. difference in form, character, or degree; incongruity.

dis·pas·sion n. lack of feeling; serenity. -ate a. impartial.

dis·patch, despatch v.t. to send away; to execute promptly; to dispose of; n.

speed; the sending out of mails, etc. -er n.

dis·pel v.t. to drive away; to scatter; to cause to disappear. pr.p. -ling. pa.p., pa.t. -led.

dis·pense v.t. to divide out in parts; v.i. to excuse from; dispensable a. dispensary n. a place where medicines are made up and distributed. dispensation n. the act of distributing; a license to do what is normally prohibited. -r n. to dispense with, to do without.

dis·perse v.t. to scatter here and there; to spread; to distribute; v.i. to separate. dispersal n. dispersedly adv. dispersedness n. dispersion n. dispersive a.

dis·pir·it v.t. to deject; to depress; to discourage. -ed a.

dis·place v.t. to put out of position; to oust from situation or office. -able a. Displaced Persons, homeless war victims. -ment n. the weight of water displaced by a floating ship.

dis·play v.t. to unfold; to set out conspicuously; n. exhibition; exaggerated expression of feeling.

dis·please v.t. and v.i. to offend; to cause dissatisfaction to. displeasure n. slight anger; dislike.

dis·pose v.t. to arrange; to regulate; to adjust; v.i. to settle; to determine. disposable a. free to be disposed of. disposal n. control; regulation. disposed a. inclined; arranged. disposedly adv. disposition n. arrangement. to dispose of, to get rid of.

dis·pos·sess v.t. to put out of possession; to deprive of property; to eject. -ion n. -or n.

dis·proof n. the act of disproving; refutation; a proving to be erroneous.

dis·pro·por·tion n. want of proportion, symmetry, proper quantity; v.t. to mismatch. -able, -al, -ate, -ed a.

dis·prove v.t. to prove to be false; to refute; to prove the opposite of.

dis·pute v.t. to debate; to argue; to discuss; n. an argument; a debate. disputable a. disputably adv. disputability n. disputant n. one who takes part in a dispute. disputation n. a controversy in words. disputatious, disputative a.

dis·qual·i·fy v.t. to make unfit for some special purpose; to make ineligible. disqualification n.

dis·qui·et v.t. to disturb; to make restless; n. apprehensiveness; -ment, -ude n. uneasiness.

dis·qui·si·tion n. a formal enquiry into a subject by argument or discussion. -al, -ary a.

dis·re·gard v.t. to take no notice of; to ignore; n. indifference.

dis·re·pair n. state of being out of repair; delapidation.

dis·re·pute n. discredit; state of being unpopular. disreputable a. disreputableness n.

dis·re·spect n. want of respect or deference; rudeness. -ful a. -fully adv.

dis·robe v.t. to undress.

dis·rupt v.t. to break; to create a schism.

disruption n. breach. **disruptive** a. **disrupture** n. a bursting asunder.

dis·sat·is·fy v.t. to fail to satisfy; to make discontented. **dissatisfaction** n.

dis·sect v.t. to cut up; to divide for minute examination of its parts. **dissection** n. -or n.

dis·sem·ble v.t. to disguise; to ignore; v.i. to give an erroneous impression; to be hypocritical. -r n.

dis·sem·i·nate v.t. to scatter abroad; to broadcast; **dissemination** n. scattering; circulation. **disseminative** a. **disseminator** n.

dis·sent v.i. to differ in opinion; to disagree; n. disagreement; nonconformity. **dissension** n. quarrelling; discord. -er n.

dis·ser·tate v.i. to discourse. **dissertation** n. a formal treatise or discourse.

dis·serve v.i. to serve badly another's interests. **disservice** n. injury; harm.

dis·sev·er v.t. to separate; to disunite. -ance, -ation, -ment n.

dis·si·dent a. differing; disagreeing; n. a dissenter. **dissidence** n.

dis·sim·i·lar a. unlike. **dissimilarity**, **dissimilitude** n.; **difference**. -ly adv.

dis·sim·u·late v.t. to feign; v.i. to conceal one's true feelings; to be hypocritical. **dissimulation** n. the act of pretending.

dis·si·pate v.t. to scatter; to squander; to dispel; v.t. to disappear. -d a. dissolute. **dissipation** n. **dissipative** a.

dis·so·ci·ate v.t. to separate; to disunite; to disclaim connection with. **dissociability** n. **dissociable** a. incongruous. **dissocial** a. anti-social. **dissociation** n. separation. **dissociative** a.

dis·sol·u·ble a. capable of being dissolved, liquefied, melted, or decomposed.

dis·so·lute a. lax in morals; dissipated. -ly adv. -ness n. **dissolution** n. act of dissolving or passing into solution; disintegration; termination.

dis·solve v.t. to break up, esp. a solid by the action of a liquid; to terminate; to annul; v.i. to melt; to waste away. **dissolvability**, **dissolvableness** n. **dissolvable** a. **dissolvent** a.

dis·so·nant a. discordant; harsh; unharmonious. **dissonance** n. Also **dissonancy**.

dis·suade v.t. to persuade not to; to advise against. -r n. **dissuasion** n. **dissuasive** a.

dis·taff n. a cleft stick for holding the fiber from which thread is made in the process of hand spinning. **the distaff side**, the female line.

dis·tance n. the space between two objects; the interval between two events; remoteness; v.t. to outstrip; to surpass. **distant** a. far off; aloof. **distantly** adv.

dis·taste n. dislike; aversion. -ful a. unpleasant.

dis·tem·per n. a method of painting (also called *tempera*) with pigments, in powder form, mixed with any glutinous substance soluble in water; v.t. to paint in distemper.

dis·tem·per n. a disordered state of mind or body; a highly infectious inflammatory disease in young dogs.

dis·tend v.t. to stretch out; to swell; to inflate. v.i. to become swollen or puffed out. **distensible** a. **distention**, **distension** n.

dis·till v.t. to vaporize and recondense a liquid; to cause to fall in drops; to cause to trickle; v.i. to undergo distillation. -ate n. the essence produced by distilling. -ation n. -atory a. used in distilling. -er n. -ery n. a place where distilling is carried on.

dis·tinct a. of marked difference; separate; clear; well-defined; precise. **distinction** n. that which indicates individuality. -ive a. marking distinction. -ively adv. -iveness n. -ness n.

dis·tin·guish v.t. to observe the difference between; to keep apart; to give individuality to; v.i. to make distinctions. -ed a. eminent; dignified. -ing a. characteristic.

dis·tort v.t. to twist out of shape; to misrepresent. -ed a. -edly adv. **distortion** n. a twisting awry; misrepresentation.

dis·tract v.t. to divert; to bewilder; to disturb mentally. -ed a. -edly adv. -edness n. **distraction** n. -ive a. **distraught** a. perplexed; bewildered; frantic.

dis·train v.t. to seize goods, esp. to enforce payment of debt. -ment, -t n. -or, -er n.

dis·tress n. extreme pain; misfortune; extreme poverty; v.t. to cause pain or anguish to. -ful a. -fully adv. **distressed area**, a part of the country where unemployment is rife.

dis·tri·bute v.t. to divide among several; to allot or hand out. **distributable** a. **distribution** n. **distributive** a. **distributor(-er)** n.

dis·trict n. an administrative division of a country; a. local; v.t. to divide into specified areas.

dis·trust v.t. to have no faith in; to suspect; n. doubt.

dis·turb v.t. to upset the normal condition of; to disquiet; to agitate. -ance n. confusion.

dis·un·ion n. discord; dissension. **disunite** v.t. to cause a breach between. **disunity** n.

dis·use n. cessation of use or practice.

di·syl·la·ble n. a word of two syllables. Also **dissyllable**.

ditch n. a trench dug esp. for drainage or defense; a natural waterway; v.t. to cut a ditch in; v.i. to make a forced 'landing' on the sea.

dith·er n. a state of nervous agitation or confusion.

dit·to n. that which has been said; the same; — symbol:", placed below thing to be repeated; adv. as aforesaid; v.t. to copy.

dit·ty n. a song; a short poem to be sung.

dit·ty bag n. a small bag used by soldiers and sailors for holding needles, thread, etc. **ditty box** n.

di·u·ret·ic a. exciting the discharge of urine; n. a medicine which tends to increase the flow of urine. **diuresis** n. excessive urinary excretion.

di·ur·nal *a.* belonging to the day; daily. -ly *adv.*

di·va *n.* a popular female singer.

di·va·lent *a.* (*Chem.*) capable of combining with two radicals; bivalent.

di·van *n.* a long cushioned seat; a council room; a smoking room.

dive *v.i.* to plunge into water head first; to remain under water; to penetrate deeply into; *n.* a plunge head-first. **diving bell** *n.* an apparatus by which deep-sea divers can work under water.

di·verge *v.i.* to turn in different directions; to differ. -ment, -nce, -ncy *n.* -nt *a.* branching off. -ntly *adv.*

di·vers *a.* several; sundry. **diverse** *a.* of different kinds. **diversely** *adv.* **diversity** *n.*

di·ver·si·fy *v.t.* to give variety to.

di·vert *v.t.* to turn aside; to alter the direction of; to amuse or entertain. **diversion** *n.* -ing *a.* **divertissement** *n.* a diversion; a short ballet or interlude between the acts of a play.

di·vest *v.t.* to strip; to dispossess. -iture, -ment *n.*

di·vide *v.t.* to separate into parts; to share; to keep apart; to find how many times one number is contained in another; *v.i.* to be separated. *n.* a watershed. -rs *n.pl.* compasses for measuring or dividing lines.

div·i·dend *n.* the sum to be divided by the divisor to obtain the quotient; interest payable on loans; the share of profits paid to holders of stocks, insurance, etc.

di·vine *a.* belonging to or having the nature of God, or a god; holy; sacred; heavenly; *n.* a clergyman; *v.t.* and *v.i.* to forecast by supernatural means. **divination** *n.* the art or act of foretelling the future by non-rational methods. **divinator, diviner** *n.* -ly *adv.* -ness *n.* **divining rod**, a forked twig used to locate underground water. **divinity** *n.* God; the study of theology.

di·vi·sion *n.* part of a whole; a section; difference in opinion. **divisibility** *n.* **divisible** *a.* -al, **divisionary** *a.* pert. to or belonging to a division. **divisor** *n.* the number by which another is divided.

di·vorce *n.* the legal dissolution of a marriage contract; *v.t.* to separate; to sever. **divorcee** *n.* a divorced person. -ment *n.*

div·ot *n.* (*Golf*) a piece of turf cut out accidentally by golfer.

di·vulge *v.t.* to disclose something secret or unknown; **divulgate** *v.t.* to publish. -ment, -nce *n.*

Dixie *n.* the Southern States of the U.S.

diz·zy *a.* giddy; light-headed; stupid; *v.t.* to make dizzy. **dizzily** *adv.* **dizziness** *n.* vertigo.

do (*Mus.*) the first tone of the major diatonic scale.

do *v.t.* to perform; to execute; to finish; to prepare; *v.i.* to act. *pr.p.* -ing. *pa.t.* did. *pa.p.* done. *n.* to do away with, to destroy. -er *n.* an agent. to do in, to murder. -ings *n.pl.* things done; activities. **done-out** *a.* exhausted.

dob·bin *n.* a name for patient, quiet workhorse.

do·cent *n.* a teacher in a university below professorial rank.

doc·ile *a.* easily instructed or managed. -ly *adv.*

dock *v.t.* to cut short; to deduct; *n.* the part of tail left after clipping.

dock *n.* wharf, or row of piers where ships are berthed; enclosed space in a law court where accused stands. -age *n.* space available in docks for ships; charge made for use of docks. -er *n.* one who works at the docks. -yard, *n.* **dry dock**, *n.*

dock·et *n.* a list of cases for trial; a memorandum; a bill or label affixed to goods giving instructions; *v.t.* to summarize.

doc·tor *n.* one who holds the highest degree granted by any faculty of a university; a medical practitioner; *v.t.* to falsify; *v.i.* to practice medicine; to take medicine. -ate *n.* -ship *n.* -ial *a.*

doc·trine *n.* principle of belief; instruction. **doctrinal** *a.* **doctrinally** *adv.* **doctrinaire** *n.* a theorist who tends to urge the application of a doctrine beyond all practical considerations; *a.* impracticable.

doc·u·ment *n.* an official paper containing information, giving instructions, or establishing facts; *v.t.* to furnish with written evidence of. -al, **documentary** *a.* -ation *n.* -ed *a.*

dod·der *v.t.* or *v.i.* to totter or tremble, as with age. -ing *a.*

do·dec·a·gon *n.* a plane figure with twelve sides and twelve angles. -al *a.*

dodge *v.t.* to evade or escape by a sudden turning; *v.i.* to twist aside; *n.* a quick, evasive movement; a trick; -r *n.*

do·do *n.* an extinct flightless bird. *pl.* -(e)s.

doe *n.* the female of the fallow deer; antelope, rabbit, goat, rat, mouse. -skin *n.* a fine close-woven cloth.

does *3rd pers. sing. pr. ind.* of verb **do**.

doff *v.t.* to take off; to rid oneself of.

dog *n.* a common, carnivorous quadruped of the same genus as the wolf, mainly domesticated; a worthless fellow; one of the two constellations of stars (*Canis Major, Canis Minor*); a metal bar for holding logs of wood or supporting fire-irons; *v.t.* to pursue relentlessly. *pr.p.* -ging. *pa.p.* -ged. —collar. — **days** *n.pl.* the hottest period of the northern summer. —**eared** *a.* having the corners of the pages turned down. -ged *a.* stubborn; persistent. -gedly *adv.* -gedness *n.* -gish *a.* surly. -gy *a.* -house *n.* -like *a.* faithful. —tired, *a.* completely exhausted. -tooth, *n.* a canine tooth. -watch *n.* one of the two-hour watches on board ship from 4-6 or 6-8 p.m. **a dog in the manger**, a spoil-sport. **a hot dog**, a hot sausage inside a roll. **in the doghouse**, in disfavor. **to go to the dogs**, to be ruined. **to let sleeping dogs lie**, not to stir up trouble unnecessarily.

dog·ger·el *n.* unpoetical burlesque verse; *a.*

dog·ma *n.* a philosophical tenet; a

principle or belief. **dogmatic, -al,** *a.* opinionated; authoritative. **dogmatically** *adv.* **dogmatics** *n.* doctrinal theology. **-tize** *v.i.* to express an opinion positively or arrogantly. **-tism** *n.* positive assertion. **-tist** *n.*

doi·ly *n.* a small table mat placed under dishes or put on plate.

dol·ce *a.* sweet; soft.

dol·drums *n.pl.* a belt of calms at the Equator; a state of depression.

dole *v.t.* to distribute in small portions; *n.* something given or paid out.

dole·ful *a.* grievous; melancholic. **-ly** *adv.* **-ness** *n.*

doll *n.* a puppet; a toy baby as a child's plaything; a pretty, rather brainless girl. **to doll up** to dress up smartly.

dol·lar *n.* a silver coin or paper note, the monetary unit of U.S.A. and Canada.

dol·lop *n.* a lump, a shapeless mass.

doll·y *n.* a mobile platform; a small locomotive used in quarries, etc. **dollied** *a.*

dol·man *n.* a long, loose Turkish garment; Hussar's coat worn like a cape.

dol·men *n.* a prehistoric tomb formed by a large unhewn stone resting on two or

dolmen

more unhewn uprights.

dol·or·ous *a.* full of, expressing, or causing grief. **-ly** *adv.*

dol·phin *n.* a sea mammal; a mooring buoy.

dolphin

dolt *n.* a dull, stupid fellow. **-ish** *a.* **-ishly** *adv.*

do·main *n.* that which one has dominion over; property; the scope or sphere of any branch of human knowledge. **-al, dominial** *a.*

dome *n.* a hemispherical vault reared above the roof of a building; a large cupola. **-d, domical** *a.*

do·mes·tic *a.* pert. to a house or home; tame (of animals); not foreign (of a country's policy); *n.* a household servant. **-ally** *adv.* **-ate** *v.t.* **domesticity** *n.* life in a household. **— science,** science of home management, etc.

dom·i·cile *n.* an abode; a person's permanent residence; *v.t.* to establish in a fixed residence. **domiciliary** *a.*

dom·i·nant *a.* ruling; prevailing; *n.* the fifth note of the diatonic scale. **dominance** *n.* authority. **dominancy** *n.* **-ly** *adv.* **dominate** *v.t.* and *v.i.* to influence strongly. **domination** *n.* **dominative** *a.* **dominator** *n.* **domineer** *v.i.* to rule with arbitrary sway. **domineering** *a.* arrogant. **dominion** *n.* territory under one government.

do·min·i·cal *a.* belonging to the Lord's Day.

Do·min·i·can *a.* belonging to St. *Dominic,* or to the order of preaching friars, founded by him. *n.*

dom·i·no *n.* a long cloak of black silk with a hood, worn at masquerades; a mask; one of the 28 oblong pieces marked each with a certain number of spots used in the game of *dominoes.*

don *v.t.* to put on; to assume. *pr.p.* **-ning** *pa.p., pa.t.* **-ned.**

do·na·tion *n.* act of giving; a gift; a contribution. **donate** *v.t.* **donative** *n.* **donor** *n.*

done *pa.p.* of the verb **do. done!** agreed.

don·key *n.* an ass; a foolish person. **— engine** *n.* a small auxiliary steam engine.

don't contr. of **do not.**

doo·dle *v.i.* to scribble aimlessly.

doom *n.* fate; evil destiny; judgment; ruin; *v.t.* to destine; to pass sentence on; to condemn. **-ed** *a.* under sentence. **-ful** *a.* **-sday** *n.* the Day of Judgment. **Doomsday or Domesday Book,** the census compiled by order of William the Conqueror, for purposes of taxation.

door *n.* the wooden or metal structure, hinged or sliding, giving access to house, room, passage, or cupboard. **dead as a door nail** quite dead. **-post** *n.* the jamb. **-step** *n.* the step outside a door. **-way** *n.* the entrance to a house, room, etc. **to darken one's door,** to enter one's house.

dope *n.* any thick liquid, or semi-liquid lubricant; a varnish; any narcotic; a stupid person; inside information; *v.t.* to administer dope to. **dopey** *a.* stupefied with drugs; slow-witted.

Do·ri·an *a.* pert. to *Doris,* in ancient Greece, or to its inhabitants. **Doric,** *a.* pert. to the simple style of architecture of the Dorians; (of dialect) unpolished; *n.* a mode of Greek music.

dor·mant *a.* sleeping; hibernating; not in action. **dormancy** *n.* **dormer-window** *n.* a small vertical window projecting from a roof slope. **dormitory** *n.* a building primarily containing sleeping rooms. **dormouse** *n.* a small, hibernating rodent.

dor·sal *a.* pert. to, near, or belonging to, the back.

do·ry *n.* a flat-bottomed boat.

dose *n.* the prescribed quantity of medicine to be taken at one time; anything disagreeable that must be taken or done; *v.t.* dosage *n.* the amount of a dose. **dosimeter** *n.* an instrument for measuring minute doses accurately.

dos·si·er *n.* a set of documents.

dot *n.* a small point or spot made with a pencil, or sharp instrument; a speck; *v.t.* to mark with dots; *v.i.* *pr.p.* **-ting.** *pa.p.* **-ted. -ty** *a.* **dot and dash,** in Morse code, the short and long symbols.

dot *n.* a dowry. **dotal** *a.*

dote *v.i.* to be foolishly sentimental; to be over-fond of. **dotage** *n.* childishness of old people; senility. **dotard** *n.* one whose intellect is impaired by old age.

dou·ble *a.* denoting two things of the same

kind; existing in pairs; serving for two; deceitful; ambiguous; *adv.* twice; *v.t.* to fold in two; *v.i.* to increase to twice as much; *n.* a duplicate; an actor's substitute or understudy. — **bass** *n.* the largest and lowest pitched of the stringed instruments. —**breasted** *a.* able to fasten over on either side. — **cross** *v.t.* to cheat a swindler. —**dealing** *n.* —**decker** *n.* a ship or bus with two decks. —**edged** *a.* having two edges; effective for and against. — **entry** *n.* in bookkeeping, a system by which every entry is made both on debit and credit side of an account. —**faced** *a.* hypocritical. **-r** *n.*

doublet *n.* one of a pair; a close-fitting garment for the upper part of body. — **time** *n.* the fastest marching pace next to a run.

doubt *v.t.* to disbelieve; *v.i.* to be in a state of uncertainty; to hesitate; *n.* uncertainty of mind; distrust of others. **-able** *a.* **-er** *n.* **-ful** *a.* dubious; uncertain. **-fully** *adv.* **-fulness** *n.* **-ing** *a.* **-ingly** *adv.* **-less** *adv.* without doubt; probably. **-lessly** *adv.*

douche *n.* a jet of water directed upon or into the body; an apparatus for douching.

dough *n.* a mass of flour moistened and kneaded, to be baked afterwards; money. **-boy** *n.* an infantryman. **-nuts** *n.* sweetened dough in shape of balls or rings, fried in fat and finally dipped in sugar. **-y** *a.*

dough•ty *a.* brave; valiant. **doughtily** *adv.*

dour *a.* sullen; gloomy; obstinate. **-ly** *adv.*

douse, dowse *v.t.* to dip or plunge into water; to lower a sail; to put out.

dove *n.* a pigeon; a symbol of peace or of the Holy Ghost. —**colored** *a.* soft pinkish grey. **-cot(e)** *n.* nesting box of pigeons. **-tail** *n.* a joint made by fitting

dovetail
joint

one piece toothed with wedge like projections into cavities of corresponding shape; *v.t.* to link together.

dow•a•ger *n.* widow with property or title left by her husband; a dignified elderly lady.

dow•dy *a.* untidy; lacking style. **dowdily** *adv.* **dowdiness** *n.*

dow•el *n.* a wooden or iron pin for joining two adjacent boards or stones.

dow•er *n.* a widow's share of her husband's property; gift; talent. **-ed** *a.* **-less** *a.* **dowry** *n.* goods given to the husband by the bride or her family at marriage.

down *n.* the fine, soft feathers of birds. **-y** *a.* resembling or covered with down.

down *n.* a hillock of sand by the sea; treeless land.

down *prep.* along a descent; towards a lower place; towards the mouth of a river; passing from the past to less remote times; *adv.* in a downward direction; to the bottom; *v.t.* to knock down; *n.* a reversal of fortune. **-cast** *a.* depressed. **-fall** *n.* ruin; a heavy fall of rain. **-fallen** *a.* **-hearted** *a.* despondent.

-hill *a.*; *adv.* **-pour** *n.* a heavy fall of water. **-right** *adv.* completely; *a.* unqualified. **-stairs** *adv.*; *n.* the ground floor. **-stream** *adv.* with the current. **-trodden** *a.* oppressed. **-ward** *a.* **-wards** *adv.* —**town;** towards the center of the town.

dowse *v.t.* and *v.i.* to find subterranean water supply by means of a divining rod. **-r** *n.*

dox•ol•o•gy *n.* a short hymn of praise to God.

doze *v.i.* to sleep lightly; *n.* a nap.

doz•en *n.*; *a.* twelve. **baker's dozen, devil's dozen,** thirteen.

drab *n.* a dingy, brownish-grey color; *a.* dull; monotonous.

drach•ma *n.* a Greek coin.

draft *n.* a sketch or rough copy; a current of air; an order directing payment of money by a bank; a drink. *v.t.* to compose and write; to take for military service. **-sman** *n.* **-smanship** *n.* **-y** *a.* **-iness** *n.*

drag *v.t.* to draw with main force; to trawl with a drag or net; *v.i.* to move heavily or slowly. *pr.p.* **-ging.** *pa.p.* **-ged.** *n.* a net or hook to bring up submerged things; anything that slows progress. **-ger** *n.* **-net** *n.* a fishing net for dragging along the sea floor.

drag•gle *v.t.* and *v.i.* to make or become wet and dirty by trailing on the ground.

dra•gon *n.* a fabulous winged reptile represented as breathing out fire and smoke. **-et** *n.* a little dragon. **-fly** *n.* an insect. **-'s blood,** a carmine fruit resin used for coloring varnishes and lacquers.

dra•goon *n.* a cavalryman; *v.t.* to oppress.

drain *v.t.* to filter; to make dry; to swallow down; to exhaust; *v.i.* to flow off or drip away gradually; *n.* a pipe, sewer or ditch; **-able** *a.* **-age** *n.* system of carrying away surplus water from an area. **-er** *n.* a kitchen utensil on which plates, etc. are placed to dry; a colander or sieve.

drake *n.* the male of the duck.

dram *n.* a unit of weight; ⅛ of an ounce.

dra•ma *n.* a composition to be acted on the stage; the branch of literature dealing with plays; a series of real emotional events. **dramatic** *a.* tense. **dramatically** *adv.* **dramatization** *n.* **dramatize** *v.t.* **dramatist** *n.* a writer of plays. **-turge** *n.* **-turgy** *n.* the art of writing or producing plays. **dramatis personae** characters of a drama.

drank *pa.t.* of drink.

drape *v.t.* to hang something loosely in folds; to adorn with drapery. **drapery** *n.*

dras•tic *a.* very powerful; harsh; thorough.

drat *interj.* a mild expletive expressing annoyance.

draught *n.* **-s** *n.pl.* the game of checkers; *a.* drawn from a barrel, as beer. **-(s)man** *n.* See **draft.**

draw *v.t.* to pull along; to haul towards oneself; to deduce; to receive (as money, salary, etc.); to inhale; to sketch; *v.i.* to attract; to pull out a weapon for action; to be equal in a match; to cast lots; to have a free passage of air (as a chimney). *pr.p.* **-ing.** *pa.t.* **drew.** *pa.p.* **-n.** *n.* a game ending with same score for both sides. -able *a*. -back *n*. a disadvantage. -bridge *n*. a bridge that can be raised or let down. -er *n*. one who or that which draws; a lidless, sliding box in a table, chest, etc. -ers *n.pl*. close fitting undergarment for lower limbs. -ing *n*. a lottery; the art of representing objects by line or color on paper, canvas, etc. -ing-room *n*. a room in which guests are entertained. **to draw a blank**, to fail to find what one is seeking. **to draw the line**, to stop. **drawn and quartered** quartered and disemboweled.

drawl *v.i*. to speak with slow and lengthened tone; *v.t*.; *n*. a manner of speech.

dray *n*. a low cart for heavy goods.

dread *n*. overwhelming apprehension; awe; terror; *a*. dreadful; *v.t*. and *v.i*. to regard with fear; -ed *a*. -ful *a*. terrifying; -fully *adv*. -fulness *n*. -nought *n*. a large-sized battleship mounting heavy guns; a thick woolen overcoat.

dream *n*. a series of images or thoughts in the mind of a person asleep; a vision; an aspiration; *v.i*. to have yearnings; *v.t*. to see in a dream; *pa.t*. and *p.p*. -ed or -t. -er *n*. -ily *adv*. -iness *n*. -land *n*. an imaginary land seen in dreams. -less *a*. -like *a*. -y *a*.

drear•y *a*. dismal; gloomy; bleak. **drearily** *adv*. **dreariness** *n*. (*Poetic*) **drear** *a*.

dredge *v.t*. to sprinkle. -r *n*. a flour can with perforated lid.

dredge *n*. a machine like a large scoop for taking up mud from a river bed; a dragnet for oysters or zoological specimens.

dregs *n.pl*. sediment in a liquid that falls to the bottom; the most worthless class.

drench *v.t*. to wet thoroughly; to soak.

dress *v.t*. and *v.i*. to put clothes on; to adorn; *n*. clothes. -er *n*. a dressing table or bureau. -ing *n*- a sterile substance for a wound; manure; substance used to stiffen fabrics; a sauce; stuffing for a fowl. -ing-down *n*. a scolding. -ing gown *n*. a robe worn while dressing. -ing table *n*. -maker *n*. -making *n*. -y *a*. fashionable.

drew *pa.t*. of draw.

drib•ble *v.i*. to trickle down, esp. of saliva; to bounce the ball repeatedly. **driblet** *n*. a small drop.

dried *pa.t*. and *pa.p*. of verb **dry**.

drift *n*. the state or process of being driven; the accumulation of substance driven by the wind; a slow surface current in the sea caused usually by the prevailing wind; tendency; *v.t*. to drive into heaps; to cause to float in a certain direction; *v.i*. to follow unconsciously. -age *n*. deviation of a ship from its course. — **anchor** *n*. an anchor for keeping a ship's head to the wind during a storm. -er *n*. an aimless wanderer. -wood *n*. wood cast on shore by tide.

drill *v.t*. to pierce; to bore a hole through; to instruct thoroughly; *n*. revolving tool for boring holes; an implement for making holes for seed; instruction. **drilling** *n*.

drink *v.t*. to swallow; to empty as a glass; to

breathe in. *pa.t*., *pa.p*. **drunk**. *n*. intoxicating liquor. -able *a*. -er *n*. a tippler. **to drink in**, to absorb through the senses.

drip *v.t*.; *v.i*. to ooze; to trickle. *pr.p*. -ping. *pa.t*., *pa.p*. -ped. *n*. a drop; the sound made by water dripping. -ping *a*. thoroughly wet; *n*. that which falls in drops; *pl*. fat, from meat while roasting. -stone *n*. a projecting molding over doors to deflect rain water.

drive *v.t*. to urge on; to guide the course of; to cause to work; to strike in, as a nail; to hit a ball with force; *v.i*. to be forced along. *pr.p*. **driving**. *pa.t*. **drove**. *pa.p*. **driven**. *n*. the capacity for getting things done. -r *n*. a golf club for hitting ball from the tee. **to drive at**, to hint at.

driv•el *v.i*. to dribble like a child; to talk nonsense; *n*. nonsense. -er *n*.

driz•zle *v.t*. and *v.i*. to rain gently; *n*. fine rain.

droit *n*. legal right.

droll *a*. laughable; funny; queer; *n*. a buffoon; a jester; an odd character. -ery *n*.

drom•e•dar•y *n*. a one-humped camel.

dromedary

drone *n*. the male of the honey-bee; an idler who lives on the work of others; a deep, humming sound; the largest pipe of the bagpipes; *v.t*. and *v.i*. to speak or sing in a monotone.

drool *v.i*. to drivel; to speak foolishly.

droop *v.i*. to hang down; to grow weak; to sag; to wilt (as flowers); *v.t*. to lower.

drop *n*. a globular particle of fluid that falls; a minute quantity of fluid in medical dose; *v.t*. to let fall; to dismiss or break off; (of animals) to give birth to prematurely; *v.i*. to sink to a lower level. *pr.p*. -ping. *pa.t*. and *pa.p*. -ped. — **curtain** *n*. a painted curtain lowered in front of theater stage between scenes in a play. —**kick** *n*. a kick effected by letting the ball fall from the hands to the ground to be kicked immediately on the rebound. -let *n*. a tiny drop. -per *n*. a small glass tube from which liquid is measured out in drops. -pings *n.pl*. dung. **to drop in**, to make an informal visit. **a drop in the bucket**, a small amount.

drop•sy *n*. a morbid collection of fluid in any part of body. **dropsical** *a*.

dross *n*. the scum of metals thrown off in smelting; refuse.

drought, drouth *n*. dryness; absence of rain over a prolonged period. -iness *n*. -y *a*.

drove *n*. a herd or flock, esp. on the move. -r *n*. one who drives cattle or sheep.

drown *v.t*. to suffocate by submerging in water; to deluge; to render inaudible; *v.i*.

drowse *v.t*. to make sleepy; *v.i*. be heavy with sleep; *n*. a doze. **drowsy** *a*. **drowsily**

adv. **drowsiness** *n.*

drub *v.t.* to beat; *v.i.* to defeat. *pr.p.* -**bing.** *pa.p., pa.t.* -**bed.** -**bing** *n.* a thrashing.

drudge *v.i.* to labor at menial tasks; *n.* one who must do menial work. **drudgery** *n.* hard, monotonous, toil. **drudgingly** *adv.*

drug *n.* any substance used in the composition of a medicine; a narcotic; *v.t.; v.i.* to take drugs habitually and in excess. *pr.p.* -**ging.** *pr.p.* -**ged.** -**gist** *n.* a pharmaceutical chemist.

drum *n.* a percussion instrument comprising a hollow, parchment-covered cylinder beaten with a drumstick; the middle portion of ear; *v.t.* to teach by constant repetition; *v.i.* to beat rhythmically. *pr.p.* -**ming** *pa.p., pa.t.* -**med.** — **major** *n.* the leader of a marching drum corps or band. -**mer** *n.* -**stick** *n.* lower part of leg of cooked fowl.

drunk *pa.p.* of **drink;** *a.* intoxicated; *n.* a drunk person. -**ard** *n.* one who habitually drinks to excess. -**en** *a.* given to excessive drinking. -**enness** *n.*

drupe *n.* a fleshy fruit, such as peach, with a stone or kernel containing the seed.

dry *a.* free from moisture; not giving milk, as a cow; thirsty; unsweetened, as wines; uninteresting; sarcastic; plain; pert. to a district subject to prohibition laws; *v.t.* to drain; *v.i.* to evaporate; to become void of ideas. **drier** *n.* — **battery** *n.* a battery composed of *dry cells* sealed in a container to prevent leakage. **to dry clean,** to clean garments with chemicals. — **goods** *n.pl.* textile fabrics. -**ly, drily** *adv.* — **measure,** a measure of bulk, used for grain, etc. -**ness** *n.* — **rot** *n.* a decay caused by fungous disease. —**shod** *a.* with dry feet.

dry•ad *n.* in Greek mythology a spirit of the trees.

du•al *a.* consisting of two; *n.* the dual number. **duad** *n.* pair of things regarded as one. -**ism** *n.* the belief in the existence of good and evil as separate entities. -**ist** *n.* -**ity** *n.* state of being double.

dub *v.t.* to knight; to give a nickname to; to make smooth; to provide a film with a sound track not in the original language. *pr.p.* -**bing.** *pa.p.* and *pa.t.* -**bed.**

du•bi•ous *a.* doubtful; liable to turn out well or ill; shady. -**ly** *adv.* -**ness** *n.* **dubiety** *n.* hesitancy; uncertainty. **dubitable** *a.* doubtful. **dubitancy, dubitation** *n.*

du•cal *a.* pert. to a duke. -**ly** *adv.* in a ducal manner. **ducat** *n.* a coin. **duce** *n.* leader, **duchess** *n.* the wife or widow of a duke. **duchy** *n.* dominions of dukes.

duch•ess *n.* See **ducal.**

duck *n.* a coarse cloth or light canvas. -**s** *n.pl.* trousers made of this.

duck *n.* any broad-beaked, web-footed, short-legged water bird; female duck; a sudden lowering of head; *v.i.* to cringe; *v.i.* to dodge. -**board** *n.* planking to cross swampy areas. **duckling** *n.* a young duck. -**pins,** small bowling pins. -**weed** *n.* minute, floating, green plants growing on all standing waters.

duct *n.* a canal or tube for conveying fluids.

-**less glands** endocrine glands which discharge their secretions directly into the blood.

duc•tile *a.* (of metals) capable of being drawn out in fine threads or hammered thin; easily influenced. **ductility** *n.*

dud *n.* anything defective or worthless; *n.pl.* clothes, esp. old and sloppy.

dudg•eon *n.* anger; resentment.

due *a.* fitting to be paid or done to another; appointed to arrive; attributable; *adv.* directly; *n.* that which is owed. **duly** *adv.* properly.

du•el *n.* any two-sided contest; *v.i.* to fight a duel. -**ist** *n.*

du•et *n.* a musical composition for two performers. -**ist** *n.*

duff *v.t.* to make old things look like new; to fake. -**er** *n.* a poor player.

duf•fel, duffle *n.* a coarse woolen cloth with a thick nap. — **bag** *n.* a canvas bag used for carrying clothes, etc.

dug *n.* a teat, esp. of an animal.

dug *pa.t.* and *pa.p.* of **dig.** -**out** *n.* a canoe hollowed out of a tree trunk; covered shelter for players not on field.

duke *n.* (*fem.* **duchess**) the highest order of nobility in the British peerage. -**dom** *n.* possessions of a duke. See **ducal.**

dul•cet *a.* sweet to the ear; melodious.

dul•ci•mer *n.* an old musical instrument probably like a small harp; a modern instrument related to the guitar.

dull *a.* stupid; slow of hearing or seeing; tedious; uninspired; dim or cloudy; blunt; *v.t.* to stupefy; to mitigate; *v.i.* to become dull. -**ard** *n.* a slow-witted person. -**ness** *n.*

dulse *n.* an edible reddish-brown seaweed.

du•ly See **due.**

dumb *a.* lacking permanently the power of speech; mute; *v.t.* to silence. -**bell** *n.* two heavy iron balls connected by a bar for a handle, used in gymnastic exercises; moron. -**ly** *adv.* in silence. -**ness** *n.* —**waiter** *n.* a hand-operated elevator. **dum(b)found** *v.t.* to amaze; -**ed** *a.* **dummy** *a.* sham; *n.* a tailor's mannequin.

dum-dum *n.* a soft nosed bullet.

dump *v.t.* to deposit; to unload; *n.* refuse or scrap heap; a poorly kept up place. -**ling** *n.* a ball of dough boiled in water. -**y** *a.* short; thick; squat. -**iness** *n.* — **truck** *n.* a truck whose body tilts and end opens for unloading.

dun *a.* greyish-brown color; dark; *n.*

dun *v.t.* to importune for payment of a debt. *pr.p.* -**ning.** *pa.p.* -**ned.**

dunce *n.* one who is slow at learning.

dune *n.* a low hill of sand in desert areas or on the seacoast.

dung *n.* the excrement of animals; *v.t.* to treat with manure; *v.i.* -**hill** *n.* a mound of dung.

dun•ga•ree *n.* a coarse hard-wearing cotton cloth. -**s** *n.pl.* trousers of this material.

dun•geon *n.* orig. the principal tower or 'keep' of a castle; a damp subterranean prison cell; *v.t.* to confine in a dungeon.

dunk *v.t.* to dip into tea, coffee, soup, etc.

du•o *n.* a duet; a pair of stage artists.

du•o•de•cen•ni•al *a.* occurring every

D

twelve years. **duodenary** *a.* pert. to 12.
du•o•dec•i•mo *n.* a 12 mo. book.
duodecimal *a.* proceeding by twelves; *n.*
duodecimals *n.pl.* a method of
computation by denominations of 12
instead of 10. **duodecimally** *adv.*
du•o•de•num *n.* upper part of intestines;
pl. **duodena. duodenal** *a.*
dupe *n.* one who is easily cheated; *v.t.* to
cheat; to mislead. **-ry** *n.*
du•plex *a.* twofold; *n.* a house consisting of
two family units. **duple** *a.* double.
du•pli•cate *a.* double; *n.* an exact copy;
facsimile; *v.t.* to make a copy.
duplication *n.* **duplicator** *n.* a machine for
making copies of written matter.
duplicity *n.* deception.
du•ra•ble *a.* lasting; able to resist wear and
tear. **-ness, durability** *n.* **durably** *adv.*
durance *n.* confinement. **duration** *n.*
continuance in time.
du•ress *n.* compulsion; coercion.
dur•ing *prep.* in the time of; in course of.
dusk *a.* tending to darkness; *n.* twilight. **-y**
a. partially dark; dim; dark-skinned.
dust *n.* very fine particles of matter; *v.t.* to
remove dust from. **— jacket** *n.* a book
cover. **-er** *n.* a tin with perforated lid for
sprinkling; a light garment used as a
robe. **-ily** *adv.* **-iness** *n.* **-ing** *n.*
Dutch *a.* pert. to Holland; *n.* the language,
people of Holland. **-man** *n.* **— treat,** an
entertainment for which each person
pays his own share.
du•ty *n.* that which is due; military service;
a period of work set down for each
person on a roster. **duteous** *a.* obedient.
duteously *adv.* **dutiable** *a.* subject to
customs duties. Also **dutied. dutiful** *a.*
attentive to duty; submissive. **dutifully**

adv. **dutifulness** *n.* **—free** *a.* exempt from
customs duty.
dwarf *n.* abnormally small in size; *v.t.* to
hinder the growth of. **dwarf, -ish** *a.*
undersized.
dwell *v.i.* to abide; to be domiciled; to deal
with in detail. **-er** *n.* **-ing** *n.*
dwin•dle *v.i.* to shrink; *v.t.* to lessen.
dye *v.t.* to give a new color to; to stain; *v.i.*
to undergo change of color. *pr.p.* **-ing.**
pa.p. **-d** *n.* **-r** *n.* **-stuff** *n.* substance used
for dyeing.
dy•ing *pr.p.* of die.
dyke *n.* See dike.
dy•nam•ic *a.* possessing energy and
forcefulness. Also **-al. -s** *n.* branch of
mechanics which deals with *force in
motion.* **dynamism** *n.* a school of
scientific thought which explains
phenomena of universe as resulting from
action of natural forces. **dynamist** *n.*
dynamite *n.* a powerful high explosive,
with great disruptive force; *v.t.*
dynamiter *n.* one who uses dynamite.
dynamo *n.* a generator for transforming
mechanical energy into electrical energy;
pl. **dynamos. dynamo-graph** *n.*
dynamometer *n.* an instrument for
measuring force.
dy•nas•ty *n.* a line of kings of the same
family; the period of a family's rule.
dynast *n.* a ruler. **dynastic** *a.*
dyne *n.* a centimeter-gram-second unit of
force.
dys- *prefix* fr. Gk. meaning bad, ill,
difficult.
dys•en•ter•y *n.* inflammation of the
mucous membrane of the large intestine.
dysenteric, -al *a.*
dys•pep•sia *n.* indigestion. **dyspeptic** *a.*; *n.*

each *a.* and *pron.* denoting every one of a number, separately considered. Abbrev. **ea.**

ea•ger *a.* yearning; earnest. **-ly** *adv.* **-ness** *n.*

ea•gle *n.* large bird of prey; *(Golf)* a hole played in two under par. **—eyed** *a.* sharp-sighted. **-t** *n.* a young eagle.

ear *n.* the organ of hearing, esp. external part of it; sensitiveness to musical

ear

sounds. **-ache** *n.* acute pain in ear. **-drum** *n.* the middle ear or tympanum. **-ed** *a.* **-lobe** *n.* **-mark** *v.t.* to reserve for a particular purpose. **-shot** *n.* distance at which sounds can be heard. **-splitting** *a.* exceedingly loud and piercing. **-wax** *n.* cerumen, a waxy secretion of glands of ear.

earl *n.* a nobleman ranking between a marquis and a viscount. **-dom** *n.* territory of an earl.

ear•ly *a.* and *adv.* in the beginning of a period of time; belonging far back in time. **earliness** *n.*

earn *v.t.* to gain money by labor; to merit by service; to get. **-ings** *n.pl.* wages; savings.

ear•nest *a.* sincere; zealous; *n.* seriousness. **-ly** *adv.* **-ness** *n.*

ear•nest *n.* a pledge.

earth *n.* the planet on which we live; the soil, dry land, on the surface of the earth. **-bound** *a.* worldly. **-en** *a.* **-enware** *n.* crockery made of earth. **-iness** *n.* **-ling** *n.* a dweller on the earth. **-ly** *a.* terrestrial. **-quake** *n.* disturbance of the earth's surface due to contraction of a section of the crust of the earth. **-worm** *n.* the common worm. **-y** *a.*

ease *n.* leisure; freedom from anxiety, bodily effort; facility; natural grace of manner; *v.t.* to free from pain. **-ful** *a.* **-ment** *n.(Law)* right of way. **easily** *adv.* **easiness, easing** *n.* **easy** *a.* moderate; comfortable. **stand at ease!** military term to relax. **easy chair** *n.* an armchair. **easygoing** *a.*

ea•sel *n.* a wooden frame to support pictures.

east *n.* one of the four cardinal points; the part of the horizon where the sun rises; **-ern** *a.* toward, in, or from the east; oriental. **-ing** *n.* distance eastward from a given meridian. **-ward** *adv.* or *a.* **-wards** *adv.* **Far East**, China, Japan, etc. **Middle East**, Iran, Iraq, etc. **Near East**, Turkey, Syria, Palestine, etc.

Eas•ter *n.* a festival commemorating Christ's resurrection.

eas•y See **ease.**

eat *v.t.* to chew and swallow; gnaw; corrode; wear away; *v.i.* to take food. **ate** *pa.t.* **-en** *pa.p.* **-able** *a.* or *n.*

eaves *n.pl.* the lower edges of a sloping roof overhanging the walls of a building. **-drop** *v.i.* to listen furtively to a conversation. **-dropper** *n.*

ebb *n.* a decline; growing less; *v.i.* to flow back; to sink. **— tide** *n.* the retiring tide.

eb•on *a.* black as ebony. **-y** *n.* a cabinet wood which is jet black. **-ite** *n.* hard rubber or form of a vulcanite.

e•bul•lient *a.* overflowing; exuberant; enthusiastic. **ebullience** *n.* **ebullition** *n.* act of boiling; outburst of feeling; agitation.

ec•cen•tric *a.* departing from the center; irregular; odd; *n.* a whimsical person; one who defies the social conventions. **-ally** *adv.* **-ity** *n.* departure from normal way of conducting oneself.

ec•cle•si•a *n.* a church; a religious assembly. **-stic** *n.* a clergyman. **-stical** *a.* **-sticism** *n.* **ecclesiology** *n.* the science and study of church architecture and decoration. **ecclesiologist** *n.*

ech•e•lon *n.* a level of command; formation of airplanes in which each plane flies slightly above and to the right or left of the one in front.

e•chi•nus *n.* a sea urchin; a rounded molding.

ech•o *n.* repetition of sound produced by sound waves reflected from an obstructing object; close imitation of another's remarks or ideas; repetition; *pl.* **-es. -ism** *n.* forming words to imitate natural sounds.

é•clair *n.* a pastry filled with cream and frosted with chocolate.

é•clat *n.* splendor; renown; acclamation.

e•clec•tic *a.* and *n.* a thinker who selects and reconciles principles, opinions, belonging to different schools of thought. **-ally** *adv.*

e•clipse *n.* an interception of the light of one heavenly body by another; *v.t.* to obscure or hide; to surpass.

e•clip•tic *n.* the great circle on the celestial sphere which lies in the plane of the sun's apparent orbit around the Earth. Also **-al** *a.*

ec•logue *n.* a short poem of a pastoral nature.

e•col•o•gy *n.* a study of relations between animals, plants, people and their environment.

e•con•o•my *n.* wise expenditure of money; careful use of materials. **economic(al)** *a.* **economically** *adv.* **economics** *n.pl.* **political economy** *n.* the science which deals with the production, distribution, and consumption of the world's resources and the management of state income and expenditure. **economize** *v.i.* **economist** *n.*

ec•ru *n.* beige.

ec•sta•sy *n.;* a sense of uplift and joyfulness and increased well-being; excessive joy. **ecstatic** *a.* to be in a state of rapture; overjoyed. **-ally** *adv.*

ec•to-, ect- *pref.* implying *outside, without.*

ec•to•plasm *n. (Zool.)* exterior protoplasm of a cell. **-ic** *a.*

ec‧u‧men‧ic, ecumenical a. universal; representative of the Church. Also oecumenic.

ec‧ze‧ma n. disease of the skin, characterized by itchiness and inflammatory eruption.

ed‧del‧weiss n. a small white flowering plant found in the Swiss Alps.

ed‧dy n. a current of air, smoke, or water, swirling back contrary to the main current; a vortex; v.i. to move in a circle.

E‧den n. the garden where Adam and Eve lived: (lc.) a place of delight; a paradise.

e‧den‧tate a. lacking teeth.

edge n. the thin cutting side of the blade of an instrument; rim; keenness; v.t. to sharpen; to move almost imperceptibly; v.i. to move sideways. -d a. sharp. -less a. -ways, -wise adv. in the direction of the edge. edging n. border or fringe; narrow lace. edgy a. irritable.

ed‧i‧ble a. fit for eating. edibility n.

e‧dict n. a law or decree.

ed‧i‧fy v.t. to instruct in moral and religious knowledge. edified pa.t. and pa.p. edification n. improvement of the mind or morals. edifice n. a fine building. edifier n. -ing a.

ed‧it v.t. to prepare for publication; to revise and alter or omit. -ion n. the form in which a book is published. -or n. -orial n. an article in a newspaper presenting the newspaper's point of view.

ed‧u‧cate v.t. to cultivate and discipline the mind and other faculties by teaching. educable a. able to absorb education. educability n. education n. process of training. educational a. educationally adv. educative a. educator n.

e‧duce v.t. to draw or bring out that which is latent; to elicit; to extract. educible a. educt n. that which is educed. eduction n.

eel n. a group of fish with elongated bodies.

ee‧rie, eery a. weird, superstitiously timid; frightening. eerily adv. eeriness n.

ef‧face v.t. to erase or scratch out. -ment n.

ef‧fect n. that which is produced by an agent or cause; result; v.t. to bring about. -s n.pl. property. -ive a. in a condition to produce desired result; powerful. -ively adv. -iveness n. -ual a. -uality n. -ually adv. -uate v.t. to achieve. in effect, for practical purposes. to take effect, to become operative.

ef‧fem‧i‧nate a. unmanly; womanish.

ef‧fer‧ent a. conveying away from the center.

ef‧fer‧vesce v.i. to bubble, to seethe; to be in a state of excitement. -nce n. -nt a. bubbling; lively; sparkling.

ef‧fete a. no longer capable of bearing young; sterile; unfruitful; worn-out; spent.

ef‧fi‧ca‧cious a. producing the desired effect. -ly adv. -ness, efficacity, efficacy n.

ef‧fi‧cient a. producing results; capable; able; effective. efficiency n. competency. -ly adv.

ef‧fi‧gy n. an image or representation of a

person. hang in effigy, to hang an image of a person as a public expression of hatred.

ef‧flo‧resce v.i. to burst into bloom; to blossom. -nce, -ncy n. -nt a.

ef‧flu‧ent a. flowing out; n. a stream which flows out from another river or lake. effluence n. issue; emanation.

ef‧flu‧vi‧um n. an exhalation with a disagreeable smell; pl. effluvia. effuvial a.

ef‧flux n. that which flows out.

ef‧fort n. putting forth an exertion of strength or power, bodily or mental; attempt. -less a.

ef‧fron‧ter‧y n. brazen impudence; audacity.

ef‧fulge v.i. to shine brightly. -nce n. -nt a. diffusing a flood of light; radiant.

ef‧fuse v.t. to pour out or forth. effusion n. that which is poured out. effusive a. gushing.

e‧gad interj. a mild imprecation.

egg v.t. to urge on; to encourage one to take action.

egg n. an oval body laid by birds and a few animals in which the embryo continues development apart from parent body; matured female germ cell or ovum; anything egg-shaped. — cell n. the ovum. -nog n. a drink made of egg, milk, sugar, and alcoholic liquor. -shell n. -plant n. an edible plant with somewhat egg-shaped purple fruit.

e‧gis See aegis.

eg‧lan‧tine n. the sweetbrier; honeysuckle.

e‧go n. I; self; the personal identity. -centric a. self-centered. -centricism, -centricity n. -ism n. theory that bases morality on self-interest. -ist n. -istical a. -mania n. abnormal self-esteem. -tism n. selfishness. -tist n. -tistical a. -tistically adv.

e‧gre‧gious a. remarkably flagrant. -ly adv.

e‧gress n. act of leaving an enclosed place; exit; the right of departure. -ion n.

e‧gret n. several species of heron.

E‧gyp‧tian a. pert. to Egypt. Egyptology, Egyptologist n.

ei‧der n. a species of sea ducks. -down n. the breast down of the eider.

eight n. and a. one more than seven; written as 8 or VIII. -een n. and a. eight more than ten; written 18 or XVIII. -eenth n. and a. written 18th. -fold a. eight times quantity -h n. one of eight equal parts; 8th; the interval of an octave. -ieth a. written 80th; n. written 1/80. -y n. and a. fourscore.

ei‧ther a. or pron. one or the other; one of two.

e‧jac‧u‧late v.t. to utter suddenly and briefly; to eject. ejaculation n. a sudden emission. ejaculatory a.

e‧ject v.t. to throw out; to cast forth; to turn out. -a n. waste matter. -ion n. -ment n. explosion; (Law) the forcible removal of a defaulting tenant by legal process from land or house. -or n.

eke v.t. to add or augment. — out, to supplement; to use makeshifts.

e‧lab‧o‧rate v.t. to work out in detail; to

take pains with; *v.i.* to give fuller treatment; *a.* highly finished; complicated. -ly *adv.* -ness, elaboration *n.*

é•lan *n.* dash; impetuosity.

e•land *n.* the largest of the antelopes, found in Africa.

e•lapse *v.i.* of time, to pass by; to slip away.

e•las•tic *a.* possessing the property of recovering the original form when a distorting or constraining force has been removed; springy; *n.* a fabric whose threads are interwoven with strands of rubber; a rubber band. -ity *n.*

e•late *v.t.* to raise or exalt the spirit of; make proud. -d *a.* elation *n.* exultation.

el•bow *n.* the joint between the arm and forearm; any sharp bend or turn; *v.t.* and *v.i.* to jostle. — grease *n.* hard work. -room *n.* ample room for free movement.

el•der *a.* older; senior; prior; *n.* one who is older. -liness *n.* -ly *a.* up in years. eldest *a.*

el•der *n.* a flowering shrub which yields berries.

e•lect *v.t.;* to choose by vote; to select; *v.i.* to determine on a course of action; *a.* chosen; *n.* those predestined to eternal life. -ion *n.* the act of electing. -ioneer *v.i.* to work for the election of a candidate. -ive *a.* appointed by. -ively *adv.* -or *n.* one with right to vote at election. -oral *a.* -oral college *n.* a body of electors chosen by voters in the states to elect the president and vice-president of the U.S. -orate *n.* the whole body of electors.

e•lec•tric *a.* pertaining to, worked by, producing electricity; thrilling. — chair *n.* — eel *n.* a freshwater fish of S. America which is capable of inflicting powerful shocks. -al *a.* -ally *adv.* -ity *n.* a form of energy generated by friction, induction, or chemical change.

e•lec•tri•cian *n.* a mechanic who makes or repairs electrical apparatus.

e•lec•tri•fy *v.t.* to charge with electricity; to thrill, startle, excite by an unexpected statement or action.

e•lec•tro- *pref.* referring to some phase of electricity. -analysis *n.* chemical analysis by electrolysis. -cardiogram *n.* a tracing of electrical changes of contractions of heart. -cardiograph *n.* machine which makes the tracing.

e•lec•tro•cute *v.t.* to cause death by electric shock. electrocution. *n.*

e•lec•trode *n.* a metallic conductor of an open electric circuit in contact with some other kind of conductor.

e•lec•tro•dy•nam•ics *n.* a branch of the science of electricity which treats of the laws of electricity in motion or of electric currents and their effects. Also electrokinetics.

e•lec•trol•y•sis *n.* the resolution of dissolved or fused chemical compounds into elements by passing a current of electricity through them; destruction of hair roots, tumors, by an electric current. electrolyze *v.t.* electrolyte *n.* the liquid which carries the electric current between two electrodes.

e•lec•tro•mag•net *n.* a mass of soft iron temporarily magnetized by a current of electricity. -ic *a.* -ism *n.* branch of electrical science which deals with the relation of magnetism and electricity.

electromagnet

e•lec•trom•e•ter *n.* an instrument for measuring electricity.

e•lec•tro•mo•tion *n.* the flow of an electric current in a voltaic circuit. electromotive *a.* producing motion by means of electricity.

e•lec•tron *n.* the lightest known particle, a constituent of all atoms. -ics *n.* the branch of physics which deals with the behavior of free electrons. — microscope, and instrument of immense magnifying power in which controlled rays of electrons are used instead of light rays.

e•lec•tro•neg•a•tive *a.* carrying a negative charge of electricity.

e•lec•trop•a•thy *n.* treatment of disease by means of electricity. Also electrotherapy. electrotherapeutics *n.*

e•lec•tro•plate *v.t.* to cover with a coating of metal by means of electrolysis.

e•lec•tro•pos•i•tive *a.* carrying a positive charge of electricity.

e•lec•tro•type *n.* a facsimile printing plate of type or illustrations.

e•lec•trum *n.* an alloy of gold and silver.

el•ee•mos•y•nar•y *a.* given in charity.

el•e•gant *a.* graceful; refined; luxurious. -ly *adv.* elegance *n.* grace; beauty.

el•e•gy *n.* a poem of mourning. elegiac *a.* elegiacs *n.pl.* elegiacal *a.* elegiast, elegist *n.* a writer of elegies.

e•lek•tron *n.* a magnesium alloy of unusual lightness.

el•e•ment *n.* the first principle or rule; a component part; the habitation most suited to a person or animal; a substance which cannot be separated into two or more substances. -s *n.pl.* the physical forces of nature which determine the state of the weather. -al *a.* of the powers of nature; basic; fundamental. -ary *a.* rudimentary; simple.

el•e•phant *n.* the largest four-footed animal, having a long flexible trunk, two ivory tusks, and exceedingly thick skin. -ine *a.* huge; unwieldy. -oid *a.* like an elephant.

el•e•phan•ti•a•sis *a.* disease in which there is gross enlargement of the affected parts.

el•e•vate *v.t.* to lift up; to raise to a higher rank or station. -d *n.* a railroad on elevated tracks. elevation *n.* elevated place, a hill, a height. elevator *n.* a lift or hoist. elevatory *a.* tending or having power to elevate.

e•lev•en *n.* and *a.* one more than ten,

written as 11 or XI. -th n. one of 11 equal parts of a whole.

elf n. a supernatural, diminutive being of folklore with mischievous traits; a dwarf; pl. elves. -in n. a little elf. -ish a.

e•lic•it v.t. to draw out; to extract; to bring to light facts by questioning or reasoning.

el•i•gi•ble a. legally qualified; fit and worthy to be chosen; desirable. eligibility n.

e•lim•i•nate v.t. to remove; get rid of; leave out of consideration. elimination, eliminator n.

e•lite n. a choice or select body.

e•lix•ir n. a cure-all; a medicine.

E•liz•a•be•than a. pert. to Queen Elizabeth I or her times; n. a writer or distinguished person of her reign.

elk n. the largest member of the deer family in the N. of Europe.

elk

el•lipse n. a regular oval; the plane section across a cone not taken at right angles to the axis. **ellipsoid** n. a closed solid figure of which every plane section is an ellipse. **elliptic(al)** a. oval. See ellipsis.

el•lip•sis n. in English syntax a term denoting the omission of a word or words from a sentence whereby the complete meaning is obtained by inference. elliptic(al) a.

elm n. a genus of trees.

el•o•cu•tion n. art of effective public speaking from the point of view of enunciation, voice-production, delivery. -ary a. -ist n.

e•lon•gate v.t. to lengthen; to extend. elongation n. the act of stretching out.

e•lope v.i. to run away with a lover; to marry secretly; to bolt unexpectedly. -ment n.

el•o•quence n. oratory; rhetoric; fluency. eloquent a. eloquently adv.

else adv. besides; other; otherwise; instead. -where adv. in or to some other place.

e•lu•ci•date v.t. to make clear; to throw light upon; to explain. elucidation n. elucidative, elucidatory a. elucidator n.

e•lude v.t. to keep out of sight; to evade; to baffle. elusion n. evasion. elusive, elusory a.

el•van, elves, elvish See elf.

E•ly•si•um n. any place of perfect happiness. Elysian a. like a paradise.

em- pref. in or with; or adding a transitive or casual force in the composition of verbs.

em n. typographical unit of width (approx. 1/6th of an in.) used for measuring the length of a line of type.

e•ma•ci•ate v.t. to reduce one to flesh and bones; v.i. to waste away; to become extremely thin. -d a. emaciation n.

em•a•nate v.i. to issue from; to originate; to proceed from. emanant a. flowing from. emanation n. a flowing out from. emanative, emanatory a.

e•man•ci•pate v.t. to set free from any restraint or restriction. emancipation, emancipator n.

e•mas•cu•late v.t. to castrate; to render effeminate. emasculation n. emasculatory a.

em•balm v.t. to preserve a corpse from decay by means of antiseptic agents, balm, aromatic oils and spices. -er, -ing, -ment n.

em•bank v.t. to enclose or defend with a bank, mound, or earthwork. -ment n.

em•ar•go n. in international law, an order by which a government prevents a foreign ship from entering or leaving port; a general prohibition; pl. -es.

em•bark v.t. or v.i. to put on board a ship; to enter on some business or enterprise. -ation n.

em•bar•rass v.t. to perplex; to impede; to involve one in difficulties. -ed, -ing a. -ment n.

em•bas•sy n. the person sent abroad as an ambassador along with his staff; the residence of an ambassador.

em•bat•tle v.t. to furnish with battlements. -ment n.

em•bed v.t. to lay as in a bed; to bed in soil. Also imbed.

em•bel•lish v.t. to make beautiful or elegant with ornaments; to add fanciful details to a report or story. -er n. -ingly adv. -ment n.

em•ber n. a live piece of coal or wood; pl. red-hot ashes.

em•bez•zle v.t. to misappropriate fraudulently. -ment, -r n.

em•bit•ter v.t. to make bitter. -ed a.

em•bla•zon v.t. to adorn with heraldic figures; to deck in blazing colors. -ment, -ry n.

em•blem n. sign; badge; symbol; device. -atical a. -atically adv. -atize v.t. to represent by an emblem.

em•bod•y, imbody v.t. to form into a body; to incorporate; to represent. embodiment n.

em•bold•en v.t. to give boldness or courage to; to encourage.

em•bo•lism n. the insertion of days between other days to adjust the reckoning of time; (Med.) the result of the presence in the bloodstream of a solid foreign substance, as a clot. -al a.

em•bos•om, imbosom v.t. to clasp or receive into the bosom; to enclose; to shelter; to foster.

em•boss v.t. to raise or form a design above the surrounding surface. -ed a. -ment n.

em•bow•el v.t. to disembowel.

em•bow•er v.t. to surround (with flowers).

em•brace v.t. to press to the bosom; to accept; to encircle; n. a hug.

em•bro•cate v.t. to moisten and rub with lotion, etc. embrocation n.

em•broi•der v.t. to ornament fabrics with threads of silk, linen, etc. to form a design. -er n. -y n. ornamental needlework.

em•broil v.t. to involve in a quarrel or strife; to entangle; to confound. -ment n.

em•bry•o, embryon n. fetus during first months of gestation; a plant in rudimentary stage of development within seed; a. rudimentary. -logical a. -logist n. -logy n. science which deals with the growth and structure of the embryo. -nic a. at an early stage of development.

mend v.t. to remove faults or blemishes from; to alter for the better. -ate v.t. -ation n. correction of errors or blemishes. -ator n. -atory a.

em•er•ald n. precious stone of beryl species, transparent and bright green in color.

emerge v.i. to come forth; -nce n. coming into view; an outgrowth from a plant. -ncy n. state of pressing necessity; difficult situation; urgent need. -nt a. rising into view.

emer•i•tus n. and a. one who has honorably resigned or retired from a position of trust or responsibility but is retained on the rolls.

emer•sion n. an emerging.

em•er•y n. a naturally occurring mixture of corundum and iron oxide, used as an abrasive for polishing; v.t. to rub with emery.

emet•ic a. and n. any agent which causes vomiting.

em•i•grate v.i. to leave one's country to settle in another. emigrant a. and n. one who emigrates. emigration. n.

em•i•nent a. exalted in rank, office, or public estimation; prominent. eminence n. elevation; official dignity; fame.

em•is•sar•y n. agent sent on a mission.

emit v.t. to send forth; to utter (a declaration). -ting pr.p. -ted pa.p. and pa.t. emission n. emissive a.

emol•lient a. softening; relaxing; a soothing agent or medicine.

emol•u•ment n. profit arising from office or employment; gain; pay; salary; fee.

emo•tion n. strong, generalized feeling. -al a. easily excited or upset. -alism n. -ally adv. -less a. emotive a. causing emotion.

em•pa•thy n. intellectual identification of oneself with another.

em•per•or n. the title assumed by the ruler of an empire.

em•pha•sis n. stress on anything. pl. emphases. emphasize v.t. to stress. emphatical n.

em•pire n. a country with its satellite states under the rule of an emperor or some other supreme control.

em•pir•ic, em•pir•i•cal a. having reference to actual facts. empiric n. one who depends for his knowledge entirely on experience. -ally adv. empiricism n. the formulation of scientific laws by the process of observation and experiment. empiricist n.

em•place•ment n. the place or site of a building; placing in position.

em•ploy v.t. to make use of; to hire or engage; to exercise; to occupy; n. paid service. -able a. -ce n. one who is employed at a wage or salary. -er, -ment n.

em•po•ri•um n. a place of extensive commerce or trade; a big shop. pl. -s, emporia.

em•pow•er v.t. to authorize.

em•press n. the wife of an emperor; a female who exercises similar supreme power to that of an emperor.

emp•ty a. containing nothing; void; vacant; hollow; senseless; v.t. to drain; v.i. to discharge. emptiness n.

em•py•e•ma n. a collection of pus in body cavity, esp. in pleura.

em•py•re•al a. of pure fire or light; pert. to highest and purest regions of heaven. empyream a. and n. the firmament.

e•mu, emeu a. a large flightless bird.

em•u•late v.t. to strive to equal or surpass; to imitate. emulation n. emulative a. emulator n. emulous a. anxious to outdo another.

e•mul•sion n. a liquid mixture in which a fatty or oily substance is suspended in water and by aid of a mucilaginous medium forms a smooth milky white fluid; the coating of silver salts on a photographic film or plate. emulsic a. emulsification n. emulsify v.t. emulsive a. yielding a milklike substance.

en- pref. in; with; or adding transitive or causal force in verb composition.

en•a•ble v.t. to make able; to authorize to empower; to fit; to qualify.

en•act v.t. to make into a law; to act the part of. -ing, -ive a. -ment n.

e•nam•el n. a vitreous compound fused into surface of metal, pottery, or glass for utility and ornament; the hard, glossy surface of teeth; paint with glossy finish; v.t. to enamel.

en•am•or v.t. to inflame with love; to charm.

en•camp v.t. to form into a camp; v.i. to settle down temporarily. -ment n. campsite.

en•caus•tic a. pertaining to the fixing of colors by burning; n. an ancient style of decorative art, consisting in painting on heated wax.

en•ceinte a. pregnant; n. the precincts within the walls of a fort.

en•ceph•a•lon n. the brain. encephalic a. cerebral. encephalitis n. inflammation of the brain.

en•chain v.t. to fasten with a chain. -ment n.

en•chant v.t. to charm by sorcery. -ed a. held by a spell. -er n. (fem. -ress). -ingly adv. -ment n. magic; delight.

en•chase v.t. to set with jewels. -d a.

en•cir•cle v.t. to enclose in a circle; to surround. -ment n.

en•clave n. a country entirely surrounded by territories of another power; anything entirely enclosed into something else.

en•close, inclose v.t. to shut in; to

surround; to envelop; to contain. **enclosure** n.

en•co•mi•um n. high commendation; formal praise. pl. -s, **encomia**. **encomiast** n. eulogist. **encomiastic(al)** a. **encomiastically** adv.

en•com•pass v.t. to include; to encircle. -ment n.

en•core n. a recall awarded by an audience;

en•coun•ter v.t. to meet face to face; to confront; n. an unexpected meeting; a fight or combat.

en•cour•age v.t. to give courage to; to inspire with hope. -ment n. **encouraging** a.

en•croach v.i. to invade the rights or possessions of another. -er n. -ingly adv. -ment n.

en•cum•ber v.t. to load; to burden. **encumbrance** n. a burden; a dependent person.

en•cyc•li•cal a. intended to circulate among many people and in many places. Also **encyclic**.

en•cy•clo•pe•di•a, **encyclopaedia** n. works which give detailed account, in alphabetical order, of field of human knowledge. -n a. embracing all forms of knowledge. **encyclopedia** a. having universal knowledge; full of information. **encyclopedist** n.

en•cyst v.t. or v.i. to enclose or become enclosed in a sac or cyst.

end n. termination; conclusion; limit; extremity; final condition; result; purpose; v.t. to bring to conclusion; to destroy, to put to death; v.i. to finish; to cease. -ed a. -ing n. -less a. -lessly adv. -lessness n. to make both ends meet, to keep out of debt.

en•dan•ger v.t. to place in jeopardy; to expose to loss or injury.

en•dear v.t. to render more beloved. -ed, -ing a. -ingly adv. -ment n. tender affection; loving word; a caress.

en•deav•or v.i. to attempt; to strive; n. effort; struggle.

en•dem•ic, **endemical** a. terms applied to recurring diseases confined to certain people or localities and which arise from local causes.

en•dive n. an annual plant of the family *Compositae*, used for salads.

en•do- pref. indicating *within*.

en•do•car•di•tis n. inflammation of the lining membrane of the heart.

en•do•car•di•um n. the lining membrane of the heart. **endocardiacal** a.

en•do•crine a. describing the tissues and organs giving rise to an internal secretion; n. any such secretion. **endocrinology** n. study of internal secretions of ductless glands.

en•dog•a•my n. the custom of compulsory marriage within the limits of a tribe or between members of the same race. **endogamous** a.

en•do•plasm n. inner portion of cytoplasm of a cell.

en•dorse, indorse v.t. to sign one's name on back of a check; to sanction; to confirm; to vouch for **endorsable** **endorsee** n. the person to whom a bil exchange is assigned by endorseme -ment, -r n.

en•do•sperm n. the nutritive starchy tis which surrounds the embryo in m seeds. -ic a.

en•dow v.t. to enrich or furnish. -er -ment n. grant; bequest; natural capac

en•dure v.t. to remain firm under; to b with patience; to put up with; to susta to suffer; to tolerate; v.i. to continue; last. **endurable** a. can be endur **endurableness** n. **endurably** a **endurance** n. patience; fortitu stamina. -r n. **enduring** a. and **enduringly** adv.

en•e•ma n. a liquid solution injected i intestine through rectum; device for th

en•e•my n. an armed foe; opposing sta something harmful; a. due to an enem

en•er•gy n. vigor; force; activity; power of doing mechanical wo **energetic(al)** a. active; forcib **energetically** adv. **energize** v.t. to gi energy to.

en•er•vate v.t. to deprive of ner strength, or courage; a. spiritle **enervating, enervative** a. **enervation** n

en•fee•ble v.t. to render feeble.

en•fi•lade n. a line or straight passage; f from either flank along a line.

en•force v.t. to give strength to; to put force; to compel; to urge on; to execu -able a. **enforcedly** adv. under threat compulsion. -ment n.

en•fran•chise v.t. to set free from slave to extend political rights to; to grant t privilege of voting. -ment n.

en•gage v.t. to bind by contract, pledge, promise; to hire; to order; to attract; interlock; v.i. to begin to fight; to empl oneself. -d a. -ment n. obligation contract or agreement; pledge; betroth occupation; affair of business or pleasu **engaging** a. attractive; pleasing.

en•gen•der v.t. to beget; to cause to exi to sow the seeds of; to breed.

en•gine n. any mechanical contrivance producing and conveying motive powe a machine. -er n. one who construc designs, or is in charge of engine military works, or works of publ utility; v.t. to direct or design work as skilled engineer; to bring about. -erin n. the art of constructing and usin machines or engines.

En•glish a. belonging to England or inhabitants; n. the people or th language of England; v.t. to angliciz -man n.

en•gorge v.t. to swallow greedily and large quantities; v.i. to devour. -ment n.

en•graft, ingraft v.t. to graft on; incorporate; to add to. -ation, -ment n.

en•grave v.t. to imprint; to make a dee impression; v.i. to practice the art engraving. -r n. **engraving** n. the art cutting designs, etc. on wood, metal, stone; a print. See **grave**.

en•gross v.t. to occupy wholly; to absor to copy in legal form; to monopolize. -e

-ing, -ment n.

n·gulf, ingulf v.t. to swallow up or absorb as in a gulf; to encompass wholly.

n·hance v.t. to intensify; to increase in value or worth; to add to the effect. -ment n.

n·har·mon·ic, enharmonical a. having the same pitch but written in different notation, as G# and Ab.

·nig·ma n. an obscure question or saying difficult of explanation; anything or anybody puzzling; a riddle. -tic(al) a. -tically adv.

n·jamb·ment n. in verse, continuation of a sentence from one line into the next.

en·join v.t. to direct with authority; to order; to prohibit by judicial order; -ment n.

en·joy v.t. to delight in; to have the use or benefit of. -able a. pleasurable. -ably adv. -ment n.

en·large v.t. and v.i. to make or become larger; to broaden. -d a. -ment n.

en·light·en v.t. to give information to; to instruct; to make clear; to free from superstition, etc. -ment n.

en·list v.t. to enter on a list; to enroll; to secure support of; v.i. to enter heartily into a cause. -ment n.

en·liv·en v.t. to give life, action, or motion to; to quicken; to make merry. -er n.

en masse adv. in a group.

en·mesh, immesh, inmesh v.t. to catch in a mesh or net; to entangle; to trap.

en·mi·ty n. the quality of being an enemy; hatred; rancor; hostility.

en·noble v.t. to exalt; to dignify. -ment n.

en·nui n. boredom; listlessness due to satiety or lack of interest.

e·nor·mous a. huge; vast; immense. enormity n. -ly adv. ness n.

e·nough a. as much or as many as need be; sufficient; adequate. n. a sufficiency; adv. sufficiently; fully.

e·nounce v.t. to state; to declare; to pronounce; to proclaim. -ment n.

en·rage v.t. to fill with rage; to provoke to frenzy or madness. -d a.

en·rap·ture v.t. to transport with pleasure, to delight excessively. -d, enrapt a.

en·rich v.t. to make rich; to add to; to enhance; to embellish. -ment n.

en·robe v.t. to dress; to clothe.

en·roll v.t. to enter a name in a roll or register; to enlist; to record. -ment n.

en·sconce v.t. to shelter; to hide securely.

en·sem·ble n. all the parts taken together; general effect; an entire costume.

en·shrine v.t. to enclose in a shrine; to treasure with affection. -ment n.

en·shroud v.t. to hide from view.

en·sign n. a badge of rank or insignia of office; a flag or banner; an emblem.

ensign

en·si·lage n. a process of storing crops to serve as winter food for cattle.

en·slave v.t. to reduce to slavery or bondage. -ed a. -ment n.

en·snare, insnare v.t. to entrap; to entangle.

en·sue v.i. to follow; to happen after; to be the consequence of. ensuing a.

en·sure v.t. to make sure, safe, or certain.

en·tail n. a predetermined order of succession; an estate; v.t. to involve as a result; to bring about or cause. -ment n.

en·tan·gle v.t. to twist or interweave so as not to be easily separated; to ensnare. -ment n.

en·tente n. cordial agreement or understanding.

en·ter v.t. to go or come into; to invade; to join; v.i. to make a beginning; to take a part or interest in. to enter on, upon, to begin.

en·ter- Gk. pref. used in the construction of compound words relating to the intestine. -a n.pl. -ic a. -itis n. inflammation of the intestines.

en·ter·prise n. that which is undertaken or attempted; daring spirit. enterprising a. adventurous; energetic. enterprisingly adv.

en·ter·tain v.t. to show hospitality to; to amuse; to consider favorably. -er n. -ing a. -ment n.

en·thrall v.t. to thrill; to hold spellbound.

en·throne v.t. to place on a throne; to raise to sovereignty; to exalt. -ment n.

en·thu·si·asm n. passionate zeal; keen interest. enthusiast n. enthusiastic(al) a. enthusiastically adv.

en·tice v.t. to draw on by exciting hope or desire; to lead astray. -able a. -ment n. allurement. enticing a. enticingly adv.

en·tire a. whole; unimpaired; not castrated. -ly adv. -ness, -ty n. completeness.

en·ti·tle v.t. to give a title to; to name; to qualify; to fit for; to give claim to.

en·ti·ty n. a real being; reality; existence.

en·tomb v.t. to deposit in a tomb; to inter; to bury. -ment n.

en·to·mol·o·gy n. scientific study, classification, and collection of insects. entomological a. entomologically adv. entomologize v.t. entomologist n.

en·tou·rage n. one's habitual associates.

en·trails n.pl. the internal parts of anything.

en·trance n. the act of entering; a door, gateway, or passage to enter by; the beginning. entrant n. one who enters; a competitor.

en·trance v.t. to ravish with delight and wonder. -ment n. entrancing a.

en·trap v.t. to catch; to ensnare. -ment n.

en·treat v.t. to ask earnestly; to implore; v.i. to make an earnest request. -y n. supplication.

en·tree n. right of access; a dish served as a main course, or between main courses.

en·trench, intrench v.t. to dig a trench; to surround; v.i. to encroach. -ment n. any fortification or defense.

en·tre·pre·neur n. a contractor; an organizer.

en·trust, intrust v.t. to charge with a

E

responsibility; to confide to the care of.

en·try n. the act of entering; a place to enter by; an item noted down in a ledger.

en·twine, intwine v.t. to twist together; to plait; to encircle.

e·nu·mer·ate v.t. to count, one by one; to give in detail. **enumeration, enumerator** n.

e·nun·ci·ate v.t. to state clearly; to announce; to pronounce each syllable distinctly. **enunciable** a. **enunciation** n. articulation or pronunciation. **enunciator** n.

en·vel·op v.t. to cover by folding or wrapping; to surround. **-e** n. a cover or wrapper. **-ment** n.

en·ven·om v.t. to impregnate with venom; to poison; to embitter.

en·vi·a·ble, envious See envy.

en·vi·ron v.t. to surround; to encompass. **-ment** n. external conditions. **-s** n.pl. neighborhood; suburbs.

en·vis·age v.t. to face; to imagine; to visualize.

en·voy n. a diplomatic agent of a country below the rank of ambassador; messenger.

en·vy v.t. to grudge another person's good fortune; to feel jealous of. **-ing** pr.p. **envied** pa.p. **eviable, envious** a. **enviously** adv.

en·wrap, inwrap v.t. to wrap up; to envelop.

en·zyme, enzym n. a complex organic substance which in solution produces fermentation and chemical change in other substances apparently without undergoing any change itself; a form of catalyst. **enzymatic** a.

e·o·lith n. the oldest known stone implement used by prehistoric men. **-ic** a. pertaining to the earliest stage of human culture.

e·pact n. the excess of a solar over a lunar month or year in number of days.

ep·au·let, epaulette n. an ornamental shoulder-piece or badge of rank.

é·pée n. a dueling sword with a sharp point but no cutting edge, used in fencing.

e·pergne n. an ornamental table centerpiece.

ep·ex·a·ge·sis n. a further explanation of a previous statement. **epexegetical** a.

e·phed·rine n. an alkaloid drug, derived from plants of the genus *Ephedra*.

e·phem·er·a n. anything of temporary interest and value; a genus of insects, which as adults, live only for one day; pl. **ephemerae. -l** a. transitory.

e·phem·er·is n. a table or calendar giving for successive days the positions of heavenly bodies; pl. **ephemerides.**

epi- Gk. pref. meaning upon, at, in addition to, etc., used in the construction of compound terms.

ep·ic n. a long narrative poem in the grand style, usually dealing with the adventures of great soldiers or heroes whose deeds are part of the history of a nation; a. in the grand style; lofty in conception; memorable; heroic.

ep·i·car·di·um n. the serous membrane the pericardium, the sac which envelo the heart. **epicardial** a.

ep·i·cene a. common to both sexes; n. person having characteristics of bot sexes; a hermaphrodite.

ep·i·cen·ter n. the point on the uppe crust of the earth below which a earthquake has originated.

ep·i·crit·ic a. pert. to fine sensitivity, e. to the slightest sensation of heat or touc

Ep·i·cu·rus n. a Greek philosophe **epicure** n. one with a refined taste i food and drink. **epicurean** a. and n. sensualist. **epicureanism** n. the doctrin that the chief end of man was physic and mental happiness.

ep·i·cy·cle n. a circle whose center move around in the circumference of a greate circle.

ep·i·dem·ic, epidemical a. common to c affecting a whole people or communit prevalent. **epidemic** n. the temporar appearance of infectious diseas attacking whole communities.

ep·i·der·mis n. the outer protective laye of skin; a sheath which forms a layer ove surface of leaves. **epidermatoid epidermic, epidermal, epidermidal** a.

ep·i·glot·tis n. a covering of tissue which closes the opening leading into the larynx during the act of swallowing **epiglottic** a.

ep·i·gram n. a neat, witty, pointed saying **-matical** a. **-matically** adv. **-matize** v.t **-matist** n.

ep·i·graph n. an inscription, esp. on building, statue, etc.; an appropriate motto or saying at the beginning of book or chapter.

ep·i·lep·sy n. a nervous diseas characterized by sudden convulsions an unconsciousness. **epileptic** n. one subjec to epilepsy.

ep·i·logue n. conclusion of a literary work.

E·piph·a·ny n. a church festival held o the twelfth day after Christmas.

ep·i·phyte n. a plant which grows on bu does not draw nourishment from anothe plant.

e·pis·co·pa·cy n. the government of the church by bishops; the office of a bishop prelacy. **episcopal** a. governed by bishops. **Episcopalian** a. or n. a membe or adherent of an episcopal church **Episcopalianism** n. **episcopally** adv episcopate n. the office or order o. bishop.

ep·i·sode n. an incident; a digression, only remotely relevant to the plot. **episodal episodical** a. **episodically** adv.

e·pis·tle n. a letter, written for effect or fo instruction. **epistolary** a.

ep·i·taph n. an inscription placed on a tombstone in commemoration of the dead.

ep·i·tha·la·mi·um n. a nuptial song.

ep·i·the·li·um n. cellular tissue covering cutaneous, mucous, and serous surfaces.

ep·i·thet n. phrase or word used adjectivally to express some quality or attribute of its object; a designation; title. **epithetical** *a.*

e·pit·o·me *n.* a brief summary; synopsis; digest. **epitomize** *v.t.* to make or be a short abstract of.

p·och *n.* a fixed point or duration of time from which succeeding years are reckoned; era; date; period; age. **-al** *a.*

q·ua·ble *a.* uniform in action or intensity; not variable. **equability, -ness** *n.* **equably** *adv.*

·qual *a.* having the same magnitude, dimensions, value, degree, or the like; identical; *n.* a person of the same rank, age, etc. **-ization** *n.* **-ize** *v.t.* **-itarian** *n.* one who holds that all men are equal in status. **-ity** *n.* **-ly** *adv.*

:·qua·nim·i·ty *n.* evenness of mind or temper; composure; calmness.

·quate *v.t.* to make or treat as equal. **equation** *n.* the act of making equal; allowance for any inaccuracies; the sign of equality (=). **equational** *a.* **equationally** *adv.*

e·qua·tor *n.* a great circle supposed to be drawn around the earth 90° from each pole and dividing the globe into the N. & S. hemispheres. **-ial** *a.* of or pertaining to the equator; *n.* an astronomical telescope. **ially** *adv.*

eq·uer·ry *n.* one charged with the care of horses.

e·ques·tri·an *a.* pertaining to horses or horsemanship; mounted on a horse (*fem.* **equestrienne**). **-ism** *n.*

:·qui- *pref.* denoting equal, used in the construction of compound words.

e·qui·an·gu·lar *a.* having equal angles.

e·qui·dis·tance *n.* an equal distance from some point. **equidistant.** *a.*

e·qui·lat·er·al *a.* having all the sides equal.

e·quil·i·brate *v.t.* to balance exactly. **equilibrant, equilibration** *n.* **equilibrator** *n.* in aviation the stabilizing fin which controls the balance of an airplane.

e·qui·lib·ri·um *n.* (*Mech.*) the state of rest of a body produced by action and reaction of a system of forces; a state of balance.

e·quine, equinal *a.* pert. to a horse; *n.* a horse.

e·qui·noc·tial *a.* pert. to the equinoxes; *n.* a great circle in the heavens corresponding to the plane of the equator when extended. /

e·qui·nox *n.* the time at which the sun crosses the plane of the equator. Approx. March 21 and Sept. 22, when day and night are equal.

e·quip *v.t.* to supply with all requisites for service; to furnish. **-ping** *pr.p.* **-ped** *pa.p.* and *pa.t.* **-age** *n.* furniture, accoutrements. **-ment** *n.* outfit; apparatus.

e·qui·poise *n.* the state of equality of weight or force; even balance.

eq·ui·ta·ble *a.* giving each his due; just. **-ness** *n.* **equitably** *adv.* fairly; justly.

eq·ui·ta·tion *n.* skill in horsemanship.

eq·ui·ty *n.* fairness; equal adjustment or distribution.

e·quiv·a·lent *a* and *n.* equal in value, power, import, etc. **equivalence** *n.* identical value. **equivalency** *n.*

e·quiv·o·cal *a.* of double or doubtful meaning; questionable; ambiguous. **-ly** *adv.* **-ness** *n.* **equivocate** *v.i.* to use words of doubtful signification to mislead. **equivocation, equivocator** *n.*

e·ra *n.* a fixed point of time from which a series of years is reckoned; epoch; time; age; a memorable date or period.

e·rad·i·cate *v.t.* to pull up by the roots; to destroy. **eradicable** *a.* **eradication** *n.*

e·rase *v.t.* to rub or scrape out; to efface. **erasable, -d** *a.* **-r, -ment, erasure** *n.*

ere *adv.* before; sooner; *prep.* before; *conj.* sooner than.

e·rect *v.t.* to set upright; to elevate; to construct; *a.* upright. **-ion, -or** *n.*

erg *n.* the absolute unit of measurement of work and energy in the metric system.

er·go *adv.* therefore; consequently.

er·got *n.* a dried fungus used as a drug to stop bleeding and contract muscles.

Er·in *n.* Ireland.

er·mine *n.* a member of weasel family the white winter coat of which is highly prized as a fur; the robe of a judge in England.

ermine

e·rode *v.t.* to eat into; to wear away. **-nt** *n.* a caustic drug. **erose** *a.* appearing as if gnawed or worn irregularly. **erosion** *n.* act or operation of eating away; corrosion. **erosive** *a.*

E·ros *n.* the Greek god of love. **erotic** *a.* pertaining to love; *n.* a love poem; **erotics** *n.pl.* science and art of love. **erotica** *n.* literature dealing with sexual love. **eroticism, erotism** *n.*

err *v.i.* to commit a mistake; to go astray; to sin. **-atic(al)** *a.* wandering; eccentric; changeable; not dependable. **-atic** *n.* a wanderer. **-atically** *adv.* **-atum** *n.* an error in writing or printing; *pl.* **-ata.**

er·rand *n.* commission; message.

er·rant *a.* roving; wild; abandoned. **-ly** *adv.* **-ry** *n.* a state of wandering about, esp. of a knight-errant in search of adventures.

er·ror *n.* a deviation from right or truth; a mistake. **erroneous** *a.* wrong; incorrect; false. **erroneously** *adv.* **erroneousness** *n.*

er·satz *a.* substituted for articles in everyday use; artificial; makeshift.

erst *adv.* formerly; of old. **-while** *adv.* former.

e·ruct, e·ruc·tate *v.t.* to belch. **eructation** *n.* belching.

er·u·dite *a.* learned; deeply read; scholarly. **-ly** *adv.* **erudition** *n.* learning; scholarship.

e·rupt *v.i.* to throw out; to break through. **-ion** *n.* outburst of lava, ashes, gas, etc. from the crater of a volcano; a rash on the skin. -ive *a.*

er•y•sip•e•las *n.* contagious disease causing acute inflammation of the skin.

es•ca•lade *n.* mounting the walls of a fortress by means of ladders; *v.t.* to scale.

es•ca•la•tor *n.* continuous, moving stairway.

es•cape *v.t.* to gain freedom; to evade; to pass unnoticed; *v.i.* to hasten away; to avoid capture; *n.* flight from danger; evasion. escapable *a.* escapade *n.* a wild prank or exploit. -ment *n.* the act or means of escaping. escapism *n.* morbid desire to escape from the realities of life by concentrating on some other interest. escapist *n.*

es•carp *v.t.* to make into a steep slope. -ment *n.* a steep, sloping bank.

es•cha•tol•o•gy *n.* the department of theology which treats of the last things, such as death, the return of Christ, the resurrection, the end of the world, etc.

es•cheat *n.* the legal process of property reverting to the crown or government on the tenant's death without heirs; *v.t.* to forfeit; to confiscate.

es•chew *v.t.* to shun; to abstain from.

es•cort *n.* a person or persons accompanying another on a journey for protection or as an act of courtesy; *v.t.* to accompany.

es•cri•toire *n.* a writing desk with drawers.

Es•cu•la•pi•an *a.* pertaining to the art of healing.

es•cu•lent *a.* suitable as a food for man; edible.

es•cutch•eon *n.* that part of a vessel's stern on which her name is inscribed; an ornamental plate or shield placed around a keyhole opening. -ed *a.*

Es•ki•mo, Esquimau *n.* and *a.* one of an aboriginal people thinly scattered along the northern seaboard of America and Asia and in many of the Arctic islands; *pl.* -s, -x.

e•soph•a•gus *n.* the gullet.

es•o•ter•ic *a.* secret; profound.

es•pe•cial *a.* distinguished; preeminent; more than ordinary; particular. -ly *adv.*

Es•pe•ran•to *n.* a universal auxiliary language.

es•pi•o•nage *n.* the practice of employing secret agents; spying.

es•pla•nade *n.* a level space, esp. for a promenade.

es•pouse *v.t.* to marry; to support. espousal *n.* espousals *n.pl.* nuptials. -r *n.*

es•prit *n.* spirit; wit; liveliness. — de corps *n.* loyalty and attachment to the group of which one is a member.

es•py *v.t.* to catch sight of.

-esque *suff.* in the manner or style of.

es•quire *n.* originally, a squire or shield bearer, one of two attendants on a knight; now a courtesy title.

es•say *n.* a literary composition; a trial; *v.t.* to try; to attempt. -ist *n.* a writer of essays.

es•sence *n.* the very being or power of a thing; the formal cause of being; essential part; a perfume. **essential** *a.* necessary to the existence of a thing;

inherent; *n.* something indispensable; chief point; a leading principl• **essentiality** *n.* **essentially** *ad•* **essentialness** *n.*

es•tab•lish *v.t.* to make stable or firm; set up; to prove; to substantiate. -ed fixed; settled. -er *n.* -ment *n.* a institution; settlement; place of busines residence, etc. -mentarian *a.* and supporting church establishment.

es•tate *n.* a piece of landed property; ran• position; quality. the Fourth Estate *n.* satirical term for the press. real estate property in land.

es•teem *v.t.* to regard with respect affection; to set a value on; *n.* hig regard; favorable opinion.

es•thet•ic See aesthetic.

es•ti•ma•ble *a.* able to be estimated worthy of regard. estimably *adv.*

es•ti•mate *v.t.* to calculate; *v.i.* to offer complete certain work at a stated cost; appraisement. estimator *n.*

es•ti•va•tion, aestivation *n.* a state torpor, affecting some insects, during th dry summer months. estival *a.* pertainin to the summer aestival. estivate *v.i.*

Es•to•ni•an, Esthonian *a.* pert. t Est(h)onia, a country on the Baltic; the Finnish-Ugrian language.

es•top *v.t.* to impede; to bar by one' own act.

es•trange *v.t.* to alienate; to divert from it original use. -d *a.* -ment *n.*

es•tu•ar•y *n.* a narrow arm of the sea at the mouth of a river. estuarine *a.*

e•su•ri•ent *a.* hungry; voraciou• gluttonous.

et cet•er•a *n.* phrase meaning "and the others"; and so on; (*abbrev.*) etc.

etch *v.t.* to make an engraving by eatin• away the surface of a metal plate wit• acid; *v.i.* to practice this art. -er *n.* -ing *n* the printed impression taken from a• etched plate.

e•ter•nal *a.* without beginning or end in relation to time; everlasting. -ize eternize *v.t.* to perpetuate. -ly *adv* **eternity** *n.* the infinity of time; the future state after death.

eth•ane *n.* a colorless, odorless inflammable gas.

e•ther *n.* the higher regions beyond the earth. -eal *a.* celestial; airy; delicate -ealization *n.* -alize *v.t.* to render ethereal or spiritual. -eality *n.* -eally *adv*

e•ther *n.* a volatile liquid, prepared by the action of sulfuric acid on alcohol, used as a solvent and as an anesthetic.

eth•ic, eth•i•cal *a.* relating to morals or moral principles. -ally *adv.* -s *n.pl.* philosophy which treats of human character and conduct, of distinction between right and wrong, and moral duty and obligations to the community.

E•thi•o•pi•a *n.* a kingdom in E. Africa; Abyssinia. -n *a.* pertaining to Ethiopia.

eth•nic, eth•ni•cal *a.* pert. to races or peoples; heathen; pagan. ethnography *n.* detailed study of the physical characteristics and social customs of racial groups. **ethnographer** *n.*

ethnographic *a.* **ethnology** *n.* the science which traces the origin and distribution of races, their peculiarities and differences. **ethnological** *a.* **ethnologist** *n.*

thos *n.* the character, customs, and habits which distinguish a people or community from another.

h•yl *n.* the univalent radical C₂H₅; an antiknock fluid. **— alcohol** *n.* common alcohol.

ti•o•late *v.t.* to render pale or unhealthy by denying light and fresh air. **etiolation** *n.*

ti•ol•o•gy *n.* the study of the causes of diseases. Also **aetiology**.

t•i•quette *n.* the conventional code of good manners which governs behavior in society.

tude *n.* a short musical composition.

t•y•mol•o•gy *n.* the investigation of the origins and meanings of words and word forms. **etymological** *a.* **etymologically** *adv.* **etymologist** *n.*

u•caine *n.* a synthetic drug, resembling cocaine, used as a local anesthetic.

u•ca•lypt *n.* any member of the genus Eucalyptus. **-us** *n.* the gum tree of Australia with tough and durable wood. **-ol** *n.* eucalyptus oil.

eucalyptus

Eu•cha•rist *n.* Holy Communion; the consecrated elements at the sacrament of the Lord's Supper. **-ic(al)** *a.*

eu•chre *v.t.* to outwit; to get the best of.

Eu•clid•e•an *a.* pert. to Euclid of Alexandria; geometric; three-dimensional.

eu•de•mo•nism, eudaemonism *n.* the doctrine that the attainment of personal happiness, power and honor is the chief end and good of man. **eudemonist** *n.*

eu•gen•ic *a.* relating to the production of fine offspring. **-s** *n.pl.* the scientific application of the findings of the study of heredity to human beings with the object of perpetuating those inherent and hereditary qualities which aid in the development of the human race. **eugenist** *n.*

eu•ge•nol *n.* an aromatic acid, obtained from the oil of cloves.

eu•lo•gy, eu•lo•gi•um *n.* a speech or writing in praise, especially a speech praising a dead person. **eulogic(al)** *a.* commendatory. **eulogize** *v.t.* to speak in flattering terms. **eulogist** *n.* **eulogistic** *a.* **eulogistically** *adv.*

eu•nuch *n.* a castrated male.

eu•pep•sia *n.* healthy normal digestion — opposed to *dyspepsia*. **eupeptic** *a.*

eu•phe•mism *n.* a figure of speech where a less disagreeable word or phrase is substituted for a more accurate but more offensive one. **euphemize** *v.t.* or *v.i.* **euphemistic** *a.*

eu•pho•ny *n.* pleasantness or smoothness of sound; assimilation of the sounds of syllables to facilitate pronunciation and to please the ear. **euphonic, euphonious** *a.* **euphoniously** *adv.*

eu•pho•ri•a *n.* a sense of health and well-being which may, however, be misleading; state of irrational happiness. **euphoric** *a.*

eu•phu•ism *n.* an affected, elaborate, bombastic prose style; a stilted expression. **euphuist** *n.* **euphuistic** *a.*

Eur•a•sian *n.* offspring of mixed European and Asiatic parentage.

eu•rhyth•mics *n.pl.* an art of rhythmical free movement to music.

Eu•rope *n.* the continent which extends from the Atlantic Ocean to Asia. **European** *n.* a native or inhabitant of Europe.

eu•tec•tic *a.* easily melted or fused; *n.* alloy of metals whose melting point is lower than other mixtures of the same ingredients.

eu•tha•na•sia *n.* an easy, painless death; the putting of a person to death painlessly. Also **euthanasy**.

e•vac•u•ate *v.t.* to make empty; to withdraw from; to excrete; *v.i.* to quit. **evacuant** *n.* **evacuation** *n.* the act of emptying out. **evacuative** *a.* **evacuator** *n.* **evacuee** *n.* a person temporarily removed from dangerous area.

e•vade *v.t.* to avoid by dexterity, artifice, or stratagem; to elude; to avoid. **evadable** *a.*

e•val•u•ate *v.t.* to appraise or determine the value of. **evaluation** *n.* estimation of worth.

ev•a•nesce *v.i.* to vanish; to fade or melt away. **-nce** *n.* **-nt** *a.* vanishing; fleeting; transitory; scarcely perceptible. **-ntly** *adv.*

e•van•gel *n.* good tidings; one of the first four books of the New Testament. **-ic(al)** *a.* consonant with the Gospel; orthodox; *n.* one who holds the views of the evangelical school. **-ically** *adv.* **-ical, -ness, -icism, -icalism, -ism** *n.* **-ization** *n.* conversion. **-ize** *v.t.* and *v.i.* to convert, by preaching the Gospel. **-ist** *n.* **-istic** *a.*

e•vap•o•rate *v.t.* and *v.i.* to pass off in vapor; to disperse; to disappear. **evaporable, evaporative** *a.* **evaporation** *n.*

e•va•sion *n.* the act of eluding; excuse; dodge. **evasible** *a.* **evasive** *a.* not straightforward. **evasively** *adv.*

eve *n.* evening; the period immediately preceding an event or important occasion. **evensong** *n.* evening prayer. **eventide** *n.*

e•ven *a.* level; equal in surface; uniform in quality; balanced; equable; unruffled; impartial; exactly divisible by two; *v.t.* to smooth; to equalize; *adv.* just; still. **-handed** *a.* fair, impartial, just. **-ly** *adv.* **-ness** *n.* **— tempered** *a.*

E

eve·ning n. the close of day. — dress n. formal dress worn at evening functions.

e·vent n. that which happens; a notable occurrence. -ful a. momentous. -ual a. happening as a consequence; ultimate. -uality n. force of circumstances. -ually adv. -uate v.i. to happen.

ev·er adv. at any time; constantly; unceasingly. -glade n. a swampy, grassy tract. -green a. always green; n. nondeciduous tree or shrub which remains green throughout the year. -more adv. eternally. for ever and a day, always.

ev·er·last·ing a. enduring forever; eternal; n. eternity; a flower which does not lose shape or color when dried.

e·vert v.t. to turn inside out. eversible a. eversion n.

ev·er·y a. each of all; all possible. -body n. every person. -day a. ordinary. -where adv. universally. — other, alternately.

e·vict v.t. to dispossess by a judicial process; to turn out. -ion n. ejectment. -or n.

ev·i·dent a. visible; obvious. evidence n. ground for belief; testimony; proof; v.t. to render evident. -ial, -iary a. proving conclusively. -ly adv. apparently; plainly. to turn State's evidence, to give evidence, on the part of one accused, against an accomplice.

e·vil a. having bad natural qualities; harmful; disagreeable; vicious; corrupt; wicked; unfortunate; n. harm; misfortune; wickedness; sinfulness; wrong; adv. in an evil manner. — eye n. the power of bewitching others by the glance of the eyes. -ly adv. -ness n.

e·vince v.t. to prove beyond any reasonable doubt; to show clearly. evincible a. evincibly adv. evincive a. tending to prove.

e·vis·cer·ate v.t. to disembowel; to take out the entrails or viscera. evisceration n.

e·voke v.t. to call up; to summon forth; to draw out; to bring to pass. evocation n.

ev·o·lu·tion n. gradual unfolding or growth; the scientific theory according to which the higher forms of life have gradually developed from simple and rudimentary forms. -al, -ary a. -ism, -ist n.

e·volve v.t. to develop gradually; to unfold; v.i. to open out.

ewe n. a female sheep.

ew·er n. a large jug with a wide spout.

ex- pref. used in the construction of compound terms, signifying out of, from, former.

ex·ac·er·bate v.t. to render more bitter; to increase the violence of; to exasperate; to irritate; to aggravate. exacerbation n.

ex·act a. accurate; correct; precise; v.t. to insist upon. -ing a. making severe demands on. -ion n. -itude n. extreme accuracy. -ly adv. precisely.

ex·ag·ger·ate v.t. to magnify in the telling. -dly adv. exaggeration n. a statement going beyond the facts. exaggerative a. exaggerator n. exaggeratory a.

ex·alt v.t. to elevate as in rank; to praise; to elate with joy. -ation n. -ed a.

ex·am·ine v.t. to inquire into and determine; to try to assay by the appropriate tests; to inspect; to investigate. exam n. examination. -e n. one who undergoes an examination test. examination n. interrogation; scholastic test of knowledge, written or oral. -r n.

ex·am·ple n. a thing illustrating a general rule; a specimen; sample.

ex·as·per·ate v.t. to rouse angry feelings to provoke beyond endurance exasperating a. extremely trying exasperation n. -r n.

ex·ca·vate v.t. to form a cavity or hole in; to dig out. excavation, excavator n.

excavator

ex·ceed v.t. to pass or go beyond the limit of; v.i. to surpass; to excel. -ing a. excessive. -ingly adv. very.

ex·cel v.t. to be better than; to exceed; to outdo; v.i. to be very good -ling pr.p. -led pa.t. and pa.p. -lence n. -lency n. complimentary title borne by ambassadors, etc. -lent a. worthy; remarkably good. -lently adv.

ex·cept v.t. to leave out; to exclude; v.i. to object; prep. leaving out; all but; conj. with the exception (that). -ing prep. excluding. -ion n. that which is not included in a rule. -ionable a. objectionable. -ionably adv. -ional a. outstanding; superior. -ionally adv.

ex·cerpt v.t. to extract; n. a passage quoted or culled from a book, speech, etc.

ex·cess n. that which goes beyond a definite limit; extravagance. -ive a. more than enough.

ex·change v.t. to give or take in return for; to barter; n. the act of giving or taking one thing in return for another; the transfer of goods between countries. -able a.

ex·cheq·uer n. the public treasury.

ex·cise n. a tax or duty upon certain articles of home production and consumption; v.t. to impose an excise duty on. excisable a. liable to excise duty.

ex·cise v.t. to cut out; to cut off. excision n. act of cutting; surgical operation.

ex·cite v.t. to rouse; to call into action; to stir up; to stimulate. excitability n. excitable a. capable of being easily excited. excitant n. a stimulant. excitation n. the act of exciting; the excitement produced. excitative, excitatory, -d a. -dly adv. -ment n. agitation; commotion. exciting a. rousing to action; thrilling. **excitingly** *adv*.

ex·claim *v.i.* and *v.t.* to utter loudly and vehemently; to declare suddenly. **exclamation** *n*. vehement utterance. **exclamation mark**, the mark (!) used to suggest sudden emotion. **exclamatory** *a*.

ex·clude *v.t.* to shut out; to eject. **exclusion** *n*. **exclusive** *a*. limited to a special favored few. **exclusively** *adv*. **exclusiveness** *n*.

ex·cog·i·tate *v.t.* to find out by thinking; to think out. **excogitation** *n*.

ex·com·mu·ni·cate *v.t.* to expel from the communion and membership of the church by an ecclesiastical sentence; to deprive of spiritual privileges. **excommunication** *n*.

ex·co·ri·ate *v.t.* to strip, wear, or rub the skin off; to flay. **excoriation** *n*.

ex·cre·ment *n*. matter excreted; feces. **-al** *a*. **-itious** *a*. resembling feces.

ex·cres·cence *n*. an abnormal protuberance which grows out of anything, as a wart or tumor; a normal outgrowth, such as hair. **excrescent** *a*. growing out unnaturally.

ex·crete *v.t.* to eject waste matter. **excreta** *n.pl.* the normal discharges from the animal body as urine, feces, and sweat. **excretion** *n*. **excretive**, **excretory** *a*.

ex·cru·ci·ate *v.t.* to inflict the severest pain on; to torture. **excruciating** *a*.

ex·cul·pate *v.t.* to clear from a charge or imputation of fault or guilt. **exculpation** *n*. vindication. **exculpatory** *a*.

ex·cur·sion *n*. a short trip for a special purpose; deviation. **-ist** *n*. one who makes a journey for pleasure. **excursive** *a*. prone to wander; rambling. **excursus** *n*. a dissertation appended to a book and containing a fuller exposition of some relevant point.

ex·cuse *v.t.* to free from fault or blame; to pardon; *n*. a pretext; an apology. **excusable** *a*.

ex·e·crate *v.t.* to feel or express hatred for; to curse; to loathe. **execrable** *a*. **execrably** *adv*. **execration** *n*. a curse; imprecation.

ex·e·cute *v.t.* to accomplish; to perform; to complete; to enforce a judgment of a court of law; to put to death by sentence of a court. **executable** *a*. **executant** *n*. a performer, esp. of music. **execution** *n*. death penalty inflicted by law; performance. **executioner** *n*. hangman. **executive** *a*. administrative; *n*. a body appointed to administer the affairs of a corporation, a company, etc.; a high official of such a body. **executively** *adv*. **executor** *n*. (*fem*. **executrix**, **executress**) a person appointed under a will to fulfill its terms and administer the estate. **executorial** *a*.

ex·e·ge·sis *n*. literary commentary. **exegete**, **exegetist** *n*. one versed in interpreting the text of the Scriptures. **exegetic**, **exegetical** *a*.

ex·em·plar *n*. a person or thing to be imitated; model. **-ily** *adv*. in a manner to be imitated. **-iness** *n*. **-y** *a*. commendable.

ex·em·pli·fy *v.t.* to show by example; to illustrate. **-ing** *pr.p*. **exemplified** *pa.t*. and *pa.p*. **exemplification** *n*.

ex·empt *v.t.* to free from; to grant immunity from; *a*. not included; freed from; not affected by. **-ible** *a*. **-ion** *n*. immunity.

ex·er·cise *n*. use of limbs for health; practice for the sake of training; *pl*. a ceremony; *v.t.* to exert; to apply; to practice; *v.i.* to take exercise.

ex·ert *v.t.* to put forth; to exercise; to strive; to labor. **-ion** *n*. **-ive** *a*.

ex·hale *v.t.* to breathe out; to discharge; *v.i.* to rise or be given off as vapor. **exhalable**, **exhalant** *a*. **exhalation** *n*.

ex·haust *v.t.* to empty; to weaken; to tire; to use up; *n*. conduit through which steam, waste gases and the like, pass to the outer air; the steam or gases themselves. **-ed** *a*. tired out; emptied; consumed. **-ible** *a*. **-ion** *n*. state of being completely deprived of strength or vitality. **-ive** *a*. comprehensive; thorough. **-ively** *adv*.

ex·hib·it *v.t.* to show; to display; to express; *n*. anything displayed at an exhibition. **-er**, **-or** *n*. one who sends articles to an exhibition for display. **-ion** *n*. display; a public show. **-ionism** *n*. a tendency to show off before people. **-ionist** *n*. **-ory** *a*.

ex·hil·a·rate *v.t.* to make cheerful; to animate. **exhilarant** *a*. exciting joy, mirth, or pleasure; *n*. **exhilarating** *a*. **exhilaration** *n*.

ex·hort *v.t.* to advise strongly; to admonish earnestly. **-ation** *n*. **-ative**, **-atory** *a*.

ex·hume *v.t.* to dig up; to unearth; to disinter. **exhumation**, **-r** *n*.

ex·i·gent *a*. calling for immediate action or aid; pressing; urgent. **exigence**, **exigency** *n*. emergency. **exigible** *a*.

ex·i·gu·i·ty *n*. smallness; slenderness. **exiguous** *a*.

ex·ile *n*. separation or enforced banishment; one living away from his native country; *v.t.* to banish or expel.

ex·ist *v.t.* to be; to live; to subsist; to occur. **-ence** *n*. state of being actual; life; **-ential** *a*. consisting in existence. **-entialism** *n*. a school which describes, analyzes and classifies the experiences of an individual mind. **-ibility** *n*.

ex·it *n*. a departure; a way out of a place. **exeunt**, stage direction.

ex·o- *pref*. outside, without.

ex·o·dus *n*. a departure. **Exodus** *n*. the second book of the Old Testament.

ex·og·a·my *n*. a custom compelling a man to marry outside his tribe or clan. **exogamous** *a*.

ex·on·er·ate *v.i.* to declare free from blame or responsibility; to relieve of a charge or obligation. **exoneration**, **exonerator** *n*.

ex·o·ra·ble *a*. capable of being moved by entreaty.

ex·or·bi·tant *a*. very excessive; extravagant. **exorbitance**, **exorbitancy** *n*. **-ly** *adv*.

ex·or·cise *v.t.* to free a person of evil spirits. **exorcism** *n*.

ex·or·di·um *n*. a beginning; the introduction part of a discourse or treatise. **exordial** *a*.

E

ex•o•skel•e•ton n. external hard supporting structure such as scales, nails, feathers. exoskeletal a.

ex•o•ter•ic, extrical a. capable of being understood by many; not secret; the opposite to *esoteric*.

ex•ot•ic a. introduced from a foreign country; unusual or colorful. -ism n.

ex•pand v.t. to enlarge; to increase in volume or bulk; to stretch. expanse n. a wide extent of surface. -able, expansible a. expansibly adv. expansion n. spreading; distension. expansive a. widely extended; communicative. expansively adv. expansiveness n.

ex•pa•ti•ate v.i. to speak or write at great length. expatiation n. expatiative a.

ex•pa•tri•ate v.t. to banish from one's native land; to exile. expatriation n.

ex•pect v.t. to look forward to; to anticipate; to suppose. -ance, -ancy n. that which is expected. -ant a. waiting; hopeful. -antly adv. -ation n. -ations n.pl. prospects in life.

ex•pec•to•rate v.t. or v.i. to spit; to cough up. expectorant a. aiding expectoration. expectoration n. sputum; spittle.

ex•pe•di•ent a. suitable; fitting; advisable; desirable; useful; n. suitable means to accomplish an end. expediency n. -ly adv.

ex•pe•dite v.t. to free from hindrance or obstacle; to hurry forward; a. quick; ready. expedition n. a journey for a specific purpose. expeditionary a. expeditious a. prompt; speedy. expeditiously adv.

ex•pel v.t. to drive or force out; to eject. -ling pr.p. -led pa.t. and ; a.p.

ex•pend v.t. to use up; to exhaust. -able a. -iture n. expense; cost. expense n. cost. expensive a. costly; dear.

ex•pe•ri•ence n. practical knowledge gained by trial or practice; personal proof; continuous practice; an event in one's life; v.t. to undergo; to feel. -d a. skilled; expert; wise; capable. experiential a. empirical.

ex•per•i•ment n. the action of trying anything; practical test; v.i. to make an experiment. -al a. founded on or known by experiment. -alist n. -ally adv. -ation n. -ative a. -er, -ist n.

ex•pert a. adroit; dexterous; skillful. n. an authority; a specialist. -ly adv. -ness n.

ex•pi•ate v.t. to atone for; to make amends for. expiable a. expiation n.

ex•pire v.t. to exhale; v.i. to die; to come to an end. expirant n. one who is dying. expiration n. the exhalation of air from the lungs; termination. expiratory, expiring a. expiry n. conclusion.

ex•plain v.t. to elucidate; to define. -able a. explanation n. the meaning of or reason given for anything. explanative, explanatory a.

ex•ple•tive a. serving only to fill out a sentence; n. a word inserted to fill up or to add force to a phrase; an exclamation.

ex•pli•cate v.t. to unfold the meaning of; to explain; to interpret. explicable a. explication n. explicative, explicatory a.

ex•plic•it a. stated in detail; unambiguous; clear; unequivocal. -ly adv. -ness n.

ex•plode v.t. to cause to blow up; v.i. to become furious with rage. -d a. rejected; debunked. explosion n. sudden release of gases, accompanied by noise and voilence; a manifestation of rage. explosive a. liable to explode; n. a chemical intended to explode.

ex•ploit n. a brilliant feat; a heroic deed; v.t. to utilize for personal gain. -able a. -age, -ation n. -er n.

ex•plore v.t. to search through with the view of making discovery; to investigate; to examine. exploration n. exploratory a. -r n.

ex•po•nent n. one who expounds, demonstrates, or explains; in algebra, index number or quantity, written to the right of and above another to show how often the latter is to be multiplied by itself, e.g. $a^3 = a \times a \times a$.

ex•port v.t. to send goods or produce out of a country. -able a. -ation, -er n.

ex•pose v.t. to leave unprotected; to exhibit; to disclose. exposé n. an exposure or disclosure of discreditable facts. exposition n. exhibition; display. expositor n. expository a. exposure n. the state of being laid bare.

ex•post•u•late v.i. to remonstrate with; to reason earnestly. expostulation n. expostulative, expostulatory a.

ex•pound v.t. to explain; to interpret.

ex•press v.t. to make known one's opinions or feelings; to put into words; to represent by pictorial art; a. explicit; clear; plain; speedy; adv. posthaste; by express messenger or train; n. a messenger sent on a special errand; a fast train making few stops en route. -ible a. -ion n. utterance; declaration; phrase; term; remark; aspect; look; a quantity denoted by algebraic symbols. -ionism n. an antirealistic art theory that all art depends on the expression of the artist's creative self. -ionist n. -ionless a. -ive a. full of expression. -ively adv. -iveness n. -ly adv. plainly; explicitly; specially.

ex•pro•pri•ate v.t. to dispossess; to take out of the owner's hand. expropriation n.

ex•pul•sion n. the act of expelling or casting out; banishment. expulsive a.

ex•punge v.t. to erase; to obliterate; to cancel.

ex•pur•gate v.t. to cleanse; to purify; to purge. expurgation n. expurgator n.

ex•qui•site a. of extreme beauty or delicacy; of surpassing excellence. -ly.

ex•sic•cate v.t. to dry up; to evaporate. exsiccation n.

ex•tant a. still existing.

ex•tem•po•re a. or adv. without previous study or meditation; on the spur of the moment. extemporal, extemporaneous, extemporary a. impromptu. extemporization n. extemporize v.i.

ex•tend v.t. to prolong in duration; to offer; to enlarge; v.i. to be continued in length or breadth; to stretch. -ible, extensible, extensile a. capable of being stretched, expanded, or enlarged. extensibility,

extension n. **extensional** a. **extensive** a. large; spacious. **extensively** adv. **extensiveness** n. **extensor** n. a muscle which straightens or extends a limb.

extent n. size; scope; area; degree; volume; length; expanse.

x•**ten•u•ate** v.t. to mitigate; to make less blameworthy. **extenuating** a. **extenuation** n.

x•**te•ri•or** a. outer; external; n. outer surface; outward appearance.

x•**ter•mi•nate** v.t. to root out; to destroy utterly. **extermination, exterminator** n.

x•**ter•nal** a. not inherent or essential; outward; exterior; superficial; apparent. -s n.pl. outward appearances. -**ly** adv.

x•**tinct** a. no longer existing. -**ion** n.

x•**tin•guish** v.t. to put out; to quench; to destroy. -**able** a. -**er** n.

x•**tir•pate** v.t. to pull or pluck up by the roots; to destroy utterly. **extirpative** a. **extirpation, extirpator** n.

x•**tol** v.t. to praise highly. -**ling** pr.p. -**led** pa.t. and pa.p.

x•**tort** v.t. to obtain by force or threats; to extract. -**ive** a. -**ion** n. illegal compulsion; unjust exaction. -**ionary, -ionate** a. -**ioner, -ionist** n.

x•**tra-** pref. meaning beyond, on the other side of, on the outside of; denoting excess. a. extraordinary; additional; adv. unusually; n. additional item. -**curricular** a. pert. to the studies or activities which are not included in the curriculum. -**judicial** a. out of the proper court or the ordinary legal procedure. -**mural** a. beyond the walls, as outside a university. -**sensory** a. beyond the senses. -**sensory perception** (abbrev. E.S.P.), an awareness of events not presented to the physical senses. -**territorial** a. outside the limits of a country or its jurisdiction.

x•**tract** v.t. to take out, esp. by force; to obtain against a person's will; to quote; to calculate; n. matter obtained by distillation; a passage from a book, speech, etc. -**able, -ible** a. -**ion** n. parentage; ancestry; lineage; descent. -**ive** a. -**or** n.

x•**tra•dite** v.t. to deliver up a fugitive to another nation or authority. **extradition** n.

x•**tra•ne•ous** a. not naturally belonging to; not essential; foreign. -**ly** adv.

x•**traor•di•nar•y** a. beyond or out of the common order or method. **extraordinarily** adv. **extraordinariness** n.

x•**trav•a•gant** a. profuse in expense; excessive; wasteful. **extravagance** n. **extravagate** v.i. to wander beyond proper limits.

x•**trav•a•gan•za** n. an extravagant, farcical, or fantastic composition, literary or musical.

ex•**trav•a•sate** v.t. to let out of the proper vessels, as blood; a. let out of its proper vessel.

ex•**treme** a. at the utmost point, edge, or border; outermost; severe; excessive; most urgent; n. the utmost point or degree; the first and last of a series. -**ly** adv. **extremism** n. holding extreme views or doctrines. **extremist** n. **extremity** n. the most distant point or side. **extremities** n.pl. hands and feet; arms and legs.

ex•**tri•cate** v.t. to free from difficulties or perplexities. **extricable** a. **extrication** n.

ex•**trin•sic, extrinsical** a. developing or having its origin from outside the body; not inherent.

ex•**tro•vert** n. in psychology, a person whose emotions express themselves readily in external actions and events, as opposed to an introvert. **extroversion** n.

ex•**trude** v.t. to thrust out; to press out. **extrusion** n.

ex•**u•ber•ant** a. effusive; vivacious; exuberance, exuberancy n. -**ly** adv.

ex•**ude** v.t. to discharge through the pores, as sweat; v.i. to ooze out; to escape slowly.

ex•**ult** v.i. to rejoice exceedingly; to triumph. -**ance, -ancy** n. -**ant** a. -**tation** n.

ex•**u•vi•ae** n.pl. cast off skin, teeth, shells, etc. of animals. **exuvial** a. **exuviate** v.i.

eye n. the organ of sight or vision; sight; bud; shoot; view; keen sense of value; a small staple or ring to receive a door hook; an aperture for observing; v.t. to look at; to view. -**eying** or -**ing** pr.p. -**d** pa.t. and pa.p. -**ball** n. the globe of the eye. -**brow** n. the arch of hairs above the eyes. -**d** a. having eyes. -**glass** n. the eyepiece of an optical instrument; pl. spectacles. -**lash** n. one of the hairs which edge the eyelid. -**let** n. a small eye or hole for a lace or cord, as in garments, sails, etc.; v.i. to make eyelets. -**lid** n. folds of skin which may be drawn at will over the eye. —**opener** n. revealing statement. -**piece** n. lens in an optical instrument by means of which the observer views the image of the object formed in the focus of the other lenses. -**sight** n. power of vision. -**sore** n. an object offensive to the eye. -**tooth** n. either of the two canine teeth of the upper jaw. -**wash** n. eye lotion. -**witness** n. one who gives testimony as to what he actually saw. **to see eye to eye**, to agree; to think alike.

ey•rie n. the nest of a bird of prey.

E

fa•ble n. a short tale or prolonged personification, often with animal characters, intended to convey a moral truth; a myth; legendary.

fab•ric n. structure; woven, knitted or felted cloth. **-ate** v.t. to frame; to fake; to concoct. **-ation, -ator** n.

fab•u•lous a. amazing; exaggerated.

fa•cade n. the front view of a building.

face n. the front of the head; the outer appearance; the outer or upper surface of anything; the dial of a clock, etc.; the front; v.t. to confront; to stand opposite to; to admit the existence of (as facts); to put a layer of different material on to, or to trim an outer surface; v.i. to turn. — **value** n. apparent worth. **facial** a. pert. to the face; n. a beauty treatment for the face. **facing** n. material applied to the edge of a garment.

fac•et n. a small surface, as of a crystal or precious stone; aspect. a. having facets.

fa•ce•tious a. witty; jocular.

fac•ile a. easy. **-ly** adv. **-ness** n. **facilitate** v.t. to make easy; to expedite. **facilitation** n. **facility** n. ease; deftness; aptitude; easiness of access.

fac•sim•i•le n. an exact copy; a. identical; v.t. to make a facsimile.

fact n. anything done; anything actually true; that which has happened. **-ual** a. pert. to facts; actual. **matter-of-fact** a. prosaic; unimaginative.

fac•tion n. a group of people working together, esp. for subversive purposes; dissension; party clique. **factious** a. **factiously** adv.

fac•ti•tious a. oppos. of natural; artificial; manufactured.

fac•tor n. one of numbers which, multiplied together, give a given number; a contributory element or determining cause; v.t. to express as a product of two or more quantities. **-ial** a. pert. to a factor. v.t. to find the factors of a given number. **-ship** n. **-y** n. a building where things are manufactured.

fac•ul•ty n. ability or power to act; mental aptitude; talent; natural physical function; the teaching body. **facultative** a. optional.

fad n. a pet whim; a fancy or notion.

fade v.i. to lose freshness, brightness, or strength gradually; to disappear slowly. **-less** a. not liable to fade; fast (of dye).

Fahr•en•heit n. a type of thermometer graduated so that freezing point of water is fixed at 32° and boiling point at 212°.

fail v.i. to be lacking; to diminish; to deteriorate; to miss; to be unsuccessful in; v.t. to disappoint or desert; to omit; **-ing** pr.p. **-ed** pa.p. **-ing** n. a fault; a weakness; a shortcoming; prep. in default of. **-ure** n. bankruptcy; lack of success.

faint a. lacking strength; indistinct; giddy; timorous; v.i. to become weak; to grow discouraged; to swoon; n. a swoon.

fair a. clear; light-colored; blond; not cloudy; hopeful; just; plausible; middling; adv. in a fair or courteous manner; according to what is just. **-ly**

adv. justly; tolerably; wholly. **-ness** n. — **play** n. straightforward justice. **-way** n. a navigable channel on a river. **fair and square,** honest; honestly.

fair n. periodic competitive exhibition for showing produce of a district; a sale of fancy articles to raise money for charitable purposes.

fair•y n. an imaginary creature in the form of a diminutive human being, supposed to meddle with the affairs of men; a. fairylike. **-land** n. land of the fairies; wonderland. — **tale** n. a story about fairies and magic.

faith n. belief, esp. in a revealed religion; trust or reliance; a system of religious doctrines believed in; loyalty; pledged word. **-ful** a. loyal; reliable; honorable; exact. **-fully** adv. **-fulness** n.

fake v.t. to conceal the defects of, by artifice; to copy, as an antique, and pass it off as genuine; v.i. to pretend; n. a fraud; a deception; a forgery; a faker. **-r** n.

fal•con n. a subfamily of birds of prey, allied to the hawk, with strong curved beaks and long sickle-shaped claws. **-er** n. one who breeds and trains falcons or hawks for hunting wildfowl. **-ry** n. the sport of flying hawks in pursuit of game.

fal•de•ral See **folderol.**

fall v.i. to drop; to collapse; to decline in value; to become degraded; to be captured; n. the act of falling; a drop; the amount (of rain, snow, etc.) deposited in a specified time; a cascade; a wrestling bout; diminution in value, amount, or volume; the autumn. **-ing** pr.p. **fell** pa.t. **-en** pa.p. **-en** a. prostrate; degraded; of loose morals. **-ing star** n. a meteor. **-out** n. radioactive particles which descend to earth after a nuclear explosion.

fal•la•cy n. deceptive appearance; a delusion; an apparently forcible argument which is really illogical. **fallacious** a. misleading; illogical.

fal•li•ble a. liable to error; not reliable.

fal•low a. left untilled for a season; untrained; n. land which has lain untilled and unsown for a year or more; v.t. to plow without sowing.

false a. untrue; inaccurate; dishonest; deceptive; artificial. — **face** n. a mask. **-hood** n. an untruth; a lie. **-ly** adv. **-ness** n. **falsifiable** a. capable of being falsified. **falsification** n. **falsifier** n. one who falsifies. **falsify** v.t. to distort the truth; to forge; to tamper with; to prove to be untrue.

fal•set•to n. forced high notes esp. of a male voice.

fal•ter v.i. to stumble; to hesitate.

fame n. good repute. **-d** a. celebrated. **famous** a. celebrated; noted. **famously** adv.

fa•mil•iar a. intimate; well-known; n. a close acquaintance. **-ize** v.t. to make familiar; to get to know thoroughly. **-ity** n. intimacy; forwardness. **-ly** adv.

fam•i•ly n. parents and their children; the children of the same parents; descendants of one common ancestor. — **tree,** a diagram representing the genealogy of a family.

fam·ine *n.* large-scale scarcity of food. **famish** *v.t.* to starve; *v.i.* to feel acute hunger.

fan *n.* an instrument to produce currents of air or assist ventilation; a decorative folding object, made of paper, silk, etc. used to cool face; *v.t.* to cool with a fan; to ventilate; to cause to flame (as a fire); to excite; to spread out like a fan. **-ning** *pr.p.* **-ned** *pa.p.*

fa·nat·ic *n.* a person inspired with excessive and bigoted enthusiasm, esp. a religious zealot; *a.* over-enthusiastic. **-al** *a.* **-ally** *adv.* **-ism** *n.* violent enthusiasm.

fan·cy *n.* a whim; a notion; partiality; *a.* pleasing to the taste; guided by whim; elaborate; *v.t.* to imagine; to have a liking for; to desire.

fan·fare *n.* a flourish of trumpets; a showy display.

fang *n.* the canine tooth of a carnivorous animal.

fan·ta·sy *n.* mental image; hallucination. Also **phantasy**. **fantasia** *n.* a composition not conforming to the usual rules of music. **fantasied** *a.* fanciful. **fantastic, fantastical** *a.* fanciful; wild. **fantastically** *adv.*

far *a.* distant; remote; more distant of two; *adv.* to a great extent or distance; *n.* a distant place. **-ther** *a.* (*comp.*). **-thest** *a.* (*superl.*) and *adv.* **Far East,** that part of Asia including India, China, Japan. **-sighted** *a.* seeing to a great distance; taking a long view; prudent.

far·ad *n.* the unit of electrostatic capacity — the capacity of a condenser which requires one coulomb to raise its potential by one volt. **-ay,** *n.* the quantity of electricity required to liberate 1 gram-equivalent of an ion. **-aic, -ic** *a.* pert. to induced electrical currents.

farce *n.* a style of comedy marked by boisterous humor and extravagant gesture; absurd or empty show; a pretense.

fare *n.* the sum paid by a passenger on a vehicle; a passenger; food and drink at table. **-well** *interj.* good-bye; *n.* a parting wish for someone's welfare; *a.* parting.

fa·ri·na *n.* flour or meal of cereal grains, used for cereal and puddings; starch.

farm *n.* a tract of land set apart for cultivation or for other industries, as dairy farm, etc.; the buildings on this land; *v.t.* cultivate land for agricultural purposes; *v.i.* and *v.t.* to cultivate; to operate a farm. **-er** *n.* **-ing** *n.* the occupation of cultivating the soil. **-yard** *n.* enclosure surrounded by farm buildings.

far·row *n.* a litter of pigs; *v.t.* to give birth to (pigs).

far·ther *a.* more far; more remote; *adv.* to a greater distance. **-most** *a.*

fas·ci·nate *v.t.* to enchant; to deprive of the power of movement, by a look. **fascinating** *a.* **fascination** *n.* enchantment; irresistible attraction. **fascinator** *n.*

fas·cism *n.* a centralized autocratic national regime with extremely nationalistic policies with an economic system based on state-controlled capitalism. **Fascist** *n.*

fash·ion *n.* the style in which a thing is made or done; pattern; *v.t.* to form; to shape. **-able** *a.* **-ably** *adv.*

fast *v.i.* to abstain from food; to deny oneself certain foods as a form of religious discipline; *n.* abstinence from food; a day of fasting.

fast *a.* rapid; securely fixed; firm; permanent, as a dye; in advance of the correct time, as a clock; *adv.* firmly; soundly; securely; rapidly. **-ness** *n.* security; a stronghold.

fas·ten *v.t.* to fix firmly; to hold together; *v.i.* to fix itself; to catch (of a lock). **-er** *n.* a contrivance for fixing things firmly together. **-ing** *n.* that by which anything fastens, as a lock, bolt, nut, screw.

fas·tid·i·ous *a.* difficult to please; discriminating. **-ly** *adv.* **-ness** *n.*

fat *a.* **-ter** (*comp.*). **-test** (*superl.*). fleshy; plump; oily; yielding a rich supply; *n.* an oily substance found in animal bodies; solid animal or vegetable oil; the best or richest part of anything; *v.t.* to make fat; *v.i.* to grow fat. **-ting** *pr.p.* **-ted** *pa.p.* **-ten** *v.t.* to make fat; to make fertile; *v.i.* to grow fat. **-tener, -tiness** *n.* **-ty** *a.* resembling or containing fat; greasy.

fate *n.* an inevitable and irresistible power supposedly controlling human destiny; appointed lot; death; doom. **fatal** *a.* causing death. **fatalism** *n.* the doctrine that all events are predetermined and unavoidable. **fatalist** *n.* **fatalistic** *a.* **fatality** *n.* accident causing death; the state of being fatal. **-d** *a.* destined; preordained; doomed. **-ful** *a.* momentous; irrevocable. **-fully** *adv.* **-fulness** *n.*

fa·ther *n.* a male parent; *v.t.* to make oneself the father of; to adopt; to assume or admit responsibility for. **-hood** *n.* the state of being a father; paternity. **—in-law** *n.* (*pl.* **-s-in-law**) the father of one's wife or husband. **-less** *a.* without a father living. **-liness** *n.* **-ly** *a.* and *adv.* like a father in affection and care; paternal; benevolent.

fath·om *n.* a nautical measure of depth, 6 ft.; *v.t.* to ascertain the depth of; to sound; to understand.

fa·tigue *n.* weariness from bodily or mental exertion; *v.t.* to weary by toil; to exhaust the strength of; to tire out. **-ing** *pr.p.* **-d** *pa.p.*

fau·cet *n.* a fixture for controlling the flow of liquid from a pipe, etc.; a tap.

fault *n.* a failing; blunder; mistake; defect; flaw; responsibility for error; a dislocation of rock strata; a defect in electrical apparatus. **-ed** *a.* broken by one or more faults. **-ily** *adv.* **-iness** *n.* **-less** *a.* without flaws; perfect. **-lessly** *adv.* **-lessness** *n.* perfection. **-y** *a.* imperfect.

fa·vor *n.* a gracious act; kind regard; goodwill; partiality; token of generosity or esteem; a gift; *v.t.* to regard with kindness; to show bias towards; to resemble in feature. **-able** *a.* friendly; propitious; advantageous; suitable; satisfactory. **-ableness** *n.* **-ably** *adv.* **-ed** *a.*

fortunate; **-ite** *n.* a person or thing regarded with special favor; the likely winner; *a.* regarded with particular affection; most esteemed. **-itism** *n.* undue partiality.

fawn *n.* a young deer; its color; *a.* delicate yellowish-brown; *v.i.* to give birth to a fawn.

fawn *v.i.* to flatter unctuously; to curry favor. **-er** *n.* **-ing** *n.* servile flattery; *a.* over-demonstrative. **-ingly** *adv.* **-ingness** *n.*

fear *n.* alarm; dread; anxiety; reverence towards God; *v.t.* to regard with dread or apprehension; to anticipate (as a disaster); to hold in awe; *v.i.* to be afraid; to be anxious. **-ful** *adv.* **-fulness** *n.* **-less** *a.* without fear; intrepid; dauntless. **-lessly** *adv.* **-lessness** *n.* courage; intrepidity. **-some** *a.* causing fear; terrifying.

fea·si·ble *a.* capable of being done; suitable. **-ness**, feasibility *n.* feasibly *adv.*

feast *n.* a day of joyful or solemn commemoration; a banquet; *v.t.* to feed sumptuously; *v.i.* to eat sumptuously; to be highly gratified or delighted. **-er** *n.*

feat *n.* an exploit or action of extraordinary strength, courage, skill, or endurance.

feath·er *n.* one of the epidermal growths forming the body covering of a bird; a

feather

plume. **-weight** the lightest weight that may be carried by a racehorse; a boxer weighing not more than 126 lbs. **-y** *a.* pert. to, covered with, or resembling feathers.

fea·ture *n.* any part of the face; distinctive characteristic; main attraction; *v.t.* to portray; to outline; to present as the leading attraction. **-less** *a.* void of striking features. **-s** *pl.* the face.

Feb·ru·ar·y *n.* the second month of the year.

fe·ces, fae·ces *n.pl.* dregs; the solid waste matter from the bowels. fecal *a.*

fe·cund *a.* prolific; fruitful; fertile. **-ate** *v.t.* to make fruitful; to impregnate.

fed *pa.t.* and *pa.p.* of the verb feed.

fed·er·al *a.* pert. to a league or treaty, esp. between states; of an association of states which, autonomous in home affairs, combine for matters of wider national and international policy. federacy *n.* **-ize** *v.t.* to form a union under a federal government. **-ism** *n.* **-ist** *n.* a supporter of such a union. federate *v.t.* to unite states into a federation. *a.* united; allied. federation *n.* a federal union. federative *a.*

fee *n.* orig. land held from a lord on condition of certain feudal services; remuneration for professional services; *v.t.* to pay a fee to.

fee·ble *a.* weak; deficient in strength; frail; faint. **—minded** *a.* mentally subnormal. **-ness** *n.* feebly *adv.*

feed *v.t.* to give food to; to supply with nourishment; *v.i.* to eat; to subsist; *n.* that which is consumed, esp. by animals; **-ing** *n.* act of eating; that which is consumed; grazing. fed *pa.p.* and *pa.t.*

feel *v.t.* to perceive by the touch; to be sensitive to; to experience emotionally; *v.i.* to know by the touch; *n.* the sensation of touch; the quality of anything touched. **-er** *n.* one of the tactile organs (antennae, tentacles, etc.) of certain insects and animals; a tentative remark. **-ing** *n.* sense of touch; intuition; sensibility; sympathy. **-ings** *n.pl.* emotions; *a.* kindly; responsive. **-ingly** *adv.* felt *pa.p.* and *pa.t.*

feet *n.pl.* of foot.

feign *v.t.* to invent; to pretend; to counterfeit. **-ed** *a.* pretended; disguised. **-edly** *adv.* **-edness** *n.* **-ing** *n.* pretense; invention. feint *n.* an assumed appearance; *v.i.* to make a deceptive move.

feld·spar *n.* a constituent of granite and other igneous rocks.

fe·lic·i·ty *n.* happiness. felicitate *v.t.* to express joy or pleasure to; to congratulate. felicitation *n.* congratulation; the act of expressing good wishes. felicitous *a.* happy; appropriate; aptly expressed.

fe·line *a.* pert. to cats; catlike.

fell *a.* cruel; ruthless; deadly.

fell *n.* an animal's skin or hide.

fell *pa.t.* of the verb fall.

fell *v.t.* to cause to fall; to cut down. **-er** *n.*

fel·low *n.* a man; boy; a person; **-ship** *n.* companionship.

fel·on *n.* one who has committed felony; *a.* fierce; traitorous. **-ious** *a.* **-iously** *adv.* **-iousness** *n.* **-y** *n.* a crime more serious than a misdemeanor (as murder, manslaughter, etc.).

felt *pa.t.* and *pa.p.* of feel.

felt *n.* a closely matted fabric of wool, hair, etc.: *v.t.* to make into felt; to cover with felt; *v.i.* to become matted like felt. **-ing** *n.* the art or process of making felt; the felt itself.

fe·male *n.* one of the sex that bears young; a plant which produces fruit; *a.* feminine. feminine *a.* pert. to or associated with women; womanly; tender. femininely *adv.* feminineness, femininity *n.* the nature of the female sex; womanliness. feminism *n.* the doctrine that maintains the equality of the sexes; advocacy of women's rights. feminist *n.*

fe·mur *n.* the thighbone. femoral *a.*

fence *n.* a wall or hedge for enclosing; the art of fencing; *v.t.* to enclose with a fence; to guard; *v.i.* to practice the art of swordplay; to evade a direct answer to an opponent's challenge. **-r** *n.* one who is skilled in fencing. fencing *n.* the art or practice of self-defense with the sword, foil, etc.; the act of enclosing by a fence; the materials of which a fence is made.

fend *v.t.* to ward off; *v.i.* to resist; to provide. **-er** *n.* that which acts as a protection; the metal part over wheels of an automobile.

fen·nel n. a perennial umbelliferous plant with yellow flowers.

fer·al a. wild; not domesticated; run wild (of plants). **ferine** a.

fer·ment n. a substance which causes fermentation, as yeast; fermentation; v.t. to induce fermentation in; v.i. to undergo fermentation; to work (of wine). **-ability** n. **-able** a. **-ation** n. the decomposition of organic substances produced by the action of a living organism, or of certain chemical agents. **-ative** a.

fern n. plant characterized by fibrous roots, and leaves called fronds. **-y** a.

fe·roc·i·ty n. cruelty; savage fierceness of disposition. **ferocious** a. fierce; violent; wild. **ferociously** adv. **ferociousness** n.

fer·ric a. pert. to or extracted from iron; applied to compounds of trivalent iron. — **acid**, an acid containing iron and oxygen.

fer·ro- containing or made of iron, occurring in compound words. **ferroconcrete** n. reinforced concrete; concrete with inner skeleton of iron or steel. **ferromagnetic** a. reacting like iron in a magnetic field. **-us** a. pert. to iron.

fer·ry v.t. to transport over stretch of water by boat; n. a place where one is conveyed across a river, etc. by boat; the ferryboat.

fer·tile a. producing or bearing abundantly; prolific; fruitful. **-ly** adv. **-ness**, n. **fertilization** n. the act of fertilizing; enrichment of soil, by natural or artificial means; union of the female and male cells. **fertilize** v.t. to make fruitful; to fecundate; to pollinate. **fertilizer** n. one who, or that which, fertilizes; material to enrich soil. **fertility** n.

fer·vent a. glowing; ardent; zealous, enthusiastic. **fervency** n. ardor; intensity of devotion. **-ly** adv. **fervid** a. burning; vehement; intense. **fervidity** n. **fervidly** adv. **fervidness** n. zeal; enthusiasm. **fervor** n. heat; ardor; passion.

fes·ter v.t. to cause to putrefy; v.i. to become inflamed; to rot; n. an ulcer; a sore.

fes·tive a. joyous, convivial. **festival** n. a feast or celebration; an annual competition or periodic gathering of musical or dramatic societies. **-ly** adv. **festivity** n. merriment; merrymaking; festival.

fetch v.t. to go for and bring; to summon; v.i. to go and bring things; n. the act of bringing; a trick or artifice. **-ing** a. attractive; alluring.

fete n. a festival; a holiday; v.t. to honor with celebrations. **-d** a. honored.

fe·tish, fetich, fetiche n. anything regarded with exaggerated reverence. **-ism**, n. fetish worship. **-istic**, a.

fe·tus, foetus n. the young of vertebrate animals between the embryonic and independent states. **fetal, foetal** a. **fetation, foetation** n. pregnancy. **feticide** n. destroying of the fetus;

abortion.

feud n. a lasting hereditary strife between families or clans.

feud n. an estate or land held on condition of service; a fief. **-al** a. pert. to feuds or to feudalism. **-alism** n. a system which prevailed in Europe in the Middle Ages, by which vassals held land from the king and the tenants-in-chief in return for military service. Also **feudal system.** **-ary**, **-atory** a. holding land by feudal tenure; n. a vassal holding land in fee.

fe·ver n. bodily disease marked by unusual rise of temperature and usually a quickening of pulse; v.t. to put into a fever; v.i. to become fevered. **-ed** a. affected with fever; frenzied. **-ish** a. slightly fevered. **-ishly** adv.

few a. not many; n. and pron. a small number. **-ness** n.

fi·an·cé n. a betrothed man.

fi·as·co n. any spectacular failure.

fib n. a falsehood; a mild lie; v.i. to tell a petty lie. **-bing** pr.p. **-bed** pa.p. and pa.t.

fi·ber n. one of the bundles of threadlike tissue constituting muscles, etc.; any threadlike substance used for weaving fabric. **-ed, -less, fibriform** a. **fibril** n. a very small fiber. **fibrillose** a. covered with fibers. **fibrillous** a. composed of small fibers. **fibrin** n. a protein formed in coagulation of blood. **fibroid** a. of a fibrous nature; n. a fibrous tumor. **fibrous** a. composed of fibers. **fibrousness** n.

fib·u·la n. the slender outer bone of the leg between knee and ankle. **-r** a.

fick·le a. inconstant; capricious; unreliable. **-ness** n.

fic·tion n. literature dealing with imaginary characters and situations; something invented, or imagined. **-al** a. **fictitious** a. imaginary; feigned; false. **fictitiously** adv.

fid·dle n. a stringed musical instrument; a violin; v.t. and v.i. to play on a fiddle. — **bow** n. the bow used in playing a violin. **-dee-dee** n. nonsense. **-faddle** v.i. to trifle; to dawdle; n. triviality; interj. rubbish. **-sticks** nonsense. **fiddling** a. trifling.

fi·del·i·ty n. faithfulness; loyalty; devotion to duty; adherence to marriage vows.

fid·get v.i. to move restlessly; to be uneasy; n. uneasiness. **-s** n.pl. nervous restlessness. **-y** a.

fi·du·ciar·y a. holding or held in trust; n. a trustee. **fiducial** a. having faith or confidence.

field n. cleared land; a division of farmland; scene of a battle; any wide expanse; sphere of influence within which magnetic, electrostatic, or gravitational forces are perceptible; the background of a flag, coin, etc. on which a design is drawn; area of ground used for sports; v.t. to catch the ball; v.i. to act as fielder. — **artillery** n. light guns for active operations. — **battery** n. battery of field guns. — **book** n. book used for notes by land surveyor or naturalist. — **day** n. a day for athletic contests; a gala day. **-er** n. one who fields at cricket, baseball, etc.

fiend n. a demon; the devil; a malicious

foe; one who is crazy about something, as, *a fresh-air fiend.* -ish *a.*

fierce *a.* ferocious; violent; savage; intense. -ly *adv.* -ness *n.* ferocity; rage.

fi•er•y *a.* flaming; hot; ardent; fierce; vehement; irritable. fierily *adv.* fieriness *n.*

fife *n.* a high-pitched flute. -r *n.* one who plays the fife.

fif•teen *a.* and *n.* five and ten; the symbol, 15 or XV.

fifth *a.* next after the fourth; *n.* one of five equal parts of a whole.

fif•ty *a.* and *n.* five times ten; the symbol 50 or L. fiftieth *a.* next in a series of forty-nine others; *n.* a fiftieth part. to go fifty-fifty, share and share alike.

fig *n.* a Mediterranean tree or its fruit.

fight *v.t.* to wage war against; to contend against; to oppose; *v.i.* to take part in single combat or battle; to resist; *n.* a combat; a battle; a struggle. fought *pa.p.* -er *n.* one who fights; an aircraft designed for fighting. -ing *a.* able to, or inclined to, fight; pert. to a fight.

fig•ment *n.* an invention, fiction, or fabrication.

fig•ure *n.* outward form of anything; the form of a person; a diagram, drawing, etc.; the sign of a numeral, as 1, 2, 3; *v.t.* to note by numeral characters; to calculate; to symbolize; to image in the mind; *v.i.* to make a figure. figurative *a.* not literal. figuratively *adv.* figurativeness *n.* -head *n.* the nominal head of an organization, without real authority; ornamental figure under the bowsprit of a ship. figurine *n.* a statuette. figure of speech, an unusual use of words to produce a desired effect, such as metaphor, simile, etc.

fil•a•ment *n.* a slender thread; a fiber, the stalk of a stamen. -ous *a.* threadlike.

fil•bert *n.* the nut of the hazel tree.

file *n.* an orderly line; a cabinet, wire, or portfolio for keeping papers in order; the papers or cards thus kept; *v.t.* to set in order in a public record office; *v.i.* to march in a file; to make application. Indian or single file, a single line of men marching one behind the other. rank and file, noncommissioned soldiers; the general mass of people as distinct from well-known figures.

file *n.* a steel instrument for smoothing rough surfaces or cutting through metal; *v.t.* to cut or abrade with a file. filing *pr.p.* -d *pa.p.* filing *n.* a particle of metal rubbed off by a file; *v.t.* the action of abrading stone or cutting metal.

fil•i•al *a.* pert. to or befitting a son or daughter. -ly *adv.*

fil•i•bus•ter *n.* one who deliberately obstructs legislation, esp. by making long speeches; *v.i.* to act as a filibuster.

Fil•i•pi•no *n.* a native of the Philippine Islands.

fill *v.t.* to make full; to replenish; to occupy as a position; to stop up (a tooth); *v.i.* to become full; *n.* a full supply. -er *n.* one who, or that which, fills. -ing *n.* that which fills up a space, as gold, etc. used by dentists; a mixture put into sandwiches, cakes, etc.; *a.* satisfying; ample.

fil•let *n.* piece of meat cut from the thigh; a piece of meat boned and rolled; fish after bones are removed; *v.t.* to bone.

fil•ly *n.* a young mare.

film *n.* a thin coating or membrane; a delicate filament; a roll of flexible, sensitized material used for photography; pictures taken on this roll; *pl.* a movie show; *v.t.* to cover with a film; to take a moving picture of; to reproduce on a film. -iness *n.* -y *a.* composed of or covered with film; membranous; sheer.

fil•ter *n.* a device for separating liquids from solids, or for straining impurities from liquids; a device for removing dust from the air; a piece of colored glass placed in front of the lens, passing certain rays only; *v.t.* to purify by passing through a filter; to filtrate; *v.i.* to pass through a filter. filtrate *v.t.* to filter; *n.* the liquid which has been strained through a filter. filtration *n.*

filth *n.* foul matter; dirt; pollution; immorality; obscenity. -ily *adv.* -iness *n.* -y *a.*

fin *n.* a paddle-like organ of fishes and other aquatic forms serving to balance and propel; a vertical surface, fixed usually on the tail of an aircraft to aid lateral and directional stability.

fi•nal *a.* pert. to the end; last; *n.* the last stage of anything; *pl.* the last examination or contest in a series. -ist *n.* a competitor who reaches the finals of a contest. -ity *n.* the state of being final; conclusiveness. -ize *v.t.* to give a final form to. -ly *adv.*

fi•na•le *n.* the end; the last movement of a musical composition; final scene.

fi•nance *n.* the management of money affairs; *pl.* the income of a state or person; resources; funds; *v.t.* to provide funds for; to supply capital. financial *a.* pert. to finance; fiscal. financially *adv.* financier *n.* one who deals in large-scale money transactions.

finch *n.* the name applied to various species of small, seed-eating birds, including the *chaffinch, bullfinch.*

find *v.t.* to come to by searching; to meet with; to discover; *n.* a discovery, esp. of unexpected value. found *pa.t.* and *pa.p.* -er *n.* -ing *n.* the act of one who finds; a legal decision arrived at by a jury after deliberation; a discovery.

fine *a.* excellent; thin; refined; *v.t.* to make fine; to refine or purify; *v.i.* to become fine, pure, or slender; delicately thin (of wire). -ly *adv.* -ness *n.* the state of being fine; the amount of gold in an alloy. -r *n.* refiner. -ry *n.* ornament; gay clothes; a furnace for making wrought iron. finesse *n.* subtlety of contrivance to gain a point; *v.i.* and *v.t.* to use artifice; to try to take a trick by finesse.

fine *n.* a sum of money imposed as a penalty for an offense; *v.t.* to impose a fine on.

fi•nesse See fine.

fin•ger *n.* any one of the extremities of the

hand, excluding thumb; *v.t.* to touch with fingers; to handle; to perform with fingers; *v.i.* to use the fingers. -ing *n.* the act of touching or handling lightly with fingers; the manner of manipulating the fingers in playing an instrument.

fin•i•cal *a.* affectedly fine; overfastidious. -ly *adv.* finicking, finicky, *a.* overparticular.

fin•ish *v.t.* to bring to an end; to terminate; *v.i.* to conclude; *n.* that which finishes, or perfects; last stage; the final coat of paint, etc. -ed *a.* terminated. -er *n.* one who or that which finishes or gives the final touches. -ing school, a school for completing the education of young women.

fi•nite *a.* limited in quantity, degree, or capacity. -ly *adv.* -ness, finitude *n.*

Finn *n.* a native of Finland. -ic, -ish *a.* Finlander *n.* a Finn.

fir *n.* cone-bearing evergreen tree, yielding valuable timber. — cone *n.* fruit of the fir.

fire *n.* heat and light caused by combustion; burning; flame; *v.t.* to set on fire; to kindle; to supply with fuel; *v.i.* to be ignited. — alarm *n.* an alarm giving warning of an outbreak of fire. — brigade *n.* men specially trained to deal with fire. — escape *n.* iron stair used as emergency exit from burning building. -fly *n.* a type of beetle which has light-producing organs. -man *n.* a member of a fire-fighting unit. -place *n.* hearth or grate. -plug *n.* a hydrant for drawing water by hose to extinguish a fire. -proof *a.* -r *n.* — screen *n.* a movable protective screen in front of a fire. -side *n.* the hearth. -wood *n.* wood for fuel; kindling. -work *n.* a preparation containing gunpowder, sulfur, etc. for making spectacular explosions. firing line *n.* the area of a battle zone within firing range of the enemy. firing party or squad, soldiers detailed to fire the final salute at a military funeral, or to shoot a condemned person.

firm *a.* fixed; solid; compact; rigid; steady; unwavering; stern; inflexible. -ly *adv.* -ness *n.*

firm *n.* the name, title, or style under which a company transacts business.

fir•ma•ment *n.* the expanse of the sky; the heavens.

first *a.* preceding all others in a series or in kind; foremost (in place); earliest (in time); *adv.* before anything else in time, place, degree, or preference; *n.* beginning. — aid *n.* preliminary treatment given to injured person before the arrival of a doctor. -born *n.* eldest child. — class *a.* first-rate; of highest worth; of superior accommodation; *adv.* in the firstclass. -hand *a.* obtained direct from the source. -ly *adv.* —rate *a.* of highest excellence.

fis•cal *a.* pert. to the public treasury or revenue; pert. to financial matters generally.

fish *n.* a cold-blooded, aquatic vertebrate animal, with limbs represented by fins, and breathing through its gills; *pl.* fish, -es; *v.t.* to catch by fishing; *v.i.* to follow the occupation of a fisherman, for business or pleasure. -er *n.* one who fishes. -erman *n.* one whose employment is to catch fish; one who fishes for pleasure; an angler. -ery *n.* the business of fishing; a fishing ground; the legal right to fish in a certain area. -hook *n.* a barbed hook for catching fish by line. -ily *adv.* -iness *n.* -ing *n.* the act of fishing. -ing rod *n.* a long supple rod with line attached, used by anglers. -ing tackle *n.* an angler's gear comprising, rod, lines, hooks, etc. -y *a.* abounding in fish; pert. to fish; expressionless; dubious.

fish

fis•sion *n.* the process of splitting or breaking up into parts; cell cleavage; *v.t.* and *v.i.* to split into two parts. -able *a.*

fis•sure *n.* a cleft, crack, or slit.

fist *n.* the hand clenched with fingers doubled into the palm.

fis•tu•la *n.* a narrow duct; an infected channel in the body leading from an internal abscess to the surface. -r, fistulous *a.* hollowed like a pipe.

fit *a.* -ter. -test. suitable; qualified; proper; vigorous; *v.t.* to make suitable; to qualify; to adapt; to adjust; to fashion to the appropriate size; *v.i.* to be proper or becoming. -ting *pr.p.* -ted *pa.t.* -ly *adv.* -ness *n.* the state of being fit; appropriateness; sound bodily health. -ter *n.* one who or that which makes fit; a tailor or dressmaker who fits clothes on a person. -ting *a.* appropriate; suitable; *n.* a trial of a garment to see that it fits. -tings *n.pl.* fixtures; equipment. -tingly *adv.*

fit *n.* a sudden and violent attack of a disorder; a seizure. -ful *a.* spasmodic; intermittent. -fully *adv.*

five *n.* four and one; the symbol 5 or V; *a.* one more than four. -fold *a.* five times repeated; quintuple. -r *n.* a five-dollar bill.

fix *v.t.* to make firm; to establish; to secure; to immobilize; to gaze at; to repair; to put in order; *v.i.* to settle permanently; to become hard; *n.* dilemma; predicament. -ation *n.* the act of fixing; steadiness; in psychoanalysis, an emotional arrest of part of the psychosexual development. -ative *n.* a fixing agent; a chemical which preserves specimens in a lifelike condition. -ed *a.* settled, permanent, not apt to change; steady. -edly *adv.* -edness *n.* -er *n.* one who, or that which, fixes. -ity *n.* fixedness; immobility. -ings *n.pl.* apparatus, trimmings. -ture *n.* that which is fixed or attached; anything of an accessory nature considered a part of the real property.

fizz *v.i.* to effervesce; *n.* a hissing sound; any effervescent liquid. -le *v.i.* to fizz or splutter.

flab•ber•gast *v.t.* to overcome with

amazement.

flab·by *a.* soft; yielding to the touch; drooping; weak. **flabbily** *adv.* **flabbiness** *n.*

flag *v.i.* to hang loosely; to grow spiritless or dejected; to become languid; to lose vigor. **-ging** *pr.p.* **-ged** *pa.p.*

flag *n.* a flat paving stone; a type of sandstone which splits easily into large slabs. Also **-stone.**

flag *n.* an ensign or colors; a standard; a banner as a mark of distinction, rank, or nationality; *v.t.* to decorate with flags or

flags

bunting; to convey a message by flag signals. **-ship** *n.* the ship flying the admiral's flag. **white flag,** the symbol of truce or surrender. **yellow flag,** a flag indicating that a ship is in quarantine. **to fly a flag half-mast,** to hoist flag halfway as token of mourning.

fla·grant *a.* glaring; notorious; scandalous. **flagrance, flagrancy** *n.* **-ly** *adv.*

flair *n.* instinctive discernment; a keen scent.

flake *n.* a scalelike particle; *v.t.* to form into flakes, to cover with flakes; *v.i.* to scale; to fall in flakes. **flaky** *a.* consisting of flakes.

flam·boy·ant *a.* florid; showy; ornate. **flamboyance, flamboyancy** *n.*

flame *n.* a mass of burning vapor or gas; a blaze of light; fire in general; *v.i.* to blaze; to blush; to become violently excited, fervent, or angry. **flaming** *a.* blazing; gaudy; fervent. **flamingly** *adv.* **flammability** *n.* **flammable** *a.*

fla·min·go *n.* tropical wading bird.

flan *n.* a pastry shell or cake filled with fruit filling.

flange *n.* a projecting edge, as of a railway-car wheel to keep it on the rails, or of castings to fasten them together.

flank *n.* the fleshy part of side of animal between ribs and hip; *v.t.* to stand at the side of; to protect the flank of an army, etc.; to border.

flan·nel *n.* a soft-textured, loosely woven woolen cloth; *a.* made of flannel; *v.t.* to cover or rub with flannel. **-s** *n.pl.* clothes made of this, esp. sports garments; woolen undergarments. **-ette** *n.* a cotton material like flannel.

flap *n.* a piece of flexible material attached on one side only and usually covering an opening, as of envelope; anything hinged and hanging loose; *v.t.* to cause to sway or flutter; *v.i.* to flutter; to fall like a flap; to move, as wings. **-ping** *pr.p.* **-ped** *pa.p.* **-jack** *n.* a broad, flat pancake.

flare *v.i.* to burn with a glaring, unsteady or fitful flame; to burst out with flame, anger, etc.; *n.* an unsteady, blazing light; a brilliant, often colored, light used as a signal; a sudden burst of flame, passion, etc. **-d** *a.* (of a skirt) spreading gradually out toward the bottom. **flaring** *a.*

flash *n.* a sudden brief burst of light; an instant or moment; a news story; *a.* showy; tawdry; *v.i.* to blaze suddenly and die out; to pass swiftly; *v.t.* to cause to flash; to transmit instantaneously, as news by radio, telephone, etc. **-back** *n.* momentary turning back to an episode in a story. **-bulb** *n.* *(Photog.)* an electric bulb giving brilliant flash for night picture. **-ily** *adv.* **-iness** *n.* **-light** *n.* a portable light powered by batteries or a small generator. **-y** *a.* showy; tawdry; cheap.

flask *n.* a narrow-necked, usually flat bottle easily carried in the pocket.

flat *a.* **-ter. -test.** level; even; tasteless; monotonous; dull; below the true pitch; *n.* a level surface; low-lying sometimes flooded, tract of land; a note, a semitone below the natural; the symbol for this; *adv.* prone; in a manner below true pitch. **—finish** *n.* a flat surface in paint work. **—footed** *a.* having fallen arches in the feet. **-ly** *adv.* peremptorily. **-ness** *n.* **— rate,** uniform rate. **-ten** *v.t.* to make flat; to lower the true musical pitch of. **-ware** *n.* silver knives, forks, etc.

flat·ter *v.t.* to praise unduly and insincerely; to pay fulsome compliments to. **-er** *n.* **-ing** *a.* **ingly** *adv.* **-y** *n.* the act of flattering; undue praise.

flaunt *v.t.* to display ostentatiously or impudently; *v.i.* to wave or move in the wind; to parade showily; *n.* a vulgar display.

fla·vor *n.* savor; quality affecting taste or smell; distinctive quality of a thing; *v.t.* to season; to give zest to. **-ous** *a.* **-ing** *n.* substance to add flavor to a dish, e.g. spice, essence.

flaw *n.* a crack; a defect; a weak point as in an argument; *v.t.* to break; to crack. **-less** *a.* perfect.

flax *n.* the fibers of an annual blue-flowered plant, used for making linen; the plant itself. **-en** *a.* pert. to or resembling flax; loose or flowing; of the color of unbleached flax, hence yellowish or golden.

flea *n.* a small, wingless, very agile insect with irritating bite. **—bitten** *a.* bitten by a flea; mean; worthless.

fleck *n.* a spot; a streak; *v.t.* to spot; to dapple.

fled *pa.t.* and *pa.p.* of **flee.**

flee *v.i.* to fly or retreat from danger; *v.t.* to hasten from. **-ing** *pr.p.* **fled** *pa.p.* and *pa.t.*

fleece *n.* the coat of wool covering a sheep or shorn from it; anything resembling wool; *v.t.* to shear wool. **fleecy** *a.* woolly;

resembing wool.

fleet *n.* a group of ships; a force of naval vessels under one command.

fleet *a.* swift; nimble; *v.t.* to pass swiftly; *v.t.* to make to pass quickly. **-ing** *a.* transient; ephemeral; passing. **-ingly** *adv.* **-ness** *n.* swiftness. —**footed** *a.* swift of foot.

Flem·ing *n.* a native of Flanders. **Flemish** *a.* pert. to Flanders.

flesh *n.* the body tissue; kindred; the pulpy part of fruit; *v.t.* to incite to hunt, as a hound, by feeding it on flesh; to remove flesh from the underside of hides preparatory to tanning process. — **color** *n.* the pale pink color of the human skin (of white races). **-iness** *n.* state of being fleshy; plumpness. **-less** *a.* **-liness** *n.* **-ly** *a.* corporeal; worldly; sensual. — **wound** *n.* **-y** *a.* pert. to flesh; corpulent; gross; thick and soft.

fleur-de-lis *n.* a design based on the shape of an iris; the royal insignia of France.

flew *pat.* of verb **fly.**

flex *v.t.* and *v.i.* to bend. **-ibility** *n.* quality of being pliable; adaptability; versatility. **-ible** *a.* **-ibly** *adv.* **-ile** *a.* bendable. **-ion, flection** *n.* a bend; a fold; an inflection. **-or** *n.* a muscle. **-uose, -uous** *a.* bending; tortuous. **-ure** *n.* act of bending; a bend.

flick *v.t.* to strike lightly, as with whip; *n.* light, smart stroke.

flick·er *v.i.* to flutter; to waver; to quiver; to burn unsteadily; *n.* act of wavering; quivering.

flight *n.* the act or power of flying; the distance covered in flying; a journey by airplane; a flock of birds. — **deck,** *n.* the deck of an aircraft carrier for planes to land or take off. **-y** *a.* capricious; giddy; volatile.

flight *n.* the act of fleeing; retreat. **to put to flight,** to rout.

flim·sy *a.* thin; fragile; unsubstantial; *n.* thin, transfer paper. **flimsily** *adv.* **flimsiness** *n.*

flinch *v.i.* to shrink from pain or difficulty; to wince. **-ing** *n.* the act of flinching.

fling *v.t.* to throw from the hand; *v.i.* to flounce; to throw oneself violently; *n.* a cast or throw; a gibe; abandonment to pleasure; lively dance. **flung** *pat.* and *pa.p.* **-er** *n.*

flint *n.* quartz, which readily produces fire when struck with steel; a prehistoric stone weapon; *a.* made of flint. **-lock** *n.* a gunlock with a flint fixed on the hammer for firing the priming. **-y** *a.* made of, or resembling, flint; hardhearted; cruel.

flip *v.t.* to flick; to jerk; *n.* a flick; a snap. **-ping** *pr.p.* **-ped** *pat.* and *pa.p.* **-per** *n.* the limb of an animal which facilitates swimming.

flip·pant *a.* smart or pert in speech. **flippancy** *n.* **-ly** *adv.*

flirt *v.t.* to jerk, as a bird's tail; to move playfully to and fro, as a fan; *v.i.* to move about briskly; *n.* a jerk; a philanderer; a flighty girl. **-ation** *n.* **-atious** *a.*

flit·ter *v.i.* to flutter.

float *v.i.* to flutter.

float *v.i.* to rest or drift on the surface of

a liquid; to be buoyed up; to be suspended in air; to wander aimlessly; *v.t.* to cause to stay on the surface of a liquid; *n.* anything which is buoyant; a raft; cork or quill on a fishing line, or net; a hollow floating ball of metal indicating depth of liquid in tank or cistern. **-able** *a.* **-age** *n.* See **flotage. -ation** *n.* See **flotation. -er** *n.* **-ing** *a.* buoyant on surface of the water or in air; movable; fluctuating; in circulation. **-ing dock,** a floating dry dock. **-ingly** *adv.*

flock *n.* a small tuft of wool; refuse of wool in cloth-making, used for stuffing cushions, etc.

flock *n.* a collection of animals; a crowd of people; *v.i.* to come together in crowds.

flog *v.t.* to beat or strike, as with a rod or whip; to thrash. **-ging** *pr.p.* **-ged** *pa.t.* and *pa.p.*

flood *n.* an overflow of water; an inundation; a deluge; a torrent; *v.t.* to overflow; to drench; to overwhelm; *v.i.* to spill over; to rise (as the tide). **-lighting** *n.* artificial lighting by lamps fitted with special reflectors.

floor *n.* the horizontal surface of a room upon which one walks; any level area; minimum level, esp. of prices; *v.t.* to cover with a floor; to strike down; to perplex; to stump. **-ing** *n.* materials for floors. — **show** *n.* a show at a nightclub.

flop *v.t.* to flap; to set down heavily; *v.i.* to drop down suddenly or clumsily; *n.* a fall, as of a soft, outspread body. **-ping** *pr.p.* **-ped** *pa.t.* and *pa.p.* **-py** *a.* slack.

flo·ra *n.* the plants native to a certain geographical region or geological period; a classified list of such plants. **-l** *a.* **-lly** *adv.* adorned with flowers. **floriated,** *a.* **floret** *n.* a single flower in a cluster of flowers; a small compact flower head. **florist** *n.* a grower or seller of flowers.

flo·res·cence *n.* a bursting into flower. **florescent** *a.*

floss *n.* untwisted threads of very fine silk. — **silk** *n.* very soft silk thread. **-y** *a.*

flo·tage *n.* state or act of floating; the floating capacity of anything.

flo·ta·tion *n.* the act of floating; act of launching, esp. a business venture, loan, etc. Also **floatation.**

flo·til·la *n.* a fleet of small vessels.

flounce *v.i.* to turn abruptly; to flounder about; *n.* a sudden, jerky movement.

floun·der *n.* a small, edible flatfish.

floun·der *v.i.* to struggle helplessly, as in marshy ground; to tumble about; to stumble hesitatingly, as in a speech.

flour *n.* the finely ground meal of wheat, etc.; *v.t.* to turn into flour; to sprinkle with flour. **-y** *a.*

flour·ish *v.t.* to decorate with flowery ornament or with florid diction; *v.i.* to grow luxuriantly; to prosper; *n.* ornament; a fanciful stroke of the pen. **-ing** *a.* thriving; vigorous.

flout *v.t.* to mock; *v.i.* to jeer; *n.* a gibe; an insult.

flow *v.i.* to run, as a liquid; to rise, as the tide; to circulate, as the blood; to glide along; *v.t.* to overflow; *n.* a stream; a current; the rise of the tide; any easy expression of thought, diction, etc.; output. -ing *a.* moving; running; fluent; curving gracefully, as lines; falling in folds, as drapery. -ingly *adv.*

flow•er *n.* the reproductive organ in plants; a blossom. -s *n.pl.* a substance in the form of a powder, as *flowers of sulfur; v.t.* to adorn with flowers or flowerlike shapes; *v.i.* to produce flowers; to bloom;

flower

to come to prime condition. -ed *a.* decorated with a flower pattern, as fabric. -et *n.* a small flower; a floret. -ing *a.* having flowers. -y *a.* abounding in or decorated with flowers; highly ornate; euphuistic.

flown *pa.p. of* fly.

flu *n.* influenza.

fluc•tu•ate *v.i.* to move up and down, as a wave; to be unstable; to be irresolute. fluctuant *a.* fluctuation *n.* a vacillation.

flue *n.* a shaft or duct in a chimney.

flu•ent *a.* flowing; ready in the use of words. fluency *n.*

fluff *n.* light, floating down; *v.t.* to give a fluffy surface to; *v.i.* to become downy; -y *a.*

fluid *n.* a substance which flows; a nonsolid; *a.* capable of flowing; liquid; gaseous; shifting. -ify *v.t.* to make fluid. -ity, -ness *n.* the state or quality of being a nonsolid; -ly *adv.*

fluke *n.* the flounder; a parasitic worm.

fluke *n.* any lucky chance.

flung *pa.t.* and *pa.p.* of fling.

flunk *v.i.* to fail as in an examination or course; *v.t.* to fail in.

flu•or *n.* a mineral, fluoride of source of fluorine. -esce *v.i.* to exhibit calcium, usually called *fluorite;* principle fluorescence. -escense *n.* the property of some substances which emit surface reflections of light different in color from the mass of the material upon exposure to external radiation. -escent *a.* -ide *n.* a compound of fluorine with another element. -ine *n.* a pale yellow very active gaseous element. -escent lighting, *a.* form of artificial diffused lighting, giving the effect of permanent daylight.

flur•ry *n.* a sudden, brief gust of wind; bustle; commotion; *v.t.* to agitate; to fluster.

flush *v.i.* to turn red in the face; to blush; to cause to blush or turn red; to cleanse with a rush of water; *n.* a flow of water; a rush of blood to the face.

flush *n.* a run of cards of the same suit.

flush *v.t.* to level up; *a.* being in the same plane; well-supplied, as with money; full; even with margins.

flus•ter *v.t.* to make agitated; to flurry; *v.i.* to be confused and flurried; *n.* confusion; nervous agitation. -ed *a.*

flute *n.* a musical tubular wind instrument; a stop in the pipe organ; a vertical groove in the shaft of a column; *v.i.* to play the flute; *v.t.* to play (tune) on the flute; to make flutes or grooves in. -d *a.* ornamented with grooves, channels, etc. fluting *n.* action of playing a flute; the ornamental vertical grooving on a pillar, on glass. flutist *n.* one who plays a flute. Also flautist. fluty *a.*

flut•ter *v.t.* to throw into confusion; *v.i.* to flap the wings; *n.* quick and irregular motion; nervous hurry; confusion.

flux *n.* the act of flowing; fluidity; *v.t.* to fuse; to melt; *v.i.* to flow. -ion *n.* a flow or flux.

fly *v.t.* to cause to fly; to flee from; *v.i.* to move through the air, as a bird or an aircraft; to become airborne; to travel by airplane; to move rapidly; to flee; *n.* a winged insect, esp. of the order *Diptera;* a housefly; a fishhook in imitation of a fly; a flap on a garment covering a row of buttons or other fastener; a ball sent high in the air (*pa.t.* and *pa.p.* in baseball, flied). -ing *pr.p.* flew *pa.t.* flown *pa.p.* -ing *n.* moving through the air; air navigation; *a.* capable of flight; streaming; swift. -ing saucer *n.* name given to a saucerlike object reputedly seen flying at tremendous speeds and high altitudes. -paper *n.* a paper smeared with sticky substance to trap flies. -wheel *n.* a heavy-rimmed wheel attached to the crankshaft of an engine to regulate its speed or accumulate power.

flywheel

foal *n.* the young of a mare, a colt or a filly; *v.t.* and *v.i.* to bring forth a foal.

foam *n.* froth; the bubbles of air on surface of effervescent liquid; *v.i.* to froth; to bubble; to gather foam. -ing *a.* ingly *adv.* — rubber *n.* latex made into a soft, elastic, and porous substance, resembling a spong. -y *a.* frothy.

fo•cus *n.* the point at which rays of light meet after reflection or refraction; one of two points connected linearly to any point on a curve; any point of concentration; *v.t.* to bring to a focus; to adjust; to concentrate; *v.i.* to converge. -es, foci *pl.* -ing *pr.p.* -ed *pa.p.* focal *a.* pert. to a focus. focalize *v.t.* to bring into focus; to cause to converge; to concentrate. focalization *n.* in focus, clearly outlined; well-defined. out of

F

focus, distorted.

foe n. an enemy.

foe·tus See fetus.

fog n. thick mist; mental confusion; v.t. to shroud in fog; to perplex the mind. v.i. to become cloudy or obscured. **-bank** n. a mass of fog. **-gily** adv. **-giness** n. **-gy** a. **-horn** n. a loud siren used during fog for warnings.

fo·gy, fogey n. dull, old fellow; an elderly person whose ideas are behind the times.

foi·ble n. weakness of character; a failing.

foil v.t. to frustrate; to baffle.

foil n. a thin leaf of metal, as tinfoil.

foist v.t. to palm off. **-er** n.

fold n. a doubling over of a flexible material; a pleat; a crease or a line made by folding; a dip in rock strata caused originally by pressure; v.t. to double over; to enclose within folds or layers; to embrace; v.i. to be pleated or doubled. **-er** n. the one who or that which folds; a folded, printed paper; a file for holding papers, etc.

fold n. an enclosure for sheep; a flock of sheep; v.t. to confine in a fold.

fol·der·ol n. the refrain to a song.

fo·liage n. leaves of a plant in general; leafage. **-d** a. having leaves.

fo·li·o n. the two opposite pages of a ledger used for one account and numbered the same; page number in a book; a. pert. to or formed of sheets folded so as to make two leaves; v.t. to number the pages of a book on one side only.

folk n. people in general, or as a specified class; a. originating among the common people. **-s** n.pl. one's own family and near relations. — **dance** n. a traditional country dance. **-lore** n. popular superstitions or legends.

fol·li·cle n. a one-celled seed vessel; a small sac; a gland, as in hair follicle. **follicular** a. pert. to a follicle.

fol·low v.t. to go after; to move behind; to succeed (in a post); to adhere to (a belief); to watch carefully; to keep in touch with; v.i. to come after; to pursue; to occur as a consequence; n. the act of following. **-er** n. one who comes after; adherents; vocation; a. coming next after.

fol·ly n. weakness of mind; a foolish action; (pl.) a theatrical revue.

fond a. loving; doting; very affectionate. **fond of,** much attached to. **-le** v.t. to caress; to stroke tenderly. **-ly** adv. **-ness** n.

fon·dant n. a thick, creamy sugar candy.

font n. a stone basin for holding baptismal water.

food n. matter which one feeds on; solid nourishment as contrasted with liquids; mental or spiritual nourishment. **-stuff** n. edible commodity with nutritional value.

fool n. one who behaves stupidly; one devoid of common sense; v.t. to make a fool of, to impose on; to trick; v.i. to behave like a fool; to trifle. **-ery** n. silly behavior; foolish act. **-hardily** adv. **-hardiness** n. **-hardy** a. recklessly daring; venturesome. **-ish** a. weak in intellect.

-ishly adv. **-ishness** n. **-ing** n. foolery. **-proof** a. (of machines) so devised that mishandling cannot cause damage to machine or personnel.

foot n. the extreme end of the lower limbs, below the ankle; a base or support, like a foot; the end of a bed, couch, etc. where the feet would normally lie; a measure of length = 12 inches; v.t. to traverse by walking; v.i. to dance; to walk. pl. **feet** **-age** n. the length expressed in feet. **-ball** n. a game played by two teams of eleven each trying to carry or pass the ball over the opponents' goal line; the elongated inflated leather ball used in the game. **-ed** a. having feet or a foot. **-ing** n. ground to stand on; the part of a construction contacting the ground; status. **-lights** n.pl. a row of screened lights along the front of the stage. **-note** n. a note of reference or explanation at foot of a page.

for prep. in place of; instead of; because of; during; as being; considering; in return for; on behalf of; in spite of; in respect to; intended to belong to; suited to; with the purpose of; conj. because. **as for,** regarding.

for·as·much as conj. seeing that; because; since.

for·ay n. a raid to get plunder; v.t. to pillage.

for·bade pa.t. of forbid.

for·bear v.t. to abstain from; to avoid; to bear with; v.i. to refrain from; to control one's feelings. **forbore** pa.t. **forborne** pa.p. **-ing.** a. long-suffering.

for·bid v.t. to prohibit. **forbade** or **forbad** pa.t. **-den** pa.p. **-den** a. prohibited. **-ding** a. repellent; menacing; sinister. **-dingly** adv.

force n. strength; energy; coercion; power; body of soldiers, police, etc.; v.t. to compel; to strain. **-s** n.pl. Army, Navy and Air Force. **-d** a. achieved by great effort, or under compulsion; lacking spontaneity, as forced laugh. **-ful** a. full of energy; vigorous. **-fully** adv. **-less** a. weak; inert. **-r** n. **forcible** a. having force; compelling; cogent; effective. **forcibly** adv. **forcing** n. the action of using force or applying pressure.

for·ceps n. a surgical instrument like tongs.

ford n. a shallow part of a stream, etc. where a crossing can be made on foot; v.t. to cross by a ford. **-able** a.

fore a. in front; forward; prior; adv. in front, as opp. to aft; n. the front. interj. a warning cry to person in the way.

fore- prefix meaning in front or beforehand.

fore·arm n. the part of the arm between the elbow and the wrist.

fore·arm v.t. to take defensive precautions.

fore·bear, forbear n. an ancestor.

fore·bode v.t. to predict; to prognosticate. **-ment** n. **foreboding** n. an intuitive sense of impending evil or danger.

fore·cast n. a prediction; v.t. and v.i. to conjecture beforehand; to predict.

fore·close v.t. to prevent; to exclude; to deprive of the right to redeem a mortgage or property. **foreclosure** n.

fore·fa·ther n. an ancestor.

fore•fin•ger n. the finger next to the thumb; the index finger.

fore•front n. the foremost place.

fore•go v.t. to precede. -ing a. preceding; just mentioned. -ne a. predetermined or inevitable, as in a foregone conclusion.

fore•ground n. the part of a picture which seems nearest the observer.

fore•hand n. (Tennis) used of a stroke played forward on the right or natural side, as opp. to backhand. -ed a.

fore•head n. the upper part of the face above the eyes; the brow.

for•eign a. situated outside a place or country; alien; irrelevant. -er n. a native of another country; an alien. -ism n.

fore•man n. the principal member and spokesman of a jury; the overseer of a group of workmen.

fore•mast n. the mast in the forepart of a vessel, nearest the bow.

fore•most a. first in place or time; first in dignity or rank.

fo•ren•sic a. pert. to the law courts, public discussion, or debate. -ally adv.

fore•see v.t. to see beforehand; to foreknow. foresaw pa.t. -n pa.p. foresight n. wise forethought; prudence; front sight on gun.

fore•shad•ow v.t. to shadow or indicate beforehand; to suggest in advance.

fore•skin n. the skin covering the glans penis.

for•est n. a tract of wooded, uncultivated land; the trees alone; v.t. to cover with trees. -er n. one who practices forestry; one who has forestland, game etc. under supervision. -ry n. the science of growing timber.

fore•stall v.t. to thwart by advance action; to buy up goods before they reach the market, so as to resell at maximum price; to get in ahead of someone else. -er, -ment n.

fore•tell v.t. to predict; to prophesy. -ing pr.p. foretold pa.t. and pa.p.

fore•thought n. anticipation; provident care; a thinking beforehand.

for•ev•er adv. always; n. eternity. -more adv.

fore•warn v.t. to warn or caution in advance.

fore•word n. a preface; an introductory note to a book.

for•feit v.t. to be deprived of, as a punishment; n. that which is forfeited; a fine or penalty. -able a. -ure n. the act of forfeiting; the state of being deprived of something as a punishment; the thing confiscated.

for•gave pa.t. of verb forgive.

forge v.t. to fabricate; to counterfeit; v.i. to work with metals; to commit forgery. -r n. -ry n. the making of an imitation of money, work of art, etc., and representing it as genuine; the act of falsifying a document, or illegally using another's signature; that which is forged.

forge v.i. to move forward steadily.

for•get v.t. to lose remembrance of; to neglect inadvertently; to disregard. -ting pr.p. forgot pa.t. forgot or forgotten pa.p.

-table a. -ful a. apt to forget; heedless; oblivious. -fully adv. -fulness n.

for•give v.t. to pardon; to exercise clemency; to grant pardon. forgave pa.t. -n pa.p. forgivable a. -ness n. forgiving a. ready to pardon.

for•go v.t. to renounce; to abstain from possession or enjoyment. forewent pa.t. -ne pa.p.

fork n. a table utensil of silver, etc. usually with four prongs; each part into which anything divides, as a road, river, etc.; v.i. to divide into branches; v.t. to pitch with a fork, as hay; to lift with a fork (as food); to form a fork. -ed, -y a. shaped like a fork; cleft.

for•lorn a. deserted; forsaken. -ly adv. -ness n.

form n. shape or appearance; a mold; style; v.t. to give shape to; to construct; to devise; to arrange to conceive; v.i. to assume position; to develop. -al a. according to form; conventional; ceremonious. -alization n. -alize v.t. and v.i. to give form to; to make formal. -alism n. the quality of being formal. -alist n. quality of being conventional or pedantically precise; propriety. -ally adv. -ation n. structure; an arrangement, of troops, aircraft, etc. -ative a. giving form; conducive to growth. -less a.

form•al•de•hyde n. a colorless, pungent gas, soluble in water, used as a disinfectant and preservative.

for•mat n. the general makeup of a book, its size, shape, style of binding, quality of paper, etc.

for•mer a. preceding in time; long past; first mentioned. -ly adv.

for•mi•da•ble a. exciting fear or apprehension; overwhelming. formidability, -ness n. formidably adv.

for•mu•la n. a prescribed form; a general rule or principle expressed in algebraic symbols; the series of symbols denoting the component parts of a substance. pl. -s, -e. -te, formulize v.t. to reduce to a formula; to express in definite form.

for•ni•cate v.i. to indulge in unlawful sexual intercourse. fornication n. sexual intercourse between unmarried persons. fornicator n.

for•sake v.t. to abandon. forsaking pr.p. forsook pa.t. -n pa.p. -n a. deserted.

for•syth•i•a n. a spring-flowering shrub with bright yellow blossoms.

fort n. a stronghold; a small fortress; outpost.

forte a. and adv. loud; loudly; n. a loud passage. fortissimo adv. very loudly.

forth adv. forwards, in place of time; into view; away. -coming a. ready to come forth or appear; available.

for•ti•fy v.t. to strengthen, as by forts, batteries, etc. -ing pr.p. fortified pa.t. and pa.p. fortification n. the art or act of strengthening; a defensive wall; a fortress.

for•ti•tude n. power to endure pain or confront danger; resolute endurance; fortitudinous a. courageous.

for•tress n. a fortified place; a stronghold.

for•tu•i•tous *a.* happening by chance; accidental. **-ness, fortuity** *n.*

for•tune *n.* chance; good luck or ill luck; possessions, esp. money or property. **fortunate** *a.* lucky; propitious. **fortunately** *adv.* **fortunateness** *n.* —**teller** *n.* one who reveals the future by palmistry, crystal-gazing, etc.

for•ty *a.* and *n.* four times ten; a symbol expressing this, as 40 or XL. **fortieth** *a.* fortieth part.

fo•rum *n.* the marketplace of ancient Rome where legal as well as commercial business was conducted; a public discussion of questions of common interest.

for•ward *adv.* towards a place in front; onwards in time; *a.* toward or at the forepart, as in a ship; eager; progressive; bold; *n.* a player in the front line; *v.t.* to promote; to redirect (letter, parcel) to new address; to send out or dispatch. **-ness** *n.* the state of being advanced; precocity; presumption.

fos•sil *n.* any portion of an animal or vegetable organism or imprint of such, which has undergone a process of petrifaction and lies embedded in the rock strata. **-iferous** *a.* bearing or containing fossils. **-ize** *v.t.* to turn into a fossil; to petrify; *v.t.* to become a fossil.

fos•ter *v.t.* to rear; to promote; to cherish. — **child** *n.* a child reared by one who is not the parent.

fought *pa.t.* and *pa.p.* of verb **fight.**

foul *a.* filthy; obscene; wicked; stormy of weather; *n.* the breaking of a rule (in sports); *v.t.* to make foul; to obstruct deliberately; to clog or jam; *v.i.* to become foul, clogged, or jammed; to come into collision. **-ly** *adv.*

found *pa.t.* and *pa.p.* of verb **find. -ling** *n.* a small child who has been found abandoned.

found *v.t.* to lay the basis or foundation of; to establish; to endow; *v.i.* to rely; to depend. **-ation** *n.* the base or substructure of a building; groundwork; underlying principle; an endowment; an endowed institution. **-er** *n.*

found *v.t.* to melt and pour into a mold; to cast. **-er** *n.* **-ing** *n.* metal casting. **-ry** *n.* works for casting metals; the process of metal-casting.

foun•tain *n.* a natural spring; an artificial jet of water. **-head** *n.* source of a stream.

four *a.* one more than three; twice two; *n.* the sum of four units; the symbol representing this sum, 4 or IV. **-fold** *a.* quadruple; folded or multiplied four times. —**in-hand** *n.* a necktie. **-some** *n.* a group of four persons. **-teen** *n.* the sum of four and ten; the symbol representing this, 14 or XIV; *a.* four and ten. **-teenth** *a.* making one of fourteen equal parts. **-th** *a.* next after third; *n.* one of four equal parts. **-thly** *adv.*

fowl *n.* barnyard cock or hen; a similar game bird; *v.i.* to catch or kill wild fowl. *pl.* **-s, fowl. -ern.** one who traps wild fowl.

fox *n.* an animal of the canine family, genus *Vulpes*, reddish-brown or gray in color,

with large, bushy tail and erect ears; a wily person; *v.t.* to trick; to mislead. **-hole** *n.* a small trench; a dugout for one or more men. **-iness** *n.* the quality of being foxy. — **terrier** *n.* a popular breed of dog sometimes trained for unearthing foxes.

fox terrier

—**trot** *n.* a social dance. **-y** *a.* pert. to foxes; cunning; reddish-brown in color. **-ily** *adv.* slyly.

foy•er *n.* an entrance hall.

fra•cas *n.* a noisy quarrel; a disturbance; a brawl.

frac•tion *n.* a small portion; a fragment; a division of a unit. **decimal fraction,** a fraction expressed with numerator above and denominator below the line. **-al** *a.* **fractious** *a.* quarrelsome; peevish. **fractiously** *adv.* **fracture** *n.* the act of breaking; the breaking of a bone; *v.t.* to break; to crack; *v.i.* to become broken. **compound fracture,** a fracture of a bone, the jagged edge of which protrudes through the skin. **simple fracture,** a fracture where the bone is broken, but surrounding tissues and skin are undamaged.

frag•ile *a.* easily broken; frail; brittle. **fragility** *n.*

frag•ment *n.* a part; an unfinished portion, as of a literary composition. **-al** *a.* composed of fragments of different rocks. **-ary** *a.* broken.

fra•grant *a.* sweet-smelling. **fragrance, fragrancy** *n.* sweet scent; perfume; pleasant odor. **-ly** *adv.*

frail *a.* fragile; infirm; morally weak. **-ly** *adv.* **-ness, -ty** *n.* quality of being weak.

frame *v.t.* to construct; to contrive; to provide with a frame; to bring a false charge against; *v.i.* to take shape; *n.* anything made of parts fitted together; the skeleton of anything; a structure; the case or border around a picture; a mood of the mind; a structure upon which anything is stretched. **-work** *n.* the fabric which supports anything. **framing** *n.*

franc *n.* a coin and monetary unit of France, Belgium and Switzerland.

fran•chise *n.* the right to vote; permission by a manufacturer to sell his products.

Fran•cis•can *n.* one of the order of friars founded by St. Francis of Assisi.

frank *a.* open; candid; unreserved; *v.t.* to exempt from charge, esp. postage; *n.* a signature on outside of a letter authorizing its free delivery. **-ly** *adv.* candidly. **-ness** *n.* openness; honesty; candor.

Frank•en•stein *n.* any creation which brings disaster or torment to its author.

frank•furter *n.* a smoked sausage.

Frank•lin *n.* a type of open iron stove.

fran·tic *a.* frenzied; wild. **-ally** *adv.*

fra·ter·nal *adv.* brotherly. **fraternization** *n.* **fraternize** *v.i.* to associate with others in a friendly way. **fraternizer** *n.* **fraternity** *n.* a student society, designated by letters of the Greek alphabet; brotherhood; a group of men associated for a common purpose.

fraud *n.* deception deliberately practiced; trickery; a cheat; imposter. **-ulence**, **-ulency** *n.* trickery, deceitfulness. **-ulent** *a.* pert. to or practicing fraud; dishonest. **-ulently** *adv.*

fraught *a.* loaded; charged.

fray *n.* a brawl; a contest.

fray *v.t.* to wear through by friction; to ravel the edge of cloth; to irritate, as the nerves, or temper; *v.i.* to become frayed.

fraz·zle *v.t.* to fray; to exhaust; *n.* exhaustion.

freak *n.* a sudden whim; a prank; capricious conduct; something or someone abnormal; *a.* odd; unusual. **-ish** *a.* **-ishly** *adv.* **-ishness** *n.*

freck·le *n.* a small brownish spot on the skin; any small spot; *v.t.* to color with freckles; *v.i.* to become covered with freckles. **freckly**, *a.*

free *a.* having political liberty; unrestricted; loose; independent; open; liberal; spontaneous; exempt from impositions, duties, or fees; *adv.* without hindrance; *v.t.* to set at liberty; to emancipate; to clear; to disentangle. **-ing** *pr.p.* **-d** *pa.p.* **-man** *n.* one who has been freed from slavery. **-dom** *n.* liberty; immunity; indecorous familiarity. **-hand** *a.* unrestricted authority; drawn by hand without instruments, etc. **-handed** *a.* generous; liberal. **— lance** *n.* orig. a mercenary soldier who sold his services to any country, esp. said of a journalist, not attached to a particular staff. **— love** *n.* doctrine that sexual relations should be unhampered by marriage, etc. **-ly** *adv.* **-thinker** *n.* one who professes to be independent of all religious authority; a rationalist. **-thinking**, **— thought** *n.* **— will** *n.* the power of the human will to choose without restraint; *a.* voluntary.

freeze *v.t.* to harden into ice; become congealed or stiff with cold; *n.* frost. **freezing** *pr.p.* **froze** *pa.t.* **frozen** *pa.p.* **freezing point** *n.* the temperature at which a liquid turns solid, esp. that at which water freezes, marked 32°F. or 0° C.

freight *n.* the cargo of a ship, etc; charge for conveyance of goods; *v.t.* to load a ship, etc. **-age** *n.* charge for transport of goods; freight. **-er** *n.* cargo boat.

French *a.* pert. to France or its inhabitants; *n.* the inhabitants or the language of France. **— horn** *n.* a musical wind instrument with mellow note like a hunting horn. **-man** *n.* a native of France.

fren·zy *n.* violent agitation of the mind; madness; *v.t.* to render frantic. **frenzied** *a.* **frenetic** *a.* mad; frenzied.

fre·on *n.* gas used in refrigeration and for air-conditioning.

fre·quent *a.* happening at short intervals; constantly recurring; repeated.

fre·quent *v.t.* to visit often. **frequency** *n.* the state of occurring repeatedly; periodicity; number of vibrations per second of a recurring phenomenon. **-ation** *n.* the practice of visiting repeatedly. **-ative** *a.* denoting the repetition of an action; *n.* a word, usually a verb, expressing frequency of an action. **-er** *n.* **-ly** *adv.* **-ness** *n.*

fres·co *n.* a method of mural decoration on walls of fresh, still damp, plaster; *v.t.* to paint in fresco.

fresh *a.* vigorous; unimpaired; new; not stale; *n.* a stream of fresh water. **-en** *v.t.* to make fresh; *v.i.* to grow fresh; to become vigorous. **-ness** *n.* **-water** *a.* pert. to or living in water which is not salty.

fret *v.t.* to wear away by friction; to eat away; to ruffle; to irritate; *v.i.* to wear away; to be corroded; to be vexed or peevish; *n.* irritation; erosion. **-ting** *pr.p.* **-ted** *pa.t.* and *pa.p.* **-ful** *a.* querulous. **-fully** *adv.* **-fulness** *n.*

fret *n.* a small piece of wood or wire fixed on the fingerboard, as of a guitar, under the strings.

Freud·i·an *a.* pert. to *Sigmund Freud* (1856-1939), the Austrian psychoanalyst, or to his theories.

fric·as·see *n.* a dish of fowl, rabbit, etc. stewed with rich gravy sauce; *v.t.* to make a fricassee.

fric·tion *n.* the act of rubbing one thing against another; unpleasantness. **fricative** *a.* produced by friction. **-al** *a.* caused by friction. **-ally** *adv.*

Fri·day *n.* the sixth day of the week.

fried *pa.t.* and *pa.p.* of verb fry.

friend *n.* one attached to another by esteem and affection; an intimate associate; a supporter. **Friend** *n.* a member of the Quakers. **-less** *a.* without friends. **-liness** *n.* **-ly** *a.* having the disposition of a friend; kind; propitious. **-ship** *n.* attachment; comradeship. **Society of Friends**, the Quaker sect.

frieze *n.* decoration on the upper part of the wall, around a mantel, etc.

frieze

frig·ate *n.* a fast 2-decked sailing ship of war of the 18th and 19th centuries.

frigate

fright *n.* sudden and violent fear; extreme terror; alarm; an ugly or grotesque person or object; *v.t.* to make afraid. **-en** *v.t.* to terrify; to scare. **-ened** *a.* **-ful** *a.* terrible; calamitous; shocking. **-fully** *adv.* terribly. **-fulness** *n.* **-some** *a.* frightful.

frig·id *a.* very cold; unfeeling; passionless. **-ity** *n.* coldness. **-ly** *adv.* **-ness** *n.* **Frigidaire** *n.* a brand of refrigerator.

frill *n.* a gathered cloth or paper edging; a ruffle; excessive ornament; *v.t.* to ornament with a frill; *v.i.* to become crinkled like a frill.

fringe *n.* loose threads as ornamental edging of cloth; *v.t.* to adorn with fringe; to border.

frisk *v.i.* to leap; to skip; *n.* a frolic. **-ily** *adv.* playfully. **-iness** *n.* **-y** *a.* lively.

frit·ter *n.* a slice of fruit, vegetable or meat dipped in batter and fried to form a cake.

frit·ter *v.t.* to waste in a futile way. **-er** *n.*

friv·ol *v.t.* and *v.i.* to squander, esp. time or energy; to fritter away. **-ity** *n.* the act or habit of idly wasting time; lack of seriousness. **-ous** *a.* **-ously** *adv.* **-ousness** *n.*

frizz *v.t.* to curl; to crisp; *n.* a row of small curls. **-le** *v.t.* to curl; *n.* curled hair.

fro *adv.* from; back, as in *to and fro.*

frock *n.* a woman's dress; a monk's long, wide-sleeved garment.

frog *n.* an amphibious, tailless animal (developed from a tadpole); hoarseness caused by mucus in the throat; ornamental braiding on uniform, or ornamental fastening of loop and button; *v.t.* to ornament with frogs.

frol·ic *n.* a merrymaking; *a.* full of pranks; merry; *v.i.* to play merry pranks; to have fun. **-king** *pr.p.* **-ked** *pa.t.* and *pa.p.* **-some** *a.*

from *prep.* away; forth; out of; on account of; at a distance.

frond *n.* an organ of certain flowerless plants, such as ferns, in which leaf and stem are combined and bear reproductive cells.

front *n.* the forepart, the forehead; firing line; battle zone; outward appearance; *a.* pert. to, or at the front of, anything; *adv.* to the front; *v.t.* and *v.i.* to have the face or front towards any point. **-age** *n.* the front part of general exposure of a building; land abutting on street, river, or sea. **-al** *a.* pert. to the forehead or foremost part; direct, as an attack, without flanking movement; *n.* a bone of the forehead; an ornamental cloth for altar front.

fron·tier *n.* border of a country; the undeveloped areas of a country; *a.* bordering; pioneering. **-sman** *n.* one who settles on a frontier.

frost *n.* condition when water turns to ice, i.e. when temperature falls below 32° F.; severe cold; *v.t.* to ice a cake. **-bite** *n.* freezing of the skin and tissues due to exposure to extreme cold. **-bitten** *a.* **-ed** *a.* covered with frost. **-ily** *adv.* **-iness** *n.* **-y** *a.* accompanied with frost; chilly; white.

froth *n.* foam; trivial things or ideas; *v.t.* to cause to froth; *v.i.* to bubble. **-iness** *n.*

-y *a.*

frown *v.i.* to wrinkle the brow; *v.t.* to rebuke by a stern look; *n.* a wrinkling of the brow to express disapproval.

fro·zen *pa.p.* of the verb freeze.

fru·gal *a.* sparing; thrifty; economical. **-ly** *adv.* **-ity** *n.*

fruit *n.* the produce of the earth used for man's needs; the edible produce or seed of a plant; offspring; *v.i.* to produce fruit. **-er** *n.* fruit-grower. **-ful** *a.* producing fruit; abundant; profitable. **-fully** *adv.* **-fulness** *n.* **-ing** *n.* the process of bearing fruit. **-less** *a.* having no fruit; profitless; empty. **-lessly** *adv.* **-lessness** *n.* **-y** *a.* resembling fruit; mellow.

frus·trate *v.t.* to bring to nothing; to balk; to thwart; to circumvent. **frustration** *n.* disappointment; defeat. **frustrative** *a.*

fry *v.t.* to cook with fat in a pan over the fire; *v.i.* to be cooked in a frying pan; to sizzle. **-ing** *pr.p.* **fried** *pa.t.* and *pa.p.* **-er**, **frier** *n.*

fry *n.* young fish just spawned; young children.

fuch·sia *n.* a genus of flowering plants, with drooping bright purplish-red flowers.

fud·dle *v.t.* to make confused.

fudge *interj.* stuff; nonsense; *n.* a soft chocolate candy; space reserved in a newspaper for last-minute news.

fuel *n.* anything combustible to feed a fire, as wood, coal; *v.t.* to provide with fuel.

fu·gi·tive *a.* escaping; fleeing; fleeting; wandering; *n.* a refugee; one who flees from justice.

ful·crum *n.* the pivot of a lever. *pl.* **-s, fulcra.**

ful·fill *v.t.* to carry into effect; to execute; to discharge; to satisfy. **-er** *n.* **-ment** *n.* accomplishment; completion.

full *a.* filled to capacity; replete; crowded; complete; plump; abundant; showing the whole surface (as the moon); ample (of garments, etc.); clear and resonant (of sounds); *n.* the utmost extent; highest degree; *adv.* quite; completely; exactly.
—**blooded** *a.* of pure race; vigorous.
—**blown** *a.* fully developed, as a flower.
— **dress** *n.* dress worn on ceremonial occasions. — **dress** *a.* formal. **-y** *adv.* completely.

ful·some *a.* excessive; insincere. **-ly** *adv.* **-ness** *n.*

ful·vous *a.* tawny; dull yellow.

fu·ma·role *n.* a small fissure in volcano.

fum·ble *v.i.* to grope blindly or awkwardly; *v.t.* to handle clumsily.

fume *n.* pungent vapor from combustion or exhalation; rage; *v.i.* to smoke; to be in a rage; *v.t.* to send forth as fumes.

fu·mi·gate *v.t.* to expose to poisonous gas or smoke, esp. for the purpose of destroying germs. **fumigator** *n.* apparatus or substance used in fumigation.

fun *n.* merriment; hilarity; sport. **-nies** *n.pl.* comic strips. **-nily** *adv.* **-niness** *n.* **-ny** *a.* full of fun.

func·tion *n.* performance; the special work done by an organ or structure; a quantity the value of which varies with that of another quantity; a social entertainment;

v.i. to operate; to fulfill a set task. -al *a.* having a special purpose; pert. to a duty or office. -ally *adv.* -ary *n.* an official.

fund *n.* permanent stock or capital; an invested sum, the income of which is used for a set purpose; ample supply; *pl.* money in hand; *v.t.* to establish a fund for the payment of interest or principal. -ed *a.*

fun·da·men·tal *a.* pert. to the foundations; basic; essential; original; *n.* a primary principle. -ism *n.* belief in literal truth of the Bible. -ist *n.* -ly *adv.*

fu·ner·al *n.* the ceremony of burying the dead; *a.* pert. to or used at burial. funerary, funereal *a.* gloomy.

fun·gus *n.* any of a group of thallophytes (molds, mushrooms, mildews, puffballs, etc.). *pl.* fungi, -es. **fungicide** *n.* any preparation which destroys molds or fungoid growths. **fungoid, fungous** *a.* pert. to or caused by fungus.

fungi

fun·nel *n.* an inverted hollow metal cone with tube, used for filling vessels with narrow inlet; the smokestack of a steamship.

fur *n.* the short, fine, soft hair of certain animals; animal pelts used for coats; *v.t.* to line, face, or cover with fur. -ring *pr.p.* -red *pa.p.* -rier *n.* a dealer in furs. -ry *a*

fur·bish *v.t.* to polish; to burnish; to renovate.

fu·ri·ous *a.* raging; violent; savage. -ly *adv.*

furl *v.t.* to roll, as a sail.

fur·long *n.* eighth of mile; 220 yards.

fur·lough *n.* leave of absence; *v.t.* to grant leave.

fur·nace *n.* an enclosed structure for the generating of heat required for smelting ores, warming houses, etc.

fur·nish *v.t.* to supply; to equip; to fit out. -er *n.* -ings *n.pl.* fittings, of a house, esp. furniture, curtains, carpets, etc.

fur·ni·ture *n.* equipment; that which is put into a house, office, etc. for use or ornament.

fu·ror *n.* wild excitement; enthusiasm.

fur·row *n.* a trench made by a plow; channel; groove; deep wrinkle; *v.t.* to plow; to mark with wrinkles. -y *a*

fur·ther *a.* more remote; additional; *adv.* to a greater distance; moreover. -more *adv.* moreover; besides. -most *a.* most remote. **furthest** *adv.* and *a.* most remote. (farther, farthest are preferred as *comp.* and *superl.* of far.)

fur·ther *v.t.* to help forward; to promote. -ance *n.* the act of furthering.

fu·ry *n.* rage; passion; frenzy.

fuse *v.t.* to melt by heat; to amalgamate; *v.i.* to become liquid; *n.* a tube filled with combustible matter, used in blasting or discharge of bombs, etc.; a device used as a safety measure in electric lighting and heating systems. **fusibility** *n.* **fusible** *a.* **fusion** *n.* the act or process of melting; the state of being melted or blended; coalition.

fu·se·lage *n.* the body of an airplane.

fuss *n.* bustle; unnecessary ado; needless activity; *v.i.* to become nervously agitated; *v.t.* to bother another with excessive attentions. -budget *n.* a fussy person. -ily *adv.* -iness *n.* -y *a.*

fu·tile *a.* ineffectual, unavailing, useless. -ly *adv.* futility *n.* uselessness; fruitlessness.

fu·ture *a.* about to happen; that is to come hereafter; *n.* time to come. **futurism** *n.* a modern aesthetic movement marked by complete departure from tradition. **futurist** *n.* **futuristic** *a.* **futurity** *n.* time to come.

fuzz *n.* fine, light particles; fluff. -iness *n.* -y *a.*

gab *n.* trifling talk; *v.i.* to chatter. *pr.p.*
-bing. *pa.t.* -bed. -by *a.* -ble *n.*, *v.i.*

gab·ar·dine *n.* a firm, woven twilled fabric
of cotton, rayon or wool. Also **gaberdine**.

gad *v.i.* to go about idly; to ramble. *pr.p.*
-ding. *pa.p.* and *pa.t.* -ded. -about *v.i.* to
wander idly; *n.* a pleasure seeker.

gadg·et *n.* a general term for any small
mechanical contrivance or device.

Gael *n.* a Scottish Highlander of Celtic
origin. -ic *a.* *n.* the language of the Gaels.

gaff *n.* a barbed fishing spear; a stick with
an iron hook for landing fish; *v.t.* to seize
with a gaff.

gag *n.* something thrust into or over the
mouth to prevent speech; *v.t.* to apply a
gag to; to silence by force; *v.i.* to heave
with nausea. *pr.p.* -ging. *pa.t.*, *pa.p.* -ged.

gag *n.* a joke.

gag·gle *v.i.* to crackle like geese; *n.* a flock
of geese.

gai·e·ty *n.* mirth; merriment; glee; jollity.
gaily *adv.* merrily.

gain *v.t.* to attain to, or reach; to get by
effort; to get profit; to earn; to win; *v.i.* to
have advantage or profit; to increase; to
improve; to make an advance; *n.* profit;
advantage; incease. -ful *a.* profitable;
lucrative. -fully *adv.* -fulness *n.*

gait *n.* manner of walking or running; pace.

ga·la *n.* a show or festivity; *a.* festive.

gal·ax·y *n.* a band of stars encircling the
heavens; the Milky Way. **galactic** *a.*

gale *n.* a wind between a stiff breeze and a
hurricane.

gall *n.* bile secreted in the liver; anything
bitter; bitterness; rancor. —**bladder** *n.* a
small sac on the under side of the liver,
in which the bile is stored. -**stone** *n.* a
concretion formed in the gall bladder.

gall *v.t.* to fret and wear away by rubbing;
to vex, irritate, or harass; *n.* a skin wound
caused by rubbing. -ing *a.* irritating.

gal·lant *a.* splendid or magnificent; brave;
chivalrous; courteous to women;
amorous. *n.* a brave, high-spirited man;
-ly *adv.* -ry *n.* bravery; chivalry.

gal·ler·y *n.* a long corridor, hall, or room; a
room or series of rooms in which works
of art are exhibited; a balcony; the
uppermost tier of seats, esp. in theater;
audience or spectators.

gal·ley *n.* a low, one-decked vessel,
navigated both with oars and sails; a

galley

large rowboat; the kitchen of a ship.

Gal·lic *a.* pert. to ancient Gaul, or France;
French. **gallicize** *v.t.* to make French in
opinions, manners.

gal·li·um *n.* a soft grey metal of extreme
fusibility.

gal·li·vant *v.i.* to gad about.

gal·lon *n.* a measure of capacity both for
liquid and dry commodities, containing
four quarts.

gal·lop *n.* fastest gait of horse, when it lifts
forefeet together, and hind feet together;
a ride at a gallop; *v.i.* to ride at a gallop;
to go at full speed; *v.t.* to cause to gallop.
-ing *a.* speedy; swift.

gal·lows *n.* a frame from which criminals
are hanged.

gal·lore *adv.* abundantly; in plenty.

ga·losh, golosh *n.* a rubber overshoe.

gal·va·nism *n.* the branch of science which
treats of the production of electricity by
chemical action. **galvanic** *a.* **galvanize**
v.t. to apply galvanic action to; to
stimulate by an electric current; to coat
metal with zinc. **galvanization** *n.*
galvanizing *n.* coating with zinc.
galvanized iron, iron coated with zinc to
prevent rust.

gam·bit *n.* in chess, opening move
involving sacrifice of pawn.

gam·ble *v.i.* to play for money; to risk esp.
by financial speculation; *v.t.* to lose or
squander in speculative ventures; *n.* a
risky undertaking; a reckless speculation.
-r *n.*

game *n.* any sport; a pastime; a contest for
amusement; a trial of strength, skill, or
chance; animals and birds protected by
law and hunted by sportsmen; *a.* pert. to
animals hunted as game; brave; plucky;
v.i. to gamble. *n.pl.* athletic contests. -ly
adv. -ness *n.* -ster *n.* a gambler. **gamy** *a.*
having the flavor of dead game which
has been kept uncooked for a long time.
— **preserve**, land stocked with game for
hunting or shooting. — **warden** *n.* an
official who enforces game laws. **big
game**, all large animals hunted for sport.
to play the game, to act in a
sportsmanlike way.

gam·ete *n.* a protoplasmic body, ovum, or
sperm, which unites with one of opposite
sex for conception.

gam·ma *n.* the third letter of the Greek
alphabet. — **rays**, electro-magnetic
radiations, of great penetrative powers,
given off by radioactive substances, e.g.
radium.

gam·ut *n.* the whole series of musical
notes; a scale; the compass of a voice;
the entire range.

gan·der *n.* a male goose.

gang *n.* people banded together for some
purpose, usually bad; body of laborers
working together. *v.i.* to act as a gang
-ster *n.* one of a gang of criminals.

gan·gli·on *n.* a globular, hard tumor,
situated on a tendon. *pl.* -s, **ganglia**.
gangliate *a.* furnished with ganglia. -ic *a.*

gang plank *n.* a moveable plank bridge
between a ship and the shore.

gan·grene *n.* the first stage of mortification
or death of tissue in the body; *v.t.* and *v.i.*
to affect with, or be affected with,
gangrene. **gangrenous** *a.* mortified;
putrefying.

gang·way *n.* a passageway; a platform and
ladder slung over the side of a ship; *interj.*
make way, please!

gap n. an opening.

gape v.i. to open wide, esp. the mouth; to stare with open mouth; to yawn. n. a wide opening; the act of gaping.

ga·rage n. a covered enclosure for motor vehicles; a fuel and repair station for motor vehicles; v.t. to place in a garage.

garb n. clothing; mode or style of dress; v.t. to dress.

gar·bage n. kitchen refuse; anything worthless.

gar·ble v.t. to pervert or mutilate, as a story, a quotation, an account, etc. by picking out only certain parts.

gar·den n. ground for cultivation of flowers, vegetables, etc. generally attached to a house; v.i. to cultivate, or work in, a garden. -er n. -ing n. the act of tending a garden.

gar·den·nia a. a genus of tropical trees and shrubs with sweet-scented, beautiful white flowers.

gar·gan·tu·an a. immense, emormous, esp. of appetite.

gar·gle v.t. to rinse; v.i. to make a sound of gargling; to use a gargle; n. a throat wash.

gar·goyle n. a projecting spout, often in the form of a grotesque carving, found on old

gargoyle

buildings and intended to carry off the water.

gar·ish a. gaudy; showy; glaring; dazzling. -ly adv.

gar·land n. a wreath of flowers; v.t. to ornament with a garland.

gar·lic n. a plant having a bulbous root, a strong smell like onion, and a pungent taste. -ky a.

gar·ment n. any article of clothing.

gar·net n. a semi-precious stone, usually of a dark-red color and resembling a ruby; a dark-red color.

gar·nish v.t. to adorn; to embellish; to ornament; to make food attractive or appetizing; n. ornament; decoration; -ment n. **garniture** n. that which garnishes.

gar·ri·son n. a body of troops stationed in a fort, town, etc.; the fort or town itself; v.t. to occupy with a garrison.

gar·ru·lous a. talkative; loquacious. -ly adv. -ness n. garrulity n.

gar·ter n. a string or band worn near the knee to keep a stocking up; v.t. to support with a garter.

gas n. an elastic fluid such as air, esp. one not liquid or solid at ordinary temperatures; mixture of gases, used for heating or lighting; an anesthetic; a chemical substance used to poison or incapacitate the enemy; v.t. to poison with gas; v.i. pr.p. -sing. pa.p. and pa.t. -sed. -eous a. like, or in the form of gas. -ification n. -fy v.t. to convert into gas, as by the action of heat, or by chemical processes. -sy a. full of gas. — **burner** n. a gas jet or stove. — **jet** n. a nozzle or burner of a gas burner; the burner itself. —**mask** n. a respirator worn to protect against poisonous gases. —**meter** n. a metal box used to measure the amount of gas consumed. **-ometer** n. an apparatus for measuring or storing gas. —**range** n. a gas cooking stove.

gash v.t. to make a long, deep cut in; n. a deep cut.

gas·ket n. washer between parts such as the cylinder head and cylinder block.

gas·o·line, gasolene, n. a volatile, inflammable, liquid mixture produced by the distillation of petroleum, used as a fuel solvent, etc.

gasp v.i. to struggle for breath with open mouth; to pant; v.t. to utter with gasps; n. the act of gasping; a painful catching of the breath.

gas·tric a. pert. to the stomach. **gastritis** n. inflammation of the stomach. **gastro-enteritis** n. inflammation of the stomach and intestines. **gastrology** n.

gas·tro·pod n. a class of molluscs, e.g. snails and whelks, having a fleshy, ventral disk, which takes the place of feet.

gate n. an opening into an enclosure, through a fence, wall, etc.; -way n. an entrance.

gath·er v.t. to bring together; to collect; to pick; in sewing, to draw into puckers; to infer or deduce; to harvest; v.i. to come together; to congregate; to increase; n. a pucker or fold in cloth. -ing n. an assemblage; a crowd.

Gat·ling·gun n. machine gun invented by R. J. *Gatling.*

gauche a. awkward; clumsy; tactless. **gaucherie.**

gau·cho n. a cowboy of the S. American pampas.

gaud n. a piece of worthless finery; a trinket. -ily adv. -y a.

gauge v.t. to ascertain the capacity of; to measure the ability of; to estimate; n. an instrument for determining dimensions or capacity; a standard of measure; test; criterion; -r n. one who gauges.

Gaul n. an old name for France; a Frenchman.

gaunt a. lean and haggard; pinched and grim; desolate. -ly adv. -ness n.

gauss n. the unit of density of a magnetic field.

gauze n. a thin, transparent fabric. **gauziness** n. **gauzy** a.

gave pa.t. of give.

gav·el n. a mallet; a small wooden hammer used by a chairman or auctioneer.

gawk n. an awkward person; a simpleton; v.i. to stare stupidly. -y a.

gay a. lively; merry; light-hearted. -ly, **gaily** adv. -ety, **gaiety** n.

gaze *v.i.* to look fixedly; to stare; *n.* a fixed, earnest look; a long, intent look. -r *n.* one who gazes.

ga·ze·bo *n.* a summerhouse commanding a wide view.

ga·zelle *n.* a small, swift, graceful antelope.

gazelle

ga·zette *n.* a newspaper. **gazetteer** *n.* formerly a writer for a gazette; now, a geographical dictionary.

gear *n.* apparatus; equipment; tackle; utensils; a set of toothed wheels working together, esp. by engaging cogs; *v.t,* to provide with gear; to put in gear; *v.i.* to be in gear. -ing *n.* the series of toothed wheels for transmitting power, changing speed, etc.

gee *interj.* exclamation of surprise.

geese *n.* plural of goose.

Gei·ger counter *n.* a hypersensitive instrument for detecting radio-activity, cosmic radiation, etc.

gei·sha *n.* a Japanese dancing girl.

gel *n.* a colloidal solution which has set into a jelly; *v.i.* to become a gel. -ling. *pa.t., pa.p.* -led. -ation *n.* a solidifying by means of cold.

gel·a·tin, gelatine *n.* a glutinous substance gotten by boiling parts of animals (bones, hoofs, etc.) which is soluble in hot water and sets into a tremulous jelly. -ous *a.* of the nature of consistency of gelatin; like jelly. -age, ize *v.t.* to convert into gelatine. -ation *n.*

gem *n.* a precious stone of any kind; a jewel; anything of great value; *v.t.* to adorn with gems. *pr.p.* -ming. *pa.p., pa.t.* -med.

gem·i·nate *a.* doubled; existing in pairs; *v.i.* and *t.* to make or become paired or doubled. **gemination** *n.*

Gem·i·ni *n.pl.* the third sign of the Zodiac; a constellation containing the two bright stars Castor and Pollux, twin heroes of Greek legend.

gen·der *n.* sex, male or female; the classification of nouns according to sex or animateness.

gene *n.* the hereditary factor which is transmitted by each parent to offspring and which determines hereditary characteristics.

ge·ne·al·o·gy *n.* a record of the descent of a person or family from an ancestor; lineage. **genealogist** *n.* one who traces the descent of persons or families. **genealogical** *a.*

gen·er·a *n.* See genus.

gen·er·al *a.* pert. to a whole class or order; not precise, particular, or detailed; usual, embracing the whole, not local or partial;

n. **-ly** *adv.* as a whole; for the most part; commonly; extensively. **generality** *n.* indefiniteness; vagueness; a vague statement; the main body. **-issimo** *n.* the chief commander of all the country's forces in China and the U.S.S.R. **in general,** in most respects. **general practitioner,** a doctor whose work embraces all types of cases.

gen·er·al·ize *v.t.* to make universal in application; *v.i.* to draw general conclusions from particular instances; to speak vaguely. **generalization** *n.* a general conclusion from particular instances.

gen·er·ate *v.t.* to bring into being; to produce; **generation** *n.* a bringing into being; the act of begetting; the act of producing; all persons born about the same time; family. **generative** *a.* having the power of generating or producing; prolific. **generator** *n.* one who, or that which, generates; an apparatus for producing steam, etc.; a machine for converting mechanical into electrical energy.

ge·ner·ic *a.* pert. to a genus; of a general nature in regard to all members of a genus. **-ally** *adv.*

gen·er·ous *a.* liberal, free in giving; **-ly** *adv.* **generosity** *n.* magnanimity; liberality in giving.

gen·e·sis *n.* origin; creation; production; birth. *pl.* **geneses. Genesis** *n.* the first book of the Old Testament.

ge·net·ic *a.* pert. to origin, creation, or reproduction. **-s** *n.* the scientific study of the heredity of individuals, esp. of inherited characteristics. **geneticist** *n.*

Ge·ne·van *a.* pert. to *Geneva,* in Switzerland. **Geneva Conventions,** international agreements, signed at Geneva in 1864, 1868, 1906 and 1949, to lessen sufferings of the wounded in war by providing for the neutrality of hospitals, amubulances, etc.

gen·ial *a.* kindly; sympathetic; cordial. **geniality** *n.* the quality of being genial; friendliness; sympathetic cheerfulness. **-ly** *adv.*

gen·i·tal *a.* pert. to generation, or to the organs of generation. **-s** *n.pl.* the external sexual organs. Also **genitalia.**

gen·i·tive *a.* pert. to, or indicating, source, origin, possession, etc.; *n.* the case used to indicate source, origin, possession and the like.

gen·ius *n.* one's mental endowment or individual talent; a person endowed with the highest mental gifts.

gen·o·cide *n.* race murder. **genocidal** *a.*

gen·re *n.* a kind; sort; style.

gen·teel *a.* possessing the qualities belonging to high birth and breeding; well-bred; stylish; refined. **-y** *adv.* **-ness** *n.* **gentility** *n.*

gen·tian *n.* the common name of Gentiana, plants whose root is used medicinally as a tonic and stomachic; its flower is usually of a deep, bright blue.

gen·tile *n.* one who is not a Jew.

gen·tle *a.* kind and amiable; mild and

refined in manner; v.t. to tame; to make docile. **gently** adv. **-ness** n. **gentry** n. people of birth and good breeding.

gen•tle•man n. a man of good breeding and refined manners; pl. **gentlemen. -ly** a. **-like** a. **-'s** agreement, one binding in honor but not legally.

gen•u•flect v.i. to bend the knee, esp. in worship. **genuflection, genuflexion** n. **-or** n. **-ory** a.

gen•u•ine a. real; true; pure.

ge•nus n. a class; an order; a subdivision ranking next above species, and containing a number of species having like characteristics. pl. **genera.**

ge•o-, ge- combining forms from Gk. *ge*, meaning earth, ground, soil. **geocentric** a. having reference to the earth as center.

ge•ode n. in mineralogy, a rounded nodule of stone, containing a cavity, usually lined with crystals.

ge•og•ra•phy n. the science of the earth's form, its physical divisions into seas, rivers, mountains, plains, etc.; a book on this. **geographer** n. one versed in geography. **geographic, geographical** a. pert. to geography. **geographically** adv.

ge•ol•o•gy n. the science of the earth's crust, the rocks, their strata, etc. **geological** a. **geologically** adv. **geologist** n.

ge•om•e•try n. the mathematical study of the properties of lines, angles, surfaces, and solids. **geometric(al)** a. pert. to geometry. **geometrically** adv. **geometric progression** a series of quantities in which each quantity is obtained by multiplying the preceding term by a constant factor, e.g. 2, 6, 18, 54, etc.

ge•ot•ro•pism n. the tendency of a growing plant to direct its roots downwards. **geotropic** a.

ge•ra•ni•um n. plant having showy flowers.

ger•i•at•rics n. science of the diseases and care of the old.

germ n. the rudimentary form of a living things, whether animal or plant; a microbe; **-icide** n. a substance for destroying disease-germs. **germicidal** a. — warfare waged with bacteria for weapons.

Ger•man a. belonging to *Germany;* n. a native of Germany; the German language. **Germanic** a. pert. to Germany; Teutonic. **Germanize** v.t. to make German. **German measles,** a disease like measles, but less severe.

ger•ma•ni•um n. a rare metallic element.

ger•mi•nate v.i. to sprout; to bud; to shoot; to begin to grow; v.t. to cause to grow. **germinative** a. pert. to germination. **g tion** n.

ger•on•tol•o•gy n. the science that studies the decline of life of man.

ger•ry•man•der v.t. to arrange or redistribute electoral districts to private advantage.

ger•und n. part of the Latin verb used as a verbal noun; used to **ger•und** n. part of the Latin verb used as a verbal noun; used to express **ger•und** n. part of the Latin verb used as a verbal noun; used to express purpose. **gerundial** a. of the nature of a gerund. **gerundive** n. the future passive participle of a Latin verb expressing the action of having to be done.

Ge•sta•po n. the secret police of the German Nazi party.

ges•ta•tion n. carrying young in womb; pregnancy.

ges•tic•u•late v.i. to make violent gestures or motions, esp. with hands and arms, when speaking. **gesticulation** n. a gesture.

ges•ture n. a motion of the head, hands, etc. as a mode of expression; an act indicating attitude of mind; v.i. to make gestures.

get v.t. to procure; to obtain; to gain possession of; to come by; to receive; to earn; to induce or persuade; to understand; v.i. to become; to reach or attain; to bring one's self into a condition. pr.p. **-ting.** pa.t. **got.** pa.p. **got, gotten. -away** n. escape. **get-up** n. equipment; dress; energy.

gey•ser n. a hot spring which spouts water intermittently.

ghast•ly a. horrible; shocking. Also adv. **ghastliness** n.

gher•kin n. a small species of cucumber used for pickling.

ghet•to n. a section to which Jews were restricted; a section of a city in which members of a national or racial group live or are restricted.

ghost n. the apparition of a dead person; semblance or shadow; a person who does literary or artistic work for another, who takes the credit for it. **-ly** a. **-liness** n. **-like** a. **Holy Ghost,** the Holy Spirit; the third element in the Trinity.

ghoul n. imaginary evil being. **-ish** a.

gi•ant n. a man of extraordinary bulk and stature; a person of unusual powers, bodily or intellectual; a. like a giant. **-ism** n. abnormal development.

gib•ber v.i. and t. to speak rapidly and inarticulately; to chatter. **-ish** n. meaningless speech; nonsense.

gibe, jibe v.i. to taunt; to sneer at; to scoff at; n. an expression of contempt; a taunt.

gib•lets n. pl. the internal edible parts of poultry, e.g. heart, liver, gizzard, etc.

gid•dy a. dizzy; feeling a swimming sensation in the head; liable to cause this sensation; whirling; flighty; frivolous. **giddily** adv. **giddiness** n.

gift n. a present; a thing given; a donation; natural talent; faculty; power; v.t. to endow; to present with; to bestow. **-ed** a. possessing natural talent. **-edness** n.

gi•gan•tic a. like a giant; of extraordinary size; huge. **-ally** adv.

gig•gle v.i. to laugh in a silly way, n. such a laugh. **-r** n. **giggling** n.

gild v.t. to overlay with gold-leaf or gold-dust; to make gold in color; to brighten; to give a fair appearance to; to embellish.

gill n. a measure of capacity containing one fourth of a pint.

gill *n.* the organ of respiration in fishes and other water animals.

gilt *n.* a thin layer of gold, or something resembling gold; *a.* yellow like gold; gilded. **-edged** *a.* having the edges gilded; of the best quality.

gim‧mick *n.* a gadget.

gimp *n.* a narrow fabric or braid used as an edging or trimming.

gin *n.* a distilled alcoholic beverage, flavored with juniper berries, orange peel, etc.

gin *n.* a machine for separating the seeds from cotton; *v.t.* to clear cotton of seeds by a gin; *pr.p.* **-ning.** *pa.p.* and *pa.t.* **-ned.**

gin‧ger *n.* a plant of the Indies with a hot-tasting spicy root; *v.t.* to flavor with ginger. **-ale** *n.* an effervescent beverage. **-bread** *n.* a. cake, flavored with ginger and molasses; showy ornamentation. **-y** *a.* hot and spicy.

gin‧ger‧ly *adv.* cautiously; carefully.

ging‧ham a kind of cotton cloth, usually checked or striped.

gin rum‧my *n.* a card game for two or more players.

gip‧sy See Gypsy.

gi‧raffe *n.* an African animal with spotted coat and very long neck and legs.

gird **-er** *n.* an iron or steel beam used as a support in constructional engineering.

gir‧dle *n.* a tight-fitting undergarment worn for support of the lower part of the body; *v.t.*

girl *n.* a female child; **-hood** *n.* the state, or time, of being a girl. **-ish** *a.* like a girl. **-ishly** *adv.* **-ishness** *n.*

girth *n.* band to hold a saddle, blanket, etc. in place on a horse; a girdle; the measurement around a thing.

gist *n.* the main point of a question; the substance or essential point of any matter.

give *v.t.* to bestow; to make a present of; to grant; to deliver; to pledge, as one's word; *v.i.* to yield; to give away; to move; *n.* elasticity; a yielding to pressure; *pr.p.* **giving.** *pa.p.* **given.** *pa.t.* **gave. -n** *a.* granted; admitted; supposed; certain; particular; addicted to; inclined to. **-r** *n.*

giz‧zard *n.* a bird's strong muscular second stomach.

gla‧cé *a.* of a cake, iced; of a kind of leather, polished or glossy; of fruits, candied.

gla‧cier *n.* a mass of ice, formed by accumulated snow in high cold regions, which moves very slowly down a mountain. **glacial** pert. to ice or its action; pert. to glaciers; icy; frozen; crystallized. **glaciate** *v.t.* to cover with ice; to turn to ice. **glaciology** *n.* the scientific study of the formation and action of glaciers.

glad *a.* pleased; happy; joyous. **-den** *v.t.* to make glad; to cheer; to please. **-ly** *adv.* with pleasure; joyfully; cheerfully. **-ness** *n.*

glad‧i‧a‧tor *n.* a combatant who fought in the arena.

glad‧i‧o‧lus *n.* a plant of the iris family, with long sword-shaped leaves.

glam‧our *n.* deceptive or alluring charm; **-ous** *a.* Also **glamor.**

glance *n.* a quick look; a glimpse; *v.t.* to cast a glance; *v.i.* to give a swift, cursory look. **glancing** *a.*

gland *n.* an organ or collection of cells secreting and abstracting certain substances from the blood and transforming them into new compounds. **-ular, -ulous** *a.* consisting of or pert. to glands.

glare *n.* a strong, dazzling light; an overwhelming glitter; a fierce, hostile look or stare; *v.i.* to shine with a strong dazzling light; to stare in a fierce and hostile manner. **glaring, glary** *a.* brilliant; open and bold.

glass *n.* a hard, brittle, generally transparent substance formed by fusing silica with fixed alkalis; articles made of glass; *a.* made of glass; *v.t.* to cover with glass; to glaze. **-es** *n.pl.* spectacles. **-y** *a.* made of glass; vitreous; like glass; dull or lifeless. **-ily** *adv.* **-iness** *n.* **-ful** *n.* the contents of a glass. **—blowing** *n.* the art of shaping and fashioning glass by inflating it through a tube, after heating. **—blower** *n.* **-ware** *n.* articles made of glass.

glau‧co‧ma *n.* a serious eye disease causing tension and hardening of the eyeball with progressive loss of vision.

glaze *n.* the vitreous, transparent coating of pottery or porcelain; any glossy coating; *v.t.* to furnish with glass, as a window; to overlay with a thin, transparent surface, as earthenware; to make glossy. **-r** *n.* a workman who glazes pottery, cloth, etc. **glazier** *n.* one who sets glass in windows, etc.

gleam *n.* a faint or transient ray of light; brightness; glow *v.i.* to shoot or dart, as rays of light; to flash; to shine faintly.

glee *n.* mirth; merriment; joy; a part song for three or more voices. **-ful** *a.* **-fully** *adv.* **-fulness** *n.* **—club** *n.* a group of singers.

glen *n.* a valley, usually wooded and with a stream.

glib *a.* smooth; fluent. **-ly** *adv.* **-ness** *n.*

glide *v.i.* to move gently or smoothly; of an airplane, to move, or descend, usually with engines shut off; *n.* a sliding movement. **-r** *n.* one who or that which, glides; a plane capable of flight without motive power, by utilizing air currents.

glim‧mer *v.i.* to shine faintly and unsteadily; to flicker; *n.* a faint, unsteady light; a faint glimpse; an inkling. Also **-ing** *n.* and *a.*

glimpse *n.* a momentary view; a passing appearance; *v.t.* to catch a glimpse of; *v.i.* to look briefly.

glis‧ten *v.i.* to glitter; to sparkle; to shine; *n.*

glit‧ter *v.i.* to shine with a bright; quivering light; to sparkle; to be showy and attractive; *n.* a bright, sparkling light; brilliance.

gloat *v.i.* to gaze with adulation; to think about with evil satisfaction. **-ing** *a.*

globe *n.* a sphere; a sphere with a map of

the earth or the stars; anything approximately of this shape, e.g. a fish bowl, a lamp shade, etc. **global** a. taking in the whole world. **globate, globated** a. spherical. **globoid** a. globe-shaped. **globose, globous** a. round, spherical (or nearly so). **globosity** n. **globular** a. globe-shaped (or nearly so). **-trotter** n. traveler; tourist.

glob•u•lin n. one of the proteins of the blood. -

glock•en•spiel n. a musical instrument consisting of a row of bells suspended from a rod, or of a series of flat bars, which when struck with a mallet give forth a bell-like sound; a carillon.

gloom n. thick shade; partial or almost total darkness; melancholy; v.i. to become dark or threatening; to be dejected. **-y** a. dark and dreary; melancholy. **-ily** adv. **-iness** n.

glo•ry n. renown; whatever brings honor; praise and adoration; splendor or brilliance; v.i. to be proud; boast; to exult triumphantly. **glorious** a. illustrious; conferring renown; splendid; noble. **gloriously** adv. **gloriousness** n. **glorify** v.t. to exalt; to praise esp. in worship; to make eternally blessed; to shed radiance on; to magnify. **glorifier** n. **glorification** n.

gloss n. luster from a smooth surface; polish; v.t. to make smooth and shining; **-y** a. smooth and shining.

glos•sa•ry n. a vocabulary of obscure or technical words; vocabulary to a book. **glossarial** a.

glove n. a cover for the hand and wrist with a sheath for each finger; v.t. to cover with a glove. **-r** n. one who makes or sells gloves.

glow v.i. to shine with an intense heat; to feel hot, as the skin; to burn; to rage; n. incandescence; warmth or redness; sensation of warmth; ador. **-ing** a. bright; warm; excited; enthusiastic. **-ingly** adv.

glu•cose n. a white crystalline sugar obtained from fruits and honey.

glue n. an adhesive, gelatinous substance made by boiling skins, hoofs, etc. of animals; v.t. to join with glue; to cause to stick as with glue. **-y** a.

glum a. sullen; moody; morose. **-ness** n. **-ly** adv.

glut v.t. overindulge; to fill to excess. pr.p. **-ting.** pa.p., pa.t. **-ted** n. an oversupply.

glut•ton n. one who eats too much; **-ize** v.i. to eat to excess. **-ous** a. **-ously** adv. **-y** n.

glyc•er•ine n. a sweet, colorless, odorless, syrupy liquid. Also **glycerol**.

gly•co•gen n. the form in which the body stores carbohydrates.

gly•col n. an artificial compound linking glycerine and alcohol used as an antifreeze.

gnarl n. a knot in wood or on the trunk of a tree. **-ed, -y** a. knotty; knobby.

gnat n. a kind of small biting insect.

gnaw v.t. to wear away by scraping with the teeth; to bite steadily, as a dog a bone; to fret; to corrode; v.i. to use the teeth in biting; to cause steady pain. **-er** n. **-ing** a., n.

go v.i. to pass from one place or condition to another; to move along; to be in motion; to proceed; to depart; to be able to be put; to result; to contribute to a result; to tend to; to pass away; to become; pr.p. **-ing** pa.p. **gone.** pa.t. **went** n. a going; **-ings on** usually in a bad sense, behavior; conduct. **gone** a. lost; beyond recovery; weak and faint. **-between** n. an intermediary. **to go in for,** to indulge in. **to go off,** to depart; to explode.

goad n. a sharp, pointed stick for driving cattle; anything that urges to action; v.t. to drive with a goad; to urge on; to irritate.

goal n. an object of effort; an end or aim; in a race, the winning post; in football, hockey, etc., the space marked by two upright posts and a cross-bar; the act of kicking or driving the ball between these posts.

goat n. a long-haired, ruminant quadruped with cloven hoofs and curving horns; the 10th sign of the Zodiac, Capricorn.

gob n. a lump or mass.

gob•ble v.t. to eat hurriedly or greedily. **-r** n. a greedy eater.

gob•ble n. the throaty, gurgling cry of the turkey cock; v.i. to make such a noise. **-r** n. a turkey.

gob•let n. a drinking glass with a stem and foot.

gob•lin n. an evil or mischievous sprite or elf.

god n. a being of more than human powers; a divinity; an idol; n.pl. false deities; the Supreme Being; Jehovah. **-dess** n. a female god or idol. **godly** a. reverencing God; pious; devout. **godliness** n. holiness; righteousness. **-less** a. wicked; impious; acknowledging no God. **godsend** n. an unexpected piece of good fortune. **-forsaken** a. dreary; dismal.

god•child n. one for whom a person become sponsor, guaranteeing his religious education. Also **-daughter, -son, -parent, -mother, -father,** the sponsor.

god•wit n. a long-billed wading bird.

gog•gle v.i. to roll the eyes; to stare; n. a rolling of the eyes; a. rolling; bulging; **-s** n.pl. spectacles to protect the eyes.

gold n. a precious metal of a bright yellow color; money; riches; a bright yellow color; a. made of gold; of color of gold. **-en** a. made of gold; having the color of gold; precious. **-finch** n. a beautiful bird, so named from its color. **-fish** n. a small fish of the carp family named from its color. **-smith** n. one who manufactures vessels and ornaments of gold. **-dust** n. gold in very fine particles. **-mine** n. a mine from which gold is due; a source of wealth. **-rush** n. the mad scramble to reach a new goldfield. **—standard,** a currency system under which banknotes are exchanged for gold at any time. **-en age,** the most flourishing period in the history of a nation. **-enrod,** a plant with branching clusters of small yellow flowers. **-en rule,** the rule of doing as you would be done by.

golf *n.* out door game played with set of clubs and a ball, in which the ball is driven with the fewest possible strokes, into a succession of holes. *v.i.* to play this game. **-er** *n.* **—course,** tract of land for playing golf.

gol•ly *interj.* to express joy, sorrow, surprise, etc.

go•losh See galosh.

gon•ad *n.* a gland that produces reproductive cells; ovary or testis. **-al** *a.*

gon•do•la *n.* a long, narrow, flat-bottomed boat, used in the canals of Venice. **gondolier** *n.* the boatman.

gone *pa.p.* of the verb go. **-r** *n.*

gong *n.* a circular metal plate which gives out a deep note when struck with a soft mallet; anything used in this way.

gon•o•coc•cus *n.* microbe of gonorrhea. **gonorrhea** *n.*

good *a.* commendable; right; proper; suitable; virtuous; honest; just; kind; adequate; *comp.* better. *superl.* best *n.* that which is good; welfare; well-being; profit; advantage; *n.pl.* property; wares; commodities; merchandise; textiles; *interj.* well! right! so be it! **-ly** *a.* pleasant; of considerable size. **-liness** *n.* **-ness** *n.* the quality of being good; *interj.* used for emphasis; *pl.* **-ies** candy; sweets. **— turn,** a kindly action. **— will** *n.* benevolence; kindly disposition; the right, on transfer or sale of a business, to the reputation, trade, and custom of that business.

goose *n.* a web-footed bird like a duck but larger; *pl.* **geese. gosling** *n.* a young goose. **— flesh** *n.* a bristling state of the skin due to cold or fright.

go•pher *n.* in N. America, the ground squirrel; a kind of rat with pouched cheeks.

gopher

gore *n.* thick or clotted blood; blood. **gory** *a.* bloody.

gore *v.t.* to pierce with a spear, horns, or tusks.

gore *n.* a tapering piece of material inserted in a garment or a sail, to widen it; *v.t.* to cut into a wedge shape.

gorge *n.* a narrow pass between mountains; *v.t.* to swallow with greediness; *v.i.* to feed greedily and to excess.

gor•geous *a.* splendid; showy; magnificent; **-ly** *adv.*

go•ril•la *n.* an ape inhabiting W. Africa, of great size and strength.

gor•y See gore.

gosh *interj.* a minced and very mild oath.

gos•pel *n.* glad tidings; the revelation of the Christian faith; story of Christ's life as found in first four books of New Testament; doctrine; belief accepted as infallibly true; *a.* pert. to, or in accordance with, the gospel.

gos•sa•mer *n.* a filmy substance, like cobwebs; think gauzy material; *a.* light, thin and filmy.

gos•sip *n.* idle talk about others, regardless of fact; idle talk or writing; one who talks thus; *v.i.* to talk gossip; to chat.

got *pa.pa.* and *pa.t.* of get.

Goth *n.* a member of ancient Teutonic tribe; a barbarian. **-ic** *a.* pert. to Goths; barbarous; pert. to pointed-arch style of architecture; *n.* the language of Goths; a printing type Gothic.

got•ten *pa.p.* of get.

Gou•da *n.* a well-known Dutch cheese.

gouge *n.* a chisel with a curved cutting edge, for cutting grooves or holes; *v.t.* to cut or scoop out with a gouge; to hollow out; to force out, as the eye of a person, with the thumb or finger.

gou•lash *n.* a Hungarian stew.

gourd *n.* trailing or climbing plant: pumpkin, squash, etc.; large fleshy fruit of this plant.

gour•mand *n.* one fond of eating; a judge of fine foods. Also **gormand, gourmet.**

gout *n.* a disease characterized by acute inflammation and swelling of the smaller joints. **-iness** *n.* **-y** *a.*

gov•ern *v.t.* to rule; to direct; to guide; to control; to regulate by authority; *v.i.* to exercise authority; to administer the laws. **-able** *a.* **-ance** *n.* directions; control; management. **-ess** *n.* woman with authority to control and direct; a lady, usually resident in a family, in charge of children's education. **-ment** *n.* act of governing; the system of governing in a state or community; the administrative council or body; **-mental** *a.* **-or** *n.* the executive head of a state; regulating mechanical device for velocity, pressure, etc.

gown *n.* a losse, flowing garment; outer dress of a woman; *v.t.* to dress in a gown; *v.i.* to put on a gown.

grab *v.t.* to grasp suddenly; to snatch; to clutch; to seize. *pr.p.* **-bing.** *pa.p.* and *pa.t.* **-bed.** *n.* a sudden clutch; unscrupulous seizure.

grace *n.* charm; attractiveness; easy and refined motion, a short prayer of thanksgiving before or after a meal; a period of delay granted as a favor; *v.t.* to adorn; to honor; to add grace to. **-ful** *a.* displaying grace or charm in form or action; elegant; easy. **-fully** *adv.* **-fulness** *n.* **-less** *a.* lacking grace. **gracious** *a.* favorable; kind; friendly; merciful; pleasing; proceeding from divine grace; **graciously** *adv.* **graciousness** *n.*

gra•da•tion *n.* successive stage in progress; degree; a step, or series of steps. **gradate** *v.t.* to cause to change by imperceptable degrees, as from one color to another.

grade *n.* a step or degree in rank, merit, quality, etc.; a mark or rating of a student's work; a gradient; *v.t.* to arrange in order, degree, or class; to gradate.

gra•di•ent *n.* an incline.

grad•u•al *a.* proceeding by steps or degrees; progressive; **-ly** *adv.*

grad·u·ate v.t. to grant a diploma or university degree; v.i. to receive a diploma or university degree; n. one who has received a diploma or degree upon completing a course of study. **graduation** n.

graft, graff v.t. to insert a bud or small branch of a tree into another; to transplant living tissue, from one part of the body to another; n. a bud, etc. so inserted, or a piece of tissue so transplanted.

gra·ham a. made of whole-wheat flour.

grail n. a cup. **The Holy Grail**, in medieval legend, the cup or vessel used by Jesus at the Last Supper.

grain n. a kernel, esp. of corn, wheat, etc.; any small, hard particle; that arrangement of the particles of any body which determines its roughness, markings or texture; v.t. to paint in imitation of the grain of wood; to form into grains, as sugar, powder, etc. **-ed** a. **against the grain**, i.e. against the fiber of the wood.

gram n. unit of weight in metric system = 15.432 grains. Also **gramme**.

gram·mar n. a system of general principles for speaking and writing according to the forms and usage of a language; n. a philologist; **grammatical** a. pert to grammar; according to the rules of grammar.

gramme See gram.

gram·o·phone n. a phonograph.

gran·a·ry n. a storehouse for threshed grain; a barn.

grand a. great; high in power and dignity; eminent; distinguished; superior; splendid; lofty; noble; dignified; majestic; indicating family relationship of the second degree; n. **-child** n. a son's or daughter's child. **-daughter, -son** n. a son's or daughter's daughter. **-eur** n. nobility of action; majesty; splendor; magnificence. **-father (-mother)** n. a father's or mother's father (mother). **-iosely** adv. **-iosity** n. **-ly** adv. in a grand manner, splendidly. **- ness** n. greatness; magnifence. **-stand** n. main seating structure for spectators at a sporting event.

grange n. a farm; an association of farmers.

gran·ite n. a hard igneous rock, consisting of quartz, feldspar, and mica; gray or pink in color.

grant v.t. to allow; to yield; to concede; to bestow; to confer; to admit as true; n. a bestowing; a gift; an allowance. **-er, -or** n. the person who transfers property.

gran·ule n. a little grain; a small particle. **granular** a. consisting of grains or granules. **granulate** v.t. to form into grains; to make rough on the surface; v.i. to be formed into grains. **granulated** a. **granulation** n. the process of forming into grains; the development of new tissue in a wound, characterized by the formation of grain-like cells.

grape n. the fruit of the vine. **-ry** n. a place for the cultivation of grapes.

graph n. a diagram of curve representing the variation in value of some phenomenon or relationship of two or more things, according to stated conditions; v.t. to show variation by

graph

means of a diagram. **-ic(al)** a. pert. to writing or delineating; truly descriptive; vivid. **-ically** adv. ic **arts**, drawing, engraving, and painting. **-ics** n. the art of drawing, esp. mechanical drawing. **-ite** n. a natural form of carbon used in the making of the 'lead' of pencils.

grasp v.t. to seize firmly; to clutch; to take possession of; to understand. v.i. to endeavor to seize; to catch at; n. a firm grip of the hand; the power of seizing and holding; reach of the arms; mental power or capacity. **-ing** a. seizing; greedy of gain.

grass n. ground covered with grass; v.t. to cover with grass; to feed with grass. **-y** a. **-hopper** n. a jumping, chirping insect, allied to the locust family. **—roots** a. close to, or from, the people.

grate n. a framework of crossed bars. **grating** n. a partition of parallel or cross bars.

grate v.t. to rub or scrape into small bits; v.i. sound harshly; to irritate. **-r** n. an instrument with a rough surface for rubbing off small particles.

grate·ful a. thankful; pleasant.

gra·ti·fy v.t. to give pleasure to; to satisfy. **-ing** a. **gratifier** n. one who gratifies. **gratification** n. the act of pleasing; satisfaction.

grat·in n. a dish prepared with a covering of bread crumbs or cheese. **au gratin** a. food so cooked.

gra·tis adv. free.

grat·i·tude n. thankfulness.

gra·tu·i·ty n. a gift of money for services rendered; a tip. **gratuitous** a. free; voluntary; granted without obligation; asserted without cause or proof. **gratuitously** adv.

grave n. a hole dug for a dead body; a place of burial; **-stone** n. a memorial stone set at a grave. **-yard** n. a burial ground.

grave a. solemn; serious; weighty; important. **grave** n. the 'grave' accent in French or its sign (`). **-ly** adv.

grave v.t. to engrave; to impress deeply. **-n image**, an idol.

grav·el n. small stones; v.t. to cover with gravel; to puzzle. **-ly** a.

grav·i·tate v.i. to obey the law of gravitation; to tend towards a center of attraction; **gravitation** n. the act of gravitating; the tendency of all bodies to attract each other. **gravitational**, gravitative a.

grav·i·ty n. weight; seriousness; the force of attraction of one body for another, esp. of objects to the earth.

gra·vy n. the juices from meat in cooking; sauce made with this. —boat n. a dish for holding gravy.

gray, grey a. between black and white in color, as ashes or lead; clouded; dismal; v.t. to cause to become gray; v.i. to become gray. -ish a. somewhat gray. —matter the gray nerve tissue of the brain and spinal cord; -ness n.

graze v.t. to touch lightly in passing; n. a light touch in passing; a grazing.

graze v.t. to feed, as cattle, with grass; v.i. to eat grass or herbage.

grease n. soft melted fat of animals; thick oil as a lubricant; v.t. to apply grease to; greasy a. like grease; oily; fat; -r n. greasiness n.

great a. large in size or number; admirable; eminent; uncommonly gifted; -ly adv. -ness n. great-grandchild n. the child of a grandchild. Great Britain England, Wales and Scotland.

Gre·cian a. Greek; pert. to Greece; n. a native of Greece.

greed n. an eager and selfish desire; -y a. having a keen desire for food, drink, wealth, etc.; ravenous. -ily adv. -iness n.

Greek a. pert. to Greece; Grecian; n. a native of Greece; the language of Greece.

green a. of color between blue and yellow; grass-colored; emerald-colored; unripe; easily deceived; n. the color; n.pl. fresh leaves or branches; wreaths; green leafy vegetables. -ery n. a place where plants are cultivated; vegetation. -ish a somewhat green. -ness n. the quality of being green; freshness. -house n. a glass building for keeping or growing plants. — light traffic signal to go; — thumb apparent skill in growing plants.

Greenwich time, the basis for calculating standard time everywhere.

greet v.t. to welcome; to receive. -ing n. a salutation; expression of good wishes.

gre·gar·i·ous a. living in flocks or herds; fond of company. -ly adv. -ness n.

gre·nade n. an explosive shell or bomb, thrown by hand or shot from a rifle; grenadier n. formerly, a soldier trained to throw grenades.

gren·a·dine n. a syrup for flavoring drinks.

grew pat. of grow.

grey See gray.

grey·hound n. a swift, slender dog, used in racing.

grid n. a frame of bars; a grating.

grid·dle n. flat utensil for cooking over direct heat; v.t. to cook on a griddle.

grid·i·ron n. a framework of metal bars, for broiling meats, fish, etc.; a football field.

grief n. deep sorrow.

grieve v.t. to cause grief; to afflict; v.i. to feel grief; to be distressed; to lament. grievance n. a real or imaginary complaint; a cause of grief or uneasiness. -r n. grievous a. causing sadness; atrocious. grievously adv.

grill v.t. to broil on a gridiron; to question relentlessly; n. a cooking utensil for broiling meat, fish, etc.

grille n. a metal grating screening a window, doorway, etc. grillwork n.

grim a. stern; severe; of forbidding aspect; fierce; surly. -ly adv. -ness n.

gri·mace n. a distortion of the face to express contempt, dislike, etc.; a wry face; v.i. to make a grimace.

grime n. ingrained dirt; soot; v.t. to soil deeply; to dirty. grimy a. dirty.

grin v.i. to show the teeth as in laughter derision, or pain. pr.p. -ning. pa.t., pa.p. -ned. n. a wide smile.

grind v.t. to crush to powder between hard surfaces; to sharpen by friction; v.i. to grind; to work hard. pa.p. and pa.t. ground. n. the action of grinding.

grip n. a firm hold; a grasp or pressure of the hand; a clutch; mastery of a subject, etc. a handle; a suitcase; v.t. to grasp or hold tightly; -ping. pa.p., pa.t. -ped. -per n.

gripe v.t. to grip; to oppress; to afflict with sharp pains; v.i. to grasp at gain; to suffer griping pains; to complain constantly; n. grasp; clutch; severe intestinal pain. griping a.

grippe n. influenza.

gris·ly a. grim; horrible. grisliness n.

gris·tle n. a smooth, solid, elastic substance in animal bodies; cartilage.

grit n. the coarse part of meal; particles of sand; coarse sandstone; pl. grain coarsely ground; v.t. to grind; to grate; v.i. to cover with grit. pr.p. -ti g. pa.t., pa.p. -ted. -ty a.

griz·zle n. gray hair. -d a. gray; grayhaired. grizzly a. gray; n. a large ferocious bear of N. Amer.

groan v.i. to make a low deep sound of grief or pain; n. the sound. -er n. -ing n.

gro·cer n. storekeeper. -y n. a store. groceries n.pl. goods sold by a grocer.

grog n. a mixture of spirits, esp. rum and cold water. -gy a. drunk; unsteady; shaky.

groin n. the depression where the abdomen joins the thigh.

groom n. a bridegroom; v.t. to dress with neatness and care; to tend a horse.

groove n. a channel or hollow, esp. one cut by a tool; a rut; a routine; v.t. to cut a groove in.

grope v.t. to feel about; to search blindly as if in the dark.

gros·grain n. corded ribbon or cloth.

gross a. coarse; indecent; crude; thick; not net; n. twelve dozen; mass; bulk; v.t. to earn a total of. -ly adv. -ness n.

gro·tesque a. wildly formed; irregular in design or form; n. a whimsical figure; a caricature. -ness.

ground pa.p. and pa.t. of grind.

ground n. the surface of the earth; dry land; territory; reason; motive; basis; a conducting line between electrical equipment and the ground; v.t. to establish; to place on the ground; to run ashore; v.i. to come to the ground. -s n.pl. dregs; sediment; lands around a house.

G

-less *a.* without reason. -ed *a.* of aircraft, unable to fly because of weather conditions. -ing *n.* the background; thorough knowledge of the essentials of a subject. -work *n.* foundation; basis; —rent *n.* rent paid to a landlord for the privilege of building on his ground.

group *n.* a number of persons or things near, placed, or classified together; *v.t.* to arrange in groups; *v.i.* to fall into groups. -ing *n.*

grout *n.* coarse meal; thin mortar to fill cracks; plaster; *v.t.* to fill with grout.

grow *v.t.* to produce by cultivation; to raise; *v.i.* to develop naturally; to increase in size, height, etc.; *pa.p.* -n. *pa.t.* grew. -er *n.* -th *n.* the process of growing; something already grown; a morbid formation; a tumor. grown-up *n.* an adult.

growl *v.i.* to make a low guttural sound, of anger or menacing like an animal; to grumble; *n.* such a sound. -er *n.*

grub *v.t.* to dig superficially; to root up; *v.i.* to dig; to rummage; that which is dug up for food; *pr.p.* -bing. *pa.p.*, *pa.t.* -bed. -ber *n.* -biness *n.* the state of being grubby. -by *a.* unclean; dirty; grimy.

grudge *v.t.* to be reluctant to give or allow; to envy; *n.* a feeling of ill will; resentment. grudging *a.*

gru·el -ing *a.* exhausting.

grue·some *a.* causing horror, fear or loathing.

grum·ble *v.i.* to murmur with discontent; to complain; to make growling sounds; *n.* grumbling; a complaint.

grump·y *a.* surly; irritable; gruff. grumpily *adv.* grumpiness *n.*

grunt *v.i.* of a pig, to make its characteristic sound; to utter a sound like this; *n.* a deep, guttural sound; a pig's sound. -er *n.* -ing *a.*

Gru·yère *n.* a whole-milk cheese.

guar·an·tee *n.* formal assurance given by way of security; an assurance of the truth, genuineness, permanence, etc. of something, the one who receives such promise or assurance; guaranty; *v.t.* to promise; to answer for. guaranty *n.* a pledge of commitment; security; basis of security. guarantor *n.*

guard *v.t.* to protect from danger; to accompany for protection; *v.i.* to keep watch; to take precautions; *n.* he who, or that which, guards; a protective device. -ed *a.* cautious; wary. -edly *adv.* -ian *n.* a keeper; a protector; one who has custody of a minor. -ianship *n.*

gu·ber·na·to·ri·al *a.* pert. to a governor.

guer·ril·la guerilla *n.* a member of a band of irregular troops taking part in a war independently of the principal combatants; *a.* pert. to this kind of warfare.

guess *v.t.* and *i.* to estimate without calculation or measurement; to judge at random; to suppose; *n.* a rough estimate; a random judgment.

guest *n.* a visitor received or entertained.

guide *n.* one who shows the way; a sign, mark, or device to indicate direction; *v.t.*

to lead; to direct; to influence; to act as a guide to. **guidance** *n.* direction. **guided missile**, powered rocket or other projectile which can be directed by remote control.

guild *n.* a society for mutual help, or with a common object.

guil·lo·tine *n.* a machine for beheading by the descending stroke of a heavy blade; *v.t.* to use a guillotine upon.

guilt *n.* the fact or state of having offended; criminality and consequent liability to punishment. -y *a.* judged to have committed a crime. -ily *adv.* -iness *n.* -less *a.* innocent.

guin·ea *n.* a former Brit. gold coin. —**pig** *n.* a small rodent, used frequently in scientific experiments; a person used as a subject for experimentation.

guise *n.* external appearance, semblance; pretense.

gui·tar *n.* a six-stringed musical instrument

guitar

resembling the lute. -ist *n.* a player of the guitar.

gulch *n.* a ravine; a deep-walled valley.

gulf *n.* a large bay; a sea extending into the land; *v.t.* to swallow up.

gull *n.* a long-winged, web-footed seabird.

gull *n.* a dupe; *v.t.* to deceive; to trick; to defraud. -ible *a.* easily imposed on; credulous. -ibility *n.*

gul·let *n.* the tube from mouth to stomach; the throat.

gul·ly *n.* a channel or ravine worn by water; a ravine; a ditch.

gulp *v.t.* to swallow eagerly; to swallow in large amounts; *v.t.* to gasp; to choke; *n.* an act of gulping; an effort to swallow; a large mouthful.

gum *n.* the firm flesh in which the teeth are set.

gum *n.* a sticky substance issuing from certain trees; this substance used for stiffening or adhesive purposes; resin; an adhesive; chewing gum; *v.t.* to coat with gum; *v.i.* to exude gum; to become clogged. *pr.p.* -ming. *pa.p.*, *pa.t.* -med. -miness *n.* -my *a.* consisting of gum; sticky.

gum·bo *n.* okra; soup thickened with this.

gump·tion *n.* resourcefulness; courage; common sense; courage.

gun *n.* a weapon consisting of a metal tube from which missiles are thrown by explosion; *v.i.* to shoot with a gun. *pr.p.* -ning. *pa.pa.*, *pa.t.* -ned. -ner *n.* one who works a gun. -nery *n.* the firing of guns;

the science of artillery. **-powder** *n.* an explosive. *n.* the range of a gun; a shot fired from a gun. **-smith** *n.* one who makes, repairs, deals in guns.

gup·py *n.* tiny fresh-water fish.

gur·gi·ta·tion *n.* a surging rise and fall.

gur·gle *n.* a bubbling noise; *v.i.* to make a gurgle.

gush *v.i.* to flow out suddenly and copiously; to display exaggerated and effusive affection; *n.* a sudden copious flow; **-er** *n.* a gushing person; an oil-well with a natural flow. **-iness** *n.* **-ing, -y** *a.* effusive.

gus·set *n.* a triangular piece of material inserted in a garment to strengthen or enlarge it.

gust *n.* a sudden blast of wind; an outburst of passion. **-y** *a.*

gus·to *n.* keen enjoyment; zest; artistic style.

gut *n.* a material made from animal intestines, as violin strings, etc.; *n.pl.* entrails; intestines; courage; pluck; determination; *v.t.* to remove the entrails from; to destroy the interior as by fire. *pr.p.* **-ting.** *pa.p.* and *pa.t.* **-ted.**

gut·ter *n.* a passage for water; a trough or pipe for conveying rain from the eaves of a building; a channel at the side of a road for carrying water; *v.t.* to make channels in; *v.i.* to flow in streams.

gut·tur·al *a.* pert. to or produced in the throat; *n.* a guttural sound.

guz·zle *v.t.* and *i.* to drink greedily. **-r** *n.*

gym·kha·na *n.* a place for athletic games; a sports meet.

gym·na·sium *n.* a building or room equipped for physical training or sports; *pl.* **gymnasia** or **-s. gymnast** *n.* an expert in gymnastics. **gymnastic** *a.* **gymnastics** *n.pl.* muscular and bodily exercises. **gym** *n.* a gymnasium; a school athletic course.

gy·ne·col·o·gy *n.* the science which deals with the diseases and disorders of women, esp. the organs of generation. **gynecologist** *n.*

gyp·sum *n.* a mineral, consisting mostly of sulfate of lime, used for making plaster of Paris.

Gyp·sy *n.* one of a nomadic tribe of Indian origin; a person who resembles or lives like a Gypsy; *a.* of or like a Gypsy.

gy·rate *v.i.* to revolve around a cent-al point; to move in a circle; to move spirally. **gyratory** *a.* **gyration** *n.* a circular or spiral motion.

gy·ro·scope *n.* a wheel so mounted that its axis can turn freely in any direction when set rotating and left undisturbed, it will maintain the same direction in space, independently of its relation to the earth.

G

gyroscope

H

ha *interj.* denoting surprise, joy, or grief.

ha·be·as cor·pus *n.* writ requiring that a prisoner be brought to court to determine legality of confinement.

ha·ber·dash·er *n.* a dealer in men's furnishings. -y *n.*

ha·bil·i·ment *n.* (usually in *pl.*) dress.

hab·it *n.* custom; usage; tendency to repeat an action in the same way; *v.t.* to dress; to clothe. -ual *a.* formed by habit. -ually *adv.* habituate *v.t.* to accustom to a practice or usage; to familiarize; (*Colloq.*) to frequent. -uation *n.* -ude *n.* customary manner of action; confirmed practice. -ué *n.* a frequenter (of a place).

hab·it·a·ble *n.* fit to live in. -ness, habitability *n.* habitably *adv.* habitant *n.* an inhabitant. habitat *n.* the natural home of an animal or plant; place of residence. habitation *n.*

hack *v.t.* to cut irregularly; to notch; *v.i.* to make cuts or notches; to give harsh dry coughs; *n.* a cut; a notch; an ax, a pick; a short cough.

hack *n.* a horse for ordinary riding; a horse worn out by over work; a drudge, esp. literary; *a.* hackneyed; hired; a hired carriage.

hack·ney *n.* a horse for riding or driving; a horse (and carriage) kept for hire; *a.* to let out for hire; *v.i.* to use often; to make trite or commonplace. -ed *a.*

had *pa.p.* and *pa.t.* of **have.**

had·dock *n.* a fish of the cod family.

Ha·des (*Myth.*) the underworld.

haft *n.* a handle, esp. of a knife; a hilt; *v.t.* to set in a handle.

hag *n.* an ugly old woman; a witch. -gish *a.* -gishly *adv.* -ridden troubled with nightmares.

hag·gard *a.* wild-looking; lean and gaunt; *n.* untrained hawk. -ly *adv.*

hag·gle *v.t* to hack; to mangle; *v.i.* to dispute terms; to be difficult in bargaining; *n.* act of haggling. -r *n.*

Hag·i·og·ra·pha *n.pl.* the last of the three divisions of the Old Testament.

hag·i·ol·o·gy *n.* a history of the lives of saints. hagiologist *n.* hagiography *n.*

hail *n.* frozen rain falling in pellets; *v.i.* to rain hail; *v.t.* to pour down like hail. -stone *n.* frozen raindrops.

hail *v.t.* to greet, salute or call; *n.* an exclamation of respectful salutation.

hair *n.* a filament growing from the skin of an animal; such filaments collectively, esp. covering the head; bristles; anything small or fine. -ed *a.* having hair. -iness *n.* -y *a.* covered with, made of, resembling hair. -brush *n.* a brush for the hair. -cloth *n.* cloth made wholly or partly of hair. -dresser *n.* one who dresses or cuts hair; a barber. -pin *n.* a special two-legged pin for controlling hair.

hal·cy·on *n.* the kingfisher; *a.* calm. — days, peaceful, tranquil days; calm weather just before and after the winter solstice.

hale *a.* robust; sound; healthy, esp. in old age. -ness *n.*

hale *v.t.* to haul.

half *v.t.* either of two equal parts of a thing. *pl.* halves *a.* forming a half; *adv.* to the extent of half. -back *n.* (*Football*) a player, or position, behind the forward line. —breed *n.* one whose parents are of different races. — brother *n.* a brother by one parent only. —caste *n.* a half-breed. — mast *n.* the position of a flag lowered halfway down the staff, as a signal of distress, or as a sign of mourning. — measure *n.* inadequate means to achieve an end. — moon *n.* the moon when half its disk appears illuminated; a semicircle. — title *n.* the name of a book, or subdivision of a book, occupying a full page. —tone *n.* an illustration printed from a relief plate, showing light and shade by minute dots.

half-tone

halve *v.t.* to divide into two equal portions; to reduce to half the previous amount.

hal·i·but *n.* a large, flat sea fish.

hal·i·to·sis *n.* foul or offensive breath.

hall *n.* a corridor in a building; a place of public assembly; a room at the entrance of a house; a building belonging to a collegiate institution, guild, etc. -mark *n.* the mark used to indicate the standard of tested gold and silver; any mark of quality.

Hal·le·lu·jah, Halleluiah *n.* and *interj.* used in songs of praise to God.

hal·liard See halyard.

hal·low *v.t.* to make holy; to consecrate; to treat as sacred; to reverence. -ed *a.* Hallowe'en *n.* the evening before All Hallows' or All Saints' day.

hal·lu·ci·nate *n.* to produce illusion in the mind of. hallucination *n.* hallucinative, hallucinatory *a.*

ha·lo *n.* a circle of light around the moon, sun, etc.; a ring of light around a saint's head in a picture. *pl.* -s, -es.

hal·o·gen *n.* (*Chem.*) one of the elements chlorine, bromine, iodine, and fluorine.

halt *n.* a stoppage on a march or journey; *v.t.* to cause to stop; *v.i.* to make a stop.

halt *v.i.* to falter in speech or walk; to hesitate; *n.* cripple. -ing.

hal·ter *n.* a rope or strap with headstall to fasten or lead horses or cattle.

halve *v.t.* to divide into two equal parts.

hal·yard, halliard *n.* (*Naut.*) a rope for hoisting or lowering yards or sails.

ham *n.* the thigh of any animal, esp. a hog's thigh cured by salting and smoking. -string *n.* a tendon at the back of the

149

knee; *v.t.* to cripple by cutting this.

ham•burg•er *n.* ground beef, seasoned and formed into cakes.

ham•let *n.* a small village.

ham•mer *n.* a tool, usually with a heavy head at the end of a handle, for beating metal, driving nails, etc.; a contrivance for exploding the charge of a gun; *v.t.* and *i.* to beat with, or as with, a hammer; to work hard at. **-head** *n.* a rapacious kind of shark.

ham•mock *n.* a kind of hanging bed, consisting of a piece of canvas, and suspended by cords from hooks.

ham•per *n.* a large covered basket for conveying goods.

ham•per *n.* (*Naut.*) cumbrous equipment; *v.t.* to impede.

ham•shack•le *v.t.* to fasten the head of an animal to one of the forelegs.

ham•ster *n.* a species of rodent.

ham•string See ham.

hand *n.* the extremity of the arm beyond the wrist; a pointer on a dial, e.g. on a watch; a measure of the hand's breadth, four inches; a style of handwriting; cards dealth to a player; a manual worker; *a.* belonging to, worn on, carried in, the hand; *v.t.* to give with the hand; to deliver; to pass; to hold out. **-y** *a.* convenient. **-ily** *adv.* **-iness** *n.* **-bag** *n.* bag for carrying in the hand. **-bill** *n.* printed sheet for circulation by hand. **-book** *n.* a short treatise; a manual. **-breath** *n.* the breadth of a hand (about four inches). **-cart** *n.* a small cart drawn or pushed by hand. **-cuff** *n.* shackle around wrist connected

handcuff

by a chain with one on other wrist; a manacle; *v.t.* to manacle. **-ful** *n.* as much as the hand will grasp or contain. **-maid(en)** *n.* female servant.

hand•i•cap *n.* a race or contest in which competitors' chances are equalized by starts given, weights carried, etc.; a condition so imposed; *v.t.* to hinder or impede.

hand•i•craft *n.* manual occupation or skill.

hand•ker•chief *n.* a small square of fabric carried in the pocket for wiping the nose, etc.

han•dle *v.t.* to touch or feel with the hand; to manage; to wield; to deal with. *n.* the part of a thing by which it is held.

hand•some *a.* of fine appearance; generous. **-ly** *adv.* **-ness** *n.*

hang *v.t.* to suspend; to put to death by suspending from gallows; to cover with, as wallpaper, curtains, pictures, etc.; to display; *v.i.* to be suspended; to incline; to be in suspense; to linger; to cling to. *pa.p.* and *p.t.* **-ed** or **hung**. *n.* **-er** *n.* that by which a thing is suspended. **-man** *n.* one who hangs another; a public executioner. **-nail** *n.* piece of skin hanging from root of fingernail. **-over** *n.* depressing after-effects of drinking.

han•gar *n.* a shed for aircraft.

hank *n.* a coil, esp. as a measure of yarn.

han•ker *v.i.* to long for; to crave. **-ering** *n.* an uneasy longing for; a craving.

han•som *n.* a light two-wheeled cab with the driver's seat at the back.

hap•haz•ard *n.* chance; accident; *a.* ransom; without design. **-ly** *adv.* **-ness** *n.*

hap•less *a.* unlucky. **-ly** *adv.*

hap•pen *v.i.* to come by chance; to occur; to take place. **-ing** *n.* occurrence; event.

hap•py *a.* glad; content; lucky; fortunate; apt; fitting. **happily** *adv.* **happiness** *n.*

ha•rangue *n.* a loud, passionate speech; *v.i.* to deliver a harangue; *v.t.* to speak vehemently to. **-r** *n.*

har•ass *v.t.* to attack repeatedly; to worry; to trouble. **-ed** *a.* **-er** *n.* **-ing** *a.* **-ment** *n.*

har•bing•ger *n.* one who announces another's approach; a forerunner.

har•bor *n.* shelter for ships; a port; any shelter; *v.t.* to give shelter to; to protect; *v.i.* to take shelter.

hard *a.* firm; solid; resisting pressure; difficult; harsh; unfeeling; difficult to bear; strenuous; bitter, as winter; keen, as frost; of water, not making lather well with soap; strong; said of alcoholic liquors; *adv.* vigorously; intently; solidly. **-en** *v.t.* to make hard or more hard; to strengthen; to confirm in wickedness or obstinacy; to make less sympathetic; *v.i.* to become hard. **-ly** *adv.* with difficulty; not quite; scarcely; severly. **-ness** *n.* **ship** *n.* severe toil or suffering; ill-luck; privation; suffering. **-ware** *n.* articles made of metal, e.g. tools, locks, fixtures, etc.

har•dy *a.* robust; vigorous; bold; brave; daring; able to bear exposure. **-ily** *adv.* **-ihood** *n.* **-iness** *n.*

hare *n.* a rodent with long hind legs, long ears, short tail, and divided upper lip, noted for its speed. **-lip** *n.* (*Med.*) a congenital fissure in the upper lip. **-lipped** *a.*

har•em *n.* apartment for females in a Mohammedan household; the occupants.

hark *v.i.* to listen; *interj.* listen! hear!

har•lot *n.* a prostitute. **-ry** *n.*

harm *n.* injury; hurt; misfortune; *v.t.* **-ful** *a.* **-fully** *adv.* **-fulness** *n.* **-less** *a.* **-lessly** *adv.* **-lessness** *n.*

har•mo•ny *n.* agreement; concord; friendliness; peace; the science that treats of musical sounds in their combination and progression. **harmonic, harmonical** *a.* **harmonically** *adv.* **harmonica** *n.* a mouth organ. **harmonicon** *n.* harmonics *n.* sounds. **harmonious** *a.* **harmoniously** *adv.* **harmoniousness** *n.* **harmonize** *v.t.* **harmonizer** *n.* **harmonist** *n.* **harmonium** *n.* a small reed organ. **harmonic progression,** a series of numbers whose reciprocals are in arithmetical progression.

har•ness *n.* the working gear, straps, bands, etc. of a draft horse; *v.t.* to put harness on.

harp *n.* a stringed musical instrument played by hand; *v.i.* to dwell persistently upon a particular subject. **-ist** *n.* **-sichord** *n.* a forerunner of the piano.

har•poon *n.* a barbed spear with a rope attached for catching whales, etc.; *v.t.* to

harpoon

strike with a harpoon. -er n.

Har·py n. (*Myth.*) ravenous monster, with head and breast of woman and wings and claws of vulture; (*l.c.*) a rapacious woman.

har·ri·dan n. a haggard old woman.

har·row n. a toothed agricultural implement to break clods or cover seed

harrow

when sown; *v.t.* to draw harrow over; (*Fig.*) to distress greatly. -er n. -ing a.

har·ry *v.t.* to ravage; to torment.

harsh a. rough; unpleasing to the touch or taste; severe. -ly adv. -ness n.

hart n. a male deer or stag.

harte·beest n. a large S. African antelope.

har·um-scar·um a. reckless; wild; n. a rash person.

har·vest n. (season for) gathering crops; the crop itself; *v.t.* to gather in. -er n. — moon n. the full moon nearest the autumn equinox.

has 3rd sing. pres. indic. of the verb have.

hash (hash) *v.t.* to chop into small pieces; to mince; n. a dish of hashed meat and potatoes.

hasp n. a clasp passing over a staple for fastening a door, etc.; *v.t.* to fasten with a hasp.

has·sock n. a padded cushion for kneeling.

haste n. speed; quickness. **hasten** *v.t.* **hastener** n. **hasty** a. **hastily** adv.

hat n. covering for head, usually with brim. -ter n. one who makes hats. **top hat**, a silk hat with a high crown. **to pass (round) the hat**, to make a collection.

hatch *v.t.* to bring forth; to plot; *v.i.* to come forth; n. the act of hatching; the brood hatched. -er n. -ery n. a place for hatching eggs.

hatch n. the lower half of a divided door; an opening in a floor or roof; the hatchway itself. -way n. a square opening in a ship's deck.

hatch (hach) *v.t.* to shade with lines.

hatch·et n. a small ax. — **faced** a. having a face with sharp features. **to bury the hatchet**, to make peace.

hate *v.t.* to dislike strongly; to detest; n. strong dislike; hatred. -ful a. -fully adv. -fulness n. -r n. **hatred** n.

haugh·ty a. proud. **haughtily** adv. **haughtiness** n.

haul *v.t.* to pull with force; to steer a ship closer to the wind; *v.i.* to pull; n. a catch; good profit, gain. -age n. -er n. **close-hauled** a.

haunch n. the part of the body between the ribs and thighs; the hop.

haunt *v.t.* to frequent; of ghosts, to visit regularly; *v.i.* to loiter about a place. n. a place of frequent resort. -ed a. frequently visited by ghosts.

haut·boy n. an older form of the oboe.

hau·teur n. haughtiness.

Ha·van·a n. a fine brand of cigar [named from *Havana*, the capital of Cuba].

have *v.t.* to hold or possess; to be possessed or affected with; *pr.p.* **having**. *pa.p.* and *pa.t.* **had**.

ha·ven n. a bay or inlet giving shelter for ships; any place of shelter.

hav·er·sack n. a soldier's canvas ration-bag; a similar bag for travelers.

hav·oc n. devastation; ruin.

haw n. a hesitation in speech.

hawk n. a bird of prey. *v.t.* and *i.* to hunt with hawks. **hawker** n. -ing n. falconry.

hawk *v.i.* to clear the throat noisily; n. an audible clearing of the throat.

hawk *v.t.* to carry about wares for sale; to peddle. -er n. an itinerant dealer.

hawk n. a plaster's tool for holding.

hawse n. the part of a ship's bows.

haw·ser n. a large rope or small cable.

hay n. grass mown and dried for fodder. — **fever** n. irritation of the mucous membrane of the nose. -rick n. -stack n. a large pile of hay with ridged or pointed top.

haz·ard n. chance; a chance; risk; danger; *v.t.* to expose to risk; to run the risk of. -ous a.

haze n. a misty appearance in the air; mental obscurity. **hazy** a. **hazily** adv.

haze *v.t.* to torment or punish.

ha·zel n. a nut-bearing bush or small tree; the reddish-brown color of the nuts; a. of this color. -nut n. the nut of the hazel tree.

he pron. the 3rd pers. sing. masc. pronoun.

head n. the upper part of a man's or animal's body; the brain; intellectual capacity; upper part of anything; the top; the chief part, a chief; something the shape of a head; progress; a section of a chapter; the source of a stream; a cape or headland; a crisis; freedom to go on; a. chief; principal; of wind, contrary; *v.t.* to lead; to be at the head of; to direct; to go in front, so as to hinder. *v.i.* to originate; to form a head; to make for. -y a. impetuous; apt to intoxicate. -ily adv. -iness n. -ache n. a nerve-pain in the head. -achy a. -gear n. a hat; the harness about an animal's head. -ing n. -land n. a cape; a promontory. -light n. a strong light carried on the front of a locomotive, motor vehicle, etc. —line n. a summary of news in large print in a newspaper; a caption. -quarters n.pl. (*Mil.*) a center of operations. -sman n. an executioner. -stone n. a memorial stone placed at the head of a grave. -strong a. obstinate; stubborn; self-willed. -way n. progress.

heal *v.t.* to make whole; to restore to health; to make well; *v.i.* to become sound. -er n. -ing a.

health n. soundness of body; general condition of the body; a toast drunk in a person's honor. -y a. -ily adv. -iness n. -ful a.

heap n. a number of things lying one on

another; a pile; a mass; *v.t.* to throw or lay in a heap; to amass.

hear *v.t.* to perceive with the ear; to listen to; to heed; (*Law*) to try (a case); *v.i.* to perceive sound; to learn by report. *pr.p.* -ing. *pa.p.* and *pa.t.* **heard.** -er *n.* -ing *n.* -say *n.* rumor; common talk.

hearse *n.* a vehicle to carry a coffin to the place of burial.

heart *n.* the hollow, muscular organ which makes the blood circulate; the seat or

heart

source of life; the seat of emotions and affections; the inner part of anything; courage; warmth or affection; a playing-card marked with a figure of a heart. -y *a.* cordial; friendly; vigorous; in good health; of a meal, satisfying the appetite. -ily *adv.* -iness *n.* -less *a.* unfeeling. -en *v.t.* to encourage; to stimulate. -blood *n.* life; essence. -break *n.* overpowering sorrow. -burn *n.* a form of dyspepsia.

hearth *n.* the fireside; the house itself.

heat *n.* hotness; a sensation of this; hot weather or climate; warmth of feeling; anger; excitement; sexual excitement in animals, esp. female; *v.t.* to make hot; to excite; *v.i.* to become hot. -ed *a.* -edly *adv.* -er *n.*

heath *n.* waste land; moor; shrub of genus Erica. -y *a.*

hea·then *n.* one who is not an adherent of a religious system; and infidel.

heath·er *n.* a small plant of the genus Erica.

heave *v.t.* to lift with effort; to utter (a sigh); to pull on a rope, etc.; to haul; *v.i.* to rise and fall in alternate motions; *n.* a heaving; an effort to lift something; a rise and fall. *pr.p.* **heaving.** *pa.p.* and *pa.t.* **heaved or hove.**

heav·en *n.* the sky; the upper air; the abode of God; God Himself; a place of bliss; supreme happiness. -ly *a.* -liness *n.* -ward, -wards *adv.* toward heaven.

Heav·i·side lay·er *n.* the upper part of the atmosphere, which reflects radio waves.

heav·y *a.* weighty; striking or falling with force; large in amount, as a debt. **heavily** *adv.* **heaviness** *n.*

heb·do·mad *n.* a group of seven things; a week.

He·brew *n.* one of the ancient inhabitants of Palestine; an Israelite; a Jew; the language. **Hebraic** *a.*

hec·a·tomb *n.* any large number of victims.

heck·le *n.* a comb for cleaning flax; *v.t.* to comb flax; to ask awkward questions of a speaker at a public meeting.

hec·to- *prefix* combining to form derivatives used in the metric system.

-gram, -gramme *n.* a weight of 1·0 grammes. -liter *n.* a unit of capacity, containing 100 liters. -meter *n.* a unit of length.

hec·tic *a.* exciting; wild.

hec·to·graph *n.* an apparatus for multiplying copies of writings.

Hec·tor *n.* the chief hero of Troy in war with Greeks.

hedge *n.* a fence of bushes; a protecting barrier; *v.t.* to enclose with a hedge; to obstruct; to hem in; *v.i.* to bet on both sides so as to guard against loss: to shift; to shuffle; to skulk. **hedging** *n.* **hedgy** *a.* -hog *n.* a small quadruped.

hedgehog

he·don·ism *n.* the doctrine that pleasure is the chief good. **hedonist** *n.*

heed *v.t.* to take notice of; to care for; to mind; to observe; *n.* attention; notice; care; caution. -ful *a.* -fully *adv.* -fulness *n.* -less *a.*

heel *n.* back part of foot, shoe, boot, or stocking; *v.t.* to add a heel to, as in knitting; to touch ground, or a ball, with the heel.

heel *v.i.* of a ship; to lean to one side; to incline; *v.t.* to cause to do this.

heft *v.t.* to try the weight by lifting; -y *a.* heavy; vigorous.

he·gem·o·ny *n.* leadership; predominance. **hegemonic** *a.*

He·gi·ra, hejira *n.* Mohammed's flight from Mecca to Medina, A.D. 622.

heif·er *n.* a young cow.

height *n.* measurement from base to top; quality of being high; a high position; a hill; eminence. -en *v.t.*

hei·nous *a.* extremely wicked; atrocious; odious.

heir *n.* (*fem.* -**ess**) a person legally entitled to succeed to property or rank. — apparent *n.* the person who is first in the line of succession to an estate, crown, etc. -loom *n.* article of personal property which descends to heir along with inheritance.

held *pa.p.* and *pa.t.* of hold.

hel·i·cal *a.* pert. to a helix; spiral. **helicopter** *n.* an airplane which can rise or descend vertically.

he·li·o·graph *n.* signaling apparatus employing a mirror to reflect the sun's rays; *v.t.* to signal by means of a heliograph. -ic *a.* **heliography** *n.*

he·li·o·trope *n.* a plant with fragrant purple flowers. **heliotropism** *n.* (*Bot.*) the tendency of plants to direct their growth towards light.

he·li·um *n.* (*Chem.*) an inert non-inflammable, light gas.

he·lix *n.* a spiral. **helical** *a.* spiral.

hell *n.* the abode of the damned; the lower regions; a place or state of vice, misery, or torture. -ish *a.* -ishly *adv.* -ishness *n.* -ion *n.* troublemaker.

Hel·lene *n.* ancient Greek; a subject of modern Greece. **Hellenic** *a.* **Hellenism** *n.* Grecian culture; a Greek idiom. **Hellenist** *n.* Greek scholar. **Hellenistic** *a.*

hel·lo *interj.* a greeting or call to attract attention.

helm *n.* (*Naut.*) a tiller or wheel for turning the rudder of a ship; *v.t.* to steer; to control.

hel·minth *n.* an intestinal worm.

help *v.t.* to aid; to succor; to relieve; to prevent; *v.i.* to lend aid; to be useful; *n.* one who, or that which, helps; aid; assistance; support; a domestic servant. -er *n.* -ful *a.* -fulness *n.* -ing *n.* a portion of food. -less *a.* not able to take care of oneself; weak; dependent. -lessly *adv.* -lessness *n.* -mate *n.* an assistant; a partner; a wife or husband.

hel·ter-skel·ter *adv.* in disorder; in hurry and confusion.

Hel·ve·tia *n.* the Latin, and political, name for Switzerland.

hem *n.* border, esp. one made by sewing; *v.t.* to fold over and sew down. *pr.p.* -ming. *pa.p.* and *pa.t.* -med.

he·ma-, hemo- a word element meaning "blood."

he·mal, haemal *a.* of the blood.

hem·a·tin, haematin *n.* the constituent of hemoglobin containing iron.

hem·i- *prefix* meaning half.

hem·i·sphere *n.* a half sphere; half of the celestial sphere; half of the earth. **hemispheric, hemispherical** *a.*

hem·i·stich *n.* half a line of verse.

hem·lock *n.* a poisonous umbelliferous plant; a coniferous spruce.

he·mo·glo·bin, haemoglobin *n.* the coloring matter of the red blood corpuscles.

he·mo·phil·i·a, haemophilia *n* (*Med.*) tendency to excessive bleeding due to a deficiency in clotting power of blood; *n.* a bleeder.

hem·or·rhage, haemorrhage *n.* (*Med.*) a flow of blood. **hemorrhagic** *a.*

hem·or·rhoids, haemorrhoids *n.pl.* dilated veins around anus; piles.

he·mo·stat·ic, haemostatic *n.* an agent which stops bleeding; a styptic. Also *a.*

hemp *n.* a plant whose fiber is used in the manufacture of coarse cloth, ropes,

hemp

cables, etc. -en *a.*

hen *n.* the female of any bird, esp. the domestic fowl.

hence *adv.* from this point; for this reason;

interj. go away! begone! -forth, -forward *adv.* from now.

hench·man *n.* a servant; a loyal supporter.

hen·dec·a·gon *n.* a plane figure having eleven sides.

hen·na *n.* a shrub or small tree of the Near East; a dye made from it.

he·pat·ic *a.* pert. to the liver. **hepatitis** *n.*

hep·ta- *prefix* meaning seven. **-1** *n.* a group of seven. **-gon** *n.* a plane figure with seven sides. **-gonal** *a.* **-meter** *n.* a line of verse of seven feet.

hep·tar·chy *n.* government by seven persons.

her *pron.* the objective case of the pronoun she; also, the possessive case used adjectivally. **hers** *pron.* the absolute possessive case. **herself** *pron.* emphatic and reflexive form.

her·ald *n.* an officer who makes royal proclamations; a messenger; an envoy; a forerunner. **heraldic** *a.* **-ry** *n.* the science of recording genealogies and blazoning armorial bearings.

heraldry

herb *n.* a plant of which parts are used for medicine, food, or scent. -aceous *a.* -age *n.* herbs; nonwoody vegetation.

Her·cu·les *n.* (*Myth.*) Latin name of Greek hero Heracles distinguished for his prodigious strength; hence any person of extraordinary strength and size. **Herculean** *a.*

herd *n.* a number of animals feeding or traveling together; *v.i.* to go in a herd; *v.t.* to tend (a herd); to drive together. -er *n.* -sman *n.* one who tends cattle.

here *adv.* in this place; at or to this point (opposed to *there*). -about, -abouts *adv.* about this place. -after *adv.* after this; *n.* a future existence. -by *adv.* by means of this; by this. -in *adv.* in this. -on *adv.* hereupon. -to *adv.* to this. -tofore *adv.* up to the present; formerly. -with *adv.* with this.

he·red·i·ty *n.* the transmission of characteristic traits and qualities from parents to offspring. **herditable** *a.* **hereditament** *n.* (*Law*) property that may be inherited. **hereditary** *a.*

her·e·sy *n.* opinion contrary to orthodox opinion, teaching, or belief. **heresiarch** *n.* the originator or leader of a heresy. **heretic** *n.* one holding opinions contrary to orthodox faith. **heretical** *a.*

her·it·a·ble *a.* that can be inherited; attached to the property or house, as opposed to movable. **heritage** *n.* **heritor** *n.*

her·maph·ro·dite *n.* and *a.* animal or

flower with the characteristics of both sexes. **hermaphroditic, hermaphroditical** *a.* **hermaphrodism, hermaphroditism** *n.*

her·met·ic *a.* pert. to alchemy; magical; sealed. — **sealing,** the airtight closing of a vessel by fusion.

her·mit *n.* a person living in seclusion. **-age** *n.* the abode of a hermit.

her·ni·a *n. (Med.)* the external protrusion of any internal part through the enclosing membrane; rupture.

he·ro *n. (fem.* **heroine)** one greatly regarded for his achievements or qualities; the chief man in a poem, play, or story; an illustrious warrior. *pl.* **-es. heroic** *a.* **heroical** *a.* **heroically** *adv.* **heroics** *n.pl.* high-flown language; bombastic talk. **heroism** *n.* courage; valor; bravery.

her·o·in *n. (Med.)* habit-forming drug used as a sedative.

her·on *n.* a long-legged wading bird.

heron

her·pes *n.* a skin disease. **herpetic** *a.*

her·pe·tol·o·gy *n.* the study of reptiles.

her·ring *n.* a familiar sea-fish, moving in shoals, much used as a food. **-bone** *n.* a zig-zag pattern.

hers See **her.**

hes·i·tate *v.i.* to feel or show indecision; to hold back; to stammer. **hesitant** *a.* **hesitance, hesitancy** *n.* **hesitation** *n.* **hesitantly, hesitatingly** *adv.*

Hes·per·us *n.* the planet Venus as the evening star. **Hesperian** *a.* western.

het·er·o·dox *a.* contrary to accepted opinion. **-y** *n.*

het·er·o·ge·ne·ous *a.* composed of diverse elements. **heterogeneity, -ness** *n.*

het·er·o·gen·e·sis *n. (Biol.)* spontaneous generation. **heterogenetic** *a.*

het·er·o·sex·u·al *a.* directed towards the opposite sex.

hew *v.t.* to chop or cut with an ax or sword; to cut in pieces; to shape or form. *pa.p.* **-ed** *or* **-n. -er** *n.*

hex *n.* a witch.

hex·a- *prefix* meaning six **-gon** *n.* a plane figure having six sides and six angles. **-gonal** *a.* **-hedron** *n.* solid figures having six faces. e.g. a cube.

hex·ad *n.* a group of six.

hex·am·e·ter *n.* a verse of six feet.

hex·a·pod *n.* a six-footed insect.

hey *interj.* used to call attention, or to express joy, wonder, or interrogation. **-day** *n.* the time of fullest strength and greatest vigor.

hi·a·tus *n.* a gap in a series; an opening; a lacuna.

hi·ber·nate *v.i.* to winter; to pass the

winter, esp. in a torpid state. **hibernation** *n.*

Hi·bis·cus *n. (Bot.)* a genus of shrubs or tree with large flowers.

hic·cup *n.* a spasm of the breathing organs with an abrupt cough-like sound; the sound itself; *v.i.* to have this. *pr.p.* **-ping.** *pa.p.* and *pa.t.* **-ped.**

hick·ory *n.* a nut-bearing tree.

hide *v.t.* to put or keep out of sight; to keep secret; *v.i.* to lie concealed. *pa.p.* **hidden, hid.** *pa.t.* **hid. hidden** *a.* **hiddenly** *adv.* **hiding** *n.*

hide *n.* skin of an animal; the dressed skin of an animal.

hid·e·ous *a.* repulsive; revolting; horrible; frightful. **ly** *adv.*

hie *v.i.* and *refl.* to go quickly; to hurry on; to urge on.

hi·er·arch *n.* one who has authority in sacred things; a chief priest. **-al, -ical** *a.* **-ically** *adv.* **-y** *n.* a graded system of people or things.

hi·er·at·ic *a.* priestly; pert. to a cursive style of ancient Egyptian writing.

hi·er·o- *prefix* meaning holy. **hierograph** *n.* a sacred inscription. **hierology** *n.* the science or study of sacred things.

hi·er·o·glyph·ic (usually *pl.*) *n.* ancient Egyptian characters or symbols used in place of letters; picture-writing. Also **hieroglyph. hieroglyphic, hieroglyphical** *a.*

hig·gle *v.i.* to dispute about terms.

high *a.* elevated; tall; elevated in rank, etc.; chief; eminent; proud; loud; strongly marked, as color; dear; costly; extreme; sharp, as tone or voice; *adv.* far up; strongly; to a great extent. **-ly** *adv.* **-ball** *n.* mixed whisky and soda. —**born** *a.* of noble birth. **-bred** *a.* of superior breeding, thoroughbred. —**flown** *a.* elevated; extravagant. —**lands** *n.pl.* a mountainous region. **-lights** *n.pl. (Art.)* the brightest parts of a painting; *(Fig.)* moments of crisis; persons of importance. **-ness** *n.* the quality of being high; a title of honor to princes and princesses. — **school,** a school following grammar school. — **seas,** the sea or ocean beyond the three-mile belt of coastal waters. **-spirited** *a.* bold; daring. —**strung** *a.* in a state of tension. — **water** *n.* tide at its highest elevation. **-way** *n.* a main road. **-wayman** *n.* a robber on a public road.

hike *v.i.* to walk; to tramp; *v.t.* to hoist or carry on one's back; *n.* a journey on foot. **-r** *n.*

hi·lar·i·ous *a.* mirthful; joyous. **-ly** *adv.* **hilarity** *n.*

hill *n.* a natural elevation of land; a small mountain; a mound; *v.t.* to heap up. **-y** *a.* **-iness** *n.* **-ock** *n.* a small hill.

hilt *n.* the handle of a sword, dagger, etc.

him *pron.* the objective case of the pronoun **he. -self** *pron.* emphatic and reflexive form of he and him.

hind *n.* the female of the deer.

hind, hind·er *a.* at the back; placed at the back.

hin·der *v.t.* to prevent from progressing; to

stop. -er n. hindrance n.

Hin•du•stan n. (Geog.) the name applied to the country of the upper valley of the R. Ganges, India. Hindi, Hindes n. an Indo-Germanic language spoken in N. India. Hindu, Hindoo n. a native of Hindustan. Hindustani, Hindoostanee n. chief language of Hindu India.

hinge n. a movable joint; point on which thing depends; v.t. to turn on; to depend on.

hint n. a slight allusion; an indirect suggestion; v.t. and i. to allude to indirectly.

hin•ter•land n. the district inland from the coast or a river.

hip n. the upper part of the thigh.

hip n. the fruit of the rose.

Hip•poc•ra•tes n. a Greek physician, the 'Father of Medicine,' born about 460 B.C. Hippocratic a.

hip•po•drome n. in ancient Greece and Rome, a stadium for horse and chariot races; an arena.

hip•po•pot•a•mus n. a very large pachydermatous African quadruped frequenting rivers. pl. -es or hippopotami.

hir•cine a. pert to a goat; strong-smelling.

hire n. payment for the use of a thing; a hiring or being hired; v.t. to pay for the use of a thing; to contract with for wages; to take care or give on hire. -r n. -ling n. one who serves for wages.

hir•sute a. hairy; (Bot.) set with bristles.

his pron. and a. the possessive case of the pronoun he, belonging to him.

his•pid a. (Bot.) bristly; having rough hairs.

hiss v.i. to make a sound like that of ss to express strong dislike or disapproval; n. the sound. -ing n.

hist interj. a word used to command attention or silence.

his•ta•mine n. substance released by the tissues in allergic reactions.

his•to- prefix meaning a web or tissue. — histology n. the science that treats of the minute structure of the tissues of animals, plants, etc.

his•to•ry n. the study of past events; a record of events in the life of a nation, state, institution, epoch, etc.; a description of animals, plants, minerals, etc. existing on the earth, called natural history. historian n. historic a. historically adv. historicity n. the historical character of an event; the genuineness of it.

his•tri•on•ic a. theatrical; affected. -al a. -ally adv. -s n.pl. theatrical representation.

hit v.t. to strike with a blow or missile; v.i. to strike; to light (upon). pr.p. -ting. pa.p. and pa.t. hit. n. a blow; a stroke; a success.

hitch v.t. to raise or move with a jerk; to fasten with a loop, etc.; to harness; v.i. to be caught or fastened; n. a jerk; a fastening, loop, or knot; a difficulty; -er n. to -hike, to travel by begging rides from motorists, etc.

hith•er adv. to or toward this place; a.

situated on this side. -most a. nearest in this direction. -to adv. up to now.

hive n. a place where bees live; place of great activity; v.t. to gather or place bees in a hive.

hive

hives n. an eruptive skin disease.

hoar a. gray with age; grayish-white. -y a. -frost n. white frost.

hoard n. a stock or store, esp. if hidden away; v.t. to store secretly; v.i. to lay up a store. -er n.

hoarse a. rough and harsh sounding; husky. -ly adv. -ness n.

hoax v.t. to deceive by an amusing or mischievous story; n. a practical joke. -er n.

hob n. the flat-topped casing of a fireplace where things are placed to be kept warm. -nail n. a large-headed nail for boot soles.

hob n. an elf.

hob•ble v.i. to walk lamely; to limp; v.t. to tie the legs together of a horse, etc.; to impede; n. a limping gait; a fetter; a rope for hobbling.

hob•by n. formerly a small horse; a favorite pursuit or pastime.

hob•nail See hob.

hob•nob v.i. to drink together; to be very friendly with.

ho•bo n. a vagrant; a tramp.

hock n. the joint of a quadruped's hind leg between the knee and the fetlock.

hock v.t., n. pawn.

hock•ey n. a game played with a ball or disk and curved sticks.

ho•cus v.i. to hoax; to stupefy with drugs.

hod n. a small trough on a staff used by builders.

hodge-podge n. a medley or mixture.

hoe n. a tool for breaking ground, scraping out weeds, etc.; v.t. to break up or weed with a hoe. -r n.

hog n. a swine; a pig, esp. if reared for fattening; (Colloq.) a greedy or dirty fellow; v.i. to arch the back. -gish a. -back, -s-back n. a crested hill-ridge.

hogs-head n. a large cask; a liquid measure.

hoist v.t. to raise aloft, esp. of flags; to raise with tackle, etc.; n. a hoisting; an elevator.

hold v.t. to keep fast; to grasp; to support in or with the hands, etc.; to own; to occupy; to detain; to celebrate; to believe; to contain; v.i. to cling; not to give way; to abide (by); to adhere (to); to proceed; to be in force. pa.p. and pa.t. held. n. a grasp; grip; handle; binding power and influence; a prison. -er n. -ing n. land, farm, etc. rented from another;

stocks held.

hold n. the space below the deck of a ship, for cargo.

hole n. a hollow; cavity; pit; den; lair; burrow; opening; a perforation; mean habitation; v.t. to make a hole in; to perforate; to put into a hole; v.i. to go into a hole.

hol·i·day n. a day of rest from work esp. in memory of an event or a person.

hol·low n. a cavity; a hole; a depression; a valley; a. having a cavity; not solid; empty; v.t. to make a hollow in. —**toned** a. deep toned. **-ware** n. silver serving dishes.

hol·ly n. an evergreen shrub.

hol·ly·hock n. a tall garden plant.

hol·o- a combining form meaning whole, used in many derivatives. **-caust** n. a burnt offering; destruction, or slaughter. **-graph** n. and a. any writing, as a letter, deed, will, etc. wholly in the handwriting of the signer of it. **-graphic** a.

hol·ster n. a leather case for a pistol.

ho·ly a. belonging to, or devoted to, God; morally perfect; divine; sacred; pious; religious. **holily** adv. **holiness** n.

hom·age n. in feudal times, service due by a vassal to his over-lord; tribute; respect paid.

hom·burg n. a type of men's soft, felt hat.

home n. one's fixed residence; a dwelling-place; a native place or country; an institution for the infirm, sick, poor, etc.; a. pert. to, or connected with, home; not foreign; domestic; adv. to or at one's home; to the point aimed at; close. **-ly** a. belonging to home; plain; ugly. **-liness** n. **-land** n. **-sick** a. depressed in spirits through absence from home. **-sickness** n. **-spun** a. spun or made at home; anything plain or homely. **-stead** n. a house with land and buildings. **-work** n. schoolwork to be done outside of class.

home v.i. of a pigeon, to fly home; v.t. in naval warfare, to guide by radio to the attack of a target.

ho·me·op·a·thy n. the treatment of disease by the administration of very small doses of drugs which would produce in a healthy person effects similar to the symptoms of the disease. Also **homeotherapy**, **homeopath**, **homeopathist** n. **homeopathic** a.

hom·i·cide n. manslaughter; the one who kills. **homicidal** a.

hom·i·ly n. a discourse on a religious or moral subject; a sermon. **homilist** n.

hom·i·ny n. maize porridge.

ho·mo- a combining form meaning same, used in derivatives. **-centric** a. having the same center.

ho·mog·e·ne·ous a. of the same kind or nature; similar; uniform. **-ness**, **homogeneity** n. sameness; uniformity. **homogenize** v.

hom·o·graph n. a word having the same spelling as another, but different meaning and origin.

ho·mol·o·gate v.t. to approve; to confirm. **homologous** a. having the same relative

value, position, etc. **homologation** n.

hom·o·nym n. a word having the same pronunciation as another but a different meaning, e.g. air and heir. Also **homophone**.

ho·mo·sex·u·al·ity n. attraction between individuals of the same sex. **homosexual** n.

hone n. a stone for sharpening knives, etc. v.t. to sharpen on one.

hon·est a. upright; dealing fairly; just; faithful; free from fraud; unadulterated. **-ly** adv. **-y** n. (Bot.) a small flowering plant.

hon·ey n. the sweet, thick fluid collected by bees from flowers; anything very sweet; sweetness; (Colloq.) sweetheart; darling; a. sweet; luscious; v.t. to sweeten. pa.p. and a. **-ed**. Also **honied** a. sweet; (Fig.) flattering. **-bee** n. the common hive-bee. **-comb** n. the structure of wax in hexagonal cells in which bees place honey, eggs, etc.; v.t. to fill with cells or perforations. **-combed** a. **-dew** n. a sweet sticky substance found on plants; a melon. **-moon** n. the holiday taken by a newlywed couple. Also, v.i. **-suckle** n. a climbing plant with yellow flowers.

honk n. the cry of the wild goose; any sound resembling this.

hon·or n. high respect; renown; glory; reputation; sense of what is right or due; v.t. to respect highly; to confer a mark of distinction on; to accept or pay (a bill, etc.) when due. **-s** n.pl. public marks of respect or distinction. **-able** a. **-ably** adv. **-ableness** n.

hon·or·ary a. conferred for the sake of honor only. **honorarium** n. a sum of money granted voluntarily to a person for services rendered. **honorific** a. conferring honor; n. term of respect.

hood n. covering for the head and neck; the cover of an automobile engine; v.t. to cover with a hood. **-wink** v.t. to blindfold; to deceive.

hood·lum n. a hooligan.

hoof n. the horny casing of the foot of a horse, ox, sheep, etc.; pl. **-s**, **hooves**.

hook n. a bent piece of metal, etc. for catching hold, hanging up, etc.; anything curved or bent like a hook; v.t. and i. to fasten, draw, catch, etc. with a hook.

hook·ah, **hoo·ka** n. a tobacco pipe in which the smoke is drawn through water.

hook·worm n. (Med.) a parasitic worm.

hoo·li·gan n. one of a gang of street roughs.

hoop n. a band for holding together the staves of casks, etc.; a circle of wood or metal.

hoot n. the cry of an owl; a cry of disapproval; v.t. to assail with hoots; v.i. to cry as an owl; to cry out in disapproval. **-er** n.

hooves pl. of hoof.

hop v.i. of persons, to spring on one foot; of animals or birds, to leap or skip on all feet at once. pr.p. **-ping**. pa.p. and pa.t. **-ped**. n. an act or the action of hopping. **-per** n. a device for feeding material into a mill or machine; a railroad car with dumping device for coal, sand, etc.

op *n.* a climbing plant with bitter cones used to flavor beer, etc.; *v.t.* to flavor with hops. **-s** *n.pl.* the cones of the hop plant.

ope *n.* a desire combined with expectation; *v.t.* to desire, with belief in possibility of obtaining; *v.i.* to feel hope. **-ful** *a.* **-fully** *adv.* **-fulness** *n.* **-less** *a.* **-lessly** *adv.*

op•scotch *n.* a child's game.

o•ral *a.* of or pert. to an hour.

orde *n.* a great multitude; a troop of nomads or tent-dwellers.

ore•hound *n.* a plant with bitter juice. Also **hoarhound.**

o•ri•zon *n.* the boundary of the part of the earth seen from any given point; the line where earth (or sea) and sky seem to meet. **horizontal** *a.* parallel to the horizon; level. **horizontally** *adv.*

or•mone *n.* a substance secreted by certain glands.

orn *n.* a hard projecting organ growing from heads of cows, deer, etc.; substance forming this organ; a wind instrument of music; a drinking cup; a utensil for holding gunpowder; a sounding contrivance on motors as warning; either of the extremities of the crescent moon; *v.t.* to furnish with horns; to gore. **-y** *a.* of, or made of, horn; hard or callous. **-beam** *n.* a small tree or shrub. **-book** *n.* a primer

hornbook

for children, formerly covered with horn to protect it. **-pipe** *n.* an old musical instrument; a vigorous dance; the lively tune for such a dance.

or•net *n.* a large insect.

oro•ro- time; used as a combining form, e.g. **—horologe** *n.* an instrument of any kind for telling the time. **horologer, horologist** *n.* **horology** *n.*

or•o•scope *n.* a chart of the heavens which predicts character as well as future events. **horoscopic** *a.*

or•ri•ble *a.* tending to excite horror, fear, dread. **horribly** *adv.* **-ness** *n.* **horrid** *a.* frightful; shocking; abominable. **horrify** *v.t.* **horrific** *a.*

or•ror *n.* painful emotion of fear, dread and repulsion.

horse *n.* a large hoofed quadruped used for riding, drawing vehicles, etc.; *v.t.* to

horse

provide with a horse, or horses; to carry or support on the back; *v.i.* to mount on a

horsefly

horse. **-fly** *n.* a stinging fly troublesome to horses. **-hair** *n.* hair from the tail or mane of a horse, haircloth. **-man** *n.* a man on horseback; a skilled rider. **-manship** *n.* the art of riding or of training horses. **-pistol** *n.* an old kind of large pistol, **-play** *n.* rough and boisterous play. **-power** *n.* (abbrev. **h.p.**), the power a horse is capable of exerting. **-radish** *n.* a cultivated plant used for sauces, salads, etc. **-shoe** *n.* a curved, narrow band of iron for nailing to the underpart of the hoof.

hor•ta•tive, hor•ta•tory *a.* tending or serving to exhort; advisory.

hor•ti•cul•ture *n.* gardening; the art of cultivating a garden.

ho•san•na *n.* a cry of praise to God.

hose *n.* stockings; socks; tight-fitting breeches or pants; a flexible tube or pipe for conveying water; *v.t.* to water with a hose. **hosier** *n.* dealer in hosiery. **hosiery** *n.* a collective word for stockings and similar garments.

hos•pice *n.* a traveler's house of rest kept by a religious order.

hosp•i•ta•ble *a.* receiving and entertaining guests in a friendly and liberal fashion. **hospitality** *n.*

hos•pi•tal *n.* an institution for the care of the sick. **-ization** *n.* being in the hospital. **-ize** *v.t.*

host *n.* one who lodges or entertains another; an animal or plant which has parasites living on it. **-ess** *n.* a woman who entertains guests. **hostel** *n.* a lodging place for young people who are hiking or traveling by bicycle; (*Arch.*) an inn.

host *n.* a large number; a multitude; a crowd.

Host *n.* the bread consecrated in the Eucharist.

hos•tage *n.* one handed over to the enemy as security.

hos•tel See host.

hos•tile *a.* of, or pert. to, an enemy; unfriendly; opposed. **-ly** *adv.* **hostility** *n.*

hot *a.* of high temperature; very warm; of quick temper; ardent or passionate. **-ly** *adv.* **-ness** *n.*

ho•tel *n.* a large and superior kind of inn. **-keeper** *n.*

Hot•ten•tot *n.* a member of a native race of S. Africa.

hound *n.* a dog used in hunting, esp. in hunting by scent; *v.t.* to chase with, or as with, hounds; (with 'on') to urge or incite; to pursue, to nag.

hound

hour *n.* the twenty-fourth part of a day, or 60 minutes; the time of the day; an appointed time or occasion; *pl.* the fixed times of work, prayers, etc. **-glass** *n.* a sand-glass running for an hour. **-ly** *adv.*

hou·ri *n.* a nymph of the Mohammedan paradise.

house *n.* a dwelling-place; a legislative or other assembly; a family; a business firm; audience at theater, etc.; dynasty; *v.t.* to shelter; to receive; to store; *v.i.* to dwell. **housing** *n.* shelter; the providing of houses; a support for part of a machine, etc. **-ful** *n.* **-less** *a.*

hous·ing *n.* a saddle-cloth; *pl.* the trappings of a horse.

hove *pa.p.* of **heave.**

hov·el *n.* a small, mean house; *v.t.* to put in a hovel.

hov·er *v.i.* to hang fluttering in the air, or on the wing; to loiter; to waver.

how *adv.* in what manner; by what means; to what degree or extent; in what condition. **-beit** *adv.* nevertheless. **-ever** *adv.* in whatever manner or degree; *conj.* in spite of how.

how·itz·er *n.* a form of gun.

howitzer

howl *v.i.* to utter a prolonged, wailing cry such as that of a wolf or dog; to cry; *v.i.* to utter with howling; *n.* a wail or cry. **-er** *n.* one who howls.

hoy·den, hoiden *n.* a rude, bold girl; a tomboy. **-ish** *a.* romping; bold; boisterous.

hub *n.* the central part, or nave, of a wheel; center of activity.

hub·bub *n.* a commotion.

huck·a·back *n.* a kind of coarse linen with an uneven surface, much used for towels. Also **huck.**

huck·le·ber·ry *n.* an American shrub.

huck·le·bone *n.* the hopbone; the anklebone.

huck·ster *n.* retailer of small articles; a street peddler; a mean, mercenary fellow; *(Colloq.)* an advertising man; *v.i.* to peddle.

hud·dle *v.t.* to crowd together; to heap together confusedly; *v.i.* to press together.

hue *n.* color; tint. **-d** *a.* having a color.

huff *n.* a fit of petulance or anger; *v.t.* to bully; *v.i.* to take offense. **-y** *a.*

hug *v.t.* to clasp tightly in the arms; to embrace; to cling to. *pr.p.* **-ging.** *pa.t.*, *pa.p.* **-ged.** *n.*

huge *a.* very large; immense; enormous. **-ly** *adv.* **-ness** *n.*

Hu·gue·not *n.* a 16th cent. French Protestant.

hu·la *n.* native Hawaiian dance.

hulk *n.* the body of a ship, esp. dismantled ship; anything big and unwieldy; *v.i.* to be bulky. **-ing, -y** *a.*

hull *n.* husk of any fruit, seed, or grai frame or body of a vessel; *v.t.* to remo shell or husk.

hul·la·ba·loo *n.* uproar; outcry.

hum *v.t.* to sing with the lips closed; *v.i.* make droning sound, as bee. *n.* the noi of bees or the like. *pr.p.* **-ming.** *pa.p.* a *pa.t.* **-med.**

hu·man *a.* belonging to, or having t qualities of, man or mankind. **-ly** *ad* **-ness** *n.* **humane** *a.* having the mo qualities of man; kind; benevolent. **-** *n.* **-ism** *n.* a philosophic mode of thoug devoted to human interests; litera culture. **-ist** *n.* **-istic** *a.* **-ize** *v.t.* humani *n.* the quality of being human; hum nature; the human race; kindss benevolence. **humanities** *n.pl.* languag literature, art, philosophy, e **humanitarian** *n.* one who denies t divinity of Jesus; a philanthropist. **-ki** *n.* the whole race of man.

hum·ble *a.* lowly; meek; *v.t.* to bring lo to make meek. **humbly** *adv.* **-ness** *n.*

hum·bug *n.* a hoax; sham; nonsense; imposter; *v.t.* to hoax; to deceive.

hum·drum *a.* commonplace.

hu·mer·al *a.* belonging to the should **humerus** *n.* the long bone of the upp arm.

hu·mid *a.* damp; moist. **-ly** *adv.* **humidi** *v.t.* **humidity, -ness** *n.* **humidor** *n.* device for keeping the air moist in a j case, etc.

hu·mil·i·ate *v.t.* to humble; to lower t dignity of. **humilating** *a.* **humiliation humility** *n.*

hum·mock *n.* a hillock.

hu·mor *n.* quality of imagination quick perceive the ludicrous or to express itse in an amusing way; disposition; moo the fluids of animal bodies; *v.t.* indulge; to comply with mood or whi of. **-ous** *a.* **-ously** *adv.*

hump *n.* the protuberance or hunch forme by a crooked back; a hillock; *v.t.* to ber into a hump shape.

hu·mus *n.* a brown or black constituent the soil, composed of decayed vegetab or animal matter.

Hun *n.* a barbarian.

hunch *n.* a hump; *v.t.* to bend or arch into hump; *v.i.* to move forward in jerks.

hun·dred *n.* a cardinal number, th product of ten times ten. **-th** *a.* last, one, of a hundred; *n.* one of a hundre equal parts. **-weight** *n.*

hung *pa.p.* and *pa.t.* of **hang.**

hun·ger *n.* discomfort or exhaustion cause by lack of food; a craving for food; an strong desire; *v.i.* to feel hunger; to lor for; *v.t.* to starve. **hungry** *a.* feelin hunger. **hungrily** *adv.*

hunk *n.* a lump.

hunt *v.t.* to pursue and prey on (as anima on other animals); to pursue animals game for food or sport; to searc diligently after; *v.i.* to go out in pursuit game; to search; *n.* the act of huntin chase; search; an association huntsmen. **-er** *n.*

hur·dle *n.* a barrier in a race course; a

obstacle; *v.t.* to enclose with hurdles.

hur·dy-gur·dy *n.* an old-fashioned musical instrument.

hurl *v.t.* to send whirling; to throw with violence; *n.* a violent throw.

hur·ly-bur·ly *n.* tumult; bustle; confusion.

hur·ri·cane *n.* a wind of 60 m.p.h. or over; a violent cyclonic storm of wind and rain.

hur·ry *v.t.* to hasten; to impel to greater speed; to urge on; *v.i.* to move or act with haste; *n.* the act of pressing forward in haste; quick motion. **hurried** *a.* **hurriedly** *adv.*

hurt *v.i.* to cause pain; to wound or bruise; to impair or damage. *v.i.* to give pain; *n.* wound, injury, or harm. **-ful** *a.*

hur·tle *v.t.* to fling, to dash against; *v.i.* to move rapidly; to rush violently.

hus·band *n.* a married man; *v.t.* to manage with economy. **-ry** *n.* farming; thrift.

hush *interj.* or *imper.* be quiet! silence! *n.* silence or stillness; *v.t.* to make quiet.

husk *n.* the dry, external covering of certain seeds and fruits; *v.t.* to remove the outer covering. **-y** *a.* rough in tone; hoarse; (*Colloq.*) big and strong. **-ily** *adv.* **-iness** *n.*

husk·y *n.* an Eskimo sled-dog.

hus·sar *n.* one of the light cavalry of European armies.

hus·sy *n.* an ill-behaved woman.

hus·tings *n.* any platform from which political campaign speeches are made.

hus·tle *v.t.* to push about; to jostle; *v.i.* to hurry; to bustle; *n.* speed; jostling. **-r** *n.*

hut *n.* a small house or cabin.

hutch *n.* a chest or box; a grain-bin; a pen for rabbits, etc.

hy·a·cinth *n.* a bulbous plant; a purplish-blue color.

hy·a·line *a.* glassy; transparent.

hy·brid *n.* the offspring of two animals or plants of different species; a mongrel.

hy·dra *n.* (*Myth.*) a monstrous water-serpent with many heads, slain by Hercules; (*Zool.*) a small fresh-water polyp.

hy·dran·gea *n.* a genus of shrubs.

hy·drant *n.* a water-pipe with a nozzle to which a hose can be attached.

hy·drate *n.* (*Chem.*) a compound of water with another compound or an element; *v.t.* to combine with water. **hydrated** *a.* **hydration** *n.*

hy·drau·lic *a.* relating to the conveyance of water.

hy·dro- *prefix* meaning water, combining to form derivatives; in many compounds used to indicate hydrogen. **-carbon** *n.* a compound of hydrogen and carbon. **-cephalus** *n.* (*Med.*) an excess of cerebrospinal fluid in the brain. **-cephalic, -cephalous** *a.* **-chloric** *a.* containing hydrogen and chlorine.

hy·dro·dy·nam·ics *n.pl.* the branch of physics which deals with the flow of fluids.

hy·dro·e·lec·tric *a.* pert. to the generation of electricity by utilizing water power.

hy·dro·gen *n.* an inflammable, colorless, and odorless gas, the lightest of all known substances. **hydrogenous** *a.*

— bomb *n.* atom bomb of enormous power.

hy·drol·o·gy *n.* the science of the properties, laws, etc. of water. **hydrolysis** *a.* **hydrolytic** *a.*

hy·drom·e·ter *n.* a graduated instrument for finding the specific gravity, and thence the strength of liquids.

hydrometer

hy·drop·a·thy *n.* the treatment of diseases with water. Also **hydrotherapy**.

hy·dro·pho·bi·a *n.* an acute infectious disease in man caused by the bite of a mad dog; rabies; an extreme dread of water.

hy·dro·plane *n.* an airplane designed to land on and take off from water; a kind of flat-bottomed boat.

hy·drous *a.* containing water; containing hydrogen.

hy·e·na *n.* a carnivorous mammal of Asia and Africa, allied to the dog.

hy·giene *n.* medical science which deals with the preservation of health. **hygienic, hygienist** *n.*

hy·gro- *prefix* meaning moist, combining to form derivatives.

hy·gro·scope *n.* an instrument which indicates variations of humidity.

hygroscope

Hy·men *n.* (*Myth.*) the god of marriage; (*l.c.*) membrane fold at entrance to female sex organs. **hymeneal** *a.* pert. to marriage.

hy·me·nop·ter·ous *a.* belonging or pert. to an order of insects as the bee, the wasp, etc.

hymn *n.* an ode or song of praise, esp. a religious one; *v.t.* to praise in song; *v.i.* to sing in worship. **-al** *n.* a hymn book.

hy·per·bo·la *n.* (*Geom.*) a curve. **hyperbolic** *a.*

hy·per·bo·le *n.* (*Gram.*) a figure of speech

which expresses much more or much less than the truth, for the sake of effect; exaggeration. **hyperbolic, hyperbolical** a. **hyperbolically** adv.

hy‧per‧crit‧ic n. one who is critical beyond measure or reason. **-al** a. **-ally** adv.

hy‧per‧phys‧i‧cal a. supernatural.

hy‧per‧sen‧si‧tive a. abnormally sensitive. **-ness, hypersensitivity** n.

hy‧per‧tro‧phy n. (Med.) abnormal enlargement of organ or part of body.

hy‧phen n. a mark (-) used to connect syllables or compound words; v.t. to connect with a hyphen. **-ated** a.

hyp‧no‧sis n. the state of being hypnotized; abnormal sleep. **hypnotic** a. **hypnotize** v.t. to produce a mental state resembling sleep. **hypnotism** n. **hypnotist** n.

hy‧po- prefix meaning under, beneath, below.

hy‧po‧chon‧dri‧a n. a mental disorder, in which one is tormented by melancholy and gloomy views, especially about one's own health. **hypochondriac** a. and n.

hy‧poc‧ri‧sy n. stimulation or pretense of goodness; feigning to be what one is not; insincerity. **hypocrite** n. **hypocritical** a.

hy‧po‧der‧mic a. pert. to parts underlying the skin; n. the injection of a drug beneath the skin by means of a needle and small syringe. **-ally** adv.

hy‧pos‧ta‧sis n. essential nature of anything; the substance of each of the three divisions of the Godhead; (Med.) a deposit of blood in an organ; pl. **hypostases.**

hy‧pot‧e‧nuse n. (Geom.) the side of a right-angled triangle which is opposite the right angle.

hy‧poth‧e‧cate v.t. to give in security; to mortgage.

hy‧poth‧e‧sis n.pl. **hypotheses,** a supposition used as a basis from which to draw conclusions; a theory. **hypothesize** v.i. and v.t. **hypothetic, hypothetical** a.

hys‧te‧ri‧a, hysterics n. an affection of the nervous system, characterized by excitability and lack of emotional control. **hysteric, hysterical** a. **hysterically** adv.

I *pron.* the pronoun of the first person singular.

i·am·bus *n.* a metrical foot of two syllables, the first unaccented, and the second accented. **iamb** *n.* **iambic** *a.*

i·at·ric, iatrical *a.* pert. to physicians, medicine.

I·ber·ri·an *a.* pert. to Iberia, viz. Spain and Portugal.

i·bex *n.* variety of wild goat.

i·bis *n.* a stork-like wading bird.

ibis

I·car·i·an *a.* adventurous in flight; rash.

ice *n.* frozen water; a frozen dessert made with fruit juices and water; *v.t.* to freeze; to chill with ice; to frost a cake; *pr. p.* **icing**. **icily** *adv.* coldly. **iciness** *n.* **icing** *n.* a covering of sugar on cakes, etc. **icy** *a.*

Ice·land·er *n.* a native of Iceland. **Icelandic** *a.*

ich·nol·o·gy *n.* the classification of fossil footprints.

i·chor *n.* (*Gk. Myth*) the fluid which flowed in the veins of the Gods; the colorless, watery discharge from ulcers. **-ous** *a.*

ich·thy·ol·o·gy *n.* the branch of zoology which treats of fishes. **ichthyological** *a.* **ichthyologist** *n.* **ichthyic** *a.* **ichthyoid** *a.*

i·ci·cle *n.* a pendent conical mass of ice.

i·con *n.* any sign which resembles the thing it represents; a venerated representation of Christ, an angel, or a saint, found in Greek and Orthodox Eastern Churches. **-ic, -ical** *a.* **-oclasm** *n.* act of breaking images; an attack on the cherished beliefs or enthusiasms of others. **-oclast** *n.* **-ography** *n.* **-olator** *n.* an image worshipper. **-olatry** *n.* image worship.

ic·ter·us *n.* jaundice. **icteric, icterical** *a.*

id *n.* in psycho-analysis, the primary source in individuals of instinctive energy.

i·de·a *n.* a product of intellectual action; way of thinking; a thought; belief; plan; aim; principle at the back of one's mind. **ideal** *a.* existing in fancy only; perfect; satisfying desires; *n.* an imaginary type or norm of perfection to be aimed at. **idealization** *n.* **idealize** *v.t.* **idealizer** *n.* an idealist. **idealism** *n.* tendency to seek the highest spiritual perfection; imaginative treatment in comparative disregard of the real. **-list** *n.* **-listic** *a.*

i·den·ti·cal *a.* the very same; not different. **-ly** *adv.* **-ness** *n.*

i·den·ti·fy *v.t.* to establish the identity of; to recognize; to associate (oneself) in interest, purpose, use, etc. **identifiable** *a.* **identification** *n.*

i·den·ti·ty *n.* state of having the same nature or character with; absolute sameness, as opposed to mere similarity; individuality.

id·e·o·graph *n.* a picture, symbol, diagram, etc., suggesting an idea or object without specifically naming it. **ideogram** *n.* an ideograph. **-ic, -ical** *a.* **ideography** *n.*

i·de·ol·o·gy *n.* the body of beliefs of any group. **ideologic, ideological** *a.* **ideologist** *n.* a theorist.

ides *n. pl.* in the Roman calendar, the 15th day of March, May, July, and October, and the 13th day of the other months.

id·i·o·cy *n.* See idiot.

id·i·om *n.* a peculiar mode of expression; the genius or peculiar cast of a language. **-atic, -atical** *a.* **-atically** *adv.*

id·i·o·syn·cra·sy *n.* a peculiarity in a person; peculiar view. **idiosyncratic, idiosyncratical** *a.*

id·i·ot *n.* one mentally deficient; a born fool. **idiocy** *n.* extreme and permanent mental deficiency. **-ic, -ical** *a.* **-ically** *adv.* **-ism** *n.* natural imbecility.

i·dle *a.* doing nothing; inactive; *v.t.* to spend in idleness; *v.i.* to be idle or unoccupied. **-ness** *n.* **-r** *n.* **idly** *adv.*

i·dol *n.* an image of a diety as an object of worship. **-ater** *n.* (*fem.* **idolatress**) a worshipper of idols. **-atrize** *v.t.* to worship as an idol. **-atrous** *a.* **-atrously** *adv.* **-atry** *n.* worship of idols. **-ization -ize** *v.t.* **-izer** *n.*

i·dyl, idyll *n.* a short pastoral poem; a picture of simple perfection and loveliness. **-lic** *a.* of a perfect setting; blissful.

if *conj.* on the condition or supposition that; whether; in case that.

ig·loo *n.* a dome-shaped house built of blocks of hard snow by Eskimos.

ig·ne·ous *a.* resembling fire.

ig·nite *v.t.* to set on fire; to kindle; *v.i.* to catch fire. **ignitible** *a.* **ignition** *n.*

ig·no·ble *a.* of humble birth or family; mean; base; inferior. **ignobility, -ness** *n.* **ignobly** *adv.*

ig·no·min·y *n.* public disgrace of dishonor; infamous conduct. **ignominious** *a.* **ignominiously** *adv.* **ignominiousness** *n.*

ig·no·ra·mus *n.* an ignorant person.

ig·no·rant *a.* uninstructed; uninformed; unlearned. **ignorance** *n.* **-ly** *adv.*

ig·nore *v.t.* to refuse to take notice of.

i·gua·na *n.* a family of lizards, found in tropical America.

iguana

ilk *a.* the same.

ill *a.* bad or evil in any respect; sick; *n.* evil of any kind; misfortune; misery; pain, *adv.* not well; faultily; unfavorably. **-ness** *n.* sickness.

ill- *prefix,* used in the construction of

compound words, implying badness in some form or other.

il·le·gal *a.* unlawful. -ize *v.t.* to render unlawful. -ity *n.* unlawful act. -ly *adv.*

il·leg·i·ble *a.* incapable of being read or deciphered. -ness, illegibility *n.* illegibly *adv.*

il·le·git·i·mate *a.* unlawful; not authorized by good usage; born out of wedlock. illegitimacy *n.* -ly *adv.*

il·lib·eral *a.* not liberal; niggardly; narrow-minded; intolerant. illiberality *n.*

il·lic·it *a.* not permitted; unlawful. -ly *adv.* -ness *n.*

il·lim·it·a·ble *a.* incapable of being limited or bounded.

il·lit·er·ate *a.* unable to read or write; *n.* a person unable to read or write; *adv.* -ness, illiteracy *n.*

il·log·i·cal *a.* not according to the rules of logic; unsound; fallacious. -ly *adv.* -ness, illogicality *n.*

il·lu·mi·nate *v.t.* to enlighten literally and figuratively; to light up; to embellish, as a book or manuscript with gold and colors. illuminable *a.* illuminant *a.* and *n.* illumination *n.* act of giving light; instructions; enlightenment; decoration on manuscripts and books. illuminative *a.* illuminator *n.* illumine *v.t.* and *v.i.*

il·lu·sion *n.* an erroneous interpretation or unreal image. illusionist *n.* a professional entertainer who produces illusions. illusive, illusory *a.* illusively *adv.* illusiveness *n.*

il·lus·trate *v.t.* to make clear or bright; to exemplify, esp. by means of figures, diagrams, etc.; to adorn with pictures. illustration *n.* illustrative, illustratory *a.* illustratively *adv.* illustrator *n.*

il·lus·tri·ous *a.* conferring honor; possessing honor or dignity. -ness *n.*

im·age *n.* a mental picture of any object; a representation of a person or object; a symbol; idol; figure of speech; *v.t.* to form an image of; to reflect; to imagine; *n.* images regarded collectively; figures of speech.

im·ag·ine *v.t.* to form in the mind an idea or image; to conjecture; to picture; to believe; to suppose; *v.i.* to form an image of; to picture in the mind. imaginable *a.* imaginableness *n.* imaginably *adv.* imaginary *a.* existing only in imagination or fancy; fanciful; unreal. imaginative *a.* gifted with the creative faculty; fanciful. imagination *n.* the mental faculty which apprehends and forms ideas of external objects, the poetical faculty. imaginatively *adv.* imaginativeness *n.*

i·mam, imaum *n.* a Moslem priest.

im·be·cile *a.* mentally feeble; silly; idiotic; *n.* one of feeble mentality. imbecility *n.*

im·bed *v.t.* See embed.

im·bibe *v.t.* to drink in; to absorb; to receive into the mind; *v.t.* to drink. imbiber *n.*

im·brue *v.t.* to wet, to drench.

im·bro·glio *n.* an intricate, complicated plot.

im·bue *v.t.* to inspire; to tinge deeply; to saturate.

im·i·tate *v.t.* to follow, as a pattern, model or example; to copy. imitable *a.* imitation *n.* imitative *a.* inclined to imitate; not original. imitatively *adv.* imitativeness *n.* imitator *n.*

im·mac·u·late *a.* without blemish; spotless; unsullied; pure; undefiled. -ly *adv.* -ness *n.*

im·ma·nent *a.* abiding in; inherent; intrinsic; innate. immanence, immanency *n.*

im·ma·te·ri·al *a.* not consisting of matter; incorporeal; of no essential consequence; unimportant. -ize *v.t.* to separate from matter. -ism *n.* -ist *n.*

im·ma·ture *a.* not mature or ripe; raw; unformed; undeveloped; untimely. -ness, immaturity *n.*

im·meas·ur·a·ble *a.* incapable of being measured. immeasurably *adv.*

im·me·di·ate *a.* occuring at once; present; not separated by others. immediacy *n.* -ly *adv.* -ness *n.*

im·me·mo·ri·al *a.* beyond the range of memory. immemorable *a.* -ly *adv.*

im·mense *a.* unlimited; immeasureable; very great; vast. -ly *adv.* -ness, immensity *n.*

im·merge *v.t.* to plunge into.

im·merse *v.t.* to plunge into anything, esp a fluid; to dip. immersable, immersible *a.* -d *a.* immersion *n.*

im·mi·grate *v.i.* to migrate into a country. immigrant *n.* immigration *n.*

im·mi·nent *a.* threatening immediately to fall or occur. imminence *n.* -ly *adv.*

im·mis·ci·ble *a.* not capable of being mixed. immiscibility *n.*

im·mit·i·ga·ble *a.* incapable of being mitigated or appeased; relentless.

im·mo·bile *a.* incapable of being moved. immobilize *v.t.*

im·mod·er·ate *a.* exceeding just bounds; excessive. -ness *n.* -ly *adv.* immoderation *n.*

im·mod·est *a.* wanting in modesty or delicacy. -ly *adv.* -y *n.*

im·mo·late *v.t.* to sacrifice; to offer as a sacrifice. immolation *n.* immolator *n.*

im·mor·al *a.* uninfluenced by moral principle; wicked. -ity *n.* -ly *adv.*

im·mor·tal *a.* not mortal; undying; deathless; *n.* one exempt from death or decay; a divine being. immortalize *v.t.* to make famous for all time. immortality *n.*

im·mov·a·ble *a.* incapable of being moved. -ness, immovability *n.* immovably *adv.*

im·mune *a.* exempt; protected against any particular infection; *n.* one who is so protected. immunization *n.* immunize *v.t.* immunity *n.*

im·mure *v.t.* to enclose within walls; to imprison.

im·mu·ta·ble *a.* not susceptible to any alteration; invariable; unalterable. immutability, immutableness *n.*

imp *n.* a little demon; a mischievous child. -ish *a.*

im·pact *v.t.* to press or drive forcibly together. impact *n.* impulse communicated by one object striking another.

im·pair v.t. to diminish in quantity, value, excellence, or strength.

im·pale v.t. to fix on a sharpened stake; to put to death by fixing on an upright sharp stake. -ment n.

im·pal·pa·ble a. not capable of being felt or perceived by the senses, esp. by touch. impalpability n. impalpably adv.

im·pan·el v.t. to place a name on a panel or list. -ment n.

im·part v.t. to bestow a share or portion or.

im·par·tial a. not partial; without prejudice. impartiality, impartialness n.

im·pas·sa·ble a. incapable of being passed; impervious. impassability, impassableness n.

im·passe n. deadlock; dilemma.

im·pas·sion v.t. to move or affect strongly with passion. -ed a.

im·pas·sive a. not susceptible of pain or suffering; showing no emotion; calm. -ly adv. -ness, impassivity n.

im·pa·tient a. uneasy or fretful under trial or suffering; averse to waiting; restless. impatience n. -ly adv.

im·pav·id a. fearless.

im·peach v.t. to charge with a crime or misdemeanor; to call to account; to denounce; to challenge. -able a. -er n. -ment n.

im·pec·ca·ble a. not liable to sin or error; perfect. impeccability, impeccancy n.

im·pe·cu·ni·ous a. having no money; poor; hard up. impecuniosity n.

im·pede v.t. to stop the progress of; to hinder; to obstruct. impedance n. impedible a. impediment n. impedimenta n.pl. baggage, esp. military; encumbrances. impedimental a.

im·pel v.t. to drive or urge forward; to induce; to incite. pr. p. -ling. pa. t. and pa. p. -led. -lent a.

im·pend v.i. to hang over; to threaten; to be imminent. -ence, -ency n. -ent a.

im·pen·e·tra·ble a. incapable of being penetrated or pierced; obscure. impenetrability n.

im·pen·i·tent a. not repenting of sin; not contrite; obdurate.

im·per·a·tive a. expressive of command; authoritative. -ly adv.

im·per·cep·ti·ble a. not discernible by the senses; minute. -ness, imperceptibility n. imperceptibly adv. imperceptive a.

im·per·fect a. wanting some part or parts; defective; faulty; n. -ly adv. imperfection n.

im·per·fo·rate, imperforated a. not perforated or pierced.

im·pe·ri·al a. pertaining to an empire or to an emperor. -ism n. -istic a.

im·per·il v.t. to bring into peril; to endanger.

im·pe·ri·ous a. commanding; domineering; dictatorial. -ly adv. -ness n.

im·per·ish·a·ble a. not liable to decay. -ness n. imperishability n.

im·per·ma·nence n. want of permanence or stability.

im·per·me·a·ble a. not permitting passage. impermeability n. -ness n.

impermeably adv.

im·per·son·al a. having no personal reference; objective. -ly adv.

im·per·son·ate v.t. to represent in character or form. impersonation n. impersonator n.

im·per·ti·nent a. having no bearing on the subject; irrelevant; impudent. impertinence n.

im·per·turb·a·ble a. incapable of being disturbed or agitated. imperturbability n. imperturbably adv. imperturbation n.

im·per·vi·a·ble, im·per·vi·ous a. not admitting of entrance or passage through; impenetrable; impassable. -ness, imperviability n. imperviously adv.

im·pe·ti·go n. (med.) a pustulous skin disease.

im·pet·u·ous a. rushing with force and violence; vehement; hasty. -ly adv. -ness, impetuosity n.

im·pe·tus n. the force with which a body moves; momentum.

im·pi·e·ty n. lack of reverence.

im·pinge v.i. to fall or dash against; to touch on; to infringe.

im·pi·ous a. not pious; proceeding from or manifesting a want of reverence. -ly adv. -ness, impiety n.

im·pla·ca·ble a. inexorable; not to be appeased; urelenting. -ness, implacability n.

im·plant v.i. to set in; to insert; to sow (seed).

im·plead v.t. to sue at law.

im·ple·ment n. a weapon, tool, or instrument; a utensil; v.t. to fulfill an obligation or contract which has been entered into. -al a. -ation n.

im·pli·cate v.t. to involve; to include; to entangle; to imply. implication n. the implied meaning. implicative a. implicatively adv. implicit a. implied; without questioning. implicity adv.

im·plore v.t. to entreat earnestly; to beseech. imploration n. -r n. imploringly adv.

im·ply v.t. to contain by implication; to signify; to insinuate.

im·po·lite a. rude; discourteous. -ly adv. -ness n.

im·pol·i·tic a. ill-advised; not in the best interests of; inexpedient. impolicy n. injudicious action. -ly adv.

im·pon·der·a·ble a. without perceptible weight; not able to be weighed. -ness, imponderability n.

im·port v.t. to bring in from abroad; to convey a meaning; to be of consequence. -ance n. consequence; moment. a. -antly adv. -ation n. act of bringing from another country.

im·por·tune v.t. to request with urgency; to entreat; to solicit. importunacy, importunateness n. importunate a. earnestly solicitous; troublesome. importunately adv.

im·pose v.t. to lay on; to levy; to lay, as a charge or tax; to force oneself upon others; v.i. (with upon) to deceive; to take undue advantage of a person's

good-nature; to impress. **imposable.** *a.*
imposing *a.* adapted to impress
considerably; commanding; grand.
imposition *n.*
im·pos·si·ble *a.* that which cannot be
done. **impossibility** *n.*
im·post *n.* tax duty.
im·pos·tor *n.* one who assumes a false
character. **imposture** *n.* deception.
im·po·tent *a.* powerless; wanting natural
strength. **impotence, impotency** *n.*
im·pound *v.t.* to confine cattle in a pound
or pen; to restrain within limits.
im·pov·er·ish *v.t.* to reduce to poverty; to
exhaust the strength, richness, or fertility
of land. **-er** *a.* **-ment** *n.*
im·prac·ti·ca·ble *a.* not able to be
accomplished; unfeasible. **impractica-
bility, impracticableness** *n.* **impractical** *a.*
im·pre·cate *v.t.* to invoke by prayer (evil)
upon; to curse. **imprecation** *n.*
imprecatory *a.*
im·preg·na·ble *a.* not to be stormed or
taken by assault; not to be moved,
impressed, or shaken. **impregnability** *n.*
impregnably *adv.*
im·preg·nate *v.t.* to make pregnant; to
render fertile; to saturate; to imbue.
impregnable *a.* **impregnation** *n.*
im·pre·sa·ri·o *n.* an organizer of public
entertainments.
im·press *v.t.* to take forcibly, persons or
goods, for public service; to
commandeer. **-ment** *n.*
im·press *v.t.* to press in or upon; to make a
mark or figure upon; to fix deeply in the
mind; to stamp. *n.* a mark made by
pressure. **-ibility** *n.* susceptibility. **-ible** *a.*
-ibly *adv.* **impression** *n.* **impressionable**
a. **-ive** *a.* **-ively** *adv.* **-iveness** *n.*
im·pres·sion·ism *n.* a revolutionary
modern movement, originating in
France, in art, literature and music,
aiming at reproducing the *impression*
which eye and mind gather, rather than
representing actual fact. **impressionist** *n.*
im·pri·ma·tur *n.* a license to print a book.
im·print *v.t.* to mark by pressure; to fix
indelibly *n.* an impression.
im·prob·a·ble *a.* unlikely. **improbability** *n.*
improbably *adv.*
im·pro·bi·ty *n.* want of integrity or
rectitude; dishonesty.
im·promp·tu *adv.* or *a.* offhand.
im·prop·er *a.* unsuitable to the end or
design; unfit; indecent; inaccurate. **-ly**
adv. **impropriety** *n.*
im·prove *v.t.* to make better; *v.i.* to grow
better. **improvability, improvableness** *n.*
improvable *a.* **improvably** *adv.* **-ment** *n.*
improvingly *adv.*
im·prov·i·dent *a.* not prudent or
foreseeing. **improvidence** *n.*
im·pro·vise *v.t.* to extemporize; to make
the best of materials at hand; to compose,
speak or perform without preparation.
improvisation *n.* **-r** *n.*
im·pru·dent *a.* lacking in discretion.
imprudence *n.* **-ly** *adv.*
im·pu·dent *a.* brazen; boldfaced; rude.
impudence *n.* **-ly** *adv.*

im·pugn *v.t.* to call in question; to
contradict. **-able** *a.* **-er** *n.* **-ment** *n.*
im·pulse *n.* the motion or effect produced
by a sudden action or applied force.
impulsion *n.* **impulsive** *a.* **impulsively**
adv. **impulsiveness** *n.*
im·pu·ni·ty *n.* exemption from punishment.
im·pure *a.* not pure; mixed; adulterated;
foul; unchaste. **-ly** *adv.* **impurity,
impureness** *n.*
im·pute *v.t.* to ascribe to (in a bad sense); to
attribute to. **imputable** *a.* **imputableness,
imputability** *n.* **imputation** *n.* **imputative**
a. **imputatively** *adv.*
in *prep.* within; inside of; indicating a
present relation to time, space, or
condition; *adv.* inside; closely.
in·a·bil·i·ty *n.* want of strength, means, or
power.
in·ac·cu·rate *a.* not correct; not according
to truth or reality; erroneous. **inaccuracy**
n. **-ly** *adv.*
in·ac·tive *a.* not disposed to action or
effort; idle. **inaction** *n.* **inactivate** *v.t.* to
make inactive. **inactivation** *n.* **-ly** *adv.*
inactivity *n.*
in·ad·e·quate *a.* insufficient. **inadequacy**
n. **-ly** *adv.* **-ness** *n.*
in·ad·mis·si·ble *a.* not allowable;
improper. **inadmissibly** *adv.*
in·ad·vert·ent *a.* not turning the mind to a
matter; inattentive; thoughtless; careless.
inadvertence, inadvertency *n.* **-ly** *adv.*
in·al·ien·a·ble *a.* incapable of being separated or transferred.
in·ane *a.* empty; void; foolish; silly.
inanition *n.* **inanity** *n.*
in·an·i·mate *a.* destitute of life or spirit.
inanimation *n.* **-ness** *n.*
in·ap·pli·ca·ble *a.* unsuitable; irrelevant.
in·ap·pre·ci·a·ble *a.* not worth reckoning.
in·ap·pro·pri·ate *a.* unsuitable; at the
wrong time. **-ly** *adv.* **-ness** *n.*
in·apt *a.* inappropriate; unsuitable;
awkward. **-itude** *n.* **-ly** *adv.*
in·ar·tic·u·late *a.* unable to put one's ideas
in words; not uttered distinctly. **-ly** *adv.*
-ness *n.* **-inarticulation** *n.*
in·au·di·ble *a.* not able to be heard.
inaudibility, inaudibleness *n.* **inaudibly**
adv.
in·au·gu·rate *v.t.* to induct into an office in
a formal manner. **inaugural, inauguratory**
a. **inauguration** *n.* **inaugurator** *n.*
in·aus·pi·cious *a.* ill-omened. **-ly** *adv.*
-ness *n.*
in·born *a.* born in or with; innate; natural;
inherent.
in·bred *a.* bred within; innate. **inbreed** *v.t.*
to mate animals of the same blood stock;
to marry within the family or tribe.
inbreeding *n.*
in·cal·cu·la·ble *a.* countless; beyond
calculation; uncertain. **incalculability,
-ness** *n.*
in·can·des·cent *a.* glowing with white
heat and providing light. **incandescense**
n.
in·can·ta·tion *n.* a formula or charm-words
used to produce magical or supernatural
effect. **incantatory** *a.*

in•ca•pa•ble *a.* wanting ability or capacity. incapability *n.*

in•ca•pa•ci•tate *v.t.* to render incapable. incapacitation *n.* incapacity *n.*

in•car•cer•ate *v.t.* to confine; to imprison. incarcerator, incarceration *n.*

in•car•na•dine *a.* flesh-colored; of a carnation color; crimson; *v.t.* to dye crimson.

in•car•nate *v.t.* to put into concrete form; to embody in flesh; *a.* embodied in flesh; typified. incarnation *n.*

in•cen•di•ar•y *n.* one who maliciously sets fire to property; an agitator who inflames passions. incendiarism *n.*

in•cense *v.t.* to inflame to violent anger.

in•cense *n.* a mixture of aromatic gums and spices which, when burned produces a sweet-smelling smoke.

in•cen•tive *a.* inciting; provoking; *n.* motive; stimulus.

in•cep•tion *n.* beginning; start; origin. inceptive *a.* inceptively *adv.*

in•ces•sant *a.* continuing or following without interruption. incessancy *n.* -ly *adv.*

in•cest *n.* sexual intercourse of kindred within the forbidden degrees. -uous *a.*

inch *n.* twelfth part of a linear foot; *v.i.* to push forward by slow degrees.

in•cho•ate *a.* just begun; rudimentary; incipient. -ly *adv.* inchoation *n.* inchoative *a.*

in•ci•dent *a.* liable to happen; subordinate to; *n.* that which takes place; event. incidence *n.* -al *a.* and *n.* -ally *adv.* -alness *n.*

in•cin•er•ate *v.t.* to consume by fire. incineration *n.* incinerator *n.* furnace for consuming refuse.

in•cip•i•ent *a.* beginning; originating. incipience, incipiency *n.*

in•cise *v.t.* to cut into. incision *n.* the act of cutting with a sharp instrument; a cut; gash. incisive *a.* having the quality of cutting or penetrating; sharp; biting. incisively *adv.* incisiveness *n.* incisor *n.* one of the eight front cutting teeth.

in•cite *v.t.* to move the mind to action. incitant *n.* and *a.* incitation *n.* -ment *n.*

in•clem•ent *a.* severe; harsh; stormy. inclemency *n.*

in•cline *v.t.* to cause to deviate from a line or direction; to give a tendency to, as to to the will or affections; to bend; *v.i.* to deviate from the vertical; to be disposed; *n.* an ascent or descent; a slope. inclination *n.*

in•clude *v.t.* to confine within; to comprise. inclusion *n.* inclusive *a.* inclusively *adv.*

in•cog•ni•to *a.* and *adv.* in a disguise; *n.* (fem incognita) the state of being unknown; a person who conceals his identity.

in•co•her•ent *a.* not connected or clear; confused. incoherence *n.* -ly *adv.* incoherency *n.*

in•com•bus•ti•ble *a.* not capable of being burned. incombustibility, incombustibleness *n.* incombustibily *adv.*

in•come *n.* the gain or reward from one's labors or investments. incoming *n.* and *a.*

in•com•men•su•ra•ble *a.* having no common measure or standard of comparison. -ness *n.* incommensurably *adv.* incommensurate *a.* incommensurately *adv.*

in•com•mode *v.t.* to put to inconvenience or discomfort; to hinder. incommodious *a.* incommodiously *adv.* incommodity *n.*

in•com•mu•ni•ca•ble *a.* incapable of being communicated or shared. incommunicability *n.* -ness *n.* incommunicably *adv.* incommunicative *a.* reserved.

in•com•pa•ra•ble *a.* not admitting any degree of comparison; unequaled. incomparability *n.* -ness *n.* incomparably *adv.*

in•com•pat•i•ble *a.* incapable of existing side by side. incompatibility, incompatibleness *n.* incompatibly *adv.*

in•com•pe•tent *a.* not efficient in the performance of function. incompetence *n.*

in•com•plete *a.* defective; unfinished; imperfect. -ly *adv.*

in•com•pre•hen•si•ble *a.* incapable of being comprehended or understood. -ness, incomprehensibility, incomprehension *n.* incomprehensibly *adv.* incomprehensive *a.* limited; not extensive.

in•com•pres•si•ble *a.* cannot be compressed or reduced in bulk.

in•con•ceiv•a•ble *a.* not capable of being conceived in the mind; unthinkable. inconceivability, inconceivableness *n.* inconceivably *adv.*

in•con•clu•sive *a.* not decisive or conclusive. -ly *adv.*

in•con•gru•ous *a.* inappropriate; not reciprocally agreeing; (Math.) not coinciding. incongruent *a.* incongruity, incongruousness *n.*

in•con•se•quent *a.* not following from the premises; illogical. inconsequence *n.* inconsequential *a.* not to the point; illogical; of no import; trivial. inconsequentially *adv.*

in•con•sid•er•a•ble *a.* unworthy of consideration; unimportant.

in•con•sid•er•ate *a.* thoughtless; careless of others' feelings.

in•con•sis•tent *a.* liable to sudden and unexpected change. inconsistency *n.* -ly *adv.*

in•con•spic•u•ous *a.* scarcely noticeable.

in•con•stant *a.* not constant or consistent; subject to change inconstancy *n.* -ly *adv.*

in•con•ti•nent *a.* morally incapable of restraint. incontinence, incontinency *n.* -ly *adv.*

in•con•tro•vert•i•ble *a.* too clear or certain to admit of dispute; unquestionable. incontrovertibly *adv.*

in•con•ven•ient *a.* awkward; unsuitable. inconvenience *v.t.* inconvenience, inconveniency *n.* -ly *adv.*

in•con•vert•i•ble *a.* cannot be changed or exchanged. inconvertibility *n.*

in•co•or•di•nate *a.* not in orderly relation with one another.

in•cor•po•rate *v.t.* and *v.i.* to combine, as different ingredients, into one body or mass. **incorporation** *n.* **incorporative** *a.* **incorporeal** *a.* not possessed of a body. **incorporeality** *n.*

in•cor•rect *a.* not in accordance with the truth; improper -ly *adv.* -ness *n.*

in•cor•ri•gi•ble *a.* beyond any hope of reform.

in•cor•rupt *a.* morally pure. -ible *a.* -ibility *n.* -ly *adv.* -ness *n.*

in•crease *v.t.* to make greater; to extend; to lengthen; *v.t.* to become greater; *n.* growth; produce; interest; progeny. **increasable** *a.* **increasingly** *adv.*

in•cred•i•ble *a.* impossible to be believed. **incredibility, -ness** *n.* **incredibly** *adv.*

in•cred•u•lous *a.* not disposed to believe; showing unbelief. **incredulity** *n.* -ness *n.* -ly *adv.*

in•cre•ment *n.* increase; matter added; growth. -al *a.*

in•crim•i•nate *v.t.* to charge with a crime; to involve one in a criminal action. **incriminatory** *a.*

in•crust, encrust *v.t.* to charge with a crime; to involve one in a criminal action. **incriminatory** *a.*

in•cu•bate *v.i.* to sit, as on eggs, for hatching; of disease germs, to pass through the stage between infection and appearance of symptoms; *v.t.* to hatch; to ponder over. **incubation** *n.* **incubative, incubatory** *a.* **incubator** *n.* a cabinet used

incubator

to hatch eggs; similar devices for premature infants or bacterial cultures.

in•cu•bus *n.* a nightmare; any burdensome or depressing influence.

in•cul•cate *v.t.* to urge forcibly and repeatedly; to impress by admonition. **inculcation** *n.* **inculcator** *n.*

in•cum•bent *a.* lying or resting upon; *n.* holder of an office. **incumbency** *n.*

in•cur *v.t.* to become liable to. *pr. p.* -ring. *pa. t.* and *pa. p.* -red.

in•cur•a•ble *a.* not able to be cured; *n.* one beyond cure. **incurability** *n.*

in•cu•ri•ous *a.* not inquisitive. -ly *adv.*

in•cur•sion *n.* a raid into a territory with hostile intention. **incursive** *a.*

in•curve *v.t.* to bend into a curve; *v.i.* to bend inward. **incurvate** *v.t.* to bend inward or upward; *a.* curved in.

in•debt•ed *a.* placed under an obligation. -ness *n.*

in•de•cent *a.* unbecoming; immodest; obscene. **indecency** *n.* -ly *adv.*

in•de•ci•pher•a•ble *a.* incapable of being deciphered; illegible.

in•de•ci•sion *n.* irresoluteness. **indecisive** *a.* **indecisively** *adv.* **indecisiveness** *n.*

in•de•clin•a•ble *a.* (*Gram.*) having no inflections or cases.

in•dec•o•rous *a.* contrary to good manners. -ly *adv.* -ness, **indecorum** *n.*

in•deed *adv.* in reality; in truth; in fact; certainly. *interj.* denotes surprise.

in•de•fat•i•ga•ble *a.* incapable of being fatigued; unwearied; untiring. -ness, **indefatigability** *n.* **indefatigably** *adv.*

in•de•fea•si•ble *a.* not to be defeated. **indefeasibility** *n.* **indefeasibly** *adv.*

in•de•fen•si•ble *a.* incapable of being maintained, vindicated, or justified; untenable.

in•de•fin•a•ble *a.* not able to be defined. **indefinably** *adv.*

in•def•i•nite *a.* having no known limits. -ly *adv.* -ness, **indefinitude** *n.*

in•del•i•ble *a.* not to be blotted out or erased; ineffaceable; ingrained. **indelibility, -ness** *n.* **indelibly** *adv.*

in•del•i•cate *a.* offensive to good manners or to purity of mind; indecorous. **indelicacy** *n.* -ly *adv.*

in•dem•ni•fy *v.t.* to reimburse; to free one from the consequences of a technically illegal act. **indemnification** *n.* **indemnitor** *n.* **indemnity** *n.* an agreement to render a person immune from a contingent liability.

in•de•mon•stra•ble *a.* cannot be demonstrated or proved.

in•dent *v.t.* to cut into points or inequalities; to make notches or holes in; (*Print.*) to begin the first line of a paragraph farther away from the margin than the remaining lines; *v.i.* to wind back and forth; to make an agreement; to make an order in duplicate. -ation *n.* a notch; a depression. -ure *n.* a contract of apprenticeship.

in•de•pen•dent *a.* not dependent; not subject to the control of others. **independence, independency** *n.* -ly *adv.*

in•de•scrib•a•ble *a.* incapable of being described.

in•de•struct•i•ble *a.* not able to be destroyed; imperishable. **indestructibility** *n.* **indestructibly** *adv.*

in•de•ter•mi•na•ble *a.* cannot be determined, classified, or fixed. -ness *n.* **indeterminably** *adv.* **indeterminate** *a.* **indeterminately** *adv.* **indeterminateness, indetermination** *n.* an unsettled or wavering state of mind.

in•dex *n.* any table for facilitating reference in a book; a directing sign; that which points out, shows, indicates, or manifests; a pointer or hand which directs to anything; the forefinger or pointing finger; *pl.* -es, **indices.** *v.t.* to provide with an index or table references.

In•di•a *n.* a country in Asia, named from river *Indus.*

In•di•an *a.* pert. to India in Asia, to the East Indies, or to the aborigines of America; *n.* a native of India in Asia, of the East Indies, or one of the aboriginal inhabitants of America. *n.*

in•di•cate *v.t.* to point out; to be a sign of; to denote. **indication** *n.* **indicative** *a.* and *n.* **indicatively** *adv.* **indicator** *n.* **indicatory** *a.*

in•dict *v.t.* to charge with a crime; to accuse; to arraign. -able *a.* -ment *n.*

in·dif·fer·ent *a.* uninterested; without concern; not making a difference; neither good not bad. indifference *n.* -ly *adv.*

in·di·gene *n.* an aborigine; a native animal or plant. Also indigen. indigenous *a.* born or originating in a country; native. indigenously *adv.*

in·di·gent *a.* destitute of property or means of subsistence. indigence *n.*

in·di·ges·ted *a.* not digested; lacking order or system. indigestibility *n.* indigestible *a.* indigestibly *adv.* indigestion *n.* dyspepsia. indigestive *a.*

in·dig·nant *a.* moved by a feeling of wrath, mingled with scorn or contempt; roused. -ly *adv.* indignation *n.* indignity *n.* affront; contemptuous treatment.

in·di·go *n.* a blue dye-stuff; *a.* of a deep-blue color.

in·di·rect *a.* not direct or straight; crooked; dishonest. -ion *n.* roundabout way; trickery. -ly *adv.* -ness *n.*

in·dis·creet *a.* imprudent; injudicious; reckless. -ly *adv.* indiscretion *n.*

ind·dis·crim·i·nate *a.* not making any distinction. -ly *adv.* indiscriminating, indiscriminative *a.* indiscrimination *n.*

in·dis·pen·sa·ble *a.* absolutely necessary. indispensability, -ness *n.* indispensably *adv.*

in·dis·pose *v.t.* to render unfit or unsuited; to render averse or disinclined (toward). -d *a.* averse; ill. indisposition *n.*

in·dis·put·a·ble *a.* too obvious to be disputed.

in·dis·sol·u·ble *a.* perpetually binding or obligatory; inviolable. -ness. indissolubility *n.* indissolubly *adv.*

in·dis·tinct *a.* not distinct or distinguishable. -ive *a.* -ly *adv.*

in·dis·tin·guish·a·ble *a.* may not be distinguished. -ness *n.* indistinguishably *adv.*

in·dite *v.t.* to compose; to write. -ment *n.*

in·di·vid·u·al *a.* not divided; peculiar to single person or thing; *n.* a single being, or thing. -ization *n.* -ize, individuate *v.t.* -ism *n.* theory which asserts the rights of the individual as against those of the community. -ist *n.* -istic *a.* -ity *n.* -ly *adv.*

in·di·vis·i·ble *a.* not divisible; not separate. indivisibility, -ness *n.* indivisibly *adv.*

in·doc·tri·nate *v.t.* to instruct; to imbue with political or religious principles and dogmas. indoctrination *n.*

in·do·lent *a.* habitually idle or lazy. indolence, indolency *n.* -ly *adv.*

in·dom·i·ta·ble *a.* not to be subdued. indomitably *adv.*

In·do·ne·sia *n.* Republic of S.E. Asia (since 1945). -n *a.*

in·door *a.* being within doors. indoors *adv.*

in·dorse, in·dorse·ment See en·dorse.

in·du·bi·ta·ble *a.* too obvious to admit of doubt. indubitably *adv.*

in·duce *v.t.* to overcome by persuasion or argument; to produce or cause (as electricity). -ment *n.* -r *n.* inducible *a.*

in·duct *v.t.* to bring in or introduce; to install or put formally into office. -ion *n.*

-ional *a.* -ive *a.* -ively *adv.* -or *n.*

in·dulge *v.t.* to give freedom or scope to; to allow one his own way; to gratify; to give oneself to the habit or practice of. -nce *n.* -nt *a.* yielding; compliant; very forbearing. -ntly *adv.*

in·du·rate *v.t.* to make hard; to deprive of sensibility; *v.i.* grow hard.

in·dus·try *n.* habitual diligence in any employment, bodily or mental; a particular branch of trade or manufacture. industrial *a.* pert. to industry or manufacture. industrialism *n.* industrially *adv.* industrious *a.* diligent. industriously *adv.* industriousness *n.*

in·e·bri·ate *v.t.* to make drunk; to exhilarate; *a.* intoxicated; *n.* a habitual drunkard. inebriation, inebriety *n.* inebrious *a.*

in·ed·i·ble *a.* not eatable. inedibility *n.*

in·ef·fa·ble *a.* incapable of being expressed in words. -ness, ineffability *n.* ineffably *adv.*

in·ef·face·a·ble *a.* incapable of being rubbed out. ineffaceably *adv.*

in·ef·fec·tive *a.* incapable of producing any effect or the effect intended. -ly *adv.* ineffectual *a.* ineffectuality, ineffectualness *n.* ineffectually *adv.*

in·ef·fi·ca·cy *n.* want of power to produce the proper effect. inefficacious *a.* inefficaciously *adv.*

in·ef·fi·ci·ent *a.* not fitted to perform work in a capable, economical way. inefficiency *n.* -ly *adv.*

in·e·las·tic *a.* not elastic. inelasticity *n.*

in·el·e·gant *a.* lacking in form or beauty inelegance, inelegancy *n.* -ly *adv.*

in·el·i·gi·ble *a.* unsuitable; legally disqualified. ineligibility *n.*

in·e·luc·ta·ble *a.* inevitable. ineluctability *n.*

in·ept *a.* not apt or fit; inexpert. -itude, -ness *n.* -ly *adv.*

in·e·qual·i·ty *n.* want of equaltiy; disparity.

in·eq·ui·ta·ble *a.* not fair or just.

in·e·rad·i·ca·ble *a.* incapable of being rooted out; deep-seated.

in·ert *a.* without the power of action or resistance; sluggish. inertia *n.* -ly *adv.* -ness *n.*

in·es·cap·a·ble *a.* inevitable.

in·es·sen·tial *a.* not necessary.

in·es·ti·ma·ble *a.* not possible to be estimated. inestimably *adv.*

in·ev·i·ta·ble *a.* unavoidable. -ness, inevitability *n.* inevitably *adv.*

in·ex·act *a.* not exact; not strictly true. -itude, -ness *n.*

in·ex·cus·a·ble *a.* not admitting excuse of justification; unpardonable.

in·ex·haust·i·ble *a.* incapable of being exhausted, emptied, or spent; unfailing. inexhaustibility *n.* inexhaustibly *adv.* inexhaustive *a.*

in·ex·o·ra·ble *a.* not to be persuaded or moved by entreaty; unyielding. -ness, inexorability *n.* inexorably *adv.*

in·ex·pe·di·ent *a.* not advisable; impolitic; undesirable at the moment. inexpedience, inexpediency *n.*

IJ

in•ex•pen•sive *a.* cheap.

in•ex•pe•ri•ence *n.* absense or want or experience. -d *a.*

in•ex•pert *a.* unskilled; clumsy. -ness *n.*

in•ex•pi•a•ble *a.* admitting of no atonement; implacable; inexorable.

in•ex•pli•ca•ble *a.* incapable of being explained. inexplicability *n.* inexplicably *adv.*

in•ex•plic•it *a.* not explicit; not clearly stated; equivocal.

in•ex•press•i•ble *a.* cannot be expressed; indescribable. inexpressibly *adv.*

in•ex•pres•sive *a.* not expressive; lacking emphasis; insignificant.

in•ex•ten•si•ble *a.* not capable of extension. inextensibility *n.*

in•ex•tin•guish•a•ble *a.* cannot be extinguished; unquenchable.

in•ex•tri•ca•ble *a.* not to be extricated or disentangled. inextricably *adv.*

in•fal•li•ble *a.* incapable of error. infallibilism, infallibility *n.* infallibly *adv.*

in•fa•my *n.* total loss of reputation; public disgrace; ill-fame. infamous *a.* infamously *adv.*

in•fant *n.* a young baby. infancy *n.* infanticide *n.* the killing of a newly-born child. -ile *a.* pert. to infants; extremely childish.

in•fan•try *n.* foot-soldiers.

in•fat•u•ate *v.t.* to render foolish; to inspire with a foolish passion. -d *a.* infatuation *n.* excessive and foolish love.

in•fea•si•ble *a.* not capable of being done or accomplished; impracticable.

in•fect *v.t.* to affect (with disease); to make noxious; to corrupt. -ion *n.* -ious. -ive. -iously *adv.*

in•fe•li•i•ty *n.* unhappiness; anything not appropriate. infelicitous *a.*

in•fer *v.t.* to draw as a conclusion; to deduce. *pr. p.* -ring. *pa. t.* and *pa. p.* -red. -able *a.* -ence *n.* -ential *a.* deduced or deducible by inference. -entially *adv.*

in•fe•ri•or *a.* lower in rank, order, or excellence; *n.* a person of a lower rank or station. -ity *n.* -ly *adv.*

in•fer•nal *a.* pert. to the lower regions; hellish. -ity *n.* -ly *adv.* inferno *n.* hell.

in•fest *v.t.* to inhabit; to swarm in such numbers as to be a source of annoyance. -ed *a.* -ation *n.*

in•fi•del *a.* unbelieving; *n.* one who is without religious faith; unbeliever. -ity *n.* unfaithfulness to the marriage contract.

in•field *n.* (*Baseball*) the three basemen and the short stop, or the diamond; a field in close proximity to a farmhouse. -er *n.*

in•fil•trate *v.t.* and *v.i.* to filter into; to enter gradually. infiltration *n.*

in•fi•nite *a.* unlimited in time or space; *n.* the boundlessness and immeasurableness of the universe. -ly *adv.* -ness *n.* infinitestimal *a.* infinitestimally *adv.* infinitude *n.* boundlessness. infinity *n.* unlimited and endless extent.

in•fin•i•tive *n.* the simple form of the verb which can be preceded by *to* (*to be*); *a.* not defined or limited.

in•firm *a.* not strong; feeble. -ary *n.* a hospital. -ity disease; failing. -ly *adv.*

in•flame *v.t.* to set on fire; to arouse, as desire. imflammable *a.* combustible. inflammability, inflammableness *n.* inflammably *adv.* inflammation *n.* inflaming; disease condition characterized by heat, redness and pain. inflammatory *a.* tending to arouse passions.

in•flate *v.t.* to swell with air or gas; to raise (price) artificially. -d *a.* swollen; bloated; bombastic. inflatable *a.* inflation *n.* swelling; increase in the amount of fiduciary money issued, beyond what is justified by the country's tangible resources; a rise in prices. inflationary *a.*

in•flect *v.t.* to bend; to modulate the voice. -ion *n.* a bending inwards or deviation; a variation in the tone of the voice. -ional *a.* -ive *a.* inflexibility *n.* inflexible *a.* incapable of being bent; unyielding to influence of entreaty. inflexibly *adv.*

in•flict *v.t.* to lay on; to afflict with something painful. -ion *n.* pain; burden. -ive *a.*

in•flu•ence *n.* power over men or things; effect on the mind; *v.t.* to act on the mind; to induce. influential *a.* influentially *adv.*

in•flu•en•za *n.* (*Med.*) an acute, infectious epidemic catarrhal fever.

in•flux *n.* act of flowing in; the mouth of a stream.

in•fold, enfold *v.t.* to wrap up; to enclose; to encircle.

in•form *v.t.* and *v.i.* to give information.

in•form *a.* without form. -al *a.* without formality, unceremonious. ation *n.* knowledge; intelligence; news. -ative, -atory *a.* educational. -ed *a.* -er *n.* one who gives information.

in•frac•tion *n.* breach; violation.

in•fran•gi•ble *a.* not capable of being broken; not to be violated. infrangibility *n.*

in•fra•red *a.* of the longer invisible heat rays below the red end of the visible spectrum.

in•fre•quent *a.* seldom happening. infrequence, infrequency *n.* -ly *adv.*

in•fringe *v.t.* to violate; to transgress. -ment *n.*

in•fu•ri•ate *v.t.* to enrage; to madden. infuriation *n.*

in•fuse *v.t.* to pour into; to instill; to inspire; to steep in order to extract soluble properties. infusible *a.* infusibility *n.* infusion *n.* act of infusing, instilling, or inspiring; aqueous solution containing the soluble parts of a substance.

in•gen•ious *a.* skilled in inventing new ideas; curious or clever in design. -ly *adv.* -ness, ingenuity *n.*

in•ge•nue *n.* an artless, naive, girl; *a.* frank; artless; innocent. -ly *adv.* -ness *n.*

in•got *n.* a metal casting, esp. of unwrought silver or gold.

in•grain, engrain *v.t.* to fix firmly in the mind; *a.* firmly fixed; dyed, before manufacture into articles. -ed *a.*

in•grate *n.* an ungrateful person. **ingratitude** *n.*

in•gra•ti•ate *v.t.* to work oneself into favor with another. **ingratiation** *n.*

in•gre•di•ent *n.* a component part of any mixture.

in•gress *n.* entrance.

in•grow•ing *a.* growing inwards, esp. of a toenail. **ingrowth** *n.* **ingrown** *a.*

in•gur•gi•tate *v.t.* to swallow up greedily or hastily; to engulf. **ingurgitation** *n.*

in•hab•it *v.t.* to live or dwell in; to occupy. **-able** *a.* **-ant** *n.* **-ation** *n.*

in•hale *v.t.* to breath in. **inhalation** *n.*

in•here *v.i.* (usu. followed by *in*) to exist in. **-nce, -ncy** *n.* **-nt** *a.* **-ntly** *adv.*

in•her•it *v.t.* to receive by descent, or by will; to fall heir to; *v.i.* to succeed as heir. **-able** *a.* **-ance** *n.* **-or** *n* (*fem.* **-ress, -rix**).

in•hib•it *v.t.* to hold back; to restrain. **inhibition** *n.* a subconscious repressed emotion which controls attitude or behavior. **-ory** *a.*

in•hos•pi•ta•ble *a.* averse to showing kindness to guests; discourteous. **-ness, inhospitality** *n.* **inhospitably** *adv.*

in•hu•man *a.* not human or humane; without feeling or pity. **inhumane** *a.* cruel. **-ity** *n.*

in•hume *v.t.* to put into the ground; to bury. **inhumation** *n.*

in•im•i•cal *a.* like an enemy. **-ly** *adv.*

in•im•i•ta•ble *a.* defying imitation; incomparable. **inimitably** *adv.*

in•iq•ui•ty *n.* gross injustice. **iniquitous** *a.* **iniquitously** *adv.*

in•i•tial *a.* occurring at the beginning; *v.t.* to put one's initials to; *n.* the first letter of a word. **initiate** *v.t.* to begin; to instruct in the rudiments of; to admit into a society, etc., with formal rites; *n.* one who is initiated. **initiation** *n.* **initiative** *a.* serving to initiate; *n.* the first step; the quality of being able to set things going. **initiator** *n.* **initiatory** *a.*

in•ject *v.t.* to throw in; to force in; to introduce (a fluid) under the skin by means of a hollow needle. **-ion** *n.* **-or** *n.*

in•ju•di•cious *a.* ill-advised; inprudent; lacking in judgment. **injudicial** *a.* not according to the form of law. **-ly** *adv.*

in•junc•tion *n.* an order of command; an exhortation.

in•jure *v.t.* to do wrong, injury, damage, or injustice to. **injurious** *a.* **injuriously** *adv.* **injury** *n.*

in•jus•tice *n.* an unjust act.

ink *n.* a fluid for writing, printing and sketching. **-iness** *n.* **-y** *a.*

ink•ling *n.* a hint or whisper.

in•land *a.* remote from the sea; *n.* the interior part of a country. **-er** *n.*

in•lay *v.t.* to ornament, by cutting out part of a surface and inserting pieces of pearl, ivory, wood, etc., to form a pattern. *pa. p.* **inlaid.** *n.*

in•let *n.* an entrance; a small bay or creek.

in•mate *n.* a dweller in a house or institution; a fellow-lodger.

inn *n.* a house which provides lodging accomodation for travelers.

in•nate *a.* inborn; native; natural. **-ly** *adv.*

in•ner *a.* farther in; interior; private; not obvious; **-most, inmost** *a.* farthest in.

in•ner•vate Also **innerve,** *v.t.* to give nervous strength to; to stimulate. **innervation** *n.*

in•ning *n.* in games, a side's turn of batting; the ingathering of grain.

in•no•cent *a.* free from guilt; *n.* an innocent person, exp. a child. **innocence, innocency** *n.* **-ly** *adv.*

in•noc•u•ous *a.* producing no ill effects; harmless. **-ly** *adv.* **-ness.**

in•no•vate *v.t.* to make changes by introducing something new. **innovation** *n.*

in•nox•ious *a.* innocuous.

in•nu•en•do *n.* an allusive remark (usually deprecatory).

in•nu•mer•a•ble *a.* not able to be numbered. **innumerability** *n.* **innumerably** *adv.*

in•nu•tri•tion *n.* want of nutrition. **innutritious** *a.*

in•ob•serv•ant *a.* not observant; heedless. **inobservance** *n.*

in•oc•u•late *v.t.* (*Med.*) to introduce into the body pathogenic bacteria or living virus to secure immunity. **inoculation** *n.*

in•op•er•a•ble *a.* (*Surgery*) not in a condition for operating on. **inoperative** *a.* not operating; without effect.

in•op•por•tune *a.* unseasonable in time; untimely. **-ly** *adv.* **inopportunity** *n.*

in•or•di•nate *a.* not limited; disordered. **-ness** *n.* **-ly** *adv.* excessively.

in•or•gan•ic *a.* devoid of an organized structure; not derived from animal or vegatable life. **-ally** *adv.*

in•os•cu•late *v.t.* and *v.i.* to join by openings (arteries, etc.).

in•pa•tient *n.* a patient who is lodged and fed in a hospital.

in•put *n.* (*Elect.*) the power supplied to batter, condenser, etc.

in•quest *n.* a judicial inquiry.

in•qui•e•tude *n.* uneasiness either of body or of mind; restlessness.

in•quire, enquire *v.i.* to ask questions; to seek information; *v.t.* to ask about. **-r** *n.* **inquiring** *a.* **inquiringly** *adv.* **inquiry** *n.* investigation; a question.

in•qui•si•tion *n.* a strict investigation; official inquiry. **-al** *a.* **inquisitive** *a.* apt to ask questions; prying. **inquisitively** *adv.* **inquisitiveness** *n.* **inquisitor** *n.* **inquisitorial** *a.* **inquisitorially** *adv.*

in•road *n.* a sudden incursion into enemy territory.

in•sane *a.* unsound in mind; mentally diseased; lunatic. **-ly** *adv.* **-ness, insanity** *n.*

in•sa•tia•ble *a.* incapable of being satisfied; voracious; rapacious. **-ness, insatiability** *n.* **insatiably** *adv.*

in•sa•ti•ate *a.* not to be satisfied. **-ly** *adv.* **-ness** *n.*

in•scribe *v.t.* to write upon; to engrave; to address or dedicate. **inscribable** *a.* **-r** *n.* **inscription** *n.* **inscriptional, inscriptive** *a.*

in•scru•ta•ble *a.* incapable of being searched into and understood by inquiry or study; mysterious. **inscrutability, -ness**

IJ

n. **inscrutably** *adv.*

in·sect *n.* one of a class of invertebrate animals called the *Insecta.* **insecticide** *n.* killing insect pests. **-ivorous** *a.* living on insects.

in·se·cure *a.* not securely fixed; unguarded; having doubts and fears. **insecurity** *n.*

in·sem·i·nate *v.t.* to sow; to impregnate. **insemination** *n.*

in·sen·sate *a.* destitute of sense; without power of feeling. **-ly** *adv.*

in·sen·si·ble *a.* without bodily sensation; not perceived by the senses; unconscious; callous; imperceptible. **-ness** *n.* **insensibility, insensibly** *adv.*

in·sen·si·tive *a.* not sensitive; callous. **-ness, insensitivity** *n.*

in·sen·ti·ent *a.* not having perception; inanimate.

in·sep·a·ra·ble *a.* not divisible or separable. **inseparably** *adv.*

in·sert *v.t.* to put in; to place among; to introduce. *n.* anything inserted. **-ion** *n.*

in·side *prep.* or *adv.* within the sides of; in the interior; *a.* internal; interior; *n.* the part within.

in·sid·i·ous *a.* lying in wait; treacherous. **-ly** *adv.* **-ness** *n.*

in·sight *n.* view of the interior of anything; mental penetration.

in·sig·ni·a *n. pl.* symbols of authority, dignity, or office.

in·sig·ni·fi·cant *a.* having little importance, use or value; trifling. **insignificance, insignificancy** *n.* **-ly** *adv.*

in·sin·cere *a.* not sincere; dissembling; hypocritical. **-ly** *adv.* **insincerity** *n.*

in·sin·u·ate *v.t.* to introduce gently and adroitly; to suggest by remote allusion; to work oneself into favor; *v.i.* to ingratiate oneself. **insinuating** *a.* **insinuatory** *a.*

in·sip·id *a.* destitute of taste; deficient in spirit, life, or animation. **-ly** *adv.* **-ness, -ity** *n.*

in·sip·i·ent *a.* not wise; foolish. **insipience** *n.*

in·sist *v.i.* to dwell upon as a matter of special moment; to be urgent or pressing. **-ence** *n.* **-ency** *n.* **-ent** *a.*

in·so·bri·e·ty *n.* drunkeness.

in·so·lent *a.* proud and haughty. **insolence** *n.* contemptuous rudeness or arrogance. **-ly** *adv.*

in·sol·u·ble *a.* incapable of being dissolved; inexplicable. **insolubility, -ness** *n.* **insolvable** *a.*

in·sol·vent *a.* not able to pay one's debts; bankrupt. **insolvency** *n.*

in·som·ni·a *n.* chronic sleeplessness.

in·so·much *adv.* so that; to such a degree; in such wise that.

in·sou·ci·ance *n.* carelessness of feeling or manner. **insouciant** *a.*

in·spect *v.t.* to view narrowly and critically; to examine officially. **-ingly** *adv.* **inspection** *n.* **inspectional, -ive** *a.* **-or** *n.* official examiner. **-orate** *n.* **-orial** *a.*

in·spire *v.t.* to breathe in; to infuse thought or feeling into; to arouse; *v.i.* to give inspiration; to inhale. **inspirable** *a.* **inspiration** *n.* **inspirational** *a.* **inspiratory**

a. **inspired** *a.*

in·sta·bil·i·ty *n.* want of stability or firmness.

in·stall *v.t.* to place in position; to induct, with ceremony, a person into an office. **installation** *n.* complete equipment of a building for hearing, lighting, etc.; generally, placing in position for use. **-ment** *n.* act of installing; a periodical payment.

in·stance *n.* case in point; example; *v.t.* to mention as an example; to cite. **instant** *a.* urgent; pressing; immediate; *n.* a particular point of time; moment. **instantaneity** *n.* **instantaneous** *a.* **instantaneously** *adv.* **instantaneousness** *n.* **instantly** *adv.* at once.

in·stead *adv.* in the stead, place, or room.

in·step *n.* the arched upper part of the human foot; that part of a shoe.

in·sti·gate *v.t.* to goad or urge forward; to incite, esp. to evil; to bring about. **instigation** *n.* **instigator** *n.*

in·still *v.t.* to put in by drops; to infuse slowly. **-ed. -ation, -ment** *n.*

in·stinct *n.* intuition; an innate train of reflexes; inborn impulse or propensity. **instinctively, instinctly** *adv.* **instinctivity** *n.*

in·sti·tute *v.t.* to establish; to set going; to originate; *n.* a society or organization established for promoting some particular work, scientific, educational, etc. **institution** *n.* the act of instituting or establishing; an established law, custom, or public occasion; an institute; **institutional** *a.* **institutionally** *adv.* **institutive** *a.* **institutively** *adv.* **institutor, -r** *n.*

in·struct *v.t.* to teach; to inform; to order or command. **-ible** *a.* **-ion** *n.* **-ional** *a.* **-ive** *a.* **-ively** *adv.* **-iveness** *n.* **-or** *n.*

in·stru·ment *n.* a tool or implement; a person or thing made use of; a means of producing musical sounds; *(Law)* a formal or written document. **-al** *a.* **-alist** *n.* one skilled in playing upon a musical instrument. **-ality** *n.* **-ally** *adv.* **-ation** *n.*

in·sub·or·di·nate *a.* disobedient; unruly. **insubordination** *n.*

in·suf·fer·a·ble *a.* not able to be endured; intolerable. **insufferably** *adv.*

in·suf·fi·cient *a.* not enough; deficient. **insufficiency** *n.* **-ly** *adv.*

in·su·lar *a.* pert. to or like an island. **-ism, -ity** *n.* **-ly** *adv.*

in·su·late *v.t.* to keep rigidly apart from contact with other people; to bar the passage of electricity, heat, sound, light, dampness, or vibration by the use of nonconducting materials. **insulation** *n.*

in·su·lin *n.* a hormone; organic drug for the treatment of diabetes.

in·sult *v.t.* to treat with insolence or contempt; *n.* gross abuse.

in·su·per·a·ble *a.* not able to be overcome or surmounted. **insuperability** *n.* **insuperably** *adv.*

in·sup·port·a·ble *a.* incapable of being borne or endured. **-ness** *n.*

in·sure *v.t.* to make sure or certain; to secure the payment of a sum in event of loss. **insurable** *a.* **insurance** *n.*

in·sur·gent *a.* rising in opposition to lawful authority; rebellious; *n.* one in revolt; a rebel. **insurgency** *n.* Also **insurgence.**

in·sur·mount·a·ble *a.* not able to be surmounted or overcome. **insurmountability** *n.* **insurmountably** *adv.*

in·sur·rec·tion *n.* a rising against civil or political authority. **-al, -ary** *a.* **-ist** *n.*

in·sus·cep·ti·ble *a.* not susceptible. **insusceptibility** *n.*

in·take *n.* that which is taken in; inlet of a tube or cylinder.

in·tan·gi·ble *a.* not perceptible to the touch; not clear to the mind. **-ness, intangibility** *n.* **intangibly** *adv.*

in·te·ger *n.* the whole of anything; whole number. **integral** *a.* constituting an essential part of a whole. **integrally** *adv.* **integrate** *v.t.* to make entire. **integration** *n.* **integrator** *n.* **integrity** *n.* the state of being entire; wholeness; probity; honesty.

in·teg·u·ment *n.* the outer protective layer of tissue which covers a plant or animal. **integumentary** *a.*

in·tel·lect *n.* the faculty of reasoning and thinking. **ive** *a.*

in·tel·lect·u·al *a.* of high mental capacity; *n.* one well endowed with intellect. **-ism** *n.* **-ly** *adv.*

in·tel·li·gent *a.* having or showing good intellect; quick at understanding. **intelligence** *n.* **-ly** *adv.* **-sia** *n.* the intellectual or cultured classes. **intelligible** *a.* that can be readily understood; rational. **intelligibleness, intelligibility** *n.* **intelligibly** *adv.*

in·tem·per·ate *a.* immoderate; indulging to excess any appetite or passion; extreme in climate. **intemperance** *n.* **-ly** *adv.*

in·tend *v.t.* and *v.i.* to design; to purpose; to mean; to have in mind. **-ant** *n.* one who has the charge of some public business. **-ancy** *n.* **-ed** *a.* and *n.*

in·tense *a.* to an extreme degree; very strong or acute; emotional. **-ly** *adv.* **-ness, intensity** *n.* **intensification** *n.* **intensify** *v.t.* and *v.i.* *pa. t.* and *pa. p.* **intensified. intensive** *a.* giving emphasis; unrelaxed; increasing in force. **intensively** *adv.*

in·tent *a.* havint the mind bent on an object; absorbed; *n.* intention. **-ion** *n.* design; aim; purpose. **-ional, -ioned** *a.* done purposely. **-ionally** *adv.* **-ly** *adv.* **-ness** *n.*

in·ter- *prefix*, between, among, with, amid.

in·ter·act *v.i.* to act mutually on each other. **-ion** *n.*

in·ter·cede *v.i.* to act as peacemaker; to plead in favor of one; to mediate. **-r** *n.* **intercession** *n.* **intercessor** *n.* **intercessorial, intercessory** *a.*

in·ter·cept *v.t.* to stop or obstruct passage. **-er, -or** *n.* **-ion** *n.* **-ive** *a.*

in·ter·ces·sion, intercessor See **intercede.**

in·ter·change *v.t.* to exchange; to reciprocate; *v.i.* to succeed alternately; to exchange places; *n.* access to a freeway; a mutual exchange. **-able** *a.* **-ability,**

-ableness *n.*

in·ter·communicate *v.t.* to exchange conversations or messages. **intercommunication** *a., n.* **intercommunicative** *a.*

in·ter·con·nect *v.t.* and *v.i.* to connect mutually and intimately.

in·ter·cos·tal *a.* (*Anat.*) between the rigs.

in·ter·course *n.* communication between individuals; exchange of goods; coition.

in·ter·cur·rent *a.* running between or among; occurring during the course of another (disease).

in·ter·de·pend *v.i.* to depend mutually. **-ence** *n.* **-ent** *a.* **-ently** *adv.*

in·ter·dict *v.t.* to forbid; to prohibit; *n.* prohibition. **-ion** *n.* **-ive, -ory** *a.*

in·ter·est *v.t.* to engage and keep the attention of; *n.* special attention; regard to personal profit or advantage; curiosity; the profit per cent derived from money lent. **-ed** *a.* having a share in; feeling an interest in. **-edly** *adv.* **-edness** *n.* **-ing** *a.* appealing to or exciting one's interest or curiosity. **-ingly** *adv.*

in·ter·fere *v.i.* to be in or come into, opposition; to enter into or take part in the concerns of others; to intervene. **-nce** *n.* meddling with other people's business; uncalled-for intervention. **-r** *n.* **interferingly** *adv.*

in·ter·im *n.* the time between; the meantime; *a.* for the time being; temporary.

in·te·ri·or *a.* innter; internal; inland, away from coast or frontiers; *n.* the inside part or portion. **-ly** *adv.*

in·ter·ject *v.t.* to throw between; to insert; to exclaim abruptly. **-ion** *n.* act of throwing between; a word which expresses strong emotion or passion when suddenly uttered. **-ional, -ionary, -ory** *a.* **-ionally** *adv.*

in·ter·lace *v.t.* to lace together; to entwine.

in·ter·lard *v.t.* to diversify by mixture (of words, etc.).

in·ter·line *v.t.* to write or mark between the lines; to put an inner lining in a garment. **-al, -ar** *a.* **-ate** *v.t.*

in·ter·lock *v.t.* to unite by locking together; to fasten together so that one part cannot move without the other; *v.i.* to be locked or jammed together.

in·ter·lo·cu·tion *n.* dialogue; a conference; speaking in turn.

in·ter·lope *v.i.* to traffic without a proper license; to intrude into other people's affairs. **-r** *n.*

in·ter·lude *n.* a dramatic or musical performance given between parts of an independent play; an interval.

in·ter·mar·ry *v.i.* to connect families or races by a marriage between two of their members. **intermarriage** *n.*

in·term·me·di·ate *a.* lying or being between two extremes; intervening; *n.* anything in between; *v.i.* to mediate; to intervene. **intermediacy** *n.* **intermediary** *a.* and *n.* **intermedium** *n.* **intermediation** *n.*

in·ter·ment See **inter.**

in·ter·mez·zo *n.* a light dramatic entertainment between the acts; (*Mus.*) a

IJ

short movement connecting more important ones.

in·ter·mi·na·ble *a.* endless; unlimited. **-ness** *n.* **interminably** *adv.*

in·ter·min·gle *v.t.* to mingle or mix together.

in·ter·mit *v.t.* to give up or forbear for a time; to interrupt; *v.i.* to cease for a time. *pr. p.* **-ting.** *pa. t., pa. p.* **-ted.** **intermission** *n.* intervening period of time. **intermissive.** *a.* coming after temporary cessations. **-tence, -tency** *n.* **-tent** *a.* occurring at intervals. **-tently** *adv.*

in·ter·mix *v.t.* and *v.i.* to mix together. **-ture** *n.*

in·tern *v.t.* to confine, esp. aliens or suspects in time of war; *n.* a resident doctor in a hospital. Also **interne.** **internee** *n.* one who is confined to a certain place. **-ment** *n.* **-ship** *n.*

in·ter·nal *a.* interior; inward; domestic, as opposed to foreign. **-ly** *adv.*

in·ter·na·tion·al *a.* pert. to the relations between nations. **-ist** *n.* **-ly** *adv.*

in·ter·ne·cine *a.* mutually destructive; deadly.

in·ter·nee See **intern.**

in·ter·nist *n.* a specialist in internal medicine.

in·ter·pel·late *v.t.* to interrupt a speaker in a legislative assembly by demanding an explanation. **interpellation** *n.* **interpellator** *n.*

in·ter·pen·e·trate *v.t.* to grow through one another; to penetrate thoroughly. **interpenetration** *n.*

in·ter·plan·e·tar·y *a.* situated between the planets.

in·ter·play *n.* reciprocal action of two things.

in·ter·po·late *v.t.* to insert new (esp. misleading) matter into a text; to interpose with some remark. **interpolation** *n.* **interpolator** *n.*

in·ter·pose *v.t.* and *i.* to place or come between; to offer, as aid or service; to interrupt. **interposal** *n.* **-r** *n.* **interposition** *n.*

in·ter·pret *v.t.* to explain the meaning of; to translate orally for the benefit of others. **-able** *a.* **-ation** *n.* **-ative** *a.* **-er** *n.*

in·ter·reg·num *a.* the time a throne is vacant between the death or abdication of a king and the accession of his successor; any interruption in continuity.

in·ter·re·la·tion *n.* reciprocal or mutual relation. **-ship** *n.*

in·ter·ro·gate *v.t.* to question. **interrogation** *n.* **interrogative** *a.* **interrogatory** *a.*

in·ter·rupt *v.t.* to break in upon; to break continuity of. **-edly** *adv.* **-er** *n.* **-ion** *n.* **-ive** *a.*

in·ter·sect *v.t.* to cut into or between; to divide into parts; to cross on another. **-ion** *n.* **-ional** *a.*

in·ter·sperse *v.t.* to scatter or place here and there. **interspersion** *n.*

in·ter·stel·lar *a.* passing between, or situated among, the stars. **-y.**

in·ter·stice *a.* a small gap or chink; a crevice. **interstitial** *a.*

in·ter·twine *v.t.* to twine or twist together.

in·ter·val *n.* time or distance between; a pause; a break.

in·ter·vene *v.i.* to come or be between; to interfere. **-r** *n.* **intervention** *n.* **interventionist** *n.* or *a.*

in·ter·view *n.* a meeting or conference; *v.t.* to have an interview with. **-er** *n.*

in·tes·tate *a.* not having made a valid will; *n.* a person who dies intestate. **intestacy** *n.*

in·tes·tine *a.* internal; domestic; *n. pl.* the bowels; the entrails. **intestinal** *a.*

in·ti·mate *a.* innermost; familiar; closely-related; *n.* an intimate friend; *v.t.* **intimate** to hint; to imply. **intimacy** *n.*

in·tim·i·date *v.t.* to force or deter by threatsl to inspire with fear. **intimidation** *n.* **intimidator** *n.*

in·to *prep.* expresses motion to a point within, or a change from one state to another.

in·tol·er·a·ble *a.* insufferable; unbearable. **-ness** *n.* **intolerably** *adv.* **intolerance** *n.* **intolerant** *a.* **intolerantly** *adv.*

in·tone *v.t.* to tuter or recite with a long drawn out musical note or tone; to chant; *v.i.* to modulate the voice; to give forth a deep protracted sound. **intonate** *v.t.* **intonation** *n.*

in·tox·i·cate *v.t.* to make drunk; to excite beyond self-control. **intoxicating** *a.* **intoxicant** *n.* **intoxication** *n.*

in·tra- *prefix,* within, inside of, used in the construction of many compound terms.

in·trac·ta·ble *a.* not to be managed or governed. **intractability, intractably** *adv.*

in·tra·mu·ral *a.* pert. to a single college or its students; within the walls or limits.

in·tran·si·gent *a.* refusing in any way to compromise; *n.* one who adopts this attitude. **intransigence,** *n.* **-ly** *adv.*

in·tran·si·tive *a.* (*Gram.*) denoting such verbs as express an action or state which is limited to the agent.

in·trep·id *a.* free from fear or trepidation. **-ity** *n.* undaunted courage. **-ly** *adv.*

in·tri·cate *a.* involved; entangled; complicated; difficult. **intricacy, -ness** *n.* **-ly** *adv.*

in·trigue *n.* a plot to effect some purpose by secret artifices; *v.i.* to scheme secretly; *v.t.* to fascinate; to arouse interest in. *pr. p.* **intriguing. intrigant, -r** *n.* **intriguing** *a.* **intriguingly** *adv.*

in·trin·sic *a.* from within; having internal value; inherent. **-ality** *n.* **-ally** *adv.*

in·tro- *prefix,* inwards, used in compound terms.

in·tro·duce *v.t.* to lead or bring in; to make known formally (one person to another); **introduction** *n.* **introductory, introductive** *a.* **introductively, inductorily** *adv.*

in·tro·spect *v.t.* to look within; to inspect; *v.i.* to pre-occupy oneself with one's own thoughts, emotions and feelings. **-ion** *n.* **-ive** *a.* **-ively** *adv.*

in·tro·vert *v.t.* to turn inward; *n.* a self-centered, introspective individual. **introversion** *n.* **introversive, -ive** *a.*

in·trude *v.i.* to thrust oneself in; to enter unwelcome or uninvited; *v.t.* to force in. **-r** *n.* **intrusion** *n.* **intrusive** *a.* **intrusively**

adv. **intrusiveness** *n.*

in•trust See entrust.

in•tu•i•tion *n.* immediate and instinctive perception of a truth; direct understanding without reasoning. **intuit** *v.t.* and *v.i.* to know intuitively. **-al** *a.* **-alism, -ism** *n.* the doctrine that the perception of good and evil is by intuition. **-alist** *n.* **intuitive** *a.* **intuitively** *adv.*

in•tu•mesce *v.i.* to swell; to enlarge or expand, owing to heat. **-nce** *n.*

in•twine See entwine.

in•un•date *v.t.* to overflow; to flood; to overwhelm. **inundation** *n.*

in•ure *v.t.* to accustom (to); to habituate by use; to harden (the body) by toil, etc. **-ment** *n.*

in•vade *v.t.* to attack; to enter with hostile intentions; to encroach upon. **-r** *n.* **invasion** *n.* **invasive** *a.*

in•val•id *a.* not valid; void; *v.t.* to render invalid. **-ate** *v.* **-ation** *n.* **-ity, -ness** *n.*

in•va•lid *n.* a person enfeebled by sickness or injury; *a.* ill; sickly; weak; *v.t.* and *v.i.* to make invalid.

in•val•u•a•ble *a.* incapable of being valued; priceless.

in•var•i•able *a.* not displaying change. **-ness, invariability** *n.* **invariably** *adv.* **invariant** *n.*

in•va•sion *n.* See invade.

in•vec•tive *n.* violent outburst of censure; abuse; *a.* abusive.

in•veigh *v.i.* to exclaim or rail against. **-er** *n.*

in•vei•gle *v.t.* to entice by deception or flattery. **-ment** *n.* **-r** *n.*

in•vent *v.t.* to devise something new or an improvement; to originate; to think out something untrue. **-ion** *n.* **-ive** *a.* **-ively** *adv.* **-or** *n.*

in•ven•to•ry *n.* a detailed list of articles comprising the effects of a house, etc.; *v.t.* to make a list.

in•verse *a.* inverted; opposite in order or relation. **-ly** *adv.* **inversion** *n.* **inversive** *a.*

in•vert *v.t.* to turn over; to put upside down; to place in a contrary order. **-edly** *adv.*

in•ver•te•brate *a.* not having a vertebral column or backbone; *n.* animal with no spinal column.

in•vest *v.t.* to lay out capital with a view to profit; to clothe, as with office or authority; *v.t.* to make a purchase or an investment. **-iture** *n.* ceremony of installing anyone in office. **-ment** *n.* **-or** *n.*

in•ves•ti•gate *v.t.* to inquire into; to examine thoroughly. **investigable** *a.* **investigation** *n.* **investigator** *n.* **investigatory** *a.*

in•vet•er•ate *a.* firmly established by long continuance. **-ly** *adv.* **-ness, inveteracy,** *n.*

in•vid•i•ous *a.* likely to provoke envy, ill-will or hatred; offensive. **-ly** *adv.* **-ness** *n.*

in•vig•or•ate *v.t.* to animate with life and energy. **invigoration** *n.* **-d** *a.*

in•vin•ci•ble *a.* unconquerable; insuperable. **-ness, invincibility** *n.* **invincibly.**

in•vi•o•la•ble *n.* not to be violated; sacred. **inviolably** *adv.* **inviolate** *a.* **inviolately** *adv.* **inviolateness** *n.*

in•vis•i•ble *a.* incapable of being seen. **invisibility, -ness** *n.* **invisibly** *adv.*

in•vite *v.t.* to ask by invitation; to attract. **invitation** *n.* act of inviting; the spoken or written form with which a request for a person's company is extended. **-r** *n.* **inviting** *a.* **invitingly** *adv.*

in•vo•ca•tion *n.* act of addressing in prayer. **invocatory** *a.* [See invoke.].

in•voice *n.* a detailed list of goods, with prices, sold or consigned to a purchaser; *v.t.* to make such a list.

in•voke *v.t.* to address (esp. God) earnestly or solemnly in prayer.

in•vol•un•ta•ry *a.* outside the control of the will; unintentional; instinctive. **involuntarily** *adv.* **involuntariness** *n.*

in•vo•lute *a.* (*Bot.*) rolled inwardly or spirally; *n.* the locus of the far end of a flexible thread unwound from a circle. **involution** *n.* that in which anything is involved; entanglement; complication. [See involve].

in•volve *v.t.* to envelop; to wrap up; to include; to comprise; to embrace; to implicate (a person); to complicate (a thing). **-ment** *n.*

in•vul•ner•a•ble *a.* incapable of being wounded or injured. **invulnerability** *n.* **invulnerably** *adv.*

in•ward *a.* placed within; towards the inside; interior; internal; seated in the mind or soul; *adv.* toward the inside; into the mind. Also **inwards. -ly** *adv.*

i•o•dine *n.* a non-metallic chemical element belonging to the halogen group. **iodiferous** *a.* yielding iodine. **iodize** *v.t.* to treat with compounds of iodine.

i•on *n.* electrically charged atom. **ionic** *a.* **-ization** *n.* **-ize** *v.t.* **ionosphere** *n.* the layer of ionized molecules in the upper atmosphere.

i•on•ic *a.* pert. to section of Greece; (*Archit.*) denoting type of column with fluted molding and ram's horn design.

ionic column

i•o•ta *n.* a very small quantity or degree.

ir- *prefix* for *in*; not, before 'r.'

i•ras•ci•ble *a.* easily provoked; hot-tempered, **irascibility** *n.* **irascibly** *adv.*

i•rate *a.* angry; incensed.

ire *n.* anger; wrath. **-ful** *a.* **-fully** *adv.* **-fully** *adv.* **-fulness** *n.*

irid-, irido-, *prefix* used in the construction of compound terms, pertaining to the iris of the eye or to the genus of plants, as **iridescence** *n.* rainbow-like display of colors. **iridescent** *a.*

IJ

iris n. (Anat.) the thin colored membrane between the cornea and the lens of the eye; (Bot.) a genus of flowering plants; an appearance resembling the rainbow.

I•rish a. pert. to Ireland; n. the early language spoken in Ireland. -ism n.

irk v.t. to weary; to trouble; to distress. -some a. -somely adv.

i•ron n. the most common and useful of the metallic elements; something hard and unyielding; an instrument or utensil made of iron; an instrument used, when heated, to press and smooth cloth; in golf, an ironheaded club. -s n. pl. fetters; mannacles; a. made of iron; inflexible; v.t. to smooth with a heated flat iron; v.i. to furnish or arm with iron; to fetter.

i•ro•ny n. a mode of speech in which the meaning is the opposite of that actually expressed. ironic, ironical a. ironacally adv.

ir•ra•di•ate v.t. to shine upon, throw light upon; v.t. to emit rays; to give forth light; a. illumined with beams of light. irradiance, irradiancy n. irradiant a. irradiation n. exposure to X-rays, ultra-violet rays, solar rays, etc.; illumination; enlightenment. irradiative a. irradiator n.

ir•ra•tion•al a. incompatible with or contrary to reason. -ity n. -ly adv.

ir•re•claim•a•ble a. incapable of being reclaimed. irreclaimably adv.

ir•rec•on•cil•a•ble a. incapable of being reconciled. -ness, irreconcilability n. irreconcilably adv.

ir•re•cov•er•a•ble a. cannot be recovered; irreparable; irretrievable. -ness n. irrecoverably adv.

ir•re•deem•a•ble a. not redeemable; incorrigible. -ness, irredeemability n. irredeemably adv.

ir•re•duc•i•ble a. that which cannot be reduced or lessened. -ness, irreducibility n. irreducibly adv.

ir•ref•u•ta•ble a. that cannot be refuted. irrefutability n. irrefutably adv.

ir•reg•u•lar a. not regular; deviating from the moral standard. -ity n. -ly adv.

ir•rel•a•tive a. not relative; unconnected. -ly adv.

ir•re•li•gion n. state of indifference or opposition to religious beliefs. irreligious a. irreligiously adv. irreligiousness n.

ir•re•me•di•a•ble a. not to be remedied or redressed. -ness n. irremediably adv.

ir•re•place•able a. that cannot be passed by or forgiven; unpardonable.

ir•rep•a•ra•ble a. that cannot be repaired or rectified. -ness n. irreparability n. irreparably adv.

ir•re•place•able a. that cannot be replaced.

ir•re•press•i•ble a. not able to be kept under control. irrepressibility n. -ness n. irrepressibly adv.

ir•re•proach•a•ble a. free from blame; faultless. irreproachably adv.

ir•re•sist•i•ble a. incapable of being resisted. -ness, irresistibility n. irresistibly adv.

ir•res•o•lute a. infirm or inconstant in purpose; vacillating. -ly adv. -ness,

irresolution n.

ir•re•spec•tive a. and adv. without regard to; apart from. -ly adv.

ir•re•spon•si•ble a. not liable to answer (for consequences); without a due sense of responsibility. irresponsibility n. irresponsibly adv.

ir•re•spon•sive a. not responsive (to); unanswering; taciturn. -ness n.

ir•re•triev•a•ble a. incapable of recovery or repair. -ness n. irretrievability n. irretrievably adv.

ir•rev•er•ent a. not reverent; disrespectful. irreverence n. -ly adv.

ir•re•vers•i•ble a. that cannot be reversed. irreversibly adv.

ir•rev•o•ca•ble a. incapable of being recalled or revoked. -ness, irrevocability n. irrevocably adv.

ir•ri•gate v.t. to water (by artificial channels). irrigable, irrigative a. irrigation n.

ir•ri•tate v.t. to excite to anger; to annoy; to excite heat and redness in the skin by friction. irritability n. irritable a. easily provoked or annoyed; able to be acted upon by stimuli. irritableness n. irritably adv. irritant a. and n. irritation n. irritative a.

ir•rup•tion n. a sudden invasion; a violent incursion into a place. irruptive a. irruptively adv.

is v. the third pers. sing. pres. idic. of the verb to be.

is•land n. a piece of land surrounded by water. -er n.

isle n. an island. islet n. a tiny island.

i•so- prefix, equal, used in the construction of compound terms.

i•so•dy•nam•ic a. having equal force or power.

i•so•gon n. a plane figure having equal angles. isogonal a. -ic a.

i•so•late v.t. to place in a detached position. isolation n. isolationist n.

i•so•met•ric a. of equal measurement.

i•sos•ce•les a. having two sides which are equal (said of a triangle).

i•so•topes n. pl. (physics) of most of the elements, atoms with nuclei of slightly different weights.

Is•ra•el n. since 1948, the name of the Jewish State in Palestine. Israeli n. an inhabitant of Israel. -ite n. (Bib.) a descendant of Israel or Jacob; a Jew. -itic, -itish, a.

is•sue n. act of passing or flowing out; the act of sending out; a topic of discussion or controversy; a morbid discharge from the body; outlet; edition; consequence; progeny; v.t. to send out (a book, etc.); to put into circulation; to proclaim or set forth with authority; to supply with equipment, etc.; v.i. to pass or flow out; to come out; to proceed; to be born or spring from. -less a. -er n.

isth•mus n. a narrow neck of land connecting two larger portions. isthmian a.

it pron. the neuter pronoun of the third person.

I•tal•ian a. pert. to Italy, its inhabitants or

their language.

i·tal·ics n. pl. a printing type having the type sloping from the right downwards, *as these letters.* **italicization** n. **italicize** v.t.

itch n. an irritation in the skin; v.i. to feel uneasiness or irritation in the skin. **-iness** n. **-y** a.

i·tem n. a piece of news, as in a newspaper; a detail. **itemize** v.t. to list.

it·er·ate v.t. to repeat; to do again. **iteration** n. **iterative, iterant** a.

i·tin·er·ant a. traveling from place to place; of notsettled abode. n. one who goes from place to place, esp. on business. **itineracy, itinerancy** n. **-ly** adv. **itinerary** n. a record of travel; a guide-book for travelers. **itinerate** v.i. to travel up and down a country, exp. in a regular circuit. **itineration** n.

its the *possessive case of pron.* **it. itself** pron. the neuter reciprocal pronoun applied to things; the reflexive form of it.

i·vo·ry n. the hard, white, opaque, dentine constituting tusks of elephant, walrus, etc.; as carving of ivory; creamy white color; a. made of or like ivory.

i·vy n. a climbing evergreen plant. **ivied** a.

IJ

jab v.t. to poke sharply; n. a sharp poke, stab, or thrust. -**bing** pr.p. -**bed**. pa.t. and pa.p.

jab·ber v.i. to speak quickly and indistinctly; vt. to utter indistinctly; n. rapid, incoherent talk. -**er** n. -**ingly** adv.

Jack n. a popular nickname and diminutive of *John. lc* the knave in a pack of cards; a device to facilitate removal of boots, as a *bootjack;* a portable apparatus for raising heavy weights, esp. for raising a motor vehicle to change a tire; the male of certain animals, as *jackass;* v.t. to raise with a jack. Also **jack up.** —**in-the-box** n. a child's toy comprising a small figure which springs out of a box when the lid is lifted. -**knife** n. a strong clasp knife. —**o'-lantern,** a latern made from hollowed-out pumpkin, with holes cut to make a face. —**of-all-trades** n. one who can turn his hand to anything. -**pot** n. a pool, in poker, which cannot be opened except by player holding two jacks or better. -**rabbit** n. a hare with very long ears. **yellow jack** n. yellow fever.

jack·al n. bushy-tailed carnivorous animal of Asia and Africa; wild dog.

jack·ass n. a male ass; a stupid fellow.

jack·daw n. a glossy, black bird of the crow family.

jack·et n. a short, sleeved coat; outer covering or skin (as of potatoes); an outer casing; a loose dustcover for a book; v.t. to cover with a jacket.

Ja·cob's lad·der n. a rope ladder with wooden rungs.

jac·quard n. a pattern woven into fabrics.

jacquard

jade n. an overworked, worn-out horse; v.t. to wear out. **jading** pr.p. -**d** pa.p. -**d** a. tired; sated.

jade n. a very hard, compact silicate of lime and magnesia, of various colors, carved for ornaments.

jag n. a ragged protuberance; (Bot.) cleft or division; v.t. to slash. -**ging** pr.p. -**ged** pa.p. -**ged**, -**gy** a. notched; rough-edged; sharp. -**gedness** n.

jag·uar n. a large spotted yellowish beast of prey.

jail n. a prison; v.t. to take into custody. -**bird** n. a prisoner; a criminal. -**er**, -**or**

n. one who has charge of prisoners in the cells.

jal·ou·sie n. a blind or shutter with slats at an angle. -**d** a.

jam n. preserve made from fruit, boiled with sugar. -**my** a.

jam v.t. to wedge in; to block up; v.i. to cease to function because of obstruction; n. a crush; a holdup (as of traffic); a tight corner. -**ming** pr.p. -**med** pa.p. -**ming** n. (Radio) to interfere with signals by sending out others of like frequency.

jamb n. the sidepiece of a door, fireplace, etc.

jam·bo·ree n. a large, usually international, rally of Boy Scouts.

jan·gle v.t. to ring with a discordant sound; v.i. to sound out of tune; n. a discordant sound; a dispute. **jangling** n.

jan·i·tor n. a caretaker of a building; a porter.

Jan·u·ar·y n. the first month, dedicated by Romans to *Janus,* the god with two faces.

Ja·pan n. a N.E. Asiatic insular country. -**ese** n. a native of Japan; a. pert. to Japan, the people or language.

japan v.t. to lacquer with black varnish. n. the black laquer japanned. -**ning** pr.p. -**ned** pa.p.

jar n. vessel narrower at top than at base, with or without handles.

jar to give forth a discordant sound; to affect the nerves, feelings, etc. unpleasantly; v.t. to cause to vibrate by sudden impact; to shake physically or mentally; n. a jolting movement. -**ring** pr.p. -**red** pa.p. -**ringly** adv.

jar·gon n. confused speech; slang; technical phraseology.

jas·mine n. a shrub with fragrant white, yellow or pink flowers. Also **jessamine.**

jas·per n. an opague form of quartz, often highly colored.

jaun·dice n. a disease, characterized by yellowness of skin and eyes; v.t. to affect with jaundice. -**d** a. affected with jaundice.

jaunt v.i. to make an excursion; n. an outing; a ramble. -**ing** a. rambling.

jaun·ty a. sprightly; trim. **jauntily** adv.

jav·e·lin n. a light hand-thrown spear.

jaw n. one of the two bones forming framework of mouth and containing the teeth; part of any device which grips object held by it, as a vise; v.t. bone of the mouth in which teeth are set.

jay n. a chattering bird with gay plumage. -**walker** n. a careless pedestrian who disregards traffic rules.

common jay

jazz n. syncopated music played as accompaniment to dancing; a. pert. to jazz; v.t. and v.i. to dance to or play jazz music. -**y** a.

jeal·ous *a.* envious; apprehensively watchful; zealously careful. **-y** *n.*

jean *n.* a strong, twilled cotton cloth; *n.pl.* trousers.

jeep *n.* light motor utility truck designed in World War II.

jeer *v.i.* to mock; *v.t.* to treat scoffingly; *n.* a railing remark. **-er** *n.*

Je·ho·vah *n.* Hebrew name of the supreme God.

jel·ly *n.* gelatinous substance; juice of fruit boiled with sugar. **jell** *v.i.* to stiffen. **jellied** *a.* of the consistency of jelly. **jellify** *v.t.* to make into jelly; *v.i.* to become set like a jelly. **-fish** *n.* name given certain marine animals of gelatinous structure.

jen·ny *n.* a spinning machine; a female ass; a female bird, the wren.

jeop·ar·dy *n.* danger; risk. **jeopardize** *v.t.* to imperil.

Jer·e·mi·ah *n.* a Hebrew prophet and author of the Book of Lamentations.

jerk *v.t.* to give a sudden pull, twist, or push; *n.* a short, sudden thrust, pull, etc.; a twitching. **-er** *n.* **-ily** *adv.* **-iness** *n.* **-y** *a.* fitful; spasmodic; lacking rhythm.

jerk *v.t.* to cure (meat) by cutting in long slices and drying in the sun. **-ed** *a.*

jer·kin *n.* a close-fitting jacket.

Jer·sey *n.* the largest of the Channel Islands; *a.* pert. to State of New Jersey. **jersey** *n.* a close-fitting, knitted vest, or pullover.

jest *n.* a joke; an object of ridicule; *v.i.* to joke; to scoff. **-er** *n.* one who jests; a professional fool, originally attached to the court. **-ful** *a.* **-ingly** *adv.*

Je·su·it *n.* one of a religious order founded by Ignatius Loyola in 1534 under the title of The Society of Jesus.

jet *n.* a variety of very hard, black lignite, capable of a brilliant polish and used for ornaments; *a.* having the glossy blackness of jet. **— black** *a.* black like jet. **-tiness** *n.* **-ty** *a.*

jet *n.* a sudden rush, as of water or flame, from a pipe; the spout emitting water, gas, etc.; a jet airplane; *v.t.* to spout; *v.i.* to shoot forth. **— propulsion** *n.* propulsion of a machine by the force of a jet of fluid or of heated gases, expelled backwards from the machine. **-ting** *pr.p.* **-ted** *pa.t.*

jet·sam *n.* goods washed ashore from a wrecked ship. **jettison** *n.* act of throwing overboard; *v.t.* to throw overboard, as cargo.

jet·ty *n.* a structure of piles, stones, built to protect a harbor; a landing pier.

Jew *n.* a Hebrew or an Israelite. **-ish** *a.* of or belonging to Jews. **-ishness** *n.* **-ry** *n.* the Jewish people.

jew·el *n.* a precious stone; an ornament set with gem(s); *v.t.* to adorn with jewels; to fit (as a watch) with a jewel for pivot bearings. **-er** *n.* one who makes or deals in jewels. **-ery** *n.* jewels collectively.

jib *n.* (*Naut.*) a triangular staysail in front of forward mast.

jibe *v.t.* to swing (the sail) from one side of the ship to the other; *v.i.* to alter the course so that the sail shifts; *n.* a jeer.

jig *n.* a lively dance; a tool used to guide cutting tools in the making of duplicate parts; *v.t.* to jerk up and down; *v.i.* to bob up and down. **-ging** *pr.p.* **-ged** *pa.p.* **-saw** *n.* a narrow saw in a frame for cutting curves, etc. **-saw puzzle**, a picture cut into irregular pieces for putting together again.

jig·ger *n.* one who or that which jigs; any mechanical device which operates with jerky movement, esp. an apparatus for washing and separating ores by shaking in sieves under water; a bridge for a billiard cue; (*Naut.*) a sail nearest the stern; a 1½ oz. measure for liquor.

jig·ger *n.* a flea, the female of which burrows under the human flesh to lay its eggs. Also **chigger.**

jig·gle *v.i.* and *v.t.* to move with repeated short, quick jerks; *n.* a short, quick movement.

jilt *n.* one who capriciously disappoints a lover; *v.t.* to disappoint in love; to break an engagement to marry.

jim·my *n.* a small crowbar, as used by burglars; *v.t.* to force open.

jin·gle *v.t.* to cause to give a sharp, tinkling sound; *v.i.* to tinkle; to give this effect in poetry; *n.* correspondence of sounds, rhymes, etc., in verse to catch the ear.

jin·rik·i·sha *n.* a small, two-wheeled hooded carriage pulled by one or more men, commonly used in Japan.

jinx *n.* a person or thing of ill omen.

jit·ney *n.* public bus traveling a regular route.

jiu·jit·su See jujitsu.

job *n.* a piece of work; labor undertaken at a stated price; *a.* lumped together (of miscellaneous articles); *v.i.* to do odd jobs; to use influence unscrupulously; *v.t.* to buy and sell as a jobber; to let out work in portions. **-bing** *pr.p.* **-bed** *pa.p.* **-ber** *n.* a wholesale dealer who sells to retailers; one who transacts public business to his own advantage; one who does odd jobs. **-bery** *n.* underhand means to gain private profit at the expense of public money. **-bing** *a.* **— lot** *n.* a large amount of goods. as handled by a jobber. **— printing,** **— work,** the printing of handbills, circulars, etc.

Job *n.* (*Bib.*) a Hebrew patriarch of the Old Testament regarded as a monument of patience.

jock·ey *n.* a professional rider in horse races; *v.t.* to ride as a jockey; to maneuver for one's own advantage; *v.i.* to cheat. **-ism, -ship** *n.*

jo·cose *a.* given to jesting; waggish. **-ly** *adv.* **-ness, jocosity** *n.* the quality of being jocose. **jocular** *a.* given to jesting; facetious.

jo·cund *a.* merry; genial. **-ity, -ness** *n.* **-ly** *adv.*

jodh·purs *n.pl.* long riding breeches, close-fitting from knee to ankle.

jog *v.t.* to push with the elbow or hand; to stimulate (as the memory); *v.i.* to move on at a slow jolting pace; to plod on; *n.* a nudge; a slow walk, trot, etc. **-ging** *pr.p.*

-ged *pa.p.*

jog *n.* a projecting part.

jog‧gle *v.t.* to shake slightly; to join by notches to prevent sliding apart; *v.i.* to shake; *n.* a jolt; a joint of two bodies so

joggle-joints

constructed that sliding apart is prevented.

John *n.* a proper name; a familiar appellation. — **Doe** *n.* fictitious plaintiff in a law case. **johnnycake** *n.* corn bread.

join *v.t.* to bring together; to unite; to become a member of; to become united in marriage, partnership; *n.* a junction; a fastening. **-er** *n.* one who or that which joins; a carpenter. **-ery** *n.* the trade of a joiner. **to join battle**, to begin fighting. **to join issue**, to take different sides on a point in debate.

joint *n.* the place where two things are joined; the articulation of two or more bones in the body; a hinge; *v.t.* to unite; to provide with joints; *v.i.* to fit like joints; *a.* jointed; held in common. **-ed** *a.* having joints. **-ly** *adv.* cooperatively. — **stock company**, a mercantile, banking, or cooperative association with capital made up of transferable shares. **out of joint**, dislocated; disordered.

joist *n.* a beam to which the boards of a floor or the laths of a ceiling are nailed.

joke *n.* something said or done to provoke laughter; a witticism; *v.t.* to make merry with; *v.i.* to make sport; to be merry. **-r** *n.* one who plays pranks; *(Cards)* an extra card in the pack, used in some games. **jokingly** *adv.*

jol‧ly *a.* jovial; cheerful; *v.t. (Colloq.)* to humor a person with pleasant talk; to tease. **jollification** *n.* a celebration; a noisy party. **jolliness**, **jollity** *n.* mirth.

jol‧ly boat *n.* a ship's small boat.

jolt *v.t.* to shake with a sudden jerk; *v.i.* to shake, as a vehicle on rough ground; *n.* a sudden jerk.

Jo‧nah *n. (Bib.)* a Hebrew prophet.

Jon‧a‧than *n.* a variety of eating apple.

jon‧quil *n.* variety of narcissus.

josh *v.t. and v.i.* to make fun of, to tease.

jos‧tle *v.t.* to push against, esp. with the elbow; *v.i.* to push; *n.* a pushing against.

jot *n.* an iota; something negligible; *v.t.* to make a memorandum of. **-ting** *pr.p.* **-ted** *pa.p.*

joule *n. (Elect.)* the energy expended in 1 sec. by 1 ampere flowing through a resistance of 1 ohm.

jour‧nal *n.* a book recording daily transactions of a business firm; a daily newspaper; a periodical. **-ize** *v.i.* to write for a journal; to keep a daily record of events. **-ism** *n.* **-ist** *n.* one who writes professionally for a newspaper or periodical. **-istic** *a.*

jour‧ney *n.* travel from one place to another; *v.i.* to travel. **-ing** *pr.p.* **-ed** *pa.p.* **-man** *n.* a skilled mechanic or artisan who has completed his apprenticeship.

joust *n.* a tournament; *v.i.* to tilt.

Jove *n.* Jupiter. **Jovial** *a.* orig. born under the influence of the planet Jupiter; *lc* convivial. **joviality**, **jovialness** *n.* **jovially** *adv.*

jowl *n.* the cheek; the dewlap, of cattle.

joy *n.* exhilaration of spirits; *v.i.* to rejoice; to exult. **-ing** *pr.p.* **-ed** *pa.p.* **-ful** *a.* **-fully** *adv.* **-fulness** *n.* **-less** *a.* dismal. **-lessly** *adv.* **-lessness** *n.* **-ous** *a.* full of joy. **-ously** *adv.* **-ousness** *n.*

ju‧bi‧lant *a.* rejoicing. **-ly** *adv.* **jubilate** *v.i.* to rejoice; to exult. **jubilation** *n.* rejoicing; exultation.

ju‧bi‧lee *n.* the fiftieth anniversary of any outstanding event; a time of rejoicing. **silver jubilee**, the twenty-fifth anniversary. **diamond jubilee**, the sixtieth anniversary.

Ju‧da‧ism *n.* the religious doctrines of the Jewish people. **Judaical** *a.* pert. to the Jews. **Judaically** *adv.*

Ju‧das *n. (Bib.)* the disciple of Christ who betrayed him; a traitor.

judge *n.* officer authorized to hear and determine civil or criminal cases, and to administer justice; an arbitrator; *v.t.* to hear and try a case in a court of law; to give a final opinion or decision; *v.i.* to act as a judge; to come to a conclusion. **-ship** *n.* the office of a judge. **judgment** *n.* a legal decision arrived at by a judge in a court of law; discernment; an opinion.

ju‧di‧ca‧ture *n.* the power of justice; a judge's period of office. **judicable** *a.* capable of being judged. **judicative** *a.* having the power to judge. **judicatory** *a.* dispensing justice. **judicial** *a.* pert. to a court or to a judge; impartial. **judicially** *adv.* **judiciary** *n.* judicial branch of government; *a.* pert. to the courts of law; passing judgment. **judicious** *a.* prudent; showing discrimination.

ju‧do *n.* a form of jujitsu.

jug *n.* a vessel of earthenware, with handle and narrow neck; vessels for holding liquids; *v.t.* to put in a jug. **-ging** *pr.p.* **-ged** *pa.p.*

jug‧ger‧naut *n.* any fanatical idea for which people are prepared to sacrifice their lives.

jug‧gle *v.t.* to toss up and keep in motion; *v.i.* to perform tricks with the hands; to use trickery; *n.* a trick by sleight of hand. **-r** *n.* one who juggles. **-ry** *n.*

jug‧u‧lar *a.* pert. to the neck or throat; *n.* one of the large veins of the neck.

juice *n.* the liquid constituent of fruits or vegetables. **juiciness** *n.* **juicy** *a.*

ju‧jit‧su *n.* a form of wrestling, originating in Japan.

juke‧box *n.* a coin-operated phonograph.

ju‧li‧enne *n.* a clear soup containing vegetables finely shredded; *a.* of vegetables in thin strips.

Ju‧ly *n.* the seventh month of the year.

jum‧ble *v.t.* to mix in a confused mass; *v.i.* to be in a muddle; *n.* a chaotic muddle.

jum‧bo *n.* a huge person, animal, or thing.

jump *v.t.* to spring over; to skip (as page of a book); *v.i.* to lift feet from ground and alight again; *n.* a leap; a sudden, nervous

IJ

start. **-er** n. **-iness** n. nervous twitching. **-y** a. **-ing bean** n. the seed of a Mexican plant containing larva which make it appear to jump.

jum-per n. a one-piece sleeveless dress.

junc-tion n. the act of joining; a connection. **juncture** n. a joint; an exigency.

June n. the sixth month of the year.

jun-gle n. land covered with trees, tangled undergrowth, esp. the dense forests of equatorial latitudes. — **fever** n. a severe form of malaria.

ju-nior a. younger, esp. of a son with the same name as his father; n. a young person; one in a subordinate position; a student in the next to last year of study.

ju-ni-per n. a genus of evergreen coniferous shrub.

junk n. useless, discarded articles; v.t. to turn into junk. — **dealer, -man** n. one who buys and sells junk.

jun-ket n. a dessert of milk curded with flavored rennet; a pleasure excursion; v.i. to feast; to go on a pleasure trip; v.t. to entertain.

jun-ta n. a meeting; a council of state in Spain or Italy.

jun-to n. a group of conspirators.

Ju-pi-ter n. in Roman mythology, the superme ruler of heaven; the brightest of the outer planets. Also **Jove**.

ju-rid-i-cal a. the administration of justice. **-ly** adv.

ju-ris-dic-tion n. the administration of justice; legal authority; extent within which this authority may be exercised. **jurisdictive** a.

ju-ris-pru-dence n. study of the fundamental principles underlying any legal system.

ju-rist n. one versed in the law.

ju-ry n. a body of citizens selected and sworn to give a verdict from the evidence produced in court. **juror** n. one who serves on a jury.

jus-sive a. expressing a command; n. a grammatical form expressing a command.

just a. founded on fact; fair; adv. exactly; scarcely. **-ly** adv. deservedly. **-ness** n. fairness.

jus-tice n. equity; merited reward or punishment; administration of the law. **-ship** n. the office of a judge. **justiciary** a. pert. to the administration of the law.

justice of the peace (J.P.), a local officer authorized to try minor cases, administer oaths, perform marriages, etc.

jus-ti-fy v.t. to prove the justice of; to excuse. **-ing** pr.p. **justified** pa.p. **justifiable** a. defensible; excusable. **justifiableness** n. **justifiably** adv. **justification** n. vindication.

jut v.i. to project. **-ting** pr.p. **-ted** pa.t. and pa.p.

jute n. fiber of an Indian plant.

jute

ju-ve-nes-cent a. becoming young. **juvenescence** n.

ju-ve-nile a. young; youthful; n. a young person; a book written for children. **-ness, juvenility** n. **juvenilia** n.pl. works of author produced in childhood.

jux-ta-pose v.t. to place side by side. **juxtaposition** n. the act of placing side by side; contiguity.

K

kai·nite *n.* hydrated compound of the chlorides and sulfates of magnesium and potassium.

kale *n.* a hardy member of the mustard family with curled leaves.

ka·lei·do·scope *n.* an optical instrument, varying symmetrical, colorful patterns being displayed on rotation. **kaleidoscopic** *a.* ever-changing in beauty and form.

kame *n.* a high narrow ridge of gravel and sand left by a glacier.

ka·mi·ka·ze *n.* a suicide attack by Jap. pilot.

kam·pong *n.* a native of any South Sea island.

kan·ga·roo *n.* a ruminating marsupial found in Australia.

kangaroo

ka·o·lin *n.* fine porcelain clay chiefly produced from feldspar.

kar·at *n.* in fineness of gold, a twenty-fourth part (pure gold being 24 karats fine). also **carat**.

kath·ode See **cathode**.

kat·i·on, cation *n.* an electropositive ion which, in electrolysis, travels towards the cathode.

ka·ty·did *n.* a green insect of the grasshopper family.

ka·va *n.* an intoxicating Polynesian beverage.

kay·ak *n.* Eskimo sealskin canoe.

keck *v.i.* to show disgust.

keck·le *v.t.* to protect a cable from damage by fraying, by wrapping old rope around the length.

kedge *n.* a small anchor; *v.t.* to move a ship by means of small anchors.

keel *n.* the lengthwise beam of a ship on which the frames of the ship rest; *v.i.* to turn up the keel; to provide with a keel. **-haul** *v.t.* to haul under the keel of a ship by ropes attached to the yardarms. **to keel over,** *(Colloq.)* to fall over; to capsize.

keen *a.* sharp; penetrating; intense; shrewd; discerning. **-ly** *adv.*

keep *v.t.* to retain possession of; to detain; to have the care of; to cause to continue; *v.i.* to remain (in good condition); *n.* guardianship; maintenance; a stronghold. **kept** *pa.p.* and *pa.t.* **-er** *n.* one who guards; an attendant; a gamekeeper. **-ing** *n.* care; support; harmony. **-sake** *n.* anything given to recall the memory of the giver.

keg *n.* a small barrel.

kelp *n.* the calcined ash of certain seaweeds, used as a source of iodine.

Kelt, Keltic Same as **Celt, Celtic.**

kelt *n.* a salmon which has just spawned.

kemps *n.pl.* coarse rough hairs in wool.

ken *n.* range of sight.

ken·nel *n.* a shelter for dogs; an establishment where dogs are bred or lodged; *v.t.* to confine in a kennel; *v.i.* to live in a kennel. **-ling** *pr.p.*

kent·ledge *n.* pig iron placed in a ship's hold for permanent ballast.

kept *pa.t.* and *pa.p.* of **keep.**

ker·at(o)-, a horn, used in the formation of compound terms. **keratin** *n.* an essential constituent of horny tissue. **keratoid** *a.* horny. **keratosis** *n.* *(Med.)* a skin disease characterized by abnormal thickening.

ker·chief *n.* any cloth used in dress, esp. on the head or around the neck. **-ed** *a.*

ker·mis, kermess *n.* affair, usually for charitable purposes; originally a dedication service at the opening of a new church.

kern *n.* *(Print.)* a part of the face of a type projecting beyond the body, as an italic *f*.

ker·nel *n.* edible part of a nut; the body of a seed; central part.

ker·o·sene *n.* an illuminating or burning oil.

ker·sey *n.* coarse woolen cloth, usually ribbed.

ketch *n.* a small two-masted vessel.

ketch·up, catch·up, cat·sup *n.* a sauce made from mushrooms, tomatoes or walnuts.

ket·tle *n.* a metal vessel, with spout and handle, used for heating and boiling water or other liquids. **-drum** *n.* a musical percussion instrument made of a hemispherical copper shell covered with vellum. **-drummer** *n.*

key *n.* a low-lying island or reef near the coast, used esp. of Spain's former possessions off the coast of Florida.

key *n.* an instrument which shuts or opens a lock; a spanner; a lever in a musical instrument, depressed by the fingers in playing; a lever on a typewriter for actuating the mechanism; a switch adapted for making and breaking contact in an electric circuit; *(Mus.)* the keynote of a scale, or tonality; the pitch of a voice; explanation; a translation of a book, or solutions to questions set; *a.* critical; of vital importance; controlling. **-board** *n.* the whole range of keys on a keyed instrument. **-hole** *n.* a hole in a door or lock for receiving a key. **— industry** *n.* an industry on which vital interests of the country or other industries depend. **-man** *n.* an indispensable employee. **-note** *n.* *(Mus.)* the first tone of the scale in which a passage is written; the essential spirit of speech, thought, etc. **— ring** *n.* a ring for keeping a number of keys together. **— signature** *n.* *(Mus.)* the essential sharps and flats placed at the beginning of a piece after the clef to indicate the tonality. **all keyed up,** agog with excitement and expectation.

kha·ki *a.* dust-colored or buff; *n.* a cloth of this color, used for the uniforms of soldiers.

khan *n.* a title of respect in various Mohammedan countries among Mongol

181

races. **-ate** *n.* the dominion of a Khan.
khe·dive *n.* the title of the Turkish ruler of Egypt.
kick *v.t.* to strike or hit with the foot; *v.i.* to strike out with the foot; to recoil violently (of a rifle, etc.); *n.* a blow with the foot; the recoil of a gun. **-er** *n.* **-off** *n.* the commencement of a game of football. **to kick over the traces,** to throw off all restraint; to rebel openly. **dropkick** *n.* *(football)* a kick made as the ball, just dropped from the hand, rebounds from the ground. **placekick** *n.* kicking a football placed on the ground.
kid *n.* a young goat; leather made from the skin of a goat; *pl.* gloves of smooth kid leather; *a.* made of kid leather.
kid *v.t.* and *v.i.* to fool; **-ded** *n.* teasing. **-ding** *pr.p.* **-ded** *pa.p.* and *pa.t.* **-der** *n.*
kid·nap *v.t.* to carry off, abduct, or forcibly secrete a person (esp. a child). **-per** *n.* **-ping** *n.*
kid·ney *n.* one of two glandular organs in the lumbar region of the abdominal

kidney

cavity which excrete urine. **— bean,** the kidney-shaped seed of a bean plant.
kill *v.t.* to deprive of life; to put to death; to destroy; to weaken or dilute; *n.* the act of killing; animal killed. **-er** *n.* **-er whale** *n.* the grampus, a whale capable of swallowing seals, porpoises, whole. **-ing** *a.* depriving of life; *n.* the act of destroying life; game killed on a hunt; a profitable business deal. **-ingly** *adv.*
kiln *n.* furnace for burning, baking or drying something.
ki·lo- in the metric system denoting a thousand. **kilocycle** *n.* unit for measuring vibrations, esp. the frequency of electromagnetic waves, 1,000 oscillations per second. **kilogram** *n.* 1,000 grams, equal to 2.2046 lb. avoirdupois. **kiloliter** *n.* 1,000 liters. **kilometer** *n.* 1,000 meters, 3280.899 feet or nearly ⅗ of a mile. **kilowatt** *n.* an electric unit of power equal to 1,000 watts. **kilowatt-hour** *n.* one kilowatt expended for one hour.
kilt *n.* a short skirt usually of tartan cloth, deeply pleated.
ki·mo·no *n.* a flowered overgarment with short wide sleeves, worn in Japan by men and women.
kin *n.* family relations; relationship; *a.* of the same kind. **next of kin,** the person closest in relationship to a deceased person.
kind *n.* genus; variety; *a.* having a sympathetic nature; obliging. **-hearted** *a.* **-heartedness** *n.* **-liness** *n.* benevolence. **-ly** *a.* and *adv.* **-ness** *n.* kind feeling or action.

kin·der·gar·ten *n.* a school for young children.
kin·dle *v.t.* to set on fire; to excite (the passions); *v.i.* to catch fire; to become bright or glowing. **kindling** *n.* the act of starting a fire; the material for starting a fire.
kin·dred *n.* relatives by blood or marriage; *a.* related; of like nature; congenial.
ki·ne·mat·ic, ki·ne·mat·i·cal *a.* relating to pure motion. **-s** *n.pl.* branch of mechanics dealing with problems of motion.
kin·es·the·sia *n.* the perception of muscular effort. **kinesthetic** *a.* Also **kinaesthesia, kinesthesis.**
ki·net·ic, kinetical *a.* imparting or growing out of motion. **-s** *n.* the science which treats of changes in movements of matter produced by forces.
king *n.* *(fem.* **queen)** supreme ruler of a country; a playing card in each suit with a picture of a king; the chief piece in the game of chess; in checkers, a man which is crowned. **-craft** *n.* **-dom** *n.* domain; one of the great divisions (animal, vegetable, and mineral) of natural history. **-fisher** *n.* a stout-billed bird, with brilliant plumage. **-hood** *n.* kingship. **-like, -ly** *a.* **-pin** *n.* *(Fig.)* in bowling, the pin at the front apex when the pins are set up.
kink *n.* a short twist, accidentally formed, in a rope, wire, chain, etc; in the neck, a crick; a whim; *v.i.* and *v.t.* to twist spontaneously; to form a kink (in).
kins·folk *n.* blood relations; members of the same family; also **kinfolk. kinship** *n.* state of being related by birth. **kinsman, kinswoman** *n.*
kip *n.* the untanned hide of young cattle.
kip·per *n.* herring, salmon, etc. split, then smoked; *v.t.* to cure fish by splitting, salting, smoking, or drying.
kis·met *n.* fate or destiny
kiss *v.t.* and *v.i.* to touch with the lips, in affection or reverence; *n.* a salute by touching with lips. **-able** *a.* **-er** *n.* one who kisses.
kit *n.* a set of tools or implements.
kitch·en *n.* a room in which food is prepared and cooked. **-ette** *n.* a small kitchen. **— garden** *n.* a garden for raising vegetables for the table. **— police** (abbrev. **(K.P.)** *n.* soldiers on kitchen duty. **-ware** *n.* cooking utensils.
kite *n.* a sheet of paper, silk, etc., stretched over a light frame and flown by a cord attached and held from ground.
kith *n.* in phrase **kith and kin,** friends and acquaintances.
kit·ten *n.* a young cat; *v.i.* to bring forth young cats. **-ish** *a.* like a kitten; playful. **kitty** *n.* a pet name for a cat.
kit·ty *n.* the pool in card games.
Klax·on *n.* electric horn on automobiles.
klep·to·ma·ni·a *n.* an uncontrollable impulse to steal things. **-c** *n.*
klick See click.
knack *n.* inborn dexterity; adroitness; habit.
knag *n.* a knot in wood; *a.* knotty; rough.
knap·sack *n.* a bag for food and clothing, borne on the back.
knave *n.* a dishonest person; *(Cards)* a jack.

-ry *n.* trickery; sharp practice. **knavish** *a.* fraudulent; 'oguish. **knavishly** *adv.*

knead *v.t.* to 'vork dough by pressing with the heel of the hands, and folding over; to massage. **-er** *n.*

knee *n.* the joint formed by the articulation of the femur and the tibia, the two principal bones of the leg; *v.t.* to touch with the knees. **— breeches** *n.pl.* breeches fastened just below the knee. **-cap** *n.* the patella, a flattened bone in front of knee joint.

kneel *v.i.* to bend a knee to the floor; to rest on the knees as in prayer. **-ed** *or* **knelt** *pa.t.* and *pa.p.* **-ing** *n.*

knell *n.* the stroke of a bell rung at a death; a portent of doom; *v.i.* to toll; *v.t.* to summon by tolling bell.

knew *pa.t.* of **know.**

knick·er·bock·ers *n.pl.* loose breeches gathered in at the knees. Also **knickers.**

knick·knack *n.* a trifle or trinket. **-ery** *n.* knickknacks collectively.

knife *n.* a cutting instrument; *pl.* **knives;** *v.t.* to stab with a knife. **—edge** *n.* anything with a thin, sharp edge.

knight *n.* in feudal times, a young man admitted to the privilege of bearing arms; a minor piece in chess bearing a horse's head; *v.t.* to dub a knight. **-hood** *n.* the order of knights. **-liness** *n.* **-ly** *a.* and *adv.*

knit *v.t.* to form fabric by interlooping yarn by means of needles or a machine; to cause to grow together, as a fractured bone; *v.i.* to be united closely. **-ting** *pr.p.* **-ted** *pa.t.* and *pa.p.* **-ter, -ting** *n.* **-wear** *n.* knitted garments.

knives *pl.* of **knife.**

knob *n.* a rounded lump; a hard protuberance or swelling; small round handle of a door. **-bed** *a.* set with knobs. **-biness** *n.* **-by** *a.* full of knobs; lumpy.

knock *v.t.* and *v.i.* to strike with something hard or heavy; to make a periodic noise, due to a faulty bearing in a reciprocating engine or too much ignition advance in a gasoline engine; to criticize adversely; *n.* a stroke with something heavy; a rap on a door; the noise of a faulty engine. **-er** *n.* an ornamental metal attachment on a door. **— kneed** *a.* having the knees bent inward.

knoll *n.* the top of a hill; a mound.

knot *n.* a complication of threads, cords, or ropes, formed by entangling; in cordage, a method of fastening a rope to an object or to another rope; a hard lump, esp. of wood where a branch has sprung from the stem; *(Naut.)* a measure of speed of ships, equal to one nautical mile (6,080 ft.) per hour; *v.t.* to form a knot in; *v.i.* to form knots. **-ting** *pr.p.* **-ted** *pa.t.* and *pa.p.* **-hole** *n.* a hole in a board where a piece of a knot has fallen out. **-tiness** *n.* **-ty** *a.* full of knots; puzzling.

know *v.t.* to be aware of; to have information about; to have experience; *v.i.* to have information or understanding. **knew** *pa.t.* **-n** *pa.p.* **-ing** *a.* professing to know; clever. **-ingly** *adv.* **to know the ropes,** to know from experience what to do.

knowl·edge *n.* direct perception; acquaintance with; learning. **-able** *a.* well-informed.

knuck·le *n.* the joint of a finger; *v.t.* to strike with the knuckles; *v.i.* to hold the knuckles close to the ground in the game of marbles. **brass knuckles** *n.pl.* iron or brass rings fitting across the knuckles, used to deliver murderous blows. **to knuckle down,** to tackle a job vigorously. **to knuckle down** or **under,** to submit.

knurl *n.* a series of rough indentations on the edge of a thumbscrew, coin, etc.; *v.t.* to roughen edges of a circular object; to indent. **-ed** *a.*

ko·a·la *n.* a small marsupial of arboreal habit, native to Australia.

koala

Ko·dak *n.* a trademark for photographic film, apparatus and supplies.

kohl *n.* powdered lead sulfide used in the East for darkening eyebrows and eyelashes.

kohl·ra·bi *n.* a cabbage with an edible turnip-shaped stem.

ko·la *n.* an African tree whose seeds contain a large quantity of caffeine and are used as a stimulant.

kook·a·bur·ra *n.* the great kingfisher with a laugh-like cry.

Ko·ran *n.* sacred book of Islam, containing revelations received by Mohammed.

ko·sher *a.* (of food) pure, clean, esp. meat, made ceremonially clean according to Jewish ordinances.

krem·lin *n.* the citadel of a Russian city; *(cap.)* the citadel of Moscow, seat of Soviet government.

kreut·zer *n.* an Austrian monetary unit. Also **kreuzer.**

kro·ne *n.* a silver coin of Denmark and Norway; *pl.* **kroner.**

kryp·ton *n.* a nonmetallic chemical element belonging to the group of rare gases.

ku·dos *n.* fame; credit.

Ku Klux Klan *n.* a lawless secret society, founded c. 1865, to oppose granting of privileges to the freed Negroes.

knot

ku•lak *n.* a prosperous landholder in Russia who resisted the efforts of the Soviet to nationalize agriculture.

küm•mel *n.* a liqueur flavored with cumin and caraway seeds.

kum•quat *n.* a shrub, native to China and Japan, produces a small orange-like fruit.

ky•pho•sis *n.* humpback, angular deformity of the spine.

ky•ir•e *n.* the words and music of part of the service in the R.C. Church; the response in the Anglican communion service after each of the Ten Commandments.

la n. syllable for sixth tone of scale in tonic sol-fa notation.

lab•da•num n. a fragrant resin used in perfumes, etc.

la•bel n. paper, card, etc., affixed to anything, denoting its contents, nature, ownership, destination, etc.

la•bel•lum n. the posterior petal of a flower of the orchid type.

la•bi•al a. pert. to the lips; formed by the lips, as certain speech sounds such as p, b, w, o; n. a sound formed by the lips. **labiate, -d** n. with calyx or corolla formed in two parts, resembling lips.

la•bi•o•den•tal a. pert. to the lips and teeth; n. a sound made with the lips and teeth, as f and v. **labium** n. a lip or lip-like structure.

la•bor n. exertion of body or mind; toil; work demanding patience and endurance; manual workers collectively or politically; (Med.) the pains of childbirth; v.i. to work strenuously; to take pains; to move with difficulty. — **union** n. an organization of workers for mutual aid and protection and for collective bargaining.

lab•o•ra•to•ry n. a place used for experiments or research in science, pharmacy, etc.

la•bret n. an ornament inserted into a hole pierced in the lip, worn by some primitive tribes. **labral** a. **labrose** a. having thick lips.

la•bur•num n. a small, hardy deciduous tree.

lab•y•rinth n. a system of intricate winding passages; a maze.

lac, lakh n. one hundred thousand, as a lac of rupees.

lac n. a deep-red, resinous substance, the excretion of an insect, found especially on trees in southern Asia, and used as a dye, in varnishes, sealing wax, etc.

lace n. a string or cord used for fastening dress, shoes, etc.; a net-like fabric of linen, cotton or silk with ornamental design interwoven by hand or machine. **lacing** n. a fastening formed by a lace threaded through eyeholes.

lac•er•ate v.t. to tear; to rend; to injure; to afflict sorely.

lach•ry•mal a. pert. to or producing tears, as lachrymal duct, the tear duct.

lack v.t. and v.i. to be destitute of; to want; n. deficiency; shortage; need; want. **-luster** a. dim; wanting in brightness.

lack•a•dai•si•cal a. affectedly pensive or languid.

lack•ey n. a liveried manservant; a footman; a follower.

la•con•ic a. brief; concise; expressing maximum meaning in the minimum of words.

lac•quer, lacker n. a varnish consisting of a solution of shellac in alcohol.

la•crosse n. an outdoor ball game played with a crosse or stick which has a net at the end.

lac•te•al a. pert. to milk; milky; resembling chyle. **lactate** n. a salt of lactic acid; v.i. to produce milk. **lactation** n. the act of giving or secreting milk. **lacteous** a. resembling milk. **lactic** a. pert. to milk; procured from milk or whey, as lactic acid. **lactose** n. milk-sugar.

la•cu•na n. a hollow; a hiatus; an omission.

lad n. a young man; a boy.

lad•der n. a frame of wood, steel, ropes, etc., consisting of two sides connected by rungs for climbing.

lade v.t. to load; to burden; to draw by means of a ladle.

la•dle n. a long-handled spoon.

la•dy n. a well-bred woman; orig. a woman having authority over a household or estate; a woman of social distinction, position.

lag v.t. to bind round, as pipes, boiler, etc., with non-conducting material to prevent loss of heat.

lag n. time lapse; retardation; v.i. to move slowly; to fall behind.

la•ger-beer n. a light German beer.

la•goon n. a shallow pond or lake.

la•ic a. lay; secular; n. a layman.

laid pa.t. and pa.p. of the verb lay; a. put down; (of paper) having a slightly ribbed surface showing the marks of the close parallel wires on which pulp was laid.

lain pa.p. of verb lie.

lair n. a den or bed of a wild animal; a place to rest.

lais•sez-faire n. a policy of non-interference.

la•i•ty n. the people, as distinct from those specially skilled; lay.

lake n. a large sheet of water within land.

lake n. a deep-red coloring matter.

lakh Same as lac.

la•ma n. a Buddhist priest in Tibet. **Lamaism** n. form of Buddhist religion practiced in Tibet.

lamb n. the young of a sheep; the flesh of lamb as food; a young and innocent person.

lam•bent a. playing on the surface; gleaming; flickering.

lame a. crippled in a limb; hobbling; (Fig.) unsatisfactory, as an excuse; imperfect; v.t. to cripple.

lam•é n. a textile containing metal threads giving a gold or silver effect.

la•mel•la n. a thin, plate-like structure or scale.

la•ment v.i. to utter cries of sorrow; to bemoan; to mourn for; v.t. to deplore; n. a heartfelt expression of sorrow; an elegy or dirge. **lamentable** a. grievous; sad. **Book of Lamentations** (Bib.) one of the poetical books of the Old Testament.

lam•i•na n. a thin plate or scale lying over another; (Bot.) the blade of a leaf. pl. **laminae, laminable, laminar, laminary** a. consisting of, or resembling, thin plates. **laminate** v.t. to cause to split into thin plates; to make into thin layers (as metal).

lamp n. a vessel containing combustible oil to be burned by a wick, or inflammable gas from a jet; any light-giving contrivance.

lam•poon n. a bitter personal satire, usually in verse; abusive or scurrilous publication.

la·nate *a.* wooly; *(Bot.)* covered with fine hairs resembling wool.

lance *n.* a former war weapon consisting of a spearhead on a long wooden shaft. *v.t.* to pierce with a lance; to open with a lancet. **lancet** *n.* a small two-edged surgical knife. **lancet arch** *n.* narrow, pointed arch. **a free lance**, one who acts on his own initiative; a journalist not attached to the staff of any particular newspaper.

lan·ci·nate *v.t.* to tear; to lacerate.

land *n.* earth; the solid matter of surface of globe; any area of the earth; ground; soil; the inhabitants of a country; real estate. **-fall** *n.* sighting of land by a ship at sea. **— grant** *n.* a grant of land from the government esp. for colleges, railroads, etc. **-holder** *n.* a proprietor of land. **-ing** *n.* the act of coming to land; disembarkation; the level part of a staircase between two flights of steps. **-ing gear** *n.* the wheeled under-carriage of an airplane on which it rests when landing or taking off. **-lady** *n.* the owner of property who leases land, buildings, etc. to tenants. **-locked** *a.* enclosed by land. **-lord** *n.* the owner of houses rented to tenants; the proprietor of an inn, etc. **-mark** *n.* a mark to indicate a boundary; any outstanding or elevated object indicating general direction or distinguishing a particular locality. **— mine** *n.* military high-explosive bomb. **-scape** *n.* that portion of land which the eye can comprehend in a single view. **-scape architecture** *n.* art of aesthetically arranging or changing features of the landscape. **-scape gardener**, one who is employed professionally to lay out gardens, etc. **-scapist** *n.* a painter of landscape. **-slide** *n.* a fall of rock from a hillside or cliff.

lan·dau *n.* a carriage, the top of which may be opened and thrown back. **landaulet**, **landaulette** *n.* an automobile with folding hood.

land·grave *n.* a German nobleman.

lane *n.* a narrow track between hedges or across fields; a narrow street or road; a specified route followed by ships or airplanes; part of a street or highway for one line of traffic.

lan·guage *n.* speech; expression of ideas by words or written symbols; mode of speech peculiar to a nation, a class, profession, etc.; communication of animals, etc.

lan·guid *a.* indifferent; listless; flagging from exhaustion. **languish** *v.i.* to become languid; to droop with weariness; to pine or suffer; to become wistful. **languor** *n.* lassitude; sentimental softness.

lan·gur *n.* a long-tailed Indian monkey.

lank *a.* drooping; gaunt and thin; long and straight, as hair. **-y** *a.* tall and slender.

lan·o·lin, **lanoline** *n.* an oily substance obtained from wool.

lan·tern *n.* something portable or fixed, enclosing a light and protecting it from wind, rain, etc.

lan·yard, **laniard** *n.* a short rope or line for fastening; a cord, with knife attached, worn round the neck.

La·od·i·ce·an *a.* like the Christians of *Laodicea*; lukewarm in religion; lacking strong feeling on any subject.

lap *n.* that part of the clothing between waist and knees of a person who is sitting; the part of the body thus covered; an, overlying part of any substance or fixture; a course or circuit, as in bicycle-racing, etc. **-el** *n.* that part of a coat or dress which laps over the facing. **-pet** *n.* a part of a garment which hangs loose; a fold of flesh.

lap *v.i.* to take up food or drink by licking; to make a sound like an animal lapping its food.

lap·i·dar·y *a.* pert. to stones or to the art of cutting stones. **lapidate** *v.t.* to stone (to death). **lapillus** *n.* a small, rounded fragment of lava. *pl.* **lapilli**, **lapis lazuli** *n.* an opaque mineral, sapphire-blue in color, much used in jewelry, ornaments, mosaics, etc.

Lapp *n.* a native of Lapland.

lapse *v.i.* to slip or fall; to fail to maintain a standard of conduct; to pass from one proprietor to another because of negligence; to pass slowly or by degrees. **lapsable** *a.* **-d** *a.* no longer valid or operative.

lar·ce·ny *n.* theft. **larcenist** *n.* a thief. **larcenous** *a.* thieving; pilfering.

larch *n.* a genus of cone-bearing, deciduous trees.

lard *n.* the clarified fat of swine; *v.t.* to smear with fat; to stuff, as meat or fowl, with bacon or pork.

lard·er *n.* a pantry where meat and food stuffs are kept; supply of provisions.

large *a.* of great size; spacious; extensive; liberal; numerous; extravagant.

lar·gess *n.* a generous gift; a donation.

lar·ghet·to *a.* *(Mus.)* rather slow; less slow than *largo*. **largo** *(Mus.)* *a.* and *adv.* slow and stately.

lar·i·at *n.* a lasso; a rope or thong of leather, with a noose for catching wild horses, etc.

lark *n.* a frolic; a prank; *v.i.* to play practical jokes.

lark *n.* a small songbird.

lar·rup *v.t.* to thrash.

lar·va *n.* an insect in the caterpillar, grub, or maggot stage.

lar·ynx *n.* the upper part of the trachea or windpipe; a cartilaginous cavity

larynx

containing the vocal cords. **laryngitis** *n.* inflammation of the larynx.

las·civ·i·ous *a.* loose; lustful; wanton.

lash *n.* the thong of a whip; a cord; a stroke with a whip; a satirical or sarcastic reproof; an eyelash.

lass *n.* a young woman; a girl; a sweetheart. **lassie** *n.* a little girl.

las·si·tude *n.* exhaustion of body or mind; languor.

las·so *n.* a long rope with a noose, used for catching wild horses.

last *a.* following all the rest; most recent; most unlikely; final; supreme. **the Last Supper,** the memorial supper celebrated by Jesus on the eve of his betrayal.

last *n.* a model of the human foot in wood on which shoes are made or repaired.

last *v.i.* to continue in time; to endure; to remain unimpaired in strength or quality; to suffice.

las·tex *n.* a fine rubber thread wound with cotton, rayon, or silk and woven into cloth or knitted into fabrics.

lat·a·ki·a *n.* a superior quality of Turkish tobacco from *Latakia* in Syria.

latch *n.* a small piece of iron or wood used to fasten a door; a catch.

late *a.* behindhand; coming after; delayed; earlier than the present time; occurring at the close of a period of time; no longer in office; deceased. **latter** *a.* later or more recent; the second of two just mentioned; modern. **latterly** *adv.* **of late,** recently.

la·tent *a.* not visible or apparent; dormant; hid; concealed. — **heat,** heat which is absorbed in changing a body from solid to liquid, or liquid to gas, without increasing its temperature.

lat·er·al *a.* relating to the side.

Lat·er·an *n.* the Pope's cathedral Church in Rome.

la·tex *n.* the milky sap of trees, plants; the milky juice of the rubber tree.

lath *n.* a thin, narrow slip of wood to support plaster, slates, etc. **-er** *n.* **-ing** *n.* the process of constructing with laths; the work done.

lathe *n.* a machine-tool for turning articles of wood, metal, etc.

lath·er *n.* foam or froth made with soap and water; froth from sweat.

Lat·in *a.* pert. to *Latium,* a part of ancient Italy with Rome as its chief center, or its inhabitants; written or spoken in Latin. — **America,** parts of Central and South America where Romance languages are spoken. — **Church,** the Roman Catholic Church using Latin as its official language.

lat·i·tude *n.* distance, measured in degrees, north or south of the equator; any region defined according to latitude; the angular distance of a heavenly body from the ecliptic. **latitudinarian** *a.* broad; liberal, esp. in religious principles; *n.* one who departs from, or is indifferent to, strictly orthodox religious principles.

la·trine *n.* a toilet, esp. in barracks, hospitals, etc.

lat·ten *n.* a metallic alloy of copper and zinc, with appearance of brass; metal in thin sheets.

lat·tice *n.* framework of wood, metal, etc., formed by strips, laths, or bars crossing each other; a gate, trellis, or window thus formed.

Lat·vi·an *a.* pert. to the Baltic state of Latvia; Lettish.

laud *v.t.* to praise in words or singing; to extol; *n.* a eulogy; praises.

laugh *v.i.* to express mirth spontaneously; to make an involuntary explosive sound of amusement; to be merry or gay. **-ing gas** *n.* nitrous oxide gas used as anesthetic in dental operations. **-ing hyena** *n.* the spotted hyena with a peculiar cry like a human laugh. **-ing stock** *n.* object of ridicule.

launch, lanch *v.t.* to throw as a lance; to let fly; to cause to slide into the water for the first time, as a ship. — **vehicle** *n.* a rocket used to place a satellite or space vehicle in orbit. **-ing pad** *n.* platform from which a missile is fired by remote control.

launch *n.* the largest boat carried on a warship; an open boat driven by steam, gasoline, or electricity.

laun·dry *n.* a place where clothes are washed, dried, and ironed; the process of washing clothes, etc. **launder** *v.t.* to wash clothes; *n.* (*Mining*) a long hollow trough for conveying powdered ore from the box where it is bruised.

lau·rel *n.* evergreen shrub, much used formerly to make wreaths symbolic of honor. **laureate** *a.* crowned with laurel.

la·va *n.* the molten rock, ejected by a volcano, hardening as it cools.

la·va·bo *n.* ceremonial washing of a celebrant's hands after the offertory and before the eucharist.

lave *v.t.* (*Poetic*) to wash; to bathe; *v.i.* to bathe; to wash oneself. **lavatory** *n.* a place for washing.

lav·en·der *n.* an aromatic plant of mint family, yielding an essential oil; pale-lilac color of lavender flowers; dried flowers used as a sachet.

lav·ish *a.* over-generous; extravagant; ample.

law *n.* a rule established by authority; a body of rules the practice of which is authorized by a community or state; legal science; established usage; a rule, principle, or maxim of science, art, etc. **—abiding** *a.* well-behaved; conforming to the law. — **court** *n.* a court in which lawcases are heard and judged. **-ful** *a.* allowed by law. — **officer** *n.* a policeman. **-suit** *n.* a process in law for recovery of a supposed right. **-yer** *n.* a practitioner of law. **common law,** body of laws established more by custom than by definite legislation. **written law,** statute law, codified and written down, as distinct from *Common law.*

lawn *n.* a stretch of closely-cut, carefully-tended grass. — **mower** *n.* a machine for cutting grass.

lawn *n.* a fine linen or cambric.

lax *a.* slack; flabby; loose, esp. in moral sense; careless; not constipated. **-ative** *a.* having purgative effect.

lay *v.t.* to place or put down; to apply; to beat down, as corn; to cause to subside; to exorcise, as an evil spirit; to spread on a surface; to wager; to produce, to

L

prepare; to station, as an ambush; to form, as a plot; to set out dishes, etc. (on a table). **laid**. *n.* a situation; disposition. **-erage** *n.* the artificial propagation of plants by layers.

lay *pa.t.* of **lie** (to recline).

lay *n.* a song; a narrative poem such as was recited by minstrels.

lay *a.* pert. to the laity, as distinct from the clergy; unprofessional. **laicize** *v.t.* to deprive of clerical character.

lay•ette *n.* a complete outfit for a new-born baby.

laz•ar *n.* a person afflicted with a loathsome disease, like *Lazarus*, the beggar.

laze *v.i.* to be lazy; to lounge.

la•zy *a.* disinclined to exertion; slothful.

lea *n.* a meadow; land left untilled; pasturage.

leach *v.t.* to wash by causing water to pass through; *(Bot.)* to remove salts from soil by percolation.

lead *n.* a well-known malleable bluish-grey metal, ductile and heavy, used for roofing, pipes, etc.; a plummet for sounding ocean depths; a thin strip of type metal to separate lines of print; graphite for pencils; bullets. **— poisoning** *n.* a form of poisoning called plumbism caused by lead being absorbed into the blood and tissues.

lead *v.t.* to show the way; to guide; to direct; to persuade; to precede. **-er** *n.* a guide; a conductor; a commander. **-ership** *n.* the state or function of a leader. **-ing** *n.* direction; the act of guiding. **-ing-article** *n.* a leader or editorial in a newspaper. **-ing-lady, -man** *n.* the actress (or actor) playing the principal role. **-ing-question** *n.* *(Law)* a question so phrased as to suggest the answer expected. **to lead astray**, to tempt from virtue.

leaf *n.* thin deciduous shoot from the stem or branch of a plant; one of the sections

leaf

of a dropleaf or extension table; a hinged flap; a very thinly beaten plate, as of gold. **-age** *n.* leaves collectively; foliage. **-iness** *n.* **-less** *a.* devoid of leaves. **-let** *n.* a tiny leaf; a printed sheet advertisement, notice of meeting, etc. **— mold** *n.* leaves decayed and reduced to mold, used as manure.

league *n.* an old nautical measure equal to three geographical miles.

league *n.* a compact made between nations or individuals for mutual aid and the promoting of common interests.

lea•guer *n.* a military camp, esp. a siege camp.

leak *n.* a crack, crevice, fissure, or hole in a vessel; the oozing of liquid from such; *(Elect.)* an escape of electrical current from a faulty conductor.

lean *v.t.* to incline; to cause to rest against; *v.i.* to deviate from the perpendicular; to

incline. **-ing** *n.* inclination (of body or mind). **— to** *n.* a shed built against a wall or side of a house or supported at one end by posts or trees.

lean *a.* thin; wanting in flesh or fat; *(Fig.)* empty; impoverished.

leap *v.i.* to spring; to jump up or forward; to vault. **-frog** *n.* a game, in which one stoops down, and another vaults over his head. **— year** *n.* a year of 366 days.

learn *v.t.* to acquire knowledge; to get to know; to gain skill by practice.

lease *n.* a contract renting lands, houses, farms, etc., for a specified time; time covered by lease; any tenure. **— hold** *a.* held on lease.

leash *n.* a line by which a hawk, dog, or other animal is held.

least *a.* *(superl.* of **little**) smallest; faintest; most minute. **at least,** at any rate.

leath•er *n.* the skin of an animal dressed and prepared for use. **-back** *n.* a large sea turtle. **— bound** *a.* (of a book) bound in calf, morocco, or other leather. **patent leather,** leather with shiny, varnished surface.

leave *n.* liberty granted; formal good-bye; furlough; permission to be temporarily absent from duty.

leave *v.t.* to quit; to forsake; to omit; to remove; to allow to remain unaltered; to bequeath; to permit; to entrust; to refer.

leav•en *n.* a substance due to fermentation which causes bread dough to rise.

lech•er *n.* a man given to lewdness; a fornicator. **-ous** *a.* lascivious; lustful.

lec•tern *n.* a reading desk in a church.

lec•tion *n.* a variation in copies of a manuscript; a portion of scripture read during a church service. **lector** *n.* a reader; a minor ecclesiastic in the early church; a lecturer in a college or university.

lec•ture *n.* a discourse on any subject; a formal reproof. **-r** *n.* one who lectures; an assistant to a professor in a university department.

led *pa.t.* and *pa.p.* of verb **lead.**

ledge *n.* a projection, as from a wall or cliff; a shelf; a ridge of rock near the surface of the sea.

ledg•er *n.* a book in which a business firm enters all debit and credit items in summary form; a cash book; a flat stone lying horizontally as on a grave. **— line** *n.* a line with hook and sinker to keep it stationary.

lee *n.* a place protected from the wind; shelter. **-board** *n.* a plank lowered on the side of a boat to diminish its drifting to leeward. **-gage** *n.* the sheltered side. **-ward** *a.* pert. to, or in, the direction towards which the wind is blowing. **-way** *n.* the side movement of a vessel to the leeward of her course; loss of progress.

leech *n.* a blood-sucking worm used for bloodletting.

leek *n.* a biennial bulbous plant allied to the onion; also, the national emblem of Wales.

leer *n.* a sly or furtive look expressive of malignity, lasciviousness, or triumph.

leer•y *a.* wary; suspicious.

lees *n.pl.* the sediment which settles at the bottom of a wine-cask; dregs.

left *a.* on the side of the body which is westward when one is facing north. **—handed** *a.* using the left hand more easily than the right; awkward. **— wing** *n.* a political group with extremist views.

leg *n.* the limb of an animal used in supporting the body and in walking, esp. that part of the limb between the knee and the foot. **-ging** *n.* a garment to cover the legs.

leg•a•cy *n.* a bequest; a gift of personal property by will. **legatee** *n.* one who receives a legacy.

le•gal *a.* pert. to, or according to, the law; defined by law; statutory; binding; constitutional. **— tender**, the form of money, coin, or notes, which may be lawfully used in paying a debt.

leg•ate *n.* Pope's highest diplomatic envoy; a diplomatic minister below ambassadorial rank. **legation** *n.* a minister and his staff.

le•ga•to *adv.* (*Mus.*) in a smooth, gliding manner.

leg•end *n.* orig. a chronicle of the lives of the saints; any traditional story of ancient times; an inscription on a coin, medal, etc.

le•ger•de•main *n.* a sleight of hand; trickery.

Leg•horn *n.* a plaited straw, from Leghorn in Italy; a hat made of this straw; a breed of domestic fowl.

leg•i•ble *a.* capable of being read.

le•gion *n.* in ancient Rome, a body of infantry of from three to six thousand; a military force; a great number.

leg•is•late *v.i.* to make or enact laws. **legislation** *n.* act of legislating; laws made. **legislative** *a.* having power to make laws; constitutional. **legislature** *n.* the body empowered to make and repeal laws.

le•git•i•mate *a.* lawful; in accordance with the law; born in lawful wedlock; justifiable; reasonable; genuine. **legitimation** *n.* the act of investing with the rights and privileges of lawful birth.

leg•ume *n.* a seed pod with two valves and having the seeds attached at one suture, as the pea; a plant bearing seed-pods.

lei *n.* a garland of flowers worn around the neck.

lei•sure *n.* freedom from occupation; spare time; *a.* unoccupied.

leit•mo•tif *n.* (*Mus.*) a theme associated with a person or idea, constantly recurring in a composition.

lem•ma *n.* (*Math.*) a subsidiary proposition; (*Logic*) a premise taken for granted; a theme; a heading of an entry.

lem•on *n.* an oval-shaped fruit with rind pale yellow in color and containing very acid pulp and juice.

le•mur *n.* one of a family of nocturnal monkey-like mammals found in Madagascar.

lend *v.t.* to grant the temporary use of, to give in general; to let out money at interest.

lend-lease *v.t.* to grant (material aid) to a foreign country in accordance with the Lend-Lease Act of March 11, 1941.

length *n.* the measurement of anything from end to end; extension; duration of time.

le•ni•ent *a.* clement; acting without severity.

lens *n.* (*Optics*) a piece of glass or other transparent substance ground with one or both sides curved so as to refract rays

lens

of light, and thereby modify vision; the crystalline biconvex tissue between the cornea and retina of the eye.

Lent *n.* the season of 40 days from Ash Wednesday until Easter Day.

len•tic•u•lar *a.* shaped like a lens or lentil; resembling a double-convex lens.

len•til *n.* a Mediterranean plant allied to the bean.

l'en•voi *n.* a kind of postscript to a poem; a short, final stanza.

Le•o *n.* the lion, the fifth sign of the Zodiac which the sun enters about July 22nd.

leo•pard *n.* a large carnivorous member of the cat family, of a yellow or fawn color with black spots.

le•o•tard *n.* a one-piece, tight-fitting garment worn by dancers.

lep•er *n.* a person afflicted with leprosy; (*Fig.*) an outcast. **leprosy** *n.* a chronic contagious disease affecting skin, tissues and nerves.

Lep•i•dop•ter•a *n.pl.* an order of insects having four wings covered with gossamer scales, as moths, butterflies, etc.

lep•re•chaun *n.* a sprite; a brownie commonly referred to in Irish folk-stories.

Les•bi•an *a.* pert. to the island of Lesbos (Mytilene) in the Aegean Sea, or to the ancient school of lyric poets there; amatory; *n.* a woman who is sexually attracted to another woman; a homosexual woman.

lese maj•es•ty *n.* (*Law*) a crime committed against the sovereign, or sovereign power of a state; high treason.

le•sion *n.* (*Med.*) any morbid change in the structure or functioning of the living tissues of the body; injury.

less *a.* smaller in size; not equal to in number; lower; inferior.

les•see *n.* one to whom a lease is granted.

les•son *n.* a reading; a piece of instruction; something to be learned by pupils.

let *v.t.* to allow; to give permission.

le•thal *a.* deadly; mortal.

leth•ar•gy *n.* unnaturally heavy drowsiness; overpowering lassitude; inertia.

le•the *n.* oblivion.

let•ter *n.* a mark or symbol used to represent an articulate, elementary sound; a written or printed communication. — **file** *n.* a device for holding letters for reference. **-head** *n.* printed heading on business stationery. **-press** *n.* printed matter as distinct from illustrations, diagrams, etc.; print. **letter of credit,** a letter authorizing money to be paid by a bank to the bearer. **letters patent,** a document under seal of the state, granting some property privileges or authority, or conferring the exclusive right to use an invention or design.

Let•tic *a.* pert. to the Letts or to their language. **Letts** *n.pl.* the inhabitants of Lithuania and Latvia.

let•tuce *n.* a common garden plant, used in salads.

leu•co•cyte *n.* one of the white corpuscles of the blood, destroying bacteria.

leu•ke•mi•a, leukaemia *n.* a disease characterized by an excessive number of white corpuscles in the blood.

Le•vant *n.* Eastern Mediterranean countries.

le•va•tor *n.* a muscle in the body which raises any part, as the eyelid, lips, etc.

lev•ee *n.* a reception; orig. a reception held by royal personage on rising from bed.

lev•ee *n.* a river embankment to prevent flooding.

lev•el *n.* a line or plane which is everywhere parallel to the horizon; the horizontal plane on which a thing rests; a state of equality; an instrument for finding or drawing a true horizontal line. **-ing rod** *n.* a graduated rod used in surveying.

lev•er *n.* a bar used to exert pressure or sustain a weight at one point of its length by receiving a force or power at a second, and turning at a third on a fixed point called a fulcrum; a crowbar for forcing open.

le•vi•a•than *n.* a huge aquatic animal; a whale; a sea-monster; anything of colossal size.

lev•i•ta•tion *n.* the act of making buoyant or light; the phenomenon of heavy bodies being made to float in air by spiritual agencies.

Le•vite *n.* one of the tribe of Levi; lesser priest in ancient Jewish synagogue. **Leviticus** *n.* (*Bib.*) third book of Old Testament.

lev•i•ty *n.* lightness; buoyancy; lack of seriousness.

le•vo•ro•ta•tion *n.* counterclockwise or left-hand rotation.

lev•u•lose *n.* fruit sugar found in honey and certain fruits.

lev•y *v.t.* to raise by assessment, as taxes; to enlist or collect, as troops; to impose, as a fine.

lewd *a.* obscene; indecent; given to unlawful indulgence.

lew•is *n.* an iron clamp dove-tailed into a stone block to raise it.

lex•i•con *n.* a dictionary, esp. of Greek, Latin, or Hebrew. **lexicographer** *n.* one who compiles a dictionary.

li•a•ble *a.* obliged in law or equity; subject; answerable; responsible. **liability** *n.* the state of being liable;

responsibility; obligation.

li•ai•son *n.* a union; connection; illicit intimacy between a man and a woman.

li•a•na *n.* a climbing tropical plant.

li•ar *n.* one who tells lies.

li•ba•tion *n.* the ceremonial pouring of wine in honor of some deity.

li•bel *n.* a defamatory writing or printed picture; (*Law*) a written statement by the plaintiff of his allegations in a law case.

lib•er•al *a.* open-minded; generous; catholic; unbiased; (in politics) favoring democratic or progressive ideals, and freedom of religion. **liberate** *v.t.* to set free. **liberator** *n.* one who sets others free, esp. from tyranny.

lib•er•ty *n.* freedom from bondage or restraint; power to act according to one's natural rights as an individual; privilege; undue freedom of act or speech. **libertine** *n.* one who leads a dissolute life.

li•bi•do *n.* in psychology, the emotional craving behind all human impulse; esp. used by Freud to denote the sex-urge.

Li•bra *n.* the balance, the 7th sign of the Zodiac.

li•brar•y *n.* a collection of books; the room or building which contains it. **librarian** *n.* the person in charge of a library. **— science** *n.* the knowledge and skills required for library service.

li•brate *v.i.* to be poised; to oscillate. **libration** *n.* balancing; a quivering motion.

li•bret•to *n.* the words of an opera or oratorio.

Lib•y•an *a.* pert. to *Libya* in N. Africa or to the language of the district.

li•cense *n.* authority granted to do any act; a legal permit; excess of liberty; *v.t.* to permit by grant of authority. **licentiate** *n.* one who has a license to practice a profession.

li•chen *n.* one of an order of cellular flowerless plants; (*Med.*) a skin eruption.

lic•it *a.* lawful; allowable.

lick *v.t.* to pass or draw the tongue over; to lap; to take in by the tongue; to touch lightly. **-ing** *n.* a lapping with tongue; a flogging; a beating.

lic•o•rice, liquorice *n.* a Mediterranean plant, the root of which contains a sweet juice; the brittle, black substance extracted from the roots of this plant, and used medicinally and in candy.

lic•tor *n.* an officer who attended a Roman magistrate, bearing the fasces.

lid *n.* a cover of a vessel or box; the covering of the eye.

lie *v.i.* to utter untruth; to misrepresent; to deceive; to make false statement.

lie *v.i.* to be recumbent; to be in a horizontal position or nearly so.

lie•der *n.pl.* German lyrics set to music; *sing.*

lief *adv.* gladly; willingly.

li•en *n.* (*Law*) a legal claim upon real or personal property for the satisfaction of some debt or duty.

lieu *n.* place; stead, as in phrase 'in *lieu of*'.

lieu•ten•ant *n.* a deputy; an officer who takes the place of a superior in his absence. — **governor** n. state official ranking below a governor.

life n. existence; vitality; condition of plants, animals, etc. in which they exercise functional powers; the span between birth and death; mode of living; narrative of a person's history; animation. — **assurance** or **insurance** n. insurance of a person's life. — **belt** n. a belt either inflated, or made buoyant with cork, for keeping person afloat in case of shipwreck. **-boat** n. a special type of boat, designed for stability in stormy seas, for

lifeboat

saving of human lives — **expectancy** n. probable life span. **-guard** n. someone employed at a swimming pool, etc. to prevent accidents. — **history** n. the cycle of life of a person, organism, etc. — **interest** n. interest in an estate or business which continues during one's life, but which cannot be bequeathed by will. — **jacket** n. a life belt. **-less** a. inanimate; dead; inert. **-like** a. like a living creature; resembling closely. **-long** a. lasting a lifetime. — **preserver** n. any apparatus (as life belt, -buoy, -line) for preserving or rescuing life. **-saver** n. someone who rescues a person, esp. from drowning. **-size** a. resembling in proportions the living model. **-time** n. the duration of person's life. **-work** n. any task, usually creative, demanding a lifetime's work.

lift v.t. to raise; to take up and remove; to elevate socially; to exalt spiritually.

lig•a•ment n. anything which binds one thing to another; (*Anat.*) strong fibrous tissue bands connecting the bones of the body; a bond.

light v.i. to come to by chance; to alight; to settle.

light a. having little weight; not heavy; easy; active; nimble. **-en** v.t. to make less heavy; to jettison; to enliven. **—fingered** a. dexterous, esp. in picking pockets. **—footed** a. agile. **—handed** a. delicate of touch; empty-handed. **—headed** a. delirious; frivolous. **—hearted** a. carefree; gay. **—minded** a. frivolous. **—s** n.pl. the lungs of a slaughtered animal. **-some** a. lively; cheerful.

light n. that form of radiant energy which stimulates visual perception; anything which has luminosity; day; illumination; a source of illumination. **-er** n. a mechanical device for producing a flame, as a cigarette-lighter. **-house** n. a tower-like structure built at danger points on seacoast and provided with very powerful light to serve as warning

to ships. — **year** n. (*Astron.*) the distance in a year (calculated at 5,878,000,000,000 miles) light travels. **Northern Lights,** aurora borealis.

lighthouse

light•ning n. a flash produced by an electrical discharge between two clouds, or between cloud and ground. — **bug** n. a firefly. — **rod** n. a rod serving, by a connected wire called a **lightning-conductor,** to carry electric current into the earth or water.

lig•ne•ous a. woody; resembling wood. **lignify** v.t. to convert into wood. **lignin** n. an organic substance formed in the woody tissues of plants. **lignite** n. coal of recent origin still showing ligneous texture; brown coal.

lig•ure n. a precious stone.

like a. equal; similar; n. an equal; a person or thing resembling another; an exact resemblance. **-lihood** n. probability. **-ly** a. probable; credible; of excellent qualities; adv. probably.

like v.t. to be pleased with or attracted by; to enjoy; to approve.

li•lac n. a shrub, with delicately perfumed flower clusters, purple, pale mauve, or white in color.

lilt n. a light or rhythmic tune; v.t. and v.i. to sing.

li•ly n. a bulbous plant, with fragrant and showy bell-shaped flowers; a. resembling a lily; pure; pale; delicate. **—livered** a. cowardly. **—white** a. pure white; unsullied.

limb n. an extremity of the human body, as an arm or leg; a branch of a tree.

limb n. an edge or border.

lim•ber a. easily bent; pliant; supple.

lim•bo n. a region intermediate between heaven and hell in which the souls of unbaptized children etc., are confined after death.

lime n. a tree which produces a small sour kind of lemon; the fruit of this tree.

lime n. birdlime; oxide of calcium; white, caustic substance obtained from limestone, shells, marble, etc.; a calcium compound to enrich soil. **-kiln** n. a furnace in which limestone is heated to produce lime. **-light** n. a powerful light, as on a stage; the public view. **-stone** n. a rock consisting chiefly of carbonate of lime.

li•men n. the threshold of consciousness.

lim•er•ick n. a five-lined nonsense verse.

lim•it n. boundary; edge; utmost extent. **-able** a. that may be bounded or restricted. **-ary** a. of, pert. to, or serving as

L

a limit; restricted. **limited liability,** said of a joint stock company in which liability of the shareholder is in proportion to the amount of his stock.

limn *v.t.* to draw or paint; to illuminate a manuscript. **limner** *n.* painter; one who decorates books with pictures.

lim·ou·sine *a.* pert. to a type of closed automobile with roof over the driver's head; *n.* a closed car.

limp *v.i.* to walk lamely; *n.* lameness.

limp *a.* wanting in stiffness, as covers of a book; flaccid; flexible.

lim·pet *n.* a small, univalve conical shaped shellfish which clings firmly to rocks.

limpet

lim·pid *a.* clear; translucent; crystal.

linch·pin *n.* a pin used to prevent a wheel from sliding off the axle tree.

lin·den *n.* a tree with yellowish flowers and heart-shaped leaves.

line *n.* a rope, wire or string; a slender cord; a thread-like mark; an extended stroke; a boundary; a row or continued series; progeny; a verse; a short letter or note; a course of conduct, thought, or policy; a trend; a department; a trade, business or profession. **lineage** *n.* descendants in a line from common progenitor; pedigree. **lineation** *n.* the act of marking with lines; the lines marked or engraved. **-d** *a.* marked with lines; ruled. — **engraving** *n.* a process of engraving lines on a copper plate. **-r** *n.* a steamship or passenger aircraft belonging to a regular transport line. **linesman** *n.* one who installs and repairs telephone and electric lines, etc.; an official (at football or tennis match) who determines whether ball has crossed the outside line or not.

line *v.t.* to cover on the inside, as a garment, pan, etc. **lining** *n.* the material used.

lin·en *n.* thread or cloth made from flax; underclothing; napery; *a.* made of flax or linen.

lin·ger *v.i.* to delay; to dally; to loiter.

lin·ge·rie *n.* orig. linen goods; women's underclothing.

lin·go *n.* language; a dialect.

lin·gual *a.* pert. to the tongue; *n.* a sound or letter made by the tongue, as *d, l, n.* **-ly** *adv.* **linguiform** *a.* shaped like a tongue. **linguist** *n.* fluent speaker of several languages; an expert in linguistics. **linguistic** *a.* **linguistically** *adv.* **linguistics** *n.* study of human speech including its sounds, history, nature, structure, etc.; comparative philology.

lin·i·ment *n.* a lotion or soft ointment.

link *n.* a single ring of a chain; anything doubled and closed like a link. **-age** *n.* a system of connections. **missing link,** a connection without which a chain of argument is incomplete.

links *n.pl.* a golf course.

lin·net *n.* a small song bird of the finch family.

li·no·le·um *n.* a hard floor covering of burlap impregnated with a cement of linseed oil, cork, etc.

lin·o·type *n.* a type-setting machine in which the matter is cast in solid lines of type.

lin·seed *n.* flaxseed. — **cake,** compressed mass of husks of linseed, after oil has been pressed out, much used for cattle feeding.

lin·sey-wool·sey *a.* made of wool and linen mixed.

lint *n.* a linen material, one side with a soft, wooly surface formerly used for dressing wounds; scraps of thread; fluff from cloth.

lin·tel *n.* a horizontal beam or stone over a doorway or window.

li·on *n.* (*fem.* **-ess**) the largest of the cat tribe, tawny-colored, with powerful, tufted tail, the male having a shaggy mane.

lip *n.* one of the two fleshy, outer edges of the mouth; a liplike part; the edge of anything; brim. — **reading** *n.* the art of hearing by reading the motions of a speaker's lips; this system as taught to the deaf. **-stick,** a salve, in the form of a small stick, used by women to redden the lips.

li·quate *v.t.* to melt; to separate or purify solids or gases by liquefying.

liq·ue·fy *v.t.* to transform a liquid; to melt.

li·queur *n.* a preparation of distilled liquors flavored with fruits or aromatic substances.

liq·uid *a.* fluid; in a state intermediate between a solid and a gas; flowing smoothly; (of sounds) pleasing to the ear. **-ate** *v.t.* to settle a debt; to wind up the affairs of business, etc.; to convert into cash; to destroy; *v.i.* (of business) to be wound up.

liq·uor *n.* any liquid or fluid, esp. alcoholic.

li·ra *n.* the monetary unit and a silver coin of Italy; a monetary unit and gold coin of Turkey.

lisle *n.* a fine hard-twisted cotton or linen thread.

lisp *v.i.* to speak imperfectly, esp. to substitute the sound *th* for *s*.

lis·some *a.* supple; flexible; lithe.

list *n.* the outer edge or selvage of woven cloth; a row or stripe; a roll; a catalogue; a register; a boundary line enclosing a field of combat at a tournament.

list *v.i.* (*Naut.*) to lean or incline (of a ship).

lis·ten *v.i.* to attend closely; to yield to advice.

list·less *a.* indifferent; languid; apathetic.

lit *p.a.t.* and *p.a.p.* of verb **light.**

lit·a·ny *n.* an earnest prayer of supplication.

li·ter *n.* a unit of volume in the metric system, equal to 1.0567 quarts. Also **litre.**

li·te·ral *a.* according to the letter; real; not figurative; word for word, as a translation.

lit·er·ar·y *a.* pert. to letters or literature; versed in literature. **literate** *a.* versed in learning and science; educated.

lit·er·a·ture *n.* the body of writings of a language, period, subject, etc.

lithe *a.* capable of being easily bent; supple; pliant.

li·thog·e·nous *a.* rock-producing, as certain corals.

lith·o·glyph *n.* an engraving on a precious stone.

lith·o·graph *v.t.* to trace on stone, zinc, or aluminium, and transfer to paper by special printing process. **lithography** *n.* the art of tracing designs on stone or other media, and taking impressions of these designs.

lith·oid, -al *a.* resembling a stone.

li·thol·o·gy *n.* the science which treats of the characteristics of rocks.

lith·o·tint *n.* the lithographic production of a tinted picture; the picture itself.

lith·o·tome *n.* a stone resembling an artificially cut gem; (*Surg.*) an instrument for performing a lithotomy. **lithotomy** *n.* (*Surg.*) the operation by which stones are removed from the bladder.

lith·o·type *n.* a stereotype plate; print from this plate.

Lith·u·a·ni·an *n.* a native of Lithuania; the language. Also **Lett.**

lit·i·gate *v.t.* to contest in law. *a.* **litigant** *n.* a person engaged in a lawsuit.

lit·mus *n.* a bluish purple vegetable dye (obtained from lichens) which turns red with an acid, and blue with an alkali. — **paper**, used to test solutions.

li·to·tes *n.* a figure of speech which expresses a strong affirmative.

lit·ter *n.* a heap of straw as bedding for animals; a vehicle containing bed carried on men's shoulders; a stretcher; odds and ends left lying about; state of disorder.

lit·tle *a.* small in size, extent, or quantity; brief; slight; mean.

lit·to·ral *a.* pert. to a lake or seashore.

lit·ur·gy *n.* the established ritual for public worship in a church, esp. the Mass. **liturge** *n.* a leader in public worship.

live *v.i.* to have life; to subsist; to be conscious; to dwell; to enjoy life; to keep oneself (as on one's income). **livable** *a.* habitable.

live *a.* having life; quick; active; vital; unexploded, as a mine; burning, as coal; full of zest; dynamite. —**circuit** *n.* a circuit through which an electric current is passing. — **wire** *n.* a wire carrying an electric current.

live·li·hood *n.* a means of living; sustenance.

live·ly *a.* animated; active; gay; exciting; light; *adv.* briskly.

liv·er *n.* (*Anat.*) glandular organ in body secreting bile; the flesh of this organ in animals or fowls used as food. **-wort** *n.* a moss-like plant with liver-shaped leaves. **-wurst** *n.* a sausage with a large amount of liver.

liv·er·y *n.* orig. the special dress or food *delivered* by a lord to his household retinue. — **stable** *n.* a stable where horses and vehicles are kept for hire.

liv·id *a.* black and blue; discolored, as flesh, by bruising.

liv·ing *a.* having life; active; flowing (of water); resembling closely; contemporary; *n.* livelihood.

liz·ard *n.* an order of four-footed scale-clad reptiles.

lizard

lla·ma *n.* a S. America two-toed ruminant, used as a beast of burden.

loach a small river fish.

load *n.* a burden; the amount normally carried at one time; any heavy weight; a cargo. to charge (a gun); to weight (as dice); to insert a spool into (as a camera). — **line** *n.* a line painted on the side of a vessel to indicate maximum immersion when loaded. **-stone** *n.* a metal which attracts other metals.

loaf *n.* shaped portion of dough baked in the oven; a lump of sugar.

loaf *v.i.* to spend (time) idly; to lounge. **-er** *n.* one who loafs; a moccasin style of shoe.

loam *n.* a rich, fertile soil of clay, sand, oxide of iron, and carbonate of lime.

loan *n.* the act of lending; that which is lent, esp. money for interest. — **office** *n.* a pawnbroker's shop.

loath, loth *a.* unwilling; reluctant; disinclined.

loathe *v.t.* to detest; to abominate; to be nauseated by. **loathing** *n.* disgust; repulsion. **loathly** *a.* **loathsome** *a.* detestable; repugnant.

lob *n.* (*Tennis*) a ball rising high in air over opponent's head; *v.t.* to bowl underhand; to hit (tennis ball, shuttle-cock) high into air.

lob·by *n.* a passage, or hall, forming the entrance to a public building or private dwelling; a waiting-room; a pressure group seeking to influence members of a legislature.

lobe *n.* a rounded division of an organ; the lower, fleshy, rounded part of human ear; a division of the lung.

lo·bel·ia *n.* a genus of herbaceous plants (including the blue dwarf variety).

lob·lol·ly *n.* a pine tree of the southern U.S.

lob·ster *n.* an edible, marine, long-tailed crustacean, with pincer-claws.

lo·cal *a.* pert. to a particular place; confined to a definite spot, district, or part. **locale** *n.* the scene of an occurrence; the scene of a film-shot.

L

localize *v.t.* to assign to a definite place; to decentralize. **locality** *n.* position of a thing; site; neighborhood. -ly *adv.* **locate** *v.t.* to set in a particular place; to find the exact position of. **location** *n.* act of locating; situation; geographical position; the out-of-doors site of a film production.

loch *n.* a lake, esp. in Scotland; an arm of the sea.

lock *n.* a strand or tress of hair.

lock *n.* a device for fastening a door, box, case, etc.; a mechanism on a gun to keep it from firing; an appliance to check the revolution of a wheel. -er *n.* a drawer, small chest, etc. where valuables may be locked. -et *n.* a small case containing portrait, lock of hair, worn on a chain. -jaw *n.* a contraction of the muscles of the jaw; tetanus. -smith *n.* one who makes and repairs locks.

lo·co·mo·tion *n.* the act or process of moving from place to place. **locomotive** *a.* capable of moving from one place to another.

lo·cus *n.* the exact position of anything; (*Math.*) the path traced out by a point moving in accordance with some mathematical law.

lo·cust *n.* a winged insect, allied to the grasshopper and found in N. Africa, Asia,

locust

and the U.S.; a thorny-branched N. American tree with very durable wood.

lo·cu·tion *n.* speech; mode or style of speaking.

lode *n.* a metallic vein; a body of ore. -star, **loadstar** *n.* a star by which one steers, esp. the Pole-star.

lodge *n.* a small country-house; a cottage at the entrance to an estate; a branch of a society, as of Freemasons, or the building where such a society meets. **lodg(e)ment** *n.* lodgings; accumulation of something deposited. **lodging(s)** *n.* room(s) let temporarily.

loft *n.* an upper room; an attic in space between top story and roof; the gallery in a church, as the *organ-loft*; *v.t.* (*Golf*) to strike a ball high.

log *n.* an unhewn piece of timber; an apparatus to measure the speed of a ship and distance covered; the tabulated record of a ship's voyage. -ger *n.* a lumberjack. -ging *n.* the process of cutting trees and getting the logs to a sawmill to be cut for lumber.

lo·gan·ber·ry *n.* a shrub, a cross between raspberry and blackberry.

log·a·rithm *n.* the index of the power to which a fixed number or base must be raised to produce the number; a method of reducing arithmetical calculations to a minimum by substituting addition and subtraction for multiplication and division.

log·ger·head *n.* a blockhead; a dunce; a kind of turtle.

log·gia *n.* a kind of open elevated gallery with pillars, common in Italian buildings.

log·ic *n.* the science of reasoning; the science of pure and formal thought; (*Colloq.*) commonsense. -al *a.* pert. to formal thought; skilled in logic; reasonable.

lo·gis·tic, -al *a.* pert. to calculating. -s *n.pl.* (used as *sing.*); (*Mil.*) branch of military science which deals with the moving of and providing for troops.

log·o·gram *n.* a symbol representing a whole word or phrase.

lo·go·gra·pher *n.* a speech-writer in ancient Greek times. **logography** *n.* a method of printing in which words cast in a single type are used instead of single letters.

loin *n.* part of animal or man above hips and on either side of spinal column.

loi·ter *v.i.* to linger; to be slow in moving; to spend time idly.

loll *v.i.* to lounge about lazily; to hang out.

lol·li·pop lollipop *n.* a piece of flavored toffee or hard candy on a stick.

lone *a.* solitary; standing by itself.

long *a.* extended in distance or time; drawn out in a line; protracted; slow in coming; continued at great length; *v.i.* to be filled with a yearning to desire. -boat *n.* the largest boat carried by a sailing ship. -bow *n.* a bow drawn by hand, and usually 5½-6 feet long—so called to distinguish it from the *Cross*-bow. **longevity** *n.* length of life. -hand *n.* ordinary handwriting. -horn *n.* a kind of cattle of Mexico and U.S. — house *n.* a long communal dwelling of the Iroquois Indians. -ing *a.* yearning; a craving. -ingly *adv.* -ish *a.* rather long. **longitude** *n.* angular distance east or west of a given meridian, measured in degrees. — measure *n.* linear measure. -shore *a.* existing or employed on the shore. -shoreman *n.* a dock laborer. -sightedness *n.* (*Med.*) hypermetropia, an abnormal eye condition whereby the rays of light are focused *beyond* and not on the retina. -wise, -ways *a.* lengthwise.

loo *n.* a card-game.

look *v.i.* to turn one's eyes upon; to seem to be; to consider; to seem; to face. -ing glass *n.* a mirror. -out *n.* a watch; a place from which a careful watch is kept; person stationed to keep watch.

loom *n.* a machine for weaving cloth from thread.

loom *v.i.* to emerge indistinctly and larger than the real dimensions; to appear over the horizon.

loom *n.* a kind of guillemot; a puffin; a loon.

loon *n.* a large fish-eating diving bird of the

loon

northern regions.

loop n. a doubling of string or rope, through which another string may run; anything with a similar shape.

loop·hole n. a narrow slit or opening as in the walls of a fortification; (Fig.) a way out of a difficult situation.

loose v.t. to free from constraint; to untie; to disconnect; to relax; to discharge. **—jointed** a. loosely built. **—leaf** a. having sheets of paper which can be removed and rearranged.

loot n. plunder; the act of plundering.

lop v.t. to cut off, esp. top of anything; to cut away superfluous parts.

lop v.i. to hand down loosely. **—eared** a. having drooping ears. **—sided** a. heavier on one side than the other.

lope v.i. to run with a long, leisurely gait.

lo·qua·cious a. talkative; babbling; garrulous.

lo·quat n. a low-growing Japanese plum tree; the fruit itself.

lo·ran n. (Flying) a navigational device which locates the position of an airplane.

lord n. a master; a ruler; a king; (Cap.) the Supreme Being; Jehovah; God; Christ. **-ship** n. the state of being a lord; authority; estate owned by a lord.

lore n. learning; erudition; traditional knowledge.

lor·gnette n. a pair of eyeglasses attached to a long handle; an opera glass.

lo·ri·ca n. a cuirass; (Zool.) a protective covering of bony plates, scales, etc., like a cuirass.

lorn a. (Arch.) lost; forsaken; desolate.

lor·ry n. (esp. Brit.) a wagon for transporting heavy loads; a car on rails, used in factories, mines, etc.; (Brit.) a truck.

lose v.t. to be deprived of; to mislay; to forfeit; to fail to win; to miss; to waste, as time; to destroy.

lot n. what happens by chance; destiny; object used to determine something by chance; the choice thus determined; a separate part; a large number of articles such as at an auction sale. **-tery** n. a scheme by which prizes are given to people, not on merit, but by drawing lots.

Lo·thar·i·o n. libertine, rake.

lo·tion n. a fluid with healing, antiseptic properties esp. for the skin.

lot·to n. a game of chance.

lo·tus n. the Egyptian water lily; a decorative representation, as in Egyptian

lotus

and Hindu art; a genus of plants including the British bird'sfoot trefoil.

loud a. making a great sound; noisy; flashy; obtrusive; vulgar. **-speaker** n. a device which makes speech, music, etc. audible at a distance.

lou·is n. an obsolete French gold coin worth 20 francs. Also **— d'or**. **— quatorze**, **— quinze**, **— seize**, applied to architecture, furniture, style of interior decoration characteristic of the reigns of the French Kings Louis XIV, VX, XVI [Fr.].

lounge v.i. to recline at ease; to loll; to spend time idly; n. the act of lounging; a room in which people may relax; a kind of sofa.

louse n. a small wingless parasitic insect infesting hair and skin of human beings; a sucking parasite found on mammals or plants.

lout n. a clumsy fellow; a bumpkin.

lou·ver n. an opening in the roof of ancient buildings for the escape of smoke or for ventilation.

love n. affection; strong liking; goodwill; benevolence; charity; devoted attachment to one of the opposite sex; passion. **— affair** n. a passionate attachment between two members of the opposite sex. **— apple** n. the tomato. **-bird** n. a small parrot with bright-colored plumage. / **knot** n. bow of ribbon tied in a special way, as a token of love. **—lies-bleeding** n. a garden flower with reddish-purple spike flowers. **-liness** n. **-lock** n. a curl worn on the forehead or over the temple. **— match** n. a marriage founded on true love. **— philter** or **— potion** n. a drink supposed to induce the emotion of love towards a chosen person. **— seat** n. a seat for two. **-sick** a. pining because of love. **—song** n. lyric inspired by love. **—token** n. an object, as a ring, given as a symbol of love. **loving** a. affectionate; loyal.

low a. not high; lying near the ground; depressed below the adjacent surface; near the horizon; shallow; not loud, as a voice; moderate, as prices. **-boy** n. a chest about three feet high usu. with two tiers of drawers and on slender legs. **-brow** n. a non-intellectual. **Low Countries**, the Netherlands, Belgium, and Luxemburg. **-down** a. mean; underhand. **-land** n. country which is relatively flat in comparison with surrounding hilly district. **—pressure**, having only a small expansive force (less than 50 lbs. to the square inch) said of steam and steam engines.

low v.i. to bellow as an ox or cow.

low·er v.i. to frown; to look gloomy or threatening, as the sky.

lox n. liquid oxygen. n. salty smoked salmon.

loy·al a. faithful to the lawful government, the sovereign, a cause, or a friend.

loz·enge n. a figure with two acute and two obtuse angles; small (often medicated) confection orig. lozenge-shaped.

lub·ber n. a heavy, clumsy fellow.

lu·bri·cate v.t. to make smooth or slippery; to smear with oil, grease, etc., to reduce friction.

L

luce *n.* a fresh-water fish, the pike when full grown.

lu·cent *a.* shining; bright.

lu·cid *a.* shining; clear; easily understood, as of style; normally sane.

Lu·ci·fer *n.* the planet Venus, when appearing as the morning star; Satan.

lu·cite *n.* a very clear plastic compound.

luck *n.* accidental fortune, good or bad; fate; chance.

lu·cre *n.* material gain; profit, esp. ill-gotten.

lu·cu·brate *v.i.* to study by lamp or candlelight, or at night.

lu·cu·lent *a.* clear; self-evident.

lu·di·crous *a.* provoking laughter; ridiculous; droll.

luff *v.i.* to turn the head of a ship towards the wind; to sail nearer the wind.

Luft·waf·fe *n.* the German Air Force.

lug *v.t.* to pull with force; to tug; to haul.

lug *n.* a projecting piece by which an object may be grasped, supported, etc.

lu·gu·bri·ous *a.* mournful; woeful; dismal.

lug·worm a large earthworm.

luke·warm *a.* moderately warm; tepid; indifferent.

lull *v.t.* to soothe to sleep; to quiet.

lum·ba·go *n.* a painful rheumatic affection of the lumbar muscles. **lumbaginous, lumbar, lumbral** *a.* pert. to the lower part of the back.

lum·ber *n.* anything useless and cumbersome; odds and ends hoarded; timber cut and split for market.

lum·ber *v.i.* to move heavily.

lu·mi·nar·y *n.* any body which gives light, esp. one of the heavenly bodies.

lump *n.* a small mass of matter of indefinite shape; a swelling; the gross.

lu·nar *a.* pert. to the moon; measured by revolutions of the moon. Also **lunary. lunacy** *n.* madness, formerly supposed to be influenced by changes of moon. **lunatic** *a.* insane; *n.* a mad person. **lunation** *n.* the period from one new moon to the next. **lunar month,** period of the moon's revolution, about 29½ days. **lunar year,** period of twelve synodic lunar months (354⅓ days).

lunch *n.* a light meal taken between breakfast and dinner.

lune *n.* anything in the shape of a half-moon.

lung *n.* one of the two main organs of respiration in a breathing animal.

lunge *n.* in fencing, a sudden thrust.

lu·pine *n.* a genus of leguminous plants, some cultivated for their flowers, others for cattle fodder.

lu·pus *n.* a spreading tubercular condition affecting the skin.

lurch *n.* a sudden roll of a ship to one side; a staggering movement; *v.i.* to stagger.

lurch *n.* a critical move in the game of cribbage.

lure *n.* a decoy used by the falconer to recall the hawk; an artificial bait.

lu·rid *a.* extravagantly colored.

lurk *v.i.* to lie hidden; to lie in wait.

lus·cious *a.* excessively sweet.

lush *a.* luxuriant; juicy.

lust *n.* longing desire; sexual appetite; craving.

lus·ter *n.* clearness; glitter; gloss; renown; radiance; chandelier with drops or pendants of cut glass; a cotton dress fabric with glossy, silky surface; a pottery glaze.

lus·trine *n.* a glossy silk fabric.

lus·trum *n.* a period of five years; purification. **lustration** *n.* the act of purifying; the sacrifice or ceremony by which cities, fields, armies, or people were purified.

lute *n.* a stringed instrument with a pear-shaped body. **lutanist, luter, lutist** *n.* a lute-player.

Lu·ther·an *n.* a follower of Martin Luther; a member of the Lutheran Church. **-ism, Lutherism.**

lu·thern *n.* a dormer-window.

lux·ate *v.t.* to put out of joint; to dislocate.

lux·u·ry *n.* indulgence in the pleasures which wealth can procure; that which is not a necessity of life.

Ly·ce·um *n.* orig. a place in Athens where Aristotle taught his pupils.

lydd·ite *n.* picric acid; a powerful explosive used in shells.

lye *n.* alkaline solution of wood ashes and water; used in soap making.

ly·ing *a.* untruthful; *n.* habit of being untruthful. **-ly** *adv.*

lymph *n.* an alkaline fluid, watery in appearance, contained in the tissues and organs of the body.

lynch *v.t.* to inflict capital punishment (on an accused) illegally.

lynx *n.* an animal of the cat tribe with abnormally keen sight.

lynx

ly·on·naise *a.* prepared with onions.

lyre *n.* a stringed, musical instrument in use among ancient Greeks, esp. to accompany minstrels. **lyrate** *a.* shaped like a lyre. **-bird** *n.* an Australian bird

lyrebird

with tail feathers which curve upward in the shape of a lyre. **lyric.** *n.* orig. a poem sung to music; a short, subjective poem expressing emotions of poet. **lyricism** *n.* lyrical quality of a poem; emotional expression.

M

ma'am *n*. contr. of **madam**.

ma•ca•bre *a*. gruesome; ghastly; grim.

mac•a•dam *n*. a road-surface material of crushed stones.

ma•caque *n*. a genus of Asian monkeys.

mac•a•ro•ni *n*. a paste of wheat flour made in long slender tubes; a dandy of the 18th cent. -c *a*. affected; burlesque verse in modern words with Latinized endings.

mac•a•roon *n*. a small cookie made of white of egg, ground almonds or coconut, and sugar.

ma•caw *n*. a long-tailed S. Amer. parrot.

mace *n*. a heavy club of metal; a staff carried as an emblem of authority; a billiard cue.

mace *n*. a spice made from nutmeg.

mac•er•ate *v.t.* to soften by soaking; to cause to grow thin.

ma•chet•e *n*. a heavy knife or cleaver used to cut down sugar canes, and as a weapon.

Ma•chi•a•vel•lian *a*. pert. to Machiavelli; unscrupulous; crafty.

mach•i•nate *v.t.* to contrive, usually with evil or ulterior motive. **machinator** *n*. one who plots.

ma•chine *n*. (*Mech.*) any contrivance for the conversion and direction of motion; an apparatus for doing some kind of work; an engine; a vehicle. — gun *n*. an automatic small-arms weapon capable of continuous firing. -ry *n*. machines collectively; the parts of a machine. machinist *n*. one who makes machinery; one who works at a machine.

mack•er•el *n*. an edible sea fish with blue and black stripes above and silver color below.

mack•i•naw *n*. a short woolen coat, usually plaid.

mack•in•tosh *n*. a waterproof coat.

mac•ra•me *n*. a coarse fringe.

mac•ro•bi•ot•ic *a*. long-lived. **macrobiosis** *n*. long life.

mac•ro•cosm *n*. the great universe.

ma•cron *n*. short line put over vowel to show it is long in quantity or quality, as *fate*.

mac•ro•scop•ic *a*. visible to the naked eye; opp. of *microscopic*.

mac•u•la *n*. a spot; *pl*. -e. -te *v.t.* to spot.

mad *a*. (*comp.* -der; *superl.* -dest) deranged in mind; insane; crazy; frenzied; angry; infatuated; irrational, as a scheme. -den *v.t.* to enrage; to drive mad; to annoy.

mad•am *n*. a formal mode of address in speaking to a married or elderly woman. madame *n*. French form.

Ma•dei•ra *n*. a rich amber-colored wine from *Madeira*; port.

ma•de•moi•selle *n*. French mode of addressing unmarried lady.

Ma•don•na *n*. the Virgin Mary; a statue of the Virgin.

mad•ras *n*. a fine cotton cloth, usu. striped or plaid.

mad•re•pore *n*. white perforate coral.

mad•ri•gal *n*. a short love poem; an unaccompanied part-song.

mael•strom *n*. a whirlpool.

mae•sto•so *a*. and *adv*. (*Mus.*) with dignity.

mae•stro *n*. master, esp. an eminent composer, conductor, or teacher of music.

Mae West *n*. an inflatable life jacket.

ma•fi•a *n*. a criminal Sicilian secret society; hostility to the law.

mag•a•zine *n*. a military storehouse; part of a ship where ammunition is stored; a periodical containing miscellaneous articles.

ma•gen•ta *n*. a purplish dye from coal tar.

mag•got *n*. a grub; larva of a housefly.

ma•gi *n.pl.* a class of priests among the ancient Persians. Magi *n*. in the N.T. the Wise Men who came to visit the infant Jesus.

mag•ic *n*. the feigned art of influencing nature or future events by occult means; sorcery; charm. -ian *n*. one skilled in magic; a conjurer.

mag•is•te•ri•al *a*. pert. to or conducted by a magistrate; authoritative; judicial; overbearing.

mag•is•trate *n*. a person vested with public judicial authority; a justice of the peace.

mag•ma *n*. a paste of mineral or organic matter; (*Geol.*) the molten rock beneath the earth's crust; (*Pharm.*) a salve.

Mag•na Car•ta (Charta) *n*. great charter of English public and private liberties signed by King John in 1215.

mag•na•nim•i•ty *n*. greatness of mind; generosity of heart, esp. in forgiveness.

mag•nate *n*. an eminent person, esp. a wealthy businessman.

mag•ne•si•um *n*. the silvery-white metallic base of magnesia, burning with an intensely brilliant white light and used for fireworks, flashbulbs, etc.

mag•net *n*. the loadstone; a bar of iron having property of attracting iron or steel and, when suspended, of pointing N. and S.; a person or thing with powers of attraction. -ize *v.t.* to give magnetic properties to; to attract. -ism *n*. the natural cause of magnetic force; the science of the phenomena of magnetic force; attraction. -o *n*. a magnetoelectric machine, esp. used to generate ignition spark in internal-combustion engine. -ic field *n*. the sphere of influence of magnetic forces.

mag•ni•fy *v.t.* to make greater; to cause to appear greater. Magnificat *n*. the song of the Virgin Mary. **magnificent** *a*. splendid; brilliant.

mag•nil•o•quent *a*. speaking pompously; boastful.

mag•ni•tude *n*. greatness; size; importance.

mag•no•lia *n*. a species of tree bearing large perfumed flowers.

mag•num *n*. a wine bottle holding two quarts. — opus *n*. one's best artistic or literary work.

mag•pie *n*. a bird of the crow family, with a harsh chattering cry.

Mag•yar *n*. dominant people of Hungary; the language of Hungary.

ma•ha•ra•jah *n*. (*fem*. **maharani** or

M

maharanee) the title of an Indian prince.

ma•hat•ma n. a man of saintly life with supernatural powers derived from purity of soul.

ma•hog•a•ny n. a tree of hard, reddish wood used for furniture; the red-brown color of mahogany.

maid n. a girl or unmarried woman; a female domestic servant. -en name n. surname of a woman before marriage.

mail n. defensive armor composed of steel rings or plates.

mail n. letters, packages, etc., carried by post; the person or means of conveyance for transit of letters, parcels, etc.

maim v.t. to deprive of the use of a limb; to disable; to disfigure.

main a. principal; first in size, importance, etc.; sheer; n. the principal pipe or line in water, gas, or electricity system. -land n. a continent, as distinct from islands.

main•tain v.t. and v.i. to hold or keep in any state; to sustain; to preserve; to defend, as an argument; to support.

maize n. Indian corn, a cereal; yellow.

maj•es•ty n. grandeur; exalted dignity; royal state; the title of a sovereign.

ma•jol•i•ca n. a decorative, enameled pottery.

ma•jor a. greater in number, quality, quantity, or extent; (Mus.) greater by a semitone; pert. to a field of study; n. an officer in the army ranking below a lieutenant colonel. — general n. an army officer in rank below a lieutenant-general. -ity n. the greater part; more than half; full legal age (21).

make v.t. to cause to be or do; to create; to constitute; to compel; to appoint; to secure; to arrive at; to reckon; to perform; n. structure; texture; form; style; brand.

mal•a•chite n. a green carbonate of copper, used for inlaid work.

mal•ad•just•ment n. faulty adjustment; inability to adjust to one's environment.

mal•ad•min•is•tra•tion n. faulty administration, esp. of public affairs.

mal•a•droit a. clumsy, awkward.

mal•a•dy n. a disease; ailment.

Mal•a•gas•y n. a native of, or the language of, Madagascar.

mal•aise n. a physical discomfort.

mal•a•prop(ism) n. the ludicrous misuse of a word.

ma•lar•i•a n. a febrile disease transmitted by the bite of mosquito.

Ma•lay n. a native of the Malay Peninsula.

mal•con•tent a. discontented; rebellious.

male a. pert. to the sex which begets young; masculine; (Bot.) having stamens; n. a male animal.

mal•e•dic•tion n. evil-speaking; a curse.

mal•e•fac•tor n. an evil-doer; a criminal.

ma•lev•o•lent a. evilly disposed; malicious.

mal•fea•sance n. misconduct, esp. in public affairs.

mal•for•ma•tion n. irregular formation. malformed a. deformed.

mal•func•tion v.i. to fail to operate correctly or normally.

ma•lic a. from the apple.

mal•ice n. ill will; spite; desire to injure others; (Law) criminal intention. malicious a. spiteful; showing malice.

ma•lign a. malicious; evil; spiteful. -ant a. being evilly disposed; harmful; (of disease) virulent; likely to prove fatal.

ma•lin•ger v.i. to feign illness in order to avoid duty. -er n. a shirker.

mall n. a level, shaded walk; a heavy mallet used in game of pall-mall.

mal•lard n. a wild drake or duck.

mal•le•a•ble a. capable of being hammered or extended by beating; amenable; tractable.

mal•let n. any of various types of wooden hammer.

mal•low n. plant with downy leaves, and having emollient properties.

mal•nu•tri•tion n. the state of being undernourished.

mal•od•or•ous a. having an offensive odor.

mal•prac•tice n. professional impropriety or negligence.

malt n. barley or other grain steeped in water until it germinates, then dried in a kiln for use in brewing.

Mal•tese n. native of Malta; its dialect and people.

mal•treat v.t. to ill-treat; to abuse; to handle roughly.

mal•ver•sa•tion n. corruption in office; fraudulent handling of public funds.

mam•bo n. rhythmic music and dance of Sp. Amer. origin.

mam•ma n. child's name for mother.

mam•ma n. milk-secreting gland in females; pl. -e. mammary a.

Mam•ma•li•a n.pl. (Zool.) the class of mammals or animals which suckle their young.

mam•mon n. wealth personified and worshipped.

mam•moth n. a huge extinct elephant; a. colossal.

mam•my n. a Negro woman who took care of white children, esp. in the South.

man n. a human being; an adult male; a manly person. — hour n. work performed by one man in one hour. -kind n. human beings. —of-war n. a warship. — power n. a unit of power equal to one-eighth of a horsepower; the total number of people in industry, the armed forces, etc. -slaughter n. culpable homicide without malice aforethought.

man•a•cle n. a handcuff.

man•age v.t. to direct; to control; to carry on; to cope with. -ment n. the act of managing; administration; body of directors controlling a business.

Man•chu n. one of the original inhabitants of Manchuria.

man•ci•ple n. a steward; a caterer.

man•da•mus n. a written order.

man•da•rin n. a European name for a Chinese provincial governor; the language used in Chinese official circles; a small orange; a long brocade coat with loose sleeves.

man•date *n.* an official order; a precept; a prescript of the Pope; a commission to act as representative of a body of people. **mandatory** *a.* containing a mandate; obligatory.

man•di•ble *n.* a jaw; in vertebrates, the lower jaw; in birds, the upper or lower beak.

man•do•lin *n.* a musical instrument with a rounded pear-shaped body.

man•drake *n.* a narcotic plant, the root thought to resemble human form.

man•drel *n.* a shaft on which objects may be fixed for turning, milling, etc.; the spindle of a lathe.

man•drill *n.* a large African baboon.

mandrill

mane *n.* long hair on the neck of an animal.

ma•nege *n.* the art of horsemanship; a riding school.

ma•neu•ver *n.* a controlled strategic movement; scheme; artifice.

man•ga•nese *n.* a grayish, hard, brittle metal which oxidizes rapidly in humid atmosphere.

mange *n.* a parasitic disease affecting the skin of animals, causing hair to fall out.

man•ger *n.* a trough for holding fodder for cattle.

man•gle *n.* a machine for pressing linen between rollers.

man•gle *v.t.* to hack; to mutilate; to spoil the beauty of.

man•go *n.* a tropical tree, the unripe fruit used in making chutney.

mango

man•grove *n.* a tropical tree the bark of which is used in tanning.

man•hat•tan *n.* a cocktail containing whiskey, vermouth, bitters.

ma•ni•a *n.* madness; a violent excitement; extravagant enthusiasm; an obsession. **-c** *n.* a madman; *a.* raving; frenzied.

man•i•cure *n.* the care of the hands and nails.

man•i•fest *a.* clearly visible; apparent to the mind or senses. **-ation** *n.* the act of revealing; the state of being revealed; display; disclosure. **-o** *n.* a public declaration of the principles or policy of a leader or party.

man•i•fold *a.* many and varied; numerous; *v.t.* to make many copies of, as letters, by a machine, such as a duplicator; *n.* (*Mech.*) a pipe fitted with several lateral outlets.

man•i•kin *n.* a little man; a dwarf; a model of the human body used in medical schools; a mannequin.

ma•nil•a *n.* a cigar made in Manila, capital of the Philippine Islands. **— paper** *n.* a stout buff-colored paper.

man•i•ple *n.* part of a Roman legion; a scarf worn by celebrant at mass.

ma•nip•u•late *v.t.* to operate with the hands; to manage (a person) in a skillful, esp. unscrupulous, way; to falsify.

man•na *n.* the food supplied miraculously to the Israelites in the wilderness; sweetish juice of the ash; spiritual nourishment.

man•ne•quin *n.* one employed to model new fashions; figure for a similar purpose.

man•ner *n.* way of doing anything; custom; style; a person's habitual bearing; *pl.* social behavior; customs.

man•or *n.* the land belonging to a lord; a unit of land in feudal times over which the owner had full jurisdiction.

man•sard roof *n.* roof in which lower slope is nearly vertical and upper much inclined.

manse *n.* a minister's residence.

man•sion *n.* a large, imposing house; a manor house.

man•sue•tude *n.* gentleness; tameness.

man•tel *n.* the shelf above a fireplace; the framework around a fireplace.

man•til•la *n.* a veil covering head and shoulders, worn esp. by Spanish women.

man•tis *n.* a genus of insects holding the forelegs folded as if praying.

mantis

man•tis•sa *n.* the decimal part of a logarithm.

man•tle *n.* a loose outer garment; a cloak; a covering. **-t** *n.* a bulletproof shelter.

man•tu•a *n.* a woman's loose gown.

man•u•al *a.* pert. to, made by or done with the hand; *n.* a handbook or small textbook; a keyboard of a pipe organ.

man•u•fac•ture *n.* making goods either by hand or by machine.

man•u•mit *v.t.* to give freedom to a slave; to emancipate.

ma•nure *v.t.* to enrich soil with fertilizer; *n.* animal excrement used as fertilizer.

man•u•script *a.* written, or typed, by hand; *n.* a book written by hand; an author's

M

script or typewritten copy for perusal by publisher.

man•y *a.* comprising a great number *n.* and *pron.* a number of people or things.

map *n.* a representation, esp. on a plane surface, of the features of the earth, or of part of it.

ma•ple *n.* a deciduous tree, valuable for its timber and the sap from which sugar is extracted.

mar•a•bou *n.* a kind of stork; the feathers of this bird used as trimming.

ma•ra•ca *n.* gourd-shaped rattle.

mar•a•schi•no *n.* a sweet liqueur distilled from cherries.

mar•a•thon *n.* a foot race (approx. 26 miles); endurance contest.

ma•raud *v.i.* to rove in quest of plunder; to loot.

mar•ble *n.* hard limestone which takes on a brilliant polish and is used for ornaments, statuary, etc.

mar•ca•site *n.* white iron pyrite used in jewelry because of its brilliance.

mar•cel *n.* an artificial hair wave.

March *n.* third month of year, named after *Mars,* Roman god of war.

march *v.i.* to move in order, as soldiers; to proceed at a steady pace.

mar•chio•ness *n.* the wife of a marquis; lady, holding in her own right, the rank of marquis.

mare *n.* the female of the horse, mule, donkey, etc.

mar•ga•rine *n.* pearly waxlike substance obtained from animal fat; a fatty extract of certain vegetable oils.

mar•gin *n.* a border; a blank space at top, bottom and sides, of a written or printed page; allowance made for contingencies.

mar•gue•rite *n.* a large oxeye daisy.

mar•i•gold *n.* name applied to a plant bearing yellow or orange flowers.

ma•ri•jua•na *n.* a type of hemp dried and used as tobacco, having a narcotic effect.

ma•rim•ba *n.* a jazz-band instrument resembling the xylophone.

ma•ri•na *n.* a small harbor or boat basin.

mar•i•nade *n.* a seasoned vinegar or wine used for steeping meat, fish, vegetables.

ma•rine *a.* pert. to the sea; found in, or near, the sea.

mar•i•o•nette *n.* a puppet worked by strings.

mar•i•tal *a.* pert. to a husband or to marriage.

mar•i•time *a.* pert. to the sea; bordering on the sea; living near the sea; pert. to overseas trade or navigation.

mar•jo•ram *n.* an aromatic plant of the mint family used in cookery.

mark *n.* a visible sign; a cross; a character made by one who cannot write; a stamp; a proof; a target; a point. **-sman** *n.* one who is expert at hitting a target. **trademark** *n.* a special symbol marked on commodities to indicate the maker.

mark *n.* unit of exchange of various countries.

mar•ket *n.* a public meeting place for the purchase and sale of commodities; a trading center.

marl *n.* a crumbly soil used for fertilizer and in brickmaking.

mar•lin *n.* a large slender deep-sea fish.

mar•line *n.* a small rope used to secure a splicing. **-spike** *n.* a pointed tool used to separate strands of a rope in splicing.

mar•ma•lade *n.* a preserve made of the pulp and peel of fruit.

mar•mo•set *n.* a small monkey of S. America.

marmoset

mar•mot *n.* a bushy-tailed rodent; the prairie dog.

ma•roon *n.* orig. a fugitive slave of the W. Indies; a marooned person; *v.t.* to put ashore on a desolate island; to isolate, cut off.

ma•roon *a.* a brownish-crimson.

marque *n.* seizure by way of retaliation.

mar•quee *n.* a roof-like structure or awning outside a public building.

mar•que•try *n.* decorative, inlaid wood; the process of inlaying wood with designs.

mar•quis *n.* noble ranking next below a duke; pointed oval diamond.

mar•qui•sette *n.* thin, lightweight fabric.

mar•row *n.* the soft substance in the cavities of bones; the essence of anything.

mar•ry *v.t.* to unite, take, or give in wedlock. **marriage** *n.* the legal union of husband and wife; the ceremony, civil or religious, by which two people become husband and wife.

Mars *n.* the Roman god of war; the planet nearest to the earth.

Mar•seil•laise *n.* the French national anthem.

marsh *n.* a tract of low, swampy land. **— gas** *n.* a gaseous product of decomposing organic matter. **-mallow** *n.* a red-flowered plant growing in marshes; a confection made from the root of this, or from gelatin.

mar•shal *n.* a civil officer of a district with powers of a sheriff; a person in charge of arrangements for ceremonies, etc.

mar•su•pi•al *a.* having an external pouch, to carry the young.

mart *n.* a market.

mar•ten *n.* a kind of weasel, valued for its fur.

mar•tial *a.* pert. to war or to the armed services; warlike; military. **— law** *n.* law enforced by military authorities and mar·tin n. a bird of the swallow family.

martin

mar·ti·net n. a strict disciplinarian.

mar·tin·gale n. a strap fastened to a horse's girth to keep its head down.

mar·ti·ni n. a cocktail of dry vermouth and gin.

mar·tyr n. one who suffers punishment or the sacrifice of his life for adherence to principles or beliefs.

mar·vel n. anything wonderful; v.i. to wonder exceedingly. -ous a. wonderful; astonishing.

Marx·ism n. the doctrines of Karl Marx, which profoundly influenced socialists and communists of Europe in latter part of 19th cent.

mar·zi·pan n. a paste of ground almonds, sugar and egg white made into confections.

mas·car·a n. a cosmetic preparation for eyelashes.

mas·cot n. a person or thing reputed to bring good luck.

mas·cu·line a. male; strong; virile; (of a woman) mannish.

mash v.t. to beat to a pulp or soft mass; to mix malt with hot water.

mash·ie n. a golf club with short iron head.

mask n. a covering for the face; an impression of a human face, as a death mask; a respirator to be worn as protection against poison gas; a false face, as worn by children at Halloween.

mas·och·ism n. a form of sex gratification by endurance of physical or mental pain.

ma·son n. a builder in stone, brick, etc.; a Freemason. -ry n. the work of a mason; stonework; freemasonry.

ma·son·ite n. a fiberboard made from pressed wood fibers used in building.

mas·quer·ade n. an assembly of masked persons; disguise.

mass n. the quantity of matter in a body; a shapeless lump; magnitude; crowd; chief portion. -ive a. forming a mass; bulky; weighty. — production n. cheap production in great quantities.

Mass n. the communion service in the R.C. Church; the music to accompany High Mass. High Mass n. Mass celebrated with music. Low Mass n. a simple celebration of Mass without music.

mas·sa·cre n. general, ruthless slaughter; carnage.

mas·sage n. a treatment of physical disorders by kneading, rubbing, carried out by specialists. massagist, masseur n. specialist in massage.

mast n. upright pole supporting rigging and sails of a ship.

mast n. fruit of oak, beech, esp. as food for swine.

mas·ter n. one who directs and controls; an employer of labor; male head of a household; a ship captain; a graduate degree in arts, or science (abbrev. M.A., M.Sc.). -ful a. compelling; domineering. — key n. a key which opens several locks. — switch n. an electric switch which must be turned on before other switches will function.

mas·ti·cate v.t. to chew; to reduce to a pulp.

mas·tiff n. a powerful breed of dog.

mastiff

mas·ti·tis n. (Med.) inflammation of the breast.

mas·to·don n. an extinct mammal resembling an elephant.

mas·toid a. nipple-shaped; n. the prominence on the temporal bone behind the human ear.

mas·tur·bate v.i. to practice self-excitation; autoeroticism.

mat n. a coarse fabric of twine, rope, or rushes for wiping the shoes on; a rug; a border or frame for a picture.

mat, matte a. having a dull finish; not shiny.

mat·a·dor, matadore n. the man who kills the bull in a bullfight.

match n. splint of wood or taper tipped with a substance capable of ignition by friction with a rough surface; a piece of rope for firing a gun; a fuse.

match n. a person or thing equal to or resembling another; a sporting contest; a marriage; a mate. -less a. having no match; peerless; unique.

mate n. a companion; a spouse; one of a pair; an assistant.

mate v.t. to checkmate (chess).

ma·te·ri·al a. consisting of matter corporeal; (of persons) not spiritually minded; the substance out of which something is fashioned; fabric. -ize v.t. to render material; to give bodily form to. -ism n. the theory that matter, and matter only, exists in the universe.

ma·te·ri·a med·i·ca n. (Med.) the substances used in the making of medicines, drugs, etc.

ma·ter·nal pert. to a mother; motherly; related on the mother's side.

math·e·mat·ics n. the science of quantity and space, including arithmetic, algebra, trigonometry, geometry.

mat·in n. a morning song; a morning service.

ma·tri·cide n. the murder of a mother.

ma·tric·u·late v.t. and v.i. to enroll as a student, esp. of a college.

mat·ri·mo·ny n. marriage; wedlock.

ma·trix n. the womb; the cavity where anything is formed; a mold, esp. for casting printer's type; rock where minerals are embedded.

M

ma•tron n. a married woman; a woman in charge of domestic affairs of an institution.

mat•ter n. that which occupies space and is the object of the senses; substance.

mat•ting n. mat work; coarse material used as floor covering.

mat•tock n. a kind of pickaxe with only one end pointed.

mat•tress n. a casing of strong fabric filled with hair, foam rubber, cotton, etc.

mat•u•rate v.i. to mature.

ma•ture a. ripe; fully developed; (Med.) come to suppuration; resulting from adult experience; due for payment, as a bill.

ma•tu•ti•nal a. morning; early.

maud•lin a. over-sentimental; tearful.

maul n. a heavy wooden hammer; v.t. to maltreat; to handle roughly.

maun•der v.i. to mutter; to talk or to wander aimlessly.

mau•so•le•um n. a large imposing tomb.

mauve n. a delicate purple color.

mav•er•ick n. an unbranded calf; an independent.

maw n. the stomach of an animal; in birds, the craw.

mawk•ish a. loathsome; sickly sweet; maudlin.

max•il•lar•y a. pert. to the upper jawbone or jaw.

max•im n. an accepted principle; an axiom; a proverb or precept.

max•i•mum a. greatest; n. the greatest number, quantity or degree.

may v.i. expressing possibility, permission, contingency; uncertainty; hope.

May n. the fifth month of the year; (Fig.) youthful prime. -pole n. a pole with streamers, around which people dance on May Day.

may•hem n. (Law) the offense of maiming by violence.

may•on•naise n. a sauce or dressing for salads.

may•or n. the chief official of a city or town.

maze n. a network of intricate paths; a labyrinth; confused condition; mental perplexity.

me pron. the objective case of first pers. pronoun, "I".

mead n. a fermented drink made of honey, yeast and water.

mead•ow n. a low, level tract of grassland; pasture. -lark n. a yellow-breasted Amer. songbird.

mea•ger a. scanty; having little flesh; gaunt.

meal n. the food served at one time; a repast.

meal n. edible grain coarsely ground. -worm n. an insect found in meal.

mean a. humble in rank or birth; sordid; lacking dignity; stingy; malicious.

mean a. in a middle position; average; n. the middle point of quantity, rate, position, or degree.

mean v.t. to have in view; to intend; to signify. -t, -ing n. that which is meant; sense; signification; a. expressive.

me•an•der v.i. to flow with a winding course; to saunter aimlessly.

mea•sles n. (Med.) a highly contagious disease, characterized by rash of bright red spots. German measles, a disease resembling measles but less severe.

mea•sure n. dimension reckoned by some standard; an instrument for measuring; a vessel of predetermined capacity; (Mus.) tempo; the notes between two bars in staff notation. -ment n. dimension, quantity, etc., ascertained by measuring with fixed unit.

meat n. flesh used as food; food of any kind.

Mec•ca n. the reputed birthplace of Mohammed; a holy city.

me•chan•i•cal a. pert. to machines, mechanism, or mechanics; produced or operated by machinery; automatic. mechanic n. one who works with or repairs machines or instruments. mechanics n. that branch of applied mathematics which deals with force and motion; the science of machines. mechanism n. the structure of a machine; machinery; a piece of machinery.

med•al n. a piece of metal, struck like a coin, as a memento or reward. -lion n. a large medal; a metal disk, usually round, with portrait in bas-relief. -ist n. a maker of medals; one who has been awarded a medal.

med•dle v.i. to interfere officiously; to tamper with.

me•di•al a. in, or through, the middle; pert. to a mean or average. median a. situated in the middle; n. (Geom.) a line drawn from vertex of a triangle to the middle point of the opposite side.

me•di•ate a. being between two extremes; intervening; depending on an intermediary; not direct. mediation n. the act of mediating; the steps taken to effect a reconciliation. mediatize v.t. to annex a small state, still leaving the ruler his title.

med•ic n. a leguminous plant with leaves like clover, used as fodder.

med•i•cal a. pert. to medicine or the art of healing; medicinal. medicate v.t. to treat with medicine.

med•i•cine n. any substance used in the treatment of disease; the science of healing and prevention of disease. medicinal a. pert. to medicine; remedial.

me•di•e•val, mediaeval a. pert. to or characteristic of the Middle Ages. -ist n. one who makes a special study of the Middle Ages.

me•di•o•cre a. middling; neither good nor bad; second-rate.

med•i•tate v.t. to consider thoughtfully; to intend; v.i. to ponder, esp. on religious matters. meditative a. given to reflection.

med•i•ter•ra•ne•an a. (of water) encircled by land. Mediterranean a. pert. to the almost landlocked water between S. Europe and N. Africa. Mediterranean climate, a climate of warm wet winters, hot dry summers.

me•di•um n. that which is in the middle; a

means; an agency; *pl.* -s or media; *a.* middle; average; middling.

med•ley *n.* a miscellaneous collection of things.

me•dul•la *n.* marrow in a bone; inner tissue of a gland; pith of hair or plants.

me•du•sa *n.* a kind of jellyfish, with tentacles.

meed *n.* reward; recompense.

meek *a.* submissive; humble; mild.

meer•schaum *n.* a fine, white clay used for the bowl of tobacco pipes.

meet *a.* fit; suitable.

meet *v.t.* to encounter; to join; to find; to satisfy; to pay, as a debt; to await arrival.

me•ga- *Gk. pref.* meaning great, mighty.

meg•a•cy•cle *n.* (*Elect.*) one million cycles.

meg•a•lith *n.* a huge stone.

meg•a•lo•ma•ni•a *n.* a form of insanity in which the patient has grandiose ideas of his own importance; lust for power.

meg•a•phone *n.* a large funnel-shaped device to increase the volume of sounds.

meg•a•ton *n.* a unit for measuring the power of thermonuclear weapons.

meg•ohm *n.* one million ohms.

me•grim *n.* a severe headache, usu. on one side.

mei•o•sis *n.* (*Rhet.*) a figure of speech which makes a deliberate understatement to achieve emphasis; a form of litotes.

mel•an•chol•y *n.* depression of spirits; morbidity; *a.* gloomy; depressed; pensive. **melancholia** *n.* morbid state of depression; abnormal introspectiveness bordering on insanity.

Mel•a•ne•sian *a.* pert. to *Melanesia*, a S. Pacific dark-skinned island group; *n.* a native.

mé•lange *n.* a mixture; a medley.

mel•a•nin *n.* a black pigment found in the eye, hair and skin. **melanism** *n.* an excess of coloring matter in the skin

mel•ba toast *n.* thin slice of toast.

meld *v.t.* and *v.i.* to blend; merge; a combination of cards melded.

me•lee *n.* a confused, hand-to-hand fight.

me•lio•rate *v.t.* to improve; *v.i.* to become better.

mel•lif•er•ous *a.* producing honey. **mellifluence** *n.* a flowing sweetly or smoothly.

mel•low *a.* soft and ripe; well-matured; genial; jovial; resonant, as a voice.

me•lo•de•on *n.* a small hand keyboard organ; a kind of accordion.

mel•o•dra•ma *n.* a dramatic entertainment, sensational and emotional; a play of romantic sentiment and situation.

mel•o•dy *n.* a rhythmical succession of single sounds forming an agreeable musical air; a tune.

mel•on *n.* a kind of gourd with a sweet, juicy pulp, and a center full of seeds.

melt *v.t.* to reduce to a liquid state; to dissolve; to soften; to make tender.

mem•ber *n.* a limb, esp. of an animal body; a constituent part of a complex whole; one of a society, group, etc. **-ship** *n.* the state of being a member, or one of a group; members collectively.

mem•brane *n.* (*Anat.*) a thin, flexible tissue forming or lining an organ of the body; a sheet of parchment.

me•mem•to *n.* anything which serves as a reminder of a person or event; a souvenir.

mem•oir *n.* a short, biographical sketch; a scientific record of personal investigations on a subject.

mem•o•ry *n.* the faculty of retaining and recalling knowledge; recollection; remembrance. **memorial** *a.* serving as a reminder; contained in the memory. **memorialize** *v.t.* to commemorate; to present a memorial. **memorize** *v.t.* to commit to memory.

men *n.pl.* of **man**.

men•ace *n.* a threat or threatening; potential danger; *v.t.* to threaten.

mé•nage *n.* a household; housekeeping.

me•nag•er•ie *n.* a collection of caged wild animals for exhibition.

mend *v.t.* to repair; to set right; to improve.

men•da•cious *a.* given to telling lies; untruthful.

men•di•cant *a.* begging; living as a beggar; *n.* a beggar.

me•ni•al *a.* pert. to domestic service; servile; *n.* a servant; a servile person.

me•nin•ges *n.pl.* the three membranes enveloping the brain and spinal cord.

me•nis•cus *n.* a lens convex on one side and concave on the other; the curved surface of a liquid in a vessel; (*Math.*) a crescent.

Men•non•ite *n.* a member of or pert. to a Protestant sect favoring plain dress and plain living.

men•o•pause *n.* female change of life.

men•sal *a.* monthly.

men•ses *n.pl.* the monthly discharge from the uterus of the female. **menstrual** *a.* monthly; pert. to the menses. **menstruate** *v.i.* to discharge the menses.

men•stru•um *n.* a solvent.

men•su•ra•ble *a.* capable of being measured.

men•tal *a.* pert. to, or of, the mind; performed in the mind. **-ity** *n.* intellectual power; mental attitude.

men•thol *n.* a camphor obtained from oil of peppermint. **-ated** *a.* treated or flavored with menthol.

men•tion *n.* a brief notice; a casual comment; *v.t.* to notice; to name.

men•tor *n.* an experienced and prudent adviser.

men•u *n.* a bill of fare; the food served.

me•phi•tis *n.* noxious exhalation, esp. from the ground or from decaying matter.

mer•can•tile *a.* pert. to commerce. **mercantilism** *n.* the mercantile system. — **system**, the economic theory that money alone is wealth and that a nation's exports should far exceed its imports.

mer•ce•nar•y *a.* working merely for money or gain; hired; greedy; *n.* a hired soldier.

mer•cer•ize *v.t.* to treat cotton fabrics with caustic lye to impart a silky finish.

mer•chant *n.* one who engages in trade; a storekeeper. **merchandise** *n.*

M

commodities bought and sold.
— marine n. the ships and men engaged in commerce.

Mer•cu•ry n. the planet of the solar system nearest to the sun. mercury n. a metallic chemical element, silvery-white in color, with very low melting point, used in barometers, thermometers, etc.

mer•cy n. forbearance; clemency; leniency shown to a guilty person; compassion. merciful a. full of mercy; compassionate.

mere a. nothing but; simple. -ly adv. simply; solely.

mer•e•tri•cious a. tawdry; cheap.

mer•gan•ser n. a diving fish-eating bird.

merganser

merge v.t. to cause to be swallowed up; to plunge or sink. -r n. a combine of commercial or industrial firms.

me•rid•i•an n. an imaginary line passing through the poles at right angles to the equator.

me•ringue n. a mixture of sugar and white of egg whipped until stiff, and baked in a cool oven.

me•ri•no n. a breed of sheep with very fine, thick fleece, orig. from Spain; a dress fabric of this wool.

mer•it n. quality of deserving reward; excellence; worth.

mer•lin n. a species of falcon.

mer•maid n. an imaginary sea creature with the upper body and head of a woman, and the tail of a fish. merman n. the male equivalent.

mer•ry a. gay; hilarious; lively. —go-round n. a revolving platform with horses, cars, etc.

mer•thi•o•late n. an antiseptic and germicide.

me•sa n. a high plateau.

mes•dames n.pl. of madam, Mrs.

mes•en•te•ry n. a fold of abdominal tissue keeping the intestines in place.

mesh n. the space between the threads of a net; network; v.i. to become interlocked, as gears of a machine.

mes•mer•ism n. exercising an influence over will and actions of another; hypnotism.

mesne a. middle; (Law) intermediate.

mes•o•lith•ic a. of period between paleolithic and neolithic ages.

me•son n. a particle equal in charge to, but having greater mass than, an electron or positron, and less mass than a neutron or proton.

Mes•o•po•ta•mi•a n. the land between Euphrates and Tigris; now Iraq.

Mes•o•zo•ic a. pert. to the second geological period.

mess n. unpleasant mixture; disorder; a muddle.

mess n. a dish of food served at one time;

the meal; a number of people who eat together, esp. in army, navy, etc. — kit n. a soldier's portable eating equipment.

mes•sage n. a communication, verbal or written, sent by one person to another; an inspired utterance. messenger n. one who delivers a communication; one employed to deliver goods.

mes•si•ah n. an expected savior or liberator.

mes•suage n. (Law) a dwelling house with lands and outbuildings.

mes•ti•zo n. a half-caste, esp. the offspring of a Spaniard and an Amer. Indian.

met pa.t. and pa.p. of the verb meet.

me•tab•o•lism n. the name given to the chemical changes continually going on in the cells of living matter.

me•ta•car•pus n. the hand between the wrist and fingers; the bones of this part.

met•age n. official weighing, as of coal; the price paid for this.

met•al n. a mineral substance, opaque, fusible and malleable, capable of conducting heat and electricity; molten glass. -lic a. pert. to, like, or consisting of, metal. -loid n. an element with both metallic and nonmetallic properties, as arsenic; a. pert. to a metal.

met•al•lur•gy n. the art of working metals or of obtaining metals from ores.

met•a•mor•pho•sis n. a change of form or structure; evolution.

met•a•phor n. a figure of speech which makes an implied comparison between things which are not literally alike. -ically adv. -ist n. mixed metaphor n. a combination of metaphors drawn from different sources.

met•a•phrase n. literal, word for word translation from foreign language.

met•a•phys•ics n. the science which investigates first causes of all existence and knowledge; speculative philosophy.

me•tas•ta•sis n. change of position, state, or form; shift of malignant cells from one part of the body to another.

met•a•tar•sus n. the front part of the foot excluding the toes.

me•tath•e•sis n. the transposition of a letter or letters in a word, as in curl, orig. crul.

met•a•zo•a n.pl. multicellular organisms.

mete v.t. to distribute by measure; to allot, as punishment.

me•te•or n. any rapidly passing, luminous body seen in the atmosphere; a shooting star. -ite n. a mass of stone or metal from outer space which lands on earth. -ograph n. an instrument for automatically recording weather conditions. -ological a. -ologist n. -ology n. the science which treats of atmospheric phenomena, esp. in relation to weather forecasts.

me•ter n. a unit of length in the metric system, 39.37 U.S. inches. metric a. metric system n. a decimal system based on the French meter. metrology n. the science of weights and measures.

me•ter n. an instrument for recording the consumption of gas, electricity, water, etc.

me•ter *n.* in poetry, the rhythmical arrangement of syllables, these groups being termed *feet;* verse; stanza form; *(Music)* rhythmical structure indicated by measures; time or beat.

meth•ane *n.* an inflammable, hydrocarbon gas.

meth•od *n.* manner of proceeding, esp. in scientific research; orderliness; system; technique.

Meth•od•ist *n.* a member of Protestant sect founded in 18th century by Charles and John Wesley.

meth•yl *n.* the chemical basis of wood.

me•tic•u•lous *a.* orig. afraid to make a mistake; overscrupulous as to detail; over-exact.

me•ton•y•my *n.* a figure of speech in which the name of one thing is put for another associated with it.

met•ro•nym•ic *a.* a name derived from a female ancestor.

me•trop•o•lis *n.* the chief city of an area; a large city; a diocese.

met•tle *n.* spirit; courage. **-some** *a.*

mew *v.t.* to shed or cast; to confine, as in a cage; *n.pl.* stables around a court or alley.

mewl *v.i.* to whimper or whine.

Mex•i•can *n.* a native or inhabitant of Mexico.

mez•za•nine *n.* *(Archit.)* a low story between two main ones; in a theater usu. the first few rows in the balcony.

mez•zo *a.* middle; moderately.

mi•as•ma *n.* noxious exhalations from decomposing matter.

mi•ca *n.* a group of mineral silicates capable of cleavage into very thin, flexible, and often transparent laminae.

mi•crobe *n.* a minute organism; a bacterium or disease germ.

mi•cro•ceph•a•lous *a.* *(Med.)* having a very small head.

mi•cro•coc•cus *n.* a spherical or oval organism or bacterium.

mi•cro•cosm *n.* miniature universe; man, regarded as the epitome of the universe.

mi•cro•film *n.* film used to make reduced photographic copies of books, etc.

mi•cro•graph *n.* an instrument for producing microscopic engraving; a microphotograph. **micrographer** *n.* **micrography** *n.* the study of microscopic objects; the art of writing or engraving on a minute scale.

mi•crol•o•gy *n.* the science which deals with microscopic objects.

mi•crom•e•ter *n.* an instrument for measuring very small distances or angles.

mi•cron *n.* the millionth part of a meter.

mi•cro•or•gan•ism *n.* a microscopic organism.

mi•cro•phone *n.* an instrument for turning sound waves into electrical waves, so enabling them to be transmitted.

mi•cro•pho•tog•ra•phy *n.* the art of producing minute photographs.

mi•cro•scope *n.* an optical instrument for magnifying minute objects. **micro-**

scopic, -al *a.* visible only with a microscope; very minute.

mi•cro•zo•a *n.pl.* microscopic animals.

mic•tu•ri•tion *n.* *(Med.)* the passing of urine.

mid *a.* situated between extremes; middle, as in *midair, mid-Atlantic.* **-shipman** *n.* rank in U.S. Navy and Coast Guard held by young men attending service academies.

mid•dle *a.* equidistant from the extremes; intermediate; *n.* middle point. **-man** *n.* an agent acting between producer and consumer; a go-between. **-weight** *n.* *(Boxing)* a boxer of a weight not more than 160 lbs. **— class** *n.* that section of the community between the very wealthy higher social classes and the laboring classes; the bourgeoisie.

midge *n.* a gnat; a very small person. **-t** *n.* a dwarf; *a.* miniature.

mid•riff *n.* the diaphragm; body part between chest and abdomen.

midst *n.* the middle; *prep.* amidst.

mid•wife *n.* a woman who assists another at childbirth.

mien *n.* manner; bearing; general appearance.

miff *v.t.* and *v.i.* to offend or take offense.

might *pa.t.* of verb **may.**

might *n.* power; strength; energy. **-iness** *n.* the state of being powerful; greatness.

mi•gnon•ette *n.* a sweet-scented, greenish-gray flowered plant.

mi•graine *n.* severe headache often accompanied by nausea.

mi•grate *v.i.* to remove one's residence from one place to another; (of birds) to fly to another place in search of warmer climate. **migrant** *n.* a person or creature who migrates.

mil *n.* .001 in., a unit of measurement in calculating the diameter of wire.

milch *a.* giving milk.

mild *a.* gentle; kind; placid; calm, or temperate, as weather.

mil•dew *n.* whitish coating of minute fungi on plants; a mold on paper, cloth, leather caused by dampness.

mile *n.* a measure of length equal to 5,280 ft. **geographical** or **nautical mile** *n.* 1/60 of 1 degree of the earth's equator, 6,080.2 ft. **-age** *n.* distance in miles; rate of travel calculated in miles; traveling expenses calculated on the number of miles traveled.

mil•i•ar•y *a.* like millet seeds. **miliaria** *n.* *(Med.)* a fever, accompanied by a rash resembling millet seeds (heat rash).

mi•lieu *n.* environment.

mil•i•tant *a.* aggressive; serving as a soldier. **militancy** *n.* warlike, fighting spirit. **militarist** *n.* one who upholds the doctrine of militarism; a student of military science. **military** *a.* pert. to soldiers, arms, or war; warlike; *n.* the army.

mi•li•tia *n.* a citizen army, liable to be called out in an emergency.

milk *n.* a white fluid secreted by female mammals for nourishment of their young and in some cases used for humans; the

M

juice of certain plants. **Milky Way** *n.* the galaxy, an irregular, luminous belt in the heavens, from the light of innumerable stars. **condensed milk** *n.* milk with sugar added and evaporated to the consistency of syrup. **evaporated milk** *n.* unsweetened condensed milk.

mill *n.* a building equipped with machinery to grind grain into flour; an apparatus for grinding, as *coffee mill;* a factory or machinery used in manufacture. **-board** *n.* stout pasteboard used in bookbinding. **-dam** *n.* a dam built to provide water for turning a mill wheel. **-race** *n.* the current of water which turns mill wheel. **-stone** *n.* one of the flat stones used in grinding grain; a burden.

mill *n.* one-thousandth of a dollar; one-tenth of a cent.

mil•len•ni•um *n.* a thousand years; a future time or perfect peace on earth. **millennarian** *n.* one who believes in the millennium. **millennary** *a.* comprising a thousand; *n.* a period of a thousand years.

mil•li- *pref.* one-thousandth of. **-gram** *n.* one-thousandth of a gram. **-meter** *n.* one-thousandth of a meter.

mil•liard *n.* a thousand millions; a billion.

mil•li•ner *n.* one who makes or sells ladies' hats.

mil•lion *n.* a thousand thousands (1,000,000); **-aire** *n.* one whose wealth amounts to a million (or more) dollars.

mil•li•pede *n.* an insect with many legs.

milt *n.* the spleen; the reproductive glands or secretion of the male fish; *v.t.* to impregnate the female roe.

mime *n.* a farce in which scenes of real life are expressed by gesture only; an actor in such a farce. **-tic(al)** *a.* imitative. **mimic** *v.t.* to imitate; to burlesque; to ridicule by imitating another.

mim•e•o•graph *n.* a form of duplicating machine.

mi•mo•sa *n.* any of a genus of leguminous plants, shrubs, or trees, with small, fluffy flowers.

min•a•ret *n.* a turret on a Mohammedan mosque.

mi•na•to•ry *a.* threatening; menacing.

mince *v.t.* to cut or chop into very small pieces. **-meat** *n.* currants, raisins, spices, apple, suet and sugar, chopped and mixed together, used as pie filling; *(Fig.)* anything chopped up.

mind *n.* the intellectual faculty; the understanding; memory; opinion; inclination. purpose; a person regarded as an intellect. **— reader** *n.* one who can sense another's thoughts.

mine *n.* a pit in the earth from which minerals are excavated; a hidden explosive to blow up a wall, vessel, etc.; a profitable source. **-field** *n.* an area of land or stretch of the sea where mines have been placed.

mine *poss. pron.* belonging to me.

min•er•al *n.* any substance, generally inorganic, taken from the earth by mining; a chemical element or compound occurring in nature. **-ization**

n. **-ize** *v.t.* to convert into or impregnate with minerals. **-ogy** *n.* the science of minerals and their classification.

min•e•stro•ne *n.* thick vegetable soup.

min•gle *v.t.* to mix; to blend; to join in.

min•i•a•ture *n.* a small-sized painting done on ivory, vellum, etc.; anything on a small scale; *a.* minute.

min•i•fy *v.t.* to lessen; to minimize.

min•im *n.* anything very minute; *(Med.)* 1/60 of a fluid dram; a drop; *(Mus.)* a half note. **-al** *a.* smallest possible. **-um** *n.* the least to which anything may be reduced.

min•ion *n.* a favorite; a servile flatterer; *(Print.)* a small type.

min•is•ter *n.* an agent or instrument; a clergyman; *(Brit.)* one entrusted with a govt. department; to serve. **ministration** *n.* the act of performing a service.

min•i•ver *n.* fine white fur.

mink *n.* a semiaquatic animal of the weasel tribe; its fur.

mink

min•now *n.* a small freshwater fish.

mi•nor *a.* lesser; inferior in bulk, degree, importance, etc.; *n.* a person under 21.

mi•nor•ca *n.* a breed of fowl.

min•ster *n.* church cathedral.

min•strel *n.* a medieval poet or wandering singer; an entertainer in a minstrel show.

mint *n.* the place where money is coined; a great amount of money.

mint *n.* an aromatic plant used for medicinal and culinary purposes.

min•u•end *n.* the number from which another is to be subtracted.

min•u•et *n.* a slow, stately dance.

mi•nus *prep.* less by; *a.* showing subtraction; negative; *n.* the sign (−) of subtraction; an amount less than nothing. **-cule** *a.* small; *n.* a lowercase letter.

mi•nute *a.* very small; slight; particular; exact.

min•ute *n.* the 60th part of an hour or degree; a moment; *pl.* the official record of a meeting.

minx *n.* a pert, saucy girl.

mir•a•cle *n.* a wonder; a supernatural happening; a prodigy. **miraculous** *a.* supernatural; extraordinary.

mi•rage *n.* an optical illusion; a delusion.

mire *n.* slimy soil; mud; defilement.

mir•ror *n.* a looking glass; a brilliantly polished reflecting surface.

mirth *n.* gaiety; merriment; joyousness; laughter.

mis- *pref.* wrong; ill.

mis•ad•ven•ture *n.* an unlucky adventure; a mishap.

mis•ad•vise *v.t.* to advise wrongly.

mis•al•li•ance *n.* an unfortunate alliance, esp. in marriage.

mis•an•thrope *n.* a hater of mankind.

mis•ap•ply v.t. to apply wrongly or dishonestly.

mis•ap•pre•hend v.t. to apprehend wrongly; to misconceive.

mis•ap•pro•pri•ate v.t. to use wrongly, esp. to embezzle money.

mis•be•got•ten a. unlawfully conceived; illegitimate.

mis•be•have v.i. to behave badly, improperly or dishonestly.

mis•be•lieve v.t. to believe wrongly.

mis•cal•cu•late v.t. to calculate wrongly.

mis•car•riage n. failure; premature birth.

mis•ce•ge•na•tion n. a mixture of races by interbreeding.

mis•cel•la•ne•ous a. mixed; heterogenous.

mis•chance n. a mishap; ill luck.

mis•chief n. harm; damage; conduct intended to annoy. mischievous a. tending to stir up trouble; playfully annoying.

mis•ci•ble a. capable of being mixed.

mis•con•ceive v.t. to misunderstand.

mis•con•duct n. bad management; dishonest conduct.

mis•con•strue v.i. to interpret wrongly; misunderstand.

mis•count v.t. to count wrongly; to miscalculate.

mis•cre•ant n. unprincipled person.

mis•cue n. (Billiards) a stroke spoiled by the cue slipping; a mistake.

mis•date v.t. to put a wrong date on; n. a wrong date.

mis•deal v.t. and v.i. to deal cards wrong; n. wrong deal. -t pa.t.

mis•deed n. an evil deed, a crime.

mis•de•mean•or n. dishonest conduct; (Law) a crime less than felony.

mis•di•rect v.t. to direct or advise wrongly.

mi•ser n. one who hoards money and lives in wretched surroundings.

mis•er•a•ble a. unhappy; causing misery; worthless; deplorable.

mis•er•y n. great unhappiness; extreme pain of body or mind.

mis•fire n. (of internal combustion engine, gun, etc.) failure to start or go off.

mis•for•tune n. ill luck.

mis•give v.t. to fill with doubt; to cause to hesitate; v.i. to fail.

mis•guide v.t. to lead astray; to advise wrongly.

mis•han•dle v.t. to maltreat; to bungle.

mis•in•form v.t. to give wrong information to.

mis•in•ter•pret v.t. to interpret or explain wrongly.

mis•join•der n. (Law) introduction into court of parties or causes not belonging.

mis•judge v.t. to judge wrongly.

mis•lay to lay down something in a place which cannot later be recollected.

mis•lead v.t. to lead astray.

mis•man•age v.t. to manage incompetently.

mis•no•mer n. a wrong name; incorrect designation.

mi•sog•a•my n. hatred of marriage.

mi•sog•y•ny n. hatred of women.

mis•place v.t. to place wrongly; to mislay.

mis•print v.t. to make an error in printing.

mis•pro•nounce v.t. to pronounce incorrectly.

mis•quote v.t. to quote incorrectly.

mis•reck•on v.t. to estimate or reckon incorrectly.

mis•rep•re•sent v.i. to represent falsely; to report inaccurately.

mis•rule n. disorder; misgovernment.

Miss n. title of unmarried women; girl.

miss v.t. to fail to hit, reach, find, catch, notice; to be without; to feel the want of.

mis•sal n. a book containing the R.C. service of the mass for a year.

mis•sel n. the large European thrush, supposed to eat mistletoe berries.

mis•shape v.t. to shape badly; to deform. -en a.

mis•sile n. that which is thrown or shot. guided missile n. a projected unmanned object which travels above the earth and performs some specific function, such as communication.

mis•sion n. the act of sending; the duty on which one is sent. -ary a. pert. to missions or missionaries; n. one sent to preach religion.

mis•sive n. a letter or message.

mis•spell v.t. to spell incorrectly.

mis•spend v.t. to spend foolishly; to squander.

mist n. visible vapor in the lower atmosphere; droplets of rain; a cloudiness or film.

mis•take v.t. to misunderstand; to take one person for another; v.i. to err.

mis•ter n. sir; title of courtesy to a man (abbrev. Mr.).

mis•tle•toe n. a parasitic, evergreen plant with white berries.

mis•tral n. a cold, often violent, N.W. wind which blows over S. France.

mis•tress n. (fem.of master) a woman in authority (as over a household, animal, institution); a kept woman.

mis•tri•al n. a trial made invalid by an error in proceedings.

mis•trust n. lack of confidence; v.t. to suspect; to lack faith in.

mis•un•der•stand v.t. to interpret incorrectly; to form a wrong judgment.

mis•use v.t. to use improperly; to maltreat.

mite n. any very small thing or person; a kind of arachnid, as cheese mite.

mi•ter n. a bishop's headdress, a tall cap; in carpentry, a joint made by two pieces of wood fitting into each other at an angle of 45°.

mit•i•gate v.t. to relieve; to alleviate; to temper. mitigable a. capable of being lessened. mitigation n. alleviation.

mi•to•sis n. (Biol.) method of cell division in which chromatin divides into chromosomes.

mitt n. a covering for wrist and hand leaving fingers exposed; a baseball glove, with palm heavily padded.

mix v.t. to unite into a mass; to blend; to combine a mixture; to associate. -ed marriage n. a marriage between two people of different religions or different races.

M

miz•zen, mizen *n.* fore-and-aft sail of a vessel.

mne•mon•ic -al *a.* assisting the memory.

moan *n.* a low cry of grief or pain; *v.i.* to utter a low, wailing cry.

moat *n.* a deep trench around a castle, usu. filled with water.

mob *n.* a disorderly crowd of people; a rabble; the populace; *v.t.* to attack in a disorderly crowd; to jostle.

mob•cap *n.* a frilled cap, tied under the chin, worn by women in the 18th cent.

mo•bile *a.* easily moved; changing; facile; (of troops) mechanized; capable of moving rapidly from place to place; *n.* an artistic arrangement of wires, etc., easily set in motion. **mobilization** *n.* the wartime act of calling up men and women for active service.

moc•ca•sin *a.* shoe of soft leather worn by N. American Indians, trappers, etc.; a bedroom slipper of similar shape; a poisonous water snake.

mo•cha *n.* a coffee orig. from *Mocha* in Yemen; *a.* flavored with coffee.

mock *v.t.* to laugh at; to ridicule; to make a fool of; to defy; to mimic; substitute. **-ing bird** *n.* a N. Amer. bird which imitates

mock

other birds. **— orange** *n.* shrub with fragrant white flowers. **— turtle** *n.* a soup made of calf's head and spices to imitate turtle soup.

mode *n.* manner, form, or method; custom; fashion; *(Mus.)* one of the two classes of keys (major or minor); *(Gram.)* the *mood* of the verb. **modal** *a.* relating to mode or form. **modality** *n.* **modish** *a.* fashionable. **modishly** *adv.*

mod•el *n.* an exact, three-dimensional representation of an object, in miniature; a pattern or standard to copy; one who poses for an artist; a mannequin; *a.* serving as a model or criterion.

mod•er•ate *a.* restrained; temperate; average; not extreme; *v.t.* to restrain; to control; to decrease the intensity or pressure of; *v.i.* to become less violent or intense; to act as moderator; *n.* a person of moderate opinions in politics, etc.

mod•ern *a.* pert. to present or recent time; up-to-date.

mod•est *a.* unassuming; restrained; decent; retiring in manner; not excessive, as *modest* means.

mod•i•cum *n.* a small amount.

mod•i•fy *v.t.* to moderate; to alter the form or intensity of. **modifiable** *a.* **modification** *n.* the act of modifying; the state of being modified; a change of form, manner, or intensity.

mod•u•late *v.t.* to regulate, esp. the pitch of the voice; to adapt; *(Mus.)* to change

the key of; *v.i. (Mus.)* to pass from one key to another. **modular** *a.* of a mode, modulation, or module. **modulation** *n.* the act of modulating; the changing of the pitch or key; *(Elect.)* the variation of the amplitude or frequency of continuous waves, usu. by a lower frequency. **module** *n.* a unit of measurement; *(Archit.)* the radius of a shaft at its base.

mo•gul *n.* a powerful or important person.

mo•hair *n.* the silky hair of the Angora goat.

Mo•ham•me•dan *a.* of Mohammed or the Moslem religion.

Mo•ha•ve *n.* a tribe of Amer. Indians.

Mo•hawk *n.* the name of a N. Amer. Indian tribe.

Mo•hi•can *n.* a N. Amer. Indian tribe of Algonquin stock.

moire *n.* watered fabric; *a.* having a wavy pattern.

moist *a.* damp; humid; rather wet.

mo•lar *a.* grinding or able to grind, as back teeth; a back double-tooth.

mo•las•ses *n. sing.* a dark-colored syrup obtained from sugar; treacle.

mold *n.* a pattern, form or matrix for giving shape to something in a plastic or molten state.

mold *n.* fine, soft soil; the upper layer of the earth.

mold *n.* a downy fungus which grows on leather, cheese, bread, etc.

mole *n.* a slightly raised, dark spot on the skin.

mole *n.* a small burrowing animal.

mole

mole *n.* a breakwater.

mol•e•cule *n.* the smallest portion of a substance which can retain the characteristics of that substance. **molecular** *a.* **molecular weight** *n.* the weight of a molecule of a substance in relation to the weight of a hydrogen atom.

mo•lest *v.t.* to trouble; to accost with sinister intention.

mol•i•fy *v.t.* to appease; to placate; to soften.

mol•lusk, mol•lusc *n.* an invertebrate animal with soft, pulpy body and a hard outer shell (oyster, snail, etc.).

molt *v.t.* and *v.i.* to shed feathers, as of birds, or skins, as of snakes; *n.* the act of shedding.

mol•ten *a.* melted; of metals, liquified.

mo•lyb•de•num *n.* a rare metal, used in alloys.

mo•ment *n.* a short space of time; interval; importance; the measure of a force by its effect in causing rotation. **-ous** *a.* very important. **-um** *n.* the impetus in a body; increasing force.

mo•nad *n. (Biol.)* a single-celled organism; *(Chem.)* an atom with the valence of one;

(Philos.) an individual thought of as a microcosm.

mon·arch *n.* a hereditary sovereign; the supreme ruler of a state. **-y** *n.* government by a single ruler; a kingdom or empire.

mon·as·ter·y *n.* a settlement of monks.

mon·au·ral *a.* of sound reproduction from one source only.

Mon·day *n.* the second day of the week.

mon·e·tary *a.* concerning money or coinage.

mon·ey *n.* any form of token, as coin, banknote, used as medium of exchange, and stamped by state authority; currency; wealth.

mon·ger *n.* *(Brit.)* a dealer, usu. in compound words, as *fishmonger, ironmonger.*

Mon·gol *n.* a native of Mongolia (Asia); *a.* also **Mongolian. -ism** *n.* arrest of physical and mental development with Asiatic features.

mon·goose *n.* a small weasel-like animal, a snake-killer.

mongoose

mon·grel *a.* and *n.* impure; hybrid of mixed breed.

mo·nism *n.* the philosophical doctrine which seeks to explain varied phenomena by a single principle.

mo·ni·tion *n.* cautionary advice; admonition; notice; *(Law)* a summons. **monitive** *a.* expressing warning.

monk *n.* a hermit; a member of a religious community living in a monastery.

mon·key *n.* a long-tailed mammal of the order of Primates resembling man in organization; mischievous child; the weighted head of a pile driver; a hammer for driving home bolts.

mon·o·bloc *n.* the cylinders of the internal-combustion engine in one casting.

mon·o·car·pous *a.* bearing fruit only once.

mon·o·chord *n.* a one-stringed instrument; a one-stringed device for measuring musical intervals.

mon·o·chrome *n.* a painting in different tones of the same color. **monochromatic, monochromic** *a.* **monochromatism** *n.* color-blindness.

mon·o·cle *n.* a single eyeglass.

mo·noc·ra·cy *n.* government by a single person.

mon·o·dy *n.* an elegy expressive of mourning; a monotonous tone.

mo·nog·a·my *n.* the state of being married to one person at a time.

mon·o·gen·e·sis *n.* the descent of an organism or all living things, from a single cell.

mon·o·gram *n.* two or more letters, as initials of a person's name.

mon·o·graph *n.* a specialized treatise on a single subject.

mo·nog·y·nous *a.* *(Bot.)* having single pistil; *(Zool.)* mating with a single female. **monogyny** *n.* the custom of having only one female mate.

mon·o·lith *n.* a monument or column fashioned from a single block of stone.

mon·o·logue *n.* a dramatic scene in which an actor soliloquizes; a dramatic entertainment by a solo performer.

mon·o·ma·ni·a *n.* a form of mental derangement in which sufferer is irrational on one subject only, or is obsessed by one idea.

mo·no·mi·al *a.* *(Math.)* comprising a single term or expression; *n.* an algebraic expression containing a single term.

mon·o·nym *n.* a name comprising a single term.

mon·o·pho·bi·a *n.* *(Path.)* a morbid fear of being alone.

mon·o·plane *n.* an aircraft with only one set of wings.

mo·nop·o·ly *n.* the sole right to trade in certain commodities; exclusive possession or control; a commodity so controlled; a controlling company.

mon·o·syl·la·ble *n.* a word of one syllable.

mon·o·the·ism *n.* the doctrine which admits of one God only.

mon·o·tint *n.* a sketch or painting in one tint.

mon·o·tone *n.* a single, unvaried tone or sound. **monotonous** *a.* uttered or recited in one tone; dull; unvaried.

mon·o·type *n.* *(Biol.)* a genus with one species; *(Print.)* a two-part machine for setting and casting type in individual letters, as distinct from *linotype.*

mon·ox·ide *n.* oxide containing one oxygen atom in a molecule.

Mon·sei·gneur *n.* my lord; a title given in France to princes, bishops, etc. *pl.* **Messeigneurs. Monsignor** *n.* an Italian title given to prelates.

mon·soon *n.* a seasonal wind of S. Asia; the very heavy rainfall season in summer, esp. in India.

mon·ster *n.* a creature of unnatural shape; a person of abnormal callousness, cruelty, or wickedness. **monstrosity** *n.* an unnatural production; an abnormal creature; a freak.

mon·strance *n.* a shrine for the consecrated host in R.C. services.

mon·tage *n.* *(Motion pictures)* assembling various shots of a film into one well-arranged series; a picture made by superimposing various elements from several sources.

Mon·tes·so·ri Sys·tem *n.* educational system to give free scope to child's individuality and creative powers.

month *n.* one of the twelve divisions of the year. **lunar month** *n.* about 29 days; a period of 28 days, or four complete weeks. **-ly** *a.* lasting, performed in, a month.

mon·u·ment *n.* any structure, as a tombstone, building tablet, erected to the memory of person, or event.

mooch *v.t.* and *v.i.* *(Colloq.)* to loiter; to sponge from another.

mood *n.* *(Gram.)* the inflection of a verb expressing its function, as *indicative,* *imperative, subjunctive, infinitive.*

mood *n.* disposition; frame of mind; temper.

moon *n.* the satellite which revolves around the earth in the period of a lunar month; any secondary planet; a month; anything crescent-shaped or shining like the moon. **-stone** *n.* an almost pellucid form of feldspar. **-struck** *a.* dazed.

Moor *n.* a native of the Barbary States; one of the conquerors of Spain in the 8th cent.

moor *n.* (*Brit.*) marshy wasteland.

moor *v.t.* to secure by cables and anchors, as a vessel.

moose *n.* largest species of deer; elk.

moot *v.t.* to debate; to discuss. — **court** *n.* a mock court.

mope *v.i.* to be dull or depressed; to sulk.

mo•raine *n.* rock debris which accumulates along the sides or at the end of a glacier.

mor•al *a.* pert. to right conduct or duties of man; ethical; virtuous; chaste; *n.* the underlying meaning implied in a fable, allegory, etc. **-istic** *a.* **-ity** *n.* the practice of moral duties; virtue; ethics; an early form of drama, in which the characters were the virtues and vices of men personified. **-ly** *adv.* — **victory** *n.* a defeat, which in a deeper sense, is a victory.

mo•rale *n.* the disposition or mental state which causes a man or body of people to face an emergency with spirit.

mo•rass *n.* marshy ground; difficult state of affairs.

mor•a•to•ri•um *n.* a law to delay payment of debts for a given period of time.

mo•ray *n.* a sharp-toothed marine eel.

mor•bid *a.* diseased; unhealthy; (of the mind) excessively gloomy.

mor•dant *n.* any substance, metallic or vegetable, which fixes dyes; a corrosive acid used in etching; *a.* biting; corrosive; sarcastic.

more *a.* greater in amount, degree, quality, etc.; in greater number; additional.

mo•rel *n.* an edible mushroom.

mo•rel *n.* the common and deadly nightshade.

mo•rel•lo *n.* a variety of dark-red cherry used in manufacture of brandy.

more•o•ver *adv.* besides; also; further.

mo•res *n.pl.* customs.

mor•ga•nat•ic *a.* applied to a marriage between a man of high, esp. royal rank, and a woman of lower station, the issue having no claim to his rank or property.

morgue *n.* a place where bodies of people killed in accidents, etc., are taken to await identification.

mor•i•bund *a.* at the point of death.

Mor•mom *n.* a member of The Church of Jesus Christ of Latter-day Saints founded by Joseph Smith in 1830 in Utah and professing theocracy and, formerly, polygamy.

morn•ing *n.* the first part of the day between dawn and midday. — **glory** *n.* a twining vine with flowers. — **coat** *n.* a tailcoat with cutaway front. — **star** *n.* a planet visible before sunrise.

mo•ron *n.* an adult with the mental development of an 8- to 12-yr.-old child.

mo•rose *a.* sullen; gloomy; soured in nature.

mor•pheme *n.* (*Gram.*) the smallest meaningful linguistic unit.

mor•phine *n.* an alkaloid of opium; a drug used to induce sleep and to deaden pain.

Morse *n.* a system of telegraphic signals in which the alphabet is represented by combinations of dots and dashes.

Morse

mor•sel *n.* a mouthful; a small piece.

mor•tal *a.* subject to death; fatal; meriting damnation, as sin.

mor•tar *n.* a thick bowl of porcelain, glass, etc., in which substances are pounded with a pestle; a mill for pulverizing ores; (*Mil.*) a short-barreled cannon for short-distance firing of heavy shells; a cement made of lime, sand and water, used in building.

mort•gage *n.* (*Law*) a conveyance of property in security of a loan; the deed effecting this; *v.t.* to pledge as security.

mor•ti•cian *n.* an undertaker.

mor•ti•fy *v.t.* to discipline the flesh; to humiliate; to vex; *v.i.* (*Med.*) to become gangrenous.

mor•tise *n.* a hole in a piece of wood to receive the projection or tenon of another piece, made to fit it.

mort•main *n.* an inalienable bequest; the holding of land by a corporation, which cannot be transferred.

mor•tu•ar•y *n.* a place for the temporary reception of dead bodies.

mo•sa•ic *a.* pert. to or made of mosaic; *n.* inlaid work of colored glass or marble.

Mo•selle *n.* a light wine.

Mos•lem *n.* a Mohammedan; *a.* pert. to the Mohammedans or their religion.

mosque *n.* a Mohammedan temple.

mos•qui•to *n.* an insect which draws blood, leaving a raised, itchy spot.

moss *n.* a small, thickly growing plant which thrives on moist surfaces.

most *a.* the greatest number or quantity; greatest; *adv.* in the greatest degree; *n.* the greatest quantity, number, etc.

mot *n.* pithy, witty saying.

mote *n.* a small particle; a speck of dust.

mo•tel *n.* lodging for travelers.

mo•tet *n.* a musical composition for (usu. unaccompanied) voices.

moth *n.* a nocturnal winged insect; larva of this insect which feeds on cloth, esp. woolens.

moth•er *n.* a female parent; the head of a

convent; the origin of anything; *a.* characteristic of a mother; native; original — of-pearl *n.* the iridescent lining of several kinds of shells. **Mother Superior** *n.* the head of a convent.

mo•tif *n.* the dominant theme in a literary or musical composition.

mo•tion *n.* the act of moving; movement; a gesture; a proposal made in an assembly. **-less** *a.* still; immobile.

mo•tive *n.* that which incites to action; inner impulse; motif; *a.* causing movement or motion; *v.t.* to impel; to motivate. **motivate** *v.t.* to incite. **motivation** *n.* **-less** *a.* without purpose or direction.

mot•ley *a.* varicolored; diversified.

mo•tor *n.* that which imparts motion; a machine which imparts motive power, esp. the internal-combustion engine; *a.* causing motion. **-cade** *n.* procession of automobiles.

mot•tle *v.t.* to mark with spots of different colors; to dapple.

mot•to *n.* a maxim or principle of behavior.

moue *n.* a pout.

mou•lage *n.* the making of molds.

mound *n.* an artificial elevation of earth; a knoll; an earthwork for defensive purposes; a heap.

mount *n.* a mountain or hill; that on which anything is mounted for exhibition; a horse for riding; *v.t.* to raise up; to ascend; to get on a horse or bicycle; to frame (a picture); to set (gemstones).

moun•tain *n.* a high hill; *a.* pert. to a mountain — **ash** *n.* any of a variety of small trees. **-eer** *n.* one who lives on or climbs high mountains. — **range** *n.* a series or system of mountains.

moun•te•bank *n.* a quack doctor; a charlatan.

Mount•ie *n.* a member of the Canadian N.W. Mounted Police.

mourn *v.t.* to grieve over; to lament; *v.i.* to express grief; to wear mourning.

mouse *n.* a small rodent found in fields, or houses; a timid person.

mousse *n.* a lightly frozen dessert.

mouth *n.* an opening between lips of men and animals through which food is taken; lips, as a feature; the cavity behind the lips containing teeth, tongue, palate, and vocal organs; an opening as of a bottle, cave, etc.; the estuary of a river; a wry face. — **organ** *n.* harmonica. **-piece** *n.* the part of a musical instrument, pipe, etc., held in mouth.

move *v.t.* to set in motion; to stir emotions of; to prevail on; to incite; to propose for consideration; *v.i.* to change one's position, posture, residence, etc.; to march; to make a proposal or recommendation; *n.* the act of moving; a change of residence; a movement, as in game of checkers. **moving** *a.* causing motion; affecting the emotions; pathetic.

mow *v.t.* to cut down with a scythe or machine; to cut down in great numbers.

mow *n.* a heap of hay, or corn, in a barn.

much *a.* great in quantity or amount; abundant; *n.* a great quantity.

mu•cid *a.* moldy, musty.

mu•ci•lage *n.* a gummy substance extracted from plants and animals; an adhesive.

muck *n.* moist manure; anything vile or filthy.

muck•rake *n.* one, esp. a reporter, who searches for corruption, scandal.

mu•cus *n.* a viscid fluid secreted by the mucous membranes; slimy.

mud *n.* soft, wet dirt. — **flat** *n.* a stretch of mud below high water. **-guard** *n.* a shield to protect from mud splashes.

mud•dle *v.t.* to make muddy; to confuse; to bewilder; to mix up.

muff *n.* a warm covering for both hands, usu. of fur, shaped like a cylinder and open at both ends.

muf•fin *n.* a small cup-shaped bread.

muf•fle *v.t.* to wrap up for warmth or to hide something; to deaden (sound of); *n.* something used to deaden sound or provide warmth.

mug *n.* a straight-sided earthenware or metal cup with or without a handle; the contents of this.

mug•gins *n.* (*Brit.*) a simpleton; a game of dominoes.

mug•gy *a.* warm and humid, as weather; close; enervating.

mug•wump *n.* one who holds independent political views.

mu•lat•to *n.* offspring of white person and Negro.

mul•ber•ry *n.* a deciduous tree on the leaves of which the silkworm feeds.

mulch *n.* a protective covering of straw, manure, etc., for plants.

mulct *n.* a fine imposed as a penalty; *v.t.* to punish with a fine; to deprive of.

mule *n.* the hybrid offspring of a donkey or horse; a small tractor for hauling, in mines, along canals, etc.; a heelless bedroom slipper; an obstinate person.

mull *v.t.* to heat, sweeten and spice.

mull *v.i.* to muse upon; to cogitate.

mul•let *n.* an edible fish.

mullet

mul•li•gan *n.* a stew made from leftover meat and vegetables.

mul•li•ga•taw•ny *n.* a rich soup flavored with curry.

mul•lion *n.* a dividing upright between the lights of windows, panels.

mul•ti•col•or *a.* having many colors. **-ed** *a.*

mul•ti•far•i•ous *a.* manifold; made up of many parts.

mul•ti•form *a.* having many forms. **-ity** *n.*

mul•ti•lat•er•al *a.* having many sides. **-ly** *adv.*

mul•ti•par•tite *a.* having many parts.

mul•ti•ped *n.* and *a.* (animal) with many feet. Also **multipede.**

mul•ti•ple *a.* manifold; of many parts; repeated many times; *n.* (*Math.*) a quantity containing another an exact number of times. — **fission** *n.* repeated division.

mul‧ti‧ply *v.t.* to increase in number; to add a number to itself a given number of times. **multipliable, multiplicable** *a.* **multiplicand** *n.* the number to be multiplied. **multiplication** *n.* the act of multiplying. **multiplicative** *a.* **multiplicator** *n.* a multiplier. **multiplier** *n.* a number by which another, the **multiplicand**, is multiplied.

mul‧ti‧tude *n.* a great number; numerousness; a crowd; an assemblage.

mul‧ti‧va‧lent *a. (Chem.)* having a valency of more than two.

mum *a.* silent; *n.* silence.

mum‧ble *v.t., v.i.* to utter, speak indistinctly; *n.* an indistinct utterance.

mum‧my *n.* a dead body preserved by embalming.

mumps *n.* a highly infectious disease causing painful swelling of face and neck glands.

munch *v.t.* and *v.i.* to chew noisily.

mu‧nic‧i‧pal *a.* pert. to local government or to internal affairs (not international). **-ity** *a.* town or district with its own local self-government.

mu‧nif‧i‧cence *n.* liberality; generosity.

mu‧ni‧ment *n.* means of protection; *pl.* title deeds; charter.

mu‧ni‧tion *v.t.* to equip with the weapons of war.

mu‧ral *n.* a wall painting.

mur‧der *n.* homicide with premeditated and malicious intent; *v.t.* to commit a murder; to kill.

mu‧ri‧ate *n.* a chloride. **-d** *a.* briny. **muriatic acid** *n.* hydrochloric acid.

murk *a.* dark; *n.* darkness; gloom.

mur‧mur *n.* a low, unbroken sound, as of wind, water, etc.; a complaint expressed in subdued tones; softly uttered speech.

mur‧rain *n.* a disease affecting cattle, foot-and-mouth disease.

mus‧cat *n.* a sweet grape.

mus‧cle *n.* a band of contractile fibrous tissue which produces movement in an animal body; strength. **muscular** *a.* pert. to muscle; brawny; strong.

mus‧coid *a. (Bot.)* like moss. **muscology** *n.* the study of mosses.

Mus‧co‧vite *n.* a native or inhabitant of Moscow or of Russia.

muse *v.i.* to think over dreamily; to ponder; to consider meditatively.

mu‧sette *n.* a small bagpipe; a melody for this instrument; a reed stop on an organ; a country dance.

mu‧se‧um *n.* a building or room housing a collection of works of art, antiques, objects of natural history, the sciences, etc.

mush *n.* a pulp; (U.S.) porridge of cornmeal; a soft mass.

mush *v.t.* to journey on foot with dogs over snowy wastes.

mush‧room *n.* an edible fungus of very quick growth; *(Fig.)* an upstart; *a.* of rapid growth; shaped like a mushroom.

mu‧sic *n.* the art of combining sounds or sequences of notes into harmonious

patterns pleasing to the ear and satisfying to the emotions. — **box** *n.* a box which when wound up plays a tune. **-al comedy** *n.* a form of light entertainment in which songs, dialogue, dancing, humor are combined. **-ian** *n.* a composer or skilled performer of musical compositions.

musk *n.* a fragrant substance obtained from a gland of the musk deer. **—ox** *n.* a sheeplike ox with brown, long-haired

muskox

shaggy coat. **-rat** *n.* a large N. Amer. water rat with musk gland, valued for its fur. — **rose** *n.* a climbing rose with white blossoms faintly perfumed with musk.

mus‧ket *n.* (formerly) a handgun or matchlock.

mus‧lin *n.* a thin cotton cloth of open weave; *a.* made of muslin.

mus‧quash *n.* the muskrat.

mus‧sel *n.* a class of marine bivalve shellfish.

mussel

must *v.i.* to be obliged, by physical or moral necessity.

must *n.* wine newly pressed from grapes but not fermented.

mus‧tache *n.* the hair on the upper lip.

mus‧tang *n.* a wild horse of the Amer. prairies; a bronco.

mus‧tard *n.* a plant with yellow flowers and pungent seeds; a powder or paste made from the seeds, used as a condiment.

mus‧ter *v.t.* to assemble, as troops for a parade; to gather together.

mus‧ty *a.* moldy; stale.

mu‧ta‧ble *a.* subject to change; inconstant. **mutation** *n.* change; the process of vowel change; *(Biol.)* a complete divergence from racial type which may ultimately give rise to a new species.

mute *a.* dumb; silent; unexpressed in words; not sounded, as *e* of *cavé*; *n.* a person who cannot speak.

mu‧ti‧late *v.t.* to maim; to cut off.

mu‧ti‧ny *n.* insurrection against lawful authority, esp. military or naval.

mut‧ter *v.t.* to speak indistinctly or in a low voice; to grumble.

mut‧ton *n.* the flesh of sheep.

mu‧tu‧al *a.* reciprocally acting or related; interchanged.

mu•zhik n. a Russian peasant.

muz•zle v.t. the snout; the mouth and nose of an animal; a cage-like fastening for the mouth to prevent biting; the open end of a gun.

my poss. a. belonging to me.

my•col•o•gy n. the science of fungi.

my•e•lin n. (Zool.) the fatty substance forming the sheath of nerve fibers. **myelitis** n. inflammation of the spinal cord or bone marrow.

my•na(h) n. a tropical starling.

my•o•car•di•tis n. (Med.) inflammation of the heart muscle.

my•o•ma n. tumor of muscle tissue.

my•o•pi•a n. nearsightedness.

my•o•sis n. prolonged contraction of the pupil of the eye.

my•o•so•tis n. a genus of herbs including the forget-me-not.

myr•i•ad n. an indefinitely large number.

myr•i•a•pod n. (Zool.) an animal with great number of legs, as centipede.

myr•me•col•o•gy n. the scientific study of ants and ant life.

myrrh n. a transparent yellow-brown aromatic gum resin formerly used as incense, now used in antiseptics.

myr•tle n. an evergreen plant with fragrant flowers and glossy leaves.

my•self pron. I or me, used emphatically, or reflexively.

mys•ter•y n. anything strange and inexplicable; a puzzle; a religious truth beyond human understanding; secrecy; a medieval drama based on Scripture.

mys•tic a. pert. to a mystery, to secret religious rites, or to mysticism. **mystification** n. **mystify** v.t. to perplex; to puzzle.

myth n. a fable; a legend embodying primitive faith in the supernatural. **-iologist** n. one who has studied myths of various countries; a writer of fables. **-ology** n. a collection of myths.

myx•e•de•ma n. (Med.) a disease caused by deficiency of secretion from thyroid gland.

M

nag *n.* a small horse; an old horse; any horse.

nag *v.t.* and *v.i.* to worry by constant faultfinding. *pr.p.* **-ging.** *pa.t.* and *pa.p.* **-ged. -ger** *n.*

nai·ad *n.* a nymph of the streams.

nail *n.* the horny shield covering the ends of the fingers or toes; a strip of pointed metal provided with a head, for fastening

nails

wood, etc.; *v.t.* to fasten with a nail; to fix or secure.

na·ïve *a.* having native or unaffected simplicity; childishly frank. **-ly** *adv.* **naïveté** *n.* childlike ingenuousness. Also **naivety.**

na·ked *a.* having no clothes; exposed; bare; nude; uncovered. **-ly** *adv.* **-ness** *n.*

name *n.* the term by which any person or thing is known; *v.t.* to give a name to; to call or mention by name; to nominate; **-less** *a.* without a name. **-lessly** *adv.* **-ly** *adv.* by name; that is to say. **-sake** *n.* a person who bears the same name as another.

nan·ny *n.* a child's nurse. — **goat** *n.* a she-goat.

nap *n.* a short sleep; a doze; *v.i.* to indulge in a short sleep. *pr.p.* **-ping** *pa.t.,* *pa.p.* **-ped.**

nap *n.* the pile of velvet.

na·palm *n.* jellied gasoline used in flame throwers.

nape *n.* the back part of the neck.

nap·kin *n.* a cloth used for wiping the hands or lips at table.

na·po·le·on *n.* a pastry of several cream-filled layers. **-ic** *a.* pert. to Napoleon I or III.

Nar·cis·sus *n.* bulbous plant genus including the daffodil, jonquil, narcissus; **narcissim** *n.* in psychoanalysis, an abnormal love and admiration for oneself. **narcissist** *n.*

nar·cot·ic *n.* a substance which relieves pain and induces sleep, and in large doses, insensibility and stupor; one addicted to the habitual use of narcotics. **narcosis** *n.* a state of unconsciousness or stupor with deadening of sensibility to pain, produced by narcotics.

nar·rate *v.t.* to relate; to tell (story) in detail; to give an account of; to describe. **narration** *n.* an account. **narrative** *n.* a tale; a detailed account of events; *a.* pert. to, containing, narration. **narratively** *adv.* **narrator** *n.*

nar·row *a.* of little breadth; not wide or broad; limited; bigoted; *n.pl.* straits. **-ly** *adv.* **—minded** *a.* bigoted; prejudiced.

nar·whal *n.* a cetacean mammal, closely related to the white whale, with one

large protruding tusk.

na·sal *a.* pert. to the nose; *n.* a nasal sound or letter, such as *m* or *n.*

na·stur·tium *n.* a common trailing garden plant of the genus Tropaeolum.

nas·ty *a.* very dirty; filthy; disgusting; offensive; repulsive; unpropitious (of the weather, etc.); ill-natured; indecent. **nastily** *adv.* **nastiness** *n.*

na·tal *a.* pert. to one's place of birth or date of birth; **-ity** *n.* birth rate.

na·tion *n.* a people inhabiting a country under the same government; an aggregation of persons of the same origin and language.

na·tion·al *a.* belonging to or pertaining to a nation; public; general; **-ization** *n.* **-ize** *v.t.* to make national; to acquire and manage by the state; to make a nation of. **-ism** *n.* devotion to the interests of one's nation, often to the detriment of common interests of all nations. **-ity** *n.* the quality of being a nation or belonging to a nation; one's nation; patriotism. **-ly** *adv.* — **anthem,** a hymn or song expressive of patriotism, praise, or thanksgiving, commonly sung by people of a nation at public gatherings. — **debt,** the debt due from a nation to individual creditors. **National Guard,** State military force which can be called to active duty.

na·tive *a.* pert. to one's birth; belonging by birth; innate; indigenous; natural; *n.* a person born in a place; **-ly** *adv.* **nativity** *n.* the time or circumstances of birth; in astrology, the position of the stars at a person's birth.

nat·u·ral *a.* in accordance with, belonging to, or derived from, nature; inborn; unconstrained; unaffected; unassuming; true to life. **-ization** *n.* **-ize** *v.t.* to give to an alien the rights of a native subject; **-ism,** *n.* natural condition or quality; theory of art, etc. which holds that any artistic creation must be a reproduction of nature or reality. **-ist** *n.* one versed in or interested in natural history. **-istic** *a.* in accordance with nature. **-istically** *adv.* **-ly** *adv.* **-ness** *n.* — **gas,** an inflammable product, usually methane, occurring in association with mineral oil deposits. — **history,** the science which deals with the earth's crust and its productions, but applies more especially to biology or zoology. — **science,** the science of nature as distinguished from mental and moral science and mathematics.

na·ture *n.* the world, the universe, known and unknown; the innate or essential qualities of a thing; the environment of man; **good-, bad-natured** *a.* showing one's innate disposition.

naught *n.* nothing; figure 0; zero. Also **nought.** **-y** *a.* not behaving well; mischievous; bad. **-ily** *adv.* **naughtiness** *n.*

nau·se·a *n.* any sickness of the stomach accompanied with a propensity to vomit. **-te** *v.i.* to feel nausea; *v.t.* to fill with disgust. **nauseous** *a.* loathsome; disgusting; producing nausea. **nauseously** *adv.*

nau•ti•cal *a.* pert. to ships, seamen, or to navigation. **-ly** *adv.* — **mile**, 6,080.2 ft.

na•val *a.* pert. to ships, esp. warships; belonging to or serving with the navy.

nave *n.* the middle or body, of a church.

na•vel *n.* the umbilicus, place of attachment of the umbilical cord to the body of the embryo, marked by a rounded depression in the center of the lower part of the abdomen.

nav•i•gate *v.t.* and *v.i.* to steer or manage a ship or aircraft; **navigable** *a.* may be sailed over or upon; seaworthy; **navigability, navigableness** *n.* **navigably** *adv.* **navigation** *n.* the science of directing course of seagoing vessel and of ascertaining its position at any given time; the control and direction of aircraft in flight; **navigator** *n.*

na•vy *n.* a fleet; the warships of a country with their crews and organization. — **blue** *n.* and *a.* dark blue.

Naz•a•rene *n.* a native of *Nazareth;* name given to Jesus; *pl.* an early Christian sect.

Na•zi *n.* and *a.* a member of the National Socialist Party of Germany (1922-1945). **-sm, -ism** *n.*

Ne•an•der•thal *a.* denoting a man of the earliest long-headed race in Europe which became extinct at least 20,000 years ago.

neap *a.* low; *n.* neap tide. — **tide** *n.* the tide whose rise and fall is least marked.

Ne•a•pol•i•tan *a.* and *n.* pert. to Naples or its inhabitants.

near *adv.* at or to a short distance; *prep.* close to; *a.* close; closely related; *v.t.* and *v.i.* to approach. **-by** *a.* in close proximity; adjacent. — **East**, part of Asia nearest Europe, from Asia Minor to Persia. **-ly** *adv.* closely; intimately; almost. **-ness** *n.* **-sighted** *a.* myopic; short-sighted. **-sightedness** *n.*

neat *a.* orderly; clean; trim; in good taste; **-ly** *adv.* **-ness** *n.*

nec•es•sar•y *a.* needful; requisite indispensable; that must be done; *n.* a needful thing; essential need. **necessarily** *adv.*

ne•ces•si•ty *n.* pressing need; indispensability; compulsion; urgency; a requisite; an essential. **necessitate** *v.t.* to make necessary or indispensable. **necessitous** *a.* needy; destitute.

neck *n.* the part of the body joining the head to the trunk, the narrower part of a bottle, etc. **-erchief** *n.* a band of cloth or kerchief worn round the neck. **-lace** *n.* a string of beads or precious stones worn round neck. **neck and neck**, just even.

nec•tar *n.* the fabled drink of the gods; honey-like secretion of the nectary gland of flowers. **-ine** *n.* a smooth-skinned variety of peach.

need *n.* a constitutional or acquired craving or want, appeased by recurrent satisfactions; necessity; poverty; urgency; *v.t.* to be in want of; to require; *v.i.* to be under a necessity. **-ful** *a.* necessary; requisite **-fully** *adv.* **-fulness** *n.* **-ily** *adv.* **-iness** *n.* condition of need. **-less** *a.* unnecessary; not needed. **-lessly**

adv. **-lessness** *n.* **-y** *a.* in need; indigent.

nee•dle *n.* a slender pointed instrument with an eye, for passing thread through cloth, etc.; a slender rod for knitting; **-point** *n.* canvas with a design worked in yarn. **-work** *n.* **-ly** *a.* thorny.

ne•gate *v.t.* to deny; to prove the contrary. **negation** *n.* the act of denying; negative statement; disavowal; contradiction.

neg•a•tive *a.* expressing denial, prohibition, or refusal; not positive; minus; *n.* a proposition in which something is denied; a negative word; *v.t.* to refuse to sanction; to reject. **-ly** *adv.* **-ness** *n.*

neg•lect *v.t.* to disregard; to take no care of; to fail to do; to slight; *n.* omission; disregard; careless treatment. **-edness** *n.* **-er** *n.* **-ful** *a.* careless; inclined to be heedless. **-fully** *adv.*

neg•li•gee *n.* a woman's loose dressing gown.

neg•li•gence *n.* carelessness; habitual neglect. **negligent** *a.* careless; inattentive; untidy. **negligently** *adv.* **negligible** *a.* hardly worth noticing.

ne•go•ti•ate *v.t.* to settle by bargaining; to arrange; to transfer; *v.i.* to discuss with a view to finding terms of agreement; to bargain. **negotiable** *a.* capable of being negotiated; transferable. **negotiability** *n.* **negotiation** *n.* **negotiant, negotiator** *n.*

Ne•gro *n.* member of one main ethnological group of human race, with dark skin. *a.* pert. to black African race. **Negress** *n.* Negro woman.

neigh *v.i.* to whinny, like horse; *n.* cry of horse.

neigh•bor *n.* a person who lives, works, near another; *a.* neighboring; *v.t.* to adjoin; to be near. **-hood** *n.* adjoining district and its people; proximity; vicinity. **-ing** *a.* close by. **-ly** *a.* friendly; sociable. **-liness** *n.*

nei•ther *a.* and *pron.* not the one or the other; *adv.* not on the one hand; not either; *conj.* nor yet; not either.

nem•e•sis *n.* inevitable retributive justice.

ne•o•dym•i•um *n.* a metallic element belonging to the group of rare earth metals.

ne•o•lith•ic *a.* pert. to the late Stone Age.

ne•on *n.* a non-metallic chemical element belonging to the group of the rare gases. — **light**, — **sign**, or — **tube**, one containing neon gas and glowing with a characteristic reddish-orange light.

ne•o•pho•bi•a *n.* a dread of the unknown.

ne•o•phyte *n.* a novice; a convert.

neph•ew *n.* a brother's or sister's son.

nephr- (or **nephro-**) prefix used in the construction of compound terms, from Greek *nephros*, a kidney. **-algia, -algy** *n.* pain in the kidney. **-ic** *a.* pert. to the kidneys. **-itic(al)** *a.* pert. to (diseases of) the kidneys. **-itis** *n.* Bright's disease, non-infective inflammation of the kidney.

nep•o•tism *n.* undue favoritism in awarding public appointments to one's relations.

Nep•tune *n.* the Roman god of the sea;

second most remote planet of solar system.

nerve n. one of the bundles of fibers which convey impulses either *from* brain (motor nerves) to muscles, etc., producing motion, or *to* brain (sensory nerves) from skin, eyes, nose, etc., producing sensation; courage; *pl.* irritability; unusual sensitivity to fear, annoyance, etc.; *v.t.* to give courage or strength to. **-d** a. **-less** a. lacking in strength or will; **-lessness** n.

nerv·ous a. pert. to, containing, or affecting nerves; uneasy; apprehensive. **-ly** adv. **-ness** n. — **breakdown** n. a condition of mental depression.

nest n. the place in which a bird or other animal lays and hatches its eggs; v.t. to form to place in a nest; v.i. to occupy or build a nest. **-ling** n. a bird too young to leave the nest. — **egg** n. an egg left in a nest to induce a bird to lay; a small sum of money put aside for some later purpose.

nes·tle v.i. to settle comfortably and close to one another; to lie snugly, as in a nest.

net n. an open-work fabric of meshes of cord, etc.; sections of this used to catch fish, protect fruit, etc.; lace formed by netting; a snare. a. made of netting; caught in a net; v.t. to cover with, or catch in, a net; to veil; pr.p. **-ting.** pa.t. and pa.p. **-ted. -ted** a. **-ting** n. the act or process of forming network; net like fabric; snaring by means of a net. **-work** n. anything made like, or resembling, a net.

net a. left after all deductions; v.t. to gain or produce as clear profit; pr.p. **-ting.** pa.p. **-ted.** — **price**, net price without discount.

neth·er a. lower; low-lying; lying below; belonging to the lower regions. **-most** a. lowest.

net·tle n. a common weed covered with fine stinging hairs; v.t. to irritate; to provoke; to make angry; to rouse to action.

neu·ral a. pert. to the nerves or nervous system.

neu·ral·gia n. a spasmodic or continuous pain occurring along the course of one or more distinct nerves. **neuralgic** a.

neu·rax·is n. the cerebrospinal axis, or central nervous system, including the brain and spinal cord.

neu·ri·tis n. an inflammatory condition of a nerve.

neu·rol·o·gy n. the study of the structure, function and diseases of the nervous system. **neurological** a. **neurologist** n.

neu·ron n. a nerve cell and all its processes.

neu·ro·sis n. a psychic or mental disorder resulting in partial personality disorganization. pl. **neuroses. neurotic** a. pert. to the nerves; n. a highly strung person.

neu·ter a. neither masculine nor feminine; n. the neuter gender.

neu·tral a. taking neither side in a war, dispute, etc.; indifferent; without bias; grey; intermediate (shade of color); neither acid nor alkaline; asexual; n. nation, person, not taking sides in a dispute; **-ize** v.t. to render neutral; to make ineffective; to counterbalance. **-izer** n. nonintervention by a state or third-party in a dispute; the state of being neutral. **-ly** adv. **-ity** n.

neu·tron n. one of the minute particles composing the nucleus of an atom.

nev·er adv. at no time; not ever; in no degree; **-more** adv. **-theless** conj. none the less; in spite of that; notwithstanding.

new a. not existing before; lately discovered or invented; adv. recently; freshly; **-ly** adv. **-ness** n. **-born** a. recently born. **New Deal,** a campaign initiated in 1933 by President Franklin Roosevelt involving social reforms. — **moon,** the period when the first faint crescent of the moon becomes visible. **New Testament,** later of the two main divisions of Bible. **New World,** N. and S. America.

news n.sing. report of recent happenings; fresh information; — **bulletin** n. the latest news, esp. as disseminated by radio or television. **-paper** n. a regular publication giving latest news. **-print** n. cheap paper for newspapers. **-reel** n. a short film depicting items of news and topical features.

next a. nearest; immediately following in place or time; adv. nearest or immediately after; on the first future occasion; prep. nearest to. — **of kin,** n. nearest blood relative. **-door** a.

nib·ble v.t. to bite a little at a time; v.i. to catch at (as a fish); to bite gently; n. a tiny bite.

nice agreeable; attractive; kind; **-ly** adv. **-ness** n. **-ty** n. precision; delicacy; exactness; refinement.

niche n. one's ordained position in life or public estimation; v.t. to place in a niche. **-d** a.

nick v.t. to make a notch in; to indent; n. a notch; a slit; the opportune moment as *in the nick of time.*

nick·el n. a silver white metallic element, malleable and ductile, and much used in alloys and plating; a five-cent piece; v.t. to plate with nickel.

nick·el·o·de·on n. a player phonograph operated by the insertion of a nickel.

nick·nack See **knickknack.**

nick·name n. a name given in contempt, derision, or familiarity to some person, nation, or object.

nic·o·tine n. a colorless, highly poisonous alkaloid present in the tobacco plant.

niece n. the daughter of a brother or sister or of one's husband's or wife's brother or sister.

nif·ty a. fine; smart.

nigh a. near; direct. adv. near.

night n. the time of darkness from sunset to sunrise; end of daylight; **-ly** a. happening or done every night; of the night; adv. every night; by night. — **club** n. establishment for dancing and entertainment remaining open until early morning. **-dress, -gown** n. a loose

N

gown worn in bed. -fall n. the close of day. -light n. bulb of low wattage kept burning all night. -mare n. a frightening dream. — owl n. one who habitually keeps late hours.

night·in·gale n. a bird of the thrush family, the male being renowned for its beautiful song at night.

ni·hil, nil n. nothing; zero. nihilism n. the rejection of all religious and moral principles as the only means of obtaining social progress; the denial of all reality in phenomena. nihilist n. nihilistic a.

nim·ble a. light and quick in motion. -ness n. nimbly adv.

nin·com·poop n. a foolish person.

nine a. and n. one more than eight; the symbol 9 or IX. -teen a. and n. nine and ten. -teenth a. and n. ninetieth a. the tenth after the eightieth. -ty a. and n. ninth a. the first after the eighth; n. ninthly adv. the Nine, the Muses.

nip v.t. to pinch sharply; to detach by pinching; to check growth (as by frost); pr.p. -ping. pa.t. and pa.p. -ped. n. a pinch; sharp touch of frost; a sip. -piness n. -pingly adv. -py a. sharp in taste; curt; smarting.

nip·ple n. the protuberance in the center of a breast by which milk is obtained from the female during breast-feeding; the mouthpiece of a nursing bottle.

Nip·pon n. Japan. -ese n., a.

Nir·va·na n. in Buddhism, that state of blissful repose or absolute existence reached by one in whom all craving is extinguished.

ni·ter n. potassium nitrate; saltpeter, a white crystalline solid used in the manufacture of gunpowder, acids, etc. nitrate n. a salt of nitric acid; a fertilizer. nitrated a. combined with nitric acid. nitration n. the conversion of nitrites into nitrates by the action of bacteria; the introduction of a nitro-group (NO_2) into an organic substance. nitric a. containing nitrogen. nitric acid, a powerful, corrosive acid. nitride n. a compound of a metal with nitrogen. nitrify v.t. to treat a metal with nitric acid; to oxidize to nitrates or nitrites, esp. by action of bacteria. nitrite n. a salt of nitrous acid. nitrous oxide, laughing gas, used as an anaesthetic in dentristry.

ni·tro·gen n. a non-metallic gaseous chemical element, colorless, odorless and tasteless, forming nearly four-fifths of the atmosphere. nitrogenous a.

nit·wit n. a fool. -ted a.

no a. not any; adv. expresses a negative reply to a question or request; not at all; n. a refusal; a denial; a negative vote. -es n.pl. term used in parliamentary proceedings, the noes have it.

No·bel Prize n. one of a series of five prizes awarded annually to persons who have distinguished themselves in physics, chemistry, medicine, literature, or the promotion of peace.

no·bil·i·ty n. the class holding special rank, usually hereditary, in a state.

no·ble a. distinguished by deeds,

character, rank, or birth; of lofty character; titled; n. a nobleman; -man n. (fem. -woman). -ness n. nobly adv.

no·bod·y n. no one; a person of no importance.

nock n. notch, esp. of bow or arrow; upper end of fore-and-aft sail.

noc·turn n. a service held during the night. -al a. pertaining to night; happening or active by night. -ally adv.

noc·u·ous a. hurtful; noxious. -ly adv.

nod v.t. and v.i. to incline the head forward by a quick motion, signifying assent or drowsiness; pr.p. -ding. pa.t. and pa.p. -ded. n. an act of nodding. -der n.

nod·al See node.

node n. a knot or knob; the part of a stem to which a leaf is attached; an articulation. nodal, nodical a. pert. to nodes. nodated a. knotted. nodation n. the knots. nodular a. like a nodule. nodulated a. having nodules. nodule n. a small node or act of making knots. nodiferous a. having nodes. nodose, nodous a. full of swelling.

No·ël n. Christmas.

nog n. a wooden peg or block.

nog n. a beverage made with eggs and usually liquor; eggnog; a kind of strong ale.

no·how adv. in no way; not at all; ability.

noise n. sound; din; loud outcry; v.t. to spread by rumor; v.i. to sound loud. -less a. making no noise; silent. -lessly adv. -lessness n. noisy a. making much noise; noisily adv. noisiness n.

no·mad a. roaming from pasture to pasture; n. a wanderer; a member of a wandering tribe. nomadic a. pert. to nomads; having no fixed dwelling place. nomadically adv. -ism n.

no·men·cla·tor n. one who gives names to things. nomenclatural a. nomenclature n. a system of naming; the vocabulary of a science, etc.

nom·i·nal a. pert. to a name; existing only in name; pert. to a noun. -istic a. -ly adv. in name only; not really.

nom·i·nate v.t. to put forward the name of, as a candidate; to propose; to designate. nomination n. act of nominating; power or privilege of nominating. nominative a. (Gram.) denoting the subject; n. a noun or pronoun which is the subject of a verb. nominator n. one who nominates. nominee n. one who is nominated.

non- prefix from L. non = not, used in the formation of compound terms signifying absence or omission.

non·a·ge·nar·i·an n. one who is ninety years old or upwards; a. relating to ninety.

non·cha·lance n. unconcern; coolness; indifference; nonchalant a. nonchalantly adv.

non·con·form·ist n. one who refuses to comply with the usages and rites of an established church, etc. nonconforming a. nonconformity n.

non·de·script a. lacking in distinction; hard to classify; n.

none a. and pron. no one; not anything. -such, nonsuch n. a person or thing without a rival or equal. **nonetheless,** nevertheless; all the same.

nones *n.pl.* one the canonical hours of the R.C. Breviary, the *ninth* hour after sunrise at the equinox, viz. 3 p.m., or the appropriate mass celebrated at this time.

non•en•ti•ty *n.* a thing not existing; nonexistence.

non•pa•reil *n.* a person or thing without an equal; *a.* unrivalled; peerless; matchless.

non•sense *n.* lack of sense; language without meaning; silly conduct. **nonsensical** *a.* **nonsensically** *adv.*

non•such See **none.**

noo•dle *n.* a strip of dough, made of flour and eggs, baked and served in soups.

nook *n.* a corner; a recess; a secluded retreat.

noon *n.* midday; twelve o'clock by day; the exact instant when, at any given place, the sun crosses the meridian. **-day, -tide** *n.* and *a.* midday.

noose *n.* a running loop with a slip knot which binds closer the more it is drawn; tight knot; *v.t.* to tie, catch in noose.

nor a particle introducing the second clause of a negative proposition; and not.

Nor•dic *a.* of or pert. to peoples of Germanic, esp. Scandinavian, stock.

norm *n.* a rule or authoritative standard; a unit for comparison; a class-average test score. **-a** *n.* a rule, pattern, or standard; **-al** *a.* conforming to type or natural law; the standard; the average. **-alcy** *n.* normality. **normality** *n.* normal state or quality. **-ly** *adv.* **-ative** *a.* setting up a norm; regulative.

Nor•man *n.* a native of Normandy; *a.* pert. to Normandy or the Normans. **— architecture,** a style of medieval architecture characterized by rounded arch and massive simplicity.

Norse *a.* pert. to ancient Scandinavia, esp. Norway, its language, or its people; *n.* Norwegians or ancient Scandinavians; the old Scandinavian language.

north *n.* the region or cardinal point in the plane of the meridian to the left of a person facing the rising sun; the part of the world, of a country, etc., towards this point; *adv.* towards or in the north; *a.* to, from, or in the north. **northerly** *a.* towards the north; of winds, coming from the north. **northern** *a.* pert. to the north; in or of the north. **northerner** *n.* an inhabitant of the northern parts of a country. **northernly** *adv.* in a northern direction. **northernmost** *a.* situated at the most northerly point. **-ward, -wardly** *a.* situated towards the north; *adv.* in a northerly direction. **-wards** *adv.* **northern lights,** aurora borealis. **North Pole,** northern extremity of earth's axis. **North Star** *n.* polar star, the only star which does not change its apparent position.

Nor•we•gian *a.* pert. to Norway; *n.* a native or language of Norway.

nose *n.* the organ for breathing and smelling; *v.t.* to detect by smell; to nuzzle; to sniff; to move forward; *v.i.* to smell; to pry; to push forward. **— dive** *n.* in aviation, a sudden steep plunge

directly towards an objective, usually from a great height; *v.i.* to perform this evolution. **-gay** *n.* a bunch of sweet-smelling flowers; a bouquet. **nosy** *a.* inquisitive.

nos•tal•gia *n.* honesickness; a phase of melancholia due to the unsatisfied desire to return home. **nostalgic** *a.*

nos•tril *n.* one of the external openings of the nose.

not *adv.* a word expressing denial, negation, or refusal.

no•ta•ble *a.* worthy of notice; remarkable; *n.* a person of distinction. **notabilia** *n.pl.* things worth noting; famous remarks. **notability** *n.* an eminent person. **-ness** *n.* **notably** *adv.*

no•ta•ry *n.* a *notary-public,* a person authorized to record statements, to certify deeds, to take affidavits, etc., on oath.

no•ta•tion *n.* any system of figures, signs and symbols which conveys information; a note.

notch *n.* a V-shaped cut or indentation; nick; a groove formed in a piece of timber to receive another piece; *v.t.* to make notches in; to indent.

note *n.* a brief comment; *pl.* a record of a lecture, speech, etc.; a memorandum; a short letter; a written or printed promise of payment; a musical tone; a character to indicate a musical tone; notice; *v.t.* to observe; to set down in writing; to attend to; to heed. **-book** *n.* a book for jotting down notes, memoranda, etc. **-d** *a.* well-known by reputation or report; celebrated; **-dly** *adv.* **-dness** *n.* **— paper** *n.* a small size of writing paper. **-worthy** *a.* worthy of notice; remarkable.

noth•ing *n.* not anything of account, value, note, or the like; non-existence; nonentity; zero; *adv.* in no degree; not at all. **-ness** *n.*

no•tice *n.* act of noting; remarking, or observing; note; consideration; news; a notification; *v.t.* to observe; to remark upon; to treat with regard. **-able** *a.* **-ably** *adv.* **to give notice,** to warn beforehand.

no•ti•fy *v.t.* to report; to give notice of or to; to announce; to inform. **notifiable** *n.* **notification** *n.* act of making known or giving notice; official notice or announcement.

no•tion *n.* apprehension; idea; conception; opinion; belief; sentiment; fancy; *pl.* small articles such as sewing supplies, etc.

no•to•ri•e•ty *n.* the state of being generally known, esp. in a disreputable way. **notorious** *a.* infamous. **notoriously** *adv.* **notoriousness** *n.*

not•with•stand•ing *adv.* nevertheless; however; yet; *prep.* in spite of; despite; *conj.* although.

nou•gat *n.* a confection of almonds, pistachio-nuts, or other nuts, in a sugar and honey paste.

noun *n.* a word used as a name of a person, quality, or thing; a substantive.

nour•ish *v.t.* to supply with food; to feed and cause to grow. **-ing** *a.* nutritious.

N

-ment n. food; nutriment.

nov•el a. new; unusual; n. a fictitious prose tale dealing with the adventures or feelings of imaginary persons so as to portray, by the description of action and thought, the varieties of human life and character. -ette n. a shorter form of novel. -ist n. a writer of novels. -ty n. newness; something new or unusual.

No•vem•ber n. the eleventh month of the year.

no•ve•na n. devotions on nine consecutive days.

nov•ice n. a candidate for admission to a religious order; one new to anything.

no•vo•caine n. a nonirritant drug which has replaced cocaine as a local anesthetic.

now adv. at the present time; conj. this being the case; n. the present time. -adays adv. in these days.

no•where adv. not in any place.

nox•a n. anything harmful to the body; pl. -e. noxal a. noxious a. hurtful; pernicious; unwholesome. noxiously adv. noxiousness n.

noz•zle n. a projecting spout or vent; the outlet end of a pipe, hose, etc.

nu•ance n. a shade or subtle variation in color, tone of voice, etc.

nub n. a knob; lump; protuberance.

nu•cle•us n. a central part of anything; the inner essential part of a living cell; the core of the atom, composed of protons and neutrons. pl. nuclei. nuclear a. nuclear energy, a more exact term for atomic energy; energy freed or absorbed during reactions taking place in atomic nuclei. nuclear fission, a process of disintegration which breaks up into chemically different atoms. nucleolus n. a minute body of condensed chromatin inside a nucleus.

nude a. bare; naked; n. a picture or piece of sculpture in the nude. -ly adv. -ness, nudity, n. nakedness. nudism n. cult emphasizing practice of nudity for health. nudist n.

nudge v.t. to touch slightly with the elbow; n. a gentle push.

nug•get n. rough lump or mass, esp. of native gold.

nui•sance n. something harmful, offensive, or annoying; a troublesome person; a pest; an inconvenience.

null a. of no legal validity; void; non-existent; of no importance; v.t. to annul; to render void. -ify v.t. to render useless; to invalidate; -fication n. -ifier n. -ity n. state of being null and void.

numb a. insensible; insensitive; chilled; v.t. to benumb; to paralyze. -ness n.

num•ber n. a word used to indicate how great any quantity is when compared with the unit quantity, one; a sum or aggregate of quantities; v.t. to give a number to; to count; v.i. to amount to. -s n.pl. fourth book of Pentateuch. -er n. -less a. innumerable. numerability, numerableness n. numerable a. may be numbered or counted.

nu•mer•al a. designating a number; n. a sign or word denoting a number. numerable a. able to be counted. numerably adv. -ly adv. according to number. numerate v.t. to count; to read figures according to their notation. numeration n. numerator n. top part of a fraction, figure showing how many of the fractional units are taken. numerically adv. numerous a. many. numerously adv. numerousness n.

nu•mis•mat•ic a. pert. to coins and medals, esp. as an aid to study of archaeology. numismatist n.

nun n. a female member of a religious order, vowed to celibacy, and dedicated to active or contemplative life. -nery n. convent of nuns.

nup•tial a. pert. to or constituting ceremony of marriage; pl. wedding ceremony; marriage.

nurse n. a person trained for the care of the sick or injured; v.t. to tend, as a nurse; nursery n. a room set aside for children; a place for the rearing of plants. nursery rhymes, jingling rhymes written to amuse young children. nursery school, a school for children of 2-5 years of age.

nur•ture n. rearing; breeding; nourishment; v.t. to nourish; to cherish; to tend; to train; to rear; to bring up. -r n.

nut n. a fruit consisting of a hard shell enclosing a kernel; v.i. to gather nuts; pr.p. -ting. pa.t. and pa.p. -ted. -cracker n. an instrument for cracking nuts; -shell n. the hard shell enclosing the kernel of a nut. -ting n. -ty a. abounding in nuts; having a nut-flavor.

nu•tant a. hanging with the apex of the flower downwards; nodding. nutation n. nodding.

nut•meg n. an aromatic flavoring spice.

nu•tri•ent a. nourishing; n. something nutritious. nutriment n. that which nourishes; food; sustenance. nutrition n. the act of nourishing. nutritional, nutritious, nutritive, nutritory a. nourishing; promoting growth.

nuz•zle v.t. and v.i. to rub with the nose; to nestle.

nyc•ta•lo•pi•a n. night blindness.

ny•lon n. an artificial fabric the yarn of which is produced synthetically; n.pl. stockings made of nylon yarn.

nymph n. a lesser goddess inhabiting a mountain, grove, fountain, river, etc.; -al, -ean, -ic, -ical a. -like a. -omania n. a morbid and uncontrollable sexual desire in women. -omaniac n.

O, oh *interj.* an exclamation of address, surprise, sorrow, wonder, entreaty.

oaf *n.* a changeling; simpleton. *pl.* **oafs** or **oaves.**

oak *n.* a familiar forest tree yielding a hard, durable timber and acorns as fruit.

oar *n.* a wooden lever with a broad blade worked by the hands to propel a boat; *v.t.* and *v.i.* to row. **-ed** *a.* having oars.

o•a•sis *n.* a fertile spot in the desert. *pl.* **oases.**

oat *n.* but usually in *pl.* **oats,** the grain of a common cereal plant, used as food. **-meal** *n.* meal made from oats.

oath *n.* confirmation of the truth by naming something sacred, esp. God; *pl.* **oaths.**

ob•du•rate *a.* hard-hearted; stubborn; unyielding. **-ly** *adv.* **obduracy** *n.*

o•be•di•ent *a.* willing to obey. **-ly** *adv.* **obedience** *n.* submission to authority; doing what one is told.

ob•e•lisk *n.* a tall, four-sided, tapering pillar, ending in a small pyramid; in

obelisk

printing, a reference mark (†) also called 'dagger'; an **obelus,** the marks – or ÷.

o•bese *a.* fat. **obesity** *n.* excessive fatness.

o•bey *v.i.* to be obedient; *v.t.* to comply with the orders of; to yield submission to; to be ruled by.

o•bit•u•ar•y *a.* pert. to death of person; *n.* a notice, often with a biographical sketch, of the death of a person.

ob•ject *n.* a material thing; an end or aim; *(Gram.)* a noun, pronoun, or clause governed by, and dependent on, a transitive verb or a preposition. **-less** *a.* having no aim or purpose.

ob•ject *v.t.* to offer in opposition; to put forward as reason against; *v.i.* to make verbal opposition; to protest against; to feel dislike or reluctance. **objection** *n.* act of objecting; adverse reason; argument against. **objectionable** *a.* **objectionably** *adv.* **-or** *n.*

ob•jec•tive *a.* pert. to the object; relating to that which is external to the mind; unbiased. **-ly** *adv.* **objectivity** *n.* the quality of being objective.

ob•li•gate *v.t.* to bind, esp. by legal contract. **obligation** *n.* the binding power of a promise or contract; indebtedness for a favor of kindness; a duty. **obligatory** *a.* binding legally or morally; compulsory. **obligatorily** *adv.*

o•blige *v.t.* to constrain by physical, moral, or legal force; to do a favor to; to compel.

-d *a.* grateful; indebted. **-ment** *n.* a favor. **obliging** *a.* helpful; courteous. **obligingly** *adv.* **obligingness** *n.*

ob•lique *a.* slanting; inclined; indirect; obscure; not straightforward. **-ly** *adv.* **-ness, obliquity** *n.* slant or inclination; deviation from moral uprightness; dishonesty.

ob•lit•er•ate *v.t.* to blot out; to efface or destroy. **obliteration** *n.* the act of blotting out; destruction; extinction. **obliterative** *a.*

ob•liv•i•on *n.* a forgetting, or being forgotten; forgetfulness; heedlessness. **oblivious** *a.* forgetful; causing to forget; heedless. **obliviously** *adv.* **obliviousness** *n.*

ob•long *a.* longer than broad; *n.* a rectangular figure with adjacent sides unequal.

ob•nox•ious *a.* offensive; objectionable. **-ly** *adv.* **-ness** *n.*

o•boe *n.* a woodwind instrument, long and slender, with tone produced by a double reed. **oboist** *n.*

ob•scene *a.* indecent; filthy. **-ly** *adv.* **-ness** *n.* **obscenity** *n.* lewdness; indecency.

ob•scure *a.* dark; hidden; dim; uncertain; *v.t.* to dim; to conceal; to make less intelligible; to make doubtful. **-ly** *adv.* **-ness** *n.* **obscurity** *n.* absence of light; lack of clear expression or meaning.

ob•serve *v.t.* to watch; to perform or keep religiously; *v.i.* to take notice; to make a remark; to comment. **observable** *a.* **observance** *n.* a paying attention; the keeping of a law, custom, religious rite; a religious rite; a rule or practice. **observant** *a.* quick to notice; alert; carefully attentive; obedient to. **observantly** *adv.* **observation** *n.* the action or habit of observing; the result of watching, examining, and noting; a comment; a remark. **observatory** *n.* a building for the observation and study of astronomical, meteorological, etc., phenomena. **-r** *n.*

ob•sess *v.t.* to haunt; to fill the mind completely; to preoccupy. **-ion** *n.* complete domination of the mind by one idea; a fixed idea.

ob•sid•i•an *n.* vitreous lava or glassy volcanic rock.

ob•so•lete *a.* no longer in use; out of date. **-ly** *adv.* **-ness** *n.* **obsolescent** *a.* becoming obsolete; going out of use. **obsolescence** *n.*

ob•sta•cle *n.* anything that stands in the way; an obstruction; a hindrance.

ob•stet•rics *n.* *(Med.)* the science dealing with the care of pregnant women. **obstetric, obstetrical** *a.* **obstetrician** *n.*

ob•sti•nate *a.* stubborn. **-ly** *adv.* **-ness** *n.* **obstinacy** *n.* unreasonable firmness; stubbornness.

ob•strep•er•ous *a.* noisy; clamorous; vociferous; unruly; *adv.* **-ness** *n.*

ob•struct *v.t.* to block up; to impede; to hinder the passage of; **-er, -or** *n.* **-ion** *n.* the act of obstructing; that which obstructs or hinders. **-ive** *a.* **-ively** *adv.*

ob•tain *v.t.* to gain; to acquire; to procure;

v.i. to be customary or prevalent. **-able** *a.* procurable. **-ment** *n.* Also **obtention**.

ob•trude *v.t.* to thrust forward unsolicited; to push out; *v.i.* to intrude. **-r** *n.* **obtrusion** *n.* the act of obtruding. **obtrusive** *a.* **obtrusively** *adv.*

ob•tuse *a.* blunt; dull of perception; greater than a right angle, but less than 180°. **-ly** *adv.* **-ness** *n.*

ob•vi•ous *a.* easily seen or understood; evident; apparent. **-ly** *adv.* **-ness** *n.*

oc•ca•sion *n.* opportunity; a time of important occurrence; *v.t.* to cause; to bring about. **-al** *a.* occurring now and then; incidental; meant for a special occasion. **-ally** *adv.* from time to time.

oc•ci•dent *n.* part of the horizon where the sun sets, the west. **occidental** *a.* western; *n.* native of Europe or America.

oc•cult *a.* secret; mysterious; magical; supernatural; **-ly** *adv.* **-ism** *n.* the doctrine or study of the supernatural, magical, etc.

oc•cu•py *v.t.* to take possession of; to inhabit; to fill; to employ. **occupancy** *n.* the act of having or holding possession; tenure. **occupant** *n.* one who occupies or is in possession. **occupation** *n.* occupancy; possession; employment; trade; calling; business, profession. **occupational** *a.*

oc•cur *v.i.* to happen; to be met with. *pr.p.* **-ring.** *pa.p.* and *pa.t.* **-red. -rence** *n.* a happening; an event.

o•cean *n.* great body of salt water surrounding land of globe; *a.* pert. to the great sea. **oceanic** *a.* pert. to, found, or formed in the ocean. **-ography** *n.* the scientific description of ocean phenomena. **-ographer** *n.* **-ographic, -ographical** *a.* **-ology** *n.* science which relates to the ocean.

o•ce•lot *n.* a S. Amer. quadruped of the leopard family.

ocelot

o'clock *adv.* by the clock.

oct-, octa-, octo- *prefix* fr. Gk. *okto*, eight, combining to form derivatives. **-agon** *n.* a plane figure with 8 sides and 8 angles. **-agonal** *a.* **-ahedron** *n.* a solid figure with 8 plane faces. **-ahedral** *a.* **-ane** *n.* a hydrocarbon of the paraffin series, obtained from petroleum and used as a fuel, esp. for airplanes.

oc•tave *n.* a stanza of 8 lines.

oc•tet *n.* a group of 8 musicians or singers; a composition for such a group; a group of 8 lines, esp. the first 8 lines of a sonnet. Also **octette**.

Oc•to•ber *n.* tenth month.

oc•to•ge•nar•i•an *a.* and *n.* between 80 and 90 years of age.

oc•to•pus *n.* a mollusk with 8 arms or tentacles covered with suckers.

oc•u•lar *a.* pert. to the eye, or to sight; visual; *n.* the eyepiece of an optical instrument. **oculist** *n.* a specialist in the defects and diseases of the eye.

odd *a.* not even; not divisible by two; extra; surplus; out-of-the-way; strange. **-ity** *n.* quality of being odd; peculiarity; **-ly** *adv.* **-ness** *n.* **odds** *n.pl.* the difference in favor of one as against another; advantage or superiority; the ratio by which one person's bet exceeds another's; likelihood or probability.

ode *n.* a lyric poem of exalted tone.

o•dont- *prefix* from the Gk. *odous, odontos,* a tooth. **odontalgia** *n.* toothache. **odontology** *n.* the science of the teeth.

o•dor *n.* smell; fragrance; perfume; repute or estimation.

O•dys•seus *n.* hero of Homer's **Odyssey** *n.* a Greek epic poem glorifying the adventures and wanderings of Odysseus; hence, any long, adventurous journey.

Oed•i•pus *n.* a king of Thebes who unwittingly slew his father and married Jocasta, his mother. **Oedipus complex,** in psychoanalysis, a complex involving an abnormal love by a person for the parent of opposite sex.

of *prep.* belonging to; from; proceeding from; relating to; concerning.

off *adv.* away; in general, denotes removal or separation, also completion, as in *to finish off; prep.* not on; away from; *a.* distant; on the farther side; *interj.* begone! depart! **-hand** *a.* without preparation; free and easy; curt; *adv.* without hesitation; impromptu. **-shoot** *n.* that which shoots off or separates from a main branch or channel; a descendant. **— side** *a.* of a player, being illegally ahead of the ball, etc. **-spring** *n.* children; **off and on,** intermittently.

of•fend *v.t.* to displease; to make angry; to wound the feelings of; *v.i.* to cause displeasure; to do wrong; to sin. **-er** *n.*

of•fense *n.* transgression; sin; insult; wrong; resentment; displeasure; **offensive** *a.* causing or giving offense; insulting; unpleasant; *n.* attack; onset; aggressive action. **offensively** *adv.* **offensiveness** *n.*

of•fer *v.t.* to present for acceptance or refusal; to tender; to bid, as a price; to propose; to attempt; to express readiness to do; *v.i.* to present itself or to occur; *n.* an act of offering; a presentation; a price bid; a proposal, esp. of marriage. **-ing** *n.* that which is offered, as a contribution through the church; a sacrifice; a gift. **-er** *n.*

of•fer•to•ry *n.* a part of the mass during which the elements are offered up.

of•fice *n.* a place for doing business; an official position; **-r** *n.* a person who holds an official position; one who holds commissioned rank in the navy, army, air force, etc.

of•fi•cial *a.* pert. to an office; vouched for by one holding office; authorized; *n.* one holding an office, esp. in a public body. **-ly** *adv.*

of•fi•ci•ate *v.i.* to perform the duties of an officer; to perform a divine service.

of•ten *adv.* frequently; many times.

o•gle *v.i.* to make eyes; *v.t.* to make eyes

at; to cast amorous glances at; *n.* an amorous glance. **-r** *n.*

oh *interj.* an exclamation of surprise, sorrow, pain, etc.

ohm *n.* the standard unit of electrical resistance. **-meter** *n.* an instrument for measuring electrical current and resistance.

oil *n.* one of several kinds of light viscous liquids, obtained from various plants, animal substances, and minerals, used as lubricants, illuminants, fuel, medicines, etc.; *v.t.* to apply oil to; *v.i.* to take oil aboard as fuel. **-y** *a.* consisting of, or resembling, oil; greasy; **-ily** *adv.* **-iness** *n.* **-s** *n.pl.* (*Paint.*) short for 'oil-colors'; **-cloth** *n.* coarse canvas cloth coated with oil and pigment to make waterproof, used for table coverings, etc. **— colors** *n.pl.* colors made by grinding pigments in oil. **— painting** *n.* one done in oil colors. **— well** *n.* boring made in district yielding petroleum.

oint·ment *n.* an unguent.

o·kay *a.* and *adv.* abbrev. to **O.K.,** an expression signifying approval.

old *a.* advanced in age; having lived or existed long; not new or fresh. **-en** *a.* old; ancient; pert. to the past. **—fashioned** *a.* out of date; not modern. **— school** *a.* old-fashioned. **Old Testament,** the first division of Bible. **Old World,** the Eastern hemisphere.

o·le·o·mar·ga·rine *n.* a butter substitute. *Abbrev.* oleo.

ol·fac·tion *n.* smelling; sense of smell. olfactory *a.* pert. to smelling.

ol·i·gar·chy *n.* government in which supreme power rests with a few; those who constitute the ruling few. oligarch *n.* a member of an oligarchy. oligarchal *a.* Also oligarchic(al).

ol·i·go·cene *a.* pert. to a geological period between the eocene and miocene.

ol·ive *n.* an evergreen tree, long cultivated in the Mediterranean countries for its

olive

fruit; its oval, oil-yielding fruit; *a.* of the color of an unripe olive, or of the foliage.

O·lym·pi·a a plain in ancient Greece, the scene of the Olympic Games. **Olympiad** *n.* the name given to period of four years between each celebration of Olympic Games. **Olympic** *a.* pert. to Olympia, or to the games. **Olympics** *n.pl.* the Olympic Games.

om·e·let, omelette *n.* a dish of eggs beaten with milk and seasonings and cooked in a frying pan.

o·men *n.* a sign of future events; a foreboding; *v.t.* to foreshadow by means of signs.

o·mit *v.t.* to leave out; to neglect; to fail to perform. *pr.p.* **-ting** *pa.p., pat.* **-ted.** omission *n.* the act of omitting; neglect; failure to do; that which is omitted or left undone. **omissible** *a.* that may be omitted. **omissive** *a.*

om·ni·po·tent *a.* all-powerful, esp. of God; almighty. **-ly** *adv.* **omnipotence** *n.* unlimited power.

om·ni·pres·ent *a.* present in all places at the same time. omnipresence *n.*

om·nis·cience *n.* infinite knowledge. omniscient *a.* all-knowing.

om·niv·o·rous *a.* all-devouring; eating every kind of food. **-ly** *adv.*

on *prep.* above and touching; in addition to; following from; referring to; at; near; towards, etc.; *adv.* so as to be on; forwards; continuously.

once *adv.* at one time; on one occasion; formerly; ever; *n.* one time. **at once,** immediately.

on·com·ing *a.* approaching; *n.* approach.

one *a.* single; only; *n.* the number or figure 1, I; the lowest cardinal number; unity; a single specimen; *pron.* a particular but not stated person; any person. **-ness** *n.* unity; uniformity; singleness. **-self** *pron.* one's own self or person. **—sided** *a.* esp. of a contest, game, etc., limited to one side; considering one side only; partial; unfair. **—way** *a.* denoting a system of traffic circulation in one direction only.

on·go·ing *n.* a going on; advance; procedure; *a.* continuing.

on·ion *n.* an edible, bulbous plant with pungent odor. **— skin** *n.* thin, glazed paper.

on·ly *a.* being the one specimen; single; sole; *adv.* solely; singly; merely; exclusively; *conj.* but then; except that.

on·o·mat·o·poe·ia *n.* the formation of a word by using sounds that resemble or suggest the object to be named; e.g. *hiss, ping-pong.* onomatopoeic, onomatopoetic *a.*

on·shore *a.* towards the land, esp. of a wind.

on·slaught *n.* attack; an onset; an assault.

on·to *prep.* upon; on the top; to.

on·tol·o·gy *n.* the science that treats of reality of being; metaphysics. ontological *a.* ontologist *n.*

o·nus *n.* burden; responsibility.

on·ward *a.* and *adv.* advancing; going on; forward. **-s** *adv.* in a forward direction; ahead.

on·yx *n.* a variety of quartz.

ooze *n.* soft mud or slime; a gentle flow; *v.i.* to flow gently as if through pores; to leak or percolate; *v.t.* to exude or give out slowly. oozy *a.*

o·pal *n.* a mineral much used as a gem owing to its beautiful and varying hues of green, yellow and red.

o·paque *a.* not transparent; impenetrable to light; not lucid; dull-witted. **-ly** *adv.* **-ness** *n.* opacity *n.*

o·pen *a.* not shut or blocked up; allowing passage in or out; without restrictions; available; exposed; frank and sincere; *n.*

O

clear, unobstructed space; *v.t.* to set open; to uncover; to give access to; to cut or break into; *v.i.* to become open; to begin. **-er** *n.* one who or that which opens. **-ing** *a.* first in order; initial; *n.* a hole or gap; an open or cleared space; an opportunity; a beginning. **-ly** *adv.* publicly; frankly. **-ness** *n.*

op•er•a *n.* a musical drama; the theater where opera is performed. **operatic** *a.* pert. to opera. **operetta** *n.* a short light opera. **grand opera**, opera in which no spoken dialogue is permitted.

op•er•ate *v.t.* to cause to function; to effect; *v.i.* to work; to perform an act of surgery; **operation** *n.* the act of operating; a method or mode of action; treatment involving surgical skill. **operational** *a.* **operative** *a.* having the power of acting; exerting force; producing the desired effect; efficacious; **operator** *n.*

o•phid•i•an *n.* a snake; *a.* snake-like.

oph•thal•mi•a *n.* inflammation of the eye. **ophthalmic** *a.* of the eye. **ophthalmologist** *n.* a physician skilled in the study and treatment of the eye. **ophthalmology** *n.* the science dealing with the structure, functions, and diseases of the eye. **ophthalmoscope** *n.* an instrument for viewing the interior of the eye.

o•pi•ate *n.* any preparation of opium; a narcotic; *a.* containing opium; inducing sleep. **opiatic** *a.*

o•pin•ion *n.* judgment or belief; formal statement by an expert. **-ated** *a.* dogmatic.

o•pi•um *n.* narcotic used to induce sleep or allay pain.

o•pos•sum *n.* a small marsupial animal. Also **possum.**

opossum

op•po•nent *a.* opposite; opposing; antagonistic; *n.* one who opposes.

op•por•tune *a.* well-timed; convenient. **-ly** *adv.* **-ness** *n.* **opportunism** *n.* the policy of doing what is expedient at the time regardless of principle. **opportunist** *n.* **opportunity** *n.* a fit or convenient time; a good chance.

op•pose *v.t.* to set against; to resist; to compete with. **opposable** *a.* **-r** *n.*

op•po•site *a.* contrary; *n.* the contrary; *prep.* and *adv.* in front of; on the other side; across from; **-ly** *adv.* facing each other. **-ness** *n.* **opposition** *n.* the state of being opposite; resistance; contradiction; a party opposed to that in power.

op•press *v.t.* to govern with tyranny; to treat severely; to lie heavily on. **-ion** *n.* harshness; tyranny; dejection. **-ive** *a.* unreasonably burdensome; hard to bear. **-ively** *adv.* **-iveness** *n.* **-or** *n.*

opt *v.i.* to make a choice; to choose. **-ative** *a.* expressing wish or desire.

op•tic *a.* pert. to the eye or to sight; pert. to optics; *n.* the eye. **-s** *n.* the science which deals with light and its relation to sight. **-al** *a.* pert. to vision; visual. **-ally** *adv.* **optician** *n.* a maker of, or dealer in, optical instruments, esp. spectacles.

op•ti•mism *n.* belief that everything is ordered for the best; disposition to look on bright side. **optimist** *n.* believer in optimism; one who takes hopeful view. **optimistical** *a.*

op•tion *n.* the power or right of choosing; choice. *a.* left to one's free choice. **-ally** *adv.*

or *conj.* introducing an alternative; if not.

or•a•cle *n.* shrine where ancient Greeks consulted deity; response given, often obscure; a person of outstanding wisdom.

o•ral *a.* spoken; pert. to the mouth. **-ly** *adv.*

or•ange *n.* a juicy, gold-colored citrus fruit; tree bearing it; reddish yellow color like an orange; *a.* reddish yellow in color. **-ade** *n.* drink of orange juice, sugar, and water.

o•rang•u•tan, o•rang•ou•tang *n.* a large long-armed ape.

o•rate *v.i.* to talk loftily; **oration** *n.* a formal and dignified public speech. **orator** *n.* one who delivers an oration; one distinguished for gift of public speaking. **oratorical** *a.* pert. to orator(y); rhetorical. **oratorically** *adv.* **oratorio** *n.* a religious musical composition for voices and orchestra. **oratory** *n.* the art or exercise of speaking in public; eloquence.

orb *n.* a sphere or globe. **-it** *n.* path traced by one heavenly body in its revolution round another; range of influence or action. **-ital** *a.*

or•chard *n.* a garden or enclosure containing fruit trees.

or•ches•tra *n.* the space in a theater occupied by musicians; the main floor of a theater; a group of performers on various musical instruments. **orchestral** *a.* **orchestrate** *v.t.* to arrange music for performance by an orchestra. **-tion** *n.*

or•chid, orchis *n.* a genus of plants with fantastically-shaped flowers of varied and brilliant colors.

orchid

or•dain *v.t.* to decree; to destine; to appoint; **ordination** *n.* the act of ordaining admission to the ministry.

or•deal *n.* a trying experience; a test of endurance.

or•der *n.* rank; class; group; regular arrangement; sequence; succession; method; regulation; a command or direction; one of the five styles of architecture; a subdivision of a class of plants or animals, made up of genera. *v.t.* to arrange; to command; to require; to regulate; to systematize; to give an order for. **-ly** *a.* methodical; tidy; well regulated; *n.* a soldier following an officer to carry orders; in a hospital, an attendant; *adv.* in right order. **-liness** *n.* **in order to,** for the purpose of.

or·di·nal *a.* and *n.* showing order or position in a series, e.g. *first, second,* etc.; pert. to an order, of plants, animals, etc.

or·di·nance *n.* an established rule, religious rite, or ceremony; a decree.

or·di·nar·y *a.* usual; regular; normal, commonplace; plain; *n.* something customary; **ordinarily** *adv.*

or·di·na·tion See **ordain.**

ore *n.* a native mineral from which metal is extracted.

or·gan *n.* a musical instrument of pipes worked by bellows and played by keys; a member of an animal or plant exercising a special function. **organic** *a.* pert. to or affecting bodily organs; having either animal or vegetable life; derived from living organisms; **organically** *adv.* **-ism** *n.* an organized body or system; a living body. **-ist** *n.* a player on the organ. **organic chemistry,** the branch of chemistry dealing with the compounds of carbon.

or·gan·dy *n.* a muslin of great transparency and lightness. Also **organdie.**

or·gan·ize *v.t.* to give a definite structure; to get up, arrange, or put into working order; **organizable** *a.* **organization** *n.* act of organizing; the manner in which the branches of a service, etc., are arranged; individuals systematically united for some work; a society. **-r** *n.*

or·gasm *n.* immoderate action or excitement, esp. sexual. **orgastic** *a.*

o·ri·ent *a.* rising, as the sun; lustrous; *n.* the east; Eastern countries; *v.t.* to place so as to face the east; to determine the position of, with respect to the east; to take one's bearings. **oriental** *a.* eastern; pert. to, coming from, of, the east; *n.* an Asiatic. **orientate** *v.t.* and *i.* to orient; to bring into clearly understood relations. **orientation** *n.* the act of turning to, or determining, the east; sense of direction.

or·i·fice *n.* a mouth or opening.

or·i·gin *n.* beginning; starting point; a source. **original** *a.* earliest; first; new, not copied or derived; thinking or acting for oneself; *n.* origin; model; a pattern. **originally** *adv.* **originality** *n.* the quality of being original; initiative. **originate** *v.t.* to bring into being; to initiate; *v.i.* to begin; to arise. **originative** *a.* **origination** *n.* **originator** *n.*

o·ri·ole *n.* bird of the thrush family.

oriole

or·na·ment *n.* decoration; any object to adorn or decorate; *v.t.* to adorn; to beautify; to embellish. **ornamental** *a.* serving to decorate. **ornamentally** *adv.* **ornamentation** *n.* decoration. **ornate** *a.* richly decorated. **ornately** *adv.* **ornateness** *n.*

or·ni·tho- *prefix* fr. Gk. *ornis, ornithos,* a bird, used in derivatives. **ornithology,** the scientific study of birds. **ornithological** *a.* **ornithologist** *n.*

or·phan *n.* and *a.* a child bereft of one or both parents; *v.t.* to make an orphan. **-age** *n.* a home or institution for orphans.

or·ris *n.* a kind of iris. **-root** *n.* the dried root, used as a powder in perfumery and medicine.

or·tho·dox *a.* having the correct faith; sound in opinions or doctrine; conventional. **-ly** *adv.* **-y** *n.* soundness of faith, esp. in religion. **-ness** *n.*

or·thog·ra·phy *n.* correct spelling. **orthographer** *n.* **orthographic, orthographical** *a.* **orthographically** *adv.*

or·tho·pe·dics, orthopaedics *n.* treatment and cure of bodily deformities, esp. in children. Also **orthop(a)edia, orthop(a)edy. orthopedic** *a.* **orthopedist** *n.*

os·cil·late *v.i.* to swing to and fro; to vibrate; **oscillation** *n.* a pendulum-like motion; variation between extremes. **oscillator** *n.* **oscillatory** *n.*

os·cu·late *v.t.* and *i.* to kiss; *a.* of species sharing characteristics. **osculant, osculation** *n.* kissing; contact. **osculatory** *a.*

os·mo·sis *n.* the tendency of fluid substances, if separated by a porous membrane, to filter through it and become equally diffused. **osmotic** *a.*

os·ten·si·ble *a.* professed; apparent. **ostensibly** *adv.* **ostensibility** *n.*

os·ten·ta·tion *n.* vain-glorious display; showing off. **ostentatious** *a.* fond of display; characterized by display. **ostentatiously** *adv.* **ostentatiousness** *n.*

os·te·o- *prefix* fr. Gk *osteon,* bone, used in derivatives mainly medical. **-arthritis** *n.* chronic inflammation of a joint. **osteoid** *a.* resembling bone. **osteology** *n.* that branch of anatomy dealing with bones, their structure, etc. **osteologist** *n.*

os·te·op·a·thy *n.* a system of healing, based on the belief that the human body can effect its own cure with the aid of manipulative treatment of the spinal column, joints, etc. **osteopath** *n.* a practitioner of this system. **osteopathic** *a.*

os·tra·cise *v.t.* to exclude from society; to exile; **ostracism** *n.* exclusion from society; social boycotting.

os·trich *n.* a large flightless bird, native of Africa.

oth·er *a.* and *pron.* not this; not the same; different; opposite; additional; *adv.* otherwise. **-wise** *adv.* differently; in another way; *conj.* else; if not. **every other,** every second (one); each alternate.

o·ti·ose *a.* at ease; at leisure; superfluous; futile.

o·ti·tis *n.* inflammation of the ear. **otology** *n.*

ot•ter n. an aquatic, fish-eating animal of the weasel family.

Ot•to•man a. pert. to the Turks; n. a cushioned seat without back or arms.

ought auxil. v. to be bound by moral obligation or duty.

oui•ja n. board with letters, used at seances to answer questions.

ounce n. a unit of weight, abbrev. oz.; in avoirdupois weight = 1/16 of a pound; in troy weight 1/12 of a pound; a fluid measurement.

our n. belonging to us. -s poss. pron. used with a noun. -self pron. myself. -selves pron. pl. we, i.e. not others.

oust v.t. to put out; to expel; to dispossess, esp. by unfair means.

out adv. on, at, or to, the outside; from within; from among; away; in bloom; on strike; unemployed; a. outlying; remote; prep. outside; out of; interj. away! begone! v.t. to put out; to knock out; -er a. being on the outside; away from the inside. -ermost, -most a.

out•board a. projecting beyond and outside the hull of a ship, e.g. of a ladder; also, of a detachable motor.

out•break n, a sudden breaking out; a burst, esp. of anger; the beginning, esp. of an epidemic of disease, of war, etc.

out•burst n. a bursting out, esp. of anger, laughter, cheering, etc.

out•cast a. cast out as useless; n. one rejected by society.

out•come n. issue; result.

out•do v.t. to excel; surpass.

out•door a. out of doors; in the open air. -s adv. outside.

out•field n. the part of the field beyond the diamond or infield; the players there.

out•fit n. a supply of things, esp. clothes, tools, etc., required for any purpose; equipment; kit; v.t. to supply with equipment, etc. -ter n. one who supplies equipment.

out•go v.t. to go beyond; n. expenditure; outlay. -ing a. sociable; departing; going out.

out•grow v.t. to surpass in growth; to become too large or old for; to grow out of. -th n. what growth out of anything.

out•ing n. a going out; an excursion; a trip.

out•land•ish a. remote; barbarous; not according to custom.

out•law n. one placed beyond the protection of the law; a bandit; v.t. to declare to be an outlaw. -ry n. defiance of the law.

out•lay n. expenditure; expenses.

out•let n. a passage or way out; an exit; a vent; an opening.

out•line n. the lines that bound a figure; a boundary; a sketch without details; a rough draft; a general plan; v.t. to draw in outline; to give a general plan of.

out•look n. a looking out; a prospect; a person's point of view; prospects.

out•ly•ing a. remote; isolated; detached.

out•mod•ed a. out of fashion.

out•pa•tient n. a patient who comes to a hospital, infirmary, etc., for treatment but is non-resident.

out•put n. production; the amount of goods produced in a given time.

out•rage n. excessive violence; gross insult or indignity; v.t. to do grievous wrong or violence to; to insult grossly. outrageous a. violent; atrocious. outrageously adv.

out•set n. a beginning; start.

out•side n. the outer surface; the exterior; a. pert. to the outer part; exterior; external; outdoor; adv. not inside; out of doors; in the open air; prep. on the outer part of. -r n. one not belonging to a particular party, set, circle, etc.

out•skirt n. generally in pl. the border; the suburbs of a town.

out•spo•ken a. not afraid to speak aloud one's opinions; freedom of speech.

out•stand•ing a. standing out; prominent; conspicuous; of debts, unpaid; of work, etc., still to be done.

out•ward a. pert. to the outside; external; exterior; adv. towards the outside. -s adv. outward; toward the outside. -ly adv.

out•wit v.t. to defeat by cunning, stratagem, etc.; to get the better of.

o•va n.pl. eggs; the female germ cells; sing. ovum. ovary n. one of two reproductive organs in female animal in which the ova are formed and developed. ovarial, ovarian a. pert. to the ovary.

o•val a. egg-shaped; elliptical; n. an oval figure. -ly adv.

o•va•tion n. an enthusiastic burst of applause; a triumphant reception.

ov•en n. an enclosed chamber in a stove, for baking or heating.

o•ver prep. above; on; upon; more than; in excess of; across; from side to side of; throughout; etc.; adv. above; above and beyond; going beyond; in excess; too much; past; finished; across; a. upper; outer; covering; n. -all a. inclusive.

o•ver•act v.t. and i. to play a part in an exaggerated manner.

o•ver•all n. loose trousers worn over the ordinary clothing as a protection against dirt, etc. Also n.pl.

o•ver•arm a. and adv. in swimming, ball, etc., with the hand and arm raised.

o•ver•bear v.t. to bear down; to repress; to overpower. -ing a. domineering.

o•ver•board adv. over the side of a ship; out of a ship into the water.

o•ver•cast v.t. to cast over; to cloud; to darken. overcast a. cloudy; dull.

o•ver•coat n. an outdoor garment for men worn over ordinary clothing.

o•ver•do v.t. to do too much; to fatigue; to exaggerate. pa.t. overdid. pa.p. overdone a. exaggerated; over-acted; over-cooked.

o•ver•dose v.t. to give an excessive dose; n. to take too great a dose.

o•ver•draw v.t. and i. to exaggerate; to draw money in excess of one's credit. overdraft n. act of overdrawing; amount drawn from bank in excess of credit.

o•ver•due a. unpaid at right time; not having arrived at right time.

o•ver•flow v.t. to flow over; to flood; to fill too full; v.i. to flow over the edge, bank, etc.; to abound. n. what flows over; flood; excess; superabundance; surplus.

o•ver•hand *a.* and *adv.* with the hand raised.

o•ver•haul *v.t.* to examine thoroughly and set in order; overhaul *n.* a thorough examination, esp. for repairs; repair.

o•ver•head *a.* and *adv.* over the head; above; aloft; in the sky; the permanent expenses of running a business.

o•ver•hear *v.t.* to hear by accident. *pa.p.* and *pa.t.* overheard.

o•ver•lay *v.t.* to spread over, to cover completely; to span. *n.* a covering, as a transparent sheet, superimposed on another.

o•ver•load *v.t.* to place too heavy a load on. *n.* an excessive load.

o•ver•look *v.t.* to look over; to inspect; to superintend; to fail to notice by carelessness; to excuse; to pardon.

o•ver•night *adv.* through and during the night.

o•ver•ride *v.t.* to ride over; to ride too much; to set aside; to cancel. *n.* a gear; larger than usual payment.

o•ver•run *v.t.* to run over; to grow over, e.g. as weeds; to take possession by spreading over, e.g. as an invading army.

o•ver•seas *a.* and *adv.* from or to a country or place over the sea; foreign.

o•ver•see *v.t.* to superintend; to supervise. overseer *n.* a supervisor.

o•ver•shoe *n.* a shoe made of rubber, felt, etc., worn over the ordinary shoe.

o•ver•sight *n.* failure to notice; unintentional neglect; management.

o•ver•state *v.t.* to exaggerate, -ment *n.* exaggeration.

o•vert *a.* open to view. -ly *adv.*

o•ver•take *v.t.* to come up with; to catch; to take by surprise.

o•ver•throw *v.t.* to throw over or down; to upset; to defeat. *pa.t.* overthrew; *pa.p.* overthrown. overthrow *n.* the act of throwing over; defeat; ruin; fall.

o•ver•time *n.* time at work beyond the regular hours; the extra wages paid for such work.

o•ver•ture *n.* an orchestral introduction.

o•ver•turn *v.t.* and *i.* to throw down or over; to upset; to turn over.

o•ver•weight *n.* excess weight; extra weight beyond the just weight.

o•ver•whelm *v.t.* to crush; to submerge; to overpower. -ing *a.* decisive; irresistible. -ingly *adv.*

o•vi- *prefix* fr. L. *ovum*, an egg, used in derivatives. oviduct *n.* a passage for the egg, from the ovary. oviferous *a.* egg-bearing. oviform *a.* egg-shaped. oviparous *a.* producing eggs.

o•vo- *prefix* fr. L. *ovum*, an egg, used in derivatives. ovoid *a.* egg-shaped; oval.

o•vum See ova.

owe *v.t.* to be bound to repay; to be indebted for. owing *a.* requiring to be paid.

owl *n.* a night bird of prey. -et *n.* a young owl; a small owl. -ish *a.* owl like in appearance.

own *a.* is used to emphasize possession, e.g. my *own* money; *v.t.* to possess; to acknowledge; to admit; *v.i.* to confess. -er *n.* the rightful possessor. -ership *n.* right of possession.

ox *n.* a large cloven-footed and usually horned farm animal; a male cow. *pl.* -en.

ox•ford *n.* a low shoe laced over the instep.

ox•ide *n.* a compound of oxygen and one other element. oxidize, oxidate *v.t.* and *i.* to combine with oxygen to form an oxide; of metals, to rust, to become rusty. oxidization *n.*

ox•y- *prefix* fr. Gk. *oxus* sharp, used in derivatives. -acetylene *a.* denoting a very hot blowpipe flame, produced by a mixture of oxygen and acetylene, and used in cutting steel plates, etc.

ox•y•gen *n.* a colorless, odorless, and tasteless gas, forming about ½ by volume of the atmosphere, and essential to life, combustion, etc. -ate, -ize *v.t.* to combine or treat with oxygen. -ation *n.* -ous *a.* pert. to or obtained from, oxygen.

oys•ter *n.* an edible, bivalve shellfish.

o•zone *n.* a condensed and very active form of oxygen with a pungent odor.

O

pace *n.* a step; the length of a step in walking (about 30 inches); gait; rate of movement; *v.t.* to measure by steps; to set the speed for; *v.t.* to walk with measured fashion. **-d** *a.* having a certain gait. **-r** *n.* one who sets the pace for another.

pach•y; **-derm** *n.* a thick-skinned, nonruminant quadruped, e.g. the elephant. **-dermatous** *a.* thick-skinned; insenitive.

pac•i•fy *v.t.* to appease; to tranquilize. **pacifism** *n.* a doctrine which advocates abolition of war. **pacifist** *n.* **pacific** *a.* peaceful; calm or tranquil. **pacification**. *n.* **pacificatory** *a.* tending to make peace. **pacifier** *n.*

pack *n.* bundle for carrying, esp. on back; a band (of animals); a set of playing cards; *v.t.* to arrange closely in a bundle, box or bag; to fill, press together; to carry; to load. **-age** *n.* a bundle or parcel. **-er** *n.* **-et** *n.* a small package. **— horse** *n.* a horse for carrying burdens, in packs. **-ing** *n.* any material used to pack, fill up, or make close.

pact *n.* an agreement; a compact.

pad *n.* anything stuffed with soft material, to fill out or protect; a cushion; sheets of paper fastened together in a block; the foot or sole of certain animals; *v.t.* to furnish with a pad; to stuff; *pr.p.* **-ding.** *pa.p.* and *pa.t.* **-ded.** **-ding** *n.* the material used in stuffing; unnecessary matter inserted in a book, speech, etc., to expand it.

pad•dle *n.* a short oar with a broad blade at one or each end; a balance or float of a paddle wheel, a flipper; *v.t.* and *i.* to propel by paddles.

pad•dock *n.* a small grass field or enclosure where horses are saddled before race.

pad•dy *n.* rice in the husk.

pad•lock *n.* a detachable lock with a hinged hoop to go through a staple or ring.

pa•dre *n.* priest; chaplain.

pa•gan *n.* a heathen; *a.* heathenish.

page *n.* one side of a leaf of a book or manuscript; *v.t.* to number the pages of.

page *n.* formerly a boy in service of a person of rank; a uniformed boy attendant esp. in a hotel; *v.t.* to summon by sending a page to call.

pag•eant *n.* a show of persons in costume in procession, dramatic scenes, etc. a spectacle. **-ry** *n.* a brilliant display; pomp.

pa•go•da *n.* a temple or sacred tower in India, Burma, etc.

paid *pa.p.* and *pa.t.* of the verb **pay.**

pail *n.* a round, open vessel of wood, tin, etc., for carrying liquids; a bucket.

pain *n.* bodily or mental suffering; distress; *pl.* trouble; exertion; *v.t.* to inflict bodily or mental suffering upon. **-ful** *a.* full of pain; causing pain; difficult; **-fully** *adv.* **-fulness** *n.* **-less** *a.* **-lessly** *adv.* **-lessness** *n.* **-staking** *a.* carefully laborious.

paint *n.* coloring matter for putting on surface with brush, etc.; *v.t.* to cover or besmear with paint; to make a picture with paint; to adorn with, or as with, paint.

paint•er *n.* a rope at the bow of a boat used to fasten it to any other object.

pair *n.* two things of a kind; a single article composed of two similar pieces, e.g. a pair of scissors; a courting, engaged, or married couple; a mated couple of animals or birds; *v.t.* to unite in couples.

pa•ja•mas *n.pl.* loose trousers, worn by Mohammedans; a sleeping suit.

pal *n.* a close friend.

pal•ace *n.* the house in which a great personage resides; any magnificent house.

pal•ate *n.* the roof of the mouth; sense of taste; relish; liking. **palatable** *a.* agreeable to the taste or mind. **palatably** *adv.* **palatal** *a.* of a sound, produced by placing tongue against palate.

pal•a•tine *a.* having royal privileges; *n.* one who possesses royal privileges. **palatinate** *n.* the office or dignity of a palatine; the territory under his jurisdiction.

pa•lav•er *n.* idle talk.

pale-, palae-, paleo-, palaeo- *prefix* ancient. **-ography** *n.* ancient writings. **-ographic** *a.* **-ographer** *n.* **-olith** *n.* an unpolished stone implement of the earlier stone age. **-olithic** *a.* **-ology** *n.* study of antiquities; archaeology. **-ologist** *n.* **ontology** *n.* a study of fossils. **-ontologist** *n.* **-ontological** *a.* **-ozoic** *a.* denoting the lowest fossiliferous strata and the earliest forms of life.

pale *a.* faint in color; whitish; dim; *v.t.* to make pale; *v.i.* to become pale. **-ly** *adv.* **-ness** *n.* **palish** *a.* somewhat pale.

pal•ette *n.* a thin oval board on which a painter mixes his colors.

Pa•li *n.* the sacred language of the Buddhists.

pal•in•drome *n.* a word or sentence that is the same when read backward or forward, e.g. *level.*

pal•i•sade *n.* fence of pales or stakes; (*pl.*) an expanse of high cliffs; *v.t.* to enclose with palisades.

pall *n.* a large, ususally black cloth laid over the coffin at a funeral.

pall *v.t.* to make tedious or insipid.

Pal•la•di•an *a.* denoting a classical style of architecture.

pal•la•di•um *n.* a rare metal of the platinum group.

pal•la•di•um *n.* a safeguard; *pl.* **paladia.**

pal•let *n.* a tool with a flat blade used by potters, etc.

pal•li•ate *v.t.* to lessen or abate without curing; to excuse or extenuate. **palliation** *n.* **palliative** *a.* to mitigate. *n.* that which mitigates, alleviates.

pal•lid *a.* pale; wan, **-ly** *adv.* **-ness** *n.* **pallor** *n.* paleness.

palm *n.* the inner, slightly concave surface of hand, between wrist and fingers; flat, expanding end of any arm-like projection, esp. blade of oar; *v.t.* to conceal in the palm. **palmate** *a.* having shape of hand; (*Zool.*) web-footed. **-ist** *n.* one who claims to tell fortunes by the lines on the palm of the hand. **-istry** *n.*

palm n. a branchless, tropical tree; a branch or leaf of this tree used as a symbol of victory; prize or honor. **-er** n. in the Middle Ages, one who visited the Holy Land, and bore a branch of palm in token thereof; an itinerant monk. **-etto** n. a species of palm tree. (Cap.) — **Sunday**, Sunday before Easter.

pal•my•ra n. a tall E. Indian palm.

pal•pa•ble a. capable of being touched or felt; certain; obvious. **palpably** adv. **-ness** n. **palpate** v.t. to examine with the hand. **palpation** n.

pal•pi•tate v.i. to throb; to pulsate. **palpitation** n.

pal•sy n. paralysis; v.t. to paralyze. **palsied** a.

pal•ter v.i. to deal evasively; to use trickery; to dodge. **-er** n. **paltry** a. mean; worthless. **paltriness** n.

pam•per v.t. to gratify unduly; to over-indulge; to coddle. **-er** n.

pam•phlet n. a thin, paper-covered, unbound book; a short treatise or essay on a current topic. **-eer** n. a writer of pamphlets.

pan n. a broad, shallow metal vessel for house hold use; of an old type of gun, part of the flintlock that held the priming; v.t. and i. to wash gold-bearing soil in a pan in order to separate earth and gold.

pan- prefix, all, used in such words as **Pan-American** a. pert. to movement of the American republics to foster collaboration between N. and S. America.

pan•a•ce•a n. a cure for all diseases; a universal remedy.

pa•nache n. plume of feathers used as an ornament on a cap, etc.

Pan•a•ma n. a hat made of fine, pliant strawlike material.

pan•cake n. a thin cake of batter fried in a pan.

pan•cre•as n. (Anat.) digestive gland behind stomach; in animals, the sweetbread. **pancreatic** a.

pan•da n. a racoon-like animal; the bearcat.

panda

pan•dem•ic a. of a disease, universal; widely distributed; affecting a nation.

pan•de•mo•ni•um n. the abode of evil spirits; any disorderly, noisy place or gathering; a riotous uproar.

pan•der n. a go-between in base love intrigues; v.i. to act as a pander; to help to satisfy any unworthy desires.

pane n. a sheet of glass in a window; a square in a pattern. **-d** a.

pan•e•gyr•ic n. a speech or writing of praise; a eulogy. **-al** a. **panegyrist** n. one who writes or pronounces a eulogy. **panegyrize** v.t. to praise highly.

pan•el n. a rectangular piece of cloth, parchment, or wood; a sunken portion of a door, etc.; a list of jurors; a group of speakers, etc. v.t. to divide into, or decorate with panels. **-ing** n. paneled work. **-ist** n. member of a panel.

pang n. a sudden pain, physical or mental.

pan•ic n. sudden terror, often unreasoning; infectious fear; v.i. to be seized with sudden, uncontrollable fright. pr.p. **panicking.** pa.p. and pa.t. **panicked.** **panicky** a. affected by panic. — **stricken**, — **struck** a. seized with paralyzing fear.

pan•ier n. one of a pair of baskets carried on each side of a pack animal; a puffing-out round hips of a lady's skirt.

pan•o•ply n. a complete suit of armor; anything that covers or envelopes completely. **panoplied** a. fully armed.

pan•o•ram•a n. a complete view in every direction; a picture exhibited by being unrolled and made to pass continuously before the spector. **panoramic** a.

pan•sy n. a cultivated species of violet with richly colored flowers.

pant v.i. to breathe quickly and in a labored manner; to gasp for breath; v.i. to utter gaspingly; n. a gasp.

pan•ta•loon n.(pl.) tight trousers.

pan•the•ism n. the doctrine that identifies God with the universe, everything being considered as part of or a manifestation of Him. **pantheist** n. **pantheistic** (al) a. **pantheology** n. a system which embraces all religions and all gods.

pan•ther n. (fem. **-ess**) a variety of leopard.

pan•to- prefix, all, used in derivatives. **-graph** n. an instrument for copying drawings, maps, etc.

pantograph

pan•to•mime n. a gesture without speech; v.t. and i. to act or express by gestures only. **pantomimic** a. **pantomimist** n.

pan•try n. a small room for storing food or kitchen utensils.

pants n.pl. trousers.

pa•pa•cy n. the office and dignity of the Pope; Popes collectively. **papal** a.

pa•per n. a material made by pressing pulp of rags, straw, wood, etc., into thin flat sheets; a newspaper; an article or essay; a document; wall covering; a set of examination questions; n.pl. document(s) establishing one's identity; a. consisting of paper; v.t. to cover with paper. — **clip** n. a device for holding together sheets of paper. — **hanger** n. one who hangs paper on walls. **— money** n. official pieces of paper issued by a government or bank for circulation. **-weight** n. small, heavy object to prevent loose sheets of paper from being displaced.

pa•pier•mâ•ché n. paper pulp, mixed with glue, etc., shaped or molded into articles.

pa•pil•la n. a small nipple-shaped protuberance in a part of the body, e.g. on surface of tongue.

pa•pist n. a supporter of the papal system; a Roman Catholic. **papistic(al)** a. **-ry** n.

pa•poose n. a N. Amer. Indian baby.

pap•pus n. down, as on the seeds of the thistle, dandelion, etc. **pappose** a. downy.

pa•py•rus n. a species of reed, the pith of which was used by the ancients for making paper; a manuscript on. papyrus. *pl.* **papyri.**

papyrus

par n. equality of value or circumstances; face value (of stocks and shares); (*Golf*) the number of strokes for hole or course in perfect play.

par•a•ble n. a story or allegory with a moral. **parabolical** a. **parabolically** adv.

pa•rab•o•la n. (*Geom.*) a conic section made by a plane parallel to side of cone. **parabolic** a. **paraboloid** n. solid formed when parabola is revolved round its axis.

par•a•chute n. a collapsible umbrellalike device used to retard the descent of a falling body. **parachutist** n.

par•a•clete n. (*Bib.*) the name given to the Holy Spirit; one called to aid or support; an advocate.

pa•rade n. a public procession; a muster of troops for drill or inspection; show; v.t. to make a display or spectacle of; to marshal in military order.

par•a•digm n. an example; a model. **-atic** a. **-atically** adv.

par•a•dise n. the garden of Eden; Heaven; a state of bliss. **paradisaic, paradisaical** a.

par•a•dox n. a statement seemingly absurd or self-contradictory, but really founded on truth. **-ical** a. **-ically** adv.

par•af•fin n. a white wax-like substance obtained from crude petroleum, shale, coal tar, wood, etc.

par•a•gon n. a pattern of excellence.

par•a•graph n. a section or subdivision of a passage, indicated by the sign **P**, or begun on a new line.

par•a•keet n. a small long-tailed parrot.

par•al•de•hyde n. a powerful hypnotic.

par•al•lel a. continuously at equal distance apart; similar; n. a line equidistant from another at all points; a thing exactly like

another; a line of latitude; **-ism** n. the state of being parallel; comparison, resemblance. **— bars,** horizontal bars for gymnastic exercises.

par•al•lel•o•gram n. a four-sided plane figure with both pairs of opposite sides parallel.

pa•ral•y•sis n. (*Med.*) loss of power of movement or sensation. **paralyze** v.t. to affect with paralysis; to make useless; to cripple. **paralytic** n. one affected with paralysis. **infantile paralysis,** inflammation of grey matter in spinal cord, usually in children; poliomyelitis.

par•a•mount a. superior; of highest importance; **-cy** n. **-ly** adv.

par•a•noi•a, paranoea n. (*Med.*) a form of chronic insanity, often characterized by delusions of grandeur, persecution, etc. **paranoiac** a. and n.

par•a•pher•na•li•a n.pl. personal belongings; furnishings or accessories.

par•a•phrase n. a restatement of a passage; a free translation into the same or another language.

par•a•site n. formerly, one who habitually ate at the table of another, repaying with flattery; a plant or animal that lives on another. **parasitic** a. **parasitically** adv. **parasitology** n. the study of parasites, esp. as causes of disease. **parasitological** a. **parasitologist** n.

par•a•sol n. a small, light sun umbrella.

par•a•troops n.pl. (*World War 2*) troops organized to descend by parachute with their equipment from airplanes and gliders. **paratrooper** n.

par•boil v.t. to boil partially.

par•cel n. (*Arch.*) a part or portion, a bundle or package (wrapped in paper); a number of things forming a group or lot; a piece of land; v.t. to divide into portions; to distribute; to wrap up.

parch v.t. to search; to shrivel with heat.

parch•ment n. the skin of a sheep or goat, etc., prepared for writing on; a document written on this.

par•don v.t. to forgive; to free from punishment; to excuse; n. forgiveness; remission of a penalty. **-able** a. excusable.

pare v.t. to remove the outer skin; to peel. **-er** n. **paring** n. the action of peeling; that which is pared off.

par•e•gor•ic a. soothing; assuaging pain; n. a soothing medicine.

par•ent n. a father or mother; one who, or that which, brings forth or produces. **-age** n. descent from parents; birth. **parental** a. pert. to, or becoming, parents; tender; affectionate. **parentally** adv.

pa•ren•the•sis n. a word or sentence inserted in a passage independently of the grammatical sequence and usually marked off by brackets, dashes, or commas; **parentheses** n.pl.; round brackets ( ), used for this. **parenthetic, parenthetical** a.

pa•ri•e•tal a. pert. to a wall; pert. to the wall of the body or its cavities.

par•ish n. an ecclesiastical district under a priest or clergyman; a local church and

P

its area of activity. **parishioner** *n.* an inhabitant of a parish; a member of a parish church.

par•i•ty *n.* equality; analogy; close correspondence.

park *n.* a large piece of ground, usually with grass and trees for public use and recreation; a sports' ground; grounds around a country house; *v.t.* to enclose in a park; to leave an automobile in a certain place.

par•ka *n.* an Eskimo garment of undressed skin; a hooded outer garment.

par•lance *n.* a way of speaking; **parley** *n.* a meeting between leaders of opposing forces to discuss terms.

par•lia•ment *n.* (*usually cap.*) the supreme legislature of the United Kingdom, composed of the House of Lords and House of Commons; any similar assembly. **-ary** *a.* pert. to, enacted by, or according to, the established rules of parliament; of language, admissible in parliamentary debate, hence, decorous and non-abusive. **-arian** *n.* a skilled debater in parliament.

par•lor, parlour *n.* living room; a semi-private room in an inn.

pa•ro•chi•al *a.* pert. to a parish; provincial; narrow-minded **-ly** *adv.* **-ism** *n.*

par•o•dy *n.* an imitation of a poem, song, etc., where the style is the same but the theme ludicrously different; a feeble imitation; *v.t.* to write a parody of; to burlesque in verse. **parodist** *n.*

pa•role *n.* release of a prisoner on condition of good behavior; word of honor, esp. a promise given by a prisoner of war not to attempt to escape.

par•o•no•ma•si•a *n.* a play on words; a pun. **paronym** *n.* a word similar to another in having the same derivation or root. **paronymous** *a.*

pa•rot•id *a.* near the ear; *n.* a large salivary gland, in front of and below the ear.

par•ox•ysm *n.* sudden, violent attack of pain, rage, laughter; fit; convulsion.

par•quet *n.* flooring of wooden blocks; *v.t.* to lay such a floor. **-ry** *n.*

parr *n.* a young salmon.

parr

par•ri•cide *n.* one who murders his parent, a near relative, or a person who is venerated; the crime itself.

par•rot *n.* tropical bird; one who repeats words, actions, ideas, etc. of another.

par•ry *v.t.* to ward off; to turn aside; to avoid.

parse *v.t.* to classify a word or analyze a sentence in terms of grammar. **parsing** *n.*

par•si•mo•ny *n.* stinginess; undue economy. **parsimonious** *a.* **parsimoniously** *adv.* **parsimoniousness** *n.*

pars•ley *n.* a garden herb, used as a flavoring or garnish in cookery.

pars•nip *n.* a root vegetable, carrot-like in shape.

par•son *n.* a clergyman; the incumbent of a parish. **-age** *n.* the residence of a parson.

part *n.* a portion, fragment, or section of a whole; a share or lot; a division; an actor's role; duty; interest; a melody in a harmonic piece; *pl.* accomplishments or talents; region; *v.t.* to divide; to separate; to share; *v.i.* to separate; to take leave; to part with or give up. **-ing** *n.* the act of separating; leave-taking; division; dividing line; *a.* given on taking leave. **-ly** *adv.* in part; in some measure or degree. **-ible** *a.* divisible. **-ibility** *n.*

par•take *v.t.* and *i.* to have or take a share in; to take food or drink. *pr.p.* **partaking.** *pa.p.* **-n** *pa.t.* **partook. -r** *n.*

Par•the•no•gen•e•sis *n.* reproduction without sexual union.

Par•the•non *n.* famous Doric temple of Athena.

par•tial *a.* affecting only a part; not total; inclined to favor unreasonably. **-ly** *adv.* **partiality** *n.* quality of being partial; favoritism; fondness for.

par•tic•i•pate *v.t.* and *i.* to share in; to partake (foll. by 'in'). **participant** *n.* a partaker; *a.* sharing. **participator** *n.* **participation** *n.*

par•ti•ci•ple *n.* (*Gram.*) an adjective formed by inflection from a verb. **participial** *a.*

par•ti•cle *n.* a minute portion of matter.

par•tic•u•lar *a.* relating to a single person or thing, not general; considered apart from others; minute in details; fastidious in taste; *n.* a single point or circumstance; a detail or item. **-ly** *adv.* especially; with great attention. **particularity** *n.* quality or state of being particular; individual characteristic. **-ize** *v.t.* and *i.* to mention one by one; to give in detail; to specify. **-ization** *n.*

par•ti•san, partizan *n.* adherent, often prejudiced, of a party or cause; a member of irregular troops engaged in risky enterprises; *a.* adhering to a faction. **-ship** *n.*

par•ti•tion *n.* division or separation; any of the parts into which a thing is divided; that which divides or separates, as a wall, etc.; *v.t.* to divide into shares; to divide by walls. **partitive** *n.* a word expressing partition; a distributive; *a.* denoting a part. **partitively** *adv.*

part•ner *n.* a partaker; a sharer; an associate, esp. in business; a husband or wife; one who dances with another; in golf, tennis, etc., one who plays with another; *v.t.* in games, to play with another against opponents. **-ship** *n.* the state of being a partner; the association of two or more persons for business.

par•tridge *n.* a small game bird of the grouse family.

partridge

par•ty n. a number of persons united in opinion; a political group; a social assembly; a participator; an accessory; a litigant; a. pert. to a party or faction.

pas•quin n. a writer of lampoons or satires; a lampoon or satire. -ade n. a lampoon.

pass v.t. to go by, beyond, through etc.; to spend; to exceed; to approve; to disregard; to circulate; to send through; to move; v.i. to go; to elapse; to undergo examination successfully; to happen; to die; to circulate. pa.p. -ed, past. pa.t. -ed. n. a passage or way, esp. a narrow and difficult one; a permit; success in an examination, test, etc.; in football, hockey, etc., the passing of the ball from one player to another. -able a. that may be passed or crossed; fairly good; admissible. -ably adv. -book n. a bankbook. -key n. a masterkey. -port n. an official document, issued by a State Department, granting permission to travel abroad.

pas•sage n. the act, time, or right of passing; movement from one place to another; a voyage across the sea; fare for a voyage; an entrance or exit; part of a book, etc.; the passing of a law.

pas•sé a. past one's best; faded; rather out of date; antiquated.

pas•sen•ger n. a traveller, esp. by some conveyance; a. adapted for carrying passengers.

pas•sion n. intense emotion, as of grief, rage, love; eager desire; (Cap.) the story of Christ's suffering and last agony. -ate a. moved by strong emotions; vehement. -agely adv. -ateness n. -less a. — play n. a theatrical representation of Christ's passion.

pas•sive a. inactive; submissive; acted upon, not acting; n. (Gram.) (or passive voice) the form of the verb which expresses that the subject is acted upon. -ly adv. -ness n.

Pass•o•ver n. a feast of the Jews to commemorate the time when God, smiting the first-born of the Egyptians, passed over the houses of Israelites.

past a. pert. to former time; gone by; elapsed; ended; n. former state; bygone times; one's earlier life; prep. beyond; after; exceeding; beyond the scope of; adv. by; beyond.

paste n. a soft composition, as of flour and water; dough prepared for pies, etc.; any soft plastic mixture or adhesive; v.t. to fasten with paste. pastry n. the crust of pies and tarts; articles of food made of paste or dough. pastry-cook n. one who makes and sells pastry. -board n. a stiff, thick paper; flimsy or unsubstantial.

pas•tel n. a colored chalky crayon; a drawing made with such crayons. — shades, delicate and subdued colors.

Pas•teur n. a French chemist and biologist. pasteurization n. the sterilization of milk, etc. by heating to 140° F. or over and then cooling. pasteurize v.t.

pas•time n. that which amuses and makes time pass agreeably; recreation; diversion.

pas•tor n. a minister of the gospel. -al a. pert. to shepherds or rural life; relating to a pastor and his duties. -ally adv. -ate n. the office or jurisdiction of a spiritual pastor. -ship n.

pas•ture n. grass for food of cattle; ground on which cattle graze. pasturable a. pasturage n. pasture land; the business of grazing cattle.

pat n. a light, quick blow, esp. with hand or fingers; a small lump, esp. of butter; pr.p. -ting. pa.p. and pa.t. -ted.

patch n. a piece of material used to mend a hole, rent, etc.; a covering for a wound. -y a. full of patches; unequal. -work n. work made by sewing together pieces of cloth of different material and color.

pa•tel•la n. the kneecap.

pat•ent a. open; evident; protected by a patent; n. short for letters patent, an official document granting a right or privilege, or securing the exclusive right to invention; the invention itself. v.t. to secure or protect by a patent. -ee n. one who has secured a patent. — leather, leather with a varnished or lacquered surface.

pa•ter•nal a. pert. to a father; fatherly; hereditary. -ly adv. paternity n. the relation of a father to his offspring.

path n. a way, course, or track of action, conduct, or procedure. -finder n. a pioneer. -way n. a narrow footway.

pa•thet•ic a. affecting or moving the tender emotions; causing pity; touching.

path•o- prefix, suffering, feeling, used in derivatives. -genesis, pathogeny n. the origin and development of disease. -genetic, -genic a. causing disease. -logy n. the science and study of diseases, their causes, nature, cures, etc. -logic, -logical a. -logically adv. -logist n.

pa•thos n. the power of exciting tender emotions; deep feeling.

pa•tient a. not easily made angry; calm; not hasty; n. a person under medical treatment. -ly adv. patience n. the quality of enduring with calmness; quiet perseverance.

pa•tri•arch n. the father and ruler of a family, esp. in Biblical history; the highest dignitary in the Eastern church; a venerable old man. -al a. -ate n. dignity or jurisdiction of a patriarch. -y n. government by the head or father of a tribe.

pa•tri•ot n. one who loves his country and upholds its interests. -ic a. filled with patriotism. -ically adv. -ism n. love for, and loyalty to, one's country.

pa•trol v.t. and i. to go or walk around a camp, garrison, etc. in order to protect it. pr.p. -ling. pa.p. and pa.t. -led. n. a going of the rounds by a guard; the man or men who go to the rounds.

pa•tron n. a man who protects or supports a person, cause, entertainment, artistic production, etc.; a guardian saint. a regular customer. -age n. countenance, support, or encouragement given to a person or cause; condescending manner; in trade, regular customer. -ize *v.t.* to act as a patron to; to assume the air of a superior towards; to frequent, as a customer. **patronizing** *a.* **patronizingly** *adv.* — **saint**, a saint who is regarded as the special protector of a person, city, trade, etc.

pat•ter *v.i.* to make a quick succession of small taps or sounds, like those of rain falling.

pat•tern *n.* a model, example, or guide; a decorative design; *v.t.* to design from a pattern; to imitate.

pat•ty *n.* a little pie.

pau•ci•ty *n.* fewness; scarcity; smallness of quantity.

paunch *n.* the belly. **-iness** *n.* **-y** *a.*

pau•per *n. (fem.* **-ess)** a very poor person, esp. one supported by the public. **-ize** *v.t.* to reduce to pauperism.

pause *n.* a temporary stop or rest; cessation; hesitation; a break in speaking, reading, or writing; in music, a sign . or . placed under or over a note to indicate the prolongation of a note or rest.

pave *v.t.* to form a level surface with stone, brick, etc.; to make smooth and even; **-ment** *n.* a paved floor, road, or sidewalk; material used.

pa•vil•ion *n.* orig. a tent; hence, anything like a tent, e.g. a garden summerhouse.

paw *n.* the foot of an animal having claws; *v.t.* and *i.* to scrape with the paws.

pawn *n.* something deposited as security for money borrowed; a pledge; the state of being pledged; *v.t.* to deposit as security for a loan; to pledge. **-broker** *n.* one who lends money on something deposited with him.

pawn *n.* a piece of the lowest rank in the game of chess.

pay *v.t.* to discharge one's obligations to; to give money, etc., for goods received or services rendered. *pa.p.* and *pa.t.* **paid** *n.* reward; compensation; wages; salary. **-able** *a.* justly due; profitable. **-ment** *n.* the act of paying; discharge of a debt; recompense.

pea *n.* the fruit, growing in pods, of a leguminous plant; the plant itself. **-nut** *n.* the earth nut. — **soup** *n.* soup made of dried peas.

peace *n.* calm; repose; freedom from disturbance, war, or hostilities. **-able** *a.* in a state of peace; disposed to peace; not quarrelsome. **-ably** *adv.* **-ableness** *n.* **-ful** *a.* free from war, tumult, or commotion; mild; undisturbed. **-fully** *adv.* **-fulness** *n.* **-maker** *n.* one who makes peace.

peach *n.* a juicy fruit with light orange flesh, and a velvety skin; the tree which bears this fruit; a pale orange-pink color. **-y** *a.* peach-like.

pea•cock *n. (fem.* **peahen)** *a.* bird remarkable for the beauty of its plumage, and for its large tail.

peak *n.* the sharp top of a hill; the pointed top of anything; the projecting part of a cap brim.

peal *n.* a loud sound, or succession of loud sounds, as of thunder, bells, laughter, etc.; a set of bells attuned to each other.

pear *n.* a sweet, juicy fruit of oval shape; tree on which it grows.

pearl *n.* a hard, smooth, lustrous substance, found in several mollusks, particularly pearl oyster, and used as a gem; something very precious; a creamy grey; *a.* made of pearls; pert. to pearls; *v.t.* to adorn with pearls; to take a round form like pearls. **-y** *a.* of the color of pearls; like pearls; abounding in pearls; clear; pure. **-iness** *n.*

peas•ant *n.* a rural laborer; a rustic; *a.* rural. **-ry** *n.* peasants collectively.

peat *n.* a brown, fibrous turf, formed of decayed vegetable matter, which is used as fuel. **-y** *a.* like peat, in texture or color.

peb•ble *n.* a small, roundish stone; transparent and colorless rock crystal used pebbles.

pe•can *n.* **-d, pebbly** *a.* full of oval nut with edible kernel; the tree on which it grows.

pec•ca•ble *a.* liable to sin. **peccability** *n.* liability to sin. **peccant** *a.* sinful; offensive; causing trouble.

pec•ca•dil•lo *n.* a trifling offense; an indiscreet action.

peck *n.* a measure of capacity for dry goods =2 gallons, or the fourth part of a bushel.

peck *v.t.* and *i.* to strike with the beak; to dab; to eat little quantities at a time. *n.*

pec•tin *n.* a carbohydrate from fruits which yields a gel.

pec•to•ral *a.* pert. to the breast or chest.

pe•cul•iar *a.* belonging solely to; appropriate; particular; singular; strange. **-ly** *adv.* **peculiarity** *n.* something that belongs to only one person, thing, class, people; a distinguishing feature; characteristic.

pe•cu•ni•ar•y *a.* pert. to or consisting of, money. **pecunniarily** *adv.*

ped•a•gogue *n.* a schoolteacher; a pedantic person. **pedagogic, pedagogical** *a.* **pedagogy, pedagogics** *n.* science of teaching.

pe•dal *a.* pert. to the foot; *n.* a mechanical contrivance to transmit power by using foot as a lever, e.g. on bicycle, sewing-machine.

ped•dle *v.t.* to travel from place to place selling small articles; *v.t.* to sell or hawk goods thus. **-r; pedlar** *n.* one who peddles goods.

ped•es•tal *n.* anything that serves as a support or foundation; the base of a column, statue, etc.

pe•des•tri•an *a.* going on, performed on, foot; of walking; commonplace; *n.* a walker; one who journeys on foot.

pe•di•at•rics *n. (Med.)* the branch dealing with the diseases and disorders of children. **pediatric** *a.* **pediatrician** *n.*

pe•dic•u•lar *pert.* to lice.

ped•i•cure *n.* treatment of the feet.

ped•i•gree *n.* a line of ancestors; genealogy; *a.* having a line of ancestors.

ped•i•ment *n. (Archit.)* the triangular ornamental facing of a portico door, or window, etc. **pedimental** *a.*

pe•dom•e•ter *n.* an instrument which measures the distance walked by recording the number of steps.

pe•dun•cle *n.* a flower stalk; *(Zool.)* a stalk or stalklike process in an animal body, **peduncular** *a.*

peek *v.i.* to peep; to peer; *n.* a glance.

peel *v.t.* to strip off the skin, bark, or rind; to free from a covering; *n.* the outside skin of a fruit; rind or bark.

peep *v.i.* to look through a crevice; to look furtively or slyly; to emerge slowly; *n.* a furtive or sly glance. **— show** *n.* a small exhibit, viewed through an aperture containing a magnifying glass.

peep *v.i.* to cry, as a chick.

peer *n.* *(fem.* -ess) an equal in any respect; a nobleman; an associate. **-less** *a.* having no equal. **-lessly** *adv.* **-lessness** *n.*

peer *v.i.* to look closely and intently; to peer.

pee•vish *a.* fretful; irritable; hard to please; childish. **-ly** *adv.* **-ness** *n.* **peeve** *v.t.* to annoy.

peg *n.* a nail or pin of wood or other material. *v.t.* to fix or mark with a peg; *pr.p.* **-ging** *pa.t.*, *pa.p.* **-ged.**

Pe•king•esé *n.* a breed of Chinese lapdog.

pe•koe *n.* a black tea of superior quality.

pel•i•can *n.* a large water fowl.

pelican

pel•let *n.* a little ball; a pill; small shot.

pelt *n.* raw hide; undressed skin of furbearing animal.

pel•vis *n.* *(Anat.)* the bony basin-shaped cavity at the base of the human trunk. **pelvic** *a.*

pelvis

pen *n.* an instrument for writing with ink; a large wing feather (a quill) used for writing. *pr.p.* **-ning** *pa.p.* and *pa.t.* **-ned.** **-knife** *n.* a pocketknife. **-man** *n.* one who writes a good hand; an author. **-manship** *n.* **— name** *n.* an assumed name of author.

pen *n.* a small enclosure, as for sheep; a coop. *v.t.* to confine in a pen; to shut in. *pr.p.* **-ning** *pa.p.*, *pa.t.* **-ned.**

pe•nal *a.* pert. to; prescribing, incurring, inflicting, punishment. **-ize** *v.t.* to make penal; to impose a penalty upon; to handicap. **-ly** *adv.* **penalty** *n.* punishment for a crime or offense; in games, a handicap imposed for infringement of rule, etc.; **penology** *n.* study and arrangement of prisons and prisoners.

pen•ance *n.* suffering submitted to in penitence; act of atonement.

pen•cil *n.* a stick of graphite encased in wood, used for writing or drawing; *v.t.* to draw, write with pencil. **-ed** *a.* marked, as with pencil; having pencils or rays. **-ing** *n.* the work of a pencil.

pend•ant *n.* a hanging ornament, esp. a locket or earring; a lamp or chandelier hanging from the ceiling. **pendent** *a.* suspended; hanging; projecting. **pendently** *adv.* **pending** *a.* awaiting settlement; in suspense; undebted; *prep.* during; until.

pen•du•lous *a.* hanging loosely; swinging. **-ly** *adv.* **-ness** *n.* **pendulum** *n.* a body suspended from a fixed point, and swinging freely; the swinging rod with weighted end which regulates movements of a clock, etc.

pen•e•trate *v.t.* to enter into; to pierce; to pervade or spread through; to touch with feeling; to arrive at the meaning of; *a.* **penetrable** *a.* capable of being entered or pierced.

pen•guin *n.* a flightless sea bird inhabiting the S. temperate and Antarctic regions.

penguin

pen•i•cil•lin *n.* an antibacterial agent produced from the fungus *penicillium.*

pen•in•su•la *n.* a portion of land nearly surrounded by water, and connected with the mainland by an isthmus **-r** *a.*

pe•nis *n.* the male organ of generation. **penial** *a.*

pen•i•tent *a.* deeply affected by sense of guilt; contrite; repentant; *n.* one who repents of sin. **-ly** *adv.* **penitence** *n.* sorrow for having sinned; repentance. **penitential** *a.* pert. to or expressing penitence; *n.* among R.C.s, a book containing rules of penance. **penitentially** *adv.* **penitentiary** *a.* pert. to punish by confinement; *n.* a prison.

pen•nant *n.* a very long, narrow flag tapering to a point.

pen•ny *n.* the U.S. and Canadian cent; an English coin (about 2 U.S. cents); a small sum. *pl.* **pennies. pennilesss** *a.* without money; poor.

pen•sion *n.* an annual grant of money for past services; an annuity paid to retired officers, soldiers, etc.; *v.t.* to grant a pension to.

pen•sive *a.* thoughtful; deep in thought; somewhat melancholy **-ly** *adv.* **-ness** *n.*

pent *a.* closely confined; shut up.

pen•ta- *prefix,* five, used in derivatives. **-gon, -gram** *n.*

pen•tane *n.* a paraffin hydrocarbon, a very inflammable liquid.

Pen•ta•teuch *n.* the first five books of the Old Testament.

Pen•te•cost *n.* a Jewish festival, celebrated on the 50th day after the Passover; a Christian festival (Whitsunday) commemorating the descent of the Holy Ghost on the Apostles. **Pentecostal** *a.*

pent•house *n.* an apartment, or structure, on the roof of a building; a shed attached to a main building, its roof sloping down from the wall.

pen•to•thal *n.* sometimes called the 'truth' drug; an anesthetic.

pe•nult *n.* the next to last syllable of a word.

pe•num•bra *n.* in an eclipse, the partially shadowed region which surrounds the full shadow.

pe•on *n.* in Mexico, a day laborer or serf; in India, a foot soldier, or messenger. **-age** *n.*

pe•o•ny *n.* plant having beautiful showy flowers.

peo•ple *n.* the body of persons that compose a community, tribe, nation, or race; the populace as distinct from rulers.

pep•per *n.* a pungent, spicy condiment obtained from an E. Indian plant; *v.t.* to sprinkle with pepper; to pelt with missiles. **—corn** *n.* the berry or fruit of the pepper-plant. **-mint** *n.* a pungent plant which yields a volatile oil; essence gotten from this oil; a lozenge flavored with this essence.

pep•sin, pepsine *n.* a ferment formed in gastric juice of man and animals, and serving as an aid to digestion. **peptic** *a.* pert. to pepsin and to digestion; *n.pl.* medicines that promote digestion. **peptone** *n.* one of the soluble compounds due to the action of pepsin, etc. on proteins.

per•an•num L. by the year; annually.

per•cale *n.* closely woven cotton cloth.

per•ceive *v.t.* to obtain knowledge of through the senses; to see, hear, or feel; to understand. **perceivable** *a.* **perceivably** *adv.* **-r** *n.* **perceptible** *a.* capable of being perceived; discernible. **perceptibly** *adv.* **perceptibility** *n.* **perception** *n.* the faculty of perceiving; intuitive judgment. **perceptive** *a.* having perception; used in perception. **perceptual** *a.* involving perception.

per•cent•age *n.* proportion or rate per hundred. **per centum** *(abbrev.* **per cent)** by, in, or for, each hundred; portion.

perch *n.* an edible fresh-water fish.

perch *n.* roosting bar for birds; high place; lineal measure (also 'pole' or 'rod') = 5½ yards; a measure of area = 30¼ square yards; *v.t.* to place on a perch; *v.i.* to alight or settle on a perch.

per•chance *adv.* perhaps; by chance.

per•cip•i•ent *a.* having the faculty of perception; perceiving; *n.* one who has the power of perceiving. **percipience, percipiency** *n.*

per•co•late *v.t.* and *i.* to pass slowly through small openings, as a liquid; to

filter. **percolation** *n.* **percolator** *n.* a coffee pot fitted with a filter.

per•cuss *v.t.* to strike sharply. **percussion** *n.* a collision; an impact; *(Med.)* tapping the body to determine condition of internal organ. **-ive** *a.*

per•di•em L. daily.

per•emp•to•ry *a.* authoritative; dictatorial; non-debatable; decisive; absolute. **peremptorily** *adv.* **peremptoriness** *n.*

per•en•ni•al *a.* lasting through the year; lasting; everlasting; lasting more than two years; *n.* a plant lasting for such a time. **-ly** *adv.*

per•fect *a.* complete; faultless; correct; excellent; of the highest quality; *(Gram.)* a tense denoting completed action; **perfect** *v.t.* to finish or complete; to make perfect; to improve; to make skillful. **-ly** *adv.* **perfectible** *a.* capable of becoming perfect. **perfectibility** *n.* **perfection** *n.* state of being perfect. **perfectionist** *n.* one who believes that moral perfection is attainable, or that he has attained it.

per•fo•rate *v.t.* to pierce; to make a hole or holes in. **perforation** *n.* act of perforating; a hole, or series of holes.

per•form *v.t.* to do; to accomplish; to fulfill; to represent on the stage; *v.i.* to do; to play, as on a musical instrument. **-ing** *a.* trained to act a part or do tricks. **-er** *n.* **-ance** *n.* act of performing; execution or carrying out.

per•fume *n.* a sweet scent or fragrance; a substance which emits an agreeable scent. *v.t.* to fill or imbue with an agreeable odor; to scent.

per•func•to•ry *a.* done as a duty, carelessly and without interest; indifferent; superficial. **perfunctorily** *adv.*

per•haps *adv.* it may be; possibly; perchance.

per•i•car•di•um (Anat.) the double membranous sac which encloses the heart. **pericardiac, pericardial** *a.*

per•i•gee *n.* that point in the moon's orbit nearest to the earth. opp. to *apogee.*

per•il *n.* danger; hazard; exposure to injury or loss; *v.t.* to expose to dangers, etc. **-ous** *a.* full of peril. **-ously** *adv.* **-ousness** *n.*

per•im•e•ter *n.* (Geom.) the outer boundary of a plane figure; the sum of all its sides; circumference. **perimetrical** *a.*

pe•ri•od *n.* a particular portion of time; the time in which a heavenly body makes a revolution; a series of years; a cycle; conclusion; a punctuation mark (.), at the end of a sentence; menstruation; *a.* of furniture, dress, a play, etc., belonging to a particular period in history. **periodic** *a.* recurring at regular intervals. **periodical** *a.* periodic; pert. to a periodical; *n.* a publication, esp. a magazine issued at regular intervals.

pe•riph•er•y *n.* circumference; perimeter; the outside. **peripheral** *a.*

per•i•scope *n.* an optical instrument which enables an observer to view surrounding objects from a lower level.

per•ish *v.t.* and *i.* to die; to waste away; to decay; to be destroyed. **-able** *a.* liable to perish, decay, etc., e.g. fish, fruit, etc.

per·i·to·ne·um n. membrane which lines abdominal cavity, and surrounds intestines, etc. peritonitis n. inflammation of peritoneum.

per·i·wig n. a wig; a peruke. -ged a.

per·i·win·kle n. an edible shellfish.

per·i·win·kle n. a trailing shrub with blue flowers; myrtle.

per·jure v.t. to violate one's oath (used reflex.). -d a. guilty of perjury. perjury n. false testimony; the crime of violating one's oath. -r n.

per·ma·nent a. remaining unaltered; lasting. n. a wave put into the hair to last several months. -ly adv. permanence n.

per·man·ga·nate n. a salt of an acid of manganese, which, dissolved in water, forms a disinfectant and antiseptic.

per·me·ate v.t. to penetrate and pass through; to diffuse itself through; to saturate. permeable a. admitting of passage of fluids. permeably adv. permeability a. capable of permeating.

per·mit v.t. to allow; to give leave or liberty to; v.t. to give leave. permit n. written permission. pr.p. -ting. pa.p. and pa.t. -ted. permission n. authorization; leave or license granted. permissible a. allowable. permissibly adv. permissive a. allowing. permissively adv.

per·mute v.t. .to change the order of permutable a. permutably adv. permutableness, permutability n. permutation n. (Math.) the arrangement of a number of quantities in every possible order.

per·ni·cious a. having the quality of destroying or injuring; wicked. -ly adv. -ness n.

per·o·ra·tion n. the concluding part of an oration. perorate v.i. to deliver a speech.

per·ox·ide (Chem.) oxide containing more oxygen than the normal oxide of an element.

per·pen·dic·u·lar a. exactly upright or vertical; at right angles to the plane of the horizon; at right angles to a given line or surface; n. a line at right angles to the plane of the horizon or to any line or plane.

per·pe·trate v.t. to commit (something bad, esp. a crime). perpetration n. perpetrator n.

per·pet·u·al a. continuing indefinitely; everlasting. -ly adv. perpetuate v.t. to make perpetual; not to allow to be forgotten. perpetuation n. perpetuity n. the state or quality of being perpetual.

per·plex v.t. to make intricate, or difficult; to puzzle; to bewilder. -ed a. puzzled; bewildered. -ing a. -ity n. bewilderment; a confused state of mind.

per·se·cute v.t. to oppress unjustly for the holding of an opinion; to subject to persistent ill-treatment; to harass. persecution n. persecutor n.

per·se·vere v.i. to persist; to maintain an effort; not to give in. persevering a. perseveringly adv. perseverance n.

per·sian a. pert. to Persia (now Iran) its people, or the language. — cat, a breed of cat with long, silky fur.

per·sim·mon n. an American tree with plumlike fruit.

per·sist v.i. to continue firmly in a state or action in spite of obstacles or objections. -ent a. persisting; steady; persevering; lasting. -ently adv. -ence, -ency a.

per·sim·mon n. an American tree with plumlike fruit.

per·sist v.i. to continue firmly in a state or action in spite of obstacles or objections. -ent a. persisting; steady; persevering; lasting. -ently adv. -ence, -ency a.

per·son n. a human being; an individual; the body of a human being; a character in a play; (Gram.) one of the three classes of personal pronouns (first, second, or third) showing the relation of the subject to a verb, as speaking, spoken to, or spoken of. -able a. attractive in appearance. -age n. a person, esp. of rank or social position. -al a. pert. to, peculiar to, or done by, a person; pert. to bodily appearance; directed against a person; (Gram) denoting the pronouns, I, you, he, she, it, we, you, and they. -ally adv. in person; individually. -ality n. individuality; distinctive personal qualities. personalty n. (Law) personal effects; movable possessions. -ate v.t. to assume character of; to pretend to be. -ator n. -ation n.

per·son·i·fy v.t. to endow inanimate objects or abstract ideas with human attributes; to be an outstanding example of personification n.

per·son·nel n. the persons employed in a public service, business, office, etc.; staff.

per·spec·tive n. the art of drawing objects on a plane surface to give impression of the relative distance of objects, indicated by the convergence of their receding lines; relation of parts of a problem, etc. in the mind.

per·spire v.t. to emit through the pores of the skin; v.i. to evacuate the moisture of the body through the pores of the skin; to sweat. perspiration n. the process of perspiring; the moisture emitted.

per·suade v.t. to influence by argument, entreaty, etc.; to win over. persuasive a. having the power of persuading. persuasively adv. persuasiveness n. persuasion n. the act of persuading; the quality of persuading; conviction; belief; sect. persuasible a.

per·tain v.i. to belong; to concern.

per·ti·na·cious a. adhering to an opinion, etc. with obstinacy; persevering; resolute. -ly adv. -ness n. pertinacity n.

per·ti·nent a. related to the subject or matter in hand. -ly adv. pertinence, pertinency n.

per·turb v.t. to disturb; to trouble greatly. -ation n. mental uneasiness or disquiet; disorder.

Pe·ru n. a republic on the west coast of S. America. -vian n. a native of Peru; a. pert. to Peru.

pe·ruse v.t. to read through, esp. with care. perusal n. the act of perusing.

per·vade v.t. to spread through the whole

of; to be diffused through all parts of. **pervasion** *n*. **pervasive** *a*.

per•verse *a*. obstinately or unreasonably wrong; refusing to do the right, or to admit error; self-willed. -ness, **perversity** *n*.

per•ver•sion *n*. a turning from the true purpose, use, or meaning; corruption; unnatural manifestation of sexual desire. **perversive** *a*. tending to pervert.

per•vert *v.t.* to turn from its proper purpose; to misinterpret; to lead astray; to corrupt. **pervert** *n*. one who has deviated from the normal, esp. from right to wrong.

per•vi•ous *a*. giving passage to; penetrable. -ness *n*.

pes•si•mism *n*. the doctrine that the world is fundamentally evil; the tendency to look on the dark side of things; melancholy. **pessimist** *n*. **pessimistic** *a*. **pessimistically** *adv*.

pest *n*. a plague or pestilence; a troublesome or harmful thing or person; nuisance. -iferous *a*. pestilential; carrying disease.

pes•ter *v.t.* to trouble or vex persistently; to annoy.

pest•i•cide *n*. a pest killer.

pes•ti•lence *n*. any infectious or contagious, deadly disease. **pestilent** *a*. producing disease; noxious; harmful to morals.

pes•tle *n*. an instrument for pounding substances in a mortar.

pet *n*. an animal or person kept or regarded with affection; a favorite; *a*. favorite; *v.t.* to make a pet of; to indulge. *pr.p.* -ting. *pa.p.* and *pa.t.* -ted.

pet *n*. a sudden fit of peevishness.

pet•al *n*. a colored flower-leaf. -ed, -led *a*. having petals.

pet•it (*Law*) small; minor. *fem.* **petite** small, dainty, trim of figure. — **Point** *a*. slanting stitch used in embroidery and tapestry.

pe•ti•tion *n*. a formal request or earnest prayer; *v.t.* and *i*. to present a petition to; to entreat. -ary *a*. -er *n*.

pet•ri•fy *v.t.* to turn into stone; to make hard like stone; to make motionless with fear. **petrified** *a*, **pertifactive** *a*.

pe•tro•le•um *n*. a mineral oil drawn from the earth by means of wells.

pet•ti•coat *n*. a woman's underskirt.

pet•tish *a*. petulant; easily annoyed. -ly *adv*. -ness *n*.

pet•ty *a*. small; unimportant; trivial; small-minded; of lower rank. **pettily** *adv*. **pettiness** *n*. — **cash**, small items of expenditure, esp. in an office. — **officer**, a non-commissioned officer in the Navy.

pet•u•lant *a*. given to small fits of temper; irritable. -ly *adv*. **petulance, petulancy** *n*. peevishness; crossness; fretfulness.

pe•tu•ni•a *n*. a common garden plant with showy flowers.

pew *n*. a long, fixed bench in a church.

pe•wee *n*. a small bird, the phoebe.

pew•ter *n*. an alloy of tin and lead or some other metal, esp. copper; ware made of this; *a*. made of pewter.

pha•lanx *n*. in ancient Greece, a company of soldiers in close array; hence, any compact body of people; (*Anat.*) a small bone of a toe or finger. *pl.* -es, **phalanges**.

phal•lus *n*. sexual organs. *pl.* **phalli. phallic** *a*.

phan•tasm *n*. an imaginary vision; a phantom; a specter. -al, -ic *a*. **phantasmagoria** *n*. an exhibition of optical illusions; a shifting scene of dim or unreal figures. **phantasmagoric** *a*. **phantasy** *n*.

Phar•aoh *n*. 'The Great House' a title of the kings of ancient Egypt.

phar•ma•ceu•ti•cal *a*. pert. to pharmacy. **pharmaceutics** *n.pl.* the science of pharmacy. **pharmaceutist** *n*.

phar•ma•cy *n*. the science of preparing, compounding, and dispensing drugs and medicines; a drugstore. **pharmacist** *n*. one skilled in pharmacy. **pharmacology** *n*. the study of drugs and their action. **pharmacologist** *n*. one skilled in pharmacy. **pharmacopoeia** *n*. an authoritative book containing information on medicinal drugs.

phar•ynx *n*. the cavity at back of mouth, opening into the gullet. *pl.* **pharynges**. **pharyngeal** *a*. Also **pharyngal**. **pharyngitis** *n*. (*Med.*) inflammation of pharynx. **pharyngoscope** *n*. instrument for examing throat.

phase *n*. (*Astron.*) an aspect of moon or a planet; a stage in development; an aspect of a subject or question. **phasic** *a*.

pheas•ant *n*. a gamebird with brilliant plumage.

pheasant

phe•nom•e•non *n*. anything appearing or observed, esp. if having scientific interest; a remarkable person or thing; (*Philos.*) sense appearance as opposed to real existence. *pl.* **phenomena. phenomenal** *a*. pert. to a phenomenon; remarkable; extraordinary. **phenomenally** *adv*.

phi•al *n*. a small glass bottle; a vial.

phi•lan•der *v.i.* to flirt. -er *n*.

phi•lan•thro•py *n*. love of mankind, esp. as shown in acts of charity; an act of charity. **philanthropic, philanthropical** *a*. **philanthropically** *adv*. **philanthropist** *n*. one who loves and seeks to do good to his fellowmen. Also **philanthrope**.

phi•lat•e•ly *n*. stamp collecting. **philatelic** *a*. **philatelist** *n*.

phil•har•mon•ic *a*. loving harmony or music; musical.

Phi•lis•tine *n*. one with no love of music, painting, etc.; an uncultured person.

phi•lol•o•gy *n*. scientific study of origin, development, etc. of languages. **philological** *a*. **philogian philologist** *n*. one versed in philology.

phi•los•o•phy n. originally, any branch of investigation of natural phenomena; now, the study of beliefs regarding God, existence, conduct, etc. and of man's relation with the universe; a calmness of mind; composure. philosopher n. a student of philosophy. philosophic, philosophical a. pert. to philosophy; wise; calm. philosophically adv. philosophize v.i. to reason like a philosopher; to theorize; to moralize.

phle•bi•tis n. (Med.) inflammation of a vein. phlebitic a. phlebotomy n. (Surg.) blood-letting.

phlegm n. a secretion of thick mucous substance discharged from throat by expectoration; calmness; apathy; sluggishness. phlegmatic a. cool and collected; unemotional.

phlox n. a genus of garden plants.

pho•bi•a n. a morbid dread of anything; used esp. as a suffix, e.g. claustrophobia, hydrophobia, etc.

phone n. a sound made in speaking. phonic a. pert. to sound, esp. to speech sounds. phonics n. method of teaching reading, etc. on basis of speech sounds.

pho•net•ic a. pert. to the voice; pert. to, or representing, vocal sounds. Also -al a. -ally adv. -s n. the branch of the study of language which deals with speech sounds, and their production. -ize v.t. to represent phonetically. — spelling, a simplified system of spelling in which same letter or symbol is always used for same sound, e.g. cat = kat.

pho•no- prefix, sound, used in many derivatives. -gram n. a character or symbol, esp. in shorthand, used to represent a speech sound. -graph n. an instrument for reproducing sounds from records. phonography n. a system of shorthand. phonology n. study of speech sounds; phonetics. -logic(al) a.

phos•phate n. a salt of phosphoric acid. phosphatic a. — of lime, commercially, bone-ash. phosphide n. a compound of phosphorus with another element, e.g. copper.

phos•pho•rus n. a non-metallic element, a yellowish waxlike substance giving out a pale light in the dark. phosphorous a. pert. to phosphorus.

pho•to prefix, light, used in derivatives. -chemistry n. the branch of chemistry which treats of the chemical action of light. -electron n. an electron liberated from a metallic surface by the action of a beam of ultraviolet light. — finish, in racing, a photo taken at the finish to show correct placing of contestants. -genic a. producing light; of a person, having features, etc. that photograph well.

pho•tog•ra•phy n. the art of producing pictures by the chemical action of light on a sensitive plate or film. photograph n. a picture so made; v.i. to take a photograph of. photographer n. photographic(al) a. pert. to resembling, or produced by, photography. photographically adv.

pho•tol•o•gy n. the science of light. photometer n. an instrument for measuring the intensity of light.

pho•ton n. the unit of measurement of light intensity.

pho•to•stat n. a photographic apparatus for making copies of documents, etc. directly on paper; v.t. to copy thus. photostatic a.

pho•to•syn•the•sis n. the process by which a plant, under the influence of sunlight, can build up, in its chlorophyll-containing cells, carbohydrates from the carbon dioxide of the atmosphere and from the hydrogen of the water in the soil.

phrase n. a small group of words forming part of a sentence; a short pithy expression; a characteristic mode of expression; (Mus.) a short, distinct part of a longer passage; v.t. to express suitably in words.

phre•net•ic a. having the mind disordered; frenzied; frantic.

phre•nol•o•gy n. character reading from the shape of the head. phrenologic(al) a. phrenologically adv. phrenologist n.

phthi•sis n. (Med.) a wasting away of the lungs; consumption.

phy•log•e•ny n. (Bot.) the evolution of an animal or plant type. phylum n. one of the primary divisions of the animal or plant kingdoms. pl. phyla.

phys•i•cal a. pert. to physics; pert. to nature; bodily, as opposed to mental or moral; material. -ly adv.

phys•ics n. sciences (excluding chemistry and biology) which deal with natural phenomena, e.g. motion, force, light, sound, electricity, etc. physicist n.

phys•i•og•no•my n. art of judging character from contours of face; face itself; expression of the face. physiognomic, physiognomical a. physiognomist n.

phys•i•og•ra•phy n. the study and description of natural phenomena; physical geography. physiographer n.

phys•i•ol•o•gy n. science which deals with functions and life processes of plants, animals, and human beings. physiological a. physiologist n.

phys•i•o•ther•a•py n. the application of massage, manipulation, light, heat, electricity, etc., for treatment of certain disabilities.

phy•sique n. bodily structure and development.

phy•to prefix, a plant. phytogenesis, phytogeny n. the evolution of plants.

pi n. the Greek letter π, esp. as a mathematical symbol for the ratio of the circumference of a circle to its diameter, approx. 3 1/7, or 3.14159.

pi•a•no adv. (Mus.) softly. pianissimo adv. very softly.

pi•a•no n. abbrev. of pianoforte n. a musical instrument having wires of graduated tension, struck by hammers moved by notes on a keyboard. pianist n. one who plays the piano.

pi•az•za n. a porch of a house; a public

square.

pi‧ca n. (Print.) a size of type, having 6 lines to the inch.

pic‧a‧dor n. a mounted bullfighter armed with a lance to prod the bull.

pic‧co‧lo n. (Mus.) a small flute, sounding an octave higher than the ordinary flute.

pick v.t. to peck at, like birds with their bills; to pierce with a pointed instrument; to open with a pointed instrument, as a lock; to pluck, or cull, as flowers, etc.; to raise or lift (with 'up'); to choose or select; to rob; to pluck the strings of a musical instrument; n. a sharp-pointed tool; the choicest or best of anything. -ax n. an instrument for digging. -pocket n. one who steals from pockets.

pick‧a‧nin‧ny a small child; a Negro baby.

pick‧et n. a sharpened stake (used in fortifications, etc.); a peg or pale; a guard posted in front of an army; a party sent out by trade unions to dissuade men from working during a strike; v.t. to fence with pickets.

pick‧le n. brine or vinegar in which fish, meat, or vegetables are preserved; any food preserved in brine or vinegar; v.t. to preserve with salt or vinegar. n.pl. vegetables in vinegar and spices.

pic‧nic n. pleasure excursion with meal out of doors; agreeable situation; v.i. to go on a picnic. pr.p. -king. pa.p. and pa.t. -ked.

pic‧to‧graph n. a picture representing an idea.

pic‧to‧ri‧al a. pert. to pictures; expressed by pictures; illustrated. -ly adv.

pic‧ture n. a representation of objects or scenes on paper, canvas, etc., by drawing, painting, photography, etc.; a mental image; a likeness or copy; an illustration; picturesque object; a graphic or vivid description in words; v.t. to draw or paint an image or representation of; to describe graphically; to recall vividly. **picturesque** a. making effective picture; vivid in description. -squely adv. -squeness n. — **gallery** n. a hall containing a collection of pictures for exhibition.

pid‧dle v.i. to trifle. **piddling** a. trifling.

pie n. (Cookery) a dish of meat or fruit covered with upper or lower pastry crust or both; (Print.) a confused mass of type.

piece n. a part of anything; a bit; a portion; a single object; a separate example; a coin; a counter in chess, checkers, etc.; a literary work; a musical composition; a gun; a plot of land; v.t. to mend; to put together. — **goods** n.pl. textile fabrics sold by measured lengths of the material. — **meal** adv. little by little; gradually. — **work** n. work paid for by the amount done, and not by the hour, day, etc.

pier n. a piece of solid, upright masonry, as a support or pillar for an arch, bridge, or beam; a structure built out over the water as a landing.

pierce v.t. to thrust into, esp. with a pointed instrument; to make a hole in; to penetrate; v.i. to enter; to penetrate.

piercing a. penetrating; sharp; keen. **piercingly** adv.

pi‧e‧ty n. the quality of being pious; devotion to religion; affectionate respect for one's parents. **pietist** n. an ultrapious person; a sanctimonious person. **pietistic** a. **pietism** n.

pig n. a hoofed domestic animal, reared for its flesh; oblong mass of smelted metal, as pig iron; -**gish** a. pert. to, or like, pigs; dirty; greedy; stubborn. -**tail** n. the tail of a pig; a braid of hair hanging from the back of the head; a roll of twisted tobacco. -**headed** a. obstinate; stupidly perverse. —**iron**, —**lead**, iron, lead, cast in rough oblong bars. -**skin** n. strong leather made from the pig's skin, and used for saddles, etc. -**sty** n. a covered enclosure for keeping pigs; a dirty house or room.

pi‧geon n. any bird of the dove family, both wild and domesticated; a simpleton or dupe. —**hearted** a. timid. -**hole** n. a little division in a desk or case, for holding papers, etc.; v.t. to place in the pigeonhole of a desk, etc.; to shelve for future reference; to classify. —**toed** a. having turned-in toes.

pig‧ment n. paint; coloring matter; coloring matter in animal tissues and cells. -**ation** n. (Biol.) coloring matter.

pile n. a mass or collection of things; a heap; a large building or mass of buildings; to throw into a pile or heap; to accumulate.

pile n. fur or hair; nap of a fabric; esp. if thick and close-set, as in velvet.

piles n.pl. a disease of the rectum; hemorrhoids.

pil‧fer v.t. and i. to steal in small quantities.

pil‧grim n. a traveler, esp. one who journeys to visit a holy place. -**age** n. journey to a holy place; any long journey.

pill n. a small ball of medicine, to be swallowed whole; anything disagreeable that has to be endured.

pil‧lar n. a slender upright structure of stone, iron, etc.; a column; a support. -**ed** a.

pil‧low n. a cushion, esp. for the head of a person in bed; v.t. to place on a pillow. -**case**, -**slip** n. a removable covering for a pillow.

pi‧lot n. a person qualified to take charge of a ship entering or leaving a harbor, or where knowledge of local waters is needed; one qualified to operate an aircraft; a steersman; a guide; a small jet of gas kept burning in order to light a stove, etc.; v.t. to direct the course of; to guide through dangers or difficulties. — **engine** n. a locomotive sent on ahead to clear the way for a train.

pi‧men‧to n. allspice; pimiento, a reddish pepper.

pimp n. a procurer; a pander; v.i. to pander.

pim‧per‧nel n. an annual plant of the primrose family.

pim‧ple n. a small, red, pustular spot on the skin. -**d**, **pimply** a.

pin n. a short, thin piece of stiff wire with a

point and head for fastening soft materials together; a wooden or metal peg or rivet; an ornament that fastens on cloth; (Golf) a thin metal or wooden stick (with a flag) to mark the position of the hole; a rolling pin; a clothespin; a trifle; pl. v.t. to fasten with pins; to seize and hold fast. pr.p. -ning. pa.p. and pa.t. -ned. -cushion n. a small pad in which pins are stuck. — money n. an allowance for incidental or personal expenses. -point v.t. to locate (a target) with great accuracy.

pin•a•fore n. an apron for a child or young girl.

pin•cers n.pl. a tool for gripping, composed of two limbs crossed and pivoted; nippers; pliers; the claw of a lobster, crab, etc.

pinch v.t. to nip or squeeze, e.g. between the thumb and finger; to stint; to make thin, e.g. by hunger; v.i. to press hard; to be miserly; n. as much as can be taken up between the thumb and finger; a nip; an emergency. -ed a. (Fig.) thin and hungry looking.

pine n. a coniferous tree with evergreen, needlelike leaves; the wood of this tree; -y, piny a. -apple n. tropical plant and its fruit resembling a pine cone; the ananas; — cone n. fruit of the pine.

pine v.t. to waste away from grief, anxiety, want, etc.; to languish; to wither; to desire eagerly.

ping n. the sound that a bullet makes —pong n. table tennis.

pink n. a carnation, a garden flower of various colors; a light crimson color; that which is supremely excellent; a. of a pale crimson color.

pink v.t. to pierce with small holes; to pierce with a sword, etc.; to ornament the edge with notches, etc.

pin•na•cle n. a slender turret elevated above the main building; a rocky mountain peak; a summit; (Fig.) the climax.

pinnacle

pint n. a liquid and a dry measure equal to ½ quart.

pin•to n. a piebald horse.

pi•o•neer n. one who originates anything or prepares the way for others; v.i. to open a way or originate; an explorer; (Mil.) one of an advance body clearing or repairing a road for troops.

pi•ous a. having reverence and love for God; marked by pretended or mistaken devotion; -ly adv.

pipe n. a tubular instrument of music; any long tube; a tube of clay, wood, etc. with a bowl for smoking; a bird's note; a pipeful of tobacco; a pipe-like vein of ore; pl. bagpipes; v.t. to perform on a pipe; to utter in a shrill tone; to convey by means of pipes; to ornament with a piping or fancy edging; v.i. to play on a pipe, esp. the bagpipes; to whistle. **piped** a. furnished with a pipe; tubular; conveyed by pipes. **piping** a. giving forth a shrill sound; n. the act of playing on a pipe; a system of pipes (for gas, water, etc.); a kind of cord trimming for ladies' dresses; ornamentation made on cakes — **clay** n. a fine, whitish clay used in the manufacture of tobacco pipes; v.t. to whiten with pipe clay. — **line** n. a long line of piping for conveying water, oil, etc.

pi•pette n. a thin, glass tube used for withdrawing small quantities of a liquid from a vessel.

pi•quant a. agreeably pungent to the taste; arousing interest. -ly adv. **piquancy.**

pique v.t. to irritate; to hurt the pride of; to displease; to stimulate; to pride oneself. pr.p. **piquing.** pa.p. and pa.t. **piqued,** n. annoyance from a slight; vexation.

pi•qué n. a ribbed cotton fabric.

pi•rate n. a sea robber; a vessel manned by sea robbers; a publisher, etc. who infringes copyright; v.t. and v.i. to act as a pirate; to plunder; to publish or reproduce regardless of copyright. **piratical** a. **piratically** adv. **piracy** n.

pir•ou•ette n. a spinning round on the toes of one foot.

Pis•ces n.pl. (Astron.) the Fishes, the twelfth sign of the zodiac.

pis•ta•chi•o n. the nut of an Asiatic tree, whose kernel is used for flavoring.

pis•til n. the seed-bearing organ of a flower, consisting of the stigma, style, and ovary. -late a. having a pistil but sometimes no stamen.

pis•tol n. a small handgun; v.t. to shoot with a pistol.

pistol

pis•ton n. a closely fitting metal disk moving to and fro in a hollow cylinder, e.g. as in a steam engine, automobile, etc. — rod n. a rod which connects the piston with another part of the machinery.

pit n. a deep hole in the ground, esp. one from which coal etc. is dug or quarried; the abyss of hell; a hollow or depression; an area for cock-fighting, etc.; in the theater, the section for musicians in front of stage; in motor racing, the base where cars are refilled, etc.; pr.p. -ting. pa.p. and pa.t. -ted; a. marked with small

P

hollows. **-fall** *n.* a pit lightly covered, intended to entrap animals; any hidden danger.

pitch *n.* a thick, black, sticky substance obtained by boiling down tar; *v.t.* to cover over, smear with pitch. **-iness** *n.* **—black, —dark** *a.* very dark.

pitch *v.t.* to throw, toss, fling; to set up (a tent, camp, wickets, etc.); *(Music)* to set the keynote of; to plunge or fall forward; to slope down; of a ship, to plunge. *n.* the act of tossing or throwing; a throw or toss; steepness of a roof; downward slope; the highest point; the plunging motion of a vessel lengthwise; degree of acuteness of musical note. **-ed** *a.* **-er** *n.* **-fork** *n.* a fork for tossing hay, etc.

pitch•er *n.* a jug; a vessel for pouring liquids, usually with a handle and a lip or spout.

pith *n.* the soft, spongy substance in the center of plant stems; the essential substance; force or vigor. **-y** *a.* consisting of pith; terse and forceful; energetic. **-ily** *adv.* **-iness** *n.* **-less** *a.*

pi•tu•i•tar•y *a.* pert. to the pituitary gland. **— gland**, a ductless gland at base of the brain, secreting an endocrine influencing growth.

pit•y *n.* sympathy or sorrow for others' suffering; a cause of grief or regret; *v.t.* to feel grief or sympathy for. **-ing** *a.* expressing pity. **-ingly** *adv.* **pitiable** *a.* deserving pity. **pitiably** *adv.* **pitiful** *a.* full of pity; tender; woeful; exciting pity. **pitifully** *adv.* **pitifulness** *n.* **pitiless** *a.* feeling no pity; hardhearted. **pitilessly** *adv.* **pitilessness** *n.* **piteous** *a.* fitted to excite pity; sad or sorrowful.

piv•ot *n.* a pin or shaft on which a wheel or other body turns; that on which important results depend.

pla•ca•ble *a.* readily appeased or pacified; willing to forgive. **-ness, placability** *n.* **placate** *v.t.* to appease, conciliate. **placatory** *a.*

place *n.* a particular part of space; a spot; a locality; a building; rank; position; priority of position; stead; duty; office or employment; *(Sport)* a position among the first three competitors to finish; *v.t.* to put in a particular spot; to find a position for; to appoint; to fix; to put; to identify. **-d** *a.* in a race, etc., to be first, second, or third at the finish. **— kick** *n.* *(Football)* one made by kicking the ball after it has been placed on the ground for the purpose.

pla•cen•ta *n.* *(Med.)* the soft, spongy substance (expelled from the womb after birth) through which the mother's blood nourishes the fetus.

plac•id *a.* calm; peaceful. **-ly** *adv.* **-ity** *n.* mildness; sweetness; serenity.

pla•gi•a•rize *v.t.* to steal the words, ideas, etc. of another and use them as one's own. **plagiarism** *n.* the act of plagiarizing; literary theft. **plagiarist** *n.* **plagiary** *n.*

plague *n.* a deadly, epidemic, and infectious disease; a pestilence; a nuisance.

plaid *n.* a long, woolen garment, usually with a tartan pattern, worn as a wrap by Scottish Highlanders; *a.* marked with strips. **-ed** *a.*

plain *a.* evident; clear; unobstructed; not intricate; simple; ordinary; without decoration; not beautiful; level; flat; even; *adv.* clearly; *n.* a tract of level country. **-ly** *adv.* **-ness** *n.*

plaint *n.* *(Poet.)* a lamentation; *(Law)* a statement in writing of the complaint, accusation, etc. **-iff** *n.* the one who sues in a court of law.

plan *n.* a drawing representing a thing's horizontal section; a diagram; a map; a project; a design; a scheme; *v.t.* to make a plan of; to arrange beforehand. *pr.p.* **-ning** *pa.p.* and *pa.t.* **-ned.**

plane *n.* a flat, level surface; *(Geom.)* a surface such that, if any two points on it be joined by a straight line, that line will lie wholly on the surface; *a.* perfectly level; pert. to, or lying in, a plane.

plane

— geometry, branch of geometry which deals with plane, not solid, figures.

plan•et *n.* a celestial body revolving round the sun (e.g. Venus, Mars, etc.) as distinct from the fixed stars. **-arium** *n.* a working model of the planetary system; a projected representation of the heavens on a dome. **-ary** *a.* pert. to planets; of the nature of a planet; erratic; wandering.

plank *n.* a thick, heavy board; an article of policy in a political program; *v.t.* to lay with planks. **-ing** *n.* planks collectively.

plank•ton *n.* *(Biol.)* the minute animal and vegetable organisms floating in the ocean.

plant *n.* a living organism belonging to the vegetable kingdom, generally excluding trees and shrubs; a slip or cutting; machinery, tools, etc., used in an industrial undertaking; *v.t.* to set in ground for growth; to implant (ideas, etc.). **-ation** *n.* large estate for growing a certain crop. **-er** *n.* one who plants; the owner of a plantation.

plaque *n.* a thin, flat, ornamental tablet hung on a wall or inserted into a wall or furniture.

plas•ma *n.* *(Biol.)* protoplasm; the fluid part of the blood, as opposed to the corpuscles. Also **plasm.** **-tic, plasmic** *a.*

plas•ter *n.* a composition of lime, water, and sand, for coating walls; gypsum, for making ornaments, molds, etc.; *(Med.)* an adhesive, curative application; *(Surg.)* a composition used to hold a limb, etc. rigid; *v.t.* to cover with plaster; to smooth over or conceal. **-er** *n.*

plas•tic *a.* capable of molding or of being

molded; pliable; capable of change; *n.* a substance capable of being molded; a group of synthetic products derived from casein, cellulose, etc. which may be molded into any form. — **surgery,** the art of restoring lost or damaged parts of the body by grafting on sound tissue.

plat *n.* map.

plate *n.* a shallow, round dish from which food is eaten; a plateful; a flat; thin sheet of metal, glass, etc.; *(Dentistry)* a thin sheet of vulcanic, or metal, to hold artificial teeth; *(Photog.)* short for 'photographic plate'; a separate page of illustrations in a book; *v.t.* to cover with a thin coating of gold, silver, or other metal; to protect with steel plates, *e.g.* as a ship. **-r** *n.* — **glass** *n.* thick glass, rolled in sheets and used for windows, mirrors, etc.

pla•teau *n.* a tract of level, high ground. *pl.* **plateaus, plateaux.**

plat•form *n.* a wooden structure raised above the level of the floor, as a stand for speakers; a landing area at a railway-station; *(Mil.)* a stage on which a gun is mounted; policy of a political party.

plat•i•num *n.* a hard, silvery-white, malleable metal. **platinic, platinous.**

Pla•to *n.* a famous Greek philosopher (427-347 B.C.). **Platonic,** **-nical** *a.* pert. to Plato or to his philosophy. **-nism** *n.* the doctrines of Plato. **-nist** *n.* **Platonic love,** spiritual affection between man and woman without sexual desire.

pla•toon *n. (Mil.)* a small body of soldiers employed as a unit.

plat•ter *n.* a large shallow plate or dish.

plat•y•pus *n.* a small, acquatic, furred animal of Australia; the duckbill.

plau•si•ble *a.* having the appearance of being true; apparently right; fairspoken. **plausibly** *adv.* **plausibility** *n.*

play *v.t.* and *i.* to move with light or irregular motion; to frolic; to flutter; to amuse oneself; to take part in a game; to gamble; to act a part on the stage; to perform on a musical instrument; to operate; to trifle with; *n.* a brisk or free movement; activity; action; amusement; fun; frolic; sport gambling; a dramatic piece or performance. **-er** *n.* **-able** *a.* **-ful** *a.* fond of play or fun; lively. **-fully** *adv.* **-bill** *n.* a bill or poster to advertise a play. **-boy** *n.* a habitual pleasure-seeker. **-ground** *n.* an open space or courtyard for recreation. **-house** *n.* a theater. **-mate** *n.* a companion in play. **-pen** *n.* a portable enclosure for small children to play in. **-thing** *n.* a toy. **playwright** *n.* a writer of plays; a dramatist. **-ing card** *n.* one of a set of cards, usually 52 in number, used in card games.

plea *n. (Law)* the defendant's answer to the plaintiff's declaration; an excuse; entreaty.

plead *v.t.* to allege in proof or vindication; *(Law)* to argue at the bar; to urge reasons in support of or against; to beg or implore. *pa.p.* and *pa.t.* **-ed.**

please *v.t.* to excite agreeable sensations or emotions in; to gratify; to delight; to satisfy; *v.i.* to give pleasure. **pleasant** *a.* fitted to please; cheerful; lively; merry; agreeable. **pleasantly** *adv.* **pleasantness** *n.* **pleasantry** *n.* playfulness in conversation; a joke; a humorous act; *pl.* **pleasantries. pleasing** *a.* agreeable; gratifying. **pleasingly** *adv.* **pleasingness** *n.* **pleasure** *n.* agreeable sensation or emotion; gratification of the senses or mind; amusement, diversion, or self-indulgence; choice; a source of gratification. **pleasurable** *a.* **pleasurably** *adv.*

pleat *n.* a flattened fold fastened in position.

ple•be•ian *a.* pert. or belonging to the common people; vulgar; uncultured; *n.* a common person.

pleb•i•scite *n.* a vote of the whole community or nation.

pledge *n.* something deposited as a security; a sign or token of anything; a drinking to the health of; a solemn promise; *v.t.* to deposit in pawn; to leave as security; to engage for, by promise or declaration; to drink to the health of.

plen•ty *n.* a full supply; abundance; quite enough; sufficiency.

pleth•o•ra *n.* an excess of red corpuscles in the blood; superabundance. **plethoric** *a.*

pleu•ra *n. (Med.)* the membrane lining the chest and covering the lungs. *pl.* **-e.** **-l** *a.* **pleurisy** *n. (Med.)* inflammation of the pleura.

plex•us *n.* a network, esp. of nerves, blood vessels, fibers, etc. **plexal** *a.*

pli•a•ble *a.* easily bent; easily influenced. Also **pliant pliably, pliantly** *adv.* **pliability, pliancy** *n.*

pli•ers *n.pl.* small pincers with a flat grip.

plight *n.* a state or condition of a distressing kind; predicament.

plight *v.t.* to pledge, as one's word of honor; to betroth.

plod *v.t.* to tread with a heavy step; *v.i.* to walk or work laboriously; to toil or drudge *pr.p.* **-ding** *pa.t., pa.p.* **-ded.**

plot *n.* a small patch of ground; a plan of a field, farm, etc. drawn to scale; the plan of a play, novel, etc.; a secret scheme; a conspiracy. *v.t.* to draw a graph or plan of; to plan or scheme. *v.i.* to conspire. *pr.p.* **-ting** *pa.t., pa.p.* **-ted.**

plow *n.* an implement with a heavy cutting blade for turning up the soil; *v.t.* to turn up with the plow; to furrow; to advance laboriously; *v.i.* to till the soil with a plow. **-share** *n.* the heavy iron blade of a plow.

pluck *v.t.* to pull off; to pick as flowers; to strip off feathers, as a fowl; to snatch, or pull with sudden force; *n.* a pull or jerk; the act of plucking; courage or spirit.

plug *n.* anything used to stop a hole; a cake of compressed tobacco; *(Elect.)* a device for connecting and disconnecting of a circuit; *abbrev.* for spark plug; *v.t.* to stop with a plug; to insert a plug in.

plum *n.* a round or oval fruit; the tree that bears it; a particularly good appointment or position; a dark purplish color.

P

plum•age n. a bird's feathers, collectively.

plumb n. a weight of lead attached to a line, and used to determine perpendicularity; the perpendicular position; a. perpendicular; adv. perpendicularly; v.t. to adjust by a plumb line; to sound or take the depth of water with a plummet. **-er** n. one who installs or repairs water and sewage systems. **-ing** n. the trade of a plumber; the system of water and sewage pipes in a building. **— line** n. a weighted string for testing the perpendicular.

plume n. a feather or tuft of feathers; a crest on a helmet; a token of honor; v.t. to furnish with plumes.

plump a. of rounded form; moderately fat. **-ness** n.

plun•der v.t. to rob systematically; to take by force; n. the act of robbing by force; property so obtained.

plunge to immerse suddenly in a liquid; n. the act of plunging; a dive; a sudden rush. **-r** n. one who plunges; a solid, cylindrical rod used as a piston in pumps.

plu•ral a. more than one; (Gram.) denoting more than one person or thing; n. (Gram.) a word in its plural form. **-ly** adv. **-ism** n. (Philos.) doctrine that existence has more than one ultimate principle. **-ist** n. **-istic** a. **-ity** n. large number; a majority of votes; state of being plural.

plus n. symbol of addition (+); positive quantity; extra quantity; a. to be added; (Math., Elect., etc.) positive; prep. with the addition of.

plush n. a fabric with a long, velvet-like nap.

Plu•to n. (Myth.) god of the lower world; the planet farthest from the sun. **-nic rocks** (Geol.) name given to igneous rocks formed by action of intense subterranean heat. **-nium** n. a metal of high atomic weight made by bombarding atoms of uranium with neutrons.

ply v.t. to wield; to work at steadily; to use or practice with diligence; to urge.

ply n. a fold; a strand of yarn; thickness. pl. **plies. -wood** n. board made of two or more thin layers of wood cemented together.

pneu•mat•ic a. pert. to air or gas; inflated with wind or air; operated by compressed air. **-s** n.pl. the branch of physics dealing with the mechanical properties of gases.

pneu•mo•nia n. acute inflammation of a lung.

poach v.t. to cook eggs, by breaking them into a pan of boiling water.

pock n. pustule on skin, as in smallpox. **— mark** n. pit left in skin by pock.

pock•et n. a small pouch or bag inserted into a garment; a cavity or hollow; (Mil.) isolated area held by the enemy. to accept without resentment, as an insult. **-book** n. a small bag or case for holding money or papers. **— money** n. money for small, personal expenses, e.g. allowance to child.

pod n. a seed vessel of a plant, esp. a legume, as peas, beans, etc.

po•em n. a composition in verse; any composition written in elevated and imaginative language; opp. to 'prose.' **poesy** n. poetry. **poetically** adv. **poetics** n. principles of art of poetry; criticism of poetry. **poetry** n. language of imagination expressed in verse; metrical composition. **poetic justice**, ideal justice, in which crime is punished and virtue rewarded. **poetic license**, latitude in grammar or facts, allowed to poets. **poet laureate**, official poet.

poign•ant a. acutely painful; strongly appealing; pungent. **-ly** adv. **poignancy** n.

point n. sharp or tapering end of anything; dot or mark; dot in decimal system; punctuation mark; full stop; (Geom.) that which has position but no magnitude; item or detail; gist of argument; striking or effective part of a speech, story, etc.; moment of time; purpose; a fine lace made with a needle; of a dog, to indicate the position of game by standing facing it. **-ed** a. having a sharp point; direct; telling; aimed; **-edly** adv. **-edness** n. **-less** a. having no point; blunt; irrelevant; insipid.

poise v.t. to place or hold in a balanced or steady position; n. equilibrium; carriage of the head, body, etc.; self-possession.

poi•son n. any substance which kills or injures when introduced into a living organism; that which has an evil influence on health or moral purity; **-er** n. **-ous** a. having a deadly or injurious quality; corrupting. **-ously** adv. **— ivy** n. a vine which, if touched, causes a skin rash.

poke v.t. to push or thrust against with a pointed object, e.g. with a finger, stick, etc.; to thrust in; to tease.

pok•er n. a card game in which the players bet on the value of their hands. **—faced** a. having an expressionless face.

po•lar a. pert. to, or situated near, the North or South Poles; pert. to the magnetic poles (points on the earth's surface where a magnetic needle dips vertically); pert. to either pole of a magnet; directly opposed; having polarity. **— bear**, a large, white bear, found in the Arctic regions.

po•lar•ize v.t. to give polarity to; (Elect.) to reduce the electromotive force (E.M.F.) of a primary cell by the accumulation of certain electrolytic products on the plates; (Chem.) to separate the positive and negative charges on a molecule; (Light) to confine the vibrations of light waves to certain directions, e.g. to a plane. **polarization** n. **polaroid** n.

pole n. a long, rounded piece of wood or metal.

pole n. either of the ends of the axis of a sphere, esp. of the earth (in the latter case called the North Pole and South Pole); either of the opposite ends or terminals of a magnet, electric battery, etc.

Pole n. a native of Poland. **Polish** a. pert. to

Poland or the Poles.

pole•cat n. a small, carnivorous animal, resembling the weasel; a skunk.

po•lice n. the civil force which maintains public order; the members of the force; v.t. to control with police; to keep in order. **-man, — officer** n. (fem. **-woman**) member of a police force. **— court** n. a court for the trial of minor offenses. **— station** n. the headquarters of the police.

pol•i•cy n. a course of action adopted, esp. in state affairs; prudent procedure.

pol•i•cy n. a document containing a contract of insurance.

pol•i•o•my•e•li•tis n. (Med.) inflammation of the grey matter of the spinal cord; infantile paralysis. abbrev. **polio.**

pol•ish v.t. to make smooth and glossy; to make polite and cultured; n. the act of polishing; a smooth, glassy surface; a substance used in polishing; refinement; elegance of manners. **-er** n.

po•lite a. elegant in manners; well-bred; courteous; refined. **-ly** adv. **-ness** n.

pol•i•tic a. prudent; wise; shrewd; cunning; advisable. **-s** n.pl. the art of government; political affairs, life, or principles. **-ly** adv. **-al** a. pert. to the state or its affairs; pert. to politics. **-ally** adv. **politician** n. a holder of a political position; a statesman; a member of a political party. **political economy,** the science dealing with the nature, production, distribution, and consumption of wealth.

pol•ka n. a lively dance of Bohemian origin; music for it.

poll n. a register of persons; a list of persons entitled to vote; (the place) of voting; number of votes recorded; v.t. to cut off the top of, e.g. tree; to canvass; to receive (votes); to cast a vote.

pol•len n. the fertilizing dust of a flower. **pollinate** v.t. to fertilize a flower by conveying pollen to the pistil.

pol•lute v.t. to make foul or unclean; to defile; to desecrate. **pollution** n.

po•lo n. a game like hockey played on horseback.

po•lo•ni•um n. a metallic, radio active chemical.

pol•troon n. a coward. **-ery** n.

pol•y- prefix, many words used in derivatives. **-chrome** n. a picture, statue, etc. in several colors. **-chromatic, -chromic, -chromous** a. many-colored.

po•lyg•a•my n. the practice of having more than one wife at the same time. **polygamous** a. **polygamist** n.

pol•y•gon n. a plane figure with more than four sides or angles. **polygonal** a.

pol•y•he•dron n. (Geom.) a solid figure with many faces, usually more than six.

polyhedra

pol•y•mor•phous a. assuming many forms. Also **polymorphic. polymorphism** n.

Pol•y•ne•sia n. (Geog.) a group of islands in the S. Pacific, east of Australia. **-n** a.

pol•y•no•mi•al n. (Alg.) a quantity having many terms.

pol•y•syl•a•ble n. a word of three or more syllables. **polysyllabic** a.

pol•y•tech•nic a. pert. to many arts and sciences; n. a school or college of applied arts and sciences.

pol•y•the•ism n. belief in the existence of many gods, or in more than one. **polytheist** n. **polytheistic** a.

po•made n. scented ointment for the hair. Also **pomatum. pomander** n. ball of or case for mixture of perfumes.

pome•gran•ate n. a large fruit containing many seeds in a red pulp.

pom•er•a•ni•an n. a small breed of dog with bushy tail, sharp pointed muzzle, pointed ears and long silky hair.

pomp n. splendid display or ceremony; magnificence. **-ous** n. showy with grandeur; of a person, self-important; of language, inflated. **-ously** adv. **-ousness** n. **-osity** n.

pom•pa•dour n. woman's high swept hairstyle; man's hair style with hair brushed up from forehead.

pond n. a pool of water, either naturally or artificially enclosed.

pon•der v.t. to weigh in the mind; to consider attentively; v.i. to mediate. **-er** n. **-ing** a.

pon•der•ous a. very heavy; weighty; massive; unwieldy; dull or lacking in spirit. **-ly** adv. **-ness** n. **ponderosity** n.

pon•tiff n. the Pope; a bishop; a high priest. **pontifical** a. belonging to a high priest; popish; pompous and dogmatic; n.pl. the garb of a priest, bishop, or pope. **pontifically** adv. **pontificate** n. the state, dignity, or term of office of a priest, bishop, or pope.

po•ny n. a small breed of horse.

poo•dle n. one of a breed of dogs with thick, curly hair, often clipped into ornamental tufts.

poodle

pool n. a small body of still water; a deep place in a river.

pool n. the collective stakes in various games; the place where the stakes are put; a variety of billiards; a combination of capitalists to fix prices and divide into a common fund.

poop n. the stern of a ship; raised deck at the stern.

poor a. having little or no money; without means; needy; miserable; wretched; unfortunate; feeble; deserving of pity; unproductive; of inferior quality. **-ly** adv.

P

inadequately; with little or no success; without spirit.

pop n. an abrupt, small explosive sound; a shot; an effervescing drink; v.i. to make a sharp, quick sound; to go or come unexpectedly or suddenly; to dart; v.t. to put or place suddenly; adv. pr.p. -ping pa.p. and pa.t. -ped. -corn n. Indian corn exposed to heat causing it to burst open.

Pope n. the Bishop of Rome and head of the R.C. Church. **popish** a. pert. to the Pope or the papacy. -dom n. the office, dignity, or jurisdiction of the Pope.

pop•lar n. a tree noted for its slender tallness.

pop•py n. a bright flowered plant, one species of which yields opium.

pop•u•lace n. the common people; the masses. **populate** v.t. to people. **population** n. the total number of people in a country, town, etc. **populous** a. thickly inhabited.

pop•u•lar a. pert. to the common people; finding general favor; -ly adv. -ize v.t. to make popular; to make familiar, plain, easy, etc. to all. -ization n. -ity n. public favor.

por•ce•lain n. the finest kind of earthenware—white, glazed and semi-transparent; china.

porch n. a covered entrance to a doorway.

por•cu•pine n. a large quadruped of the rodent family, covered with spines.

pore n. a minute opening in the skin for the passage of perspiration. **porous** a. full of pores.

pork n. the flesh of swine used for food.

por•nog•ra•phy n. obscene literature or pictures. **pornographer** n. **pornographic** a.

por•poise n. a blunt-nosed cetacean mammal 5 to 8 feet long, frequenting the northern seas.

porpoise

por•ridge n. (Brit.) a soft breakfast food.

port n. a harbor; a town with a harbor.

port n. the way in which a person carries himself.

port n. a strong, sweet, dark-red wine.

port n. the left side of a ship, looking towards the bow.

port•a•ble a. capable of being easily carried.

por•tal n. a gate or entrance.

por•tend v.t. to foretell; to give warning in advance; to be an omen of. **portent** n. an omen, esp. of evil.

por•ter n. a door- or gatekeeper; railway sleeping-car attendant.

por•ter n. one employed to carry baggage esp. at stations or hotels.

por•ter•house n. place where beer (porter) was served. — **steak** choice cut of beef next to the sirloin.

port•fo•li•o n. case for holding loose documents, drawings, etc.

port•hole n. window in side of ship.

por•ti•co n. (Archit.) a row of columns in front of the entrance to a building; a covered walk.

por•tion n. a piece; a part; a share; a helping of food; v.t. to divide into shares.

por•tray v.t. to represent by drawing, painting, acting, or imitating; to describe vividly in words. -al n. the act of portraying; the representation. -er n. **portrait** n. picture of a person, esp. of the face; a graphic description of a person in words.

Por•tu•guese a. pert. to Portugal, its inhabitants, or language.

pose n. attitude or posture of a person, natural or assumed; a mental attitude or affectation; v.t. to place in a position for the sake of effect; to lay down or assert.

po•si•tion n. place; situation; the manner in which anything is arranged; posture; social rank or standing; employment.

pos•i•tive a. formally laid down; clearly stated; absolute; dogmatic; of real value; confident; not negative; plus; (Math.) pert. to a quantity greater than zero; n. the positive degree of an adjective or adverb, i.e. without comparison; in photography, a print in which the lights and shadows are not reversed (as in the negative). -ly adv. -ness n. **positivism** n. the philosophical system which recognizes only matters of fact and experience. **positivist** n. a believer in this doctrine. — **pole**, of a magnet, the northseeking-pole. — **sign**, the sign (+ read plus) of addition.

pos•i•tron n. particle differing from an electron in that it has positive electrical charge.

pos•se n. a company or force, usually with legal authority; men under orders of the sheriff, maintaining law and order.

pos•sess v.t. to own or hold as property; to have as an attribute; to enter into and influence, as an evil spirit or passions. -ed a. influenced, as by an evil spirit; demented. -ion n. the act of possessing; ownership; actual occupancy; the state of being possessed; the thing possessed. -ive a. denoting possession.

pos•si•ble a. capable of being or of coming into being; feasible.

post n. a piece of timber or metal, set upright as a support; a prop or pillar; -er n. one who posts bills; a large placard for posting.

post n. a fixed place; a military station or the soldiers occupying it; an office or position of trust, service, or emolument; a trading settlement; -age n. the cost of conveyance by mail. -al a. pert. to the post office or mail service. -man n. one who delivers mail. -mark n. a post office mark which cancels the postage stamp and gives place and time of mailing. -master n. the manager of a post office. -master general n. the chief of the post office department of a government. — **card** n. a stamped card on which a message may be sent through the mail. — **office** n. an office where letters and parcels are received for distribution; the government postal department. -age stamp n. an adhesive stamp, affixed to mail to indicate payment.

post- adv. and prefix after, behind, used in many compound words. -date v.t. to put on a document, letter, etc., a date later than the actual one. -graduate a. of academic study, research, etc., undertaken after taking a university degree. —mortem a. n. the dissection of a body after death; an autopsy.

pos•te•ri•or a. coming after; n. the rump. -ly adv. -ity n. posterity future generations.

post•hu•mous a. born after the death of the father; published after the death of the author.

post•pone v.t. to put off till a future time; to defer; to delay. -ment n. -r n.

post•script n. something added to a letter after the signature; abbrev. P.S.

pos•tu•late v.t. to assume without proof; to lay down as self-evident; to stipulate; n. a prerequisite; a proposition assumed without proof.

pos•ture n. the position of a body, figure, etc. or of its several members; attitude; v.i. to assume an artificial or affected attitude.

po•sy n. a bouquet; a flower.

pot n. a rounded vessel of metal, earthenware, etc., used for cooking, holding fluids. plants, etc.; the contents of a pot; v.t. to plant in pots; -hole n. cavity formed in rock by action of stones in the eddy of a stream; a hole in the roadway. -luck n. whatever may happen to have been provided for a meal.

po•ta•ble a. drinkable. potation n. a drinking; a draft.

pot•ash n. a powerful alkali obtained from wood ashes. potassium n. metallic base of potash.

po•ta•to n. an edible tuber widely grown for food. pl. -es.

po•tent a. having great authority or influence; powerful; mighty; procreative. -ly adv. potency n. moral or physical power; influence; energy; efficacy. a. latent; existing in possibility but not in actuality; n. inherent capability of doing anything; (Elect.) the level of electric pressure. -ially adv. -iality n. possibility as distinct from actuality. -ial difference (Elect.) the difference of pressure between two points; voltage.

po•tion n. a dose, esp. of liquid, medicine, or poison.

pot•pour•ri n. a mixture of dried rose petals, spices, etc.; a musical or literary medley.

pot•tage n. soup or stew; (Bib.) a dish of lentils.

pot•ter n. a maker of earthenware vessels. -y n. pots, vessels, etc. made of earthenware; the place where it is made; the art of making it.

pouch n. a small bag or sack; a baglike receptacle in which certain animals; e.g. the kangaroo, carry their young.

poult n. a young fowl. poultry n. domestic fowls. -erer n. a dealer in poultry.

pounce v.i. to spring upon suddenly; to swoop; n. a swoop or sudden descent.

pound n. a measure of weight (abbrev. lb.), 16 ounces avoirdupois, or 12 ounces troy; a unit of British money (abbrev. £), -age n. charge of so much per pound. -al n. a unit of force.

pound v.t. and i. to beat or strike; to crush to pieces or to powder; to walk, run, etc., heavily.

pound n. an enclosure for animals; v.t. to shut up in one.

pour v.i. to come out in a stream, crowd, etc.; to flow freely; to rain heavily; v.t. to cause to flow, as a liquid from a vessel; to shed; to utter.

pout v.i. to thrust out the lips, as in displeasure, etc.; to look sullen or sulky; n. the act of pouting; a protrusion of the lips. -er n. one who pouts.

pov•er•ty n. the state of being poor; poorness; lack of means.

pow•der n. dust; a solid matter in fine dry particles; a medicine in this form; short for gunpowder, face powder, etc.; v.t. to reduce to powder; to pulverize; to sprinkle with powder.

pow•er n. a capacity for action, physical, mental, or moral; energy; might; agency or motive force; authority; one in authority; influence or ascendancy; a nation; mechanical energy; (Math.) the product arising from the continued multiplication of a number by itself. -ful a. having great power; capable of producing great effect. -fully adv. -fulness n. -less a. -lessly adv. -lessness.

pox n. a disease attended with pustules on the skin, as smallpox, chickenpox, etc.; syphilis.

prac•tice n. performance or execution, as opposed to theory; custom or habit; systematic exercise for instruction; training; exercise of a profession. practicable a. capable of being accomplished or put into practice; capable of being used, e.g. a weapon, a road, etc. n. practitioner n. one engaged in a profession, esp. law or medicine.

prag•mat•ic, pragmatical a. pert. to state affairs; concerned with practical consequences; matter-of-fact. -ally adv. -alness n. pragmatize v.t. to represent an imaginary thing as real. pragmatism n. a philosophy based on the conception that the truth of a doctrine is to be judged by its practical consequences. pragmatist n.

prai•rie n. a large tract of grassland, destitute of trees.

praise v.t. to express approval or admiration; to glorify; n. approval of merit; commendation; worship. —worthy a. deserving of praise.

prance v.i. to spring or bound like a high-spirited horse; to swagger; to caper, esp. of children; n. a prancing movement.

prank n. a mischievous trick; a practical joke.

prawn n. an edible crustacean of the shrimp family.

pray v.i. to ask earnestly; to entreat; to petition; v.i. to make a request or confession, esp. to God; to commune with God. -er n. one who prays; the act of praying; an earnest entreaty; the words used; the thing asked for; a petition.

pre- prefix, before, beforehand, used with many nouns and verbs.

preach v.i. and t. to deliver a sermon; to speak publicly on a religious subject, esp. as a clergyman; to advocate.

pre•am•ble n. the introductory part of a discourse, story, document, etc.; a preface.

pre•ar•range v.t. to arrange beforehand. -ment n.

pre•car•i•ous a. depending on the will or pleasure of another; depending on circumstances; uncertain; dangerous; perilous. -ly adv. -ness n.

pre•cau•tion n. care taken beforehand; v.t. to forewarn. -ary a. characterized by precaution.

pre•cede v.t. to go before in place, time, rank, or importance. -nt a. preceding; -nt n. something done, or said, that may serve as an example in similar cases. -ntly adv. -nce n. the act of preceding; priority in position, rank, or time. **preceding** a.

pre•cept n. an instruction intended as a rule of conduct, esp. moral conduct; (Law) a written warrant or mandate given to an administrative officer. -ive a.

pre•ces•sion n. a going before. -al a.

pre•cinct n. a division of a city for police protection, voting, etc.; a boundary or limit; a minor territorial division.

pre•cious a. of great value or price; costly; highly esteemed; over-refined; fastidious; adv.

pre•cip•i•tate v.i. to throw headlong; to urge on eagerly; to hasten the occurrence of; (Chem.) to cause to separate and fall to the bottom, as a substance in solution; of vapor, to condense. **precipitant** n. falling headlong; too hasty; unexpectedly hastened. **precipitation** n. the act of precipitating; rash haste; a falling headlong; condensation of vapor, rain, snow, etc.

pre•cise a. exact; definite; distinct; prim. -ly adv. -ness n. precision n. accuracy; definiteness; a. done with great accuracy.

pre•clude v.t. to shut out; to hinder; to prevent from happening **preclusion** n. **preclusive** a.

pre•co•cious a. having the mental powers or bodily growth developed at an early age; premature; forward. -ly adv. -ness, **precocity** n.

pre•con•ceive v.t. to form an opinion or idea of beforehand. **preconception** n. a prejudice.

pre•cur•sor n. a person or thing going before; a forerunner; a harbinger. -y, **precursive** a.

pre•da•cious a. living on prey; predatory. **predatory** a. living by preying on others; plundering; pillaging.

pre•date v.t. to date earlier than the true date.

pred•e•ces•sor n. one who has preceded another in an office, position, etc.

pre•des•tine v.t. to destine beforehand; to foreordain. **predestinate** v.t. to determine beforehand; to foreordain. **predestination** n. (Theol.) the doctrine that the salvation or damnation of individuals has been foreordained by God; the determination beforehand of future events; destiny; fate.

pre•de•ter•mine v.t. to determine beforehand. **predeterminate** a. determined beforehand. **predetermination** n.

pre•dic•a•ment n. an awkward plight; a trying situation.

pred•i•cate v.t. to affirm; to assert; to declare; n. that which is predicated; (Gram.) a statement made about the subject of the sentence. **predication** n. **predicative** a. **predicatively** adv.

pre•dict v.t. to tell beforehand; to foretell; to prophesy. -able a. -ion n. the act of foretelling; prophecy. -ive a. -or n.

pre•di•lec•tion n. a prepossession of mind in favor of something; partiality.

pre•dis•pose v.t. to incline beforehand; to give a tendency or bias to; to render susceptible to. **predisposition** n.

pre•dom•i•nate v.i. to surpass in strength, influence, or authority; to rule; to have ascendancy; to prevail. **predominance, predominancy** n. ascendancy; superiority. **predominant** a. superior in influence, authority, etc.; having ascendancy. **predominantly** adv.

pre•em•i•nent a. distinguished above others; outstanding. -ly adv.

pre•emp•tion n. the act or right of purchasing before others. **pre-empt** v.t. to appropriate beforehand.

pre•ex•ist v.i. to exist beforehand, or before something else. -ence n. -ent a.

pre•fab n. a prefabricated house.

pre•fab•ri•cate v.t. to build houses and ships in standardized units in factories for rapid assembly. **prefabrication** n.

pref•ace n. introductory remarks at beginning of book, or spoken before a discourse; foreword; v.t. to furnish with a preface. **prefatory** a. introductory.

pre•fer v.t. to like better; to choose rather; to promote to an office or dignity. -able a. worthy of preference; more desirable. -ably adv. -ence n. what is preferred; choice. -ential a. giving or receiving a preference.

pre•fix n. a letter, syllable, or word put at the beginning of another word to modify its meaning, e.g. predigest, underground.

preg•na•ble a. able to be taken by assault or force.

preg•nant a. being with child. **pregnancy.**

pre•hen•sile a. (Zool.) capable of grasping.

pre•his•to•ry n. the period before written records were kept; **prehistoric** a.

prej•u•dice n. an opinion, favorable or unfavorable, formed without fair examination of facts; bias; **prejudicial** a. injurious.

prel•ate n. a bishop, or other church

dignitary of equal or higher rank.

pre·lect v.i. to deliver a lecture or discourse in public. **prelection** n. a lecture.

pre·lim·i·nary a. introductory; preparatory; n. an introduction.

prel·ude n. an introductory performance or event; a musical introduction; v.t. to serve as a prelude or forerunner to. **prelusive, prelusory** a. introductory.

pre·ma·ture a. ripe before the natural or proper time; untimely. **-ly** adv. **-ness, prematurity** n.

pre·med·i·tate v.t. to consider, or revolve in the mind beforehand.

pre·mier a. first; chief or principal; n. the prime minister. **-ship** n.

pre·miere n. a first public performance of a play.

prem·ise v.t. to set forth beforehand, or as introductory to the main subject. **premise** n. Also **premiss**, a proposition previously supposed or proved; n.pl. a building with its adjuncts.

pre·mi·um n. a prize; money paid for insurance; the amount exceeding the par value of shares of stock. **at a premium,** in great demand.

pre·mo·ni·tion n. previous warning. **premonitory** a. **premonitorily** adv.

pre·na·tal a. previous to birth.

pre·oc·cu·py v.t. to take possession of before another. **preoccupied** a. occupied previously; engrossed in thought. **preoccupancy** n. **preoccupation** n.

pre·or·dain v.t. to ordain beforehand. **preordination** n.

pre·paid a. paid in advance.

pre·pare v.t. to make ready for use; to fit for a particular purpose; to provide; to fit out; v.i. to make things ready; to make oneself ready. **preparation** n. the act of making ready for use; readiness; a substance, esp. medicine or food, made up for use. **preparatory** a. preparing the way; preliminary; introductory. **preparedness** n.

pre·pay v.t. to pay beforehand.

pre·pon·der·ate v.i. to exceed in power, influence, numbers, etc.; to outweigh. **preponderance** n. superiority of power, numbers, etc. **preponderant** a. **preponderantly** adv.

prep·o·si·tion n. (Gram.) a word, e.g. with, by, for, etc., used before a noun or pronoun to show the relation to some other word in the sentence. **-al** a.

pre·pos·sess v.t. to possess beforehand; to influence a person's mind, heart, etc. beforehand; to prejudice favorably. **-ing** a. tending to win a favorable opinion; attractive. **-ingly** adv. **prepossession** n.

pre·pos·ter·ous a. contrary to nature, truth, reason, or common sense; utterly absurd. **-ly** adv. **-ness** n.

pre·rog·a·tive n. an exclusive right or privilege by reason of rank, position, etc.

Pres·by·te·ri·an n. one belonging to Presbyterian Church. **-ism** n. **presbytery** n. a body of elders; court of pastors.

pre·sci·ence n. knowledge of events before they take place. **prescient** a.

pre·scribe v.t. to lay down authoritatively for direction; to set out rules for; (Med.) to order or advise the use of. **-r** n. **prescript** n. direction; ordinance. **prescription** n. the act of prescribing or directing; a doctor's direction for use of medicine. **prescriptive** a.

pres·ent a. being in a certain place; here or at hand; now existing; (Gram.) pert. to time that now is; n. present time; (Gram.) the present tense. **presence** n. the state of being present; nearness or proximity; the person of a superior; mien or appearance; apparition. **-ly** adv. at once; soon; by and by.

pre·sent v.t. to introduce into the presence of; to exhibit or offer to the notice; to offer as a gift; to bestow; to aim, as a weapon; n. a gift. **-able** a. fit to be presented. **-ation** n. the act of presenting; the state of being presented; that which is presented.

pre·sen·ti·ment n. a previous notion or opinion.

pre·serve v.t. to keep from injury or destruction; n. that which is preserved, as fruit, etc. a place for the preservation of game, fish, etc. **-r** n. **preservable** a. **preservation** n. the act of keeping safe. **preservative** n. that which preserves. **preservatory** a.

pre·side v.i. to be chairman of a meeting; to direct. **president** n. the head of a society, company, association, etc.; the elected head of a republic. **presidency** n. the office, or term of office, of a president. **presidential** a. pert. to a president.

press v.t. to push or squeese; to crush; to smooth by pressure; n. an instrument or machine for squeezing; a printing machine; newspapers collectively; **-ing** a. urgent; persistent. **— agent** n. one employed to advertise and secure publicity for any person or organization. **to go to press,** of a newspaper, to start printing.

press v.t. to force to serve in the navy or army.

pres·sure n. the act of pressing.

pres·su·ri·za·tion n. maintenance of pressure inside aircraft at great altitudes. **pressurize** v.t.

pres·ti·dig·i·ta·tion n. conjuring; sleight of hand. **prestidigitator** n. a conjurer, a magician.

pres·tige n. influence resulting from past achievement, character, reputation, etc.

pres·to adv. (Mus.) quickly.

pre·sume v.t. to take for granted; to suppose to be true without proof. **presumable** a. probable. **presumably** adv. **presumption** that which is taken for granted; **presumptive** a. based on probability; **presumptively** adv. **presumptuous** a. forward; taking liberties.

pre·sup·pose v.t. to assume or take for granted beforehand.

pre·tend v.t. to assert falsely; to make believe; n. one who simulates or feigns; **pretense** n. simulation; the act of laying claim; **pretentious** a. given to outward show; **pretentiously** adv. **pretentiousness** n.

pre·ter- prefix meaning beyond, above, more than, etc., used in combining forms. **-natural** a. beyond or different from what is natural.

pre·text n. ostensible reason or motive which cloaks the real reason; pretense.

pret·ty a. of a beauty that is charming and attractive, but not striking or imposing; neat and tasteful; pleasing; fine or excellent in an ironical sense; adv. in some degree; moderately; fairly; rather.

pre·vail v.i. to gain the upper hand or mastery; to succeed; to be current; to be in force; to persuade or induce (with 'on' or 'upon'). **-ing** a. **prevalent** a. most generally; extensively existing; rife. **prevalently** adv. **prevalence** n.

pre·vent v.t. to keep from happening; to stop. **-able** a. **-ion** n. obstruction; hinderance; preventive. **-ive** a. tending to prevent or ward off; n. that which prevents; antidote to keep off disease.

pre·view n. a private showing of works of art, films, etc. before being exhibited.

pre·vi·ous a. preceding; happening before.

prey n. any animal hunted and killed for food by another animal; a victim; to seize and devour; to weigh heavily; to pillage.

price n. the amount at which a thing is valued, bought, or sold; value; cost; v.t. to fix the price of; to ask the cost of. **-less** a. beyond any price.

prick n. a sharp-pointed instrument; a puncture made by a sharp point; the act of pricking; a sharp, stinging pain; v.t. to pierce slightly with a sharp point; to incite; to affect with sharp pain; to sting.

prick·le n. a small sharp point; a thorn; a spike; a bristle; v.t. to prick slightly; v.i. to feel a tingling sensation. **prickly** a. full of prickles; stinging; tingling.

pride n. the state or quality of being proud; too high an opinion of oneself; worthy self-esteem.

priest n. (fem. -ess) a clergyman; in R.C. and Episcopal churches; in pagan times, one who officiated at the altar, or performed the rites of sacrifice. **-like**, **-ly** a. **-liness** n. **-hood** n.

prim a. formal and precise; affectedly nice; prudish. **-ly** adv. **-ness** n.

pri·ma a. first. **— donna**, the principal female singer in an opera.

pri·mal a. first, original; chief. **primary** a. first in order of time, elementary; n. that which stands highest in rank or importance; a preliminary election (often pl.); **primarily** adv. in the first place. **primary colors**, red, yellow and blue.

pri·mate n. (Brit.) the chief dignitary in a church; an archbishop. **primacy** n. the chief dignitary in a national church.

prime a. first in time; original; of highest quality; (Math.) that cannot be separated into factors; n. the best portion; v.t. to prepare a firearm by charging with powder; to prepare wood with a protective coating before painting it; to fill with water, etc., as a pump, to make it start working; **-r** n. one who, or that which, primes; a small elementary book used in teaching. **-ly** adv. **-ness** n.

priming n. **— minister**, the first minister of state in some countries. **— number**, a number divisible without remainder only by itself or one.

pri·me·val a. original; primitive; **-ly** adv.

prim·i·tive a. pert. to the beginning or origin; (Biol.) rudimentary; undeveloped; **-ly** adv. **-ness** n.

pri·mo·gen·i·ture n. the state of being the first-born child. **primogenital**, **primogenitary** a. **primogenitor** n. the earliest ancestor.

pri·mor·di·al a. existing from the beginning.

prim·rose n. a plant bearing pale-yellow and other colored flowers in spring.

prince n. (fem. **princess**) a ruler or chief; the son of a king or emperor. **-dom** n. the jurisdiction. **-ly** a. stately. **-liness** n. **Prince Consort**, the husband of a reigning queen.

prin·ci·pal a. chief in importance; first in rank; n. the chief person in authority; the head of certain institutions, esp. a school; the chief actor in a crime; a chief debtor; a sum of money lent and yielding interest. **-ly** adv. **-ship** n. **principality** n. the territory of a prince; sovereignty.

prin·cip·i·a n. pl. first principles; beginnings.

prin·ci·ple n. a fundamental truth or law; a moral rule.

print v.t. to reproduce words, pictures, etc. by pressing inked types on paper, etc.; to write in imitation of this; to publish; n. a photograph. **-er** n. one engaged in the setting of type for, and the printing of books, newspapers, etc. **-ing press** n. a machine for reproducing on paper, etc. impressions made by inked type.

pri·or a. previous; former; earlier; preceding in time; n. the state of being antecedent in time; precedence; preference in regard to privilege.

prism n. (Geom.) a solid whose bases or ends are any similar, equal, and parallel plane figures, and whose sides are parallelograms; (Optics) a transparent figure of this nature, ususally with triangular ends. **colors**, the seven colors, red, orange, yellow, green, blue indigo, violet, into which a ray of light is separated by a prism.

pris·on n. building for confinement of criminals; jail; any place of confinement or restraint.

private a. not public; belonging to or concerning an individual; peculiar to oneself; personal; secluded; secret; of a soldier, not holding any rank; n. a common soldier. **-ly** adv. **-ness** n. **privacy** n. the state of being in retirement from company; solitude; seclusion; secrecy.

pri·va·teer n. an armed private vessel commissioned by a government to attack enemy ships.

pri·va·tion n. the state of being deprived, esp. of something required; destitution;

want.

priv·i·lege n. a special right or advantage; v.t. to grant some special favor to. **-d** a. enjoying a special right or immunity.

priv·y a. private; admitted to knowledge of a secret; n. a person having an interest in a law suit; a latrine.

prize n. a reward given for success in competition; a reward given for merit; a thing striven for; a thing won by chance, e.g. in a lottery. v.t. to value highly; to esteem. **— fight** n. a professional boxing match.

pro- prefix meaning for; instead of; on behalf of; in front of; before; forward; according to.

prob·a·ble a. likely; to be expected; having more evidence for than against. **probably** adv. **probability** n. likelihood.

pro·bate n. the process by which a last will and testament is legally authenticated after the testator's death; an official copy of a will.

pro·ba·tion n. a trial or test of a person's character, conduct, ability, etc.; the testing of a candidate before admission to full membership of a body, esp. a religious sect or order; a system of releasing offenders, esp. juveniles, and placing them under supervision of.

probe n. (Med.) instrument for examining a wound, ulcer, cavity, etc.; an investigation; v.t. to explore a wound, etc. with a probe; to examine thoroughly.

prob·lem n. a matter proposed for solution; a question difficult of solution; a puzzle. **-atical** a. questionable; uncertain.

pro·ceed v.i. to move onward; to advance; to renew progress; to pass from one point or topic to another; to come forth; to carry on a series of acts; to take legal proceedings. **-ing** n. going forward; movement or process; pl. (Law) the several steps of prosecuting a charge, claim, etc. **proceeds** n.pl. yield; sum realized by a sale. **procedure** n. act, method of proceeding.

pro·cess n. continued forward movement; lapse of time; a series of actions or measures; a method of operation; (Anat.) a projecting part or growth; (Law) procedure; v.t. to subject to some process, as food or material. **procession** n. a moving line of people, cars, animals, etc.; regular progress. n. **-ional** a hymn sung during a church procession.

pro·claim v.t. to make known by public announcement; to declare. **proclamation** n. the act of announcing publicly; an official public announcement.

pro·cras·ti·nate v.i. to put off till some future time. **procrastination** n. **procrastinator** n.

pro·cre·ate v.t. to bring into being; to beget; to generate. **procreation** n. **procreative** a. having the power to beget; productive.

proc·tor n. (Law) one who manages the affairs of another in a court; one who supervises students in an examination.

proc·u·ra·tion n. management of another's affairs; power of attorney.

pro·cure v.t. to acquire; to obtain; to get; to bring about; v.i. to act as a procurer. **procurable** a. obtainable. **-ment** n. **-r** n.

prod v.t. to poke with something pointed; to goad; n. a pointed instrument; a poke.

prod·i·gal a. wasteful; spending recklessly; n. one who spends recklessly; a spendthrift.

prod·i·gy n. a person or thing causing wonder; a marvel; a very gifted person; a monster; a portent.

pro·duce v.t. to bring forth; to exhibit; to give birth to; to yield; to make; to cause; of a play, to present it on the state. **produce** n. that which is produced; product; agricultural products; crops. **-r** n.

prod·uct n. that which is produced; (Arith.) a number resulting from the multiplying of two or more numbers.

pro·fane a. not sacred; irreverent; blasphemous; vulgar; v.t. to treat with irreverence; to put to a wrong or unworthy use; to desecrate. **-ly** adv. **-ness** n. **-r** n. **profanity** n. profaneness; irreverence; the use of bad language.

pro·fess v.t. to make open declaration of; to confess publicly; to affirm belief in; to pretend to knowledge or skill in. **-ed** a. openly acknowledged. **-ion** n. occupation or calling, esp. one requiring learning. **-ional** a. engaged in for money, as opposed to amateur; n. one who makes a livelihood in sport or games.

pro·fes·sor n. a teacher of the highest rank in a university. **professorial** a. **-ially** adv. **professoriate** n. the office of a professor; his period of office; body of professors. **-ship** n.

pro·fi·cient a. thoroughly versed or qualified in any art or occupation; skilled; n. an expert. **-ly** adv. **proficience**, **proficiency** n.

pro·file n. an outline or contour; a portrait in a side view; the side face; short biographical sketch; v.t. to draw the outline of.

prof·it n. advantage or benefit; the excess of returns over expenditure; pecuniary gain in any transaction or occupation. **-able** a. yielding profit or gain; advantageous; helpful. **-ably** adv. **-ableness** n. **profiteer** n. one who makes excessive profits.

prof·li·gate a. abandoned to vice; dissolute; extravagant; n. a depraved person. **-ly** adv. **-ness** n.

pro·found a. deep; intellectually deep; learned; deeply felt. **-ly** adv. **profundity** n. depth of place, knowledge, skill, feeling.

pro·fuse a. giving or given generously; lavish; extravagant. **-ly** adv. **-ness**, **profusion** n. great, abundance.

prog·e·ny n. descendants; offspring; children.

prog·no·sis n. a forecast; (Med.) foretelling the course of a disease.

pro·gram, **programme** n. a plan or detailed notes of intended proceedings at a public entertainment, ceremony, etc.; a party policy at election time.

prog•ress *n.* a moving forward; advancement; development. **progress** *n.* the act of moving forward; onward movement; progress. **-ively** *adv.* **-iveness** *n.* **arithmetical progression,** a series of numbers increasing or decreasing by the same amount, e.g. 3, 6, 9, 12, 15, etc. **geometrical progression,** a series of numbers increasing or decreasing by a common ratio, e.g. 3, 9, 27, 81, etc.

pro•hib•it *v.t.* to forbid; to prevent; to hinder. **-er, -or** *n.* **-ion** *n.* the act of forbidding; interdict; the forbidding by law of manufacture, importation, sale, or purchase of alcoholic liquors. **-ionist** *n.* one in favor of prohibition. **-ive, -ory** *a.* tending to forbid, prevent, or exclude; exclusive. **-ively** *adv.*

pro•ject *v.t.* to throw or cast forward; to plan; to contrive; to throw a photographic image on a screen; *n.* a plan; a scheme; a task. **-ile** *a.* capable of being thrown; *n.* a heavy missile, esp. a shell or cannon ball. **-ion** *n.* the act of projecting; something that juts out; a plan; delineation; the representation on a plane of a curved surface or sphere; in psychology, mistaking for reality something which is only an image in the mind. **-ive** *a.* **-or** *n.* an apparatus for throwing photographic images, esp. films, on a screen.

pro•lapse *n.* (*Med.*) the falling down on a part of the body from its normal position, esp. womb or rectum.

pro•le•tar•i•an *a.* pert. to the proletariat; belonging to the working class; *n.* one of the proletariat. **proletariat** *n.* propertyless wage-earners who live by sale of their labor.

pro•lif•er•ous *a.* (*Biol.*) reproducing freely by cell division; developing anthers. **-ly** *adv.* **proliferate** *v.t.* to bear.

pro•lif•ic *a.* bringing forth offspring; fruitful, abundantly productive; bringing about results. **-ally** *adv.*

pro•lix *a.* long drawn out; diffuse; wordy. **-ly** *adv.* **-ity** *n.*

pro•loc•u•tor *n.* a chairman of an assembly.

pro•logue *n.* the preface or introduction to a discourse, poem, book, or performance, esp. the address spoken before a dramatic performance.

pro•long *v.t.* to lengthen out; to extend the duration of.

prom•e•nade *n.* a leisurely walk, generally in a public place; a place adapted for such a walk; a march of dancers.

prom•i•nent *a.* sticking out; projecting; conspicuous; distinguished. **-ly** *adv.* **prominence, prominency** *n.*

pro•mis•cu•ous *a.* mixed without order or distinction; indiscriminate. **-ly** *adv.*

prom•ise *n.* an undertaking to do or not to do something; cause or grounds for hope; *v.t.* to give one's word to do or not to do something; to give cause for expectation; to agree to give. **promising** *a.* likely to turn out well or to succeed; hopeful.

prom•is•so•ry *a.* containing a promise. **— note,** written agreement to pay sum to named person at specified date.

pro•mote *v.t.* to move forward; to move up to a higher rank or position; to encourage the growth or development of; to help organize a new business venture or company. **-r** *n.* a supporter; an initiator. **promotion** *n.* advancement; preferment; a higher rank, station, or position.

prompt *a.* ready and quick to act; done at once; punctual; *v.t.* to excite to action; to suggest; to help out (actor or speaker) by reading, suggesting next words. **-ly** *adv.*

pro•mul•gate *v.t.* to proclaim; to publish; to make known officially. **promulgation** *n.*

prone *a.* lying face downward; sloping; inclined; naturally disposed. **-ly** *adv.* **-ness** *n.* inclination; tendency.

prong *n.* one of the pointed ends of a fork; a spike.

pro•noun *n.* (*Gram.*) a word used instead of a noun.

pro•nounce *v.t.* to speak with the correct sound and accent; to speak distinctly; to utter formally or officially; to declare or affirm. **-d** *a.* strongly marked; very definite or decided. **-able** *a.* **-ment** *n.* a formal declaration. **-r** *n.* **pronouncing** *a.* teaching or indicating pronounciation. **pronunciation.**

proof *n.* something which proves; a test or trial; demonstration; evidence that convinces the mind and produces belief; argument; standard strength of alcoholic spirits; (*Print.*) a trial impression from type, on which corrections may be made; *a.* firm in resisting; impenetrable; serving as proof or designating a certain standard or quality. **-reader** *n.* one who corrects printer's proofs.

prop *v.t.* to support by placing something under or against; to sustain.

prop•a•gan•da *n.* the propagating of doctrines or principles. **propagandize** *v.t.* and *i.* to spread propaganda. **propagandist** *n.*

prop•a•gate *v.t.* to cause to multiply or reproduce by generation; to breed; to spread the knowledge of; to transmit or carry forward; *v.i.* to have young; to breed. **propagator** *n.* **propagation** *n.*

pro•pel *v.t.* to drive forward; to press onward by force; to push. *pr.p.* **-ling.** *pa.p.* **-led.** **-ler** *n.* one who, or that which, propels; a revolving shaft with blades for driving a ship or airplane.

pro•pen•si•ty *n.* bent of mind; leaning or inclination.

prop•er *a.* fit; suitable; correct or according to usage. **-ly** *adv.* **— fraction** (*Arith.*) one in which the numerator is less than the denominator.

prop•er•ty *n.* an inherent or essential quality or peculiarity; ownership; the thing owned; possessions; land; *pl.* theatrical requisites, as scenery, costumes, etc.

proph•e•cy *n.* the foretelling of future events; prediction; revelation of God's will. **prophesy** *v.t.* to predict; to utter by divine inspiration; **prophet** *n.* one who foretells future events; an inspired teacher or revealer of the Divine Will.

pro•phy•lac•tic *a.* *(Med.)* tending to prevent disease, preventive; *n.* medicine or treatment tending to prevent disease. **prophylaxis** *n.* preventive treatment of disease.

pro•pi•ti•ate *v.t.* to appease; to conciliate; to gain the favor of.

pro•po•nent *n.* one who supports or makes a proposal.

pro•por•tion *n.* relative size, number, or degree; comparison; relation between connected things or parts; *(Arith.)* equality of ratios; the rule of three; *n.pl.* dimensions; **-al** *a.* *n.* a number of quantity in arithmetical or mathematical proportion. **-ally** *adv.* **-ality** *n.* **-ate** *a.* **-ed** *a.* **-ment** *n.*

pro•pose *v.t.* to offer for consideration; to suggest; to nominate; *v.i.* to form a plan; to intend; to offer oneself in marriage. **proposal** an offer, esp. of marriage. **-r** *n.* **proposition** *n.* a proposal; a statement or assertion. **propositional** *a.*

pro•pri•e•tor *n.* one who is the owner of property, a business, restaurant, etc. made and sold by an individual or firm having the exclusive rights of manufacture and sale.

pro•pri•e•ty *n.* properness; correct conduct.

pro•pul•sion *n.* the act of driving forward. **propulsive, propulsory** *a.* tending, or having power, to propel.

pro•rate *v.t.* and *i.* to divide or distribute proportionally.

pro•scribe *v.t.* to put outside the protection of the law; to outlaw; to prohibit. **-r** *n.* **proscription** *n.* **proscriptive** *a.*

prose *n.* ordinary language in speech and writing; language not in verse; *a.* pert. to prose; not poetical; *v.i.* to write prose; to speak or write in a dull, tedious manner.

pros•e•cute *v.t.* to follow or pursue with a view to reaching or accomplishing something; *(Law)* to proceed against judicially; *v.i.* to carry on a legal suit. **prosecution** *n.* *(Law)* the institution and carrying on of a suit in a court of law; the party by which legal proceedings are instituted, as opposed to the *defense*.

pros•pect *n.* a wide view; anticipation; reasonable hope; promise of future good. *v.t.* and *i.* to search or explore (a region), esp. for precious metals, oil, etc. **-ive** *a.* looking forward; relating to the future. **-ively** *adv.* **-or** *n.* **-us** *n.* a preliminary statement of an enterprise.

pros•per *v.t.* to cause to succeed; *v.i.* to succeed; to do well. **-ity** *n.* **-ous** *a.* **-ously** *adv.*

pros•tate *n.* a small gland at the neck of the bladder in males.

pros•ti•tute *n.* a harlot; *v.t.* to make a prostitute of; to put to base, infamous, or unworthy use. **prostitution** *n.*

pros•trate *a.* lying on the ground, esp. face downwards; mentally or physically exhausted; *v.t.* to lay flat, as on the ground; to bow down in adoration; to overcome. **prostration** *n.*

pro•tag•o•nist *n.* the principal actor in a drama; a leading character.

pro•tect *v.t.* to defend; to guard; to put a tariff on imports to encourage home industry. **-ion** *n.* defending from injury or harm; state of being defended; that which defends. **-ive** *a.* affording protection; sheltering. **-ively** *adv.* **-or** *n.* one who defends.

pro•te•in *n.* a nitrogenous compound required for all animal life processes.

pro•test *v.i.* to assert formally; to make a declaration against; *v.t.* to affirm solemnly; to object to. **protest** *n.* a declaration of objection. **-ant** *n.* one who holds an opposite opinion.

Protestant *a.* pert. or belonging to any branch of the Western Church outside the Roman communion; *n.* a member of such a church. **Protestantism** *n.* **protestation** *n.* a solemn declaration, esp. of dissent.

pro•to- *prefix* first; hence, original; primitive. **-plasm** *n.* a semi-fluid substance forming the basis of the primitive tissue of animal and vegetable life; living matter. **-plasmatic, -plasmic** *a.* **-type** *n.* original or model from which anything is copied; a pattern. *a.* **Protozoa** *n.pl.* first or lowest division of animal kingdom, consisting of microscopic, unicellular organisms. **-zoon** *n.* a member of this division. **-zoal, -zoan, -zoic** *a.*

pro•to•col *n.* an original copy; a rough draft, esp. a draft of terms signed by negotiating parties as the basis of a formal treaty or agreement; rules of diplomatic etiquette.

pro•ton *n.* in physics, the unit of positive electricity, found in the nuclei of all atoms.

pro•tract *v.t.* to lengthen; to draw out; to prolong; to draw to scale. **-ed** *a.* prolonged; long drawn out; tedious. **-ion** *n.* **-ive** *a.* **-or** *n.* a mathematical instrument for measuring angles; *(Anat.)* a muscle which draws forward or extends a limb.

pro•trude *v.t.* and *i.* to stick out; to project; to thrust forward. **protrusion** *n.* **protrusive** *a.*

pro•tu•ber•ant *a.* bulging; swelling out; prominent. **-ly** *adv.* **protuberance** *n.*

proud *a.* haughty; self-respecting. **-ly** *adv.*

prove *v.t.* to try by experiment; to ascertain as fact, by evidence; to demonstrate; to show; to establish the validity of; to be found by trial. **pr.p. proving. pa.p. -d** or **-n. pa.t. provable** *a.* able to be proved.

prov•e•nance *n.* source or place of origin.

proverb *n.* a short pithy saying to express a truth or point a moral; an adage. **Proverbs** *n.pl.* *(Bib.)* book of Old Testament. **-ial** *a.* well-known. **-ially** *adv.*

pro•vide *v.t.* to supply; to furnish; to get or make ready for future use. **providence** *n.* prudence; wise economy; God's care; an event regarded as an act of God. **Providence** *n.* God Himself. **provident** *a.* prudent; thrifty. **providently** *adv.*

prov•ince *n.* a division of a country or empire; an administrative district; a district under the jurisdiction of an archbishop; a department of knowledge; *n.* an inhabitant of a province.

pro•vi•sion *n.* the act of providing; measures taken beforehand; store esp. of food (generally in *pl.*); a condition or proviso; **-al** *a.* temporary; adopted for the time being. **-ally** *adv.*

pro•vi•so *n.* a condition or stipulation in a deed or contract. *pl.* **-s** or **-es.** **-ry** *a.* containing a proviso or condition.

pro•voke *v.t.* to excite or stimulate to action, esp. to arouse to anger or passion; to bring about or call forth. **provoking** *a.* **provocation** *n.* the act of provoking. **provocative** *a.* serving or tending to provoke. **provocatively** *adv.* **provocativeness** *n.*

prow•ess *n.* bravery, esp. in war; valor.

prowl *v.i.* to roam about stealthily.

prox•i•mate *a.* next or nearest; closest; immediately following or preceding. **-ly** *adv.* **proximity** *n.* being next in time, place, etc.

prox•y *n.* an authorized agent or substitute; one deputed to act for another; a writing empowering one person to vote for another.

prude *n.* a woman of affected or over-sensitive modesty or reserve. **prudish** *a.*

pru•dent *a.* cautious and judicious; careful; not extravagant. **-ly** *adv.* **prudence** *n.* **prudential** *a.* **-ially** *adv.*

prune *n.* a dried plum.

prune *v.t.* to cut off dead parts, excessive branches.

Prus•sia *n.* (*Geog.*) formerly the leading state of Germany, and the recognized home of German militarism. **-n** *n./a.* **-n blue,** a deep blue salt of potassium and iron, used as a pigment.

pry *v.i.* to look curiously; to peer; to nose about.

psalm *n.* a sacred song or hymn. **the Psalms** (*Bib.*) a book of the Old Testament. **psalmnist** *n.* a writer of psalms.

pseu•d(o)- *prefix* false, used in many derivatives to signify, false; pretended; sham; not real; wrongly held to be, etc. **-nym** *n.* a fictitious name; a pen name.

pso•ri•a•sis *n.* (*Med.*) chronic skin disease.

psy•che *n.* the soul personified; the principle of life.

psy•chi•a•try *n.* study and treatment of mental disorders. **psychiatrist** *n.* a specialist in mental disorders.

psy•chic(al) *a.* pert. to soul, spirit, or mind; spiritualistic.

psy•cho•a•nal•y•sis *n.* process of studying the unconscious mind; **psychoanalyze** *v.t.* **psychoanalyst** *n.* **psychoanalytic(al).**

psy•chol•o•gy *n.* the scientific study of the mind, its activities, and human and animal behavior. **psychological** *a.* **psychologically** *adv.* **psychologist** *n.*

psy•cho•pa•thol•o•gy *n.* the science or study of mental diseases. **psychopathy** *n.* mental affliction. **psychopath** *n.* one so afflicted. **psychopathic** *a.*

psy•cho•sis *n.* a general term for any disorder of the mind. *pl.* **psychoses.**

psy•cho•so•mat•ic *a.* of mind and body as

a unit; treatment of physical diseases as having a mental origin.

psy•cho•ther•a•py *n.* the treatment of disease through the mind, e.g. by hypnotism, auto-suggestion, etc. **psychotherapeutic (-al)** *a.*

pto•maine *n.* substance, usually poisonous, found in putrefying organic matter.

pu•ber•ty *n.* the earliest age at which an individual is capable of reproduction. **pubescence** *n.* the period of sexual development; puberty. **pubescent** *a.*

pub•lic *a.* of, or pert. to, the people; not private or secret; open to general use; accessible to all; serving the people; *n.* community or its members; a section of community. **-ly** *adv.* **ation** *n.* making known to the public; proclamation; printing a book, etc. for sale or distribution; a book, periodical, magazine, etc. **publicize** *v.t.* to make widely known; to advertize. **publicist** *n.* one versed in, or who writes on, international law, or matters of political or economic interest. **publicity** *n.* the state of being generally known; notoriety; advertisement. **— prosecutor,** the legal officer appointed to prosecute criminals in serious cases on behalf of the state. **— school,** one of a system of schools, maintained at public expense.

pub•lish *v.t.* to make general known; to proclaim; to print and issue for sale (books, music, etc.); to put into circulation. **-er** *n.*

puck *n.* a rubber disk used in ice hockey.

puck•er *v.t.* and *i.* to gather into small folds or wrinkles; *n.* a wrinkle; a fold; **-y** *a.*

pud•ding *n.* name of various forms of cooked foods, usually in a soft mass, served as a dessert.

pud•dle *n.* a small pool of dirty water; a mixture of clay and water used as rough cement.

puff *n.* a short blast of breath or wind; its sound; a small quantity of smoke, etc.; a swelling; a light pastry; a soft pad for applying powder; *v.i.* to send out smoke, etc. in puffs; to breathe hard; to pant; to swell up; *v.t.* to send out in a puff; to blow out; to smoke hard; to cause to swell.

pug *n.* a small, snub-nosed dog; *a.* **— nose** *n.* a turned-up nose.

pu•gil•ism *n.* the art of fighting with the fists; boxing. **pugilist** *n.* a boxer. **pugilistic** *a.*

pug•na•cious *a.* given to fighting; quarrelsome. **-ly** *adv.*

pull *v.t.* to draw towards one; to drag; to haul; to tug at; to pluck; to row a boat; *v.i.* to draw with force; to tug; *n.* act of pulling; force exerted by it; a tug; a means of pulling; effort.

pul•ley *n.* a small wheel with a grooved rim on which runs a rope, used for

pulley

hauling or lifting weights.

Pull•man•car *n.* a railway car.

pul•mo- *prefix*, the lung. **-nary** *a.* pert. to or affecting the lungs.

pulp *n.* a soft, moist, cohering mass of animal or vegetable matter; the soft, succulent part of fruit; the material of which paper is made.

pul•pit *n.* elevated place in a church for preacher.

pul•sate *v.t.* to beat or throb, as the heart; to vibrate; to quiver. **pulsation** *n.*

pulse *n.* the beating or throbbing of the heart or blood vessels, esp. of the arteries; the place, esp. on the wrist, where this rhythmical beat is felt; any measured or regular beat. *v.i.* to throb or pulsate.

pul•ver•i•ze *v.t.* to reduce to a fine powder; to smash or demolish; *v.i.* to fall down into dust. **pulverization** *n.* **-r** *n.*

pu•ma *n.* a large American carnivorous animal of the cat family; cougar.

pum•ice *n.* Also — **stone,** a light, porous variety of lava, used for cleaning, polishing, etc.

pump *n.* an appliance used for raising water, putting in or taking out air or liquid, etc.; *v.t.* to raise with a pump, as water; to free from water by means of a pump; to extract information by artful questioning.

pump *n.* a low, thin-soled shoe.

pump•kin *n.* a plant of the gourd family; its fruit, used as food.

pun *n.* a play on words similar in sound but different in sense; *v.i.* to use puns. *pr.p.*

punch *n.* a drink made of fruit juices, sugar, and water, sometimes carbonated or with liquor.

punch *n.* a tool used for making holes or dents; a machine for perforating or stamping; *v.t.* to perforate, dent, or stamp with a punch.

punch *v.t.* to strike with the fist; to beat; to bruise.

punc•tu•al *a.* arriving at the proper or fixed time; prompt; not late.

punc•tu•ate *v.t.* to separate into sentences, clauses, etc. by periods, commas, colons, etc.; to emphasize in some significant manner; to interrupt at intervals. **punctuation** *n.* the act or system separating by the use of punctuation marks (the period, comma, colon, semi-colon, etc.).

punc•ture *n.* an act of pricking; a small hole made by a sharp point; a perforation; *v.t.* to make a hole with a sharp point.

pun•gent *a.* sharply affecting the taste or smell; stinging; sarcastic; caustic. **-ly** *adv.* **pungency** *n.*

pun•ish *v.t.* to inflict a penalty for an offense; to chastise. **-able** *a.* **-ment** *n.* **punitive** *a.* pert. to or inflicting punishment.

punt *v.t.* and *i.* to kick a football, when dropped from the hands, before it touches the ground; *n.* such a kick.

pu•ny *a.* small and feeble; petty. **puniness** *n.*

pup *n.* a puppy or young dog; a young seal; *v.i.* to bring forth puppies or whelps. *pr.p.* **-ping.** *pa.p., pa.t.* **-ped.**

pu•pil *n.* a student; a boy or girl under the care of a guardian; the small circular opening in the center of the iris of the eye.

pup•pet *n.* a marionette; a person whose actions are completely controlled by another. **-ry** *n.* a puppet show.

pur•chase *v.t.* to buy; to obtain by any outlay of labor, time, sacrifice, etc.; *(Law)* to obtain by any means other than inheritance; *n.* acquisition of anything for a price or equivalent; a thing bought.

pure *a.* free from all extraneous matter; untainted; spotless; blameless; unsullied; chaste; innocent; absolute; theoretical, not applied. **-ly** *adv.* entirely; solely. **-ness** *n.* **purity** *n.* freedom from all extraneous matter; freedom from sin or evil.

pu•rée *n.* a thick soup.

purge *v.t.* to purify; to cleanse; to clear out; to clear from guilt, accusation, or the charge of a crime, etc.; to cleanse the bowels by taking a cathartic medicine; *n.* a cleansing, esp. of the bowels; a purgative. **purgative** *a.* having the power of purging; *n.* any medicine which will cause evacuation of bowels. **purgatory** *a.* tending to cleanse; purifying; expiatory; *n.* in R.C. faith, place where souls of dead are purified by suffering; *(Fig.)* a place or state of torment.

pu•ri•fy *v.t.* to make pure, clear, or clean; to free form impurities; to free from guilt or defilement. **purification** *n.* **purificative** *a.* **purifier** *n.*

pur•ist *n.* an advocate of extreme care or precision in choice of words, etc.; a stickler for correctness.

Pu•ri•tan *n.* a member of the extreme Protestant party, who desired further *purification* of the Church after the Elizabethan reformation; *(l.c.)* a person of extreme strictness in morals or religion. **-ically** *adv.* **-ism** *n.* doctrine and practice of Puritans; narrow-mindedness.

purl *n.* an embroidered border; a knitting stitch that is reverse of plain stitch.

pur•loin *v.i.* to steal; to pilfer.

pur•ple *n.* a color between crimson and violet; robe of this color, formerly reserved for royalty; royal dignity; *a.* purple-colored; dark red; *v.i.* to make or dye a purple color; *v.i.* to become purple. **born to the purple,** of princely rank.

pur•port *n.* meaning; apparent meaning; import; aim.

pur•pose *n.* object in view; aim; end; plan; intention; effect; purport; *v.t.* to intend; to mean to. **-ly** *adv.* intentionally; expressly. **-ful** *a.* determined resolute. **-fully** *adv.* **-less** *a.* aimless. **-lessly** *adv.* **purposive** *a.* done with a purpose.

pur•pu•ra *n.* *(Med.)* the appearance of purple patches under the skin, caused by hemorrhage; shellfish, yielding purplish fluid.

purr *n.* a low, murmuring sound made by a cat; *v.i.* to utter such a sound.

purse *n.* a small bag or pouch to carry money in; money offered as a prize, or collected as a present; money.

pur•sue *v.t.* to follow with the aim of overtaking; to run after; to chase; to aim at; to seek; to continue; *v.i.* to go on; to proceed; -r *n.* **pursuance** *n.* the act of pursuing. **pursuant** *a.* done in consequence, or performance, of anything. **pursuit** *n.* the act of pursuing; a running after; chase; profession occupation. **pursuivant** *n.* an attendant.

pur•vey *v.t.* (*Brit.*) to furnish or provide; to supply, esp. provisions. **-ance** *n.* act of purveying; supplies; former royal prerogative of requisitioning supplies, or enforcing personal service. **-or** *n.*

pus *n.* the yellowish-white matter produced by suppuration.

push *v.t.* to move or try to move away by pressure; to drive or impel; to press hard; to press or urge forward; to shove; *v.i.* to make a thrust; to press hard in order to move; *n.* a thrust; any pressure or force applied; emergency; enterprise; (*Mil.*) an advance or attack on a large scale. **-er** *n.* **-ing** *a.* given to pushing oneself or one's claims; self-assertive. **-ingly** *adv.*

pus•tule *n.* a small swelling or pimple containing pus. **pustular, pustulous** *a.*

put *v.t.* to place; to set; to lay; to apply; to state; to propose; to throw; *v.i.* to go. *pr.p.* **-ting.** *pa.p.* and *pa.t.* **put.** *n.* a throw, esp. of a heavy weight. **to put about** (*Naut.*) to alter a ship's course.

pu•ta•tive *a.* commonly thought; supposed; reputed. **-ly** *adv.* **putation** *n.*

pu•tre•fy *v.t.* and *i.* to make or become rotten; to decompose; to rot. **putrefaction** *n.* the rotting of animal or vegetable matter; rottenness; decomposition. **putrefactive** *a.*

putt *v.t.* and *i.* (Golf) to hit a ball in the direction of the hole; *n.* the stroke so made in golf; the throw of the weight. **-er** *n.* one who putts; a short golf club.

put•ter *v.i.* to work or act in a feeble, unsystematic way; to dawdle.

put•ty *n.* a kind of paste or cement, used by plasterers; *v.t.* to fix, fill up, etc. with putty.

puz•zle *n.* a bewildering or perplexing question; a problem, etc. requiring clever thinking to solve it; a conundrum; *v.t.* to perplex; to bewilder; (with 'out') to solve after hard thinking; (with 'over') to think hard over; -r *n.* **puzzling** *a.* bewildering, perplexing.

Pyg•my, Pigmy *n.* one of a race of dwarf Negroes of C. Africa. (*l.c.*) a very small person or thing; a dwarf; *a.* diminutive.

py•or•rhe•a *n.* (*Med.*) a dental discharge of pus from the gums. Also **pyorrhoea.**

pyr•a•mid *n.* a solid figure on a triangular, square, or polygonal base, and with sloping sides meeting at an apex; a structure of this shape. **-al** *a.* pert. to, or having the form of a pyramid. **-ally** *adv.*

pyre *n.* a pile of wood for burning a dead body; funeral pile.

py•ret•ic *a.* (*Med.*) pert. to producing, or relieving, fever; feverish. **pyrexia** *n.* fever.

py•rite *n.* a yellow mineral formed of sulphur and iron; iron pyrites. **pyrites** *n.pl.* a name for many compounds of metals with sulphur, esp. iron pyrites, or copper pyrites. **pyritic, pyritiferous, pyritous** *a.* pert. to, or yielding, pyrites.

py•ro- *prefix,* fire, used in many derivatives. — **electricity** *n.* the property possessed by some crystals, of becoming electrically polar when they are heated.

py•ro•ma•ni•a *n.* a mania for setting things on fire. **pyromaniac** *n.*

py•ro•tech•nics *n.pl.* the art of making fireworks; the art of displaying them. Also **pyrotechny. pyrotechnic, pyrotechnical** *a.*

Py•thag•o•ras *n.* a Greek philosopher and mathematician (582-507 B.C.).

py•thon *n.* a large, non-poisonous snake that kills its prey by crushing it; a spirit.

quack v.i. to cry like a duck; n. cry of duck or like sound; one who pretends to skill in medicine; a charlatan; a. pert. to quackery. **-ery** n. **-salver** n. a quack doctor.

quad·ran·gle n. in geometry, a plane figure having four sides and angles; a square surrounded by buildings. **quadrangular** a.

quad·rant n. the fourth part of the area of a circle; an arc of 90°; in gunnery, an instrument to mark the degrees of a gun's elevation.

quad·rate a. having four sides and four right angles; divisible by four (used in antaomical names); n. square; v.i. to suit. **quadratic** a. pert. to, or resembling, a square; (Alg.) involving the second power of the unknown quantity, esp. in **quadratic equation. quadrature** n. the act of squaring or reducing to a square.

quad·ri·cen·ten·ni·al a. pert. to a period of four hundred years; n. the four-hundredth anniversary.

quad·ri·lat·er·al a. having four sides; n. (Geom.) a plane figure having four sides.

qua·dril·lion n. a number represented in the Fr. and U.S. notation by one with 15 ciphers annexed.

quad·ri·no·mi·al a. (Alg.) consisting of four terms.

quad·ri·par·tite a. divided into four parts.

quad·ru·mane n. an animal which has all four feet formed like hands. **quadrumanous** a. four-handed.

quad·ru·ped n. an animal having four feet; a. having four feet.

qua·dru·ple a. fourfold; n. a sum four times as great as another; v.t. to multiply by four; v.i. to be multiplied by four. **-t** n. one of four children born at a birth. **quadruplicate** v.t. to multiply by four; n. one of four things corresponding exactly; a. fourfold. **quadruplication** n.

quaff v.t. and v.i. to swallow in large drafts; n. a drink.

quag·mire n. soft, wet land, yielding under feet. **quaggy** a. boggy.

quail v.i. to lose spirit; to flinch.

quail n. a game bird.

quaint a. interestingly old-fashioned or odd; whimsical. **-ly** adv. **-ness** n.

quake v.i. to shake with emotion; to quiver or vibrate; n. a trembling.

Quak·er n. a member of a religious sect founded in the 17th cent. **-ism** n.

qual·i·fy v.t. to describe (as); to prepare by requisite training for special duty; to furnish with the legal title to; v.i. to show oneself fit for. **qualifier** n. **qualifiable** a. **qualification** n. condition of being qualified; any acquirement that fits a person for an office or employment; restriction.

qual·i·ty n. a particular property inherent in a substance; an essential attribute, distinguishing feature, or characteristic; superiority of sound, tonal color. **qualitative** a. relating to quality; concerned with quality.

qualm n. a sudden attack of illness, distress; a scruple of conscience.

quan·da·ry n. a state of perplexity; a dilemma.

quan·ti·fy v.t. to measure. **quantification** n.

quan·ti·ty n. property of things ascertained by measuring; number; pl. profusion. **quantitative** a. relating to quantity.

quan·tum n. amount; a specified or required amount. pl. **quanta.**

quar·an·tine n. isolation of infected persons to prevent spread of serious disease; v.t. to put under quarantine.

quar·rel n. rupture of friendly relations; an angry altercation; v.i. to dispute; to disagree. **-er** pr.p. and n. **-some** a. contentious.

quar·ry n. an excavation whence stone is dug for building; v.t. to dig from a quarry. **quarried** pa.p. and pa.t.

quar·ry n. prey; victim.

quart n. the fourth part of a gallon.

quar·ter n. fourth part; (U.S. and Canada) one fourth of a dollar, or the coin valued at this amount; one of the four cardinal points of the compass; a territory; pl. assigned position; lodgings, esp. for soldiers; v.t. to divide into four equal parts; to furnish with shelter; v.i. to have temporary residence. **-ing** n. an assignment of quarters for soldiers. **-ly** a. occurring every quarter of a year; n. a magazine published four times a year; adv. by quarters; once in a quarter of a year. **-deck** n. a part of deck of a ship which extends from stern to mainmast. **-master** n. (Mil.) an officer in charge of quarters, clothing. **-master -sergeant** n. the N.C.O. assistant to the quartermaster.

quar·tet, quartette n. (Mus.) a composition of four parts, each performed by a single voice or instrument; a. denoting the size of a book in which the paper is folded to give four leaves to the sheet.

quartz n. kinds of mineral, consisting of pure silica or silicon dioxide.

quash v.t. to quell; (Law) to annul, or make void.

qua·si as if; as it were; in a certain sense or degree.

qua·train n. (Pros.) a stanza of four lines.

qua·ver v.i. to tremble, or vibrate; to sing with tremulous modulations; n. a trembling, esp. of the voice.

quay n. a landing place for loading and unloading of ships. **-age** n. payment for use of a quay.

quea·sy a. affected with nausea; fastidious. **queasily** adv. **queasiness** n.

queen n. woman who is the sovereign of a kingdom; the sovereign of a swarm of bees, ants, etc.; one of the chief pieces in a game of chess; v.i. to act the part of a queen. **-ly** a. majestic. **-liness** n. **-hood** n. position of a queen. **— dowager** n. the widow of a king. **— mother** n. a queen dowager who is also mother of reigning monarch. **— regent** n. a queen reigning in her own right.

queer a. odd; of a questionable character. **-ly** adv. **-ish** a. somewhat queer. **-ness** n.

quell v.t. to subdue; to suppress forcibly. **-er** n.

quench v.t. to put out, as fire or light; to

slake (thirst). -able, -less *a.* -er *n.*

quer·u·lous *a.* peevish; fretful. -ly *adv.* -ness *n.*

que·ry *n.* an inquiry; a mark of interrogation; *v.t.* to inquire into.

quest *n.* search; the thing sought; *v.i.* to search; to seek.

ques·tion *n.* interrogation; inquiry; that which is asked; subject of debate; a problem; *v.t.* to inquire of by asking questions; to take objection to. -able *a.* suspicious. -ably *adv.* -ableness, -er *n.* — mark *n.* a mark of interrogation (?). out of the question, not to be thought of.

ques·tion·naire *n.* a list of questions.

queue *n.* a pigtail.

quib·ble *n.* an evasion of the point in question by a play upon words; equivocation; *v.i.* to use quibbles. -r *n.*

quick *a.* prompt; rapid; hasty; impatient; *n.* sensitive flesh under nails; *(Fig.)*one's tenderest susceptibilities. -ly *adv.* rapidly; promptly. -ness *n.* -en *v.t.* to make sprightly; to hasten; to stimulate; *v.i.* to move with greater rapidity. -ener *n.* -ening *n.* becoming quick. -sand *n.* sand, readily yielding to pressure, esp. if loose and mixed with water. -silver *n.* mercury. -step *n.* a lively dance step.

quid *n.* a portion suitable for chewing, esp. of tobacco; a cud.

quid·di·ty *n.* a trifling nicety; the essence of anything.

qui·es·cent *a.* motionless; at rest. -ly *adv.* quiescence, quiescency *n.*

qui·et *a.* peaceful; not agitated; of gentle disposition; *n.* calm; tranquillity; *v.t.* to reduce to a state of rest; to calm; to allay or appease; *v.i.* to become quiet. -en *(Dial.) v.t.* and *v.i.* to quiet. -ly *adv.* -ness *n.* -ude *n.* freedom from noise, alarm; tranquillity; repose. -us *n.* final acquittance, of debt.

quill *n.* a large, hollow feather used as a pen; a prickle, as of a porcupine; an implement for striking the strings of certain instruments.

quilt *n.* any thick, warm coverlet; *v.t.* to stitch together, like a quilt, with a soft filling; to pad. -ed. *a.*

qui·na·ry *a.* consisting of, or arranged in, fives.

quince *n.* a hard, yellow, acid fruit, somewhat like an apple.

qui·nine *n.* a bitter alkaloid obtained from various species of cinchona bark; a tonic and febrifuge. quinic *a.*

Quin·qua·ge·si·ma *n.* the Sunday before Ash Wednesday, so-called because fifty days before Easter.

quin·sy *n.* a severe inflammation of the throat and tonsils.

quin·tes·sence *n.* the perfect embodiment of a thing. quintessential *a.*

quin·tet, quintette *n. (Mus.)* a composition for five voices or instruments; a set of five.

quin·til·lion *n.(U.S. and France)* a number represented by one with 18 ciphers following.

quin·tu·ple *a.* multiplied by five; to multiply by five. -ts *n.pl.* five children at a birth *(Colloq.* quints).

quip *n.* a sarcastic turn of phrase; a witty saying. -ster *n.*

quire *n.* 24 sheets of paper of the same size, the twentieth part of a ream.

quirk *n.* sudden twist; a quibble; a peculiarity. -y *a.*

quit *v.t.* to cease from; to give up; *v.i.* to stop doing a thing; *a.* released from obligation. -ting *pr.p.* quit or -ted *pa.p.* and *pa.t.* -tance *n.* discharge from a debt or obligation. -ter *n.* a person easily discouraged.

quite *adv.* completely; entirely.

quiv·er *n.* a sheath for holding arrows.

quiv·er *v.i.* to shake with a tremulous motion; *n.* the act of quivering; a tremor.

Qui·xo·te *n.* the hero of the great romance of Miguel Cervantes. quixotic *a.* like Don Quixote; ideally and extravagantly romantic. quixotically *adv.* quixotism, quixotry *n.*

quiz *n.* a test or examination; a hoax; *v.t.* to question. -zing *pr.p.* -zed *pa.p.* and *pa.t.* -zer *n.* -zical *a.* odd; teasing.

quoin *n.* a cornerstone; *(Gun.)* a metallic wedge inserted under the breech of a gun to raise it; *(Print.)* a small wooden wedge used to lock the types in the galley etc.

quoit *n.* a flat, iron ring to be pitched at a fixed object in play; *pl.* game of throwing these onto a peg; *v.i.* to play at quoits.

quon·dam *a.* that was once; sometime.

quo·rum *n.* number of members present at a meeting to make its transactions valid.

quo·ta *n.* a proportional share.

quote *v.t.* to repeat a passage from; to state a price for; *pl.* quotation marks. quotation *n.* — marks *n.pl.* marks ("—") to indicate beginning and end of a quotation.

quo·tid·i·an *a.* daily; *n.* thing returning daily, esp. fever.

quo·tient *n.* number resulting from division of one number by another.

rab·bet n. a groove made to form, with a corresponding edge, a close joint; v.t. to cut such an edge.

rab·bi n. a Jewish teacher of the Law. **-nic (al)** a.

rab·bit n. a small, burrowing rodent mammal, like the hare, but smaller. **— hutch** n. an enclosure for rearing tame rabbits.

rab·ble n. a noisy, disorderly crowd; v.t. to mob.

ra·bid a. affected with rabies. **-ly** adv. **-ness, -ity** n.

ra·bies n. canine madness; hydrophobia.

rac·coon, racoon n. one of a genus of plantigrade carnivorous mammals of N. America.

raccoon

race n. distinct variety of human species; a peculiar breed, as of horses, etc.; lineage; descent. **racial** a. pert. to race or lineage. **racially** adv. **racialism, racism** n. animosity shown to peoples of different race.

race n. rapid motion; a contest involving speed; v.t. to cause to run rapidly; v.i. to run swiftly; of an engine, pedal, to move rapidly without control. **-r** n. one who races; a racehorse, yacht, car, etc. used for racing. **—horse** n. a horse bred to run for a price. **—track** n. a track used for horse-racing, etc. **racing** n.

ra·chis n. an axial structure, such as vertebral column in animals; pl. **rachides**. **rachitic** a. having rickets. **rachitis** n. rickets.

rack n. an instrument for stretching; an open framework for displaying; a straight cogged bar to gear with a toothed wheel to produce linear motion from rotary motion, or vice versa; v.t. to stretch almost to breaking point; to overstrain; to place in a rack. **-ed** a. **-ing** a. agonizing (pain). **— and ruin**, destruction.

rack·et, racquet n. bat used in tennis, etc.; pl. a ball game played in a paved court with walls.

rack·et n. a confused, clattering din; v.i. to make clatter.

ra·cy a. lively; pungent. **racily** adv. **raciness** n.

ra·dar n. radiolocation or apparatus used in it.

ra·di·al a. pert. to a ray; branching out like spokes of a wheel.

ra·di·an n. angle subtended by an arc of a circle equal in length to the radius.

ra·di·ant a. emitting rays; beaming; n. (Astron.) point in sky from which a shower of meteors appears to come. **radiance, radiancy** n. brilliancy; splendor. **-ly** adv.

ra·di·ate v.i. to shine; v.t. to emit rays, as heat, etc.; a. with rays diverging from a center. **radiation** n. emission and diffusion of rays from central point.

radiator n. any device which emits rays of heat or light; in motoring, apparatus to split up and cool circulating water in water-cooling system.

rad·i·cal a. pert. to the root; thorough; of extreme or advanced liberal views; n. (Gram.) a root; a politician who advocates thorough reforms; (Bot.) a radicle; (Math.) a quantity expressed as the root of another. **-ly** adv. **-ness** n.

rad·i·cle n. (Med.) the initial fibril of a nerve; (Bot.) primary root of an embryo plant.

ra·di·o- used in forming compound terms with the meaning of "rays", as in **radioactive** a. emitting from an atomic nucleus invisible rays which penetrate matter. **radioactivity** n. **radioelement** n. metallic chemical element having radioactive properties. **radiograph** n. an instrument for measuring and recording the intensity of the heat given off by the sun. **radiographer, radiography** n. **radiology** n. the science of radioactivity in medicine. **radiologist** n. **radioscopy** n. examination by X rays. **radiotherapy, radiotherapeutics** n. treatment of disease by X rays.

ra·di·o n. wireless telegraphy; apparatus for reception of broadcast. **-gram** n. a telegram transmitted by radio.

rad·ish n. an herb with pungent edible root.

ra·di·um n. a metallic, radioactive element.

ra·di·us n. a straight line from center of circle to circumference; distance from any one place; pl. **-es, radii**.

ra·dix n. a root; (Anat.) the point of origin of a structure, as the root of a tooth; (Math.) fundamental base of a system of logarithms; pl. **-es, radices**.

ra·don n. a gaseous, radioactive element.

raf·fi·a n. fiber from a cultivated palm used for baskets.

raf·fle n. a lottery; v.t. to sell by raffle. **-r** n.

raft n. a mass of logs chained together for transportation down a river; v.i. to proceed by raft.

raf·ter n. a sloping beam, from the ridge to the eaves, to which the roof covering is attached; v.t. to provide with rafters.

rag n. a fragment of cloth; pl. tattered attire; a. made of rags. **-man** n. one who collects rags. **-time** n. dance music marked by strong syncopation. **-weed** n. a widespread weed, common cause of hay fever.

rag v.t. to tease. **-ging** pr.p. **-ged** pa.t. and pa.p.

rage n. extreme anger; fashion; v.i. to be furious with anger; to proceed violently and without check. **raging** a. **ragingly** adv.

rag·ged a. worn to tatters; imperfectly performed. **-ly** adv. **-ness** n.

rag·lan n. wide sleeves running up to the neck, not to the shoulders.

raid n. a hostile incursion depending on surprise and rapidity; v.t. to make a sudden attack upon. **-er** n.

rail n. bars of steel on which the flanged

wheels of vehicles run; a horizontal bar for support; v.t. to enclose with rails; to send by railway. -ing n. material for rails; a construction of rails. -road n. a road on which steel rails are laid for wheels to run on; a system of such rails and all equipment.

rail n. wading bird.

rail v.i. to use insolent language; to utter abuse. -er n. -lery n. good-humored banter; ridicule.

rain n. condensed moisture, falling in drops from clouds; v.t. and v.i. to pour down like rain. -bow n. arch showing seven prismatic colors and formed by refraction and reflection of sun's rays in falling rain. — check n. a ticket for a future performance, when one is stopped by rain. -coat n. a light, rainproof overcoat. -fall n. the amount of rain, in inches, which falls in a particular place. -iness n. -less n. -proof a. impervious to rain. -y a.

raise v.t. to cause to rise; to elevate; to produce by cultivation; to rear; to heighten (voice). -d a. elevated. raising n.

rai·sin n. a dried grape.

rake n. a long-handled garden implement; v.t. and v.i. to scrape with a toothed implement; sweep over.

rake n. a dissolute man of fashion. rakish a. rakishly adv.

rake n. inclination of masts from the perpendicular; v.i. to incline from perpendicular. rakish a. having a backward inclination of the masts. rakishly adv.

ral·ly v.t. and v.i. to reassemble; to collect and restore order; to recover (health); to return a ball (in tennis); n. outdoor demonstration; lively exchange of strokes in tennis.

ram n. male sheep; a swinging beam with a metal head for battering; (Astron.) Aries, one of the signs of zodiac; v.t. to drive against with violence. -ming pr.p. -med pa.t. and pa.p. -er n.

ram·ble v.i. to walk without definite route; to talk or write incoherently; n. a short walk. -r n. one who rambles. rambling a. wandering.

ram·i·fy v.t. and v.i. to branch out in various directions. ramification n. subdivision proceeding from a main structure.

ramp v.i. to rear up on hind legs; n. a gradual slope.

ram·page n. a state of excitement, as on the rampage; v.i. to rush about, in a rage; to act violently. -ous a.

ram·pant a. rearing; violent; rank. rampancy n.

ram·part n. mound of earth around fortified place; v.t. to strengthen with ramparts.

ram·rod n. a rod for cleaning barrel of a rifle, etc.

ram·shack·le a. tumbledown; beyond repair.

ran pa.t. of run.

ranch n. prairie land for sheep- and cattle-rearing; v.i. to keep a ranch. -er n. man who owns or works on a ranch.

ran·cid a. having a rank smell. -ly adv.

-ness, -ity n.

ran·cor n. bitter and inveterate ill-feeling. -ous a. evincing intense hatred; malignant. -ously adv.

ran·dom a. done haphazardly; n. in phrase, at random, haphazard.

rang pa.t. of ring.

range n. to set in a row; to rove over; v.i. to roam; to fluctuate between, as prices, etc.; n. limits, within which something is possible; a large kitchen stove; line of mountains; place for practice shooting; pastureland. -er n. keeper of park or forest. rangy a. roaming; long-limbed.

rank n. soldiers standing side by side; grade in armed services; relative position; pl. enlisted soldiers; v.t. to arrange in order, or division; to place abreast; v.i. to be placed in a class; to possess social distinction. -er n. -ing n. arrangement.

rank a. offensively strong of smell; rancid. -le v.i. to remain a sore point with. -ly adv. -ness n.

ran·sack v.t. to search thoroughly.

ran·som n. a price paid for release of prisoner; v.t. to redeem from captivity.

rant v.i. to talk wildly and noisily; n. noisy and meaningless declamation. -er n.

rap n. a smart, light blow; v.t. and v.i. to deliver a smart blow. -ping pr.p. -ped pa.t. and pa.p.

ra·pa·cious a. subsisting on prey; grasping. -ly adv. -ness, rapacity n.

rape n. carnal knowledge of a female against her will; v.t. to ravish or violate.

rape n. an annual of the cabbage family.

rap·id a. very quick; hurried; descending steeply. -s n.pl. part of a river where current rushes over rocks. -ity n. -ly adv. -ness n.

ra·pi·er n. a light, slender, pointed sword, for thrusting only.

rap·ine n. act of plundering; pillage; plunder.

rap·port n. harmony; agreement.

rapt a. intent; in a state of rapture. -ure n. extreme joy; exultation. -urous a. exulting. -urously adv.

rare a. underdone (of meat).

rare a. uncommon; thin, not dense, as air; extremely valuable. -faction n. decrease of quantity of a gas in fixed volume. -fy v.t. to make less dense; v.i. to become less dense. -ly adv. -ness n. rarity n. state of being rare; something seldom seen.

ras·cal n. a rogue; a. dishonest; low. -ity n. base villainy. -ly a.

rash a. without reflection; precipitate. -ly adv. -ness n.

rash n. a temporary eruption of the skin.

rash·er n. a thin slice of bacon.

rasp v.t. to file; to scrape (skin) roughly; to speak in grating manner; a rough, grating sound. -ing a. irritating. -ingly adv.

rasp·ber·ry n. a plant, cultivated for its fruit; a small drupe, the fruit of the plant.

rat n. large rodent; v.i. to hunt rats; to abandon associates in times of difficulty. -ting pr.p. -ted pa.t. and pa.p. -ter n. a terrier which kills rats. -ting n.

ratch·et n. a piece of mechanism turning at

one end upon a pivot, while the other end falls into teeth of wheel, allowing the latter to move in one direction only.

ratchet

rate *n.* established measure; proportion; value; movement, as fast or slow; *v.t.* to estimate value; to settle relative rank, price or position of; *v.i.* to be set in a class; to have rank. **-able, ratable** *a.* **ratability** *n.* **rating** *n.* assessment; amount set as a rate.

rate *v.i.* to take to task; to chide.

rath•er *adv.* preferably; on the other hand; somewhat.

rat•i•fy *v.t.* to sanction officially; to make valid. **ratification** *n.*

rat•ing See rate.

ra•tio *n.* relation one quantity has to another; proportion.

ra•ti•oc•i•nate *v.i.* to reason logically. **ratiocination** *n.* deductive reasoning. **ratiocinative** *a.*

ra•tion *n.* fixed allotted portion; *pl.* provisions; *v.t.* to limit to fixed amount.

ra•tio•nal *a.* reasonable; (*Math.*) a quantity expressed in finite terms. **-e** *n.* logical basis; exposition of principles. **-ization** *n.* in psychology, the attempt to square one's conscience by inventing reasons for one's own conduct. **-ize** *v.t.* **-ism** *n.* philosophy which makes reason the sole guide. **-ist, -istic(al)** *a.* **-istically** *adv.* **-ity** *n.* the faculty of reasoning; soundness of mind. **-ly** *adv.*

rat•tan, ratan *n.* a species of palm found in India and the Malay Peninsula; the stems used for wickerwork, etc.

rat•tle *v.i.* to clatter; to move along quickly and noisily; *v.t.* to shake briskly; *n.* a rapid succession of clattering sounds; a toy for making a noise; rings at the end of a rattlesnake's tail. **-brained, -headed, -pated** *a.* empty-headed; lacking stability. **-snake** *n.* an American poisonous snake. **rattling** *n.* clattering; *a.* brisk; *adv.* extremely.

rau•cous *a.* hoarse; rough. **-ly** *adv.*

rav•age *v.t.* to lay waste; to plunder; *n.* destruction.

rave *v.i.* to talk in delirium. **-r** *n.* **raving** *n.* incoherent talk; *a.* delirious; exceptional. **ravingly** *adv.*

rav•el *v.t.* to entangle; to fray out; *v.i.* to become twisted and involved; *n.* complication.

ra•ven *n.* crow with glossy black plumage, predatory in habit; *a.* glossy black.

rav•en, ravin *v.t.* and *v.i.* to prowl for prey; *n.* rapine; spoil. **-er** *n.* a plunderer. **-ous** *a.* famished; eager for prey. **-ously** *adv.*

ra•vine *n.* a deep, narrow gorge.

rav•ish *v.t.* to seize and carry away by violence. **-er** *n.* **-ing** *a.* entrancing; captivating. **-ingly** *adv.* **-ment** *n.*

raw *a.* not cooked; not covered with skin; not manufactured; *n.* naked state. **-boned** *a.* having little flesh; gaunt. **-hide** *n.* compressed untanned leather. **-ly** *adv.* **-ness** *n.* — **deal,** unfair and undeserved treatment.

ray *n.* beam of light; the path along which light and electromagnetic waves travel in space; a gleam (of hope, truth, etc.); *v.t.* and *v.i.* to radiate; to send forth rays. **-ed** *a.* having rays.

ray•on *n.* a synthetic fibrous material in imitation of silk.

raze, rase *v.t.* to level to the ground; to demolish.

ra•zor *n.* a keen-edged cutting appliance for shaving.

razz *v.t.* to ridicule.

reach *v.t.* to stretch; to touch by extending hand; to come to; *v.i.* to stretch out the hand; to arrive; *n.* easy distance; scope; grasp. **-able** *a.*

re•act *v.i.* to respond to stimulus; to exercise a reciprocal effect on each other; (*Chem.*) to undergo a chemical or physical change when brought in contact with another substance. **-ance** *n.* (*Elect.*) resistance in a coil to an alternating current due to capacity in the circuit. **-ion** *n.* response to stimulus, events, etc. **-ionary** *a.* tendency to reaction; *n.* one opposed to progressive ideas in politics, thought, etc. **-ionist** *n.* **-ivation** *n.* restoration to an activated state. **-ive** *a.*

re•act *v.t.* to act again.

re•ac•tor *n.* apparatus for generating heat by nuclear fission.

read *v.t.* to peruse and understand printed matter; to understand any indicating instrument (as a gas meter); *v.i.* to perform the act of reading; to find mentioned in print; to surmise. **read** *pa.t.* and *pa.p.; a.* versed in books; learned. **-able** *a.* informative; interesting; legible. **-ably** *adv.* **-er** *n.* one who reads; one who determines suitability for publication of manuscripts offered to publisher; corrector of printer's proofs. **-ing** *a.* pert. to reading; *n.* a public recital of passages from books.

read•i•ly, readiness See ready.

re•ad•just *v.t.* to put in order again. **-ment** *n.*

read•y *a.* prepared; fitted for use; willing; *v.t.* to prepare. *n.* position of fighting unit. **readily** *adv.* **readiness** *n.*

re•a•gent *n.* substance to bring about a characteristic reaction in chemical analysis. **reagency** *n.*

re•al *a.* actual; not fictitious or imaginary; denoting property not movable or personal, as lands and tenements. **-ity** *n.* actuality; truth. **-ly** *adv.* actually; *interj.* is that so? **-ty** *n.* real estate. — **estate,** — **property** *n.* immovable property.

re•al•i•ty, re•al•al•ty See real.

re•al•ize *v.t.* to make real; to yield (profit); to apprehend the significance of. **realization** *n.* **realism** *n.* interest in things as they are; practical outlook on life. **realist** *n.* **realistic** *a.* factual; true to life. **realistically** *adv.*

realm *n.* kingdom.

R

ream n. a paper measure containing usually 500 sheets.

ream v.t. to enlarge a tapered or conical hole with a reamer. -er n. a machine tool for enlarging a hole.

reap v.t. to cut down ripe grain for harvesting; to receive as fruits of one's labor. -er n. a harvester; a reaping machine.

rear n. back of hindmost part. -most a. at the very back.

rear v.t. to bring to maturity, as young; v.i. to rise up on the hind legs, as a horse.

re•arm v.t. to equip the fighting services with new weapons. -ament n.

re•ar•range v.t. to set in a different order. -ment n.

rea•son n. a faculty of thinking; power of understanding; cause; purpose; v.i. to exercise rational faculty; to deduce from premises; v.t. to discuss by arguments. -able a. rational; fair. -ableness n. -ably adv. -er, -ing n.

re•as•sure v.t. to allay anxiety; to restore confidence. reassurance n. reassuring a.

re•bate v.t. to allow as discount; n. deduction.

re•bate See rabbet.

reb•el n. one who resists the lawful authority; revolutionist; one who is defiant; a. rebellious; v.i. to revolt. -ling pr.p. -led pa.t. and pa.p. -lion n. organized resistance to authority; mutiny. -lious a.

re•birth n. state of being born again, spiritually; renaissance.

re•bound v.i. to leap back; v.t. to cause to fly back; n. rebounding; recoil.

re•buff n. a blunt contemptuous refusal; v.t. to beat back.

re•buke v.t. to censure; to reprove; n. reprimand; reproof.

re•but v.t. to disprove. -ting pr.p. -ted pa.t. and pa.p. -table a. -tal n. refutation of an argument.

re•cal•ci•trate v.i. to be refractory. recalcitrant n. one who defies authority; a. willfully disobedient. recalcitrance, recalcitration n.

re•call v.t. to take back (a gift, etc.); to revoke; to remember; n. a summons to return.

re•cant v.t. to take back, words or opinions. -ation n.

re•ca•pit•u•late v.t. to relate in brief the matter of a previous discourse; v.i. to sum up what has been previously said. recapitulation n.

re•cap•ture v.t. to capture back; n. act of retaking.

re•cast v.t. to remodel; to throw back.

re•cede v.i. to retreat; to ebb. receding a.

re•ceipt n. a written acknowledgment of money.received; pl. money received; v.t. to give a receipt for.

re•ceive v.t. to accept; to get (an offer, etc.); to welcome. receivable a. -r n. one who receives; receptacle, place of storage, etc.; earpiece of a telephone. receiving n.

re•cent a. that has lately happened. -ly adv. -ness n.

re•cep•ta•cle n. a vessel—that which receives, or into which anything is received and held.

re•cep•tion n. receiving; ceremonial occasion when guests are personally announced; the quality of signals received in broadcasting. receptible a. receivable. -ist n. person in hotel, office, who receives guests or clients. receptive a. able to grasp ideas quickly. receptiveness, receptivity n.

re•cess n. a withdrawing from usual activity; vacation, as of legislative body or school; a niche in a wall; (Zool.) a small indentation in an organ; v.i. to go on a recess. -ed a. fitted with recess. -ion n. act of withdrawing; a period of reduced business; a procession at the close of a service. -ional a. pert. to recession; n. hymn sung as clergyman leaves chancel. -ive a. iveness n.

rec•i•pe n. a prescription; a cookery receipt.

re•cip•i•ent a. receptive; n. one who receives.

re•cip•ro•cal a. moving backwards and forwards; mutual; n. idea alternating with another by contrast. -ly adv. -ness n. reciprocate v.t. to interchange; v.i. to move backwards and forwards; to alternate. reciprocating, reciprocatory a. reciprocation n. mutual giving and receiving. reciprocative a. reciprocity n. action and reaction; in international trade, equal advantages gained by abolition of protective duties.

re•ci•sion n. the act of cutting.

re•cite v.t. and v.i. to repeat aloud before an audience. recital n. detailed narration; a musical or dramatic performance by one person. recitation n. repetition of something from memory. recitative n. declamation to musical accompaniment, as in opera; a. in the style of recitative. -r n.

reck v.t. and v.i. (Arch.) to heed. -less a. rashly negligent. -lessly adv. -lessness n.

reck•on v.t. and v.i. to calculate; to estimate; to be of opinion. -er n. table of calculations. -ing n. computing; a bill.

re•claim v.t. to win back from error or sin. -able a. able to be reformed. reclamation n.

re•claim v.t. to demand the return of.

re•cline v.t. to lean back; v.i. to rest. -r n.

re•cluse a. secluded from the world; n. a hermit.

rec•og•nize v.t. to identify; to acknowledge. recognizable a. recognizably adv. recognizance n. acknowledgment of a person or thing; sum pledged as surety. recognition n. acknowledgment. recognitive, recognitory a.

re•coil v.i. to roll, bound, fall back; n. return motion.

rec•ol•lect v.t. to recall; to remember. -ion n. power of recalling ideas to the mind; things remembered.

rec•om•mend v.t. to speak well of; to advise. -able a. worthy of recommendation. -ation n. statement that one is worthy of favor.

rec•om•pense *v.t.* to reward, to make an equivalent return for service; *n.* repayment; requital.

rec•on•cile *v.t.* to conciliate; to make agree; to adjust or compose. **reconcilable** *a.* **-ment, reconciliation** *n.* harmonizing of apparently opposed ideas. **reconciliatory** *a.*

re•con•dite *a.* hidden from view or mental perception. **-ness** *n.*

re•con•di•tion *v.t.* to restore to sound condition; to repair.

re•con•nais•sance *n.* an examination by land or air, for military operations.

re•con•sid•er *v.t.* to take up for renewed discussion.

re•con•sti•tute *v.t.* to constitute anew; to reconstruct.

re•con•struct *v.t.* to rebuild. **reconstruction** *n.*

re•cord *v.t.* to commit to writing; to make a note of; to inscribe; to make a sound record; *v.i.* to speak, sing, etc. for reproduction on a record; *n.* register; authentic copy of any writing; finest performance or highest amount ever known; a disk, cylinder, for mechanical reproduction of sound; *pl.* public documents. **-er** *n.* one who registers transactions; instrument which transforms sounds into disk impressions. **-ing** *n.* reproduction of sound by mechanical means. **off the record,** unofficial.

re•count *v.t.* to relate; to enumerate; *n.* a second enumeration.

re•coup *v.t.* to recover equivalent for what has been lost.

re•course *n.* application made to another in distress; person or thing resorted to.

re•cov•er *v.t.* to get back; to reclaim; *v.i.* to regain health or a former state. **-able** *a.* **-y** *n.* regaining, or obtaining possession; restoration to health.

re•cov•er *v.t.* to cover again.

rec•re•ant *a.* cowardly; *n.* a craven; an apostate. **recreancy** *n.*

re•cre•ate *v.t.* to give fresh life to; to refresh from weariness. **recreation** *n.* any pleasurable interest; amusement. **recreational** *a.*

re•crim•i•nate *v.t.* and *v.i.* to charge an accuser with a similar crime. **recrimination** *n.* a coun009charge brought by the accused against the accuser. **recriminative, recriminatory** *a.*

re•cruit *v.t.* to enlist persons for army, navy, etc.; *v.i.* to gain health, spirits, etc.; *n.* a newly enlisted soldier. **-ing, -ment** *n.*

rect•an•gle *n.* a four-sided figure with four right angles. **rectangular** *a.*

rec•ti•fy *v.t.* to correct; to convert an alternating current of electricity into a direct current. **rectifiable** *a.* **rectification** *n.* **rectifier** *n.* one who corrects; a device which rectifies.

rec•ti•lin•e•al, rectilinear *a.* bounded by straight lines.

rec•ti•tude *n.* honesty of purpose.

rec•to *n.* the right-hand page of an open book.

rec•tor *n.* clergyman (as of Episcopal Church) who has charge of a parish. **-y** *n.* house of a rector.

rec•tum *n.* lower end of the large intestine; *pl.* **recta. rectal** *a.*

re•cum•bent *a.* reclining; lying on back.

re•cu•per•ate *v.i.* to win back health and strength. **recuperation** *n.* convalescence. **recuperative** *a.*

re•cur *v.i.* to happen again. **-ring** *pr.p.* **-red** *pa.t.* and *pa.p.* **-rence, -rency** *n.* **-rent** *a.* returning periodically.

re•curve *v.t.* to bend backwards.

red *a.* (*comp.* **-der;** *superl.* **-dest**) of the color of arterial blood, rubies, glowing fire, etc.; connected with bloodshed, revolution, left-wing politics, etc.; *n.* color of blood; a danger signal. **-den** *v.t.* to make red; *v.t.* to become red; to blush. **-ness** *n.* quality of being red. **—blooded** *a.* vigorous; manly. **-breast** *n.* the robin. **-coat** *n.* a British soldier, because of the bright scarlet tunic. **— corpuscle** *n.* a colored blood corpuscle, containing hemoglobin and carrying oxygen. **Red Cross** *n.* international emblem of organization for relief of sick and wounded in wartime and for helping distressed persons in emergencies, as floods. **— hat** *n.* cardinal's hat. **— heat** *n.* temperature of a body emitting red rays, about 700-800° C. **— herring** *n.* the common herring, cured by drying, smoking and salting. **— hot** *a.* heated to redness; enthusiastic. **— pepper** *n.* seasoning, such as cayenne. **— tape** *n.* adherence to official regulations, fr. red tape used for tying up government documents. **-wing** *n.* a blackbird with a red patch on wings. **-wood** *n.* the sequoia tree of California, a gigantic evergreen coniferous tree.

re•dact *v.t.* to digest or reduce to order, literary or scientific materials. **-ion** *n.* **-or** *n.* an editor.

re•deem *v.t.* to regain, as mortgaged property, by paying principal, interest and costs of mortgage; to deliver from sin; to recover. **-able** *a.* **-ableness** *n.* **-er** *n.*

re•demp•tion *n.* buying back; salvation. **-er** *n.* one who has redeemed himself. **redemptive** *a.* redeeming. **redemptory** *a.*

red•in•te•grate *v.t.* to make whole again. **redintegration** *n.*

re•di•rect *v.t.* to readdress a communication. **-ion** *n.*

re•dis•trib•ute *v.t.* to apportion again. **redistribution** *n.*

red•o•lent *a.* diffusing a strong or fragrant odor. **redolence** *n.*

re•doubt *n.* a central part within fortifications for a final stand by the defenders.

re•doubt•able *a.* dreaded; valiant.

re•dound *v.i.* to turn to; to conduce (to); to recoil.

re•draft *v.t.* to draw up a second time; *n.* a new bill of exchange.

re•dress *v.t.* to make amends for; *n.* reparation; remedy. **-er** *n.* **-ible** *a.*

re•duce *v.t.* to diminish in number, length, quantity, value, price, etc.; (*Chem.*) to remove oxygen or add hydrogen; to

R

decrease valency number. -d a. **reducible** a. **reduction** n. subjugation; diminution; amount by which something is reduced. **reductive** a. having the power of reducing. **reductively** adv. reducing **agent** n. a reagent for abstracting oxygen or adding hydrogen.

re•dun•dant a. superfluous; using more words than necessary for complete meaning. **redundance, redundancy** n. -ly adv.

re•ech•o v.t. to echo back.

reed n. a tall hollow-stemmed grass growing in marshes; in certain wind instruments, a thin strip of metal which vibrates and produces a musical sound; a musical instrument made of the hollow joint of some plant; pl. a molding; v.t. to fit with a reed. -ed a. covered with reeds; molded like reeds. -iness n. — **instrument** n. (Mus.) a wind instrument played by means of a reed. — **pipe** n. organ pipe whose tone is produced by vibration of metal tongue. — **stop** n. organ stop owing its tone to vibration of little metal tongues. -y a.

reef n. a portion of square sail which can be rolled up and made fast to the boom; v.t. to reduce the area of sail by taking in a reef. -er n. a sailor's close-fitting jacket.

reef n. a ridge of rock near the surface of the sea.

reek n. fume; v.i. to smell strongly unpleasant. -ing, -y a.

reel n. bobbin on which yarn is wound; in motion pictures, a flanged spool on which film is wound; a portion of film; v.t. to draw (in) by means of a reel.

reel v.i. to stagger; to be dizzy.

re•fec•tion n. a simple repast. **refectory** n. a hall in a monastery, convent, or college where meals are served.

re•fer v.t. and v.i. to have relation to; to offer, as testimony in evidence of character; to allude (to). -ring pr.p. -red pa.t. and pa.p. -able, -rable a. may be assigned to. -ee n. a neutral judge in various sports. -ence n. appeal to the judgment of another; a passage in a book to which reader is referred; a testimonial. -endum n. vote for ascertaining the public will on a single definite issue. -ential a. used for reference.

re•fine v.t. to reduce crude metals to a finer state; to improve; to free from coarseness; v.i. to improve in accuracy, or good taste. -d a. clarified; well-bred. -dly adv. -ment n. -ry n. place where process of refining sugar, oil, is effected.

re•flect v.t. to throw back rays of light, heat or sound, from surfaces; to mirror; v.i. to consider attentively; to disparage. -ed a. -ing a. thoughtful; throwing back rays of light, etc. -ingly adv. -ion n. return of rays of heat or light, or waves of sound, from a surface; image given back from mirror or other reflecting surface; contemplation. -ive a. meditative; reciprocal. -ively adv. -iveness n. -or n. a reflecting surface.

re•flex a. turned, bent, or directed backwards; produced by reaction; (Anat.) denoting the involuntary action of the motor nerves under a stimulus from the sensory nerves; involuntary; n. a reflex action; v.t. to bend back; to reflect. -ible a. -ibility n. -ive a. bending or turned backwards. -ively, -ly adv. **conditioned reflex**, reflex action due to power of association and suggestion.

re•flux n. a flowing back; ebbing.

re•form v.t. to amend; to improve; v.i. to amend one's ways; to improve; n. improvement; correction. -able a. -ation n. reforming; change for the better. -ative a. aiming at reform. -atory a. tending to reform; n. institution for reforming young lawbreakers. -ed a. amended; reclaimed. -er n. an advocate of reform.

re•fract v.t. to cause to deviate from a direct course, as rays of light on passing from one medium to another. -able, -ed a. -ing a. serving to refract; refractive. -ion n. -tive a. -or n.

re•frac•to•ry a. suitable for lining furnaces because of resistance to fusion at very high temperatures; (Med.) resistant to treatment. **refractorily** adv.

re•frain v.i. to abstain. -ment n.

re•frain n. chorus recurring at end of each verse of song.

re•fran•gi•ble a. able to be refracted.

re•fresh v.t. to revive; to freshen up. -er n. one who, or that which, refreshes. -ing a. invigorating. -ment n. that which adds fresh vigor, as rest, drink, or food—hence, pl. food and drink.

re•frig•er•ate v.t. to preserve food by cooling; v.i. to become cold. **refrigerant** a. **refrigeration** n. **refrigerative, refrigeratory** a. cooling. **refrigerator** n. apparatus and plant for the manufacture of ice; chamber for preserving food by mechanical production of low temperatures.

ref•uge n. shelter; retreat. -e n. one who flees to a place of safety.

re•ful•gent a. shining. **refulgence** n. splendor. Also **refulgency.**

re•fund v.t. to return compensation for; to repay. **refund** n. repayment.

re•fur•bish v.t. to furbish up again; to renovate.

re•fuse v.t. to deny or reject; v.i. not to comply. **refusal** n. act of refusing; the first chance of accepting or declining an offer.

ref•use a. worthless; n. waste matter.

re•fuse v.t. of metals, to fuse again. **refusion** n.

re•fute v.t. to prove to be false. **refutable** a. capable of being refuted. **refutably** adv. **refutation** n.

re•gain v.t. to retrieve; to reach again.

re•gal a. pert. to a king; royal. -ia n.pl. insignia of royalty. -ity n. sovereignty -ly adv.

re•gale v.t. to entertain in sumptuous manner; v.i. to feast.

re•gard v.t. to consider; to pay respect to; n. aspect; esteem; concern; pl. good wishes. -able a. -ful a. heedful. -fully adv. -ing prep. concerning—also in, with, regard to, as regards. -less *a*. without regard; neglectful. -lessly *adv*.

re•gat•ta *n*. boat races.

re•gen•cy See regent.

re•gen•er•ate *v.t.* and *v.i.* to give fresh life or vigor to; to cause to be born again; *a*. born anew; changed from a natural to a spiritual state; regenerated. **regeneracy, regeneration** *n*. **regenerative** *a*.

re•gent *a*. holding the office of regent; *n*. one who governs a kingdom during the minority, absence, or disability of sovereign. **regency** *n*. office of a regent.

reg•i•cide *n*. one who kills, or the killing of, a king. **regicidal** *a*.

re•gime *n*. style of rule or management.

reg•i•men *n*. orderly government; systematic method of dieting, exercising.

reg•i•ment *n*. a body of soldiers commanded by a senior officer; *v.t.* to systematize. **-al** *a*. **-ation** *n*. thorough systemization.

re•gion *n*. territory of indefinite extent; part of body. **-al** *a*. **-ally** *adv*.

reg•is•ter *n*. an official record; book in which a record is kept; an alphabetical index; a metal damper to close a heating duct; *v.t.* to record; to indicate, by cash register, scales, etc., by facial expression. **registrable, -ed** *a*. **registrant** *n*. one who registers. **registrar** *n*. an official who keeps a record. **registration** *n*. record; total entries registered. **registry** *n*. office for registering births, deaths and marriages. **-ed mail**, a method of postal delivery by which mail is insured against loss or damage in transit.

reg•nal *a*. pert. to reign of monarch. **regnancy** *n*. reign.

re•gress *n*. the power of passing back; reentry; *v.i.* to fall back; to return to a former state. **-ion** *n*. returning; retrogression. **-ive** *a*.

re•gret *v.t.* to grieve over; *n*. grief; sorrow; remorse. **-ting** *pr.p.* **-ted** *pa.t.* and *pa.p.* **-ful** *a*. **-fully** *adv*. **-table** *a*. lamentable. **-tably** *adv*. **-ter** *n*.

reg•u•lar *a*. conforming to, governed by rule; periodical; habitual. **-ization** *n*. **-ity** *n*. uniformity. **-ly** *adv*.

reg•u•late *v.t.* to adjust by rule, method, etc.; to control. **regulation** *n*. state of being reduced to order; a law. **regulator** *n*.

re•gur•gi•tate *v.t.* to throw, flow, or pour back in great quantity; *v.i.* to be thrown back. **regurgitation** *n*.

re•ha•bil•i•tate *v.t.* to restore to former position; to recondition. **rehabilitation** *n*.

re•hash *v.t.* to mix together and use a second time.

re•hearse *v.t.* and *v.i.* to repeat aloud; to recite; to narrate. **rehearsal** *n*. trial performance of a play, opera, etc.

re•i•fy *v.t.* to make concrete. **reification** *n*.

reign *n*. the period during which a sovereign occupies throne; *v.i.* to possess sovereign power.

re•im•burse *v.t.* to refund; to give the equivalent of. **-ment** *n*. **-r** *n*.

rein *n*. strap of bridle to govern a horse; restraint; *pl*. means of exercising power.

re•in•car•nate *v.t.* to embody again in the flesh. **reincarnation** *n*.

rein•deer *n*. large deer of colder regions.

reindeer

re•in•force *v.t.* to strengthen with new force; to increase. **-ment** *n*.

re•in•state *v.t.* to restore to former position. **-ment** *n*.

re•is•sue *v.t.* to republish; *n*. a reprint.

re•it•er•ate *v.t.* to repeat again and again. **reiterant** *a*. **reiteration** *n*.

re•ject *v.t.* to throw away; to refuse; *n*. a person or thing rejected as not up to standard. **-ion** *n*.

re•joice *v.t.* to give joy to; to cheer; *v.i.* to triumph. **rejoicing** *n*. act of expressing joy; *pl*. festivities.

re•join *v.t.* to unite again; to meet again; *v.i.* to become united again; to reply. **-der** *n*. an answer to a reply.

re•ju•ve•nate *v.t.* to make young again. **rejuvenation, rejuvenator** *n*. **rejuvenesce** *v.i.* to grow young again. **rejuvenescence** *n*. **rejuvenescent** *a*.

re•lapse *v.i.* to slide back, esp. into state of ill health, evil ways; *n*. a falling back.

re•late *v.t.* to establish relation between; *v.i.* to refer (to). **-d** *a*. connected by blood or marriage; akin. **relation** *n*. telling; *pl*. dealings between persons or nations; connection between things; a relative. **relational** *a*. indicating some relation. **relationship** *n*.

rel•a•tive *a*. dependent on relation to something else, not absolute; *n*. a person connected by blood. **-ly** *adv*. comparatively. **-ness** *n*. **relativity** *n*. doctrine that all observable motion, and time, are relative.

re•lax *v.t.* to make less stern; to loosen; *v.i.* to unbend; to ease up. **-ation** *n*. recreation. **-ing** *a*.

re•lay *n*. supplies conveniently stored at successive stages of a route; a device for making or breaking a local electrical circuit; a low-powered broadcasting station which broadcasts programs originating in another station; *v.t.* to pass on, as a message, broadcast, etc. **— race**, a race between teams of which each runner does a part of the distance.

re•lease *v.t.* to set free; to exempt from obligation; *n*. liberation; exemption; a catch for controlling mechanical parts of a machine; *(Law)* a surrender of a claim. **releasable** *a*.

rel•e•gate *v.t.* to send away; to demote. **relegation** *n*.

re•lent *v.i.* to give up harsh intention. **-less** *a*. showing no sympathy. **-lessly** *adv*. **-lessness** *n*.

rel•e•vant *a*. pertinent. **relevance,**

R

relevancy n. -ly adv.

re·li·a·ble a. trustworthy; creditable. -ness, reliability n. reliably adv. reliance n. trust; dependence. reliant a.

rel·ic n. something surviving from the past.

re·lief n. alleviation of pain, distress; one who relieves another at his post. — map n. a map showing the elevations and depressions of a country in relief.

re·lieve v.t. to alleviate; to remedy. relieving a. serving to relieve.

re·li·gion n. recognition of God as object of worship; any system of faith and worship. -ist, -ary, -er n. one who makes inordinate professions of religion. religiosity n. sense of, or tendency towards, religiousness. religious a. pert. to religion; pious. religiously adv.

re·lin·quish v.t. to give up; to yield. -er, -ment n.

rel·i·quar·y n. a shrine.

rel·ish v.t. to taste with pleasure; v.t. to have a pleasing taste; n. savor; what is used to make food more palatable, as sauce.

re·luc·tant a. unwilling; disinclined. reluctance n. reluctancy n. -ly adv.

re·ly v.i. to trust; to depend; relier n.

re·main v.i. to stay; to continue or endure; n.pl. a corpse. -der n. what remains; remnant.

re·mand v.t. to send back; n. such a recommital.

re·mark v.t. to take notice of; to express in words or writing; to comment. -able a. extraordinary. -ableness n. -ably adv.

rem·e·dy n. a means of curing or relieving a disease; legal means to recover a right; antidote; v.t. to restore to health; to put right; a. curable. remedial a. affording a remedy.

re·mem·ber v.t. to retain in the memory; v.i. to have in mind. -able a. remembrance n. act of remembering; recollection; keepsake.

re·mind v.t. to cause to remember. -er n. that which reminds.

rem·i·nis·cence n. a recollection of past events; pl. memoirs. reminiscent a.

re·mise v.t. to remit; to surrender (property, etc.) by deed; n. (Law) a surrender.

re·miss a. not exact in duty; careless. -ful a. -ible a. able to be remitted. -ion n. act of remitting; abatement; period of moderation of intensity of a disease; pardon. -ive a. -ly adv. -ness n.

re·mit v.t. to send back; to transmit to a distance, as money bills; to slacken (efforts); v.i. to slacken off. -ting pa.p. -ted pa.t. and pa.p. -tal n. act of remitting to another court. -tance n. transmitting money, bills, to a distant place; the money sent. -tent a. increasing and decreasing at periodic intervals.

rem·nant n. fragment of cloth; remainder.

re·mon·strate v.t. to make evident by strong protestations; v.i. to speak strongly against. remonstrance n. protest. remonstrant n. one who remonstrates; a. expostulatory. remonstration n. remonstrative, remonstratory a.

re·morse n. self-reproach excited by sense

of guilt; repentance. -ful a. repentant -fully adv. -less a. relentless.

re·mote a. far back in time or space; -ly adv. -ness n. — control, control o apparatus from a distance.

re·move v.t. to take or put away; to extract v.i. to change residence; n. removal; a step in any scale of gradation. removable a. not permanently fixed. removal n dismissal from a post. -d a. denoting distance of relationship. -r n.

re·mu·ner·ate v.t. to reward for services to compensate. remunerable a. that may or should be, remunerated. remuneration n. recompense; salary. remunerative a.

ren·ais·sance (Cap.) n. a rebirth; a period of intellectual revival; a. pert. to renaissance. Also renascence.

re·nal a. pert. to kidneys.

re·nas·cent a. regaining lost vigor renascence n. See renaissance.

rend v.t. to pull to pieces; to lacerate. ren pa.t. and pa.p.

ren·der v.t. to give in return; to deliver up to portray; to extract animal fats by heating. -able a. -er, -ing n. rendition n rendering.

ren·dez·vous n. an appointed place fo meeting.

ren·di·tion See render.

ren·e·gade n. one faithless to principle o party; a. false. renege v.t. and v.i. to brea a promise.

re·new v.t. and v.i. to restore; to renovate -able a. -al n. restoration.

ren·net n. preparation used for curdlin milk and in preparation of cheese junket, etc.

re·nounce v.t. to disavow; to give up -ment, renunciation n.

ren·o·vate v.t. to make as good as new; t overhaul and repair. renovation n.

re·nown n. great reputation. -ed a eminent.

rent n. pa.t. and pa.p. of rend; n. an openin made by rending; a split; a rift.

rent n. a periodical payment at an agreed rate for use of something; v.t. to lease v.i. to be leased. -able a. -al n. th amount of rent; a. pert. to rent. -er n. on who rents.

re·nun·ci·a·tion n. a surrender of claim o interest; repudiation. Also renunciance renunciative, renunciatory a.

re·or·ga·nize v.t. to organize anew.

re·pair v.t. to restore to a sound state afte injury; n. mending. -able a. -er n.

rep·a·ra·ble a. that can be made good reparably adv. reparation n. makin amends; compensation. reparative a.

rep·ar·tee n. apt, witty reply.

re·past n. a meal.

re·pa·tri·ate v.t. to restore to one's ow country. repatriation n.

re·pay v.t. to pay back; to make return fo to require. repaid pa.t. and pa.p. -able a -ment n.

re·peal v.t. to revoke, rescind, annul, as law, or statute; to abrogate; n. revocation abrogation. -able a.

re·peat v.t. to say or do again; to reiterate frequent; recurring. -edly adv. -er n. on *n.* repetition; encore. **-able** *a.* **-ed** *a.* who, or that which, repeats; fire alarm which may be discharged many times. **ing** *n.*

re•pel *v.t.* to drive back; to repulse; *v.i.* to cause repugnance. **-ling** *pr.p.* **-led** *pa.t.* and *pa.p.* **-lence, -lency** *n.* **-lent** *a.* driving back; *n.* that which repels. **-ler** *n.*

re•pent *v.t.* and *v.i.* to desire to change one's life as a result of sorrow for one's sins. **-ance** *n.* sorrow for a deed; penitence. **-ant** *a.*

re•per•cus•sion *n.* reverberation; indirect effect.

rep•er•toire *n.* list of musical works, dramatic roles, within sphere of an individual. **repertory** *n.* a repertoire; *a.* pert. to the stock plays of a resident company.

rep•e•ti•tion *n.* act of repeating; a copy. **repetitious** *a.* full of repetitions. **repetitive** *a.* involving much repetition.

re•pine *v.i.* to fret. repining *n.*

re•place *v.t.* to put back into place; to substitute for. **-able** *a.* **-ment** *n.* substitution.

re•plen•ish *v.t.* to fill up again; to supply. **-ment** *n.*

re•plete *a.* completely filled; surfeited. **-ness, repletion** *n.* satiety.

rep•li•ca *n.* exact copy of work of art by the artist of the original; facsimile. **-te** *v.t.* to duplicate. **-tion** *n.* an answer; a copy.

re•ply *v.t.* and *v.i.* to return an answer; to respond; *n.* answer; response.

re•port *v.t.* to take down in writing; to give an account of; *v.i.* to make official statement; to present oneself as to superior officer; *n.* an official statement of facts; reputation. **-er** *n.* one who reports, for newspapers.

re•pose *v.t.* to put trust (in). **reposit** *v.t.* to lodge, in a place of safety. **repository** *n.* place where valuables are deposited for safety.

re•pose *v.i.* to sleep; to recline; *v.t.* to lay at rest; *n.* sleep; relaxation. **reposal** *n.* **-ful** *a.* **-fully** *adv.*

rep•re•hend *v.t.* to find fault with; to rebuke. **reprehensible** *a.* blameworthy. **reprehensibly** *adv.* **reprehension** *n.* reproof.

rep•re•sent *v.t.* to express the image of; to be the agent for; to personate; to be the member for. **-able** *a.* **-ation** *n.* that which represents, as a picture; the act of representing. **-ational** *a.* **-ative** *a.* typical; exhibiting a likeness; *n.* an agent, delegate, or substitute.

re•press *v.t.* to keep under control; to quell. **-er, -or** *n.* **-ible** *a.* **-ibly** *adv.* **-ion** *n.* restraint; in psychoanalysis, the rejection from consciousness of anything unpleasant. **-ive** *a.*

re•prieve *v.t.* to commute a sentence; to grant temporary relief; *n.* temporary suspension of execution of sentence; relief.

rep•ri•mand *v.t.* to reprove severely; *n.* a sharp rebuke.

re•print *v.t.* to print again; *n.* new edition of any printed work.

rep•pri•sal *n.* an act of retaliation.

re•proach *v.t.* to rebuke; *n.* reproof; an object of scorn. **-ful** *a.* expressing censure. **-fully** *adv.* **-fulness** *n.*

rep•ro•bate *v.t.* to disapprove with signs of extreme dislike; cast off by God; *n.* scoundrel. **reprobation** *n.* condemnation; censure.

re•pro•duce *v.t.* to produce over again; *v.i.* to propagate; to generate. **reproducible** *a.* **reproduction** *n.* a facsimile; process of multiplication of living individuals whereby the species is perpetuated. **reproductive** *a.* pert. to reproduction; yielding profits.

re•proof *n.* reprimand; admonition. **reprove** *v.t.* to charge with a fault; to rebuke. **reprovable** *a.* deserving censure. **reproval** *n.*

rep•tile *n.* animal of class Reptilia, cold-blooded, air-breathing vertebrates which move on their bellies or by means of small, short legs.

re•pub•lic *n.* a state, in which supremacy of the people or its elected representatives is formally acknowledged; commonwealth. **-an** *a.* pert. to republic; (*Cap.*) one of the two traditional political parties of the U.S.A. **-anism** *n.*

re•pu•di•ate *v.t.* to reject; to disown. **repudiation** *n.*

re•pug•nance *n.* condition of being repugnant. **repugnancy** *n.* habitual feeling of aversion. **repugnant** *a.* distasteful in a high degree; adverse.

re•pulse *v.t.* to drive back; to repel decisively; *n.* act of driving off; rejection. **repulsion** *n.* act of driving back. **repulsive** *a.* loathsome. **repulsively** *adv.*

re•pute *v.t.* to account or consider; to reckon; *n.* good character; reputation; esteem. **reputation** *n.* estimation in which a person is held; reported character; good name; renown. **reputable** *a.* held in esteem; respectable; creditable. **reputably** *adv.* **reputedly** *adv.* generally believed.

re•quest *v.t.* to ask for earnestly; to petition; *n.* expression of desire for; demand. **-er** *n.*

re•qui•em *n.* (R.C.) celebration of the mass for soul of a dead person.

re•quire *v.t.* to claim as by right; to need. **-ment** *n.* what is required; an essential condition.

req•ui•site *a.* necessary; essential; *n.* something indispensable. **requisition** *n.* a written order for supplies; *v.t.* to demand certain supplies; to request formally; to seize. **requisitionist** *n.* one who makes a requisition.

re•quite *v.t.* to return an equivalent in good or evil; to make retaliation. **requital** *n.* that which repays; compensation.

re•scind *v.t.* to annul; to cancel; to abrogate. **-able** *a.* **recission** *n.* act of rescinding. **rescissory** *a.*

re•script *n.* an edict or decree.

res•cue *v.t.* to free from danger, or restraint; to deliver; *n.* deliverance. **-r** *n.*

re•search *n.* diligent inquiry; scientific investigation and study to discover facts;

a. pert. to research; *v.i.* to examine with care. -er *n.*

re·seat *v.t.* to provide with a new seat; to patch (trousers, etc.).

re·sem·ble *v.t.* similar to. **resemblance** *n.* similarity. **resembling** *a.*

re·sent *v.t.* to consider as an affront; to be angry at. -er *n.* -ful *a.* full of resentment. -fully *adv.* -ment *n.* deep sense of affront.

re·serve *v.t.* to set apart; to keep for future use; *a.* acting as a reserve; *n.* what is reserved; troops, held back from line of battle to assist when necessary. **reservation** *n.* booking of a hotel room, etc.; a condition; land reserved for some public use. -d *a.* booked; self-restrained; uncommunicative. -dly *adv.* -dness *n.* **reservist** *n.* a member of the armed forces belonging to reserves.

res·er·voir *n.* area for storage and filtering of water; a large supply.

reservoir

re·set *v.t.* to set again. -ting *pr.p.* reset *pa.p.* and *pa.t.*

re·side *v.i.* to dwell permanently; to be inherent in. -nce *n.* place where one resides; house. -ncy *n.* a residence. -nt *a.* dwelling; *n.* one who resides in a place. -ntial *a.* pert. to a part of a town consisting mainly of dwelling houses.

res·i·due *n.* balance. **residual** *a.* remaining after a part is taken away. **residuary** *a.* pert. to part remaining. **residuum** *n.* what is left after any process of separation.

re·sign *v.t.* and *v.i.* to relinquish formally (office, etc.); to give up. -ation *n.* giving up, as a claim, office, or place; endurance. -ed *a.* relinquished; patient. -edly *adv.*

re·sile *v.i.* to draw back from a previous offer; to recoil. **resilience, resiliency** *n.* elasticity, esp. of mind. **resilient** *a.* possessing power of quick recovery.

res·in *n.* term for brittle, thickened juices exuded by certain plants; *v.t.* to coat with resin.

re·sist *v.t.* and *v.i.* to oppose; to withstand; to strive against. -ance *n.* hindrance; power possessed by an individual to resist disease. -ant *n.* one who, or that which, resists; *a.* offering resistance. -er *n.* -ibility, -ibleness *n.* the quality of being resistible. -ible *a.* -ibly, -ingly *adv.* -less *a.* irresistible; unable to resist. -lessly *adv.* -lessness *n.* -or *n.* apparatus possessing resistance to electrical current. -ance movement, the organized, underground movement.

res·o·lute *a.* having a decided purpose; determined; *n.* a determined person. -ly *adv.* -ness *n.* determination. **resolution** *n.* intention; motion or declaration.

re·solve *v.t.* to solve and reduce to a different form; to make clear; to unravel *v.i.* to purpose; to determine unanimously; *n.* act of resolving; firm determination. **resolvable** *a.* -d *a.* determined; resolute. -dly *adv.* -dness *n.*

res·o·nant *a.* resounding; ringing **resonance** *n.*

re·sort *v.i.* to have recourse; *n.* a frequented place; vacation spot; aid.

re·sound *v.i.* to send back sound; *v.i.* to reverberate.

re·source *n.* that on which one depends for supply or support; skill in improvising; *pl.* wealth. -ful *a.* clever in devising fresh expedients. -fully *adv* -fulness *n.*

re·spect *v.t.* to esteem; to relate to; *n.* consideration; *pl.* expression of esteem -able *a.* worthy of respect; reputable -ability, -ableness *n.* -ably *adv.* -ful *a.* polite. -fully *adv.* -fulness *n.* -ing *prep.* concerning. -ive *a.* relative; not absolute -ively *adv.* each.

re·spire *v.t.* and *v.i.* to breathe. **respirable** *a.* fit to be breathed. **respiration** *n.* process of breathing. **respirational** *a.* respiratory. **respirator** *n.* a device to produce artificial respiration. **respiratory** *a.* serving for, pert. to, respiration.

re·spite *n.* a temporary intermission; *v.t.* to reprieve.

re·splen·dent *a.* shining with brilliant luster. **resplendence, resplendency** *n.* -ly *adv.*

re·spond *v.i.* to reply; to correspond to; to react. -ent *a.* giving response; *n.* one who refutes in a debate.

re·sponse *n.* answer or reply. **responsibility** *n.* state of being responsible; duty; an obligation. **responsible** *a.* accountable rational. **responsibly** *adv.* **responsive** *a.* able, ready, or inclined, to respond **responsively** *adv.* **responsiveness** *n.*

rest *n.* repose; a cessation from motion or labor; a pause; *v.t.* to lay at rest; *v.i.* to cease from action; to repose; to be undisturbed. -ful *a.* soothing; quiet. -fully *adv.* -fulness *n.* -less *a.* continually on the move; uneasy. -lessly *adv.* -lessness *n.*

rest *v.i.* to continue to be; *n.* that which is left over or remainder.

res·tau·rant *n.* a place where customers are provided with meals on payment.

res·ti·tu·tion *n.* reparation; compensation **restitutive** *a.* **restitutor** *n.*

res·tive *a.* impatient; stubborn. -ly *adv.* -ness *n.*

re·store *v.t.* to give back or return; to recover from decay; to reinstate; to cure **restorable** *a.* **restoration** *n.* reconstruction; reestablishment. **restorative** *a.* having power to renew strength; *n.* a remedy for restoring health and vigor

re·strain *v.t.* to hinder; to check. -able *a.* -edly *adv.* with restraint. -ment *n.* -t *n.* curb; imprisonment.

re·strict *v.t.* to restrain within bounds; to limit. -ed *a.* limited. -edly *adv.* -ion *n.*

state of being restricted; restraint. -ive *a.*
-ively *adv.*

re·sult *v.i.* to follow, as a consequence; *n.*
issue; outcome; *a.* following as a result.

re·sume *v.t.* to renew; to take again.
resumable *a.* resumption *n.* act of taking
back or taking again; a fresh start.
resumptive *a.* resuming.

re·surge *v.i.* to rise again. -nce *n,* -nt *a.*
rising again (from the dead).

res·ur·rect *v.t.* to restore to life; to use
again. -ion *n.* rising of the body after
death; a revival. -ion, -ionary *a.* -ionist *n.*
a believer in resurrection.

re·sus·ci·tate *v.t.* to restore to life one
apparently dead; to revive; *v.i.* to come
to life again. resuscitable *a.* resuscitation
n. resuscitative *a.* tending to reanimate.
resuscitator *n.*

re·tail *v.t.* to sell to consumer, in small
quantities; *a.* denoting sale to consumer,
as opposed to wholesale; *n.* sale in small
quantities. -er, -ment *n.*

re·tain *v.t.* to continue to keep in
possession; to engage services of. -able *a.*
-er *n.* follower; a fee paid to secure
services of, esp. lawyer. -ment *n.*

re·tal·i·ate *v.t.* and *v.i.* to repay in kind; to
requite. retaliation *n.* retaliative,
retaliatory *a.* retaliator *n.*

re·tard *v.t.* to hinder progress; to impede,
-ation *n.* delaying; delayed mental
development in children. -ment *n.*

retch *v.i.* to strain at vomiting. -ing *n.*

re·ten·tion *n.* power of retaining; memory.
retentive   *a.*   retentively   *adv.*
retentiveness *n.*

ret·i·cent *a.* uncommunicative. reticence
n.; also reticency. -ly *adv.*

ret·i·cle *n.* a group of lines in the focus of
an optical instrument. reticule *n.* a little
bag. reticular, reticulary *a.* intricate.
reticulate *v.t.* to cover with netlike lines.
reticulated *a.* reticulation *n.*

ret·i·na *n.* innermost, semitransparent,
sensory layer of the eye.

re·tire *v.t.* to withdraw from circulation
notes or bills; *v.i.* to give up one's work
or office; to go to bed. retiral *n.* occasion
when one retires from office, etc. -d *a.*
secluded; withdrawn permanently from
work. -dly *adv.* -ment, -dness *n.* state of
being retired. retiring *a.* reserved;
modest.

re·tort *v.t.* to repay in kind; *v.i.* to make a
smart reply; *n.* vigorous reply.

re·trace *v.t.* to go back the same way.
-able *a.*

re·tract *v.t.* and *v.i.* to take back, as a
statement. -able *a.* -ation *n.* recalling of
opinion; recantation. -ile *a.* (*Zool.*)
capable of being drawn back or inwards,
as claws, etc. -ion *n.* retractile power. -ive
a. -ively *adv.*

re·tread *v.t.* to replace a worn tread on the
outer cover of a rubber tire with a new
tread.

re·treat *n.* withdrawing; a military signal
for retiring; *v.i.* to move back; to retire
before an enemy. -ing *a.* sloping
backward, as forehead or chin.

re·trench *v.t.* to curtail; *v.i.* to economize.

-ment *n.* dimunition of expenditure;
economy.

ret·ri·bu·tion *n.* just or suitable return;
repayment. retributive, retributory *a.*

re·trieve *v.t.* to gain back. retrievable *a.*
retrievably *adv.* -ment, retrieval *n.* -r *n.*
dog trained to find and bring back game.

retriever

ret·ro·act *v.i.* to act backwards; to react.
-ion *n.* -ive *a.* acting in regard to past
events; retrospective. -ively *adv.*

ret·ro·cede *v.t.* to go or move back.
retrocession *n.* going back.

ret·ro·grade *v.i.* to move backward; to
deteriorate;   *a.*   deteriorating.
retrogradation *n.* retrogress *v.i.* to
deteriorate. retrogression *n.* a decline
into an inferior state of development.
retrogressive *a.* degenerating; assuming
baser characteristics. retrogressively *adv.*

re·trorse *a.* pointing backwards, as feathers
of birds. Also retroverse. -ly *adv.*

ret·ro·spect *n.* survey of past events; a
review. -ion *n.* -ive *a.* applicable to past
events; of laws, rules, having force as if
authorized at earlier date. -ively *adv.*

ret·ro·verse *a.* bent backwards; retrorse.
retroversion *n.* retrovert *v.t.* to turn back.

re·turn *v.t.* to bring, give, or send back; to
restore; to yield (a profit); *v.i.* to go or
come back; *n.* coming back to the same
place; profit; restitution. -able *a.* — match
n. second game played by same
opponents. — ticket *n.* ticket for journey,
there and back.

re·u·nion *n.* union formed anew after
separation; a social gathering. reunite *v.t.*
and *v.i.* to join after separation.

re·veal *v.t.* to disclose; to show. -able *a.* -er
n. -ment *n.* revelation.

rev·eil·le *n.* the bugle call or roll of drums
sounded in military establishments at
daybreak to rouse inmates.

rev·el *v.i.* to carouse; to delight in; *pr.p.,*
pa.t., *pa.p.* and *n.* noisy celebration; *pl.*
entertainment, with music and dancing.
-er, -ment, -ry *n.*

rev·e·la·tion *n.* act of revealing; God's
disclosure of himself to man; (*Cap.*) last
book of New Testament. -al, revelatory
a.

re·venge *v.t.* to make retaliation for; to
avenge; *n.* infliction of injury in return
for injury; passion for vengeance. -ful *a.*
-fully *adv.* -fulness *n.*

rev·e·nue *n.* income derived from any
source, esp. annual income of a state or
institution; profits.

re·ver·ber·ate *v.t.* and *v.i.* to send back, as
sound; to reflect, as light or heat; to
resound. reverberant *a.* beating back.
reverberation *n.* reverberative *a.* tending
to reverberate.   reverberator   *n.*

reverberatory *a.* producing reverberation.

re•vere *v.t.* to regard with mingled fear, respect and affection. **-nce** *n.* awe mingled with respect and esteem; *(Cap.)* a title applied to a clergyman; *v.t.* to venerate. **-nd** *a.* worthy of reverence; a title of respect given to clergy. **-nt** *a.* showing, behaving with, reverence. **-ntial** *a.* respectful. **-ntially, -ntly** *adv.*

rev•er•ie, revery *n.* state of mind, akin to dreaming.

re•verse *v.t.* to turn in an opposite direction; to give a contrary decision; to invert; *v.i.* to change direction; *n.* side which appears when object is turned around; contrary; gear to drive a car backward; *a.* turned backward; opposite. **reversal** *n.* changing, annulling. **-d** *a.* turned in opposite direction; annulled. **-ly** *adv.* **reversibility** *n.* property of being reversible. **reversible** *a.* capable of being used on both sides or in either direction. **reversibly** *adv.* **reversion** *n.* returning or reverting; a deferred annuity; reverting or hope of future possession; atavism. **reversional, reversionary** *a.* involving a reversion. **reversive** *a.*

re•vert *v.i.* to return to former state or rank; to come back to subject; *v.t.* to turn back or reverse. **-ible** *a.*

re•view *v.t.* to reexamine; to consider critically (book); to inspect troops, etc.; *n.* revision; survey; inspection, esp. of massed military forces; a critical notice of a book. **-er** *n.* one who writes critical reviews; inspector.

re•vile *v.t.* to abuse with opprobrious language; to defame. **-ment, -r** *n.*

re•vise *v.t.* to review, alter and amend; *n.* a revised form. **revisal** *n.* reexamination. **revision** *n.* revisal; revised copy of book or document. **-r** *n.* revisional, revisionary *a.* pert. to revision. **revisory** *a.* having power to revise.

re•vive *v.i.* to come back to life; to awaken; *v.t.* to resuscitate; to recover from neglect; to refresh (memory). **revivability** *n.* revivable *a.* capable of being revived. **revivably** *adv.* revival *n.* reviving or being revived; renewed activity, of trade; reappearance of old, neglected play, etc. **revivalism** *n.* religious fervor of a revival. **revivalist** *n.* one who promotes religious revivals. **-r** *n.* one who, or that which, revives; a stimulant. **revivification** *n.* renewal of life and energy. **revivify** *v.t.* to reinvigorate.

re•voke *v.t.* to annul; to reverse (a decision); *v.i.* at cards, to fail to follow suit; *n.* neglect to follow suit at cards. **-r** *n.* revocable *a.* able to be revoked. **revocableness, revocability** *n.* revocably *adv.* revocation *n.* reversal. **revocatory** *a.*

re•volt *v.i.* to renounce allegiance; to rise in rebellion; *v.t.* to rebel; *n.* rebellion; loathing. **-er** *n.* **-ing** *a.* disgusting. **-ingly** *adv.*

rev•o•lu•tion *n.* motion of body around its orbit or focus; a radical change in constitution of a country after revolt. **-ary** *a.* marked by great and violent changes;

n. one who participates in a revolution. **-ize** *v.t.* to change completely.

re•volve *v.i.* to turn around on an axis; to rotate; *v.t.* to cause to turn; to reflect upon. **revolvable** *a.* **-r** *n.* pistol.

re•vue *n.* theatrical entertainment, partly musical comedy, with little continuity of structure or plot.

re•vul•sion *n.* sudden, violent change of feeling; abhorrence. **revulsive** *a.*

re•ward *v.t.* to give in return for; to recompense; *n.* what is given in return for assistance in any form. **-er** *n.* **-ing** *a.*

rhap•so•dy *n.* collection of verses. **rhapsodic(al)** *a.* in extravagant, irregular style. **rhapsodically** *adv.* **rhapsodize** *v.* and *v.i.* to recite, as a rhapsody; to be ecstatic over.

rhe•o- used in the formation of scientific compound terms. **rheometer** *n.* instrument for measuring force of flow of fluids. **rheostat** *n.* instrument for controlling and varying within limits value of resistance in electrical circuit. **rheostatic** *a.*

rhe•sus *n.* small Indian monkey. **rhesian** *a.* **— factor** *(Med.)* *n.* Rh factor; peculiarity of red cells of blood of most individuals, the so-called **rhesus positive,** rendering transfusion of their blood unsuitable for rhesus negative minority of patients.

rhet•o•ric *n.* art of persuasive speech or writing; exaggerated oratory. **-al** *a.* concerning style or effect; of the nature of rhetoric. **-al question** *n.* statement in the form of question to which no answer is expected. **-ally** *adv.* **-ian** *n.* one versed in principles of rhetoric.

rheum *n.* thin, serous fluid secreted by mucous glands and discharged from nostrils or eyes during a common cold. **-atic(al)** *a.* suffering from rheumatism. **-atism** *n.* a disease with symptoms of sharp pains and swelling in muscles and larger joints. **-atoid** *a.* resembling rheumatism. **-y** *a.* damp. **-atoid arthritis** *n.* severe chronic inflammation of joints, esp. knees and fingers.

rhi•nal *a.* pert. to the nose.

rhine•stone *n.* paste imitation of diamonds.

rhi•noc•er•os *n.* thick-skinned mammal, allied to elephant, hippopotamus, with strong horn on nose.

rhinoceros

rhod-, rhodo- used in the formation of compound terms, signifying rose-colored. **rhodocyte** *n.* red blood corpuscle. **rhododendron** *n.* evergreen shrub with magnificent red blossoms.

rhom•bus *n.* *(Geom.)* parallelogram whose sides are all equal but whose angles are not right angles. **rhomb** *n.* diamond-shaped figure. **rhombic(al), rhombiform, rhomboid(al)**

rhomboid n. parrallelogram like rhombus, but having only opposite sides and angles equal.

rhu•barb n. two species of cultivated plants, rhubarb of kitchen garden, and an eastern variety whose roots are used as a purgative.

rhyme n. identity of sound in word endings of verses; v.t. to put into rhyme; v.i. to make verses. -r, -ster n. one who makes rhymes.

rhythm n. regular flow of sound, as in music and poetry, or of action, as in dancing; measured, periodic movement, as in heart pulsations. -ic(al) a. -ically adv. -ics n. science of rhythm.

ri•ant a. laughing; genial. -ly adv.

rib n. one of arched and very elastic bones springing from vertebral column; v.t. to furnish with ribs. -bing pr.p. -bed pa.t. and pa.p. -bing n. an arrangement of ribs.

rib•ald a. vulgar; indecent. -ry n. obscenity. -ish a.

rib•bon n. woven strip of material such as silk or satin, as trimming for a dress; inked tape in a typewriter. **blue ribbon** n. first-prize award.

ri•bo•fla•vin n. chemical substance present in vitamin B_2 complex, with growth-promoting properties.

ice n. annual grass plant, cultivated in Asia, the principal food of one-third of world. — **paper** n. very thin and delicate paper used in China and Japan for drawing and painting.

ich a. wealthy; abounding in possessions; abounding in nutritive qualities; n. the wealthy classes. -es n.pl. wealth. -ly adv. -ness n.

ick•ets n. rachitis, infantile disease marked by defective development of bones. **rickety** a. affected with rickets; insecure.

ic•o•chet n. glancing rebound of object after striking flat surface at oblique angle; v.t. and v.i. to rebound.

id v.t. to free of; to disencumber. -ding pr.p. **rid** or -ded pa.t. and pa.p. -dance n. removal.

id•den pa.p. of ride.

id•dle n. large sieve for sifting gravel; v.t. to separate, as grain from chaff, with a riddle.

id•dle n. puzzling fact, thing, person; v.i. to speak in riddles.

ide v.t. to be mounted on horse, bicycle; to cover distance; v.i. to be carried on back of animal; n. act of riding; journey on horseback, in a vehicle. **riding** pr.p. **rode** pa.t. **ridden** pa.p. -r n. one who rides; addition to a document; supplement to original motion or verdict. **riding** a. used for riding on; used by a rider; n. act of riding.

dge n. line of meeting of two sloping surfaces; long narrow hill; highest part of roof; v.t. to form into ridges; v.i. to wrinkle. -d a. having ridges on its surface.

d•i•cule n. mockery; v.t. to make fun of. -r n. **ridiculous** a. exciting ridicule;

laughable.

ri•fle v.t. to search and rob. -r n. **rifling** n. pillaging.

ri•fle v.t. to make spiral grooves in; n. artillery piece whose barrel is grooved. **rifling** n. arrangement of grooves in a gun barrel or rifle tube. -**man** n. a man armed with rifle.

rift n. fissure; v.t. and v.i. to crack.

rig v.t. to provide (ship) with spars, ropes; to equip; to clothe; n. manner in which masts and sails of vessel are rigged; equipment used in installing machinery. -**ging** pr.p. -**ged** pa.t. and pa.p. -**ger** n. -**ging** n. system of ropes and tackle, esp. for supporting mast or controlling sails; adjustment of components of an aircraft.

right a. proper; in accordance with truth and duty; in politics, implying preservation of established order or of former institutions; (Geom.) applied to regular figures rising perpendicularly; adv. in a right manner; according to truth and justice; exactly; n. that which is correct; a just claim; that which is opposite to left; political party inclined towards conservatism and preservation of status quo; v.t. to do justice to; v.i. to recover natural position; to become upright. -**ful** a. legitimate; fair. -**fully** adv. -**fulness** n. -**ly** adv. in accordance with justice; correctly. -**ness** n. justice. —**about** n. the opposite direction. —**angled** a. having a **right angle**, one of ninety degrees.

righ•teous a. doing what is right; just. -**ly** adv. -**ness** n.

rig•id a. not easily bent; rigorous. -**ness**, -**ity** n. -**ly** adv.

rig•or n. strictness, stiffness; (Med.) a chill with fever. -**ism** n. austerity. -**ist** n. a person of strict principles. -**ous** a. -**ously** adv. -**ousness** n. —**mortis** n. stiffening of body after death.

rile v.t. to irritate.

rim n. border; metal ring forming outer part of a car wheel and carrying the tire; v.t. to furnish with a rim. -**ming** pr.p. -**med** pa.t. and pa.p. -**less** a.

ri•mose a. having surface covered with cracks.

rind n. external covering of trees, fruits, cheese, bacon; v.t. to strip off rind.

ring n. small circle of gold, esp. on finger; band, coil, rim; circle formed for dance or sports; v.t. to encircle; to cut a ring around trunk of a tree. -**ed** a. wearing, marked with, or surrounded by, a ring or rings. -**ing** n. -**leader** n. the leader of people associated together for a common object. -**less** a. -**master** n. one who directs performance in circus ring. -**worm** n. contagious disease of skin, scalp, leaving circular bare patches.

ring v.t. to cause to sound, by striking; v.i. to give out a clear resonant sound, as a bell; to chime; n. a resonant note; chime (of church bells); a telephone call. **rang** pa.t. **rung** pa.p.

rink n. place for skating or ice hockey; floor for roller skating, etc.

rinse v.t. to wash out, by filling with water,

R

etc. and emptying. rinsing n.

ri•ot n. tumultuous disturbance of peace; noisy festivity; profusion, as of color; v.i. to make, or engage in, riot; to disturb peace. -er n. -ing n. -ous a. boisterous. -ously adv. -ousness n. -ry n. riotous conduct.

rip v.t. to rend; to tear off or out; v.i. to tear; to move quickly and freely; n. tear. -ping pr.p. -ped pa.t. and pa.p. -pern. -ping a. — cord n. cord to withdraw parachute from pack so that ascending air forces it open. -saw n. saw with large teeth for cutting timber in direction of grain.

rip n. a stretch of broken water in river. — current, -tide n.

ri•par•i•an a. pert. to, or situated on, banks of a river.

ripe a. ready for reaping; fully developed. -ly adv. -n v.t. to mature; v.i. to grow ripe. -ness n.

rip•ple n. dimpling of surface of water; a little wave; subdued murmur or sound; v.t. to cause ripple in; v.i. to flow into little waves.

rise v.i. to ascend; to get up; to increase in value, price, power; n. that which rises or seems to rise; increase, as of price, wages, etc.; elevation. rising pr.p. rose pa.t. -n pa.p. -r n. one who, or that which, rises; vertical part of a step. rising n. insurrection; a. advancing.

ris•i•ble a. very prone to laugh. -ness, risibility n. risibly adv.

risk n. danger; peril; amount covered by insurance; v.t. to expose to danger or possible loss. -er n. -y a.

rite n. formal custom, esp. religious; ceremonial. ritual a. ceremonial; n. prescribed book of rites. ritualism n. fondness for ceremonial customs in public worship. ritualist n. ritualistic a. ritually adv.

ri•val n. opponent; a. having same claims; competing; v.t. to strive to equal or excel. -ry n. emulation.

rive v.t. to split; v.i. to be rent asunder. -d, -n pa.p.

riv•er n. natural stream of water flowing in a channel; abundance. — basin n. area drained by a river and its tributaries. -bed n. channel of a river. -side n. the bank of a river.

riv•et n. cylindrical iron or steel pin with strong flat head at one end, used for uniting two overlapping plates, by hammering down the stub end; v.t. to fasten with rivets; to fasten firmly.

riv•u•let n. a little river.

roach n. freshwater fish.

roach See cockroach.

road n. a track prepared for passengers, vehicles; direction; route. -block n. an obstruction placed across a road to stop someone. -side n. strip of ground along edge of road. -way n. a road.

roam v.t. and v.i. to wander; n. a ramble; a walk. -er n.

roan a. having coat in which the main color is thickly interspersed with another, esp. chestnut mixed with white or grey; n. a roan horse.

roar v.t. and v.i. to shout; to make loud, confused sound, as winds, waves, traffic, etc.; to laugh loudly; n. sound of roaring, deep cry. -ing n. sound of roaring. -ingly adv.

roast v.t. to cook by exposure to open fire or in oven; to expose to heat (as coffee, etc.); v.i. to become overheated; n. what is roasted, as joint of meat; a. roasted. -ing n. -er n.

rob v.t. to take by force or stealth; to steal. -bing pr.p. -bed pa.t. and pa.p. -ber n. -bery n. forcibly depriving a person of money or of goods.

robe n. a long outer garment, esp. of flowing style; ceremonial dress denoting state, office; v.t. to array; to dress. robing n.

rob•in n. brown red-breasted bird of thrush family. Also — redbreast.

ro•bot n. automaton; mechanical man.

ro•bust a. strong; muscular, vigorous. -ly adv. -ness n.

rock n. (Geol.) any natural deposit of sand, earth, or clay when in natural beds. -ery n. small artificial mound of stones planted with flowers, ferns, etc. -iness n. -y a. full of rocks; resembling rocks. — crystal n. transparent quartz used in making certain lenses. — garden n. a garden laid out with rocks and plants. — salt n. unrefined sodium chloride found in great natural deposits.

rock v.t. to sway to and fro; to put to sleep by rocking; v.i. to be moved, backward and forward; to totter. -er n. curving piece of wood on which cradle or chair rocks. -y a. shaky. -ing n. -ing chair n. chair mounted on rockers. -ing horse n. hobbyhorse.

rock•et n. cylindrical tube filled with a mixture of sulfur, niter, and charcoal, which, on ignition, hurls forward by action of liberated gases; firework; v.i. to soar up.

ro•co•co n. style of architecture, overlaid with ornamentation.

rococo

rod n. slender, straight stick, or switch lightning conductor; linear measure equal to 5½ yards or 16½ feet.

rode pa.t. of ride.

ro•dent a. gnawing; n. gnawing animal, as rabbit, rat.

ro•de•o n. exhibition in steer wrestling and bronco busting by cowboys.

roe n. small deer; female hart. -buck n. male of roe.

roe n. the eggs or spawn of fish.

roent•gen n. (Nuclear Phys.) measuring unit of radiation dose. — rays n.pl. X rays. -ize v.t. to submit to action of X rays.

ro•ga•tion n. in ancient Rome demand, by tribunes, of a law to be passed by people; supplication. **Rogation Days** three days preceding Ascension Day, on which special litanies are recited by R.C

clergy invoking a blessing on crops.
rogatory *a.* commissioned to gather
information.

ogue *n.* rascal; mischievous person.
roguery *n.* cheating; waggery. **roguishly**
adv. **roguishness** *n.*

ogue *v.t.* and *v.i.* to remove plant from
crop (potatoes, cereals, etc.) when that
plant falls short of standard; to keep
strain pure; *n.* plant that falls short of a
standard or has reverted to original type.

ois·ter *v.i.* to bully; to swagger. **-er** *n.*
-ous *a.*

ole *n.* a part played by an actor in a
drama — hence, any conspicuous part or
task in public life.

oll *v.t.* to turn over and over; to move by
turning on an axis; to level with a roller;
v.i. to move forward by turning; to
revolve upon an axis; to keep falling over
and over; to rock from side to side, as a
ship; *n.* a piece of paper, etc., rolled up;
bread baked into small oval or rounded
shapes; official list of members; a full
corkscrew revolution of an airplane
about its longitudinal fore and aft. **-able**
a. **— call** *n.* calling over list of names to
check absentees. **-er** *n.* a cylinder which
distributes ink over type in printing;
long, broad bandage; small, insectivorous
bird which tumbles about in the air. **-er
skate** *n.* skate with wheels or rollers
instead of steel runner. **-ing** *a.* moving on
wheels; turning over and over; *n. (Naut.)*
reeling of a ship from side to side. **-ing
pin** *n.* cylindrical device for rolling out
dough.

·l· lick *v.i.* to move about in a boisterous,
careless manner; *n.* frolicsome gaiety.
-ing *a.* jovial; high-spirited.

·· ly-po· ly *a.* plump and rounded.

o· man *a.* pert. to Rome or Roman people;
in printing, upright letters as
distinguished from *italic* characters;
expressed in letters, not in figures, as I,
IV. **-ic** *a.* **-ize** *v.t.* to introduce many
idioms derived from Latin; *v.i.* to use
Latin expressions. **— candle** *n.* a firework
which throws out differently colored
stars. **— Catholic**, a member of section of
Christian Church which acknowledges
supremacy of Pope.

o· mance *n.* languages; *a.* pert. to these
languages. **romance** *n.* historical novel;
story depending mainly on love interest;
romantic quality; *(Mus.)* composition
sentimental and expressive in character;
v.i. to write or tell romances; embroider
one's description with extravagances.
romantic *a.* fanciful; sentimental;
imaginative. **romantically** *adv.*
romanticism *n.* the reactionary
movement in literature and art against
formalism and classicism. **romanticist** *n.*

mp *v.i.* to leap and frisk about in play; a
boisterous form of play. **-ers** *n.pl.* a
child's overall, with leg openings. **-ish** *a.*

n· deau *n.* poem, thirteen lines with only
two rhymes, the opening words recurring
additionally, after eighth and thirteenth
lines. **rondel** *n.* poem of thirteen or
fourteen iambic lines, first two lines of

which are repeated in middle and at
close. **rondo** *n.* sonata movement in
music in which a principal theme is
repeated two or three times.

roof *n.* outside structure covering building;
framework supporting this covering;
ceiling; *v.t.* to cover with a roof; to
shelter. **— garden** *n.* miniature garden
on flat roof. **-tree** *n.* the ridgepole or roof
itself.

rook *n.* in chess, one of the four pieces
placed on corner squares of the board;
also known as a castle.

rook *n.* blue-black, hoarse-voiced bird of
crow family; swindler; *v.t.* to swindle.
-ery *n.* colony of rooks and their nests.

room *n.* (enough) space; apartment or
chamber; *pl.* lodgings; *v.i.* to lodge. **-ful**
a. **-ily** *adv.* **-iness** *n.* spaciousness. **-y** *a.*

roost *n.* pole on which birds rest at night;
perch; *v.i.* to settle down to sleep, as
birds on a perch; to perch. **-er** *n.* a cock.

root *n.* part of plant which grows down into
soil seeking nourishment for whole
plant; origin; vital part; basis; *v.t.* to
plant and fix in earth; to establish firmly;
to pull out by roots; *v.i.* to enter earth, as
roots; to be firmly established. **-ed** *a.*
firmly established. **-stock** *n.* a rhizome.

root *v.t.* and *v.i.* to turn up with the snout,
as swine; to uncover (with *up*).

rope *v.t.* stout cord of several twisted
strands of fiber or metal wire; *v.t.* to
mark off a rack track, with ropes; to lasso.
— ladder, **— bridge**, etc. *n.* one made of
ropes.

Roque· fort *n.* a cheese of ewe's milk.

Ro· sa· ceae *n.pl.* order of plants including
rose, strawberry, blackberry, spiraea.
rosaceous *a.* belonging to rose family.
rosarium *n.* rose garden.

ro· sa· ry *n.* string of prayer beads.

rose *pa.t.* of rise.

rose *n.* genus of plant family of Rosaceae;
shade of pink. **-ate** *a.* blooming;
optimistic. **-bud** *n.* the bud of the rose;
-water *n.* water tinctured with roses by
distillation. **— window** *n.* circular
window with a series of mullions
diverging from center. **-wood** *n.* rich,
dark-red hardwood from S. America,
used for furniture-making. **rosily** *adv.*
rosiness *n.* **rosy** *a.* blooming; red;
favorable.

rose· mar· y *n.* a small fragrant evergreen
shrub.

ro· sette *n.* something fashioned to
resemble a rose, as ribbon; a rose-shaped
architectural ornament.

ros· in *n.* resin in solid state; *v.t.* to cover
with rosin. **-y** *a.*

ros· ter *n.* a list showing turns of duty;
register of names.

ros· trum *n.* beak of a ship; raised platform;
pulpit. **rostral** *a.* pert. to a rostrum.
rostrate, rostrated *a.* beaked.

ros· y See rose.

rot *v.t.* and *v.i.* to decompose naturally; to
become morally corrupt; to molder away;
n. decomposition; decay. **-ting** *pr.p.* **-ted**
pa.t. and *pa.p.*

ro· ta· ry *a.* turning, as a wheel; rotatory; *n.*

R

(*Cap.*) international association of businessmen's clubs. **Rotarian** *n.* member of Rotary Club. **— engine** *n.* (*Aero.*) engine in which cylinder and crankcase rotate with propeller.

ro•tate *v.t.* to cause to revolve; *v.i.* to move around pivot; *a.* (*Bot.*) wheel-shaped, as a calyx. **rotation** *n.* turning, as a wheel or solid body on its axis; serial change, as rotation of crops. **rotational** *a.* **rotator** *n.* **rotatory** *a.* turning on an axis, as a wheel; following in succession.

rote *n.* mechanical repetition.

ro•tis•ser•ie *n.* grill with a turning spit.

ro•tor *n.* revolving portion of dynamo, motor, or turbine.

rot•ten *a.* putrefied; decayed; corrupt. **-ly** *adv.* **-ness** *n.*

ro•tund *a.* round; plump. **-a** *n.* circular building or hall, covered by dome. **-ity,** **-ness** *n.* globular form; roundness.

rouge *n.* cosmetic for tinting cheeks; *v.t.* and *v.i.* to tint (face) with rouge.

rough *a.* not smooth; uneven; uncut; unpolished; stormy; *adv.* in rough manner; *n.* crude, unfashioned state; *v.t.* to make rough; to roughen; to shape out in rough-and-ready way. **-age** *n.* fibrous, unassimilated portions of food which promote intestinal movement. **— diamond** *n.* uncut diamond; a person of ability and worth, but uncouth. **-en** *v.t.* to make rough; *v.i.* to become rough. **—hew** *v.t.* to give first form to a thing. **-ly** *adv.*

rou•lette *n.* game of chance, played with a revolving disk and a ball.

round *a.* circular; spherical; not fractional, as a number; plump; *n.* circle; circuit; cycle; series; a course of action performed by persons in turn; beat of policeman, milkman, etc.; one of successive stages in competition; 3-minute period in boxing match; circular dance; *adv.* on all sides; circularly; back to the starting point; *v.t.* to make circular, spherical, or cylindrical; to finish; *v.i.* to become round or full in form. **-about** *a.* indirect; circuitous. **-er** *n.* a tool for rounding off objects. **-house** *n.* circular building for locomotives. **-ly** *adv.* vigorously; open. **-ness** *n.* **—table conference** *n.* one where all participants are on equal footing. **-up** *n.* collecting cattle into herds; *v.t.* to collect and bring into confined space.

rouse *v.t.* to wake from sleep; to startle or surprise; *v.i.* to awake from repose. **-r** *n.* **rousing** *a.*

rout *n.* tumultous crowd; confusion of troops in flight; *v.t.* to defeat and throw into confusion.

rout *v.i.* to roar; to snore.

rout *v.t.* to turn up with the snout; to cut grooves by gouging; *v.i.* to poke about.

route *n.* course which is traveled or to be followed.

rou•tine *n.* regular course of action adhered to by habit; *a.* in ordinary way of business; according to rule.

rove *v.t.* to wander over; *v.i.* to wander about; to ramble. **-r** *n.* wanderer; roving machine. **roving** *n.* and *a.*

row *n.* persons or things in straight line a file; a line.

row *v.t.* to impel (a boat) with oars; *v.t.* to labor with oars; *n.* spell of rowing; a tri in a rowboat. **-boat** *n.* boat impelle solely by oars.

row *n.* riotous, noisy disturbance. **-dy** *a* noisy. **-dyism, -diness** *n.*

row•el *n.* wheel of a spur, furnished wit sharp points.

roy•al *a.* pert. to the crown; worthy o patronized by, a king or queen; *n.* a size of paper. **-ism** *n.* principles o government by king. **-ist** *n.* adherent t sovereign, or one attached to kingly government. **-ly** *adv.* **-ty** *n.* kingly office person of king or sovereign; members o royal family; payment to inventor for us of his invention, or to author dependin on sales of his book.

rub *v.t.* to subject to friction; to chafe; t wipe; *v.i.* to come into contac accompanied by friction; *n.* difficulty impediment; a sore spot from rubbing **-bing** *pr.p.* **-bed** *pa.t.* and *pa.p.* **-ber** *n* **-bing** *n.* applying friction to a surface.

rub•ber *n.* coagulated sap of certai tropical trees; *pl.* overshoes; galoshes; *a* made of rubber. **-ized** *a.* mixed wit rubber, as rubberized fabrics.

rub•bish *n.* anything worthless; refuse nonsense.

rub•ble *n.* upper fragmentary decompose mass of stone overlying a solid stratum o rock; rough stones used to fill up space between walls, etc. **-rubbly** *a.*

ru•bi•cund *a.* ruddy; florid; reddish. **-ity** *n*

ru•bid•i•um *n.* rare silvery metalli element, one of the alkali metals.

ru•ble *n.* Russian monetary unit.

ru•bric *n.* medieval manuscript or printe book in which initial letter wa illumined in red; heading or portion o such a work, printed in red — hence, th title of a chapter, statute, etc. originall in red; *v.t.* to illumine with red. **-al** *a* colored in red; to formulate as a rubri **-ian** *n.* one versed in the rubrics. **-is** *n.* a strict adherent to rubrics; a formalist

ru•by *n.* a red variety of corundum value as a gem; *a.* having the dark-red color o a ruby.

ruck *v.t.* to wrinkle; *v.i.* to be drawn int folds; *n.* fold; wrinkle.

ruck *n.* rank and file; common herd.

ruck•sack *n.* pack carried on back b climbers, etc.

rudd *n.* British freshwater fish allied to th roach.

rud•der *n.* flat frame fastened vertically t stern of ship, which controls direction anything which guides, as a bird tail feathers.

rud•dle red ocher, used for marking sheep *v.t.* to mark (sheep) with ruddle.

rud•dy *a.* of a red color; of healthy fles color. **ruddiness** *n.*

rude *a.* uncivil; roughly made. **-ly** *adv* **-ness** *n.*

ru•di•ment *n.* beginning; vestige; (*Biol* imperfectly developed or formed orga *pl.* elements, first principles, beginning. -al, -ary *a.* -arily *adv.*

ue *v.t.* and *v.i.* to grieve for; to repent of. -ing *pr.p.* -ful *a.* woeful; sorrowful. -fully *adv.*

ue *n.* aromatic, bushy, evergreen shrub.

uff *n.* broad, circular collar, plaited, or fluted; light-brown mottled bird, the male being ringed with ruff of long, black, red-barred feathers during breeding season; *(fem.)* reeve; neck fringe of long hair or feathers on animal or bird. -ed *a.*

uf‧fi‧an *n.* a rough, lawless fellow; *a.* brutal. -ism *n.* conduct of a ruffian. -ly *a.*

uf‧fle *v.t.* to draw into wrinkles, open plaits, or folds; to roughen surface of; to put out (of temper); *v.i.* to be at variance; *n.* a strip of gathered cloth, attached to a garment, a frill; commotion.

ug *n.* piece of carpeting.

ug‧by *n.* English form of football, played with teams of 15 players each.

ug‧ged *a.* rough; uneven; unpolished; vigorous. -ly *adv.* -ness *n.*

u‧gose *a.* wrinkled; ridged. -ly *adv.* rugosity *n.*

u‧in *n.* downfall; remains of demolished city, work of art, etc.; state of being decayed; *v.t.* to bring to ruin; to spoil; to cause loss of livelihood to. -s *n.pl.* ruined buildings, etc. -ation *n.* state of being ruined. -er *n.* -ous *a.* dilapidated; destructive. -ously *adv.*

ule *n.* act, power, or mode of directing; authority; prescribed law; established principle or mode of action; *v.t.* to govern; to decide authoritatively; to mark with straight lines, using ruler; *v.i.* to have command. -r *n.* sovereign; instrument with straight edges for drawing lines. ruling *a.* governing; predominant; *n.* an authoritative decision; a point of law settled by a court of law.

am *n.* spirit distilled from sugarcane skimmings or molasses.

am‧ba *n.* Cuban dance.

am‧ble *v.i.* to make a low, vibrant, continuous sound; to reverberate; *n.* vibrant, confused noise, as of thunder; seat for footmen at back of carriage. -r *n.*

a‧mi‧nant *n.* animal which chews cud, as sheep, cow; *a.* chewing cud. ruminate *v.t.* to chew over again; *v.i.* to chew cud; to meditate. ruminatingly *adv.* rumination *n.* ruminative *a.* ruminator *n.*

am‧mage *v.t.* to search thoroughly into or through; to ransack; *v.i.* to make a search; *n.* careful search; odds and ends. -r *n.*

am‧my *n.* a simple card game for any number of players.

a‧mor *n.* current but unproved report; *v.t.* to spread as a rumor.

mp *n.* end of backbone of animal with the parts adjacent; buttocks.

am‧ple *v.t.* to muss; crumple; *n.* an irregular fold.

n *v.i.* to move rapidly on legs; to hurry; to contend in a race; to stand as candidate for; to flee; to continue in operation; to be worded; *v.t.* to cause to run; to drive, push, or thrust; to manage; to maintain regularly, as bus service; to incur (risk); *n.* flow; act of running; course run; regular, scheduled journey; pleasure trip by car; unconstrained liberty; point gained in baseball; a great demand. -ning *pr.p.* ran *pa.t.* run *pa.p.* -about *n.* motorboat. -away *n.* fugitive; horse which has bolted. -ner *n.* one taking part in a race; messenger; one of curved pieces on which sleigh, skate, slides; device for facilitating movement of sliding doors, etc.; smuggler. -ner-up *n.* one who gains second place. -ning *a.* flowing; entered for a race, as a horse; successive (numbers); *n.* flowing quickly; chance of winning; operation of machine, business, etc. -ning board *n.* narrow, horizontal platform running along locomotive, car, to provide step for entering or leaving. -ning commentary *n.* broadcast description of event by eyewitness. -ning knot *n.* knot made so as to tighten when rope is pulled. -way *n.* prepared track on airfields for landing and taking off.

run‧dle *n.* a step of a ladder; something which rotates like a wheel.

rung *pa.p.* of ring.

rung *n.* rounded step of a ladder; spoke.

run‧nel *n.* small brook.

runt *n.* small, weak specimen of any animal, person or thing.

rup‧ture *n.* breaking or bursting; state of being violently parted; hernia; *v.t.* to part by violence; to burst.

ru‧ral *a.* pert. to the country; pert. to agriculture; pastoral. -ize *v.t.* to make rural; *v.i.* to live in the country; to become rural. -ism *n.* -ly *adv.*

ruse *n.* trick; strategem.

rush *v.t.* to carry along violently and rapidly; to hasten forward; *v.i.* to speed; *n.* heavy current of water, air, etc.; haste. -er *n.*

rush *n.* name of plants of genus Juncus, found in marshy places; straw. —bottomed *a.* of chair with seat made of rushes. -y *a.*

rus‧set *a.* of reddish-brown color; *n.* apple of russet color.

Rus‧sian *a.* pert. to Russia; *n.* inhabitant of Russia; Russian language.

rust *n.* coating formed on iron or various other metals by corrosion; reddish fungus disease on plants; *v.t.* to corrode with rust; *v.i.* to dissipate one's potential powers by inaction. -ily *adv.* -iness *n.* -proof *a.* not liable to rust. -y *a.*

rus‧tic *a.* pert. to the country; rural; *n.* a simple country person. -ally *adv.* -ate *v.t.* to make rustic; *v.i.* to live in the country. -ation, -ity *n.*

rus‧tle *v.i.* to make soft, swishing sounds, like rubbing of dry leaves; *v.t.* (U.S.) to steal, esp. cattle; *n.* a soft whispering sound. -r *n.* one who, or that, which rustles. rustling *n.*

rut *n.* furrow made by wheel; settled way of living; *v.t.* to form ruts in. -ting *pr.p.* -ted *pa.t.* and *pa.p.*

ruth‧less *a.* pitiless; cruel. -ly *adv.* -ness *n.*

rye *n.* a kind of grass allied to wheat; whiskey made from rye.

R

Sab·bath *n.* seventh day of week; Sunday; Lord's Day.

sa·ber *n.* sword with broad and heavy blade; *v.t.* to wound or cut down with saber.

Sa·bine *n.* one of an ancient tribe of Italy who became merged with the Romans; *a.* pert. to the Sabines.

sa·ble *n.* small carnivorous mammal of weasel tribe; sable fur; *pl.* mourning garments; *a.* black.

sable

sab·ot *n.* a wooden shoe.

sab·o·tage *n.* willful damage or destruction of property perpetrated for political or economic reasons. **saboteur** *n.*

sac *n.* pouch-like structure or receptacle.

sac·cha·rin, saccharine *n.* a white crystalline solid substance, with an intensely sweet taste. **saccharine** *a.* pert. to sugar; cloying; sickly sentimental. **saccharify** *v.t.* to convert into sugar. **saccharinity** *n.* **saccharize** *v.t.* to convert into sugar. **saccharoid, -al** *a.* having granular texture resembling that of loaf sugar.

sac·cule *n.* a small sac. **saccular** *a.*

sac·er·do·tal *a.* pert. to priests, or to the order of priests. **-ism** *n.* **-ist** *n.* **-ly** *adv.*

sa·chet *n.* a small scent bag.

sack *n.* a large bag, usually of coarse material; contents of sack; also **sacque**, loose garment or cloak; any bag; *v.t.* to put into sacks. **-ing** *n.* coarse cloth or canvas.

sack *n.* old name for various kinds of dry wines.

sack *v.t.* to plunder or pillage; to lay waste; *n.* pillage of town. **-ing** *n.*

sac·ra·ment *n.* one of the ceremonial observances in Christian Church. **-al** *n.* **-ally** *adv.* **-arian** *n.* **-arianism** *n.*

sac·ri·fice *v.t.* to consecrate ceremonially offering of victim by way of expiation or propitiation to deity; to surrender for sake of obtaining some other advantage; *v.i.* to make offerings to God of things consumed on the altar; *n.* anything consecrated and offered to divinity; anything given up for sake of others. **-r** *n.* **sacrificial** *a.* **sacrificially** *adv.*

sac·ri·lege *n.* profanation of sacred place or thing; church robbery. **sacrilegious** *a.* violating sacred things; profane; desecrating. **sacrilegiously** *adv.* **sacrilegiousness** *n.*

sac·ris·tan *n.* officer in church entrusted with care of sacristy or vestry; sexton. **sacristy** *n.* vestry.

sac·ro·sanct *a.* inviolable and sacred in the highest degree. **-ity** *n.*

sa·crum *n.* a composite bone at the base of the spinal column. *pl.* **sacra.**

sad *a.* sorrowful; affected with grief; deplorably bad; somber-colored. **-den** *v.t.* to make sad or sorrowful; *v.i.* to become sorrowful and downcast. **-ly** *adv.* **-ness** *n.*

sad·dle *n.* rider's seat to fasten on horse, or form part of a cycle, etc.; part of a shaft; joint of mutton or venison containing part of backbone with ribs on each side; ridge of hill between higher hills; *v.t.* to put a saddle upon; to burden with; to encumber. **-r** *n.* one who makes saddles and harness for horses. **saddlery** *n.*

sad·ism *n.* insatiate love of inflicting pain for its own sake. **sadist** *n.* **sadistic** *a.*

sa·fa·ri *n.* hunting expedition.

safe *a.* free from harm; sound; protected; sure; *n.* a fireproof chest for protection of money and valuables; case with wire gauze panels to keep meat, etc. fresh. **-guard** *n.* protection; precaution; convoy; escort; passport; *v.t.* to make safe; to protect. **-ly** *adv.* **-ness** *n.* **-ty** *n.*

saf·fron *n.* plant of iris family, used in medicine and as a flavoring and coloring in cookery; *a.* deep yellow.

sag *v.i.* to sink in middle; to hang sideways or curve downwards under pressure; to give way; to tire. *pr.p.* **-ging.** *pa.p.* **-ged.** *n.* a droop.

sa·ga *n.* a prose narrative, written in Iceland in the 12th and 13th centuries, concerning legendary and historic people and actions of Iceland and Norway; novels describing life of a family.

sa·ga·cious *a.* quick of thought; acute; shrewd. **-ly** *adv.* **-ness** *n.* **sagacity** *n.*

sage *n.* dwarf shrub of mint family.

sage *a.* wise; discerning; solemn; *n.* wise man. **-ly** *adv.* **-ness** *n.*

sage-brush *n.* a shrub smelling like sage and found chiefly on western plains of U.S.

Sa·git·ta *n.* a constellation north of Aquila—the Arrow. **sagittal, sagittate** *a.* shaped like an arrow or arrowhead. **sagittally** *adv.* **Saggitarius** *n.* the Archer, 9th sign of zodiac; constellation in Milky Way.

sa·go *n.* dry, granulated starch.

said *pa.t.* and *pa.p.* of **say**; the before-mentioned; already specified; aforesaid.

sail *n.* sheet of canvas to catch wind for propelling ship; sailing vessel; a journey upon the water; arm of windmill; *v.t.* to navigate; to pass in a ship; to fly through; *v.i.* to travel by water; to glide in stately fashion. **-able** *a.* navigable. **-boat** *n.* a boat propelled by sails. **-less** *a.* **-or** *n.* mariner; seaman; tar.

saint *n.* outstandingly devout and virtuous person; one of the blessed in heaven; one formally canonized by R.C. Church; *v.t.* to canonize. **-ed** *a.* pious; hallowed; sacred; dead. **-hood** *n.* **—like, -ly** *a.* **-liness** *n.*

sake *n.* cause; behalf; purpose; account; regard.

sal *n.* salt (much used in compound words pert. esp. to pharmacy).

sa·la·cious *a.* lustful; lewd; lecherous. **-ly** *adv.* **-ness, salacity** *n.*

sal·ad *n.* green vegetables raw or cooked, meat, fish, fruit, dressed with various seasonings or dressings.

sal·a·man·der *n.* small, tailed amphibian, allied to newt. **salamandriform,**

common
salamander

salamandrine *a.* pert. to or shaped like a salamander; fire-resisting.

sa·la·mi *n.* Italian salted sausage.

sal·a·ry *n.* fixed remuneration, usually monthly, for services rendered; stipend. **salaried** *a.*

sale *n.* exchange of anything for money; demand (for article); public exposition of goods; a special disposal of stock at reduced prices. **-able, salable** *a.* capable of being sold. **-ableness** *n.* **-ably** *adv.* **-sman** *n.* **-smanship** *n.*

sal·i·cin *n.* a bitter white crystalline glucocide used as drug. **salicylate** *n.* any salt of salicylic acid. **salicylic** *a.*

sa·li·ent *a.* moving by leaps; projecting angle in line of fortifications, etc. **-ly** *adv.*

sa·lif·er·ous *a.* bearing or producing salt.

sal·i·fy *v.t.* to form a salt by combining an acid with a base; to combine with a salt. **salifiable** *a.*

sa·line *a.* of or containing salt; salty; *n.* a saline medicine. **salina** *n.* salt marsh; saltworks. **saliniferous** *a.* **salinity** *n.*

sa·li·va *n.* digestive fluid or spittle. **-ry** *a.* **-te** *v.t.* to produce abnormal secretion of saliva.

sal·low *a.* of sickly yellow color. **-ish** *a.* **-ness** *n.*

sal·ly *n.* sudden eruption; sortie; witticism; *v.i.* to issue suddenly.

salm·on *n.* silver-scaled fish with orange-pink flesh.

salmon

sa·lon *n.* spacious apartment for reception of company.

sa·loon *n.* public dining room; principal cabin in steamer; a place where liquor is sold and drunk.

sal·si·fy, salsafy *n.* hardy, biennial, composite herb with edible root.

salt *n.* sodium chloride or common salt; compound resulting from reaction between acid and a base; savor; piquancy; wit; *a.* containing or tasting of salt; preserved with salt; pungent; *v.t.* to season or treat with salt. **-er** *n.* **-ern** *n.* saltworks. **-ing** *n.* land covered regularly by tide. **-less** *a.* **-ness** *n.* **-y** *a.*

sal·tant *a.* leaping; jumping; dancing. **saltation** *n.*

sal·tire, saltier *n.* cross in the shape of an X, or St. Andrew's cross.

salt·pe·ter *n.* common name for niter or potassium nitrate.

sa·lu·bri·ous *a.* wholesome; healthy. **-ly** *adv.* **-ness, salubrity** *n.*

sal·u·tar·y *a.* wholesome; healthful; beneficial. **salutarily** *adv.* **salutariness** *n.*

sa·lute *v.t.* to address with expressions of kind wishes; to recognize one of superior rank by a sign; to honor by a discharge of cannon or small arms, by striking colors, etc.; to greet; *n.* greeting showing respect. **salutation** *n.* **salutatory** *a.* welcoming. **salutatorian** *n.*

salvage See salve.

sal·va·tion *n.* preservation from destruction; redemption; deliverance.

salve *v.t.* to save or retrieve property from danger or destruction. **salvability** *n.* **salvable** *a.* **salvage** *n.* compensation allowed to persons who assist in saving ship or cargo, or property in general, from destruction; property, so saved; *v.t.* to save from ruins, shipwreck, etc. **-r, salvor** *n.*

salve *n.* healing ointment applied to wounds or sores; *v.t.* to anoint with such; to heal; to soothe.

sal·ver *n.* a tray for visiting cards.

sal·vo *n.* guns fired simultaneously, or in succession as salute; sustained applause or welcome from large crowd. *pl.* **salvo(e)s.**

Sa·mar·i·tan *a.* pert. to Samaria in Palestine; *n.* native or inhabitant of Samaria; kind-hearted, charitable person.

sam·ba *n.* a dance of S. American origin.

sam·bo *n.* offspring of black person and mulatto.

Sam Browne *n.* military belt.

same *a.* identical; not different; of like kind; unchanged; uniform; aforesaid. **-ly** *adv.* **-ness** *n.*

sam·ite *n.* rich silk material; any lustrous silk stuff.

sam·o·var *n.* Russian tea urn.

Sam·o·yed *n.* Mongolian race inhabiting N. shores of Russia and Siberia; breed of dog, orig. a sledge dog.

sam·pan *n.* a Chinese light river vessel. Also **sanpan.**

sam·phire *n.* European herb found on rocks and cliffs, St. Peter's wort.

sam·ple *n.* specimen; example; *v.t.* to take or give a sample of; to try; to test; to taste. **-r** *n.*

san·a·tive *a.* having power to cure or heal. **-ness** *n.* **sanatorium** *n.* (*pl.* **sanatoria**) institution for open air treatment of tuberculosis; institution for convalescent patients. Also **sanitarium.** See **sanitary.** **sanatory** *a.*

sanc·ti·fy *v.t.* to set apart as sacred or holy; to consecrate; to purify. **sanctification** *n.* **sanctified** *a.* **sanctifiedly** *adv.* **sanctimonious** *a.* hypocritically pious. **sanctimoniously** *adv.* **sanctimoniousness, sanctimony** *n.* affected piety. **sanctitude** *n.* saintliness; holiness. **sanctity** *n.*

sanc·tion *n.* solemn ratification; express permission; legal use of force to secure obedience to law; *v.t.* and *v.i.* to confirm; to authorize; to countenance. **sanctions** *n.pl.* measures to enforce fulfillment of international treaty obligations.

sanc·tu·ar·y *n.* holy place; shrine; the chancel; a church or other place of protection for fugitives. **sanctum** *n.* sacred place; private room or study. **sanctum sanctorum**, holy of holies in Jewish temple.

sand *n.* fine, loose grains of quartz or other mineral matter formed by disintegration of rocks; *n.pl.* sandy beach; desert region; moments of time; *v.t.* to sprinkle or cover with sand; to smooth with sandpaper. **-iness** *n.* **-piper** *n.* small wading bird of plover family. **-y** *a.*

sand-piper

san·dal *n.* a shoe consisting of flat sole, bound to foot by straps or thongs. **-led** *a.*

san·dal·wood *n.* fragrant heartwood of santalum.

sand·er·ling *n.* a wading bird.

sand·wich *n.* two thin pieces of bread with slice of meat, etc., between them. *v.t.* to make into sandwich; to form of alternating layers of different nature; to insert or squeeze in between, making a tight fit.

sane *a.* of sound mind; not deranged; rational; reasonable; lucid. **-ly** *adv.* **-ness** *n.*

sang *pa.t.* of sing.

san·guine *a.* hopeful; confident; cheerful; deep red; florid; *n.* a crayon; blood-red color. **sanguinarily** *adv.* **sanguinariness** *n.* **sanguinary** *a.* bloody; blood-thirsty; murderous. **-ly** *adv.* **-ness** *n.* **-ous** *a.* bloody; blood-red; containing blood.

San·he·drin *n.* supreme court of Ancient Jerusalem. Also **Sanhedrim**.

san·i·tar·y *a.* pert. to health; hygienic; clean; free from dirt, germs, etc. **sanitarian** *n.* one interested in the promotion of hygienic reforms. **sanitarily** *adv.* **sanitation** *n.* **sanitarium**, *n.* private hospital for treatment of special or chronic diseases.

san·i·ty *n.* state of being sane.

sank *pa.t.* of the verb **sink**.

sans·cu·lotte *n.* ragged fellow.

San·skrit, **Sanscrit** *n.* classic literary language of ancient India.

San·ta Claus *n.* traditional 'Father Christmas' of children.

sap *n.* watery juice of plants. **-less** *a.* **-ling** *n.* young tree. **-py** *a.* **-wood** *n.* alburnum, exterior part of wood of tree next to bark.

sap *n.* tunnel driven under enemy positions for purpose of attack; *v.t.* and *v.i.* to undermine. *pr.p.* **-ping**. *pa.t.* and *pa.p.* **-ped**.

sap·id *a.* savory; palatable; tasty. **-ity** *n.*

sa·pi·ent *a.* discerning; wise; sage. **sapience** *n.* **-ly** *adv.*

sap·o·na·ceous *a.* resembling soap; slippery, as if soaped. **saponify** *v.t.*

sa·por *n.* taste; savor; flavor. **-oific** *a.* **-osity** *n.*

Sap·phic *a.* pert. to Sappho, lyric poetess of Greece of 7th cent. B.C.; denoting verse in which three lines of five feet each are followed by line of two feet; *n.* Sapphic verse. **sapphism** *n.* unnatural sexual relations between women.

sap·phire *n.* translucent precious stone of various shades of blue; *a.* deep, pure blue.

sar·a·band *n.* slow, stately dance.

Sar·a·cen *n.* Arab or Mohammedan who invaded Europe and Africa; an infidel. **-ic**, **-ical** *a.*

sar·casm *n.* taunt; scoffing gibe; veiled sneer; irony; use of such expressions. **sarcastic**, **-al** *a.* **sarcastically** *adv.*

sar·coph·a·gus *n.* kind of limestone used by Greeks for coffins and believed to consume flesh of bodies deposited in it; stone coffin; monumental chest or case of stone, erected over graves. *pl.* **sarcophagi**.

sar·dine *n.* small fish of herring family.

sar·don·ic *a.* (of laugh, smile) bitter, scornful, derisive, mocking. **-ally** *adv.*

sar·do·nyx *n.* semiprecious stone.

sar·gas·sum *n.* genus of seaweeds. **sargasso** *n.* gulfweed.

sargasso

sa·ri *n.* long outer garment of Hindu women. Also **saree**.

sa·rong *n.* garment draped round waist by Malayans.

sar·sa·pa·ril·la *n.* several plants of genus Smilax, with roots yielding a mild diuretic; a soft drink flavored with the extract.

sar·to·ri·al *a.* pert. to tailor, tailoring.

sash *n.* silken band; belt or band, usually decorative.

sash *n.* frame of window which carries panes of glass.

sas·sa·fras *n.* a tree of the laurel family.

sat *pa.t.* and *pa.p.* of sit.

Sa·tan *n.* the devil. **-ic**, **-al** *a.* devilish; infernal; diabolical. **-ically** *adv.*

satch·el *n.* small bag for books, etc.

sate *v.t.* to satisfy appetite of; to glut.

sa·teen *n.* glossy cloth for linings.

sat·el·lite *n.* one constantly in attendance upon important personage; an obsequious follower; (*Astron.*) a

S

secondary body which revolves round planets of solar system; a moon. **satellitic** *a.*

sa•ti•ate *v.t.* to satisfy appetite of; to surfeit; to sate. **satiability** *n.* **satiable** *a.* capable of being satisfied. **satiation** *n.* state of being satiated. **satiety** *n.*

sat•in *n.* soft, rich, usually silk fabric with smooth, lustrous surface; *a.* made of satin; smooth; glossy. **-et** *n.* thin kind of satin. **-wood** *n.* beautiful hard yellow wood. **-y** *a.*

sat•ire *n.* literary composition holding up to ridicule vice or folly of the times. **satiric, -al** *a.* **satirically** *adv.* **satiricalness** *n.* **satirize** *v.t.* **satirist** *n.*

sat•is•fy *v.t.* to gratify fully; to convince; to content; to answer; to free from doubt; *v.i.* to give content; to supply to the full; to make payment. **satisfaction** *n.* **satisfactorily** *adv.* **satisfactoriness** *n.* **satisfactory** *a.* **-ing** *a.* **-ingly** *adv.*

sa•trap *n.* governor of province under ancient Persian monarchy; petty, despotic governor. **-al** *a.* **-y** *n.*

sat•u•rate *v.t.* to soak thoroughly; to steep; to drench. **-d** *a.* **saturation** *n.* **saturator** *n.* contrivance for saturating air with water-vapor.

Sat•ur•day *n.* seventh day of week.

Sat•urn *n.* old deity, father of Jupiter; sixth of major planets in order of distance from sun. **saturnalian** *a.* **Saturnian** *a.* pert. to epoch of Saturn; golden; distinguished for prosperity and peacefulness. **saturnine** *a.* gloomy, sluggish in temperament.

sat•yr *n.* woodland deity in Greek mythology, part human and part goat, fond of sensual enjoyment; lecherous person. **satyriasis** *n.* excessive and morbid desire for sexual intercourse exhibited by men. **-omaniac** *n.* **-ical** *a.*

sauce *n.* liquid or soft seasoning for food; condiment; relish; *v.t.* to season with sauce; to give flavor or interest to; *(Colloq.)* to be rude in speech or manner. **saucy** *a.* bold; pert; cheeky. **saucily** *adv.* **sauciness** *n.*

sau•cer *n.* small plate put under cup.

sauer•kraut *n.* cabbage cut fine and allowed to ferment in brine.

saun•ter *v.i.* to stroll. *n.* leisurely walk or stroll. **-er** *n.* **-ing** *n.*

sau•ri•an *n.* lizard-like reptile.

sau•sage *n.* meat minced and seasoned and enclosed in thin membranous casing obtained from small entrails of pig or sheep.

sau•terne *n.* a well-known white wine.

sav•age *a.* remote from human habitation; wild; uncivilized; primitive; cruel; *n.* man in native state of primitiveness; a barbarian. **-ly** *adv.* **-ry** *n.*

sa•vant *n.* a man of learning.

save *v.t.* to rescue, preserve from danger, evil, etc.; to redeem; to protect; to lay by; to spare; to except; *v.i.* to lay by money; to economize; *prep.* except; *conj.* but. **savable** *a.* **-r** *n.* **savingly** *adv.*

sav•ior *n.* one who saves or delivers from destruction or danger; *(Cap.)* the Redeemer, Jesus Christ. Also **saviour.**

sa•voir•faire *n.* the knack of knowing the right thing to do at the right time; tact.

sa•vor *n.* taste; flavor; relish; odor; *v.t.* to like; to taste or smell with pleasure; to relish; *v.i.* to have a particular smell or taste; to resemble; to indicate the presence of. **-ily** *adv.* **-less** *a.* **-y** *a.*

sa•vor•y *n.* genus of aromatic plants.

saw *pa.t.* of the verb **see.**

saw *n.* old saying; maxim; proverb; aphorism; adage.

saw *n.* hand or mechanical tool with thin blade, band, or circular disk with

saws

serrated edge, used for cutting; *v.t.* and *v.i.* to cut with a saw; *pa.t.* **sawed.** *pa.p.* **sawed** or **sawn. -er** *n.* **-yer** *n.*

sax•horn *n.* brass wind instrument.

sax•i•frage *n.* popular name of various plants, most of them true rock plants.

Sax•on *n.* one of the people who formerly dwelt in N. Germany and who invaded England in the 5th and 6th cents.; a person of English race; native of Saxony; language of Saxons.

Sax•o•ny *n.* very fine quality of wool; flannel.

sax•o•phone *n.* brass wind instrument.

say *v.t.* to utter with speaking voice; to state; to express; to allege; to recite; to take as near enough. *pa.t.* and *pa.p.* **said** *n.* something said; what one has to say; share in a decision. **-er** *n.* **-ing** *n.* proverbial expression; adage.

scab *n.* crust forming over open wound or sore; *v.i.* to heal over; to form a scab. *pa.t.* and *pa.p.* **-bed.** *pr.p.* **-bing. -bed** *a.* covered with scabs. **-bedness** *n.* **-by** *a.*

scab•bard *n.* sheath for sword or dagger; *v.t.*

sca•bies *n.* skin disease caused by parasite; the itch; the scab.

sca•bi•ous *a.* consisting of scabs; scabby; itchy.

sca•brous *a.* rough; scaly; harsh; full of difficulties; indelicate. **-ly** *adv.* **-ness** *n.*

scad *n.* a species of mackerel.

scaf•fold *n.* temporary structure for support of workmen; framework; stage; platform, esp. for execution of criminal; *v.t.* to furnish with a scaffold; to prop up. **-ing** *n.*

scal•a•wag, scallawag *n.* *(Colloq.)* scamp; worthless fellow.

scald *v.t.* to burn with moist heat or hot liquid; to cleanse by rinsing with boiling water; to heat to point approaching boiling point; *n.* injury by scalding.

scald See **skald.**

scale *n.* dish of a balance; balance itself;

machine for weighing, chiefly in *pl.*; Libra, one of signs of zodiac; *v.t.* to weigh, as in scales.

scale *n.* horny or bony plate-like outgrowth from skin of certain mammals, reptiles, and fishes; *v.t.* to deprive of scales; *v.i.* to come off or peel in thin layers. **-d** *a.* having scales. **-less** *a.* **scaliness** *n.* **scaly** *a.* covered with scales.

scale *n.* series of steps or gradations; ratio between dimensions as shown on map, etc. to actual distance, or length; basis for a numerical system, as *binary scale*; instrument for measuring, weighing, etc. *(Mus.)* succession of notes arranged in order of pitch between given note and its octave; gamut; *v.t.* to climb as by a ladder; to measure; *v.i.* to mount.

sca•lene *a.* uneven; *(Geom.)* having all three sides unequal; *n.* a scalene triangle.

scal•lion *n.* a variety of shallot.

scal•lop, scollop *n.* bivale mollusk; ornamental edge of rounded projections; *v.t.* to cut edge of material into scallops.

scalp *n.* covering dome of cranium consisting of skin and hair; skin and hair torn off by Indian warriors as token of victory; *v.t.* to deprive of integument of head; to make quick profits in buying and prompt reselling.

scal•pel *n.* small, straight surgical knife.

scamp *n.* scoundrel; rascal; rogue.

scam•per *v.i.* to run about; to run away in haste and trepidation; *n.* a hasty, impulsive flight.

scan *v.t.* to examine closely; to scrutinize; *v.i.* to be metrically correct. *pr.p.* **-ning.** *pa.t.* and *pa.p.* **-ned. -ning** *n.*

scan•dal *n.* malicious gossip; disgraceful action; disgrace; injury to a person's character. **-ize** *v.t.* to shock by disgraceful actions. **-ous** *a.* **-ously** *adv.* **-ousness** *n.*

Scan•di•na•vi•a *n.* peninsula of Norway, Sweden, and Finland. **-n** *a.*

scansion. See scan.

scant *a.* barely sufficient; inadequate; *v.t.* to put on short allowance; to fail to give full measure. **-ily** *adv.* **-iness** *n.* **-ly** *adv.* sparingly; scarcely; barely. **-ness** *n.* scantiness; insufficiency. **-y** *a.*

scant•ling *n.* a small amount.

scape•goat *n.* one who has to shoulder blame due to another. **scapegrace** *n.* graceless, good-for-nothing fellow.

scaph•oid *a.* boat-shaped.

scap•u•la *n.* shoulder blade. *pl.* **scapulae. -r** *a.* Also **-ry.**

scar *n.* permanent mark left on skin after healing of a wound, burn; *v.t.* to mark with scar; *v.i.* to heal with a scar.

scar•ab *n.* beetle regarded by ancient Egyptians as emblematic of solar power; gem cut in shape of this beetle.

scarab

scarce *a.* not plentiful; deficient; scanty. **-ly** *adv.* hardly; not quite. **-ness, scarcity** *n.*

scare *v.t.* to terrify suddenly; to alarm; to drive away by frightening; *n.* sudden alarm (esp. causeless).

scarf *n.* long, narrow, light article of dress worn loosely over shoulders or about neck; a muffler. *pl.* **-s, scarves.**

scarf *v.t.* to unite lengthways to pieces of timber; *n.* joint for connecting timbers lengthwise.

scarf joint

scar•i•fy *v.t.* to scratch or slightly cut the skin; to stir the surface soil of; to lacerate; to criticize unmercifully. **scarification** *n.* **scarifier** *n.*

scar•la•ti•na *n.* scarlet fever.

scar•let *n.* bright red color of many shades; cloth of scarlet color; *a.* of this color. **— fever** *n.* childhood disease characterized by a scarlet rash.

scarp *n.* steep inside slope of ditch in fortifications; *v.t.* to make steep. **-ed** *a.*

scar•y *a. (Colloq.)* producing fright or alarm; exceedingly timid.

scathe *v.t.* to criticize harshly. **scathing** *a.* damaging; cutting; biting. **scathingly** *adv.*

sca•tol•o•gy *n.* scientific study of fossilized excrement of animals; interest in obscene literature. **scatological** *a.*

scat•ter *v.t.* to strew about; to sprinkle around; to put to rout; to disperse; *v.i.* to take to flight; to disperse. **-er** *n.* **-ingly** *adv.*

scav•en•ger *n.* one employed in cleaning streets, removing refuse, etc.; animal which feeds on carrion; *v.i.* to scavenge. **scavenge** *v.t.* to cleanse streets, etc.

sce•nar•i•o *n.* script or written version of play to be produced by motion picture; plot of a play. **scenarist** *n.*

scene *n.* place, time of action of novel, play, etc.; a division of a play; spectacle, show, or view. **-ry** *n.* stage settings; natural features of landscape which please eye. **scenic** *a.* **scenographic, -al** *a.* drawn in perspective. **scenographically** *adv.* **scenography** *n.*

scent *v.t.* to discern or track by sense of smell; to give a perfume to; to detect; to become suspicious of; *v.i.* to smell; *n.* odor or perfume; trail left by odor. **-ed** *a.* perfumed.

sceptic. See skeptic.

scep•ter *n.* ornamental staff or baton, as symbol of royal power; royal or imperial dignity. **-ed** *a.* Also **sceptre.**

scepter

sched•ule *n.* document containing list of details forming part of principal document, deed, etc.; order of events; *v.t.* to note and enter in a schedule.

S

sche·ma *n.* plan or diagram; outline; scheme; *pl.* **-ta.** **-tic** *a.* **-tically** *adv.* **-tize** *v.t.*

scheme *n.* plan; design; system; plot; diagram; *v.t.* to plan; to contrive; to frame; *v.i.* to intrigue; to plot. *pr.p.* **scheming.** **-r** *n.* **scheming** *n.* and *a.* **schemist** *n.*

scher·zo *n.* (*Mus.*) composition of a lively, playful character.

schism *n.* split of a community into factions; crime of promoting this. **schismatic** *a.* —*n.* one who separates from a church. **-atical** *a.* schismatic. **-atically** *adv.*

schiz·o- *prefix* to cleave, used in the construction of compound terms. **schizoid** *a.* exhibiting slight symptoms of schizophrenia. **-phrenia** *n.* mental disorder known as 'split personality.' **-phrenic** *a.*

schnapps, schnaps *n.* kind of Holland gin.

schol·ar *n.* learned person; holder of scholarship. **-ly** *a.* **-ship** *n.* learning; erudition; a grant to aid a student. **scholastic** *a.* pert. to schools, scholars, or education. **scholastically** *adv.* **Scholasticism** *n.* system of philosophy during Middle Ages.

scho·li·ast *n.* ancient commentator or annotator of classical texts. **scholiastic** *a.* **scholium** *n.* — *pl.* **scholia,** marginal note or comments.

school *n.* a shoal (of fish, whales, etc.).

school *n.* institution for teaching or giving instruction in any subject; group of writers, artists, thinkers, etc. with principles or methods in common; branch of study, in a university; *v.t.* to educate; to discipline; to instruct; to train. **-room** *n.* **-teacher** *n.*

schoon·er *n.* small sharp-built vessel, having two masts, fore-and-aft rigged.

three-masted schooner

schot·tische, shottish *n.* round dance resembling polka; music in 2/4 time for this dance. **Highland schottische,** lively dance to strathspey tunes, Highland fling.

sci·at·i·ca *n.* neuralgia of sciatic nerve, with pains in region of hip. **sciatic, -al** *a.* situated in, or pert. to, hip region. **-lly** *adv.*

sci·ence *n.* systematic knowledge of natural or physical phenomena; ordered arrangement of facts known under classes or heads; scientific, **-al** *a.* **scientifically** *adv.* **scientism** *n.* **scientist** *n.* natural science, physical science, science which investigates nature and properties of material bodies and natural phenomena. **pure science,** science based on self-evident truths, as mathematics,

logic, etc.

scim·i·tar *n.* short saber with curved, sharp-edged blade.

scin·til·la *n.* spark; least particle. **-nt** *a.* emitting sparks; sparkling. **-te** *v.i.* to emit sparks; to sparkle; to glisten. **-tion** *n.*

sci·o·lism *n.* superficial knowledge used to impress other. **sciolist** *n.* **sciolistic** *a.*

sci·on *n.* slip for grafting; offshoot; a descendant; heir.

scis·sile *a.* (*Bot.*) capable of being cut, split, or divided. **scission** *n.* act of cutting; division.

scis·sors *n.pl.* instrument of two sharp-edged blades pivoted together for cutting; small shears. **scissor** *v.t.* to cut with scissors.

scle·ro- *prefix* hard, used in the construction of compound terms, implying hardness or dryness. **sclera** *n.* strong, opaque fibrous membrane forming outer coat of eyeball. **scleral** *a.* hard, bony. **scleritis** *n.* inflammation of sclera of eye. **sclerodermatous** *a.* (*Zool.*) possessing a hard, bony, external structure for protection. **scleroid** *a.* of hard texture. **scleroma** *n.* hardening of tissues. **sclerosal** *a.* pert. to sclerosis. **sclerosis** *n.* hardening of organ as a result of excessive growth of connective tissue; induration.

scoff *v.i.* to treat with derision; to mock; to jeer; *n.* expression of scorn; an object of derision. **-er** *n.* **-ingly** *adv.*

scold *v.t.* and *v.i.* to find fault (with); to chide; to reprove angrily; *n.* one who scolds. **-er** *n.* **-ing** *n.* rebuke. **-ingly** *adv.*

sconce *n.* ornamental bracket fixed to wall, for carrying a light.

scone *n.* a thin, flat cake.

scoop *n.* article for ladling; kind of shovel; hollow place; *v.t.* to ladle out, shovel, lift, dig or hollow out with scoop.

scoot *v.i.* to move off quickly; to dart away suddenly; to scamper off.

scope *n.* range of activity or application; space for action; room; play; outlet.

scor·bu·tic *a.* affected with, or relating to, scurvy.

scorch *v.t.* to burn the surface of; to parch; to char; *v.i.* to be burnt on surface; to dry up; to parch. **-er** *n.* **-ing** *a.*

score *n.* a cut, notch, line, stroke; tally mark; reckoning, bill, account; number twenty; reason; sake; *v.t.* to mark with lines, scratches, furrows; to cut; to enter in account book, to record; to make (points, etc.) in game; *v.i.* to add a point, run, goal, etc. in a game; to make a telling remark; to achieve a success. **-r** *n.* **scoring** *n.* **-book, -card, -sheet** *n.*

sco·ri·a *n.* dross or slag resulting from smelting of metal ores. *pl.* **scoriae. scorify** *v.t.* to reduce to dross or slag.

scorn *n.* extreme disdain or contempt; *v.t.* to contemn. **-ful** *a.* **-fully** *adv.*

Scor·pi·o *n.* Scorpion, 8th sign of zodiac; scorpion. **-n** *n.* insect allied to spiders having slender tail which ends in very acute sting.

scot *n.* formerly, tax, contribution, fine. **—free** *a.* unhurt; exempt from payment.

Scot n. native of Scotland.

Scotch a. pert. to Scotland or its inhabitants; n. Scots; Scots dialect; Scotch whiskey.

scotch v.t. to support, as a wheel, by placing some object to prevent its rolling; n. prop, wedge, strut.

scotch v. to wound slightly; to cut; n. scratch; mark or score.

Scots n. dialect of English spoken in lowland Scotland; a. pert. to Scotland. -man, -woman n.

Scot-tish a. pert. to Scotland or its people.

scoun-drel n. rascal; villain. -ly a.

scour v.t. to clean or polish the surface of, by hard rubbing; to purge violently; to flush out; v.i. to clean by rubbing; n. act or material used in scouring. -er n.

scour v.t. to pass rapidly along or over in search of something; to range; v.i. to scamper; to rove over; to scurry along. -er n.

scourge n. whip made of leather thongs; lash; punishment; v.t. to flog; to lash; to chastise;

scout n. one sent out to reconnoiter; lookout; v.t. to reconnoiter; to spy out.

scout v.t. to reject with contempt.

scow n. large flat-bottomed barge.

scowl v.i. to wrinkle brows in displeasure; n. an angry frown.

scrab-ble v.t. to scribble; to scrawl; v.i. to scratch with hands.

scrag n. anything thin, lean, gaunt, or shrivelled. -ged a. -gedness, -giness n. -gily adv. -gly a. rough and unkempt. -gy a.

scram-ble v.t. to move by crawling, climbing, etc. on all fours; to struggle with others for; v.t. to collect together hurriedly and confusedly; n. scrambling; disorderly proceeding. scrambling a.

scrap n. small detached piece or fragment; material left over which can be used as raw material again; pl. odds and ends; v.t. to make into scraps; to discard; pa.t. and pa.p. -ped. pr.p. -ping. -py a.

scrape v.t. to abrade; to grate; to scratch; v.i. to produce grating noise; to live parsimoniously; to bow awkwardly with drawing back of foot; to scratch in earth, as fowls; n. act or sound of scraping; scratch; predicament; embarrassing situation. -r n.

scratch v.t. to score or mark a narrow surface wound with claws, nails, or anything pointed; to erase; to scrape; to rub an itchy spot; v.i. to use claws or nails in tearing, abrading, or shallow digging; n. slight wound, mark, or sound made by sharp instrument; a. taken at random, brought together in a hurry, as a *scratch team*. -er n. -y a.

scrawl v.t. to write or draw untidily; to scribble; v.i. to write unskillfully; n. hasty, careless writing; -er n.

scraw-ny a. lean; scraggy; rawboned. scrawniness n.

scream v.t. and v.i. to utter a piercing cry; n. a shrill, piercing cry; a person who excites much laughter; laughter-provoking incident. -ing a.

scree n. pile of débris at base of cliff or hill; a talus.

screech v.i. to utter a harsh, shrill cry; n. a shrill and sudden, harsh cry. — owl n. owl with persistent harsh call.

screed n. long letter or passage; long boring speech.

screen n. covered frame to shelter from heat, light, draft, or observation; coarse, rectangular sieve for grading coal, pulverized material, etc.; white surface on which image is projected by optical means; v.t. to provide with shelter or concealment; to protect from blame or censure; to sift; to film; to project film, lantern slide, etc. on a screen; to subject a person to political scrutiny. -ing n.

screw n. in mechanics, a machine consisting of an inclined plane wound round a cylinder; cylinder with a spiral ridge running round it, used as holding

screw

agent or as mechanical power; turn of screw; twist to one side; a screw propeller; v.t. to fasten with screw; to press or stretch with screw; to work by turning; to twist round; to obtain by pressure; to extort; v.i. to assume a spiral motion; to move like a screw. -ed a. -er n. -ing a. -y a.

scrib-ble v.t. and v.i. to write carelessly; to draw meaningless lines; n. something scribbled. -r n. **scribbling** a. used for scribbling; n. careless writing.

scribe n. a writer; official or public writer; clerk; copyist; v.t. to incise wood, metal, etc. with a sharp point as a guide to cutting. scribal a.

scrim-mage n. a confused struggle.

scrimp v.t. to make too short or small; to stint. -ed a. -ily adv. -iness n. -y a.

scrim-shaw (Naut.) v.t. and v.i. to make decorative article out of bone, whale's tooth, shell, etc.; n. such work.

scrip n. a writing; interim certificate of holding bonds, stock, or shares.

script n. kind of type, used to imitate handwriting; handwriting; text of words of play, or of scenes and word of film.

scrip-ture n. anything written; sacred writing; passage from Bible. **scriptural,** **scripture** a.

scrive-ner n. rotary.

scrof-u-la n. a tuberculous condition most common in childhood. **scrofulitic,** **scrofulous** a.

scroll n. roll of paper or parchment; a list; flourish at end of signature; ornament consisting of spiral volutes. -ed a.

scro-tum n. external muscular sac which lodges testicles of the male.

scrub v.t. to clean with a hard brush, etc. and water; v.i. to clean by rubbing; pa.t.

S

and *pa.p.* -bed *pr.p.* -bing *n.*

scrub *n.* stunted growth of trees and shrubs; an animal of unknown or inferior breeding; *a.* stunted; inferior. -by *a.*

scruff *n.* the back of the neck; nape. Also skruff.

scrunch *v.t.* to crush with the teeth; to crunch; to crush.

scru‧ple *n.* very small quantity; feeling of doubt; conscientious objection; qualm; *v.i.* to hesitate from doubt; to have compunction. **scrupulous** *a.* extremely conscientious; attentive to small points. **scrupulously** *adv.* **scrupulousness, scrupulosity** *n.*

scru‧ti‧ny *n.* close search; critical examination. **scrutator** *n.* **scrutinate, scrutinize** *v.t.*

scud *v.i.* to move quickly; to run before a gale; *pr.p.* -ding. *pa.t.* and *pa.p.* -ded.

scuff *v.t.* to graze against; *v.i.* to shuffle along without raising the feet; *n.* a mark left by scuffing; a flat slipper.

scuf‧fle *v.i.* to struggle at close quarters; to fight confusedly; to shuffle along; *n.* confused fight, or struggle; a shuffling. -r *n.*

scull *n.* short light oar pulled with the one hand; light racing boat of a long, narrow build; *v.t.* to propel boat by two sculls; to propel boat by means of oar placed over stem.

sculp‧ture *n.* art of reproducing objects in relief or in the round out of hard material by means of chisel; carved work; art of modeling in clay or other plastic material; *v.t.* to represent by sculpture. **sculptor** *n.* (*fem.* **sculptress**). **sculptural** *a.*

scum *n.* impurities which rise to surface of liquids; vile person or thing, riffraff; *v.t.* to take scum off; to skim; *v.i.* to form scum. *pr.p.* -ming. *pa.t.* and *pa.p.* -med, -my *a.*

scup‧per *n.* channel alongside bulwarks of ship to drain away water from deck.

scurf *n.* dry scales or flakes formed on skin. -y *a.*

scur‧ril‧ous *a.* indecent; abusive; vile. -ness, **scurrility** *n.* -ly *adv.*

scur‧ry *v.i.* to hurry along; to run hastily. -ing *n.*

scur‧vy *n.* deficiency disease due to lack of vitamin C; (*Med.*) scorbutus; *a.* afflicted with the disease; mean; low; vile. **scurvily** *adv.* **scurviness** *n.*

scut *n.* a short tail, as that of a hare.

scu‧tate *a.* (*Bot.*) shield-shaped; (*Zool.*) protected by scales.

scutch‧eon See escutcheon.

scu‧tel‧lum *n.* horny plate or scale. **scutellate, -d** *a.* **scutelliform** *a.* **scutellate. scutiform** *a.* (*Bot.*) shield-shaped.

scut‧tle *n.* wide-mouthed vessel for holding coal.

scut‧tle *n.* hole with a cover, for light and air, cut in ship's deck or hatchway; *v.t.* to make holes in ship, esp. to sink it.

scut‧tle *v.i.* to rush away.

scythe *n.* mowing implement; *v.t.* to cut with scythe.

sea *n.* mass of salt water covering greater part of earth's surface; certain large expanses of inland water, when salt; vast expanse; flood; large quantity.

seal *n.* an aquatic carnivorous animal with flippers as limbs; *v.i.* to hunt for seals. -er

seal

n. ship, or person, engaged in seal fishing. -ery *n.* seal fishing station.

seal *n.* piece of metal or stone engraved with a device, cipher, or motto for impression on wax, lead, etc.; that which closes or secures; symbol, token, or

seal

indication; *v.t.* to affix a seal to; to confirm; to ratify; to shut up; to close up joints, cracks, etc. -ed *a.*

seam *n.* line of junction of two edges, e.g. of two pieces of cloth, or of two planks; thin layer or stratum, esp. of coal; *v.t.* to join by sewing together; to mark with furrows or wrinkles; to scar. -less *a.* -ster *n.* (*fem.* -stress, **seamstress**) one who sews by profession. -y *a.* showing seams; sordid.

sé‧ance *n.* assembly; meeting of spiritualists for consulting spirits and communicating with 'the other world.'

sear *v.t.* to scorch or brand with a hot iron; to dry up; to wither; to brown meat quickly *a.* (*Poetic.*) dry; withered.

search *v.t.* to look over or through in order to find; to probe into; *v.i.* to look for; to explore; *n.* searching; quest; investigation. -ing *a.* thorough; penetrating; keen; minute. -ingly *adv.* -ingness *n.*

sea‧son *n.* one of four divisions of year—spring, summer, autumn, winter; time of the year for certain activities, foods, etc.; convenient time; period; time; *v.t.* to render suitable; to spice; to mature; *v.i.* to grow fit for use. -able *a.* suitable or appropriate for the season. -ableness *n.* -ably *adv.* -al *a.* depending on, or varying with seasons. -ally *adv.* -ing *n.* flavoring.

seat *n.* thing made or used for sitting; right to sit (e.g. in council, etc.); sitting part of body; part of trousers which covers buttocks; locality of disease, trouble, etc.; country house; place from which a country is governed; *v.t.* to place on a seat; to fit up with seats; to establish. -ed *a.*

se‧ba‧ceous *a.* made of, or pert. to tallow or fat.

se‧cant *a.* cutting; dividing into two parts; *n.* any straight line which cuts another line, curve, or figure.

se‧cede *v.t.* to withdraw formally from

federation, alliance, etc. -er n. **secession** n.

se•clude v.t. to shut up apart. -d a. -dly adv. **seclusion** n. **seclusive** a.

sec•ond a. next to first; another; inferior; n. one who, or that which, follows the first; one next and inferior; sixtieth part of a minute; n.pl. inferior quality of commodity or article; v.t. to support, esp. a motion before a meeting or council; to back; to encourage. -ly adv. in the second place.

sec•ond•ar•y a. succeeding next in order to the first; of second place, origin, rank; second-rate; inferior; unimportant; n. one who occupies a subordinate place. **secondarily** adv.

se•cret a. kept from general knowledge; concealed; unseen; private; n. something kept secret or concealed; a mystery. **secrecy** n. -ly adv. -ness n. **secrecy**. **secretive** a. uncommunicative; reticent; underhand. -ively adv. -iveness n.

sec•re•tar•y n. one employed to deal with papers and correspondence, keep records, prepare business, etc.; official in charge of a particular department of government; a desk with bookshelves on top. **secretarial** a. **secretariat** n. administrative office or officials controlled by secretary.

se•crete to hide or conceal; of gland, etc. to collect and supply particular substance in body; a. separate; distinct. **secreta** n.pl. products of secretion. **secretion** n. **secretional** a. **secretive** a. **secretor** n. **secretory** a.

sect n. followers of philosopher or religious leader; faction. -arian a. pert. to a sect; n. one of a sect; a bigot; a partisan. -arianism n. -ary n. one of a sect.

sec•tion n. cutting or separating by cutting; part separated from the rest; (Bot. and Zool.) thin, translucent slice of organic or inorganic matter mounted on slide for detailed microscopic examination. -al a. -alism n. partial regard for limited interests of one particular class at expense of others. -ally adv. -ize v.t.

sec•tor n. portion of circle enclosed by two radii and the arc which they intercept; mathematical instrument; (Mil.) a subdivision of the combat area. -al a.

sec•u•lar a. worldly; temporal, as opposed to spiritual; lay; lasting for, occurring once in, a century or age; n. layman; clergyman, not bound by vow of poverty and not belonging to religious order. -ization n. **secularize** v.t. **secularism** n. ethical doctrine which advocates a moral code independent of all religious considerations or practices. -ist n. -ity n. worldliness; secularism. -ly adv.

se•cure a. free from care, anxiety, fear; safe; in close custody; certain; confident; v.t. to make safe, certain, fast; to close, or confine, effectually; to gain possession of; to obtain; to assure. **securable** a. **securance** n. -ly adv. -ness n. -r n. **security** n. being secure; protection; anything given as bond, caution, or pledge. **securities** n.pl. general term for shares, bonds, stocks, debentures, etc.

se•dan n. old-time closed conveyance for one, carried on two poles; a closed automobile with two full seats.

se•date a. staid; not excitable, composed; calm. -ly adv. -ness n. **sedative** a. and n.

sed•en•tar•y a. sitting much; requiring sitting posture; inactive. **sedentariness** n.

sedge n. any marshgrass. **sedgy** a.

sed•i•ment n. matter which settles to bottom of liquid; lees; dregs. -ary a. -ation n.

se•di•tion n. any act aimed at disturbing peace of realm or producing insurrection. -ary n. **seditious** a. **seditiously** adv. **seditiousness** n.

se•duce v.t. to lead astray; to draw aside from path of rectitude and duty; to induce woman to surrender chastity; to allure. -ment n. -r n. **seducible** a. **seduction** n. **seductive** a. **seductively** adv. **seductiveness** n.

sed•u•lous a. diligent; steady; industrious; persevering. **sedulity** n. -ness n. -ly adv.

see n. diocese or jurisdiction of bishop; province of archbishop.

see v.t. to perceive by eye; to form an idea; to have interview with; v.i. to have the power of sight; to pay regard; to consider; to understand. pa.t. **saw**. pa.p. **seen**. -ing conj. considering; since; n. act of perceiving.

seed n. ovule, which gives origin to new plant; that from which anything springs; origin; offspring; sperm; first principle; v.t. to sow with seed; to remove seeds from; to arrange draw for sports tournament. v.i. to produce seed. -ed a. -ily adv. in seedy manner. -iness n. being seedy; shabbiness. -less a. -ling n. young plant or tree, grown from seed. -y a. abounding with seeds; run to seed; shabby; worn out; miserable looking.

seek v.t. to make search or enquiry for; v.i. to make search. pa.t. and pa.p. **sought**. -er n.

seem v.i. to appear (to be or to do). -ing a. n. appearance; apparent likeness. -ingly adv. -liness n. -ly a. fit; becoming; adv. in a decent or proper manner.

seen pa.p. of see.

seep v.i. to ooze; to trickle. -age n.

se•er n. a prophet.

seer•suck•er n. a cotton fabric of alternating plain and crinkled stripes.

see•saw n. game in which two children sit at opposite ends of plank supported in middle and swing up and down; plank for this; a. moving up and down or to and fro; reciprocal; v.i. to move up and down.

seethe v.t. to soak; v.i. to be in a state of ebullition; to be violently agitated.

seg•ment n. part cut off from a figure by a line; section; portion; part; v.t. and v.i. to separate into segments. -al a. -ary, -ate a. -ation n. -ed a.

seg•re•gate v.t. and v.i. to set or go apart from the rest; a. set apart. **segregation** n.

seine n. open net for sea fishing. v.t. to catch fish by dragging a seine.

seism n. earthquake. -al, -ic a. -ogram n. record of earthquake made by seismograph. -ograph n. instrument which records distance and intensity of slightest earth tremors. -ologic, -al a. -ologist n. one versed in seismology. -ology n. the study of earthquakes.

seize v.t. to grasp; to take hold of; to take possession of by force or legal authority; to comprehend; v.i. to take hold. seizable a. seizure n. thing or property seized; sudden attack, as apoplectic stroke.

sel•dom adv. rarely.

se•lect v.t. to choose; to cull; to prefer; a. of choice quality; exclusive; n. the best people. -ed a. -edly adv. -ion n. selecting; things selected; variety of articles from which to select. -ive a. having power of selection; discriminating. -ively adv. -ivity n. -or n.

sel•e•nite n. a colorless and translucent crystalline form of gypsum.

self n. one's individual person; one's personal interest; ego. pl. selves. pron. affix used to express emphasis or a reflexive usage; prefix used in innumerable compounds. -ish a. concerned unduly over personal profit or pleasure; lacking consideration for others; mercenary; greedy. -less a. unselfish.

sell v.i. to dispose of for an equivalent, usually money; to betray for money or a consideration; v.t. to fetch a price; to be in demand; pa.t. and pa.p. sold. n. deception; hoax. -er n.

Selt•zer n. a carbonated mineral water.

sel•vage, selvedge n. edge of cloth finished to prevent raveling.

selves n.pl. of self.

se•man•tic a. pert. to meaning of words. -s n.pl. branch of linguistic research concerned with studying meaning and changes in meaning of words.

sem•a•phore n. a post with movable arms used for signaling.

se•ma•si•ol•o•gy n. the science of the development of the meanings of words, semantics. semasiological a.

sem•blance n. real or seeming likeness; appearance.

se•men n. male secretion containing sperm.

se•mes•ter n. one of two or three divisions of the school year.

sem•i- prefix with the meaning of half, partly, imperfectly, etc., used in the construction of compound terms, the meaning being usually obvious. a. -colon n. punctuation mark (;) used to separate clauses of a sentence requiring a more marked separation than is indicated by a comma.

sem•i•nal a. pert. to seed of plants or semen of animals; reproductive, semination n. act of sowing or disseminating; seeding. seminiferous, seminific a.

sem•i•nar n. group of advanced students pursuing research.

sem•i•nar•y n. academy; secondary school for girls; a training college for priesthood or ministry; a. trained in seminary. seminarist n.

Sem•i•nole one of a nomadic tribe of American Indians.

se•mi•ol•o•gy n. (Med.) study of signs and symptoms of disease; symptomatology. semiotics n. science or language of signs.

Sem•ite n. member of a speech family comprising Hebrews, Arabs, Assyrians, etc. Semitic a.

sem•o•li•na n. hard grains of wheat used in production of spaghetti, macaroni, etc. Also semola.

sen n. Japanese copper coin.

sen•ate n. supreme legislative and administrative assembly in ancient Rome; upper house of legislature. senator n. senatorial a.

send v.t. to cause to go; to transmit; to forward; v.i. to despatch messenger; to transmit message. pa.t. and pa.p. sent.

se•nes•cence n. the state of growing old; decay; old age. senescent a.

se•nile a. pert. to old age; aged; doting. senility n.

sen•ior a. older; superior in rank or standing; n. a person older, or of higher rank, or of longer service, than another. -ity n. state of being older; precedence in rank, or longer in service.

sen•na n. a valuable purgative drug.

sen•sa•tion n. what we learn through senses; effect produced on a sense organ by external stimulus; exciting event; strong impression. sensate a. perceived by the senses. -al a. -alist n. -ally adv.

sen•sa•tion•al•ism n. matter, language or style designed to excite and please vulgar taste; sensualism.

sense n. any of the bodily faculties of perception or feeling; ability to perceive; meaning; coherence; wisdom; prudence. pl. wits; faculties; v.t. to perceive; to suspect; (Colloq.) to understand. -less a. -lessly adv. -lessness n.

sen•si•ble a. capable of being perceived by the senses; characterized by good sense; reasonable. sensibility n. sensibly adv.

sen•si•tive a. open to, or acutely affected by, external stimuli or impressions; easily upset by criticism. -ly adv. -ness n. sensitivity n.

sen•si•tize v.t. to render sensitive. sensitizer n.

sen•so•ry a. pert. to, or serving, senses; conveying sensations.

sen•su•al a. pert. to the senses; given to pursuit of pleasures of sense; self-indulgent; voluptuous; lewd. -ization n. -ize v.t. -ism n. fleshly indulgence. -ist n. one given to lewd or loose mode of life. -istic a. -ity n. -ly adv. sensuous a. stimulating, or apprehended by, senses. sensuously adv. sensuousness n.

sent pa.t. and pa.p. of send.

sen•tence n. combination of words, which is complete as expressing a thought; judgment passed on criminal by court or judge; decision; v.t. to pass sentence upon; to condemn. sententious a. abounding with axioms and maxims.

sen•tient a. feeling or capable of feeling; perceiving by senses; sensitive. sentience, sentiency n. consciousness at a sensory level. -ly *adv.*

sen·ti·ment *n.* abstract emotion; tendency to be moved by feeling rather than idea; opinion. sentimental *a.* -alism, -ality *n.* -alist *n.*

sen·ti·nel *n.* guard; sentry; *a.* acting as sentinel.

sen·try *n.* soldier on guard; sentinel.

se·pal *n.* (*Bot.*) leaf-like member of outer covering, or calyx, of flower. -ous *a.*

sep·a·rate *v.t.* to part in any manner; to divide; *a.* disconnected; distinct; individual. separability *n.* separable *a.* -ly *adv.* -ness *n.* separation *n.* separationist *n.* separatist *n.*

se·pi·a *n.* brown pigment.

sep·sis *n.* (*Med.*) state of having bodily tissue infected by bacteria. septic *a.*

sept *n.* clan, race, or family, proceeding from common progenitor.

Sep·tem·ber *n.* ninth month of year.

sep·te·nar·y *a.* crossing of seven; lasting seven years; occurring once in seven years.

sep·tet, septette *n.* (*Mus.*) composition for seven voices or instruments.

sep·tic *a.* pert. to sepsis; infected. -emia, -aemia *n.* blood poisoning. -ally *adv.*

sep·tu·a·ge·nar·i·an *n.* person between seventy and eighty years of age. septuagenary *a.* and *n.*

Sep·tu·a·ges·i·ma *n.* third Sunday before Lent.

Sep·tu·a·gint *n.* the first and only complete version in Greek of the Old Testament. -al *a.*

sep·tu·ple *a.* sevenfold; *v.t.* to multiply by seven.

sep·ul·cher *n.* tomb; grave; burial vault; *v.t.* to place in a sepulcher. sepulchral *a.* sepulture *n.* act of burying dead.

se·qua·cious *a.* following; attendant; easily led. -ness, sequacity *n.*

se·quel *n.* that which follows; continuation, complete in itself, of a novel or narrative previously published.

se·quence *n.* connected series; succession. sequent *a.* following; succeeding; *n.* sequence. sequential *a.* sequentially *adv.*

se·ques·ter *v.t.* to put aside; to separate; to seclude.

se·quin *n.* small, ornamental metal disk on dresses, etc.

Se·quoi·a *n.* genus of gigantic coniferous evergreen trees native to California.

sequoia

ser·aph *n.* member of the highest order of angels. -s, -im *n.pl.* -ic, -ical *a.*

Serb, Serbian *a.* pert. to Serbia; *n.* native or inhabitant of Serbia, the chief constituent state of Yugoslavia.

sere *a.* dry; withered.

ser·e·nade *n.* music sung or played at night below person's window, esp. by lover; *v.t.* to entertain with serenade. -r *n.* serenata *n.* instrumental work, between suite and symphony.

ser·en·dip·ity *n.* knack of stumbling upon interesting discoveries in a casual manner.

se·rene *a.* clear and calm; fair; placid. -ly *adv.* -ness, serenity *n.*

serf *n.* under feudalism, vassal. -age, -dom, -hood *n.*

serge *n.* hard-wearing worsted fabric.

ser·geant, sergeant *n.* noncommissioned officer in army, ranking above corporal; police officer ranking above constable; officer of a law court. -ship, sergeancy *n.*

se·ri·al *a.* consisting of a series; appearing in successive parts or installments; *n.* a periodical publication. -ize *v.t.* to publish as a serial. -ly, seriately *adv.* in a regular series or order. seriatim *adv.* point by point.

se·ries *n.s.* and *pl.* succession of related objects or matters; sequence.

ser·if *n.* (*Printing*) a fine line at the end of the stems and arms of unconnected Roman type letters, as M, y, etc.

se·ri·ous *a.* grave in manner or disposition; earnest; important. -ly *adv.* -ness *n.*

ser·jeant. See sergeant.

ser·mon *n.* discourse for purpose of religious instruction. -ic, -al *a.* -ize *v.t.* to preach earnestly; to compose a sermon. -izer *n.*

se·rous *a.* pert. to, containing, or producing serum; watery; thin. serosity *n.*

ser·pent *n.* snake; treacherous or malicious person; kind of firework; (*Cap.*) constellation in northern hemisphere; *a.* deceitful treacherous. -ine *a.*; *n.* skin; *v.i.* to wind in and out like a serpent. -inely *adv.*

ser·rate, serrated *a.* notched or cut like saw, as a leaf edge. serration *n.* serrature *n.* serriform *a.*

ser·ried *a.* in close order; pressed shoulder to shoulder.

se·rum *n.* watery secretion; whey; thin straw-colored fluid, residue of plasma or liquid part of the blood.

serv·ant *n.* personal or domestic attendant.

serve *v.t.* to work for; to be a servant to; to distribute, as rations, stores, etc.; to deliver formally; *v.i.* to work under another; to be a member of a military, naval, etc. unit; to be useful, or suitable, or enough. servable *a.* -r *n.*

serv·ice *n.* state of being a servant; work done for and benefit conferred on another; act of kindness; military, naval, or air force duty; advantage; use; form of divine worship; regular supply, as water, bus, electricity, etc.; a set of dishes, etc.; *v.t.* to perform service for, e.g., automobiles, etc. -able *a.*

serv·ice *n.* a small fruit tree.

serv·i·ette *n.* a table napkin.

serv·ile *a.* pert. to or befitting a servant or slave; submissive; dependent; menial. -ly *adv.* servility *n.*

ser·vi·tor n. attendant; follower or adherent. **servitude** n.

ses·a·me n. annual herbaceous plant cultivated in India and Asia Minor for seeds.

ses·qui- prefix denoting a proportion of 3:2. **-alteral, -alterate, -alterous** a. one and a half more. **-centennial** a. pert. to a century and a half; n. the 150th anniversary. **-pedalian** a. measuring a foot and a half long; applied humorously to any long cumbersome technical word or to one given to using unnecessarily long words. **-pedalianism** n.

ses·sile a. attached by the base, as a leaf; fixed and stationary.

ses·sion n. actual sitting of a court, council, etc. for transaction of business; a period of time at school or college when a definite course of instruction is given. **-al** a.

ses·tet, seste n. (Mus.) composition for six instruments or voices; last six lines of a sonnet.

set v.t. to put; to cause to sit; to seat; to place; to plant; to make ready; to adjust; to crouch or point, as dog, to game; v.i. to pass below horizon; to go down; to strike root; to become fixed or rigid; to put forth an effort; to begin. pr.p. **-ting**. pa.t. and pa.p. **set**.

set n. a number of things or persons associated as being similar or complementary or used together, etc.; the manner in which a thing is set, hangs, or fits, as a dress; an attitude or posture; young plant, cutting, or slip for planting out; group or clique; setting of sun; equipment to form the ensemble of a scene for stage or film representation; a. fixed; firm; prescribed; regular; established; arranged; appointed; obstinate; determined. **-back** n. check to progress.

se·ta n. bristle or bristlelike structure. **setaceous, setose** a.

set·tee n. couch or sofa.

set·ter n. hunting dog trained to crouch or set when game is perceived.

english setter

set·ting n. fixing, adjusting, or putting in place; descending below horizon, as of sun; bezel which holds a precious stone, etc. in position; mounting of scene in play or film; background or surroundings.

set·tle v.t. to put in place, order, arrangement, etc.; to decide upon; to bring (dispute) to an end; to pay; to take up residence in; to colonize; v.i. to become fixed or stationary; to arrange; to (cause to) sink to bottom; to subside; to take up residence in; to dwell; to become calm; to become clear (of liquid). **-d** a. **-ment** n. **-r** n. one who

makes his home in a new country; colonist. **settling** n.

set·tle n. long high-backed bench; settee.

sev·en a. one more than six; n. number greater by one than six, symbol 7 or VII.

sev·en·teen a. one more than sixteen; n. sum of ten and seven; symbol 17, or XVII a. and n. the seventh after the tenth.

sev·enth a. constituting one of seven equal parts; n. one of seven equal parts.

sev·en·ty a. seven times ten; n. sum of seven times ten; the symbol 70 or LXX. **seventieth** a. constituting one of seventy equal parts.

sev·er v.t. to part or divide by violence; to sunder; to cut or break off; v.i. to divide. **-able** a. **-ance** n.

sev·er·al a. more than two; some; separate; pron. several persons or things. **-ly** adv.

se·vere a. serious; rigidly methodical; harsh; not flowery, as style. **-ly** adv. **-ness, severity** n.

sew v.t. to fasten together with needle and thread; v.i. to practice sewing. **-er** n. **-ing** n. and a.

sew·age n. drainage; organic refuse carried off by a regular system of underground pipes.

sew·er n. underground drain or conduit to remove waste water and organic refuse. **-age** n.

sex n. state of being male or female; sum total of characteristics which distinguish male and female organisms; function by which most animal and plant species are perpetuated; males or females collectively. **-ual** a. **-uality** n. **-ually** adv.

sex-, comb. form, six.

sex·ag·e·nar·y a. pert. to the number sixty; proceeding by sixties. **sexagenarian** n. person of age of sixty.

Sex·a·ges·i·ma n. second Sunday before Lent. **sexagesimal** a.

sex·en·ni·al a. continuing for six years; happening once every six years. Also **sextennial. -ly, sextennially** adv.

sex·tant n. an astronomical instrument used in measuring angular distances.

sextant

sex·ten·nial. See **sexennial**.

sex·tet, sex·tette n. musical composition for six voices or instruments.

sex·ton n. church lay officer acting as caretaker.

sex·tu·ple a. sixfold; v.t. to multiply by six.

shab·by a. torn or worn to rags; poorly dressed; faded; worn; mean. **shabbily** adv. **shabbiness** n.

shack n. roughly built wooden hut.

shack·le n. metal loop or staple; pl. fetters; manacles; anything which hampers; restraints; v.t. to fetter; to hamper.

shad n. name of several species of herring family.

shade *n.* partial darkness, due to interception of light; screen; darker part of anything; depth of color; tint; hue; a very minute difference. *pl. invisible world or region of the dead; Hades; v.t.* to shelter or screen, from light or a source of heat; to darken; to pass almost imperceptibly from one form or color to another. **-d** *a.* shadily *adv.* shadiness *n.* **shading** *n.* interception of light; slight variation; light and color values in a painting or drawing. **shady** *a.* providing shade; in shade; (*Colloq.*) disreputable.

shad∙ow *n.* patch of shade; dark figure projected by anything which intercepts rays of light; inseparable companion; ghost; gloom; *v.t.* to cast a shadow over; to follow and watch closely. **-er** *n.* **-iness** *n.* **-ing** *n.* gradation of light and color; shading. **-y** *a.* full of shadow; faint; obscure.

shaft *n.* straight rod, stem, or handle; shank; anything long and slender.

shag *n.* coarse, matted wool or hair; strong mixture of tobacco leaves cut and shredded for smoking; *a.* rough; shaggy. **-gedness, -giness** *n.* **-gy** *a.* covered with rough hair or wool; rough; unkempt.

shah *n. abbrev.* of Shah-in-Shah (King of Kings), the title given to the monarchs of Iran, Persia.

shake *v.t.* to cause to move with quick vibrations; to weaken stability of; *v.i.* to tremble; to totter. *pa.t.* shook. *pa.p.* **-n.** *n.* shaking; vibration; jolt; severe shock to system; friendly grasping of hands by two individuals. **-n** *a.* shakily *adv.* shakiness *n.* shaky *a.*

shak∙o *n.* military peaked headdress.

shale *n.* (*Geol.*) clay or mud become hardened.

shall *v.i.* and *aux.* used to make compound tenses or moods to express futurity, obligation, command, condition or intention.

shal∙low *a.* having little depth of water; having little knowledge; superficial; *n.* place where water is of little depth. **-ly** *adv.* **-ness** *n.*

sham *n.* any trick, fraud, or device which deludes; *a.* counterfeit; false; pretended; *v.t.* to counterfeit; to feign, to pretend; *v.i.* to make false pretenses. *pr.p.* **-ming.** *pa.t.* and *pa.p.* **-med.**

sham∙ble *v.i.* to walk unsteadily with shuffling gait.

shame *n.* emotion caused by consciousness of something wrong or dishonoring in one's conduct or state; cause of disgrace; ignominy; *v.t.* to cause to feel shame; **-ful** *a.* disgraceful. **-fully** *adv.* **-fulness** *n.* **-less** *a.* destitute of shame; brazen-faced; immodest. **-lessly** *adv.* **-lessness** *n.*

sham∙my. See chamois.

sham∙poo *v.t.* to wash (scalp); *n.* act of shampooing; preparation used. **-er** *n.*

sham∙rock *n.* small trefoil plant; national emblem of Ireland.

shang∙hai *v.t.* to drug or render a man unconscious by violence so that he may be shipped as member of a crew; to bring by deceit and force; *pa.t.* and *pa.p.* shanghaied.

shank *n.* lower part of leg, from knee to ankle; long connecting part of an appliance.

shan∙tung *n.* silk cloth with rough, knotted surface.

shan∙ty *n.* crude wooden building.

shan∙ty *n.* sailor's song. Also **chanty, chantey.**

shape *v.t.* to mold or make into a particular form; to figure; to devise; *v.i.* to assume a form or definite pattern; *n.* form; figure; appearance; outline. **-able, shapable** *a.* **-less** *a.* without regular shape or form; deformed; ugly. **-lessness** *n.* **-liness** *n.* beauty of shape or outline. **-ly** *a.*

shard *n.* broken fragment, esp. of earthenware; hard wing-case of beetle. Also **sherd.**

share *n.* pointed, wedge-shaped, cutting blade of plough.

share *n.* part allotted; unit of ownership; *v.t.* to give or allot a share; to enjoy with others; to apportion; *v.i.* to take a share; to participate. **-r** *n.*

shark *n.* general name applied to certain voracious marine fishes; swindler; rapacious fellow.

shark

sharp *a.* having keen, cutting edge or fine point; abrupt; having ready perception; acid; acrid; pungent; sarcastic; harsh; strongly marked, esp. in outline; shrill; (*Mus.*) raised a semitone in pitch; *n.* acute sound, esp. note raised semitone above its proper pitch; *v.t.* and *v.i.* to raise or sound a half tone above a given tone; *adv.* punctually. **-en** *v.t.* **-ener** *n.* one who, or that which, sharpens. **-er** *n.* swindler. **-ly** *adv.* **-ness** *n.*

shat∙ter *v.t.* to break into many pieces; to smash; to disorder; *v.i.* to fly in pieces.

shave *v.t.* to pare away; to cut close, esp. hair of face or head with razor; to miss narrowly; to graze; *v.i.* to shave oneself; *pa.p.* **-d** or **-n.** **-r** *n.* shaving *n.*

shawl *n.* cloth used as loose covering for neck and shoulders; *v.t.* to wrap in a shawl.

shay *n.* an obsolete one-horse carriage.

she *pron.* this or that female; feminine pronoun of the third person.

sheaf *n.* bundle of stalks of wheat, rye, oats, or other grain; a sheave; *pl.* **sheaves.** *v.t.* and *v.i.* to make sheaves.

shear *v.t.* to clip or cut through with shears or scissors; to deprive. *v.i.* to divide by action of shears; to reap with a sickle. *pa.t.* **-ed.** *pa.p.* **-ed, shorn** *n.*; *pl.* a cutting instrument, consisting of two blades movable on a pin. **-er** *n.* **-ing** *n.*

sheath *n.* close-fitting cover, esp. for knife or sword; scabbard; thin protective covering. **-e** *v.t.* to put into a sheath; to envelop; to encase. **-ing** *n.*

S

sheave n. grooved wheel in block, etc. on which a rope works.

sheave v.t. to bind into sheaves.

shed n. shelter used for storage or workshop.

shed v.t. to cause to emanate, proceed, or flow out; to cast off, as hair, feathers, shell; to radiate; v.i. to come off. pr.p. -ding. pa.t. and pa.p. shed.

sheen n. gloss; glitter; brightness. -y a.

sheep n. sing. and pl. ruminant mammal, valued for its flesh and its soft fleecy wool; simple, bashful person; pl. pastor's church congregation. -ish a. like a sheep; bashful; awkwardly timid and diffident. -ishly adv. -ishness n. -shank n. knot or hitch for temporarily shortening rope, halyard, etc.

sheer a. pure; unmixed; absolute; perpendicular; of linen or silk, very thin; adv. quite; completely.

sheer v.i. to deviate from the right course; to swerve.

sheet n. any broad expanse; a broad piece of cloth spread on bed; broad piece of paper; v.t. to cover, as with a sheet. — metal, etc. n. metal in broad, thin sheets. -ing a.

sheik, sheikh n. Arab chief; a title of respect to Moslem ecclesiasts.

shel•drake n. (fem. shelduck) genus of wild duck.

shelf n. board fixed horizontally on frame, or to wall, for holding things; ledge of rocks; sandbank in sea, rendering water shallow. pl. shelves.

shell n. hard, rigid, outer, protective covering of many animals, particularly mollusks; outer covering of eggs of birds; protective covering of certain seeds; hollow steel container, filled with high explosive; outer part of structure left when interior is removed; frail racing boat or skiff; group of electrons in atom all having same energy. -ed a. -fish n. aquatic animal with external covering of shell.

shel•lac n. refined, melted form of seed lac used as varnish. v.t. to cover with shellac.

shel•ter n. place or structure giving protection; v.t. to give protection to; v.i. to take shelter. -er n.

shelve v.t. to furnish with shelves; to place on a shelf; to put aside, as unfit for use; to defer consideration of; v.i. to slope gradually; to incline. shelving n.

shep•herd n. (fem. shepherdess) one who tends sheep; pastor of church; v.t. to tend sheep; to watch over and guide.

Sher•a•ton n. style of furniture design distinguished for grace and beauty.

sher•bet n. a frozen dessert.

sherd. See shard.

she•rif, shereef n. a descendant of Mohammed.

sher•iff n. chief law enforcement officer.

sher•ry n. Spanish wine of deep amber color.

Shet•land (Geog.) group of islands off N. coast of Scotland. -er n.

shib•bo•leth n. testword or password; a distinctive custom.

shield n. broad piece of armor carried on arm; buckler; anything which protects or defends; v.t. to protect; to screen; to forfend.

shift v.t. to change position (of); to change gears in an automobile; v.i. to move; to change in opinion; n. change; evasion; expedient. -er n. -iness n. trickiness of character or behavior. -ing a. -less a. lacking in resource or character. -lessness n. -y a. not to be trusted; unreliable.

shil•le•lagh, shillelah n. a club or cudgel.

shil•ling n. formerly, a British silver coin.

shil•ly-shal•ly n. vacillation; indecision; v.i. to hesitate or trifle; to waver. shilly-shallier n.

shim•mer v.i. to shine with faint, tremulous light; n. faint, quivering light or gleam. -ing n. -y a.

shim•my n. dance characterized by exaggerated wriggling; wobbling, as in wheel of a car; v.i. to wobble.

shin n. forepart of leg, between ankle and knee; shank; v.i. to climb (up) with aid of one's arms and legs. Also -ny.

shine v.i. to give out or reflect light; to perform in brilliant fashion. pa.t. and pa.p. shone. v.t. to cause to shine; to polish, shoes, etc. pa.t. and pa.p. shined. n. brightness; gloss. shining a. shininess n. shiny a.

shin•gle n. rounded water-worn pebbles. shingly a.

shin•gle n. thin, rectangular slat for roofing and house siding; small signboard (esp. of physician, lawyer); v.t. to cover with shingles.

shin•gles n.pl. (Med.) herpes zoster, viral infection of nerve ganglia, accompanied by severe pain and a vesicular eruption along the nerve course.

Shin•to n. native religion of Japan. -ism n.

ship n. a vessel for carriage of passengers and goods by sea; v.t. to engage for

ship

service on board a ship; to place object in position as oar; to take in water (over the side); v.i. to transport. pr.p. -ping. pa.t. and pa.p. -ped. -board n. deck or side of ship. -ment n. process of shipping; cargo. -per n. -ping n. -shape a. orderly, trim; adv. properly. -wright n. one engaged in building or repairing ships. -yard n. place where ships are built or repaired.

shire n. territorial division in Great Britain.

shirk v.t. to evade; to try to avoid (duty, etc.) -er n.

shirr n. in needlework, row of puckering or gathering; v.t. to gather with parallel threads; to bake eggs.

shirt n. garment for upper part of body.

shiv•er v.t. to quiver or shake from cold or fear; v.t. to cause to shake; n. shaking or shuddering. -y a.

shiv•er n. small piece or splinter; v.t. and v.i. to break into many small pieces or splinters.

shoal n. large number of fish swimming together; a crowd; v.i. to crowd together.

shoal n. a sandbank or bar; shallow water; a. shallow; v.i. to become shallow. -y a.

shoat n. a young pig.

shock n. violent impact or concussion when bodies collide; sudden depression of the system due to violent injury or strong mental emotion; paralytic stroke; effect of electric discharge through body; v.t. to strike against suddenly; to strike with surprise, horror, or disgust. -er n. -ing a. appalling; terrifying; frightful; repulsive; offensive. -ingly adv.

shock n. disordered mass of hair; a. shaggy; bushy.

shock n. group of sheaves of grain; v.t. to make into shocks.

shod pa.t. and pa.p. of verb shoe.

shod•dy n. inferior textile material; a. inferior; of poor quality.

shoe n. covering for foot, but not enclosing ankle; various protective plates or undercoverings; v.t. to furnish with shoes; to put shoes on. pr.p. -ing. pa.t., pa.p. -less a.

shone pa.t. and pa.p. of shine.

shoo interj. begone; v.t. to scare or drive away.

shook pa.t. of shake.

shoot v.t. to discharge missile from gun, etc.; to kill or wound with such a missile; to propel quickly; to thrust out; to pass swiftly over (rapids) or through (arch of bridge); to photograph episode or sequence of motion picture; v.i. to move swiftly and suddenly; to let off a gun, etc.; to sprout; to advance; to kick towards goal. pa.t. and pa.p. shot. n. shooting; young branch or stem. -er n. -ing n.

shop n. building where goods are made, or sold; workshop; store v.i. to visit shops to purchase articles. pr.p. -ping pa.t. and pa.p. -ped. -lifter n. one who makes petty thefts from shop counter. -ping n. -worn a. soiled or tarnished by long exposure in shop.

shore n. land adjoining sea or large lake; v.t. to put ashore.

shore n. strong beam set obliquely against wall of building or ship to prevent movement during alterations; v.t. to support by post or buttress; to prop. shoring n.

shorn pa.p. of shear; a. cut off; having the hair or wool cut off.

short a. having little length; not long in space; low; not extended in time; limited or lacking in quantity; hasty of temper; pronounced with less prolonged accent; concise; abrupt; adv. suddenly; abruptly;

without reaching the end; pl. short trousers reaching down to above knees. -age n. -coming n. failing; fault; defect. -cut n. quicker but unorthodox way of reaching a place or of accomplishing a task, etc. -en v.t. to make shorter; v.t. to contract; to lessen. -ening n. lard, butter, or other fat used when baking pastry, etc. -hand n. system of rapid reporting by means of signs or symbols. —handed a. not having the full complement of staff on duty. -ly adv. in a brief time; soon; in a few words; curtly. -ness n. — shrift, summary treatment.

shot pa.t. and pa.p. of shoot.

shot a. pert. to fabrics woven with warp and weft of contrasting tints or colors.

shot n. act of shooting; one of small pellets, contained in cartridge fired from sporting rifle; charge of blasting powder; stroke in billiards, tennis, etc.; a photograph; a try to attempt; v.t. to load or weight with shot. pr.p. -ting. pa.t. and pa.p. -ted. -gun n. smoothbore gun for shooting small game or birds.

should v. and aux. used in Future-in-the-Past tenses of verbs with pronouns I or we; auxiliary used after words expressing opinion, intention, desire, probability, obligation, etc.

shoul•der n. ball and socket joint formed by humerus with scapula; upper joint of foreleg of animal; anything resembling human shoulder, as prominent part of hill; v.t. to push forward with shoulders; to bear (burden, etc.); to accept (responsibility); v.i. to push forward through crowd.

shout n. loud, piercing cry; v.t. and v.i. to utter loud sudden cry.

shove v.t. to push; to press against; to jostle; v.i. to push forward; n. act of pushing.

shov•el n. spade with broad blade slightly hollowed; scoop; machine for scooping and lifting; v.t. to lift or move with a shovel; v.i. to use shovel. -ler n.

show v.t. to present to view; to disclose; to explain; to prove; to conduct; to guide; v.i. to appear; to be visible; to come into sight. pa.p. -n or -ed n. that which is shown; spectacle; exhibition; display; -er n. -ily n. -man n. one who presents a show; one who is skilled at presenting things. -manship n. -y a. gaudy; attracting attention; ostentatious.

show•er n. a brief fall of rain or hail; anything coming down like rain; great number; v.t. to wet with rain; to give abundantly; v.i. to rain; to pour down. -y a. raining intermittently.

shrank pa.t. of shrink.

shrap•nel n. shell timed to explode over, and shower bullets and splinters on, personnel; shell splinters.

shred n. long, narrow piece cut or torn off; strip; v.t. to cut or tear to shreds. pr.p. -ding. pa.t. and pa.p. -ded.

shrew n. noisy, quarrelsome woman; a termagant; mammal resembling, but unrelated to, mouse. -ish a. -ishly adv. -ishness n.

S

shrew

shrewd *a.* intelligent; discerning; cunning. -ly *adv.* -ness *n.*

shriek *v.t.* and *v.i.* to scream; to screech; *n.* a loud, shrill cry.

shrift *n.* confession made to a priest.

shrike *n.* bird which preys on birds, frogs, and insects.

shrill *a.* uttering an acute sound; piercing; high-pitched; *v.i.* to sound in a shrill tone. -y *adv.*

shrimp *n.* small edible crustacean allied to prawns; small person; *v.i.* to catch shrimps with net. -er *n.*

shrine *n.* case in which sacred relics are deposited; tomb of saint; place of worship; any sacred place.

shrink *v.i.* to contract; to dwindle; to recoil; to draw back; *v.t.* to cause to contract. *pa.t.* shrank, shrunk. *pa.p.* shrunk. -age *n.* shrunken *a.*

shrive *v.t.* to give absolution to; to confess (used reflexively); *v.i.* to receive or make confession. -d or shrove. *pa.p.* shriven.

shriv·el *v.t.* and *v.i.* to cause to contract and wrinkle; to wither.

shroud *n.* that which clothes or covers; sheet for a corpse; winding sheet; *v.t.* to enclose in winding sheet; to cover with shroud; to conceal.

shrove *pa.t.* of the verb shrive. Shrovetide *n.* period immediately before Lent.

shrub *n.* any hard-wooded plant of smaller and thicker growth than tree; bush; low, dwarf tree. -bery *n.* collection of shrubs. -by *a.*

shrug *v.i.* to raise and narrow shoulders in disdain, etc. *v.t.* to move (shoulders) thus. *pr.p.* -ging. *pa.t.* and *pa.p.* -ged. *n.* drawing up of shoulders.

shrunk, shrunken See shrink.

shuck *n.* husk or pod; shell of nut; *v.t.* to remove husk, pod, or shell from.

shud·der *v.i.* to tremble violently; *n.* trembling or shaking. -ing *n.* and *a.* trembling; shivering.

shuf·fle *v.t.* to shove one way and the other; to throw into disorder; to mix (cards); to scrape (feet) along ground; *v.i.* to change position of cards in pack; to prevaricate; to move in a slovenly manner; to scrape floor with foot in dancing or walking; *n.* act of throwing into confusion by change of places; artifice or pretext; scraping movement of foot in dancing.

shun *v.t.* to keep clear of; to avoid. *pr.p.* -ning. *pa.t.* and *pa.p.* -ned.

shunt *v.t.* to move or turn off to one side; *v.i.* to go aside; to turn off. *n.* act of shunting. -er *n.*

shut *v.t.* to close to hinder ingress or egress; to forbid entrance to; *v.i.* to close itself; to become closed. *pr.p.* -ting. *pa.t.* and *pa.p.* shut. *a.* closed; made fast. -ter

n. one who, or that which, shuts; movable protective screen for window.

shut·tle *n.* instrument used in weaving for shooting thread of woof between threads of warp; *v.t.* and *v.i.* to move backwards

shuttle

and forwards. -cock *n.* cork with fan of feathers for use with battledore or in badminton.

shy *a.* sensitively timid; reserved; easily frightened; cautious; falling short; *v.i.* to start suddenly aside. *pa.t.* and *pa.p.* shied. -ly *adv.* -ness *n.* -ster *n.* unscrupulous lawyer or person.

shy *v.t.* to throw; to fling. *pa.t.* and *pa.p.* shied. *n.* throw; cast.

Si·a·mese *a.* pert. to Siam, the people, or language; *n.* native of Siam; the language.

sib *a.* having kinship; related by blood; *n.* a blood relation.

Si·be·ri·an *a.* pert. to Siberia, part of the Soviet Union.

sib·i·lance *n.* hissing sound; quality of being sibilant. Also sibilancy. sibilant *a. n.* letter uttered with hissing of voice, as *s, x,* etc. sibilate *v.t.*

sib·yl *n.* a name applied to certain votaresses of Apollo. -lic, -line *a.*

sic *adv.* abbreviated form of *sic in originail* printed in brackets as guarantee that passage has been quoted correctly; so; thus.

sic·ca·tion *n.* act or process of drying. siccative *a.* and *n.*

Si·cil·i·an *a.* pert. to island of Sicily; *n.* native of Sicily.

sick *a.* affected with physical or mental disorder; tired of. -en *v.t.* to make sick; to disgust; *v.i.* to become sick; to be filled with abhorrence. -ening *a.* causing sickness or disgust; nauseating. -eningly *adv.* -ly *a.* -ness *n.*

sick·le *n.* reaping hook.

side *n.* one of surfaces of object, esp. upright inner or outer surface; one of the edges of plane figure; margin; border; part of body from hip to shoulder; slope, as of a hill; one of two parties, teams, or sets of opponents; line of descent traced through one parent; *a.* being on the side; lateral; indirect; incidental; *v.i.* (with) to hold or embrace the opinions of another. -board *n.* piece of furniture designed to hold dining utensils, etc. in dining room. -car *n.* small box-shaped body attached to motorcycle. — light *n.* any source of light situated at side of room, door, etc.; lantern, showing red or green, on side of a vessel; incidental information or illustration. —long *a.* lateral; oblique; not directly forward; *adv.* obliquely; on the side. -r *n.* -show *n.* minor entertainment or attraction; subordinate affair. -slip *n.* involuntary skid or slide sideways; *v.i.* to skid. -stroke *n.* style of swimming where body is turned on one side. -track *v.t.* to shunt into siding; to postpone indefinitely; to shelve; *n.* a railway siding. **siding** *n.* **sidle** *v.i.* to move sideways; to edge.

si•de•re•al *a.* relating to constellations and fixed stars.

sid•er•ite *n.* brown ironstone.

siege *n.* the surrounding of a town or fortified place by hostile troops in order to induce it to surrender; continuous effort to gain (affection, influence, etc.); *v.t.* to besiege.

si•en•na *n.* natural yellow earth which provides pigment. **burnt sienna,** pigment giving reddish-brown tint. **raw sienna,** pigment giving a yellowish-brown tint.

si•er•ra *n.* chain of mountains with saw-like ridge.

sieve *n.* utensil with wire netting or small holes for separating fine part of any pulverized substance from the coarse; *v.t.* to sift.

sift *v.t.* to separate coarser portion from finer; to sieve; to scrutinize.

sigh *v.i.* to make a deep, single respiration, as expression of exhaustion or sorrow; *v.t.* to utter sighs over; *n.* long, deep breath.

sight *n.* one of the five senses; act of seeing; that which is seen; anything novel or remarkable; exhibition; spectacle; any guide for eye to assist direction; *v.t.* to catch sight of; to see; *v.i.* to take aim by means of a sight. **-less** *a.* blind; invisible. **-lessly** *adv.* **-lessness** *n.* **-liness** *n.* comeliness. **-ly** *a.* pleasing to the eye; graceful; handsome.

sig•il *n.* seal; signet; occult sign. **sigillary** *a.*

sign *n.* movement, mark, or indication to convey some meaning; token; symbol; omen; signboard; password; *(Math.)* character indicating relation of quantities or operation to be performed; *(Mus.)* any character, as flat, sharp, dot, etc.; *v.t.* to represent by sign; to affix signature to; to ratify; *v.i.* to make a signal or gesture; to append one's signature.

sig•nal *n.* sign to give notice at a distance; that which in the first place impels any action; *v.t.* to communicate by signals; *v.i.* to make signals. *pr.p.* **-ing.** *pa.t.* and *pa.p.* **-ed** *a.* pert. to a signal; remarkable; conspicuous. **-ize** *v.t.* to make notable, distinguished, or remarkable; to point out. **-er** *n.* **-ly** *adv.* eminently; remarkably.

sig•na•to•ry *a.* and *n.* (one) bound by signature to terms of agreement.

sig•na•ture *n.* a sign, stamp, or mark impressed; a person's name written by himself; act of writing it.

sig•net *n.* seal used for authenticating documents.

sig•ni•fy *v.t.* to make known by a sign; to convey notion of; to indicate; *v.i.* to express meaning; *pa.t.* and *pa.p.* **signified. significance** *n.* **significant** *a.* fitted or designed to signify or make known something; important. **significantly** *adv.* **signification** *n.* **significative** *a.* **significatory** *a.*

si•lage *n.* compressed, acid-fermented fodder.

si•lence *n.* stillness; quietness; calm; refraining from speed; oblivion; *interj.*be quiet!; *v.t.* to cause to be still; to forbid to speak; to refute; to kill. **-r** *n.* **silent** *a.* **silently** *adv.* **silentness** *n.*

si•lex *n.* silica.

sil•hou•ette *n.* portrait or picture done in black upon a light ground; outline of object seen against the light; *v.t.* to represent in outline.

sil•i•ca *n.* silicon dioxide, main component of most rocks, occurring in nature as sand, flint, quartz, etc. **silicate** *n.* salt of silicic acid. **silicated** *a.* **siliceous** *a.* Also **silicious. silicic** *a.*

sil•i•cones *n.pl.* new family of materials—petroleum, brine, ordinary sand.

silk *n.* fine, soft, lustrous thread; fabric made from this; *a.* made of silk. **-en** *a.* made of, or resembling, silk; soft; smooth; silky. **-iness** *n.* **-screen** *a.* and *n.* (pert. to) the reproduction of a design by means of a pattern made on a screen of nylon or silk. **-worm** *n.* caterpillar of any moth which produces silk.

sill *n.* base or foundation; horizontal member at the bottom of window frame, door, or opening.

sil•ly *a.* weak in intellect; foolish; senseless; stupid; *n.* silly person. **sillily** *adv.* **silliness** *n.*

si•lo *n.* large, airtight tower, elevator, or pit in which green crops are preserved; *v.t.* to preserve in a silo.

silt *n.* fine, alluvial, soil, particles, mud; sediment; *v.t.* and *v.i.* to choke or obstruct with silt.

sil•ver *n.* soft, white, metallic element, very malleable and ductile; silverware; silver coins; anything resembling silver; *a.* made of, or resembling, silver; white or gray, as hair; bright, silvery; *v.t.* to coat or plate with silver; to tinge with white or gray; to render smooth and bright; *v.i.* to become gradually white, as hair. **-ize** *v.t.* **-plating** *n.* **-ware** *n.* articles made of silver. **-ry** *a.* like silver; lustrous; (of sound) soft and clear.

sim•i•an *a.* pert. to or like an ape generally; *n.* a monkey or ape.

sim•i•lar *a.* like; resembling; exactly corresponding. **-ity** *n.* quality or state of being similar. **-ly** *adv.*

sim•i•le *n.* figure of speech using some point of resemblance observed to exist between two things which differ in other respects.

si•mil•i•tude *n.* state of being similar or like; parable.

sim•mer *v.t.* to cause to boil gently; *v.i.* to be just bubbling or just below boiling-point; to be in a state of suppressed anger or laughter; *n.* gentle, gradual heating.

si•mo•ni•ac *n.* one guilty of simony. **-al** *a.* **-ally** *adv.* **simonist** *n.*

si•mo•ny *n.* the offense of offering or accepting money or other reward for nomination or appointment.

sim•per *v.i.* to smile in a silly, affected manner; *n.* smile with air of silliness or affectation. -er n.

sim•ple a. single; not complex; entire; mere; plain, sincere; clear; intelligible; simple-minded; (Chem.) composed of a single element; n. something not compounded. —minded a. ingenuous; open; frank; mentally weak. -ness n. -ton n. foolish person; person of weak intellect. -simplicity n. simplification n. simplificative a. simplify v.t. to make or render simple, plain, or easy. pa.t. and pa.p. simplified. simply adv.

sim•u•la•crum n. image; representation. pl. simulacra.

sim•u•lant a. simulating; having the appearance of; n. one simulating something. simular a. and n.

sim•u•late v.t. to assume the mere appearance of, without the reality; to feign. simulation n. simulator n.

si•mul•ta•ne•ous a. existing or occurring at same time. -ness, simultaneity n. -ly adv.

sin n. transgression against divine or moral law, esp. when committed consciously; iniquity; evil; v.i. to depart from path of duty prescribed by God; to do wrong. pr.p. -ning. pa.t. and pa.p. -ned. -ful a. -fully adv. -fulness n. -ner n.

since adv. from then till now; subsequently; ago; prep. at some time subsequent to; after; conj. from the time that; seeing that; because.

sin•cere a. not assumed or merely professed; straightforward. -ly adv. -ness, sincerity n.

sine n. (abbrev. sin) (Math.) perpendicular drawn from one extremity of an arc to diameter drawn through other extremity; function of one of the two acute angles in a right angle triangle; ratio of line subtending this angle to hypotenuse.

si•ne•cure n. office, position, etc. with salary but with few duties. sinecurist n.

sin•ew n. ligament or tendon which joins muscle to bone; source of strength or vigor. -ed a. -y a. well braced; muscular.

sing v.t. to utter with musical modulations of voice; to celebrate in song; v.i. to utter sounds with melodious modulations of voice; to pipe, twitter, chirp, as birds; to hum; to reverberate. pa.t. sang or sung. pa.p. sung. -ern. one who sings; vocalist. -ing n.

singe v.t. to burn the surface slightly; to burn loose fluff from yarns, etc. pr.p. -ing. n. superficial burn.

Sin•gha•lese a. pert. to Ceylon, its people, or language. n. a native of Ceylon.

sin•gle a. sole; not double; unmarried; sincere; whole-hearted; straightforward; upright; n. unit; v.t. (with out) to select from a number; to pick; to choose. -ness n. singly adv. one by one; by oneself.

sin•gle•ton n. (Cards) hand containing only one card of some suit.

sing•song n. rhythmical, monotonous fashion of uttering. a. monotonous; droning.

sin•gu•lar a. existing by itself; individual; unique; outstanding; n. single instance; word in the singular number. -ize v.t. -ity n. state of being singular; anything

unusual or remarkable; oddity. -ly adv.

Sin•ic a. Chinese. -ism n.

sin•is•ter a. on left hand; evil-looking. sinistral a. to the left; reversed.

sink v.t. to cause to descend; to submerge; to dig; to excavate; to ruin; to suppress; to invest; v.i. to subside; to descend; to penetrate (into); to become submerged. pa.t. sank or sunk. pa.p. sunk. n. a receptacle for washing up; place notoriously associated with evildoing. -er n. -ing n. operation of excavating; subsidence; settling; ebb; part sunk below surrounding surface.

Si•no-, in compounds, meaning Chinese.

Si•nol•o•gy n. that branch of knowledge which deals with the Chinese.

sin•u•ate v.i. to bend in and out; a. (Bot.) wavy; tortuous; curved on the margin, as a leaf. Also -d. sinuation n. sinuose, sinuous a. bending in and out; morally crooked; supple. sinuously adv.

si•nus n. (Anat.) opening; hollow; cavity. -itis n. inflammation of sinus.

Sioux n. member of great Siouan division of N. American aborigines; their language. pl. Sioux.

sip v.t. and v.i. to drink or imbibe in very small quantities; to taste. pr.p. -ping. pa.t. and pa.p. -ped. n. a small portion of liquid sipped with the lips.

si•phon, syphon n. a bent tube or pipe by which a liquid can be transferred by atmospheric pressure from one receptacle to another; bottle provided with internal tube and lever top, for holding and delivering aerated water; projecting tube in mantle of shell of bivalve; v.t. to draw off by means of a siphon. n. action of a siphon.

sir n. a title or respect to any man of position.

sire n. title of respect to a king or emperor; male parent of an animal (applied esp. to horses); pl. (Poetic) ancestors; v.t. to beget (of animals).

si•ren n. (Myth.) one of several nymphs said to sing with such sweetness that sailors were lured to death; seductive alluring woman; form of horn which emits series of loud, piercing notes used as warning signal; steam whistle; a. pert. to, or resembling a siren.

Sir•i•us n. (Astron.) a star of the first magnitude known as the Dog Star.

sir•loin n. the upper part of a loin of beef.

si•roc•co n. a hot, southerly, dust-laden wind from Africa.

si•sal n. fiber plant, native to Florida and Yucatan.

sis•sy n. (Colloq.) ineffective effeminate man or boy; a. effeminate.

sis•ter n. female whose parents are same as those of another person; woman of the same faith; nun; a. related; of a similar nature to, as institute, college, etc. -hood n. state of being a sister; society of women united in one faith or order. -like, -ly a.

Sis•tine a. pert. to any Pope named Sixtus. — Chapel, the Pope's private chapel in the Vatican at Rome.

sit *v.i.* to rest upon haunches, a seat, etc.; to remain; to rest; to perch, as birds; to be in session; to be representative in legislative for constituency; to fit (of clothes); *v.t.* to keep good seat, upon, as on horseback; to place upon seat; *pr.p.* **-ting.** *pa.t.* and *pa.p.* **sat.** *n.* position assumed by an object after being placed. **-ter** *n.* **-ting** *n.* and *a.*

site *n.* situation; plot of ground for, or with, building; locality; place where anything is fixed; *v.t.* to place in position; to locate.

si·tol·o·gy *n.* dietetics.

sit·u·ate *v.t.* to give a site to; to place in a particular state or set of circumstances to locate; **-d** *a.* **situation** *n.* location; place or position; site; condition; job; post; plight.

six *a.* one more than five; *n.* sum of three and three; symbol 6 or VI. **-teen** *n.* and *a.* six and ten, symbol 16 or XVI. **-teenth** *a.* sixth after the tenth; being one of sixteen equal parts into which anything is divided; *n.* one of sixteen equal parts. **-th** *a.* next in order after the fifth; one of six equal parts. **-ty** *a.* six times ten; three score; *n.* symbol 60 or LX. **-tieth** *a.* next in order after the fifty-ninth; one of sixty equal parts.

size *n.* bulk; bigness; comparative magnitude; dimensions; *v.t.* to arrange according to size. **-able, sizable** *a.* of considerate size or bulk.

size *n.* substance of a gelatinous nature, like weak glue; *v.t.* to treat or cover with size.

siz·zle *v.i.* to make hissing or sputtering noise; *n.* hissing, sputtering noise. **sizzling** *n.*

skald *n.* ancient Scandinavian poet. **-ic** *a.* Also **scald.**

skate *n.* steel blade attached to boot, used for gliding over ice; *v.i.* to travel over ice on skates. **-r** *n.* **skating** *n.* **skating-rink** *n.* stretch of ice or flat expanse for skating.

skate *n.* a large, edible, flat fish of the ray family.

skean *n.* Highland dagger or dirk.

skeet *n.* trapshooting with clay targets.

skein *n.* small hank, of fixed length, of thread, silk, or yarn.

skel·e·ton *n.* body framework providing support for human or animal body; any framework; *a.* pert. to skeleton; containing mere outlines. Also **skeletal.**

skel·ter. See helter-skelter.

skep *n.* beehive made of straw; light basket.

skep·tic *n.* one who doubts, esp. existence of God, or accepted doctrines. **-al** *a.* **-ally** *adv.* **-alness** *n.* **skepticize** *v.i.* **skepticism** *n.*

sker·ry *n.* rocky isle; reef.

sketch *n.* first rough draft or plan of any design; drawing in pen, pencil, or similar medium; descriptive essay or account, in light vein; *v.t.* to make rough draft of; *v.i.* to draw. **-er** *n.* **-ily** *adv.* **-iness** *n.* lack of detail. **-y** *a.*

skew *a.* awry; askew; turned aside; *n.* a deviation; *v.t.* to put askew; to skid.

skew·er *n.* pointed rod for fastening meat to a spit; *v.t.* to fasten with skewers.

ski *n.* long wooden runner strapped to foot, for running, sliding and jumping over snow; *v.i.* to run, slide, or jump on skis. **-er** *n.*

ski·a·graph *n.* an X-ray photograph. Also **skiagram. -er** *n.* **-ic** *a.*

skid *n.* a piece of timber to protect side of vessel from injury; inclined plane down which logs, etc. slide; low, wooden platform for holding and moving loads; *v.i.* to slide or slip sideways; *v.t.* to slide a log down a skid; to place on skids. *pr.p.* **-ding** *pa.p., pa.t.* **-ded.**

skiff *n.* a small rowboat or sailboat.

skill *n.* practical ability and dexterity; knowledge; expertness; aptitude. **-ful** *a.* **-fully** *adv.* **-fulness** *n.* **-ed** *a.*

skil·let *n.* a frying pan.

skim *v.t.* to remove from surface of liquid; to glide over lightly and rapidly; to glance over in superficial way; to graze; *v.i.* to pass lightly over. *pr.p.* **-ming.** *pa.t.* and *pa.p.* **-med.** *n.* skimming; matter skimmed off. **-mer** *n.*

skimp *v.t.* to stint; *v.i.* to be mean or parsimonious. **-y** *a.*

skin *n.* external protective covering of animal bodies; coat of fruits and plants; thick scum; *v.t.* to strip off skin or hide of. **-ner** *n.* dealer in hides; furrier. **-niness** *n.* leanness. **-ny** *a.* of skin; very lean or thin.

skip *v.t.* to leap over lightly; to omit without noticing; *v.i.* to leap lightly, esp. in frolic; to pass from one thing to another. *pr.p.* **-ping.** *pa.t.* and *pa.p.* **-ped.** *n.* **-ping** *a.*

skip·per *n.* captain of ship or team.

skirl *v.i.* to sound shrilly. *n.* shrill, high-pitched sound of bagpipe.

skir·mish *n.* irregular, minor engagement between two parties of soldiers; *v.i.*

skirt *n.* lower part of coat, gown; outer garment of a woman fitted to and hanging from waist; margin; edge; rim; *v.t.* to be on border; to go around.

skit *n.* short, usually humorous, play; *v.i.* to leap aside. **-tish** *a.* frisky; frivolous; fickle; apt to shy, of a horse. **-tishly** *adv.* **-tishness** *n.*

skit·tle *n.* game of ninepins.

skive *v.t.* in shoe-making, to pare away edges of leather.

skoal *interj.* salutation, hail!

skulk *v.i.* to lurk or keep out of sight in a furtive manner; to act sullenly; *n.* one who skulks.

skull *n.* body framework which encloses brain; cranium along with bones of face.

skull

skunk n. small N. American burrowing animal, allied to weasel, which defends itself by emitting evil-smelling fluid; (Colloq.) a base, mean person.

skunk

sky n. the apparent vault of heaven; heavens; firmament; climate. v.t.

Skye n. or Skyeterrier, breed of Scotch terrier, with long hair.

slab n. thickish, flat, rectangular piece of anything.

slack a. not taut; not holding fast; remiss about one's duties; easygoing; n. part of a rope which hangs loose; quiet time. -en v.t. and v.i. -er n. -ly adv. -ness n. -s n.pl. loose trousers worn by men or women.

slack n. the finer screenings of coal.

slag n. silicate formed during smelting of ores; v.i.

slain pa.p. of the verb slay.

slake v.t. to quench; to extinguish; to combine quicklime with water; to slacken; v.i. to become mixed with water.

slam v.t. to shut violently and noisily; to bang; to hit; to dash down. pr.p. -ming. pa.t. and pa.p. -med. n. act of slamming; bang.

slan·der n. false or malicious statement about person; calumny; v.t. to injure by maliciously uttering false report; to defame. -er n. -ous a.

slang n. word or expression in common colloquial use but not regarded as standard English.

slant v.t. to turn from a direct line; to give a sloping direction to; v.i. to lie obliquely; n. slanting direction or position; point of view or illuminating remark (on); a. sloping; oblique. -ingly adv. -ly, -wise adv.

slap n. blow with open hand or flat instrument; insulting remark; v.t. to strike with open hand or something flat. pr.p. -ping. pa.t. and pa.p. -ped. -stick n. boisterous farce of pantomime or low comedy.

slash v.t. to cut by striking violently and haphazardly; v.i. to strike violently and at random with edged weapon; n. long cut; gash. -er n.

slat n. narrow strip of wood, metal, etc. -ted a.

slate n. a form of shale which splits readily into thin leaves; dark blue-gray color; list of candidates for offices; a. made of slate; bluish-gray; v.t. to cover with slates; to put on a list for nomination, etc. slating n. act of covering with slates; roof covering thus put on. slaty n.

slat·tern n. slut; slovenly woman or girl. -liness n. -ly a. and adv. like a slattern.

slaugh·ter n. carnage; massacre; butchery; killing of animals to provide food; v.t. to kill; to slay in battle; to butcher. -er n. -ous a. -ously adv.

Slav n. a member of a group of peoples in E. and S.E. Europe, comprising Russians, Ukrainians, White Russians, Poles, Czechs, Slovaks, Serbians, Croats, Slovenes and Bulgarians; a. relating to the Slavs; Slavic; Slavonic. -ic a. -onic a.

slave n. person held legally in bondage to another; v.i. to work like a slave, to toil unremittingly. -r n. person or ship engaged in slave traffic. -ry n. slavish a. slavishly adv. slavishness n.

slav·er n. saliva running from mouth; sentimental nonsense; v.t. to smear with saliva issuing from mouth; v.i. to slobber; to talk in a weakly sentimental fashion. -er n.

slaw n. sliced cabbage served cooked, or uncooked, as a salad.

slay v.t. to kill. pa.t. slew pa.p. slain. -er n.

sleave n. knotted or entangled part of silk or thread; a fine wisp of silk made by separating a thread; v.t. to separate and divide as into threads.

slea·zy a. thin or poor in texture.

sled, sledge n. a vehicle on runners, for conveying loads over hard snow or ice; a sleigh; a small flat sled for coasting; v.t. to convey on a sled; v.i. to ride on a sled.

sledge n. large, heavy hammer.

sleek a. having a smooth surface; ingratiating; v.t. to make smooth; to calm; to soothe; adv. -ly adv. -ness n.

sleep v.i. to rest by suspension of exercise of powers of body and mind; to become numb (of limb). pa.t. and pa.p. slept. n. slumber; repose; rest; death. -er n. -ily adv. -iness n. -ing a. and n. -less a. wakeful; restless; alert; vigilant; unremitting. -lessly adv. -lessness n. -y a. inclined to sleep; drowsy.

sleet n. rain that is partly frozen; v.i. to fall as fine pellets of ice. -iness n. -y a.

sleeve n. part of garment which covers arm.

sleigh n. a sled; an open carriage on runners, usually horse-drawn; v.i. to drive in a sleigh.

sleight n. artful trick; skill.

slen·der a. thin or narrow; weak; feeble; not strong. -ly adv. -ness n.

slept pa.t. and pa.p. of sleep.

sleuth n. bloodhound; a relentless tracker; (Colloq.) detective.

slew pa.t. of slay.

slew, slue v.t. and v.i. to turn about.

slice v.t. and v.i. to cut off thin flat pieces; n. thin, flat piece cut off; share or portion. -r n.

slick a. smooth; sleek; smooth-tongued; smart; clever; slippery; adv. deftly; cleverly; v.t. to sleek; to make glossy. n. a smooth spot. See sleek.

slick·er n. waterproof coat.

slid, slidden See slide.

slide v.i. to slip smoothly along; to pass imperceptibly; to deteriorate morally; v.t. to move something into position by pushing along the surface of another body. pr.p. sliding. pa.t. slid. pa.p. slid or slidden. n. sliding; track on ice made by sliding; anything which moves freely in. or out; photographic film holder for projecting; chute. **-r** n. **— rule** n.

slight a. trifling; slim; slender; n. contempt by ignoring another; v.t. to ignore; to insult. **-ing** n. and a. **-ingly** adv. **-ly** adv. to slight extent; not seriously. **-ness** n.

slim a. of small diameter or thickness; slender; unsubstantial; v.t. and v.i. to make or become slim. pa.t., pa.p. **-med**. pr.p. **-ming. -ly** adv.

slime n. soft, sticky, moist earth or clay; viscous secretion of snails, etc.; **slimily** adv. **sliminess** n. **slimy** a.

sling n. pocket of leather, etc., with a string attached at each end for hurling a stone; hanging bandage, for supporting an arm or hand; rope, chain, belt, etc. for hoisting weights; v.t. to throw by means of sling or swinging motion of arm; to suspend. pa.t. and pa.p. **slung. -er** n.

sling n. American iced drink.

slink v.i. to move in a stealthy, furtive manner. pa.t. and pa.p. **slunk**.

slip v.t. to move an object smoothly, secretly, or furtively into another position; to escape (memory); v.i. to lose one's foothold; to move smoothly along surface of; to withdraw quietly; to make a mistake; to lose one's chance; to pass without notice. pr.p. **-ping**. pa.t. and pa.p. **-ped**. n. act of slipping; unintentional error; loose garment worn under woman's dress; covering for a pillow; skid; inclined plane from which ships are launched. **-per** n. light shoe for indoor use; dancing-shoe. **-perily** adv. **-periness** n. **-pery** a. so smooth as to cause slipping or to be difficult to hold or catch; unstable; untrustworthy; changeable.

slit v.t. to cut lengthwise; to cut open; v.i. to be slit. pr.p. **-ting**. pa.t. and pa.p. **slit**. n. straight, narrow cut or incision; narrow opening. **-ter** n.

slith·er v.i. to slide and bump (down a slope, etc.); to move in a sliding, snakelike fashion; n.

sliv·er v.t. to divide into long, thin strips; v.i. to split; to become split off; n. thin piece cut lengthwise; splinter.

slob·ber v.i. to let saliva drool from mouth; dribble; v.t. to cover with saliva. n. saliva coming from mouth; sentimental drivel. Also **slabber. -er** n.

sloe n. blackthorn; small dark fruit of blackthorn.

slog v.t. to hit wildly and vigorously; v.i. to work or study with dogged determination. pr.p. **-ging**. pa.t. and pa.p. **-ged, -ger** n.

slo·gan n. war cry of Highland clan in Scotland; catchword for focusing public interest, etc.

sloop n. one-masted sailing vessel.

slop n. liquid carelessly spilled; puddle; v.t. to spill; to soil by spilling over; v.i. to overthrow or be spilled. pr.p. **-ping**. pa.t. and pa.p. **-ped. -pily** adv. **-piness** n. **-py** a.

slope n. upward or downward inclination; v.t. to form with slope; v.i. to assume

oblique direction. **sloping** a.

slosh n. soft mud; v.t. to stir in liquid; v.i. to splash.

slot n. slit cut out for reception of object or part of machine; v.t. to make a slot in. pr.p. **-ting**. pa.t. and pa.p. **-ted**.

sloth n. lethargy; indolence. **-ful** a. **-fully** adv. **-fulness** n.

sloth n. group of edentate mammals of S. America.

sloth

slouch n. ungraceful, stooping manner of walking or standing; shambling gait; v.i. to sit or stand in a drooping position; v.t. to depress; to cause to hang down loosely. **-y** a.

slough n. bog; swamp.

slough n. cast-off outer skin; v.t. to cast off, or shed, as a slough; v.i. to separate as dead matter which forms over sore.

Slo·vak n. member of Slav people in northern Carpathians; language spoken in Slovakia; a. pert. to Slovaks. Also **Slovakian**.

slov·en n. person careless of dress, or negligent of cleanliness. **-liness** n. **-ly** a. adv.

slow a. not swift; indicating time earlier than true time; mentally sluggish; dull; adv. slowly; v.t. to render slow; to retard; v.i. to slacken speed. **-ly** adv. **-ness** n.

sludge n. mud which settles at bottom of waterways, of vessel containing water, or a shaft when drilling. **sludgy** a.

slug n. one of land snails without a shell. **-gard** n. person habitually lazy and idle; a. disinclined to exert oneself. **-gishly** adv. **-ishness** n.

slug n. small thick disk of metal.

slug (Colloq.) v.i. to strike heavily; to slog; n. heavy blow.

sluice n. valve or shutter for regulating flow; artificial channel along which stream flows; v.t. to drain through a sluice; v.i. to run through a sluice.

slum n. squalid street, or quarter of town, characterized by gross over-crowding, dilapidation, poverty, vice and dirt; v.i. to visit slums. pr.p. **-ming** pa.t. and pa.p. **-med**.

slum·ber v.i. to sleep lightly; n. light sleep; doze. **-er** n. **-ous, slumbrous** a. inducing slumber; drowsy.

slump n. act of slumping; sudden, sharp fall in prices or volume of business done; v.i. to drop suddenly.

slung pa.t. and pa.p. of **sling**.

slunk pa.t. and pa.p. of **slink**.

slur v.t. to pass over lightly; to deprecate; to insult; to pronounce indistinctly; (Mus.) to sing or play in a smooth,

S

gliding style. *pr.p.* **-ring.** *pa.t.* and *pa.p.*
-red. *n.* stigma; reproach; implied insult;
indistinct sound.

slush *n.* half-melted snow; any greasy,
pasty mass; overly sentimental talk or
writings; *v.t.* to splash or cover with
slush. **-y** *a.*

slut *n.* dirty, untidy woman; slattern. **-tish**
a.

sly *a.* artfully cunning; mischievous. **-ly**
adv. **-ness** *n.*

smack *v.t.* to make a loud, quick noise; to
slap loudly; to strike; *v.i.* to make sharp,
quick noise with lips; *n.* quick, sharp
noise, esp. with lips.

smack *v.i.* to have a taste or flavor; to give a
suggestion (of); *n.* a slight taste.

smack *n.* small sailing vessel.

small *a.* little in size, number, degree, etc.;
unimportant; slender; mean; *n.* small or
slender part, esp. of back. **-ish** *a.* **-ness** *n.*

small-pox *n.* infectious disease,
characterized into pustules.

smart *n.* sharp, stinging pain; *v.i.* to feel
such a pain; *a.* causing a sharp, stinging
pain; clever; active; well-dressed. **-ly**
adv. **-ness** *n.* **smarten** *v.t.* and *v.i.* to make
more spruce.

smash *v.t.* to break into pieces to shatter; to
hit hard; to ruin; *v.i.* to break into pieces;
n. crash; accident, wrecking vehicles;
utter ruin. **-ing** *a.*

smat-ter *v.i.* to talk superficially. **-ing** *n.*
slight, superficial knowledge.

smear *v.t.* to rub over with a greasy, oily, or
sticky substance; to daub; to impute
disgrace to. **-iness** *n.* **-y** *a.*

smell *n.* sense of perceiving odors by nose;
(unpleasant) odor; scent; perfume; *v.t.* to
perceive by nose; to detect; *v.i.* to use
nose; to give out odor. *pr.p.* **-ing.** *pa.p.*
and *pa.t.* **-ed** or **smelt. -ing** *n.* **-y** *a.* having
unpleasant smell.

smelt *n.* small, silvery fish of salmon
family.

smelt *v.t.* to melt or fuse ore in order to
extract metal. **-ing** *n.*

smi-lax *n.* genus of evergreen climbing
shrubs.

smile *v.i.* to express pleasure, approval,
amusement, contempt, irony, etc. by
curving lips; to look happy; *v.t.* to
express by smile; *n.* act of smiling.
smiling *a.* cheerful; gay; joyous.

smirch *v.t.* to dirty; to stain; to bring
disgrace upon; *n.* stain.

smirk *v.i.* to smile in an affected or
conceited manner; *n.*

smite *v.t.* to hit hard; to defeat; to afflict;
v.i. to strike. *pa.p.* **smitten.** *pa.t.* **smote. -r**
n.

smith *n.* one who shapes metal, esp. with
hammer and anvil; blacksmith. **-y** *n.*
smith's workshop.

smith-er-eens *n.pl.* (*Colloq.*) small bits.
Also **smithers.**

smit-ten *pa.p.* of smite.

smock *n.* a loose garment worn over other
clothing. **-ing** *n.* embroidered gathering
of dress, etc.

smog *n.* mixture of smoke and fog.

smoke *n.* cloudy mass of suspended

particles that rises from fire; *v.t.* to
consume by smoking; to expose to smoke
(esp. in curing fish, etc.); *v.i.* to inhale
and expel smoke of burning tobacco; to
give off smoke. **-r** *n.* **smoking** *n.*
smokiness *n.* **smoky** *a.*

smol-der *v.i.* to burn slowly without flame.

smolt *n.* young salmon.

smooth *a.* not rough; calm; steady in
motion; pleasant; easy; *v.t.* to make
smooth; *adv.* in a smooth manner. **-ly**
adv.

smor-gas-bord *n.* meal of appetizers served
buffet style.

smote *pa.p.* and *pa.t.* of smite.

smoth-er *v.t.* to destroy by depriving of air;
v.i. to be stifled; to be without air; *n.*
thick smoke or dust.

smudge *n.* smear; stain; smoky fire to drive
off insects; *v.t.* to smear; to make a dirty
mark; *v.i.* to become dirty or blurred.

smug *a.* very neat and prim; self-satisfied;
complacent. **-ly** *adv.* **-ness** *n.*

smug-gle *v.t.* to import or export goods
secretly to evade customs duties. **-r** *n.*
smuggling *n.*

smut *n.* black particle of dirt; lewd or
obscene talk or writing; *v.t.* to blacken;
to smudge. *pr.p.* **-ting.** *pa.p.* and *pa.t.*
-ted. -ty *a.* **-tily** *adv.* **-tiness** *n.*

smutch *v.t.* to blacken, as with soot, etc.; *n.*
dirty spot; stain; smudge.

snack *n.* share; slight, hasty meal.

snaf-fle *n.* horse's bridle bit jointed in
middle but without curb; *v.t.*

snag *n.* stump projecting from tree-trunk;
any obstacle, drawback, or catch; *v.t.* to
catch on a snag. *pr.p.* **-ging.** *pa.p.,* *pa.t.*

snail *n.* slow-moving mollusk with spiral
shell; slow person.

snake *n.* long, scaly, limbless reptile;
serpent; treacherous person; *v.i.* to move
like a snail. **snaky** *a.*

snap *v.t.* to break abruptly; to seize
suddenly; to snatch; to bite; to shut with
click; *v.i.* to break short; to try to bite; to
utter sharp, cross words; to make a quick,
sharp sound; to sparkle. *pr.p.* **-ping.** *pa.p.*
and *pa.t.* **-ped.** *n.;* *a.* unprepared; without
warning. **-per** *n.* one who snaps; kind of
fresh-water turtle. **-py** *a.* lively; brisk.

snare *n.* running noose of cord or wire,
used to trap animals or birds; a trap; *v.t.*
to catch with snare; to entangle.

snarl *v.i.* to growl like an angry dog; *n.*
growling sound; surly tone of voice. **-er**
n.

snarl *n.* tangle or knot of hair, wool, etc.;
complication; *v.t.* and *v.i.*

snatch *v.t.* to seize hastily or without
permission.

sneak *v.i.* to creep or steal away; to slink; *n.*
furtive, cowardly fellow. **-ing** *a.* **-ingly**
adv. **-iness, -ingness** *n.* **-y** *a.*

sneer *v.i.* to show contempt; *n.* look of
contempt or ridicule; scornful utterance.
-er *n.* **-ing** *a.*

sneeze *v.i.* to expel air through nose and
mouth with sudden convulsive spasm
and noise; *n.* a sneezing.

snick *n.* small cut; notch; nick; *v.t.* to cut;
to notch.

snick•er v.i. to laugh with small, audible catches of voice; to giggle; n. half-suppressed laugh.

sniff v.i. to draw in breath through nose with sharp hiss; to snuff; v.t. to take up through nose, to smell; n. **-le** v.i. to sniff noisily through nose; to snuffle. **-ler** n.

snip v.t. to clip off with scissors; to cut; n. a single, quick stroke, as with scissors; a bit cut off. pr.p. **-ping**. pa.p. and pa.t. **-ped**. **-per** n. **-pet** n. a fragment.

snipe n. long-billed gamebird; a shot; v.i. to shoot snipe; (Mil.) to shoot from cover; v.t. to hit by so shooting. **-r** n.

snipe

sniv•el n. running at the nose; sham emotion; whining, as a child. v.i. to run at the nose; to show real or sham sorrow; to cry or whine.

snob n. one who judges by social rank or wealth rather than merit. **-bery** n. **-bish** a. **-bishly** adv. **-bishness** n.

snood n. ribbon formerly worn to hold back hair; fillet.

snoot n. snout; nose; contemptuous. **-ily** adv. arrogantly. **-iness** n. **-y** a.

snooze n. (Colloq.) short sleep; nap; v.i. to take a snooze.

snore v.i. to breathe heavily and noisily during sleep; n. such noisy breathing. **-r** n.

snor•kel n. device for submarines and divers for air intake.

snort v.i. to force air with violence through nose, as horses; v.t. to express by snort; n. snorting sound.

snout n. projecting nose and jaws of animal, esp. of pig.

snow n. frozen vapor which falls in flakes; v.t. to let fall like snow; to cover with snow; v.i. to fall as or like snow. **-y** a. **-ily** adv. **-iness** n. **-fall** n. **-flake** n.

snub v.t. to check or rebuke with rudeness or indifference. pr.p. **-bing**. pa.p. and pa.t. **-bed**. n. intentional slight; rebuff; check; a. of nose, short and slightly turned up.

snuff n. charred part of wick of candle or lamp; v.t. to nip this off; to extinguish.

snuff v.t. to draw up or through nostrils; to smell; to inhale; v.i. to draw air or snuff into nose; n. powdered tobacco for inhaling through nose; sniff. **-er** n.

snuf•fle v.i. to breathe noisily through nose; to speak through nose; n. act of snuffling; a nasal twang. **-r** n.

snug a. cosy; trim; comfortable; sheltered; close fitting. **-ly** adv. **-ness** n. **-gle** v.i. to lie close to, for warmth or from affection.

so adv. in this manner or degree; very; the case being such; accordingly; conj. therefore; in case that; interj. well.

soak v.t. to steep; to wet thoroughly; v.i. to lie steeped in water or other fluid; n. a soaking; the act of soaking; heavy rain.

-er n. **-ing** a.

soap n. compound of oil or fat with alkali, used in washing; v.t. and v.i. to apply soap to. **-y** a. **-iness** n.

soar v.i. to fly high; to glide; to rise far above normal or to a great height.

sob v.i. to catch breath, esp. in weeping. pr.p. **-bing**. pa.p. and pa.t. **-bed**. n. convulsive catching of breath, esp. in weeping or sighing.

so•ber a. temperate; not intoxicated; subdued; v.t. and v.i. to make or become sober. **-ly** adv. **-ness** n. **sobriety** n.

soc•cer n. association football.

so•cia•ble a. inclined to be friendly; fond of company. **sociably** adv. **-iness** n. **sociability** n.

so•cial a. pert. to society; affecting public interest; living in communities, as ants; sociable; companionable; convivial; n. social meeting. **sociably** adv. **-ite** n. member of fashionable society.

so•cial•ism n. economic and political system, aiming at public or government ownership of means of production, etc. **socialize** v.t. **socialization** n. **socialist** a. **socialistic** a. **socialistically** adv.

so•ci•e•ty n. people in general; people of culture and good breeding in any community; the world of fashion; fellowship; wealthy; a company; an association; a club.

so•ci•ol•o•gy n. science of problems confronting society; social science. **sociological** a. **sociologist** n.

sock n. a short stocking.

sock•et n. opening or hollow into which anything is fitted; v.t. to provide with, or place in, socket.

sock•eye n. a red salmon.

sod n. flat piece of earth with grass; turf; v.t. to cover with turf. pr.p. **-ding** pa.p., pa.t. **-ded**.

so•da n. name applied to various compounds of sodium, e.g. baking soda, caustic soda, washing soda. (See **sodium**); (Colloq.) soda water.

so•dal•i•ty n. fellowship; an association.

sod•den a. soaked; soft with moisture; dull and heavy; stupid.

so•di•um n. silvery-white metallic alkaline element, the base of soda.

sod•o•my n. unnatural sexual intercourse, esp. between males or with an animal.

so•fa n. an upholstered couch.

soft a. yielding easily to pressure; not hard; smooth; gentle; melodious; quiet; susceptible; sentimental; weak; not astringent; containing no alcohol; in phonetics, esp. of consonants 'c' and 'g,' pronounced with a sibilant sound; adv. softly; quietly. **-ish** a. **-ly** adv. **-ness** n. **-headed** a. weak in intellect. **-hearted** a. kind; gentle.

soft•ball n. variant of the game of baseball.

soft•en v.t. to make soft or softer; to lighten; to mitigate; to tone down; to make less loud; v.t. to become soft or softer. **-ing** n. act, process, or result of becoming soft or softer.

sog•gy a. soaked with water.

soil v.t. to make dirty; to defile; dirty

marks; filth; manure; top layer of earth's surface; earth, as food for plants.

so•journ to dwell for a time; *n.* short stay.

sol•ace *n.* comfort in grief; consolation; *v.t.* to console.

so•lan *n.* large sea bird like a goose; a gannet.

so•lar *a.* pert. to, caused by, measured by sun. **-ize** *v.t.* and *v.i.* to expose to sun's rays. **solarium** *n.* a sun room or porch. *pl.* **solaria.**

sold *pa.p.* and *pa.t.* of sell.

sol•der *n.* easily melted alloy for joining metals; *v.t.* to join or mend with solder.

sol•dier *n.* man engaged in military service; an enlisted man as distinguished from commissioned officer. **-y** *n.* soldiers collectively; troops.

sole *n.* flat of the foot; lower part of anything, or that on which anything rests; small flatfish, used for food; *v.t.* to supply with a sole.

sole *a.* being, or acting, without another; alone; only. **-ly** *adv.*

sol•e•cism *n.* breach of grammar; a breach of etiquette. **solecist** *n.*

sol•emn *a.* marked, or performed, with religious ceremony; inspiring awe or dread. **-ly** *adv.* **-ness** *n.* **-ize** *v.t.* to perform with ceremony. **-ity** *n.* sacred rite; gravity; seriousness.

so•len *n.* genus of bivalve molluscs.

sol•fa *v.i.* to sing notes of scale.

so•lic•it *v.t.* to ask with earnestness; to entreat; *v.i.* to try to obtain, as trade, etc.; to accost. **-ant** *n.* **-ation** *n.* **-or** *n.* **-ous** *a.* anxious; eager; earnest. **-ously** *adv.* **-ousness, -ude** *n.* being solicitous; uneasiness; anxiety.

sol•id *a.* not in a liquid or gaseous state; not hollow; dependable; sound; *n.* a firm, compact body. **-ly** *adv.* **-arity** *n.* state of being solidly united in support of common interests, rights, etc. **-ity** *n.*

so•lid•i•fy *v.t.* to make solid or firm; to harden; *v.i.* to become solid.

sol•i•dus *n.* oblique stroke (/) in fractions, dates, etc. *pl.* **solidi.**

so•lil•o•quy *n.* talking to oneself; monologue, esp. by actor alone on stage. **soliloquize** *v.i.*

sol•i•taire *a.* living alone; done or spent alone; *n.* hermit; a single gem set by itself. **solitarily** *adv.* **solitariness** *n.* **solitude** *n.*

so•lo *n.* musical composition played or sung by one person; *a.* done or performed by one person; unaccompanied; alone. **soloist** *n.*

sol•stice *n.* either of two points in sun's path at which sun is farthest N. or S. from equator, about June 21 and December 22 respectively. **solstitial.**

sol•u•ble *a.* capable of being dissolved in a liquid; able to be solved or explained. **solubility** *n.*

so•lus *a.* as a stage direction, alone. *fem.* **sola.**

so•lu•tion *n.* process of finding answer to problem; answer itself; dissolving gas, liquid, or solid, esp. in liquid; mixture so obtained; *v.t.* to coat with solution.

solve *v.t.* to find the answer to; to explain; to make clear. **solvable** *a.* **-r** *n.* **solvent** *a.* having the power to dissolve another substance; able to pay all one's debts; *n.* substance, able to dissolve another's substance. **-ncy** *n.* state of being able to pay one's debts.

so•mat•ic *a.* pert. to the body; corporeal; physical. Also **-al.**

som•ber *a.* dark; gloomy; melancholy. **-ly** *adv.* **-ness** *n.* **sombrous** *a. (Poet.)* somber **sombrously** *adv.*

som•bre•ro *n.* broad-brimmed felt hat.

some *a.* denoting an indefinite number, amount, or extent; amount of; one or other; approximately; *(pron.)* portion; particular persons not named; *adv.* approximately. **-body** *n.* person not definitely known. **-how** *adv.* in one way or another; by any means. **-one** *pron.* **-such** *a.* denoting person or thing of the kind specified. **-thing.** **-time** *adv.* **-times** *adv.* at times; now and then; occasionally. **-what** *n.* indefinite amount or degree; *adv.* to some extent; rather. **-where** *adv.*

som•er•sault *n.* a movement in which one turns heels over head; *v.i.*

som•nam•bu•late *v.i.* to walk in one's sleep. **somnambulation** *n.* **somnambulism** *n.* **somnambulist** *n.* **somnambulistic** *a.*

som•ni•fa•cient *a.* inducing sleep; *n.* soporific. **somniferous** *a.* **somnific** *a.*

som•no•lent *a.* sleepy; drowsy. **-ly** *adv.* **somnolence** *n.* Also **somnolency.** **somnolescent** *a.*

son *n.* male child; term of affection; native of a place; disciple.

so•nant *a.* pert. to sound; *n.* a syllabic sound. **sonance** *n.*

so•na•ta *n.* a musical composition in three or four movements. **sonatina** *n.* a short sonata.

song *n.* singing; poem, or piece of poetry, esp. if set to music; musical sounds made by birds; *(Colloq.)* a mere trifle. **-ster** *n. (fem.* **songstress)** one who sings.

son•ic *a.* pertaining to sound.

son•net *n.* poem of fourteen lines. **soneteer** *n.* a writer of sonnets.

so•no•rous *a.* giving out a deep, loud sound when struck; resonant; high-sounding. *adv.* **-ness, sonority** *n.*

soon *adv.* in a short time; shortly; without delay; willingly.

soot *n.* a black powdery substance formed by burning coal, etc.; *v.t.* to cover with soot. **-y** *a.*

sooth *n. (Arch.)* truth; reality. **-sayer** *n.* one who claims to be able to foretell future. **-saying** *n.*

soothe *v.t.* to please with soft words or kind actions; to calm; to allay, as pain. **soothing** *a.* **soothingly** *adv.*

sop *n.* piece of bread, etc., dipped in a liquid; *v.t.* to steep in liquid. *pr.p.* **-ping.** *pa.p.* and *pa.t.* **-ped. -ping** *a.* **-py** *a.* soaked; rainy.

soph•ism *n.* specious argument; clever but fallacious reasoning. **sophist** *n.* **sophistry** *n.* **sophistic, sophistical** *a.* **sophistically**

adv. **sophisticate** *v.t.* to deceive by using sophisms; to make artificial; to make wise in the ways of the world. **sophisticated** *a.* **sophistication** *n.*

soph•o•more *n.* second year student.

so•por *n.* unnaturally deep sleep. **-ific** *a.* causing or inducing sleep; *n.* drug, which induces deep sleep. **-iferous, soporose** *a.*

so•pran•o *n.* highest type of female or boy's voice; soprano singer; *pl.* **-s, soprani.**

sor•cer•y *n.* witchcraft; magic; enchantment. **sorcerer** *n.; fem.* **sorceress.**

sor•did *a.* filthy; squalid; meanly avaricious. **-ly** *adv.* **-ness** *n.*

sore *a.* painful when touched; distressed; grieved; *n.* diseased, injured, or bruised spot on body. **-ly** *adv.* **-ness** *n.*

sor•ghum *n.* cereal grasses of several varieties.

so•ror•i•ty *n.* a girls' or women's society.

so•ro•sis *n.* compound fleshy fruit; women's club.

sor•rel *n.* meadow plant.

sor•rel *a.* reddish-brown; *n.* (horse of) reddish-brown color.

sor•row *n.* grief; sadness; distress; cause of grief, etc.; *v.i.* to feel pain of mind; to grieve. **-er** *n.* **-ful** *a.* **-fully** *adv.* **-fulness** *n.*

sor•ry *a.* feeling regret; mean; shabby; wretched; worthless. **sorriness** *n.*

sort *n.* kind or class; quality; character; order or rank; *v.t.* to classify; to put in order. **-er** *n.*

sor•tie *n.* sally by besieged forces to attack besiegers.

sot *n.* confirmed drunkard. **-tish** *a.*

sou *n.* former French coin.

soubriquet See **sobriquet.**

souf•flé *n.* a delicate dish made of eggs.

sough *n.* low murmuring, sighing sound; *v.i.*

sought *pa.p.* and *pa.t.* of **seek.**

soul *n.* spiritual and immortal part of human being; seat of emotion, sentiment, and aspiration; spirit. **-ful** *a.* **-fully** *adv.* **-less** *a.* without a soul; not inspired; prosaic.

sound *a.* healthy; in good condition; profound; free from error; reliable; *adv.* soundly; completely. **-ly** *adv.* **-ness** *n.*

sound *n.* long, narrow stretch of water.

sound *v.t.* to find depth of water, by means of line and lead; *(Fig.)* to try to discover the opinions of; *v.i.* to find depth of water; of a whale, to dive suddenly. **-ing** *n.*

sound *n.* that which is heard; noise; *v.t.* to cause to make a sound; to utter; to play on; *v.i.* to make a noise; to be conveyed by sound; to seem. **-ing** *a.*

soup *n.* liquid food made by boiling meat, vegetables, etc.

sour *a.* acid; having a sharp taste; pungent; rancid; cross; *v.t.* and *v.i.* to make or become sour. **-ed** *a.* **-ly** *adv.* **-ness** *n.*

source *n.* spring; origin (of stream, information, etc.).

sour•dough *n.* fermented batter of flour and water used to leaven fresh dough.

souse *v.t.* to steep in brine; to pickle; to soak; *n.* a pickle made with salt; brine; a drenching.

sou•tane *n.* gown worn by R.C. priests.

south *n.* cardinal point of compass opposite north; region lying to that side; *a.; adv.* toward or in the south; *v.i.* to move towards the south. **southerly** *a.* **-ern** *a.* **-erner** *n.* **-ernly** *adv.* towards the south. **-ernmost** (also **-ermost, —most**) *a.* lying farthest towards the south. **—ward** *a.* and *adv.*

sou•ve•nir *n.* a keepsake.

sov•er•eign *n.* ruler; British gold coin; *a.* supreme in power. **-ty** *n.* supreme power.

so•vi•et *n.* council. **Soviet** *n.* political body elected to local municipalities, regional councils, etc. and sending delegates to higher congresses. *a.* **Soviet Union**, short for the Union of Soviet Socialist Republics,' i.e. Russia; *abbrev.* **U.S.S.R.**

sow *n.* female pig.

sow *v.t.* to scatter or deposit (seed); to spread abroad; *v.i.* to scatter seed. *pa.p.* **sown** or **sowed** *pa.t.* **-ed. -er** *n.*

soy *n.* sauce made from soybean **-bean** *n.* seed of leguminous plant of Far East.

Spa *n.* inland watering place in Belgium. **spa** *n.* any place with mineral spring.

space *n.* expanse of universe; area; extent; empty place; *v.t.* to place at intervals. **spacious** *a.* roomy; capacious; extensive. **spaciously** *adv.*

spade *n.* digging tool; *v.t.* to dig with spade.

spade *n.* *(Cards)* one of two black suits, marked by figure like a pointed spade.

spa•ghet•ti *n.* foodstuff resembling macaroni.

spake *pa.t. (Arch.)* of **speak.**

span *pa.t. (Arch.)* of **spin.**

span *n.* distance between thumb and little finger, when fingers are fully extended; this distance as measure = 9 in; short distance or period of time; *v.t.* to reach from one side of to the other; to extend across. *pr.p.* **-ning** *pa.p.* and *pa.t.* **-ned. -ner** *n.*

span•drel *n. (Archit.)* the space between outer curves of arch and square head over it; ornamental design in corner of postage stamp.

span•gle *n.* a small piece of glittering metal, used to ornament dresses; *v.t.* to adorn with spangles; *v.i.* to glitter.

Span•iard *n.* native of Spain. **Spanish** *a.; n.* language of Spain.

span•iel *n.* breed of dogs, with long, drooping ears; fawning person.

spaniel

spank *v.i.* to move with vigor or spirit. **-ing** *a.* **-er** *n.*

spank *v.t.* to strike with flat of hand, esp. on buttocks as punishment; *n.* slap.

spar *v.i.* to fight with the fists; to fight with spurs, as in cock fighting; to dispute, bandy words. *pr.p.* **-ring.** *pa.p.* and *pa.t.* **-red.**

S

spar *n.* pole or beam, esp. as part of ship's rigging.

spar *n.* crystalling mineral.

spare *v.t.* and *v.i.* to use frugally; to do without; to save; to leave unhurt; *a.* frugal; scanty; parsimonious; lean; in reserve; *n.* that which is held in reserve; a duplicate part. **-ly** *adv.* **-ness** *n.* thinness; leanness. **sparing** *a.* **sparingly** *adv.*

spark *n.* small glowing or burning particle; flash of light; *v.i.* to send out sparks.

spar·kle *n.* small spark; a glitter; vivacity; *v.i.* to emit small flashes of light. **-r** *n.* **sparkling** *a.*

spar·row *n.* small brown bird of finch family.

sparse *a.* thinly scattered; scanty; rare. **-ly** *adv.* **-ness** *n.* scantiness.

Spar·ta *n.* ancient Greek city-state. **Spartan** *n.* citizen of this town; one who is frugal and faces danger, etc. without flinching; *a.*

spasm *n.* sudden, involuntary contraction of muscle(s); fitful effort. **spasmodic(al)** *a.* **spasmodically** *adv.* by fits and starts. **spastic** *a.*

spat *pa.t.* of **spit.**

spat *n.* kind of cloth gaiter. Usually in *pl.* **spats.**

spat *n.* spawn of shellfish or oyster; *v.i.* to spawn, of oysters.

spate *n.* flood in a river, exp. after heavy rain.

spathe *n.* leaflike sheath enveloping flower cluster. **spathed, spathose** *a.*

spa·tial *a.* pert. to space. **-ly** *adv.*

spat·ter *v.t.* to cast drops of water, mud, etc. over; to splash; *v.i.* to fall in drops; *n.* the act of spattering.

spat·u·la *n.* broad-bladed implement. **spatular, spatulate** *a.*

spav·in *n.* swelling on horse's leg, causing lameness. **-ed** *a.*

spawn *n.* eggs of fish, frogs; offspring; *v.t.* and *v.i.* of fish, frogs, to cast eggs; to produce offspring.

speak *v.i.* to utter words; to deliver a discourse; *v.t.* to utter; to express in words; to express silently or by signs; *pr.p.* **-ing.** *pa.p.* **spoken.** *pa.t.* **spoke. -r** *n.* **-ing** *n.* having power to utter words.

spear *n.* long, pointed weapon, used in fighting, hunting, etc.; lance; pike; *v.t.* to pierce or kell with spear.

spe·cial *a.* pert. to a species or sort; beyond the usual; distinct; intimate. **-ly** *adv.* **-ize** *v.t.* and *v.i.* **-ization** *n.* **-ist** *n.* one trained and skilled in a special branch. **-istic** *a.* **-ty** *n.* a special characteristic of a person or thing; a special product; that in which a person is highly skilled.

spe·cie *n.* coined money.

spe·cies *n.* kind; sort; subdivision of a more general class or genus.

spe·cif·ic *a.* pert. to, or characteristic of, a species; peculiar to; well defined; *n.* a specific statement, etc. **-ally** *adv.*

spec·i·fi·ca·tion *n.* act of specifying. **specify** *v.t.* to state definitely; to give details of; to indicate precisely. **specifiable** *a.*

spec·i·men *n.* part of anything, or one of a number of things, used to show nature and quality of the whole.

spe·cious *a.* having a fair appearance; apparently acceptable, esp. at first sight. **-ly** *adv.* **-ness speciosity** *n.*

speck *n.* small spot; very small thing; *v.t.* to mark with specks. **-le** *n.* a small speck or spot; *v.t.* **speckled** *a.* **-less** *a.*

spec·ta·cle *n.* sight; thing exhibited. **spectacles** *n.pl.* eyeglasses. **-ed** *a.* wearing spectacles. **spectacular** *a.* showy; making great display. **spectacularly** *adv.*

spec·ta·tor *n.* an onlooker; specter is ghost or apparition not spectator ghost; apparition. **spectral** *a.* **spectrally** *adv.*

spectrum *n.* the colored band into which a ray of light can be separated; *pl.* **spectra.**

spec·tro- *prefix* an image, used in many derivatives.

spec·u·late *v.i.* to make theories of; guesses; to meditate; to engage in risky commercial transactions. **speculation** *n.* **speculative** *a.* **speculatively** *adv.* **speculator** *n.* **speculatory** *a.*

spec·u·lum *n.* mirror. *pl.* **specula.**

sped *pa.p.* and *pa.t.* of **speed.**

speech *n.* power of speaking; what is spoken; faculty of expressing thoughts in words; language; formal address. **-less** *a.* without power of speech. **-lessly** *adv.* **-lessness** *n.*

speed *n.* swiftness of motion; velocity; *v.t.* to cause to move faster; to aid; to bid farewell to; *v.i.* to move quickly *pa.p.* and *pa.t.* **sped. -y** *a.* **-ily** *adv.* **-ometer** *n.* instrument indicating speed.

speedometer

spell *n.* word or words supposed to have magical power; fascination. **-bind** *v.t.* to hold as if by spell; to enchant; to fascinate. *pa.p., pa.t.* **-bound** *a.*

spell *n.* a brief period of time.

spell *v.t.* to read letter by letter; to mean; *v.i.* to form words with proper letters. *pa.p.* and *pa.t.* **-ed** or **spelt.**

spe·lun·ker one who explores caves.

spend *v.t.* and *v.i.* to pay out; to disburse; to pass, as time; to employ; to waste; to exhaust. *pa.p., pa.t.,* **spent** *a.* exhausted; worn out; of a fish, having deposited spawn. **-er** *n.*

sperm *n.* fertilizing fluid of male animals; the male cell. **— whale** *n.* cachalot, large

sperm whale

whale, valuable for its oil and for spermaceti. **spermaceti** *n.* waxlike substance obtained from head of sperm whale. **-atic** *a.*

sperm•a•to- *prefix* seed. **spermatoid** *a.* resembling sperm. **spermatozoon** *n.* male generative cell, found in semen. *pl.* **-zoa, -zoal, -zoan** *a.*

spew, spue *v.t.* and *v.i.* to eject from the stomach; to vomit.

sphere *n.* round, solid body, ball; globe; celestial body; range of knowledge, influence, etc.; *v.t.* to put in a sphere; to encircle. **spheral** *a.* **spheric** *a.* pert. to heavenly bodies. **spherical** *a.* **spherically** *adv.* **sphericity** *n.* **spheroid** *n.* body almost, but not quite, spherical, e.g. orange, earth, etc. **spheroidal** *a.* Also **spheroidic. spherule** *n.* a small sphere. **spherular, spherulate** *a.*

sphinc•ter *n.* (*Anat.*) circular muscle which contracts or expands orifice of an organ.

sphinx *n.* (*Myth.*) fabulous monster, with winged body of lion and head of woman, which proposed riddles.

sphinx

sphyg•mus *n.* (*Med.*) pulse. **sphygmic** *a.*

spice *n.* aromatic substance, used for seasoning; (*Fig.*) anything that adds flavor, zest, etc. *v.t.* to season with spice. **spicery** *n.* **spicy** *a.* **spicily** *adv.*

spi•der *n.* small eight-legged insect-like animal; an evil person. *a.* like a spider.

spied *pa.p.* and *pa.t.* of spy.

spig•ot *n.* peg for stopping hole in cask; a faucet.

spike *n.* sharp-pointed piece of metal or wood; (*Bot.*) flower cluster growing from central stem; *v.t.* **spiky** *a.*

spill *v.t.* to cause to flow out; to shed (blood); to throw off, as from horse, etc.; to upset; *v.i.* to flow over; to be shed; *pa.p.* and *pa.t.* **-ed** or **spilt. -er** *n.*

spill *n.* thin strip of wood or twist of paper, for lighting a fire, pipe, etc.

spin *v.t.* to twist into threads; to cause to revolve rapidly; to draw out tediously, as a story; to prolong; *n.* rapid whirling motion; short, quick run or drive. *pr.p.* **-ning** *pa.p.* and *pa.t.* **spun** or (*Arch.*) **span. -ner** *n.* **-ning jenny** *n.* machine for spinning several threads simultaneously.

spin•ach *n.* leafy vegetable. **spinaceous** *a.*

spin•dle *n.* long, slender rod, used in spinning; measure of yarn, thread, or silk; shaft; axis; *v.i.* to grow long and slender. **spindly** *a.* **spindling** *a.*

spine *n.* thorne; quill; backbone; back of book. **spinal** *a.* **-less** *a.* having no spine; weak of character. **spiny** *a.* **spinule** *n.* small spine.

spin•it *n.* musical instrument.

spin•na•ker *n.* a large triangular sail.

spin•ster *n.* unmarried woman. **-hood** *n.* **spinstress** *n.* woman who spins.

spi•ra•cle *n.* breathing-hole; blowhole of whale. **spiracular, spiraculate** *a.*

Spi•rae•a *n.* a genus of herbaceous plants.

spi•rant *n.* consonant pronounced with perceptible emission of breath.

spire *n.* winding line like threads of screw; burl; coil. **spiral** *a.* winding; coiled; *n.* spiral curve; *v.i.* to follow spiral line.

spire *n.* blade of grass; anything tall and tapering to point; steeple; *v.i.* to rise high, like spire. **spiral** *a.* **spiry** *a.*

spir•it *n.* vital force; immortal part of man; ghost; frame of mind; disposition; eager desire; courage; essential character; (*Cap.*) Holy Spirit; liquid got by distillation, esp. alcoholic; *v.t.* to carry away mysteriously; to put energy into. **spirits** *n.pl.* a state of mind; mood; distilled alcoholic liquor. **-ed** *a.* **-edly** *adv.* **-edness** *n.* **-ism** *n.* See **spiritualism.** **-less** *a.* without spirit or life; lacking energy; listless. **-essly** *adv.* **-uous** *a.* containing alcohol.

spir•it•u•al *a.* pert. to spirit or soul; not material; holy; *n.* Negro sacred song or hymn. **-ly** *adv.* **-ize** *v.t.* **-ism, spiritism** *n.* belief that spirits of dead can communicate with living people. **-ist** *n.*

spit *n.* pointed rod put through meat for roasting; narrow point of land projecting into sea; *pr.p.* **-ting.** *pa.p.* and *pa.t.* **-ted.**

spit *v.t.* to eject from mouth; *v.i.* to eject saliva from mouth; to expectorate; *pr.p.* **-ting.** *pa.p. pa.t.* **spat** *n.* **-ter** *n.* **-tle** *n.* saliva ejected from mouth; **-toon** *n.* a vessel for spittle.

spite *n.* malice; ill will; *v.t.* to treat maliciously; to annoy. **-ful** *a.* **-fully** *adv.* **-fulness** *n.*

spit•fire *n.* hot tempered person.

spitz *n.* kind of Pomeranian dog.

splash *v.t.* to spatter water, mud, etc. over; to soil thus; *v.i.* to dash or scatter, of liquids; to fall in drops; *n.* sound of object falling into liquid.

splat•ter *v.t.* and *v.i.* to splash; to spatter.

splay *v.t.* to slope; to slant; to spread outwards; *a.* turned outwards.

spleen *n.* organ lying to left of stomach; ill humor.

splen•did *a.* magnificent; gorgeous; (*Colloq.*) excellent. **-ly** *adv.* **splendor** *n.* **splendorous** *a.*

sple•net•ic *a.* pert. to spleen; morose; irritable.

splice *v.t.* to join together; to join, as wood, etc. by overlapping and binding.

splint *n.* rigid piece of material for holding broken limb in position; *v.t.* to bind with splints. **-er** *n.* thin piece of wood, metal, etc. split off; *v.t.* and *v.i.* to make or break into thin pieces. **-ery** *a.*

split *v.t.* to cut lengthwise; to cleave; to separate; *v.i.* to break asunder; to dash to pieces; to spearate; *n.* crack; fissure; a breach; a share. *pr.p.* **-ting.** *pa.p.* and *pa.t.* **split. -ing** *n.* cleaving or rending; *a.* severe; distressing.

splut•ter *v.t.* to utter incoherently with spitting sounds; *v.t.* to emit such sounds; *n.* such sounds or speech. **-er** *n.*

Spode *n.* highly decorated porcelain.

spoil *v.t.* to damage; to cause to decay; *v.i.* to decay; *n.* booty; prey; plunder. *pa.p.* and *pa.t.* **-ed** or **-spoilt.**

S

spoke *pa.t.* of the verb **speak**. *pa.p.* **spoken**. **-s-man** *n.* one deputed to speak for others.

spoke *n.* one of small bars connecting hub of wheel with rim.

spo•li•ate *v.t.* to rob; to plunder; *v.i.* to practice plundering. **spoliative** *a.* **spoliation** *n.* **spoliator** *n.*

spon•dee *n.* in poetry a foot of two long syllables. **spondaic** *a.*

sponge *n.* marine animal of cellular structure, outer coating of whose body is perforated to allow entrance of water; skeleton of this animal; *v.t.* to wipe, cleanse, with sponge; *v.i.* to live at expense of others. **-r** *n.* **spongy** *a.* **sponginess** *n.* **-cake** *n.* light, sweet cake.

spon•sor *n.* one who is responsible for another; surety; a patron; *v.t.* to support; to act as guarantor or patron of; **-ial** *a.* **-ship** *n.*

spon•ta•ne•ous *a.* of one's own free will; natural; produced by some internal cause. **-ly** *adv.* **-ness**, **spontaneity** *n.*

spook *n.* (*Colloq.*) ghost; apparition. **-ish**, **-y** *a.*

spool *n.* small cylinder for winding thread, wire, etc.; *v.t.* to wind on spool.

spoon *n.* implement with bowl at end of handle; *v.t.* and *v.i.* to use a spoon. **-bill** *n.* long-legged wading bird.

spoon•er•ism *n.* transposition of letters of spoken words, causing a humorous effect.

spoor *n.* track or trail of wild animal.

spo•rad•ic *a.* occurring singly here and there; occasional. Also **-al**. **-ally** *adv.*

spore *n.* in flowerless plants, minute cell with reproductive powers; germ; seed. **sporangium** *n.* spore case. *pl.* **sporangia**. **sporangial** *a.* **sporoid** *a.*

spor•ran *n.* large pouch worn in front of the kilt.

sport *n.* that which amuses; pastime; object of jest; outdoor game or recreation esp. of athletic nature; *v.i.* to play; to take part in outdoor recreation. **-s** *n.pl.* games; athletic meetings. **-ing** *a.* **-ive** *a.* pert. to sport; playful.

spot *n.* speck; blemish, esp. on reputation; place; *v.t.* to cover with spots; (*Colloq.*) to detect; to recognize; *v.i.* to become marked. *pr.p.* **-ting** *pa.p.* and *pa.t.* **-ted**. **-less** *a.* **-lessly** *adv.* **-lessness** *n.* **-ted**, **-ty** *a.* marked with spots or stains; irregular. **-tedness**, **tiness** *n.* **-ter** *n.*

spouse *n.* married person, husband or wife. **spousal** *a.*

spout *v.t.* to shoot out, as liquid through a pipe; *v.i.* to gush out in jet; *n.* projecting tube, pipe, etc., for pouring liquid.

sprag *n.* piece of wood or metal used to lock wheel of vehicle.

sprain *v.t.* to wrench or twist muscles *n.* such an injury.

sprang *pa.t.* of the verb **spring**.

sprat *n.* small sea fish.

sprawl *v.i.* to sit or lie with legs out-stretched or in ungainly position; to move about awkwardly; to write carelessly and irregularly; *n.*

spray *n.* twigs; small, graceful branch with leaves and blossoms; sprig.

spray *n.* fine droplets of water; atomizer; *v.t.* to sprinkle. **-er** *n.*

spread *v.t.* to stretch out; to extend; to cover surface with; to circulate, as news, etc.; *v.i.* to extend in all directions; *n.* extension; expanse; covering for bed, etc. *pa.p.* and *pa.t.* **spread**. **-ing** *n.*; *v.t.* to lie with outstretched limbs.

spree *n.* lively frolic; drinking bout.

sprig *n.* small shoot or twig; ornament in form of spray; scion; youth; small, headless nail. *pr.p.* **-ging**. *pa.p.*, *pa.t.* **-ged**.

spright•ly *a.* lively; airy; vivacious. **sprightliness** *n.*

spring *v.i.* to leap; to shoot up, out, or forth; to appear; to recoil; to result, as from a cause; *v.t.* to cause to spring up; to bend so as to weaken; to release, as catch of trap; *n.* a leap; recoil; a contrivance of coiled or bent metal with much resilience; resilience; flow of water from earth; fountain; season of year; upward curve of arch. *pa.p.* **sprung**. *pa.t.* **sprang** or **sprung**. **-er** *n.* **-y** *a.* elastic; light in tread or gait. **-iness** *n.* **-board** *n.* springy board used in jumping and diving.

springe *n.* snare with a spring noose; *v.t.* to catch in a springe.

sprin•kle *v.t.* to scatter small drops of water, sand, etc.; *v.i.* to scatter (a liquid or any fine substance); *n.* small quantity scattered; occasional drops of rain. **-d** *a.* **-r** *n.* **sprinkling** *n.*

sprint *v.i./n.* short run at full speed. **-er** *n.*

sprit *n.* (*Naut.*) small spar set diagonally across fore-and-aft sail to extend it.

sprite *n.* elf; a fairy; a goblin.

sprock•et *n.* toothlike projection on outer rim of wheel.

sprout *v.i.* to begin to grow; to put forth shoots; *n.* shoot; bud.

spruce *a.* neat in dress; *v.t.* and *v.i.* to dress smartly. **-ly** *adv.* **-ness** *n.*

spruce *n.* common name of some coniferous trees.

sprung *pa.p.* and *pa.t.* of **spring**.

spry *a.* nimble; agile.

spud *n.* small spadelike implement.

spue. See **spew**.

spume *n./v.i.* froth; foam; scum. **spumous** *a.* **spumy** *a.*

spun *pa.p.* and *pa.t.* of verb **spin**.

spunk *n.* wood that readily takes fire; (*Colloq.*) spirit **-y** *a.* (*Colloq.*) plucky.

spur *n.* pricking instrument worn on horseman's heels, used as goad; anything that incites to action; mountain projecting from range; projection; *v.t.* to apply spurs to; to urge to action; *pr.p.* **-ring** *pa.p.* and *pa.t.* also *a.* **-red**.

spurge *n.* plant of several species, having milky juice.

spu•ri•ous *a.* not genuine or authentic; false. **-ly** *adv.*

spurn *v.t.* to reject with disdain; to scorn; *n.* disdainful rejection.

spurt *v.t.* to force out suddenly in a stream; *v.i.* to gush out with force; *n.* a sudden, strong flow or effort. Also **spirt**.

sput•ter *v.t.* to throw out in small particles

with haste and noise; *v.i.* to scatter drops of saliva, as in excited speech; to fly off with crackling noise; *n.* act of sputtering; sound made. -er *n.*

spu•tum *n.* spittle; saliva. *pl.* sputa.

spy *n.* one who enters enemy territory secretly, to gain information; one who keeps watch on others. *v.t.* to catch sight of; *v.i.* to act as a spy. -glass *n.* small telescope.

squab *a.* fat and short; *n.* nestling pigeon used for food.

squab•ble *v.i.* to wrangle; to dispute noisily; *n.* petty, noisy quarrel.

squad *n.* (*Mil.*) smallest unit of soldiers, etc.

squad•ron *n.* a military tactical unit; an athletic team.

squal•id *a.* mean and dirty, esp. through neglect; filthy; foul. *adv.* -ity, -ness, squalor *n.* filth; foulness.

squall *v.t.* and *v.i.* to scream or cry out violently; *n.* loud scream; sudden gust of wind. -y *a.*

squa•ma *n.* scale; scalelike part *pl.* squamae.

squan•der *v.t.* to waste; to dissipate. -er *n.* spendthrift.

square *n.* plane figure with four equal sides and four right angles; in town, open space of this shape; (*Math.*) product of a number or quantity multiplied by itself; *a.* square shaped; at right angles; giving equal justice; balanced or settled, as account or bill; *adv.* squarely; directly; *v.t.* to make like a square; to place at right angles; (*Math.*) to multiply by itself; to balance; to settle; *v.i.* to agree exactly; -ly *adv.* -ness *n.* squarish *a.*

squash *v.t.* to beat or crush flat; to suppress; *v.i.* to fall into a soft, flat mass; *n.* anything soft and easily crushed; packed crowd; game played with rackets. -iness *n.* -y *a.*

squash *n.* gourdlike fruit.

squat *v.i.* to sit on heels; to settle on land without having title to it, or in order to acquire title; *a.* short and thick *pr.p.* -ting. *pa.p.* and *pa.t.* -ted. -ter *n.*

squaw *n.* N. American Indian woman.

squeak *n.* short, sharp, shrill sound; sharp, unpleasant, grating sound; *v.i.* to utter, or make, such sound. -y *a.*

squeal *n.* long, shrill cry; *v.i.* to utter long, shrill cry. -er *n.*

squeam•ish *a.* easily made sick; easily shocked. -ly *adv.* -ness *n.*

squee•gee *n.* implement with rubber edge for clearing water from deck of ship, etc. Also squilgee.

squeeze *v.t.* to press or crush; to extract by pressure; to force into; *v.i.* to force one's way; to press; *n.* pressure; close hug or embrace. squeezable *a.*

squelch *n.* crushing blow; suppression; sound made when withdrawing feet from sodden ground; *v.t.* to crush down; *v.i.* to make sound of a squelch.

squid *n.* kind of sea mollusc.

squil•gee *n.* Same as squeegee.

squill *n.* plant of lily family. -s *n.pl.* drug from bulb of squill.

squint *a.* looking obliquely; having eyes turned in; *v.i.* to look with eyes partly closed; *n.* act, habit of squinting.

squire *n.* (*Brit.*) rural landowner; lady's escort; *v.t.* to escort.

squirm *v.i.* to move like a snake, eel, worm, etc.; to wriggle. -iness *n.* -y *a.*

squir•rel *n.* small graceful animal with bushy tail.

squirt *v.t.* and *v.i.* to eject, or be ejected, in a jet; *n.* instrument for squirting; thin jet of liquid. -er *n.*

stab *v.t.* to pierce or wound with pointed instrument; to hurt feelings of; *v.i.* to strike with pointed weapon; *n.* blow or wound so inflicted; sudden pain. *pr.p.* -bing. *pa.p.* and *pa.t.* -bed. -ber *n.*

sta•bi•lize *v.t.* to make stable, fixed, etc. stabilization *n.* stabilizer *n.* stability *n.*

sta•ble *a.* firmly fixed, established; steady; resolute. stably *adv.* Also stabile.

sta•ble *n.* building for horses; *v.t.* and *v.i.*

stac•ca•to *a.* and *adv.* (*Mus.*) short, sharp, and distinct.

stack *n.* large heap or pile; a chimney; (*Colloq.*) a great number; *pl.* book shelves; *v.t.* to heap or pile up; to arrange cards for cheating.

sta•di•um *n.* arena for sports events, entertainments, etc.

staff *n.pl.* -s or staves: pole or stick used in walking, climbing, etc. or for support or defense; flagpole; body of persons working in office, school, etc., *v.t.* to provide with staff.

stag *n.* male of red or other large deer; man who attends party without a woman.

stage *n.* raised floor or platform esp. of theater, etc.; dramatic art of literature; scene of action; degree of progress; *v.t.* to put (a play) on stage. staging *n.* scaffolding.

stag•ger *v.i.* to walk or stand unsteadily; to hesitate; *v.t.* to cause to reel; to shock; to distribute in overlapping periods; to arrange in zigzag fashion; *n.* -ing *a.* amazing.

stag•nate *v.i.* to be motionless; to be dull. stagnant *a.* of water, not flowing; hence, foul; impure. stagnantly *adv.* stagnation *n.*

staid *a.* of sober and quiet character. -ly *adv.* -ness *n.*

stain *v.t.* and *v.i.* to discolor; to spot; to dye; to mark with guilt; *n.* discoloration; dye; taint of guilt; disgrace. -less *a.* not liable to stain or rust, esp. of a kind of steel.

stair *n.* steps one above the other for connecting different levels. -s *n.pl.* flight of steps. -case *n.* flight of steps with railings, etc. Also -way.

stair case

stake *n.* sharpened stick or post; post to which one condemned to be burned, was tied; interest in result of enterprise; *pl.* money in contention; *v.t.* to mark out with stakes.

sta·lac·tite *n.* deposit of carbonate of lime, hanging like icicle from roof of cave. **stalactic, stalactitic** *a.* **stalactical** *a.*

sta·lag·mite *n.* deposit of carbonate of lime from floor of cave. **stalagmitic(al).**

stale *a.* not fresh; tasteless; musty; trite; common; *v.i.* to lose freshness. **-ly** *adv.* **-ness** *n.*

stale *v.i.* of horses, to make water.

stale·mate *n.* (*Chess*) position, resulting in drawn game; standstill.

stalk *n.* stem of plant, leaf, etc.

stalk *v.i.*, *v.t.* to steal up to game cautiously; to walk in stiff and stately manner; *n.* act of stealing up to game; stiff and stately gait. **-er** *n.*

stall *n.* compartment for animal in stable; erection for display and sale of goods; *v.t.* and *v.i.* to place or keep in stall; to come to a standstill; of engine or automobile, to stop running unintentionally.

stal·lion *n.* an uncastrated male horse kept for breeding.

stal·wart *a.* sturdy; brave; steadfast; *n.* strong, muscular person; staunch supporter. **-ly** *adv.*

sta·men *n.* (*Bot.*) male organ of flowering plant, pollen-bearing part. **staminal** *a.*

stam·i·na *n.* power of endurance.

stam·mer *v.i.* to speak with repetition of syllables or hesitatingly; to stutter; *n.* halting enunciation; stutter. **-er** *n.* **-ing** *n.*

stamp *v.i.* to put down a foot with force; *v.t.* to set down (a foot) heavily or with force; to make an official mark on; to affix postage stamp; to brand; *n.* act of stamping; instrument for making imprinted mark; mark imprinted; piece of gummed paper printed with device. **-er** *n.*

stam·pede *n.* sudden, frightened rush, esp. of herd of cattle, crowd, etc.; *v.t.* to put into a state of panic; *v.i.* to take part in a stampede.

stance *n.* position of feet in certain games.

stanch *v.t.* to stop or check flow (of blood). *a.* firm; loyal; trustworthy. **-ly** *adv.* **-ness** *n.* Also **staunch.**

stan·chion *n.* upright support; iron bar, used as prop.

stand *v.i.* to remain at rest in upright position; to become or remain stationary; to endure; to adhere to principles; to have a position, order, or rank; to place oneself; to persist; to be of certain height; *v.t.* to endure; to sustain; to withstand; to set. *pa.p.* and *pa.t.* **stood.** *n.* place where one stands; structure for spectators; piece of furniture on which things may be placed; stall for display of goods; position on some question. **-by** *n.* something in reserve. **-point** *n.* a point of view.

stand·ard *n.* weight, measure, model, quality, etc. to which others must conform; criterion; pole with a flag; royal banner; *a.* serving as established rule, model, etc.; standing upright. **-ize** *v.t.* **-ization** *n.*

stand·ing *a.* established by law, custom, etc.; settled; permanent; not flowing; erect; *n.* duration; existence; reputation.

stank *pa.t.* of the verb **stink.**

stan·za *n.* group of lines or verses of poetry having definite pattern. **stanzaic** *a.*

sta·ple *n.* chief product of a country or district; unmanufactured material; *a.* established in commerce; principal; chief; *v.t.* of textiles, to grade according to length and quality of fiber. **-r** *n.*

sta·ple *n.* U-shaped piece of metal with pointed ends; piece of wire to hold sheets of paper together. **-r** *n.* mechanical device for fastening papers together.

star *n.* shining celestial body, seen as twinkling point of light; five or six-pointed figure asterisk; *v.t.* to set or adorn with stars; *v.i.* to shine, as star. *pr.p.* **-ring.** *pa.p.*, *pa.t.* **-red.** **-let** *n.* small star; **-lit** *a.* **-red** *a.* **-ry** *a.* **-riness** *n.* **-fish** *n.* marine animal shaped like a star.

starfish

star·board *n.* and *a.* right-hand side of a ship, looking forward; *v.t.* to put (the helm) to starboard.

starch *n.* substance forming main food element in bread, potatoes, etc. and used, mixed with water, for stiffening linen, etc.; formality; primness; *v.t.* to stiffen with starch. **-y** *a.* **-ily** *adv.* **-iness** *n.*

stare *v.i.* to look fixedly; to gaze; *v.t.* to abash by staring at; *n.* fixed, steady look. **-r** *n.* **staring** *n. a.*

stark *a.* stiff; desolate; naked; downright; *adv.* completely. **-ly** *adv.*

star·ling *n.* bird, bluish-black and speckled.

start *v.i.* to make sudden movement; to spring; to begin, esp. journey; *v.t.* to cause to move suddenly; to begin; to loosen; *n.* sudden involuntary movement, spring or leap; act of setting out. **-er** *n.*

star·tle *v.t.* to cause to start; to give a fright to; *v.i.* to move abruptly, esp. from fright, apprehension, etc. **startling** *a.* **startlingly** *adv.*

starve *v.i.* to suffer from hunger; to be short of something necessary; *v.t.* to cause to suffer or die from lack of food, etc. **starvation** *n.*

state *n.* condition of person or thing; formal dignity; politically organized community; *a.* pert. to state; governmental; ceremonial; *v.t.* to express in words; to specify. **-d** *a.* fixed; regular; settled. **-ly** *a.* dignified; imposing; majestic. **-liness** *n.* **-ment** *n.*

stat·ic *a.* pert. to bodies at rest, or in equilibrium; motionless; *n.* *(Radio)* crackling noises during reception. **-al** *a.*

sta·tion *n.* place where thing or person stands; situation; rank; regular stopping place for trains, etc.; local or district office for police force, fire-brigade, etc.; *v.t.* to put in a position; to appoint to place of duty. **-ary** *a.* not moving; fixed.

sta·tion·er *n.* one who deals in writing materials. **-ery** *n.*

sta·tis·tics *n.pl.* numerical data collected systematically. **statistic(al)** *a.* **statistically** *adv.* **statistician** *n.*

stat·ue *n.* image carved out of solid substance or cast in metal. **statuary** *n.* collection of statues. **statuesque** *a.* **statuette** *n.*

stat·ure *n.* the height of a person or animal.

sta·tus *n.* position; rank.

stat·ute *n.* law passed by legislature. **statutory** *a.*

staunch. See **stanch.**

stave *n.* one of curved strips of wood forming cask; rung of ladder; staff; *v.t.* to fit with staves; to ward off; to deter. *pa.p.* and *pa.t.* **-d** or **stove.**

staves *n.pl.* See **staff** and **stave.**

stay *v.t.* to restrain; to check; to support; to last; *v.i.* to remain; to dwell.

stead *n.* place which another had; use; service; frame of bed.

stead·fast *a.* firmly fixed; steady; constant. **-ly** *adv.* **-ness** *n.*

stead·y *a.* firm; uniform; temperate; reliable; *v.t.* to make steady; to support; *v.i.* to become steady. **steadily** *adv.* **steadiness** *n.*

steak *n.* slice of meat, esp. beef.

steal *v.t.* to take by theft; to win gradually by skill, affection, etc.; *v.i.* to move silently, or secretly. *pa.p.* **stolen.** *pa.t.* **stole. stealth** *n.* secret means used to accomplish anything. **stealthy** *a.* **stealthiness** *n.*

steam *n.* vapor rising from boiling water; any exhalation of heated bodies; *a.* worked by steam; *v.t.* to apply steam; to; *v.i.* to give off steam; to move under power of steam. **-y** *a.* **-iness** *n.* **-er** *n.* steamship; vessel for cooking or washing by steam; something operated by steam. **-roller** *n.* heavy roller, driven by steam.

ste·a·rin *n.* hard, waxy solid used in manufacture of candles. Also **stearine.** **stearic** *a.*

steed *n.* horse.

steel *n.* hard and malleable metal; tool or weapon of steel; *a.* made of steel; inflexible; unfeeling; *v.t.* to harden; to make obdurate. **-y** *a.* **-iness** *n.*

steel·yard *n.* balance with unequal arms and movable weight.

steelyard

steep *a.* having abrupt or decided slope; *n.* steep place; precipice. **-ly** *adv.* **-en** *v.t.* and *v.i.* to make, or become, steep.

steep *v.t.* to soak in a liquid; to saturate; *n.* act or process of steeping.

stee·ple *n.* a church tower with a spire. **-chase** *n.* a cross-country horse race.

steer *n.* a young male ox.

steer *v.t.* to guide or direct the course of (a ship, car, etc.) by means of a rudder, wheel, etc. **-age** *n.* the part of a ship allotted to passengers paying the lowest fare. **-er, -sman** *n.*

stel·lar *a.* pert. to, or like, stars. **stellate, stellated** *a.* arranged in the form of a star; star-shaped; radiating. **stelliform** *a.* **stellular** *a.*

stem *n.* the principal stalk of a tree or plant; any slender shaft resembling a stalk; part of word to which inflectional endings are added; *v.t.* to remove the stem of; *v.i.* to originate. *pr.p.* **-ming** *pa.p.* and *pa.t.* **-med.**

stem *v.t.* to check; to stop; to dam up. *pr.p.* **-ming.** *pa.p.* and *pa.t.* **-med.**

stench *n.* strong, offensive odor.

sten·cil *n.* thin sheet of metal, paper, etc. pierced with pattern or letters; *v.t.* to mark or paint with a stencil. *pr.p.* **-ing.** *pa.p.* and *pa.t.* **-ed.**

ste·nog·ra·phy *n.* shorthand writing. **stenograph** *n.* character used in stenography; stenographic machine; *v.i.* to write in shorthand. **stenographer, stenographist** *n.* **stenotype** *n.* a machine for writing shorthand. **stenographic, stenographical** *a.*

step *v.i.* to move and set down the foot; *n.* act of stepping; complete movement of foot in walking, dancing, etc.; manner of walking; tread of stair; degree of progress. *pr.p.* **-ping.** *pa.p.* and *pa.t.* **-ped. -per** *n.*

step- *prefix,* showing relation acquired by remarriage. **-father** *n.* second, or later, husband of one's mother. Similarly **-mother, -brother, -sister.**

steppe *n.* vast, treeless plain.

ster·e·o- solid, used in referring to hardness solidity, three-dimensionality. **-phonic** *a.,* of or denoting a system of placing microphone to impart greater realism of sound.

ster·e·o·scope *n.* optical instrument. **-scopic(al)** *a.* **-scopically** *adv.* **-scopy** *n.*

ster·e·o·type *n.* in printing, plate made by pouring metal into mold of plaster or papier maché made from original type; fixed form. *a.* pert. to stereotypes; *v.t.* to make a stereotype from; to make always the same. **-d** *a.* **-r, stereotypist** *n.*

ster·ile *a.* barren; not fertile; *(Med.)* entirely free from germs of all kinds. **sterilize** *v.t.* **sterilization** *n.* **sterilizer** *n.* **sterility** *n.* barrenness.

ster·ling *a.* pert. to standard value, weight, or purity of silver 922/ pure; of solid worth.

stern *a.* severe; strict; rigorous. **-ly** *adv.* **-ness** *n.*

stern *n.* after part of ship.

ster·num *n.* breastbone. *pl.* **sterna. sternal** *a.*

S

ster·nu·ta·tion n. act of sneezing.

ster·tor n. heavy, sonorous breathing. -ous a. -ously adv.

stet v.i. word used by proofreaders as instruction to printer to cancel previous correction. pr.p. -ting. pa.p., pa.t. -ted.

steth·o·scope n. instrument for listening to action of lungs or heart.

ste·ve·dore n. one who loads and unloads ships.

stew v.t. to cook slowly in a closed vessel; v.i. to be cooked slowly; n. stewed meat, etc. -ed a.

stew·ard n. one who manages another's property; on ship, attendant on passengers. -ess n. -ship n.

stib·i·um n. antimony stibial a.

stich n. verse or line of poetry. -ic a. -ometry n. measurement of manuscript by number of lines it contains. -ometric, -ometrical a.

stick n. small branch cut off tree or shrub; staff; rod.

stick v.t. to stab; to puncture; to cause to adhere; to thrust; v.i. to pierce; to adhere closely; to hesitate. pa.p. and pa.t. stuck. -er n. -y a. adhesive; viscous. -iness n.

stick·le v.i. to hold out stubbornly. -r n.

stick·pin n. necktie pin.

stiff a. not easily bent; moved with difficulty. -ly adv. -ness n. -en v.t. and v.i. to make or become stiff or stiffer. -ener n.

sti·fle v.t. and v.i. to smother. stifling a.

stig·ma n. brand; mark of disgrace; (Bot.) top of pistil of a flower. pl. -s or -ta. stigmata n.pl. marks resembling five wounds of Christ, said to have been miraculously impressed on bodies of certain saints. -tic(al) a. -tization n. -tizer n.

stile n. arrangement of steps for climbing fence or wall.

sti·let·to n. small dagger; pointed instrument.

still a. motionless; quiet; of wine, not sparkling; n. stillness; v.t. to quiet; adv. to this time; yet; even; conj. yet; however. -ness n. -birth n. state of being dead at time of birth. -born a.

still n. apparatus for distilling.

stilt n. pole with footrest for walking raised from ground; v.i. to walk on stilts. -ed a. formal; pretentious.

stim·u·lus n. goad; incentive. pl. stimuli. stimulate v.t. to rouse to activity. stimulater n. stimulant a. and n. (Med.) any agent which temporarily increases action of any organ of body. stimulation n. stimulative a., n.

sting n. pointed organ often poisonous, of certain animals, insects, or plants; thrust, wound, or pain of one; v.t. to thrust sting into; v.i. to use a sting. pa.p. and pa.t. stung. -er n. -ing a. -ingly adv.

stin·gy a. meanly avaricious; miserly. stinginess n.

stink v.i. to give out strongly offensive smell. pa.p. stunk pa.t. stank. n. stench. -er n. -ing a.

stint v.t. to limit; to skimp; v.i. to be frugal; n. limitation of supply or effort; allotted task. -ed a.

sti·pend n. money paid for a person's services; regular payment. -iary a.

stip·ple v.t. and v.i. to engrave, draw, or paint by using dots instead of lines; n. this process. -r n. stippling n.

stip·u·late v.i. to arrange; to settle definitely. stipulation n. stipulator n.

stir v.t. to set or keep in motion; to mix up ingredients, materials, etc.; to incite; v.i. to begin to move; to be emotionally moved. pr.p. -ring. pa.p. and pa.t. -red. n. act of stirring; commotion. -rer n. -ring a.

stir·rup n. metal loop hung from strap, for foot of rider on horse.

stitch n. in sewing, a single pass of needle; bit of clothing; sharp, sudden pain in the side; v.t. and v.i. to form stitches; to sew. -er n. -ing n.

stith·y n. anvil; forge.

stoat n. ermine or weasel.

stock n. stump or post; stem or trunk of tree or plant; piece of wood to which the barrel, lock, etc. of firearm are secured; ancestry; domestic animals on farm; supply of goods merchant has on hand; capital of company or corporation; quantity; juices of meat, etc. to form a liquid used as foundation of soup; v.t. to lay in supply for future use; a. used, or available, for constant supply; commonplace; pert. to stock. -breeder n. one who raises cattle, horses, etc. -broker n. one who buys and sells stocks or shares for others. -broking n. -still a. still as stock or post; motionless.

stock·ade n. enclosure or pen made with posts and stakes; v.t. to surround by erecting line of stakes.

stock·fish n. codfish, hake, etc., split and dried in open air.

stock·ing n. woven or knitted covering for foot and leg.

stock·y a. short and stout; thickset. stockily adv.

stodge v.i. to stuff; to cram. stodgy a. heavy; lumpy; indigestible; (Fig.) dull and uninteresting. stodginess n.

sto·ic n. disciple of Greek philosopher Zeno; one who suffers without complaint; one indifferent to pleasure or pain. -al a. -ally adv. -ism n.

stoke v.t. and v.i. to stir up, feed, or tend (fire). -r n.

stole pa.t. of steal.

stole n. long, narrow scarf.

stol·en pa.p. of steal.

stol·id a. dull or stupid. -ly adv. -ness, -ity n.

stom·ach n. chief digestive organ in any animal; appetite; desire; v.t. to put up with; to endure.

stone n. hard, earthy matter of which rock is made; hard center of certain fruits; gem; concretion in kidneys or bladder; a. made of stone; v.t. to pelt with stones; to remove stones from, as from fruits. stony a. stonily adv. stoniness n. -crop n. creeping plant.

stood pa.p. and pa.t. of stand.

stool n. chair with no back; low backless seat for resting feet on; discharge from bowels.

stoop *v.i.* to bend body; to lean forward; to condescend; *n.* act of stooping; stooping carriage of head and shoulders.

stoop *n.* raised entrance landing in front of doorway.

stop *v.t.* to fill up opening; to keep from going forward; to obstruct; to impede; to desist from; to bring to an end; *v.i.* to cease; to halt. *pr.p.* **-ping.** *pa.p.* and *pa.t.* **-ped;** *n.* act of stopping; halt; halting place; any device for checking movement, e.g. peg, pin, plug, etc. **-page** *n.* **-per** *n.* **-cock** *n.* valve for regulating flow of liquid.

store *n.* great quantity; reserve supply; shop; *pl.* supplies; *v.t.* to collect; to place in a warehouse. **storage** *n.* act of placing goods in a warehouse.

stork *n.* large wading bird.

common stork

storm *n.* violent wind or disturbance of atmosphere with rain, snow, etc.; assault on fortified place; outburst of emotion; *v.t.* to take by storm; to assault; *v.i.* to raise tempest; to scold violently. **-y** *a.* **-ily** *adv.* **-iness.** *n.*

sto•ry *n.* history or narrative of facts or events. **storied** *a.* **-teller** *n.*

sto•ry *n.* horizontal division of building. **storied** *a.*

stoup *n.* holy water basin.

stout *a.* strong; vigorous; thickset; *n.* strong, dark-colored beer; porter. **-ly** *adv.* **-ness** *n.* **-hearted** *a.* brave.

stove *n.* apparatus for cooking, warming room, etc.; oven of blast furnace. **-pipe** *n.* metal pipe for carrying off smoke.

stove *pa.p.* and *pa.t.* of **stave.**

stow *v.t.* to fill by packing closely. **-age** *n.* act of packing closely; space for stowing goods. **-away** *n.* one who hides on ship to obtain free passage.

strad•dle *v.i.* to spread legs wide; *v.t.* to bestride something; *n.* act of straddling; **astraddle** *adv.*

Strad•i•var•i•us *n.* a violin, usually of great value, made at Cremona, Italy, by Antonio *Stradivari.*

strag•gle *v.i.* to wander from direct course; to lag behind. **-r** *n.* **straggling** *a.*

straight *a.* passing from one point to another by nearest course; without a bend; honest; frank; *adv.* in a direct line or manner; without ambiguity; at once. **-ly** *adv.* **-en** *v.t.* to make straight. **-en** *n.* **-away** *a.* straight forward. **-forward** *a.* proceeding in a straight course; honest; frank; simple.

strain *n.* race; inherited quality.

strain *v.t.* to stretch to the full or to excess; to exert to the utmost; to injure by overexertion, as muscle; to wrench; to pass through sieve; *v.i.* to make great effort; to filter; *n.* stretching force; violent effort; injury caused by over-exertion; tune; manner; tone of speaking or writing. **-ed** *a.* **-er** *n.* filter; sieve.

strait *n.* narrow channel of water connecting two larger areas; financial embarrassment. **-en** *v.t.* to narrow; to put into position of difficulty or distress.

strand *n.* *(Poetic)* edge of sea or lake; the shore; *v.t.* to cause to run aground; to leave in helpless position; *v.i.* to run aground. **-ed** *a.*

strand *n.* single string or wire of rope; any string, e.g. of hair, pearls, etc.

strange *a.* unaccustomed; uncommon; extraordinary. **-ly** *adv.* **-ness** *n.* **-r** *n.* unknown person; newcomer; one unaccustomed (to).

stran•gle *v.t.* to kill by squeezing throat; to stifle; **strangulate** *v.t.* to constrict so that circulation of blood is impeded. **strangulation** *n.*

strap *n.* long, narrow strip of leather, cloth, or metal; strop; *v.t.* to fasten, bind, chastize with strap. *pr.p.* **-ping.** *pa.p.* and *pa.t.* **-ped. -ping** *n.*

stra•ta *n.pl.* See stratum.

strat•a•gem *n.* artifice in war; scheme for deceiving enemy.

strat•e•gy *n.* skillful management in getting the better of an adversary. **strategic** *a.* pert. to, based on, strategy. **strategics** *n.pl.* strategy. **strategical** *a.* **strategically** *adv.* **strategist** *n.*

strat•i•fy *v.t.* to form or deposit in strata or layers. **stratification** *n.*

strat•o•sphere *n.* upper part of atmosphere.

stra•tum *n.* bed of earth, rock, coal, etc. in series of layers; class in society. *pl.* **strata.** **stratus** *n.* cloud form, in low, horizontal layers or bands. *pl.* **strati.**

straw *n.* stalk of wheat, rye, etc. after grain has been thrashed out; hollow tube for sipping beverage; *a.* made of straw.

straw•ber•ry *n.* a red berry.

stray *v.i.* to wander from path; *a., n.* stray animal.

streak *n.* stripe; flash of lightning; trait; strain; *v.t.* to mark with streaks. **-ed, -y** *a.*

stream *n.* flowing body of water, or other liquid; river, brook, etc.; steady flow of air or light, or people; *v.i.* to issue in stream; to float or wave in air. **-y** *a.* **-er** *n.* **-let** *n.* little stream. **-line** *n.* shape of a body calculated to offer least resistance to air or water when passing through it; *v.t.* to design body of this shape.

street *n.* road in town or village, usually with houses or buildings at the side.

strength *n.* quality of being strong; ability to endure; physical, mental, or moral force; potency of liquid, esp. of distilled or malted liquors; vigor of style; security. **-en** *v.t.* and *v.i.* **-ener** *n.*

stren•u•ous *a.* eagerly pressing; full of, requiring effort. **-ly** *adv.* **-ness** *n.* **strenuosity** *n.*

S

strep•to•coc•cus n. (Med.) bacterium of chain formation, the organism responsible for serious infections. pl. streptococci.

strep•to•my•cin n. (Med.) antibiotic drug.

stress n. force; strain; emphasis; accent; v.t. to lay stress on.

stretch v.t. to pull out; to reach out; to exaggerate; v.i. to be drawn out; to spread; n. extension; effort; expanse. -er n. one who, or that which, stretches; a frame or litter for carrying sick or wounded.

strew v.t. to scatter over surface; to spread loosely. pa.p. -ed or -n, pa.t. -ed.

stri•a n. line or small groove. pl. -e thread-like lines. -te, -ted a. -tion n.

strick•en a. struck; smitten; afflicted.

strict a. stern; exacting; rigid; without exception; accurate. -ly adv. -ness n. -ure n. severe criticism; (Med.) morbid contraction of any passage of body.

stride n. long step, or its length; v.i. to walk, with long steps. pa.p. stridden pa.t. strode.

stri•dent a. harsh in tone. stridence, stridency n. -ly adv.

strife n. conflict; struggle.

strike v.t. to hit; to collide; to sound; to occur to; to afflict; to stamp; to cancel; v.i. to hit; to stop work for increase of wages, etc.; to take root, of a plant; n. a stoppage of work to enforce demand; find, esp. in prospecting for gold; stroke of luck. pa.p. struck, or -n pa.t. struck. striking a. affecting with strong emotions; impressive. strikingly adv.

string n. cord; thick thread; chain; succession; stretched cord of gut or wire for musical instrument; pl. stringed musical instruments collectively; v.t. to furnish with strings; to put on string, as beads, pearls, etc. pa.p. and pa.t. strung. -ed a. -y a. fibrous; of person, long and thin. -iness n.

strin•gent a. binding strongly; severe. -ly adv. -ness, stringency n.

strip v.t. to pull or tear off; to peel; to lay bare; to rob; v.i. to take off one's clothes; n. long, narrow piece of anything. pr.p. -ping. pa.p. and pa.t. -ped. -ling n. youth.

stripe n. narrow line, band, or mark; v.t. to mark with stripes. -d a.

strive v.i. to make an effort; to struggle. pa.p. -n. pa.t. strove. n.

strode pa.t. of stride.

stroke n. blow; paralytic fit; sound of bell or clock; mark made by pen, pencil, brush, etc.; completed movement of club, stick, racquet, etc.; in swimming, completed movement of arm; in rowing, sweep of an oar; single, sudden effort, esp. if successful, in business, diplomacy, etc.; piece of luck.

stroke v.t. to pass hand gently over; n.

stroll v.i. to walk leisurely from place to place; n. a leisurely walk. -er n.

strong a. having physical force; muscular; healthy; violent; intense; not easily broken; positive. -ly adv.

stron•ti•um n. (Chem.) a yellowish, reactive, metallic element.

strop n. strip of leather for sharpening razor; v.t. to sharpen on strop. pr.p. -ping. pa.p. and pa.t. -ped.

stro•phe n. in ancient Greek drama, song sung by chorus while dancing from right to left of orchestra; stanza. strophic a.

strove pa.t. of strive.

struck pa.p. and pa.t. of strike.

struc•ture n. that which is built; organization. structural a. structurally adv.

stru•del n. type of Ger. pastry.

strug•gle v.i. to put forth great efforts, esp. accompanied by violent twistings of body; n. violent physical effort; any kind of work in face of difficulties; strife. n.

strum v.t. and v.i. to play badly and noisily on (stringed instrument). pr.p. -ming. pa.p. and pa.t. -med.

strum•pet n. prostitute; harlot.

strung pa.p. and pa.t. of string.

strut v.i. to walk pompously; n. stiff, proud and affected walk. pa.p. -ting. pa.p. and pa.t. -ted.

strut n. rigid support, usually set obliquely; v.t. to brace.

strych•nine n. highly poisonous alkaloid; stimulant. Also strychnin.

stub n. stump of a tree; short, remaining part of pencil, cigarette, etc.; v.t. to strike toe against fixed object. pr.p. -bing. pa.p. and pa.t. -bed. -bed a. short and blunt like stump; obtuse. -by a. -biness n.

stub•ble n. short ends of cornstalks left after reaping; short growth of beard. -d a. stubbly a.

stub•born a. fixed in opinion; obstinate. adv. -ness n.

stuc•co n. plaster of lime, sand, etc. used on walls; v.t. to make stucco.

stud n. a movable, double-headed flat-headed nail; upright wooden support, as in wall; v.t. to furnish with studs; to set thickly in, or scatter over. pr.p. -ding. pa.p. and pa.t. -ded.

stud n. collection of horses, kept for breeding, or racing.

stu•dent n. one who studies.

stu•di•o n. workroom of artist, sculptor, or professional photographer.

stu•di•ous a. given to, or fond of, study; contemplative. -ly adv.

stud•y n. application of the mind to books, etc. to gain knowledge; subject of such application; meditation; room for study; v.t. to set the mind to; to ponder over; v.i. to read books closely in order to gain knowledge. studies also a. examined closely; carefully considered.

stuff n. essential part; material; goods; worthless things, trash, esp. in stuff and nonsense; v.t. to fill by pressing closely. -ing n. material used to stuff or fill.

stuff•y a. badly ventilated; conceited. stuffiness n.

stul•ti•fy v.t. to make to look ridiculous; to make ineffectual.

stum•ble v.i. to trip in walking and nearly fall; to fall into error; n. stumblingly adv.

stump n. part of tree left after trunk is cut down; part of limb, tooth, etc. after main part has been removed; remnant; v.t. to reduce to a stump; to puzzle or perplex; *v.i.* to walk noisily or heavily. -y *a.*

stun *v.t.* to knock senseless; to amaze. *pr.p.* -ning. *pa.p.* and *pa.t.* -ned. -ner *n.* -ning *a.*

stung *pa.p.* and *pa.t.* of **sting.**

stunk *pa.p.* and *pa.t.* of **stink.**

stunt *v.t.* to check the growth of. -ed *a.*

stunt *n.* (*Colloq.*) any spectacular feat of skill or daring.

stu•pe•fy *v.t.* to deprive of full consciousness; to amaze. **stupefier** *n.* **stupefaction** *n.* **stupefactive** *a.* **stupefacient** *a.* and *n.*

stu•pen•dous *a.* astonishing, esp. because of size, power, etc.; amazing. -ly *adv.* -ness *n.*

stu•pid *a.* unintelligent; foolish; dull. -ly *adv.* -ness, -ity *n.*

stu•por *n.* complete or partial loss of consciousness. -ous *a.*

stur•dy *a.* hard; vigorous; strongly built; firm. **sturdily** *adv.* **sturdiness** *n.*

stur•geon *n.* large fish, whose roe is made into caviar.

sturgeon

stut•ter *v.i.* and *v.t.* to stammer; *n.* the act or habit of stuttering. -er *n.* -ing *a.*

sty *n.* place to keep pigs; hence, any filthy place.

sty, stye *n.* small abscess on edge of eyelid.

styg•i•an *a.* pert. to river *Styx* in Hades; gloomy; dismal.

style *n.* engraving tool; manner of expressing thought in writing, speaking, acting, painting, etc.; mode of dress; fine appearance; title; sort, kind, make, shape, etc. of anything; (*Bot.*) stem-like part of pistil of flower, supporting stigma. -t *n.* stiletto; probe. **stylize** *v.t.* to make conform to convention. **stylish** *a.* fashionable; elegant. **stylishly** *adv.* **stylishness** *n.* **stylist** *n.* writer, who is attentive to form and style. **stylistic** *a.* **stylistically** *adv.* **stylus** *n.* style.

sty•mie *n.* to thwart.

styp•tic *a.* contracting; astringent; *n.* (*Med.*) any substance used to arrest bleeding.

sua•sion *n.* persuasion.

suave *a.* smoothly polite. -ly *adv.* **suavity** *n.*

sub- *prefix*, meaning under, lower, inferior, about, slightly, moderately.

sub•al•tern (*Mil.*) *a.* of lower rank.

sub•a•que•ous *a.* living, lying, or formed under water. **subaquatic** *a.*

sub•arc•tic *a.* pert. to region immediately next to the Arctic.

sub•con•scious *a.*; *n.* subconscious mind. -ly *adv.*

sub•cu•ta•ne•ous *a.* under the skin. -ly *adv.*

sub•di•vide *v.t.* to divide again; *v.i.* to be subdivided. **subdivision** *n.*

sub•duc•tion *n.* withdrawal; deduction.

sub•due *v.t.* to bring under one's power; to bring under control; to soften. -d *a.* -r *n.* **subdual** *n.*

sub•head•ing *n.* division of main heading.

sub•hu•man *a.* less than human.

sub•ject *a.* under power or control of another; subordinate; liable to; exposed; *n.* one owing allegiance to a sovereign, state, government, etc.; topic; theme. **subject** *v.t.* to bring under power or control of; to cause to undergo. **ion** *n.* act of bringing under power or control. -ive *a.* existing in the mind; relating to, or reflecting, thoughts and feelings of person. -ively *adv.* -iveness *n.* -ivity *n.*

sub•join *v.t.* to append; to annex. -der *n.* something added at end.

sub•ju•gate *v.t.* to force to submit. **subjugation** *n.* **subjugator** *n.*

sub•junc•tive *a.* mood of verb implying condition, doubt, or wish.

sub•lease *n.* lease granted to another tenant by one who is himself a tenant; *v.t.* to grant or hold a sublease.

sub•let *v.t.* to let to another tenant property of which one is a tenant; *pr.p.* -ting. *pa.t.*, *pa.p.* **sublet.**

sub•li•mate *v.t.* to direct repressed impulses, esp. sexual, towards new aims and activities. **sublimation** *n.*

sub•lime *a.* exalted; eminent; majestic; grandiose; *n.* that which is sublime; *v.t.* to sublimate; to purify; to exalt; to ennoble. -ly *adv.* -ness, **sublimity** *n.*

sub•lim•i•nal *a.* in psychology, below level of consciousness.

sub•ma•chine gun *n.* (*Mil.*) light, portable machine gun.

sub•ma•rine *a.* situated, living, or able to travel under surface of sea; *n.* submersible boat.

sub•merge *v.t.* to put under water; *v.i.* to go under water. -nce *n.*

sub•merse *v.t.* to submerge; to put under water. **submersible** *a.* **submersion** *n.*

sub•mit *v.t.* to put forward for consideration; to surrender; *v.i.* to yield oneself to another. *pr.p.* -ting. *pa.p.* and *pa.t.* -ted. **submission** *n.* **submissive** *a.* **submissively** *adv.* **submissiveness** *n.*

sub•mul•ti•ple *n.* number or quantity that divides into another exactly.

sub•nor•mal *a.* below normal.

sub•or•di•nate *a.* lower in rank, importance, power, etc.; *n.* one of lower rank, importance, etc. than another; *v.t.* to make or treat as subordinate; to make subject. -ly *adv.* -ness, **subordinacy** *n.* **subordination** *n.*

sub•orn *v.t.* to induce (person) to commit perjury; to bribe to do evil. -ation *n.* -er *n.*

sub•poe•na *n.* (*Law*) writ summoning person to appear in court; *v.t.* to issue such an order.

sub•rep•tion *n.* concealment or misrepresentation of truth. **subreptitious** *a.*

sub•scribe *v.t.* to write underneath; to sign at end of paper or document; to contribute; *v.i.* (with *to*) to pay in advance for regular supply of issues of newspaper, magazine, etc.; to agree with or support. -r *n.* **subscript** *a.* written underneath. **subscription** *n.*

sub•se•quent *a.* following or coming after

S

in time; happening later. -ly *adv*.

sub•serve *v.t.* to serve in small way; to promote. **subservient** *a.* submissive; servile. **subserviently** *adv*. **subservience, subserviency** *n*.

sub•side *v.i.* to sink or fall to the bottom; to abate. **subsidence, subsidency** *n*.

sub•sid•i•ar•y *a.* aiding, helping, supplementary, secondary; auxiliary; *n*. one who, or that which, helps; auxiliary.

sub•si•dy *n.* financial aid; government grant for various purposes, e.g. to encourage certain industries, to keep cost of living steady, etc. **subsidize** *v.t.*

sub•sist *v.i.* to continue to be; *v.t.* to support with food; to feed. **-ent** *a.* having real being; existing. **-ence** *n*.

sub•soil *n.* the layer of earth lying just below the top layer.

sub•son•ic *a.* pert. to speeds less than that of sound; below 700-750 m.p.h.

sub•stance *n.* essence; material, etc. of which anything is made; property. **substantial** *a.* **substantiation** *n*. **substantive** *a.* having independent existence; real; fixed. **substantively** *adv*.

sub•sti•tute *v.t.* to put in place of another; to exchange. *v.i.* to take place of another; *n.* **substitution** *n.* **substitutional, substitutionary** *a.* **substitutionally** *adv*.

sub•stra•tum *n.* underlying stratum or layer of soil, rock, etc.; a basic element. *pl.* **substrata. substrative** *a*.

sub•sume *v.t.* to include under a class as belonging to it. e.g. 'all sparrows are birds.' **subsumption** *n.* **subsumptive** *a*.

sub•ten•ant *n.* tenant who rents house, farm, etc. from one who is himself a tenant. **subtenancy** *n*.

sub•tend *v.t.* (*Geom.*) of line, to extend under or be opposite to, e.g. angle.

sub•ter•fuge *n.* that to which a person resorts in order to escape from a difficult situation.

sub•ter•ra•ne•an *a.* being or lying under surface of earth. Also **subterraneous, subterrene, subterrestrial**.

sub•ti•tle *n.* additional title of book.

sub•tle *a.* delicate; discerning; clever; making fine distinctions. **subtly** *adv*. **-ness, -ty** *n.* quality of being subtle.

sub•tract *v.t.* to take away (part) from rest; to deduct one number from another. **-ion** *n.* **-ive** *a.* **subtrahend** *n.* quantity or number to be subtracted from another.

sub•trop•i•cal *a.* designating zone just outside region of the tropics.

sub•urb *n.* residential district on outskirts of town; *pl.* outskirts. **suburban** *a.* and *n*. **-ia** *n*.

sub•ven•tion *n.* act of coming to the help of; subsidy.

sub•vert *v.t.* to overthrow, esp. government; to destroy. **-er** *n.* **subversion** *n.* **subversive** *a*.

sub•way *n.* underground passage; underground railway.

suc•ceed *v.t.* to come immediately after; to take place of, esp. of one who has left or died; *v.i.* to come next in order; to become heir (to); to achieve one's aim to prosper. **-er** *n.* **success** *n.* favorable

accomplishment; prosperity; **successful** *a.* **successfully** *adv*. **successfulness** *n*.

succession *n.* sequence; act or right of entering into possession of property, place, office, title, etc., of another, esp. of one near of kin. **successional** *a.* **successionally** *adv*. **successive** *a.* **successively** *adv*. **successor** *n*.

suc•cinct *a.* expressed in few words; concise. **-ly** *adv*. **-ness** *n*.

suc•cor *v.t.* to help esp. in great difficulty or distress; *n.* aid; support. **-er** *n*.

suc•cu•lent *a.* full of juice; juicy. **-ly** *adv*. **succulence** *n*.

suc•cumb *v.i.* to yield; to submit; to die.

such *a.* of like kind; of degree, quality, etc. mentioned; *pron.* used to denote a certain person or thing; these or those. **-like** *a.* similar; *pron.* similar things.

suck *v.t.* to draw into mouth (by using lips and tongue); to absorb; *v.i.* to draw in with mouth; *n.* act of drawing with the mouth; milk drawn from mother's breast. **-er** *n.* shoot of plant from roots or lower part of stem. **-ing** *a.* **-le** *v.t.* to give suck to; to feed at mother's breast. **-ling** *n.* young child or animal not yet weaned.

su•crose *n.* cane sugar, beet sugar, etc.

suc•tion *n.* act of sucking or drawing in; 'force' that causes one object to adhere to another when air between them is exhausted.

sud•den *a.* happening without notice or warning. **-ly** *adv*. **-ness** *n*.

suds *n.pl.* water in which soap has been dissolved.

sue *v.t.* (*Law*) to seek justice by taking legal proceedings; *v.i.* to begin legal proceedings.

suede *n.* soft, undressed kid leather; *a.* made of undressed kid.

su•et *n.* hard animal fat around kidneys and loins. **-y** *a*.

suf•fer *v.t.* to endure; to tolerate; *v.i.* to undergo pain, punishment, etc. **-able** *a.* **-ableness** *n.* **-ably** *adv*. **-ance** *n*.

suf•fice *v.t.* to satisfy; *v.i.* to be enough; to meet the needs of. **sufficient** *a.* enough; satisfying the needs of. **sufficiently** *adv*. **sufficiency** *n*.

suf•fix *n.* letter or syllable added to end of word; affix. *v.t.* to add to end of. **-al** *a.* **-ion** *n*.

suf•fo•cate *v.t.* to kill by choking; to stifle; *v.i.* to be choked, stifled, or smothered. **suffocating** *a.* **suffocatingly** *adv*. **suffocation** *n*.

suf•frage *n.* vote; right to vote. **-tte** *n*. **suf•fuse** *v.t.* to spread over, as fluid. **suffusion** *n.* **suffusive** *a*.

sug•ar *n.* sweet, crystalline substance; (*Fig.*) sweet words; *v.t.* to sweeten with sugar; *v.i.* to turn into sugar; *a.* made of, tasting of, or containing sugar; sweet; flattering. **-iness** *n*.

sug•gest *v.t.* to bring forward; to propose; to insinuate. **-er** *n.* **-ion** *n.* **-ive** *a.* **-ively** *adv*. **-iveness** *n*.

su•i•cide *n.* one who kills himself intentionally; act of doing this. **suicidal** *a.* (*Fig.*) disastrous; ruinous. **suicidally** *adv*.

suit *n.* act of suing; request; courtship;

series or set of things of same kind or material; set of clothes; *v.t.* to fit; to appropriate; to meet desires of; *v.i.* to agree; to be convenient. -able *a.* -ably *adv.* -ability, -ableness *n.* -or *n.*

suite *n.* a number of things used together, e.g. set of apartments, furniture; *(Mus.)* series of dances.

sul•cus *n.* groove; a furrow. sulcate, sulcated *a.* sulcation *n.*

sul•fa *n.* abbrev. for sulfa drugs, a group of antibacterial compounds.

sul•fate *n.* salt of sulfuric acid. sulfide *n.* compound of sulfur with metal or other element. sulfite *n.* salt of sulfurous acid.

sul•fur *n.* yellow, nonmetallic element. -ous *a.* -y *a.* -ic acid, colorless acid.

sulk *v.i.* to be silent owing to ill humor, etc.; *n.* sullen fit or mood. -y *a.*; *n.* light two-wheeled carriage for one person. -ily *adv.* -iness *n.*

sul•len *a.* gloomily ill-humored. -ly *adv.* -ness *n.*

sul•ly *v.t.* to soil; to disgrace; *v.i.* to be sullied.

sul•tan *n.* Mohammedan prince or ruler. -a *n.* wife, mother, or daughter of sultan; kind of raisin.

sul•try *a.* hot, close, and oppressive; sweltering. sultrily *adv.* sultriness *n.*

sum *n.* result obtained by adding together two or more things, quantities, etc.; quantity of money; *v.t.* (generally with up) to add up; to make summary of main parts. *pr.p.* -ming. *pa.p.* and *pa.t.* -med. -mation *n.*

sum•ma•ry *a.* expressed in few words; *n.* abridgment or statement of chief points of longer document, speech; etc.; epitome. summarily *adv.* summarize *v.t.* summarist *n.* summarization *n.* summarizer *n.*

sum•mer *n.* warmest of four seasons of year, season between spring and autumn; *a.* pert. to period of summer. -y *a.*

sum•mit *n.* highest point.

sum•mon *v.t.* to demand appearance of, esp. in court of law; to gather up (energy, etc.). -er *n.*

sump *n.* lowest part of excavation; well in crankcase of motor vehicle for oil.

sump•tu•ar•y *a.* pert. to, or regulating, expenditure. sumptuous *a.* costly; lavish; magnificent. sumptuously *adv.* sumptuousness *n.*

sun *n.* luminous body round which earth and other planets revolve; its rays; any other heavenly body forming the center of system of planets; *v.t.* to expose to sun's rays; to bask. *pr.p.* -ning. *pa.p.* and *pa.t.* -ned. -ny *a.* -niness *n.* -bathe *v.i.* to expose body to sun. -beam *n.* -burn *n.* darkening of skin, due to exposure to sun; *v.t.* and *v.i.* to darken by exposure to sun. -burned, burnt *a.* -down *n.* sunset. -flower *n.* tall plant with yellow-rayed flowers. -light *n.* -lit *a.* lighted by sun. -rise *n.* dawn. -set *n.* descent of sun below horizon. -shine *a.* -spot *n.* dark, irregular patch on surface of sun. -stroke *n.* feverish prostration caused by undue

exposure to strong sunlight.

sun•dae *n.* ice-cream served with topping.

Sun•day *n.* first day of week.

sun•der *v.t.* to separate; *v.i.* to come apart.

sundry *a.* separate; various. sundries *n.pl.* sundry things; odd items.

sung *pa.p.* of sing.

sunk *pa.p.* and alt. *pa.t.* of sink.

sunk•en alt. *pa.p.* of sink.

sup *v.t.* to take in sips; *v.i.* to have supper; to sip; *n.* small mouthful; sip. *pr.p.* -ping. *pa.p.* and *pa.t.* -ped.

su•per *n.* *(Colloq.)* short for superfine, super-excellent, etc.

su•per- *prefix*, above, over, higher, superior, to extra, etc.

su•per•a•ble *a.* capable of being overcome.

su•per•a•bound *v.i.* to be exceedingly abundant. superabundant *a.* superabundantly *adv.* superabundance *n.*

su•per•an•nu•ate *v.t.* to pension off because of age or infirmity. superannuation *n.* pension.

su•perb *a.* grand; splendid. -ly *adv.* -ness *n.*

su•per•car•go *n.* ship's officer who takes charge of cargo.

su•per•charge *v.t.* to charge or fill to excess.

su•per•cil•i•ar•y *a.* pert. to eyebrow. supercilious *a.* lofty with pride; haughty and indifferent. superciliously *adv.*

su•per•cool *v.t.* *(Chem.)* to cool (liquid) below its freezing point without solidifying it. -ing *n.*

su•per•e•go *n.* in psychoanalysis, that unconscious morality which directs action of censor.

su•per•er•o•ga•tion *n.* doing more than duty or necessity requires.

su•per•fi•cial *a.* on surface; understanding only what is obvious. -ly *adv.* -ity.

su•per•fine *a.* fine above others.

su•per•flu•ous *a.* more than is required or desired; useless. -ly *adv.* superfluity *n.* -ness *n.*

su•per•heat *v.t.* to heat (steam) above boiling point of water.

su•per•het•er•o•dyne *n.* *(Radio)* receiving set of great power and selectivity. *abbrev.* superhet.

su•per•hu•man *a.* more than human; divine; excessively powerful.

su•per•im•pose *v.t.* to lay upon another thing. superimposition *n.*

su•per•in•tend *v.t.* to manage; to supervise; *v.i.* to supervise. -ence, -ency *n.* -ent *a.* and *n.*

su•pe•ri•or *a.* higher in place, position, rank, quality, etc.; *n.* one who is above another, esp. in rank or office. superiority *n.*

su•per•la•tive *a.* of or in the highest degree; *n.* superlative degree of adjective or adverb. -ly *adv.*

su•per•man *n.* one endowed with powers beyond those of the ordinary man.

su•per•nal *a.* pert. to things above; celestial; heavenly.

su•per•nat•u•ral *a.* beyond powers or laws of nature; miraculous.

su•per•nu•mer•ar•y over and above; *n.*

S

person or thing in excess of what is necessary or usual.

su•per•scribe v.t. to write or engrave on outside or top of. superscription n.

su•per•sede v.t. to set aside; to replace by another person or thing. supersession n.

su•per•son•ic a. pert. to soundwaves of too high a frequency to be audible.

su•per•sti•tion n. belief in, or fear of, what is unknown or supernatural. superstitious a. superstitiously adv.

su•per•struc•ture n. structure built on top of another. superstructive, superstructural a.

su•per•vene v.i. to happen in addition, or unexpectedly; to follow closely upon. supervenient a. supervenience, supervention n.

su•per•vise v.t. to oversee; to direct and control. supervision n. Also supervisal n. supervisor n. supervisory a.

su•pine a. lying on one's back; indolent; inactive.

sup•per n. the last meal of the day.

sup•plant v.t. to displace (person) esp. by unfair means. -er n.

sup•ple a. easily bent; limber; obsequious; v.t. and v.i. to make or become supple. -ly adv. -ness n.

sup•ple•ment n. something added to fill up or supply deficiency. supplement v.t. -al a. -ary a.

sup•pli•ant a. asking humbly and submissively; n. one who supplicates. -ly adv. supplicant a. and n. supplicate v.t. and v.i. supplication n.

sup•ply v.t. to provide what is needed; n. act of supplying; what is supplied; stock; store. supplies n.pl. food or money. supplier n.

sup•port v.t. to keep from falling; to bear or tolerate; to furnish with means of living; n. act of sustaining; maintenance or subsistence; one who, or that which, supports. -er n.

sup•pose v.t. to assume as true without proof; to imagine. -d a. supposedly adv. supposable a.

sup•po•si•tion n. act of supposing; assumption; that which is supposed; -ally adv. supposititious a.

sup•pos•i•to•ry n. medicinal substance, cone-shaped, introduced into a body canal.

sup•press v.t. to put down or subdue. suppression n. -ive a. -or n.

sup•pu•rate v.i. to form pus; to fester. suppurative a. suppuration n.

su•pra- prefix, meaning above.

su•preme a. holding highest authority; greatest possible. -ly adv. -ness n. supremacy n.

sur- prefix, meaning over, above, upon, in addition.

sur•cease v.t. (Arch.) to cause to cease; v.i. to cease; n. cessation.

sur•charge v.t. to make additional charge; to overload or overburden. surcharge n. excessive charge, load, or burden.

sur•cin•gle n. girth for holding something on a horse's back.

sur•coat n. long and flowing cloak worn by knights over armor.

surd a. (Math.) not capable of being expressed in rational numbers.

sure a. certain; admitting of no doubt; firmly established; strong or secure. -ly adv. certainly; undoubtedly; securely. -ness n. -ty n. certainty; that which makes sure.

surf n. foam or water of sea breaking on shore or reefs, etc.

sur•face n. external layer or outer face of anything; a. involving the surface only; v.t. to cover with special surface; v.i. to come to the surface.

sur•feit v.t. to overfeed; to fill to satiety; n. excess in eating and drinking. -er n. -ing n.

surge n. rolling swell of water, smoke, people; v.i. to swell. surging a.

sur•geon n. medical man qualified to perform operations. surgery n. branch of medicine dealing with cure of disease or injury by manual operation. surgical a. surgically adv.

sur•ly a. of unfriendly temper. surlily adv. surliness n.

sur•mise v.t. to imagine or infer something without proper grounds; n. supposition; a guess or conjecture.

sur•mount v.t. to rise above; to conquer or overcome. -able a.

sur•name n. family name.

sur•pass v.t. to go beyond; to outstrip. -ing a.

sur•plice n. white linen vestment worn over cassock by clergy.

sur•plus n. excess beyond what is wanted; excess of income over expenditure; a. more than enough.

sur•prise v.t. to fall or come upon unawares; to strike with astonishment; n. astonishment; unexpected event, piece of news, gift, etc. surprisal n. surprising a. surprisingly adv.

sur•re•al•ism n. 20th cent. phase in art and literature of expressing subconscious in images without order or coherence, as in dream. surrealist n. surrealistic a.

sur•ren•der v.t. to yield or hand over to power of another; to yield to emotion, etc.; v.i. to cease resistance; to capitulate; n. act of surrendering. -er n.

sur•rep•ti•tious a. done by stealth. -ly adv.

sur•rey n. lightly built, four-wheeled carriage.

sur•ro•gate n. deputy who acts for bishop or chancellor of diocese. -ship n.

sur•round v.t. to be on all sides of. -ings n. that which surrounds; pl. things which environ.

sur•tax n. additional tax; v.t. to impose extra tax on.

sur•veil•lance n. close watch; supervision.

sur•vey v.t. to look over; to view as from high place. survey n. general view, as from high place; measured plan or chart of any tract of country. -or n. one who surveys.

sur•vive v.t. to live longer than; v.i. to remain alive. survival n. survivor n. surviving a.

sus•cep•ti•ble a. capable of; readily

impressed; sensitive. **susceptibly** *adv.* **-ness** *n.* **susceptibility** *n.* **susceptive** *a.* receptive. **susceptivity, susceptiveness** *n.*

sus•pect *v.t.* to imagine existence or presence of; to imagine to be guilty; to mistrust. **suspect** *n.* suspected person; *a.* inspiring distrust. **-er** *n.*

sus•pend *v.t.* to cause to hang; to bring to a stop temporarily; to debar from an office or privilege; to defer or keep undecided. **-er** *n.* one who suspends; *pl.* pair of straps for holding up trousers, skirt, etc. **suspense** *n.* state of uncertainty or anxiety; indecision. **suspension** *n.* **suspensive** *a.* **suspensively** *adv.* **suspensor** *n.* **suspensory** *a.*

sus•pi•cion *n.* act of suspecting; imagining of something being wrong, on little evidence; doubt; mistrust; slight trace or hint. **suspicious** *a.* **suspiciously** *adv.*

sus•tain *v.t.* to keep from falling or sinking; to nourish or keep alive; to endure or undergo. **-able** *a.* **-er** *n.* **sustenance** *n.* that which sustains (life); food, nourishment. **sustentation** *n.* **sustentative** *a.* **sustention** *n.*

su•ture *n.* sewing up of wound; connection or seam, between bones of skull; *v.t.* to join by stitching. **sutural** *a.*

su•ze•rain *n.* feudal lord; paramount ruler. **-ty** *n.* authority or dominion of suzerain.

svelte *a.* supple; lithe; slender.

swab *n.* mop; bit of cotton on stick for applying medicine; *v.t.* to clean with mop or swab. *pr.p.* **-bing.** *pa.t.* and *pa.p.* **-bed. -ber** *n.*

swad•dle *v.t.* to bind or wrap as with bandages; *n.* the cloth wrapping.

swage *n.* tool for bending, marking, or shaping metal. *v.t.*

swag•ger *v.i.* to walk with a conceited or defiant strut; to boast or brag; *n.* defiant or conceited bearing. **-er** *n.* **-ing** *a.*

Swa•hi•li *n.* people of mixed Bantu and Arab stock, occupying Zanzibar and adjoining territory; their language. *(Poetic)* **-an** *a.*

swain *n.* *(Poetic)* country lad; rustic lover.

swal•low *n.* small migratory, passerine, insectivorous bird. **-tail** *n.* forked tail.

swallow

swal•low *v.t.* to receive into stomach through mouth and throat; *(Colloq.)* to accept without criticism or scruple; *v.i.* to perform act of swallowing; *n.* act of swallowing; amount taken down at one gulp. **-er** *n.*

swam *pa.t.* of swim.

swamp *n.* tract of wet, low-lying ground; marsh; *v.t.* to cause to fill with water, as boat; *v.i.* to overwhelm; to sink. **-y** *a.*

swan *n.* large, web-footed bird of goose family. **-nery** *n.* place where swans are bred.

swap *v.t.* and *v.i.* to exchange; to barter; *n.* exchange. *pr.p.* **-ping.** *pa.p.* and *pa.t.* **-ped.** Also swop.

sward *n.* land covered with short green grass; turf; *v.t.* to cover with sward. **-ed** *a.*

swarm *n.* large number of insects esp. in motion; crowd; *v.i.* to collect in large numbers.

swarm *v.i.* to climb with arms and legs.

swarth•y *a.* dark in hue; of dark complexion.

swash•buck•ler *n.* swaggering bully. **swashbuckling** *a.*

swas•ti•ka *n.* symbol in form of Greek cross with ends of arms bent thus 卐

swat *v.t.* *(Colloq.)* to hit smartly; to kill, esp. insects. *pr.p.* **-ting.** *pa.t.*, *pa.p.* **-ted.**

swatch *n.* piece of cloth, cut as a sample of quality.

swath *n.* line of hay or grain cut by scythe or mowing machine. Also swathe.

swathe *v.t.* to bind with bandage; *n.* bandage; folded or draped band.

sway *v.t.* to cause to incline to one side or the other; *v.i.* to incline to one side or the other; to totter; *n.* swaying or swinging movement; control. **-er** *n.* **-back** *a.* having inward curve of the spine.

swear *v.t.* to utter, affirm or declare on oath; *v.i.* to utter solemn declaration with appeal to God for truth of what is affirmed; to curse. *pa.p.* **sworn.** *pa.t.* **swore. -er** *n.* **-ing** *n.*

sweat *n.* perspiration; moisture exuding from any substance; *v.t.* to cause to excrete moisture from skin; *v.i.* to excrete moisture; *(Colloq.)* to toil or drudge at. **-er** *n.* warm knitted jersey or jacket. **-y** *a.* damp with sweat. **-ily** *adv.* **-iness** *n.*

Swede *n.* native of Sweden. **Swedish** *a.* pert. to Sweden; *n.* language of Swedes.

sweep *v.t.* to pass brush or broom over to remove loose dirt; to scan rapidly; *v.i.* to pass with swiftness or violence; to move with dignity; to extend in a curve; to effect cleaning with a broom; *n.* act of sweeping. *pa.p.* and *pa.t.* **swept. -er** *n.* **-ing** *a.* of great scope; comprehensive. **-ingly** *adv.*

sweet *a.* tasting like sugar; having agreeable taste; melodious; gentle; dear or beloved; likeable; *pl.* confections. **-en** *v.t.* **-ening** *n.* **-ly** *adv.* **-ness** *n.* **-bread** *n.* pancreas or thymus of animal, as food. **-pea** *n.* climbing plant with fragrant flowers. **-potato** *n.* sweet, starchy tuber.

swell *v.t.* to increase size, sound, etc.; *v.i.* to grow larger; to rise in waves; to be filled to bursting point with some emotion. *n.* act of swelling. *pa.p.* **swollen** or **swelled.** *pa.t.* **-ed. -ing** *n.*

swel•ter *v.i.* to be oppressive, or oppressed, with heat; *n.* heated or sweaty state. **-ing** *a.* **sweltry** *a.*

swept *pa.t.* and *pa.p.* of sweep.

swerve *v.i.* to depart from straight line; *v.t.* to cause to bend or turn aside; *n.* act of swerving.

swift *a.* quick; prompt. **-ly** *adv.* **-ness** *n.*

swig *v.t.* and *v.i.* *(Colloq.)* to gulp down; to drink in long drafts; *n.* long draft. *pr.p.* **-ging.** *pa.p.,* *pa.t.* **-ged.**

swill *v.t.* and *v.i.* to drink greedily; *n.* act of swilling; pig food; hogwash slops. **-er** *n.*

swim *v.i.* to propel oneself in water by means of hands, feet, or fins, etc.; to float on surface; *v.t.* to cross or pass over by swimming; *n.* act of swimming. *pr.p.* **-ming.** *pa.p.* **swum.** *pa.t.* **swam. -mer** *n.* **-mingly** *adv.* easily, successfully.

swim *v.i.* to be dizzy or giddy; *n.* dizziness or unconsciousness. *pr.p.* **-ming.** *pa.p.* **swum.** *pa.t.* **swam.**

swin•dle *v.t.* and *v.i.* to cheat or defraud; *n.* act of defrauding.

swine *n.sing.* and *pl.* thick-skinned domestic animal, fed for its flesh; pig; hog. **—herd** *n.* one who tends swine. **swinish** *a.*

swing *v.i.* to move to and fro, esp. as suspended body; *v.t.* to attach so as to hang freely; to move to and fro; to brandish; *n.* act of swinging or causing to swing. *pa.p.* and *pa.t.* **swung. -er** *n.* **-ing** *a.* **-ingly** *adv.*

swing *n.* *(Mus.)* kind of jazz music.

swipe *v.t.* and *v.i.* to strike with a wide, sweeping blow, as with a bat, racket, etc.

swirl *n.* eddy of wind or water; whirling motion; *v.i.* to whirl; *v.t.* to carry along with whirling motion.

swish *n.* *v.i.* to move with hissing or rustling sound.

Swiss *n.sing.* and *pl.* native of Switzerland; *a.* pert. to Switzerland or the Swiss.

switch *n.* flexible twig or rod; tress of false hair; *(Elect.)* device for making, breaking, or transferring, electric current; act of switching; *v.t.* to strike with switch; to wisk; *(Elect.)* to turn electric current off or on with switch; to transfer one's thoughts to another subject; to transfer. **-er** *n.* **—like** *a.* **-back** *n.* zigzag method of ascending slopes. **-board** *n.* set of switches at telephone exchange.

swiv•el *n.* ring turning on pivot, forming connection between two pieces of mechanism and enabling one to rotate independently of the other; *v.i.* to swing on pivot; *v.t.* to turn as on pivot.

swol•len *a.* swelled. *pa.p.* of **swell.**

swoon *v.i.* to faint; *n.* fainting fit.

swoop *v.t.* to catch up with sweeping motion (with 'up'); *v.i.* to sweep down swiftly upon prey, as hawk or eagle; *n.*

swop. See **swap.**

sword *n.* **-fish** *n.* large fish with sword-like

sword-fish

upper jaw. **-play** *n.* fencing. **-sman** *n.* one skillful with sword. **—smanship** *n.*

swore *pa.t.* of **swear.**

sworn *pa.p.* of **swear.**

swum *pa.p.* of **swim.**

swung *pa.p.* and *pa.t.* of **swing.**

syb•a•rite *n.* person devoted to luxury and pleasure. **sybaritic, sybaritical** *a.*

syc•a•more *n.* tree with broad leaves.

syc•o•phant *n.* flatterer, or one who fawns on rich or famous; parasite; *a.* servile; obsequious. **sychophancy, -ism** *n.* **-ic, -ical, -ically** *adv.* **-ish** *a.*

syl•la•ble *n.* sound uttered at single effort of voice, and constituting word, or part of word; *v.t.* to utter in syllables; to articulate. **syllabic, syllabical** *a.* **syllabically** *adv.* **syllabicate, syllabify, syllabize,** *v.t.* to divide into syllables.

syl•la•bus *n.* outline or program of main points in a course of lectures, etc.

syl•lo•gism *n.* formal statement of argument, consisting of three parts, major premise, minor premise, and conclusion. **syllogize** *v.t.* and *v.i.* **syllogization** *n.* **syllogizer** *n.* **syllogistic, syllogistical** *a.*

sylph *n.* elemental spirit of the air; fairy or sprite; graceful girl. **-id** *n.* little sylph. **-like** *a.*

syl•van *a.* forest-like; pert. to or inhabiting the woods.

sym•bi•o•sis *n.* *(Biol.)* living together of different organisms for mutual benefit. **symbiotic** *a.* **symbiont** *n.*

sym•bol *n.* something that represents something else; emblem; type character or sign used to indicate relation or operation in mathematics. **-ic, -ical** *a.* **-ically** *adv.* **-ize** *v.t.* to stand for, or represent. **-ism** *n.* representation by symbols; system of symbols. **-ist** *n.* one who uses symbols.

sym•me•try *n.* due proportion between several parts of object. **symmetric, symmetrical** *a.* **symmetricalness** *n.* **symmetrize** *v.t.*

sym•pa•thy *n.* fellow feeling, esp. feeling for another person in pain or grief; compassion or pity. **sympathetic(al)** *a.* **sympathetically** *adv.* **sympathize** *v.i.* **sympathizer** *n.*

sym•pho•ny *n.* *(Mus.)* composition for full orchestra. **symphonic** *a.* **symphonist** *n.* composer of symphonies.

sym•po•si•um *n.* gathering, esp. one at which interchange or discussion of ideas takes place. *pl.* **symposia.**

symp•tom *n.* *(Med.)* perceptible change in body or its functions, which indicates disease. **-atic, -atical** *a.*

syn- *prefix,* meaning with, together, at the same time; becomes *sym-,* before *p, b,* and *m,* and *syl-* before *l.*

syn•a•gogue *n.* congregation of Jews meet for worship. **synagogical** *a.*

syn•chro•nize *v.i.* to agree in time; to be simultaneous; *v.t.* to cause to occur at the same time. **synchronization** *n.* **synchronism** *n.* **synchronal** *a.* **synchronous** *a.*

syn•chro•tron *n.* scientific machine for accelerating electrons to very high speeds.

syn•co•pate *v.t.* *(Gram.)* to contract, as a word, by taking one or more sounds or syllables from middle; in music, to alter rhythm by accenting a usually unaccented note. **syncopation** *n.*

syn•cope *n.* the omission of one or more letters from the middle of a word; *(Med.)* a fainting or swooning. **syncopal,**

syncopic *a.* (See syncopate).

syn·dic *n.* legal representative chosen to act as agent for corporation or company. -ate *n.* council of syndics; body of persons associated to carry out enterprise; *v.t.* to control by a syndicate; to publish news, etc. simultaneously in several periodicals owned by one syndicate.

syn·ed·do·che *n.* (*Rhet.*) figure of speech by which the whole is put for the part, or a part for the whole. synecdochic, synecdochical *a.*

syn·od *n.* an assembly of ecclesiatus; convention or council. -al, -ic, -ical, *a.* -ically *adv.*

syn·o·nym *n.* -ous *a.* -ously *adv.*

syn·op·sis *n.* general outlook, view; summary. *pl.* synopses. synoptic, synoptical *a.* synoptically *adv.*

syn·tax *n.* rules governing sentence construction. syntactic, syntactical *a.* syntactically *adv.*

syn·the·sis *n.* combination or putting together; (*Chem.*) uniting of elements to form compound. *pl.* syntheses. synthetic, synthetical *a.* not derived from nature;

artificial. synthetically *adv.*, synthesize, synthetize *v.t.* synthesist, synthetist *n.*

syph·i·lis *n.* contagious venereal disease. syphilitic *a.*

sy·phon. See siphon.

Syr·i·a *n.* country in W. Asia. -c *n.* language of Syria. -n *n.* and *a.*

syr·inge *n.* tube and piston serving to draw in and then expel fluid; *v.t.* to inject by means of syringe Panpipe.

syr·inx *n.* (*Mus.*) (*Anat.*) the Eustachian tube; vocal organ of birds. *pl.* -ed, syringes. syringeal *a.*

syr·up, sirup *n.* fluid separated from sugar in process of refining. -y *a.*

sys·tem *n.* assemblage of objects arranged after some distinct method, usually logical or scientific; universe; organization; classification; set of doctrines or principles; the body as functional unity. -atic, -atical *a.* -atically *adv.* -atize, -ize *v.t.* to reduce to system; to arrange methodically. -atization, -ization *n.*

sys·to·le *n.* contraction of heart and arteries for expelling blood and carrying on circulation. systolic *a.*

tab n. small flap; a label.

tab•by n. stout kind of watered silk; striped cat, esp. female; a. striped; v.t. to give watered finish to, as silk.

tab•er•nac•le n. movable shelter for religious worship by Israelites; place for worship.

tab•la•ture n. painting on ceiling or wall; mental picture.

ta•ble n. smooth flat surface of wood, etc. supported by legs, as furniture for working at, or serving meals; systematic arrangement of figures, facts, as *multiplication table*; index, schedule; a. pert. to a table; v.t. to form into a catalog; to postpone for subsequent consideration. **-spoon** n. a large spoon for serving, measuring, holding ½ fluid ounce. **— tennis** n. game of indoor tennis played on a table; Ping-Pong. **-ware** n. utensils (incl. china, glass and silver) for table use.

tab•leau n. vivid representation of scene in history, literature, art, by group of persons appropriately dressed and posed.

tab•let n. anything flat on which to write; slab of stone with inscription; small, compressed solid piece of medication.

tab•loid n. illustrated newspaper, giving topical and sensational events in compressed form.

ta•boo n. system by which certain objects and persons are set aside as accursed; political, social, or religious prohibition; a. prohibited; v.t. to forbid the use of; to ostracize.

ta•bor n. small drum, like a tambourine. **-et** n. small tabor; low cushioned stool.

tab•u•lar a. having a broad, flat top; arranged systematically in rows or columns. **-ize** v.t. to tabulate. **-ly** adv. **tabulate** v.t. to form into a table, scheme or synopsis.

ta•chom•e•ter n. instrument for measurement of speed.

tac•it a. implied, but not expressed; silent. **-ly** adv. **-urn** a. reserved of speech. **-urnity** n. **-urnly** adv.

tack n. small sharp-pointed nail; long stitch; course of action; v.t. to fasten with long, loose stitches; to nail with; v.t. to change policy. **-er** n. **-iness** n. stickiness. **-y** a. sticky; viscous.

tack n. food; fore.

tack•le n. mechanism of ropes and pulleys for raising heavy weights; gear; (Football) move by player to grasp and stop opponent; v.t. to undertake; (Football) to seize and stop. **tackling** n. rigging of a ship. **— block** n. pulley.

tact n. awareness of right thing to say to avoid giving offense. **-ful** a. **-fully** adv. **-ile** a. capable of being felt; tangible. **-less** a. wanting in tact. **-ual** a. pert. to sense of touch.

tac•tics n. sing. adroit management of situation. **tactical** a. **tactically** adv. **tactician** n.

tad•pole n. young of frog in its first state before gills and tail are absorbed.

taf•fe•ta n. lightweight glossy silk of plain weave.

tag n. tie-on label; appendage; game in which one player chases and tries to touch another; v.t. to fit with tags; to add on. **-ging** pr.p. **-ged** pa.t. and pa.p.

tail n. flexible prolongation of animal's spine; back, inferior part of anything; (Aero.) group of stabilizing fins at rear of airplane; v.t. to furnish with tail; to extend in line; to trail. **-ed** a. **-less** a. **-light** n. red rear light of vehicle. **— plane** n. (Aero.) stabilizing surface at rear of aircraft.

tai•lor n. one who makes clothes; v.t. and v.i. to make men's suits, women's costumes, etc. **-ing** n. work of a tailor. **-less** a. **— made** a. plain in style and fitting perfectly.

taint v.t. to contaminate; v.i. to be infected with incipient putrefaction; n. touch of corruption.

take v.t. to grasp; to capture; to win; to photograph; v.i. to be effective; to please; to direct course of; to resort to; n. quantity of fish caught at one time; one of several movie shots of same scene; receipts. **taking** pr.p. **took** pa.t. **-n** pa.p. **taking** n. act of gaining possession; pl. cash receipts of shop, theater, etc.; a. infectious. **takingly** adv. **takingness** n. quality of being attractive.

talc n. fine, slightly perfumed powder. **-ose** a. composed of talc. **-um** n. powdered talc, as toilet powder.

tale n. narrative; false report. **-bearer** n. one who spitefully informs against another.

tal•ent n. special or outstanding ability. **-ed** a. gifted.

tal•is•man n. object endowed with magical power of protecting the wearer from harm. **-ic**, **-al** a.

talk v.t. and v.i. to converse; to speak; n. short dissertation; gossip. **-ative** a. chatty. **-atively** adv. **-ativeness**, **-er** n. **-ing** a. capable of speaking.

tall a. high in stature; lofty. **-ness** n.

tal•low n. animal fat melted down and used in manufacture of candles, etc.; v.t. to smear with tallow. **-ish** a. pasty; greasy. **-like**, **-y**, a.

tal•ly n. something on which a score is kept; identity label; v.t. to score; v.i. to agree. **tallied** pa.t. and pa.p.

Tal•mud n. collection of texts on Jewish religious law. **-ic(al)** a. **-ist** n. student of the Talmud. **-istic** a.

tal•on n. hooked claw of bird of prey. **-ed** a. having talons.

tam•bour n. small flat drum; piece of embroidery worked in metal threads on tambour.

tam•bou•rine n. round, shallow, single-sided drum with jingling metal disks, used to accompany Spanish dances.

tame a. domesticated; subdued; v.t. to domesticate. **-ability**, **tamability**, **-ableness** n. **able** a. **-ly** adv. **-ness**, **-r** n.

tam•per v.i. to meddle; to alter with malicious intent. **-er** n.

tan n. bark of oak, etc. bruised to extract tannic acid for tanning leather; yellowish-brown color; v.t. to convert skins into leather by soaking in tannic acid; *v.i.* to become sunburned. -ning *pr.p.* -ned *pa.t.* and *pa.p.* -nate *n.* (*Chem.*) salt of tannic acid. -ner *n.* one who works in tannery. -nery *n.* place where leather is made. -nic *a.* pert. to tannin. -nin *n.* now called tannic acid. -ning *n.*

tan•dem *adv.* one behind the other; *n.* a bicycle for two people.

tang *n.* a prong (of a tool) which connects with the handle; a pungent smell or taste; *v.t.* to furnish (a tool) with a tang. -ed, -y *a.*

tan•gent *n.* (*Geom.*) line which touches curve but, when produced, does not cut it; *a.* touching but not intersecting. tangency, tangence *n.* state of touching. tangential *a.* digressing. tangentially *adv.*

tan•ger•ine *n.* small sweet orange originally grown near Tangiers.

tan•gi•ble *a.* perceptible by the touch; concrete. tangibility *n.* tangibly *adv.*

tan•gle *n.* knot of raveled threads, hair; *v.t.* to form into a confused mass; to muddle.

tan•go *n.* dance of Spanish origin in two-four time.

tank *n.* large basin or reservoir for storing liquids or gas; a mechanically propelled bulletproof armored vehicle with

tank

caterpillar treads; *v.t.* to store in a tank. -age *n.* storage of water, oil, gas, in a tank. -er *n.* vessel designed to carry liquid cargo.

tan•kard *n.* large drinking vessel, with lid and handle.

tan•nin See tan.

tan•sy *n.* common perennial plant used in medicine.

tan•ta•lize *v.t.* to tease. tantalizing *a.* provocative.

tan•ta•lum *n.* (*Chem.*) rare metallic element, symbol Ta, used for filaments of electric lamps, chemical apparatus, and surgical instruments.

tan•ta•mount *a.* equivalent in significance.

tan•trum *n.* fit of bad temper.

tap *v.t.* to strike lightly; *v.i.* to strike gentle blow; *n.* a rap; *pl.* military signal for lights out; leather patch on shoe sole. -ping *pr.p.* -ped *pa.p.* — dance *n.* a dance step audibly tapped out with the feet. — dance *v.i.*

tap *n.* hole, pipe, or screw device with valve, through which liquid is drawn; *v.t.* to pierce to let fluid flow out, as from a cask, tree, etc.; (*Surg.*) to draw off fluid from body, as from lung, abdomen, etc. -ping *pr.p.* -ped *pa.p.* -per *n.* one who taps. -root *n.* the root of a plant which goes straight down into earth without dividing.

tape *n.* narrow piece of woven material used for tying, fastening clothes, etc.; strip of paper used in a printing

telegraph instrument; strip of paper marked off in units used for measuring; *v.t.* to fasten with tape; to measure. — measure *n.* strip marked in units for measuring. -worm *n.* parasite found in alimentary canal of vertebrates.

ta•per *n.* long wick for lighting candles; *v.i.* to narrow gradually toward one end; *v.t.* to cause to narrow. -ing *a.* narrowing gradually.

tap•es•try *n.* fabric covering for furniture, walls, woven by needles, not in shuttles.

tap•i•oc•ca *n.* starchy granular substance used for desserts, thickening, etc.

ta•pir *n.* ungulate mammal with piglike body and flexible proboscis.

tapir

ta•pis *n.* carpeting.

tar *n.* black viscid liquid, used for waterproofing, road-laying; *v.t.* to cover, or treat with tar. -ring *pr.p.* -red *pa.t.* and *pa.p.* -ry *a.* pert. to, or smelling of, tar.

ta•ran•tu•la *n.* large, hairy, venomous spider.

tar•dy *a.* slow; late. tardily *adv.* tardiness *n.*

tare *n.* plant grown for fodder; a weed.

tar•get *n.* mark to aim at in shooting, esp. flat circular board with series of concentric circles; object of attack.

tar•iff *n.* list of goods (imports and exports) on which duty is payable; the duty imposed.

tar•nish *v.t.* to lessen luster of; to sully, as one's reputation; *v.i.* to become dull.

ta•ro *n.* plant of Pacific islands, cultivated for edible leaves and root.

tar•pau•lin *n.* canvas sheet treated with tar to make it waterproof.

tar•pon *n.* large edible fish of herring family.

tar•ra•gon *n.* perennial herb cultivated for its aromatic leaves.

tar•ry *v.i.* to linger; to stay behind.

tar•sus *n.* ankle. *pl.* tarsi. tarsal *a.*

tart *a.* sour to taste; acid. -ish *a.* rather sour. -ly *adv.* -ness *n.*

tart *n.* small pastry cup containing fruit.

tar•tan *n.* woolen cloth of colored plaids, each genuine Scottish clan possessing its own pattern; *a.* made of tartan.

tar•tar *n.* crust deposited in wine cask during fermentation; acid incrustation on teeth. -ous *a.* containing tartar. -ic *a.* pert. to, or obtained from, tartar. tartrate *n.* a salt of tartaric acid. cream of tartar, purified form of tartar used medicinally and as raising agent in baking.

task *n.* specific amount of work apportioned and imposed by another; *v.t.* to impose task on; to exact. -er *n.* — force *n.* body of soldiers sent to do specific operation. -master *n.* overseer.

Tass *n.* official news agency of the U.S.S.R.

tas•sel *n.* ornamental fringed knot of silk,

wool. -ed *a.*

taste *v.t.* to perceive by tongue or palate; *v.i.* to eat or drink very small quantity; to have specific flavor; *n.* one of five senses; aesthetic appreciation; small amount. **-ful** *a.* having or showing good taste. **-fully** *adv.* **-fulness** *n.* **-less** *a.* insipid. **-lessly** *adv.* **-lessness** *n.* **-r** *n.* one whose palate is trained to discern subtle differences in flavor. **tastily** *adv.* with good taste. **tasty** *a.* savory.

tat•ter *n.* rag; shred of cloth hanging loosely; *v.t.* and *v.i.* to hang in tatters. **-demalion** *n.* ragged fellow. **-ed, -y** *a.*

tat•tle *v.i.* to tell a secret; *n.* chatter. **-r** *n.*

tat•too *v.t.* to prick colored designs, initials, into skin with indelible inks; *n.* such design. **-er** *n.*

taught *pa.t.* and *pa.p.* of verb **teach.**

taunt *v.t.* to reproach with insulting words; *n.* sarcastic remark. **-er** *n.* **-ing** *a.*

Tau•rus *n.* bull, 2nd sign of zodiac, which sun enters about April 21st. **taurian** *a.* pert. to a bull. **taurine** *a.* bovine.

taut *a.* fully stretched. **-en** *v.t.* to make tight or tense. **-ness** *n.*

tau•tol•o•gy *n.* repetition of same idea in different words in same sentence. **tautological** *a.* **tautologically** *adv.* **tautologism** *n.* superfluous use of words.

tav•ern *n.* licensed house for sale of liquor; inn.

taw *n.* large marble for children's game.

taw•dry *a.* showy but cheap. **tawdrily** *adv.* **tawdriness** *n.*

taw•ny *a.* of yellow-brown color. **tawniness** *n.*

tax *n.* levy imposed by state on income, property; *v.t.* to impose tax on; to subject to strain. **-able** *a.* **-ness, -ability** *n.* **-ably** *adv.* **-ation** *n.* act of levying taxes; assessing of bill of costs.

tax•i *n.* (*abbrev. of* **taximeter cab**) automobile for hire, fitted with a taximeter; *v.i.* to travel by taxi. **-ing** *pr.p.* **-ed** *pa.p.* **-cab** *n.* automobile for public hire. **— driver, -man** *n.* **-meter** *n.* instrument which automatically registers mileage and corresponding fare of journey by taxi.

tax•i•der•my *n.* art of preserving pelts of animals and stuffing them for exhibition. **taxidermist** *n.* **taxidermal, taxidermic** *a.*

tea *n.* dried and prepared leaves of tea plant, native to China and Japan; infusion of dry tea in boiling water. **-spoon** *n.* small spoon used with teacup. **-spoonful** *n.* ⅓ tablespoon.

teach *v.t.* to impart knowledge of; *v.i.* to follow profession of a teacher. **taught** *pa.t.* and *pa.p.* **-ability** *n.* **-able** *a.* capable of being taught; willing to learn. **-ableness** *n.* **-er** *n.* one who instructs.

teak *n.* tree of E. Indies yielding very durable timber.

team *n.* people working together for common purpose; side of players in game, as *football team.* **-ster** *n.* one who drives a truck as an occupation. **-work** *n.* cooperation among members of a group.

tear *n.* small drop of fluid appearing in and flowing from eyes, due to emotion; *pl.*

sorrow. **-drop** *n.* tear. **-ful** *a.* weeping. **-fully** *adv.* **-fulness** *n.* **— gas** *n.* irritant gas causing abnormal watering of eyes and temporary blindness. **-less** *a.* dry-eyed.

tear *v.t.* to pull apart forcibly; *v.i.* to become ragged; *n.* fissure. **-ing** *pr.p.* **tore** *pa.t.* **torn** *pa.p.* **-er** *n.*

tease *v.t.* to annoy in fun; to chaff. **-r** *n.* **teasing** *a.*

teat *n.* nipple of female breast.

tech•ni•cal *a.* pert. to mechanical arts; connected with particular science; accurately defined. **-ity** *n.* term peculiar to specific art; point of procedure. **-ly** *adv.* **-ness** *n.* **technician** *n.* expert in particular branch of knowledge. **technics** *n.pl.* industrial arts. **technique** *n.* skill acquired by thorough mastery of subject. **technological** *a.* pert. to technology. **technologically** *adv.* **technologist** *n.* **technology** *n.* science of mechanical and industrial arts, as contrasted with fine arts.

te•di•ous *a.* wearisome; irksome. **-ness** *n.* **-ly** *adv.* **tedium** *n.* wearisomeness.

tee *n.* wooden peg, etc. on which golf ball is placed for first drive of each hole; *v.t.* to place (ball) on tee.

teem *v.i.* to bring forth, as animal; to be stocked to overflowing. **-ing** *a.* prolific.

teens *n.pl.* the years of one's age, thir*teen* through nine*teen.* **-ager** *n.* a young person of this age.

teeth. See **tooth.**

teeth•ing *n.* the process, in babyhood, of cutting the first teeth. **teethe** *v.i.* to cut the first teeth.

tee•to•tal *a.* pert. to teetotalism; abstemious. **-er** *n.* one who abstains from intoxicating liquors. **-ism** *n.*

teg•u•ment *n.* covering, esp. of living body. **-al, -ary** *a.*

tel•e•cast *v.i.* to transmit program by television.

tel•e•gram *n.* message sent by telegraph. **-mic** *a.*

tel•e•graph *n.* electrical apparatus for transmitting messages by code to a distance; a message so sent; *v.i.* to send a message by telegraph. **-er, -ist** *n.* one who operates telegraph. **-ic(al)** *a.* **-ically** *adv.* **-y** *n.* electrical transmission of messages to a distance.

tel•e•ol•o•gy *n.* science of final causes. **teleological** *a.* **teleologically** *adv.* **teleologist** *n.*

te•lep•a•thy *n.* occult communication of facts, feelings, impressions between mind and mind at a distance. **telepathic** *a.*

tel•e•phone *n.* electrical instrument by which sound is transmitted and reproduced at a distance; *v.t.* and *v.i.* to communicate by telephone. **telephonic** *a.* **telephonically** *adv.* **telephony** *n.* process of operating telephone.

tel•e•pho•to *a.* pert. to a camera lens which makes distant objects appear close.

Tel•e•Promp•Ter *n.* in television, a device to enable the speaker to refer to his script out of sight of the cameras, giving viewers the impression of a talk without script.

tel·e·scope n. optical instrument for magnifying distant objects; v.i. to be impacted violently, as cars in railway collision. **telescopical** a. pert. to a telescope.

Tel·e·type n. automatically printed telegram.

tel·e·vi·sion n. transmission of scenes, persons, etc. at a distance by means of electromagnetic radio waves. **televise** v.t.

tell v.t. to recount or narrate; v.i. to produce marked effect; to report. **told** pa.t. and pa.p. **-er** n. bank clerk who pays out money; enumerator. **-ing** a. striking. **-ingly** adv. **-tale** n. one who betrays confidence; a. warning.

te·mer·i·ty n. rashness; audacity.

tem·per v.t. to mingle in due proportion; to moderate; n. consistency required and achieved by tempering; attitude of mind; irritation. **-ed** a. having a certain consistency, as clay, or degree of toughness, as steel; having a certain disposition. **-edly** adv. **-ing** n. **-er** n.

tem·per·a n. process of painting using pigments mixed with size, casein, or egg instead of oil.

tem·per·a·ment n. physical, moral and mental constitution peculiar to individuals. **-al** a. liable to moods. **-ally** adv.

tem·per·ance n. moderation; sobriety.

tem·per·ate a. moderate; not extreme. **-ly** adv. **-ness** n. **temperative** a. **temperature** n. degree of heat or cold of atmosphere or of a human or living body; fevered condition. — **zones** n. areas of earth between polar circles and tropics.

tem·pest n. violent commotion. **-uous** a. violent. **-uously** adv. **-uousness** n.

tem·ple n. place of worship.

tem·ple n. part of forehead between outer end of eye and hair. **temporal** a.

tem·po n. degree of speed at which passage should be played or sung.

tem·po·ral a. pert. to time or to this life; secular. **-ity** n. concept of time; pl. material possessions, esp. ecclesiastical revenues. **-ly** adv. **temporariness** n. **temporarily** adv. only for a time. **temporary** a. fleeting. **temporization** n. **temporize** v.i. to hedge; to compromise. **temporizer** n. **temporizing** n.

tempt v.t. to entice. **-ation** n. inducement to do evil. **-er** n. one who tempts, esp. Satan. **-ing** a. seductive. **-ingly** adv. **-ingness** n.

ten a. one more than nine; n. the number nine and one; the symbol representing this, as 10 or X. **-fold** a. ten times repeated; adv. ten times as much. **-th** a. being one of ten equal divisions of anything; n. tenth part of anything; tithe. **-thly** adv.

ten·a·ble a. capable of being held, logically maintained. **-ness, tenability** n.

te·na·cious a. holding fast; pertinacious. **-ly** adv. **-ness, tenacity** n.

ten·ant n. one who occupies property for which he pays rent; v.i. to occupy as tenant. **tenancy** n. act of holding property

as tenant; property held by tenant. **-able** a. fit for occupation. **-ry** n. tenants collectively on estate.

tend v.i. to hold a course; to have a bias. **-ency** n. inclination. **-entious** a. (of writings) having a biased outlook.

tend v.t. to minster to. **-er** n. one who tends; small vessel supplying larger one with stores, or landing passengers.

ten·der v.t. to offer for acceptance; n. an offer, esp. contract to undertake specific work, or to supply goods at fixed rate.

ten·der a. expressive of gentler passions; considerate; not tough (of meat).

ten·der·loin n. choice cut of meat between loin and ribs.

ten·don n. a tough fibrous cord attaching muscle to bone. **tendinous** a.

ten·dril n. spiral shoot of climbing plant by which it clings to another body for support; curl, as of hair. **-lar, -ous** a.

ten·e·brous a. dark; obscure. **tenebrosity** n.

ten·e·ment n. building divided into separate apartments, of very poor quality, and let to different tenants. **-al, -ary** a.

te·net n. any opinion or principle which a person holds as true.

ten·nis n. game for two or four players, played on a court by striking a ball with rackets, across a net. — **court** for specially marked enclosed court for tennis.

ten·or n. (Mus.) highest male adult voice; one who sings tenor; a. pert. to tenor voice.

tense n.. (Gram.) form of verb which indicates time of action, as present, past or future tense.

tense a. strained almost to breaking point; unrelaxed. **-ly** adv. **-ness** n. **tensibility, -ness** n. the quality of being tensile. **tensible, tensile** a. capable of being subjected to stress. **tension** n. strain; a state of being nervously excited or overwrought.

tent n. portable canvas shelter stretched and supported by poles and firmly pegged ropes; v.i. to pitch tent. **-ed** a. covered with tents.

ten·ta·cle n. long flexible appendage of head or mouth in many lower animals for exploring, touching, grasping; feeler. **tentacular** a. **—like** a.

ten·ta·tive a. experimental; done as a trial. **-ly** adv.

ten·ter n. machine for stretching cloth by means of hooks; v.t. to stretch on hooks. **-hook** n. one of the sharp hooks stretched on a tenter.

te·nu·i·ty n. thinness. **tenuous** a. slender; unsubstanial. **tenuously** adv. **tenuousness** n.

ten·ure n. holding of office, property.

te·pee n. Indian wigwam.

tep·e·fy v.t. to make moderately warm. **tepefaction** n.

tep·id a. moderately warm; lukewarm. **-ity, -ness** n.

ter·cen·te·na·ry n. the 300th anniversary of an event; a. pert. to a period of 300 years.

ter·cet n. (Mus.) triplet; (Pros.) group of three lines or verses.

ter·gi·ver·sate v.i. to make use of subterfuges; to be vacillating. **tergiversation, tergiversator** n.

term n. limit, esp. of time; expression with specific meaning; (Math.) member of compound quantity; pl. stipulation; v.t. to call. **-inological** a. pert. to terminology. **-inologically** adv. **-inologist** n. **-inology** n. technical words; nomenclature.

ter·mi·nate v.t. to set limit to; to end; v.i. to finish. **terminable** a. liable to cease. **terminal** n. extremity; a. pert. to end; occurring in, or, at end of, a term; (Bot.) growing at tip. **terminally** adv. **termination** n. conclusion; ending of word. **terminational** a. **terminative** a. **terminatively** adv. **terminus** n. farthest limit; railway station, airport, at end of line; pl. **termini, -es.**

ter·mite n. insect, very destructive to wood.

tern n. seabird allied to gull.

tern n. that which consists of three; a. threefold. **-al, -ary** a. consisting of three; (Chem.) comprising three elements, etc. **-ate** a. (Bot.) having three leaflets. **-ion** n. group of three.

Terp·sich·o·re n. (Myth.) Muse of choral song and dancing. **terpsichorean** a. pert. to dancing.

ter·ra n. earth as in various Latin phrases. **— cotta** n. reddish, brick-like earthenware, porous and unglazed. **-nean** a. belonging to surface of earth. **-neous** a. growing on land. **-queous** a. comprising both land and water, as the globe.

ter·race n. level shelf of earth, natural or artificial; flat roof used for open-air activities; v.t. to form into terraces.

ter·rain n. tract of land, considered for suitability for various purposes.

ter·ra·pin n. edible tortoise found in eastern U.S.

ter·res·tri·al a. pert. to earth; earthly, as opp. to celestial; n. inhabitant of earth.

ter·ri·ble a. frightful; formidable. **-ness** n. **terribly** adv.

ter·ri·er n. breed of small or medium-sized dog, originally trained for hunting foxes, badgers, etc.

ter·ri·fy v.t. to frighten greatly; to inspire with terror. **terrified** pa.t. **terrific** a. causing alarm. **terrifically** adv.

ter·ri·to·ry n. part of country which has not yet attained political independence. **territorial** a. limited to certain district. **territoriality** n.

ter·ror n. extreme fear; one who causes terror. **-ization** n. **-ize** v.t. to rule by intimidation. **-izer** n. **-ism** n. mass-organized ruthlessness. **-ist** n. one who rules by terror.

ter·ry cloth n. cotton fabric with pile of uncut loops on both sides.

terse a. (of speech, writing) concise; brief. **-ly** adv. **-ness** n.

ter·tian a. (Med.) occurring every other day; n. fever, with paroxysms occurring at intervals of forty-eight hours.

ter·ti·ar·y a. of third formation or rank; (Geol.) (Cap.) pert. to era of rock formation following Mezozoic; n. (Geol.) (Cap.) the Tertiary era.

test n. critical examination; substance used to analyze compound into its several constituents; v.i. to make critical examination of; (Chem.) to analyze properties of a compound. **— case** n. (Law) case tried for purpose of establishing a precedent. **-er** n. **-ing** n. and a. demanding endurance. **— paper** n. examination paper; litmus paper used to test acid or alkaline content of chemical solution. **— tube** n. glass tube rounded and closed at one end, used in chemical tests.

tes·ta·ment n. solemn declaration of one's will; one of the two great divisions of the Bible, as the Old Testament, or the New Testament. **-al -ary** a. pert. to testament or will; bestowed by will.

tes·tate a. having left a valid will. **testacy** n. state of being testate. **testator** n. one who leaves a will.

tes·ti·cle n. one of the two male reproductive glands. **testicular** a. **testiculate, -d** a. having testicles; resembling testicle in shape. **testis** n. a testicle; pl. **testes**

tes·ti·fy v.i. to bear witness; to give evidence upon oath; v.t. to manifest. **testifier** n.

tes·ti·mo·ny n. solemn affirmation; proof of some fact; in Scripture, the two tables of the law; divine revelation as a whole. **testimonial** a. containing testimony; n. written declaration testifying to character and qualities of person, esp. of applicant for a position.

tes·ty a. fretful; irascible.

tet·a·nus n. a disease in which a virus causes spasms of violent muscular contraction; lockjaw. **tetanic** a.

tetch·y a. peevish; fretful. **techily** adv. Also **techy.**

teth·er n. rope fastened to grazing animal to keep it from straying; v.t. to restrict movements of.

tet·rad n. group of four things.

tet·ra·gon n. a plane figure, having four angles. **-al** a.

tet·ra·gram n. (Geom.) figure formed by four right angles.

tet·ra·he·dron n. solid figure enclosed by four traingles. **tetrahedral** a.

te·tral·o·gy n. group of four dramas, connected by some central character.

tet·ter n. skin disease; ringworm; v.t. to affect with this. **-ous** a.

Teu·ton n. member of one of Germanic tribes. **-ic** a. pert. to Teutons or their language.

text n. original words of author, orator; passage of Scripture chosen as theme of sermon. **-book** n. manual of instruction. **-ual** a. based on actual wording; literal. **-ually** adv.

tex·tile a. capable of being woven; n. fabric made on loom.

tex·ture n. quality of surface of a woven material; that which is woven.

T

tha•las•sic *a.* pert. to the sea; living in the sea.

thal•lus simple plant organism which shows little or no differentiation into leaves, stem, or root as in *fungi, algae,* etc. *pl.* thalli.

than *conj.* introducing adverbial clause of comparison and occurring after comparative form of an adjective or adverb.

thank *v.t.* to express gratitude to; *n.* expression of gratitude (usually in *pl.*). -fulness *n.* -less *a.* unappreciated by others. -lessly *adv.* -lessness *n.* -sgiving *n.* service held as expression of thanks for Divine goodness.

that *demons. pron.* or *a.* (*pl.* those) pointing out a person or thing, or referring to something already mentioned; *rel. pron.* who or which; *conj.* introducing a noun clause, adjective clause, or adverbial clause of purpose, result, reason.

thatch *n.* straw, rushes, used to roof cottage; *v.t.* to roof with thatch. -er, -ing *n.*

thaw *v.t.* to cause to melt by increasing temperature; *n.* melting of ice or snow.

the *a.* or *def. ar.,* placed before nouns, and used to specify general conception, or to denote particular person or thing; *adv.* by that amount.

the•ar•chy *n.* government by gods. thearchic *a.*

the•a•ter *n.* building for plays or motion pictures; field of military, naval operations. theatrical *a.* theatrically *adv.* theatricals *n.pl.* dramatic performances, esp. by amateurs.

theft *n.* act of stealing.

their *a.* and *pron.* of them; *poss. case* of they. -s *poss. pron.* form of their used absolutely.

the•ism *n.* belief in existence of personal God who actively manifests Himself in world. theist *n.* theistical *a.*

them *pron.* ob. and dat. case of they.

theme *n.* subject of writing, or discussion; (*Mus.*) groundwork melody recurring at intervals and with variations. thematic *a.* thematically *adv.* — song *n.* recurring melody in play, film.

them•selves *pron. pl.* of himself, herself, and itself; emphatic form of them or they; reflexive form of them.

then *adv.* at that time (past or future); immediately afterwards; in consequence of; *conj.* moreover; *a.* acting at particular time.

thence *adv.* from that place; from that time; for that reason. -forth *adv.* from that time on.

the•oc•ra•cy *n.* government professedly in the name of God; government by priests. theocrat, theocratist *n.* ruler under this system. theocratical *a.* theocratically *adv.*

the•od•o•lite *n.* instrument for measuring angles, used in surveying.

the•ol•o•gy *n.* science of facts and phenomena of religion, relations between God and man. theologian *n.* one learned in theology. theological *a.* pert. to theology. theologically *adv.* theologize

v.t. to theorize upon theological matters. theologist *n.*

the•oph•a•ny *n.* manifestation of God to men, in human form. theophanic *a.*

the•o•rem *n.* established principle; (*Math.*) propostion to be proved by logical reasoning. -atic, -atical *a.*

the•o•ry *n.* supposition put forward to explain something; speculation. theoretical *a.* speculative as opp. to *practical.* theoretics *n.pl.* speculative side of science. theorize *v.t.* to speculate. theorizer, theorist *n.* theorization *n.*

ther•a•peu•tic *a.* pert. to healing. -ally *adv.* -s *n.* branch of medicine concerned with treatment and cure of diseases. therapeutist *n.*

ther•a•py *n.* remedial treatment.

there *adv.* in that place; an introductory adverb; *interj.* expressing surprise. -after *adv.* after that time. -by *adv.* in consequence. -fore *conj.* and *adv.* accordingly. -of *adv.* of that or this. -to *adv.* to that or this. -upon *adv.* upon that or this; immediately.

therm *n.* a unit of heat; unit of 1.000 large calories. -al *a.* pert. to heat. -ic *a.* caused by heat.

therm•i•on *n.* positively or negatively charged particle emitted from incandescent substance. -ic *a.* pert. to thermions. -ics *n.* branch of science dealing with thermions.

ther•mo•chem•is•try *n.* branch of science which deals with heat in relation to chemical processes.

ther•mo•dy•nam•ics *n.* branch of science which deals with the conversion of heat into mechanical energy.

ther•mo•e•lec•tric•i•ty *n.* electricity developed by action of heat alone on two different metals. thermoelectrical *a.*

ther•mo•gen•e•sis *n.* production of heat, esp. in body. thermogenetic, thermogenic *a.*

ther•mom•e•ter *n.* instrument for measuring temperature, usually consisting of graduated and sealed glass tube with bulb containing mercury. thermometrical *a.* thermometrically *adv.* thermometry *n.*

ther•mo•pile *n.* instrument for measuring minute variations in temperature.

Ther•mos *n.* double-walled bottle which substantially retains temperature of liquids by the device of surrounding interior vessel with a vacuum jacket.

ther•mo•scope *n.* instrument for detecting fluctuations in temperature without actual measurement.

ther•mo•stat *n.* instrument which controls temperature automatically. -ic *a.* -ics *n.* science dealing with equilibrium of heat.

ther•mot•ic *a.* pert. to heat. Also -al *n.* the science of heat.

the•sau•rus *n.* treasury of knowledge; lexicon.

these *demons. a.* and *pron. pl.* of this.

the•sis *n.* dissertation. *pl.* theses. thetic *a.* dogmatic.

the•ur•gy *n.* art of working so-called miracles by supernatural agency.

theurgical *a.* **theurgically** *adv.* **theurgist** *n.*

they *pers. pron. pl.* of he, she, it; indefinitely, for a number of persons.

thi•a•mine *n.* Vitamin B, complex compound, deficiency of which causes beriberi.

thick *a.* dense; not thin; packed; *n.* thickest part; *adv.* to a considerable depth. **-en** *v.t.* to make thick; *v.i.* to become thick. **-ening** *n.* something added to thicken. **-et** *n.* dense growth of shrubs, trees, etc. **-ly** *adv.* **-ness** *n.* measurement of depth between opposite surfaces; layer.

thief *n.* (*pl.* **thieves**) one who steals the goods of another. **thieve** *v.i.* to steal. **thievery** *n.* **thievish** *a.* addicted to stealing. **thievishness** *n.*

thigh *n.* fleshy part of leg between knee and trunk.

thim•ble *n.* metal cap for tip of middle finger, in sewing. **-ful** *n.* very small amount.

thin *a.* (*comp.*) **-ner.** (*superl.*) **-nest.** having little thickness; slim; *adv.* sparsely; *v.t.* to make thin; *v.i.* to grow or become thin. **-ning** *pr.p.* **-ned** *pa.p.* and *pa.t.* **-ly** *adv.* **-ness, -ning** *n.*

thing *n.* entity; specimen; commodity; *pl.* belongings; clothes, furniture.

think *v.t.* to conceive; to surmise; to believe; *v.i.* to reason; to deliberate; to recollect. **thought** *pa.t.* and *pa.p.* **-able** *a.* **-ing** *a.* reflective; rational.

thi•o- word element used in chemistry to illustrate the replacement by sulfur of part or all of the oxygen atoms in a compound.

third *a.* forming one of three equal divisions; *n.* one of three equal parts; (*Mus.*) interval of three diatonic degrees of the scale. **— class** *a.* accommodation for passengers not traveling first or second class. **-ly** *adv.* **—rate** *a.* inferior.

thirst *n.* desire to drink; craving; *v.i.* to wish for earnestly. **-er** *n.* **-ily** *adv.* **-iness** *n.* **-y** *a.* having a desire to drink; parched; eager for.

thir•teen *a.* ten and three; *n.* symbol representing thirteen units, as 13 or XIII, **-th** *a.* being one of thirteen equal parts; *n.* one of these parts.

thir•ty *a.* three times ten; *n.* symbol representing this, as 30 or XXX. **thirtieth** *a.* being one of thirty equal parts; *n.* thirtieth part.

this *demons. pron.* and *a.* denoting a person or thing near at hand, just mentioned, or about to be mentioned.

this•tle *n.* one of the numerous prickly plants of the genus *Carduus,* with yellow or purple flowers. **thistly** *a.*

thith•er *adv.* to that place; to that point, result.

thole *v.t.* pin in gunwale of boat to keep oar in oarlock. Also **-pin.**

thong *n.* narrow strap of leather used for reins, whiplash, etc.

tho•rax *n.* chest cavity containing heart, lungs, etc. **thoracic** *a.*

thorn *n.* sharp, woody shoot on stem of tree or shrub; prickle; (*Fig.*) anything which causes trouble. **-y** *a.* prickly; beset with difficulties.

thor•ough *a.* absolute. **-bred** *a.* (of animals) purebred from pedigree stock; (of people) aristocratic; *n.* animal of pure breed. **-fare** *n.* highway. **-ly** *adv.* **-ness** *n.*

those *a.* and *pron. pl.* of **that.**

though admitting; even if; however.

thought *pa.t.* and *pa.p.* of **think.**

thought *n.* act of thinking; that which one thinks; reflection; opinion; serious consideration. **-ful** *a.* contemplative; considerate. **-fully** *adv.* **-fulness** *n.* **-less** *a.* without thought; inconsiderate. **-lessly** *adv.* **-lessness** *n.*

thou•sand *a.* consisting of ten hundred; *n.* symbol for this, 1,000 or M. **-fold** *a.* multiplied by a thousand. **-th** *a.* constituting one of thousand equal parts; *n.* thousandth part.

thrall *n.* slave; servitude. **-dom, thraldom** *n.* bondage.

thrash *v.t.* to flog; to defeat soundly. **-er** *n.* **-ing** *n.* flogging.

thra•son•i•cal *a.* bragging. **-ly** *adv.*

thread *n.* very thin twist of wool, cotton, linen, silk, etc.; filament as of gold, silver; consecutive train of thought; *v.t.* to pass thread through eye of needle. **-bare** *a.* worn away with wear; shabby. **-worm** *n.* threadlike parasitic worm often found in intestines of children. **-y** *a.*

threat *n.* declaration of determination to harm another; menace. **-en** *v.t.* to menace; to portend. **-ener** *n.* **-ening** *a.* menacing; portending.

three *a.* two and one; *n.* symbol of this sum, 3 or III. **-fold** *a.* triple. **— ply** *a.* having three layers or thicknesses; **-score** *a.* and *n.* sixty. **-some** *n.* group of three people.

thren•o•dy *n.* song of lamentation; dirge. Also **threnode. threnodial, threnodic** *a.* funereal.

thresh *v.t.* to separate grain from chaff by use of machine; to beat. **-er** *n.*

thresh•old *n.* doorsill; point of beginning.

threw *pa.t.* of **throw.**

thrice *adv.* three times; repeatedly.

thrift *n.* economical management. **-ily** *adv.* **-iness** *n.* frugality. **-less** *a.* extravagant; wasteful. **-lessly** *adv.* **-y** *a.*

thrill *n.* emotional excitement; *v.t.* to arouse tingling emotional response; *v.i.* to feel a glow of enthusiasm. **-ing** *a.* **-ingly** *adv.*

thrive *v.i.* to prosper; to develop healthily. **throve** and **-d** *pa.t.* **thriven, -d** *pa.p.* **thriving** *a.* **thrivingly** *adv.*

throat *n.* passage connecting back of mouth with lungs, stomach. **-iness** *n.* quality of having throaty voice. **-y** *a.* guttural.

throb *v.i.* to pulsate; *n.* pulsation; palpitation (of heart, etc.); beat. **-bing** *pr.p.* **-bed** *pa.t.* and *pa.p.*

throe *n.* suffering; pains of childbirth.

throm•bo•sis *n.* formation of blood clot in vein or artery.

throne *n.* royal seat; sovereign power and dignity; *v.t.* to place on royal seat; to exalt. **throning** *pr.p.* **-d** *pa.p.*

throng *n.* multitude; crowd; *v.t.* to press in crowds.

throt•tle *n.* windpipe; valve controlling

amount of vaporized fuel delivered to cylinders in internal-combustion engine; *v.i.* to choke by external pressure on windpipe; to silence; *v.i.* to pant for breath, as if suffocated.

through *prep.* from end to end of; along; by means of; as consequence of; *adv.* from one side to the other; from beginning to end; *a.* passing from one to another without stops; unobstructed. **through and through** *adv.* completely. **-ly** *(Arch.) adv.* thoroughly. **-out** *adv.* and *prep.* wholly; during entire time of.

throve *pa.t.* of **thrive.**

throw *v.t.* to fling, cast, or hurl; to send; to unseat, as of a horseman; to spread carelessly; *v.i.* to hurl; *n.* distance something can be thrown; light blanket. **-ing** *pr.p.* **threw** *pa.t.* **-n** *pa.p.* **-er** *n.* **-n** *a.*

thrum *n.* fringe of threads left on loom after web is cut off.

thrum *v.t.* to strum on instrument; to drum with fingers. **-ming** *pr.p.* **-med** *pa.p.* and *pa.t.*

thrush *n.* songbird.

thrush *n. (Med.)* inflammatory disease affecting mouth, tongue and lips, commonly found in young children.

thrust *v.t.* to drive with sudden force; *v.i.* to make a push; to attack with a pointed weapon; *n.* assault; stress acting horizontally, as in machinery. **thrust** *pa.t.* and *pa.p.* **-er** *n.*

thud *n.* dull sound made by heavy fall; *v.i.* to make sound of thud.

thug *n.* ruffian; gangster. **-gery** *n.*

thumb *n.* short, thick finger of human hand; *v.t.* to manipulate awkwardly. **-ed** *a.* having thumbs; soiled with thumb marks. **-less** *a.* **-like** *a.* **-nail** *n.* nail on human thumb. **-nail sketch,** miniature; succinct description.

thump *n.* sudden fall of heavy weight; *v.t.* to beat with something heavy; *v.i.* to fall with a thud. **-er** *n.* **-ing** *a.* very large.

thun·der *n.* rumbling sound which follows lightning flash; *v.t.* to rage with loud voice; *v.i.* to roar. **-bolt** *n.* flash of lightning followed by peal of thunder. **-clap** *n.* a peal of thunder. **-ing** *n.* thunder; booming, as of guns; *a.* making a loud noise. **-ous** *a.* **-ously** *adv.* **-storm** *n.* storm of thunder and lightning with torrential rain. **-struck** *a.* speechless with amazement. **-y** *a.*

thu·ri·ble *n.* a metal censer.

Thurs·day *n.* fifth day of week, after *Thor,* Scandinavian god of thunder.

thus *adv.* in this or that manner; to this extent; so; in this wise. **— far,** so far.

thwack *v.t.* to flog; *n.* a hard slap.

thwart *a.* lying across; *v.t.* to hinder; to frustrate; *n.* seat athwart a rowboat; *adv.* and *prep.* across. **-er** *n.* **-ing** *a.*

thyme *n.* small flowering shrub cultivated for its aromatic leaves for flavoring in cookery.

thy·mus *n.* small ductless gland in upper part of the chest.

thy·roid *a.* signifying cartilage of a gland of trachea. **— gland,** ductless gland situated in neck on either side of trachea,

secreting hormone which profoundly affects physique and temperament of human beings.

ti·ar·a *n.* gem-studded coronet worn by ladies.

tib·i·a *n.* shinbone; inner, larger of two bones of leg, between knee and ankle. *pl.* **-s, tibiae. -l** *a.*

tic *n.* spasmodic twitching of muscle, esp. of face.

tick *n.* a parasitic bloodsucking insect.

tick *n.* cover of mattress, pillow, etc. **-ing** *n.* specially strong material used for mattress covers.

tick *v.i.* to make small, recurring, clicking sound; *n.* sound made by watch. **-er** *n.* anything which ticks regularly.

tick *v.t.* to dot lightly; *n.* small mark placed after word, entry.

tick·et *n.* piece of paper entitling admission to anything, to travel by public transport; *(U.S.)* list of candidates in an election; *v.t.* to mark with ticket. **season ticket** *n.* ticket entitling holder to attend a series of concerts, lectures, etc.

tick·le *v.t.* to touch skin lightly to excite nerves and cause laughter; *v.i.* to feel sensation of tickling; to be gratified. **-r** *n.* **ticklish** *a.* easily tickled; requiring skillful handling. **ticklishly** *adv.* **ticklishness** *n.*

tid·bit *n.* choice morsel.

tid·dly·winks *n.pl.* game in which players try to snap small disks into cup.

tide *n.* time; periodical rise and fall of ocean due to attraction of moon and sun; *(Fig.)* trend. **tidal** *a.* pert. to tide. **tidal basin** *n.* harbor which is affected by tides. **tidal wave** *n.* mountainous wave as caused by earthquake, atom bomb explosion, etc. **-less** *a.* having no tides. **ebb** or **low tide** *n.* the falling level of the sea. **flood** or **high tide** *n.* the rising level of the sea.

tid·ings *n.pl.* news; information.

ti·dy *a.* neat; orderly; *n.* chair-back cover; *v.t.* to put in order.

tie *v.t.* to fasten by rope, string, etc.; to fashion into knot; to bind together, by connecting piece of wood or metal; *v.t.* *(Sport)* to make equal score, etc.; *n.* knot; necktie; connecting link; equality of score; traverse supports for railroad tracks. **tying** *pr.p.* **tied** *pa.t.* and *pa.p.* **— beam** *n.* horizontal timber connecting two rafters. **-r** *n.*

tier *n.* row when two or more rows are arranged behind and above the other.

tierce *n.* cask containing third of pipe or 42 wine gallons; in fencing, particular thrust (third position).

tiff *n.* slight quarrel; *v.i.* to quarrel.

ti·ger *n.* fierce carnivorous quadruped of cat tribe, with tawny black-striped coat. **— cat** *n.* wildcat; ocelot or margay.

tight *a.* compressed; not leaky; fitting close to body; *adv.* firmly. **-en** *v.t.* to make tighter; to make taut; *v.i.* to become tight. **-ener** *n.* **-ly** *adv.* **-ness** *n.* **-rope** *n.* a strong, taut rope, or steel wire on which acrobats perform. **-s** *n.pl.* close-fitting woven hose and trunks worn by acrobats, dancers, etc.

tile *n.* a thin piece of slate, plastic, asphalt, used for roofs, walls, floors, drains; *v.t.* to cover with tiles. -r *n.* **tiling** *n.*

till *n.* a cash register.

till *prep.* until; *conj.* to the time when.

till *v.t.* to plow the soil, sow seeds, etc. -age *n.* the act of preparing soil for cultivation; the cultivated land. -er *n.*

til·ler *n.* a bar used as a lever, for turning a rudder.

tilt *v.t.* to raise one end of; *v.i.* to slant; *n.* inclination. -er *n.* — **hammer** *n.* a heavy hammer used in ironworks and tilted by a lever.

tilt *n.* canvas covering of a cart; *v.t.* to cover with a tilt.

tim·bal *n.* kettledrum.

tim·ber *n.* trees or wood suitable for building purposes; *v.t.* to furnish with timber. -ed *a.* -line *n.* tree line, above which altitude trees will not grow.

tim·bre *n.* special tone quality in sound of human voice or instrument.

tim·brel *n.* kind of drum.

time *n.* particular moment; period of duration; conception of past, present, and future, as sequence; opportunity; (*Mus.*) rhythmical arrangement of beats within measures or bars; *pl.* period characterized by certain marked tendencies; term indicating multiplication; *v.t.* to ascertain time taken, as by racing competetitor; (*Mus.*) to measure; *v.i.* to keep time. — **bomb** *n.* delayed-action bomb. **-keeper** *n.* one who keeps a record of men's hours of work; clock. -less *a.* eternal; unending. -lessly *adv.* -liness *n.* -ly *a.* opportune. -piece *n.* clock. -r *n.* a stopwatch. **timing** *n.* control of speed of an action or actions for greatest effect.

tim·id *a.* lacking self-confidence; shy. -ness, -ity *n.* -ly *adv.*

ti·moc·ra·cy *n.* government in which possession of property is qualification for holders of offices.

tim·pa·num *n.* kettledrum, part of percussion section of orchestra. *pl.* **timpani. timpanist, tympanist** *n.*

tin *n.* soft, whitish-gray metal, used for plating, as consituent of alloys and for food containers in canning industry; *a.* made of tin; *v.t.* to plate with tin -ning *pr.p.* -ned *pa.p.* and *pa.t.* -foil *n.* wafer-thin sheets of tin. -ned *a.* preserved in a tin. -ning *n.* -ny *a.* making a sound like tin when struck. -type *n.* (*Photog.*) ferrotype; positive on varnished tinplate. -ware *n.* utensils, etc. made of tinplate.

tinc·ture *n.* tinge of color; (*Pharm.*) solution of a substance in alcohol; *v.t.* to affect to a small degree.

tin·der *n.* anything inflammable used for kindling fire from a spark.

tine *n.* prong of fork; branch of deer's antler.

ting *n.* sharp, ringing sound, as of bell; *v.t.* and *v.i.* to tinkle.

tinge *v.t.* to color or flavor slightly; *n.* a faint touch.

tin·gle *v.i.* to feel faint prickling sensation; *n.* pricking sensation.

tin·ker *n.* mender of pots, kettles, who travels around countryside; jack-of-all trades; *v.i.* to attempt to mend.

tin·kle *v.t.* to cause to make small, quick, metallic sounds; *v.i.* to jingle; *n.* small, sharp, ringing sound. **tinkling** *n.* **tinkly** *a.*

tin·sel *n.* very thin, glittering, metallic strips for decorations; *a.* showy and cheap; *v.t.* to decorate with tinsel; to make gaudy. -ly *a.*

tint *n.* hue or dye; color with admixture of white; *v.t.* to give faint coloring to; to tinge. -er *n.*

ti·ny *a.* very small; diminutive.

tip *n.* point of anything slender; end; *v.t.* to form a point on. -ping *pr.p.* -ped *pa.p.* -toe *adv.* on tips of toes; *v.t.* to walk stealthily.

tip *v.t.* to tilt; to weigh down, as scales; to recompense with small gratuity; *n.* light stroke; advice; gratuity. -ping *n.*

tip·ple *v.i.* to drink small quantities of intoxicating liquor frequently; *n.* strong drink. -r *n.*

tip·sy *a.* intoxicated; staggering. -tipsily *adv.* tipsiness *n.*

ti·rade *n.* long denunciatory speech; volley of abuse.

tire *v.t.* to fatigue; *v.i.* to become wearied, impatient. -d *a.* wearied; bored. -dness *n.* -less *a.* -lessly *adv.* -some *a.*

tire *n.* hoop of iron, rubber, or rubber tube, placed around a wheel.

tis·sue *n.* (*Biol.*) cellular structures which make up various organs of plant or animal body; fine cloth interwoven with gold or silver; *a.* made of tissue. -d *a.* made of tissue. — **paper** *n.* very thin, white or colored semi-transparent paper.

tit *n.* teat.

tithe *n.* orig. tenth part of produce of land and cattle given to the church, later paid in form of tax; small portion; *v.t.* to levy a tithe; *v.i.* to give a tithe. -r *n.* -less *a.*

ti·tian *a.* rich auburn; color of hair in many portraits by Titian, Italian painter.

tit·il·late *v.t.* to tickle, usually in sense of stimulating mind, palate, etc. — **titillation** *n.* any pleasurable sensation. **titillative** *a.*

ti·tle *n.* designation; appellation denoting rank or office; just claim or right; title deed. -d *a.* having title, esp. aristocratic title. — **deed** *n.* document giving proof of legal ownership of property. — **page** *n.* page of book on which is inscribed name of book, author and publication data. — **role** *n.* part in play from which it takes its name.

tit·mouse *n.* small bird which builds in holes of trees. *pl.* **titmice.**

titmouse

ti‧trate *v.t.* to determine amount of ingredient in solution by adding quantities of standard solution until required chemical reaction is observed. **titration** *n.*

tit‧ter *v.i.* to give smothered laugh; *n.* such a laugh. **-er** *n.*

tit‧tle *n.* minute particle; jot.

tit‧u‧lar *a.* pert. to a title; ruling in name but not in deed. **-ity** *n.* **-y** *a.* titular; *n.* nominal holder of title.

to *prep.* expressing motion towards; as far as; compared with; preceding infinitive mood of the verb; *adv.* forward.

toad *n.* amphibian resembling frog, but brownish with dry warty skin and short legs. **-stool** *n.* fungus resembling mushroom, but poisonous. **-y** *n.* obsequious flatterer; *v.i.* to fawn on. **-ying** *pr.p.* **-ied** *pa.t.* and *pa.p.* **-yish** *a.* **-yism** *n.* sycophancy.

toast *v.t.* to warm by exposure to fire; to crisp and brown (as bread) before fire, under grill; to drink in honor of; *v.i.* to drink a toast; *n.* slice of bread crisped and browned by heat; person in whose honor toast is drunk; the drink itself. **-er** *n.* **-master** *n.* one who presides at luncheon or dinner, proposes toasts, introduces speakers, etc.

to‧bac‧co *n.* plant, dried leaves of which are used for chewing, smoking, or as snuff. *pl.* **-s, -es**

to‧bog‧gan *n.* flat-bottomed sled used for coasting down snow-clad hill slopes; *v.i.* to slide down hills on toboggan. **-ing** *n.*

to‧by *n.* small jug in shape of an old man wearing a three-cornered hat.

to‧day *n.* this day; present time; *adv.* on this day; at the present time.

tod‧dle *v.i.* to walk with short, hesitating steps; *n.* unsteady gait. **-r** *n.* child just learning to walk.

tod‧dy *n.* drink of whisky, sugar, and hot water.

toe *n.* one of five small digits of foot; part of boot, shoe, or stocking covering toes; *v.t.* to reach with toe; *v.i.* to tap with toes. **-d** *a.* having toes.

tof‧fee, tof‧fy *n.* hard candy made of sugar, butter, flavoring, etc. boiled together. Also **taffy.**

to‧geth‧er *adv.* in company; in or into union; simultaneously.

toil *v.i.* to labor; *n.* exhausting labor; task. **-er** *n.* **-ful, -some** *a.* laborious. **-somely** *adv.* **-someness** *n.*

toi‧let *n.* process of dressing; a lavatory. **— articles** *n.pl.* objects used in dressing, as comb, brush, mirror, toothbrush, etc. **— paper** *n.* thin paper for lavatory use. **— powder** *n.* talcum powder.

to‧ken *n.* symbol; concrete expression of esteem; coin-like piece of metal for special use, as *bus token, etc.* **— payment** *n.* deposit paid as token of later payment of full debt.

told *pa.t.* and *pa.p.* of verb tell.

tol‧er‧ate *v.t.* to put up with. **tolerable** *a.* endurable; passably good. **tolerability, tolerableness** *n.* **tolerably** *adv.* **tolerance** *n.* forbearance. **tolerant** *a.* broad-minded.

tolerantly *adv.* **toleration** *n.* practice of allowing people to worship as they please; granting to minorities political liberty. **tolerationist** *n.* **tolerator** *n.*

toll *n.* tax, esp. for right to use bridge, ferry, public road, etc.; charge for long-distance telephone call. *v.i.* to exact toll.

toll *v.t.* to cause to ring slowly, as bell, esp. to signify death; *v.i.* to peal with slow, sonorous sounds; *n.* sound of such bell.

tom *n.* used to denote male animal, as tomcat. **-boy** *n.* girl of boyish behavior; romping, mischievous girl.

tom‧a‧hawk *n.* war hatchet used by N. Amer. Indians; *v.t.* to wound or kill with tomahawk.

tomahawk

to‧ma‧to *n. pl.* **-es.** plant with red or yellow fruit much-used in salads.

tomb *n.* a grave; underground vault; any structure for a dead body. **-stone** *n.* stone erected over grave.

to‧mor‧row *n.* day after today; *adv.* on the following day.

tom-tom *n.* small drum used by Indian and African natives.

ton *n.* weight consisting of 2,000 lb.; measure of capacity varying according to article being measured. **-nage** *n.* cubical content (100 cu. ft.) of ship in tons; shipping collectively assessed in tons.

tone *n.* quality or pitch of musical sound; modulation of speaking or singing voice; color values of picture; *(Med.)* natural healthy functioning of bodily organs; *v.t.* to give tone or quality to; to modify color or general effect of, as in photograph; to tune (instrument); *v.i.* to blend (with). **tonal** *a.* **tonality** *n.* quality of tone or pitch; system of variation of keys in musical composition. **tonally** *adv.* **-deaf** *a.* unable to distinguish musical intervals.

tongs *n.pl.* implement consisting of pair of pivoted levers, for grasping.

tongue *n.* flexible muscular organ in mouth used in tasting, swallowing, and for speech; facility of utterance; language; clapper of bell; *v.t.* to modulate with tongue as notes of flute; to chide. **-d** *a.* having a tongue. **—tied** *n.* having tongue defect causing speech impediment.

ton‧ic *a.* pert. to tones or sounds; having an invigorating effect bodily or mentally; *n.* a medicine which tones up the system; *(Mus.)* a keynote. **-ally** *adv.* **-ity** *n.*

to‧night *n.* this night; night following this present day; *adv.* on this night.

ton‧nage *n.* See ton.

ton‧sil *n.* one of two oval-shaped lymphoid organs on either side of pharynx. **-litis** *n.* inflammation of the tonsils.

ton‧sure *n.* act of shaving part of head as

token of religious dedication; shaved crown of priest's head. **tonsor** *n.* barber.

too *adv.* in addition; more than enough.

took *pa.t.* of take.

tool *n.* implement operated by hand, or by machine; cutting or shaping part of a machine; *v.t.* to cut, shape, or mark with a tool. **-ing** *n.*

toot *v.t.* to cause to sound, as an automobile horn or wind instrument; *n.* sound of horn; hoot.

tooth *n.* hard projection in gums of upper and lower jaws of vertebrates, used in mastication; prong of comb, rake. *pl.* **teeth.** *v.t.* to provide with teeth; *v.i.* to interlock. **-ache** *n.* pain in tooth. **-brush** *n.* small brush for cleaning teeth. **-ed** *a.* **-some** *a.* pleasant to taste. **-y** *a.* having prominent teeth; toothed.

teeth

top *n.* highest part of anything; highest rank; first in merit; *a.* highest; most eminent; best; *v.t.* to cover on the top; to rise above; *v.i.* to surpass; *v.i.* to be outstanding. **— heavy** *a.* having top too heavy for base. **-per** *n.* something placed on the top; topcoat. **-ping** *n.* act of lopping off top of something; something put on top of a thing as decoration. **-pingly** *adv.* **-soil** *n.* surface layer of soil.

to·paz *n.* gem stone, translucent and of varied colors.

tope *v.i.* to drink to excess. **-r** *n.*

to·pi·a *n.* mural decoration comprising landscapes. **-ry** *a.* cut into ornamental shapes, as trees, hedges, etc.; *n.* topiary work or art; a garden or single shrub so trimmed. **-rist** *n.*

top·ic *n.* subject of essay, discourse, or conversation; branch of general subject. **-al** *a.* pert. to a place; concerning local matters. **-ally** *adv.*

to·pog·ra·phy *n.* description of a place; physical features of region. **topographer** *n.* **topographical** *a.*

top·ple *v.t.* to overturn; *v.i.* to overbalance.

top·sy-tur·vy *adv.* upside down; *a.* turned upside down; *n.* disorder; chaos.

torch *n.* piece of wood with some substance at the end soaked in inflammable liquid, and used as portable light. **-bearer** *n.*

tore *pa.t.* of tear.

to·re·a·dor *n.* bullfighter.

tor·ment *n.* extreme pain of body; anguish of mind; *v.t.* to inflict pain upon; to tease. **-ing** *a.* **-ingly** *adv.* **-or,** **-er** *n.*

torn *pa.p.* of tear.

tor·na·do *n.* whirling progressive windstorm causing widespread devastation.

tor·pe·do *n.* cigar-shaped underwater projectile with high explosive charge; *pl.* **-es;** *v.t.* to attack, sink with torpedoes. **-ist** *n.* expert in handling and firing torpedoes.

tor·pid *a.* dormant, as hibernating animal; physically or mentally inert. **-ity** *n.* lethargy. **-ly** *adv.* **-ness** *n.* **torpor** *n.* inertia. **torporific** *a.*

tor·re·fy *v.t.* to roast, as metals. **torrefaction** *n.*

tor·rent *n.* downpour; rapid flow, as of words. **-ial** *a.* pert. to, resembling torrent; overwhelming.

tor·rid *a.* extremely hot, dry or burning; passionate. **-ness,** **-ity** *n.* **-ly** *adv.* **—zone,** broad belt lying between Tropics of Cancer and Capricorn.

tor·sion *n.* act of turning or twisting; *(Mech.)* force with which twisted wire tends to return to original position. **-al** *a.* **— balance,** scientific instrument for measuring minute forces by small bar suspended horizontally at end of very fine wire.

tor·so *n.* trunk of human body.

tort *n. (Law)* private injury to person or property for which damages may be claimed in court of law. **-ious** *a.* **-iously** *adv.*

tor·toise *n.* land reptile or turtle. **-shell** *n.* mottled brown outer shell of tortoise used for combs; *a.* mottled like tortoiseshell.

tortoise

tor·tu·ous *a.* full of twists; deceitful. **tortuosity** *n.* **-ly** *adv.* **-ness** *n.*

tor·ture *n.* act of deliberately inflicting extreme pain as punishment or reprisal; *v.t.* to inflict agony. **torturing** *a.* **torturous** *a.*

To·ry *n.* and *a.* supporter of Britain in the American Revolution. **-ism** *n.*

toss *v.t.* to throw upwards with a jerk; *v.i.* to roll and tumble; *n.* fling; distance anything is tossed. **-er,** **-ing** *n.* **— up,** *n.* tossing of coin to decide issue.

tot *n.* anything small, esp. a child.

to·tal *a.* complete; *n.* the whole; sum; *v.t.* to add; *v.i.* to amount to. **-izator,** *n.* machine which registers totals. **-ity** *n.* entirety. **-ly** *adv.* **-ness** *n.*

to·tal·i·tar·i·an *a.* open-party dictatorial form of government. **-ism** *n.*

tote *v.t. (Colloq.)* to carry; to transport.

to·tem *n.* natural object, taken by primitive tribe as emblem of hereditary relationship with that object; image of this. **-ic** *a.* **-ism** *n.* **-ist** *n.* member of tribe. **-istic** *a.* **— pole** *n.* pole with totems carved on it, one above the other.

tot·ter *v.i.* to walk with faltering steps; to reel. **-er** *n.* **-ing** *a.* **-ingly** *adv.* **-y** *a.* unsteady.

tou·can *n.* bird of tropical Amer.

touch *v.t.* to come in contact with; to

finger; to move deeply; *v.i.* to be in contact; to take effect on; *n.* contact; sense of feeling; unique quality; tinge; mild attack. **-able** *a.* **-ableness** *(Football)* scoring by having ball behind goal line. **-er** *n.* **-ily** *adv.* **-iness** *n.* **-ing** *a.* emotionally moving; *prep.* referring to. **-ingly** *adv.* **-ingness** *n.* **-y** *a.* hypersensitive.

tough *a.* flexible but not brittle; not easily broken; difficult to chew; difficult to solve; *n.* a bully; a ruffian. **-en** *v.t.* to make hardy; *v.i.* to become tough. **-ly** *adv.* **-ness** *n.*

tou·pee *n.* artificial lock of hair.

tour *n.* journey from place to place in a country; *v.t.* to travel around; to visit as part of tour. **-ism** *n.* **-ist** *n.* sightseer.

tour·na·ment *n.* any sports competition or championship. **tourney** *n.* a tournament.

tour·ni·quet *n.* surgical device for arresting hemorrhage by compression of a blood vessel, as a bandage tightened by twisting.

tous·le *v.t.* to make untidy by pulling, as hair; *a.* untidy.

tout *v.i.* and *v.t.* to solicit business; to praise highly; *n.* one who pesters people to be customers. **-er** *n.*

tow *v.t.* to drag by rope or chain; *n.* act of pulling; rope or chain used for towing. **-age** *n.* act of or charge for towing.

to·ward(s) *prep.* in direction of; regarding.

tow·el *n.* cloth or paper for drying skin, or for domestic purposes. **-ing** *n.* soft fabric for making towels.

tow·er *n.* lofty round or square structure; *v.i.* to soar. **-ed** *a.* having towers. **-ing** *a.* lofty; violent.

town *n.* collection of houses, etc., larger than village; *a.* pert. to town. **— clerk** *n.* official of administrative side of a town's affairs.

tox·i·col·o·gy *n.* science of poisons, their effects. **toxemia,** *n.* blood poisoning. **toxemic** *a.* **toxical** *a.* poisonous. **toxically** *adv.* **toxicant** *a.* poisonous; *n.* poison. **toxicological** *a.* **toxicologist** *n.* **toxin** *n.* poison of bacterial origin.

tox·oph·i·lite *n.* student of, or expert in, archery. **toxophilitic** *a.*

toy *n.* child's plaything; *v.i.* to trifle.

trace *n.* mark; outline; barely perceptible sign; *v.t.* to draw exactly on a superimposed sheet; to follow track of; to work out step by step; *v.i.* to move. **-able** *a.* capable of being detected. **-ableness** *n.* **-ably** *adv.* **-r** *n.* **tracing** *n.* traced copy of drawing. **tracing paper** *n.* transparent paper for tracing design.

trace *n.* strap, rope, by which horse pulls vehicle.

tra·che·a *n.* windpipe between lungs and back of throat. *pl.* **tracheae.** **-l** *a.* **tracheotomy** *n.* *(Surg.)* operation by which opening is made in windpipe.

track *n.* mark left by something; footprint; laid-out course for racing; (railway) metal rails forming a permanent way; *(Fig.)* evidence; *v.t.* to make a track of footprints on; *v.i.* to follow a trail; to be in alignment. **-er** *n.* **—meet,** athletic contest held on a track.

tract *n.* region of indefinite extent; continuous period of time. **-ability** *n.* state of being tractable. **-able** *a.* amenable to reason. **-ableness** *n.* **-ably** *adv.* **-ile** *a.* capable of being drawn out. **-ility** *n.* **-ion** *n.* gripping power, as of a wheel on a road. **-ional** *a.* **-ion engine** *n.* locomotive, steam-driven, for haulage. **-ive** *a.* pulling. **-or** *n.* motor vehicle for drawing agricultural machinery.

trade *n.* the business of buying and selling; occupation, esp. in industry, shopkeeping, etc.; employees collectively in a particular trade; *v.t.* to engage in commerce; *v.i.* to exchange. **-mark** *n.* registered name on maker's goods. **— name** *n.* name given by manufacturer to proprietary article. **-r** *n.* merchant (wholesale or retail). **— union** *n.* legally recognized association of workmen. **— unionist** *n.* member of trade union. **trading** *n.*

tra·di·tion *n.* belief, custom, transmitted by word of mouth from age to age. **-al, -ary** *a.* **-alism,** **-alist** *n.* **-alistic** *a.*

tra·duce *v.t.* to defame the character of; to calumniate. **-r** *n.* a slanderer.

traf·fic *n.* business dealings; movement of people, vehicles, to and fro, in streets; coming and going of ships, trains, aircraft; *v.i.* to carry on trade. **-king** *pr.p.* **-ked** *pa.t.* and *pa.p.* **-ker** *n.*

trag·e·dy *n.* serious and dignified dramatic composition in prose or verse with unhappy ending; sad or calamitous event. **tragedian** *n.* actor in or writer of tragedy. **tragical** *a.* pert. to tragedy; calamitous. **tragically** *adv.* **tragicalness** *n.*

trail *v.t.* to draw along ground or through water; to follow track of; to carry rifle in hand with butt close to the ground; *v.i.* to drag one foot wearily after other; *n.* visible trace left by anything; scent of hunted animal. **-er** *n.* vehicle towed by another. **-less** *a.*

train *v.t.* to instruct or educate; to submit person to arduous physical exercise, for athletics; to cause plant to grow in certain way; *v.i.* to exercise body or mind to achieve high standard of efficiency; *n.* retinue; line of cars drawn by locomotive on railway track; sequence of events, ideas. **-ed** *a.* **-ee** *n.* one who is training. **-er,** **-ing** *n.*

traipse *v.i.* *(Colloq.)* to walk aimlessly.

trait *n.* distinguishing feature, esp. in character.

trai·tor *n.* one who betrays person, country, or cause. **-ous** *a.* guilty of treachery; pert. to treason or to traitors. **-ously** *adv.*

tra·jec·to·ry *n.* curve of projectile in its flight through space.

tram·mel *n.* long net for catching birds or fish; anything which impedes movement; *v.t.* to confine. **-er,** *n.*

tramp *v.t.* to hike over or through; *v.i.* to plod; *n.* homeless vagrant; cargo boat with no regular route. **-er** *n.*

tram·ple *v.t.* to tread heavily underfoot; *n.* act of trampling. **-r** *n.*

tram·po·line *n.* canvas springboard.

trampolinist n.

trance n. a fit of complete mental absorption; semiconscious condition.

tran•quil a. serene; undisturbed. -ly adv. tranquillity, -ness n.

trans- pref. meaning across, beyond, on the other side of.

trans•act v.t. to negotiate; v.i. to do (business). -or n. -ion n. act of transacting business; pl. records of a society. -ional a.

trans•at•lan•tic a. across the Atlantic.

tran•scend v.t. to go beyond; to surpass. -ence, -ency n. (Theol.) supremacy of God above all human limitations. -ent a. surpassing all; beyond all human knowledge. -ently adv. -entness n. -ental a. supernatural; intuitive. -entalism, -entalist n. -entally adv.

trans•con•ti•nen•tal a. crossing a continent.

tran•scribe v.t. to write over again; to reproduce in longhand notes taken in shorthand. -r n. transcript n. written copy. transcription n. act of copying; transcript.

tran•sect v.t. to cut transversely.

trans•fer v.t. to move from one place to another; to pass an impression from one surface to another; to convey, as property, legally to another; n. ticket allowing change of vehicle during single trip without further charge; design to be, or which has been transferred. -ring pr.p. -red pa.t. and pa.p. -ability n. -able a. capable of being transferred; valid for use by another. -ence n. the act of transferring.

trans•fig•ure v.t. to change outward appearance of. -ment n. transfiguration n. change of appearance.

trans•fix v.t. to pierce through; to stun. -ion n.

trans•form v.t. to change form, nature, or disposition of; v.i. to be changed. -able a. -ation n. change of outward appearance of inner nature. -ative a. -er n. an electrical device for changing voltage up or down. -ing a.

trans•fuse v.t. to pour, as liquid, from one receptacle into another; (Med.) to transfer blood from one person to vein of another. -r n. transfusible, transfusive a. transfusion n.

trans•gress v.t. to violate law; v.i. to sin. -ion n. act of violating civil or moral law. -ive a. ively adv. -or n.

tran•sient a. momentary; not permanent. transience, transiency n. -ly adv. -ness n.

tran•sit n. the act of conveying. -ion n. change from one condition to another. -ional, -ionary a. -ionally adv. -ive a. having power of passing across. -ively adv. -iveness n. -orily adv. -oriness n. state of being transitory. -ory a.

trans•late v.t. to turn from one language into another; to change from one medium to another; v.i. to be capable of translation. translatable a. translation, translator n.

trans•lit•er•ate v.t. to write words of language in alphabetic symbols of another. transliteration, transliterator n.

trans•lu•cent a. diffusing light but not revealing definite contours of object. translucence, translucency n. -ly adv. translucid a. translucent.

trans•mi•grate v.i. to pass from one country to another as permanent residence. transmigration, transmigrator n. transmigratory a.

trans•mit v.t. to send from one person to another; to communicate. -ting pr.p. -ted pa.t. and pa.p. transmissibility n. transmissible, -tible a. capable of being transmitted. transmission n. in motoring, gear by which power is transmitted from engine to axle. -tal n. transmission. -tance n. -ter n. apparatus for transmitting radio waves through space.

trans•mute v.t. to change from one nature, species, form, or substance into another. transmutable a. transmutableness, transmutability n. transmutably adv. transmutant a. transmutation n. alteration, esp. biological transformation of one species into another; in alchemy, supposed change of baser metals into gold. transmutative a. -r n.

tran•som n. windo•v over a doorway; horizontal crossbar in window.

trans•par•ent a. that may be distinctly seen through; pervious to light. transparence, transparency n. -ly adv. -ness n.

tran•spire v.t. to emit through pores of skin; v.i. to exhale; (Bot.) to lose water by evaporation. transpiration n. transpiratory a.

trans•plant v.t. to remove and plant elsewhere; (Surg.) to graft live tissue from one part of body to another. -able a. -ation, -er n.

trans•port v.t. to convey from one place to another; to overwhelm emotionally; n. vehicles collectively used in conveyance of passengers. -able a. -ability, -er n. -ation n. act or means of transporting from place to place. -ed a.

trans•pose v.t. to change respective place or order of two things. transposable a. transposal n. change of order. transposition n. transpositional a.

tran•sub•stan•ti•ate v.t. to change into another substance.

tran•sude v.i. to pass through pores of substance.

trans•verse a. lying in crosswise direction. transversal n. line which cuts across two or more parallel lines. -ly adv.

trap n. device for catching animals, vermin; U-shaped bend in pipe which, by being always full of water, prevents foul air or gas from escaping; plot to catch person unawares; v.t. to catch in a trap, or by stratagem. -ping pr.p. -ped pa.p. and pa.t. -door n. hinged door in floor. -per n.

tra•pe•zi•um n. quadrilateral with no parallel sides; (Anat.) one of wrist bones pl. -s, trapezia. trapeze n. apparatus comprising horizontal crossbar swing for gymnastics, acrobatic exhibitions, etc. trapezoid n. quadrilateral with only two of its sides parallel. trapezoidal a.

trash v.t. to lop off, as branches, leaves,

etc.; *n.* worthless refuse; rubbish. -**ily** *adv.* -**iness** *n.* -**y** *a.* worthless; shoddy.

trass *n.* volcanic material used in making cement.

trau·ma *n. (Med.)* bodily injury caused by violence; emotional shock (psychic trauma) with a lasting effect. *pl.* -**ta.** -**tic** *a.*

tra·vail *n.* painful, arduous labor; *v.i.* to labor with difficulty.

trave *n.* beam.

trav·el *v.t.* to journey over; *v.i.* to journey on foot or in a vehicle; *n.* act of traveling; journey; touring, esp. abroad; *pl.* prolonged journey, esp. abroad. -**ed** *a.* -**er** *n.* -**ing** *a.* -**ogue** *n.* travel lecture illustrated by slides, film.

tra·verse *a.* lying across; built crosswise; anything set across; lateral movement; *v.t.* to cross; to obstruct; to survey across a plot of ground; to discuss, as topic, from every angle; *v.i.* to move sideways. **traversable** *a.* -**r** *n.*

trav·es·ty *n.* parody; *v.t.* to caricature.

trawl *v.t.* to catch fish with a trawl; *v.i.* to drag with a trawl; *n.* a strong fishing net, shaped like a large bag with one end open. -**er** *n.* one who fishes with a trawl; fishing vessel. -**ing** *n.*

tray *n.* flat, shallow, rimmed vessel used for carrying dishes, food, etc.

treach·er·y *n.* violation of faith; treason; perfidy. **treacherous** *a.* **treacherously** *adv.*

tread *v.i.* to walk; to move with measured step; to crush; *v.t.* to crush with foot; to operate with foot, as treadle; *n.* that which one steps on, as surface of horizontal step of flight of stairs; part of a rubber tire in contact with ground. **trod** *pa.t.* and *pa.p.* **trodden** *pa.p.* -**ing** *n.* -**le** *n.* part of machine operated by foot pressure, as sewing machine, etc.; *v.i.* to work treadle. -**ler** *n.*

trea·son *n.* act of betrayal. -**able** *a.* treason. -**ableness** *n.* -**ably** *adv.* -**ous** *a.*

trea·sure *n.* hoard of valuables; that which has great worth; *v.t.* to hoard; to value; to cherish, as friendship. — **chest** *n.* box for storing valuables. -**r** *n.* person appointed to take charge of funds of church, club, etc. -**ship** *n.* **treasury** *n.* place where treasure or public funds are deposited; anthology. **Treasury** *n.* government department which controls management of public revenues.

treat *v.t.* to entertain with food or drink; to pay for another's entertainment or refreshment; to apply a remedy to; *v.i.* to come to terms of agreement; to give entertainment; *n.* entertainment given as a celebration or expression of regard; one's turn to pay for another's entertainment. -**er,** -**ing** *n.* -**ise** *n.* dissertation on particular theme. -**ment** *n.* mode of treating person, subject, artistic work; method of counteracting disease or injury. -**y** *n.* a negotiated agreement between states.

tre·ble *a.* triple; *(Mus.)* singing highest part; *n.* highest part; soprano part or voice; *v.i.* to become three times as much. **trebly** *adv.*

tree perennial plant, having trunk, bole, or woody stem with branches; *v.t.* to chase

up a tree; to corner. -**less** *a.* -**lessness** *n.* -**top** *n.* uppermost branches of tree.

tre·foil *n.* plant of genus *Trifolium,* with leaves comprising three leaflets; clover.

trek *v.i.* to migrate; *n.* mass migration. -**king** *pr.p.* -**ked** *pa.p.* and *pa.t.* -**ker** *n.*

trel·lis *n.* lightweight lattice structure esp. as frame for climbing plants. -**ed** *a.* -**work** *n.* latticework.

trem·ble *v.i.* to shake involuntarily; to quake; *n.* tremor. -**r** *n.* **trembling** *n.* and *adv.* **trembly** *a.* shaky. **tremulant, tremulous** *a.* fearful. **tremulously** *adv.* **tremulousness** *n.*

tre·men·dous *a.* awe-inspiring; *(Colloq.)* great. -**ly** *adv.* -**ness** *n.*

trem·o·lan·do *a. (Mus.)* tremulous. **tremolo** *n.* quivering of singing voice.

trem·or *n.* involuntary quiver; shaking, as caused by earthquake. -**less** *a.* steady.

trem·u·lous *a.* See **tremble.**

trench *v.t.* to dig, as a ditch; to fortify with ditch, using earth dug out for rampart; *v.i.* to encroach; *n.* deep ditch to protect soldiers from enemy fire. -**ancy** *n.* quality of being trenchant. -**ant** *a.* penetrating. — **coat** *n.* waterproof coat. -**ing** *n.*

trend *v.i.* to stretch in a certain direction; *n.* inclination; tendency; general direction.

tre·pan *n.* heavy tool for boring shafts.

trep·id *a.* quaking. -**ation** *n.* involuntary trembling; fluster.

tres·pass *v.i.* to cross boundary line of another's property unlawfully; to intrude. -**er** *n.*

tress *n.* long lock, curl, braid or strand of hair; ringlet. -**ed** *a.*

tres·tle *n.* frame consisting of two pairs of braced legs fixed underneath horizontal bar, used as support; similar construction supporting a bridge.

tri- *pref.* meaning three.

tri·ad *n.* union of three; *(Mus.)* the common chord, one of three notes. -**ic** *a.* -**ist** *n.* writer of triads.

tri·al *n.* act of trying, testing, or proving properties of anything; judicial examination in law court of accused person.

tri·an·gle *n. (Math.)* figure bounded by three lines and containing three angles; *(Mus.)* small percussion instrument consisting of a bar of steel bent in shape of triangle and struck with small steel rod. -**d, triangular** *a.* **triangularity** *n.* **triangularly** *adv.*

tri·ar·chy *n.* government by three persons.

tri·a·tom·ic *a.* consisting of three atoms; having valency of three.

tribe *n.* family, race, or succession of generations descending from same progenitor. **tribal** *a.* **tribalism** *n.* tribal feeling; tribal life. **tribally** *adv.* -**sman** *n.* one of a tribe.

trib·u·la·tion *n.* severe affliction; prolonged suffering, esp. of mind.

tri·bune *n.* in ancient Rome, magistrate chosen by the people to defend their rights. **tribunal** *n.* court of justice. **tribunate,** -**ship** *n;* office of tribune.

trib·ute *n.* personal testimony to achievements or qualities of another;

prearranged payment made at stated times by one state to another. **tributarily** *adv.* **tributary** *a.* paying tribute; subordinate; (of river) flowing into main river; *n.* one who pays tribute; stream flowing into larger river.

trice *n.* moment; a very short time.

tri·ceps *a.* three-headed; *n.* three-headed muscle as at back of upper arm.

trich·i·no·sis *n.* disease due to the presence of the nematode worm, trichina, in the intestines and muscular tissue.

tri·chol·o·gy *n.* study of hair and diseases affecting it.

tri·cho·sis *n.* any disease affecting the hair.

tri·chot·o·mous *a.* divided into three or threes. **trichotomy** *n.*

trick *n.* stratagem designed to deceive; conjurer's sleight of hand; dexterity; *v.t.* to deceive; to mystify; to dress, decorate. **-er** *n.* **-ery** *n.* practice of playing tricks; fraud. **-ily** *adv.* **-iness** *n.* **-sy** *a.* ingenious; neat. **-ster**, *n.* swindler. **-y** *a.* full of tricks; crafty; intricate.

trick·le *v.i.* to flow gently in a slow, thin stream; *n.* slow movement of anything.

tri·col·or *n.* national flag of three colors, esp. French national flag. **-ed** *a.*

tri·corn *a.* having three horns, or points; *n.* three-cornered hat.

tri·cot *n.* machine-made knitwear fabric. **-tine** *n.* a ribbed, fine woolen fabric, machine-made.

tri·cus·pid *a.* having three cusps or points, as certain teeth; a valve of the right ventricle of the heart.

tri·cy·cle *n.* three-wheeled cycle, esp. for children's use; *v.t.* to ride a tricycle. **tricyclist** *n.*

tri·dent *n.* any three-pronged instrument, such as fish spear. **-ate**, *a.* having three prongs.

tried See **try**.

tri·en·ni·al *a.* lasting for three years; happening once every three years. **-ly** *adv.*

tri·fle *n.* anything of little value or importance; *v.i.* to speak or act lightly; to toy, or waste time. **-r** *n.* **trifling** *a.* trivial. **triflingly** *adv.*

tri·form *a.* having a triple form. Also **-ed**. **-ity** *n.*

tri·fur·cate *a.* having three branches. **trifurcation** *n.*

trig·ger *n.* catch of firearm which, when pulled, releases hammer of lock.

trig·o·nom·e·try *n.* branch of mathematics which deals with relations between sides and angles of triangle. **trigonometer** *n.* instrument for solving plane right-angled triangles by inspection. **trigonometrical** *a.* **trigonometrically** *adv.*

tri·lat·er·al *a.* having three sides. **-ly** *adv.*

tri·lin·e·ar *a.* consisting of three lines.

tri·lin·gual *a.* expressed in three languages; speaking three languages.

trill *v.t.* and *v.i.* to sing or play (instrument) with vibratory quality; *n.* vibration of voice, in singing.

tril·lion *n.* a million million (U.S.), i.e. 1 with 12 ciphers.

tril·o·gy *n.* group of three plays, novels,

with common theme, or common central character.

trim *a.* (*comp.*) **-mer** (*superl.*) **-est.** neat; in good order; to decorate, as hat; to clip shorter; (*Naut.*) to arrange sails according to wind direction; *v.i.* to balance; *n.* dress; decoration; anything trimmed off. **-ming** *pr.p.* **-med** *pa.t.* and *pa.p.* **-ly** *adv.* **-mer** *n.* one who trims; instrument for clipping. **-ming** *n.* that which trims, edges, or decorates. **-ness** *n.* neatness; readiness for use.

trim·e·ter *n.* verse containing three measures. **trimetrical** *a.*

tri·nal *a.* threefold; three in one. **trinary** *a.* ternary. **trine** *a.* threefold; *n.* group of three; aspect of two planets distant from each other 120°, or one-third of the zodiac.

tri·ni·tro·tol·u·ene *n.* (*abbrev.* T.N.T.) high explosive.

Trin·i·ty *n.* union of one Godhead of Father, Son, and Holy Ghost; (*l.c.*) combination of three people or things as one. **Trinitarian** *a.* pert. to doctrine of the Trinity; *n.* one who believes in this doctrine. **Trinitarianism** *n.*

trin·ket *n.* small ornament of little value. **-ry** *n.*

tri·no·mi·al *a.* (*Bot. Zool.*) having three names as of *order*, *species* and *subspecies*; (*Math.*) consisting of three terms connected by sign + or −; *n.* a trinomial quantity.

tri·o *n.* group of three persons or things; (*Mus.*) composition arranged for three voices or instruments.

tri·ox·ide *n.* (*Chem.*) compound comprising three atoms of oxygen with other element.

trip *v.t.* to cause to stumble; to start up, as machine, by releasing clutch; *v.i.* to walk lightly; to stumble over an obstacle; *n.* a journey; false step; indiscretion in speech or conduct. **-ping** *pr.p.* **-ped** *pa.p.* **-per** *n.* device to start a mechanism. **-ping** *a.* light-footed. **-pingly** *adv.*

tri·par·tite *a.* having three corresponding parts; arranged or agreed to, by three nations. **tripartition** *n.*

tripe *n.* large stomach of ruminating animal, prepared for food.

triph·thong *n.* a syllable containing three vowels together.

tri·ple *a.* three times repeated; *v.t.* to make three times as many; *v.i.* to become trebled. **-t** *n.* three of a kind; (*Mus.*) three notes played in the time of two; one of three children born at a birth. **-x** *a.* threefold; *n.* (*Mus.*) triple time. **triplicate** *a.* threefold; *n.* third copy corresponding exactly to two others; *v.t.* to make three copies of. **triplication** *n.*

tri·pod *n.* three-legged, folding stand for a camera; *a.* having three legs. **-al**, **-ic** *a.*

trip·o·li *n.* mineral substance used for polishing metals, originally from *Tripoli*.

trip·tych *n.* picture in three panels.

tri·sect *v.t.* to divide into three equal parts, as a line or angle. **-ion** *n.*

tri·sul·fide *n.* (*Chem.*) chemical compound containing three sulfur atoms.

tri·syl·la·ble *n.* word of three syllables.

T

trisyllabical *a.* trisyllabically *adv.*

trite *a.* made stale by use; banal. -ly *adv.* -ness *n.*

Tri•ton *n.* (*Gk. Myth.*) god of the sea.

trit•u•rate *v.t.* to grind to a very fine powder. triturable *a.* trituration *n.*

tri•umph *n.* victory; great achievement; *v.i.* to celebrate victory with great ceremony; to exult. -al *a.* expressing joy for success. -antly *adv.*

tri•um•vir *n.* one of three men sharing governing power in ancient Rome. *pl.* -i, -s. -al *a.* -ate *n.* coalition of three men in authority.

tri•une *a.* three in one. triunity *n.*

tri•va•lent *a.* (*Chem.*) having valency of three; capable of combining with three atoms of hydrogen. trivalence *n.*

triv•et *n.* three-legged support; short-legged metal rack to put under a hot platter, etc.

triv•i•al *a.* of little consequence. -ism *n.* triviality *n.pl.* insignificant matters. -ly *adv.* -ness *n.*

trod, trodden *pa.t.* and *pa.p.* of tread.

trog•lo•dyte *n.* cave dweller; a hermit.

Tro•jan *a.* pert. to ancient Troy; *n.* inhabitant of Troy.

troll *n.* mischievous humpbacked cave-dwelling dwarf.

troll *v.t.* and *v.i.* to roll; to sing in succession the parts of a round; to fish with baited line trailing behind boat; *n.* a round or catch; act of trolling. -er *n.*

trol•ley *n.* form of truck, body of which can be tilted over; device to connect electric streetcar with wires. -bus, passengar bus not operating on rails but drawing power from overhead wires. — car *n.* electric streetcar.

trom•bone *n.* deep-toned brass musical instrument. trombonist *n.*

troop *n.* assembly of people; body of cavalry; *pl.* soldiers collectively; *v.i.* to gather in a crowd. -er *n.* policeman; horse cavalryman. -ship *n.* vessel for transporting soldiers.

trope *n.* phrase used metaphorically. tropical *a.* figurative. tropically *adv.* tropist *n.* one who uses figurative language. tropological *a.* containing figures of speech. tropology *n.* figurative language; metaphorical interpretation of the Bible.

tro•phical *a.* pert. to nutrition. trophi *n.pl.* masticating organs of insect. trophology *n.* study of nutrition.

tro•phy *n.* memorial of victory; prize, esp. for sports, etc.

trop•ic *n.* one of the two circles of celestial sphere, situated 23½° N. (*Tropic of Cancer*) and 23½° S. (*Tropic of Capricorn*) of equator. *pl.* region (*torrid zone*) between tropics of Cancer and Capricorn. tropical *a.* pert. to or within tropics; very hot. -ally *adv.*

tro•po•sphere *n.* lower layer of atmosphere below stratosphere.

trot *v.i.* to move at sharp pace; *v.t.* to cause to trot; *n.* quick walk. -ting *pr.p.* -ted *pa.p.* and *pa.t.* -ter *n.* one who trots.

troth *n.* fidelity. to plight one's troth, to

become engaged to be married.

trou•ble *v.t.* to stir up; to distress; *v.i.* to feel anxiety; *n.* disturbance; agitation of mind; inconvenience. -r *n.* -some *a.* difficult; irksome. -somely *adv.* -someness *n.*

trough *n.* long, open vessel for water or fodder for animals.

trounce *v.t.* to beat severely; (*Colloq.*) to defeat completely.

troupe *n.* company, esp. of actors, acrobats, etc. -r *n.* member of a theatrical troupe.

trou•sers *n.pl.* garment extending from waist to ankles; slacks. trousered *a.* wearing trousers. trouserless *a.*

trous•seau *n.* bride's outfit of clothes, etc.

trout *n.* fish resembling salmon.

trout

trow•el *n.* mason's tool for spreading mortar; garden tool for scooping out earth, plants; *v.t.* to smooth with trowel.

troy weight *n.* system of weight for precious metals and gems.

tru•ant *n.* one who shirks his duty; pupil who absents himself from school; *a.* idle; *v.i.* to play truant. truancy *n.*

truce *n.* temporary cessation of hostilities; lull.

truck *v.t.* to exchange; *v.i.* to deal with by exchange; *n.* exchange of commodities; garden produce. -er *n.* — farm *n.* a small farm on which vegetables are grown for market.

truck *n.* horse-drawn or automotive vehicle for hauling; barrow for heavy luggage. -age *n.* transport by trucks. -le *n.* small caster. — bed *n.* low bed on casters which may be pushed beneath another.

truc•u•lent *a.* aggressive; ruthless. truculence, truculency *n.* -ly *adv.*

trudge *v.t.* to plod along; *n.* wearisome walk.

trud•gen *n.* fast racing stroke in swimming.

true *a.* conforming with fact; genuine; loyal; *v.t.* to adjust accurately, as machine; *adv.* truly conforming to type. -ness *n.* truism *n.* self-evident truth. truly *adv.*

tru•ism See true.

trump *n.* (*Arch.*) trumpet; its sound. -et *n.* wind instrument of brass, consisting of long tube bent twice on itself, ending in wide bell-shaped mouth, and having finger stops; *v.t.* to proclaim by trumpet; *v.i.* (of elephant) to utter characteristic cry trough trunk. -eter *n.* one who plays on trumpet; wild swan of N. Amer. -eting *n.*

trump *n.* one of the suit of cards, declared by dealing, bidding of which takes any card of another suit; *v.t.* and *v.i.* to play trump card; to take a trick with trump.

trump *v.t.* to deceive. -ery *n.* anything showy but of little value.

trun•cate *v.t.* to cut off; to maim. truncated, truncation *a.* appearing as if cut off at tip; blunt.

trun•dle *n.* anything capable of being

rolled; a small caster; *v.t.* to roll on little wheels; *v.i.* to roll.

trunk *n.* stem of tree, as distinct from branches and roots; torso; main part of anything; main lines of railway, bus, or telephone system; proboscis of elephant; *pl.* short pants, esp. for swimming.

truss *n.* bundle; framework of beams constructed to bear heavy loads; (*Med.*) appliance to keep hernia in place; *v.t.* to bind or pack close; to support, as a roof, with truss.

trust *n.* confidence; implicit faith; moral responsibility; *v.t.* to have implicit faith in; to give credit; *v.i.* to be confident or to confide in; *a.* held in trust. **-ee** *n.* person or group which manages the business affairs of another. **—eeship, -er** *n.* -ful *a.* -fully *adv.* -fulness *n.* -ily *adv.* -iness *n.* quality of being trusty. **-ing** *a.* confiding. **-ingly** *adv.* **-worthiness** *n.* -worthy *a.* -y *a.* reliable; *n.* reliable prisoner given special privileges.

truth *n.* conformity to reality; true statement; undisputed fact. **-ful** *a.* -fully *adv.* -fulness *n.* -less *a.*

try *v.t.* to test; (*Law*) to examine judicially; *v.i.* to make effort; *n.* effort; attempt. **tried** *a.,* *pa.t.* and *pa.p.* **trier** *n.*

tryst *n.* appointment to meet. **-er** *n.*

tset·se *n.* African fly, its bite causing sleeping sickness.

T square *n.* ruler with crossbar at one end for drawing parallel lines.

tub *n.* vessel to bathe in; small cask. **-by** *a.* (of persons) squat and portly.

tu·ba *n.* (*Mus.*) largest brass instrument of orchestra.

tube *n.* long hollow cylinder for conveyance of liquids, gas; inner rubber tire of bicycle or automobile wheel. **tubing** *n.* tubular, tubulated, tubulous, tubulose *a.* tubule *n.* a small tube.

tu·ber *n.* fleshy, rounded underground stem or root, containing buds for new plant; (*Med.*) a swelling. **-ous, -ose** *a.*

tu·ber·cle *n.* small swelling; (*Med.*) morbid growth, esp. on lung causing *tuberculosis; a.* having tubercules. **tubercular, tuberculated, tuberculose, tuberculous** *a.* affected with tuberculosis. **tuberculin** *n.* liquid extract from tubercle bacillus used as injection in testing for, in treatment of, tuberculosis. **tuberculosis** *n.* phthisis, disease caused by infection with the tubercle bacillus. **tuberculum** *n.* tubercle.

tuck *v.t.* to make fold(s) in cloth before stitching down; to enclose snugly in bedclothes; *n.* flat fold in garment to shorten it.

Tues·day *n.* third day of week.

tuft *n.* bunch of something soft, as hair, feathers; *v.t.* to adorn with, arrange in tufts. **-ed, -y** *a.*

tug *v.t.* to pull with effort; *v.i.* to comb, as hair, with difficulty; *n.* strong pull. **-ging** *pr.p.* **-ged** *pa.t.* and *pa.p.* **-boat** *n.* a small but powerful boat used for towing larger vessel.

tu·i·tion *n.* the price for instruction. **-al, -ary** *a.*

tu·lip *n.* bulbous plant popular in Holland.

tulle *n.* fine silk net used for dresses.

tum·ble *v.i.* to fall heavily; to turn head over heels; to perform acrobatic tricks; *v.t.* to overturn; to toss about; *n.* act of tumbling; confusion. **-er** *n.* acrobat; glass drinking vessel; spring catch of a lock. **tumbling** *n.* act of turning somersault

tum·brel, tumbril *n.* low open cart in which victims of French Revolutionists were conveyed to guillotine.

tu·me·fy *v.t.* to cause to swell; *v.i.* to develop into a tumor. **tumefaction** *n.* a tumor.

tu·mid *a.* swollen; pompous. **tumescence** *n.* **tumescent** *a.* -ness, -ity *n.* -ly *adv.*

tu·mor *n.* (*Med.*) morbid overgrowth of tissue, sometimes accompanied by swelling. **-ous** *a.*

tu·mult *n.* commotion of a crowd; disturbance. **-uary, -uous** *a.* uproarious; disturbing. **-uously** *adv.* **-uousness** *n.*

tu·mu·lus *n.* artificial burial mound, erected by primitive peoples. *pl.* **-es,** **tumuli. tumulous** *a.*

tun *n.* measure of liquid, for wine, equivalent to 252 gallons; *v.t.* to store in casks.

tu·na *n.* large oceanic food and game fish.

tun·dra *n.* one of vast treeless plains of Arctic Circle.

tune *n.* melody; unison; harmony; *v.t.* to adjust to proper pitch; to make efficient, esp. part of machine; (*Radio*) to adjust circuit to give resonance at desired frequency. **tunable** *a.* **tunableness** *n.* **tunably** *adv.* -ful *a.* melodious; harmonious. **-fully** *adv.* -fulness *n.* -less *a.* without melody; discordant; silent. **-r** *n.* **tuning fork** *n.* steel two-pronged instrument giving specified note when struck.

tung·sten *n.* hard gray metallic element used in alloys, special forms of steel, and for filaments in electric lamps.

tu·nic *n.* short-sleeved knee-length garment worn by women and boys in ancient Greece and Rome.

tun·nel *n.* subterranean passage; *v.t.* and *v.i.* to excavate. **-er** *n.*

tun·ny *n.* edible fish of mackerel family; tuna fish.

tur·ban *n.* headdress comprising long strip of cloth swathed around head or cap. **-ed, -like** *a.*

tur·bid *a.* muddy; dense. **-ly** *adv.* -ness, -ity *n.*

tur·bine *n.* rotary engine driven by steam, hot air, or water striking on curved vans of wheel, or drum; high-speed prime

steam turbine

mover used for generating electrical energy. **turbinal, turbinate** *a.* coiled like a spiral. **turbojet** *n.* jet-propelled gas turbine. **turboprop** *n.* jet engine in which turbine is coupled to propeller.

tur·bot *n.* large flat sea fish.

tur·bu·lent *a.* disturbed; refractory. **-ly** *adv.* **turbulence, turbulency** *n.*

tu·reen *n.* large, deep dish with removable cover, for serving soup.

turf *n.* surface soil containing matted roots, grass; a racecourse; *v.t.* to cover with turf, as lawn. **-like** *a.* **-y** *a.* covered with turf.

turgent *a.* *(obs.)* puffing up like a tumor; bombastic. **-ly** *adv.* **turgescence, turgescency** *n.* swelling caused by congestion; **turgid** *a.* distended abnormally; bombastic. **turgidity, turgidness** *n.* **-ly** *adv.*

Turk *n.* native of Turkey; Ottoman. **-ish** *a.* pert. to Turks or Turkey. **-ish bath** *n.* steam bath after which person is massaged, etc. **-ish towel** *n.* an absorbent towel.

tur·key *n.* large bird, bred for food. — **trot** *n.* ragtime dance.

tur·moil *n.* commotion; tumult.

turn *v.t.* to cause to revolve; to change direction of; to convert; *v.i.* to rotate; to move as on a hinge; (of tides) to change from ebb to flow or the reverse; to become sour, as milk; *n.* act of turning; change of bend; an action, as *good turn*; action done in rotation with others; short walk, a subtle quality of expression; crisis. **-about** *n.* reversal of opinion. **-ing** *n.* deflection; winding. **-ing point** *n.* decisive moment; crisis. **-over** *n.* rate at which employees are replaced by others; tart of pastry folded over a filling of fruit. **-pike** *n.* **-pike road,** main highway with tollgate. **-stile** *n.* revolving gate for controlling admission of people. **-table** *n.* revolving circular platform. **to turn down,** to decline, as offer; to reject, as application.

tur·nip *n.* plant of mustard family.

tur·pen·tine *n.* oily liquid extracted by distillation of resin exuded by pine and other coniferous trees.

tur·pi·tude *n.* revolting baseness; infamy.

tur·quoise *n.* bluish-green gem stone.

tur·ret *n.* revolving gun tower on ship, tank, or aircraft. **-ed** *a.* having turrets.

tur·tle *n.* marine tortoise with hard shell and limbs like paddles.

turtle

tur·tle·dove kind of pigeon, noted for its soft cooing and its affection for its mate.

Tuscan *a.* *(Archit.)* denoting the simplest of the five classical styles in architecture.

tusk *n.* the long, protruding side tooth of certain animals such as elephant, wild boar, walrus. **-ed** *a.* **-er** *n.* animal with fully developed tusks. **-y** *a.* **-less** *a.* **-like** *a.*

tus·sle *n.* and *v.t.* struggle; scuffle.

tut *interj.* exclamation of irritation.

tu·te·lage *n.* guardianship; state or period of being under this. **tutelar, tutelary** *a.* protective.

tu·tor *n.* private teacher; *v.t.* to prepare another for special examination by private coaching. **-ial** *a.* pert. to tutor. **-ially** *adv.* **-ing, -ship** *n.*

tut·ti·frut·ti *n.* preserve of fruits; ice cream made with mixed fruits.

tu·tu *n.* ballet dancer's skirt.

tux·e·do *n.* semiformal dinner jacket.

twad·dle *n.* inane conversation; *v.i.* to talk inanely. **-r** *n.* **twaddling** *n.* twaddle. **twaddly** *a.* silly.

twang *n.* sharp, rather harsh sound made by tense string sharply plucked; nasalized speech; *v.t.* to pluck tense string of instrument; *v.i.* to speak with a twang.

tweak *v.t.* to twist and pull with sudden jerk; *n.* sharp pinch.

tweed *n.* heavy woolen fabric esp. for coats, suits; *a.* of tweed.

tweez·ers *n.sing.* small pair of pincers, esp. for pulling superfluous hairs.

twelve *a.* one more than eleven; dozen; *n.* symbol representing twelve units, as 12 **twelfth** *a.* constituting one of twelve or XII. equal parts; *n.* one of twelve equal parts. **Twelfth Day,** January 6th, twelfth day after Christmas; Feast of Epiphany. **twelfthly** *adv.*

twen·ty *a.* twice ten; *n.* score; symbol representing twenty units, as 20 or XX. **twentieth** *a.* and *n.* one of twenty equal parts. **-fold** *adv.* twenty times as many.

twice *adv.* two times; doubly.

twid·dle *v.t.* to play with; *v.i.* to trifle with. **-r** *n.*

twig *n.* small branch of tree. **-gy** *a.* covered with twigs.

twi·light *n.* half-light immediately after sunset; *a.* pert. to or like twilight.

twill *n.* fabric woven with diagonal ribbing; *v.t.* to weave with twill.

twin *n.* one of two born at birth; exact counterpart; *a.* being one of two born at birth; growing in pairs. **-ned** *a.* **— beds** *n.pl.* two single beds of identical size. **-born** *a.* born at the same birth. **— brother, sister** *n.*

twine *n.* cord composed of two or more strands twisted together; *v.t.* to twist together; *v.i.* to coil spirally, as tendrils of plant; to follow circuitous route. **twining** *a.*

twinge *n.* acute spasm of pain; *v.t.* to affect momentarily with sudden pain.

twin·kle *v.i.* to sparkle; to light up; *n.* gleam of amusement in eyes; quick movement of feet, in dancing; sparkle. **twinkling** *n.* an instant.

twirl *v.t.* to whirl around; to flourish; *v.i.* to turn around rapidly; *n.* a rapid, rotary motion; convolution. **-er** *n.* one who or that which twirls.

twist *v.t.* to contort; to form, as cord, from

several fibers wound together; *v.i.* to become tangled or distorted; to wriggle; to follow a roundabout course; *n.* turning movement; a turn in meaning; a heavy silk thread; -ed *a.* -er *n.* one who, or that which, twists. -ability *n.* -able *a.* -ingly *adv.*

twit *v.t.* to reproach; to tease; *n.* taunt. -ting *pr.p.* -ted *pa.t.* and *pa.p.*

twitch *v.t.* to pull suddenly with a jerk; *v.i.* to contract with sudden spasm, as a muscle; *n.* sudden spasmodic contraction of muscle. -ing *n.*

twit•ter *n.* chirping sound; slight trembling of nerves; *v.i.* to make succession of small light sounds; to talk rapidly. -ing *n.* -y *a.*

two *a.* one and one; *n.* symbol representing two units, as 2 or II; a pair. —edged *a.* having two sharp edges; -faced *a.* hypocritical; double-dealing. -fold *a.* doubly. —handed *a.* requiring two hands or players. —ply *a.* having two strands twisted together. —sided *a.* having two aspects; reversible.

ty•coon *n.* head of great business combine; a magnate.

tym•pa•num *n.* a drum (*Anat.*) cavity of the middle ear. *pl.* -s, tympana. tympanal, tympanic *a.* like a drum; pert. to middle ear. tympanist *n.* one who plays percussion instrument.

type *n.* model; class or group; person or thing representative of certain quality; (*Biol.*) individual specimen representative of species; (*Print.*) metal block on one end of which is raised letter; *v.t.* to represent in type; to reproduce by typewriter; to classify; *v.i.* to use a typewriter. **typal** *a.* — **cutter** *n.*

one who engraves blocks for printing types. -founder *n.* one who casts type for printing. — metal *n.* alloy of lead, antimony, and tin used for casting type. -script *n.* a typewritten document. -setting *n.* process of preparing type for printing. -writer *n.* machine with

typewriter

keyboard operated by fingers, which produces printed characters on paper; typist. -writing *n.* -written *a.* typical *a.* symbolic. typing *n.* script typed. typist *n.* one who operates typewriter. typographer *n.* printer. typographical *a.* pert. to printing. typography *n.* style of printing.

ty•phoid *a.* resembling typhus; pert. to typhoid fever. — fever *n.* infectious disease characterized by severe diarrhea, profound weakness, and rash. -al *a.*

ty•phoon *n.* cyclonic hurricane. typhonic *a.*

ty•phus *n.* highly contagious disease caused by virus and characterized by purplish rash, prostration, and abnormally high temperature. typhous *a.*

ty•rant *n.* harsh, despotic ruler. tyrannical, tyrannous *a.* tyrannically, tyrannously *adv.* tyrannicalness *n.* tyrannize *v.i.* to exert authority ruthlessly; *v.t.* to subject to tyrannical authority. tyrannizer *n.* tyrannizingly *adv.* tyranny *n.* harsh enforcement of authority.

ty•ro *n.* novice.

T

U

u·biq·ui·ty *n.* existing in all places at same time; omnipresence. **ubiquitous, ubiquitary** *a.* existing or being everywhere.

U-boat *n.* German submarine.

ud·der *n.* milk gland of certain animals, as cow.

u·dom·e·ter *n.* instrument for measuring rainfall.

ug·ly *a.* offensive to the sight; of disagreeable aspect; dangerous, of situation.

U·krain·i·an *n.* citizen of Ukraine in S.W. Russia; Slavic language related to Russian. *a.* pert. to Ukraine.

u·ku·le·le *n.* small four-stringed instrument like guitar.

ul·cer *n.* superficial sore discharging pus.

ul·lage *n.* amount which cask lacks of being full; loss of wine, grain, etc. by leakage.

ul·na *n.* the larger of two bones of forearm.

ul·ster *n.* long loose overcoat originally made in *Ulster*, Ireland. **-ed** *a.*

ul·te·ri·or *a.* situated on the farther side; beyond; (of motives) undisclosed; not frankly stated.

ul·ti·mate *a.* farthest; final; primary; conclusive. **-ly** *adv.* **-ness** *n.* **ultimatum** *n.* final proposition; final terms offered as basis of treaty.

ul·tra *a.* beyond; extreme; in combination words with or without hyphen, as **ultra modern.**

ul·tra·ma·rine *a.* situated beyond the sea; *n.* bright blue pigment obtained from powdered lapis lazuli, or produced synthetically.

ul·tra·mon·tane *a.* being beyond the mountains, esp. the Alps; pert. to absolute temporal and spiritual power of Papacy or to party upholding this claim; *n.* advocate of extreme or ultra-papal views.

ul·tra·vi·o·let *a.* beyond limit of visibility at violet end of the spectrum.

ul·u·lant *a.* howling. **ululate** *v.i.* to howl; to lament.

um·bel *n.* (*Bot.*) flower clusters, the stalks of which rise from a common center on

umbel

main stem, forming a convexed surface above.

um·ber *n.* natural earth pigment, yellowish-brown in color when raw, reddish-brown when calcined or burnt.

um·bil·i·cal *a.* pert. to umbilicus or umbilical cord. **— cord** (*Anat.*) fibrous cord joining fetus to placenta.

um·bra *n.* shadow; (*Astron.*) complete shadow cast by earth or moon in eclipse, as opposed to *penumbra*, partial shadow in eclipse.

um·brage *n.* (*Poetic*) shadow; feeling of resentment. **umbrageous** *a.* shady.

um·brel·la *n.* light-weight circular covering

of silk or other material on folding framework of spokes, carried as protection against rain (or sun).

um·laut *n.* term used to denote mutation, e.g., caused by influence of vowel *i* (earlier *j*) on preceeding vowel such as a, o, u.

um·pire *n.* person chosen to arbitrate in dispute; impartial person chosen to see that rules of game are properly enforced; referee.

un- *prefix* before nouns, adjectives, and adverbs adding negative force; before verbs, expressing reversal of the action, separation, etc.

un·a·bashed *a.* (**abash**)
un·a·bat·ed *a.* (**abate**)
un·a·bridged *a.* (**abridge**)
un·ac·cept·a·ble *a.* (**accept**)
un·ac·com·mo·dat·ing *a.* (**accommodate**)
un·ac·com·pa·nied *a.* not accompanied; sung or played on instrument without piano, organ, or orchestral accompaniment.
un·ac·cus·tomed *a.* (**accustom**)
un·ac·quaint·ed *a.* (**acquaint**)
un·a·dul·ter·at·ed *a.* (**adulterate**)
un·af·fect·ed *a.* not affected; unmoved; straightforward; sincere.
un·al·ter·a·ble *a.* not capable of alteration; fixed; permanent.
un·am·bi·tious *a.* (**ambition**)
u·nan·i·mous *a.* all of one mind; agreed to by all parties.
un·an·nealed *a.* (**anneal**)
un·ap·pre·ci·at·ed *a.* **unappreciative** *a.* (**appreciate**)
un·arm *v.t.* to disarm; to render harmless.
un·as·sail·a·ble *a.* not assailable; irrefutable; invincible. **unassailed** *a.*
un·as·sist·ed *a.* (**assist**)
un·as·sum·ing *a.* not assuming; modest; not overbearing.
un·at·tached *a.* not attached; dangling; not posted to a particular regiment; not married or engaged.
un·at·trac·tive *a.* not attractive; repellent; plain; not prepossessing.
un·au·thor·ized *a.* **unauthoritative** *a.* (**authorize**)
un·a·vail·ing *a.* not availing; fruitless; having no result. **unavailability** *n.* **unavailable** *a.* not procurable; not at one's disposal.
un·a·ware *a.* having no knowledge of; *adv.* **unawares.**
un·bal·ance *v.t.* to upset. **-d** *a.* not balanced; lacking equipoise, or mental stability; not adjusted or equal on credit and debit sides (of ledger). **unbalance** *n.*
un·bear·able *a.* not bearable; intolerable; (of pain) excruciating.
un·be·com·ing *a.* not becoming; not suited to the wearer; (of behavior) immodest; indecorous.
un·be·fit·ting *a.* (**befit**)
un·be·known *a.* not known. **-st** *adv.* without the knowledge of.
un·be·lief *n.* **unbelievability** *n.* **unbelievable** *a.* **unbelieving** *a.* **unbelievingly** *adv.* (**believe**)
un·bend *v.t.* to free from bend position; to

339

straighten; to relax; to loose, as anchor.
unbent a. straight.
un•bi•ased v.t. (bias)
un•bleached a. (bleach)
un•blem•ished a. not blemished; faultness;
(of character) pure; perfect.
un•bod•ied a. free from the body;
incorporeal.
un•bolt•ed a. (of grain) unsifted; not
fastened with a bolt. unbolt v.t.
un•born a. not yet born; future, as unborn
generations.
un•bos•om v.t. to disclose freely; to reveal
one's intimate longings.
un•bound a. not bound; free; without outer
binding, as a book; pa.p., pa.t. of unbind.
-ed a. illimitable; abundant; irrepressible. -edly adv.
un•break•a•ble a. (break)
un•bri•dle v.t. to remove the bridle from,
as a horse. -d a. unrestrained; violently
passionate.
un•bro•ken a. complete; whole; (of horse)
untamed; inviolate; continuous.
un•bur•den v.t. to relieve of a burden;
(Fig.) to relieve the mind of anxiety.
un•busi•ness•like a. (business)
un•cal•cu•la•ted v.t. (calculate)
un•called a. not summoned. uncalled for,
unnecessary or without cause.
un•can•ny a. weird; unearthly.
un•ceas•ing a. -ly adv. (cease)
un•cer•e•mo•ni•ous a. not ceremonious;
informal; abrupt.
un•cer•tain a. not certain; not positively
known; unreliable; insecure. -ty n. state
of being or that which is uncertain; lack
of assurance.
un•change•a•ble a. unchangeability, -ness
n. unchangeably adv. unchanged a.
unchanging a. unchangingly adv.
(change)
un•char•i•ta•ble a. -ness n. uncharitably
adv. (charity)
un•chart•ed a. not shown on a map; unexplored.
un•church v.t. to excommunicate; to deprive of name and status of a church.
un•ci•al a. pert. to a type of rounded script,
found in ancient MSS from 4th-9th

CⲈNⲞⲈⲤⲒⲘⲞ:

uncial letters

cents.; n. uncial letter or manuscript.
un•ci•form a. shaped like a hook. uncinal,
uncinate a. hooked; having hook-like
prickles.
un•claimed a. (claim)
un•cle n. brother of one's father or mother;
any elderly man.
un•clean a. not clean; filthy; ceremonially
unsanctified; obscene.
un•cock v.t. to let down hammer of gun
without exploding charge.
un•come•ly a. not comely; unprepos-
sessing; ugly; obscene.
un•com•fort•a•ble a. -ness n. uncom-
fortably adv. uncomforted a. (comfort)
un•com•mer•cial a. (commerce)
un•com•mu•ni•ca•tive a. not communi-

cative; discreet; taciturn. -ly adv. -ness n.
uncommunicable a. not capable of being
shared or communicated.
un•com•plain•ing a. not complaining; resigned.
un•com•pro•mis•ing a. not compromising;
making no concession; rigid.
un•con•cern n. lack of concern; apathy. -ed
a. not concerned; disinterested; apathetic; not involved.
un•con•di•tioned a. not subjected to conditions; absolute; instinctive. unconditional a. complete; absolute; without reservation. — reflexes, the instinctive responses of an animal to external stimuli.
un•con•firmed a. (confirm)
un•con•gen•i•al a. (congenial)
un•con•scion•a•ble a. beyond reason; unscrupulous; excessive.
un•con•scious a. not conscious; unaware;
deprived of consciousness; involuntary.
un•con•sti•tu•tion•al a. not constitutional;
contrary to the constitution, as of a society
or state.
un•con•tro bdla•ble a. not capable of
being controlled; unmanageable;
irrepressible.
uncontrolled a. not controlled; (of prices)
not restricted by government regulations.
un•con•ven•tion•al a. -ity n. -ly adv. not
conforming to convention, rule or
precedent.
un•con•vert•ed a. not converted; unchanged in heart; heathen; not changed
in opinion. unconversion n. un-
convertible a. not convertible.
un•count•ed a. not counted; innumerable.
un•cou•ple v.t. to loose, as a dog from a
leash; to disjoin, as railway carriages.
un•couth a. awkward in manner; strange;
unpolished; unseemly.
un•cov•a•nant•ed a. not agreed to by
covenant.
unc•tion n. act of anointing with oil, as in
ceremony of consecration or coronation;
(Med.) ointment; act of applying
ointment; that which soothes; insincere
fervor. extreme unction, R.C. rite of
anointing the dying.
un•cul•ti•va•ble a. not capable of being
cultivated; waste. uncultivated a. not
cultivated; not tilled. uncultured a. not
cultured; not educated; crude.
un•damped a. not damped; dry.
un•daunt•ed a. -ly adv. (daunt)
un•de•ceive v.t. to free from deception. -d
a.
un•de•c•d•ed a. not settled; irresolute;
vacillating. undecidable a. not capable of
being settled.
un•de•ci•pher•a•ble a. (decipher)
un•de•clared a. not declared; (of taxable
goods at customs) not admitted as being
in one's possession during customs
examination.
un•de•filed a. (defile v.)
un•dem•o•crat•ic a. not according to the
principles of democracy. undemocratize
v.t. to make undemocratic.
un•de•mon•stra•tive a. -ly adv. -ness n.
(demonstrate)
un•der prep. below; beneath; subjected

to; less than; liable to; included in; in the care of; during the period of; bound by.

un•der•act v.t. or v.i. to act a part in a play in a colorless, ineffective way.

un•der•arm a.n. under the arm; armpit; adv. from below the shoulder (as a throw).

un•der•bid v.t. to bid lower than another for a contract, etc.; to make lower bid at bridge than one's cards justify.

un•der•bred a. of inferior manners; not thoroughbred.

un•der•brush n. undergrowth of shrubs and bushes.

un•der•car•riage n. (Aero.) landing gear of aircraft.

un•der•charge v.t. to charge less than true price; n. price below the real value.

un•der•clothes n.pl. garments worn below the outer clothing, esp. next to the skin; underclothing; lingerie.

un•der•cov•er a. (Colloq.) secret; used esp. of secret service agents.

un•der•cur•rent n. current under surface of main stream, sometimes flowing in a contrary direction; hidden tendency.

un•der•cut v.t. to cut away from below, as coal seam; to strike from beneath; to sell goods cheaply in order to capture a market or monopoly; (Golf) to hit ball so it backspins.

un•der•de•vel•op v.t. (Photog.) to develop insufficiently so that the photographic print is indistinct.

un•der•es•ti•mate v.t. to miscalculate the value of; to rate at too low a figure; n. an inadequate valuation.

un•der•ex•posed a. (Photog.) insufficiently exposed to the light to impress details on a sensitive surface with clarity of outline.

un•der•feed v.t. to feed insufficiently; to undernourish. underfed a.

un•der•foot adv. beneath the feet; a. lying under the foot; in subjection.

un•der•gar•ment n. a garment worn underneath the outer clothes.

un•der•grad•u•ate n. student attending classes for his first degree at a university or college.

un•der•ground a. under the ground; subterranean; secret; n. (chiefly Brit.) a subway; (Fig.) secret organization or resistance movement.

un•der•growth n. small trees, shrubs, or plants growing beside taller trees.

un•der•hand adv. by secret means; fraudulently; a. (Sports) served or thrown, as a ball, with hand underneath and an upward swing of the arm from below the waist; sly and dishonorable.

un•der•hung a. projecting beyond upper jaw, as lower jaw.

un•der•lay v.t. to lay underneath; to support by something put below.

un•der•lie v.t. to lie underneath; to be the basis of. **underlying** a. basic; placed beneath; obscure.

un•der•line v.t. to mark with line below, for emphasis.

un•der•ling n. one who holds inferior position.

un•der•manned a. supplied (as a ship) with

too small a crew; having too small a staff.

un•der•mine v.t. to excavate for the purpose of mining, blasting, etc.; to erode; to sap, as one's energy; to weaken insidiously.

un•der•neath adv. and prep. beneath; below; in a lower place.

un•der•nour•ished a. insufficiently nourished.

un•der•pass n. road or passage (for cars, pedestrians) under a highway or railroad.

un•der•pay v.t. to pay inadequately for the work done; to exploit.

un•der•priv•i•leged a. deficient in the necessities of life because of poverty, discrimination, etc.

un•der•proof a. containing less alcohol than proof spirit.

un•der•rate v.t. to rate too low; to underestimate.

un•der•score v.t. to underline for emphasis.

un•der•sec•re•tar•y n. secretary who ranks below the principal secretary., esp. of government department.

un•der•sell v.t. to sell more cheaply than another.

un•der•set n. (Naut.) an ocean undercurrent.

un•der•side n. the surface underneath.

un•der•sign v.t. to write one's name at the foot of or underneath.

un•der•skirt n. petticoat; skirt worn or placed under another.

un•der•stand v.t. to comprehend; to grasp the significance of.

un•der•state v.t. to state less strongly than truth warrants; to minimize deliberately.

un•der•stud•y n. one ready to substitute for principal actor (or actress) at a moment's notice.

un•der•take v.t. to take upon oneself as a special duty; to agree (to do).

un•der•tone n. low, subdued tone of voice or color.

un•der•tow n. undercurrent or backwash of a wave after it has reached the shore.

un•der•wear n. underclothes.

un•der•wood n. small trees growing among larger trees.

un•der•world n. the nether regions; Hades; the antipodes; section of community which lives by vice and crime.

un•der•write v.t. to write under something else; to subscribe; to append one's signature, as to insurance policy; to undertake to buy shares not bought by the public.

un•de•sir•a•ble a. not desirable; having no appreciable virtues; n. person of ill-repute.

un•de•vi•at•ing a. not deviating; resolute in pursuing a straight course.

un•dine n. water sprite.

un•do v.t. to reverse what has been done; to annul; to loose; to unfasten; to damage character of. **-ing** n. act of reversing what has been done; ruin, esp. of reputation.

undone a. ruined; not done; not completed.

un•dress n. informal dress; off-duty

military uniform.

un·due *a.* not yet payable; unjust; immoderate; not befitting the occasion.

un·du·late *v.t.* to move up and down like waves; to cause to vibrate; *v.i.* to move up and down; to vibrate; to have wavy edge; *a.* wavy. **undulant** *a.* undulating; wavy. **-ly** *adv.* **undulating** *a.* wavy; having series of rounded ridges and depressions, as surface of landscape. **undulatingly** *adv.* **undulation** *n.* wave; fluctuating motion, as of waves; wave-like contour of stretch of land; series of wavy lines; vibratory motion. **undulatory** *a.* pert. to undulation; moving like a wave; pert. to theory of light which argues that light is transmitted through ether by wave motions.

un·du·ly *adv.* unjustly; improperly; excessively.

un·dy·ing *a.* not dying; immortal; everlasting.

un·earned *a.* not earned by personal labor. **— income,** income derived from sources other than salary, fees, etc. **— increment,** increased value of property, land, etc. due to circumstances other than owner's expenditure on its upkeep.

un·earth *v.t.* to dig up; to drive as a fox, rabbit, etc. from its burrow; to bring to light.

un·eas·y *a.* anxious; awkward; uncomfortable.

un·em·ploy·ment *n.* state of being unemployed. **— benefit,** money received by unemployed workers according to conditions laid down by insurance regulations. **— insurance,** insurance against periods of unemployment contributed to by workers, employers, etc.

U·nes·co *n.* coined word from initial letters of *United Nations Educational, Scientific and Cultural Organization,* established in November, 1945.

un·ex·pect·ed *a.* not expected; sudden; without warning.

un·fail·ing *a.* not liable to fail; ever loyal; inexhaustible.

un·fair *a.* not fair; unjust; prejudiced; contrary to the rules of the game.

un·feel·ing *a.* void of feeling; callous; unsympathetic.

un·fin·ished *a.* not finished; roughly executed; not published.

un·fledged *a.* not yet covered with feathers; immature.

un·fleshed *a.* (of sword) not yet used in fighting; not having tasted blood. **unfleshly** *a.* uncorporeal. **unfleshy** *a.* having no flesh.

un·fold *v.t.* to open the folds of; to spread out; to disclose; *v.i.* to expand.

un·fore·seen *a.* unexpected. **unforeseeable** *a.* not capable of being foreseen; unpredictable.

un·formed *a.* not formed; amorphous; immature.

un·found·ed *a.* not based on truth; not established.

un·frock *v.t.* to deprive of a frock, esp. to deprive of the status of a monk or priest.

un·fruit·ful *a.* not productive; not profitable.

un·furl *v.t.* and *i.* to open or spread out.

un·gain·ly *a.* clumsy; awkward; *adv.* in a clumsy manner.

un·god·ly *a.* not religious; sinful.

un·ground·ed *a.* having no foundation; false.

un·gual *a.* having nails, hooves, or claws. **ungulate** *a.* having hoofs, *n.* one of the hoofed mammals.

un·guent *n.* ointment. **-ary** *a.* pert. to unguents. **unguinous** *a.* oily.

un·hal·lowed *n.* unholy; not consecrated; wicked. **unhallowing** *n.*

un·hand *v.t.* to let go. **-ily** *adv.* awkwardly. **-iness** *n.* **-led** *a.* not handled. **-y** *a.* not handy; inconvenient; lacking skill.

un·heard *a.* not heard; not given hearing. **unheard of,** unprecedented.

un·hes·i·tat·ing *a.* not hesitating; spontaneous; resolute. **-ly** *adv.* without hesitation.

un·hinge *v.t.* to take from the hinges; (*Fig.*) to cause mental instability. **-d** *a.* (of the mind) unstable; distraught.

un·ho·ly *a.* not sacred.

un·horse *v.t.* to throw from a horse; to cause to fall from a horse.

un·hy·gi·en·ic *a.* not hygienic; unsanitary; unhealthy.

u·ni-, *prefix* denoting one or single.

u·ni·ax·i·al *a.* having a single axis; having one direction along which ray of light can travel without bifurcation. **-ly** *adv.*

u·ni·cam·er·al having one legislative chamber.

u·ni·cel·lu·lar *a.* having a single cell; monocellular.

u·ni·corn *n.* (*Myth.*) horselike animal with a single horn protruding from forehead.

un·i·de·al *a.* realistic; prosaic.

u·ni·form *a.* having always same form; conforming to one pattern; regular; consistent; not varying, as temperature; *n.* official dress, as a livery, etc. **-ed** *a.* wearing uniform. **-ity** *n.* conformity to pattern or standard. **-ly** *adv.* **-ness** *n.*

u·ni·fy *v.t.* to make into one; to make uniform. **unifiable** *a.* capable of being made one. **unification** *n.* act of unifying; state of being made one; welding together of separate parts. **unifier** *n.*

u·ni·lat·er·al *a.* one-sided; binding one side only, as in party agreement.

u·ni·loc·u·lar *a.* having single chamber or cavity.

un·im·ag·i·n·ble *a.* not imaginable; inconceivable.

un·im·peach·a·ble *a.* not impeachable; irreproachable; blameless.

un·in·formed *a.* having no accurate information; ignorant; not expert.

un·ion *n.* act of joining two or more things into one; federation; marriage; harmony; combination of administrative bodies for a common purpose; trade union; **-ed** *a.* joined. **-ist** *n.* one who supports union.

union flag

Union Jack, national flag of United Kingdom.

u·nip·a·rous *a.* producing normally just one at a birth; *(Bot.)* having single stem.

u·nique *a.* single in kind; having no like or equal; unusual; different.

u·ni·sex·u·al *a.* of one sex only, as a plant; not hermaphrodite or bisexual.

u·ni·son *n.* harmony; concord; *(Mus.)* identity of pitch. **in unison** with all voices singing the same note at the same time; sounding together; in agreement.

u·nit *n.* single thing or person; group regarded as one; standard of measurement; *(Math.)* the least whole number.

U·ni·tar·i·an *n.* one who rejects doctrine of the Trinity and asserts the oneness of God and the teachings of Jesus.

u·nite *v.t.* to join; to make into one; to form a whole; to associate; to cause to adhere. *(Math.)* any quantity taken as one. **unitive** *a.* **United Nations,** international organization, formed 1942. **United Nations Organization,** international organization set up after *World War 2* with Security Council as chief executive body.

u·ni·va·lent *a. (Chem.)* having a valence of one; *(Bot.)* unpaired.

u·ni·valve *a.* having only one valve; *n.* a single-shelled mollusk.

u·ni·verse *n.* all created things regarded as a system or whole; the world. **universal** *a.* pert. to universe; embracing all created things; world-wide. **Universalism** *n.* theological doctrine of the ultimate salvation of all mankind. **Universalist** *n.* **universalistic** *a.* **-ity** *n.* — **joint** (in motoring) device whereby one part of machine has perfect freedom of motion in relation to another.

u·ni·ver·si·ty *n.* institution for educating students in higher branches of learning, and having authority to confer degrees.

un·kempt *a.* dishevelled; rough.

un·kind *a.* not kind, considerate, or sympathetic; cruel.

un·know·a·ble *a.* not capable of being known; *n.* that which is beyond man's power to understand; the absolute.

un·leav·ened *a.* not leavened; made without yeast, as *unleavened bread.*

un·less *conj.* except; if not; supposing that; *prep.* except.

un·let·tered *a.* illiterate.

un·like *a.* not like; dissimilar; *prep.* different from; *adv.* in a different way from.

un·load *v.t.* to remove load from; to remove charge from, as gun; to sell out quickly, as stocks, shares, etc. before slump.

un·looked-for *a.* unexpected, unforeseen.

un·loose *v.t.* to set free.

un·make *v.t.* to destroy what has been made; to annul; to ruin, destroy; to depose.

un·marked *a.* without a mark.

un·mean·ing *a.* without meaning; unintentional; insignificant. **-ly** *adv.* **unmeant** *a.* not intended; accidental.

un·men·tion·a·ble *a.* not worthy of mention; not fit to be mentioned. **-ness** *n.* **-s** *n.pl.* facetious synonym for undergarments.

un·mer·ci·ful *a.* having or showing no mercy; cruel. **-ly** *adv.*

un·mind·ed *a.* not remembered. **unmindful** *a.* forgetful; regardless.

un·mis·tak·a·ble *a.* clear; plain; evident.

un·mit·i·gat·ed *a.* not softened or lessened; absolute; unmodified.

un·mor·al *a.* not concerned with morality or ethics. **-izing** *a.* not given to reflecting on ethical values.

un·nerve to deprive of courage, strength; cause to feel weak.

un·num·bered *a.* not counted; innumerable.

un·oc·cu·pied *a.* not occupied; untenanted; not engaged in work; not under control of troops.

un·or·gan·ized *a.* without organic structure; having no system or order; not belonging to a labor union.

un·pack *v.t.* to remove from a pack or trunk; to open by removing packing; *v.i.* to empty contents of.

un·par·al·leled *a.* having no equal; unprecedented.

un·par·lia·men·ta·ry *a.* contrary to parliamentary law or usage.

un·prec·e·dent·ed *a.* without precedent; having no earlier example; novel. **-ly** *adv.*

un·print·a·ble *a.* not printable; too shocking to be set down in print.

un·pro·fes·sion·al *a.* not professional; contrary to professional ethics.

un·qual·i·fied *a.* not qualified; not having proper qualifications; not modified; absolute. **unqualifying** *a.*

un·quote *v.t.* and *i.* to end a quotation.

un·read *a.* (of a book) not read; not having gained knowledge by reading. **-able** *a.* not readable — illegible, uninteresting or unsuitable.

un·real *a.* not real; insubstantial; illusive. **-izable** *a.* not realizable. **-izableness** *n.* **-ized** *a.* not realized; unfulfilled. **unreality** *n.* want of reality. **-ly** *adv.* **-ity** *n.*

un·rea·son *n.* lack of reason; irrationality. **-able** *a.* immoderate; impulsive; exorbitant (of prices). **-ableness** *n.* **-ably** *adv.* **-ed** *a.* not logical. **ing** *a.* irrational.

un·re·lat·ed *a.* not related; having no apparent connection; diverse.

un·re·mit·ting *a.* not relaxing; incessant; persistent. **unremitted** *a.* not remitted. **unremittedly, -ly** *adv.*

un·rest *n.* want of rest; disquiet; political or social agitation. **-ful** *a.* **-fulness** *n.* **-ing** *a.* not resting. **-ingly** *adv.*

un·ruf·fled *a.* not ruffled; placid. **unruffle** *v.i.* to become placid.

un·ruled *a.* not ruled; ungoverned; (of paper) blank; unrestrained. **unruliness** *n.* state of being unruly. **unruly** *a.* lawless; disobedient.

un·say *v.t.* to retract (what has been said).

un·scathed *a.* unharmed; without injury.

un·scram·ble *v.t.* to decode a secret message; to straighten out.

U

un·scru·pu·lous *a.* not scrupulous; ruthless; having no moral principles.

un·sea·son·a·ble *a.* untimely; out of season.

un·seat *v.t.* to throw from a horse; to deprive of official seat.

un·self·con·scious *a.* not self-conscious; natural.

un·set·tle *v.t.* to move or loosen from a fixed position; to disturb mind; to make restless or discontented. **-d** *a.* not settled; changeable, as weather; unpaid, as bills; not allocated; not inhabited.

un·shod *a.* barefoot.

un·sight·ed *a.* not sighted; not observed; (of gun) without sights; (of shot) aimed blindly. **unsightable** *a.* invisible. **unsightliness** *n.* ugliness. **unsightly** *a.* ugly; revolting to the sight.

un·sling *v.t.* *(Naut.)* to remove slings from, as from cargo; to take down something which is hanging by sling, as a rifle.

un·so·lic·i·ted *a.* not solicited; gratuitous. **unsolicitous** *a.* unconcerned.

un·so·phis·ti·cat·ed *a.* not sophisticated; ingenuous; simple.

un·sound *a.* imperfect; damaged; decayed; (of the mind) insane; not based on reasoning; fallacious.

un·speak·a·ble *a.* beyond utterance or description (in good or bad sense); ineffable.

un·sport·ing *a.* *(Colloq.)* not like sportsman; unfair. **unsportsmanlike** *a.* not in accordance with the rules of fair play.

un·sprung *a.* not fitted with springs, as a vehicle, chair, etc.

un·sta·ble *a.* unsteady; wavering; not firm; unreliable; *(Chem.)* applied to compounds which readily decompose or change into other compounds.

un·stop *v.t.* to open by removing a stopper, as a bottle; to clear away an obstruction; to open organ stops. *pr.p.* **-ping**. *pa.p.,* *pa.t.* **-ped.** *a.* not stopped; having no cork or stopper.

un·strained *a.* not strained, as through a filter; *(Fig.)* relaxed; friendly.

un·stuck *a.* not glued together.

un·suc·cess·ful *a.* not succeeding; unfortunate; incomplete.

un·sung *a.* not sung or spoken; not celebrated.

un·sup·port·ed *a.* not supported; without backing. **unsupportable** *a.* not supportable; intolerable.

un·taught *a.* *pa.p.,* *pa.t.* of **unteach**; uneducated; ignorant; natural, without teaching.

un·thank·ful *a.* ungrateful.

un·think·ing *a.* thoughtless; heedless.

un·til *prep.* till; to; as far as; as late as; *conj.* up to the time that; to the degree that.

un·time·ly *a.* not timely; premature; inopportune.

un·to *prep.* *(Poet.)* to; until.

un·touch·a·ble *a.* incapable of being touched; unfit to be touched; out of reach; belonging to non-caste masses of India; *n.* non-caste Indian whose touch or even shadow was regarded as defiling.

un·to·ward *a.* unlucky; inconvenient; hard to manage.

un·trav·eled *a.* not having traveled; unexplored.

un·tried *pa.p.,* *pa.t.* of try; not proven, attempted or tested; not tried in court.

un·true *a.* not true; false; disloyal; not conforming to a requisite standard. **-ness** *n.* **untruly** *adv.* falsely. **untruth** *n.* **untruthful** *a.* dishonest; lying.

un·used *a.* not used; not accustomed. **unusual** *a.* not usual; uncommon; strange. **unusually** *adv.* **unusualness** *n.*

un·ut·ter·a·ble *a.* unspeakable beyond utterance. **utterability** *n.*

un·war·rant·a·ble *a.* unjustifiable; improper.

un·washed *a.* not washed; dirty; not reached by the sea.

un·well *a.* ill; ailing.

un·wept *a.* not mourned or regretted.

un·will·ing *a.* loathe; reluctant.

un·wind *v.t.* to wind off; to loose what has been wound; to roll into a ball from a skein, as wool, silk, etc.; *v.i.* to become unwound.

un·wit·ting *a.* unawares; not knowing.

un·wont·ed *a.* unaccustomed; unusual.

un·writ·ten *a.* not written; oral; not expressed in writing. **unwritten Law,** law originating in custom, usage.

un·yield·ing *a.* not yielding; stubborn; implacable; not flexible.

up *adv. prep.* to or toward a higher place or degree; on high; on one's legs; out of bed; above horizon; in progress; in revolt; as far as; of equal merit or degree; thoroughly well versed in; competent.

u·pas *n.* tree of E. Indian islands, yielding sap of deadly poison.

up·braid *v.t.* to reprove severely; to chide; *v.i.* to voice a reproach.

up·bring·ing *n.* the process of rearing and training a child; education.

up·coun·try *adv.* inland; *a.* away from the sea.

up·grade *a., adv.* uphill; *n.* incline; *v.t.* to raise to a higher level.

up·heave *v.t.* to lift up, as heavy weight. **upheaval** *n.* raising up, as of earth's surface, by volcanic force.

up·hill *a.* going up; laborious; difficult; *adv.* towards higher level.

up·hold *v.t.* to hold up; to sustain; to approve; to amaintain, as verdict in law court.

up·hol·ster *v.t.* to stuff and cover furniture.

up·keep *n.* maintenance; money required for maintenance, as of a home.

up·land *n.* high land or region. *a.* pert. to or situated in higher elevations.

up·lift *v.t.* to lift up; to improve conditions of, morally, socially etc.; to exalt.

up·per *a.* higher in place, rank, or dignity; superior; more recent; *n.* the part above. **— hand** *n.* superiority; advantage over another.

up·right *a.* standing, pointed straight up; honest; *adv.* in such a position.

up·rise *v.i.* to rise up; to revolt. *pa.p.*

up·roar *n.* tumult; violent, noisy disturbance.

up·root v.t. to tear up by the roots.

up·set v.t. to turn upside down; to knock over; to defeat; to disturb or distress.

up·shot n. final issue; conclusion.

up·side n. the upper side. **—down** adv. with the upper side underneath; inverted; in disorder.

up·stage a., adv. of or toward rear of stage; v.t. to act on stage so as to minimize another actor.

up·stairs adv. in the upper story; on the stairs; a. pert. to upper story.

up·stand·ing a. erect; honorable.

up·start n. one who has suddenly risen to wealth, power, or honor; parvenu.

up·stream adv. in direction of source (of stream).

up·stroke n. the upward line in handwriting; upward stroke.

up·surge v.t. to surge upwards. n. welling, as of emotion.

up·sweep n. a curve upward.

up·swing n. a trend upward.

up·thrust n. upward thrust.

up·to·date a. modern; most recent; extending up to, pert. to, the present time.

up·town a. pert. to, or in upper part of, town; adv.

up·turn v.t. to turn up. n. an upward turn for the better.

up·ward a. directed towards a higher place; adv. upwards.

u·ra·nite n. an almost transparent ore of uranium.

u·ra·ni·um n. radio-active metallic element (symbol U), used as an alloy in steel manufacture and in the production of atom bomb.

u·ra·nog·ra·phy n. descriptive astronomy.

ur·ban a. pert. to, or living in, city or town. **urbane** a. refined; suave; courteous.

ur·chin n. sea urchin.

u·re·a n. crystalline solid, the principle organic constituent of urine.

u·re·ter n. one of two ducts of kidney conveying urine to bladder. **urethra** n. duct by which urine passes from bladder.

urge v.t. to press; to drive; to exhort; to simulate; to solicit earnestly; v.i. to press onward; to make allegations, entreaties, etc. n. act of urging; incentive; irresistible impulse. **-ncy** n. quality of being urgent; compelling necessity; importunity.

u·rine n. yellowish fluid secreted by kidneys, passed through ureters to bladder from which it is discharged through urethra. **uremia** n. toxic condi-tion of the blood caused by insufficient secretion of urine. **urology** n. branch of Med. dealing with urinogenital system.

urn n. vase-shaped vessel of pottery or metal with pedestal, and narrow neck, as used for ashes of dead after cremation.

ur·sine a. pert. to or resembling a bear.

use v.t. to make use of; to employ; to consume or expend. **use** n. act of using or employing for specific purpose; utility; custom. **usable** a. fit for use. **usability** n. **usage** n. mode of using; treatment; long-established custom. **usance** n. usual time allowed for payment of foreign bills of exchange.

ush·er n. doorkeeper; one who conducts people to seats in church, theater, etc.

us·que·baugh n. whiskey.

u·su·al a. customary; ordinary.

u·su·fruct n. right of using and enjoying produce benefit, or profits of another's property provided that the property remains undamaged.

u·surp v.t. to take possession of unlawfully or by force.

u·su·ry n. charging of exorbitant interest on money lent. **usurer** n. money lender who charges exorbitant rates of interest.

u·ten·sil n. vessel of any kind which forms part of domestic, esp. kitchen, equipment.

u·ter·ine a. pert. to uterus or womb; born of the same mother but by a different father.

u·til·i·tar·i·an n. one who accepts doctrines of utilitarianism. **-ism** n. ethical doctrine, the ultimate aim and criterion of all human actions must be 'the greatest happiness for the greatest number.'

u·ti·lize v.t. to put to use; to turn to profit.

ut·most a. situated at farthest point or extremity; to highest degree; n. most that can be; greatest possible effort.

u·to·pi·a n. any ideal state, constitution, system, or way of life.

u·tri·cle n. (Bot.) little bag or bladder, esp. of aquatic plant; (Anat.) a sac in inner ear influencing equilibrium.

ut·ter a. total; unconditional.

ut·ter v.t. to speak; to disclose; to put into circulation.

ut·ter·most a. farthest out; utmost; n. the highest degree.

u·vu·la n. fleshy tag suspended from middle of lower border of soft palate.

ux·o·ri·ous a. foolishly or excessively fond of one's wife.

U

va·cant *a.* empty; void; not occupied; unintelligent. **-ly** *adv.* **vacancy** *n.* emptiness; opening; lack of thought; place or post; unfilled. **vacate** *v.t.* to leave empty or unoccupied; to quit possession of; to make void. **vacation** *n.* act of vacating; intermission of stated employment; recess; holidays.

vac·cine *a.* pert. to, or obtained from cows; *n.* virus of cowpox, used in vaccination; any substance used for inoculation against disease. **vaccinate** *v.t.* to inoculate with cowpox, to ward off smallpox or lessen severity of its attack. **vaccination** *n.* act or practice of vaccinating; the inoculation.

vac·il·late *v.i.* to move to and fro; to waver; to be unsteady; to fluctuate in opinion.

vac·u·um *n.* space devoid of all matter; space from which air, or other gas, has been almost wholly removed, as by air pump. **— cleaner** *n.* apparatus for removing dust from carpets, etc. by suction. **— tube** used in radio, TV, and electronic equipment; a sealed tube containing metallic electrodes but (almost) no air or gas.

va·de·me·cum *n.* small handbook or manual for ready reference.

vag·a·bond *a.* moving from place to place without settled habitation; wandering; *n.* wanderer or vagrant, having no settled habitation; idle scamp; rascal.

va·gar·y *n.* whimsical or freakish notion; unexpected action; caprice.

va·gi·na *n.* (*Anat.*) canal which leads from uterus to external orifice.

va·grant *a.* wandering from place to place; moving without certain direction; roving.

vague *a.* uncertain; indefinite; indistinct; not clearly expressed.

vain *a.* useless; unavailing; fruitless; empty; worthless; conceited. **-ly** *adv.* **-ness** *n.* **vanity** *n.* conceit; something one is conceited about; worthlessness; dressing table.

vain·glo·ry *n.* excessive vanity; boastfulness.

val·ance *n.* short drapery across the top of a window, bed, etc.

vale *n.* valley.

val·e·dic·tion *n.* farewell; a bidding farewell. **valedictory** *a.* bidding farewell. **valedictorian** *n.* student in a graduating class with the highest scholastic standing who gives the valedictory at graduation exercises.

va·lence, va·len·cy *n.* (*Chem.*) the combining power of an element or atom as compared with a hydrogen atom.

va·len·tine *n.* sweetheart chosen on *St. Valentine's* day; card containing profession of love, sent on *St. Valentine's* day, Feb. 14th.

va·le·ri·an *n.* flowering herb with strong odor; its root, used as sedative drug.

val·et *n.* manservant who cares for clothing, etc. of his employer.

val·e·tu·di·nar·i·an *a.* sickly; infirm; solicitous about one's own health.

val·iant *a.* brave; heroic; courageous; intrepid.

val·id *a.* sound or well-grounded; capable of being justified; (*Law*) legally sound; executed with proper formalities.

va·lise *n.* suitcase.

val·ley *n.* low ground between hills; river basin.

val·or *n.* bravery; prowess in war; courage.

valse *n.* waltz, esp. one played as concert piece.

val·ue *n.* worth; utility; importance; estimated worth or valuation; precise significance; equivalent. **valuation** *n.* value estimated or set upon a thing; appraisal.

valve *n.* device for closing aperture (as in pipe) in order to control flow of fluid, gas, etc.

vamp *n.* upper leather of shoe or boot; new patch put on old article.

vam·pire *n.* reanimated body of dead person who cannot rest quietly in grave. **— bat** *n.* of several species of bat of S. America which sucks blood of animals.

van *n.* covered wagon or motor truck for goods.

van *n.* leaders of a movement. **-guard** *n.* detachment of troops who march ahead of army.

va·na·di·um *n.* a metallic element (the hardest known) used in manufacture of hard steel.

van·dal *n.* one who wantonly damages or destroys property of beauty or value.

van·dyke *n.* one of the points forming an edge, as of lace, ribbon, etc.

vane *n.* a device on a windmill, spire, etc. to show the direction of the wind; a weathercock; the blade of a propeller, of a windmill, etc.

va·nil·la *n.* tropical American plant of orchid family; long pod of plant, used as flavoring.

van·ish *v.i.* to pass away; to be lost to view; to disappear; (*Math.*) to become zero.

van·quish *v.t.* to conquer in battle; to defeat in any contest; to get the better of.

van·tage *n.* better situation or opportunity; advantage; in tennis, same as 'advantage.'

vap·id *a.* having lost its life and spirit; flat; insipid; dull.

va·por *n.* any light, cloudy substance which impairs clearness of atmosphere, as mist, fog, smoke, etc.; a substance converted into gaseous state; anything unsubstantial. **-ize** *v.t.* to convert into vapor; *v.i.* to pass off in vapor.

var·i·a·ble *a.* changeable; capable of being adapted; unsteady or fickle; *n.* that which is subject to change. **variant** *a.* different; diverse; *n.* different form or reading. **variation** *n.* act of varying; alteration; modification; extent to which thing varies; (*Gram.*) change of termination; in magnetism, deviation of magnetic needle from true north.

var·i·col·ored *a.* having various colors.

var·i·cose *a.* enlarged or dilated, as veins, esp. in legs.

var·i·e·gate *v.t.* to diversify by patches of different colors; to streak, spot, dapple, etc.

V

va•ri•e•ty *n.* state of being varied; diversity; collection of different things; many-sidedness; different form of something; subdivision of a species.

var•i•o•rum *n.* an edition of a work with notes by various commentators.

var•i•ous *a.* different; diverse; manifold; separate; diversified.

var•let *n.* (*Arch.*) page or attendant; scoundrel.

var•nish *n.* clear, resinous liquid laid on work to give it gloss and protection.

var•si•ty *n.* team, usu. athletic, representing a university, school, etc. in competition; *a.* designating such a team.

var•y *v.t.* to change; to make different or modify; to diversify; *v.i.* to alter, or be altered; to be different. **varied** *a.* various; diverse; diversified.

vas *n.* (*Anat.*) vessel or duct. **-cular** *a.* pert. to vessels or ducts for conveying blood, lymph, sap, etc.

vase *n.* vessel for flowers or merely for decoration; large sculptured vessel, used as ornament, in gardens, on gateposts, etc.

vas•e•line *n.* brand of petroleum used in ointments, pomades, as lubricant, etc.

vas•sal *n.* one who holds land from superior, and vows fealty and homage to him; dependant; retainer. **-age** *n.* state of being a vassal.

vast *a.* of great extent; very spacious; very great in numbers or quantity.

vat *n.* large vessel, tub, for holding liquids.

vat•ic *a.* prophetic; oracular.

Vat•i•can *n.* palace and official residence of Pope on Vatican Hill.

vaude•ville *n.* stage show with mixed specialty acts; variety show.

vault *n.* arched roof; room or passage covered with vault, esp. subterranean; cellar; sky; anything resembling a vault.

vault

vault *v.i.* to spring or jump with hands resting on something; to leap or spring, as horse.

vaunt *v.t.* to boast of; to make vain display of; *n.* boast; vainglorious display.

veal *n.* flesh of a calf killed for the table.

vec•tor *n.* (*Math.*) any quantity requiring direction to be stated as well as magnitude in order to define it properly; disease-carrying insect.

Ve•da *n.* most ancient sacred literature of Hindus.

ve•dette *n.* mounted sentinel placed in advance of outposts to give notice of danger.

veer *v.t.* and *v.i.* to turn; of wind, to change direction, esp. clockwise; (*Naut.*) to change ship's course; (*Fig.*) to change one's opinion or point of view.

veg•e•ta•ble *a.* belonging to plants; having nature of plants; *n.* plant, esp. plant used as food. **vegetal** *a.* **vegetarian** *n.* one who abstains from animal flesh and lives on vegetables, eggs, milk, etc. **vegetation** *n.* process of vegetating; vegetable growth; plants in general.

ve•he•ment *a.* acting with great force; impetuous; vigorous; passionate.

ve•hi•cle *n.* any means of conveyance (esp. on land) as carriage, etc.; liquid medium in which drugs are taken, or pigments applied; means or medium of expression or communication.

veil *n.* piece of thin, gauzy material worn by women to hide or protect face; covering; curtain; disguise.

vein *n.* each of the vessels or tubes which receive blood from capillaries and return it to heart; layer of mineral intersecting a stratum of rock; streak or wave of different color appearing in wood, marble, etc.

veld, veldt *n.* in S. Africa, open grass country.

vel•lum *n.* fine parchment made of skin; paper of similar texture.

ve•loc•i•pede *n.* a vehicle propelled by the rider, early form of bicycle or tricycle.

ve•loc•i•ty *n.* rate of motion; swiftness; speed; distance traversed in unit time in a given direction.

ve•lours *n.sing.* and *pl.* fabric resembling velvet or plush.

vel•vet *n.* soft material of silk with thick short pile on one side. **-een** *n.* a pile fabric made of cotton, or of silk and cotton mixed.

ve•nal *a.* to be obtained for money; prepared to take bribes; mercenary. **venality** *n.* quality of being purchaseable.

ve•nat•ic, ve•nat•i•cal *a.* relating to hunting.

vend *v.t.* to sell; to dispose of by sale. **-or** *n.* person who sells.

ven•det•ta *n.* blood feud, in which it was the duty of the relative of murdered man to avenge his death by killing murderer or relative of murderer.

ve•neer *n.* thin layer of valuable wood glued to surface of inferior wood.

ven•er•ate *v.t.* to regard with respect and reverence. **venerable** *a.* worthy of veneration; deserving respect by reason of age, character, etc.

ve•ne•re•al *a.* pert. to sexual intercourse; arising from sexual intercourse with infected persons.

ver•er•y *n.* (*Arch.*) hunting; sports of the chase.

Ve•ne•tian *a.* pert. to city of Venice, Italy; *n.* native, inhabitant of Venice. — **blind,** blind made of thin, horizontal slats, so hung as to overlap each other when closed.

venge•ance *n.* infliction of pain or loss on another in return for injury or offense. **vengeful** *a.* disposed to revenge; vindictive.

ve•ni•al *a.* capable of being forgiven; excusable.

ven•i•son *n.* flesh of the deer.

ven•om n. poison, esp. that secreted by serpents, bees, etc.; spite; malice. -ous a. poisonous; spiteful; malicious.

ve•nous, ve•nose a. pert. to veins or the blood in veins.

vent n. small opening; outlet; flue or funnel of fireplace; touch hole of gun; utterance; emission; voice; escape. -age, -er n. -less a. to give vent to, to pour forth.

ven•ti•late v.t. to remove foul air from and supply with fresh air; to expose to discussion; to make public. ventilation n. replacement of stale air by fresh air; free exposure to air; open discussion.

ven•tral a. belonging to belly; abdominal; opp. of dorsal; n. one of the pair of fins on belly of fish. ventricle n. (Anat. or Zool.) small cavity in certain organs, esp. one of chambers of heart.

ven•tril•o•quism n. art of speaking in such a way that words or sounds seem to come from some source other than speaker.

ven•ture n. undertaking of chance or danger; business speculation. -r n. venturous a. daring; risky.

ven•ue n. (Law) district in which case is tried; scene of an event.

ven•ule n. small vein.

Ve•nus n. (Myth.) Roman goddess of love and beauty; brightest planet of solar system; beautiful woman.

ve•ra•cious a. truthful; true. veracity n. quality of being truthful; truth; correctness.

ve•ran•da, verandah n. open porch or gallery, along side of house, often with roof.

verb n. (Gram.) part of speech which expresses action or state of being. -less a. -al a. pert. to words; expressed in words, esp. spoken words; literal or word for word.

ver•be•na n. genus of plants of family Verbenaceae, used in ornamental flower beds. Also called vervain.

ver•bi•age n. excess of words; use of many more words than are necessary; wordiness. verbose a. prolix; tedious because of excess of words.

ver•dant a. green or fresh; flourishing; ignorant or unsophisticated. verdure n. greenness or freshness; green vegetation.

ver•dict n. decision of jury in a trial; decision or judgment.

ver•di•gris n. green rust on copper, bronze, etc.; basic acetate of copper, used as pigment, etc.

verge n. border, or edge; brink; a rod of office; mace of bishop, etc.

verge v.i. to tend; to slope; to border upon.

ver•i•fy v.t. to prove to be true; to confirm truth of.

ver•i•ly adv. (Arch.) truly; certainly.

ver•i•ta•ble a. actual; genuine.

ver•i•ty n. quality of being true; truth; reality.

ver•juice n. sour juice of crab-apples, unripe grapes, etc.

ver•mi- prefix. worm. -an a. worm-like; pert. to worms. -celli n. paste made from same ingredients as macaroni, and formed into slender worm-like threads.

ver•mil•ion n. prepared red sulfide of mercury; brilliant red color.

ver•min n. collectively noxious or troublesome small animals or insects, e.g. squirrels, rats, worms, lice, etc.; low contemptible persons. -ous a. infested by vermin; caused by vermin; tending to breed vermin.

ver•mouth, vermuth n. cordial of white wine flavored with wormwood, used as aperitif.

ver•nac•u•lar a. belonging to country of one's birth.

ver•nal a. belonging to, or appearing on, spring; youthful.

ver•ni•er n. short, graduated-scale instrument, for measuring fractional parts.

Ver•o•nal n. hypnotic or sedative drug.

ve•ron•i•ca n. genus of plants, including speedwell.

ver•ru•ca n. ver•sa•tile a. having aptitude in many subjects; liable to change; capable of moving freely in all directions.

verse n. metrical line containing certain number of feet; metrical arrangement of language; short division of any literary composition; stanza; piece of poetry.

ver•sion n. translation; account from particular point of view.

ver•so n. left-hand page; reverse side of coin or medal.

ver•sus prep. (Law, Games) against; contrasted with.

ver•te•bra n. one of the small bony segments of spinal column. vertebrate a. having backbone; n. vertebrate animal.

ver•tex n. highest point; summit; top of head. vertical a. situated at vertex; directly overhead or in the zenith; upright or perpendicular. vertiginous a. revolving; giddy; causing giddiness.

verve n. enthusiasm or vigor; energy; spirit.

ver•y a. true; real; actual; genuine; now used chiefly to emphasize word following.

ves•i•cal a. (Med.) pert. to bladder. vesicant a. tending to raise blisters; n. blistering application.

Ves•per n. the evening star, Venus; (l.c.) evening; a. (l.c.) pert. to evening or vespers. -s n.pl. an evening prayer; evensong; late afternoon or evening service.

ves•sel n. utensil for holding either liquids or solids; large ship; (Anat.) tube or canal; recipient or means of conveying something.

vest n. short, sleeveless garment worn under a man's suit coat; undergarment. -ment n. ceremonial or official garment.

ves•tal a. chaste; pure. n. nun; chaste woman.

ves•ti•bule n. small room or hall between outer and inner doors at entrance to house or building.

ves•tige n. trace or sign; mark of something that has been; remains; (Biol.) trace of some part or organ formerly present in body.

ves•try n. room attached to church for holding ecclesiastical vestments, prayer meetings, etc.

vetch n. plant of bean family used for fodder.

vet•er•an n. person who has served a long time; a. long practiced.

vet•er•i•nar•y a. pert. to healing diseases and surgical treatment of domestic animals. **veterinarian** n. one skilled in medical and surgical treatment of animals.

ve•to n. power or right of forbidding.

vex v.t. to make angry; to irritate; to distress.

vi•a•ble a. born alive and sufficiently developed to be able to live; capable of living or growth.

vi•a•duct n. high bridge or series of arches for carrying road or railway over valley, etc.

vi•al n. small glass bottle; phial.

vi•and n. article of food; chiefly pl. food, victuals, provisions.

vi•at•i•cum n. supplies for a journey; Communion or Eucharist given to dying person.

vi•brate v.t. to move to and fro; to cause to quiver; to measure by vibrations or oscillations. **vibrant** a. vibrating; thrilling or throbbing; powerful.

vi•bur•num n. any of a group of shrubs of honeysuckle family.

vic•ar n. a deputy; clergyman. **-age** n. residence of vicar.

vi•car•i•ous a. delegated; substituted; done or suffered for another.

vice n. depravity or immortal conduct; blemish or defect in character, etc. **vicious** a. depraved; wicked; spiteful; not well broken, as horse.

vice- prefix in words signifying persons, denoting one who acts in place of another, or one who is second in authority.

vice•ge•rent a. exercising delegated power; n. holder of delegated authority.

vice•roy n. governor of country or province who rules as representative of his king.

vi•ce ver•sa adv. the order being reversed; the other way round.

vi•chy•ssoise n. thick cream soup of potatoes.

vi•cin•i•ty n. neighborhood; nearness or proximity.

vi•cis•si•tude n. regular change or succession; alteration.

vic•tim n. living creature sacrificed in performance of religious ceremony; person, or thing, destroyed or sacrificed; person who suffers; dupe or prey.

vic•tor n. one who defeats enemy in battle; conqueror; winner in contest. **-y** n. defeat of enemy in battle, or of antagonist in contest; conquest; triumph.

vic•to•ri•a n. low four-wheeled carriage with folding top.

Vic•to•ri•an a. of or characteristic of time of Queen Victoria; prudish; easily shocked; (of style) ornate, flowery.

vic•tro•la n. a phonograph.

vict•ual v.t. to supply with provisions.

vid•e•o n. television; a. of picture phase of television.

vie v.i. to strive for superiority; to contend.

view n. sight; inspection by eye or mind; power of seeing; range of sight; what is seen; pictured representation of scene. **— finder** n. device in camera for showing limits of picture. **-point** n. attitude or standpoint.

vig•il n. staying awake at night, either for religious exercises, or to keep watch. **-ante** n. a member of an unlawful group which sets itself up to control and punish crime.

vi•gnette n. orig. running ornament of leaves or tendrils; small designs used as headings or tail pieces in books; any engraving, woodcut, etc. not enclosed within border.

vig•or n. active strength; capacity for exertion; energy; vitality; forcefulness of style, in writing.

vi•king n. Scand. sea rover or pirate who ravaged the northwest coast of Europe (8th-10th cent.).

vile a. mean; worthless; base; depraved.

vilify v.t. to speak ill of; to try to degrade by slander; to defame or traduce.

vil•la n. country seat; large suburban residence.

vil•lage n. assemblage of houses, smaller than town and larger than hamlet.

vil•lain n. wicked, depraved or criminal person.

vil•la•nelle n. poem of 19 lines on 2 rhymes having 5 three-lined stanzas, followed by one of four lines.

vil•lein n. serf who was slave to his lord but free with respect to others.

vil•lus n. one of the small, fine, hair-like processes which cover certain membranes; any of the fine soft hairs covering certain fruits, flowers, or plants.

vin•ai•grette n. small box, containing sponge saturated with aromatic vinegar salts, etc.; a savory sauce.

vin•ci•ble a. that may be conquered.

vin•cu•lum n. bond of union; (Alg.) straight, horizontal mark placed over several members of compound quantity to be treated as one quantity.

vin•di•cate v.t. to justify; to maintain as true and correct.

vin•dic•tive a. given to revenge; revengeful.

vine n. woody, climbing plant that produces grapes; any plant which trails or climbs. **vinery** n. greenhouse for rearing vines. **-yard** n. plantation of grapevines.

vin•e•gar n. acid liquor obtained from malt, wine, cider, etc. by fermentation, and used as condiment or in pickling.

vin•tage n. gathering of grapes; season's yield of grapes or wine; wine of particular year. **— wine**, wine made from grapes of particularly good year.

vi•nyl n. man-made plastic material.

vi•o•la n. instrument larger than violin, but smaller than violoncello.

vi•o•la n. (Bot.) genus of plants including

violet and pansy.

vi•o•late v.t. to infringe or break a promise; to treat with disrespect; to outrage or rape.

vi•o•lence n. force; vehemence; intensity; assault or outrage. violent a. characterized by physical force.

vi•o•let n. flower of genus Viola, generally of bluish-purple color.

vi•o•lin n. modern musical instrument of viol family, with four strings, played with bow.

vi•o•lon•cel•lo n. bass violin, much larger than violin, held between player's knees.

vi•per n. a venomous snake; malicious person.

vi•res•cent a. turning green.

vir•gin n. girl or woman who has not had sexual intercourse; maiden. the Virgin, mother of Christ.

Vir•gin•ia creep•er climbing vine whose leaves turn bright red in autumn.

Vir•go n. (Astron.) the Virgin, one of the signs of Zodiac.

vir•gule n. short diagonal line (/) between two words indicating either may be used.

vir•ile a. pert. to man; masculine; strong; having vigor.

vir•tu n. objects of art or antiquity, collectively.

vir•tu•al a. being in essence or effect, though not in fact; potential. -ly adv. to all intents and purposes.

vir•tue n. moral excellence; merit; good quality; female chastity.

vir•tu•o•so n. one with great knowledge of fine arts.

vir•u•lent a. extremely poisonous; bitter in enmity; malignant; deadly. virus n. organism causing disease; corrupting influence.

vi•sa n. official endorsement, as on passport, in proof that document has been examined and found correct.

vis•age n. face; countenance; look or appearance.

vis•a•vis adv. face to face; n. person facing another.

vis•cer•a n.pl. internal organs of body; intestines; entrails.

vis•cid a. glutinous; sticky; tenacious. -ity n. viscose n. viscid solution of cellulose, drawn into fibers and used in making rayon, cellophane.

vis•count n. a degree or title of nobility next in rank below earl.

vise n. device with two jaws that can be brought together with screw, for holding steady anything which needs filing.

vis•i•ble a. that can be seen; perceptible; in view. visibly adv. visibility n. degree of clarity of atmosphere.

vi•sion n. act or faculty of seeing external objects; sight; thing seen; imaginary sight; phantom; imaginative insight or foresight.

vis•it v.t. to go, or come, to see; to punish; v.i. to be a guest.

vi•sor n. front part of helmet which can be lifted to show face.

vis•ta n. view, esp. distant view, as through avenue of trees.

vis•u•al a. relating to sight; used in seeing; visible.

vi•tal a. necessary to or containing life; very necessary. — statistics data concerning births, deaths, etc.

vi•ta•min n. any of a group of chemical substances present in various foods and indispensable to health and growth.

vi•ti•ate v.t. to make faulty or impure; to corrupt; to impair; to invalidate.

vit•i•cul•ture n. cultivation of grapevines.

vit•re•ous a. pert. to, or resembling, glass; glassy; derived from glass.

vit•ri•fy v.t. to convert into glass or glassy substance; v.i. to be converted into glass.

vit•ri•ol n. sulfuric acid. -ic a. pert. to, resembling, derived from, vitriol; sarcastic, caustic; bitter.

vi•tu•per•ate v.t. to ,abuse in words; to revile; to berate.

vi•va interj. long live.

vi•va•cious a. lively; sprightly; animated; having great vitality.

vi•var•i•um n. place for keeping or raising living animals or plants.

vi•va vo•ce adv. orally; a. oral.

viv•id a. animated; lively; clear; evoking brilliant images.

viv•i•fy v.t. to endue with life; to animate; to make vivid.

vi•vip•a•rous a. producing young in living state, instead of eggs.

viv•i•sec•tion n. dissection of, or experimenting on, living animals for purpose of physiological investigations.

vix•en n. she-fox; cross bad-tempered woman.

vi•zier, vi•zir n. high executive officer in Turkey and other Oriental countries.

vo•ca•ble n. a word esp. with ref. to sound rather than meaning; term.

vo•cab•u•lar•y n. list of words, usu. arranged in alphabetical order and explained; wordbook; stock of words used by language, class, or individual.

vo•cal a. pert. to voice or speech; having voice; uttered by voice.

vo•ca•tion n. divine call to religious career; profession, or occupation.

voc•a•tive a. relating to, used in, calling or address; n. (Gram.) case used in direct address.

vo•cif•er•ate v.t. to utter noisily or violently; to bawl; v.i. to cry with loud voice.

vod•ka n. in Russia and Poland alcoholic liquor distilled from cereals or potatoes.

vogue n. prevailing fashion; mode; style; current usage.

voice n. faculty of uttering audible sounds; sound produced by organs of respiration. -d a. furnished with voice or with expression.

void a. empty; being without; not legally binding; n. an empty space. -ance n. act of voiding; state of being void.

voile n. thin cotton, woolen, or silk material.

vo•lant a. borne through the air; capable of flying.

Vo•la•puk n. artificial language invented in 1879.

vol•a•tile *a.* evaporating quickly; easily passing into a vapor state; fickle; changeable.

vol•ca•no *n.* opening in crust of earth, from which heated solid, liquid, and gaseous matters are ejected.

vole *n.* mouse-like rodent living out-of-doors.

vol•i•tant *a.* volant; flying; having power of flight.

vo•li•tion *n.* act of willing or choosing; exercise of will.

vol•ley *n.* discharge of many shots or missiles at one time; missiles so discharged; rapid utterance; *(Tennis)* return of ball before it touches ground. **-ball** *n.* team game played with ball and net.

volt *n.* practical unit of electro-motive force, being the pressure which causes current of one ampere to flow through resistance of one ohm. **-age** *n.* electro-motive force reckoned in volts.

volt, volte *n.* in fencing, sudden turn or movement to avoid thrust; gait, or track, made by horse going sideways round center; circle so made.

volte•face *n.* turning round; sudden reversal of opinion or direction.

vol•u•ble *a.* having flowing and rapid utterance; fluent in speech; glib.

vol•ume *n.* formerly, roll or scroll; book; part of a work which is bound; bulk or compass; cubical content; power, fullness of voice or musical tone. **voluminal** *a.* pert. to cubical content. **voluminous** *a.* consisting of many volumes; bulky.

vol•un•tar•y *a.* proceeding from choice or free will; unconstrained; spontaneous; subject to the will.

vol•un•teer *n.* one who enters service, esp. military, of his own free will; *a.* serving as a volunteer; composed.

vo•lup•tu•ar•y *n.* one addicted to luxurious living or sensual gratification; sensualist; *a.* concerned with, or promoting, sensual pleasure.

vo•lute *n.* *(Archit.)* spiral scroll used in Ionic, Corinthian, and Composite capitals; *(Zool.)* tropical spiral shell; *a.* rolled up spiraled.

volute

vom•it *v.t.* to eject from stomach by mouth; to spew or disgorge; *v.i.* to eject contents of stomach by mouth.

voo•doo *n.* body of primitive rites and practices; one who practices such rites; evil spirit; *a.* belonging to, or connected with, system of voodoo.

vo•ra•cious *a.* greedy in eating; eager to devour; ravenous.

vor•tex *n.* whirling motion of any fluid, forming depression in center of circle; whirlpool; whirling mass of air, fire, etc. which draws with irresistable power.

vo•ta•ry *a.* consecrated by vow or promise; devoted to any service, study, etc. **votaress** *n.* *(fem.).*

vote *n.* formal expression of wish, choice, or opinion, of individual, or a body of persons; expression of will by a majority; right to vote; suffrage; what is given or allowed by vote.

vo•tive *a.* offered or consecrated by vow; given in fulfillment of vow.

vouch *v.t.* to warrant; to attest; to affirm; *v.i.* to bear witness.

vouch•safe *v.t.* to condescend to grant or do something; *v.i.* to deign.

vow *n.* solemn promise made esp. to deity; *v.t.* to consecrate or dedicate by solemn promise.

vow•el *n.* any vocal sound (such as *a, e, i, o, u*) produced with least possible friction or hindrance from any organ of speech.

voy•age *n.* journey esp. by sea; *v.i.* to sail or traverse by water.

Vul•can *n.* *(Myth.)* Roman god of fire and of metal working. **vulcanize** *v.t.* to treat rubber with sulfur at high temperature to increase durability and elasticity.

vul•gar *a.* of common people; in common use; coarse or offensive; rude; boorish. **-ness, vulgarity** *n.* commonness; lack of refinement in manners; coarseness of ideas or language.

vul•ner•a•ble *a.* capable of being wounded; offering open to criticism; assailable; in contract bridge, denoting side which has won first game in rubber and is subject to increased honors and penalties.

vul•pine *a.* pert. to fox; cunning; crafty.

vul•ture *n.* large, rapacious bird of prey; rapacious person.

vulture

vul•va *n.* fissure in external organ of generation in female.

W

wad n. little tuft or bundle; soft mass of loose, fibrous substance, for stuffing, etc.; v.t. to form into wad; to line with wadding; to pad; pr.p. -ding. pa.t. and pa.p. -ded. -ding n. soft material for wads.

wad•dle v.i. to walk like duck, with short swaying steps; n. slow, rocking gait.

wade v.i. to walk through something which hampers movement, as water, mud, etc.; v.t. to cross (stream) by wading; n. a wading.

wa•fer n. very thin biscuit; v.t. to seal or close with wafer. -y a.

waf•fle n. a thin cake of batter with criss-cross pattern. — **iron** n. hinged metal utensil for baking both sides of waffle at once.

waft v.t. to impel lightly through water or air; v.i. to float gently; n. breath or slight current of air or odor; puff. -ure n.

wag v.t. to cause to move to and fro; v.i. to shake; to swing; to vibrate. pr.p. -ging. pa.p., pa.t. -ged n. swinging motion, to and fro.

wage v.t. to carry on; n. payment paid for labor or work done.

wa•ger n. something staked on issue of future event or of some disputed point; bet; stake; v.t. to bet; to lay wager. -er n.

wag•gle v.t. and v.i. to move one way and the other; to wag.

wag•on n. four-wheeled vehicle or truck, for carrying heavy freight. -less a. -load n.

waif n. homeless person, esp. neglected child; stray article or animal.

wail v.t. and v.i. to lament (over); to express sorrow audibly; to weep; n. loud weeping; great mourning; doleful cry. -er n. -ing n. -ingly adv.

waist n. part of human body immediately below ribs and above hips. -band n. part of dress or trousers which fits round waist.

wait v.t. to stay for; v.i. to stop until arrival of some person or event; to be temporarily postponed; to be expecting; to serve at table; to attend (on); n. act, period of waiting. -er n. one who waits; a man who waits on table. -ing n. and a. -ing-list n. list of names of those wishing some article, etc. in short supply. -ing room n. room set aside for use of people waiting in public place, office, etc. -ress n. female waiter.

waive v.t. to give up claim to; to forgo; to relinquish a right, etc. -r n. relinquishment, or statement of such.

wake v.t. to rouse from sleep; to waken; to excite; to kindle; to provoke; v.i. to awaken. pa.t. and pa.p. -d or woke. pr.p. waking. n. vigil; act of sitting up overnight with corpse. -ful a. indisposed to sleep; sleepless. -fully adv. -n v.t., i. -ner n. waking a. as in waking hours, period when one is not asleep.

wale n. mark left on flesh by rod or whip; ridge in the weave of a fabric; v.t. to mark with wales. waling n. wale, piece of heavy timber fastened horizontally to tie together boards supporting sides of trench or vertical pieces of jetty.

walk v.t. to pass through, along, upon; to lead, drive, or ride (horse) at a slow pace; v.i. to go on foot; n. act of walking; characteristic gait or style of walking; path for pedestrians; avenue set with trees; stroll; distance walked over; sphere of life; conduct. -er n. -ie-talkie n. portable wireless combined transmitting and receiving set. -out n. a strike.

wall n. structure of brick, stone, etc. serving as fence, side of building, etc.; pl. fortifications; works for defense; v.t. to enclose with wall; to block up with wall. —**board** n. lining of various materials for applying to or making walls. -ed a. provided with walls; fortified. -flower n. garden plant, with sweet-scented flowers; lady left sitting at dance for lack of partners. -less a. -like a.

wal•la•by n. a small kangaroo.

wal•la•roo n. large kangaroo.

wal•let n. folding pocketbook for paper money identification, cards, etc.

wal•lop v.t. to beat soundly; to strike hard; n. stroke or blow. -ing n. a thrashing; a. tremendous; big.

wal•nut n. large tree producing rich, dark-brown wood of fine texture; fruit of tree, large nut with crinkled shell.

wal•rus n. mammal closely related to seal but with down-turned tusks.

walrus

waltz n. ballroom dance in three-four time; music for this dance; v.i. to dance a waltz. -er n. -ing n.

wan a. having a sickly hue; pale; pallid; ashy; gloomy. -ly adv. -ness n.

wand n. long, slender, straight rod.

wan•der v.i. to ramble; to go astray; to depart from subject. -er n. -ing a. rambling; unsettled; n. journeying here and there, usually in pl.

wane v.i. to decrease; to fail; n. decrease of illuminated part of moon; decline; diminution.

wan•gle v.t. to obtain by deception or trickery; v.i. to manage with difficulty. -r n. trickery; artifice.

want n. scarcity of what is needed; poverty; v.t. to be without; lack; v.t. to be without; to lack; to need; to crave; v.i. to be lacking; to have need. -ed a. desired; required; sought after; searched for (by police). -er n. -less a. -ing a. lacking; deficient. prep. without; minus. -s n.pl. requirements.

wan•ton a. dissolute; unrestrained; recklessly arrogant, malicious; n.; v.i. -ly adv. -ness n.

war n. armed conflict between two (groups of) states; state of opposition or hostility; v.i. to make war; to carry on hostilities; to contend. pr.p. -ring. pa.t. and pa.p. -red. -fare n. hostilities. -ship n. vessel

353

equipped for war. Also **-man-of-war. civil war,** war between citizens of same country. **cold war,** state of international hostility short of actual warfare.

ward *v.t.* to repel; to turn aside; *n.* division of city; room for patients in hospital; guardianship; minor legally in the care of a guardian; divisions of a prison; custody. **-en** *n.* civil defense officer; keeper; supervisor of prison. **-robe** *n.* cupboard for holding clothes; wearing apparel in general. **-ship** *n.* office of guardian; state of being under guardian.

ware *n.* article of merchandise; pottery; usually in combinations as, *earthenware, hardware,* etc.; *pl.* goods for sale; commodities; merchandise. **-house** *n.* storehouse for goods; *v.t.* to store in warehouse.

warm *a.* having heat in moderate degree; not cold; hearty; lively; of colors, suggesting heat, as red, orange, yellow; excited; passionate; affectionate; *v.t.* to communicate moderate degree of heat to; to excite interest or zeal in; *v.i.* to become moderately heated; to become animated. **—blooded** *a.* of animals with fairly high and constant body-temperature; passionate; generous. **—hearted** *a.* affectionate; kindly disposed; sympathetic. **-ly** *adv.* **-ness, -th** *n.* slight heat; cordiality; heartiness; enthusiasm.

warn *v.t.* to notify by authority; to caution; to admonish; to put on guard. **-ing** *n.* advance notice of anything; admonition; caution; *a.* cautioning.

warp *v.t.* to twist permanently out of shape; to bend; to pervert; *v.i.* to turn, twist, or be twisted; *n.* distortion of wood due to unequal shrinkage in drying. **-ed** *a.* twisted by unequal shrinkage; perverted; depraved. **-er** *n.* one who, or that which, warps. **-ing** *n.*

war•rant *v.t.* to give justification for; to authorize or sanction with assurance of safety; to guarantee to be as represented; to assure; to indemnify against loss; *n.* instrument which warrants or justifies act otherwise not permissible or legal; instrument giving power to arrest offender; authorization; guarantee. **-able** *a.* **-ably** *adv.* **-ableness** *n.* **-ed** *a.* guaranteed. **-er, -or** *n.* **-y** *n.* security; guarantee.

war•ren *n.* enclosure for breeding rabbits and other game.

war•ri•or *n.* soldier.

wart *n.* small hard conical excrescence on skin; hard, glandular protuberance on plants and trees.

war•y *a.* cautious; heedful; careful; prudent. **warily** *adv.* **wariness** *n.*

was *pa.t.* of verb **to be.**

wash *v.t.* to free from dirt with water and soap; *v.i.* to perform act of ablution; to cleanse clothes in water; to be washable; *n.* clothes, etc. washed at one time; liquid applied to surface as lotion or coat of paint. **-able** *a.* **-er** *n.* one who washes; flat ring of metal, rubber, etc. to make a tight joint, distribute pressure from nut or head of bolt, prevent leakage, etc. **-ing** *n.* act of one who washes; ablution; clothes washed at one time; *a.* used in, or intended for, washing. **-ed out, exhausted; faded.**

wasp *n.* stinging insect like bee with longer body and narrow waist.

waste *v.t.* to expend uselessly; to use extravagantly; to squander; to neglect; to lay waste; to spoil; *v.i.* to wear away by degrees; to become worn and emaciated; to decrease; to wither; *a.* lying unused; of no worth; desolate; *n.* act of wasting; that which is wasted; refuse; uncultivated country; loss; squandering. **wastage** *n.* loss by use, leakage, or decay. **-basket** *n.* container for waste materials. **-ful** *a.* full of waste; destructive; prodigal; extravagant. **-fully** *adv.* **-fulness** *n.* **-land** *n.* barrenland. **-r** *n.*

watch *n.* state of being on the look-out; close observation; vigil; one who watches; watchman; sentry; portable timekeeper for pocket, wrist, etc.; to keep in view; to guard; to observe closely; *v.i.* to be vigilant; to be on watch; to keep guard; to be wakeful; to look out (for); to wait (for). **-dog** *n.* guard dog; any watchful guardian. **-er** *n.* **-ful** *a.* vigilant; attentive; cautious. **-fully** *adv.* **-fulness** *n.* **-maker, -making** *n.* **—man** *n.* man who guards property. **-word** *n.* password; a slogan; rallying cry.

wa•ter *n.* transparent, tasteless liquid, substance of rain, rivers, etc.; body of water; *v.t.* to wet or soak with water; to cause animal to drink; to irrigate; *v.i.* to shed water; to take in or obtain water. **—color** *n.* artist's color ground up with water; painting in this medium. **-ed** *a.* diluted with water. **-fall** *n.* fall or perpendicular descent of water of river; cascade; cataract. **-fowl** *n.* any aquatic bird with webbed feet and coat of closely packed feathers or down. **— gauge** *n.* instrument for measuring height of water in boiler, etc. **-less** *a.* **— level** *n.* level formed by surface of still water; leveling instrument in which water is employed. **-lily** *n.* aquatic plant with fragrant flowers and large floating leaves. **—line** *n.* line on hull of ship to which water reaches. **—main** *n.* large pipe running under streets, for conveying water. **—mark** *n.* in paper making, faint translucent design stamped in substance of sheet of paper and serving as trademark. **-melon** *n.* large fruit with smooth, dark-green rind and red pulp. **— power** *n.* power of water used as prime mover. **-proof** *a.* impervious to water; *v.t.* to make impervious to water. **-shed** *n.* area drained by a river. **-spout** *n.* drain carrying rain water down side of building. **-tight** *a.* so fitted as to prevent water escaping or entering. **— tower** *n.* raised tank for water storage. **-way** *n.* fairway for vessels; navigable channel. **-works** *n.pl.* reservoirs, etc. for the purification, supply and distribution of water; **-y** *a.* resembling water; thin or transparent, as a liquid. **above water,**

financially sound; solvent. **mineral water,** water impregnated with mineral matter and possessing specific medicinal properties; artificially aerated water.

watt *n.* unit of power represented by current of one ampere produced by electromotive force of one volt.

wat·tle *n.* fleshy excrescence, usually red, under throat of cock or turkey. **-d** *a.*

wave *n.* waving movement or gesture of hand; advancing ridge or swell on surface of liquid; wavelike style of hair dressing; passage of sound or light through space; *pl.* the sea; *v.t.* to raise into inequalities of surface; to move to and fro; to give the shape of waves; to brandish; to beckon; *v.i.* to wave one way and the other; to flap; to undulate; to signal. **—band** *n.* range of wave lengths allotted for broadcasting, morse signals, etc. **-d** *a.* undulating. **wavily** *adv.* **— length** *n.* distance between maximum positive points of two successive waves; velocity of wave divided by frequency of oscillations. **—like** *a.* **waviness** *n.* **waving** *a.* moving to and fro. **wavy** *a.*

wa·ver *v.i.* to move to and fro; to fluctuate; to vacillate; to tremble; to totter. **-er** *n.* **-ing** *n.* and *a.* **-ingly** *adv.*

wax *n.* a fatty acid ester of a monohydric alcohol; an amorphous, yellowish, sticky substance derived from animal and vegetable substances; beeswax; sealing wax; *v.t.* to smear, rub, or polish with wax. **-en** *a.* made of or resembling wax; plastic; impressionable. **-er** *n.* **-iness** *n.* **-ing** *n.* **—paper** *n.* paper coated with wax, used for airtight packing. **-y** *a.* made of or like wax.

way *n.* street; passage; path; lane; route; progress; distance; method; mode; custom; usage; habit; means; plan; desire; momentum. **-ward** *a.* liking one's way; perverse; refractory. **-wardly** *adv.* **-wardness** *n.* **ways and means,** methods; resources. **by the way,** as we proceed; incidentally. **right-of-way** *n.* right to use path through private property; such a path.

we *pron.* plural form of I; another person, or others, and I.

weak *a.* feeble; frail; delicate; fragile; watery; diluted; inconclusive. **-en** *v.t.* to make weak; *v.i.* to become weak or less resolute. **-liness** *n.* **-ling** *n.* feeble person, physically or mentally. **-ly** *adv.* **-ness** *n.*

weal *n.* streak left on flesh by blow of stick or whip; wale.

wealth *n.* riches; affluence; opulence; abundance. **-iness** *n.* **-y** *a.*

wean *v.t.* to discontinue breast-feeding of infant gradually. **-ling** *n.* newly-weaned infant.

weap·on *n.* instrument to fight with.

wear *v.t.* to carry clothes, decorations and the like, upon the person; to consume or impair by use; to deteriorate by rubbing; *v.i.* to last or hold out; to be impaired gradually by use or exposure. *pa.t.* **wore.** *pa.p.* **worn.** *n.* act of wearing; impairment from use. **-able** *a.* **-er** *n.* **-ing** *a.* intended for wearing; exhausting; exhausting to

mind and body. **wear and tear,** loss or deterioration due to usage. **to wear off,** to disappear slowly.

wear·y *a.* fatigued; tired; bored; exhausted; tiresome; *v.t.* to exhaust one's strength or patience; to make weary; *v.i.* to become weary; to become dissatisfied with. **wearily** *adv.* **weariless** *a.* tireless. **weariness** *n.* **wearisome** *a.* tedious; causing annoyance or fatigue. **wearisomely** *adv.* **wearisomeness** *n.*

wea·sel *n.* small, long-bodied, short-legged bloodthirsty carnivore.

weasel

weath·er *n.* combination of all atmospheric phenomena existing at one time in any particular place; *v.t.* to expose to the air; to season by exposure to air; to endure; *v.i.* to decompose or disintegrate, owing to atmospheric conditions. **Weather Bureau** *n.* meterorological office directed by U.S. Department of Commerce. **— forecast** *n.* prediction of probable future weather conditions based on scientific data collected by meteorological office. **-ing** *n.* process of decomposing of rocks, wood, etc. exposed to elements. **—report,** daily report of meteorological conditions. **-vane** *n.* weather cock.

weave *v.t.* to interlace threads, etc.; to interlace threads, etc.; to construct, to fabricate, as a tale; *v.i.* to practice weaving; to move from side to side. *pa.t.* **wove.** *pa.p.* **woven.** *n.* style of weaving. **-r** *n.*

web *n.* that which is woven; membrane which unities toes of waterfowl; network spun by spider. **-bing** *n.* strong, hemp fabric woven in narrow strips, used for chairs, etc. **—footed** *a.*

wed *v.t.* to marry; *v.i.* to contract matrimony. *pr.p.* **-ding.** *pa.t.* and *pa.p.* **-ded** or **wed. -ded** *a.* married; wholly devoted (to art, etc.) **-ding** *n.* nuptial ceremony; nuptials; marriage.

wedge *n.* piece of wood or metal, tapering to thin edge at fore end, used for splitting,. lifting heavy weights, or rendering rigid two parts of structure; anything shaped like wedge; *v.t.* to jam; to compress; to force (in); to squeeze (in); to fasten with wedge. **-d** *a.* cuneiform or wedge-shaped; jammed tight.

Wedg·wood *n.* and *a.* fine Eng. pottery.

Wednes·day *n.* fourth day of week.

wee *n.* small; tiny.

weed *n.* plant growing where it is not desired; *v.t.* to free from weeds. **-y** *a.* full of weeds.

week *n.* seven successive days, usually Sunday to Sunday. **—day** *n.* any day of week except Sunday. **—end** *n.* Friday or

W

Saturday to Monday. -ly a. pert. to a week; happening once a week; n. publication issued weekly; adv. once a week.

weep v.i. to grieve for by shedding tears; to cry; to drip; v.t. to lament; to bewail. pa.t. and pa.p. wept. -er n. one who weeps. -ing a. of trees whose branches droop, as weeping willow. -y a.

wee-vil n. common name given to thousands of different kinds of small beetles, all distinguished by heads lengthened out to resemble beaks—larvae attack plants and stored grain.

weigh v.t. to find weight of; to deliberate or consider carefully; v.i. to have weight; to be considered as important. -er n. -t n. gravity as property of bodies; heavy mass; object of known mass for weighing; importance; power and influence; v.t. to make more heavy. -tily adv. -tiness n. -ty a. having great weight; important; momentous; forcible. dead weight n. heavy burden.

weird a. unearthly; uncanny; odd. -ly adv. -ness n.

wel-come a. received gladly; free to enjoy or use; n. kind or hearty reception; v.t. to greet with kindness and pleasure.

weld v.t. to join pieces of heated, plastic metal by fusion without soldering materials, etc. -er n.

wel-fare n. well-doing or well-being; prosperity.

well n. shaft or tube sunk deep in ground to obtain water, oil, etc.; spring; fountain; v.i. to issue forth in volume, as water.

well

well a. comp. better. superl. best. in good health; fortunate; comfortable; satisfactory; adv. agreeably; favorably; skillfully; intimately; satisfactorily; soundly; interj. exclamation of surprise, interrogation, resignation, etc. —being n. welfare. —meaning a. having good intentions. —spoken a. cultured in speech; favorably commented on; speaking easily, fluently, graciously.

Welsh, Welch a. relating to Wales or its inhabitants; n. language- or people of Wales. —man, —woman n. — rabbit, or rarebit, savory dish consisting of melted cheese on toast.

welt n. cord around border or seamline of upholstery, etc.; a flat, overlapping seam; ridge on flesh from whiplash, etc. v.t. to

furnish with welt; beat soundly. -ed a. -ing n.

wel-ter-weight n. in boxing or wrestling, class of contestants weighing between 135 lb. and 147 lb.; boxer or wrestler of this weight.

wench n. girl; maid.

went pa.t. of go.

wept pa.t. and pa.p. of weep.

were pa.t. plural, and subjunctive singular and plural, of be.

were-wolf, wer-wolf n. human being who, at will, could take form of wolf while retaining human intelligence.

Wes-ley-an n. pert. to Wesley or Wesleyanism. -ism n. Wesleyan Methodism, i.e. religion practiced in methodical manner.

west n. point in heavens where sun sets; one of four cardinal points of compass; region of country lying to the west; a. situated in, facing, coming from the west; adv. to the west. -erly a. situated in west; of wind, blowing from west; adv. in west direction; n. wind blowing from west. -ern a. situated in west; coming from west; n. inhabitant of western country or district; film featuring cowboys in western states of U.S. -erner n. native of the west.

wet a. comp. -ter. superl. -test. containing water; full of moisture; humid; damp; rainy; n. water; moisture; rain; v.t. to make wet; to moisten; pr.p. -ting. pa.p. wet or ted. -ness n. -tish a. humid; damp.

whack v.t. to hit, esp. with stick; to beat; v.i. to strike with smart blow; n. blow. -y a.

whale n. large fishlike mammal; v.i. to hunt for whales. -bone n. baleen, an elastic,

whale

flexible, horny product of jaws of baleen whale.— oil n. lubricating oil extracted from blubber of sperm whale.

wharf n. structure on bank of navigable waters at which vessels can be loaded or unloaded. pl. -s, wharves. v.t. to moor at, or place on, wharf. -age n. charge for use of wharf; wharf accomodation.

what pron. interrogative pronoun; relative pronoun, meaning that which; a. which; which kind; conj. that; interj. denoting surprise, anger, confusion, etc.; adv. to what degree? -ever pron. anything that; all that. -soever pron. whatever.

what-not n. piece of furniture, having shelves for books, bric-a-brac, etc.; indescribable thing.

wheat n. edible portion of annual cereal grass providing most important bread food of the world.

whee-dle v.t. to cajole; to coax.

wheel n. solid disk or circular frame with spokes; steering wheel; v.t. to convey on wheels; to furnish with wheels; v.i. to turn on, or as on, axis; to change direction by pivoting about an end unit, as in marching; to roll forward; to revolve. **-barrow** *n*. conveyance with a single wheel and two shafts for pushing.

wheeze *v.i.* to breathe audibly and with difficulty; *n*. the sound or act of wheezing. **-r** *n*. **wheezingly** *adv.* **wheezy** *a.* **wheezily** *adv.* **wheeziness** *n*.

whelm *v.t.* to cover completely; to submerge; to overpower.

when *adv.* and *conj.* at what time? at the time that; whereas; at which time. **-ever** *adv.* and *conj.* at whatever time. **-soever** *adv.* and *conj.* whenever.

where *adv.* and *conj.* at what place?; in what circumstances?; at or to the place in which. **-abouts** *adv.* and *conj.* about where; near what or which place? *n*. place where one is. **-as** *conj.* considering that; when in fact. **-by** *adv.* and *conj.* by which; how. **-in** *adv.* in which; in which, or what, respect, etc.; in what. **-of** *adv.* of which; of what. **-on** *adv.* on which; on what. **-to** *adv.* to which; to what; to what end. **-upon** *adv.* upon which; in consequence of which. **-'er**, **-ver** *adv.* at whatever place. **-with** *adv.* with what. **the wherewithal**, the money; the means.

whet *v.t.* to sharpen by rubbing; to make sharp, keen, or eager; *n*. act of sharpening. *pr.p.* **-ting**. *pa.t.* and *pa.p.* **-ted**. **-stone** *n*. fine-grained stone used for sharpening cutlery and tools; sharpener. **-ter** *n*.

wheth-er *conj.* used to introduce the first of two or more alternative clauses, the other(s) being connected by *or*.

whew *n*. or *interj.* whistling sound, expressing astonishment, dismay, or pain.

which *pron.* as interrogative, signifying *who*, or *what one*, of a number; as relative, used of things; a thing or fact that; whatever. **-ever**, **-soever** *pron.*, *a.* whether one or the other.

whiff *n*. puff of air, smoke, etc.; an odor; *v.t.* to throw out in whiffs; to blow; *v.i.* to emit whiffs, as of smoke.

Whig *n*. supporter of American Revolution; member of early political party (1834-1955).

while *n*. space of time; *conj.* during time when; as long as; whereas; *adv.* during which. **to while away**, to pass time.

whim *n*. passing fancy; caprice; fad. **-sical** *a.* capricious; freakish; fanciful; quaint. **-sicality** *n*. fanciful idea; whim. **-sically** *adv.* **-sicalness** *n*. **-sy** *n*. caprice; fancy.

whim-per *v.i.* and *v.t.* to cry, or utter, with low, fretful, broken voice; *n*. low peevish, or plaintive cry. **-er** *n*. **-ing** *n*.

whine *n*. drawing, peevish wail; unmanly complaint; *v.i.* to utter peevish cry; to complain in childish way. *n*. **whining** *n*. **whiningly** *adv.* **whiny** *a.*

whin-ny *v.i.* to neigh; *n*. sound made by horse.

whip *v.t.* to strike with lash; to flog; to overcast edges of seam, etc.; to beat into froth, as cream or eggs; to defeat decisively; *v.i.* to start suddenly. *pr.p.* **-ping**. *pa.t.* and *pa.p.* **-ped**. *n*. lash attached to handle for urging on or correction; legislative manager appointed to ensure fullest possible attendance of members of his party at important debates, etc. **-ping** *n*. flogging.

whip-poor-will *n*. nocturnal American bird.

whir *v.i.* to dart, fly, or revolve with buzzing or whizzing noise. *pr.p.* **-ring**. *pa.t.* and *pa.p.* **-red**. *n*. buzzing or whizzing sound.

whirl *v.t.* to turn round rapidly; to cause to rotate; *v.i.* to rotate rapidly; to spin; to gyrate; *n*. rapid rotation; anything which whirls; bewilderment. **-ing** *n*. and *a*. **-pool** *n*. vortex or circular eddy of water.

whish *v.i.* to move with soft, rustling sound; *n*. such a sound.

whisk *n*. rapid, sweeping motion; small bunch of feathers, straw, etc. used for brush; instrument for beating eggs, etc.; *v.t.* to sweep with light, rapid motion or with a whisk. **-er** *n*. thing that whisks; *pl.* hair on a man's face; long stiff hairs at side of mouth of cat or other animal. **-ered** *a.*

whis-key *n*. distilled alcoholic liquor made from various grains. Also **whisky**.

whis-per *v.t.* to utter in low, sibilant tone; to suggest secretly or furtively; *v.i.* to speak in whispers, under breath; to rustle; *n*. low, soft, sibilant remark. **-er** *n*. **-ing** *n*. **-ingly** *adv.*

whis-tle *n*. sound made by forcing breath through rounded and nearly closed lips; instrument or device for making a similar sound; form of horn; *v.i.* to make such sound; *v.i.* and *v.t.* to render tune by whistling; to signal, by whistling. **-r** *n*. one who whistles. **whistling** *n*.

white *a.* of the color of snow; light in color; pure; clean; bright; spotless; *n*. color of pure snow; albuminous part of an egg; white part of eyeball surrounding iris. **-cap** *n*. wave with crest of white foam. **—collar** *a.* of clerical or professional workers. **— elephant**, sacred elephant of Siam; gift entailing bother and expense; object valueless to the owners. **— fish** *n*. non-oily food fish. **— flag**, sign of truce or surrender. **— gold**, alloyed gold with platinum appearance. **— lie**, harmless fib. **-n** *v.t.* and *v.i.* to make or turn white. **-ner** *n*. **-ening** *n*. making white. **-ness** *n*. **-wash** *n*. mixture of whiting, water, and size, for coating walls; *v.t.* to cover with whitewash; to clear reputation of; to conceal errors, faults, etc. **whitish** *a.* somewhat white.

whith-er *adv.* to which, or what, place?

whit-ing *n*. edible seafish; pulverized chalk, for making putty and whitewash.

whit-tle *v.t.* and *v.i.* to cut off thin slices or shavings with knife; to pare away.

whiz, whizz *v.i.* to make hissing sound, as arrow flying through air. *pr.p.* **-zing**. *pa.t.* and *pa.p.* **-zed**. *n*. violent hissing and humming sound; person or thing regarded as excellent. **-zingly** *adv.*

who *pron.* relative or interrogative, referring to persons. **-ever** *pron.* whatever person; any one, without

W

exception. -m *pron.* objective case of *who.* -msoever *pron.* objective of -soever *pron.* any person, without exception. -se *pron.* possessive case of *who* or *which.*

whoa *interj.* stop!

whole *a.* entire; complete; not defective or imperfect; unimpaired; *n.* entire thing; complete system; aggregate; gross; sum; totality. -hearted *a.* earnest; sincere. -heartedly *adv.* -heartedness *n.* -ness *n.* -sale *n.* sale of goods in bulk to retailers; *a.* selling or buying in large quantities; extensive; indiscriminate. -saler *n.* -some *a.* tending to promote health; healthy; nourishing; beneficial. -someness *n.* wholly *adv.* completely.

whom See who.

whoop *n.* loud cry or yell; hoot, as of owl; convulsive intake of air after cough; *v.i.* to utter loud cry; to hoot; to make the sound characteristic of whooping cough. -ee *interj.* exclamation of joy or abandonment. -er *n.* one who whoops; bird with a loud harsh note. -ing cough *n.* infectious disease marked by fits of convulsive coughing, followed by characteristic loud whoop or indrawing of breath.

whore *n.* harlot; prostitute.

whose *poss.* of *who, which.* whosoever, whomsoever. See who.

why *adv.* and *conj.* for what reason? on which account? wherefore? *interj.* expletive to show surprise, indignation, protest; *n.* reason; cause; motive.

wick *n.* cotton cord which draws up oil or wax, as in lamp or candle, to be burned. -less *a.*

wick•ed *a.* addicted to vice; evil; immoral; mischievous. -ly *adv.* -ness *n.*

wick•er *n.* small flexible twig; wickerwork; *a.* made of pliant twigs.

wide *a.* broad; spacious; comprehensive; *adv.* to a distance; far. —awake *a.* fully awake. -ly *adv.* -n *v.t.* to make wide or wider; *v.i.* to grow wide or wider; to expand. -ness *n.* width. -spread *a.* extending on all sides; diffused; circulating among numerous people. width *n.* wideness; breadth. widthwise *adv.*

wid•ow *n.* woman who has lost husband by death; *v.t.* to bereave of husband; to be a widow to. -er *n.* man whose wife is dead. -hood *n.*

width See wide.

wield *v.t.* to use with full command or power; to swing; to handle; to manage; to control. -able *a.* -er *n.* -iness *n.* -y *a.* manageable; controllable.

wie•ner *n.* smoked sausage in casing; frankfurter. Also weenie.

wife *n.* married woman; spouse; *pl.* wives. -hood *n.* -less *a.* -lessness *n.* without wife; unmarried. -ly *a.* as befits a wife.

wig *n.* artificial covering for head which imitates natural hair. -ged *a.*

wig•gle *v.i.* to waggle; to wriggle; *n.* a wriggling motion. -r *n.* wiggling thing.

wig•wam *n.* Amer. Ind. conical shelter.

wild *a.* living in state of nature; not domesticated or cultivated; native;

savage; turbulent; *n.* uncultivated, uninhabited region. -cat *n.* medium-sized, undomesticated feline; *a.* reckless; financially unsound; highly speculative. -fire *n.* anything which burns rapidly or spreads fast; sheet lightning; — goosechase *n.* foolish, futile pursuit or enterprise. -ly *adv.* -ness *n.*

wil•der•ness *n.* tract of land uncultivated and uninhabited by human beings; waste; desert.

will *n.* power of choosing what one will do; volition; determination; wish; desire; declaration in writing showing how property is to be disposed of after death; *v.t.* to determine by choice; to decree; to bequeath; to devise; *v.i.* to exercise act of colition; to choose; to elect; *v.* used as an auxiliary, to denote futurity dependent on subject of verb, intention, or insistence. *pa.t.* would. -able *a.* -er *n.* -ing *a.* favorably inclined; minded; disposed; ready. -ingly *adv.* readily; gladly. -ingness *n.*

wil•low *n.* name of number of trees of genus Salix, having flexible twigs used in weaving. -er *n.* — pattern, design used in decorating chinaware, blue on white ground. -y *a.* abounding in ʼwillows; pliant; supple and slender. weeping willow *n.* tree with pendent branches.

wilt *v.i.* to fade; to droop; to wither; *v.t.* to depress; *n.* weakness; plant disease.

win *v.t.* to gain by success in competition or contest; to earn; to obtain; to reach, after difficulty; *v.i.* to be victorious; *pr.p.* -ning. *pa.p., pa.t.* won. *n.* victory. -ningly *adv.*

wince *v.i.* to shrink or flinch, as from blow or pain; *n.* act of wincing. -r *n.*

wind *n.* air in motion; current of air; gale; breath; power of respiration; point of compass; *pl.* wind instruments of orchestra; *v.t.* to follow by scent; to run, ride, or drive till breathless; to expose to wind; *v.t.* to sound by blowing. *pa.p.* -ed. -breaker *n.* a warm sports jacket. -ed *a.* breathless. -ily *adv.* -iness *n.* — instrument *n.* musical instrument played by blowing or air pressure. -less *a.* calm; out of breath. -mill *n.* mill worked by action of wind on vanes or sails. -pipe *n.* trachea; cartilaginous pipe admitting air to lungs. -storm *n.* -y *a.* consisting of, exposed to wind; tempestuous; flatulent; empty.

wind *v.t.* to twist around; to coil; *v.i.* to twine; to vary from direct course. *pa.t.* and *pa.p.* wound. -er *n.* one who, or that which, winds; step, wider at one end than the other. -ing *a.* twisting or bending from direct line; sinuous; meandering; *n.* turning; twist. -up *n.* conclusion; closing stages; baseball pitcher's preliminary swing of arm before delivery. wound-up *a.* highly excited.

win•dow *n.* opening in wall to admit air and light, usually covered with glass.

wine *n.* fermented juice of grape; similar liquor made from other fruits; *v.t.* to entertain by serving wine; *v.i.* to drink much wine at a sitting. — **cellar**, stock of wine. **-ry** place where wine is made.

wing n. organ of flight; one of two feathered fore limbs of bird; flight; main lifting surface of airplane; extension or section of a building; pl. the side parts of a stage; v.t. to furnish with wings; to enable to fly or hasten; v.i. to soar on the wing. **-ed** a. furnished with wings. **-less** a.

wink v.t. and v.i. to close and open eyelids; to blink; to convey hint by flick of eyelid; to twinkle; n. act of winking; hint conveyed by winking.

win•ner, win•ning See **win**.

win•ter n. fourth season; in northern latitudes, period between winter solstice and vernal equinox (22nd Dec.—20th-21st March); a. wintry; pert. to winter; v.t. to keep and feed throughout winter; v.i. to pass the winter. **-er** n. **-green** n. aromatic evergreen plant from which is obtained oil of winter-green, used in medicine and flavoring. **-ize** v.t, ready for winter. **-ly** adv. **wintriness** n. **wintry** a. of or like winter.

wipe v.t. to rub lightly, so as to clean or dry; to remove gently; to clear away; to efface; n. act of wiping. **-r** n. one who, or that which, wipes; in motoring, automatically operated arm to keep part of windshield free from rain or dust. **wiping** n. act of wiping. **to wipe out**, to erase; to destroy utterly.

wire n. metal drawn into form of a thread or cord; a length of this; a telegram; v.t. to bind or stiffen with wire; to pierce with wire; to fence with wire; to install (building) with wires for electric circuit; a. formed of wire. **-d** a. **—haired** a. having short, wiry hair. **-less** a. without wires; pert. to several devices operated by electromagnetic waves. n. wireless telegraphy or telephony; v.t. and v.i. to communicate by wireless. — **tapping**, act of tapping telephone wires to get information. **wirily** adv. **wiriness** n. **wiring** n. system of electric wires forming circuit. **wiry** n. stiff (as hair); lean, sinewy and strong.

wis•dom n. quality of being wise; knowledge and the capacity to make use of it; judgment. — **tooth** n. posterior molar tooth, cut about twentieth year.

wise a. enlightened; sagacious; learned; dictated by wisdom. **-crack** n. concise flippant statement; v.i. to utter one. **-ly** adv. **-ness** n.

wise adv. suffix. in the way or manner of, arranged like, as in clockwise, likewise, crosswise, etc.

wish v.t. to desire; to long for; to request; v.i. to have a desire; to yearn; n. expression or object of desire; longing; request. **(ing)-bone** n. forked bone of fowl's breast. **-er** n. **-ful** a. desirous; anxious; longing; wistful. **-fully** adv. **-fulness** n.

wisp n. twisted handful, usually of hay; whisk or small broom; stray lock of hair. **-like** a. **-y** a.

wist•ful a. pensive; sadly contemplative;

earnestly longing. **-ly** adv. **-ness** n.

wit n. intellect; understanding; humor; pleasantry; pl. mental faculties. **-ticism** n. witty remark. **-tily** adv. **-tiness** n. **-tingly** adv. with foreknowledge or design; knowingly; of set purpose. **-ty** a. possessed of wit; amusing.

witch n. woman who was supposed to practice sorcery; v.t. to bewitch; to enchant. **-craft** n. black art; sorcery. — **doctor** n. medicine man of a savage tribe. **-ery** n. arts of a witch; sorcery. **-ing** a. fascinating. **-ingly** adv.

witch haz•el n. shrub with yellow flowers and edible seeds; of dried bark and leaves of the tree used, in distilled form, as astringent drug.

with prep. in company or possession of; in relation to; against; by means of; denoting association, cause, agency, comparison, immediate sequence, etc.

with•draw v.t. to take away; to recall; to retract; v.i. to go away; to retire; to retreat; to recede. pa.t. **withdrew**. pa.p. **-n, -al** n. **~ment** n.

with•er v.i. to cause to fade and become dry; to blight; to rebuff; v.i. to fade; to decay; to languish. **-ing** a. **-ingly** adv. scathingly; contemptuously.

with•hold v.t. to hold or keep back. pa.p., pa.t. **withheld**.

with•in prep. in the inner or interior part of; in the compass of; adv. in the inner part; inwardly; at home.

with•out prep. on or at the outside of; out of; not within; beyond the limits of; exempt from; all but; adv. on the outside.

with•stand v.t. to oppose; to stand against; to resist. pa.t. and pa.p. **withstood**. **-er** n.

wit•ness n. testimony; one who, or that which, furnishes evidence or proof; one who has seen or has knowledge of incident; one who attests another person's signature to document; v.t. to be witness of or to; v.i. to give evidence; to testify. — **stand** n. place where witness gives testimony in court of law. **-er** n.

wit•ti•cism, wit•ty, etc. See **wit**.

wives pl. of **wife**.

wiz•ard n. one devoted to black art; sorcerer; magician; a. with magical powers. **-like** a. **-ly** a. **-ry** n. magic.

wob•ble, wabble v.i. to rock from side to side; to be hesitant; n. rocking; unequal motion. **-r**, n. **wobbly, wabbly** a. shaky; unsteady.

woe, wo n. grief; heavy calamity; affliction; sorrow. **-ful** a. sorrowful; pitiful; paltry. **-fully** adv.

woke. alt. pa.t. of **wake**.

wolf n. carnivorous wild animal, allied to dog; rapacious, cruel person. pl. **wolves**. v.t. to devour ravenously. **-ish** a. rapacious, like wolf; voracious; fierce and greedy. **-ishly** adv. **-ishness** n.

wolves pl. of **wolf**.

wo•man n. adult human female; the quality of being a woman. pl. **women**. **-hood** n. adult stage of women; the qualities of women. **-ish** a. like a woman; effeminate. **-ishness** n. **-liness** n. **-ly** a. befitting a mature woman; essentially feminine;

adv. in manner of a woman.

womb *n.* female organ of conception and gestation; uterus.

wo-men *pl.* of **woman**.

won *pa.t.* and *pa.p.* of **win**.

won-der *n.* astonishment; surprise; amazement; admiration; *v.i.* to feel wonder; to marvel; to speculate. **-er** *n.* **-ful** *a.* very fine; remarkable; amazing. **-fully** *adv.* **-fulness** *n.* **-ing** *a.* **-ingly** *adv.* in a wondering and expectant manner. **-land** *n.* land of marvels; fairyland. **wondrous** *a.* wonderful. **wondrously** *adv.* **wondrousness** *n.*

wont *a.* accustomed; used; *n.* habit; custom; use; *v.i.* to be accustomed. **-ed** *a.* accustomed; habitual; usual. **-edness.**

won't *v.i.* a contr. of **will not.**

woo *v.t.* to make love to; to court. **-er** *n.* **-ing** *n.*

wood *n.* land with trees growing close together; grove; forest; hard, stiffening tissue in stem and branches of tree; timber; wood-wind instrument; *v.t.* to supply with wood; to plant with trees. **— alcohol** *n.* methyl alcohol, product of dry distillation of wood, esp. beech and birch. **-cut** *n.* engraving on wood; impression from such engravings. **-ed** *a.* covered with trees. **-en** *a.* made of wood. **— engraver** *n.* **— engraving** *n.* art or process of cutting design on wood for printing; impression from this; woodcut. **-land** *n.* and *a.* wooded country. **-pecker** *n.* bird which taps and bores with bill the bark of trees in search of insects. **— pulp** *n.* wood crushed and pulped for paper making. **-sman** *n.* forest dweller; forester; woodcutter. **-shed** *n.* firewood storage place. **-sy** *a.* like the woods. **—wind** *n.* wooden musical instrument, as flute, oboe, clarinet, bassoon, etc. **-work** *n.* fittings made of wood, esp. interior moldings of a house. **-y** *a.* abounding with trees or wooded growth.

woof-er *n.* large loud-speaker that reproduces low frequency sound waves.

wool *n.* soft, curled hair of sheep, goat, etc.; yarn or cloth of this. **-(l)en** *n.* cloth made of wool; *pl.* woolen goods; *a.* made of, pert. to, wool. **-liness** *n.* **-ly** *a.* of, or like wool; muddled and confused.

word *n.* spoken or written sign of idea; term; oral expression; message; order; *pl.* speech; language, esp. contentious; wordy quarrel; *v.t.* to express in words; to phrase. **-ed** *a.* phrased; expressed. **-ily** *adv.* verbosely; pedantically. **-iness** *n.* verbosity. **ing** *n.* precise words used; phrasing; phraseology. **-less** *a.* **-ly** *a.* verbose; prolix. **word for word,** literally; verbatim. **by word of mouth,** orally.

wore *pa.t.* of **wear.**

work *n.* exertion of strength; effort directed to an end; employment; toil; labor; occupation; production; achievement; manufacture; that which is produced; result of force overcoming resistance over definite distance; *pl.* structures in engineering; manufacturing establishment; good deeds; artistic productions; mechanism of a watch, etc.; fortifications;

v.i. to exert oneself; to labor; to be employed; *v.t.* to produce or form by labor; to operate; to perform; to effect. **-able** *a.* **-aday** *a.* commonplace. **-er** *n.* **-ing** *n.* act of laboring or doing something useful; mode of operation; *pl.* a mine as a whole, or a part of it where work is being carried on, e.g. level, etc.; *a.* laboring. **-man** *n.* one actually engaged in manual labor; craftsman. **-manship** *n.* skill. **-shop** *n.* place where things are made or repaired; people meeting for intensive study in some field. **to work off,** to get rid of gradually. **to work out,** to solve (problem); to plan in detail; to exhaust (mine, etc.)

world *n.* earth and its inhabitants; universe; this life; human race; mankind. **-liness** *n.* state of being worldly. **-ling** *n.* one who is absorbed in the affairs, interests, or pleasures of this world. **-ly** *a.* relating to the world; earthly; mundane; carnal; not spiritual. **-ly-wise** *a.* experienced in the ways of people. **—wide** *a.* extending to every corner of the globe. **the New World,** N. and S. America. **the Old World.** Europe, Africa, and Asia.

worm *n.* small, limbless, invertebrate animal with soft, long, and jointed body; *pl.* disease of digestive organs or intestines of humans and animals due to parasite worms; *v.i.* to work (oneself) in insidiously; to move along like a worm; *v.t.* to work slowly and secretly; to free from worms. **-y** *a.* worm-like; abounding with worms.

worn *pa.p.* of **wear.** **—out** *a.* no longer serviceable; exhausted; tired.

wor-ry *v.t.* to cause anxiety; to torment; to vex; to plague; *v.i.* to feel undue care and anxiety; *n.* mental disturbance due to care and anxiety; trouble; vexation. **worrier** *n.* **worrisome** *a.* causing trouble, anxiety, or worry. **-ing** *a.*

worse *a. comp.* of **bad, ill;** more unsatisfactory; of less value; in poorer health; *adv.* in a manner more evil or bad. **worsen** *v.t.* to make worse; to impair; *v.t.* and *i.* to make or become worse; to deteriorate. **worsening** *n.*

wor-ship *n.* religious reverence and homage; act or ceremony of showing reverence; *v.t.* to adore; to pay divine honors to; *v.i.* to perform religious service; to attend church. **-ful** *a.* **-fully** *adv.* **-fulness** *n.* **-er** *n.*

worst *a. superl.* of **bad, ill;** most evil; of least value or worth; *adv.* in most inferior manner or degree; *n.* that which is most bad or evil; *v.t.* to get the better of; to defeat.

wor-sted *n.* yarn spun from long-fibred wools which are combed, not carded; cloth of this yarn; *a.* made of worsted.

worth *n.* quality of thing which renders it valuable or useful; value, in terms of money; merit; excellence; *a.* equal in value to; meriting; having wealth or estate to the value of. **-ily** *adv.* **-iness** *n.* **-less** *a.* of no worth or value; useless. **-while** *a.* **-lessly** *adv.* **-lessness** *n.* **-y** *a.*

having worth or excellence; deserving; meritorious; *n.* man of eminent worth; local celebrity. *pl.* **worthies.**

would *pa.t.* of **will;** expresses condition, futurity, desire. **—be** *a.* desiring or intending to be.

wound *pa.t.* and *pa.p.* of **wind.**

wound *n.* injury; cut, stab, bruise, etc.; hurt; *v.t.* to hurt by violence; to hurt feelings of; to injure. **-er** *n.* **-less** *a.*

wove *pa.t.* of **weave.** **-n** *pa.p.* of **weave.**

wow *interj.* exclamation of astonishment.

wraith *n.* apparition of person seen shortly before or after death; specter; ghost.

wrap *v.t.* to cover by winding or folding something around; to roll, wind, or fold together. *pr.p.* **-ping.** *pa.t.,* *pa.p.* **-ped** (or **-t).** *n.* a loose garment; a covering. **-per** *n.* one who, or that which, wraps. **-ping** *n.* wrapping material.

wrath *n.* violent anger; indignation; rage; fury. **-ful** *a.* **-fully** *adv.* **-fulness** *n.*

wreath *n.* circular garland or crown of flowers, leaves, etc. entwined together. **wreathe** *v.t.* to surround; to form into a wreath; to wind round; to encircle; *v.i.* to be interwoven or entwined.

wreck *n.* destruction of vessel; hulk of wrecked ship; remains of anything destroyed or ruined; *v.t.* to destroy, as vessel; to bring ruin upon; to upset completely. **-age** *n.* remains of something wrecked. **-er** *n.* one who wrecks; one employed in tearing down buildings, salvaging or recovering cargo from wreck.

wren *n.* tiny song-bird about 4 in. long, with reddish-brown plumage.

wrench *v.t.* to wrest, twist, or force by violence; to distort; *n.* sudden, violent twist; tool with fixed or adjustable jaws for holding or adjusting nuts, bolts, etc.

wres•tle *v.i.* to contend by grappling and trying to throw another down; to struggle. **-r** *n.* **wrestling** *n.* sport in which contestants endeavor to throw each other to the ground in accordance with rules.

wrig•gle *v.i.* to move sinuously, like a worm; to squirm; *v.t.* to cause to wriggle; *n.* act of wriggling; wriggling motion. **-r** *n.* **wriggling** *n.* **wriggly** *a.*

wring *v.t.* to twist and compress; to turn and strain with violence; to squeeze or press out; *v.i.* to turn or twist, as with pain. *pa.t.* and *pa.p.* **wrung.** **-er** *n.* one who wrings; machine for pressing out water from wet clothes, etc. **-ing wet,** absolutely soaking.

wrin•kle *n.* ridge or furrow on surface due to twisting, shrinking, or puckering; crease in skin; fold; corrugation; *v.i.* to make ridges, creases, etc.; *v.i.* to shrink into wrinkles. **-ling** *n.* **wrinkly** *a.*

wrist *n.* joint connecting the forearm and hand; the carpus.

writ *n.* that which is written; in law, mandatory precept issued by a court; **Holy Writ,** the Scriptures.

write *v.t.* to set down or express in letters or words on paper, etc.; to compose, as book, song, etc.; *v.i.* to form characters representing sounds or ideas; to be occupied in writing; to express ideas in writing. *pr.p.* **writing.** *p.t.* **wrote.** *pa.p.* **written.** **-r** *n.* one who writes; scribe; clerk; author. **writing** *n.* mechanical act of forming characters on paper or any other material; anything written; style of execution or content of what works; official papers, etc. **written** *a.* expressed in writing. **to write off,** to cancel, as bad debts.

wrong *a.* not right; incorrect; mistaken; immoral; injurious; unjust; illegal; unsuitable; improper; *n.* harm; evil; injustice; trespass; transgression; error; *adv.* not rightly; erroneously; *v.t.* to treat with injustice; to injure; to impute evil to unjustly. **-doer** *n.* one who injures another; one who breaks law; offender; sinner. **-ful** *a.* **-fully** *adv.* **-fulness** *n.* **wrong,** at fault; blameworthy.

wrought *pa.t.* and *pa.p.* of **work.** *a.* hammered into shape, as metal products. **—iron** *n.* purest form of commercial iron, fibrous, ductile, and malleable, prepared by puddling.

wrung *pa.t.* and *pa.p.* of **wring.**

W

X chro·mo·some *n.* chromosome which determines the sex of the future organism.

xe·nog·a·my *n.* cross-fertilization. **xenogamous** *a.*

xen·o·gen·e·sis *n.* fancied generation of organism totally unlike parent. **xenogenetic** *a.*

xe·non *n.* non-metallic element belonging to group of rare or inactive gases.

xen·o·pho·bi·a *n.* fear or hatred of strangers or aliens.

xe·rog·ra·phy *n.* a process similar to photography, but not requiring specifically sensitized paper or plates, using instead a special photoconductive plate.

X rays *n.pl.* Röntgen rays —electromagnetic rays of very short wave length, capable of penetrating matter opaque to light rays and imprinting on sensitive photographic plate picture of objects; the picture so made. *v.t.* to treat, examine, or photograph with X-rays.

xy·lo·graph *n.* a wood engraving; impression from wood block. **-er** *n.* **-ic** *a.* **-ical** *a.* **-y** *n.* the art of wood engraving.

xy·lo·phone *n.* musical instrument consisting of blocks of resonant wood, notes being produced by striking blocks of resonant wood, notes being produced by striking blocks with two small hammers. **xylophonist** *n.*

xy·lo·py·rog·ra·phy *n.* production of designs in wood by charring with hot iron.

X

yacht *n.* light sailing or power-driven vessel, for pleasure or racing; *v.i.* to sail in a yacht. **-ing** *n.* art or act of sailing a yacht; *a.* pert. to yacht. **-sman** *n.* **-smanship** *n.*

yak *n.* species of ox found in C. Asia, with a hump and long hair.

yam *n.* tuber of tropical climbing-plant; sweet potato.

Yan•kee *n.* (in U.S.A.) citizen of New England, or of Northern States; (outside U.S.A.) an American; *a.* American. **-dom** *n.*

yap *v.i.* to yelp; *n.* yelp.

yard *n.* standard measure of length, equal to three feet of thirty-six inches; *(Naut.)* spar set crosswise to mast, for supporting a sail. **-age** *n.* measurement in yards. **-arm** *n.* either half of a ship's yard. **-stick** *n.* measuring stick 36 inches long.

yard *n.* grounds surrounding a building; enclosed space used for specific purpose as *brickyard*, a *railroad yard*, etc.

yarn *n.* spun thread, esp. for knitting or weaving; thread of rope.

yar•row *n.* plant having strong odor and pungent taste.

yaw *v.i.* of ship or aircraft, to fail to keep steady course; *n.* act of yawing; temporary deviation from a straight course.

yawl *n.* small, two-masted sailing boat, with smaller mast at stern; ship's small boat.

yawn *v.i.* to open mouth involuntarily through sleepiness, etc.

yaws *n.* tropical contagious disease of the skin, usually chronic.

yean *v.t.* and *v.i.* to bring forth young; as sheep or goat. **-ling** *n.* a lamb; kid.

year *n.* time taken by one revolution of earth round sun, i.e. about 365¼ days; twelve months; scholastic session in school, university, etc.; *pl.* age; old age. **-ly** *a.* and *adv.* happening every year; annual. **-ling** *n.* young animal, esp. horse, in second year; *a.* being a year old. **-long** *a.* **-book** *n.* reference book of facts and statistics published yearly. **leap year,** year of 366 days, occurring every fourth year.

yearn *v.i.* to seek earnestly; to feel longing or desire; to long for. **-ing** *n.* earnest desire; longing; *a.* desirous.

yeast *n.* froth that rises on malt liquors during fermentation; frothy yellow fungus growth causing this fermentation, used also in bread making, as leavening agent to raise dough. **-y** *a.* frothy; fermenting. **-cake** *n.* yeast mixed with meal and formed into small cakes for use in baking.

yell *v.i.* to cry out in a loud, shrill tone; *n.* a loud, shrill cry.

yel•low *n.* primary color; color of gold, lemons, buttercups, etc. **— fever** *n.* infectious, tropical disease, characterized by a yellow skin, vomiting, etc. **— jacket** *n.* a bright yellow wasp.

yelp *n.* sharp, shrill bark or cry.

yeo•man *n.* *(Arch.)* officer of royal household; *(Navy)* petty officer. *pl.* **yeomen.**

yes *interj.* word expressing affirmation or consent.

yes•ter *a.* *(Arch.)* pert. to yesterday; denoting period of time just past, esp. in compounds, e.g. 'yester-eve.' **-day** *n.* day before today. **-year** *n.* last year.

yet *adv.* in addition; at the same time; still; *conj.* nevertheless; notwithstanding.

yew *n.* cone-bearing evergreen tree; its fine-grained wood, formerly used for making bows for archers.

Yid•dish *n.* a mixture of dialectal German, Hebrew and Slavic, spoken by Jews.

yield *v.t.* to produce; to give in return, esp. for labor, investment, etc.; to bring forth; to give way; to bear; *n.* amount produced; return for labor, investment, etc; profit; crop.

yo•del, yo•dle *v.t.* and *v.i.* to sing or warble, with frequent changes from the natural voice to falsetto tone.

yo•ga *n.* system of Hindu philosophy; strict spiritual discipline practiced to gain control over forces of one's own being, to gain occult powers, but chiefly to attain union with the Deity or Universal Spirit.

yo•gurt *n.* a thick liquid food made from fermented milk.

yoke *n.* wooden framework fastened over necks of two oxen, etc. to hold them together, and to which a plough, etc. is attached; separately cut piece of material in garment, fitting closely over shoulders.

yo•kel *n.* rustic; country bumpkin.

yolk *n.* yellow part of egg.

yore *n.* the past; old times.

York•shire *n.* country in north of England. **— pudding,** batter baked in roasting tin along with meat. **— terrier,** small, shaggy terrier, resembling Skye terrier.

you *pron. sing., pl.* of second person in nominative or objective case, indicating person or persons addressed; also used indefinitely meaning, one, they, people in general; **your, yours** *a.* possessive form of *you,* meaning belonging to you, of you, pert. to you.

young *a.* not far advanced in growth, life, or existence; not yet old; vigorous; immature; *n.* offspring of animals. **-ster** *n.* young person or animal; child.

youth *n.* state of being young; life from childhood to manhood; young persons collectively.

yowl *v.i.* to howl; *n.* cry of a dog.

yo-yo *n.* toy consisting of flat spool with string wound round in the deep groove in its edge, which when released from hand spins up and down on a string.

yuc•ca *n.* genus of lilaceous plants, having tall, handsome flowers.

Yu•go•slav *a.* pert. to *Yugoslavia,* the country of the Serbs, Croats, and Slovenes, in the N.W. of the Balkan Peninsula.

yule *n.* feast of Christmas. **-tide** *n.* season of Christmas.

YZ

za•ny *n.* formerly, buffoon who mimicked principal clown; simpleton. *a.* comical. **-ism** *n.*

zeal *n.* intense enthusiasm for cause or person; passionate ardor. **zealot** *n.* fanatic; enthusiast. **zealotry** *n.* fanaticism. **zealous** *a.* ardent; enthusiastic; earnest. **zealously** *adv.* **zealousness** *n.*

ze•bra *n.* genus of African quadrupeds of horse family, with tawny coat striped with black.

ze•brass *n.* offspring of male zebra and she-ass.

Zend *n.* interpretation of the *Avesta,* sacred writings of Zoroastrians; Iranian language in which Zend-Avesta is written. **—Avesta** *n.* sacred writings and commentary thereon (Zend) of Zoroastrians.

ze•nith *n.* point of heavens directly above observer's head; summit; height of success; acme; climax. **-al** *a.*

zeph•yr *n.* west wind; gentle breeze; fine soft woolen fabric.

zep•pe•lin *n.* cigar-shaped long-range dirigible.

ze•ro *n.* nought; cipher; symbol, 0; neutral fixed point from which graduated scale is measured, as on thermometer, barometer, etc.; lowest point. **— hour,** precise moment at which military offensive, etc. is timed to begin; crucial moment. **— in,** *v.i.* to adjust gun fire to a specific point.

zest *n.* relish; fillip; stimulus; keen pleasure.

Zeus *n.* in Greek mythology, chief deity and father of gods and men, his seat being Mt. Olympus.

zig•zag *n.* line, with short sharp turns; *a.* forming zigzag; *v.t.* and *v.i.* to form, or move with, short sharp turns.

zinc *n.* hard bluish-metal used in alloys, esp. brass, and because of its resistance to corrosion, for galvanizing iron; *v.t.* to coat with zinc, to galvanize. **— alloys** *(Met.)* alloys containing percentage of zinc, as brass, etc.

zing *n.* the high-pitched sound of something moving at great speed; pep.

zin•ni•a *n.* plant with bright-colored flowers.

Zi•on *n.* hill in Jerusalem; town of Jerusalem; the Jewish people; Church of God; heaven. **-ism** *n.* movement among Jews to further the Jewish national state in Palestine. **-ist** *n.* advocate of Zionism.

zip *n.* whizzing sound, as of bullet in air; *v.t.* to shut with a zipper; *v.i.* to move with great speed. *pr.p.* **-ping.** *pa.p., pa.t.* **-ped, -per** *n.* device of interlocking flexible teeth opened and shut by sliding clip.

zir•con *n.* silicate of zirconium occurring in crystals; transparent ones used as gems. **zirconium** *n.* metal obtained from zircon, and resembling titanium **-ic** *a.*

zith•er *n.* flat, stringed instrument comprising resonance box with strings.

zo•di•ac *n.* *(Astron.)* imaginary belt in heavens following path of sun, and divided into twelve equal areas containing twelve constellations, each represented by appropriate symbols, called the *signs of the zodiac;* namely Aries *(Ram),* Taurus *(Bull),* Gemini *(Twins),* Cancer *(Crab),* Leo *(Lion),* Virgo *(Virgin),* Libra *(Balance),* Scorpio *(Scorpion),* Sagittarius *(Archer),* Capricornus *(Goat),* Aquarius *(Water-bearer),* Pisces *(Fishes);* a circular chart representing these signs **-al** *a.*

zom•bi, zom•bie *n.* orig. in Africa, deity of the python; in West Indies, corpse alleged to have been revived by black magic; the power which enters such a body; human being without will or speech but capable of automatic movement; intoxicating drink made with rum.

zone *n.* girdle; climatic or vegetation belt; one of five belts into which earth is divided by latitude lines, as *frigid zone* of Arctic and Antarctic, *torrid zone* between Tropics of Cancer and Capricorn, *temperate zone* north of Tropic of Cancer and south of Tropic of Capricorn; division of a city, etc., for building or other purposes; *v.t.* to enclose; to divide into zones; to divide country into regional areas.

zoo *n.* zoological garden; place where wild animals are kept for showing.

zo•o•chem•is•try *n.* chemistry of constituents of animal body.

zo•o•ge•og•ra•phy *n.* science which treats the regional distribution of animals in the world.

zo•oid *a.* resembling an animal; *n.* organism capable of relatively independent existence; a compound organism.

zo•ol•o•gy *n.* natural history of animals, part of science of biology. **zoological** *a.* **zoologically** *adv.* **zoologist** *n.* one versed in zoology, **zoological gardens, zoo,** park where wild animals are kept for exhibition.

zoom *n.* *v.t.* (of prices) to become inflated; (of aircraft) to turn suddenly upward at sharp angle; to move camera rapidly toward or away from an object which thus appears to move similarly.

zo•o•phyte *n.* plant-like animal, such as sponge.

zoot suit *n.* flashy type of man's suit, generally with padded shoulders, fitted waist, knee-length jacket and tight trousers.

zuc•chi•ni *n.* a long green-skinned squash.

Zu•lu *n.* member of Bantu tribe of S. Africa; *a.* pert. to Zulus.

zwie•back *n.* a dry crisp bread, usually sweetened, that has been baked, sliced and then toasted.

zyme *n.* ferment; disease germ. **zymic** *a.* **zymogen** *n.* any substance producing an enzyme. **zymotic disease,** infectious or contagious disease caused by germs introduced into body from without.

zy•mur•gy *n.* branch of chemistry dealin' with fermentation process.

YZ

RULES OF SPELLING

The rules listed below are meant to guide you in spelling; but there are exceptions to these rules. The most common exceptions are noted.

Drop the silent "e" at the end of a word when adding a termination that begins with a vowel (*Ex: shade, shading; move, movable*). Exceptions: words ending in *ce* or *ge* before terminations beginning with *a* or *o* (*Ex: change, changeable; notice, noticeable*); where confusion would result (*Ex: dye, dyeing* [*dying*]).

Keep the silent "e" at the end of a word when adding a termination that begins with a consonant (*Ex: bare, bareness; hate, hateful*). Exceptions: *acknowledge, acknowledgment; whole, wholly.*

Repeat the final consonant at the end of a single syllable or last syllable accented word if it is preceded by a single vowel when adding a terminal beginning with a vowel (*Ex: hit, hitting; begin, beginning*).

Do not repeat the final consonant at the end of a word if it is preceded by a consonant, two vowels, or if the last syllable is unaccented when adding a terminal beginning with a vowel (*Ex: art, artful; troop, trooping; profit, profiting*).

Keep the double consonant at the end of a word when adding a terminal (*Ex: fall, falling; stiff, stiffen*). Exception: where the terminal begins with the same letter as the double consonant (*Ex: full, fully*).

Add "k" to words ending in "c" when adding a terminal beginning with *e, i,* or *y* (*Ex: picnic, picnicked; shellac, shellacking; panic, panicky*).

Drop one "e" of an "ee" ending when adding a terminal beginning with e (*Ex: agree, agreed*).

Change "ie" to "y" before adding the terminal -*ing* (*Ex: die, dying*).

Change "y" to "i" before adding a terminal other than -*ing* (*Ex: racy, raciest; twenty, twentieth*). Exceptions: where a vowel precedes the y (*Ex: gay, gayest*).

USE OF CAPITALS

Capitals (denotes capitalization of the first letter of the word) are used: (1) at the beginning of each sentence; (2) for proper names and adjectives derived from these names; (3) for words referring to the Deity; (4) for official and honorary titles; (5) at the beginning of every line of poetry; (6) for each important word in a title (book, magazine, etc.); (7) for the pronoun "I" and the exclamation "O"; (8) for the days of the week and the months of the year; (9) at the beginning of each quotation; (10) for special words.

USE OF PUNCTUATION MARKS

Period (.) Used: (1) at the end of a sentence that is not a question or explanation; (2) after abbreviations; and (3) to mark off decimals.

Question Mark (?) Used: (1) at the end of a sentence that asks a question; and (2) to denote something questionable.

Exclamation Mark (!) Used at the end of a strong exclamatory word, phrase, or sentence.

Comma (,) Used: (1) to separate words, phrases and clauses of a series; (2) to set off parenthetical expressions, non-restrictive clauses, transitional words or phrases, appositives, and nouns of direct address from the rest of the sentence; (3) to separate words in a date or address; (4) before a quotation; (5) to separate independent clauses, containing no commas, that are joined by a simple conjunction; (6) denote the omission of a word; and (7) after the salutation of an informal letter.

Semi-colon (;) Used: (1) to separate parts of a complex series; (2) to separate independent clauses not connected by co-ordinating conjunction, or which already contain one or more commas; and (3) where a comma would not afford the proper clarity.

Colon (:) Used: (1) to introduce a formal direct quotation; (2) after the salutation of a business letter; and (3) to introduce a long series.

Dash (—) Used: (1) to show an interruption or change of thought or sense; (2) to denote omission of a word or part of a word; and (3) to introduce a repetitious phrase.

Hyphen (-) Used: (1) to break a word between syllables when the word must be divided between the end of one line and the beginning of another; (2) to divide certain compound words; (3) to divide words which would be otherwise confusing; and (4) after a prefix that is before a proper noun.

Parentheses (( )) Used to set off words, phrases, clauses, or sentences which are in the text as comment or explanation.

Brackets ([ ]) Used: (1) to show editorial comment; and (2) as parentheses containing parentheses.

Apostrophe (') Used: (1) to indicate possession; and (2) to replace the missing letters in a contraction.

Quotation marks (" ") Used: (1) to enclose direct quotations [quotations within quotations are enclosed by single quotation marks (' ')]; (2) to indicate titles of plays, books, etc.; and (3) to indicate the opposite meaning of the word used.

WORDBREAK RULES

1. Division of words should be minimized in leaded matter and avoided in double-leaded matter.

2. Except in narrow measures, wordbreaks should be avoided at the ends of more than two lines. Similarly, no more than two consecutive lines should end with the same word, symbol, group of numbers, etc.

3. In two-line centerheads, the first line should be centered and set as full as possible, but it is not set to fill the measure by unduly wide spacing. Wordbreaks should be avoided. Flush sideheads are set full measure and wordbreaks are permitted if unavoidable. They are not set ragged unless so indicated on copy.

4. The final word of a paragraph should not be divided.

5. Words should preferably be divided according to pronunciation; and to avoid mispronunciation, they should be divided so that the part of the word left at the end of the line will suggest the whole word: *capac-ity*, not *capa-city; extraor-dinary*, not *extra-ordinary; Wednes-day*, not *Wed-nesday; physi-cal*, not *phys-ical; service-man*, not *serv-iceman*.

6. Although WORD DIVISION lists beginning and ending one-letter syllables for pronunciation purposes, under no circumstances are words to be divided on a single letter (e.g., *usu-al-ly*, not *u-su-al-ly; imag-i-nary*, not *i-mag-i-nar-y*).

7. Division of short words (of five or fewer letters) should be avoided; two-letter divisions, including the carry-over of two-letter endings (*ed, el, en, er, es, et, fy, ic, in, le, ly, or*, and *ty*); should also be avoided. In narrow measure, however, a sounded suffix (e.g., paint-*ed;* not rained) or syllable of two letters may be carried over— only if unavoidable. (See rule 10.)

8. Words of two syllables are split at the end of the first syllable: *dis-pelled, con-quered;* words of three or more syllables, with a choice of division possible, divide preferably on the vowel: *particu-lar, sepa-rate.*

9. In words with short prefixes, divide on the prefix; e.g., *ac, co, de, dis, ex, in, non, on, pre, pro, re, un,* etc. (e.g., *non-essential,* not *nones-sential; pre-selected,* not *prese-lected*).

If possible, prefixes and combining forms of more than one syllable are preserved intact: *anti, infra, macro, micro, multi, over, retro, semi,* etc. (e.g., *anti-monopoly,* not *antimo-nopoly; over-optimistic,* not *overop-timistic*). (For chemical prefixes, see rule 30.)

10. *Words ending in* -er.—Although two-letter carryovers are to be avoided (rule 7), many *-er* words which are derived from comparatives (*coarse, coarser; sharp, sharper*) have been listed to prevent a wrong wordbreak; e.g., *coars-er,* not *coar-ser.*

Nouns ending in *-er* (*adviser, bracer, keeper, perceiver, reader*) derived from action verbs are also listed to prevent a wrong division; e.g., *perceiv-er,* not *percei-ver.*

Except in narrow measure and if unavoidable, the above *-er* words are not divided unless division can be made on a prefix; e.g., *per-ceiver.*

11. *Words ending in* -or.—Generally, *-or* words with a consonant preceding are divided before the preceding consonant; e.g., *advi-sor* (legal), *fabrica-tor, guaran-tor, interve-nor, simula-tor,*

tai-lor; but *bail-or, bargain-or, con-sign-or, grant-or.*

12. The following suffixes are not divided: *ceous, cial, cient, cion, cious, scious, geous, gion, gious, sial, tial, tion, tious,* and *sion.*

13. The suffixes *-able* and *-ible* are usually carried over intact; but when the stem word loses its original form, these suffixes are divided according to pronunciation: *comfort-able, corrupt-ible, manage-able;* but *dura-ble, audi-ble.*

14. Words ending in *-ing,* with stress on the primary syllable, are preferably divided on the base word; e.g., *appoint-ing, combat-ing, danc-ing, engineer-ing, process-ing, program-ing, stencil-ing, trac-ing,* etc. However, present participles, such as *control-ling, forbid-ding, refer-ring,* with stress placed on the second syllable, divide between the doubled consonants (see also rule 16).

15. When the final consonant sound of a word belongs to a syllable ending with a silent vowel, the final consonant or consonants become part of the added suffix: *chuck-ling, han-dler, han-dling, crum-bling, twin-kled, twin-kling;* but *rollick-ing.*

16. When the addition of *-ed, -er, -est,* or of a similar ending, causes the doubling of a final consonant, the

added consonant is carried over: *pit-ted, rob-ber, thin-nest, glad-den, control-lable, transmit-table;* but *bless-ed* (adj.), *dwell-er, gross-est.*

17. Words with doubled consonants are usually divided between these consonants: *clas-sic, ruf-fian, neces-sary, rebel-lion;* but *call-ing, mass-ing.*

18. If formation of a plural adds a syllable ending in an *s* sound, the plural ending should not be carried over by itself: *hor-ses, voi-ces;* but *church-es, cross-es,* thus not breaking the base word (see also rule 7).

19. The digraphs *ai, ck, dg, gh, gn, ng, oa, ph, sh, tch,* and *th* are not split.

20. Do not divide contractions: *doesn't. haven't.*

21. Solid compounds are divided preferably between the members: *bar-keeper, hand-kerchief, proof-reader, humming-bird.*

22. Avoid a division which adds another hyphen to a hyphened compound: *court-martial,* not *court-mar-tial; tax-supported,* not *tax-sup-ported.*

23. A word of one syllable is not split: *tanned, shipped, quenched, through, chasm, prism.*

24. Two consonants preceded and followed by a vowel are divided on the first consonant: *abun-dant, advan-tage, struc-ture;* but *attend-ant, accept-ance, depend-ence.*

25. When two adjoining vowels are sounded separately, divide between them: *cre-ation, gene-alogy*.

26. In breaking homonyms, distinction should be given to their relative functions: *pro-ject* (v.), *proj-ect* (n.); *pro-duce* (v.), *prod-uce* (n.); *stranger* (n.), *strang-er* (comparative adjective); *rec-ollect* (recall), *re-collect* (collect again); but *proc-ess* (n., v.); *pro-test* (n., v.).

27. *Words ending in* -meter.—In the large group of words ending in *-meter*, distinction should be made between metric system terms and terms indicating a measuring instrument. When it is necessary to divide metric terms, preserve the combining form *-meter;* e.g., *centi-meter, deca-meter, hecto-meter, kilo-meter*. But measuring instruments divide after the *m: al-tim-e-ter, ba-rom-e-ter, mi-crom-e-ter, mul-tim-e-ter,* etc. Derivatives of these *-meter* terms follow the same form; e.g., *mul-tim-e-ter, mul-tim-e-try*.

For orthographic reasons, however, several measuring instruments do not lend themselves to the general rule; e.g., *flow-meter, flux-meter, gauss-meter, taxi-meter, torque-meter, volt-meter, water-meter, watt-meter,* etc.

28. *Foreign languages.*—Rules for word division in foreign languages, by

language, are printed in the 1967 GPO Style Manual (unabridged), pages 387–492.

29. *Chemical formulas.*—In chemical formulas, the hyphen has an important function. If a break is unavoidable in a formula, division is preferably made after an original hyphen to avoid the introduction of a misleading hyphen. If impractical to break on a hyphen, division may be made after an original comma, and no hyphen is added to indicate a runover. The following formula shows original hyphens and commas where division may be made. No letterspacing is used in a chemical formula, but to fill a line, a space is permitted on both sides of a hyphen.

1-(2,6,6-trimethylcyclohex-1- en -1- yl)-
3,7,12,16

30. *Chemical combining forms, prefixes, and suffixes.*—If possible, and subject to rules of good spacing, it is desirable to preserve as a unit such combining forms as follows:

aceto, anhydro, benzo, bromo, chloro, chromo, cincho, cyclo, dehydro, diazo, flavo, fluoro, glyco, hydroxy, iso, keto, methyl, naphtho, phospho, poly, silico, tetra, triazo.

The following suffixes are used in chemical printing. For patent and narrow measure composition, two-letter suffixes may be carried over.

al, an, ane, ase, ate, ene, ic, id, ide, in, ine, ite, ol, ole, on, one, ose, ous oyl, yl, yne.

31. *Mineral elements.*—When it is necessary to break mineral constituents, division should preferably be made before a center period and beginning parenthesis, and after inferior figures following a closing parenthesis; but elements within parentheses are not separated. In cases of unavoidable breaks, a hyphen is not added to indicate a runover.

$$Mg(UO_2)_2(SiO_3)_2(OH)_2 \cdot 6H_2O$$

32. The em dash is not used at the beginning of any line of type, unless it is required before a credit line or signature, or in lieu of opening quotation marks in foreign languages. (See rules 9.52, 9.53, p. 142, 1967 GPO Style Manual.)

33. Neither periods nor asterisks used as an ellipsis are overrun alone at the end of a paragraph. If necessary, run over enough preceding lines to provide a short word or part of a word to accompany the ellipsis. If a runback is possible, subject to rules of good spacing and word division, this method may be adopted.

34. Abbreviations and symbols

should not be broken at the end of a line: *A.F. of L., A.T. & T., C. Cls. R., f.o.b., n.o.i.b.n., R. & D., r.p.m., WMAL.* Where unavoidable in narrow measures and AGO's, long symbols may be broken after letters denoting a complete word. Use no hyphens. COM SUB A C LANT (Commander Submarine Allied Command Atlantic).

35. Figures of less than six digits, decimals, and closely connected combinations of figures and abbreviations should not be broken at the end of a line: *$15,000, 34,575, 31.416, £8 4s. 7d., $10.25, 5,000 kw.-hr., A.D. 1952, 9 p.m., 18° F., NW¼.* If a break in six digits or over is unavoidable, divide on the comma or period, retain it, and use a hyphen.

36. Closely related abbreviations and initials in proper names and accompanying titles should not be separated, nor should titles, such as *Rev., Mr., Esq., Jr., 2d,* be separated from surnames.

37. Avoid dividing proper names, but if inescapable, follow general rules for word division.

38. Divisional and subdivisional paragraph reference signs and figures, such as *§ 18, section (a)(1), page 363(b),* should not be divided, nor should such references be separated from the matter to which they pertain.

In case of an unavoidable break in a lengthy reference (e.g., $7(B)(1)(a)(i)$), division will be made after elements in parentheses, and no hyphen is used.

39. In dates, do not divide the month and day, but the year may be carried over.

40. In case of an unavoidable break in a land-description symbol group at the end of a line, use no hyphen and break after a fraction.

41. Avoid breaking longitude and latitude figures at the end of a line; space out the line instead. In case of an unavoidable break at end of line, use hyphen.

PRESIDENTS OF THE UNITED STATES

Name (and party)	State of Birth	Born		Died
George Washington (F)	Va.	1732	1789-97	1799
John Adams (F)	Mass.	1735	1797-1801	1826
Thomas Jefferson (D-R)	Va.	1743	1801-09	1826
James Madison (D-R)	Va.	1751	1809-17	1836
James Monroe (D-R)	Va.	1758	1817-25	1831
John Quincy Adams (D-R)	Mass.	1767	1825-29	1848
Andrew Jackson (D)	S.C.	1767	1829-37	1845
Martin Van Buren (D)	N.Y.	1782	1837-41	1862
William Henry Harrison (W)	Va.	1773	1841	1841
John Tyler (W)	Va.	1790	1841-45	1862
James Knox Polk (D)	N.C.	1795	1845-49	1849
Zachary Taylor (W)	Va.	1784	1849-50	1850
Millard Fillmore (W)	N.Y.	1800	1850-53	1874
Franklin Pierce (D)	N.H.	1804	1853-57	1869
James Buchanan (D)	Pa.	1791	1857-61	1868
Abraham Lincoln (R)	Ky.	1809	1861-65	1865
Andrew Johnson (R)	N.C.	1808	1865-69	1875
Ulysses Simpson Grant (R)	Ohio	1822	1869-77	1885
Rutherford Birchard Hayes (R)	Ohio	1822	1877-81	1893
James Abram Garfield (R)	Ohio	1831	1881	1881
Chester Alan Arthur (R)	Vt.	1830	1881-85	1886
Grover Cleveland (D)	N.J.	1837	1885-89	1908
Benjamin Harrison (R)	Ohio	1833	1889-93	1901
Grover Cleveland (D)	N.J.	1837	1893-97	1908
William McKinley (R)	Ohio	1843	1897-1901	1901
Theodore Roosevelt (R)	N.Y.	1858	1901-1909	1919
William Howard Taft (R)	Ohio	1857	1909-13	1930
Woodrow Wilson (D)	Va.	1856	1913-21	1924
Warren Gamaliel Harding (R)	Ohio	1865	1921-23	1923
Calvin Coolidge (R)	Vt.	1872	1923-29	1933
Herbert Clark Hoover (R)	Iowa	1874	1923-33	1965
Franklin Delano Roosevelt (D)	N.Y.	1882	1933-45	1945
Harry S. Truman (D)	Mo.	1884	1945-53	1972
Dwight David Eisenhower (R)	Tex.	1890	1953-61	1969
John F. Kennedy (D)	Mass.	1917	1961-63	1963
Lyndon B. Johnson (D)	Tex.	1908	1963-69	1973
Richard M. Nixon (R)	Calif.	1913	1969-74 (r)	
Gerald R. Ford (R)	Nebr.	1913	1974-77	
James Earl Carter, Jr. (D)	Ga.	1924	1977-81	
Ronald W. Reagan (R)	Calif.	1911	1981-	

VICE-PRESIDENTS OF THE UNITED STATES

Name (and party)	State of Birth	Born	Term	Died
John Adams (F)	Mass.	1735	1789-97	1826
Thomas Jefferson (D-R)	Va.	1743	1797-1801	1826
Aaron Burr (R)	N.J.	1756	1801-05	1836
George Clinton (R)	N.Y.	1739	1805-12	1812
Elbridge Gerry (R)	Mass.	1744	1813-14	1814
Daniel D. Tompkins (R)	N.Y.	1774	1817-25	1825
John U. Calhoun (R)	S.C.	1782	1825-32	1850
Martin Van Buren (D)	N.Y.	1782	1833-37	1862
Richard M. Johnson (D)	Ky.	1780	1837-41	1850
John Tyler (W)	Va.	1790	1841	1862
George M. Dallas (D)	Pa.	1792	1845-49	1864
Millard Fillmore (W)	N.Y.	1800	1849-50	1874
William R. King (D)	N.C.	1786	1853	1853
John C. Breckinridge (D)	Ky.	1821	1857-61	1875
Hannibal Hamlin (R)	Me.	1809	1861-65	1891
Andrew Johnson (R)	N.C.	1808	1865	1875
Schuyler Colfax (R)	N.Y.	1823	1869-73	1885
Henry Wilson (R)	N.H.	1812	1873-75	1875
William A. Wheeler (R)	N.Y.	1819	1877-81	1887
Chester A. Arthur (R)	Vt.	1830	1881	1886
Thomas A. Hendricks (D)	Ohio	1819	1885	1885
Levi P. Morton (R)	Vt.	1824	1889-93	1920
Adlai E. Stevenson (D)	Ky.	1835	1893-97	1914
Garrett A. Hobart (R)	N.J.	1844	1897-99	1899
Theodore Roosevelt (R)	N.Y.	1858	1901	1919
Charles W. Fairbanks (R)	Ohio	1852	1905-09	1918
James S. Sherman (R)	N.Y.	1855	1909-12	1912
Thomas R. Marshall (D)	Ind.	1854	1913-21	1925
Calvin Coolidge (R)	Vt.	1872	1921-23	1933
Charles G. Dawes (R)	Ohio	1865	1925-29	1951
Charles Curtis (R)	Kan.	1860	1929-33	1936
John N. Garner (D)	Tex.	1869	1933-41	1967
Henry A. Wallace (D)	Ia.	1888	1941-45	1965
Harry S. Truman (D)	Mo.	1884	1945	1972
Alben W. Barkley (D)	Ky.	1877	1949-53	1956
Richard M. Nixon (R)	Calif.	1913	1953-61	
Lyndon B. Johnson (D)	Tex.	1908	1961-63	1973
Hubert H. Humphrey (D)	S.D.	1911	1965-69	1978
Spiro T. Agnew (R)	Md.	1918	1969-73 (r)	
Gerald R. Ford (R)	Nebr.	1913	1973-1974	
Nelson A. Rockefeller (R)	Me.	1908	1974-77	1979
Walter F. Mondale (D)	Minn.	1928	1977-81	
George Bush (R)	Mass.	1924	1981-	

F—Federalist; D—Democratic; R—Republican; W—Whig; (r)—resigned

NOTES